Principles of Economics

Version 8.0

John B. Taylor and Akila Weerapana

S-2552311-CO

9 781453 384503

Principles of Economics Version 8.0

John B. Taylor and Akila Weerapana

Published by:

FlatWorld
175 Portland Street
Boston, MA 02114

Brief Contents

Contents

About the Authors

JOHN B. TAYLOR

John B. Taylor is one of the field's most inspiring teachers. As the Raymond Professor of Economics at Stanford University, his distinctive instructional methods have made him a legend among introductory economics students and have won him both the Hoagland and Rhodes prizes for teaching excellence.

Professor Taylor is also widely recognized for his research on the foundations of modern monetary theory and policy. One of his well-known research contributions is a rule—now widely called the Taylor Rule—used at central banks around the world.

Taylor has had an active career in public service, including a four-year stint as the head of the International Affairs division at the United States Treasury, where he had responsibility for currency policy, international debt, and oversight of the International Monetary Fund and the World Bank and worked closely with leaders and policymakers from countries throughout the world. He has also served as economic adviser to the governor of California, to the U.S. Congressional Budget Office, and to the President of the United States and has served on several boards and as a consultant to private industry.

Professor Taylor began his career at Princeton, where he graduated with highest honors in economics. He then received his Ph.D. from Stanford and taught at Columbia, Yale, and Princeton before returning to Stanford.

AKILA WEERAPANA

Akila Weerapana is an Associate Professor of Economics at Wellesley College. He was born and raised in Sri Lanka and came to the United States to do his undergraduate work at Oberlin College, where he earned a B.A. with highest honors in Economics and Computer Science in 1994. He received his Ph.D. in Economics from Stanford in 1999, writing his dissertation on monetary economics under the mentorship of John Taylor.

Since then, Professor Weerapana has taught in the Economics Department at Wellesley College. His teaching interests span all levels of the department's curriculum, including introductory and intermediate macroeconomics, international finance, monetary economics, and mathematical economics. He was awarded Wellesley's Pinanski Prize for Excellence in Teaching in 2002.

He also enjoys working with thesis students. In addition to teaching, Professor Weerapana has research interests in macroeconomics, specifically in the areas of monetary economics, international finance, and political economy.

Acknowledgments

Completing a project like this is a team effort, and we both have been blessed with good students and colleagues who have given us advice and encouragement.

JOHN B. TAYLOR

I am grateful to many colleagues and students, whom I have consulted over the years, including Don Brown, Tim Breshanan, Marcelo Clerici-Arias, Anne Kreuger, Tom McCurdy, Paul Milgrom, Roger Noll, John Pencavel, Paul Romer, Nate Rosenberg, Mark Tendell and Frank Wolak. I must acknowledge with very special gratitude Akila's partnership in this project. Akila first demonstrated his extraordinary teaching and writing skills even before completing his PhD at Stanford. After receiving his PhD, Akila joined the faculty at Wellesley College, where he has taught the Principles course for many semesters and further established his reputation for teaching excellence, and in 2002, received the Anna and Samuel Pinanski Teaching Award. His ability to get complex topics across to his students and his enthusiasm for bringing policy implications alive is clearly reflected in our new coauthored book.

AKILA WEERAPANA

I am exceedingly grateful to John for giving me the opportunity to communicate my enthusiasm for teaching economics to a broader audience than the students in my classes at Wellesley. My passion for economics stems from the inspiration I received from my economics professors: Barbara Craig and Peter Montiel at the undergraduate level, and John Taylor, Frank Wolak, and Chad Jones at the graduate level. I too have benefited immensely from working with my colleagues. The faculty members in the Economics Department at Wellesley live up to the liberal arts ideal that I aspire to, combining excellent teaching with active research. Special thanks are owed to the late Chip Case, Courtney Coile and David Lindauer for the time they spent helping me understand how best to pitch topics in microeconomics that I am less familiar with teaching than they are. The real inspirations for this book, however, are the students that I have taught over the past two decades—two years at Stanford, but especially, the last seventeen years at Wellesley. Without their enthusiasm for economics, their willingness to be continually challenged, and their need to better understand an ever-changing world, none of this would be possible. My contributions to this book are shaped by countless hours spent talking economics with my students.

TOGETHER

Together, we would also like to thank William B. Stronge of Florida Atlantic University, who provided wonderful end-of-chapter problems that are conceptually challenging and require students to think more deeply about the concepts. Bill's efforts helped us meet an incredibly demanding schedule, and we are grateful for his contributions. Numerous reviewers provided insights, suggestions, and feedback along the way—often at critical points in product and supplement development. These individuals include Mohsen Bahmani-Oskooee, University of Wisconsin, Milwaukee; Erik Craft, University of Richmond; David H. Eaton, Murray State University; Lewis Freiberg, Northeastern Illinois University; Wang Fuzhong, Beijing University of Aeronautics & Astronautics; Janet Gerson, University of Michigan; Lisa Grobar, California State University, Long Beach; Ritika Gugnani, Jaipuria Institute of Management (Noida); Gautam Hazarika, University of Texas, Brownsville; Aaron Johnson, Missouri State University; Jacob Kurien, Rockhurst University; Babu Nahata, University of Louisville; Soloman Namala, Cerritos College; Sebastien Oleas, University of Minnesota, Duluth; Greg Pratt, Mesa Community College; Virginia Reilly, Ocean County College; Brian Rosario, University of California, Davis; William B. Stronge, Florida Atlantic University; Della Lee Sue, Marist College; J. S. Uppal, State University of New York, Albany; Michele T. Villinski, DePauw University; and Laura Wolff, Southern Illinois University, Edwardsville. We are grateful to Sarah L. Stafford of the College of William and Mary and Robert J. Rossana of Wayne State University for their detailed and timely accuracy checks of the main texts and several key supplements. We are especially appreciative of the contributions of the Sixth Edition supplements authors for their creativity, dedication, and careful coordination of content; this group includes Sarah E. Culver, University of Alabama, Birmingham; David H. Eaton, Murray State University; John Kane, State University of New York, Oswego; Jim Lee, Texas A&M University, Corpus Christi; John S.Min, Northern Virginia Community College; Wm. Stewart Mounts, Jr., Mercer University; David H. Papell, University of Houston; Virginia Reilly, Ocean County College Center for Economic Education; Brian Rosario, University of California, Davis; John Solow, University of Iowa; William B. Stronge, Florida Atlantic University; Eugenio D. Suarez, Trinity University; and Laura Wolff, Southern Illinois University, Edwardsville. We would also like to thank Edward Gullason of Dowling College for reviewing many of these supplements and Matthew Berg and Julia Ong for copyediting them.

REVIEWERS

- Matthew Alford, Southeastern Louisiana University
- Charles Anderson, Kean University
- Len Anyanwu, Union County College
- Kenneth Ardon, Salem State College
- Sukhwinder Bagi, Bloomsburg University
- Gaurango Banerjee, University of Texas at Brownsville
- Kevin Beckwith, Salem State College
- Charles A. Bennett, Gannon University
- Derek Berry, Calhoun Community College
- Charles Bondi, Morgan State University
- Joyce Bremer, Oakton Community College
- Amy Chataginer, MS Gulf Coast Community College
- Paul Clement, Fashion Institute of Technology-SUNY
- Marcelo Clerici-Arias, Stanford University
- Barbara Collister-Priestley, Concordia University Ann Arbor
- Mitchell Dudley, The College of William & Mary
- Dr. J. Pat Fuller, Brevard CC
- Cynthia Gamez, The University of Texas at El Paso
- Lara Gardner, Southeastern Louisiana University
- Dale Garrett, Evangel University
- Satyajit Ghosh, University of Scranton
- Sarah Ghosh, University of Scranton
- Alan Gin, University of San Diego
- Judith Grenkowicz, Kirtland Community College
- Curry Hilton, Guilford Technical Community College
- James Holcomb, University of Texas at El Paso
- Gokhan Karahan, Delta State University
- Ghebre Keleta, Grambling State University
- Deborah Kelly, University of San Diego
- Tori Knight, Carson-Newman College
- Viju Kulkarni, Mesa College
- Sonja Langley, Prairie View A&M University
- Sang Lee, Southeastern Louisiana University
- Charles Link, University of Delaware
- Linda Loubert, Morgan State University
- Farzin Madjidi, Pepperdine University/GSEP
- Tim McCabe, Tompkins Cortland Community College
- Todd McFall ,Wake Forest University
- Daniel Morvey, Piedmont Technical College
- Shahriar Mostashari, Campbell University
- Francis Mummery, Fullerton College
- Pattabiraman Neelakantan, East Stroudsburg University
- Ogbonnaya Nwoha, Grambling State University
- Olugbenga Onafowora, Susquehanna University
- Chuck Parker, Wayne State College
- Van Pham, Salem State College
- Roxana Postolache, Capital University

- Rahim Quazi, Prairie View A&M University
- MG Quibria, Morgan State University
- David Rodgers, Northwestern Connecticut Community College
- S. Scanlon Romer, Delta College
- Daniel Saros, Valparaiso University
- Mark Scanlan, Stephen F. Austin State University
- Ted Scheinman, Mt. Hood Community College
- Virginia Shingleton, Valparaiso University
- Noel Smith, Palm Beach State College
- Donald Sparks, The Citadel
- Mark Steckbeck, Campbell University
- TaMika Steward, Tarrant County College
- Chin-Chyuan Tai, Averett University
- Robert Tansky, St. Clair Community College
- Jill Trask, Tarrant County College
- Margie Vance, North Arkansas College
- Lisa Verdon, College of Wooster
- Ann Wimmer, Iowa Lakes Community College
- Benaiah YongoBure, Kettering University

Preface

Our goal in this book is to present modern economics in a form that is intuitive, relevant, and memorable to students who have had no prior exposure to the subject. We both teach introductory economics—Taylor at Stanford, Weerapana at Wellesley—and we enjoy teaching greatly. We especially enjoy interacting with students in the classroom as we endeavor to make the basic economic ideas as clear and understandable as possible. In this book we aim for that same clarity and teacher-student interaction, often imagining that we are talking with students or responding to their questions as we write.

This edition comes to you from a new publisher, FlatWorld. We hope that the partnership with FlatWorld will help us provide access to the text to a wide audience at a more reasonable price and with more flexible formats more suited to the needs of students and teachers. The FlatWorld platform will also allow us to update the book on a regular basis and help make it seem less dated with minimal disruption to us and to you, the users of the book.

THE NEW ECONOMICS FROM GENERATION TO GENERATION

We remember what it was like when we first took introductory economics—Taylor in the 1960s, Weerapana in the 1990s. People called 1960s-vintage economics the "new economics," because many new ideas, including those put forth by John Maynard Keynes, were being applied to public policy for the first time. By the 1990s there was a "new" new economics, stressing incentives, expectations, long-run fundamentals, institutions, and the importance of stable, predictable economic policies. In the 1980s and 1990s, the United States experienced far fewer recessions than in the 1960s and 1970s and the recessions were relatively short and mild.

But instability returned with the crisis and recession of 2007–2009—one of the longest and deepest in American history. The recession, and the long drawn-out recovery from the recession, caused a great deal of harm to millions of people. In the first decade of the twenty-first century, the global financial crisis, the great recessions in the United States and Europe, and explosive growth in emerging markets required a re-examination of whether the traditional frameworks needed to be augmented to explain this new reality, presenting new challenges and opportunities for instructors of introductory economics.

Economists engaged in a vigorous debate about what caused the crisis and how best to prevent future crises. After the recession ended, they grappled with whether the slow growth in the United States was in fact "the new normal." The concerns were not restricted to the United States, China's economy showed signs of slowing from the torrid pace it has sustained for much of the past two decades. The move towards closer economic integration in Europe suffered a devastating blow in 2016 from the Brexit vote, adding to the strains that had been placed on the Eurozone by the Greek debt crisis which neared the end of its 7th year with little relief in sight for the people of Greece, experiencing a downturn that resembled the Great Depression in terms of the depth and length of economic impact.

In this edition, we give these and other recent developments a prominent, clearly explained place within the basic tradition of economics. We emphasize the central idea of economics: that people make purposeful choices with scarce resources and interact with other people when they make these choices. We explain this idea using examples of choices that students actually face. We give real-world examples of how markets work, and we explain why markets are efficient when the incentives are right and inefficient when the incentives are wrong. We stress long-run fundamentals, but we also discuss current public policy issues relating to the crisis where the short run matters. The big policy questions about the role of government being debated by economists and others today receive special attention. We know from our teaching experience that examples of how economic ideas are used in practice make economics more interesting to students, thereby making learning economics easier.

A BRIEF TOUR

Recognizing that teachers use a wide variety of sequences and syllabi, *Principles of Economics* allows for alternative plans of coverage. Furthermore, the text is also available in two self-contained volumes, *Principles of Microeconomics* and *Principles of Macroeconomics.* The following is a description of the *Principles of Economics* volume.

The basic workings of markets and the reasons they improve people's lives are the subjects of the first seven chapters. Chapter 1 outlines the unifying themes of economics: scarcity, choice, and economic interaction. The role of prices, the inherent international aspect of economics, the importance of property rights and incentives, and the difference between central planning and markets are some of the key ideas in this chapter. Chapter 2 introduces the field of economics through a case study showing how economists observe and explain economic puzzles. Chapters 3 and 4 cover the basic supply and demand model and elasticity. Here, the goal is to show how to use the supply and demand model to make sense of the world—and to learn how to "think like an economist." A trio of chapters—5, 6, and 7—explains why competitive markets are efficient, perhaps the most important idea in economics. The parallel exposition of utility maximization (Chapter 5) and profit maximization (Chapter 6) culminates in a detailed description of why competitive markets are efficient (Chapter 7). The inclusion of interesting results from experimental economics plays a dual role: to illustrate how well models work, and to make the discussion of these important topics less abstract.

A modern market economy is not static; rather, it grows and changes over time as firms add new and better machines and as people add to their skills and training. Chapters 8 and 9 describe how firms and markets grow and change over time. Chapters 10 and 11 demonstrate how economists model the behavior of firms that are not perfectly competitive, such as monopolies. The models of dynamic behavior and imperfect competition developed here are used to explain the rise and fall of real-world firms and industries. Chapter 12 reviews the policy implications. Chapter 13 considers labor markets. Chapters 14 and 15 are devoted to the role of government in the economy. Tax policy, welfare reform, environmental policy, and the role of government in producing public goods are analyzed. Different countries have taken widely different approaches to the economy. The policy of some countries has been to intervene directly in virtually every economic decision; other countries have followed more hands-off policies. The problem of government failure is analyzed using models of government behavior. Chapter 16 discusses capital markets.

The study of macroeconomics begins with Chapter 17. This chapter gives an overview of the facts, emphasizing that macroeconomics is concerned with the growth and fluctuations in the economy as a whole. The overall structure of the book is to begin by introducing students to key macroeconomic variables, how they are measured and what their limitations are, then discuss economic growth, followed by economic fluctuations before moving on to discussing financial markets and economic interconnections between countries.

Chapter 18 shows how GDP and other variables are measured. Chapter 19 starts with the first macro model to determine the long run shares of GDP, illustrating how saving and investment are interrelated in the economy. Chapter 20 gives an analysis of how the level of unemployment in the economy as a whole is determined, concluding the discussion of key macroeconomic variables.

Labor, capital, and technology are then presented in Chapter 21 as the fundamental determinants of the economy's growth path. One clear advantage of this approach is that it allows students to focus first on issues about which there is general agreement among economists. Moreover, this ordering helps students better understand short-term economic fluctuations. Similarly, the long-run treatment of money, presented in Chapter 22, sets the stage for the discussion of economic fluctuations.

Chapters 23–25 focus on how the economy fluctuates even as it grows over time. Declines in production and increases in unemployment (characteristics of recessions) have not vanished from the landscape as long-term growth issues have come to the fore. These chapters delve into the causes of these fluctuations and propose an analysis of why they end. Chapters 26 and 27 take a deep dive into the world of macroeconomic policy, first fiscal policy and then monetary policy. These chapters discuss how policy can be used to minimize the impact of economic fluctuations but also point out some of the debates that economists engage in as they assess whether policy has been successful at achieving the overall goal of smoothing out fluctuations.

The last decade and a half have taught us that financial markets and global economic linkages are key elements of the world that today's students of economics will grow up to live in. Chapter 28 discusses economic growth, development and convergence around the world while Chapters 29 and 30 aim to equip students with a better understanding of how and why goods and money are traded among countries. When issues about which there are many differing opinions arise, the text tries to explain these opinions as clearly and as objectively as possible; it also stresses the areas of agreement.

We hope you enjoy learning economics from this textbook. We are always receptive to feedback and eager to hear from users of the text (instructors and students) about their experience and welcome feedback about how to present material in a way that is more instructive to the reader.

PEDAGOGICAL FEATURES

Examples within the text. Illustrations of real-world situations help explain economic ideas and models. We have attempted to include a wide variety of brief examples and case studies throughout the text.

Examples to give real-life perspectives. Stimulating vignettes appear at the beginning of each chapter. Examples of opening vignettes include explanation of economic events such as the price of Super Bowl tickets and discussions on how the United Nations evaluated the Millennium Development Goals it established at the dawn of the new millennium. Complete captions and small conversation boxes in graphs are also included. The captions and shaded conversation boxes make many of the figures completely self-contained. In some graphs, sequential numbering of these conversation boxes stresses the dynamic nature of the curves.

Use of photos to illustrate abstract ideas. Special care has gone into the search for and selection of photos to illustrate difficult economic ideas, such as inelastic supply curves or opportunity costs. Many text photos or photo spreads have short titles and captions to explain their relevance to the text discussion.

Key term definitions. Definitions of key terms appear in the margins next to where the key term is presented in the text and are listed in the index, complete with page references.

Brief reviews appear at the end of each major section. These reviews summarize the key points in abbreviated form as the chapter evolves; they are useful for preliminary skim reading as well as for review.

Questions for review appear at the end of every chapter. These are tests of recall and require only short answers; they can be used for oral review or as a quick self-check.

Problems. An essential tool in learning economics, the problems have been carefully selected, revised, and tested for this edition. An ample supply of these problems appears at the end of every chapter and appendix. Some of the problems ask the reader to work out examples that are slightly different from the ones given in the text; others require a more critical thinking approach.

WHAT'S NEW IN VERSION 8.0?

- Updated data and content bring coverage of economics through to the beginning of 2017, including developments in the Eurozone and difficulties faced by Greece, tax rate changes, and important antitrust decisions. Introductions to each chapter have been refreshed, and graphs have been updated with new data.
- Incorporates discussion of new monetary developments since 2011, including QE3, taper, raising of interest rates and the move to negative interest rates in some countries.
- Covers the debate about whether the Fed is unwinding its extraordinary policy measures at an appropriate pace as well as whether the fiscal policy measures implemented in the 2008/09 recession worked, based on academic studies.
- Discusses labor market developments, including the fall in unemployment rates, slow improvement in the employment to population ratio, and the falling labor force participation rate of men. Expands the discussion of productivity slowdown, including Robert Gordon's claim that economic headwinds will keep U.S. productivity growth low in the foreseeable future.

CHAPTER 1
The Central Idea

At the center of **economics** is the idea that people make *purposeful choices* with *scarce resources* and interact with others when they make these choices. Sometimes those choices that people make have substantial impacts on the global economy. Consider Mark Zuckerberg, the founder and CEO of Facebook. He faced a big choice when he was in college in 2004: that is, whether to finish his degree or to drop out and devote all his time to transform a novel idea into a start-up firm. Completing college while pursuing the start-up was not an option because time is scarce, only 24 hours in a day, and he did not have enough time to do both activities and sleep a bit, so he had to make a choice. In choosing one activity, he would have to incur the cost of giving up the other activity. Dropping out of college would mean passing up a degree that would help him get a good job but staying in college would mean he could not start up a new firm.

economics

The study of how people deal with scarcity.

Mark Zuckerberg, Founder and CEO of Facebook

Source: catwalker / Shutterstock.com

Zuckerberg chose to drop out of college, and it looks like he made the right choice: His firm, Facebook, is now worth billions of dollars and provides a social media platform that connects hundreds of millions of people all over the world. Or consider the story of Elon Musk, the founder and CEO of Tesla and SpaceX among other companies. Musk chose to stay in college and earned not one but two degrees—one in economics and one in physics—at the University of Pennsylvania, choosing to extend his time spent in college to five years. He joined the PhD program in Physics at Stanford University, but then decided to leave the program in a matter of days, choosing instead to join the entrepreneurial start-up culture of neighboring Silicon Valley. The resulting companies that Elon Musk founded have expanded the technological frontier of the economy over the past decade.

Of course, not every successful choice involves dropping out of college! In most cases the choice to stay in school and pursue an education is what pays off. Consider the story of Maryam Mirzakhani. She was a mathematical prodigy growing up in Iran, where she won two gold medals at the International Mathematical Olympiad. After completing her undergraduate education in Iran, Mirzakhani had to make a choice about whether to continue her mathematical studies and also about where to pursue those further studies. She chose to pursue her PhD at Harvard, became a professor at Stanford and in 2014 was the first woman to win the prestigious Fields Medal in Mathematics, considered by some to be an achievement harder than winning a Nobel Prize in an academic discipline.

The purposeful choices that these remarkable people made were magnified by the opportunities they had to interact with people. Hundreds of millions of people around the world interact through Facebook. Facebook benefits from this interaction, too, in part because people pay to advertise products on their site. Mirzakhani's discoveries have inspired other mathematicians and researchers in other areas like physics and engineering to make more discoveries. The electric cars produced by Tesla and the positive experiences of Tesla drivers has inspired many other manufacturers to pursue the use of electric motors in cars and to pursue other forms of technological advances such as driverless cars.

scarcity

The situation in which the quantity of resources is insufficient to meet all wants.

choice

A selection among alternative goods, services, or actions.

Scarcity is a situation in which people's resources are limited. People always face a scarcity of some sort. Scarcity implies that people must make a **choice** to forgo, or give up, one thing in favor of another. The successes of Mirzakhani, Musk and Zuckerberg also reflect purposeful choices that other individuals, organizations, firms and governments made with scarce resources. Harvard University had to decide who received admission to the select few openings in their PhD program, venture capitalists in Silicon Valley had to decide which of the many hundreds of entrepreneurs asking for their financial investments were the most worthy recipients, thousands of college students had to decide that they needed to take a study break on a regular basis to connect with their friends, the government of Iran had to decide how much funding to allocate to their universities to allow young talented students like Maryam Mirzakhani to achieve their full potential, and the government of the United States had to decide how many immigrants—like the South African-born Musk and the Iranian-born Mirzakhani—should be granted the opportunity to become American citizens and make contributions to the economy and the country. As you read this text, you may find yourself reflecting on decisions that you have to make—whether to major in economics or biology, whether to take all your classes after 10:00 A.M. or to schedule them all before noon, whether to search the Internet or to study.

economic interactions

Exchanges of goods and services between people.

market

An arrangement by which economic exchanges between people take place.

Economic interactions between people occur every time they trade or exchange goods with each other. A college student buys education services from a university in exchange for tuition. A teenager sells labor services to Taco Bell in exchange for cash. Within a household, one member may agree to cook dinner in exchange for the other person agreeing to wash the dishes. Economic interactions typically take place in a **market**. A market is simply an arrangement by which buyers and sellers can interact and exchange goods and services with each other. There are many types of markets, ranging from the New York stock market to a local flea market. Interactions do not have to take place with the buyer and seller in physical proximity to each other; the Internet, for example, greatly enhances the opportunities for economic interaction.

The purpose of this book is to introduce you to the field of economics, to provide you with the knowledge that will help you understand how so much of what happens in the world is shaped by the actions of people who had to make choices when confronted by scarcity. A better understanding of economics will equip you to handle the opportunities and challenges you face—should you continue with schooling if the economy is weak and it is hard to find a job? It also will leave you better informed about the challenges that the nation faces—should the government intervene in the economy to regulate businesses, or should it provide economic stimulus packages to help the economy? Soon you will find yourself viewing the world through the lens of economics. Your friends may tell you that you are "thinking like an economist." You should take that as a compliment. The first step on this path is to understand the enormous power of the central ideas of scarcity, choice, and economic interactions. That's the purpose of this chapter.

1. SCARCITY AND CHOICE FOR INDIVIDUALS

It is easy to find everyday examples of how people make purposeful choices when they are confronted with a scarcity of time or resources. A choice that may be on your mind when you study economics is how much time to spend on these studies versus other activities. If you spend all your time on economics, you may get a 100 percent on the final exam, but a 0 percent in biology. If you spend all your time on biology, then you may get a 100 percent in biology and a 0 percent in economics. Most people resolve the choice by balancing out their time to get a decent grade in both subjects. If you are premed, then you probably will devote more time to biology. If you are interested in business, then devoting more time to economics might be appropriate.

Now let us apply this basic principle to two fundamental economic problems: individual choices about what to *consume* and what to *produce.* For each type of economic problem, we first show how scarcity forces one to make a choice, and then we show how people gain from interacting with other people.

1.1 Consumer Decisions

Consider Maria, who is going for a walk in a park on a sunny day. Maria would love to wear a hat (baseball style with her school logo) and sunglasses on the walk, but she forgot them at home. Maria has brought $20 with her, however, and there is a store in the park that is having a "two-for-one" sale. She can buy two hats for $20 or two pairs of sunglasses for $20. She would prefer to buy one hat and one pair of sunglasses, but that is not possible. Her scarcity of funds causes her to make a choice. The $20 limit on her spending is an example of a *budget constraint,* a scarcity of funds that limits her to spending no more than this amount. Her choice will depend on her tastes. Let us assume that when she is forced by scarcity to make a choice, she will choose the sunglasses.

Opportunity Cost

Maria's decision is an example of an economic problem that all people face: A budget constraint forces them to make a choice between different items that they want. Choosing one item means that you have to give up other items. The opportunity cost of a choice is the value of the next-best forgone alternative that was not chosen. The **opportunity cost** of the hats is the loss from not being able to wear the sunglasses. An opportunity cost occurs every time there is a choice. For example, the opportunity cost of waking up to attend an 8:00 A.M. class rather than sleeping in is the hours of sleep you lose when you get up early. The opportunity cost of Mark Zuckerberg's staying in college versus pursuing his start-up would have been the money he earned from Facebook. In many cases involving choice and scarcity, you have to choose from among many more than two options. If you choose vanilla ice cream out of a list of many possible flavors, then the opportunity cost is the loss from not being able to consume the *next-best* flavor, perhaps strawberry.

opportunity cost

The value of the next-best forgone alternative that was not chosen because something else was chosen.

Now, suppose Maria is not the only hiker. Also in the park is Adam, who also has $20 to spend. Adam also loves both hats and sunglasses, but he likes hats more than sunglasses. When forced to make a choice, he buys the hats. His decision is shaped by scarcity just as Maria's is: Scarcity comes from the budget constraint. He must make a choice, and each choice has an opportunity cost.

Gains from Trade: A Better Allocation

gains from trade

Improvements in income, production, or satisfaction owing to the exchange of goods or services.

Now suppose that Adam and Maria meet each other in the park. Let's consider the possibility of economic interaction between them. Maria has two pairs of sunglasses and Adam has two hats, so Maria and Adam can trade with each other. Maria can trade one of her pairs of sunglasses for one of Adam's hats, as shown in Figure 1.1. Through such a trade, both Maria and Adam can improve their situation. There are **gains from trade** because the trade reallocates goods between the two individuals in a way that they both prefer. Trade occurs because Maria is willing to exchange one pair of sunglasses for one hat, and Adam is willing to exchange one hat for one pair of sunglasses. Because trade is mutually advantageous for both Maria and Adam, they will voluntarily engage in it if they are able to. In fact, if they do not gain from the trade, then neither will bother to make the trade.

This trade is an example of an economic interaction in which a reallocation of goods through trade makes both people better off. The total quantity of goods produced does not change. The number of hats and sunglasses has remained the same. Trade simply reallocates existing goods.

The trade between Maria and Adam is typical of many economic interactions that we will study in this book. Thinking like an economist in this example means recognizing that a voluntary exchange of goods between people must make them better off. Many economic exchanges are like this, even though they are more complicated than the exchange of hats and sunglasses.

FIGURE 1.1 Gains from Trade through a Better Allocation of Goods

Without trade, Maria has more pairs of sunglasses than she would like, and Adam has more hats than he would like. By trading a hat for a pair of sunglasses, they both gain.

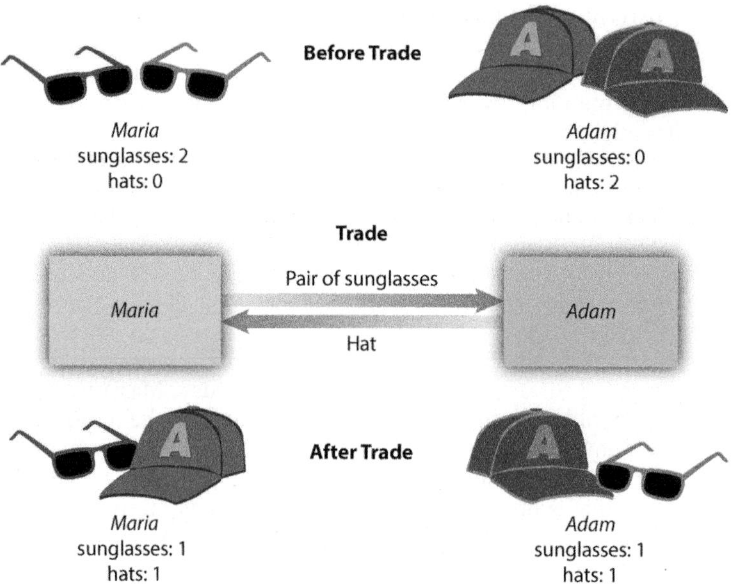

1.2 Producer Decisions

Now consider two producers—Emily, a poet, and Johann, a printer. Both face scarcity and must make choices. Because of differences in training, abilities, or inclination, Emily is much better at writing poetry than Johann is, but Johann is much better at printing greeting cards than Emily is.

If Emily writes poetry full time, she can produce 10 poems in a day; but if she wants to make and sell greeting cards with her poems in them, she must spend some time printing cards and thereby spend less time writing poems. However, Emily is not very good at printing cards; it takes her so much time to do so that if she prints one card, she has time to write only one poem rather than 10 poems during the day.

If Johann prints full time, he can produce 10 different greeting cards in a day. However, if he wants to sell greeting cards, he must write poems to put inside them. Johann is so poor at writing poems that if he writes only one poem a day, his production of greeting cards drops from 10 to one per day.

The following is a summary of the choices Emily and Johann face because of a scarcity of time and resources.

	Emily, the Poet		Johann, the Printer	
	Write Full Time	*Write and Print*	*Print Full Time*	*Write and Print*
Cards	0	1	10	1
Poems	10	1	0	1

If Emily and Johann cannot interact, then each can produce only one greeting card with a poem on the inside in a day. Alternatively, Emily could produce 10 poems without the cards and Johann could produce 10 cards without the poems, but then neither would earn anything. We therefore assume that when confronted with this choice, both Emily and Johann will each choose to produce one greeting card with a poem inside. In total, they produce two greeting cards.

Gains from Trade: Greater Production

Now consider the possibility of economic interaction. Suppose that Emily and Johann can trade. Johann could sell his printing services to Emily, agreeing to print her poems on nice greeting cards. Then Emily could sell the greeting cards to people. Under this arrangement, Emily could spend all day writing poetry, and Johann could spend all day printing. In total, they could produce 10 different greeting cards together, expending the same time and effort it took to produce two greeting cards when they could not trade.

Note that in this example the interaction took place in a market: Johann sold his print jobs to Emily. Another approach would be for Emily and Johann to go into business together, forming a firm, Dickinson and Gutenberg Greetings, Inc. Then their economic interaction would occur within the firm, without buying or selling in the market. Whether in a market or within a firm, the gains from trade in this example are huge. By trading, Emily and Johann can increase their production of greeting cards five fold, from two cards to 10 cards.

Specialization, Division of Labor, and Comparative Advantage

This example illustrates another way in which economic interaction improves people's lives. Economic interaction allows for **specialization**: people concentrating their production efforts on what they are good at. Emily specializes in poetry, and Johann specializes in printing. The specialization creates a **division of labor**. A division of labor occurs when some workers specialize in one task while others specialize in another task. They divide the overall production into parts, with some workers concentrating on one part (printing cards) and other workers concentrating on another part (writing poetry).

The writing-printing example of Emily and Johann also illustrates another economic concept, comparative advantage. In general, a person or group of people has a **comparative advantage** in producing one good relative to another good if that person or group can produce that good with comparatively less time, effort, or resources than another person or group can produce that good. For example, compared with Johann, Emily has a comparative advantage in writing relative to printing. And compared with Emily, Johann has a comparative advantage in printing relative to writing. As this example shows, production can be increased if people specialize in the skill in which they have a comparative advantage—that is, if Emily specializes in writing and Johann in printing.

specialization

A concentration of production effort on a single specific task.

division of labor

The division of production into various parts in which different groups of workers specialize.

comparative advantage

A situation in which a person or group can produce one good at a lower opportunity cost than another person or group.

1.3 International Trade

Thus far, we have said nothing about where Emily and Johann live or work. They could reside in the same country, but they also could reside in different countries. Emily could live in the United States; Johann, in Germany. If this is so, when Emily purchases Johann's printing service, **international trade** will take place because the trade is between people in two different countries.

The gains from international trade are thus of the same kind as the gains from trade within a country. By trading, people can better satisfy their preferences for goods (as in the case of Maria and Adam), or they can better utilize their comparative advantage (as in the case of Emily and Johann). In either situation, both participants can gain from trade.

international trade

The exchange of goods and services between people or firms in different nations.

REVIEW

- All individuals face scarcity in one form or another. Scarcity forces people to make choices. For every choice that is made, there is also an opportunity cost of not doing one thing because another thing has been chosen.
- People benefit from economic interactions—trading goods and services—with other people.
- Gains from trade occur because goods and services can be allocated in ways that are more satisfactory to people.
- Gains from trade also occur because trade permits specialization through the division of labor. People should specialize in the production of goods in which they have a comparative advantage.

2. SCARCITY AND CHOICE FOR THE ECONOMY AS A WHOLE

Just as individuals face scarcity and choice, so too does the economy as a whole. The total amount of resources in an economy—workers, land, machinery, and factories—is limited. Thus, the economy cannot produce all the health care, crime prevention, education, or entertainment that people want. A choice must be made. Let us first consider how to represent scarcity and choice in the whole economy and then consider alternative ways to make those choices.

2.1 Production Possibilities

To simplify things, let us suppose that production in the economy can be divided into two broad categories. Suppose the economy can produce either computers (laptops, desktops, servers) or movies (thrillers, love stories, mysteries, musicals). The choice between computers and movies is symbolic of one of the most fundamental choices individuals in any society must face: how much to invest to produce more or better goods in the future versus how much to consume in the present. Computers help people produce more or better goods. Movies are a form of consumption. Other pairs of goods also could be used in our example. Another popular example is guns versus butter, representing defense goods versus nondefense goods.

production possibilities

Alternative combinations of production of various goods that are possible, given the economy's resources.

With a scarcity of resources, such as labor and capital, a choice exists between producing some goods, such as computers, versus other goods, such as movies. If the economy produces more of one, then it must produce less of the other. Table 1.1 gives an example of the alternative choices, or the **production possibilities**, for computers and movies. Observe that six different choices could be made, some with more computers and fewer movies, others with fewer computers and more movies.

Table 1.1 tells us what happens as available resources in the economy are moved from movie production to computer production or vice versa. If resources move from producing movies to producing computers, then fewer movies are produced. For example, if all of the resources are used to produce computers, then 25,000 computers and zero movies can be produced, according to the table. If all resources are used to produce movies, then no computers can be produced. These are two extremes, of course. If 100 movies are produced, then we can produce 24,000 computers rather than 25,000 computers. If 200 movies are produced, then computer production must fall to 22,000.

2.2 Increasing Opportunity Costs

The production possibilities in Table 1.1 illustrate the concept of opportunity cost for the economy as a whole. The opportunity cost of producing more movies is the value of the forgone computers. For example, the opportunity cost of producing 200 movies rather than 100 movies is 2,000 computers.

increasing opportunity costs

A situation in which producing more of one good requires giving up an increasing amount of production of another good.

An important economic idea about opportunity costs is demonstrated in Table 1.1. Observe that movie production increases as we move down the table. As we move from row to row, movie production increases by the same number: 100 movies. The decline in computer production between the first and second rows—from 25,000 to 24,000 computers—is 1,000 computers. The decline between the second and third rows—from 24,000 to 22,000 computers—is 2,000 computers. Thus, the decline in computer production gets greater as we produce more movies. As we move from 400 movies to 500 movies, we lose 13,000 computers. In other words, the opportunity cost, in terms of computers, of producing more movies increases as we produce more movies. Each extra movie requires a loss of more and more computers. What we have just described is called **increasing opportunity costs**, with an emphasis on the word *increasing*.

Why do opportunity costs increase? You can think about it in the following way. Some of the available resources are better suited for movie production than for computer production, and vice versa. Workers who are good at building computers might not be so good at acting, for example, or moviemaking may require an area with a dry, sunny climate. As more and more resources go into making movies, we are forced to take resources that are much better at computer making and use them for movie making. Thus, more and more computer production must be lost to increase movie production by a given amount. Adding specialized computer designers to a movie cast would be quite costly in terms of lost computers, and it might add little to movie production.

TABLE 1.1 Production Possibilities

	Movies	Computers
A	0	25,000
B	100	24,000
C	200	22,000
D	300	18,000
E	400	13,000
F	500	0

2.3 The Production Possibilities Curve

Figure 1.2 is a graphical representation of the production possibilities in Table 1.1 that nicely illustrates increasing opportunity costs. We put movies on the horizontal axis and computers on the vertical axis of the figure. Each pair of numbers in a row of the table becomes a point on the graph. For example, point *A* on the graph is from row A of the table. Point *B* is from row B, and so on.

When we connect the points in Figure 1.2, we obtain the **production possibilities curve**. This curve shows the maximum number of computers that can be produced for each quantity of movies produced. Note that the curve in Figure 1.2 slopes downward and is bowed out from the origin. That the curve is bowed out indicates that the opportunity cost of producing movies increases as more movies are produced. As resources move from computer making to movie making, each additional movie means a greater loss of computer production.

production possibilities curve

A curve showing the maximum combinations of production of two goods that are possible, given the economy's resources.

FIGURE 1.2 The Production Possibilities Curve

Each point on the curve shows the maximum number of computers that can be produced when a given amount of movies is produced. The points with letters are the same as those in Table 1.1 and are connected by smooth lines. Points in the shaded area inside the curve are inefficient. Points outside the curve are impossible. For the efficient points on the curve, the more movies that are produced, the fewer computers that are produced. The curve is bowed out because of increasing opportunity costs.

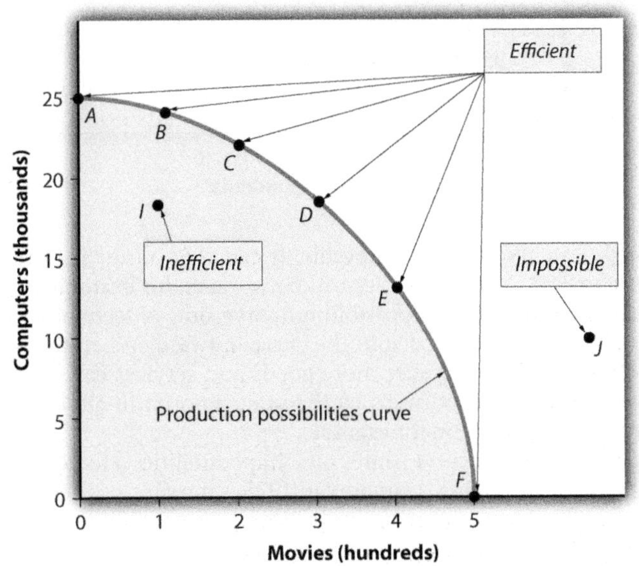

Inefficient, Efficient, or Impossible?

The production possibilities curve shows the effects of scarcity and choice in the economy as a whole. Three situations can be distinguished in Figure 1.2, depending on whether production is in the shaded area, on the curve, or outside the curve.

First, imagine production at point *I*. This point, with 100 movies and 18,000 computers, is inside the curve. But the production possibilities curve tells us that it is possible to produce more computers, more movies, or both with the same amount of resources. For some reason, the economy is not working well at point *I*. For example, a talented movie director may be working on a computer assembly line because her short film has not yet been seen by studio executives, or perhaps a financial crisis has prevented computer companies from getting loans and thus disrupted all production of computer chips. Points inside the curve, like point *I*, are *inefficient* because the economy could produce a larger number of movies, as at point *D*, or a larger number of computers, as at point *B*. Points inside the production possibilities curve are possible, but they are inefficient.

Second, consider points on the production possibilities curve. These points are *efficient*. They represent the maximum amount that can be produced with available resources. The only way to raise production of one good is to lower production of the other good. Thus, points on the curve show a *trade-off* between one good and another.

Third, consider points to the right and above the production possibilities curve, like point *J* in Figure 1.2. These points are *impossible*. The economy does not have the resources to produce those quantities.

Shifts in the Production Possibilities Curve

FIGURE 1.3 Shifts in the Production Possibilities Curve

The production possibilities curve shifts out as the economy grows. The maximum numbers of movies and computers that can be produced increase. Improvements in technology, more machines, or more labor permits the economy to produce more.

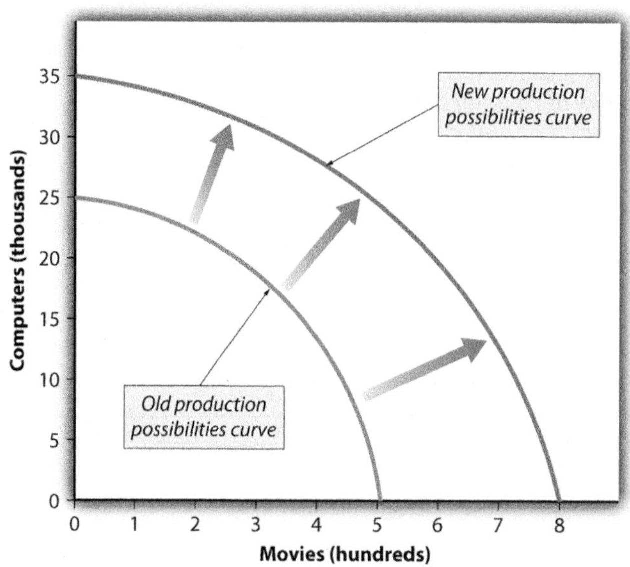

The production possibilities curve is not immovable. It can *shift* out or in. For example, the curve is shown to shift out in Figure 1.3. More resources—more workers, for example, or more cameras, lights, and studios—would shift the production possibilities curve out. A technological innovation that allowed one to edit movies faster also would shift the curve outward. When the production possibilities curve shifts out, the economy grows because more goods and services can be produced. The production possibilities curve need not shift outward by the same amount in all directions. The curve could move up more than it moves to the right, for example.

As the production possibilities curve shifts out, impossibilities are converted into possibilities. Some of what was impossible for the U.S. economy in 1975 is possible now. Some of what is impossible now will be possible in 2035. Hence, the economists' notion of possibilities is a temporary one. When we say that a certain combination of computers and movies is impossible, we do not mean "forever impossible," we mean only "currently impossible."

Scarcity, Choice, and Economic Progress

However, the conversion of impossibilities into possibilities is also an economic problem of choice and scarcity: If we invest less now—in machines, in education, in children, in technology—and consume more now, then we will have less available in the future. If we take computers and movies as symbolic of investment and consumption, then choosing more investment will result in a larger outward shift of the production possibilities curve, as illustrated in Figure 1.4. More investment enables the economy to produce more in the future.

The production possibilities curve represents a *trade-off*, but it does not mean that some people win only if others lose. First, it is not necessary for someone to lose in order for the production possibilities curve to shift out. When the curve shifts out, the production of both items increases. Although some people may fare better than others as the production possibilities curve is pushed out, no one necessarily loses. In principle, everyone can gain. Second, if the economy is at an inefficient point (like point *I* in Figure 1.2), then production of both goods can be increased with no trade-off. In general, therefore, the economy is more like a win-win situation, where everyone can achieve a gain.

FIGURE 1.4 Shifts in the Production Possibilities Curve Depend on Choices

On the left, few resources are devoted to investment for the future; hence, the production possibilities curve shifts only a little over time. On the right, more resources are devoted to investment and less to consumption; hence, the production possibilities curve shifts out by a larger amount over time.

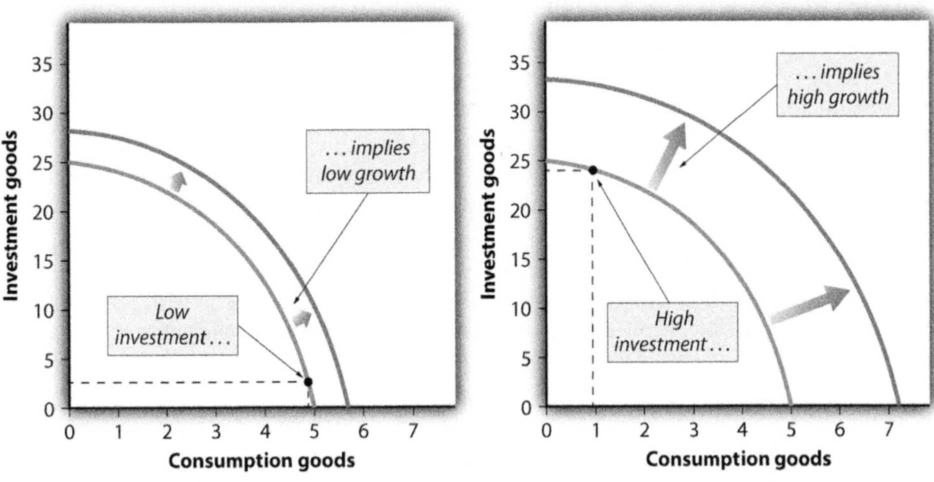

REVIEW

- The production possibilities curve represents the choices open to a whole economy when it is confronted with a scarcity of resources. As more of one item is produced, less of another item must be produced. The opportunity cost of producing more of one item is the reduced production of another item.
- The production possibilities curve is bowed out because of increasing opportunity costs.
- Points inside the curve are inefficient. Points on the curve are efficient. Points outside the curve are impossible.
- The production possibilities curve shifts out as resources increase.
- Outward shifts of the production possibilities curve or moves from inefficient to efficient points are the reasons why the economy is not a zero-sum game, despite the existence of scarcity and choice.

3. MARKET ECONOMIES AND THE PRICE SYSTEM

Any economic system has to answer three questions: What goods and services should be produced—cars, movies, or something else? How should these goods or services be produced—in what type of factory, and with how much equipment and labor? And for whom should these goods be produced?

For whom?

The Three Fundamental Economic Questions

Sources: MikeDotta / Shutterstock.com

Every economy, whether it is a small island economy or a large economy like the United States, must find a way to solve three essential questions or problems.

- *What* is to be produced: movies, computers, guns, butter, greeting cards, Rollerblades, health care, or something else? In other words, where on the production possibilities curve should an economy be?
- *How* are these goods to be produced? In other words, how can an economy use the available resources so that it is not at an inefficient point inside the production possibilities curve?
- *For whom* are the goods to be produced? We know from the hat versus sunglasses example that the allocation of goods in an economy affects people's well-being. An economy in which Maria could not trade her sunglasses for a hat would not work as well as one in which such trades and reallocations are possible. Moreover, an economy in which some people get everything and others get virtually nothing also is not working well.

market economy

An economy characterized by freely determined prices and the free exchange of goods and services in markets.

command economy

An economy in which the government determines prices and production also called a centrally planned economy.

Broadly speaking, the **market economy** and the **command economy** are two alternative approaches to answering these questions. In a market economy, most decisions about what, how, and for whom to produce are made by individual consumers, firms, governments, and other organizations interacting in markets. In a command, or centrally planned, economy, most decisions about what, how, and for whom to produce are made by those who control the government, which, through a central plan, commands and controls what people do.

Command economies are much less common in the twenty-first century than they were in the mid-twentieth century, when nearly half the world's population, including the residents of Eastern Europe, the Soviet Union, and China, lived in centrally planned economies. After many decades of struggling to make this system work, leaders of the command economies gradually grew disillusioned with the high degree of inefficiency resulting from the planned approach, which required that the state, or central planners, make critical detailed production decisions; this often resulted in shortages or surplus of products and, as a by-product, in political unrest. Since 1990, most command economies have, with varying degrees of success, tried to convert from a command to a market system. The difficulties with converting these systems are partly due to the fact that these economies have none or few of the social, legal, or political fixtures critical to the market system. China has been by far the most successful of these economies at making the transition, developing a model that the Chinese term "socialism with Chinese characteristics." Beginning in the 1970s, elements of both the command and market economies coexisted in China; in the mid-1990s, market mechanisms grew more dominant. In the twenty-first century, while its political system is still highly centralized, China's economy is much more decentralized. Many people credit China's rapid economic growth in recent years to its successful transition away from a centralized economic system.

3.1 Key Elements of a Market Economy

Let's take a closer look at some of the ingredients critical to a market economy.

Freely Determined Prices

In a market economy, most prices—such as the price of computers—are freely determined by individuals and firms interacting in markets. These **freely determined prices** are an essential characteristic of a market economy. In a command economy, most prices are set by government, and this leads to inefficiencies in the economy. For example, in the former Soviet Union, the price of bread was set so low that farmers fed bread to the cows. Feeding bread to livestock is an enormous waste of resources. Livestock could eat plain grain. By feeding the cows bread, farmers added the cost of the labor to bake the bread and the fuel to heat the bread ovens to the cost of livestock feed. This is inefficient, like point *I* in Figure 1.2.

In practice, not all prices in market economies are freely determined. For example, some cities control the price of rental apartments. We will look at these exceptions later. But the vast majority of prices are free to vary.

freely determined prices

Prices that are determined by the individuals and firms interacting in markets.

Property Rights and Incentives

Property rights are another key element of a market economy. **Property rights** give individuals the legal authority to keep or sell property, whether land or other resources. Property rights are needed for a market economy because they give people the ability to buy and sell goods. Without property rights, people could take whatever they wanted without paying. People would have to devote time and resources to protecting their earnings or goods.

Moreover, by giving people the rights to the earnings from their work, as well as letting them suffer some of the consequences or losses from their mistakes, property rights provide an **incentive**. For example, if an inventor could not get the property rights to an invention, then the incentive to produce the invention would be low or even nonexistent. Hence, there would be few inventions, and we all would be worse off. If property rights did not exist, people would not have incentives to specialize and reap the gains from the division of labor. Any extra earnings from specialization could be taken away.

property rights

Rights over the use, sale, and proceeds from a good or resource.

incentive

A device that motivates people to take action, usually to increase economic efficiency.

Freedom to Trade at Home and Abroad

Economic interaction is a way to improve economic outcomes, as the examples in this chapter indicate. Allowing people to interact freely is thus another necessary ingredient of a market economy. Freedom to trade can be extended beyond national borders to other economies.

International trade increases the opportunities to gain from trade. This is especially important in small countries, where it is impossible to produce everything. But the gains from exchange and comparative advantage also exist for larger countries.

A Role For Government

Just because prices are freely determined and people are free to trade in a market economy does not mean that there is no role for government. For example, in virtually all market economies, the government provides defense and police protection. The government also helps establish property rights. But how far beyond that should it go? Should the government also address the "for whom" question by providing a safety net—a mechanism to deal with the individuals in the economy who are poor, who go bankrupt, who remain unemployed? Most would say yes, but what should the government's role be? Economics provides an analytical framework to answer such questions. In certain circumstances—called **market failure**—the market economy does not provide good enough answers to the "what, how, and for whom" questions, and the government has a role to play in improving on the market. However, the government, even in the case of market failure, may do worse than the market, in which case economists say there is **government failure**.

market failure

Any situation in which the market does not lead to an efficient economic outcome and in which the government has a potential role.

government failure

A situation in which the government fails to improve on the market or even makes things worse.

The Role of Private Organizations

It is an interesting feature of market economies that many economic interactions between people take place in organizations—firms, families, charitable organizations—rather than in markets. Some economic interactions that take place in an organization also take place in a market. For example, many large firms employ lawyers as part of their permanent staff. Other firms simply purchase the services of such lawyers in the market; if the firm wants to sue someone or is being sued by someone, it hires an outside lawyer to represent it.

Economic interactions in firms differ from those in the market. Staff lawyers inside large firms are usually paid annual salaries that do not depend directly on the number of hours worked or their success in the lawsuits. In contrast, outside lawyers are paid an hourly fee and a contingency fee based on the number of hours worked and how successful they are.

Incentives within an organization are as important as incentives in markets. If the lawyers on a firm's legal staff get to keep some of the damages the firm wins in a lawsuit, they will have more incentive to do a good job. Some firms even try to create market-like competition between departments or workers in order to give more incentives.

Why do some economic interactions occur in markets and others in organizations? Ronald Coase of the University of Chicago won the Nobel Prize for showing that organizations such as firms are created to reduce market *transaction costs*, the costs of buying and selling, which include finding a buyer or a seller and reaching agreement on a price. When market transaction costs are high, we see more transactions taking place within organizations. For example, a firm might have a legal staff rather than outside lawyers because searching for a good lawyer every time there is a lawsuit is too costly. In a crisis, a good lawyer may not be available.

3.2 The Price System

The previous discussion indicates that in market economies, freely determined prices are essential for determining what is produced, how, and for whom. For this reason, a market economy is said to use *the price system* to solve these problems. In this section, we show that prices do a surprising amount of work: (1) Prices serve as *signals* about what should be produced and consumed when there are changes in tastes or changes in technology, (2) prices provide *incentives* to people to alter their production or consumption, and (3) prices affect the *distribution of income*, or who gets what in the economy.

Let's use an example. Suppose that there is a sudden new trend for college students to ride bicycles more and drive cars less. How do prices help people in the economy decide what to do in response to this new trend?

Signals

First, consider how the information about the change in tastes is signaled to the producers of bicycles and cars. As students buy more bicycles, the price of bicycles rises. A higher price will signal that it is more profitable for firms to produce more bicycles. In addition, some bicycle components, like lightweight metal, will also increase in price. Increased lightweight metal prices signal that production of lightweight metal should increase. As the price of metal rises, wages for metalworkers may increase. Thus, prices are a signal all the way from the consumer to the metalworkers that more bicycles should be produced. This is what is meant by the expression "prices are a signal."

It is important to note that no single individual knows the information that is transmitted by prices. Any economy is characterized by limited information, where people cannot know the exact reasons why prices for certain goods rise or fall. Hence, it is rather amazing that prices can signal this information.

Incentives

Now let's use this example to consider how prices provide incentives. A higher price for bicycles will increase the incentives for firms to produce bicycles. Because they receive more for each bicycle, they produce more. If there is a large price increase that is not merely temporary, new firms may enter the bicycle business. In contrast, the reduced prices for cars signal to car producers that production should decrease.

Distribution

How do prices affect the distribution of income? On the one hand, workers who find the production of the good they make increasing because of the higher demand for bicycles will earn more. On the other hand, income will be reduced for those who make cars or who have to pay more for bicycles. Local delivery services that use bicycles will see their costs increase.

3.3 Financial Crises and Recessions

Economies are sometimes hit by **financial crises**. When the World Trade Center was destroyed by terrorists in September 2001, the financial markets in New York had to close down because trading rooms and electronic networks for making trades were destroyed. However, backup facilities were soon made operational and the markets reopened after only a few days. Fortunately, the financial crisis was over soon after it began.

financial crises

Disruptions to financial markets which make it difficult for people and business firms to borrow and obtain loans.

In August 2007 another financial crisis began, but this one lasted much longer and its causes are more difficult to determine. Most likely a fall in home prices in 2006 and 2007 following a prior rapid rise caused people to stop making payments on their home loans; banks and other financial institutions then became reluctant to lend. As a result people throughout the economy had trouble getting loans, and they reduced their purchases of goods and services. This meant that firms had to cut production of these goods and services and they laid off people who were employed producing them. A **recession**—a period of declining production and employment—thus began in December 2007 and ended in June 2009.

recession

A decline in production and employment that lasts for six months or more.

Economies have been subject to financial crises and recessions for hundreds of years. By far the worst in the United States was the Great Depression of the 1930s, but comparably serious financial crises have occurred in other regions and countries, most recently in Latin America, Asia, and Russia in the 1990s. The 1980s and 1990s in the United States was a period of unusual financial calm with few recessions. There is a great debate about whether financial crises are inevitable—a kind of market failure where the market economy does not work well—and government has a role to play in trying to prevent them and mitigate them, or whether the crises are due to government actions which make things worse—a kind of government failure.

REVIEW

- The market economy and the command economy are two alternative systems for addressing the questions any economy must face: what to produce, how to produce, and for whom to produce.
- A market economy is characterized by several key elements, such as freely determined prices, property rights, and freedom to trade at home and abroad.
- For a market economy to work well, markets should be competitive and the government should play a role when there is a market failure.
- Prices are signals, they provide incentives, and they affect the distribution of income.
- Market economies are sometimes hit by financial crises and recessions, creating another role for government in preventing or alleviating them.

4. END-OF-CHAPTER MATERIAL

4.1 Conclusion

One basic idea lies at the center of economics: People make purposeful choices with scarce resources, and interact with other people when they make these choices.

This introductory chapter illustrates this idea, starting with decisions by Elon Musk and Mark Zuckerberg about whether to leave school and continuing with simple examples of people making choices about what to consume or produce.

From this central idea, many other powerful ideas follow, as summarized visually in Figure 1.5. An *opportunity cost* exists every time a choice is made. People *gain from trade*, both through a *better allocation* of goods and through *comparative advantage*. Every society faces trade-offs described by *production possibilities curves*. Every society faces three fundamental questions: *what*, *how*, and *for whom* to produce. Market economies—characterized by *freely determined prices, property rights, freedom to trade*, and a *role for both government and private organizations*—provide answers to these three questions. The price system helps a market economy work by providing *incentives*, sending *signals*, and affecting the *distribution* of income.

You will see this central idea again and again as you continue to study economics.

FIGURE 1.5 From One Central Idea, Many Powerful Ideas Follow

As you study economics, you will see the same central idea again and again. This figure illustrates how many powerful economic ideas are connected to the one in the center.

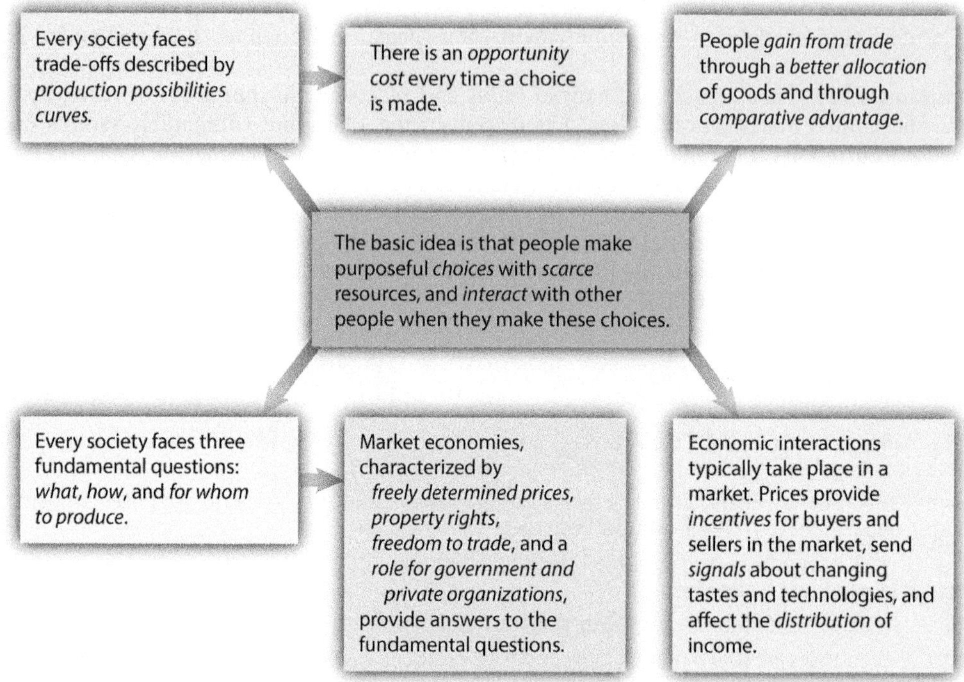

Key Points

1. Everyone faces a scarcity of something, usually time or resources.
2. Scarcity leads to choice, and choice leads to opportunity costs.
3. Trade leads to gains because it allows goods and services to be reallocated in a way that improves people's well-being.
4. Trade also leads to gains because it permits people to specialize in what they are relatively good at.
5. The production possibilities curve summarizes the trade-offs in the whole economy because of scarcity.
6. Economic production is efficient if the economy is on the production possibilities curve. Production is inefficient if the economy is inside the production possibilities curve.
7. Points outside the production possibilities curve currently are impossible. More investment, more workers, or better technology can shift the production possibilities curve out and make the impossible possible.
8. The three basic questions that any economy must face are what, how, and for whom production should take place.
9. A well-functioning market system, involving freely determined prices, property rights, freedom to trade, and a role for government and private organizations, can answer these basic questions.
10. Prices transmit signals, provide incentives, and affect the distribution of income in a market economy. If prices are set at incorrect levels by government, waste and inefficiency—such as feeding bread to livestock—will result.

QUESTIONS FOR REVIEW

1. What is the basic idea at the center of economics?
2. Why does scarcity imply a choice among alternatives?
3. What is the opportunity cost of making a choice?
4. How can gains be achieved from trade even when total production of goods and services does not change?
5. How can specialization lead to gains from trade?
6. What is the principle of increasing opportunity costs?
7. Why is the production of a combination of goods that is located inside the production possibilities curve considered to be inefficient?
8. How can financial crises cause inefficiencies?
9. What are the key ingredients of a market economy?
10. What are the three basic questions that any economic system must address?
11. What roles do prices play in a market economy?

PROBLEMS

1. Suppose that you are president of the student government, and you have to decide how to allocate a $20,000 fund for guest speakers for the year. Conan O'Brien and Will Ferrell each cost $10,000 per appearance, Stephen Colbert costs $20,000 per appearance, and former economic advisers to the government charge $1,000 per lecture. Explain the economic problem of choice and scarcity in this case. What issues would you consider in arriving at a decision?
2. Michelle Wie, a teenage golf prodigy who earned $16 million in endorsements and $4 million in prize money and appearance fees in 2006, announced that she would enroll as a student at Stanford University in the fall of 2007. What was her opportunity cost of a year of college? How does it compare to your opportunity cost of a year of college?
3. Allison will graduate from high school next June. She has ranked her three possible post-graduation plans in the following order: (1) work for two years at a consulting job in her hometown paying $20,000 per year, (2) attend a local community college for two years, spending $5,000 per year on tuition and expenses, and (3) travel around the world tutoring a rock star's child for pay of $5,000 per year. What is the opportunity cost of her choice?
4. Suppose you have two boxes of chocolate chip cookies and a friend of yours has 2 gallons of milk. Explain how you can both gain from trade. Is this a gain from trade through *better allocation* or *greater production*?
5. Suppose Tina and Julia can produce brownies and romantic poems (which can be combined to make a lovely gift) in the following combinations in a given week:

Tina		Julia	
Brownies	*Poems*	*Brownies*	*Poems*
50	0	25	0
40	1	20	1
30	2	15	2
20	3	10	3
0	4	5	4
0	5	0	5

   a. If Tina and Julia are each currently producing two poems per week, how many brownies are they producing? What is the total production of brownies and poems between them?
   b. Is there a possibility for increasing production? Why or why not?
   c. Suppose Julia completely specializes in producing poems and Tina completely specializes in producing brownies. What will be their total production of brownies and poems?

6. Suppose you must divide your time between studying for your math final and writing a final paper for your English class. The fraction of time that you spend studying math and its relation to your grade in the two classes given in the table below.

Fraction of Time Spent on Math	Math Grade	English Grade
0	0	97
20	45	92
40	65	85
60	75	70
80	82	50
100	88	0

   a. Draw a trade-off curve for the math grade versus the English grade.
   b. What is the opportunity cost of increasing the time spent on math from 80 to 100 percent? What is the opportunity cost of increasing the time spent on math from 60 to 80 percent?
   c. Are there increasing opportunity costs from spending more time on math? Explain.
   d. Suppose your parents want you to get a 92 percent in both subjects. What would you tell them?

7. A small country produces only two goods, cars and cakes. Given its limited resources, this country has the following production possibilities:

Cars	Cakes
0	200
25	180
50	130
75	70
100	0

   a. Draw the production possibilities curve.
   b. Suppose car production uses mainly machines and cake production uses mainly labor. Show what happens to the curve when the number of machines increases, but the amount of labor remains unchanged.

8. Tracy tells Huey that he can improve his economics grade without sacrificing fun activities or his grades in other courses. Can you imagine ways in which this might be possible? What does that imply about the initial situation? If Huey is taking just two courses and he can improve his economics grade without hurting his math grade, how could you represent this situation graphically?
9. Suppose decreased production of oil in the Middle East causes the price of oil to rise around the world. Explain how this change in the price signals information to U.S. producers of various goods, provides incentives to U.S. producers of various goods, and affects the distribution of income.
10. When you look at the economies of the United States, Europe, or Japan, you see most of the ingredients of a market economy. For example, consider bicycles. Prices in the bicycle market are free to vary; people have property rights to the bicycles they buy; many people sell bicycles; many bicycles sold in the United States, Europe, and Japan come from other countries; the government regulates bicycle use (no bicycles on the freeways, for example); and bicycle production takes place within firms with many workers. Replace bicycles with another good or service of your choosing and comment on whether the statement is still true.

CHAPTER 2

Observing and Explaining the Economy

Economics is a way of thinking. It entails accurately *describing* economic events, *explaining* why the events occur, *predicting* under what circumstances such events might take place in the future, and *recommending* appropriate courses of action. To make use of economics, you will want to learn to do the describing, the explaining, and even the predicting and recommending yourself—that is, to reason and think like an economist. By making use of economics in this way, you can better understand the economic challenges and opportunities you face, and thereby make improvements in your own life or the lives of those around you. Just as physicists try to explain the existence of black holes in outer space and biologists try to explain why dinosaurs became extinct, economists try to explain interesting observations and facts about the economy. One reason is pure intellectual excitement: It can be fun to solve economic puzzles. But understanding economic events or trends is also essential for making sound policy recommendations, whether in business or government. An incorrect explanation for the financial crisis in 2008, for example, could bring about harmful policy responses in the future with unintended consequences despite the best of intentions.

Source: Shutterstock.com

Are there some economic observations—from your own experience, from recent news stories, or from your history or political science courses—that you find puzzling? Some of your questions might be like these: Why is college tuition so high? Why have the wages of college graduates increased much more rapidly than the wages of high school dropouts since the 1970s? Why are there 17 different types of toothpaste? Why is the average income of people in the United States about 35 times higher than that of people in India? Why did the U.S. economy go into a recession in 2008? Why did the price of gasoline fall so much in the aftermath of the 2008/09 recession?

All these questions are based on observations about the economy. Some, like the question about college tuition, are fairly obvious and are based on casual observation. Others, like the question about the historical trends in the wages of high school and college graduates, would become evident in the course of reading a book or talking to a parent or a relative. In order to answer such questions, economists, like physicists or biologists, need to systematically document and quantify their observations and look for patterns. Learning to apply economic ideas to such real-world questions is an important part of learning economics, but it also is one of the most challenging parts because the real world is never quite as tidy as we would like and usually the explanation has several factors. In this chapter, we explain some of the ways that economists explain the facts in practice, and we point out some of the key pitfalls. We start by using a practical example to show how economists document and quantify their observations. As we will see, even documenting the facts can be tricky.

1. WHY HAS DRIVING SHIFTED INTO REVERSE

The Federal Highway Administration provides data on how many miles Americans drive in a year. A year-by-year analysis of this data shows that Americans have been driving less in recent years. Graphs are a helpful way to document and pinpoint such trends. Figure 2.1 plots the total miles traveled by all the vehicles—cars, trucks, and motorcycles—on all the streets, roads, and highways in the United States from 1993 to 2016. The vertical axis is measured in billions of miles; the horizontal axis is measured in years. Observe that after rising for many years, "vehicle miles traveled" reached a peak around 3,000 billion, or 3 trillion miles, driven in 2007 and then declined in 2008. The number of miles driven did not change very much for the next six years between 2008 and 2014. It was only in 2015 and 2016 that the number of miles driven increased again, moving past the previous peak of around 3 trillion miles driven. Why did the driving trend reverse after moving up for many years? If the reversal was connected to the recession, why did it take so long after the recession ended for the driving trend to recover?

The first thing to investigate is whether changes in the number of people in the United States may have been a factor in changes in the miles traveled. You would expect that more people would lead to more total driving and fewer people to less total driving. To test this possibility, one can simply divide vehicle miles traveled by the population of the United States. In 2007, when total miles traveled were 3,000 billion, approximately 300 million people lived in the United States; this implies that the average miles traveled per person were about 10,000, which probably is a more understandable number than 3 trillion. Vehicle miles traveled per person for the other years from 1993 to 2016 are plotted in Figure 2.2. Now note something important about Figure 2.2; compared with Figure 2.1, it reaches a peak in 2005, a few years before the recession. Thus, miles traveled started growing more slowly than the population in that year. So we should think of 2005 rather than 2007 as the turning point to try to explain the change in miles traveled. Another difference between Figure 2.1 and Figure 2.2 is that the line graph in Figure 2.2 shows a continued fall until around 2011, illustrating that, relative to the population, driving continued to decline in 2011. Finally, even though total miles driven in 2015 and 2016 exceeded the pre-recession peak, Figure 2.2 shows that adjusted for the increase in population, vehicle miles traveled per person still has not recovered to pre-recession levels.

FIGURE 2.1 "Vehicle Miles Traveled" in the United States, 1993–2016

For each year from 1993 through 2016, the total amount of miles traveled in vehicles on U.S. roads and streets is plotted; a line then connects the points to better visualize the trends and turning points.

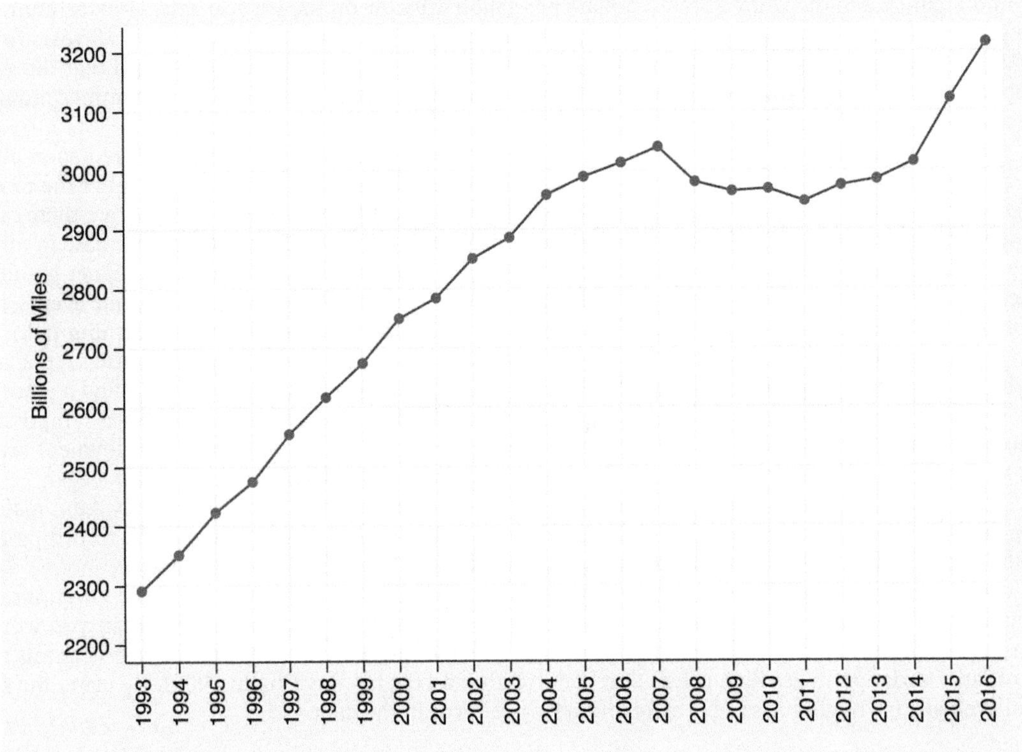

Source: Federal Highway Administration.

FIGURE 2.2 Vehicle Miles Traveled Per Person

For each year, vehicle miles traveled from Figure 2.1 is divided by the population of the United States and plotted in the graph.

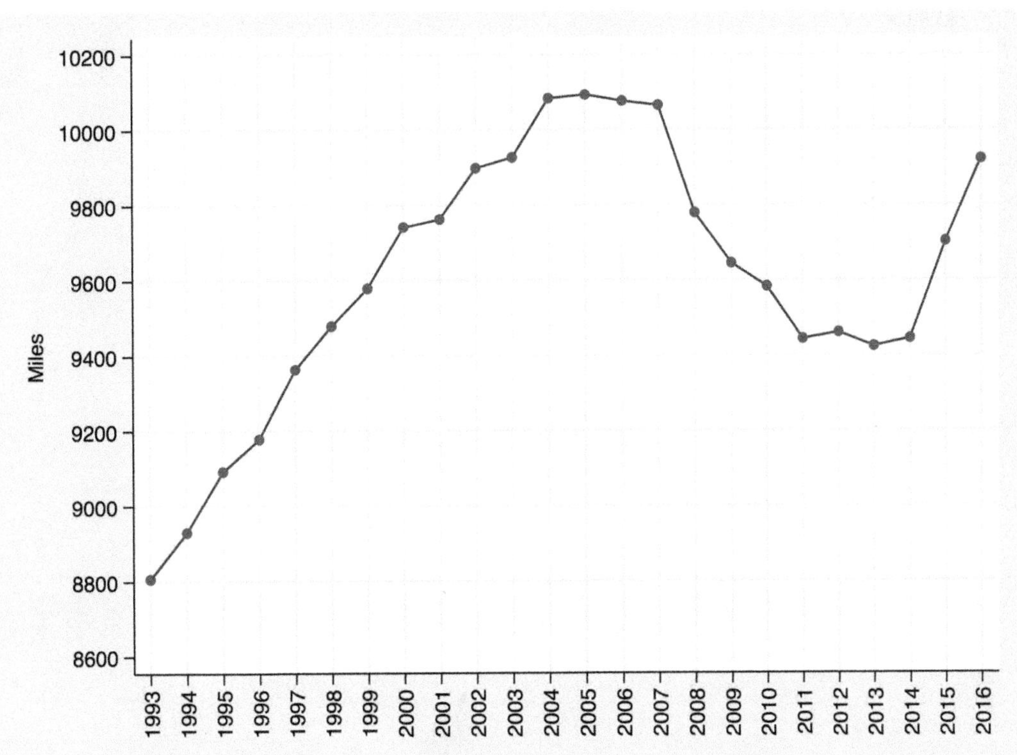

Source: Figure 2.1 and Bureau of the Census.

We can look in many places for an explanation of the reversal in this trend, but the first obvious place is the price of gasoline. If the price of gasoline increases, then people will have a greater incentive to walk or ride a bike or take a train or plane rather than drive their car, truck or motorcycle. So let's look at the price of gasoline. Figure 2.3 plots the average price of gasoline for the same years as Figure 2.1 and Figure 2.2 in the United States; dollars per gallon are now on the vertical axis. Look carefully at the pattern of the price of gasoline. Note that the price did not rise much at all for nearly 10 years from 1993 to 2002, but then it took off at a much more rapid rate, more than doubling. Recall that the data plotted in Figure 2.3 are the average prices for each year. In 2008, the price during the summer months reached more than $4 per gallon, even though the average for the year was $3.30.

By comparing Figure 2.2 and Figure 2.3 one can see that the peak in driving occurred soon after the price of gasoline started to rise rapidly. Furthermore, gasoline prices rose again right after the recession ended, which could have ended up making it more expensive for Americans to drive their cars. Only in the last two years, 2015 and 2016, did gasoline prices fall, coinciding with the increase in miles driven. Based on the data in these figures, one can begin to make a plausible case that higher gasoline prices are the explanation for the decline in driving. But, as with many real-world economic events, the explanation is not as clear and obvious as one might hope. One problem is that the turning point in driving occurred in 2005, several years after prices started rising rapidly. What could cause such a lag? Perhaps people took a while to adjust; commuters may have had to wait until they could find a place to live closer to the train station. Perhaps some people thought the high price of gasoline was temporary. Another possibility is that the recession from 2007 to 2009, and the resulting high unemployment rates, led to fewer commutes to work, although the peak in driving occurred before the recession began.

Yet another issue is the accuracy of the data. To collect the data, the Federal Highway Administration set up monitoring stations at 4,000 locations around the United States. The people recording the traffic flows could have made reporting errors or missed key intersections. In general, economic data collected via survey methods can be inaccurate; people sometimes do not understand the questions, or they do not have the correct information. Sometimes, data may be more aggregated than you would like them to be; for example, the average price of a gallon of gasoline during a given year conceals the substantial variation in gasoline prices that occur within a year (as was true in 2008). By using the annual average, one might miss potentially important patterns in the data.

FIGURE 2.3 **Average Retail Price of Gasoline in the United States, 1994–2016**

For each year, the price of a gallon of gasoline is averaged across the year and across all grades and plotted in the graph.

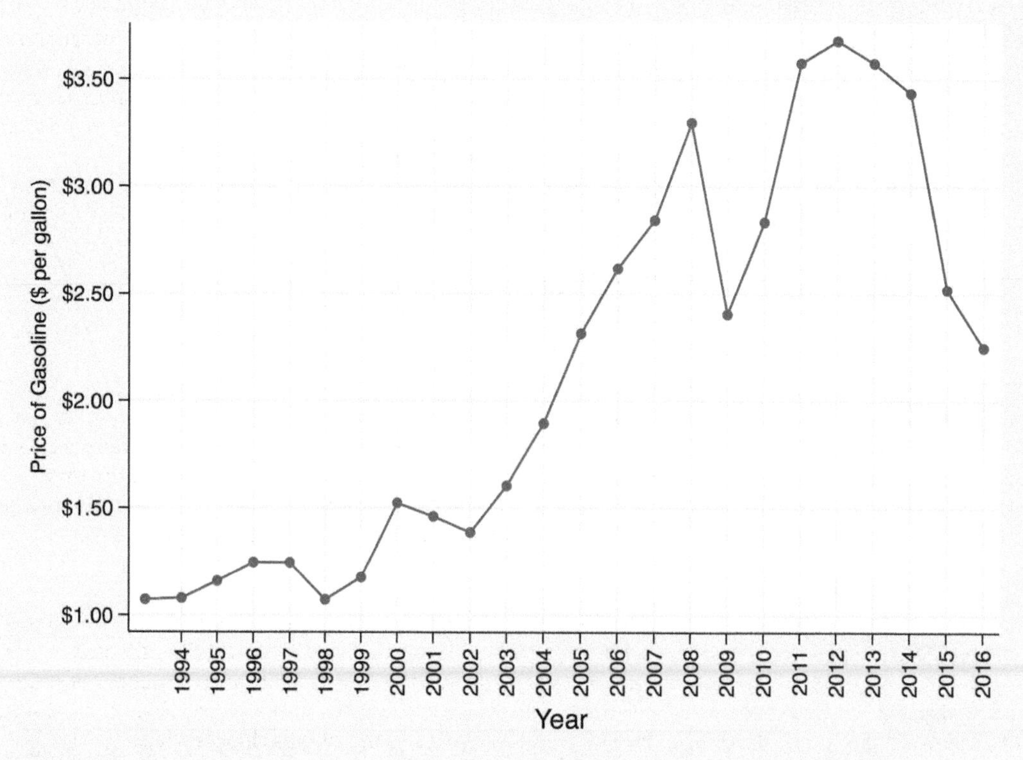

Source: Department of Energy.

It is also important to check the difference between the price of gasoline and the *relative* price of gasoline compared with other goods. If you find that the price of other forms of transportation—trains, planes, or bicycles—rose just as fast as gasoline, then the rising price of gasoline would not be a good explanation for the decline in driving. In sum, although it seems quite reasonable that an explanation for the reversal in driving trends was the rise in the price of gasoline, as always in economics, there are other possible competing views to discuss and assess.

REVIEW

- Explaining real-world economic trends and events is both interesting in its own right and essential for sound policy making. The first step is to find good data to describe the trend or event, then to identify what factors may have caused the trend, and finally to assess how changes elsewhere in the economy could affect the explanation.
- When applying economic ideas to explain real-world trends and events, it is best to recognize the limitations of the analysis and think critically about all possible causal factors. For example, when studying changes over time, it is important to take account of changes in the population which have large effects.

2. VARIABLES, CORRELATION AND CAUSATION

In examining U.S. driving trends, we focused on two economic variables: (1) vehicle miles traveled per person and (2) the price of gasoline. An **economic variable** is any economic measure that can vary over a range of values. In explaining the reversal in driving trends, we noted a relationship between these two variables. In other words, we considered the correlation between the price of gasoline and the subsequent number of miles driven; in particular, we noted that, when prices rose rapidly, driving declined.

economic variable
Any economic measure that can vary over a range of values.

Two variables are said to be *correlated* if they tend to move up or down together. A *positive correlation* exists if the two variables move in the same direction—when one goes up, the other goes up. A *negative correlation* exists if the two variables move in opposite directions—when one goes up, the other goes down.

2.1 Correlation versus Causation

Just because two variables are correlated it does not necessarily mean that one caused the other. *Causation* and *correlation* are different. *Correlation* means that one event usually occurs with another. *Causation* means that one event brings about another. But correlation does not imply causation. For example, high readings on a thermometer are correlated with hot weather: High readings occur when it is hot. But the thermometer readings do not cause the hot weather. Causation is the other way around: Hot weather causes the reading on the thermometer to be high.

In the example of miles driven, one might be concerned that the decline in vehicle miles traveled caused the higher gasoline prices, but the timing raises doubts about such a reverse causation: Gasoline prices moved first, so we have good reason to believe that gasoline prices caused the change in driving trends. In many instances, determining causation is difficult.

2.2 The Lack of Controlled Experiments in Economics

In many sciences—psychology, physics, and biology—investigators perform **controlled experiments** to determine whether one event causes another event. An example of a controlled experiment is the clinical trial of a new drug. New drugs are tested by trying them out on two groups of individuals. One group gets the new drug; the other group, the control group, gets a placebo (a pill without the drug). If the experiment results in a significantly greater number of people being cured among the group taking the drug than among the group taking the placebo, investigators conclude that the drug causes the cure.

controlled experiments
Empirical tests of theories in a controlled setting in which particular effects can be isolated.

Controlled experiments are rare in economics. When faced with a situation with limited data (say, data for one country over a particular time period), causation is hard to determine. In these circumstances, we can try to look at other countries' experiences, or we can look at the experiences of different states within the United States. But, unfortunately, no two countries or states are alike in all respects. Thus, attempting to control for other factors is not as easy as in the case of clinical trials.

experimental economics

A branch of economics that uses laboratory experiments to analyze economic behavior.

In recent years, economists have adapted some of the methods of experimental science and have begun to conduct economic experiments in laboratory settings that are similar to the real world. These experiments can be repeated, and various effects can be controlled for. **Experimental economics** is a growing area of economics. The findings of experimental economics have affected economists' understanding of how the economy works. Experiments in economics also provide an excellent way to *learn* how the economy works, much as experiments in science courses can help one learn about gravity or the structure of plant cells. But because it is difficult to replicate real-world settings as precisely as in such experiments, they have yet to be applied as widely as the clinical or laboratory experiments in other sciences.

REVIEW

- One of the most significant challenges for an economist is to identify whether one variable has a causal impact on another. Even though two variables may be strongly correlated, correlation does not imply causation.
- In the natural sciences, controlled experiments are used to establish causation. Because controlled experiments are rare in economics, establishing causation is more difficult in this field. Fortunately, experimental economics is now beginning to have a greater impact on research.

2.3 Economic Models

economic model

An explanation of how the economy or a part of the economy works.

To explain economic facts and observations, one needs an economic theory, or *model*. An **economic model** is an explanation of how the economy or a part of the economy works. In practice, most economists use the terms *theory* and *model* interchangeably, although sometimes the term *theory* suggests a general explanation and the term *model* suggests a more specific explanation. The term *law* also is used interchangeably with the terms *model* and *theory* in economics.

Economic models are always abstractions, or simplifications, of the real world. They take complicated phenomena, such as the behavior of people, firms, and governments, and simplify them. Economists like to draw an analogy between a model and a road map—both are abstractions of a much more complex reality. Some maps (like some models) can be detailed; others are just broad abstractions. No single model is "correct," just like no single map is "correct." If you wanted to drive from New York to California, you would need an interstate map, one that ignores the details of individual streets within a city to show the main highways. In contrast, if you were headed from one neighborhood of Chicago to another, an interstate map would be of no use; instead, you would need a map that showed city streets in greater detail.

Microeconomic versus Macroeconomic Models

There are two types of models corresponding to the two main branches of economics: microeconomics and macroeconomics. They each have their purpose.

microeconomics

The branch of economics that examines individual decision making at firms and households and the way they interact in specific industries and markets.

Microeconomics studies the behavior of individual firms and households or specific markets like the health care market or the college graduate market. It looks at variables such as the price of a college education or the reason for increased wages of college graduates. Microeconomic models explain why the price of gasoline varies from station to station and why airfares are discounted. The analogy in the map world is to the city street map.

Macroeconomics focuses on the whole economy—the whole national economy or even the whole world economy. The most comprehensive measure of the size of an economy is the **gross domestic product (GDP)**. GDP is the total value of all goods and services made in the country during a specific period of time, such as a year. GDP includes all newly made goods, such as cars, shoes, gasoline, airplanes, and houses; it also includes services like health care, education, and auto repair. Macroeconomics tries to explain the changes in GDP over time rather than the changes in a part of the GDP, like health care spending. It looks at questions such as, what causes the GDP to grow and why many more workers are unemployed in Europe than in the United States? The analogy in the map world is to the interstate map.

macroeconomics

The branch of economics that examines the workings and problems of the economy as a whole–GDP growth and unemployment.

gross domestic product (GDP)

A measure of the value of all the goods and services newly produced in an economy during a specified period of time.

FIGURE 2.4 A Model with Two Positively Related Variables

The upward-sloping line shows how the variables are related. When one variable increases from *A* to *B*, the other variable increases from *C* to *D*. If one variable declines from *B* to *A*, the other variable declines from *D* to *C*. We say that Variable 1 is positively related to Variable 2, or that Variable 1 varies directly with Variable 2.

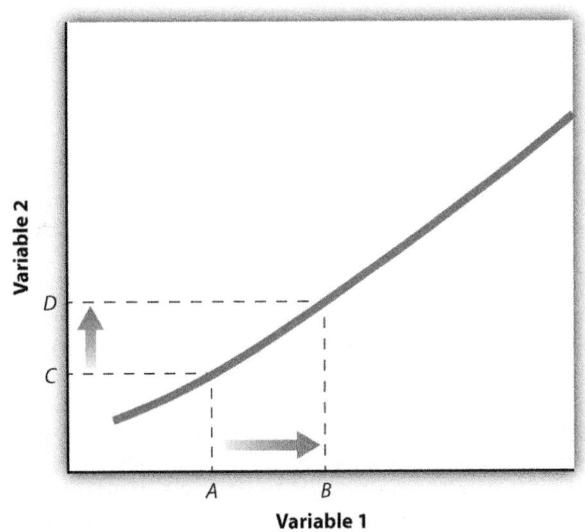

FIGURE 2.5 A Model with Two Negatively Related Variables

When one variable increases from *A* to *B*, the other variable decreases from *D* to *C*. Likewise, when one variable decreases from *B* to *A*, the other variable increases from *C* to *D*. We say that Variable 1 is negatively related to Variable 2, or that Variable 1 varies inversely with Variable 2.

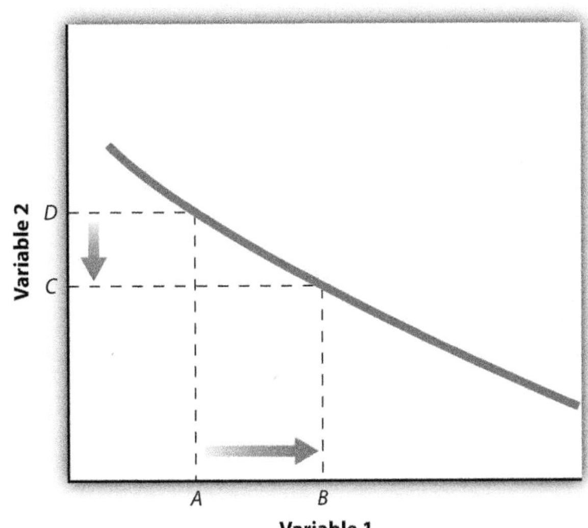

Do not be critical of economic models just because they are simplifications. In every science, models are simplifications of reality. Models are successful if they explain reality reasonably well. In fact, if they were not simplifications, models would be hard to use effectively. Economic models differ from those in the physical sciences because they endeavor to explain human behavior, which is complex and often unpredictable. It is for this reason that the brilliant physicist Max Planck said that economics was harder than physics.

Economic models can be described with words, numerical tables, graphs, or algebra. To use economics, it is important to be able to work with these different descriptions. Figure 2.4 and Figure 2.5 show how models can be illustrated with graphs. By looking at a graph, we can see quickly whether the model has an inverse or a direct relationship. If a model says that one variable varies inversely with the other, this means that if the first variable rises, then the second falls. If a model says that one variable varies directly with another, this means that if one variable rises, the other also rises. In economics, the expression "is positively related to" is frequently used in place of the phrase "varies directly with," which is more common in other sciences. Similarly, the expression "is negatively related to" is frequently used in place of "varies inversely with."

positively related

A situation in which an increase in one variable is associated with an increase in another variable; also called *directly related.*

negatively related

A situation in which an increase in one variable is associated with a decrease in another variable; also called *inversely related.*

In Figure 2.4, two variables are shown to be **positively related**. In other words, when Variable 1 increases from *A* to *B*, Variable 2 increases from *C* to *D* by the specific amount given by the curve. Likewise, when Variable 1 decreases from *B* to *A*, Variable 2 decreases from *D* to *C*. In Figure 2.5, a model with two variables that are **negatively related** is shown. Here, when Variable 1 increases from *A* to *B*, Variable 2 decreases from *D* to *C*. Likewise, when Variable 1 decreases from *B* to *A*, Variable 2 increases from *C* to *D*. Models have *constants* as well as variables. The constants in the models in Figure 2.4 and Figure 2.5 are the positions and shapes of the curves.

An Example: A Model with Two Variables

Figure 2.6 shows a model describing how doctors employed in a health maintenance organization (HMO) provide physical examinations. The model illustrates that the more doctors who are employed at the HMO, the more physical exams can be given. The model is represented in four different ways: (1) words, (2) a numerical table, (3) a graph, and (4) algebra.

A verbal description appears on the lower right of Figure 2.6: More doctors mean more physical exams, but additional doctors increase the number of exams by smaller amounts, presumably because the diagnostic facilities at the HMO are limited; for example, only so many rooms are available for physical exams.

On the upper left, a table with numbers shows how the number of examinations depends on the number of doctors. Exactly how many examinations can be given by each number of doctors is shown in the table. Clearly, this table is much more specific than the verbal description. Be sure to distinguish between the meaning of a table that presents a model and a table that presents data. They look similar, but one is a model of the real world and the other represents observations about the real world.

On the upper right, a curve shows the relationship between doctors and physical examinations. The curve shows how many exams each number of doctors can perform.

FIGURE 2.6 Economic Models in Four Ways

Each model has advantages and disadvantages; this book focuses mostly on verbal descriptions, graphs, and numerical tables, but occasionally some algebra will be used to help explain things.

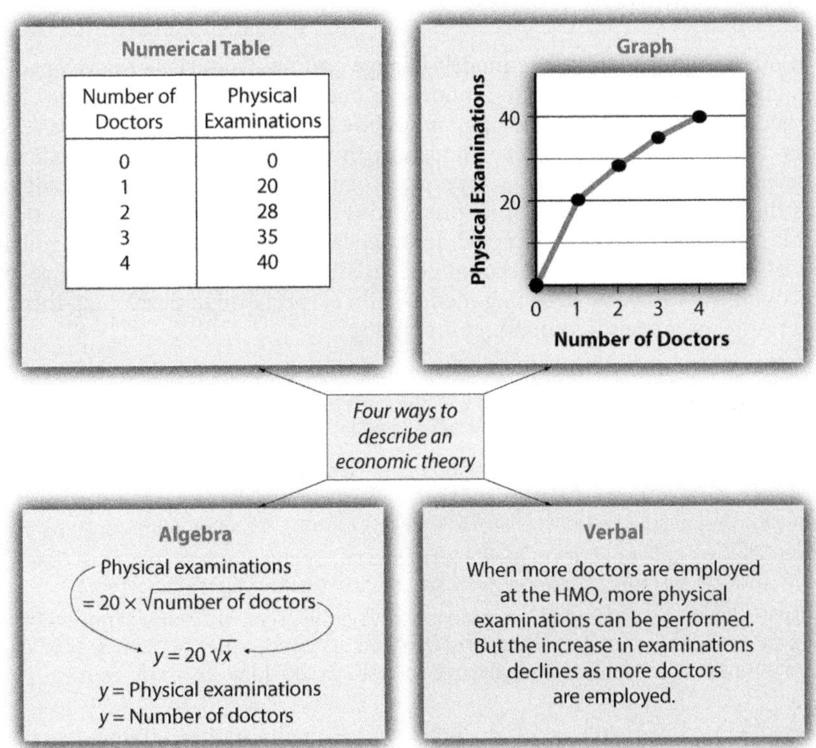

The points on the curve are plotted from the information in the table. The vertical axis has the number of examinations; the horizontal axis has the number of doctors. The points are connected with a line to help visualize the curve.

Finally, the lower left shows the doctor-examination relationship in algebraic form. In this case, the number of exams is equal to the square root of the number of doctors times 20. If we use the symbol y for the number of exams and x for the number of doctors, the model looks a lot like the equations in an algebra course.

All four ways of representing models have advantages and disadvantages. The advantage of the verbal representation is that we usually communicate with people in words, and if we want our economic models to have any use, we need to communicate with people who have not studied economics. The verbal representation, however, is not as precise as the other three models. In addition to verbal analysis, in this book we focus on tabular and graphical representations and, when appropriate, algebraic descriptions as well.

2.4 The *Ceteris Paribus* Assumption

To use models for prediction, economists use the assumption of **ceteris paribus**, which means "all other things being equal." For example, the prediction that Variable 2 will fall from *D* to *C* assumes that the curve in Figure 2.5 does not shift: The position of the curve when Variable 1 is at *A* is *equal* to the position of the curve when Variable 1 is at *B*. If other things were not equal—if the curve shifted—then we could not predict that Variable 2 would fall from *D* to *C* when Variable 1 rose from *A* to *B*. Similarly, predicting that more doctors can produce more physical exams assumes that there is no power outage that would cause the diagnostic equipment to stop operating.

ceteris paribus

"All other things being equal"; refers to holding all other variables constant or keeping all other things the same when one variable is changed.

2.5 The Use of Existing Models

Because economics has been around for a long time, many existing models can be applied to explain observations or make predictions that are useful to decision makers. In practice, whether in government or business or universities, economists use models that are already in existence.

The models are used in many different types of applications, from determining the effects of discrimination in the workplace to evaluating the gains from lower health care prices. Frequently, the models are applied in new and clever ways.

2.6 The Development of Models

Like models in other sciences, economic models change and new models are developed. Many of the models in this book are different from the models in books published 40 years ago. New economic models evolve because some new observations cannot be explained by existing models.

The process of the development of new models or theories in economics proceeds much like that in any other science. First one develops a *hypothesis*, or a hunch, to explain a puzzling observation. Then one tests the hypothesis by seeing if its predictions of other observations are good. If the hypothesis passes this test, then it becomes accepted. In practice, however, this is at best a rough description of the process of scientific discovery in economics. Existing models are constantly re-examined and tested. Some economists specialize in testing models; others specialize in developing them. The process of creating and testing of models in economics is ongoing.

REVIEW

- Economists use models to describe economic phenomena and to understand how changes in some variables affect the variable of interest. Economic models are abstractions, or simplifications, of a more complex reality. They can be extremely detailed or rather abstract, depending on the purpose or use.
- Economic models are different from models in the physical sciences because they must deal with human behavior. Models can be represented with words, numerical tables, graphs, and algebra.
- Economists also have a long-standing interest in improving the economic policy of governments. Economics can be used in a positive sense, to understand why government policies are the way they are, or in a normative sense, to identify what government policies should be enacted.

3. RECOMMENDING APPROPRIATE POLICIES

Ever since the birth of economics as a field—around 1776, when Adam Smith published the *Wealth of Nations*—economists have been concerned about and motivated by a desire to improve the economic policy of governments. In fact, economics originally was called *political economy*. Much of the *Wealth of Nations* is about what the government should or should not do to affect the domestic and international economy.

Adam Smith argued for a system of *laissez faire*—little government control—in which the role of the government is mainly to promote competition, provide for national defense, and reduce restrictions on the exchange of goods and services. More than one hundred years later, Karl Marx brought an alternative perspective to Smith's (and other classical economists') view of political economy, arguing against the laissez-faire approach. His analysis of market economies, or **capitalism**, centered on the contradictions that he saw arising out of such a system, particularly the conflict between the owners of production and the laborers. He argued that these contradictions would result in the inevitable collapse of capitalism and the emergence of a new economic system, called **socialism,** in which government essentially would own and control all production. Although Marx actually wrote little about what a Socialist or Communist economy would look like, the centrally planned economies that arose in the Soviet Union, Eastern Europe, and China in the twentieth century can be traced to Marx's ideas.

In the twenty-first century, most countries have rejected the command economy and have moved toward market economies, but the debate about the role of government continues. In many modern market economies, the government plays a large role, and for this reason, such economies are sometimes called **mixed economies**. How great should the role of government be in a market economy? Should the government provide health care services? Should it try to break up large firms? The answers to these questions are difficult to comprehend and have been debated for years.

capitalism

An economic system based on a market economy in which capital is individually owned, and production and employment decisions are decentralized.

socialism

An economic system in which the government owns and controls all the capital and makes decisions about prices and quantities as part of a central plan.

mixed economies

A market economy in which the government plays a very large role.

3.1 Positive versus Normative Economics

In debating the role of government in the economy, economists distinguish between positive and normative economics. **Positive economics** is about what *is*; **normative economics** is about what *should be*. For example, positive economics endeavors to explain why driving declined in 2008. Normative economics aims to develop and recommend policies that might prevent driving from increasing in the future, perhaps with the aim of improving the environment. In general, normative economics is concerned with making recommendations about what the government should do—whether it should control the price of gasoline or health care, for example. Economists who advise governments spend much of their time doing normative economics. In the United States, the president's **Council of Economic Advisers** has legal responsibility for advising the president about which economic policies are beneficial and which policies are detrimental to the economy.

Positive economics also can be used to explain *why* governments do what they do. Why were tax rates cut in the 1980s, increased in the 1990s, and then cut again in the 2000s? Positive analysis of government policy requires a mixture of both political science and economic science, with a focus on what motivates voters and the politicians they elect.

positive economics

Economic analysis that explains what happens in the economy and why, without making recommendations about economic policy.

normative economics

Economic analysis that makes recommendations about economic policy.

Council of Economic Advisers

A three-member group of economists appointed by the president of the United States to analyze the economy and make recommendations about economic policy.

3.2 Economics as a Science versus Partisan Policy Tool

Although economics, like any other science, is based on facts and theories, it is not always used in a purely scientific way.

In political campaigns, economists put forth arguments in favor of one candidate, emphasizing the good side of their candidate's ideas and de-emphasizing the bad side. In a court of law, one economist may help a defendant—making the best case possible—and another economist may help the plaintiff—again, making the best case possible. In other words, economics is not always used objectively. A good reason to learn economics for yourself is to see through fallacious arguments.

But economics is not the only science that is used in these two entirely different modes. For example, there is currently a great controversy about the use of biology and chemistry to make estimates of the costs and benefits of different environmental policies. This is a politically controversial subject, and some on both sides of the controversy have been accused of using science in nonobjective ways.

3.3 Economics Is Not the Only Factor in Policy Issues

Although economics can be useful in policy decisions, it frequently is not the only factor. For example, national security sometimes calls for a recommendation on a policy issue different from one based on a purely economic point of view. Although most economists recommend free exchange of goods between countries, the U.S. government restricted exports of high-technology goods such as computers during the Cold War because defense specialists worried that the technology could help the military in the Soviet Union, and this was viewed as more important than the economic argument. The government still places heavy restrictions on trade in nuclear fuels for fear of the proliferation of nuclear weapons.

3.4 Disagreement between Economists

Watching economists debate issues on television or reading their opinions in a newspaper or magazine certainly gives the impression that they rarely agree. There are major controversies in economics, and we will examine them in this book. But when people survey economists' beliefs, they find a surprising amount of agreement.

Why, then, is there the popular impression of disagreement? Because there are many economists, and one can always find an economist with a different viewpoint. When people sue other people in court and economics is an issue, it is always possible to find economists who will testify for each side, even if 99 percent of economists would agree with one side. Similarly, television interviews or news shows want to give both sides of public policy issues. Thus, even if 99 percent of economists agree with one side, the producers are able to find at least one who holds the opposing view.

Economists are human beings with varying moral beliefs and different backgrounds and political views that frequently are unrelated to economic models. For example, an economist who is concerned about the importation of drugs into the United States might appear to be more willing to condone a restriction on coffee exports from Brazil and other coffee-exporting countries to give Colombia a higher price for its coffee to offset a loss in revenue from cocaine. Another economist, who felt less strongly about drug imports, might argue forcefully against such a restriction on coffee. But if they were asked about restrictions on trade in the abstract, both economists probably would argue for government policies that prevent such restrictions.

4. END-OF-CHAPTER MATERIAL

4.1 Conclusion: A Reader's Guide

In Chapter 1, we explored the central idea of economics: scarcity, choice, and economic interaction. In this chapter, we discussed how economists observe economic events and use economic models to explain these phenomena. It is now time to move on and learn more about the models and application of the central idea. As you study economic models in the following chapters, it will be useful to keep three points in mind, which are implied by the ideas raised in this chapter.

First, *economics—more than other subjects—requires a mixture of verbal and quantitative skills.* Frequently, those who come to economics with a good background in physical science and algebra find the mix of formal models with more informal verbal descriptions of markets and institutions unusual and perhaps a little difficult. If you are one of these people, you might wish for a more cut-and-dry, or algebraic, approach.

In contrast, those who are good at history or philosophy may find the emphasis on formal models and graphs difficult and might even prefer a more historical approach that looked more at watershed events and famous individuals and less at formal models of how many individuals behave. If you are one of these people, you might wish that economic models were less abstract.

In reality, however, economics is a mixture of formal modeling, historical analysis, and philosophy. If you are good at algebra and you think the symbols and graphs of elementary economics are too simple, think of Max Planck's comment about economics and focus on the complexity of the economic phenomena that these simple models and graphs are explaining. Then when you are asked an open-ended question about government policy that does not have a simple yes or no answer, you will not be caught off guard. Or if your advantage is in history or philosophy, you should spend more time honing your skills at using models and graphs. Then when you are asked to solve a cut-and-dry economic problem with an exact answer requiring graphic analysis, you will not be caught off guard.

Second, *economics is a wide-ranging discipline.* When your friends or relatives hear that you are taking economics, they may ask you for advice about what stock to buy. Economists' friends and relatives are always asking for such advice. Some topics that you study in economics will help you answer questions about whether to invest in the stock market or put your money in a bank or how many stocks to buy. But even these areas of economics will not offer any predictions about the success of particular companies. Rather, what economics gives you is a set of tools that you can use to obtain information about companies, industries, or countries and to analyze them yourself. Furthermore, the scope of economics is vast. Even among the faculty in a small college, you will find economists who study childhood obesity, trade barriers, real estate markets, abortion policy, the formation of American corporations, economic growth, international lending agencies, social security, agricultural pollution, and school choice.

Third, and perhaps most important, *the study of economics is an intellectually fascinating adventure in its own right.* Yes, economics is highly relevant, and it affects people's lives. But once you learn how economic models work, you will find that they actually are fun to use. Every now and then, just after you have learned about a new economic model, put the book down and think of the economic model independent of its message or relevance to society—try to enjoy it the way you would a good movie. In this way, too, you will be learning to think like an economist.

Key Points

1. Economics is a way of thinking that requires observation (describing economic events), explanation (identifying variables that are potential explanatory variables of the event), prediction (building and using economic models to predict future events), and policy recommendations (courses of action for government—and business—to follow, based on these observations and models).
2. Finding the appropriate data series to explain economic events is a challenge because data often can be hard to find or incomplete, or can be misleading if they are not appropriately transformed.
3. Finding explanations for why an economic event occurred is challenging because even if you can find variables that are correlated with the variable in which you are interested, correlation does not imply causation. The inability to run controlled experiments also makes it difficult for economists to definitively establish a causal explanation for an economic event.
4. Economists have to explain the complex behavior of humans in economic situations. They often use models that are abstractions, or simplifications, of reality in their work. Economic models, like models in other sciences, can be described with words, tables, graphs, or algebra. All four ways are important and complement each other.
5. Economists use the tools of economic analysis to come up with policy insights concerning what the government is doing, or what the government should be doing, with regard to the economist's area of interest. Improving economic policy has been a goal of economists since the time of Adam Smith.
6. Economics is a discipline that requires a combination of analytical, algebraic, and verbal skills. You can apply the tools of economics to almost any problem that involves decision making by individuals. Many students are interested in studying economics because they find it relevant to events that occur in the world, but the study of economics can be an intellectually stimulating exercise in its own right.

QUESTIONS FOR REVIEW

1. How do economists typically approach an economics-related problem?
2. What are the challenges that economists face in trying to describe an economic event?
3. What is meant by a relative price, and why is it important in certain situations to look at the relative price of a good instead of the actual price of that good?
4. What does it mean for two variables to be correlated? What is the difference between positive and negative correlation?
5. Why doesn't correlation imply causation? Can you come up with your own example of why correlation does not imply causation?
6. Why do economists use economic models? Can you come up with some reasons why economists should be careful in using models?
7. What is the *ceteris paribus* assumption? Why is it so important in economics?
8. What is the difference between macroeconomics and microeconomics? Between positive and normative economics?
9. What academic disciplines do you think of as being more scientific than economics? Why do you think so? Which disciplines do you consider to be less scientific, and why?
10. Look through the research and teaching interests of the economics faculty members in your department. Collectively, how wide-ranging are those interests? Were you surprised to find that the tools of economics could be applied to a particular area?

PROBLEMS

1. Which of the following variables are studied as part of microeconomics, and which are studied as part of macroeconomics?
   a. The U.S. unemployment rate.
   b. The amount of tips earned by a waiter.
   c. The national rate of inflation.
   d. The number of hours worked by a student.
   e. The price paid to obtain this economics textbook.
2. Consider the following table, which provides the price of chicken and the price of all foods from 1996 to 2006.

Year	Price of All Foods	Price of Chicken	Relative Price
1996	92	95	
1997	93	98	
1998	96	98	
1999	97	99	
2000	100	100	
2001	103	103	
2002	104	105	
2003	108	106	
2004	111	114	
2005	113	116	
2006	116	114	

   a. Calculate the relative price of chicken for each year using the formula below
   b. Plot the relative price of chicken.
   c. What can you say about how the price of chicken has varied in comparison to the price of all foods in the decade from 1996 to 2006.

$$\text{Relative Price of Chicken} = \left(\frac{\text{Price of Chicken}}{\text{Price of All Foods}}\right) * 100$$

3. A change in the relative price of a good matters more than the change in the price of a good in analyzing the change in spending on that good. Show that the relative price of a good can fall on occasions when the price of that good is rising, falling, or remaining unchanged, using numerical examples from the table in Problem 2.
4. Indicate whether you expect positive or negative correlation for the following pairs of variables, labeled *X* and *Y*. For each pair, state whether *X* causes *Y*, *Y* causes *X*, or both.
   a. Sunrise (*X*) and crowing roosters (*Y*).
   b. The use of umbrellas (*X*) and a thunderstorm (*Y*).
   c. The price of theater tickets (*X*) and the number of theatergoers (*Y*).
   d. Weekly earnings of a worker (*X*) and the number of hours a week she works at her job (*Y*).
   e. The number of children who were vaccinated against a disease (*X*) and the number of children who currently suffer from that disease (*Y*).

5. Consider an economic model of donut production. Show how to represent this model graphically, algebraically, and verbally, as in Figure 2.6.

Number of Workers	Number of Donuts Produced
0	0
1	100
4	200
9	300
16	400

6. Suppose you decide to build a model to explain why the average worker in a particular occupation works more hours during some weeks than during others.
    a. What data would you collect to describe this phenomenon?
    b. What variable do you believe would supply the major part of the explanation of the variation in hours worked?
    c. If you graph the data with hours worked on the vertical axis and your explanatory variable on the horizontal axis, will the relationship be upward-sloping or downward-sloping?
    d. What does your answer to part c imply for whether the data on hours worked and the data on your explanatory variable are positively or negatively correlated?
7. Why is it typical for economists to make the *ceteris paribus* assumption when making predictions? Now consider the statement: "If the local McDonald's reduces the price of a Big Mac hamburger, it will sell a lot more hamburgers." What other variables are most likely being held fixed under the *ceteris paribus* assumption when this statement is being made?
8. Suppose you wanted to modify the Bertrand and Mullainathan study to focus on gender discrimination. Describe the "experiment" that you would run. Also be sure to explain how the *ceteris paribus* assumption is involved in terms of the names you would choose for the men and for the women.
9. Identify whether the following policy statements are positive or normative. Explain.
    a. The price of gasoline is too high.
    b. The average price of gasoline rose to a record high of $4.02 in June 2008.
    c. Forty-four million Americans lack access to health insurance.
    d. The government needs to provide basic health care to the uninsured.
    e. A collapse in the stock market will affect many Americans.
10. Suppose an economic study shows that increasing the tax rate on cigarettes will reduce the amount of smoking. Which of the following statements can be validly made on the basis of the study because they are positive statements, and which cannot be validly made because they are normative statements?
    a. Increasing the cigarette tax rate is a method of reducing smoking.
    b. If the government wishes to reduce smoking, it should raise the cigarette tax.
    c. If the government wishes to reduce smoking, it can raise the cigarette tax.
    d. The government should reduce smoking by raising the cigarette tax.
    e. The government should not raise the cigarette tax on low-income smokers.

5. APPENDIX: READING, UNDERSTANDING AND CREATING GRAPHS

Whether you follow the stock market, the health care market, or the whole economy, graphs are needed to understand what is going on. That is why the financial pages of newspapers contain so many graphs. Knowing how to read, understand, and even create your own graphs is part of learning to "think like an economist." Graphs help us see correlations, or patterns, in economic observations. Graphs also are useful for understanding economic models. They help us see how variables in the model behave. They help us describe assumptions about what firms and consumers do.

Computer software to create graphs is now widely available. To understand how helpful graphs can be, you might want to create a few of your own graphs. Here we provide a short review of elementary graphing techniques.

5.1 Visualizing Observations with Graphs

Cartesian coordinate system

A graphing system in which ordered pairs of numbers are represented on a plane by the distances from a point to two perpendicular lines, called axes.

time-series graph

A graph that plots a variable over time, usually with time on the horizontal axis.

Most economic graphs are drawn in two dimensions, like the surface of this page, and are constructed using a **Cartesian coordinate system**. The idea of Cartesian coordinates is that pairs of observations on variables can be represented in a plane by designating one axis for one variable and the other axis for the other variable. Each point, or coordinate, on the plane corresponds to a pair of observations.

Time-Series Graph

In many instances, we want to see how a variable changes over time. Consider the federal debt held by the public—all the outstanding borrowing of the federal government that has not yet been paid back. Table 2.1 shows observations of the U.S. federal debt. The observations are for every ten years. The observations in Table 2.1 are graphed in Figure 2.7. The graph in Figure 2.7 is called a **time-series graph** because it plots a series—that is, several values of the variable—over time.

TABLE 2.1 U.S. Federal Government Debt

Year	Debt (billions of dollars)
1960	237
1970	283
1980	712
1990	2,412
2000	3,410
2010	9,018
2020 (Projected)	16,845

FIGURE 2.7 U.S. Federal Debt

Each point corresponds to a pair of observations—the year and the debt—from Table 2.1.

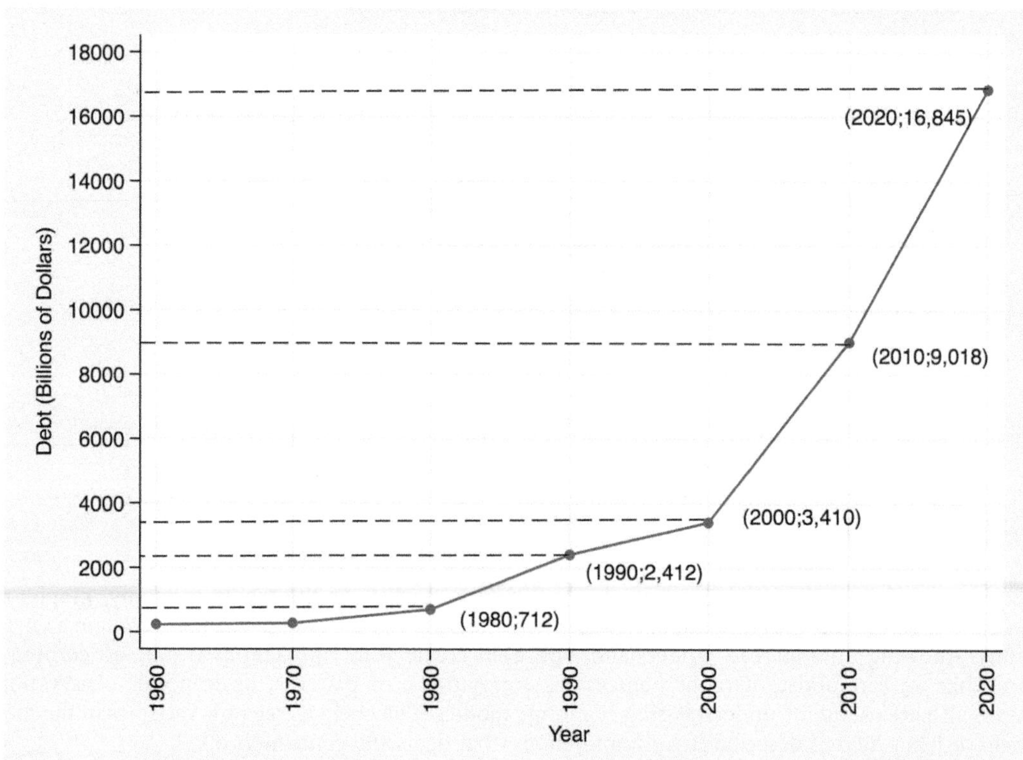

Observe the scales on the horizontal and vertical axes in Figure 2.7. The seven years are put on the horizontal axis, spread evenly from the year 1960 to the year 2020. The last year is a forecast. For the vertical axis, one needs to decide on a scale. The range of variation for the debt in Table 2.1 is wide—from a minimum of $237 billion to a maximum of $16,845 billion. Thus, the range on the vertical axis—from $0 to $18,000 billion in Figure 2.7—must be wide enough to contain all these points.

Now observe how each pair of points from Table 2.1 is plotted in Figure 2.7. The point for the pair of observations for the year 1960 and the debt of $237 billion is found by going over to 1960 on the horizontal axis, then going up to $237 billion and putting a dot there. The point for 1970 and $283 billion and all the other points are found in the same way. To better visualize the points, they can be connected with lines. These lines are not part of the observations; they are only a convenience to help in eyeballing the observations. The points for 1980, 1990, and 2000 are labeled with the pairs of observations corresponding to Table 2.1, but in general, such labels are not needed.

One could choose scales different from those in Figure 2.7, and if you plotted your own graph from the data in Table 2.1 without looking at Figure 2.7, your scales probably would be different. The scales determine the amount of movement in a time-series graph. For example, Figure 2.8 shows two ways to stretch the scales to make the increase in the debt look more or less dramatic. So as not to be fooled by graphs, it is important to look at the scales and think about what they mean.

As an alternative to time-series graphs with dots connected by a line, the observations can be shown on a bar graph, as in Figure 2.9. Some people prefer the visual look of a bar graph, but, as is clear from a comparison of Figure 2.7 and Figure 2.9, they provide the same information as time-series graphs.

The debt as a percentage of GDP is given in Table 2.2 and graphed in Figure 2.10. Note that this figure makes the debt look different from the way it looks in the first one. As a percentage of GDP, the debt fell from the end of World War II (when it was large because of the war debt) until around 1980. It increased during the 1980s and declined in the 1990s, but started to increase again in the 2000s.

Some data to be graphed have no observations close to 0, in which case including 0 on the vertical axis would leave some wasted space at the bottom of the graph. To eliminate this space and have more room to see the graph, we can start the range near the minimum value and end it near the maximum value. This is done in Figure 2.11, where the debt as a percentage of GDP is shown up to 1990. Note, however, that cutting off the bottom of the scale could be misleading to people who do not look at the axis. In particular, 0 percent is no longer at the point where the horizontal and vertical axes intersect. To warn people about the missing part of the scale, a little cut is sometimes put on the axis, as is done in Figure 2.11, but you have to look carefully at the scale.

FIGURE 2.8 Stretching the Debt Story in Two Ways

The points in both graphs are identical to those in Figure 2.7, but by stretching or shrinking the scales, the problem can be made to look either less dramatic or more dramatic.

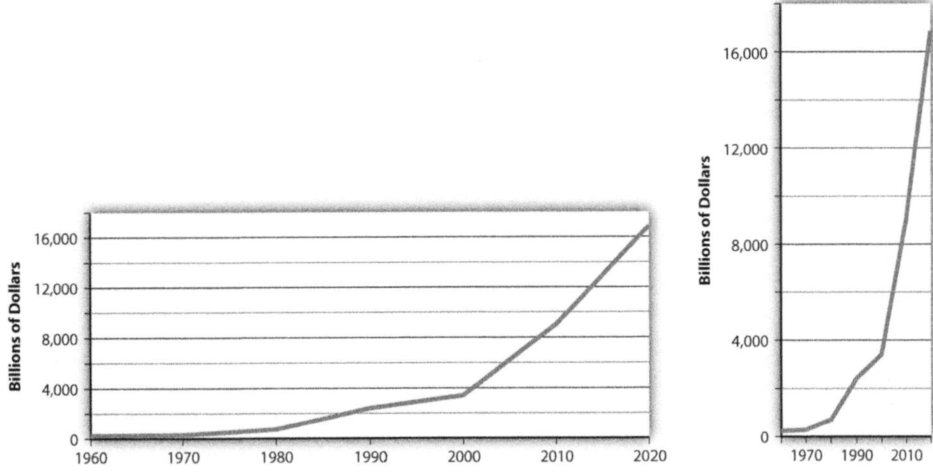

FIGURE 2.9 U.S. Federal Debt in Bars

The observations are identical to those in Figure 2.7.

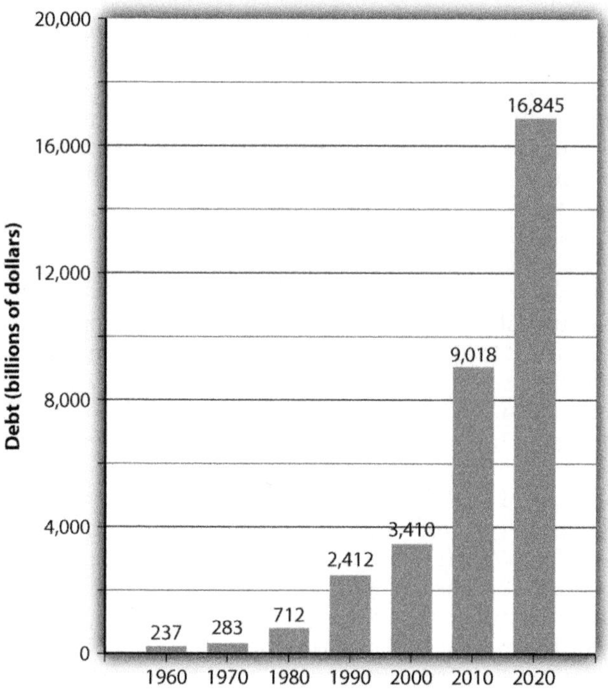

FIGURE 2.10 U.S. Federal Debt as a Percentage of GDP

Each point corresponds to a pair of observations from Table 2.2.

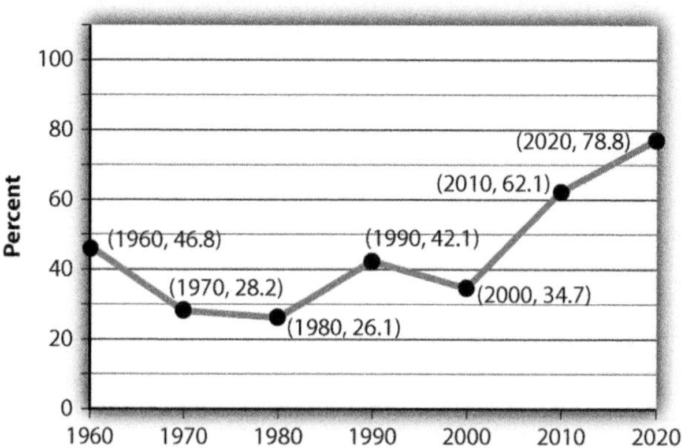

FIGURE 2.11 A Look at Debt as a Percentage of GDP from 1960 to 1990

(*Note:* To alert the reader that the bottom part of the axis is not shown, a break point is sometimes used, as shown here.)

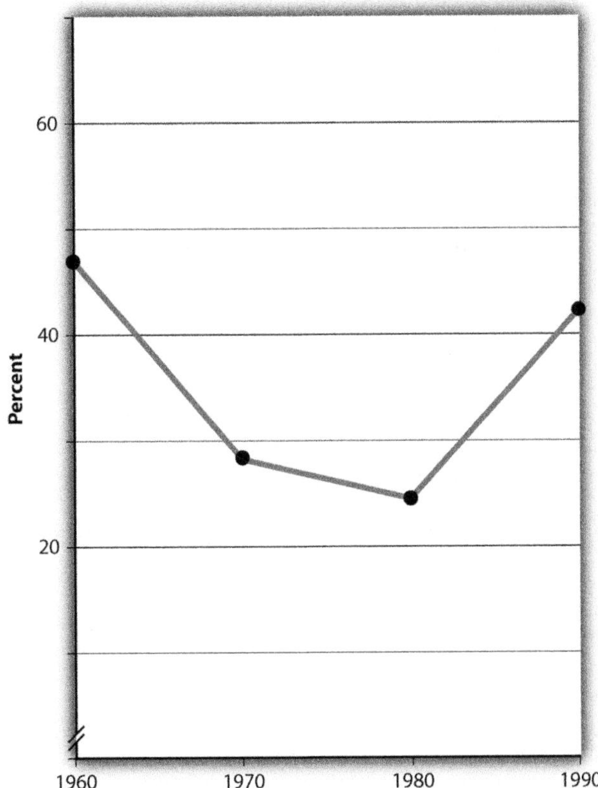

TABLE 2.2 U.S. Federal Debt as a Percentage of GDP

Year	Debt (percent of GDP)
1960	46.8
1970	28.2
1980	26.1
1990	42.1
2000	34.7
2010	62.1
2020 (Projected)	78.8

Source: Congressional Budget Office.

Time-Series Graphs Showing Two or More Variables

So far, we have shown how a graph can be used to show observations on one variable over time. What if we want to see how two or more variables change over time together? Suppose, for example, we want to look at how observations on debt as a percentage of GDP compare with the interest rate the government must pay on its debt. (The interest rate for 2020 is, of course, a forecast.) The two variables are shown in Table 2.3.

The two sets of observations can easily be placed on the same time-series graph. In other words, we can plot the observations on the debt percentage and connect the dots and then plot the interest rate observations and connect the dots. If the scales of measurement of the two variables are much different, however, it may be hard to see both. For example, the interest rate ranges between 1 and 12 percent; it would not be visible on a graph going all the way from 0 to 100 percent, a range that is fine for the debt percentage. In this situation, a **dual scale** can be used, as shown in Figure 2.12. One scale is put on the left-hand vertical axis, and the other scale is put on the right-hand vertical axis. With a dual-scale diagram, it is essential to be aware of the two scales. In Figure 2.12, we emphasize the different axes by the

dual scale

A graph that uses time on the horizontal axis and different scales on the left and right vertical axes to compare the movements of two variables over time.

color line segment at the top of each vertical axis. The color line segment corresponds to the color of the curve plotted using that scale.

Scatter Plots

scatter plot

A graph in which points in a Cartesian coordinate system represent the values of two variables.

Finally, two variables can be usefully compared with a **scatter plot**. The Cartesian coordinate method is used, as in the time-series graph; however, we do not put the year on one of the axes. Instead, the horizontal axis is used for one of the variables and the vertical axis for the other variable. We do this for the debt percentage and the interest rate in Figure 2.13. The interest rate is on the vertical axis, and the debt percentage is on the horizontal axis. For example, the point at the upper left is 26.1 percent for the debt as a percentage of GDP and 11.5 percent for the interest rate.

TABLE 2.3 Interest Rate and Federal Debt as a Percentage of GDP

Year	Debt (percent of GDP)	Interest Rate (percent)
1960	46.8	4.1
1970	28.2	7.3
1980	26.1	11.5
1990	42.1	8.6
2000	34.7	6.0
2010	62.1	3.2
2020 (Projected)	78.8	2.3

FIGURE 2.12 Comparing Two Time Series with a Dual Scale

When two variables have different scales, a dual scale is useful. Here the interest rate and the debt as a percentage of GDP are plotted from Table 2.3.

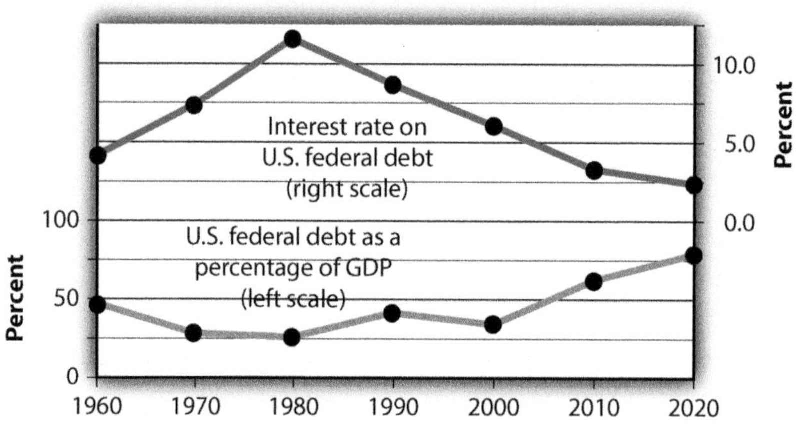

FIGURE 2.13 Scatter Plot

Interest rate and debt as a percentage of GDP are shown.

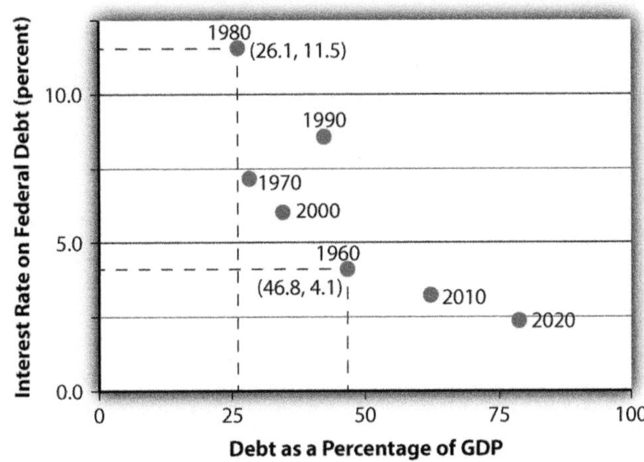

5.2 Visualizing Models with Graphs

Graphs can also represent models. Like graphs showing observations, graphs showing models usually are restricted to curves in two dimensions.

Slopes of Curves

Does a curve slope up or down? How steep is it? These questions are important to economics, as in other sciences. The **slope** of a curve tells us how much the variable on the vertical axis changes when we change the variable on the horizontal axis by one unit.

slope

A characteristic of a curve that is defined as the change in the variable on the vertical axis divided by the change in the variable on the horizontal axis.

The slope is computed as follows:

$$\text{Slope} = \frac{\text{change in variable on vertical axis}}{\text{change in variable on horizontal axis}}$$

In most algebra courses, the vertical axis is usually called the *y*-axis and the horizontal axis is called the *x*-axis. Thus, the slope is sometime described as

$$\text{Slope} = \frac{\text{change in y}}{\text{change in x}} = \frac{\Delta y}{\Delta x}$$

where the Greek letter Δ means "change in." In other words, the slope is the ratio of the "rise" (vertical change) to the run (horizontal change).

Figure 2.14 shows how to compute the slope. In this case, the slope declines as the variable on the *x*-axis increases.

Observe that *the steeper the curve, the larger the slope.* When the curve gets very flat, the slope gets close to zero. Curves can either be upward-sloping or downward-sloping. If the curve slopes up from left to right, as in Figure 2.14, it has a **positive slope**, and we say that the two variables are positively related. If the curve slopes down from left to right, it has a **negative slope**, and we say that the two variables are negatively related. Figure 2.15 shows a case where the slope is negative. When x increases by 1 unit ($\Delta x = 1$), y declines by 2 units ($\Delta y = -2$). Thus, the slope equals –2; it is negative. Observe how the curve slopes down from left to right.

positive slope

A slope of a curve that is greater than zero, representing a positive or direct relationship between two variables.

negative slope

A slope of a curve that is less than zero, representing a negative or inverse relationship between two variables.

linear

A situation in which a curve is straight, with a constant slope.

If the curve is a straight line, then the slope is a constant. Curves that are straight lines—like that in Figure 2.15—are called **linear**. But economic relationships do not need to be linear, as the example in Figure 2.14 makes clear. Figure 2.16 shows six different examples of curves and indicates how they are described.

FIGURE 2.14 Measuring the Slope

The slope between two points is given by the change along the vertical axis divided by the change along the horizontal axis. In this example, the slope declines as *x* increases. Because the curve slopes up from left to right, it has a positive slope.

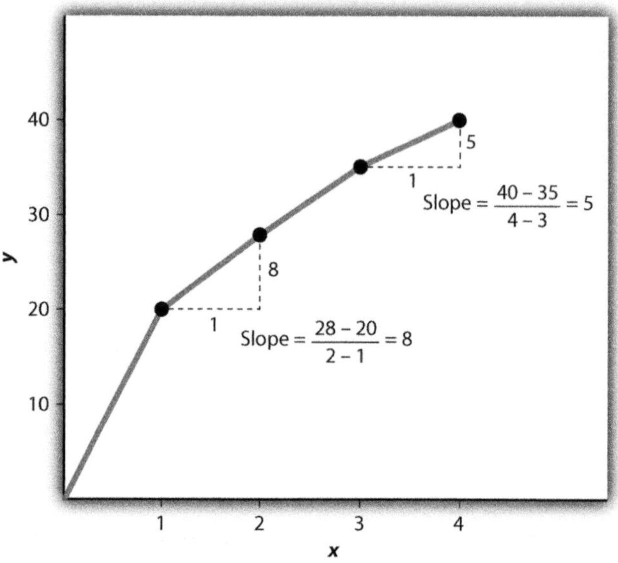

FIGURE 2.15 A Relationship with a Negative Slope

Here the slope is negative: as *x* increases, *y* falls. The line slopes down from left to right. In this case, *y* and *x* are inversely, or negatively, related.

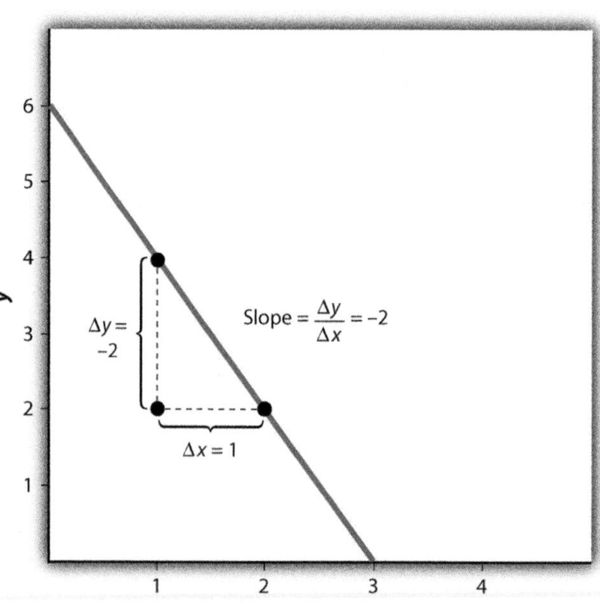

FIGURE 2.16 Six Types of Relationships

In the top row, the variables are positively related. In the bottom row, they are negatively related.

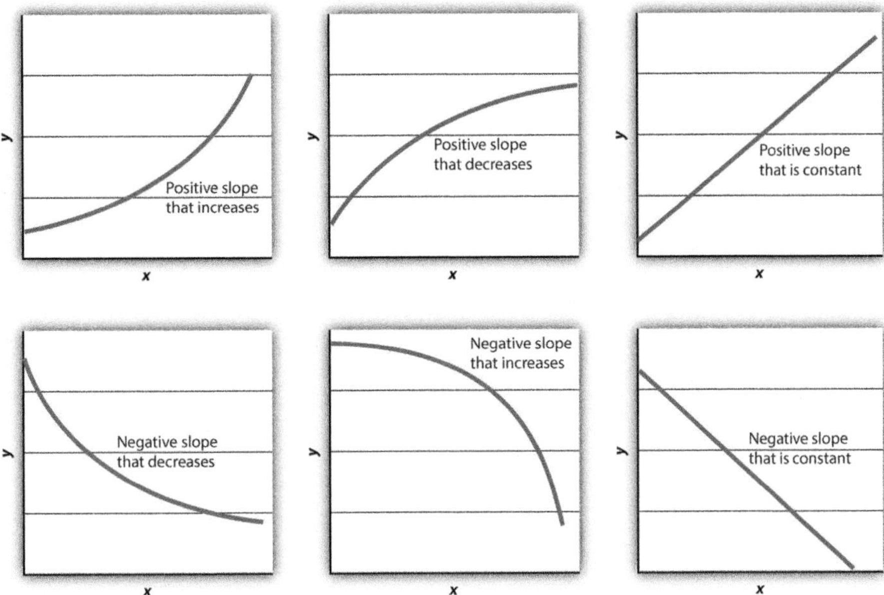

Graphs of Models with More Than Two Variables

In most cases, economic models involve more than two variables. For example, the number of physical examinations could depend on the number of nurses as well as the number of doctors. Or the amount of lemonade demanded might depend on the weather as well as on the price.

Economists have devised several methods for representing models with more than two variables with two-dimensional graphs. Suppose, for example, that the relationship between y and x in Figure 2.15 depends on a third variable z. For a given value of x, larger values of z lead to larger values of y. This example is graphed in Figure 2.17. As in Figure 2.15, when x increases, y falls. This is a **movement along the curve**. But what if z changes? We represent this as a **shift of the curve**. An increase in z shifts the curve up; a decrease in z shifts the curve down.

Thus, by distinguishing between shifts of and movements along a curve, economists represent models with more than two variables in only two dimensions. Only two variables (x and y) are shown explicitly on the graph, and when the third (z) is fixed, changes in x and y are movements along the curve. When z changes, the curve shifts. The distinction between "movements along" and "shifts of" curves comes up many times in economics.

movement along the curve

A situation in which a change in the variable on one axis causes a change in the variable on the other axis, but the position of the curve is maintained.

shift of the curve

A change in the position of a curve, usually caused by a change in a variable not represented on either axis.

FIGURE 2.17 **A Third Variable Shifts the Curve**

To represent models with three variables (*x*, *y*, and *z*) on a two-dimensional graph, economists distinguish between movements along the curve (when *x* and *y* change, holding *z* unchanged) and shifts of the curve (when *z* changes).

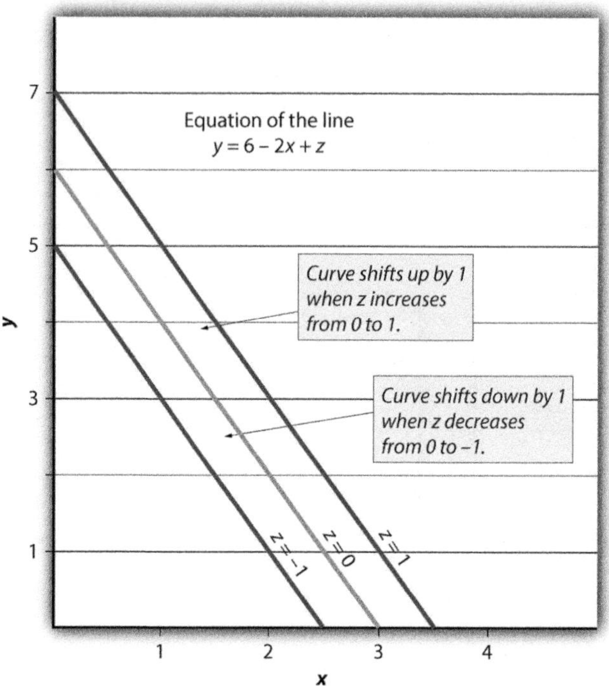

QUESTIONS FOR REVIEW

1. What is the difference between a scatter plot and a time-series graph?
2. Why are dual scales sometimes necessary?
3. What is the advantage of graphs over verbal representations of models?
4. What does a curve with a negative slope look like?
5. What is the difference between a shift in a curve and a movement along a curve?

PROBLEMS

1. Suppose the following table presents data on the debt (in billions of dollars), the debt to GDP ratio, and the interest rate predicted by the Congressional Budget Office for the United States for each year through 2021.

Year	Debt	Debt to GDP Ratio (percent)	Interest Rate
2010	9,018	62.1%	3.2
2011	10,439	69.4%	3.4
2012	11,598	73.9%	3.8
2013	12,386	75.5%	4.2
2014	12,996	75.3%	4.6
2015	13,625	74.9%	5.0
2016	14,358	75.0%	5.3
2017	15,064	75.2%	5.4
2018	15,767	75.3%	5.4
2019	16,557	75.8%	5.4
2020	17,392	76.2%	5.4
2021	18,253	76.7%	5.4

a. Construct a time-series plot of the ratio of government debt to GDP.

b. Construct a time-series plot of the debt.

c. Construct a scatter plot of the debt ratio and the interest rate.

2. The following table shows the number of physical examinations given by doctors at health maintenance organizations with three different-size clinics: small, medium, and large. The larger the clinic, the more patients the doctors can handle.

Exams per Small Clinic	Exams per Medium Clinic	Exams per Large Clinic	Number of Doctors
0	0	0	0
20	30	35	1
28	42	49	2
35	53	62	3
40	60	70	4

a. Show the relationship between doctors and physical exams given with three curves, where the number of doctors is on the horizontal axis and the number of examinations is on the vertical axis.

b. Describe how the three relationships compare with one another.

c. Is a change in the number of doctors a shift of or a movement along the curve?

d. Is a change in the size of the clinic a shift of or a movement along the curve?

CHAPTER 3
The Supply and Demand Model

In February 2017, the New England Patriots defeated the Atlanta Falcons in Super Bowl LI, widely considered to be one of the best, if not the best, game played between the last two teams left standing in the National Football League (NFL). On the field, records were smashed—the NFL counted at least 30 new records were set in a game that featured a thrilling fourth quarter comeback win by the Patriots. Records were set off the field as well—advertising rates for a 30-second television commercial topped $5 million or about $150,000 per second of television time. This was almost a 50% increase from the per-minute cost of a television advertisement in 2010 and an unfathomable 130-fold increase from the first Super Bowl, which was played 50 years previously between the Green Bay Packers and the Kansas City Chiefs.

The estimated television audience for the Super Bowl was 111 million, down slightly from the record of 114 million from the Patriots previous Super Bowl appearance in 2015. However, only around 71,000 people were able to watch the 2017 Super Bowl in person at the home arena of the Houston Texans. How does one become the fortunate one in 1,500 to attend the Super Bowl in person? It turns out that the NFL does not sell Super Bowl tickets directly to the general public. You could be one of the lucky fans to win a lottery for 1,000 tickets held directly by the NFL. Or you could be a lucky season ticket holder for one of the two participating teams, which typically get about a third of the tickets between them. If you were a season ticket holder who won the lottery you then would have to decide between going to the Super Bowl or reselling the ticket for a staggeringly high price and join the tens of millions watching the game at home. If you were lucky enough to win the lottery you would be able to buy tickets at face values ranging from $1,000 to $3,000 from the NFL but you would soon find out that plenty of people would pay $5,000 to $10,000 for those tickets, quite a temptation for even the most devoted fan. On the other hand, if you were a devoted football fan who did not win the lottery, you would find yourself having to pay several thousand dollars for a Super Bowl ticket, either to an online ticket broker or to a seller on an online auction site.

Source: U.S. Customs and Border Protection (160204-H-NI589-151) [Public domain], via Wikimedia Commons

Why does a Super Bowl ticket cost so much? Why does it cost so much to buy a 30-second television commercial to be shown during the Super Bowl? Who decides what price to charge for a Super Bowl ticket? Why do the NFL and the participating teams use a lottery system to select fans who are then permitted to buy tickets at a much lower price than that charged by a street seller or by an online ticket broker? Who ends up going to the Super Bowl, and who ends up selling their ticket and watching the game and the commercials on television? The purpose of this chapter is to show how to find the answers to such questions using the supply and demand model.

Recall from Chapter 2 that a model is a simplified description of a more complex reality. The supply and demand model is what economists use to explain how prices are determined in a market. We can use this model to understand the market for Super Bowl tickets or Final Four tickets, as well as in a variety of other settings. What causes the price of gasoline to fluctuate? What causes the price of computers to fall over time, even though the prices of most other goods seem to rise over time? Why do roses cost more on Valentine's Day? Once you understand how the model works, you will find yourself using it over and over again to understand the markets that you come across in your everyday life.

The supply and demand model consists of three elements: *demand*, describing the behavior of consumers in the market; *supply*, describing the behavior of firms in the market; and *market equilibrium*, connecting supply and demand and describing how consumers and firms interact in the market. Economists like to compare the supply and demand model to a pair of scissors. Demand is one blade of the scissors, and supply is the other. Either blade alone is incomplete and virtually useless; however, when the two blades of a pair of scissors are connected to form the scissors, they become an amazingly useful, yet simple, tool. So it is with the supply and demand model.

1. DEMAND

demand

A relationship between **price** and **quantity demanded**.

price

The amount of money or other goods that one must pay to obtain a particular good.

quantity demanded

The quantity of a good that people want to buy at a given price during a specific time period.

To an economist, the term *demand*—whether the demand for tickets or the demand for roses—has a very specific meaning. **Demand** is a relationship between two economic variables: (1) *the price of a particular good* and (2) *the quantity of that good that consumers are willing to buy at that price during a specific time period*, all other things being equal. For short, we call the first variable the **price** and the second variable the **quantity demanded**. The phrase *all other things being equal*, or *ceteris paribus*, is appended to the definition of demand because the quantity that consumers are willing to buy depends on many other things besides the price of the good; we want to hold these other things constant, or equal, while we examine the relationship between price and quantity demanded.

Demand can be represented by a numerical table or by a graph. In either case, demand describes how much of a good consumers will purchase at each price. Consider the demand for bicycles in a particular country, as presented in Table 3.1. Of course, because of the many kinds of bicycles—mountain bikes, racing bikes, children's bikes, and inexpensive one-speed bikes with cruiser brakes—you need to simplify and think about this table as describing demand for an average, or typical, bike.

Observe that, as the price rises, the quantity demanded by consumers goes down. If the price goes up from $180 to $200 per bicycle, for example, the quantity demanded goes down from 11 million to 9 million bicycles. On the other hand, if the price goes down, the quantity demanded goes up. If the price falls from $180 to $160, for example, the quantity demanded rises from 11 million to 14 million bicycles.

The relationship between price and quantity demanded in Table 3.1 is called a **demand schedule**. The relationship shows price and quantity demanded moving in opposite directions, and this is an example of the **law of demand**. The law of demand says that the higher the price, the lower the quantity demanded in the market; and the lower the price, the higher the quantity demanded in the market. In other words, the law of demand says that the price and the quantity demanded are negatively related, all other things being equal.

demand schedule

A tabular presentation of demand showing the price and quantity demanded for a particular good, all else being equal.

law of demand

The tendency for the quantity demanded of a good in a market to decline as its price rises.

1.1 The Demand Curve

Figure 3.1 represents demand graphically. The price of the good appears on the vertical axis and the quantity demanded of the good appears on the horizontal axis. It shows the demand for bicycles given in Table 3.1. Each of the nine rows in Table 3.1 corresponds to one of the nine points in Figure 3.1. For example, the point at the lower right part of the graph corresponds to the first row of the table, where the price is $140 and the quantity demanded is 18 million bicycles. The resulting curve showing all the combinations of price and quantity demanded is the **demand curve**. It slopes downward from left to right because the quantity demanded is negatively related to the price.

demand curve

A graph of demand showing the downward-sloping relationship between price and quantity demanded.

Why does the demand curve slope downward? When economists draw a demand curve, they hold constant the price of other goods: running shoes, in-line skates, motor scooters, and so on. Consumers have scarce resources and need to choose between bicycles and other goods. If the price of bicycles falls, then bicycles become more attractive to people in comparison with these other goods—some consumers who previously found the price of bicycles too high may decide to buy a bicycle rather than buy other goods. Conversely, when the price of bicycles increases, then bicycles become less attractive to people in comparison with other goods—some consumers may decide to buy in-line skates or motor scooters instead of bicycles. As a result, quantity demanded declines when the price rises and vice versa.

Plenty of real-world evidence indicates that demand curves are downward sloping. In 2016, the ride sharing firm Uber announced a cut in the per-mile travel charge in over a hundred cities that Uber had a presence in. News reports speculated that this price cut was aimed at putting pressure on their rival ride sharing firm Lyft. You might (correctly) speculate that this reduction in the price of ride sharing was intended to increase the number of potential customers switching from using Lyft vehicles to using Uber vehicles for their rides.

TABLE 3.1 Demand Schedule for Bicycles (millions of bicycles per year)

Price	Quantity Demanded	Price	Quantity Demanded
$140	18	$240	5
$160	14	$260	3
$180	11	$280	2
$200	9	$300	1
$220	7		

FIGURE 3.1 The Demand Curve

The demand curve shows that the price of a good and the quantity demanded by consumers are negatively related—the curve slopes down. For each price, the demand curve gives the quantity demanded, or the quantity that consumers are willing to buy at that price. The points along the demand curve for bicycles shown here are the same as the pairs of numbers in Table 3.1.

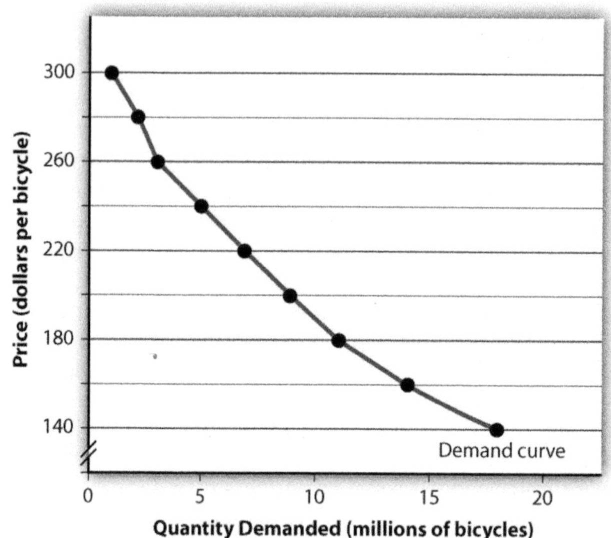

Similarly, policies designed to reduce smoking by teenagers or to cut down on drinking on college campuses often aim to do this by raising the price of cigarettes and alcohol. The idea, of course, is that teens would buy fewer cigarettes and students would buy less alcohol if these goods were more expensive.

1.2 Shifts in Demand

Price is not the only thing that affects the quantity of a good that people buy. Weather conditions, concerns about the environment, or the availability of bike lanes on roads can influence people's decisions to purchase bicycles, for example. If climate change brought on an extended period of warm weather, people would have more opportunities to ride their bicycles. As a result, more bicycles would be purchased at any given price. Or perhaps increased awareness of the health benefits of exercise might lead people to ride their bicycles to work rather than drive their cars. This also would lead to more purchases of bicycles at any given price. Alternatively, if bike lanes are taken away to allow for an extra lane of cars on the road, fewer bicycles would be purchased at any given price.

The demand curve is drawn assuming that all other things are equal, except the price of the good. A change in any one of these other things, therefore, will shift the demand curve. An increase in demand shifts the demand curve to the right—at every price, quantity demanded will increase. A decrease in demand shifts the demand curve to the left—at every price, quantity demanded will decrease.

An increase in demand is illustrated in Figure 3.2. The lightly shaded curve labeled "old demand curve" is the same as the demand curve in Figure 3.1. An extended period of warm weather will increase demand and shift the demand curve to the right. The arrow shows how this curve has shifted to the right to the more darkly shaded curve labeled "new demand curve." When the demand curve shifts to the right, more bicycles are purchased than before at any given price. For example, before the shift in demand, a $200 price led to 9 million bicycles being purchased. But when the demand curve shifts to the right because of warmer weather, that same price leads to 13 million bicycles being purchased. On the other hand, if bicycle lanes were taken away from roads, then the demand curve would shift to the left because people's purchases of bicycles would now be less at any given price.

FIGURE 3.2 A Shift in the Demand Curve

The demand curve shows how the quantity demanded of a good is related to the price of the good, all other things being equal. A change in one of these other things—the weather or people's tastes, for example—will shift the demand curve, as shown in the graph. In this case, the demand for bicycles increases; the demand curve for bicycles shifts to the right.

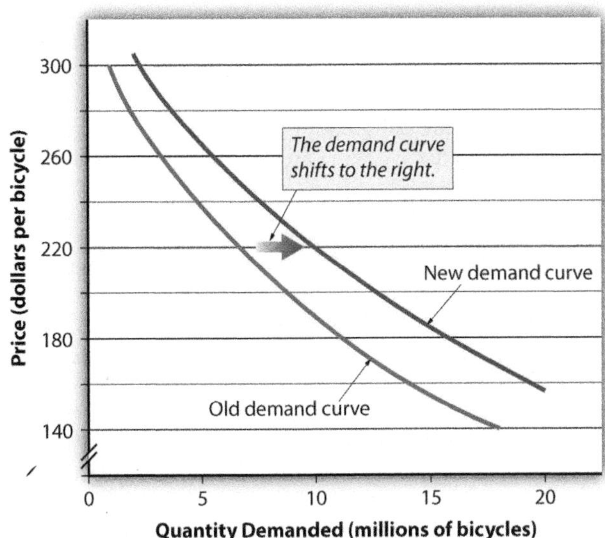

The demand curve may shift for many reasons. Most of these reasons can be attributed to one of several sources: *consumers' preferences, consumers' information, consumers' incomes, the number of consumers in the market, consumers' expectations of future prices*, and *the price of related goods.* Let us briefly consider each source of shifts in demand.

Consumers' Preferences

In general, a change in people's tastes or preferences for a product compared with other products will change the amount of the product they purchase at any given price. On many college campuses, demand for clothing that is certified as not having been produced in "sweatshops" has increased. Also, over the last couple of decades, consumers have shown a great deal of interest in buying "organically grown" fruits and vegetables, which are produced without using artificial pesticides or fertilizers.

Consumers' Information

A change in information relating to a product can also cause the demand curve to shift. For example, when people learned about the dangers of smoking, the demand for cigarettes declined. Shortly after an outbreak of *E. coli* in parts of the United States was linked to contaminated spinach, demand for spinach at grocery stores decreased. In 2015, the Environmental Protection Agency ruled that the German car-manufacturing giant Volkswagen had intentionally programmed their diesel cars to make it seem like they were emitting less pollution than they actually were. This scandal eventually led to a $4 billion fine and a recall of over 11 million cars. The fallout from this episode would lead to a sharp fall in the demand for diesel-engine automobiles made by Volkswagen.

Consumers' Incomes

If people's incomes change, then their purchases of goods usually change. An increase in income increases the demand for most goods, while a decline in income reduces the demand for these goods. Goods for which demand increases when income rises and decreases when income falls are called **normal goods** by economists. Many of the goods that people typically purchase—shoes, clothing, jewelry—fall into the category of normal goods.

normal goods

A good for which demand increases when income rises and decreases when income falls.

However, the demand for some goods may decline when income increases. Such goods are called **inferior goods** by economists. The demand for inferior goods declines when people's income increases because they can afford more attractive goods. For example, instant noodles form the basis of many college students' diets. After these students leave college and start working and earning a salary, however, many will switch over to eating microwavable meals or to eating out in restaurants. Thus, the demand for instant noodles will fall as income rises. Another example of an inferior good that is familiar to many college students in Boston and New York is the cheap bus service that runs between the

inferior goods

A good for which demand decreases when income rises and increases when income falls.

Chinatowns in the two cities; a bus ticket may cost as little as $10, whereas a plane ticket between the two cities may cost $150. As students graduate and start earning money, however, they often buy more of the $150 plane tickets and fewer of the $10 bus tickets. In this case, the plane ticket is categorized as a normal good, and the bus ticket is categorized as an inferior good.

Number of Consumers in the Market

Demand is a relationship between price and the quantity demanded by *all* consumers in the market. If the number of consumers increases, then demand will increase. If the number of consumers falls, then demand will decrease. For example, the number of teenagers in the U.S. population expanded sharply in the late 1990s. This increased the demand for *Seventeen* magazine, Rollerblades, Clearasil, and other goods that teenagers tend to buy. As the baby boom generation in the United States ages, the demand for health care, hair coloring kits, and luxury skin care products is increasing.

Consumers' Expectations of Future Prices

If people expect the price of a good to increase, they will want to buy it before the price increases. Conversely, if people expect the price of goods to decline, they will purchase fewer items and wait for the decline. One often sees this effect of expectations of future price changes. "We'd better buy before the price goes up" is a common reason for purchasing items during a clearance sale. Or, "Let's put off buying that flat-screen television until the post-holiday sales."

In general, it is difficult to forecast the future, but consumers sometimes know quite a bit about whether the price of a good will rise or fall, and they react accordingly. Thus, demand increases if people expect the *future* price of the good to rise. And demand decreases if people expect the *future* price of the good to fall.

In 2009, Congress created a program that aimed to provide incentives for U.S. consumers to buy new, more fuel-efficient cars by trading in their older, less fuel-efficient vehicles. This program, popularly known as "Cash for Clunkers," offered customers about a $4,000 discount for buying a new car. Many people moved up their planned car purchases to take advantage of the "Cash for Clunkers" program. The program, which was planned to run for five months, exhausted all the available funds allocated to it, and $2 billion more in additional allocations, in less than two months.

Prices of Closely Related Goods

substitute

A good that has many of the same characteristics as, and can be used in place of, another good.

A change in the price of a closely related good can increase or decrease demand for another good, depending on whether the good is a substitute or a complement. A **substitute** is a good that provides some of the same uses or enjoyment as another good. Butter and margarine are substitutes. In general, the demand for a good will increase if the price of a substitute for the good rises, and the demand for a good will decrease if the price of a substitute falls. Sales of CDs and downloaded music are substitutes as are DVD/Blu-Ray movie sales and streaming services like Hulu and Netflix. In the most recent decade sales of music CDs have shown a sharp downward trend as the price of downloaded music and the price of music streaming services like Spotify has decreased.

complement

A good that usually is consumed or used together with another good.

A **complement** is a good that tends to be consumed together with another good. Gasoline and sport utility vehicles (SUVs) are complements. The rapid increase in gasoline prices in 2007 and the early part of 2008 led to a decrease in demand for SUVs.

1.3 Movements Along versus Shifts of the Demand Curve

We have shown that the demand curve can shift, and we have given many possible reasons for such shifts. As you begin to use demand curves, it is important that you be able to distinguish *shifts* of the demand curve from *movements along* the demand curve. This distinction is illustrated in Figure 3.3.

A *movement along* the demand curve occurs when the quantity demanded changes as a result of a *change in the price of the good.* For example, if the price of bicycles rises, causing the quantity demanded by consumers to fall, then there is a movement along the demand curve. You can see in Figure 3.3 that at point *A*, the price is $200 and the quantity demanded is 9 million. Now suppose the price rises to $220. The quantity demanded then falls from 9 million to 7 million. This can be shown as a movement along the demand curve for bicycles from point *A* to point *B*. Conversely, if the price of a bicycle falls to $180, then the quantity demanded will increase to 11 million bicycles.

FIGURE 3.3 **Shifts of versus Movements Along the Demand Curve**

A *shift* of the demand curve occurs when a change in something (other than the good's own price) affects the quantity of a good that consumers are willing to buy. An increase in demand is a shift to the right of the demand curve. A decrease in demand is a shift to the left of the demand curve. A *movement along* the demand curve occurs when the price of the good changes, causing the quantity demanded to change, as, for example, from point *A* to point *B* or *C*.

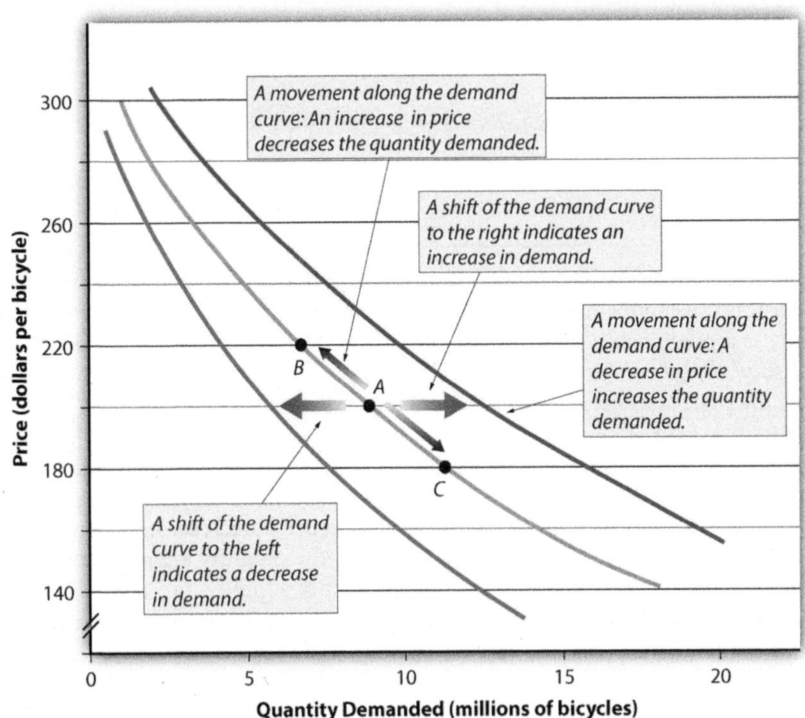

This can be shown as an increase from point *A* to point *C* in Figure 3.3. Economists refer to a movement along the demand curve as a *change in the quantity demanded.*

A *shift* of the demand curve, on the other hand, occurs when a change is caused by *any source except the price.* Remember, the term *demand* refers to the entire curve or schedule relating price and quantity demanded, whereas the term *quantity demanded* refers to a single point on the demand curve. As we discussed, if warm weather increases, people would be more likely to buy bicycles at any given price. This means that the entire demand curve would shift to the right. On the other hand, if bicycle lanes are eliminated, people would be less likely to buy bicycles at any given price. The entire demand curve would shift to the left. Economists refer to a shift in the demand curve as a *change in demand.*

You should be able to tell whether an economic event causes (1) a change in demand or (2) a change in the quantity demanded; or, equivalently, whether an event causes (1) a shift in the demand curve or (2) a movement along the demand curve. Use the following example to test your understanding of demand shifts and movement along the demand curve. Suppose that Disney's theme park attendance was lower in a recession year than in previous years because of a weak economy. Because of the fall in attendance, suppose Disney lowered the adult admission price at its California Adventure park, which helped increase attendance. Which of these was a *change in demand* and which was a *change in the quantity demanded* in the market for theme parks?

The decrease in attendance caused by the weak economy was a decrease in demand—fewer people were going to theme parks in a recession year than in prior years for any given ticket price. The demand curve for theme park visits thus shifted to the left. When Disney lowered its admission price, it hoped to entice more people to spend their money on a trip to its California Adventure park instead of on other goods. This is an increase in the quantity demanded—the park management anticipated more attendance at a lower price. This was a movement along the demand curve for theme park visits.

REVIEW

- Demand is a negative relationship between the price of a good and the quantity demanded, all other things being equal.
- The demand curve slopes down because when the price of a good rises, consumers are less likely to use their scarce resources to buy that good. Conversely, when the price of a good falls, some consumers who previously had not chosen to buy the good because the price was too high may decide to buy the good.
- It is important to distinguish shifts of the demand curve from movements along the demand curve. When the quantity demanded changes as a result of a price change, we have a movement along the demand curve. When a change in demand is brought about by something other than a price change, we have a shift of the demand curve.

2. SUPPLY

Whereas demand refers to the behavior of consumers, supply refers to the behavior of firms. The term *supply*—whether it is the supply of tickets or the supply of computers—has a specific meaning for economists. **Supply** is a relationship between two variables: (1) *the price of a particular good* and (2) *the quantity of the good that firms are willing to sell at that price*, all other things being the same. We call the first variable the price and the second variable the **quantity supplied**.

supply

A relationship between price and quantity supplied.

quantity supplied

The quantity of a good that firms are willing to sell at a given price.

Supply can be represented by a numerical table or by a graph. An example of the quantity supplied (in millions of bicycles) in the entire market by bicycle-producing firms at each price is shown in Table 3.2. For example, at a price of $180, the quantity supplied is 7 million bicycles. Observe that as the price increases, the quantity supplied increases, and that as the price decreases, the quantity supplied decreases. For example, if the price rises from $180 to $200, the quantity supplied increases from 7 to 9 million bicycles. The relationship between price and quantity supplied in Table 3.2 is called a **supply schedule**. The relationship shows price and quantity supplied moving in the same direction, and this is an example of the law of supply. The **law of supply** says that the higher the price, the higher the quantity supplied; and the lower the price, the lower the quantity supplied. In other words, the law of supply says that the price and the quantity supplied are positively related, all other things being equal.

supply schedule

A tabular presentation of supply showing the price and quantity supplied of a particular good, all else being equal.

law of supply

The tendency for the quantity supplied of a good in a market to increase as its price rises.

2.1 The Supply Curve

We can represent the supply schedule in Table 3.2 graphically by plotting the price and quantity supplied on a graph, as shown in Figure 3.4. The scales of each axis in Figure 3.4 are exactly the same as those in Figure 3.1, except that Figure 3.4 shows the quantity supplied, whereas Figure 3.1 shows the quantity demanded. Each pair of numbers in Table 3.2 is plotted as a point in Figure 3.4. The resulting curve showing all the combinations of prices and quantities supplied is the **supply curve**. Note that the curve slopes upward: At a price of $280, the quantity supplied is high—16 million bicycles. If the price were $160 a bicycle, then firms would be willing to sell only 4 million bicycles.

supply curve

A graph of supply showing the upward-sloping relationship between price and quantity supplied.

Why does the supply curve slope upward? Imagine yourself running a firm that produces and sells bicycles. If the price of the bicycles goes up from $180 to $280, then you can earn $100 more for each bicycle you produce and sell. Given your production costs, if you earn more from each bicycle, you will have a greater incentive to produce and sell more bicycles. If producing more bicycles increases the costs of producing each bicycle, perhaps because you must pay the bike assembly workers a higher wage for working overtime, the higher price will give you the incentive to incur these costs. Other bicycle firms will be thinking the same way. Thus, firms are willing to sell more bicycles as the price rises. Conversely, the incentive for firms to sell bicycles will decline as the price falls. Basically, that is why a positive relationship exists between price and quantity supplied.

When formulating economic policy, it is important to remember this supply relationship. When the price of a good increases, it leads to an increase in the quantity supplied. If U.S. agricultural policy results in the U.S. government offering to pay farmers a higher price for their corn, then the farmers will respond by increasing their production of corn. If coffee prices on the world market collapse, some coffee farmers in developing countries will switch to producing other crops instead of coffee.

TABLE 3.2 Supply Schedule for Bicycles (millions of bicycles per year)

Price	Quantity Supplied
$140	1
$160	4
$180	7
$200	9
$220	11
$240	13
$260	15
$280	16
$300	17

2.2 Shifts in Supply

The supply curve is a relationship between price and the quantity supplied drawn on the assumption that all other things are held constant. If any one of these other things changes, then the supply curve shifts. For example, suppose a new machine is invented that makes it possible to produce bicycle frames at less cost; then firms would have more incentive at any given price to produce and sell more bicycles. Supply would increase, and the supply curve would shift to the right.

FIGURE 3.4 The Supply Curve

The supply curve shows that the price and the quantity supplied by firms in the market are positively related. The curve slopes up. For each price on the vertical axis, the supply curve shows the quantity that firms are willing to sell along the horizontal axis. The points along the supply curve for bicycles match the pairs of numbers in Table 3.2.

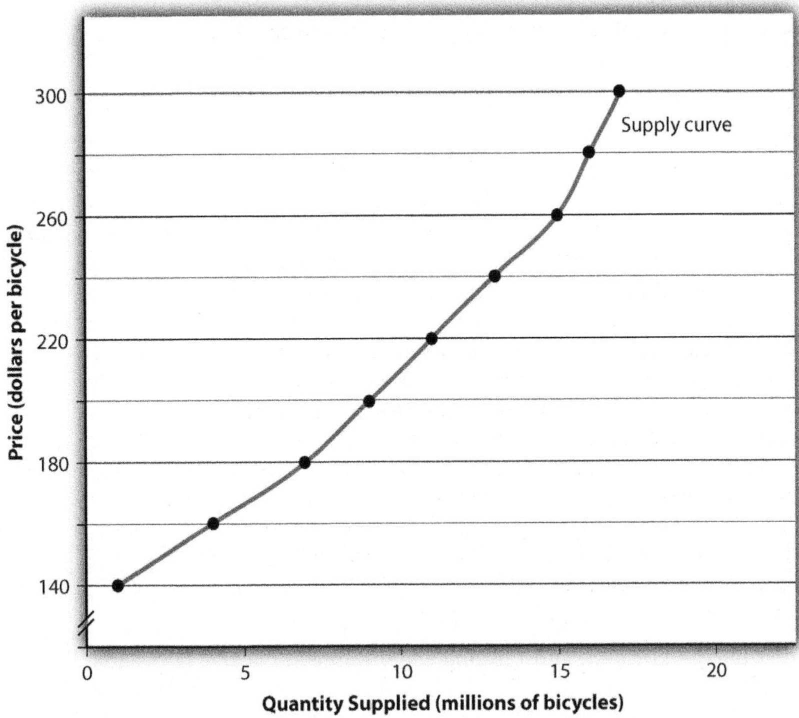

Figure 3.5 shows that the supply curve for bicycles would shift to the right because of a new cost-reducing machine. The supply curve would shift to the left if supply decreased. Supply would decrease, for example, if bicycle-producing firms suddenly found that their existing machines would break down unless they were oiled with an expensive lubricant each time a bicycle was produced. This would raise costs, lower supply, and shift the supply curve to the left.

Many things can cause the supply curve to shift. Most of these can be categorized by the source of the change in supply: *technology, weather conditions, the price of inputs used in production, the number of firms in the market*, *expectations of future prices*, and *government taxes, subsidies, and regulations.* Let us briefly consider the sources of shifts in supply.

Technology

Anything that changes the amount a firm can produce with a given amount of inputs to production can be considered a change in technology. The Harbour Report, a study that examines the number of labor hours needed to produce an automobile, calculated that in 2005, General Motors needed 34 hours per vehicle, while Toyota needed only 28 hours per vehicle. Suppose an improvement in technology enabled General Motors to reduce the time it took to produce a car by six hours per vehicle. This improvement in technology would correspond to an increase in supply, a shift in the supply curve to the right. Another way of viewing an increase in supply is that producers are willing to sell any given quantity at a lower price than before. This makes sense, because production costs are lower with the improvement in technology.

FIGURE 3.5 A Shift in the Supply Curve

The supply curve is a relationship between the quantity supplied of a good and the price of the good, all other things being equal. A change in one of these other things (other than the good's price) will shift the supply curve, as shown in the graph. In this case, the supply of bicycles increases; the supply curve for bicycles shifts to the right.

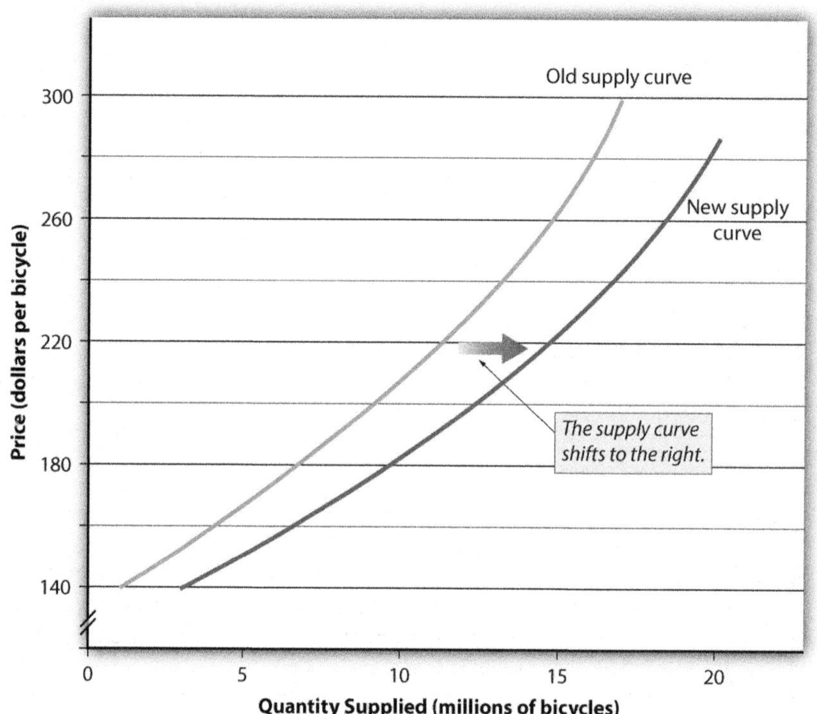

Weather Conditions

Droughts, earthquakes, and hurricanes also affect how much of certain types of goods can be produced with given inputs. A drought can reduce the amount of wheat that can be produced on a farm in the Midwest. The floods that devastated some regions in Australia in early 2011 resulted in a fall in cotton supplies on the world market, for which Australia is a leading producer and exporter. Hurricanes Katrina and Rita disrupted oil drilling and refining activities in Texas and Louisiana. Because such events change the amount that can be produced with a given amount of inputs, they are similar to changes in technology. In the examples just given, the supply curve shifted to the left, although you could have favorable weather conditions that would shift the supply curve for a particular good to the right.

The Price of Inputs Used in Production

If the prices of the inputs to production—raw materials, labor, and capital—increase, then it becomes more costly to produce goods, and firms will produce less at any given price. In this case, the supply curve will shift to the left. When the U.S. government imposed trade restrictions that caused the price of imported steel to rise in 2002, firms that used imported steel to produce household appliances were unwilling to produce the same quantity of appliances at existing price levels. So an increase in production costs causes the supply curve to shift to the left, and a decrease in production costs causes the supply curve to shift to the right.

The Number of Firms in the Market

Remember that the supply curve refers to *all* the firms producing the product. If the number of firms increases, then more goods will be produced at each price: supply increases, and the supply curve shifts to the right. A decline in the number of firms, on the other hand, would shift the supply curve to the left. For example, if a country removes barriers that prevent foreign car manufacturers from selling cars to the domestic market, then the number of firms producing cars for that country's domestic market will increase, and the supply curve for cars in that economy will shift to the right.

Expectations of Future Prices

If firms expect the price of the good they produce to rise in the future, then they will hold off selling at least part of their production until the price rises. For example, farmers in the United States who anticipate an increase in wheat prices because of political turbulence in the Russian Federation may decide to store more wheat in silos and sell it later, after the price rises. Thus, expectations of *future* price increases tend to reduce supply. Conversely, expectations of *future* price decreases tend to increase supply.

Government Taxes, Subsidies, and Regulations

The government has the ability to affect the supply of particular goods produced by firms. For example, the government imposes taxes on firms to pay for such government services as education, police, and national defense. These taxes increase firms' costs and reduce supply. The supply curve shifts to the left when a tax on what firms sell in the market increases.

The government also makes payments—subsidies—to firms to encourage those firms to produce certain goods. Such subsidies have the opposite effect of taxes on supply. An increase in subsidies reduces firms' costs and increases the supply. If the U.S. government provided subsidies for corn production to encourage the use of ethanol, an alternative fuel for cars that is produced from corn, this would increase the production of corn. On the other hand, when the U.S. government imposes a tax on cigarettes, the supply of cigarettes will decrease.

Governments also regulate firms. In some cases, such regulations can change the firms' costs of production or their ability to produce goods and thereby affect supply. For example, if a city government decides that only vendors who successfully pass a health and sanitation inspection are allowed to sell food from street carts, the supply curve for street-vendor food will shift to the left.

2.3 Movements Along versus Shifts of the Supply Curve

As with the demand curve, it is important that you understand how to distinguish between *shifts* of the supply curve and *movements along* the supply curve. This distinction is illustrated in Figure 3.6.

A *movement along* the supply curve occurs when the quantity supplied changes as a result of a *change in the price of the good.* For example, if a copper mine in Zambia increases its production because the price of copper has increased on the world market, then that indicates a movement along the supply curve. In our bicycle example, an increase in the price of bicycles from $200 to $220 would increase the quantity supplied from 9 million bicycles to 11 million bicycles. This can be shown as a movement along the supply curve for bicycles from point *D* to point *F.* Conversely, if the price of a bicycle were to fall from $200 to $180, then the quantity supplied would decrease to 7 million bicycles. This can be shown as movement from point *D* to point *E* in Figure 3.6. Economists refer to a movement along the supply curve as a *change in the quantity supplied.*

FIGURE 3.6 **Shifts of versus Movements Along the Supply Curve**

A shift of the supply curve occurs when a change in something (other than the price) affects the amount of a good that firms are willing to supply. An increase in supply is a shift to the right of the supply curve. A decrease in supply is a shift to the left of the supply curve. A movement along the supply curve occurs when the price of the good changes, causing the quantity supplied by firms to change—for example, from point *D* to point *E* or *F*.

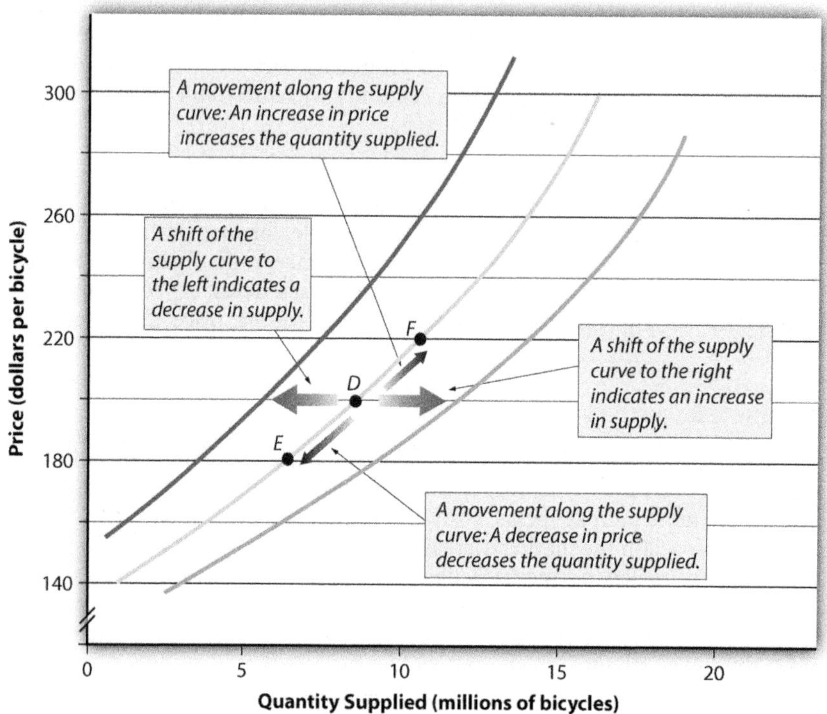

A *shift* of the supply curve, on the other hand, occurs if a change is caused by *any source except the price.* An unexpected winter freeze in California will mean that farmers will be able to produce fewer oranges at any given price. This means that the supply curve of oranges will shift to the left. When the supply curve shifts, economists call that a *change in supply.*

You should be able to tell whether a change in something causes (1) a change in supply or (2) a change in the quantity supplied; or, equivalently, if a change causes (1) a shift in the supply curve or (2) a movement along the supply curve. The following example will test your ability to distinguish between movement along a supply curve and a shift in the supply curve. Suppose that U.S. agricultural policy guarantees farmers a specific price on certain crops. An economist suggested that the government instead should pay farmers to not plant some of their fields. Which policy is describing a *change in supply* and which is describing a *change in the quantity supplied* in the market for corn?

A policy that pays farmers to leave cornfields unplanted describes a decrease in supply. The amount of corn supplied will be lower at any price. When the U.S. government guarantees the price of corn, this describes an increase in the quantity supplied—more corn will be grown in anticipation of the higher price. The increase in price leading to an increase in quantity supplied corresponds to movement along the supply curve.

REVIEW

- Supply is a positive relationship between the price of a good and the quantity supplied of the good by firms.
- The supply curve slopes upward because, all else equal, a higher price offers greater incentive for a firm to produce and sell more goods.
- It is important to distinguish shifts of the supply curve from movements along the supply curve. When the quantity supplied changes because of a change in price, we have a movement along the supply curve. Other factors—such as technology, weather, the number of firms, and expectations—can lead to a shift in the supply curve.

3. MARKET EQUILIBRIUM: COMBINING SUPPLY AND DEMAND

Figure 3.7 summarizes what you have learned thus far about consumers' demand for goods in a market and firms' supply of goods in a market. Now, we put supply and demand together to complete the supply and demand model. Consumers who want to buy goods and firms that want to sell goods interact in a market. When consumers and firms interact, a price is determined at which the transaction occurs. Recall that a market does not need to be located at one place; the U.S. bicycle market consists of all the bicycle firms that sell bicycles and all the consumers who buy bicycles.

Fascinatingly, no single person or firm determines the price in the market. Instead, the market determines the price. As buyers and sellers interact, prices may go up for a while and then go down. Alfred Marshall, the economist who did the most to develop the supply and demand model in the late nineteenth century, called this process the "higgling and bargaining" of the market. The assumption underlying the supply and demand model is that, in the give and take of the marketplace, prices adjust until they settle down at a level at which the quantity supplied by firms equals the quantity demanded by consumers. Let's see how.

3.1 Determination of the Market Price

To determine the market price, we combine the demand relationship with the supply relationship. We can do this using either a table or a diagram. First consider Table 3.3, which combines the demand schedule from Table 3.1 with the supply schedule from Table 3.2. The price is in the first column, the quantity demanded by consumers is in the second column, and the quantity supplied by firms is in the third column. Observe that the quantity that consumers are willing to buy is shown to decline with the price, whereas the quantity that firms are willing to sell is shown to increase with the price.

Finding the Market Price

Pick a price in Table 3.3, any price. Suppose the price you choose is $160. Then the quantity demanded by consumers (14 million bicycles) is greater than the quantity supplied by firms (4 million bicycles). In other words, there is a shortage of 14 - 4 = 10 million bicycles. A **shortage (excess demand)** is a situation in which the quantity demanded is greater than the quantity supplied. With a shortage of bicycles, buyers who really need a bicycle will start to offer to pay more to acquire a bicycle, while firms that are faced with an abundance of potential customers wanting to buy their bicycles will begin to charge higher prices. Thus, $160 cannot last as the market price. Observe that as the price rises above $160, the quantity demanded falls and the quantity supplied rises. Thus, as the price rises, the shortage begins to decrease. Suppose the price increases to $180. At that price, the quantity demanded falls to 11 million bicycles and the quantity supplied rises to 7 million bicycles. A shortage still exists and the price still will rise, but the shortage is now much less, at 11 – 7 = 4 million bicycles. The shortage will disappear only when the price rises to $200, as shown in Table 3.3.

shortage (excess demand)

A situation in which quantity demanded is greater than quantity supplied.

FIGURE 3.7 Overview of Supply and Demand

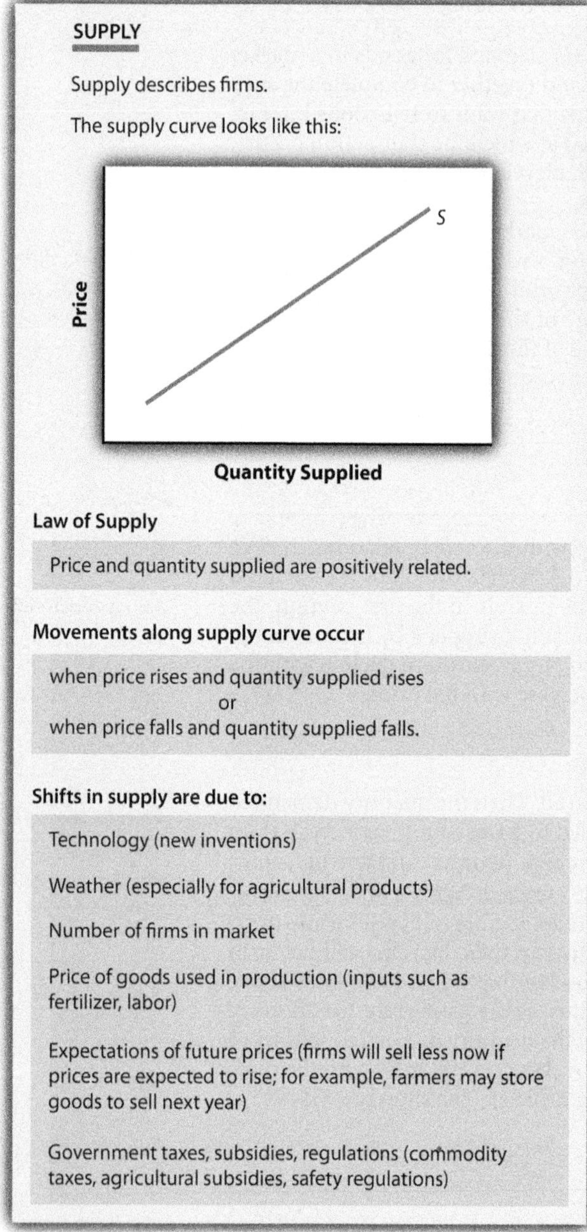

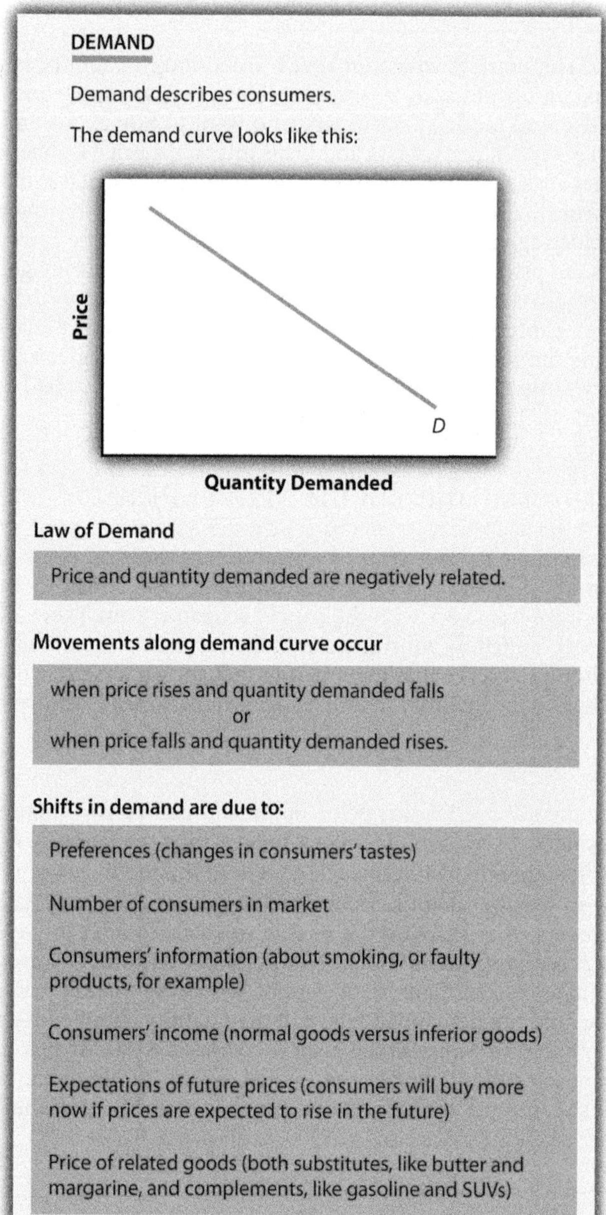

TABLE 3.3 Finding the Market Equilibrium

Price	Quantity Demanded	Quantity Supplied	Shortage, Surplus, or Equilibrium	Price Rises or Falls
$140	18	1	Shortage = 17	Price rises
$160	14	4	Shortage = 10	Price rises
$180	11	7	Shortage = 4	Price rises
$200	9*	9*	Equilibrium*	No change*
$220	7	11	Surplus = 4	Price falls
$240	5	13	Surplus = 8	Price falls
$260	3	15	Surplus = 12	Price falls
$280	2	16	Surplus = 14	Price falls
$300	1	17	Surplus = 16	Price falls

Suppose instead that you had picked a price above $200, let's say $260. Then the quantity demanded by consumers (3 million bicycles) is less than the quantity supplied by firms (15 million bicycles). In other words, there is a surplus of 12 million bicycles. A **surplus (excess supply)** is a situation in which the quantity supplied is greater than the quantity demanded. With a surplus of bicycles, buyers who really need a bicycle have an abundance of sellers who are eager to sell them a bicycle, while firms have to compete with one another to entice buyers for their products. Therefore, the price of bicycles will fall: Firms that are willing to sell bicycles for less than $260 will offer to sell to consumers at lower prices. Thus, $260 cannot be the market price either. Observe that as the price falls below $260, the quantity demanded rises and the quantity supplied falls. Thus, the surplus decreases. If you choose any price above $200, the same thing will happen: A surplus will exist, and the price will fall. The surplus disappears only when the price falls to $200.

surplus (excess supply)
A situation in which quantity supplied is greater than quantity demanded.

Thus, we have shown that for any price below $200, a shortage exists, and the price rises, while for any price above $200, a surplus exists, and the price falls. What if the market price is $200? Then the quantity supplied equals the quantity demanded; there is not a shortage or a surplus, and there is no reason for the price to rise or fall. This price of $200 is called the **equilibrium price** because, at this price, the quantity supplied equals the quantity demanded, and the price has no tendency to change. There is no other price for which quantity supplied equals quantity demanded. If you look at all the other prices, you will see either a shortage or a surplus, and thus the price has a tendency to either rise or fall.

equilibrium price
The price at which quantity supplied equals quantity demanded.

The quantity bought and sold at the equilibrium price is 9 million bicycles. This is the **equilibrium quantity**. When the price equals the equilibrium price and the quantity bought and sold equals the equilibrium quantity, economists call this a **market equilibrium**.

equilibrium quantity
The quantity traded at the equilibrium price.

market equilibrium
The situation in which the price is equal to the equilibrium price and the quantity traded equals the equilibrium quantity.

Our discussion of the determination of the equilibrium price shows how the market price coordinates the buying and selling decisions of many firms and consumers. We see that the price serves a *rationing function*. When a shortage exists, a higher price reduces the quantity demanded and increases the quantity supplied to eliminate the shortage. Similarly, when a surplus exists, a lower price increases the quantity demanded and decreases the quantity supplied to eliminate the surplus. Thus, both shortages and surpluses are eliminated by the forces of supply and demand.

Two Predictions

By combining supply and demand, we have completed the supply and demand model. The model can be applied to many markets, not just the example of the bicycle market. One prediction of the supply and demand model is that *the equilibrium price in the market will be the price for which the quantity supplied equals the quantity demanded.* Thus, the model provides an answer to the question of what determines the price in the market. Another prediction of the model is that *the equilibrium quantity bought and sold in the market is the quantity for which the quantity supplied equals the quantity demanded.*

3.2 Finding the Equilibrium with a Supply and Demand Diagram

The equilibrium price and quantity in a market can also be found with the help of a graph. Figure 3.8 combines the demand curve from Figure 3.1 and the supply curve from Figure 3.4 in the same diagram. Observe that the downward-sloping demand curve intersects the upward-sloping supply curve at a single point. At that point of intersection, the quantity supplied equals the quantity demanded. Hence, the *equilibrium price is at the intersection of the supply curve and the demand curve.* The equilibrium price of $200 is shown in Figure 3.8. At that price, the quantity demanded is 9 million bicycles, and the quantity supplied is 9 million bicycles. This is the equilibrium quantity.

FIGURE 3.8 Equilibrium Price and Equilibrium Quantity

When buyers and sellers interact in the market, the equilibrium price is at the point of intersection of the supply curve and the demand curve. At this point, the quantity supplied equals the quantity demanded. The equilibrium quantity also is determined at that point. At a higher price, the quantity demanded will be less than the quantity supplied; a surplus will exist. At a lower price, the quantity demanded will be greater than the quantity supplied; a shortage will exist.

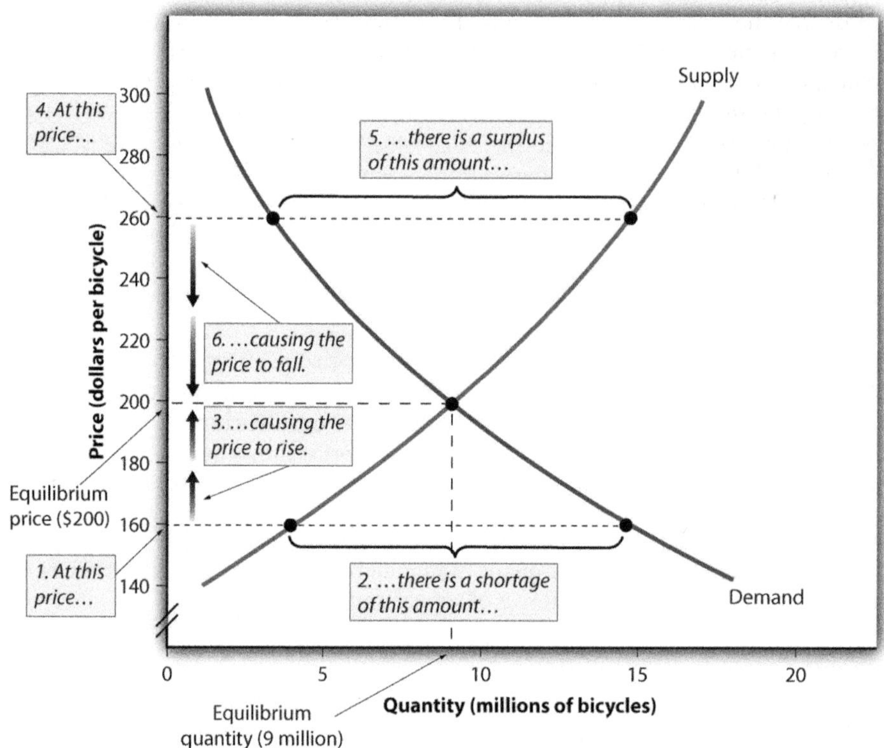

If the price were lower than this equilibrium price, say, $160, then the quantity demanded would be greater than the quantity supplied. A shortage would exist, and demand would pressure the price to increase, as shown in the graph. The increase in gasoline prices in 2007 and the early part of 2008 led to an increase in demand for hybrid automobiles. With a shortage of hybrid vehicles and long waiting lists, some automobile sellers increased the price of the hybrids.

On the other hand, if the price were above the equilibrium price, say, $260, then the quantity supplied would be greater than the quantity demanded. A surplus would exist, and excess quantity would pressure the price to fall. After September 11, 2001, a large number of vacationers canceled vacation plans that involved air travel. Caribbean hotels, with a surplus of vacant hotel rooms following this decrease in demand, began to offer big discounts.

Thus, the market price will tend to move toward the equilibrium price at the intersection of the supply curve and the demand curve. We can calculate exactly what the equilibrium price is in Figure 3.8 by drawing a line over to the vertical axis. And we can calculate the equilibrium quantity by drawing a line down to the horizontal axis.

3.3 Market Outcomes When Supply or Demand Changes

Now that you know how to find the equilibrium price and quantity in a market, we can use the supply and demand model to analyze the impact of factors that change supply or demand on equilibrium price and quantity. We first consider a change in demand and then a change in supply.

Effects of a Change in Demand

Figure 3.9 shows the effects of a shift in the demand curve for bicycles. Suppose that a shift occurs because of a fitness craze that increases the demand for bicycles. The demand curve shifts to the right, as shown in Figure 3.9(a). The demand curve before the shift and the demand curve after the shift are labeled the "old demand curve" and the "new demand curve," respectively.

If you look at the graph, you can see that something must happen to the equilibrium price when the demand curve shifts. The equilibrium price is determined at the intersection of the supply curve and the demand curve. With the new demand curve, there is a new intersection and, therefore, a new equilibrium price. The equilibrium price is no longer $200 in Figure 3.9(a); it is up to $220 per bicycle. Thus, the supply and demand model predicts that the price in the market will rise if demand increases. Note also that the equilibrium quantity of bicycles changes. The quantity of bicycles sold and bought has increased from 9 million to 11 million. Thus, the equilibrium quantity has increased along with the equilibrium price. The supply and demand model predicts that an increase in demand will raise both the price and the quantity sold in the market.

We can use the same method to find out what happens if demand decreases, as shown in Figure 3.9(b). Suppose that the elimination of dedicated bicycle lanes on roads shifts the demand curve for bicycles to the left. At the new intersection of the supply and demand curves, the equilibrium price is lower, and the quantity sold also is lower. Thus, the supply and demand model predicts that a decrease in demand will both lower the price and lower the quantity sold in the market.

In these examples, when the demand curve shifts, it leads to a movement along the supply curve. First, the demand curve shifts to the right or to the left. Then there is a movement along the supply curve because the change in the price affects the quantity of bicycles that firms will sell.

FIGURE 3.9 **Effects of a Shift in Demand**

When demand increases, as in graph (a), the demand curve shifts to the right. The equilibrium price rises, and the equilibrium quantity also rises. When demand decreases, as in graph (b), the demand curve shifts to the left. The equilibrium price falls, and the equilibrium quantity also falls.

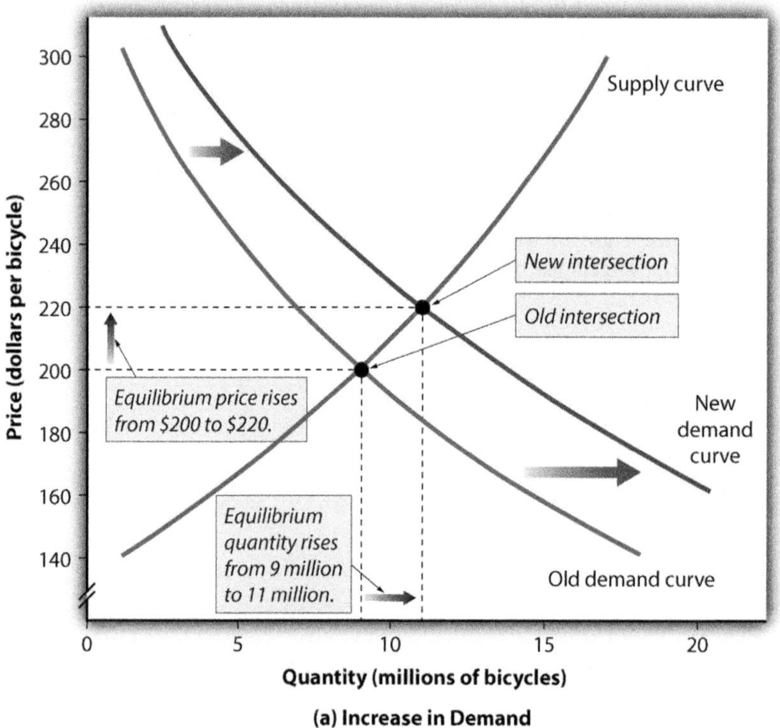

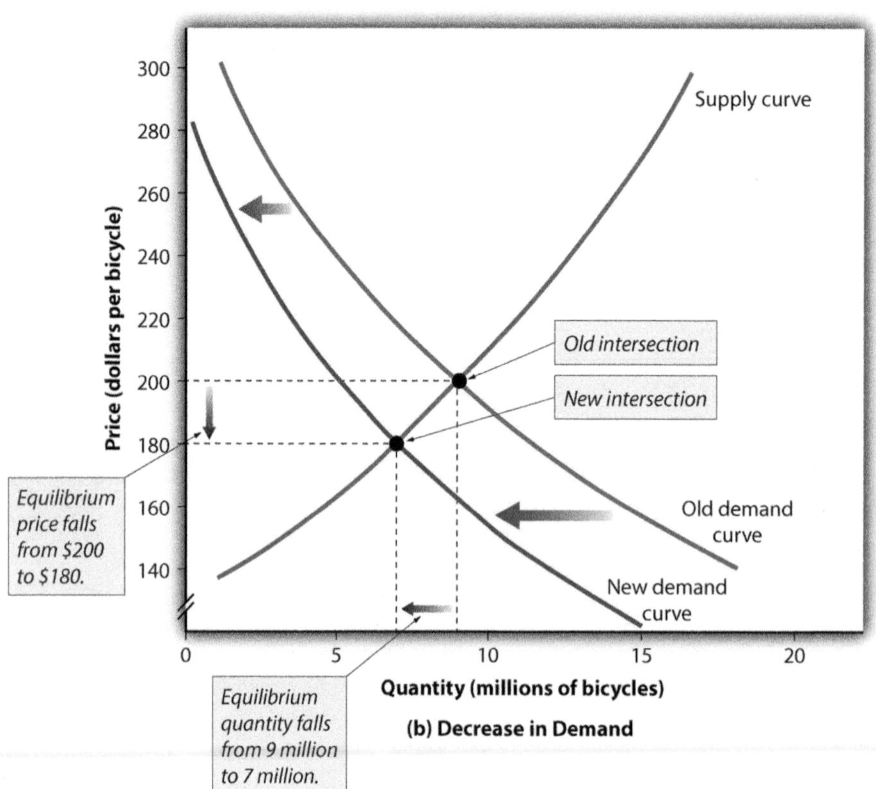

FIGURE 3.10 Effects of a Shift in Supply

When supply increases, as in graph (a), the supply curve shifts to the right, the equilibrium price falls, and the equilibrium quantity rises. When supply decreases, as in graph (b), the supply curve shifts to the left, the equilibrium price rises, and the equilibrium quantity falls.

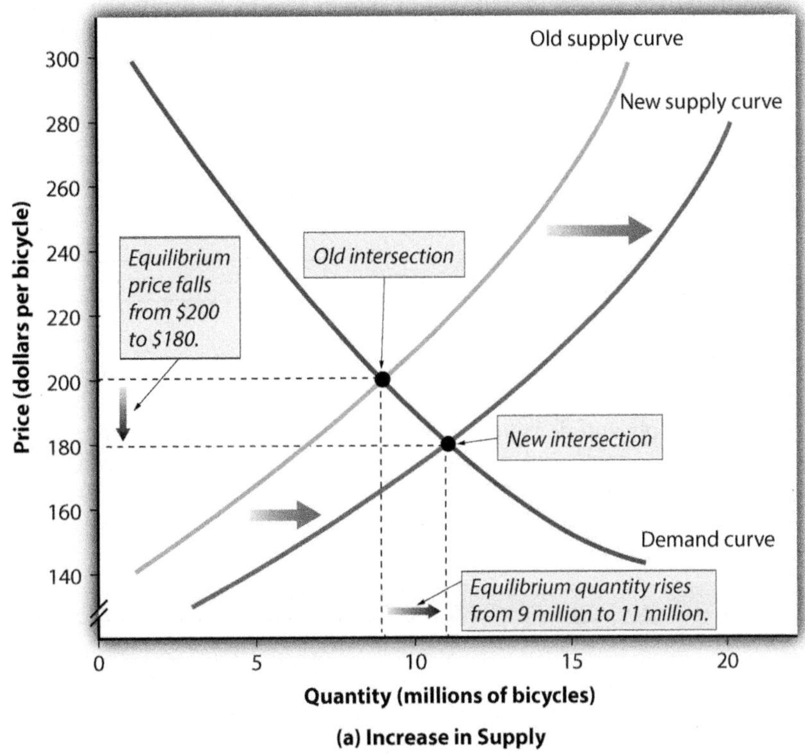

(a) Increase in Supply

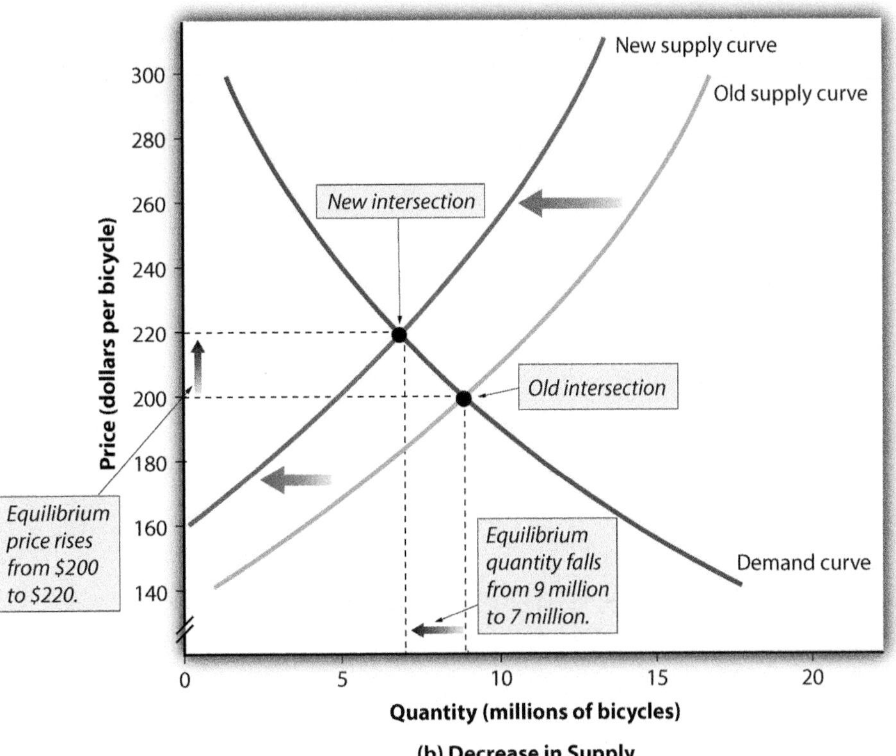

(b) Decrease in Supply

Effects of a Change in Supply

Figure 3.10 shows what happens when a change in the market shifts the supply curve. Suppose a new technology reduces the cost of producing bicycles, resulting in the supply curve for bicycles shifting to the right. Figure 3.10(a) shows that a new equilibrium price is lower than the old equilibrium price. In addition, the equilibrium quantity rises. Thus, the supply and demand model predicts that an increase in the supply of bicycles will lower the price and raise the quantity of bicycles sold.

Suppose instead that an increase in the cost of bicycle tires increases the cost of producing bicycles, resulting in the supply curve for bicycles shifting to the left. Figure 3.10(b) shows that the equilibrium price rises, and the equilibrium quantity falls. Thus, the model predicts that a decrease in the supply of bicycles will raise the price of bicycles and lower the quantity of bicycles sold.

Table 3.4 summarizes the results of this analysis of shifts in the supply and demand curves.

TABLE 3.4 Effects of Shifts in Demand and Supply Curves

Shift	Effect on Equilibrium Price	Effect on Equilibrium Quantity
Increase in demand	Up	Up
Decrease in demand	Down	Down
Increase in supply	Down	Up
Decrease in supply	Up	Down

When Both Curves Shift

The supply and demand model is easiest to use when you are analyzing a factor that shifts either demand or supply, but not both. In reality, however, it is possible for something or several different things to simultaneously shift both supply and demand. To predict whether the price or the quantity rises or falls in such cases, we need to know whether demand or supply shifts by a larger amount.

REVIEW

- The supply and demand model is used to predict the price and the quantity that result from interactions of consumers and producers in a market.
- In a market, the price will adjust upward or downward until the quantity supplied equals the quantity demanded. This price is called the equilibrium price, and the corresponding quantity is called the equilibrium quantity.
- Changes in the economy that cause the demand curve to shift to the right will raise both the equilibrium price and the equilibrium quantity. Changes that cause the demand curve to shift to the left will lower both the equilibrium price and the equilibrium quantity.
- Changes in the economy that cause the supply curve to shift to the right will lower the equilibrium price and raise the equilibrium quantity. Changes that cause the supply curve to shift to the left will raise the equilibrium price and lower the equilibrium quantity.

4. END-OF-CHAPTER MATERIAL

4.1 Conclusion

This chapter has shown how to use the supply and demand model to find out how equilibrium price and quantity are determined in markets in which buyers and sellers interact freely. The supply and demand model is probably the most frequently used model in economics, and it has been in existence for more than 100 years in pretty much the same form as economists use it now. You will come to appreciate it more and more as you study economics.

A key feature of the model is that the equilibrium price and quantity are found at the intersection of the supply and demand curves. We can use the model to analyze how a change in factors that shift either the supply curve or the demand curve (or both) will affect equilibrium price and quantity in the market.

In later chapters, we will take a closer look at the supply and demand model to understand issues like how much equilibrium price or quantity changes when the demand curve or the supply curve shifts. We also can look at whether a market in which buyers and sellers interact freely can deliver the best outcomes for society, or whether their outcomes can be improved.

We also will look at what happens when buyers and sellers are not able to interact freely because of restrictions that limit how much a seller can charge for a good or how much a buyer has to pay for a good. This examination will enable you to better understand policy debates about minimum wages and rent controls.

Key Points

1. Demand is a negative relationship between the price of a good and the quantity demanded by consumers. It can be shown graphically by a downward-sloping demand curve.
2. A movement along the demand curve occurs when a higher price reduces the quantity demanded or a lower price increases the quantity demanded.
3. A shift of the demand curve occurs when something besides a change in price changes the quantity of a good that people are willing to buy.
4. Supply is a positive relationship between the price of a good and the quantity supplied by firms. It can be shown graphically by an upward-sloping supply curve.
5. A movement along the supply curve occurs when a higher price increases the quantity supplied or a lower price decreases the quantity supplied.
6. A shift of the supply curve occurs when something besides a change in price changes the quantity of a good that firms are willing to sell.
7. The equilibrium price and equilibrium quantity are determined by the intersection of the supply curve and the demand curve. At this intersection point, the quantity supplied equals the quantity demanded—no shortages or surpluses exist.
8. The adjustment of prices moves the market into equilibrium. In situations in which a shortage or an excess demand exists for goods, price will rise, increasing the quantity supplied and reducing the quantity demanded. In situations in which a surplus or an excess supply of goods exists, price will fall, decreasing the quantity supplied and increasing the quantity demanded.
9. We can use the supply and demand model to analyze the impact of changes in factors that move the supply curve or the demand curve or both. By shifting either the supply curve or the demand curve, observations of prices can be explained and predictions about prices can be made.
10. When the demand curve shifts to the right (left), both equilibrium price and equilibrium quantity will increase (decrease). When the supply curve shifts to the right (left), the equilibrium price will fall (rise), and the equilibrium quantity will rise (fall).

QUESTIONS FOR REVIEW

1. Why does the demand curve slope downward?
2. Why does the supply curve slope upward?
3. What is the difference between a shift in the demand curve and a movement along the demand curve?
4. What are four things that cause a demand curve to shift?
5. What is the difference between a shift in the supply curve and a movement along the supply curve?
6. What are four things that cause a supply curve to shift?
7. How can one find the equilibrium price and equilibrium quantity?
8. What happens to the equilibrium price if the supply curve shifts to the right?
9. What happens to the equilibrium price if the demand curve shifts to the right?
10. If both the supply curve and the demand curve shift to the right, what happens to the equilibrium quantity? What about the equilibrium price?

PROBLEMS

1. For each of the following markets, indicate whether the stated change causes a shift in the supply curve, a shift in the demand curve, a movement along the supply curve, or a movement along the demand curve.
    a. The housing market: Consumers' incomes fall.
    b. The tea market: The price of sugar goes down.
    c. The coffee market: A freeze in Brazil severely damages the coffee crop.
    d. The fast-food market: The number of fast food restaurants in an area decreases.
    e. The peanut market in the U.S. Southeast: A drought lowers supply.
2. Determine which of the following four sentences use the terminology of the supply and demand model correctly.
    a. The price of bicycles rose, and therefore the demand for bicycles went down.
    b. The demand for bicycles increased, and therefore the price went up.
    c. The price of bicycles fell, decreasing the supply of bicycles.
    d. The supply of bicycles increased, and therefore the price of bicycles fell.
3. Use the supply and demand model to explain what happens to the equilibrium price and the equilibrium quantity for frozen yogurt in the following cases:
    a. The number of firms producing frozen yogurt expands significantly.
    b. It is widely publicized in the press that frozen yogurt is not more healthy for you than ice cream.
    c. It is widely publicized in the press that people who eat a cup of frozen yogurt a day live to be much happier in their retirement years.
    d. The price of milk used to produce frozen yogurt suddenly increases.
    e. Frozen yogurt suddenly becomes popular because a movie idol promotes it in television commercials.
4. Suppose a decrease in consumers' incomes causes a decrease in the demand for chicken and an increase in the demand for potatoes. Which good is inferior and which is normal? How will the equilibrium price and quantity change for each good?

5. Consider the following supply and demand model of the world tea market (in billions of pounds):

Price per Pound	Quantity Supplied	Quantity Demanded
$0.38	1,500	525
$0.37	1,000	600
$0.36	700	700
$0.35	600	900
$0.34	550	1,200

   a. Is there a shortage or a surplus when the price is $0.38? What about $0.34?
   b. What are the equilibrium price and the equilibrium quantity?
   c. Graph the supply curve and the demand curve.
   d. Show how the equilibrium price and quantity can be found on the graph.
   e. If there is a shortage or surplus at a price of $0.38, calculate its size in billions of pounds and show it on the graph.

6. Consider Problem 5. Suppose that there is a drought in Sri Lanka that reduces the supply of tea by 400 billion pounds at every price. Suppose demand does not change.
   a. Write down in a table the new supply schedule for tea.
   b. Find the new equilibrium price and the new equilibrium quantity. Explain how the market adjusts to the new equilibrium.
   c. Graph the new supply curve along with the old supply curve and the demand curve.
   d. Show the change in the equilibrium price and the equilibrium quantity on the graph.
   e. Did the equilibrium quantity change by more or less than the change in supply? Show how you arrived at your answer using both the table and the supply and demand diagram that you drew.

7. Suppose you notice that the prices of fresh fish have been rising while the amounts sold have been falling in recent years. Which of the following is the best explanation for this?
   a. Consumer preferences have shifted in favor of fish because it is healthier than red meat.
   b. Fishermen are prevented from using the most advanced equipment because of concerns about overfishing.
   c. Consumers' incomes have risen faster than inflation.
   d. Consumers have become worried about mercury levels in fish.

8. Suppose the prices of illegal drugs fall in your community at the same time that police drug seizures increase. Which is the best explanation for this?
   a. Fewer drugs are being supplied locally.
   b. Police arrests are removing more drug dealers.
   c. Police arrests are reducing drug consumption sharply.
   d. More drugs are being supplied locally.

9. In the United States, corn often is used as an ingredient in animal feed for livestock. Why does an increase in the use of corn to make ethanol, an additive that is used in gasoline, raise the price of meat? Use supply and demand curves for the corn market and the meat market to explain your answer.

10. Using the demand and supply diagrams (one for each market), show what short-run changes in price and quantity would be expected in the following markets if terrorism-related worries about air safety cause travelers to shy away from air travel. Each graph should contain the original and new demand and supply curves, and the original and new equilibrium prices and quantities. For each market, write one sentence explaining why each curve shifts or does not shift.
    a. The market for air travel.
    b. The market for rail travel.
    c. The market for hotel rooms in Hawaii.
    d. The market for gasoline.

CHAPTER 4
Subtleties of the Supply and Demand Model

In April of 2015, the minimum wage for workers in the city of Seattle increased to $11 per hour. This was the first in a series of increases which would result in the minimum wage reaching $15/hour for most workers (except those working for small businesses) by 2019 and rising to $18 an hour by 2025. Supporters of the legislation argued that an increase in the legally mandated minimum wage would boost the incomes of low-wage workers and help improve their lives. They also argued that the increase would be good for businesses in the city because workers who earned higher wages would be able to buy more goods and services for their family thus helping local businesses. Opponents argued that intervening in the labor market would not help these workers and might even end up hurting them. They pointed out that raising the minimum wage would result in some low-wage workers losing their jobs either because the business would not be able to survive with the higher costs or because the business owners would resort to automation—using ordering kiosks instead of hiring more cashiers, for example. They also argued that since the minimum wage only applied within the city limits of Seattle, businesses would move to nearby areas outside the city's jurisdiction and avoid paying higher wages.

Source: a katz / Shutterstock.com

The debate in Seattle mirrored a debate that was taking place all over the United States as the recovery from the 2008/09 recession gathered steam. Both New York and California passed laws that would gradually raise statewide minimum wages to $15 over the next few years (by 2018 in New York and 2023 in California). In 2015, President Barack Obama praised the decision by New York and California while expressing frustration that the federal minimum wage had not increased from the value of $7.25 that was set all the way back in June of 2009. That increase itself had been the culmination of a legislative process that began in May 2007. President George W. Bush signed a bill that raised the minimum wage to $5.85 in 2007, $6.55 in 2008 and, finally, to $7.25 in 2009. President Obama left office in January of 2017 without succeeding in persuading the Republican-controlled Congress to raise the minimum wage. Only two other presidents had previously failed to raise the minimum wage since it came into existence in the aftermath of the Great Depression.

Were the supporters of the plan correct in their claim that many poor people's lives could be improved by instituting a higher minimum wage? Or were the opponents correct to claim that a higher minimum wage could end up hurting more people than it helped? In the case of Seattle's minimum wage, a team of economists from the University of Washington closely studied the impact of the minimum wage and concluded that the impact was mixed. Wages among low-income workers in the city of Seattle increased following the passage of the law but wage increases were also seen in neighboring areas suggesting that at least some of the increases resulted from the impact of an overall improving economic climate. They also found that employment in the city of Seattle may have declined modestly following the introduction of the new minimum wage.

In this chapter, we look at more sophisticated aspects of the supply and demand model that are helpful in understanding policy debates, like the minimum-wage increase. We first look at how to use the supply and demand model in situations in which government policies do not allow price to be freely determined in a market. These interventions can take the form of a *price ceiling*, a maximum price imposed by the government when it feels that the equilibrium price is "too high," or a *price floor*, a minimum price imposed by the government when it feels that the equilibrium price is "too low," as in the case of the minimum wage. This extension of the supply and demand model also will be helpful in solidifying your understanding of the important role played by prices in the allocation of resources.

We then move on to discussing an elegant, and remarkably useful, economic concept called *elasticity* that economists use when they work with the supply and demand model. In economics, elasticity is a measure of how sensitive one variable is to another. In the case of the supply and demand model, elasticity measures how sensitive the quantity of a good that people demand, or that firms supply, is to the price of the good. In this chapter, we show how the concept of elasticity can be used to answer the question raised earlier about how much unemployment is caused when the minimum wage is raised. You will learn a formula that shows how elasticity is calculated and then learn how to work with and talk about elasticity.

1. INTERFERENCE WITH MARKET PRICES

Thus far, we have used the supply and demand model in situations in which the price is freely determined without government control. But at many times throughout history, and around the world in the twenty-first century, governments have attempted to control market prices. The usual reasons are that government leaders were not happy with the outcome of the market or were pressured by groups who would benefit from price controls.

1.1 Price Ceilings and Price Floors

In general, the government imposes two broad types of **price controls**. Controls can stipulate either a **price ceiling**, a maximum price at which a good can be bought and sold, or a **price floor**, a minimum price at which a good can be bought and sold. Why would a government choose to intervene in the market and put in a price floor or a price ceiling? What happens when such an intervention is made?

Ostensibly, the primary purpose of a price ceiling is to help consumers in situations in which the government thinks that the equilibrium price is "too high" or is inundated with consumer complaints that the equilibrium price is too high. For example, the U.S. government controlled oil prices in the early 1970s, stipulating that firms could not charge more than a stated maximum price of $5.25 per barrel of crude oil at a time when the equilibrium price was well over $10 per barrel. As another example, some cities in the United States place price controls on rental apartments; landlords are not permitted to charge a rent higher than the maximum stipulated by the **rent control** law in these cities. Tenants living in rent-controlled units pay less than the market equilibrium rent that would prevail in the absence of the price ceiling.

Conversely, governments impose price floors to help the suppliers of goods and services in situations in which the government feels that the equilibrium price is "too low" or is influenced by complaints from producers that the equilibrium price is too low. For example, the U.S. government requires that the price of sugar in the United States not fall below a certain amount. Another example can be found in the labor market, in which the U.S. government requires that firms pay workers a wage of at least a given level, called the **minimum wage**.

price controls

A government law or regulation that sets or limits the price to be charged for a particular good.

price ceiling

A government price control that sets the maximum allowable price for a good.

price floor

A government price control that sets the minimum allowable price for a good.

rent control

A government price control that sets the maximum allowable rent on a house or apartment.

minimum wage

A wage per hour below which it is illegal to pay workers.

1.2 Side Effects of Price Ceilings

Even though price ceilings typically are implemented with the idea of helping consumers, they often end up having harmful side effects that hurt the consumers that the ceiling was put in place to help. If the price ceiling that the government puts in place to prevent firms from charging more than a certain amount for their products is lower than the equilibrium price, then a shortage is likely to result, as illustrated in Figure 4.1. The situation of a persistent shortage, in which sellers are unwilling to supply as much as buyers want to buy, is illustrated for the general case of any good in the top graph in Figure 4.1 and for the specific case of rent control in the bottom graph.

Dealing with Persistent Shortages

Because higher prices are not allowed, the shortage must be dealt with in other ways. Sometimes the government issues a limited amount of ration coupons, which do not exceed the quantity supplied at the restricted maximum price, to people to alleviate the shortage. This was done in World War II when people had to present these ration coupons at stores to buy certain goods, and only those individuals who had ration coupons could buy those goods. If the price ceiling had not been in place, the shortage would have driven prices higher, and those who were willing and able to pay the higher price would have been able to buy the goods without the need for a ration coupon.

Alternatively, if ration coupons are not issued, then the shortage might result in long waiting lines. In the past, in centrally planned economies, long lines for bread frequently were observed because of price controls on bread. Sometimes black markets develop, in which people buy and sell goods outside the watch of the government and charge whatever price they want. In the past, this was typical in command economies. In the twenty-first century, black markets are common in less-developed countries when the governments in these countries impose price controls.

Another effect of price ceilings is a reduction in the quality of the good sold. By lowering the quality of the good, the producer can reduce the costs of producing it. A frequent criticism of rent control is that it can lower the quality of housing—landlords are more reluctant to paint the walls or to repair the elevator because they are prevented from charging a higher rent.

Making Things Worse

Although the stated purpose of price ceilings is to help people who have to pay high prices, the preceding examples indicate how price ceilings can make things worse. Issuing ration coupons raises difficult problems about who gets the coupons. In the case of a price ceiling on gasoline, for example, should the government give more coupons to those who use a lot of gasoline because they drive vehicles with poor gas mileage than to those who use less gasoline because they drive more fuel-efficient cars or use public transportation for their daily commute? Rationing by waiting in line also is an undesirable outcome. People who are waiting in line could be doing more enjoyable or more useful things. Similarly, black markets, being illegal, encourage people to go outside the law. People transacting in black markets also may be more vulnerable to theft or fraud. Lowering the quality of the good is also a bad way to alleviate the problem of a high price. This simply eliminates the higher-quality good from production; both consumers and producers lose. Price ceilings also are not particularly well targeted. Even though the goal of a price ceiling may be to ensure that someone who cannot afford to pay the equilibrium price still can purchase the good, there is no way to guarantee that only those who cannot afford to pay the equilibrium price end up purchasing the good. For instance, many people who end up living in rent-controlled apartments may not be poor at all.

FIGURE 4.1 Effects of a Maximum-Price Law

The top diagram shows the general case when the government prevents the market price from rising above a particular maximum price, or sets a price ceiling below the equilibrium price. The lower diagram shows a particular example of a price ceiling, rent controls on apartment units. The supply and demand model predicts a shortage. The shortage occurs because the quantity supplied is less than consumers are willing to buy at that price. The shortage leads to rationing, black markets, or lower product quality.

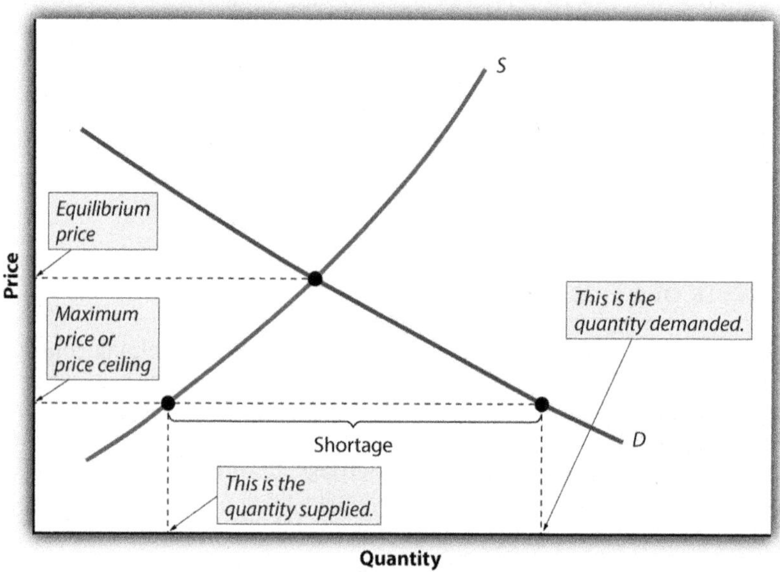

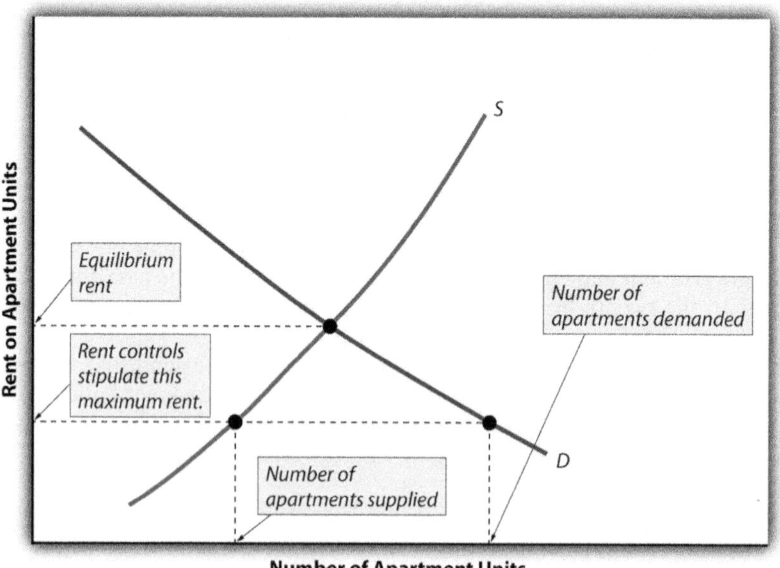

1.3 Side Effects of Price Floors

Price floors typically are enacted with the goal of helping producers who are facing low market equilibrium prices, but, as with price ceilings, they often end up having harmful side effects that hurt the people that the policy was put in place to help. If the price floor that the government imposes exceeds the equilibrium price, then a surplus will occur. The situation of a persistent surplus, in which sellers are willing to supply more output than buyers want to buy, is illustrated for the general case of any good in the top graph of Figure 4.2 and for the specific case of the minimum wage in the bottom graph.

Dealing with Persistent Surpluses

How is this surplus dealt with in actual markets? In markets for farm products, the government usually has to buy the surplus and, perhaps, put it in storage. Buying farm products above the equilibrium price costs taxpayers money, and the higher price raises costs to consumers. For this reason, economists argue against price floors on agricultural goods. As an alternative, the government sometimes reduces the supply by telling farms to plant fewer acres or to destroy crops. But government requirements that land be kept idle or crops destroyed in exchange for taxpayer's money are particularly repugnant to most people.

When the supply and demand model is applied to labor markets, the price is the price of labor (or the wage) and a minimum wage is a price floor. What does the supply and demand model predict about the effects of a minimum wage? The lower diagram in Figure 4.2 shows that a minimum wage can cause unemployment. If the minimum wage exceeds the equilibrium wage, the number of workers demanded at that wage is less than the number of workers who are willing to work. Even though some workers would be willing to work for less than the minimum wage, employers are not permitted to pay them less than the minimum wage. Therefore, there is a surplus of unemployed workers at the minimum wage.

Making Things Worse

Even though the stated purpose of price floors is to help sellers by paying them a higher price, the preceding examples indicate how price floors can make things worse. The resources allocated to building grain silos to store surplus grain could have been used to hire doctors or teachers or to build low-income houses. The land that farmers are encouraged to keep in an undeveloped yet unfarmed state could have been used for a housing development or as a high school athletic field. Price floors, like price ceilings, also are not particularly well targeted. Even though the goal of a price floor may be to ensure that a poor farmer does not suffer because crop prices are too low, the benefits of the higher price typically will accrue to extremely wealthy farmers and large agricultural businesses with lots of resources. In the case of the minimum wage, teenagers from relatively well-off families may end up earning a higher salary as a result of the minimum wage, but a poor parent may end up losing his or her job and joining the ranks of the unemployed.

FIGURE 4.2 Effects of Minimum-Price Law

The top diagram shows the general case when the government prevents the market price from falling below a particular minimum price, or sets a price floor above the equilibrium price. The lower diagram shows a particular example when the price of labor—the wage—cannot fall below the minimum wage. The supply and demand model predicts that sellers are willing to sell a greater quantity than buyers are willing to buy at that price. Thus, there is a surplus of the good or, in the case of labor, unemployment for some of those who would be hired only at a lower wage.

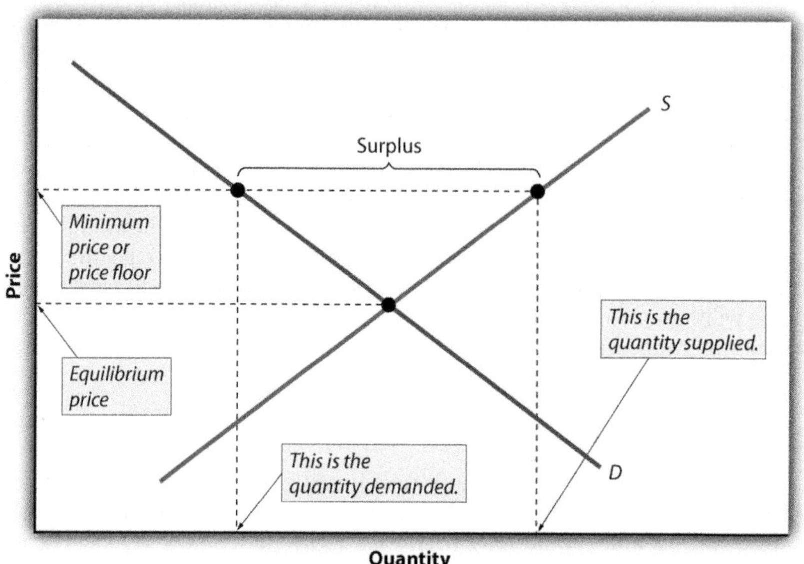

The General Case of a Price Floor

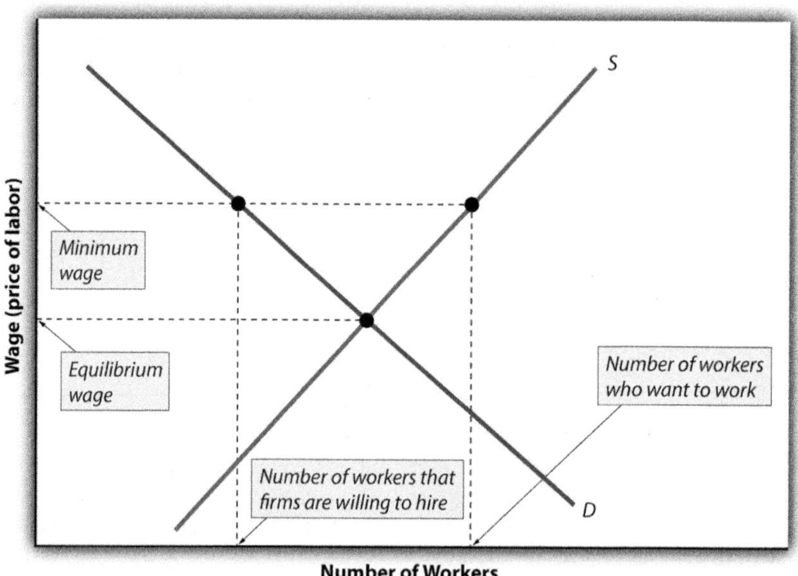

The Case of the Minimum Wage

REVIEW

- Governments occasionally will intervene in markets because they think that the equilibrium price is too high or too low. In some instances in which the government thinks the price that buyers have to pay is too high, it may impose a price ceiling. In some instances in which the government thinks the price that sellers are receiving is too low, it may impose a price floor.
- Price ceilings cause persistent shortages, which, in turn, cause rationing, black markets, and a reduced quality of goods and services. Price ceilings also may not end up helping the people that the policy was designed to benefit. In the case of rent control, for example, the people who end up in rent-controlled apartments may be more affluent than the individuals who are unable to find an apartment because of the persistent shortages.
- Price floors cause persistent surpluses, which, in turn, result in resources being diverted away from other productive activities. Price floors may not end up helping the people that the policy was designed to benefit. In the case of a minimum wage, for example, the workers who end up in jobs earning the higher minimum wage may be teenagers from relatively well-off families, while a poor worker may be unable to find a job because of the surplus of unemployed workers.

2. ELASTICITY OF DEMAND

2.1 Defining the Price Elasticity of Demand

The price elasticity of demand is a measure of the sensitivity of the *quantity demanded* of a good to the *price* of the good. "Price elasticity of demand" is sometimes shortened to "elasticity of demand," the "demand elasticity," or even simply "elasticity" when the meaning is clear from the context. The price elasticity of demand always refers to a particular demand curve or demand schedule, such as the world demand for oil or the U.S. demand for bicycles. The price elasticity of demand is a measure of *how much* the quantity demanded changes when the price changes.

For example, when economists report that the price elasticity of demand for contact lenses is high, they mean that the quantity of contact lenses demanded by people changes by a large amount when the price changes. Or if they report that the price elasticity of demand for bread is low, they mean that the quantity of bread demanded changes by only a small amount when the price of bread changes.

We can define the price elasticity of demand clearly with a formula: **Price elasticity of demand** is the percentage change in the quantity demanded divided by the percentage change in the price. That is,

price elasticity of demand
The percentage change in the quantity demanded of a good divided by the percentage change in the price of that good.

$$\text{Price elasticity of demand} = \frac{\text{percentage change in quantity demanded}}{\text{percentage change in price}}$$

We emphasize that the price elasticity of demand refers to a particular demand curve; thus, the numerator of this formula is the percentage change in quantity demanded when the price changes by the percentage amount shown in the denominator. All the other factors that affect demand are held constant when we compute the price elasticity of demand. This expression will have a negative sign because the numerator and denominator are of opposite signs. Because the demand curve slopes downward, as the price increases, the quantity demanded by consumers declines, and as the price decreases, the quantity demanded by consumers increases, all else held equal. The convention is to ignore the negative sign or, alternatively, take the negative sign for granted when we discuss the elasticity of demand.

For example, if the price elasticity of demand for gasoline is said to be about 0.2, that means that if the price of gasoline increases by 10 percent, the quantity of gasoline demanded will fall by 2 percent (0.2 x 10). If the price elasticity of demand for alcoholic beverages is said to be about 1.5, that means that when the price of alcoholic beverages rises by 10 percent, the quantity demanded will fall by 15 percent (1.5 x 10). As you can see from these examples, knowing the elasticity of demand enables us to determine how much the *quantity demanded* changes when the price changes.

2.2 The Size of the Elasticity: High versus Low

The two graphs in Figure 4.3 each show a different possible demand curve for oil in the world. We want to show why it is important to know which of these two demand curves gives a better description of economic behavior in the oil market. Each graph has the price of oil on the vertical axis (in dollars per barrel) and the quantity of oil demanded on the horizontal axis (in millions of barrels of oil a day).

FIGURE 4.3 **Comparing Different Sizes of the Price Elasticity of Demand**

Both sets of axes have exactly the same scale. In the top graph, the quantity demanded is sensitive to the price; the elasticity is high. In the bottom graph, the quantity demanded is not sensitive to the price; the elasticity is low. Thus, the same increase in price ($2, or 10 percent) reduces the quantity demanded much more when the elasticity is high (top graph) than when it is low (bottom graph).

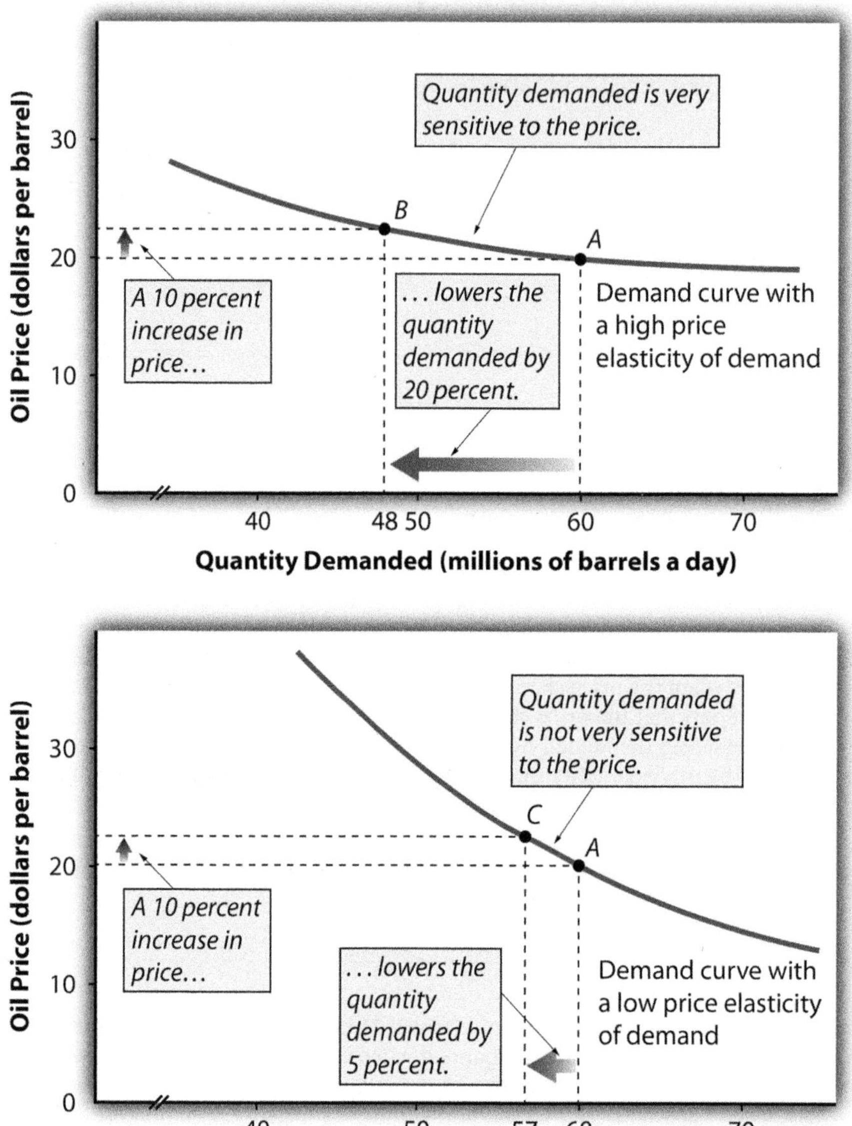

Both of the demand curves pass through the same point *A*, where the price of oil is $20 per barrel and the quantity demanded is 60 million barrels per day. But observe that the two curves show different degrees of sensitivity of the quantity demanded to the price. In the top graph, where the demand curve is relatively flat, the quantity demanded of oil is sensitive to the price; in other words, the demand curve has a high elasticity. For example, consider a change from point *A* to point *B*: When the price rises by $2, from $20 to $22, the quantity demanded falls by 12 million, from 60 million to 48 million barrels a day. In percentage terms, when the price rises by 10 percent (2/20 = 0.10, or 10 percent), the quantity demanded falls by 20 percent (12/60 = 0.20, or 20 percent).

On the other hand, in the bottom graph, the quantity demanded is not quite as sensitive to the price; in other words, the demand curve has a low elasticity. It is relatively steep. When the price rises by $2 from point *A* to point *C*, the quantity demanded falls by 3 million barrels. In percentage terms, the same 10 percent increase in price reduces the quantity demanded by only 5 percent (3/60 = 0.05, or 5 percent). Thus, the sensitivity of the quantity to the price, or the size of the elasticity, is what distinguishes these two graphs.

FIGURE 4.4 **The Importance of the Size of the Price Elasticity of Demand**

The impact on the oil price of a reduction in oil supply is shown for two different demand curves. The reduction in supply is the same for both graphs. When the price elasticity of demand is high (top graph), there is only a small increase in the price. When the price elasticity of demand is low (bottom graph), the price rises by much more.

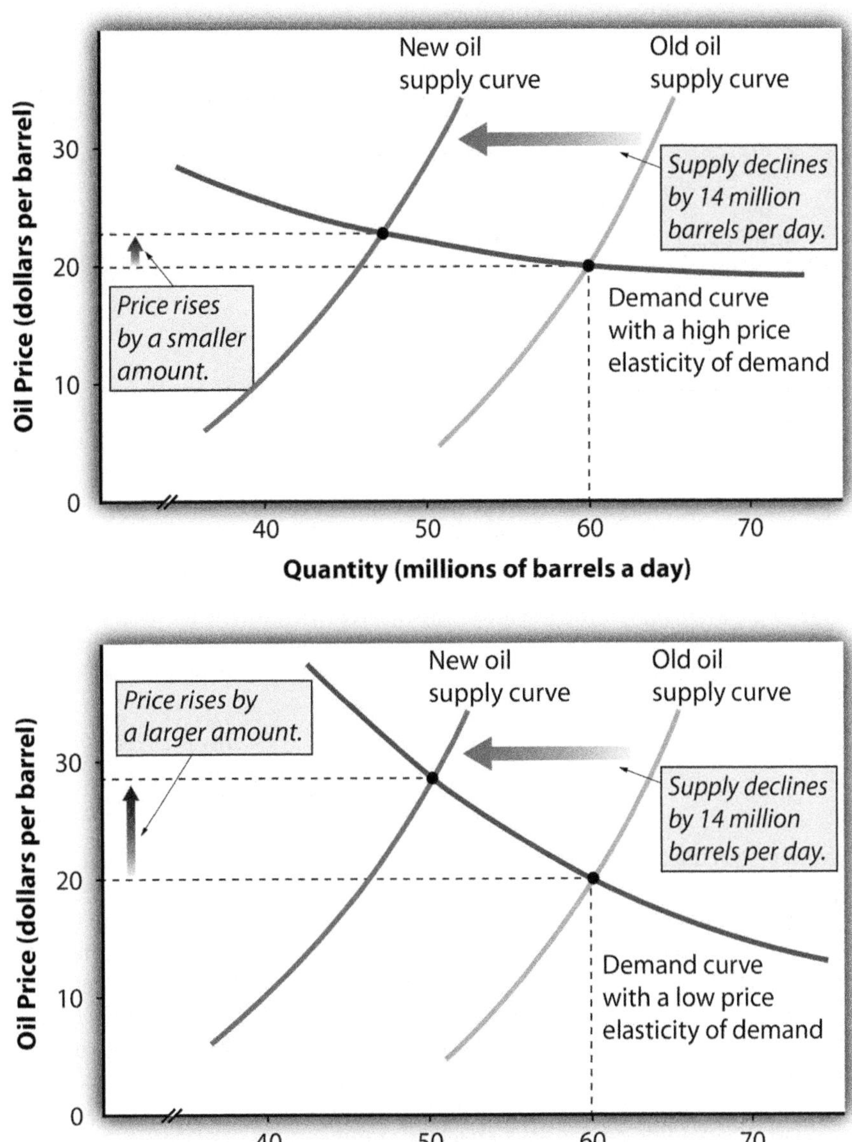

2.3 The Impact of a Change in Supply on the Price of Oil

Now consider what happens when there is a decline in supply in the world oil market. In Figure 4.4, we combine the supply curve for oil with the two demand curves for oil from Figure 4.3. Initially the oil market is in equilibrium in Figure 4.4; in both graphs, the quantity demanded equals the quantity supplied. The equilibrium price is $20 per barrel, and the equilibrium quantity is 60 million barrels a day, just like at point *A* in Figure 4.3. A reduction in the supply of oil—perhaps because of the reduction in Iraqi oil production or the shutdown of refineries following Hurricane Katrina—is also shown. The exact same leftward shift in supply is shown in the top and bottom graphs of Figure 4.4.

Now, observe how the equilibrium price changes in the two graphs. Recall that this change is our prediction—using the supply and demand model—of what would happen to the price of oil if the supply declined. We know that a decrease in supply will lead to an increase in the equilibrium price and a decrease in the equilibrium quantity. As the two graphs show, however, there is a huge difference in the size of the predicted price increase. In the top graph, the oil price increases only a little. If the elasticity is very high, then even a small increase in the price is enough to get people to reduce their use of oil and thereby bring the quantity demanded down to the lower quantity supplied. On the other hand, in the bottom diagram, the price rises by much more. Here the elasticity is very low, and thus a large increase in price is needed to get people to reduce their use of oil and bring the quantity demanded down to the quantity supplied.

Thus, to determine how much the price will rise in response to a shift in oil supply, we need to know how sensitive the quantity demanded is to the price, or the size of the elasticity of demand.

REVIEW

- We know that an increase in price will lower the quantity demanded, whereas a decrease in price will increase the quantity demanded. The price elasticity of demand is a number that tells us by how much the quantity demanded changes when the price changes.
- The price elasticity of demand, which we also refer to as "elasticity of demand" or just as "elasticity," is defined as the percentage change in the quantity demanded divided by the percentage change in the price.
- A given change in price has a larger impact on quantity demanded when the elasticity of demand is higher.
- A given shift of the supply curve will have a larger impact on equilibrium quantity (and a smaller impact on equilibrium price) when the elasticity of demand is higher.

3. WORKING WITH DEMAND ELASTICITIES

Having demonstrated the practical importance of elasticity, let us examine the concept in more detail and show how to use it. Some symbols will be helpful.

If we let the symbol e_d represent the price elasticity of demand, then we can write the definition as

$$e_d = \frac{\Delta Q_d}{Q_d} \div \frac{\Delta P}{P} = \frac{\left(\frac{\Delta Q_d}{Q_d}\right)}{\left(\frac{\Delta P}{P}\right)}$$

where Q_d is the quantity demanded, P is the price, and Δ means "change in." In other words, the elasticity of demand equals the "percentage change in the quantity demanded" divided by the "percentage change in the price." Observe that to compute the percentage change in the numerator and the denominator, we need to divide the change in the variable (or ΔQ_d) by the variable (P or Q_d).

Keep in mind again that because the quantity demanded is negatively related to the price, the elasticity of demand is a negative number: When $\Delta P/P$ is positive, $\Delta Q_d / Q_d$ is negative. But when economists write or talk about elasticity, they usually ignore the negative sign and report the absolute value of the number. Because the demand curve always slopes downward, this nearly universal convention need not cause any confusion, as long as you remember it.

It is easy to do back-of-the-envelope computations of price elasticity of demand. Suppose a study shows that when the price of Australian wine fell by 8 percent, the quantity of Australian wine demanded increased by 12 percent. The price elasticity of demand for Australian wine is

$$e_d = \frac{\left(\frac{\Delta Q_d}{Q_d}\right)}{\left(\frac{\Delta P}{P}\right)} = \frac{12}{8} \equiv 1.5$$

Suppose your university raises student season ticket prices from \$50 to \$60, which results in the quantity of season tickets sold falling from 2,000 to 1,800. The price elasticity of demand for season ticket prices would be

$$e_d = \frac{\left(\frac{\Delta Q_d}{Q_d}\right)}{\left(\frac{\Delta P}{P}\right)} = \frac{\left(\frac{200}{2000}\right)}{\left(\frac{10}{50}\right)} = \frac{0.1}{0.2} = 0.5$$

Notice that measured in percentage changes, the demand for Australian wine is responsive to changes in the price, and the demand for season tickets is not responsive to changes in the price.

3.1 The Advantage of a Unit-Free Measure

An attractive feature of the price elasticity of demand is that it does not depend on the units of measurement of the quantity demanded—whether barrels of oil or pounds of peanuts. It is a **unit-free measure** because it uses percentage changes in price and quantity demanded. Thus, it provides a way to compare the price sensitivity of the demand for many different goods. It even allows us to compare the price sensitivity of less expensive goods—like rice—with that of more expensive goods—like steak.

unit-free measure

A measure that does not depend on a unit of measurement.

For example, suppose that when the price of rice rises from \$0.50 to \$0.60 per pound, the quantity demanded falls from 20 tons to 19 tons—that is, a decline of 1 ton for a *\$0.10* price increase. In contrast, suppose that when the price of steak rises by \$1, from \$5 to \$6 per pound, the quantity demanded falls by 1 ton, from 20 tons to 19 tons of steak—that is, a decline of 1 ton for a *\$1* price increase.

Using these numbers, the price sensitivity of the demand for steak and the demand for rice might appear to be different: \$0.10 to get a ton of reduced purchases versus \$1 to get a ton of reduced purchases. Yet the elasticities are the same. The percentage change in price is 20 percent in each case (\$1/\$5 = \$0.10/\$0.50 = 0.20, or 20 percent), and the percentage change in quantity is 5 percent in each case: 1 ton of rice/20 tons of rice = 1 ton of steak/20 tons of steak = 0.05, or 5 percent. Hence, the elasticity is 5/20 = 1/4 in both cases.

Elasticity allows us to compare the price sensitivity of different goods by looking at ratios of percentage changes regardless of the units for measuring either price or quantity. With millions of different goods and hundreds of different units of measurement, this is indeed a major advantage.

3.2 Elasticity versus Slope

After looking at Figure 4.3, you might be tempted to say that demand curves that are steep have a low elasticity, and demand curves that are flat have a high elasticity. That turns out not to be the case, so you have to be careful not to simply look at a flat demand curve and say that it has a high elasticity. You need to understand why the *elasticity of the demand curve* is not the same as the *slope of the demand curve.* Remember that the slope of a curve is the change in the y variable over the change in the x variable; in the case of the demand curve, the slope is defined as the change in price divided by the change in quantity demanded. The slope is not a unit-free measure—it depends on how the price and quantity are measured. Elasticity, on the other hand, is a unit-free measure.

To illustrate the difference between slope and elasticity, we show in Figure 4.5 a demand curve for rice and a demand curve for steak. The two demand curves have different slopes because the prices are so different. When the price of rice increases by \$0.10, the quantity demanded of rice falls by 1 ton, whereas when the price of steak increases by \$1 (or 100 cents), the quantity demanded of steak falls by 1 ton. The slope of the steak demand curve is (–\$1 a ton), which is 10 times greater than the slope of the rice demand curve (–\$0.10 cents a ton). Yet the elasticity is the same for the change from A to B for both demand curves—the price of rice and the price of steak both increased by 20 percent, while the quantity demanded of rice and the quantity demanded of steak both decreased by 5 percent.

3.3 Calculating the Elasticity with a Midpoint Formula

To calculate the elasticity, we need to find the percentage change in the quantity demanded and divide it by the percentage change in the price. As we have illustrated with examples, to get the percentage change in the price or quantity, we need to divide the change in price (ΔP) by the price (P) or the change in quantity demanded (ΔQ_d) by the quantity demanded (Q_d). But when price and quantity demanded change, a question arises about what to use for P and Q_d. Should we use the old price and the old quantity demanded before the change, or should we use the new price and the new quantity demanded after the change?

FIGURE 4.5 Different Slopes and Same Elasticities

The slope of the steak demand curve in the bottom graph is greater than the slope of the rice demand curve in the top graph. The price elasticity of demand for rice and steak from point A to point B is the same, however. From point A to point B, the price rises by 20 percent and the quantity demanded decreases by 5 percent. Thus, the elasticity is one fourth for both rice and steak at these points.

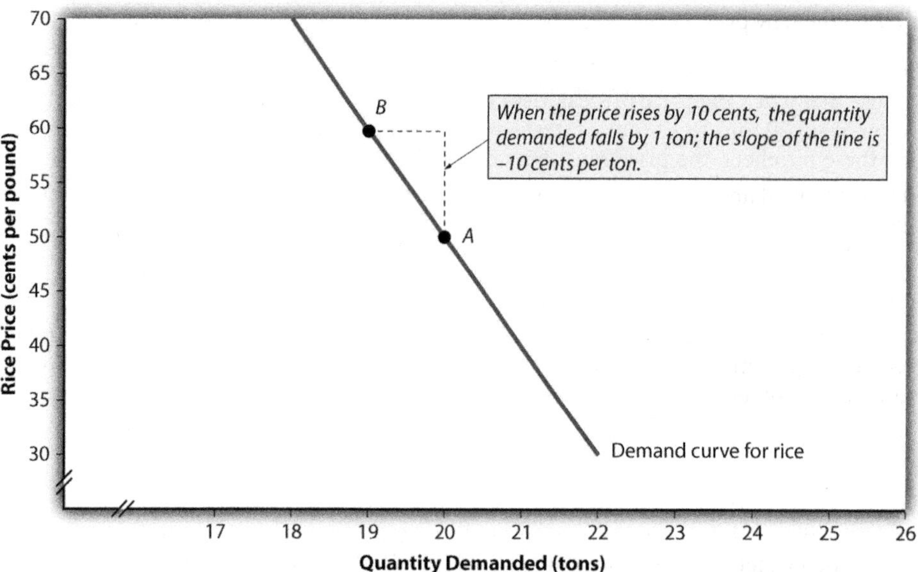

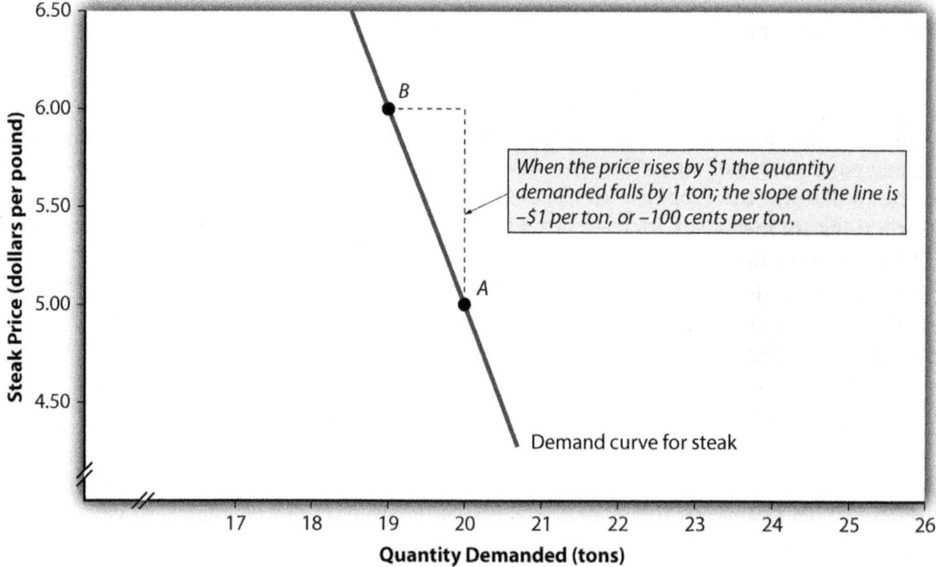

The most common convention that economists use is a compromise between these two alternatives. They take the *average,* or the *midpoint,* of the old and new quantities demanded and the old and new prices. That is, they compute the elasticity using the following formula, called the *midpoint formula:*

$$\text{Price elasticity of demand} = \frac{\text{Change in quantity}}{\text{average of old and new quantities}} \div \frac{\text{Change in price}}{\text{average of old and new prices}}$$

For example, if we use the midpoint formula to calculate the price elasticity of demand for oil when the price changes from $20 to $22 and the quantity demanded changes from 60 million to 48 million barrels a day, we get

$$\begin{aligned}\text{Price elasticity of demand} &= \frac{12}{(60+48)/2} \div \frac{2}{(22+20)/2} \\ &= \frac{2}{9} \div \frac{2}{21} = \frac{7}{3}\end{aligned}$$

That is, the price elasticity of demand is 2.33 using the midpoint formula. When we originally calculated the elasticity using the old price and the old quantity demanded, we came up with an elasticity of

$$\text{Price elasticity of demand} = \frac{12}{60} \div \frac{2}{20} = 2$$

If we had used the new price and the new quantity, we would have calculated the elasticity to be

$$\text{Price elasticity of demand} = \frac{12}{48} \div \frac{2}{22} = 2.75$$

So the elasticity calculated using the midpoint formula turns out to be in between these two values, as you would expect.

3.4 Talking about Elasticities

Economists classify demand curves by the size of the price elasticities of demand, and they have developed a very precise terminology for doing so.

Elastic versus Inelastic Demand

Goods for which the price elasticity is greater than one have an **elastic demand**. For example, the quantity of foreign travel demanded decreases by more than 1 percent when the price rises by 1 percent because many people tend to travel at home rather than abroad when the price of foreign travel rises.

Goods for which the price elasticity of demand is less than one have an **inelastic demand**. For example, the quantity of eggs demanded decreases by less than 1 percent when the price of eggs rises by 1 percent because many people do not want to substitute other things for eggs at breakfast.

elastic demand
Demand for which the price elasticity is greater than one.

inelastic demand
Demand for which the price elasticity is less than one.

Perfectly Elastic versus Perfectly Inelastic Demand

A demand curve that is vertical is called **perfectly inelastic demand**. Figure 4.6 shows a perfectly inelastic demand curve. The elasticity is zero because when the price changes, the quantity demanded does not change at all. No matter what the price, the same quantity is demanded. People who need insulin have a perfectly inelastic demand for insulin. As long as there are no substitutes for insulin, they will pay whatever they have to for the insulin.

A demand curve that is horizontal is called **perfectly elastic demand**. Figure 4.6 also shows a perfectly elastic demand curve. The elasticity is infinite. The perfectly flat demand curve is sometimes hard to imagine because it entails infinitely large movements of quantity for tiny changes in price. To better visualize this case, you can imagine that the curve is tilted ever so slightly. Goods that have a lot of comparable substitutes are likely to have high elasticities of demand.

Table 4.1 summarizes the terminology about elasticities.

perfectly inelastic demand
Demand for which the price elasticity is zero, indicating no response to a change in price and therefore a vertical demand curve.

perfectly elastic demand
Demand for which the price elasticity is infinite, indicating an infinite response to a change in price and therefore a horizontal demand curve.

3.5 Revenue and the Price Elasticity of Demand

When people purchase 60 million barrels of oil at $20 a barrel, they must pay a total of $1,200 million ($20 x 60 million). This is a payment to the oil producers and is the producers' revenue. In general, revenue is the price (*P*) times the quantity (*Q*), or *P* x *Q*. A change in price therefore will affect revenue. Although this seems obvious, it is important that you understand exactly how price affects revenue. In fact, a change in price has two opposite effects on revenue. For instance, when the price increases, people pay more for each item, which increases revenue; but they buy fewer items, which in turn reduces revenue. The price elasticity of demand determines which of these two opposite effects dominates, because elasticity is a measure of how much the quantity demanded changes when price changes.

TABLE 4.1 Terminology for Price Elasticity of Demand

Term	Value of Price Elasticity of Demand (e_d)
Perfectly inelastic	0 (vertical demand curve)
Inelastic	Less than 1
Elastic	Greater than 1
Perfectly elastic	Infinity (horizontal demand curve)

FIGURE 4.6 **Perfectly Elastic and Perfectly Inelastic Demand**

A perfectly inelastic demand curve is a vertical line at a certain quantity. The quantity demanded is completely insensitive to the price: Whatever happens to the price, the quantity demanded does not change. A perfectly elastic demand curve is a flat line at a certain price. An increase in price reduces the quantity demanded to zero; a small decrease in price raises the quantity demanded by a huge (literally infinite) amount.

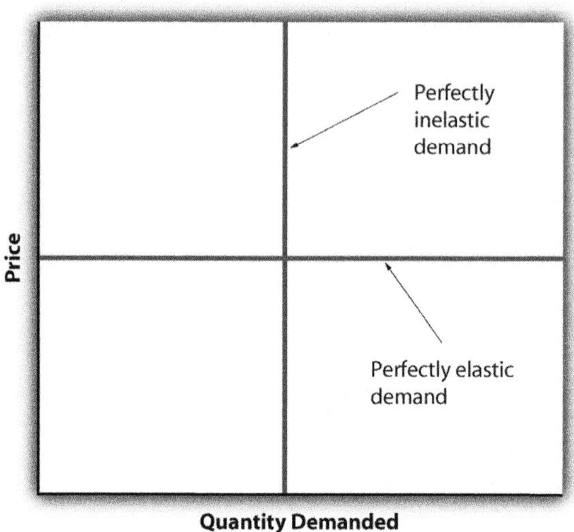

Figure 4.7, which is a replica of Figure 4.3 with the scales changed, illustrates the effects on revenue. In the top graph, revenue went from $1.2 billion (60 million x $20 = $1,200 million) to $1.056 billion (48 million x $22 = $1,056 million). In other words, revenue declined by $144 million even though price increased. Now compare this to the revenue changes in the bottom graph. There revenue went from $1.2 billion to $1.254 billion (57 million x $22 = $1,254 million), an increase of $54 million. Using the old price and the old quantity demanded, you can show that the elasticity of demand in the top graph is 2 while the elasticity of demand in the bottom graph is 0.5. We can see from this example that, following a price increase, revenue fell in the case where the elasticity was greater than one, and revenue rose when elasticity was less than one.

Is this always the case? We can illustrate the relationship between elasticity and revenue better by using a simple straight-line demand curve, as shown in Figure 4.8. Because this is a straight line, the slope is identical at all points on the demand curve—a $1 change in price will change quantity demanded by two units.

If you calculate the elasticity of demand at each point along the line, what you will find is that the elasticity of demand is equal to one at a price of $5 and a quantity demanded of 10. At this point, a $1 change in price (which is equivalent to a 20 percent change in the price) results in a two-unit change in quantity demanded (which is also equivalent to a 20 percent change in the quantity demanded). To the left of this point, the elasticity of demand is greater than one. You can see this by considering what happens at a price of $6 and a quantity demanded of eight. A $1 change in price will continue to bring about a two-unit change in quantity demanded, but the percentage change in price is smaller ($1/$6 = 16.66 percent instead of 20 percent), and the percentage change in quantity is larger (2/8 = 25 percent instead of 20 percent). Thus, the elasticity will now be greater than one. To the right of this point, the elasticity of demand is less than one. You can see this by considering what happens at a price of $4 and a quantity demanded of twelve. A $1 change in price will continue to bring about a two-unit change in quantity demanded, but the percentage change in price is larger ($1/$4 = 25 percent instead of 20 percent), and the percentage change in quantity is smaller (2/12 = 16.67 percent instead of 20 percent). Thus, the elasticity will now be less than one.

FIGURE 4.7 Effects of an Increase in the Price of Oil on Revenue

These graphs are replicas of the demand curves for oil shown in Figure 4.3, with the scale changed to show the change in revenue when the price of oil is increased. An increase in the price has two effects on revenue, as shown by the shaded rectangles. The increase in revenue (horizontal rectangle) is due to the higher price. The decrease in revenue (vertical rectangle) is due to the decline in the quantity demanded as the price is increased. In the top graph, where elasticity is greater than one, the net effect is a decline in revenue; in the bottom graph, where elasticity is less than one, the net effect is an increase in revenue.

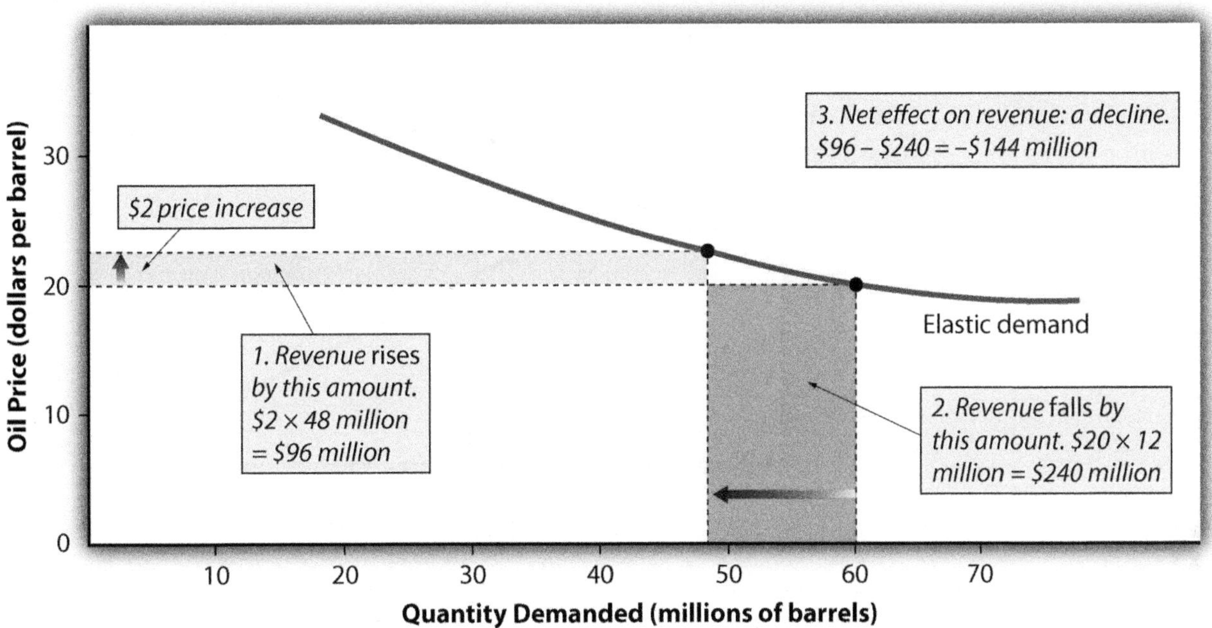

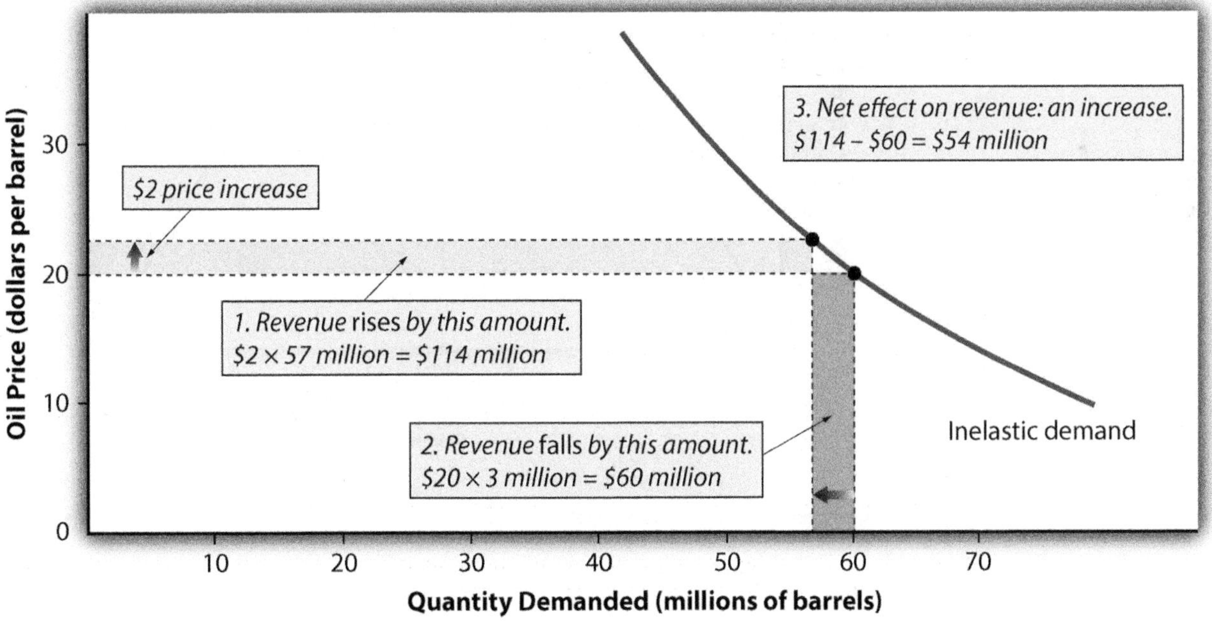

For each point along the demand curve, you can calculate revenue by simply multiplying price and quantity. The bottom panel of Figure 4.8 shows how revenue changes as the quantity demanded changes. Revenue begins at $0 (at a price of $10, quantity demanded is zero), increases for a while as quantity demanded increases, starts decreasing again, and ends up at $0 (because quantity demanded of 20 corresponds to a price of zero). Interestingly, you can see that the range over which revenue is rising with quantity demanded corresponds exactly with the range at which the elasticity is greater than one. Similarly, the range over which revenue is falling corresponds with the region of the demand curve at which the elasticity is less than one. Table 4.2 summarizes the relationship between revenue and the price elasticity of demand. An increase in price will raise revenue if the elasticity is less than one and will lower revenue if the elasticity is greater than one.

FIGURE 4.8 Revenue and Elasticity of a Straight-Line Demand Curve

Along the straight-line demand curve in the top panel, the price elasticity ranges from above 1 (to the left) to below 1 (to the right). When the price elasticity is greater than 1 an increase in the price will reduce revenue, as shown in the lower panel.

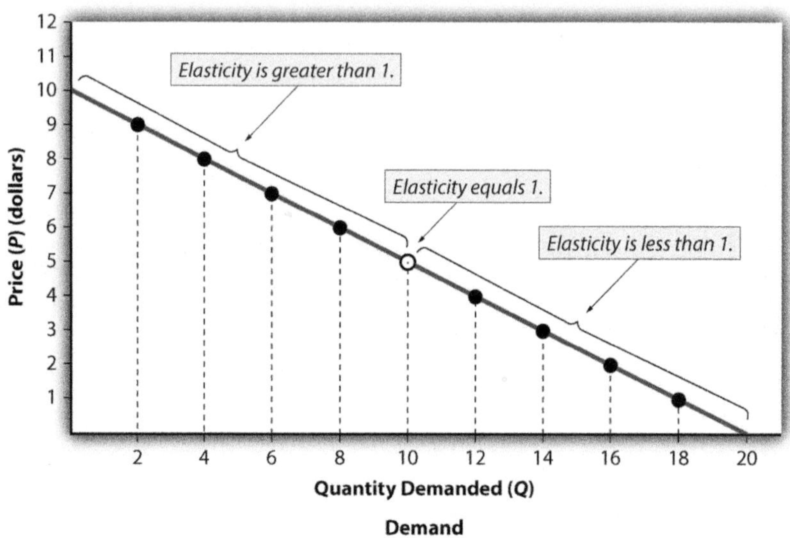

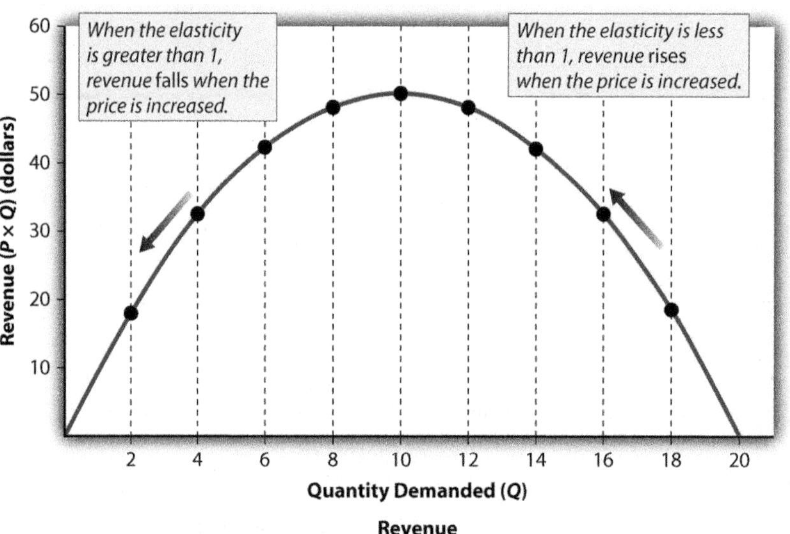

TABLE 4.2 Revenue and the Price Elasticity of Demand

Elasticity Is	Effect of a Price Increase on Revenue	Effect of a Price Decrease on Revenue
Less than 1 (<1)	Revenue increases	Revenue decreases
Equal to 1 (=1)	No change in revenue	No change in revenue
Greater than 1 (>1)	Revenue decreases	Revenue increases

This relationship between the elasticity of demand and the revenue impact of a price change is important. Businesses need to know the price elasticity of demand for their products to understand the implications of raising or lowering prices. For instance, in June 2010, Amazon.com announced that it would sharply cut the price of its new e-book reader, the Kindle, from $259 to $189, a drop of about 30 percent. Would the lower price entice more people to buy a Kindle? If so, would the increase in customers lead to an increase or a decrease in Amazon.com's revenue? The answer depends on the price elasticity of demand for Amazon's e-book readers. Similarly, in 2009, Apple, Inc. announced that it was raising the price for downloading a popular song from $0.99 to $1.29, an increase of around 26 percent using the midprice formula. Could this increase drive away many iTunes customers to rival music-downloading sites? If so, would the decrease in customers be so large as to lower Apple's revenue? The answer depends on the price elasticity of demand for music downloads on iTunes.

If demand for Amazon's e-book readers is price elastic and the demand for music downloads on iTunes is price inelastic, then both Amazon and Apple changed prices to increase revenue—Amazon cut the price of e-book readers to increase revenue, taking advantage of price-elastic demand, and Apple increased the price of music downloads to increase revenue, taking advantage of price-inelastic demand. How would Amazon or Apple know whether demand would be elastic or inelastic? The next section discusses the determinants of price elasticity of demand. You should judge as you read this chapter whether demand for business air travel and demand for pay phone calls are likely to be price elastic or price inelastic.

3.6 What Determines the Size of the Price Elasticity of Demand?

Table 4.3 shows price elasticities of demand for several different goods and services. The price elasticity for jewelry, for example, is 2.6. This means that for each percentage increase in the price of jewelry, the quantity demanded will fall by 2.6 percent. Compared with other elasticities, this is large. On the other hand, the price elasticity of eggs is very small. For each percentage increase in the price of eggs, the quantity of eggs demanded falls by only 0.1 percent.

TABLE 4.3 Estimated Price Elasticities of Demand

Type of Good or Service	Price Elasticity
Jewelry	2.6
Eggs	0.1
Telephone (first line)	0.1
Telephone (second line)	0.4
Foreign travel	1.2
Cigarettes (age 18-24)	0.6
Cigarettes (age 25-39)	0.4
Cigarettes (ages 40-older)	0.1
Gasoline (short run)	0.2
Gasoline (long run)	0.7

Why do these elasticities differ in size? Several factors determine a good's elasticity.

The Degree of Substitutability

A key factor is whether the item in question has good substitutes. Can people easily find a substitute when the price goes up? If the answer is yes, then the price elasticity will be high. Foreign travel has a high elasticity because it has a reasonably good substitute: domestic travel.

On the other hand, the low price elasticity of eggs can be explained by the lack of good substitutes. As many fans of eggs know, these items are unique; synthetic eggs are not good substitutes. Hence, the price elasticity of eggs is small. People will continue to buy them even if the price rises a lot.

The degree of substitutability depends in part on whether a good is a necessity or a luxury. If you want to easily preserve food for more than a few hours, a refrigerator has no good substitute. A fancy refrigerator with an exterior that blends in with the rest of your kitchen, however, is more of a luxury and likely will have a higher price elasticity.

Price Elasticity of Cell Phone Service in the Desert. There's probably not much of a substitute available for long-distance communication in the desert, which would make the price elasticity of the cell phone used here quite low. Do you think the caller in this picture would be equally insensitive to an increase of $0.10 per minute in the price of his calls if he were seated in his apartment in Chicago?

Source: Shutterstock.com

Big-Ticket versus Little-Ticket Items

If a good represents a large fraction of people's income, then the price elasticity will be high. If the price of foreign travel doubles, many people will not be able to afford to travel abroad. On the other hand, if the good represents a small fraction of income, the elasticity will be low. For example, if the price of eggs doubles, most people still will be able to afford to buy as many eggs as before the price increase.

Temporary versus Permanent Price Changes

If a change in price is known to be temporary, the price elasticity of demand will tend to be high, because many people can easily shift their purchases either later or earlier. For example, suppose a sewing machine store announces a discount price that will last only one day. Then people will shift their sewing machine purchase to the day of the sale. On the other hand, if the price cut is permanent, the price elasticity will be smaller. People who expect the price decrease to be permanent will not find it advantageous to buy sooner rather than later.

Differences in Preferences

Different groups of consumers may have different levels of elasticity. For example, young cigarette smokers, whose habit of smoking may not be entrenched, are more sensitive to changes in prices than older smokers. Table 4.3 shows that the price elasticity of demand for cigarettes for young adults between 18 and 24 years old is much higher than the very low price elasticity for people more than 40 years old.

Long-Run versus Short-Run Elasticity

Frequently the price elasticity of demand is low immediately after a price change, but then it increases after a period of time has passed. To analyze these changes, economists distinguish between the *short run* and the *long run.* The short run is simply a period of time before people have made all their adjustments or changed their habits; the long run is a period of time long enough for people to make such adjustments or change their habits.

Many personal adjustments to a change in prices take a long time. For example, when the price of gas increases, people can reduce the quantity demanded in the short run only by driving less and using other forms of transportation more, or by reducing the heating in their homes. This may be inconvenient or impossible. In the long run, however, when it comes time to buy a new car or a new heating system, they can buy a more fuel-efficient item or one that uses an alternative energy source. Thus, the quantity of gas demanded falls by larger amounts in the long run than in the short run (see Table 4.3).

Habits that are difficult to break also cause differences between short-run and long-run elasticity. Even a large increase in the price of tobacco may have a small effect on the quantity purchased because people cannot break the smoking habit quickly. But after a period of time, the high price of cigarettes may encourage them to break the habit, while discouraging potential new users. Thus, the long-run elasticity for tobacco is higher than the short-run elasticity.

The following examples will test your understanding of the determinants of the price elasticity of demand. The movie industry reported that its summer revenue was 3 percent higher than the previous year. A closer analysis reveals that ticket sales were down 1 percent. How could ticket revenue increase at the same time that the number of tickets sold decreased? The ticket price must have increased. Demand for movies also must be price inelastic, so that the reduction in ticket sales was more than offset by the increase in the price of the movie tickets. Does this make sense for the movie industry? It is plausible that some people feel that they *must see* the newest release and that the cost of the movie is a little-ticket item for many people who go to the movies. This would make the price elasticity of demand low and plausibly make demand price inelastic.

What Is the Price Elasticity of Demand for the Harry Potter Book Series? For loyal fans at one the 2007 book-release parties for *Harry Potter and the Deathly Hallows*, demand is price inelastic. For readers in general, the answer to that question may say a lot about the future of the book industry. If the price of books goes up, and at the same time, revenue from book sales increases, then demand for the purchase of books is price inelastic.

Source: Anton_Ivanov / Shutterstock.com

General Motors Corporation reported that revenues rose by more than 10 percent in the first half of 2010 compared with the second half of 2009. This occurred even though General Motors cut prices on many models of cars. At the same time, General Motors offered large discounts to customers purchasing cars. How could revenue increase while the price of cars was going down? It must be that more cars were sold at the lower price and that demand for these cars is price elastic. The reduction in price therefore was offset by the increase in cars sold, and revenue increased. Does this make sense for General Motors' cars? It is plausible that customers feel that cars have close substitutes and that this is a big-ticket purchase for many customers. This would make the price elasticity of demand high and demand plausibly price elastic.

3.7 Income Elasticity and Cross-Price Elasticity of Demand

Recall that the price elasticity of demand refers to movements along the demand curve. We emphasized in Chapter 3 the difference between a shift in the demand curve and a movement along the demand curve. A *shift* in the demand curve occurs when the quantity that people are willing to buy changes because of a change in anything except the price—for example, a change in income.

The concept of elasticity also can be applied to measure how changes in the quantity that consumers are willing to buy respond to changes in income. This elasticity must be distinguished from the price elasticity of demand. The **income elasticity of demand** is the percentage change in the quantity of a good demanded at any given price divided by a percentage change in income. That is,

income elasticity of demand

The percentage change in quantity demanded of a good divided by the percentage change in income.

$$\text{Income elasticity of demand} = \frac{\text{percentage change in quantity demanded}}{\text{percentage change in income}}$$

For example, if incomes rise by 10 percent and, as a result, people purchase 15 percent more health care at a given price, the income elasticity of health care is 1.5. Table 4.4 lists income elasticities of demand for several different goods and services.

TABLE 4.4 Estimated Income Elasticities of Demand

Type of Good or Service	Income Elasticity
Food	0.58
Clothing/footwear	0.58
Transport	1.18
Medical care	1.35
Recreation	1.42

As discussed in Chapter 3, the demand for most goods increases when people's incomes increase. If you have more income, your demand for movies probably will increase at each price. Recall that a normal good is a good or service whose demand increases as income increases. But not every good is a normal good; if the demand for a good declines when income increases, the good is called an inferior good. The income elasticity of demand for an inferior good is negative and is reported as a negative number by economists.

Another type of elasticity relating to shifts in the demand curve is the **cross-price elasticity of demand**, which is defined as the percentage change in the quantity demanded divided by the percentage change in the price of another good. For example, an increase in the price of Rollerblades would *increase* the quantity demanded of bicycles at every price as people shift away from Rollerblading to bicycle riding. Rollerblades are a substitute for bicycles. A cross-price elasticity also can go in the other direction. An increase in the price of bicycle helmets may *reduce* the demand for bicycles. Bicycle helmets and bicycles are complements. For a complement, the cross-price elasticity of demand is negative.

cross-price elasticity of demand

The percentage change in the quantity demanded of one good divided by the percentage change in the price of another good.

REVIEW

- The price elasticity of demand, or elasticity, is used to measure how much the quantity demanded changes when the price changes. Elasticity also helps determine how large a price increase will occur as a result of a shift in supply, and by how much revenue will change when the price rises.
- Elasticity is a unit-free measure—it is the ratio of the percentage change in quantity demanded to the percentage change in price. In other words, it measures by what percentage quantity demanded changes when the price changes by 1 percent.
- Horizontal demand curves have infinite price elasticity. Vertical demand curves have zero price elasticity. Most products have a price elasticity between these two extremes. We use the term *elastic demand*to refer to an elasticity of demand that is greater than one and *inelastic demand*to refer to an elasticity of demand that is less than one.
- Other than the horizontal and vertical cases, elasticity is different from the slope of the demand curve, however. A demand curve that is a straight line has a different elasticity of demand at each point.
- The size of the price elasticity of demand depends on the availability of substitutes for the item, whether the item represents a large fraction of income, and whether the price change is temporary or permanent.
- Whereas the price elasticity of demand refers to movements along the demand curve, the income elasticity of demand refers to shifts in the demand curve caused by changes in income. Most goods are normal and have a positive income elasticity of demand. Inferior goods have a negative income elasticity of demand.
- The cross-price elasticity of demand also relates to shifts in the demand curve, in this case, a change in the price of a complement or substitute good.

4. ELASTICITY OF SUPPLY

Knowing how sensitive the quantity supplied is to a change in price is just as important as knowing how sensitive the quantity demanded is. The price elasticity of supply measures this sensitivity. "Price elasticity of supply" is sometimes shortened to "supply elasticity" or "elasticity of supply." Supply describes the behavior of firms that produce goods. A high price elasticity of supply means that firms raise their production by a large amount if the price increases. A low price elasticity of supply means that firms raise their production only a little if the price increases.

price elasticity of supply

The percentage change in quantity supplied divided by the percentage change in price.

The **price elasticity of supply** is defined as the percentage change in the quantity supplied divided by the percentage change in the price. That is,

$$\text{Price elasticity of supply} = \frac{\text{percentage change in quantity supplied}}{\text{percentage change in the price}}$$

The price elasticity of supply refers to a particular supply curve, such as the supply curve for gasoline or video games. All other things that affect supply are held constant when we compute the price elasticity of supply. For example, suppose the price elasticity of supply for video games is 0.5. Then, if the price of video games rises by 10 percent, the quantity of video games supplied will increase by 5 percent (0.5 x 10).

4.1 Working with Supply Elasticities

All the attractive features of the price elasticity of demand also apply to the price elasticity of supply. To see this, let us first take a look at the definition of the price elasticity of supply using symbols. If we let the symbol e_s be the price elasticity of supply, then it can be written as

$$e_s = \frac{\Delta Q_s}{Q_s} \div \frac{\Delta P}{P} = \frac{\left(\frac{\Delta Q_d}{Q_d}\right)}{\left(\frac{\Delta P}{P}\right)}$$

where Q_s is the quantity supplied and P is the price. In other words, the price elasticity of supply is the percentage change in the quantity supplied divided by the percentage change in price. Observe the similarity of this expression to the analogous expression for the price elasticity of demand on page 80: The only difference is the use of quantity supplied (Q_s) rather than quantity demanded (Q_d). This means that the concepts and terminology for supply elasticity are very similar to those for demand elasticity. For example, in Table 4.1, if you replace "Demand" with "Supply," you have the terminology for the price elasticity of supply. Moreover, like the price elasticity of demand, the price elasticity of supply is a unit-free measure, and the elasticity of supply and the slope of the supply curve are not the same thing.

Because of this similarity, our discussion of supply elasticity can be brief. It is useful to consider the extreme cases of perfectly elastic supply and perfectly inelastic supply, and then to go through an example illustrating the importance of knowing the size of the price elasticity of supply.

Perfectly Elastic and Perfectly Inelastic Supply

As in the case of demand, there can be **perfectly elastic supply** or **perfectly inelastic supply**, as shown in Figure 4.9. The vertical supply curve is perfectly inelastic; it has zero elasticity. Such supply curves are not unusual. For example, only one *Mona Lisa* exists. A higher price cannot bring about a higher quantity supplied, not even one more *Mona Lisa.* But the supply curve for most goods is not vertical. Higher prices will encourage coffee producers to use more fertilizer, hire more workers, and eventually plant more coffee trees. Thus, the quantity supplied increases when the price rises.

The horizontal supply curve is perfectly elastic. In this case, the price does not change at all. It is the same regardless of the quantity supplied. It is easier to understand the horizontal supply curve if you view it as an approximation to a supply curve that is *nearly* horizontal, one with a very high elasticity. Then, only a small increase in price brings forth a huge increase in the quantity supplied by firms.

perfectly elastic supply

Supply for which the price elasticity is infinite, indicating an infinite response of quantity supplied to a change in price and therefore a horizontal supply curve.

perfectly inelastic supply

Supply for which the price elasticity is zero, indicating no response of quantity supplied to a change in price and therefor a vertical supply curve.

Why the Size of the Price Elasticity of Supply Is Important

Now let us look at the importance of knowing the size of the supply elasticity even if it is not at one of these two extremes. Figure 4.10 shows two different supply curves for coffee. The horizontal axis shows the quantity of coffee supplied around the world in billions of pounds; the vertical axis shows the price in dollars per pound of coffee. For the supply curve in the top graph, the quantity supplied is very sensitive to the price; the price elasticity of supply is high. For the supply curve in the bottom graph, the price elasticity of supply is much lower.

Perfectly Inelastic Supply. The paintings of Leonardo da Vinci provide an example of a good with a perfectly inelastic supply. The supply curve is vertical because no matter how high the price, no more *Mona Lisas* can be produced. However, what about the demand to see the *Mona Lisa* at the Louvre? Is it perfectly inelastic? Will raising the price of admission charged by the Louvre Museum in Paris reduce the number of people coming to see the painting?

Source: Nattee Chalermtiragool / Shutterstock.com

The price elasticity of supply is important for finding the response of price to shifts in demand. This is shown in Figure 4.11, in which the demand for coffee declines, perhaps because of concerns about the effect of the caffeine in coffee or because of a decrease in the price of caffeine-free substitutes for coffee. In either case, if the price elasticity of supply is high, as in the top graph, the price does not change as much as when the price elasticity of supply is low, as in the bottom graph. With a high price elasticity, a small change in price is enough to get firms to bring the quantity supplied down to the lower quantity demanded.

FIGURE 4.9 **Perfectly Elastic and Perfectly Inelastic Supply**

When the quantity supplied is completely unresponsive to the price, the supply curve is vertical and the price elasticity of supply is zero; this case is called perfectly inelastic supply. When the quantity supplied responds by large amounts to a price change, the supply curve is horizontal; economists say that supply is perfectly elastic.

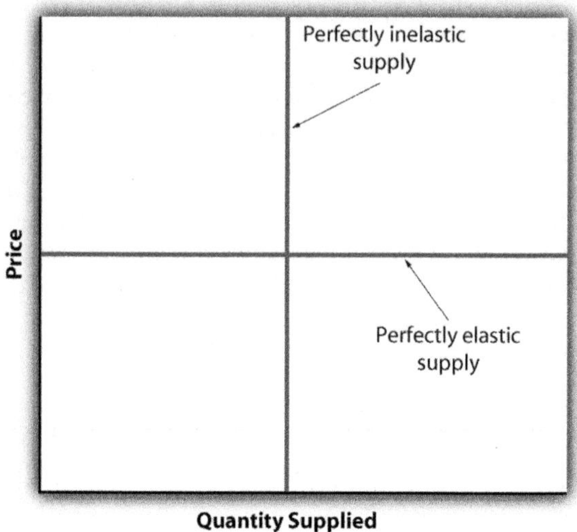

FIGURE 4.10 Comparing Different Sizes of the Price Elasticities of Supply

In the top graph, the quantity supplied is much more sensitive to price than in the bottom graph. The price elasticity of supply is greater between points *A* and *B* at the top than between points *A* and *C* at the bottom.

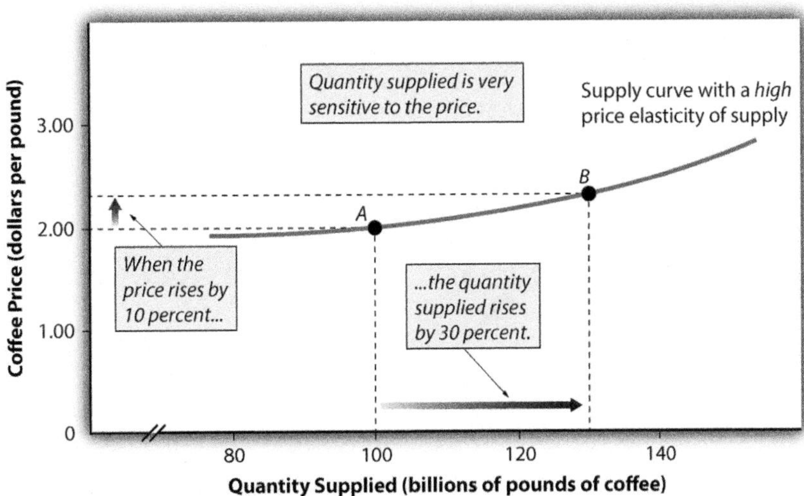

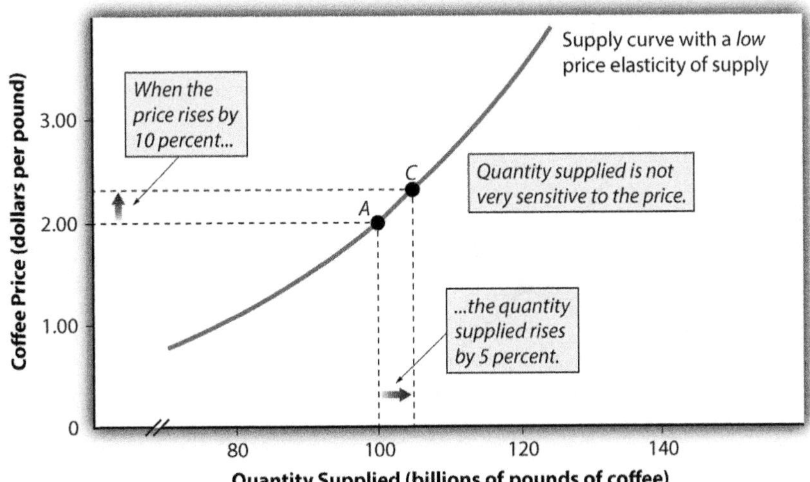

FIGURE 4.11 Importance of Knowing the Size of the Price Elasticity of Supply

When demand changes, the price also will change. If the price elasticity of supply is high, a small change in price will result. If the price elasticity of supply is low, a large change in price will result.

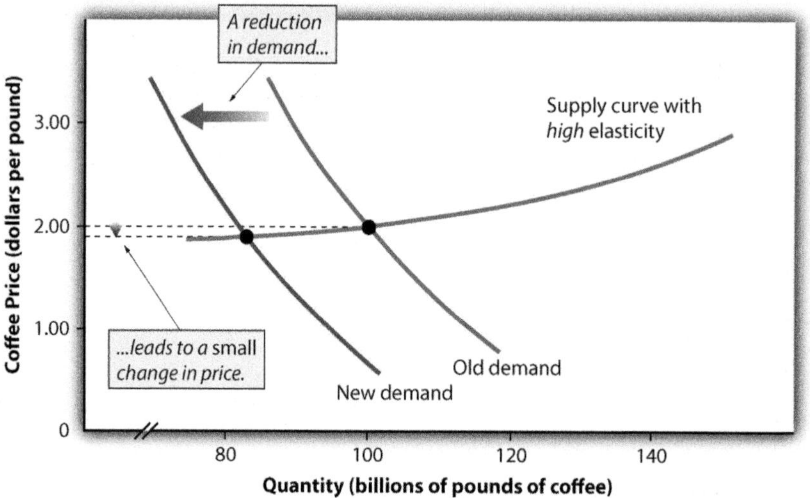

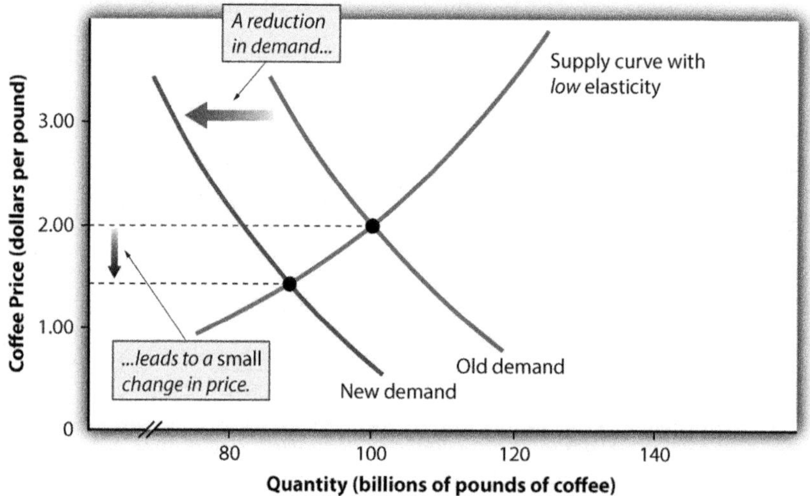

REVIEW

- The price elasticity of supply is a number that tells us how sensitive the quantity supplied is to the price. It is defined as the percentage change in the quantity supplied divided by the percentage change in the price.
- The attractive features of the price elasticity of demand are also true for the price elasticity of supply. Its size does not depend on the units of measurement of either price or quantity.
- The price elasticity of supply is useful for determining how much prices will change when demand changes.

5. END-OF-CHAPTER MATERIAL

5.1 Conclusion

In this chapter, we have extended our analysis of the supply and demand model in two directions. We first learned about what happens when the government intervenes to put a price ceiling or a price floor into the economy. Understanding how to use the supply and demand model with price floors and ceilings enables us to better understand policy debates such as the one surrounding the increase in the minimum wage.

The second extension was to develop an understanding of *how much* the equilibrium price and quantity change in response to changes in supply or demand. The concept of price elasticity of demand helps us understand what happens to the quantity demanded when price changes or when the supply of a good changes. We also can predict whether revenue will increase or decrease when prices are cut or raised. The related concept of the elasticity of supply is also useful in understanding what happens to the quantity supplied when price changes or when the demand for a good changes. We also discussed the concept of an income elasticity of demand, which can clarify how the quantity demanded for various goods will change as incomes rise, and the cross-price elasticity of demand, which tells us how much the quantity demanded of a good changes as prices for substitute or complementary goods change.

Key Points

1. Governments occasionally will intervene in markets because they think that the equilibrium price is too high or too low. When they act to impose a maximum price on a market, because they think the price that buyers have to pay is too high, they are said to be imposing a price ceiling. When they act to impose a minimum price on a market, because they think the price that sellers are receiving is too low, they are said to be imposing a price floor.
2. Price ceilings cause shortages, with the quantity supplied being less than the quantity demanded. Shortages lead to rationing or black markets. Price floors cause surpluses, with the quantity supplied being greater than the quantity demanded. Surpluses lead to resources being diverted away from other productive activities to deal with the extra output that needs to be stored or disposed of.
3. Rent controls are a classic application of a price ceiling, and minimum wages are a classic application of a price floor. The supply model helps us understand some basic issues related to these policies, which frequently appear in the news. We will develop the supply and demand model further, which will allow us to do a more sophisticated analysis of minimum-wage laws, for example, than we have done in this chapter.
4. Elasticity is a measure of the sensitivity of one economic variable to another. For example, the price elasticity of demand measures how much the quantity demanded changes when the price changes.
5. Elasticity is a unit-free measure. The price elasticity of demand is the percentage change in the quantity demanded divided by the percentage change in price. It refers to changes in price and quantity demanded along the demand curve, all other things being equal.
6. Demand is said to be elastic if the price elasticity of demand is greater than one and inelastic if the price elasticity of demand is less than one.
7. When the elasticity is greater than one, an increase in the price reduces the quantity demanded by a percentage greater than the percentage increase in the price, thereby reducing revenue. When the elasticity is less than one, an increase in the price reduces the quantity demanded by a percentage less than the percentage increase in the price, thereby increasing revenue.
8. The elasticity of demand for a good depends on whether the good has close substitutes, whether its value is a large or a small fraction of total income, and the time period of the change.
9. Whereas the price elasticity of demand refers to movements along the demand curve, the income elasticity of demand refers to shifts in the demand curve caused by changes in income, and the cross-price elasticity of demand refers to shifts in the demand curve caused by changes in the price of other goods. Most goods are normal and have a positive income elasticity of demand. Inferior goods have a negative income elasticity of demand.
10. The price elasticity of supply is defined as the percentage change in the quantity supplied divided by the percentage change in the price. If a good has a high price elasticity of supply, then a change in price will cause a big change in the quantity supplied. Conversely, if a good has a low price elasticity of supply, then a change in price will have only a small impact on the quantity supplied.

QUESTIONS FOR REVIEW

1. Why is the price elasticity of demand a unit-free measure of the sensitivity of the quantity demanded to a price change?
2. What factors determine whether the price elasticity of demand is high or low?
3. What is the difference between elastic and inelastic demand?
4. Why is the price elasticity of demand useful for finding the size of the price change that occurs when supply shifts?
5. If the price elasticity of demand for textbooks is two and the price of textbooks increases by 10 percent, by how much does the quantity demanded fall?
6. Why is the price elasticity of demand lower in the short run than in the long run?
7. For what values of the price elasticity of demand do increases in the price increase revenue?
8. What is the income elasticity of demand?
9. What is the difference between the price elasticity of demand and the income elasticity of demand?
10. What is the slope of a perfectly elastic supply curve?

PROBLEMS

1. Consider the market for automatic teller machine (ATM) services in a city. The price is the fee for a cash withdrawal.
   a. Sketch the demand curve and the supply curve for ATM transactions.
   b. How is the equilibrium price determined?
   c. If the town council imposes a ban on ATM fees— equivalent to a price ceiling in this market—what happens to quantity supplied and quantity demanded?
   d. Economists frequently argue against price controls because of the shortages and associated problems that they create. What are some of the potentially negative side effects of interference in the ATM market?
2. In 1991, the price of milk fell 30 percent. Senator Leahy of Vermont, a big milk-producing state, supported a law in the U.S. Congress to put a floor on the price. The floor was $13.09 per hundred pounds of milk. The market price was $11.47.
   a. Draw a supply and demand diagram for milk and show how the equilibrium price and quantity would be determined in the absence of the price floor.
   b. Using the diagram you just drew, explain the effects of the legislation.
   c. The dairy farmers supported the legislation, while consumer groups opposed it. Why?
   d. Economists frequently argue against price floors because of the surpluses and associated problems that they create. What are some of the potentially negative side effects of interference in the milk market?
3. More than 20 states have laws outlawing price gouging during a state of emergency, which might be declared after a hurricane or an earthquake. These laws prohibit price increases on basic necessities, such as gasoline. Which of the arguments against price ceilings might not be significant during a state of emergency?
4. Donors of organs for transplantation or medical research are prohibited from charging a price for these organs (there is a price ceiling of zero). Will this result in a shortage? How will the market cope with the shortage?

5. Consider the following data for a demand curve:

Price	Quantity
11	10
10	20
9	30
8	40
7	50
6	60
5	70
4	80
3	90

   a. Use the midpoint formula to calculate the elasticity between a price of $10 and $11.
   b. Use the midpoint formula to calculate the elasticity between a price of $3 and $4.
   c. Because this is a linear demand curve, why does the elasticity change?
   d. At what point is price times quantity maximized? What is the elasticity at that point?

6. Consider the following data for a supply curve:

Price	Quantity Supplied
2	10
3	20
4	30
5	40
6	50
7	60
8	70
9	80

   a. Use the midpoint formula to calculate the price elasticity of supply between a price of $7 and $8.
   b. Use the midpoint formula to calculate the price elasticity of supply between a price of $3 and $4.
   c. How does supply elasticity change as you move up the supply curve?
   d. Why does the supply elasticity change even though the slope of the supply curve is unchanged as you move up the supply curve?

7. Given the following income elasticities of demand, would you classify the following goods as normal or inferior goods?
   a. Potatoes: elasticity = 0.5
   b. Pinto beans: elasticity = -0.1
   c. Bottled water: elasticity = 1.1
   d. Video cameras: elasticity = 1.4

8. Calculate the cross-price elasticity for the following goods. Are they substitutes or complements?
   a. The price of movie theater tickets goes up by 10 percent, causing the quantity demanded for video rentals to go up by 4 percent.
   b. The price of computers falls by 20 percent, causing the quantity demanded of software to increase by 15 percent.
   c. The price of apples falls by 5 percent, causing the quantity demanded of pears to fall by 5 percent.
   d. The price of ice cream falls by 6 percent, causing the quantity demanded of frozen yogurt to fall by 1 percent.
9. Food items often have low elasticities of demand. Suppose excellent weather leads to bumper yields of agricultural crops. Why might farmers complain about market conditions?
10. The board of directors of an airline wishes to increase revenue. One group favors cutting airfares, and the other group favors raising airfares. What are the assumptions each group is making about the price elasticity of demand?
11. Compare a market in which supply and demand are very (but not perfectly) inelastic to one in which supply and demand are very (but not perfectly) elastic. Suppose the government decides to impose a price floor $1 above the equilibrium price in each of these markets. Compare, diagrammatically, the surpluses that result. In which market is the surplus larger?
12. In 1992, the federal government placed a tax of 10 percent on goods like luxury automobiles and yachts. The yacht-manufacturing industry had huge declines in orders for yachts and laid off many workers, whereas the reaction in the auto industry was much milder. (The tax on yachts was subsequently removed.) Explain this situation using two supply and demand diagrams. Compare the elasticity of demand for luxury autos with that for yachts based on the experience with the luxury tax.

CHAPTER 5
The Demand Curve and the Behavior of Consumers

This is a true story about a college professor who loves to teach introductory economics.

The professor is younger than most college professors but is hard of hearing and wears hearing aids in both ears. The professor teaches one of those large lecture courses, and most students are not even aware that the professor wears the hearing aids.

In the middle of one of the lectures, the professor simultaneously brings one hand to one ear and the other hand to the other ear and suddenly pulls out both hearing aids, saying, "I can't hear a thing. If it were not for these hearing aids, I wouldn't be here. I couldn't be a teacher. Do you know how much benefit I get from these hearing aids? Certainly more than from my car and maybe even more than from my house. If I had to give you a dollar amount, I would say that the benefit to me is about $60,000. Without the hearing aids, I would probably earn less, and I know my life would not be as enjoyable. Of course, I had to buy these hearing aids, and they are not very cheap. They cost me $500. But, you know, they cost me a lot less than they benefit me. The difference between $60,000 and $500 is $59,500, a huge amount. That difference is a measure of what the hearing aid market delivers to me over and above what I had to pay for the hearing aids. Most people would call that a good deal, but because I am an economics professor, I call it a *consumer surplus*."

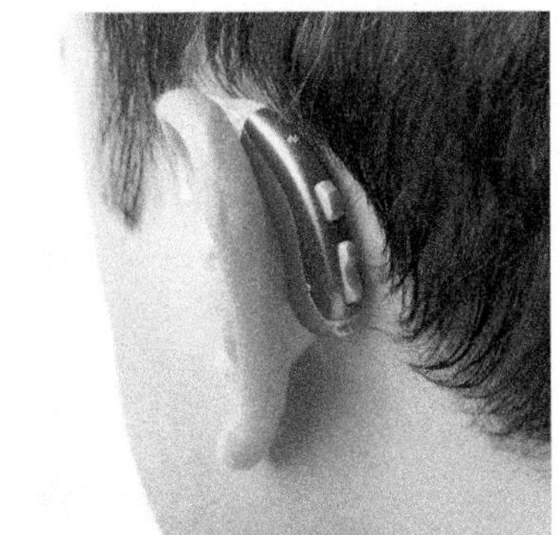

Source: © Shutterstock, Inc.

In this chapter, we show how and why the demand curve for any good—whether hearing aids, digital music players, grapes, or bananas—can be used to measure the "good deal," or the "consumer surplus," that markets deliver to people.

FIGURE 5.1 A Typical Demand Curve

Demand curves typically slope downward. In this chapter, we examine the behavior of the consumers who underline the demand curve.

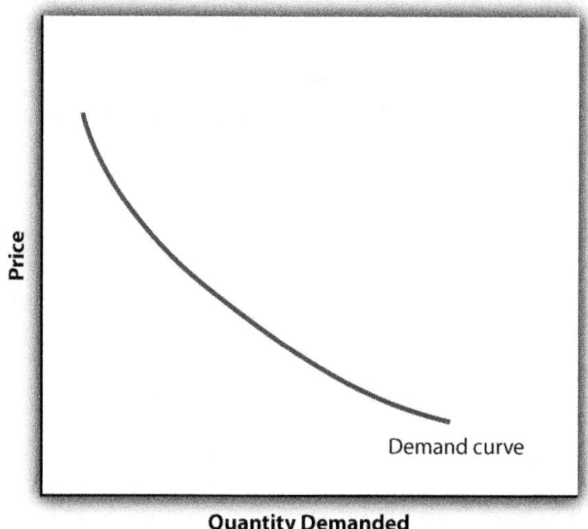

Figure 5.1 shows a typical demand curve, with price on the vertical axis and quantity demanded on the horizontal axis. The demand curve is for an entire market, which might consist of millions of consumers. But consumers do not go to the market with a demand curve; they go with certain preferences and objectives. In this chapter, we look under the surface of the demand curve and examine how a consumer's preferences and objectives, combined with the constraints that the consumer faces, determine the demand curve for a particular good for an individual.

Then we show how aggregating individual demand curves across millions of consumers generates a demand curve for the entire market for that good.

By the end of this chapter, you should better understand two important concepts. The first is exactly what determines the slope and position of the demand curve—why it slopes downward and why changes in people's preferences or incomes cause it to shift. The second is how to quantify the "good deal," or the "consumer surplus," that the market delivers to consumers. Consumer surplus is extremely important for measuring how well a market economy actually works. One of the most important conclusions of the study of economics is that, under certain circumstances, a market economy works better than alternative systems to produce and allocate goods and resources. To understand that conclusion—to question it, to criticize it, to prove it, to defend it—we must better understand how much benefit consumers are getting from a market.

1. UTILITY AND CONSUMER PREFERENCES

Our examination of consumer behavior in this chapter involves constructing a model. The main assumption of the model is that people make purposeful choices with limited resources to increase their satisfaction and better their lives. To make this assumption operational, economists have developed the idea of *utility*, which represents people's preferences for different items (products, jobs, leisure time) among a set of alternatives.

Every person has tastes and preferences for some goods relative to other goods. The millions of people who underlie a typical demand curve do not all have the same tastes and preferences, of course. Some people like brussels sprouts; some people hate brussels sprouts. We first focus on how to derive a demand curve for an individual consumer and then show how the behavior of the millions of individuals adds up to generate a market demand curve.

Utility is a numerical indicator of a person's preference for some goods compared with others. If one prefers some activity, such as eating a pizza and drinking two Cokes, to some other activity, such as eating two pizzas and drinking one Coke, then the utility from "one pizza and two Cokes" is greater than the utility from "two pizzas and one Coke." In general, if activity A is preferred to alternative B, then the utility from A is greater than the utility from B.

Utility
A numerical indicator of a person's preferences in which higher levels of utility indicate a greater preference.

Be careful not to confuse the economist's definition of utility with the everyday meaning. If you look up *utility* in the dictionary, you probably will see the word *usefulness*, but to an economist, higher *utility* does not mean greater "usefulness"; it simply means that the item is preferred to another item. Watching *The Walking Dead* or *The Office* might give you more utility than attending a review session for your economics course, even though it certainly is not as useful for studying for the final.

1.1 A Consumer's Utility Depends on the Consumption of Goods

Let us consider an example of utility. Grapes are a product with which we have a lot of experience. They have been around for more than 4,000 years (at least since 2400 B.C. in ancient Egypt), and, in one form or another, they still are consumed around the world. Bananas are another popular fruit, also consumed around the world. Let us use grapes and bananas for our example of utility.

Figure 5.2 shows an example of the utility that one individual might get from consuming different amounts of grapes and bananas. Remember that every person is different, so the utility shown in Figure 5.2 is just an example. You might imagine that the person is you, standing in front of a bin of fresh grapes and bananas in a grocery store and deciding what fruit to buy. Or it could be someone at an open-air market who is deciding how many pounds of grapes and bananas to buy with her money.

FIGURE 5.2 Example of Utility from Grapes and Bananas

The numbers inside the box give the utility from consuming the amounts of grapes and the amounts of bananas shown outside the box. For example, utility from 4 pounds of grapes and 3 pounds of bananas is 36. Combinations of grapes and bananas with higher utility are preferred to combinations with lower utility.

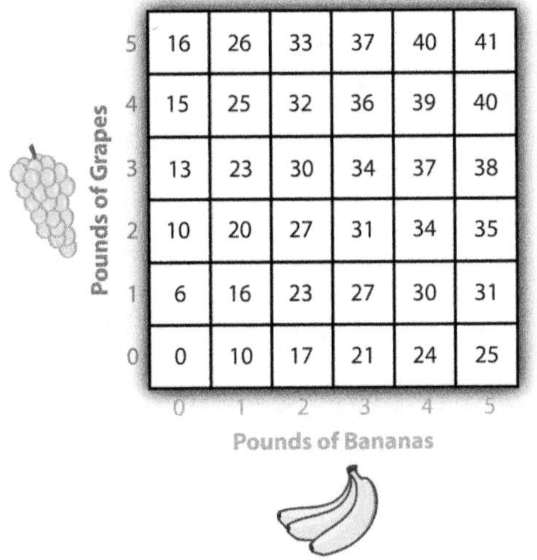

Pounds of Grapes \ Pounds of Bananas	0	1	2	3	4	5
5	16	26	33	37	40	41
4	15	25	32	36	39	40
3	13	23	30	34	37	38
2	10	20	27	31	34	35
1	6	16	23	27	30	31
0	0	10	17	21	24	25

Observe how Figure 5.2 is organized. The number of pounds of grapes is listed vertically on the left outside the box, from 0 up to 5 pounds. The number of pounds of bananas is listed horizontally below the box, from 0 to 5 pounds. The entries inside the box show the utility from consuming different combinations of grapes and bananas. The box at the intersection of a row and a column shows the utility for the consumption of that specific combination of grapes and bananas. For example, if the individual consumes 2 pounds of grapes and 2 pounds of bananas, then the utility is 27.

Remember that utility is an indicator of people's preferences, with higher utility indicating a stronger preference. As you move up a column or across a row, utility increases. This increase in utility is called **marginal utility**. In general, *marginal utility* is the increase in utility from consuming an additional unit of a good.

marginal utility
The increase in utility when consumption of a good increases by one unit.

For example, consider an individual consuming 2 pounds of grapes and 2 pounds of bananas. For this individual, at that level of consumption, consuming 1 additional pound of grapes (making her consumption 3 pounds of grapes and 2 pounds of bananas) increases utility by 3 (from 27 to 30); the marginal utility of a pound of grapes is 3.

Had she instead chosen to consume 1 more pound of bananas (making her consumption 2 pounds of grapes and 3 pounds of bananas), her utility would have increased by 4 (from 27 to 31); the marginal utility of a pound of bananas is 4.

1.2 Important Properties of Utility

We can use Figure 5.2 to illustrate some important assumptions that economists often make about utility.

diminishing marginal utility

The tendency for a consumer to derive less additional benefit from adding to the consumption of a good as consumption of that good increases.

1. *Utility can be used to rank alternative consumption combinations.* A consumer's utility describes the consumer's preference for one good compared with another. According to Figure 5.2, the consumer prefers a combination of 4 pounds of grapes and 1 pound of bananas to a combination of 1 pound of grapes and 2 pounds of bananas because the utility of the former (25) is greater than the utility of the latter (23). Other combinations can be ranked similarly. In some cases, utility levels are identical; for example, the consumer is *indifferent* as to 2 pounds of grapes and 3 pounds of bananas versus 1 pound of grapes and 5 pounds of bananas because the utility of both is 31. Of all possible combinations, the one with the highest (maximum) utility is the one that is preferred to all the others. Thus, by maximizing utility, the consumer is making decisions that lead to the most preferred outcome from her viewpoint. In this way, utility maximization implements the assumption that people make purposeful choices to increase their satisfaction.
2. *Having more of a good never makes an individual worse off.* In Figure 5.2, as you move across a row or up a column, utility is increasing, which means that marginal utility is a positive value. This implies that this individual would get more utility from 3 pounds of grapes and 2 pounds of bananas (utility = 30) or from 2 pounds of grapes and 3 pounds of bananas (utility = 31) than she would gain from 2 pounds of grapes and 2 pounds of bananas (utility = 27). This assumption seems reasonable. On occasion, an individual may derive zero marginal utility from a particular good, although that is not the case in the example in Figure 5.2. As long as you can freely dispose of goods, adding more of a good should never reduce utility, in other words, marginal utility should never be negative.
3. A corollary of statement #2. is that having more of both goods is always a more preferred option for a consumer, just as having less of both goods is always a less preferred option. For example, consider the choice of 2 pounds of grapes and 2 pounds of bananas for the individual, highlighted in Figure 5.3. All the bundles that involve the same amount or more of one fruit and more of the other (which are the upper shaded entries to the right and above) are preferred to the combination of 2 pounds each of grapes and bananas. Alternatively, the consumer prefers the 2 pounds of grapes and 2 pounds of bananas combination to all the bundles that involve the same amount or less of one fruit and less of the other (which are the lower shaded entries to the left and below). The consumer would find the remaining combinations (which involve more bananas and fewer grapes or fewer bananas and more grapes) either more preferred or less preferred or would be indifferent between them, depending on what is contained in those combinations.
4. *Marginal utility decreases as the consumption of a good increases.* If you look at Figure 5.2, you can see that marginal utility is decreasing as you consume more bananas or more grapes. For example, the marginal utility of a pound of bananas for a consumer who is consuming 2 pounds of bananas and 2 pounds of grapes is 4 (31 - 27 = 4). But the marginal utility of adding 1 more pound of bananas to her new consumption bundle of 3 pounds of bananas and 2 pounds of grapes is only 3 (34 - 31 = 3). Intuitively, what this is showing is that the more an individual is consuming of a good, the less additional benefit she will get from adding to her consumption of that good. This is known as **diminishing marginal utility**.
5. *The units that utility is measured in do not matter.* Utility is a numerical indicator of preferences, but the units used to measure it do not matter. For example, suppose we multiply the utilities from grapes and from bananas in Figure 5.2 by 10, and then re-examine what utility implies about preferences. Rather than 27 units of utility, we would have 270 units of utility from 2 pounds of grapes and 2 pounds of bananas. Instead of this combination, the consumer would still prefer 3 pounds of grapes and 3 pounds of bananas, which now would have a utility of 340 instead of 34. In fact, you can multiply utility by any positive number—even a billion or a billionth—and still get the same ordering of one combination compared with another. The fact that the description of people's preferences does not depend on the units we use to measure utility is important, because in reality economists have no way to measure utility. That is why Figure 5.2 does not give units, just a number.
6. *You cannot compare utility levels across people.* Because you can multiply the utility of any individual by any number without changing the description of that individual's preferences, the utilities of different people cannot be compared. In other words, we cannot say that one person's

utility is higher or lower than another person's utility. Only the preferences of a particular person are represented by utility.

FIGURE 5.3 Deriving Utility from Grapes and Bananas

Consuming 2 pounds each of grapes and bananas gives a utility level of 27. Combinations that have at least as much of one fruit and more of the other have a higher level of utility (upper shaded region). Combinations that have at least as much of one fruit and less of the other have a lower level of utility (lower shaded region).

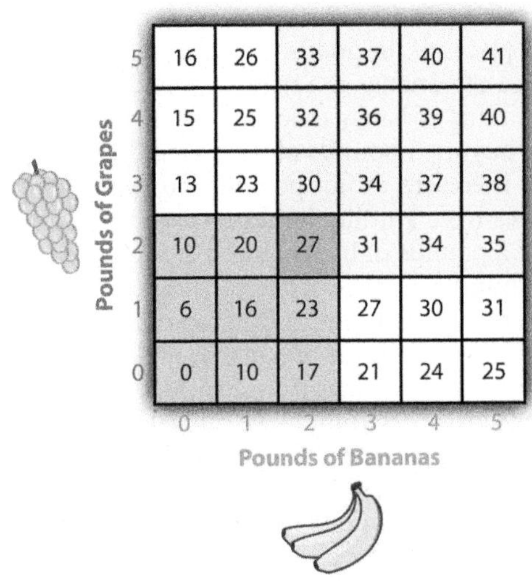

REVIEW

- Utility is a numerical indicator of a person's preferences for different goods.
- Each combination of goods has a numerical value of utility. Combinations of goods with a higher utility are preferred to combinations of goods with a lower utility.
- The change in utility from consuming one additional unit of a good is known as marginal utility. As long as you can freely dispose of goods, marginal utility never will be negative.
- Marginal utility typically will decrease as the consumption of a good increases—additional units of a good will be more valued when the consumer is not already consuming much of that good.
- The units by which utility is measured do not affect the preference for one combination compared with another.
- Utility levels cannot be compared across people. Utility is an indicator of one individual's preferences.

2. THE BUDGET CONSTRAINT AND UTILITY MAXIMIZATION

We now know how a consumer's preferences can be described by utility. We also know that the consumer wants to maximize utility—to make a purposeful choice that provides the most satisfaction. Because marginal utility is never negative for a good, you might be wondering how a consumer can ever reach a maximum level of utility. Wouldn't she always want to consume one more unit of a good? Keep in mind that economics is about how people make purposeful choices *using scarce resources.* In other words, the consumer is maximizing utility given some constraints, or limits, on her behavior. Even though she may want one more unit of a good, she may not be able to afford that additional unit. In this section, we will introduce the limits on the consumer's choice and explain how utility maximization works.

2.1 The Budget Constraint

budget constraint

An income limitation on a person's expenditure on goods and services.

Consumers are limited in how much they can spend when they choose between grapes and bananas or other goods. For example, suppose the individual choosing between grapes and bananas is limited to spending a total of $8. That is, total spending on grapes plus bananas must be less than or equal to $8. This limit on total spending is called the **budget constraint**. In general, a budget constraint tells us that total expenditures on all goods and services must be less than a certain amount, perhaps the person's income for the year. The budget constraint is what limits the consumer's choices.

Modeling a Consumer's Choice. This consumer, with a limited amount to spend, makes a choice that maximizes her utility. The combination of grapes and bananas that she prefers to other possible combinations of grapes and bananas must have a higher utility for her than the other combinations have.

Source: © Shutterstock, Inc.

How much a consumer can spend and still remain within the budget constraint depends on the prices of the goods. Suppose the price of a pound of grapes is $1 and the price of a pound of bananas is $1. Her expenditure on a combination of 2 pounds of grapes and 2 pounds of bananas would be $4, well within the budget constraint of $8. But the cost of buying 5 pounds of each would be $10, a sum that exceeds the budget constraint and, therefore, is not possible. So even though 5 pounds of bananas and 5 pounds of grapes have a utility level of 41, compared with a utility level of 27 for the combination of 2 pounds of bananas and 2 pounds of grapes, you will not see the consumer buy that bundle because of her constrained budget.

Figure 5.4 shows expenditures on grapes and bananas for two different situations. In the left panel, both the price of bananas and the price of grapes are $1. All the combinations of grapes and bananas from Figure 5.2 are shown in Figure 5.4, but several of the combinations are not within the $8 budget constraint; these are in the upper shaded area. What happens if the price of grapes is $2 instead of $1? The resulting expenditure for each combination is listed in the panel on the right. Because the price of grapes has risen from $1 to $2, each bundle is now more expensive than before. As a result, more combinations are outside the budget constraint and fewer are within the budget constraint. In general, a higher price for a good reduces consumption opportunities for the individual.

2.2 Maximizing Utility Subject to the Budget Constraint

Utility maximization

An assumption that people try to achieve the highest level of utility given their budget constraint.

Given the utility in Figure 5.2 and the budget constraint in Figure 5.4, we now can show what happens when the individual maximizes utility subject to the budget constraint. **Utility maximization** means that people choose the highest possible level of utility given their budget constraint. Figure 5.5 shows the utility combinations from Figure 5.2, but now we shade in the combinations for which expenditures are greater than the $8 budget constraint from Figure 5.4. The budget constraint means that your choices are limited to those combinations that are outside the shaded area; these are the combinations that do not violate the budget constraint.

FIGURE 5.4 The Budget Constraint and Expenditures at Two Different Prices

The numbers inside the box give the total dollar expenditures on different combinations of grapes and bananas. For example, in the left panel where the price of both bananas and grapes is $1 per pound, the total dollar expenditure would be $7 for 4 pounds of grapes and 3 pounds of bananas. If the price of grapes was $2 per pound and the price of bananas was $1 per pound, as in the right panel, that same combination would cost $11. The numbers in the shaded area are greater than the $8 budget constraint.

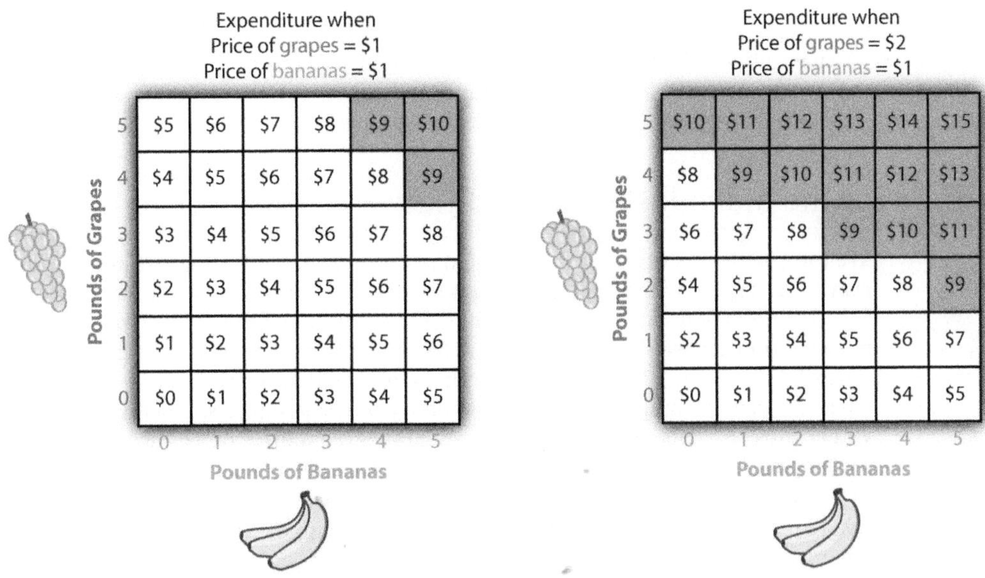

Expenditure when
Price of grapes = $1
Price of bananas = $1

Pounds of Grapes \ Pounds of Bananas	0	1	2	3	4	5
5	$5	$6	$7	$8	$9	$10
4	$4	$5	$6	$7	$8	$9
3	$3	$4	$5	$6	$7	$8
2	$2	$3	$4	$5	$6	$7
1	$1	$2	$3	$4	$5	$6
0	$0	$1	$2	$3	$4	$5

Expenditure when
Price of grapes = $2
Price of bananas = $1

Pounds of Grapes \ Pounds of Bananas	0	1	2	3	4	5
5	$10	$11	$12	$13	$14	$15
4	$8	$9	$10	$11	$12	$13
3	$6	$7	$8	$9	$10	$11
2	$4	$5	$6	$7	$8	$9
1	$2	$3	$4	$5	$6	$7
0	$0	$1	$2	$3	$4	$5

FIGURE 5.5 Maximizing Utility Subject to the Budget Constraint at Two Different Prices

The shaded areas represent combinations for which total expenditures would be greater than the $8 budget constraint. The blue number is the maximum level of utility for which spending is less than or equal to $8. In the left panel, the maximum utility of 39 represents a choice of 4 pounds of grapes and 4 pounds of bananas. In the right panel, with the higher price of grapes, the maximum utility is 34, corresponding to 2 pounds of grapes and 4 pounds of bananas.

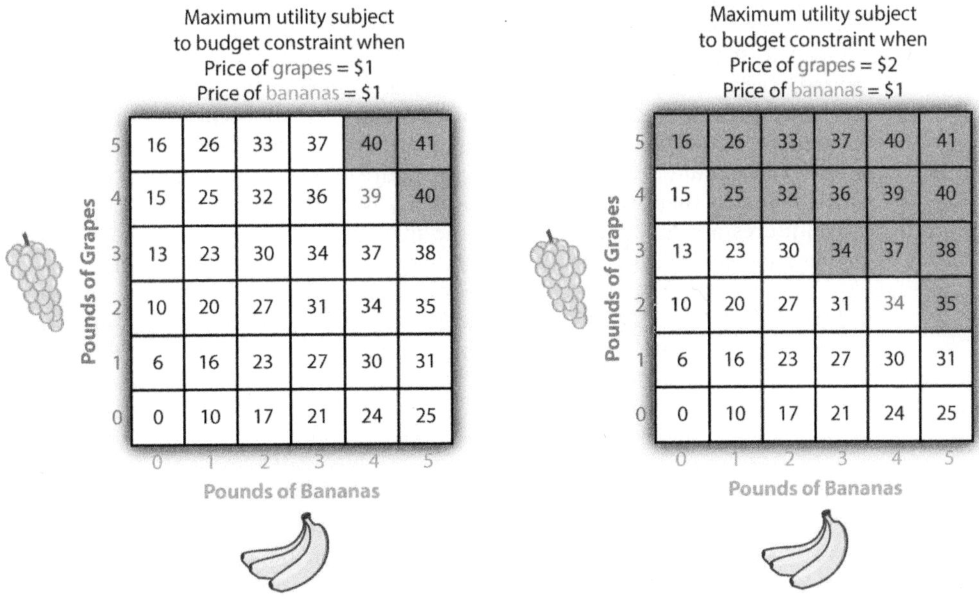

Maximum utility subject
to budget constraint when
Price of grapes = $1
Price of bananas = $1

Pounds of Grapes \ Pounds of Bananas	0	1	2	3	4	5
5	16	26	33	37	40	41
4	15	25	32	36	39	40
3	13	23	30	34	37	38
2	10	20	27	31	34	35
1	6	16	23	27	30	31
0	0	10	17	21	24	25

Maximum utility subject
to budget constraint when
Price of grapes = $2
Price of bananas = $1

Pounds of Grapes \ Pounds of Bananas	0	1	2	3	4	5
5	16	26	33	37	40	41
4	15	25	32	36	39	40
3	13	23	30	34	37	38
2	10	20	27	31	34	35
1	6	16	23	27	30	31
0	0	10	17	21	24	25

Suppose first that the price of grapes is $1 per pound and the price of bananas is $1 per pound. By looking at the left panel you can find the choice that generates the highest level of utility achievable by the consumer with an $8 budget constraint. That combination is 4 pounds of grapes and 4 pounds of bananas (with a utility level of 39). The utility-maximizing choice, and the resulting level of utility, is shown in blue boldface type. This is the most preferred combination that the individual can buy. Even though utility is higher for some combinations that lie in the shaded areas, those represent combinations for which total expenditures would be greater than the $8 budget constraint, and hence they are not possible choices.

The right panel does a similar exercise; however, as in the right panel of Figure 5.4, it assumes that the price of grapes is now higher at $2, which increases the number of unaffordable combinations. When a price changes, individuals typically will end up choosing a different utility-maximizing combination. But the reason for their switch is not because the level of utility for each combination changed; in fact, you can clearly see that the utility levels of the different combinations did not change when the price changed. Instead, what changed were the combinations that the consumer could or could not afford. For example, at the new higher price of grapes, the previous utility-maximizing choice of 4 pounds of bananas and 4 pounds of grapes is not affordable; it is in a shaded box. Now the utility-maximizing choice is 4 pounds of bananas and 2 pounds of grapes, corresponding to a utility level of 34.

2.3 Deriving the Individual's Demand Curve

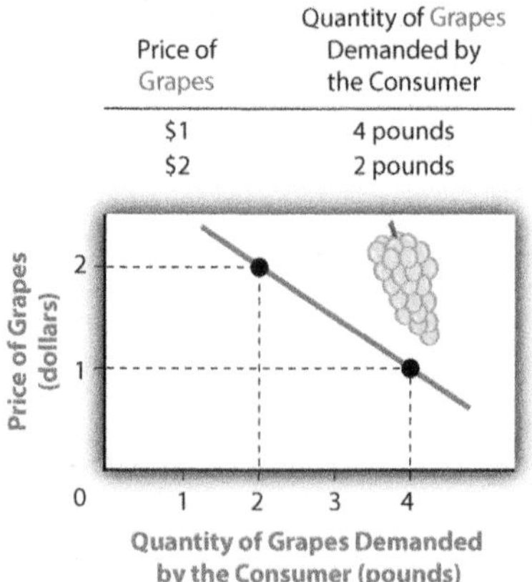

We can use the results from the utility maximization to derive the individual's demand curve for grapes. When the price of grapes was $1 (and the price of bananas was also $1), the individual would choose to consume 4 pounds of grapes (and 4 pounds of bananas). Another way of saying this is that at a price of $1 per pound of grapes, the quantity demanded of grapes by this individual would be 4 pounds. But what happened when the price of grapes rose to $2 (with the price of bananas still being $1)? The individual chose to consume only 2 pounds of grapes. At a price of $2, therefore the quantity demanded will now be 2.

These two points are plotted on the figure following. Notice that what we have derived are two points on a demand curve for the consumer. When the price goes up, the quantity demanded goes down; when the price goes down, the quantity demanded goes up. Thus, we have shown that the assumption that people maximize utility subject to a budget constraint implies that a higher price leads to a reduced quantity demanded. In other words, we have derived two points that lie along a downward-sloping demand curve. Furthermore, we have shown that changes in price lead to a *movement along* a demand curve.

Effect of a Change in Income: A Shift in the Demand Curve

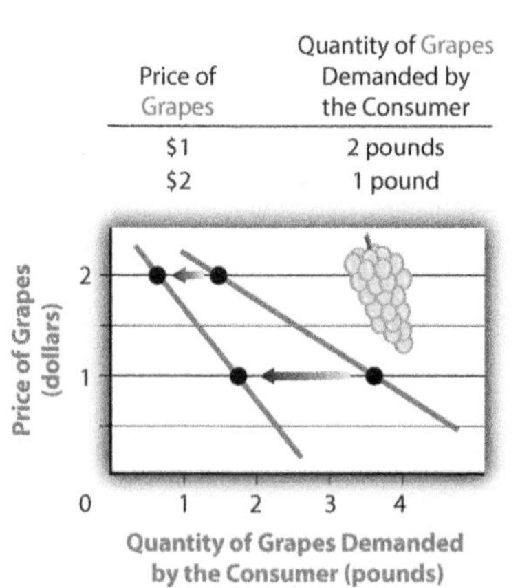

Now consider the effect of a change in the individual's income on the quantity of grapes that the individual will purchase. Suppose that the individual has only $5 to spend rather than $8; in other words, the individual's income is reduced $3. What will happen to the quantity of grapes demanded by the consumer? At a price of $1 per pound of grapes and $1 per pound of bananas (which means that the boxes on the left of Figure 5.4 and Figure 5.5 apply), the number of unaffordable combinations has increased, or, equivalently, the number of affordable combinations has shrunk. As an exercise, you should see whether you can figure out which combinations need to be shaded because they are no longer affordable, given that expenditure is limited to $5. If expenditures are limited to $5, then the maximum utility occurs when 2 pounds of grapes and 3 pounds of bananas are purchased, resulting in a utility level of 31.

We also can calculate the effects of a similar income change at a different set of prices. If the price is $2 for grapes and $1 for bananas, then the boxes on the right of Figure 5.4 and Figure 5.5 apply. (Again, you might want to shade the additional combinations of grapes and bananas that are not feasible with only $5 to spend.) With a limit of $5 to spend, the maximum utility occurs when 1 pound of grapes and 3 pounds of bananas are purchased, resulting in a utility level of 27.

With $8 to spend, the quantity of grapes demanded was 2 (at a price of $2) and 4 (at a price of $1). Now, with only $5 to spend, the quantity of grapes demanded is 1 (when the price is $2) and 2 (when the price is $1). Thus, as shown in the margin, we have derived another demand curve corresponding to the decreased amount of income. Observe that the demand curve with the lower amount of income ($5) is shifted to the left compared with the demand curve with the higher amount of income ($8). Thus, we have shown explicitly that a change in income will *shift* the consumer's demand curve.

Income and Substitution Effects of a Price Change

Using the concepts of utility and the budget constraint, economists distinguish between two separate reasons why an increase in the price leads to a decrease in the quantity demanded. When the price of grapes rises from $1 to $2 per pound, the price increase affects the quantity demanded of grapes in two ways.

First, certain combinations are no longer within the budget constraint at a grape price of $2 per pound, even though they were within the budget constraint at a grape price of $1 per pound. For instance, a total of 15 options are outside the budget constraint at a grape price of $2 per pound (in the shaded area of the right tables of Figure 5.4 and Figure 5.5), whereas only 3 are outside the budget constraint at a grape price of $1 per pound (in the shaded area of the left tables of Figure 5.4 and Figure 5.5). In other words, the purchasing power of the consumer's income is curtailed even though her income was unchanged.

Second, you can now buy 2 pounds of bananas for the same price as a pound of grapes (whereas before you could buy only 1 pound of bananas for the price of a pound of grapes). Because the relative price of grapes has risen, consumers will be more likely to buy bananas than grapes. These are the two ways in which an increase in price affects quantity demanded. The first is known as the income effect, and the second is known as the substitution effect.

The Income Effect of a Change in the Price

The **income effect** is the amount by which quantity demanded falls because of the decline in real income from the price increase. When we say that "real income" has decreased, what we mean is that income measured in terms of what goods we can buy with it has decreased. Another way to think about this is that the rise in the price of grapes reduces the number of affordable combinations; for example, the combinations of grapes and bananas that the consumer can buy have decreased *even though her actual income has not decreased.* The income effect is a general phenomenon that applies to many goods; for example, when the price of gasoline rises, people will spend less on gasoline in part because their real income has declined. With less real income, they also will spend less on most goods and services.

income effect

The amount by which the quantity demanded falls because of the decline in real income from a price increase.

The Substitution Effect of a Change in the Price

An increase in the price of grapes with no change in the price of other goods causes an increase in the relative price of grapes. Because grapes become relatively more expensive, people will switch their purchases away from grapes toward bananas, and would do so even if you were to give them additional income to make up for the income effect. A more technical way to think about this is that at the higher price of $2 per pound of grapes, the opportunity cost of consuming a pound of grapes is 2 pounds of bananas (at $1 per pound), whereas at a price of $1 per pound of grapes, the opportunity cost of consuming a pound of grapes is 1 pound of bananas. Because 2 more pounds of bananas will yield more marginal utility than 1 more pound of bananas, consumers will be more likely to consume less grapes and more bananas *even if you give them additional income to make up for the income effect.* The **substitution effect** is the amount by which the quantity demanded falls when the price rises, exclusive of the income effect.

substitution effect

The amount by which quantity demanded falls when the price rises, exclusive of the income effect.

REVIEW

- Individuals choose the combination of goods that maximizes utility, but the set of options from which to make that choice is constrained by scarce resources.
- The demand curve for an individual can be derived from the assumption that people maximize utility subject to a budget constraint. Given a certain set of prices for goods and a certain level of income, an individual will choose the combination that gives her the most utility from among the affordable combinations.
- A change in the price of a good changes the number of affordable combinations and thus changes the utility-maximizing quantity demanded. We showed that when the price of grapes rises, the utility-maximizing choice changes to a combination that contains fewer grapes. In other words, a higher price of grapes leads to a lower quantity demanded for grapes, indicating a downward-sloping demand curve.
- A change in income also changes the number of affordable combinations, and thus changes the utility-maximizing quantity demanded. We showed that a reduction in income would reduce the quantity demanded of grapes for any given price of grapes. This reduction represents a shift in of the demand curve. An increase in income would, on the other hand, lead to a shift out of the demand curve.
- The total effect of a change in the price on the quantity demanded can be divided into two parts—an income effect and a substitution effect. The income effect captures the change in demand that is brought about by the change in real income. The substitution effect captures the change in demand that is brought about by the change in relative prices, exclusive of the income effect.

3. WILLINGNESS TO PAY AND THE DEMAND CURVE

The choice between one good (grapes) and another good (bananas) in the previous section is useful for showing how to derive a demand curve from the basic idea that consumers maximize utility subject to a budget constraint. In this section, we extend the analysis to move beyond the simple choice between two goods and consider the choice between one good and all possible other goods.

3.1 Measuring Willingness to Pay and Marginal Benefit

Suppose we asked a person who is consuming a zero amount of good *X*, "How much money would you be willing to pay for one unit of *X*?" Because the money that the person would pay can be used to buy all goods, not just one good, the question implicitly asks the person to compare *X* with all other goods. In general, the answer to this question will depend on how much the person's utility would increase with one unit of *X* and how much the person's utility would decrease because less would be spent on other goods, given the budget constraint. In other words, the answer would depend on the person's preferences for *X* and all other goods, as represented by utility.

Suppose that the person gives us a truthful answer of $5. Now, we could ask, "How much would you be willing to pay for two units of *X*?" Suppose the answer is, "I would be willing to pay $8." We could then continue to ask the consumer about more and more units of *X*. We summarize the hypothetical answers in Figure 5.6. The column labeled "Willingness to Pay for *X*" tabulates the answers to the question.

marginal benefit

The increase in the benefit from, or the willingness to pay for, one more unit of a good.

Assuming that the answers to the questions are true, willingness to pay measures how much the consumer would *benefit* from different amounts of *X*. The **marginal benefit** from *X* is the increase in benefit from one more unit of a good, or the additional willingness to pay. Observe that the marginal benefit in Figure 5.6 diminishes as more is consumed. This implies that as a person consumes more and more of a good, the marginal benefit from additional amounts is likely to diminish.

You intuitively can understand this better if you suppose that *X* is pizza. Imagine that you are hungry and have no food at home, and you have a craving for pizza. At this point, you might be willing to pay $5 for a big, hot slice of pizza. Now suppose that after you have eaten that slice of pizza, you're still a little hungry. You might be willing to pay $3 for an additional slice. Now your willingness to pay for a third slice of pizza is going to be even less because you are no longer as hungry and your craving has, for the most part, been satisfied. So the more slices of pizza you eat, the less you are willing to pay for another slice of pizza.

3.2 Graphical Derivation of the Individual Demand Curve

A demand curve can be derived from the information about willingness to pay (benefit) and marginal benefit of *X* for the person described in Figure 5.6. Suppose that *X* is chocolate-covered raisins (pizza, ice cream, orange juice, DVDs, movie tickets, or any other good will serve just as well as an example). Suppose that the person has $10 to spend on chocolate-covered raisins and other goods. We want to ask how many pounds of chocolate-covered raisins the person would buy at different prices. We imagine different hypothetical prices for chocolate-covered raisins, from astronomical levels like $7 a pound to bargain basement levels like $0.50 a pound.

To proceed graphically, we first plot the marginal benefit from Figure 5.6 in Figure 5.7. Focus first on the black dots in Figure 5.7; the associated lines will be explained in the next few paragraphs. The horizontal axis in Figure 5.7 measures the quantity of chocolate-covered raisins. On the vertical axis, we want to indicate the price as well as the marginal benefit, so we measure the scale of the vertical axis in dollars. The black dots in Figure 5.7 represent the marginal benefit that an individual gets from consuming different amounts of chocolate-covered raisins.

How many pounds of chocolate-covered raisins would this person consume at different prices? First, suppose that the price is very high—$7 a pound. We are going to derive a demand curve for this individual by gradually lowering the price from this high value and asking the same question: How many pounds would the person buy at this price? To make things simple at the start, assume that the person buys only whole pounds of chocolate-covered raisins. You might want to imagine that the chocolate-covered raisins come in 1-pound cellophane packages. We consider fractions of pounds later.

FIGURE 5.6 Willingness to Pay (Benefit) and Marginal Benefit

Quantity of *X*	Willingness to Pay for *X* (Benefit from *X*)	Marginal Benefit from *X*
0	$ 0.00	
1	$ 5.00	$5.00
2	$ 8.00	$3.00
3	$ 9.50	$1.50
4	$10.50	$1.00
5	$11.00	$0.50

The connecting lines emphasize how marginal benefit is the change in benefit (or willingness to pay) as one more unit of a good is consumed.

FIGURE 5.7 Derivation of the Individual Demand Curve

The dots are exactly the same as the marginal benefit in Figure 5.6. At each dot, price equals marginal benefit. The vertical lines indicate how much is demanded at each price if the consumer is restricted to purchasing whole pounds.

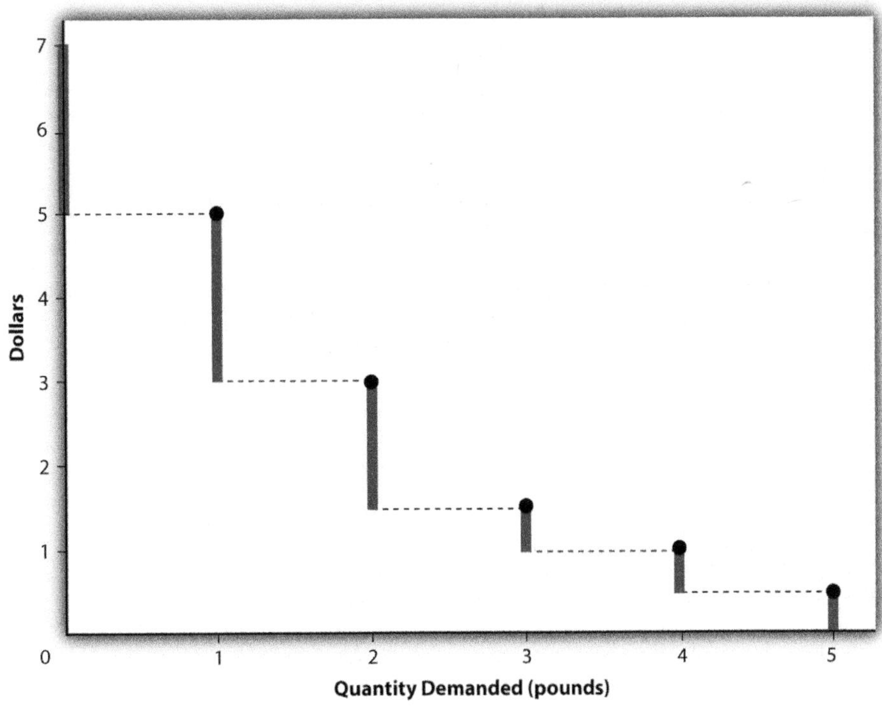

Suppose, then, that the price is $7 a pound. The marginal benefit from 1 pound of chocolate-covered raisins is $5. Thus, the price is greater than the marginal benefit. Would the person buy a pound of chocolate-covered raisins at this price? Because the price the person would have to pay is greater than the marginal benefit, *the answer would be no;* the person would not buy a pound of raisins at a price of $7. We have shown, therefore, that the quantity demanded of raisins is *zero* when the price is $7.

Now start to lower the price. As long as the price is more than $5, the person will not buy any chocolate-covered raisins because the most he is willing to pay for that first pound of chocolate-covered raisins is $5. Hence, the quantity demanded at all prices higher than $5 is 0 pounds. We indicate this by the line on the vertical axis above the $5 mark.

When the price drops to $5, the marginal benefit from a pound of chocolate-covered raisins is $5 and the price is $5, so the marginal benefit of the pound of chocolate-covered raisins is sufficient to cover the price. Because the person is willing to pay the $5 to buy 1 pound of chocolate-covered raisins, the person buys 1 pound rather than 0 pounds when the price is $5. Figure 5.7 shows that the quantity demanded is given by the black dot at 1 pound when the price equals $5.

Continue lowering the price from $5. Consider, for example, a price of $4. The person has already decided that 1 pound will be bought; the question is whether a second pound of chocolate-covered raisins is worthwhile. Another pound has a marginal benefit of $3 (willingness to pay goes from $5 to $8 as the quantity increases from 1 to 2 pounds). The person has to pay $4, which is more than the marginal benefit. Hence, *the quantity demanded stays at 1 pound when the price is $4.* In fact, the quantity demanded will stay at 1 pound as long as the price remains above the marginal benefit of buying another pound of chocolate-covered raisins, which is $3. When the price falls to $3, however, another pound is purchased. That is, when the price is $3, the quantity demanded is 2 pounds, which is shown graphically by the black dot at 2 pounds.

FIGURE 5.8 **A Smooth Individual Demand Curve**

If the consumer can buy fractions of a pound and if the marginal benefits of these fractions are between the whole pound amounts, the demand curve becomes a smooth line, as in the figure, rather than the series of steps in Figure 5.7. In some cases, such as the demand for cars, we cannot consider fractions, and so these individual demand curves will look like steps.

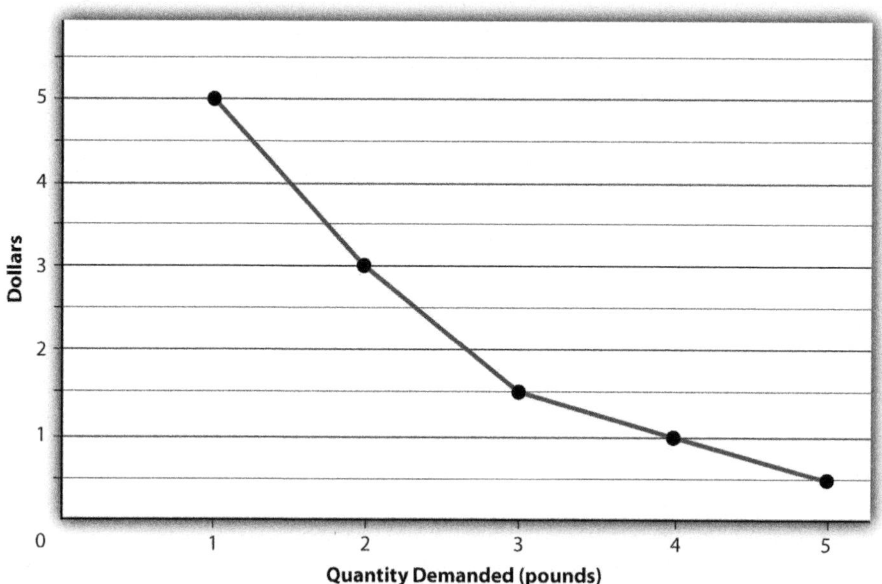

Now suppose the price falls below $3, perhaps to $2. Is a third pound purchased? The marginal benefit of a third pound is $1.50; is it worth it to buy a third pound at $2 per pound? No. The quantity demanded stays at 2 pounds when the price is between $3 and $1.50, which we denote by extending the line downward from the black dot at 2 pounds. This story can be continued. As the price continues to fall, more pounds of chocolate-covered raisins are demanded.

individual demand curve

A curve showing the relationship between quantity demanded of a good by an individual and the price of the good.

By considering various prices from more than $5 to less than $0.50, we have traced out an **individual demand curve** that slopes downward. As the price is lowered, more chocolate-covered raisins are purchased. The demand curve is downward sloping because of diminishing marginal benefit. At each black dot in the diagram, price equals the marginal benefit.

The jagged shape of the demand curve in Figure 5.7 may look strange. It is due to the assumption that the consumer can consider only 1-pound packages of chocolate-covered raisins. If it is possible to buy fractions of a pound, and if the marginal benefits of the fractions are between the values for the whole pounds, then the demand curve will be a smooth line, as shown in Figure 5.8. The price then will equal marginal benefit not only at the black dots but also on the lines connecting the dots. If you are unsure of this, imagine creating a new Figure 5.6 and Figure 5.7 with *ounces* of raisins. Each ounce will be represented with a point, and with 16 ounces per pound, there will be so many points that the curve will be as smooth as Figure 5.8.

3.3 The Price Equals Marginal Benefit Rule

We have discovered an important principle of consumer behavior. If the consumer can adjust consumption of a good in small increments—such as fractions of a pound—then the consumer will buy an amount for which the *price equals marginal benefit.* The price equals marginal benefit rule can explain a number of otherwise puzzling observations. For example, consider Adam Smith's diamond-water paradox. As Smith put it,

> "Nothing is more useful than water: but it will purchase scarce any thing; scarce any thing can be had in exchange for it. A diamond, on the contrary, has scarce any value in use; but a very great quantity of other goods may frequently be had in exchange for it."[1]

Why then are diamonds expensive and water cheap even though diamonds are less "useful" to the world's population than water?

The price equals marginal benefit rule helps explain the paradox. The price of diamonds will be high if the marginal benefit of diamonds is high. The price of water will be low if the marginal benefit of water is low. As we saw earlier, the marginal benefit of something declines the more people consume of it. Thus, water has relatively low marginal benefit because with water being so plentiful, people consume a lot of it every day. The marginal benefit is low even though the total benefit from water consumption in the world is very high. On the other hand, diamonds have a high marginal benefit because, with diamonds being so scarce, people consume relatively little of them. The marginal benefit of diamonds is high even though the total benefit of diamonds may be low. Thus, the price equals marginal benefit rule explains the diamond-water paradox.

REVIEW

- People's preferences are reflected in their willingness to pay for different amounts of a good. Because dollars can be used to buy any good, willingness to pay compares one good with all other goods.
- The marginal benefit from a good is the increase in the benefit from, or the additional willingness to pay for, one more unit of a good.
- The marginal benefit that an individual derives from a good typically will decline as the individual increases consumption of that good.
- An individual demand curve can be traced by changing the price of a good and looking at how many units consumers are willing to buy at each price.
- When the price of a good exceeds the marginal benefit of the first unit of a good, consumers will not demand any of that good. As the price falls, consumers will demand more and more units of the good as the price of each additional unit becomes equal to the marginal benefit of that unit.
- Hence, the diminishing marginal benefits from consuming more of a good results in an individual demand curve that slopes down.
- If the good is divisible into fractional quantities, the demand curve will become a smooth line instead of a series of discrete steps.

4. THE MARKET DEMAND CURVE

Thus far, we have graphically derived the demand curve for an individual. Now we consider the **market demand curve**, which is the sum of the individual demand curves. Figure 5.9 shows how we do the summing up. The figure shows the demand curves for chocolate-covered raisins for two individuals, Jim and Pam. To get the market demand curve, add up, for each given price, the total amount demanded by both Jim and Pam. For example, at a price of $5, Jim's demand is 1 pound and Pam's demand is 1 pound. The market demand is then 2 pounds. When the price is $3 a pound, the demand is 2 pounds for Jim and 2 pounds for Pam, or 4 pounds for the market as a whole. Obviously, the market for chocolate-covered raisins consists of more than just Jim and Pam. To get the whole market, you would have to sum up the demands for millions of people.

market demand curve

The horizontal summation of all the individual demand curves for a good; also simply called the demand curve.

FIGURE 5.9 Derivation of the Market Demand Curve

The market demand curve is the sum of the demand curves of many individuals. The figure shows this for only two individuals with the same preferences. As more individuals with a diversity of tastes are added, the market demand curve becomes smoother and looks more like Figure 5.1.

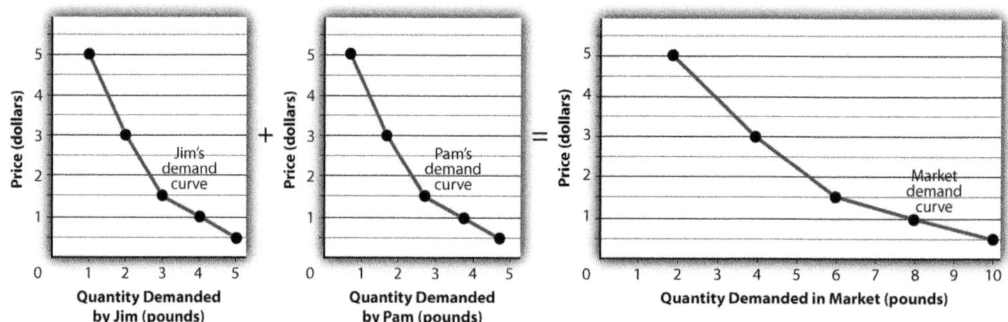

4.1 Different Types of Individuals

In Figure 5.9, Jim's and Pam's demand curves are the same. They do not have to be. In fact, it is most likely that Jim and Pam have different preferences. Jim could be a health food fan and be willing to pay less for chocolate-covered raisins than Pam would. It is incorrect to assume that everyone will be willing to pay the same amount for any good. All kinds of people in the world have different preferences. But you still can add up the demands of all these people at any given price to get the market demand curve. As you add up many individual demand curves for different types of people, the market demand curve gets smoother, even when the product cannot be bought in fractions of a unit. For example, the market demand curve for cars is smooth even though most individuals buy either zero, one, or perhaps two cars. When you add the demand curves for millions of people, the market demand curve for cars looks like the market demand curve (Figure 5.1) that we typically draw—smooth and downward sloping. To confirm your understanding of the market demand curve, make sure you work through the problems at the end of the chapter.

REVIEW

- The market demand curve is derived from individual demand curves. At each price, we add up how much is demanded by all individuals; the total is the market demand at that price.
- Even if the individual demand curves are not smooth, the market demand curve will be smooth because people have different tastes and preferences and prefer different benefits.

5. CONSUMER SURPLUS

consumer surplus

The difference between what a person is willing to pay for an additional unit of a good—the marginal benefit—and the market price of the good; for the market as a whole, it is the sum of all the individual consumer surpluses, or the area below the market demand curve and above the market price.

In many cases, people are willing to pay more for an item consumed than they have to pay for it. For example, you might be willing to pay $45 to see your favorite movie star appear in a new blockbuster movie. But like everyone else in line at the movie theater, you pay only $15, even though it is worth $45 to you. In general, **consumer surplus** is the difference between the willingness to pay for an additional item (say, $45 to see the movie)—its marginal benefit—and the price paid for it ($15 to buy a ticket that lets you see the movie). Consumer surplus is $30. The college professor who was willing to pay $60,000 for a $500 hearing aid that enabled him to lecture to a large audience of students would derive a consumer surplus of $59,500 from the hearing aid. If the hearing aid cost $5,000 instead, he still would derive $55,000 in consumer surplus.

A graphic derivation of how to find consumer surplus is shown in Figure 5.10, which shows the individual demand curve for chocolate-covered raisins that we derived in Figure 5.7. At a price of $2, the consumer will demand 2 pounds of chocolate-covered raisins. The first pound produced a marginal benefit of $5 and cost $2 to buy, thus the consumer surplus associated with the first pound would be $3. The second pound has a marginal benefit of $3 and cost $2 to buy, so the consumer surplus associated with the second pound would be $1. Overall consumer surplus is $3 + $1 = $4. Consumer surplus therefore can be defined as the sum of the differences between the marginal benefit of each unit and the price paid for the item. Graphically, consumer surplus is the area between the demand curve and the line indicating the price. In Figure 5.10, the total shaded area is equal to 4, consisting of two rectangular blocks, one with an area of 3 and the other with an area of 1. The area is the extra amount that the consumer is getting because the market price is lower than what the consumer is willing to pay.

FIGURE 5.10 Consumer Surplus for an Individual

The consumer surplus is the difference between the marginal benefit that a person gets from consuming a good and the price. It is given by the area between the demand curve and the price.

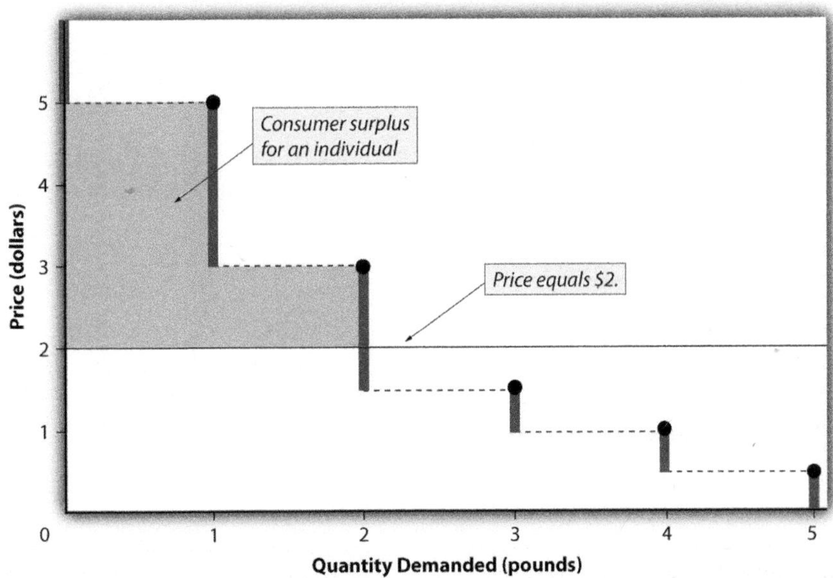

Consumer surplus for the entire market is the sum of the consumer surpluses of all individuals who have purchased goods in the market. In Figure 5.11, consumer surplus is the area between the market demand curve and the market price line.

Consumer surplus has many uses in economics. It is a measure of how well off consumers are (because it measures how much they were willing to pay above and beyond the price to acquire the good), and thus it is an important component used to gauge how well the market system works. Consumer surplus also can be used to measure the gains to consumers from an innovation. For example, if a new production technique or a policy change lowers the price of a good and increases the quantity demanded, consumer surplus for the market will increase. Those who had a high willingness to pay now will derive even more consumer surplus as a result of the lower price, and those who had a marginal benefit that was less than the old price now will demand more of the good as well. In short, when the market price of a good falls, the area between the demand curve and the market price line increases. This increase is a measure of how much the new technique or the policy change is worth to society.

FIGURE 5.11 Consumer Surplus for the Market

The sum of the consumer surplus for all individuals in the market is the area between the demand curve and the price.

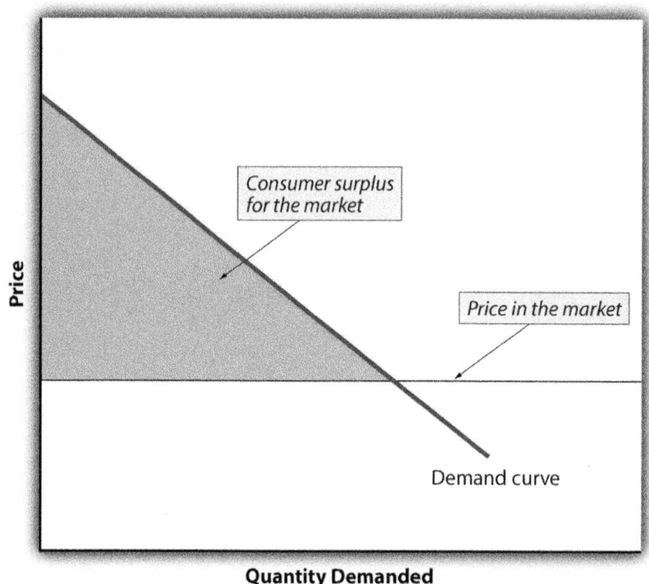

REVIEW

- Consumer surplus is the area between the individual demand curve and the market price line. It is a measure of how much the consumer gains from buying goods in the market.
- The consumer surplus for the market is the sum of the individual consumer surpluses. It can be calculated as the area between the market demand curve and the market price line. It is a measure of how much all the consumers in the economy gain from buying goods in the market.
- Consumer surplus is an important tool for measuring the performance of an economic system. Changes in consumer surplus can be used to measure the beneficial impact of a technology change or a policy change that changes the market price of a good.

6. END-OF-CHAPTER MATERIALS

6.1 Conclusion

This chapter is the first of three that looks at the individual behavior that underlies the economist's demand and supply curves. This chapter focused on consumers, Chapter 6 looks at firms, and Chapter 7 looks at the interaction of consumers and firms in markets. The payoffs in terms of understanding how and how well markets work will not be fully realized until we have completed all three chapters, but we already have derived a number of useful results.

We showed that the idea that people make purposeful choices with limited resources can be made operational with utility. In a two-good setting, we showed that utility maximization can be used to derive an individual demand curve that is downward sloping, and that individual demand curves can be aggregated to obtain a market demand curve.

In a more general setting, we showed how to derive an individual demand curve from the idea that consumers would buy an additional unit of a good only when the marginal benefit was not less than the price of the good. Because marginal benefit declines as you buy more units of a good, a lower price leads to a higher quantity demanded. Aggregating the individual demand curves would generate a market demand curve.

Finally, we derived the concept of consumer surplus for an individual, the difference between the individual's marginal benefit and the market price. Adding up individual consumer surplus generates the consumer surplus for the entire market, an important measure of how much gain people receive from the market.

Key Points

1. The idea of utility maximization subject to a budget constraint implements the assumption that people make purposeful choices with limited resources.
2. Utility indicates the preferences people have for one activity compared with other activities. The units used to measure utility do not matter, and the utility level of one person cannot be compared with the utility level of another person.
3. Economists assume—at least as an approximation—that people maximize their utility subject to a budget constraint that limits how much they can spend. This implies that they choose the feasible combination of goods that delivers the most utility.
4. An individual's demand curve can be derived from utility maximization subject to a budget constraint. Utility maximization implies that a higher price reduces the quantity demanded.
5. A higher price can reduce the quantity demanded in two ways: by reducing the purchasing power of an individual's income (income effect), and by making the relative price of that good more expensive (the substitution effect).
6. In general, the demand curve for an individual can be derived by applying the principle that the individual will demand to buy the number of units for which marginal benefit is equal to price.
7. Market demand curves are derived by adding up the quantity demanded by all individuals at each price.
8. An individual's consumer surplus is the sum of the differences between the marginal benefit the individual receives from each unit and the market price of that unit.
9. An individual's consumer surplus can be calculated as the area between the individual's demand curve and the market price line. Consumer surplus for an individual is a measure of how much benefit an individual gains from buying a product.
10. Overall consumer surplus is the sum of consumer surplus across individuals. It can be calculated as the area between the market demand curve and the market price line. Consumer surplus for a market is a measure of how much all consumers in that market gain from buying a product.

QUESTIONS FOR REVIEW

1. What is the relationship between utility and preferences?
2. Why don't the units by which utility is measured matter?
3. Why are economists typically interested in utility maximization subject to constraints?
4. Why does an increase in the price of a good typically reduce the quantity demanded by a utility maximizing consumer?
5. Why does a reduction in income typically lead to a reduction in the quantity demanded at each price?
6. Why are market demand curves usually smoother than individual demand curves?
7. What is the relationship between willingness to pay and marginal benefit?
8. Why does marginal benefit decrease as the number of units consumed of a good increases?
9. What does an individual's "consumer surplus" measure? How can you find what the individual's consumer surplus is from the demand curve?
10. What is the relationship between individual consumer surplus and consumer surplus for the market? How can you find what the consumer surplus for the market is from the demand curve?

PROBLEMS

1. Using the example of utility in Figure 5.2, find the quantity of each good the consumer will purchase in the cases shown in the table below.

Case	Budget	Price of Grapes	Price of Bananas
A	$7	$1	$1
B	$6	$2	$1
C	$8	$1	$2

2. Analyze the following data for Mara's utility from consumption of books and coffee

Quantity of Books	**4**	50	75	81	83	84
	3	46	70	76	78	79
	2	40	60	66	68	69
	1	30	40	46	48	49
	0	0	10	16	18	19
		0	**1**	**2**	**3**	**4**
	Quantity of Coffee					

a. Determine how much of each good Mara will consume if she has $20 and if the price of books is $10 and the price of coffee is $3.

b. Suppose the price of coffee goes up to $5. How much coffee will Mara consume now? Why does the amount change?

c. Multiply the utility received from books and coffee by 10. Will your answers to parts (a) and (b) change? Explain.

3. Which of the following statements are true? The income effect of a reduction in the price of gasoline refers to

a. the reduction of income incurred by gas stations.

b. the increase in the demand for other products as gasoline buyers experience increased real incomes.

c. the increase in the quantity demanded of gasoline as gasoline buyers experience increased real incomes.

d. the increase in the quantity demanded of gasoline as gasoline buyers experience increased nominal incomes.

4. Which of the following statements are true? The substitution effect of a decrease in the price of beef, with no changes in the prices of other goods, refers to

a. the decrease in the quantity demanded of beef and the increase in the quantity demanded of substitutes such as chicken.

b. the increase in the quantity demanded of beef and the decrease in the quantity demanded of substitutes such as chicken.

c. the increase in the quantity demanded of beef and the increase in the quantity demanded of substitutes such as chicken.

d. the decrease in the quantity demanded of beef and the decrease in the quantity demand for substitutes such as chicken.

5. Consider the example of willingness to pay for *X* (chocolate-covered raisins) in Figure 5.6. Assume that the price is $0.75 and that the person has $10 to spend.

a. Compute what it costs to pay for different amounts of chocolate-covered raisins from 0 to 5 pounds.

b. For each of the above amounts, calculate how much is left over from the $10 the person started out with.

c. Using the information from Figure 5.6 and your answers above, calculate the sum of the benefit plus the dollars left over for different amounts of chocolate-covered raisins from 0 to 5 pounds.

d. How many pounds of raisins will maximize the sum of the benefit plus the dollars left over? How does the answer compare with that using the price equals marginal benefit condition?

6. Individuals receive diminishing marginal benefits from consuming more of a particular good. Do you think this means that individuals receive diminishing marginal benefits from each extra dollar that they earn? Explain your answer.
7. The following table shows Carl's willingness to pay for clothing.

Quantity of Clothing	Willingness to Pay
1	$35
2	$60
3	$80
4	$97
5	$112
6	$126

   a. Calculate Carl's marginal benefit from clothing.
   b. Draw Carl's individual demand curve for clothing.
   c. Suppose the price of one item of clothing is $17. How much would Carl consume, and what is his consumer surplus? Show your answer graphically as well as numerically.
8. Suppose that the willingness to pay for hearing aids by the economics professor mentioned in the introduction to this chapter was $60,000 for one pair, $60,400 for two pairs, $60,600 for three pairs, and $60,700 for four pairs.
   a. Draw the professor's demand curve for hearing aids.
   b. If the price of a pair of hearing aids is $500, how many pairs would the professor buy?
   c. Now suppose that a technological breakthrough reduces the price of hearing aids to $150 a pair. How many pairs would the professor buy now?
9. The following table shows Margaret's and Dennis's willingness to pay for cookies.

Quantity of Cookies	Margaret	Dennis
1	$7	$15
2	$13	$25
3	$18	$34
4	$21	$42
5	$23	$45

   a. Calculate the marginal benefits for both people.
   b. Derive Margaret's and Dennis's individual demand curves for cookies. Derive the market demand curve if only Margaret and Dennis are in the market.
   c. Suppose that the price of cookies is $4.50. How many cookies will Margaret and Dennis buy? Calculate their consumer surplus. Draw a diagram to show the area representing consumer surplus.
   d. Use a diagram to show the consumer surplus for the whole market using the market demand curve.
10. Economics professors like to ask their students about the diamond-water paradox: Why is it that a good that is as essential to human existence as water costs so much less than a good like a diamond that is far less useful? Show that if we use consumer surplus, rather than price, as our measure of how "valuable" a good is to human existence, then no paradox exists—water is valued much more highly than diamonds.

7. APPENDIX: CONSUMER THEORY WITH INDIFFERENCE CURVES

Chapter 5 derives the demand curve from the assumption that consumers maximize utility subject to a budget constraint. Here we give a graphic illustration of that derivation.

Consider a single consumer deciding how much of two items to buy. Let one of the items be X and the other be Y. We first show that the consumer's budget constraint can be represented by a budget line, and then we show that the consumer's preferences can be represented by indifference curves.

7.1 The Budget Line

Suppose that the consumer has $20 to spend on X and Y, and suppose that the price of X is $2 per unit and the price of Y is $4 per unit. How much of X and Y can the consumer buy? If the consumer spends all $20 on Y, then 5 units of Y and no units of X are consumed. If the consumer buys 4 units of Y at $4 per unit, then $16 will be spent on Y and the remaining $4 can be spent buying 2 units of X. These and several other amounts of X and Y that can be bought with $20 are shown in the following table.

Units of Y	Units of X	Expenditures
5	0	(5 × $4) + (0 × $2) = $20
4	2	(4 × $4) + (2 × $2) = $20
3	4	(3 × $4) + (4 × $2) = $20
2	6	(2 × $4) + (6 × $2) = $20
1	8	(1 × $4) + (8 × $2) = $20
0	10	(0 × $4) + (10 × $2) = $20

budget line

A line showing the maximum combinations of two goods that it is possible for a consumer to buy, given a budget constraint and the market prices of the two goods.

These combinations represent the maximum amounts that can be purchased with $20. Note that the amounts are inversely related; as more is spent on X, less must be spent on Y. This inverse relationship is shown graphically in Figure 5.12. We put units of Y on the vertical axis and units of X on the horizontal axis, and then plot the pairs of points from the table. The points are then connected. The points trace a downward-sloping line starting at the upper left at $X = 0$ and $Y = 5$ and ending on the right with $X = 10$ and $Y = 0$. All the other combinations of X and Y in the table, such as $X = 4$ and $Y = 3$, are shown on the line. If it is possible to consume fractions of X and Y, then all the points on the line between the plotted points also can be purchased with the $20. (For example, 2.5 units of Y and 5 units of X would cost $20: 2.5 × $4 + 5 × $2 = $20.) Because all these pairs of X and Y on this line can be purchased with a $20 budget, we call it the **budget line**. The consumer is constrained to buy combinations of X and Y that are either on or below the budget line. Amounts of X and Y consumed below the budget line cost less than $20. Points above the line require more than $20 and are not feasible.

FIGURE 5.12 Budget Line for a Consumer

The line shows how much a consumer with $20 can consume of quantity X at a price of $2 per unit and quantity Y at $4 per unit. If $20 is spent on Y and nothing on X, then 5 units of Y can be purchased, as shown on the vertical axis. If $20 is spent on X and nothing on Y, then 10 units of X can be purchased. Other combinations are shown on the line.

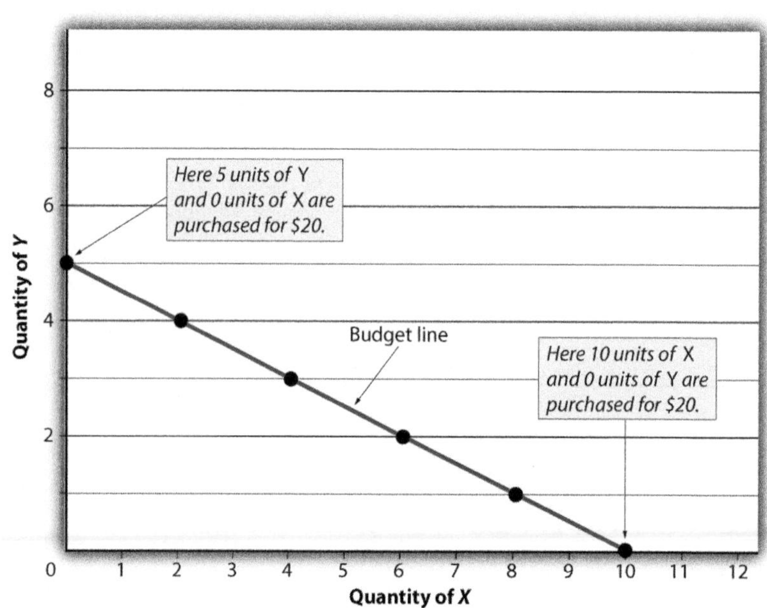

The budget line will shift out if the consumer has more to spend, as shown in Figure 5.13. For example, if the consumer has $24 rather than $20, then the budget line will shift up by 1 unit because the extra $4

permits the consumer to buy 1 more unit of *Y*. Alternatively, we could say that the budget line shifts to the right by 2 units in this case because the consumer can buy 2 more units of *X* with $4 more.

The steepness of the budget line depends on the prices of *X* and *Y*. In particular, the slope of the budget line is equal to −1 times the ratio of the price of *X* to the price of *Y*. That is, slope =−(*PX*/*PY*), which is −1/2 in this example. Why is the slope determined by the price ratio? Recall that the slope is the change in *Y* divided by the change in *X*. Along the budget line, as *X* is increased by 1 unit, *Y* must fall by 1/2 unit: Buying 1 more unit of *X* costs $2 and requires buying 1/2 unit less of *Y*. Thus, the slope is −1/2.

FIGURE 5.13 Effect of a Change in Income on the Budget Line

If the consumer has more to spend, then the budget line is farther out. If the consumer has less to spend, then the budget line is closer in. Here a higher and a lower budget line are compared with the $20 budget line in Figure 5.12.

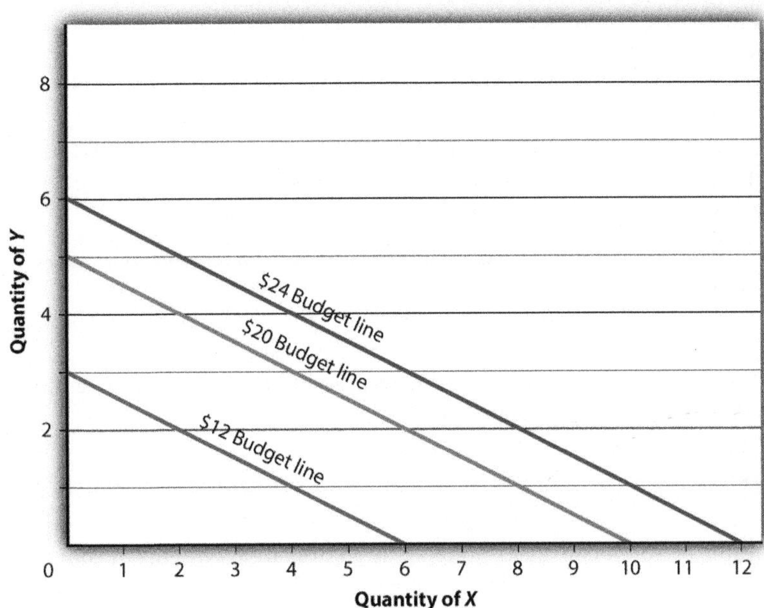

To derive the demand curve for *X*, we need to find out what happens when the price of *X* changes. What happens to the budget line when the price of *X* increases from $2 to $4, for example? The budget line twists down, as shown in Figure 5.14. The intuitive rationale for the twist is that the slope steepens to "(PX/PY) = "$4/$4 = "1, and the position of *X* = 0 and *Y* = 5 on the vertical axis does not change, because 5 units of *Y* can still be purchased. You can show this by creating a new table with pairs of *X* and *Y* that can be purchased with $20 at the new price and then plotting the points.

FIGURE 5.14 Effect of a Higher Price of *X* on the Budget Line

The budget line pivots if the price of *X* changes. Here the price of *X* rises from $2 to $4 and the budget line twists down.

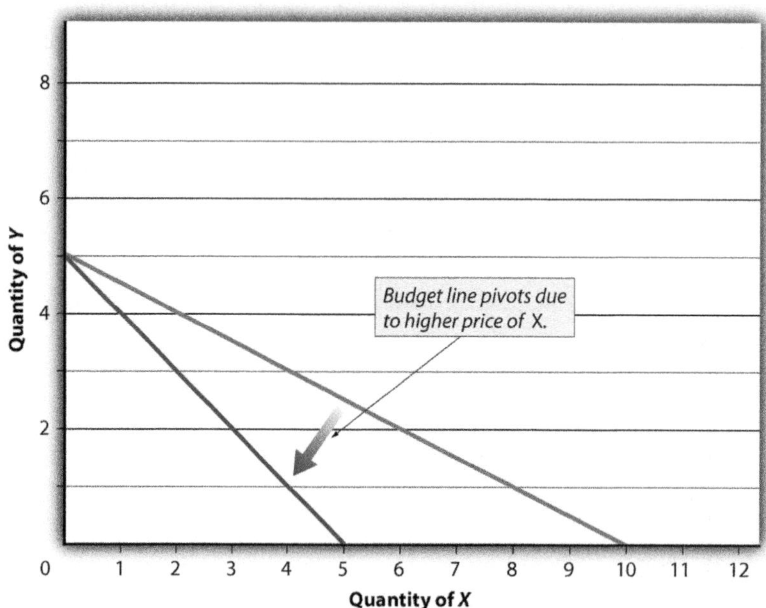

To summarize, we have shown how a budget line represents the budget constraint for the consumer; now we show how to represent the consumer's preferences.

7.2 The Indifference Curve

Utility is an indicator of how a consumer prefers one combination of items in comparison with another. If the level of utility is the same for two combinations of X and Y, then the consumer is *indifferent* between the two combinations. Suppose that the utility is the same for the combinations of X and Y that appear below.

Units of *Y*	Units of *X*
6	1
4	2
2	6
1	12

The consumer is indifferent among these combinations. Observe that these amounts are inversely related. As consumption of *Y* declines, the consumer must be compensated with more *X* if the level of utility is not to decline.

indifference curve

A curve showing the combinations of two goods that leave the consumer with the same level of utility.

We can plot these different amounts on the same type of graph we used for the budget line, as shown in Figure 5.15. The consumer is indifferent among all four points. We have connected the points with a curve to represent other combinations of *X* and *Y* about which the consumer is indifferent. The curve is called an **indifference curve** because the consumer is indifferent among all points on the curve. The indifference curve slopes downward from left to right.

FIGURE 5.15 An Indifference Curve for a Consumer

The consumer is indifferent between *A* and *B* or any other point on an indifference curve. For example, the consumer is indifferent between consuming 4 units of *Y* and 2 of *X* or 2 units of *Y* and 6 of *X*.

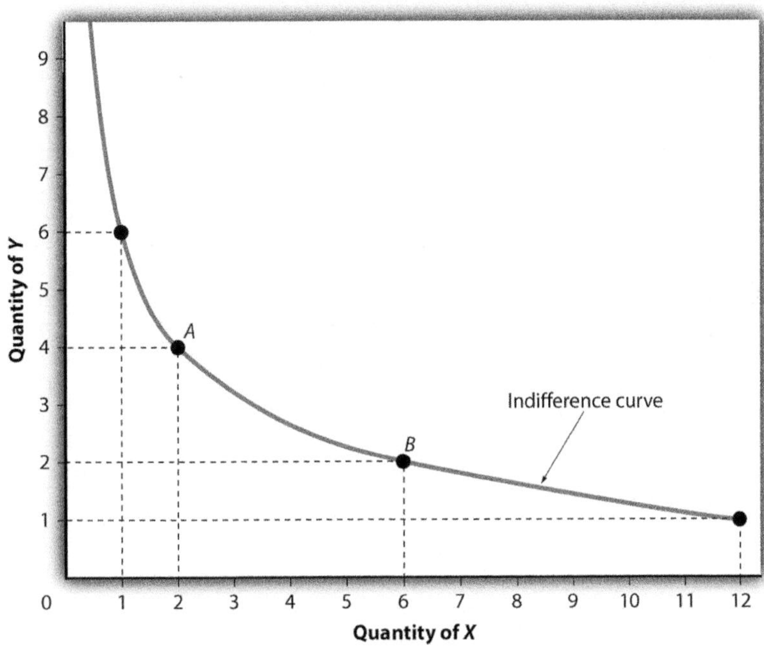

FIGURE 5.16 Higher and Lower Indifference Curves

Amounts of *X* and *Y* on indifference curves that are higher are preferred to amounts on indifference curves that are lower. Of the three combinations *C*, *D*, and *E*, the combination at *D* is the least preferred and the combination at *C* is the most preferred.

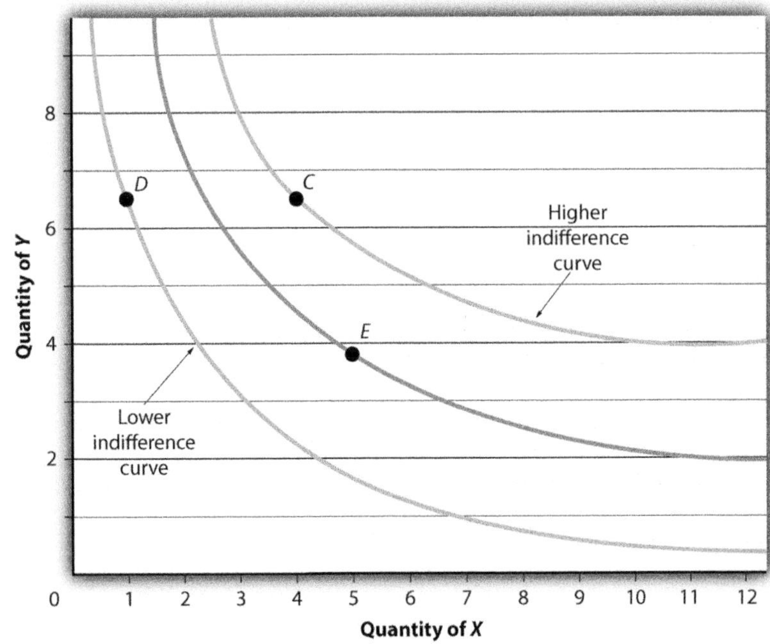

The slope of the indifference curve can be found from the marginal utilities of *X* and *Y*. Marginal utility is *the increase in utility from consuming an additional unit of a good.* For example, look back at Figure 5.2 and consider the marginal utility of increasing consumption of grapes by 1 additional pound, from 3 pounds to 4 pounds. You will see that utility increases by 2. Thus, the marginal utility of grapes is 2 at the amount of consumption. Let MU_X be the marginal utility of *X*, and let MU_Y be the marginal utility of *Y*.

The slope of the indifference curve is equal to "1 times the ratio of the marginal utility of X to the marginal utility of *Y*; that is, slope = ($-MU_X/MU_Y$). The reason is that utility is the same for all points on an indifference curve. In other words, the decline in utility as *X* falls ($-MU_X \times \Delta X$) must equal the increase in utility as *Y* rises ($MU_Y \times \Delta Y$). Thus,

$$MU_X \times \Delta X = MU_Y \times \Delta Y,$$

or,

$$-\frac{MU_X}{MU_Y} = \frac{\Delta Y}{\Delta X},$$

which is the slope of the indifference curve.

marginal rate of substitution

The amount of one good for which the consumer is willing to trade one unit of another good and still have the same utility.

The ratio of marginal utilities MU_X/MU_Y is called the **marginal rate of substitution**; it gives the number of units of one good (*Y*) for which the consumer is willing to trade 1 unit of the other good (*X*) and have the same amount of utility—or be indifferent. For example, if the marginal rate of substitution is 4, then the consumer is willing to trade 4 units of *Y* for 1 unit of *X* with utility remaining the same.

Note that the indifference curve is bowed in toward the origin. That is, the indifference curve is steep when a small amount of *X* is consumed and flat when a large amount of *X* is consumed. This curvature is due to the declining marginal rate of substitution. When the consumer is consuming only a little bit of *X*, a large amount of *Y* is required as compensation for a reduction in *X*. As *X* increases, less of *Y* is required as compensation.

We can represent higher levels of utility or more preferred combinations of *X* and *Y* by higher indifference curves, as shown in Figure 5.16. Any point on a higher indifference curve is preferred to any point on a lower indifference curve.

Getting to the Highest Indifference Curve Given the Budget Line

tangency point

The only point in common for two curves; the point at which the two curves just touch.

Now we can combine the budget line and the indifference curves on the same diagram to illustrate the model of consumer behavior. Utility maximization subject to the budget constraint means getting to the highest possible indifference curve without going above the budget line. The process is shown in Figure 5.17. The budget line from Figure 5.12 and the indifference curves from Figure 5.16 are shown in the diagram. The consumer cannot go beyond the budget line, and any point inside the budget line is inferior to points on the budget line. Thus, the combination of *X* and *Y* with the highest utility must be on the budget line. The highest indifference curve with points on the budget line is the one that just touches—is tangent to—the budget line. This occurs at point *T* in Figure 5.17. The **tangency point** is the highest level of utility the consumer can achieve subject to the budget constraint. It is the combination of *X* and *Y* that the consumer chooses. Figure 5.17 shows that, in this example, the consumer buys 2 1/4 units of *Y* and 5 1/2 units of *X*.

FIGURE 5.17 The Best Choice for the Consumer

When the budget line is tangent to the indifference curve, the consumer cannot do any better. The point of tangency is at point *T*. Compare this with the other points. Point *U* is not the best point because it is inside the budget line. Point *V* is not the best point because other points on the budget line are preferred. Point *W* is preferred to point *T*, but it is not feasible.

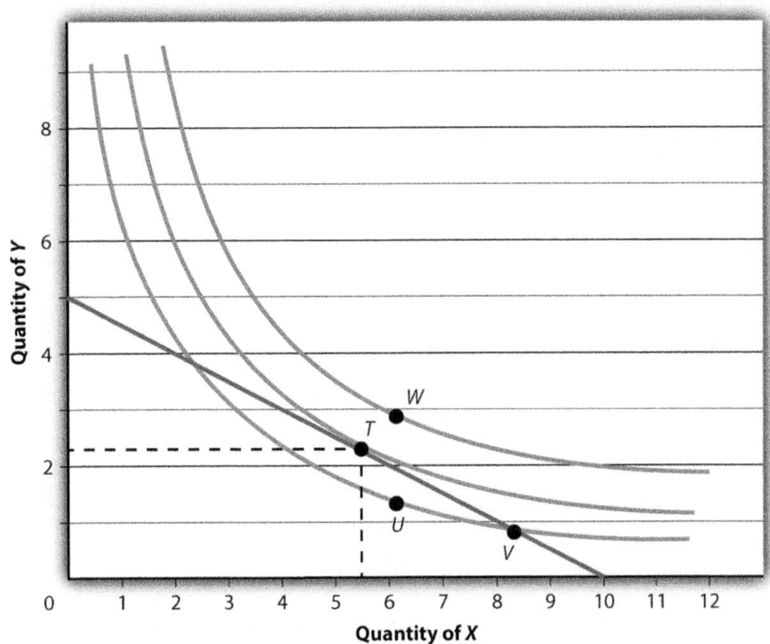

The Utility-Maximizing Rule

Observe that, at the tangency point, the slope of the budget line is equal to the slope of the indifference curve. That is, $P_X/P_Y = MU_X/MU_Y$. In other words, the ratio of the price of two goods equals the ratio of the marginal utility of the two goods as long as the consumer is maximizing utility. This equality between the price ratio and the ratio of the marginal utilities, or the marginal rate of substitution, is called the *utility-maximizing rule.*

Effect of a Price Change on the Quantity Demanded

Now suppose that the price of *X* increases; then the budget line twists down, as shown in the lower panel of Figure 5.18. With the new budget line, the old consumer choice of 2 1/4 units of *Y* and 5 1/2 units of *X* is no longer feasible: Point *S* is outside the new budget line. The highest level of utility the consumer can now achieve is at point *T* in the lower panel of Figure 5.18. At point *T*, the quantity of *X* has declined. Thus, a higher price of *X* has reduced the quantity demanded of *X*.

In the top graph in Figure 5.18, we show the relationship between the price of *X* and the quantity demanded of *X*. The price of *X* is put on the vertical axis, and the quantity demanded of *X* is put on the horizontal axis. The lower quantity demanded at the higher price shows the negative slope of the demand curve.

FIGURE 5.18 An Increase in the Price of *X*

If the price of *X* rises, the budget line pivots down and the consumer's choice changes from point *S* to point *T* in the lower panel. The quantity of *X* consumed goes down. The price of *X* and the quantity of X are plotted in the top panel, showing the negative relationship between price and quantity demanded.

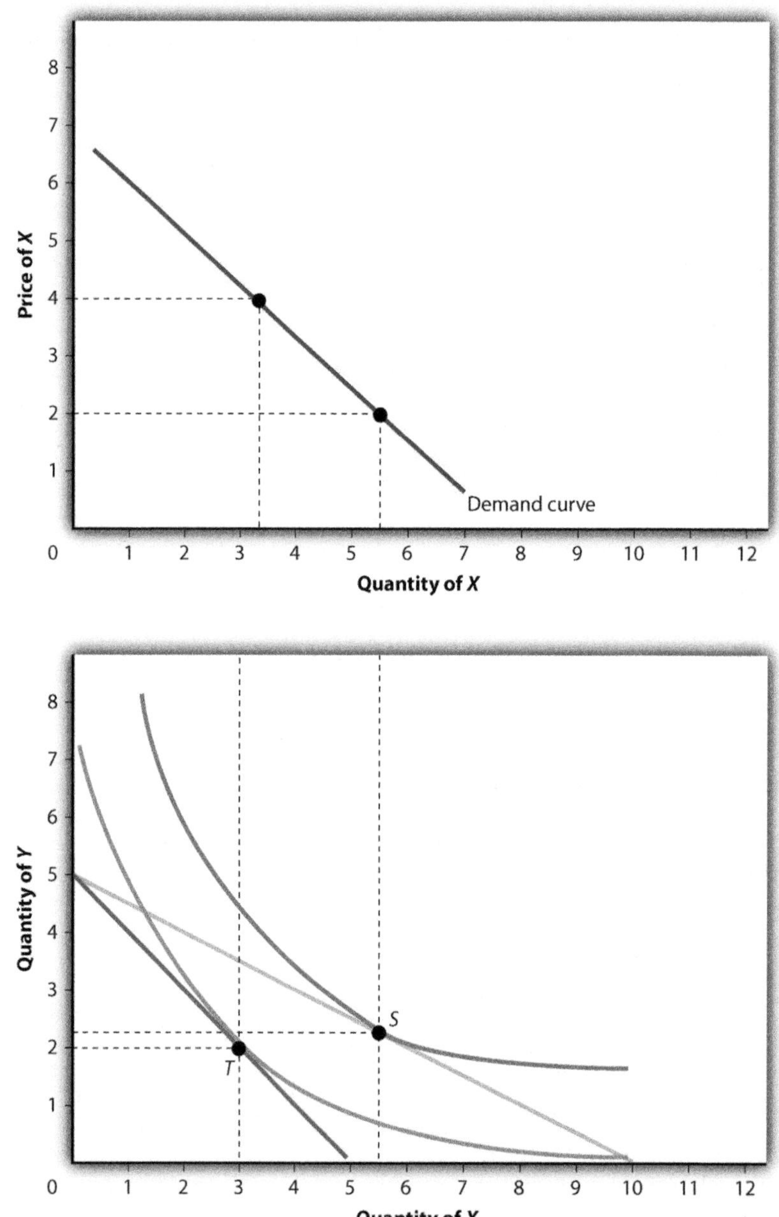

Effect of an Income Change on Demand

We also can examine what happens when the consumer's income changes but the price remains constant. This is illustrated in Figure 5.19, where income declines. The lower income leads to less consumption of both *X* and *Y*. In this case, both *X* and *Y* are normal goods because consumption goes down when income goes down. If the consumption of *X* increased as the budget curve shifted in, then *X* would be an inferior good.

Graphic Illustration of the Income Effect and the Substitution Effect

The effect of a change in the price on the quantity demanded can be divided into an income effect and a substitution effect. These two effects can be represented graphically as shown in Figure 5.20.

As in Figure 5.18, the budget line twists down due to the higher price of *X*. But now we draw in another budget line—the dashed line in Figure 5.20. This budget line has the same slope as the new budget line, but it allows the consumer to stay on the same indifference curve as she originally was. The dashed line can be used to find the substitution effect without the income effect because it has the same slope as the new budget line—the move from the dashed line to the new budget line is purely an income change rather than a relative price change.

The decline of consumption from *S* to *S'* is the substitution effect. Intuitively, you can think of this as the point that the consumer would choose if she were to (hypothetically) receive a sum of money that would compensate her for the utility loss she suffered as a result of the price increase. The remaining decline from *S'* to *T* is the income effect. Because that hypothetical sum of money never transpires, this shift clearly reflects the purchasing power that the consumer suffered as a result of the price increase.

FIGURE 5.19 A Decrease in Income

If the consumer's income falls, utility is maximized at a new point: The consumer moves from point *M* to point *N*. In this case, consumption of both *X* and *Y* declines. Neither good is an inferior good in this example.

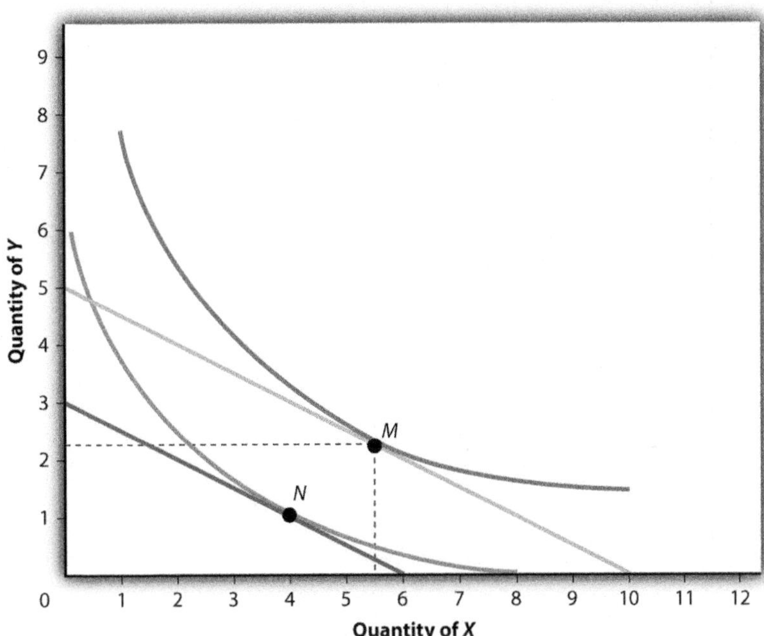

FIGURE 5.20 **Illustration of Income Effect and Substitution Effect of Price Change**

The dashed budget line has the same slope as the new budget line but allows the consumer to stay on the same indifference curve. This isolates the substitution effect. The rest of the decline is the income effect.

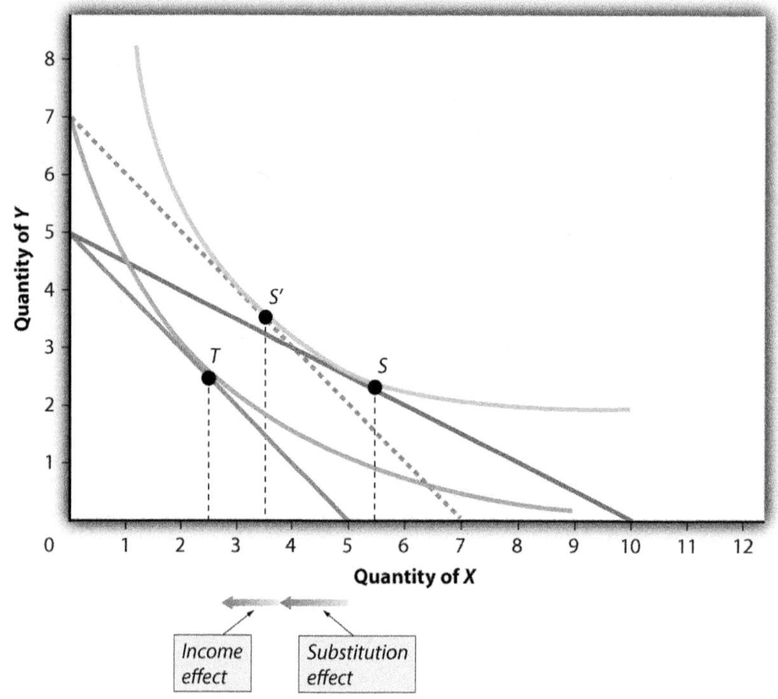

Key Points

1. The budget line represents the consumer's budget constraint in a diagram with the quantity consumed of each of two goods on the axes.
2. The budget line is downward sloping, with the slope equal to −1 times the ratio of the price of the good on the horizontal axis to the price of the good on the vertical axis.
3. A higher price of the good on the horizontal axis twists the budget line down.
4. An indifference curve shows the combinations of goods among which the consumer is indifferent.
5. Combinations of goods on higher indifference curves are preferred to combinations of goods on lower indifference curves.
6. The model of consumer behavior assumes that the consumer tries to get to the highest possible indifference curve without going beyond the budget line.
7. The consumer chooses the combination at the tangency of the budget line and the indifference curve.
8. A higher price of a good lowers the quantity demanded, according to the indifference curve and budget line diagram.

QUESTIONS FOR REVIEW

1. Why does the budget line slope downward?
2. What determines the slope of the budget line?
3. Why does the indifference curve slope downward?
4. Why does the consumer choose a point at which the indifference curve is tangent to the budget line?

PROBLEMS

1. Darnell has $30 to spend on either muffins, which cost $3 each, or cartons of orange juice, which cost$1.50 each.
   a. Graph Darnell's budget line for muffins and orange juice.
   b. What is the maximum quantity of orange juice that Darnell can buy with $30?
   c. Suppose the price of orange juice increases to $2 per carton. Show the change in the budget line.
2. Suppose you are having a party in half an hour and you have two 6-packs of beer in your refrigerator. One is an imported premium beer, and the other is a standard domestic beer. A neighbor comes to you and asks you to trade some imported premium beer for the standard domestic beer, because he is also having a party. You agree to trade two premium bottles for three standard bottles. Twenty minutes later, the neighbor comes back and asks for two more premium bottles. Will you still trade on a two premium bottles for three standard bottles basis? Suppose you demand four standard bottles for two premium bottles. What property of indifference curves is illustrated by this example?
3. Suppose that the prices of two goods consumed by an individual are reduced by the same percentage. What change will happen to the budget line? What change will happen to the consumer's indifference curves? What will happen to the consumption of the two goods? Show each of the above graphically.
4. Sarah has $20 to spend on slices of pizza and cans of diet cola. Pizza costs $1 per slice, and diet cola costs $0.50 per can.
   a. Graph Sarah's budget line for pizza and diet cola.
   b. Suppose Sarah's total budget for pizza and diet cola increases to $25. How does her budget line shift?
   c. Draw a set of indifference curves for the situation in which pizza is a normal good, and one for the situation in which pizza is an inferior good.

ENDNOTES

1. Adam Smith, *Wealth of Nations* (New York: Modern Library Edition, 1994), 31–32.

CHAPTER 6
The Supply Curve and the Behavior of Firms

Thousands of budding entrepreneurs, innovators, and inventors dream of the day that millions of people will clamor to buy their creations. The founders of a small Australian toy company decided to develop Shopkins, small plastic toys that are personifications of food items and everyday household objects. Shopkins soon developed an avid customer base among 6- to 10-year-old girls, according to a profile of the company that appeared in the Los Angeles Times. [1]

Children as consumers

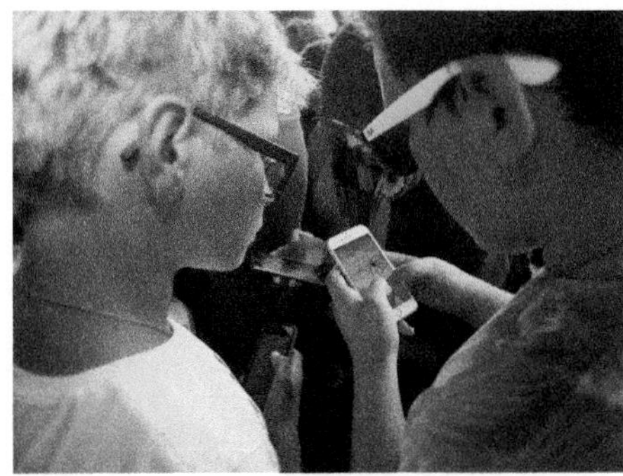

Source: © Circlephoto / Shutterstock, Inc.

FIGURE 6.1 A Typical Supply Curve for a Market
Supply curves typically slope upward. In this chapter, we look at the factors that motivate firms in the market to increase the quantity supplied as the price rises.

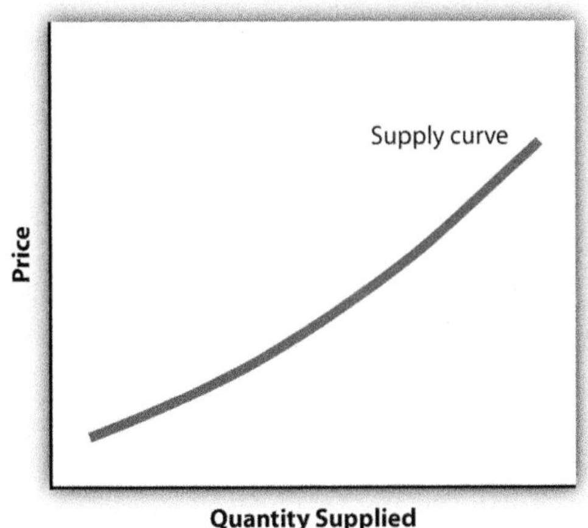

According to that news story, Shopkins became the best-selling U.S. toy in 2015, outselling household names like Barbie and Star Wars. Kids pay anywhere from $4 to $30 to buy packets of Shopkins. The little plastic pieces probably cost only pennies to make—creating, in economic terminology, a producer surplus. Moose Toys, the Australian toy company, has sold hundreds of millions of Shopkins. News stories reported that the company was no longer a small toy company—they needed four different factories to crank out the millions of Shopkins that their eager fans were demanding at retail stores.

The success of Shopkins has been a remarkable success story for Moose Toys but it is quite possible that Shopkins, like many other products that unexpectedly, and almost inexplicably, captured the minds (and wallets) of millions of consumers in a short period of time would fade away into obscurity in a few year's time. If that were to happen, then Moose Toys would see its sales fall and it would have to stop production at some of the factories and greatly reduce its workforce.

In this chapter, we examine how a firm like Moose Toys decides how many Shopkins to produce and how it responds to changing market conditions. The behavior of firms like Moose Toys can be described by supply curves like the one in Figure 6.1, which shows a typical supply curve, with price on the vertical axis and quantity supplied on the horizontal axis. The supply curve is for an entire market; it tells us how much all the firms in the market—not just a single firm like Moose Toys—would produce at each price. In this chapter, we look under the surface of the supply curve and examine how the profit-maximizing behavior of a firm determines how much of a good that firm will choose to produce at a given market price. Then we show how aggregating individual firms' supply curves generates a supply curve for the entire market for that good.

FIGURE 6.2 Applying the Central Idea of Economics

People make purposeful choices with scarce resources and interact with other people when they make these choices. In Chapter 5, the people were the consumers. In this chapter, they are the firms. In Chapter 7, the consumers and the firms interact with each other.

Basic Economic Principle	When Applied to the Behavior of Consumers	When Applied to the Behavior of Firms
People...	*Consumers...*	*Firms...*
make purposeful choices...	maximize utility...	maximize profits...
with scarce resources.	subject to a budget constraint relating expenditure to income.	subject to a production function relating output to input.

As with our study of the consumers who underlie the demand curve in Chapter 5, we have two important reasons to study the firms that underlie the supply curve. First, we want to show why the supply curve has the slope and position it does. Such information enables us to assess how a change in technology or societal trends or a new government policy affects the supply curve. Second, we want to show how and why a supply curve can be used to measure the "producer surplus" of firms. Producer surplus is a measure of how much a producer gains from participating in the market. In conjunction with consumer surplus, producer surplus is extremely useful for measuring how well a market economy actually works, and in explaining why a market economy works better than alternative systems to produce and allocate goods and resources.

1. DEFINITION OF A FIRM

firm

An organization that produces goods or services.

We start by looking at the behavior of a single firm. A **firm**, by definition, is an organization that produces goods or services. Just as no two consumers are exactly alike, no two firms are exactly alike. A firm can be a small family farm in the country or a grocery store in the city. Bakeries, restaurants, auto dealers, and bicycle shops are all examples of firms that are usually relatively small. Other firms—such as Coca-Cola—are very large, producing many different products in large volume.

The terms *firm*, *company*, and *business* are used interchangeably. A firm may include several *establishments*, which are separate physical locations, such as an office, a factory, or a store, where work is done. For example, the U.S.-based grocery chain Kroger is a firm with more than 2,500 supermarkets (most operating under the Kroger or Ralph's labels), almost 800 convenience stores (including Turkey Hill and Kwik Shop), and more than 400 jewelry stores (including Fred Meyer jewelers). Of course, not all firms are like Kroger; most small firms have only one establishment.

In the United States, about 80 percent of all firms are *sole proprietorships*, with one owner, or *partnerships*, with only a few owners, who usually manage the firm. Most of these are very small when compared with corporations like Kroger or Coca-Cola. A *corporation* is unlike a sole proprietorship or partnership in that the managers are usually somewhat removed from the owners. For example, most people who own shares of General Motors never even meet the managers of the firm. This separation of managers and owners means that the managers must be given an incentive to keep the owners' interests in mind. A common incentive is to have managers share in the profits of the firm.

You might expect that the decisions made by the managers of a firm would be more complicated—and consequently more difficult to understand—than the decisions made by consumers. Of course, many more people have had the experience of being a consumer than have had the experience of managing a firm. But if you can picture yourself as the owner or manager of your own firm, you will see that the economics of a firm's decision about how much to sell is analogous to the economics of a consumer's decision about how much to buy. The following example places you in that position.

1.1 Your Own Firm: A Pumpkin Patch

Imagine that you are the owner and manager of a firm that grows pumpkins on a pumpkin patch; the patch has good soil and gets plenty of rain. Your firm is one of many specializing in growing and selling pumpkins—in other words, you must compete with many other firms. During the spring and summer you grow the pumpkins, and in the fall you sell them. As owner and manager of the firm, you must pay rent at the start of each growing season to the landlord who owns the pumpkin patch. During the season, you hire workers to tend the patch. The more workers you have tending the pumpkins, the more pumpkins you can grow on the patch.

Your firm is typical of many small firms and has features that apply to larger firms as well. Your firm is one with a single product (pumpkins) and two factors of production—land (the patch) and labor (the workers). One of the factors of production, land, cannot be changed during the season because the rent was paid in advance; this makes land a *fixed factor*. The other factor, labor, can be varied during the season, because you can choose to hire more or fewer workers; this makes labor a *variable factor*.

1.2 Your Firm as a Price-Taker in a Competitive Market

The first task is to derive the supply curve for your pumpkin firm. *A supply curve for a single firm tells us the quantity of a good that that firm will produce at different prices.* To find the supply curve, we imagine that the firm looks at the price of the good it is selling and then decides how much to produce. For example, a baker considers the price of a loaf of bread prevailing in the market when deciding how many loaves of bread to produce. So in this case you must decide how much to produce and sell after looking at the price of pumpkins in the market. In a competitive market, any individual firm will be a **price-taker**; this means that the firm cannot influence the market price but instead has to decide how much to produce and sell at the given market price of the goods. In the case of your pumpkin firm, what this implies is that you cannot affect the price of pumpkins in the market through your decision to produce more or fewer pumpkins.

Source: © Shutterstock, Inc.

price-taker

Any firm that takes the market price as given; this firm cannot affect the market price because the market is competitive.

Many people buy pumpkins in the fall to use as Halloween decorations or to make delicious foods like pumpkin pie or pumpkin soup. As the owner of a small pumpkin firm, you are a price-taker because your pumpkins are like everyone else's pumpkins.

Source: © Shutterstock, Inc.

This description of a firm as a price-taker may seem odd to you. After all, if the firm does not set the price, then who does? Of course, in some sense, each firm does. If you go to a bakery for a loaf of bread, a price tag states the price of the loaf, so the baker is clearly determining the price. But this is not the way economists look at it; economists describe the market in a more subtle way. When many bakers are selling bread, in an important sense, the individual bakers do not have the ability to affect the price by much. If one baker charges $3 for a loaf of bread, and all the other bakers in the community charge $1.50 for the same loaf, no one will buy bread from the first baker. People will not even go to the store if they know the price is that high. They will go to other bakeries, where bread sells for $1.50 a loaf. Although in principle an individual firm has the ability to set any price it wants, in reality, a firm cannot charge a price far from the price that prevails in the market without soon losing all its customers.

competitive market

A market in which no firm has the power to affect the market price of a good.

A market in which a single firm cannot affect the market price is called a **competitive market**. Because many firms are producing pumpkins along with your pumpkin firm, the pumpkin market is competitive. A competitive market requires that there be at least several firms competing with one another. Exactly how many firms are required to make a market competitive is difficult to say without studying the market carefully—as we do in later chapters. If a market is competitive, so that firms are price takers, then we can derive a supply curve for the individual firm by asking, "How many pumpkins would the pumpkin firm produce if the price of pumpkins were $35 a crate? $70 a crate?" and so on.

1.3 Other Types of Markets

Not all markets are as competitive as the fresh bread market or the pumpkin market, and part of our job later in the book is to study these markets. The exact opposite of a competitive market is a market that has only one firm, in which case the firm is called a *monopoly*. Strictly speaking, the question "How much does the monopoly produce at a given price?" has no meaning because the monopoly is not a price-taker that has to take the price as given. Instead, it is a price-maker who can dictate the price. We consider monopolies in Chapter 10. For now we focus on the price-taking firms in a competitive market.

In deriving the demand curve in Chapter 5, we assumed that the individual consumer could not affect the price. This assumption seems natural, because we usually do not see buyers setting the price for bread or other commodities. As long as the market has at least several buyers and several sellers, we can assume that the price is taken as given by both buyers and sellers. In Chapter 7, when we study the interaction of buyers and sellers in markets, we will show how the market price is determined.

REVIEW

- A firm is an organization that produces goods or services that are sold in a market. There are a great variety of sizes and types of firms.
- In the United States, most firms take the form of sole proprietorships or partnerships, which means that they are owned by either a single owner or very few owners, respectively. Other firms, known as corporations, are owned by many individuals who typically are disconnected from the day-to-day operations of the firm, which is run by the managers of the firm.
- To understand firm behavior, we begin by focusing on a simple case of a single owner of a firm that is operating in a competitive market. A market is said to be competitive if no single firm can affect the market price.
- Not all markets are competitive. The polar opposite of a competitive market is a monopoly market, in which a single producer dictates the price that the good sells for in that market. This chapter will focus only on competitive markets.
- In a competitive market with many firms, each firm is a price-taker. The owner of the firm has to decide how much of the good or service to produce at the given price. The supply curve of an individual firm describes how the quantity produced by that firm depends on the price.

2. THE FIRM'S PROFITS

Profits

Total revenue received from selling the product minus the total costs of producing the product.

Profits for any firm—a bakery producing bread or a farm producing pumpkins—are defined as the *total revenue* received from selling the product minus the *total costs* of producing the product. That is,

$$\text{Profits} = \text{total revenue} - \text{total costs}$$

When profits are negative—total revenue is less than total costs—the firm runs a loss. When profits are zero—total revenue is equal to total costs—the firm is *breaking even.*

We assume that the firm *maximizes profits.* That is, the firm decides on the quantity of production that will make profits as high as possible. To see how this is done, we must examine how profits depend on the quantity produced. To do this, we must consider how total revenue and total costs—the two determinants of profits—depend on the quantity produced. We consider first total revenue and then total costs.

2.1 Total Revenue

Total revenue is the total number of dollars the firm receives from people who buy its product. Total revenue can be computed by multiplying the price of each unit sold by the quantity sold. That is,

Total revenue

The price per unit times the quantity the firm sells.

$$\begin{aligned} \text{Total revenue} &= \text{price} \times \text{quantity} \\ &= P \times Q \end{aligned}$$

where we use the letter *P* to stand for price and *Q* to stand for quantity. Because we are looking at an individual firm and a particular product, *P* is the price of the particular product the individual firm is selling, and *Q* is the number of items the firm sells. We can measure the quantity sold in a variety of ways: number of pumpkins, crates of pumpkins, or pounds of pumpkins. Any of these measures will suffice for our analysis.

TABLE 6.1 Total Revenue from Pumpkin Production at Three Prices

Quantity Produced (crates)	Total Revenue		
	Price = $35/crate	*Price = $70/crate*	*Price = $100/crate*
0	0	0	0
1	35	70	100
2	70	140	200
3	105	210	300
4	140	280	400
5	175	350	500

Table 6.1 uses crates of pumpkins as the measure of quantity. Note that total revenue depends both on the price of a crate of pumpkin and on the number of crates of pumpkins sold. Each row of the table shows the total revenue the firm receives from selling a specific amount of pumpkins: zero crates, one crate, and so on. Each column showing total revenue corresponds to a different price: $35 per crate, $70 per crate, and $100 per crate. For example, when the firm can get $70 per crate, it receives $280 for selling four crates.

From Table 6.1, you can see that the more items that are sold at a given price, the higher total revenue is. Thus, the firm can increase total revenue by producing and selling more goods. Total revenue therefore increases with the quantity produced for your pumpkin-producing firm.

2.2 Production and Costs

Now that we have seen how total revenue depends on the quantity produced, let's examine how total costs depend on the quantity produced. **Total costs** are what the firm has to incur to produce the product. For your pumpkin firm, total costs include the workers' salaries and the rent on the land. To see how total costs depend on the quantity produced, we must look at what happens to the quantity of labor and land used by the firm when the quantity produced increases or decreases.

Total costs

The sum of all costs incurred in producing goods or services.

The Time Period

Here, we are looking at the pumpkin firm's production decisions over a short period of time—such as one growing season—rather than over a long period of time—such as several growing seasons. Because we are focusing on the short run, we assume that only the labor input to production can be varied. Our analysis of the firm in this chapter is called a *short-run* analysis because the time is too short to change the other factors of production, such as land; only labor can be changed. We make this assumption simply because it is easier to examine the firm's decisions when only one factor of production can be changed. It is a simplifying assumption that we will modify. In Chapter 8 we take up the *long run*, in which other factors of production—such as the size of the pumpkin patch—can change as well as labor.

Reminder: *In Chapter 1, we saw that costs include opportunity costs. Thus, total costs for your pumpkin firm would include the opportunity cost of any time you spent operating the firm rather than doing something else, like studying for an exam. To emphasize that opportunity costs are included in total costs when computing profits, economists sometimes use the term economic profits rather than si mply profits.*

The Production Function

production function

A relationship that shows the quantity of output for any given amount of input.

Figure 6.3 plots the relationship between pumpkin production and labor input for a given size of pumpkin patch. The number of hours of work is on the horizontal axis, and the quantity produced is on the vertical axis. Each point in Figure 6.3 shows the number of hours of work and the quantity of pumpkins produced: To produce three crates requires 10 hours of work; to produce five crates requires 30 hours of work. Clearly, more pumpkin production requires more labor input. The graph in Figure 6.3 is called the firm's **production function** because it tells us how much is produced for each amount of labor input, given a fixed amount of land input.

FIGURE 6.3 A Production Function Relating Output to Labor Input

As more workers are employed, production increases. But the increase in production added by each additional hour of work declines as more workers are hired because the land the workers have to work with does not increase. Thus, there is a decreasing marginal product of labor, or diminishing returns to labor.

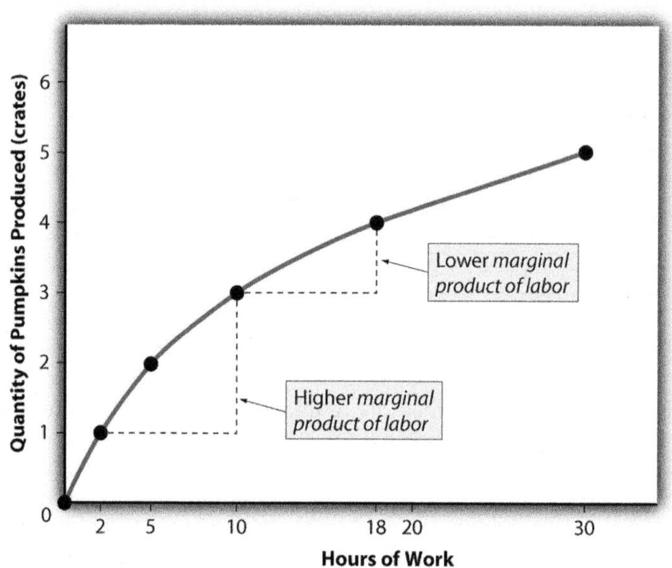

marginal product of labor

The change in production due to a one-unit increase in labor input.

The **marginal product of labor** is defined as the increase in production that comes from an additional unit of labor. Figure 6.3 shows that, because of the curvature of the production function, the marginal product of labor *declines* as labor input increases. In other words, the same increase in hours of work leads to a smaller increase in production when labor input is large than when labor input is small. In Figure 6.3, when the hours of work increase from 2 to 10, the quantity of pumpkin crates produced increases by two crates, from one to three crates. However, an increase of labor input of the identical magnitude from 10 to 18 will increase the quantity of pumpkins by only one crate, from three to four crates.

diminishing returns to labor

A situation in which the increase in output due to a unit increase in labor declines with increasing labor input; a decreasing marginal product of labor.

Another term for the phenomenon of declining marginal product of labor is **diminishing returns to labor**. In your pumpkin firm, diminishing returns to labor occur as additional workers are employed. For a given amount of land, hiring more workers initially is helpful in terms of increasing output, as the workers can water the pumpkins, pull out weeds, and harvest the pumpkins at the appropriate time. But as more and more workers are employed on a given amount of land, each worker has fewer tasks to do, and each additional worker adds less and less additional output. Diminishing returns is a general phenomenon that occurs when some inputs to production—such as land or machines—are fixed. Because the size of your pumpkin patch is fixed, additional workers must eventually add less to production. Otherwise, a single plot of land could produce all the world's pumpkins by employing huge numbers of workers. Diminishing returns to labor occur in nonagricultural examples as well.

Employing more and more workers in an automobile factory without increasing the size of the factory or adding more machines will increase the amount of cars produced by the factory by less and less.

FIGURE 6.4 Diminishing Returns to Labor

Adding the second worker to this machine in a French vineyard increased the quantity of grapes produced by much less than the first worker did. Adding a third worker to the machine would increase the quantity of grapes produced by even less than adding the second worker did. Thus, this is an example of a decreasing marginal product of labor, or diminishing returns to labor.

Source: © Shutterstock, Inc.

Costs

Table 6.2 shows how total costs depend on the quantity of pumpkins produced at your pumpkin firm. The first column shows the quantity of pumpkins produced. The second column shows the labor input required to produce that quantity of pumpkins, using the production function from Figure 6.3. The third column shows the costs of hiring the labor input at a rate of $10 per hour of work. These costs are called **variable costs** because they vary according to how much is produced; more workers are hired and more wages paid as more pumpkins are produced. We also assume that you have to pay $50 in advance for rent on the patch. The fourth column shows the cost of the land. The $50 payment for the land is considered to be a *fixed cost* because it must be paid no matter how many pumpkins are produced or even if you produce no pumpkins at all. By definition, **fixed costs** are the part of total costs that do not depend on how much is produced. Variable costs and fixed costs together constitute all the costs of producing the product. Hence, *the sum of fixed costs and variable costs equals total costs*, as shown in the last column of Table 6.2.

variable costs

Costs of production that vary with the quantity of production.

fixed costs

Costs of production that do not depend on the quantity of production.

TABLE 6.2 Example of Costs for a Single Firm

Quantity Produced (crates)	Hours of Labor Input	Variable Costs at $10 Wage (dollars)	Fixed Costs (dollars)	Total Costs (dollars)
0	0	0	50	50
1	2	20	50	70
2	5	50	50	100
3	10	100	50	150
4	18	180	50	230
5	30	300	50	350

Each row of Table 6.2 shows the costs of producing a particular quantity of pumpkins. The first row indicates that even if no pumpkins are produced, the firm will incur the fixed costs of $50. The second row shows the cost of producing one crate of pumpkins. Since two units of labor are needed for the production of this one crate, the total cost of producing one crate of pumpkins is $70, the $50 fixed costs plus the $20 in variable costs. The third row of Table 6.2 shows the costs of producing two crates of pumpkins. Because five units of labor (at a cost of $10 each) are needed for the production of these two crates, the total cost of producing two crates of pumpkins is $100, the $50 fixed costs plus the $50 in variable costs.

As more pumpkins are harvested, more workers must be hired, and the total costs increase. The remaining rows of Table 6.2 show what happens to costs as the quantity produced increases further.

marginal cost

The change in total costs due to a one-unit change in quantity produced.

Marginal cost is defined as the increase in total costs associated with an additional unit of production. Figure 6.5 shows how marginal cost is calculated for the example in Table 6.2. For example, the marginal cost of increasing production from one crate to two crates is $30 ($100 – $70 = $30), and the marginal cost of increasing production from two crates to three crates is $50 ($150 – $100 = $50).

Notice how marginal cost increases as production increases. Marginal cost is greater when we go from two crates to three crates ($50) than when we go from one crate to two crates ($30). The pattern of *increasing marginal* cost is apparent throughout the range of production in Figure 6.5.

FIGURE 6.5 Total Costs and Marginal Cost

Total Costs and Marginal Cost

Quantity Produced (crates)	Total Costs (dollars)	Marginal Cost (dollars)
0	50	—
1	70	20
2	100	30
3	150	50
4	230	80
5	350	120

The connecting lines emphasize how marginal cost is the change in total costs as the quantity produced increases by one unit.

The connecting lines emphasize how marginal cost is the change in total costs as the quantity produced increases by one unit.

Observe that *increasing marginal cost is due to the diminishing marginal product of labor*. The marginal cost of going from two crates to three crates is greater than that of going from one crate to two crates because more worker hours are required to raise production from two crates to three crates (five additional hours of labor) than are required to raise production from one crate to two crates (three additional hours of labor).

Increasing marginal cost is a general phenomenon that occurs in many production processes. It is essential for deriving the supply curve. In fact, as we will soon see, increasing marginal cost is the whole reason that the supply curve for an individual firm slopes upward.

The principle of increasing marginal cost has important exceptions. One of these exceptions is that marginal cost need not be increasing over the entire range of production. For example, a decrease in marginal cost may occur at very low levels of production. If a team of at least two workers is needed to harvest pumpkins, for example, then the marginal product of a second worker might be greater than the marginal product of a first worker. One worker might add very little, whereas the second might add a lot. But diminishing returns to labor and increasing marginal cost eventually set in as more workers are hired and more pumpkins are produced.

FIGURE 6.6 Total Costs

To produce goods, a firm incurs costs. For example, more workers must be paid to produce more goods. As more goods are produced, the firm's total costs rise, as shown here. At higher levels of production, costs increase by larger amounts for each additional item produced.

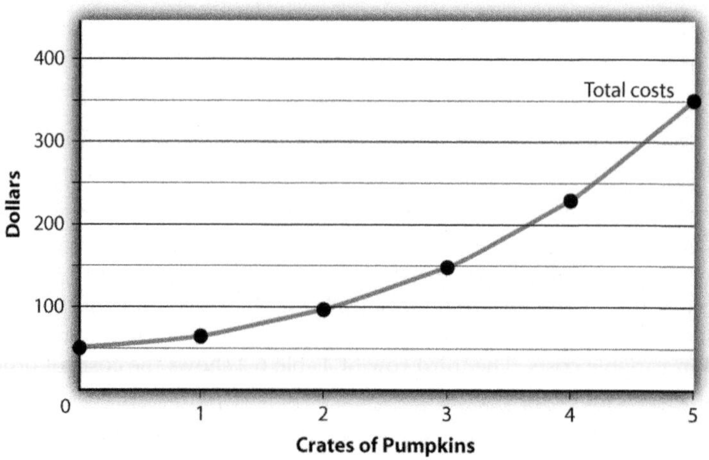

In this chapter, we assume that marginal cost increases over the whole range of production.This is a common assumption used by economists and is a good approximation except for very low levels of production.

Graphical Representation of Total Costs and Marginal cost

A better understanding of how a firm's total costs depend on production can be obtained by representing the total costs graphically. Figure 6.6 plots the pairs of numbers for total costs and quantity produced from the first two columns of Figure 6.5. Dollars are on the vertical axis, and the quantity of pumpkins produced is on the horizontal axis. Note how the total costs curve bends up: As the quantity of pumpkins produced increases, the curve gets steeper, or the slope increases. The marginal cost is the slope of the total costs curve. The increasing slope is a visual way to show the increasing marginal cost.

Figure 6.7 shows the relationship between marginal cost and the number of crates of pumpkins produced. The points in Figure 6.7 correspond to the pairs of numbers in the first and third columns of Figure 6.5. Note that the marginal cost curve slopes upward, illustrating how marginal cost increases as the quantity of pumpkins produced increases.

FIGURE 6.7 Marginal Cost

The change in total costs as more units of the good are produced is called marginal cost. Marginal cost increases as more units are produced, as illustrated here.

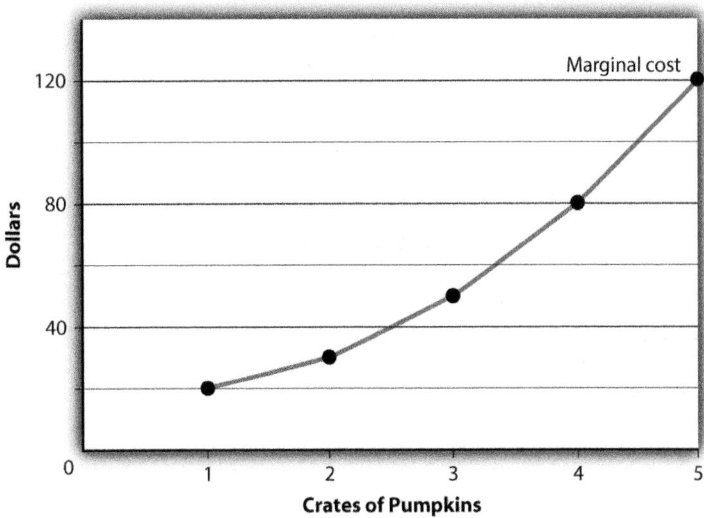

REVIEW

- Profits are defined as the difference between total revenue and total costs. Profits depend on the quantity produced because both total revenue and total costs depend on the quantity produced.
- Total revenue is defined as the price (*P*) times the quantity (*Q*) produced and sold. Total revenue increases as the quantity produced increases.
- Total costs are all the costs that the firm has to incur to produce its product. The costs that a firm incurs include opportunity costs.
- In this chapter, we look at the firm's production decisions over a short period of time. One factor of production, land, has to be held fixed whereas the other factor of production, labor, can be varied as the quantity produced varies.
- The production function describes how much output can be produced as the quantity of inputs (in this case hours of labor) varies. Typically, the marginal product of labor declines as more and more labor is employed. This phenomenon also is described as diminishing returns to labor.
- Total costs are the sum of fixed costs (which do not vary with the quantity produced) and variable costs (which vary according to how much is produced). In the pumpkin firm example, fixed costs are the cost of renting the pumpkin patch, and variable costs are the costs of hiring workers.
- Variable costs increase with the quantity produced because it takes more inputs—such as workers—to produce more output. As a result, total costs also increase with the quantity produced.
- Marginal cost is defined as the change in total costs associated with an additional unit of production. Marginal cost increases as more is produced because of diminishing returns to labor.

3. PROFIT MAXIMIZATION AND THE INDIVIDUAL FIRM

profit maximization

An assumption that firms try to achieve the highest possible level of profits—total revenue minus total costs given their production function.

To derive the firm's supply curve, we assume that the firm chooses a quantity of production that maximizes profits. This is the assumption of **profit maximization**. Now that we have seen how profits depend on the quantity produced, we can show how the firm chooses a quantity to maximize profits.

3.1 An Initial Approach to Derive the Supply Curve

Continuing with our pumpkin firm, we create a table that uses total revenue and total costs to calculate profits. Because total revenue depends on the price, we need a separate panel for each of three possible prices.

A Profit Table

TABLE 6.3 Profit Tables Showing Total Costs and Total Revenue at Different Prices

PANEL I			
If price equals $35 per crate, then production equals two crates.			
Crates	*Total Revenue*	*Total Costs*	*Profits*
0	0	50	-50
1	35	70	-35
2	**70**	**100**	**-30**
3	105	150	-45
4	140	230	-90
5	175	350	-175

PANEL II			
If price equals $70 per crate, then production equals three crates.			
Crates	*Total Revenue*	*Total Costs*	*Profits*
0	0	50	-50
1	70	70	0
2	140	100	40
3	**210**	**150**	**60**
4	280	230	50
5	350	350	0

PANEL III			
If price equals $100 per crate, then production equals four crates.			
Crates	*Total Revenue*	*Total Costs*	*Profits*
0	0	50	-50
1	100	70	30
2	200	100	100
3	300	150	150
4	**400**	**230**	**170**
5	500	350	150

Table 6.3 shows profits for your pumpkin firm. It has three panels, one for each of three possible prices. (The prices are the same as in Table 6.1.) Each panel reports total revenue and total costs for quantities ranging from zero to five crates. The last column of each panel reports profits, which are defined as total revenue less total costs.

Total revenue, shown in the second column, increases with the number of pumpkins sold. Because total revenue depends on the price, we need a separate panel showing total revenue for each price. The third column of Table 6.3 shows how total costs increase with production. This information is the same as that presented in Table 6.2. We repeat it here so that total costs can be compared easily with total revenue to calculate profits. The range of total costs is the same for all three panels because total costs do not depend on the price.

Consider Panel I, in which the price of pumpkins is $35 a crate. Total revenue equals the price ($35) times the number of crates sold. If you sell one crate, the revenue is $35; if you sell two crates, the revenue is $70, and so on. Clearly, if no pumpkins are sold, the total revenue will be zero. Panels II and III show total revenue for two higher prices—$70 per crate and $100 per crate.

The last column of Table 6.3 shows profits, which equal total revenue minus total costs. Consider the $35 per crate price in Panel I first. When no pumpkins are produced, total costs are $50 because $50 is paid for the land. Total revenue is zero. Profits, therefore, are –$50, which implies that the firm loses $50. If you produce one crate, the loss is $35; the revenue from one crate ($35) minus the total cost of producing one crate ($70) equals a profit of –$35. For two crates, profits are still negative, at –$30. Total revenue is $70; total costs are $100, leaving a loss of $30. Three crates of pumpkins yield an even greater loss of $45.

A glance down the last column in Panel I shows that profits are negative at all production levels. In this case, any production at all may seem fruitless. But remember that you already paid $50 for the use of the pumpkin patch. Hence, it is best to produce two crates and cut your losses to $30. You still lose, but not as much as by producing only zero or one crate. Even though it may seem strange because profits are negative, the profit-maximizing level of production is two crates. The maximum of profits would be –$30. Stated differently, the minimum loss would be $30.

The same type of profit-maximizing exercise with a different price is illustrated in Panel II of Table 6.3. Here the price of pumpkins is $70 per crate, and so the total revenue is higher. If you sell nothing, then total revenue is zero and the loss is $50. If you sell one crate, total revenue is $70 and profits are zero. But if you sell two crates, total costs are $100 and total revenue is $140. Finally, some positive profit can be seen. Profits can be increased further: The profit-maximizing level of production is three crates.

Panel III shows profits for a still higher price, $100 a crate. At this price, you would produce four crates. Profits would be $170. More or less production than four crates would lower profits.

In these three cases, you maximize profits by adjusting the quantity supplied. As the price rises from $35 to $70 to $100, the profit-maximizing quantity of pumpkins supplied goes from two crates to three crates to four crates. Thus, the price and the quantity supplied are positively related. This is the positively sloped supply curve.

A Profit Graph

The relationship between profits and production for your pumpkin firm given in Table 6.3 can be illustrated with a graph that compares total costs and total revenue. This comparison is shown in Figure 6.8. The curved line in the top graph of Figure 6.8 is the total costs curve. It corresponds to the total costs listed in Table 6.3 and is the same as the total costs curve in Figure 6.6. The upward-sloping straight line shows what total revenue would be for a price of $70 per crate. This line corresponds to the total revenue column in Panel II of Table 6.3.

Profits are given by the gap between the total revenue line and the total costs curve. The gap—profits—is plotted in the lower panel of Figure 6.8. Note how profits first increase and then decrease as more is produced. The profit-maximizing firm chooses the quantity to produce that leads to the biggest gap, or the biggest level of profits. That quantity is three crates of pumpkins.

3.2 The Marginal Approach to Deriving the Supply Curve

The above approach to deriving the supply curve can be involved because of the need to calculate a separate profit table for each price level. Economists use a different approach to analyzing profit maximization and deriving the supply curve. Once you know this approach, you will find that it is an easier and faster way to derive the individual firm's supply curve than using total revenue, total costs, and total profits.

Continuing with our pumpkin firm, we first plot the marginal cost from Figure 6.5 in Figure 6.9. Focus for now on the black dots in Figure 6.9; we derive the lines in the next few paragraphs. Each dot in Figure 6.9 represents the marginal cost of producing a crate of pumpkins at a different level of production (the marginal cost when production is one crate is $20, the marginal cost when production is two crates is $30, and so on).

FIGURE 6.8 An Initial Approach to Profit Maximization

The top panel shows total costs and total revenue for a price of $70 per crate of pumpkins. Profits are the gap between total revenue and total costs. The bottom panel shows explicitly how profits first increase and then decrease as production increases.

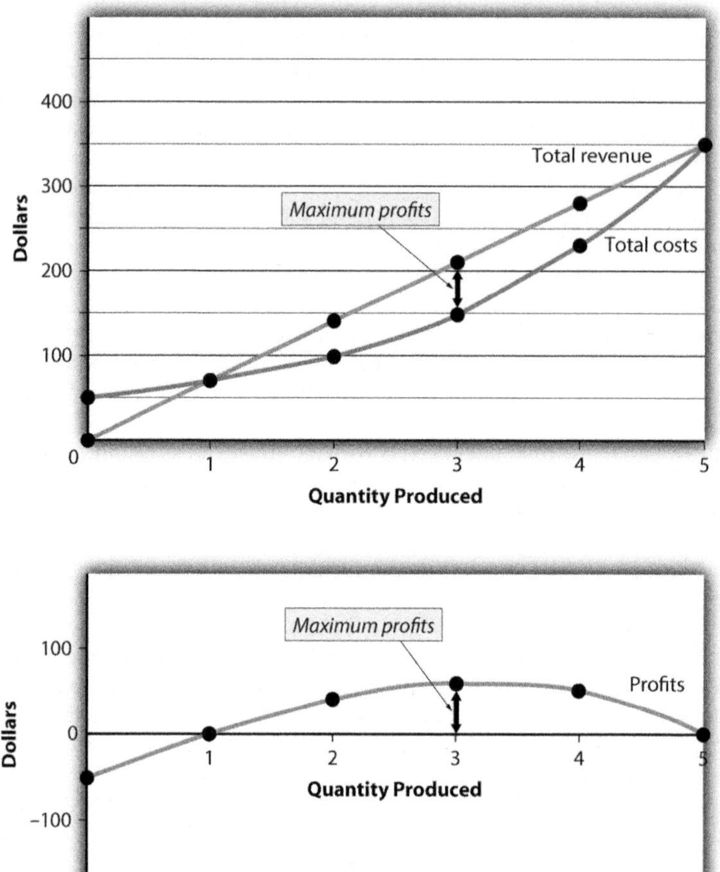

FIGURE 6.9 Derivation of the Individual Firm's Supply Curve

The dots represent the marginal cost from Figure 6.5. At each dot, price equals marginal cost. These dots and the thick vertical lines indicate the quantity the firm is willing to supply at each price. Along the vertical lines, the firm produces the quantity that keeps marginal cost closest to price without exceeding it.

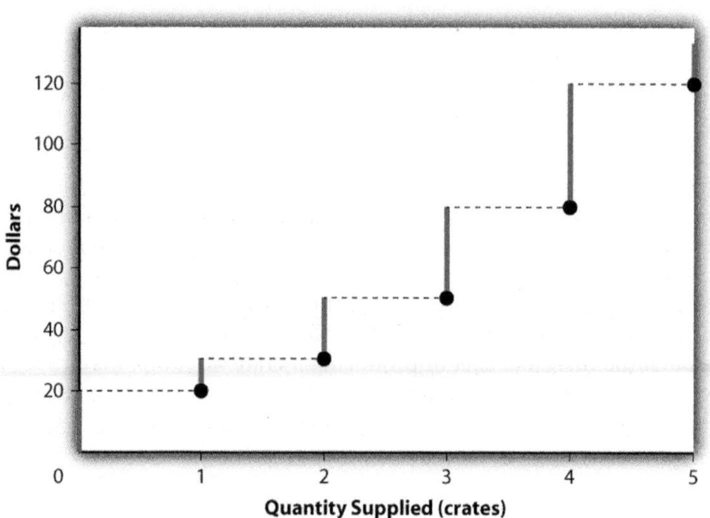

Finding the Quantity Supplied at Different Prices

Suppose the price of pumpkins is $10 a crate. At $10, the price is less than the marginal cost of producing one unit, which is $20, according to Figure 6.9. Would it make sense to produce pumpkins at this price? No, because the *additional* revenue that comes from producing one more crate, the price of a crate of pumpkins, is $10. Because laying out $20 and getting back $10 reduces profits, you would not bother to produce any pumpkins.

The additional, or extra, revenue that results from producing and selling one more unit of output is called **marginal revenue**. We can summarize the above conclusion by saying that we do not increase production from zero to one crate because the marginal cost of increasing production would be greater than the marginal revenue. Therefore, producing nothing would be the profit-maximizing thing to do.

marginal revenue

The change in total revenue due to a one-unit increase in quantity sold.

Suppose the price of pumpkins rises. As long as the price is below $20, there is no production because marginal costs exceed marginal revenue (which is the price). Thus, the amount supplied at prices from $0 to $20 is given by the thick line at the bottom of the vertical axis, indicating that quantity supplied equals zero.

Suppose the price rises to $20. Now the price equals the marginal cost, and the marginal revenue from selling a crate of pumpkins will just cover the marginal cost of producing the crate. You now have sufficient incentive to produce some pumpkins. Strictly speaking, the price would have to be a little bit greater than $20 (say, $20.01) for you to earn more by producing one crate rather than zero crates. At a price of exactly $20, you might be indifferent between producing zero crates and one crate. At a price of $19.99, you definitely would produce nothing. At a price of $20.01, you would produce one crate. The price of $20 is right between, but let's assume that you produce one crate rather than zero crates at a price of $20. We indicate this in Figure 6.9 by showing that the quantity supplied is given by the black dot at one crate and $20.

Now consider further increases in the price. At prices above $20 up to $30, you would produce one crate because the marginal revenue received for producing an extra crate (which again is the price of a crate of pumpkins) is less than the marginal cost of $30. At a price of $30, however, the quantity supplied increases to two crates because price just equals the marginal cost of increasing production from one to two crates. A supply curve is now beginning to take shape. You can complete the curve by continuing to raise the price and watching what happens.

To shorten the story, let us move toward the other end of the scale. Suppose the price of pumpkins is $100 and you are producing four crates of pumpkins. Would it make sense to produce another crate? No, because increasing production from four crates to five crates has a marginal cost of $120. The marginal revenue that comes from producing one more crate is $100. Because laying out $120 and getting back $100 is a losing proposition, you would not do it. Production would stay at four crates. If production went up to five crates, profits would go down because the marginal cost of producing the fifth crate is greater than the marginal revenue.

We have traced out the complete *individual* supply curve for your firm using Figure 6.9 with the assumption of profit maximization and the concept of marginal cost. The supply curve in Figure 6.9 is step-like; it consists of small vertical segments shooting up from the dots. At the dots, price equals marginal cost; on the vertical segments above the dots, the price is greater than the marginal cost of production, but the price is not great enough to move on to a higher level of production. What the vertical lines show is that as the price rises, the quantity supplied of pumpkins increases as well.

In reality, for most products, it is possible to divide production into smaller units—half crates, quarter crates, even a single pumpkin. As we do so, the jaggedness of the diagram disappears, as shown in Figure 6.10. In reality, the diagram would consist of hundreds of dots rather than five dots. With hundreds of dots, the vertical segments would be too small to see and the firm's supply curve would be a smooth line. Price would equal marginal cost at every single point.

The Price Equals Marginal Cost Rule

In deriving the supply curve with Figure 6.9, we have discovered the key condition for profit maximization for a firm: *The firm will choose a quantity to produce so that marginal revenue equals marginal cost.* This general rule makes intuitive sense for any profit-maximizing firm, whether it is a competitive firm or a monopoly. If the marginal revenue from producing an additional quantity of output is greater than the marginal cost, then the firm should produce that quantity; by doing so, it will increase total revenue by more than it increases total costs, and therefore it will increase profits. If the marginal revenue from an additional quantity is less than the marginal cost, however, then the firm should not produce that quantity. Thus, the firm maximizes profits by choosing the quantity of production for which marginal revenue equals marginal cost.

FIGURE 6.10 **A Smooth Individual Supply Curve**

If the firm can adjust its production by small amounts, the supply curve becomes a smooth line, as in this figure, rather than a series of steps, as in Figure 6.9. In some cases, such as the building of an airport, a dam, or a suspension bridge, fractions are not possible, and the supply curves will still have steps.

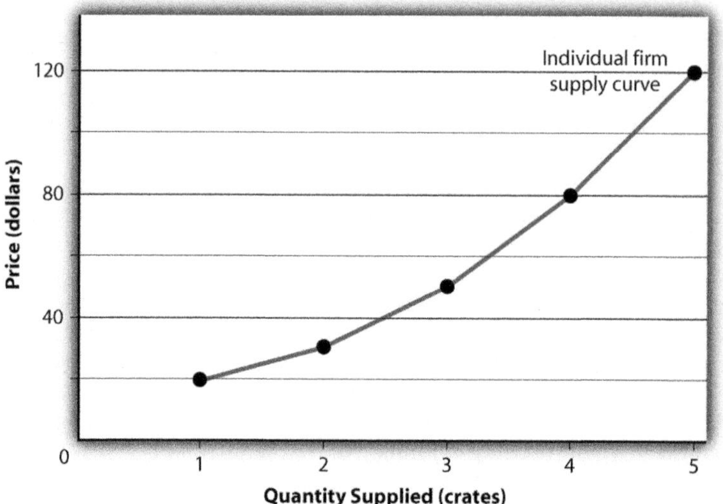

In a competitive market, we can come up with a special case of this rule that makes finding the profit-maximizing quantity even easier. *The firm will choose its quantity such that price equals marginal cost.* You can see that from Figure 6.9. When the price is $80, the firm chooses a level of production for which the marginal cost equals $80 and produces four crates. Why is the price-equals-marginal-cost rule for a competitive firm a special case of the marginal-revenue-equals-marginal-cost rule? Because *for the case of a price-taking firm in a competitive market, the marginal revenue is equal to the price.* Changes in the quantity of goods that the firm supplies do not affect the market price, so each additional unit sold brings in the same additional revenue, namely, the market price of the good. For example, as we showed above, if the price of pumpkins is $10 per crate, then the marginal, or additional, revenue from producing one crate of pumpkins is $10. Later, in Chapter 10, we will show that for a monopoly, the marginal revenue does not equal the price, so that even though marginal revenue equals marginal cost, the price does not equal marginal cost.

3.3 A Comparison of the Two Approaches to Profit Maximization

We have considered two different approaches to profit maximization. One approach looks at the explicit relationship between profits and production. The other compares the price to the marginal cost. Both give the same answer. How do the approaches compare?

In Table 6.3 we looked at several prices, and we derived the profit-maximizing level of production by looking at profits for different levels of production at these prices. To do so, we had to create a new table for each price. This process is quite time-consuming. In contrast, with the marginal cost approach, we only had to look at marginal cost for each unit of production and compare it with the price. Thus, the price-equals-marginal cost approach is considerably easier. Moreover, because marginal-cost increases as the number of items produced increases, the price-equals-marginal-cost approach tells us why the supply curve slopes upward. It is for these two reasons that economists usually use the price-equals-marginal-cost approach.

REVIEW

- The supply curve for a firm is derived by assuming that the firm chooses the quantity of production that maximizes profits. Profits are the difference between total revenue and total costs.
- As price changes, the profit-maximizing quantity changes as well. The relationship between price and the profit-maximizing quantity is the firm's supply curve.
- A profit table is an accurate if long-winded way of determining the profit-maximizing quantity produced by a firm for a given price. As the price changes, the profits calculated in the table change, providing a different profit-maximizing quantity.
- For the pumpkin-producing firm, the profit-maximizing quantity increased with price, resulting in an upward sloping supply curve.
- A less work-intensive way of calculating the profit maximizing quantity is to consider the marginal revenue and the marginal cost of an additional unit of production. If marginal revenue exceeds marginal cost, then profits would go up with the additional unit of production. If marginal revenue is less than marginal cost, then profits would go down with the additional unit of production.
- A profit-maximizing firm therefore would produce at a quantity such that marginal revenue equaled marginal cost.
- For a competitive firm, marginal revenue equals the price of the good, because the firm's production decisions do not affect the market price. Therefore, the profit-maximizing quantity easily can be found as the quantity that equates the marginal cost with the price of the good.
- Marginal cost increases as the quantity produced increases. Therefore, as price rises, the profit maximizing firm will respond by increasing the quantity it produces. In other words, the upward sloping marginal cost curve implies an upward-sloping supply curve.

4. THE MARKET SUPPLY CURVE

The *market* supply curve can be obtained by adding up the supply curves of all the *individual* firms in the market. Figure 6.11 gives an example of two individual firm supply curves for pumpkins: One curve corresponds to your pumpkin firm, and the other, which is identical to yours, corresponds to the firm of your competitor, Fred, who is growing pumpkins on the other side of town. You and Fred have the same marginal cost for pumpkin growing, so your supply curves are exactly the same. You both will choose to produce the same number of pumpkins if the price is the same.

If only you and Fred are in the market, the market supply curve is the sum of just your two supplies. You get the market curve by adding in the horizontal direction, as shown in Figure 6.11. For example, if the price is \$30, the quantity supplied by Fred will be two crates, and the quantity you supply will be two crates; thus, the quantity supplied in the market at \$30 is four crates. If the price rises to \$50, Fred will produce three crates and you also will produce three crates; thus, the quantity supplied in the market rises to six crates.

In reality, of course, a competitive market has more than two firms, and the individual supply curves for different firms in the market usually are different. But the concept of deriving the market supply curve is the same whether there are only 2 firms or 2,000 firms, and whether they are all the same or are all different. After adding up the individual supply curves for all the firms in the market, we arrive at a market supply curve like Figure 6.1. Thus, we have fulfilled one of the objectives of this chapter—deriving the market supply curve.

FIGURE 6.11 Derivation of the Market Supply Curve

The market supply curve is the sum of the individual firms' supply curves for all the firms in the market. The figure shows how the supply curves of two firms—Fred's and yours—sum to a market supply curve.

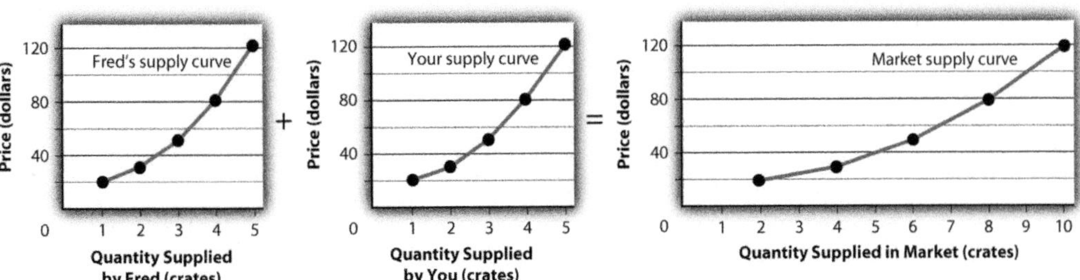

If a market has many different firms, the market supply curve can be much smoother than the individual supply curves. For example, a general contractor may be able to build only one house a year. But the market for new houses in any one year consists of many contractors with many different marginal costs. As the price of new houses rises, more and more contractors will build houses, and the market supply curve for houses will look smooth.

4.1 The Slope of the Supply Curve

We have shown that the slope and position of the individual firms' supply curves depend on the marginal cost at the different firms. If marginal cost rises very sharply with more production, then the supply curve will be very steep. If marginal cost increases more gradually, then the supply curve will be flatter.

Because the market supply curve is the sum of the individual firms' supply curves, its slope also will depend on marginal cost. The market supply curve can get steep at high levels of production because marginal cost gets high when production is high.

4.2 Shifts in the Supply Curve

Because the supply curve for the individual firm is given by its marginal cost, anything that changes marginal cost will shift the individual supply curves and therefore the market supply curve. For example, a new technology might reduce the marginal cost at every level of production. If this happens, then the marginal cost curve will shift down and the profit-maximizing quantity for each price level will increase. Observe that a downward shift of the marginal cost curve is equivalent to a rightward shift of the supply curve. Similarly, an increase in marginal cost—perhaps because of a disease affecting the pumpkins, so that more labor is required for each crate of pumpkins—would shift the supply curve upward or to the left (see Figure 6.12).

FIGURE 6.12 **Shifts in the Market Supply Curve**

An increase in marginal cost would shift the supply curve upward or to the left.

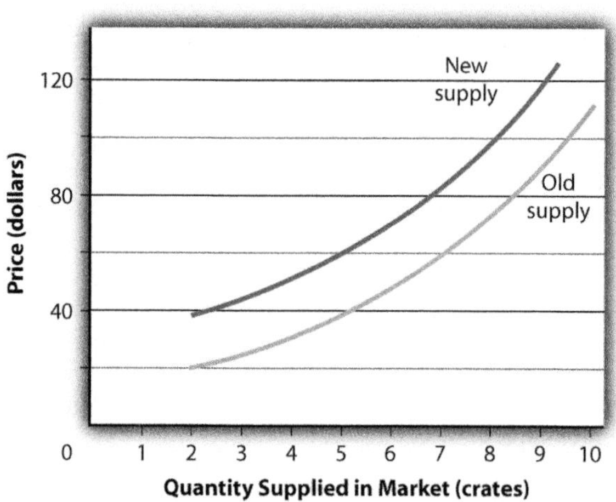

REVIEW

- The market supply curve is derived by adding up the individual supply curves of all the firms in the market.
- When the price rises, the individual firms in the market increase the quantity supplied. Hence, the market supply curve is upward sloping.
- The slope of the supply curve depends on how sharply marginal cost increases. If marginal cost rises sharply with more production, then the supply curve will be steep. If marginal cost does not change much as production increases, the supply curve will be flat.
- Anything that raises marginal cost will shift the market supply curve upward or to the left. Conversely, anything that lowers marginal cost will shift the market supply curve downward or to the right.

5. PRODUCER SURPLUS

In Chapter 5, we learned about consumer surplus, the difference between the marginal benefit derived from consuming an additional item and the price paid for it, as a measure of how well off consumers are. We can derive a similar concept for measuring how well off producers are by engaging in the production of goods for the market. **Producer surplus** is defined as the difference between the marginal cost of an item and the price received for it. For example, suppose that the price of pumpkins is $25, at which price you produce one crate of pumpkins. Then you get $25 for producing one crate and incur $20 in marginal cost. The difference, $5, is your producer surplus for producing that first crate of pumpkins. If the price of pumpkins is $35, you produce two crates and your producer surplus is $15 ($35 – $20) for the first crate plus $5 ($35 – $30) for the second crate, for a total producer surplus of $20.

Producer surplus

The difference between the price received by a firm for an additional item sold and the marginal cost of the item's production; for the market as a whole, it is the sum of all the individual firms' producer surpluses, or the area above the market supply curve and below the market price.

5.1 A Graphic Representation of Producer Surplus

Producer surplus can be represented graphically as the area above the individual firm supply curve and below the price line, as illustrated in Figure 6.13. Producer surplus in the whole market can be obtained by adding up producer surplus for all producers or by looking at the area above the market supply curve and below the price. This is illustrated in Figure 6.14. Producer surplus provides a measure of how much a producer gains from the market. The sum of producer surplus plus consumer surplus is a comprehensive measure of how well a market economy works, as we will see in Chapter 7.

5.2 The Difference between Profits and Producer Surplus

Profits and producer surplus are not the same thing. Profits are the difference between total revenue and total costs, while the producer surplus measures the difference between the price and the marginal cost of every unit. How can we compare these two measures?

Suppose the price of pumpkins is $70 per crate; then you are willing to produce three crates of pumpkins. Total revenue is $210 and total costs are $150; thus, you are making a $60 profit. (See Panel II of Table 6.3.) How much is your producer surplus when three crates are sold at $70? As just defined,

$$\text{Producer Surplus} = (P - MC_1) + (P - MC_2) + (P - MC_3)$$

$$(\$70 - \$20) + (\$70 - \$30) + (\$70 - \$50) = \$110$$

where MC_1 is the marginal cost of the first crate, MC_2 is the marginal cost of the second crate, and MC_3 is the marginal cost of the third crate. Thus, profits are $60 and producer surplus is $110.

FIGURE 6.13 Producer Surplus for an Individual Firm

As shown here, for an individual firm, the producer surplus is the area between the price line and the supply curve.

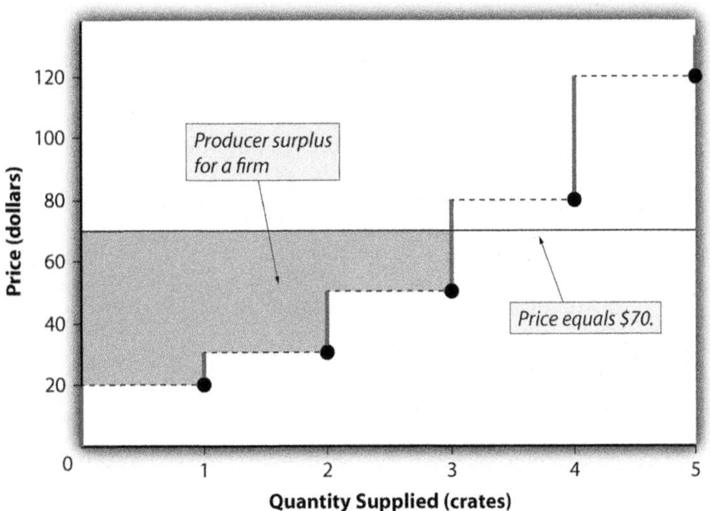

FIGURE 6.14 Producer Surplus for the Market

If we add up producer surplus for every firm, we get the producer surplus for the whole market. This surplus is given by the area between the price and the market supply curve.

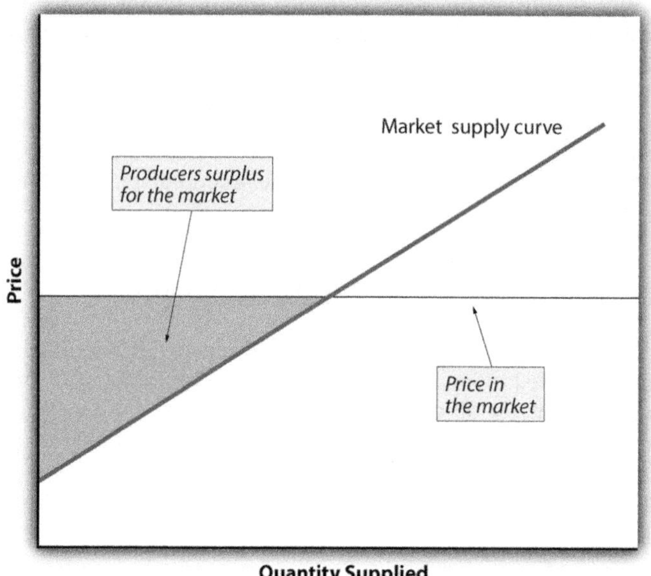

Notice the \$50 difference between producer surplus and profits. Try doing the same calculation for a price of \$100. Panel III of Table 6.3 tells us that profits are \$170, and you can calculate producer surplus to be equal to (\$80 + \$70 + \$50 + \$20) or \$220. Once again producer surplus and profits have a difference of \$50. If you try using this method for different prices and quantities sold, you will arrive at the same result. Note that \$50 is equal to the fixed costs of the firm. Producer surplus equals profit plus fixed costs. We now show that this is not a coincidence.

When the producer sells a quantity *Q*, we can say that

$$\text{Producer Surplus} = (P - MC_1) + (P - MC_2) + (P - MC_3) + \cdots + (P - MC_Q)$$

The number of terms in this sum is *Q*. For the example above, *Q* = 3 and *Q* terms were included in the sum. Thus, we can translate this definition of producer surplus into the price (*P*) of the good times the quantity (*Q*) sold minus the sum of the marginal costs of all units. That is,

$$\text{Producer surplus} = P \times Q - \text{sum of marginal costs}$$

Because P × Q is total revenue, we can write the above equation as

$$\text{Producer surplus} = \text{total revenue} - \text{sum of marginal costs}$$

The marginal cost of an additional unit is the additional costs incurred in producing that unit of output. Thus, as we sum up marginal costs for any quantity *Q* produced, we count all costs associated with increasing production from zero units to *Q* units. To obtain total costs, we would need to add fixed costs, the cost of producing zero units, to the above sum. In other words,

$$\text{Total costs} = \text{sum of marginal costs} + \text{fixed costs}$$

This can be rearranged to show that

$$\text{Sum of marginal costs} = \text{total costs} - \text{fixed costs}$$

Substituting into the definition of producer surplus, we can see therefore that

$$\text{Producer surplus} = \text{total revenue} - (\text{total costs} - \text{fixed costs})$$

This implies that

$$\text{Producer surplus} = \text{total revenue} - \text{total costs} + \text{fixed costs}$$

which gives us the result we want to understand—the difference between profits and producer surplus, namely that

Producer surplus = total profits + fixed costs

REVIEW

- Producer surplus associated with an item is the difference between the price a firm receives for selling that item and the marginal cost of producing that item. It is a measure of how well off producers are as a result of their decision to produce that item.
- Graphically, producer surplus for a firm is the area below the price line and above the firm's supply curve.
- For all the firms in a market, the producer surplus is the area below the price line and above the market supply curve.
- Producer surplus is different from profits. Producer surplus is greater than profits by the amount of fixed costs.

6. END-OF-CHAPTER MATERIALS

6.1 Conclusion

In this chapter, we derived the supply curve in a competitive market by looking at the behavior of firms. We assumed that a firm decides how much to produce at a given market price by choosing the quantity that maximizes profits. The firm makes this decision taking prices as given and considering its production function, which relates the number of hours of work at the firm to the output of the firm. The production function enters the firm's profit calculations through its effects on the firm's costs. Because the production function has diminishing returns to labor, the firm faces increasing marginal cost.

Profit maximization implies that the firm will produce the quantity for which marginal revenue equals marginal cost. In a competitive market, the marginal revenue from selling an additional unit always equals the price. Therefore the profit-maximizing quantity is the amount at which price equals marginal cost.

As the price rises, the firm will respond by increasing production until marginal cost and price are equal again. As a result, the supply curve for an individual firm will be upward sloping. The slope of the supply curve will be steep when marginal cost increases rapidly as more units are produced, and it will be flat when marginal cost does not rise by very much as more units are produced. The supply curve will shift out when marginal cost falls because of some event like a change in technology and shift in when marginal cost rises.

The connection between marginal cost and the supply curve is fundamental to understanding how markets work. We will make use of this connection many times throughout this book, especially when we consider public policy issues, such as the efficiency of markets, taxation, and regulation of firms. When economists see or draw a supply curve, they usually are thinking about the marginal cost of the firms that underlie the supply curve. The supply curve and the marginal cost curve are virtually synonymous for economists.

We have examined firm behavior in this chapter and consumer behavior in Chapter 5. In Chapter 7, we will examine the interactions of these firms and consumers. In Chapter 5 and Chapter 6, we derived two rules for characterizing individual and firm behavior: Profit maximizing firms will produce according to the price equals marginal cost rule, while utility-maximizing consumers will consume according to the price equals marginal benefit rule. In Chapter 7, we will combine these two concepts to point out an attractive feature of competitive markets.

Key Points

1. A firm is an organization that uses inputs to produce goods or services.
2. In a competitive market, no single firm can affect the price.
3. The foundations of supply are found in the profit maximizing behavior of firms, with each firm's supply curve being derived as the profit maximizing quantity that corresponds to various possible market prices.
4. Profits are defined as total revenue minus total costs. Total revenue increases as the quantity sold increases. Total costs, which are the sum of fixed costs and variable costs, also increase with production.
5. The change in total costs when production is increased is called marginal cost. How large marginal cost is depends on the production function, which shows how many inputs are needed for producing different quantities of output. Marginal cost increases as more is produced because of diminishing returns to inputs.
6. A firm produces up to the point at which marginal revenue equals marginal cost, which is the key rule for profit maximization. In a competitive market, marginal revenue always equals the price of the good. Therefore, the profit-maximizing quantity for a price-taking firm easily can be found as the quantity such that price equals marginal cost.
7. The reason the supply curve slopes upward is that marginal cost is increasing. A higher price enables the firm to produce at higher levels of marginal cost. The marginal cost curve and the supply curve are virtually synonymous.
8. The market supply curve is obtained by adding up the individual supply curves. The market supply curve can be smooth even if the individual supply curves are not.
9. Producer surplus is the difference between the price of a good and its marginal cost of production. Graphically, producer surplus for an individual firm is the area above the individual supply curve and below the price line. The producer surplus for all firms in the market is the area above the market supply curve and below the price line.
10. Producer surplus and profit are not the same thing. Producer surplus equals profits plus fixed costs.

QUESTIONS FOR REVIEW

1. What is a firm?
2. What is the definition of a competitive market?
3. Describe the relationships that exist among total costs, fixed costs, variable costs, and marginal cost.
4. Why does marginal cost increase as more is produced?
5. Why does profit maximization imply that marginal revenue equals marginal cost? Why is it that in a competitive market only, profit maximization implies that price equals marginal cost?
6. What is the relationship between an individual firm's supply curve and its marginal cost curve?
7. How is the market supply curve derived from individual supply curves?
8. Why might the market supply curve be smoother than the individual supply curves?
9. What is producer surplus and how is it calculated?
10. How does producer surplus differ from profits?

PROBLEMS

1. Name three businesses in which firms are price takers. Name three businesses in which firms are not price-takers. Suppose you set up a business through which you tutor students on campus. Would you be a price-taker or a price-maker?
2. Does the assumption that firms are price-takers in a market seem less valid than the assumption that consumers are price-takers in that market? Explain why. Would your answer change if you were told that the market included 50 firms and 50 consumers? Explain.
3. Before the Industrial Revolution, people lived in agricultural societies. What are the two primary inputs to production in an agricultural society? Which one of these inputs is variable and which one is fixed? Why is there reason to believe that the rate of growth of the food supply will slow down as the population increases?
4. Consider the example of the cost of pumpkins in Table 6.3. Compute the total revenue, total costs, and profits when the price of a crate of pumpkins is $60. How many crates of pumpkins will maximize profits? Now find the profit-maximizing quantity by using the marginal cost approach. How do your answers compare? Which approach did you find easier?
5. The following table shows the total costs of producing strawberries on a small plot of land.

Pounds of Strawberries	Total Costs (dollars)
0	10
1	11
2	14
3	18
4	25
5	34

   a. Calculate the marginal cost schedule.
   b. Draw the farmer's supply curve.
   c. Suppose the price of 1 pound of strawberries is $4. How much would this farmer produce? What are profits?
   d. Suppose the price of strawberries goes up to$7 per pound. How much will the farmer produce now? What are profits now?

6. Suppose a price-taking producer of barrels for storing wine has the following total costs schedule:

Quantity	Total Costs
0	20
1	30
2	42
3	55
4	75
5	100
6	130

   a. Calculate marginal cost. If the price of a barrel in the market is $20, how many barrels will the firm produce?
   b. Suppose the price in the market falls to $12 per barrel. How many barrels will this firm produce in order to maximize profits?
   c. Suppose an improvement in technology shifts total costs down by $8 at every level of production. How much will the firm produce and what will profits be at a price of $20 and at a price of $12?

7. Consider the following information:

Daily Production and Costs at Jill's Bread Bakers	
Quantity Produced (dozens of loaves)	*Total Cost (dollars)*
0	20
1	22
2	26
3	32
4	40
5	50
6	62
7	76

   a. Calculate the marginal cost for Jill's bread production.
   b. Draw the supply curve for this firm.
   c. Jill can sell as many loaves as she wants in the market at a price of $12 for a dozen loaves. How many loaves will she sell each day? What are her profits?
   d. Use your diagram to show how much producer surplus Jill receives.
8. Suppose you are able to mow lawns at $12 per hour. The only cost to you is the opportunity cost of your time. For the first three hours, the opportunity cost of your time is $9 per hour. But after three hours, the opportunity cost of your time rises to $15 per hour because of other commitments. Draw the marginal cost to you of mowing lawns. On that diagram, draw in the price you receive for mowing loans, indicate for how long you will mow lawns, and graphically indicate the area of your producer surplus in addition to calculating the magnitude of your producer surplus.
9. Consider the following information about a firm that sells ice cream–making machines:

Quantity	Total Costs	Total Revenue
0	500	0
1	700	500
2	1,100	1,000
3	1,500	1,500
4	2,300	2,000
5	3,500	2,500

   a. On a single diagram, plot the total revenues and total costs curves for this firm.
   b. What are the maximum profits that this firm can earn?
   c. Show this level of profits in the diagram.
   d. What is the relationship between the slopes of the two curves at the quantity that maximizes profits?
10. What is the relationship between producer surplus, profits, and fixed costs? In what types of industries would you expect producer surplus to be high while profits are low? Provide one or two examples of such industries.

ENDNOTES

1. http://www.latimes.com/business/la-fi-shopkins-20161121-story.html

CHAPTER 7
The Efficiency of Markets

This is an old but true story, going back to before the field of economics even existed. It is about an absent-minded philosophy professor who was interested in understanding human interaction. He was particularly fascinated by how the economy, consisting of the interaction of millions of people pursuing their own interests, worked. He did not have much to go on; his school, or any other school, did not have economics professors. So, although he was a gifted teacher, he quit his teaching job at the university and traveled; he interviewed business people; he visited factories; he talked to workers; he watched ships come and go; he studied the economies of other countries and of other times. Amazingly, he not only was able to pull all this material together into a coherent view, but also managed to get it down on paper for other people to read, learn, and enjoy. By doing so, he invented the field of economics and presented a view of the economy that is still the dominant view in the twenty-first century.

The professor's name was Adam Smith, and the book he wrote, called Wealth of Nations, was first published in 1776. His deepest insight, among many deep insights, is called the **invisible hand** theorem, best stated using his own words: "It is not from the benevolence of the butcher, the brewer, or the baker that we expect our dinner, but from their regard to their own interest." And whether it is the butcher, the brewer, or the baker, he is "led by an invisible hand to promote an end which was no part of his intention....By pursuing his own interest he frequently promotes that of the society more effectually than when he really intends to promote it." In other words, without any formal coordination, firms (butchers, brewers, bakers, and many others) that are pursuing their own interests interact with consumers who also are pursuing their own interests, and somehow everyone ends up producing and consuming a quantity that is efficient.

Source: © Shutterstock, Inc.

The main goal of this chapter is to state clearly and prove the invisible hand theorem. The theorem is not always true, and we want to be clear about the circumstances in which it is true. We first need to explain what is meant by efficient (the modern term for Smith's "effectual"), and then show why and under what circumstances the quantity produced and consumed is efficient. We also show how to measure the economic loss from producing more or less than the efficient quantity.

invisible hand

The idea that the free interaction of people in a market economy leads to a desirable social outcome; the term was coined by Adam Smith.

competitive equilibrium model

A model that assumes utility maximization on the part of consumers and profit maximization on the part of firms, along with competitive markets and freely determined prices.

Chapter 5 and Chapter 6 have paved the way for our goal in this chapter. In Chapter 5, we studied the behavior of consumers. We can say that consumers who maximize their utility are pursuing their own interests. In Chapter 6, we studied the behavior of firms. We can say that firms that maximize profits also are pursuing their own interests. Now we study the interactions of firms and consumers in competitive markets. Figure 7.1 is a schematic illustration of the model we use to explain this interaction and thereby explain the invisible hand theorem. The model, called the **competitive equilibrium model**, is the supply and demand model discussed in Chapter 3, now with the behavior of consumers and firms explicit.

1. INDIVIDUAL CONSUMERS AND FIRMS IN A MARKET

In our analysis of economic interaction, it is important to think about what individual consumers and firms are doing. Consider an example of consumers and producers of the same commodity: long-stemmed roses. Maria and Ken are two of many potential rose consumers who are deciding how many roses to buy. Both are willing to pay a certain amount for roses, but not necessarily the same amount. Hugo and Mimi are two of many rose producers who are deciding how many roses to produce in their gardens. They both are willing to sell roses provided the price is right, but they have different marginal costs for producing roses.

1.1 The Hard Way to Process Information, Coordinate, and Motivate

The actions of Maria, Ken, Hugo, Mimi, and all the others in the market clearly have an effect on one another. For example, an increase in Hugo's marginal costs—perhaps because of the need to use a new pesticide to ward off an insect infestation—probably will reduce the number of roses he decides to produce; either this means less rose consumption for Ken, Maria, and other consumers, or it means more rose production for Mimi and other producers. Similarly, if Ken finds a new romantic interest and decides to purchase more roses on a weekly basis, someone else must decide to decrease consumption or to increase production.

FIGURE 7.1 The Interaction of Buyers and Sellers in the Marketplace

In this chapter, we explain how individual buyers and sellers interact in a market by combining the behavior of consumers (Chapter 5) with the behavior of firms (Chapter 6) to get a model of competitive equilibrium (Chapter 7).

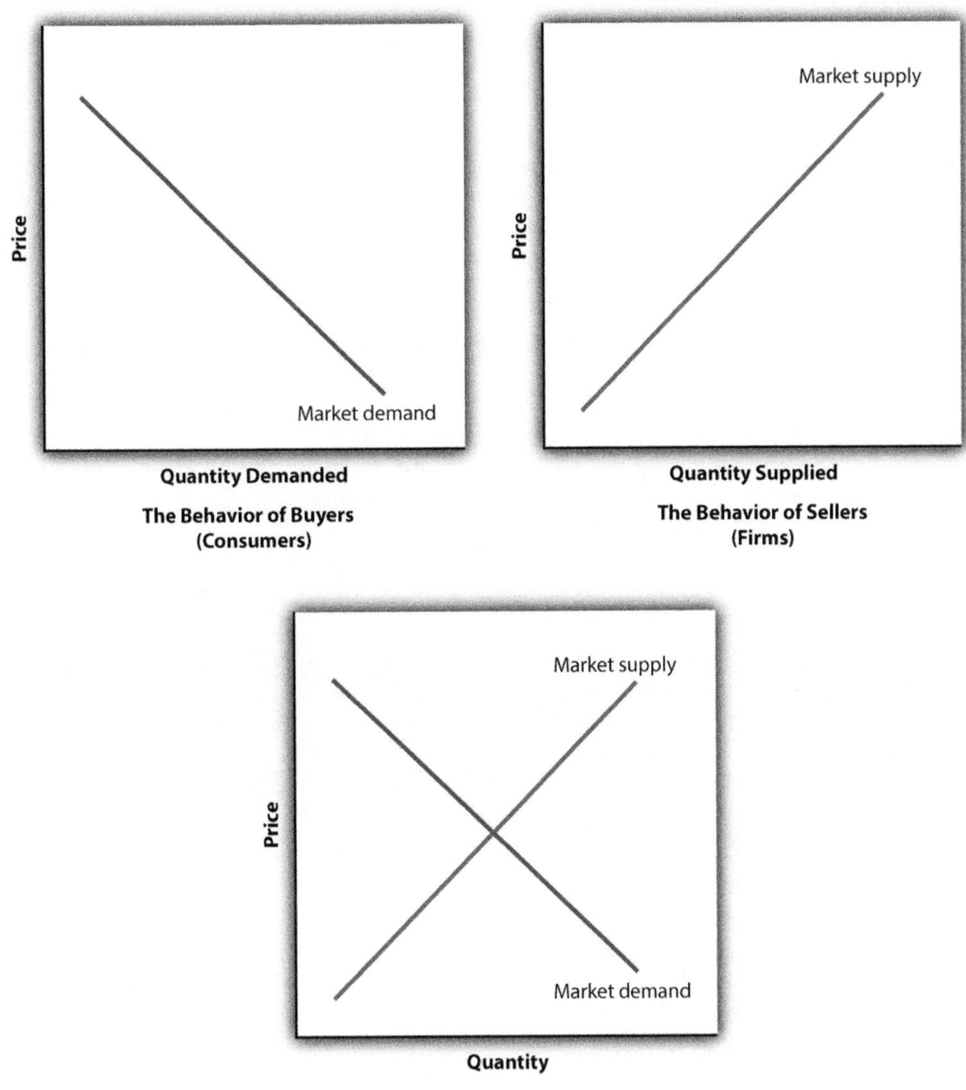

How are all these decisions worked out? What *information* is needed to determine that an increase in rose production is needed to meet the additional demand coming from Ken or to cover the shortfall in production coming from Hugo? Who *coordinates* whether the production increases needed to meet Ken's demand comes from Hugo's garden or Mimi's garden? Who decides whether Maria should cut back her consumption or Mimi should increase her production in response to Hugo's production cutbacks? What *motivates* Hugo, Mimi, and others to produce more if consumption rises, or motivates Ken, Maria, and other consumers to consume less if production falls?

Suppose you had to work out all these issues. To make your job easier, suppose that Maria, Ken, Hugo, and Mimi were the whole world as far as roses go. If you and they were all in one place together, you might imagine providing information so that they could adjust their consumption and production activities to respond to changing market conditions. When more production was needed, you would inform Mimi of the problems that Hugo was having and ask her to increase the number of roses she produces to make up for the shortfall. When Ken started buying more roses, you would have to explain to Maria about Ken's new romantic interest and ask her to cut back on her consumption, or you would have to inform Hugo and Mimi that they need to increase production to meet Ken's insatiable demand for roses.

But simply providing information is not enough. You also would have to coordinate the responses of the various consumers and firms. In response to Ken's increased purchases of roses, for example, you would have to determine how much of the extra output was being produced by Mimi and how much was being produced by Hugo. You also would have to ensure that Maria's consumption plans had not changed in the meantime. Coordinating the actions of even two consumers and two firms can be a challenge.

Even if you provided sufficient information, and in spite of your best attempts at coordinating everyone's responses, there would be no guarantee that either the consumers or the producers would change their behavior unless they had a reason for doing so. To provide motivation, you might reason with Mimi that she could sell more now that Hugo had production problems, or plead with Maria to cut back on her rose purchases until Ken's romantic fervor cools, or cajole Hugo and Mimi to increase production.

If this is not already beginning to sound ridiculously impossible, remember that if you had this job in the real world, you would have to coordinate, motivate, and know intimately millions of consumers and producers. This is an amazingly complex job even for this single, relatively simple commodity.

1.2 The Easy Way to Process Information, Coordinate, and Motivate

One-Stop Shopping for Processing Information, Coordinating, and Motivating: The Market. This flower vendor in Barcelona, Spain represents just one piece of the huge and multifaceted market for flowers that exists throughout the world.

Source: © Gordana Sermek / Shutterstock, Inc.

Fortunately, you do not need to worry about being called on to perform such an impossible task. What Adam Smith showed was that a remarkable device does the information processing, coordinating, and motivating for us. No one person invented this device; it evolved slowly over thousands of years and probably is still evolving. It is called the *market.* Of course, like many markets, the rose market does not take place in any one location. It consists of all the florists, street carts, and farmers' markets where roses are sold and all the gardens and greenhouses where roses are grown, whether in the United States, Europe, Latin America, Africa, Australia, or Asia. Fortunately, a market can serve as an information-processing, coordinating, and motivating device even if it does not take place at any one location. In fact, buyers and sellers never even have to see one another.

How does the market work? What will be the total quantity of roses consumed? Who will consume what amount? What will be the total quantity of roses produced? Which firm will produce what amount? Let us see how economists answer these questions about how people interact in a market.

1.3 The Competitive Equilibrium Model

Economists use the *individual* demand curves and the *individual* supply curves derived in Chapter 5 and Chapter 6 to describe what happens to consumers and firms when they interact in a market.

Recall that each of the individual demand curves depends on the marginal benefit—the willingness to pay for additional consumption—the individual gets from consuming a good. Together, these marginal benefits create a market demand curve for roses. The demand curve shows how much consumers in total are willing to buy at each price.

Recall also that individual supply curves depend on the marginal costs of the firms.Together, their marginal costs create a market supply curve for roses. The supply curve shows the total quantity supplied by all firms at each price.

The resulting market demand and supply curves are shown in the center of Figure 7.2, flanked by Maria's and Ken's individual demand curves and by Hugo's and Mimi's individual supply curves. We continue to assume that Maria, Ken, Hugo, and Mimi are the whole market so that we can show the market in one diagram. A competitive market typically would require more buyers and sellers. The price (*P*, measured in dollars per rose) is on the vertical axis, and the quantity (*Q*, the number of roses) is on the horizontal axis.

We have seen supply and demand curves like those in the center of Figure 7.2 before in Chapter 3. But now—after Chapter 5 and Chapter 6—we know much more about what the demand and supply curves mean. Individual consumer behavior and individual firm behavior now are seen as underlying the supply and demand model. To emphasize that the supply and demand model incorporates utility-maximizing consumers and profit-maximizing firms in competitive markets, we refer to it as the *competitive equilibrium model.* Making the behavior of consumers and firms more explicit implies that we can do more analysis with the competitive equilibrium model than we previously were able to do with the supply and demand model.

Individual Production and Consumption Decisions

A key prediction of the competitive equilibrium model is that a price will emerge from the interaction of people in the market such that the quantity supplied *equals* the quantity demanded. This is the **equilibrium price**. Graphically, the price is given at the point of intersection of the market supply curve and the market demand curve; here, the quantity supplied in the market equals the quantity demanded in the market. For the example shown in Figure 7.2, the equilibrium price is $0.90 a rose.

equilibrium price

The price at which quantity supplied equals quantity demanded.

Once we have determined the price in this way, the supply and demand curves tell us how much in total will be consumed and produced at that price. We look at the market demand curve and see how much is demanded at that price, and we look at the market supply curve and see how much is supplied at that price. Because the curves intersect at the market price, the quantity demanded and the quantity supplied are the same. They are at the point on the horizontal axis directly below the intersection. In Figure 7.2, the quantity bought and sold is eight roses.

Thus far, we have not done anything more with the competitive equilibrium model than we did with the supply and demand model. But now, armed with the price, we can go to the individual demand curves to see how much Maria and Ken will buy. Look to the left in Figure 7.2 to find the quantity demanded by Maria and by Ken when the price is $0.90 a rose. They each buy four roses. Maria and Ken are motivated to buy this amount—without any central coordinator—because, at $0.90 a rose, they maximize their respective utilities by consuming this amount. Observe that Maria and Ken do not have the same individual demand curves. Nevertheless, the quantity demanded by each still can be determined from their demand curves, as shown in Figure 7.2.

FIGURE 7.2 Prince and Quantity Determination

The market demand curve is the sum of the individual demand curves of the consumers in the market. The market supply curve is the sum of the individual supply curves for the producers. When quantity demanded equals quantity supplied, the two curves intersect. The equilibrium price and quantity will be given by this intersection. The individual firm and consumer decisions then can be read off the individual supply and demand curves at those prices.

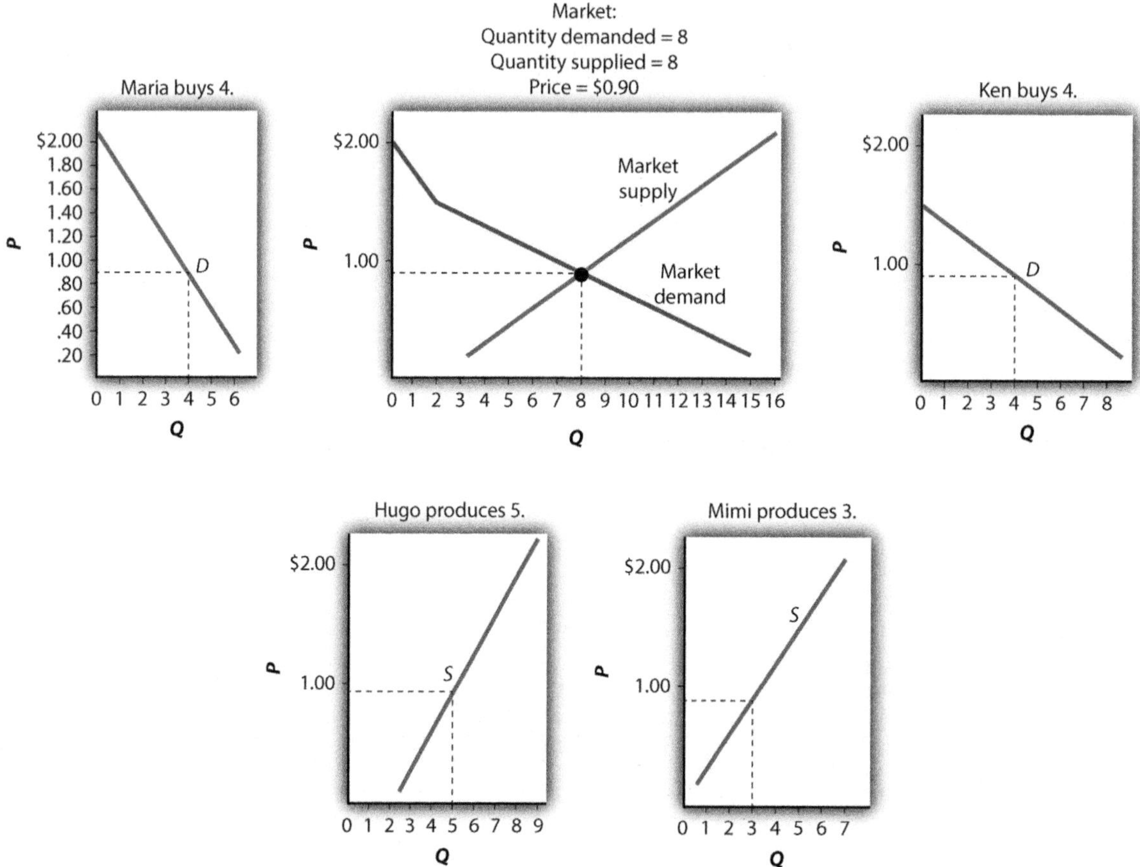

The individual supply curves tell us how much Hugo and Mimi will produce. Look to the bottom in Figure 7.2 to see how much Hugo and Mimi produce when the price is $0.90 a rose. Hugo produces five roses, and Mimi produces three roses. Hugo and Mimi are motivated to produce this amount—again without any central coordinator—because, at $0.90 a rose, they maximize their profits by producing this amount. In sum, the competitive equilibrium model, which includes the behavior of the consumers and the firms, not only predicts the equilibrium price and quantity in the market, but also predicts the quantity consumed by each person and the quantity produced by each firm.

Adjustment to the Equilibrium Price

surplus

A situation in which quantity supplied is greater than quantity demanded.

shortage

A situation in which quantity demanded is greater than quantity supplied.

In Figure 7.2, consider what would happen if the price were higher than the price at the intersection of the supply curve and the demand curve, say $1.20. At that price, utility-maximizing consumers like Ken and Maria would decrease their consumption to three units (Maria) and two units (Ken), so the quantity demanded would be five units. However, at the higher price, profit maximizers like Hugo and Mimi would increase their production, with Hugo producing six units and Mimi producing four units. The quantity supplied would exceed the quantity demanded; there would be a **surplus** in the market. When surplus appears, the price will fall, resulting in demand increasing and supply decreasing until the surplus disappears.

Conversely, suppose the price were lower than the predicted market price, say $0.60. At that price, utility maximizers like Ken and Maria would increase consumption to six units (Ken) and five units (Maria), so the quantity demanded would be 11 units. However, at the lower price, profit maximizers like Hugo and Mimi would decrease their production, with Hugo producing four units and Mimi producing two units. The quantity supplied would be much less than the quantity demanded; there would be a **shortage** in the market. When a shortage appears, the price will rise, resulting in demand decreasing and supply increasing until the shortage disappears. Thus, if the price falls when there is a surplus and rises when there is a shortage, the actions of profit-maximizing firms and utility-maximizing consumers will ensure that the price will converge to the equilibrium price.

REVIEW

- Centrally coordinating and motivating the thousands of consumers and producers of any good would be an amazingly complex task requiring a vast amount of information.
- The market is a device that provides information and coordinates and motivates consumers and producers in a decentralized way. The market does this job in a way that no one individual can.
- Economists describe the interactions of people in the market through the competitive equilibrium model, which is the supply and demand model with consumer and firm behavior made more explicit.
- According to the model, the equilibrium price and quantity are given by the intersection of the market supply and demand curves. At the equilibrium price, we can use the individual demand curves to find out each individual's decisions about consumption and use the individual firms' supply curves to figure out each firm's production decisions.

2. ARE COMPETITIVE MARKETS EFFICIENT?

We have shown how to use the competitive equilibrium model to explain *how* a market works. Now let's use the competitive equilibrium model to see *how well* the market works. Are the quantities produced and consumed in the market efficient?

2.1 The Meaning of Efficient

In general, an inefficient outcome is one that wastes scarce resources, and an efficient outcome is one that does not waste scarce resources. Extremely inefficient economic outcomes are easy to spot. Constructing 300 million new coffeehouses each year in the United States (or approximately one store per person) obviously would be wasteful. The workers building the new stores could be building other things that people wanted. If the U.S. economy produced such an outcome, everyone would say it was inefficient; shifting production to fewer coffeehouses clearly would make many people better off.

An equally inefficient situation would occur if only one new coffeehouse a year were built; at that rate, it would take more than 7,000 years to match the number of Starbucks stores that now exist in the United States. In such a situation, shifting production toward more coffeehouses clearly would make many people better off.

Both of these situations are inefficient because a change in production could make people better off. We might, therefore, define an efficient outcome as one that is so good that no change would make people better off.

The Need for a More Precise Definition

Because the economy consists of many different people, however, we need to be more careful in defining efficiency. For every economic outcome, it is possible to make someone better off at the expense of someone else. If someone takes a long-stemmed rose from Maria and gives it to Ken, then Ken is better off, but Maria is worse off. More generally, the possibility of transferring a good from one person to another, thereby making someone better off at the expense of someone else, is not an indication that an economic situation is inefficient or wasteful.

However, if a situation existed in which it was possible to change consumption or production in a way that would make someone better off without hurting someone else, then that situation would be inefficient. In such a situation, resources are being wasted, because someone, perhaps many people, could have a better life without someone else being harmed.

Based on such considerations, economists have developed the following definition of efficiency: An outcome is **Pareto efficient** if it is not possible to make someone better off without hurting someone else. The Italian economist Vilfredo Pareto is the person who developed this concept of efficiency. Economists use the term *Pareto* to distinguish this definition of efficiency from other meanings, but unless we say otherwise, when we use the term *efficient* in this chapter, we mean efficient in the sense of Pareto. If a market is not efficient in the sense of Pareto, then something is wrong with the market.

Pareto efficient

A situation in which it is not possible to make someone better off without making someone else worse off.

Three Conditions for Efficient Outcomes

Three conditions must hold if a market outcome is to be efficient in the sense of Pareto efficient.

First, the marginal benefit (MB) must equal the marginal cost (MC) of the last item produced. Why is this condition needed for efficiency? Suppose it did not hold. If the marginal cost of the last item produced is greater than the marginal benefit, then too much is being produced. In the example of producing 300 million coffeehouses a year, the marginal cost of producing the 300 millionth coffeehouse is much greater than the marginal benefit. Reducing production (by a lot) would be appropriate. If the marginal cost of the last item produced is less than the marginal benefit, then too little is being produced. In the example of producing only one coffeehouse a year, the marginal cost is certainly much less than the marginal benefit; more production would be appropriate. Only when marginal benefit is equal to marginal cost is the economic outcome efficient.

One way to better appreciate this condition is to imagine that you grow your own roses in your own garden. Clearly you would never produce more roses if the marginal cost to you was greater than the marginal benefit to you. But you would produce more roses if your marginal benefit from more roses was greater than your marginal cost. Only when marginal benefit equals marginal cost would you stop producing and consuming more.

The second condition for efficiency relates to the production of goods at different firms. It is that *the marginal cost of a good should be equal for every producer.* Again, if this were not the case, then production could be increased without increasing costs. For example, if Hugo's rose garden could produce an extra dozen roses at a marginal cost of $10 and Mimi's rose garden could produce an extra dozen roses at a marginal cost of $50, then it would make sense for Mimi to reduce her production of roses by a dozen, saving her $50, and use that money to pay Hugo to produce two dozen roses that she could then sell on the market. Both Hugo and Mimi would be better off as a result. Only when the marginal costs are the same can production increase without cost. It is not necessary for Hugo and Mimi or any other producer to be the same or even to have the same total costs; all that we require for efficiency is that the *marginal* costs be the same.

The third condition for efficiency relates to the allocation of goods to different consumers. It is that *the marginal benefit of consuming the same good should be equal for all consumers.* If the marginal benefits were not equal, then there could be a gain for some people with no loss for anyone else. For example, suppose Ken's marginal benefit from a rose was $3 and Maria's was $1; then if Maria sold a rose to Ken for $2, both would be better off. But if their marginal benefits were the same, then no improvement for one without harming the other would be possible.

In sum, three conditions are needed for efficiency: (1) the marginal benefit equals the marginal cost for the last item produced; (2) the marginal cost of producing each good is equal for all producers; and (3) the marginal benefit from consuming each good is equal for all consumers.

First efficiency condition: *MB = MC for last item produced.*
Second efficiency condition: *Every producer's MC is the same.*
Third efficiency condition: *Every consumer's MB is the same.*

2.2 Is the Market Efficient?

Now that we know the three conditions for efficiency, can we say that the market is efficient? The competitive equilibrium model provides us with a quick answer to that question.

According to the model of consumer behavior in Chapter 5, an individual consumer chooses a quantity of a good such that *price equals marginal benefit*—that is, $P = MB$. This equality holds for every consumer at every point on the market demand curve. According to the model of firm behavior in Chapter 6, a firm produces a quantity of a good such that *price equals marginal cost.* That is, $P = MC$. This equality holds for every firm at every point on the market supply curve. At a point of intersection of the supply curve and the demand curve, both of these conditions must hold because the point of intersection is on both the supply curve and the demand curve and the price P is the same. That is, $P = MB$ and $P = MC$ simultaneously. This implies that at the quantity produced by the market, *marginal benefit equals marginal cost.* That is, $MB = MC$. This is true of every good.

Thus we have proved that a competitive market satisfies the first condition of efficiency. The marginal cost of producing roses, grapes, bread, peanuts, or automobiles is equal to the marginal benefit that people get from consuming them. This occurs without any person coordinating consumers and producers.

The result is illustrated in Figure 7.3. At the market equilibrium quantity (point E), the marginal cost (the point on the supply curve) is equal to the marginal benefit (the point on the demand curve). At any other point, either marginal benefit will be greater than marginal cost or marginal benefit will be less than marginal cost.

The other two criteria for efficiency also hold in a competitive market. To see this, it will help to look back at Figure 7.2. Observe that, in a market equilibrium, the marginal cost for the producers is the same, because *they all face the same price.* Along each of their individual supply curves, all producers—Hugo, Mimi, and others—set marginal cost equal to the price. Similarly, in a market equilibrium, *all consumers*—Maria, Ken, and others—*face the same market price.* Hence, their marginal benefits are all equal, because on each of their individual demand curves the marginal benefit equals the price.

Here's the reason in a nutshell why the first condition is satisfied: P = MB and P = MC. Thus since P = P, we must have MC = MB.

Here's the reason in a nutshell why the second condition is satisfied: Hugo's MC = P. Mimi's MC = P. Thus, Hugo's MC = Mimi's MC.

Here's the reason in a nutshell why the third condition is satisfied: Maria's MB = P. Ken's MB = P. Thus, Maria's MB = Ken's MB.

FIGURE 7.3 The Efficiency of the Market: Marginal Benefit Equals Marginal Cost

Only at quantity *E* is the marginal benefit of an extra unit equal to the marginal cost of an extra unit. Point *D* is not efficient because the marginal benefit of an extra unit is greater than the marginal cost of producing it. Point *F* is also not efficient because the marginal cost of producing an extra unit is greater than the marginal benefit.

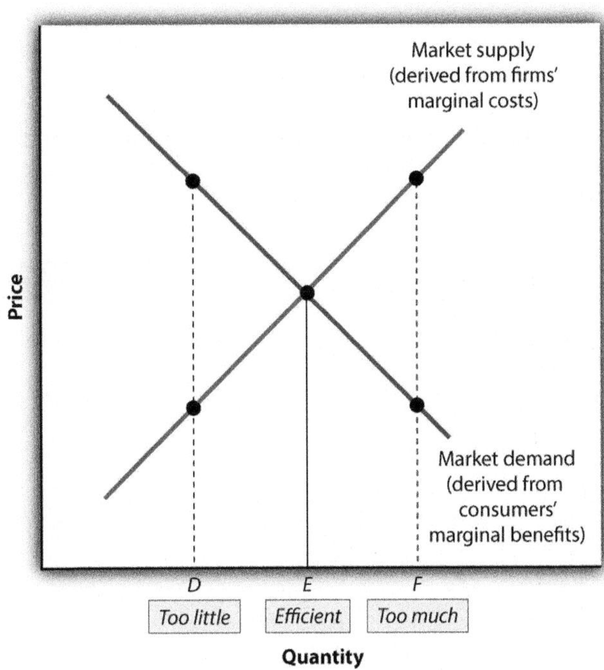

In sum, for each good produced in a competitive market, (1) the marginal benefit equals the marginal cost of the last item produced, (2) the marginal cost is equal for all producers in the market, and (3) the marginal benefit is equal for all consumers in the market. Thus, we can say that the competitive market is Pareto efficient. In a competitive market, it is not possible to make one person better off without hurting someone else.

The proposition that competitive markets are efficient is one of the most important in economics, so much so that when it is proven with the mathematics necessary to keep track of many different goods and time periods, it is called the **first theorem of welfare economics**. The word *welfare* means that the theorem is about the overall well-being of people in the economy (the word *welfare* is synonymous with "well-being," not with a transfer payment to a poor person). The word *first* is used to distinguish this theorem from the second theorem of welfare economics, which states the converse of the first: Any Pareto efficient outcome can be obtained via a competitive market.

first theorem of welfare economics

The conclusion that a competitive market results in an efficient outcome; sometimes called the "invisible hand theorem"; the definition of efficiency used in the theorem is Pareto efficiency.

2.3 Efficiency and Income Inequality

Efficiency is an important goal of an economic system, but it is not the only goal. Another goal is to avoid outcomes in which a few people earn most of the income and do most of the consumption in the economy, while the rest of the population falls into dire economic circumstances. Thus, reducing **income inequality** is another desirable goal in most economic systems.

income inequality

Disparity in levels of income among individuals in the economy.

It is important to emphasize that efficiency and income equality are not the same thing. An allocation of bread between Hugo and Mimi is efficient if their marginal benefit of bread is the same and if the marginal benefits equal the marginal cost of bread. Then no mutually advantageous trade of bread between Hugo and Mimi will make one better off without hurting the other.

However, suppose that Hugo has a low income, earning only $7,000 per year, and that Mimi has a high income, earning $70,000 per year. Suppose a severe drought raises the price of wheat and thus the price of bread. If the price of bread in the market gets very high, say, $3 a loaf, then Hugo will be able to buy few loaves of bread and may go hungry, especially if he has a family. In this case, the economy gets good marks on efficiency grounds but fails on income inequality grounds.

To remedy the situation, a common suggestion is to put price controls on bread. For example, to help Hugo and others like him, a law might be passed requiring that bread prices not exceed $0.50 a loaf. Although this may help the income inequality problem, it will cause inefficiency because it interferes with the market. At $0.50 a loaf, bread producers will not produce much, and Mimi probably will start buying bread to feed the birds, wasting scarce resources.

The temptation to deal with income inequality problems in ways that interfere with the efficiency of the market is great in all societies. Price ceilings (rent controls) on rental apartments in some U.S. cities, which we examined in Chapter 4, are one example. A better solution to the income inequality problem is to transfer income to Hugo and other low-income people from Mimi and other high-income people. With a transfer of income—say, through an income-support payment to the poor—the market would be able to function and the inefficiencies caused by price controls on bread would not occur. Even at the high price of bread, Hugo will be able to eat, perhaps buying some rice or a bread substitute, and the bread, which is so expensive to produce, will not be wasted on the birds. We will see that such transfers have advantages and disadvantages. Compared with price controls, their main advantage is that they allow the market to operate efficiently. On the other hand, such transfer programs typically will have to be financed through taxes, which often are going to create inefficiencies, as you will see in one of the sections that follows.

REVIEW

- Economic inefficiency implies a waste of resources. A Pareto efficient outcome is one in which no person's situation can be improved without hurting someone else.
- Three conditions must hold if an outcome is to be Pareto efficient. These conditions are that (1) the marginal benefit of the last item produced must equal its marginal cost, (2) the marginal cost of production for all producers must be identical, and (3) the marginal benefit for all consumers must be identical.
- If marginal benefit exceeds marginal cost, then too little of the good is being produced, whereas if marginal cost exceeds marginal benefit, too much of the good is being produced. In both cases, adjusting the quantity being produced would enhance efficiency.
- If the marginal costs of producers were not identical, then it would be possible to increase production without increasing costs, simply by making the producer with the high marginal cost produce less and the producer with the low marginal cost produce more.
- Finally, if marginal benefits are not identical, then having the person with the high marginal benefit buy the item from the person with the low marginal benefit for a price that is in between the two marginal benefits would enhance efficiency by making both parties better off.
- One of the most desirable features of competitive markets is that at the equilibrium level of production, on the demand curve, marginal benefit equals the market price, while on the supply curve, marginal cost equals the market price. Together, these imply that marginal benefit equals marginal cost.
- Similarly, because all consumers and all firms face the same market price, the marginal benefits of each consumer will be identical (and equal to the market price), as will the marginal costs of each individual producer.
- Thus, competitive markets are efficient. Any change in consumption or production that makes one person better off must make someone else worse off.
- Efficiency is not the same thing as equality. An efficient outcome can coexist with an unequal outcome.
- Attempts to remedy an unequal situation by the use of price ceilings or by rationing lead to inefficiencies in production and consumption. It may be better to redistribute resources from the more affluent to the less well off.

3. MEASURING WASTE FROM INEFFICIENCY

We know from Chapter 5 and Chapter 6 that consumer surplus and producer surplus are measures of how much consumers and producers gain from buying and selling in a market. The larger these two surpluses are, the better off people are.

3.1 Maximizing the Sum of Producer Plus Consumer Surplus

An attractive feature of competitive markets is that they maximize the sum of consumer and producer surplus. Producer and consumer surplus are shown in the market supply and market demand diagram in Figure 7.4. Recall that the producer surplus for all producers is the area above the supply curve and below the market price line, and that the consumer surplus for all consumers is the area below the demand curve and above the market price line. Both the consumer surplus and the producer surplus are shown in Figure 7.4. The lightly shaded area is the sum of consumer surplus plus producer surplus. The equilibrium quantity is at the intersection of the two curves.

3.2 Deadweight Loss

We can show that at the equilibrium price and quantity, consumer surplus plus producer surplus is maximized. Figure 7.4 also shows what happens to consumer surplus plus producer surplus when the efficient level of production does not occur. The middle panel of Figure 7.4 shows what the sum of consumer surplus and producer surplus is at market equilibrium. The top panel of Figure 7.4 shows a situation in which the quantity produced is lower than the market equilibrium quantity. Clearly, the sum of consumer and producer surplus is lower. By producing a smaller quantity, we lose the amount of the consumer and producer surplus in the darkly shaded triangular area $A + B$. The bottom panel of Figure 7.4 shows the opposite situation, in which the quantity produced is too high. In this case, we have to subtract the triangular area $C + D$ from the lightly shaded area on the left because price is greater than marginal benefit and lower than marginal cost, which means that consumer surplus and producer surplus are negative in the area $C + D$. In both the top and bottom panels of the figure, these darkly shaded triangles are a loss to society from producing more or less than the efficient amount. Economists call the loss in this darkly shaded area the **deadweight loss**. It is a measure of the waste from inefficient production.

deadweight loss

The loss in producer and consumer surplus because of an inefficient level of production.

Deadweight loss is not simply a theoretical curiosity with a morbid name; it is used by economists to measure the size of the waste to society of deviations from the competitive equilibrium. By calculating deadweight loss, economists can estimate the benefits and costs of many government programs. When you hear or read that the cost of U.S. agricultural programs is billions of dollars or that the benefit of a world-trade agreement is trillions of dollars, it is the increase or decrease in deadweight loss that is being referred to. To compute the deadweight loss, all we need is the demand curve and the supply curve.

FIGURE 7.4 Measuring Economic Loss

When production is less or more than the market equilibrium amount, the economic loss is measured by the loss of consumer surplus plus producer surplus. In the top diagram, the quantity produced is too small. In the bottom diagram, it is too large. In the middle diagram, it is efficient.

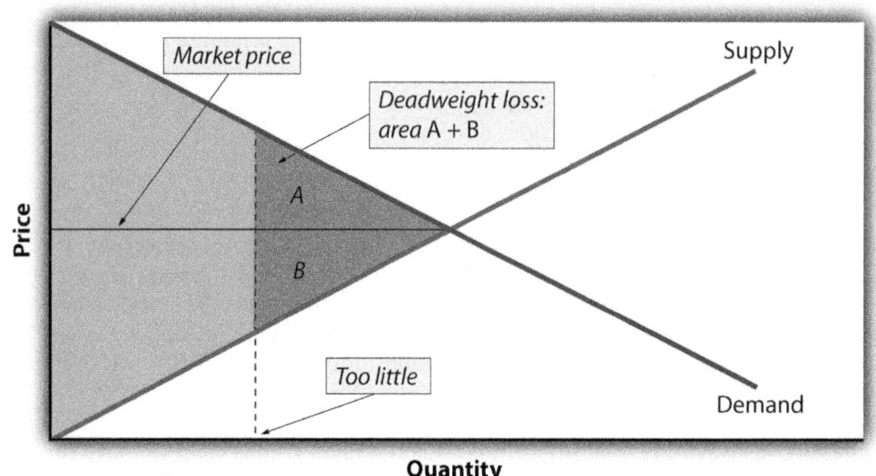

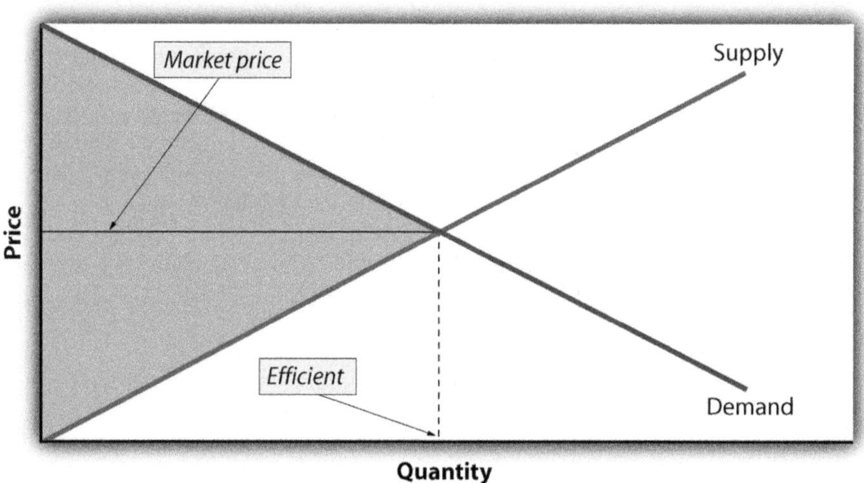

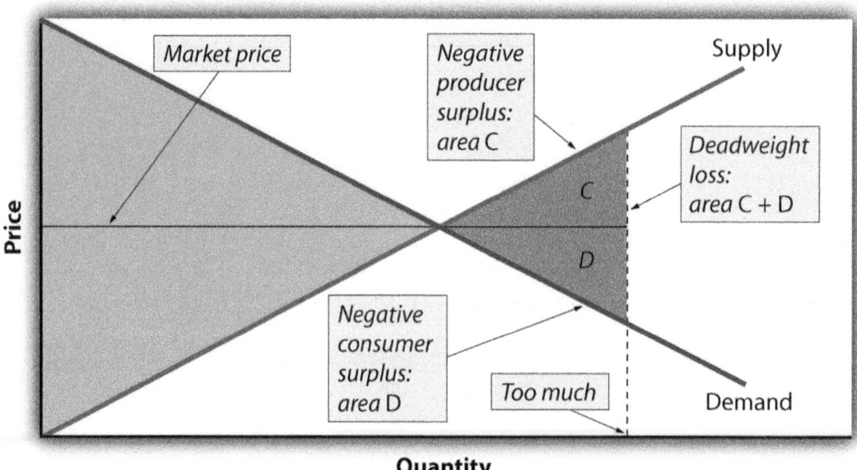

Another way to think about the lightly shaded areas in the graphs: *The sum of consumer surplus plus producer surplus is the triangular area between the demand curve and the supply curve—shown by the lightly shaded area in the middle graph of Figure 7.4. The graph shows another way to think about this*

sum: The sum of consumer surplus plus producer surplus equals the marginal benefit minus the marginal cost of all the items produced.

REVIEW

- Consumer surplus and producer surplus are measures of how well off consumers and firms are as a result of buying and selling in the market. The larger the sum of these surpluses, the better off consumers and firms (society as a whole) are.
- Competitive markets maximize producer surplus plus consumer surplus.
- If the quantity produced is either greater or less than the market equilibrium amount, the sum of consumer surplus plus producer surplus is less than at the market equilibrium. The decline in consumer plus producer surplus measures the waste from producing the wrong amount. It is called deadweight loss.

4. THE DEADWEIGHT LOSS FROM PRICE FLOORS AND CEILINGS

In Chapter 4, we used the supply and demand model to examine situations in which governments have attempted to control market prices because they were unhappy with the outcome of the market, or because they were pressured by groups who would benefit from price controls. We examined two broad types of price controls: price ceilings, which specify a maximum price at which a good can be bought or sold, and price floors, which specify a minimum price at which a good can be bought or sold. An example of a price floor was the minimum wage, and an example of a price ceiling was a rent control policy.

Using the supply and demand model, we were able to illustrate some of the problems that stemmed from the imposition of price floors or ceilings. When a price floor that is higher than the equilibrium price is imposed, the result will be persistent surpluses of the good. This situation is illustrated by Figure 7.5. The surpluses imply that an inefficient allocation of resources is going toward the good whose price has been inflated artificially. Frequently, costly government programs will be created to buy up surplus production. When a price ceiling that is lower than the equilibrium price is imposed on a market, then the result will be persistent shortages of the good. These shortages mean that mechanisms like rationing, waiting lines, or black markets will be used to allocate the now scarce good. This situation is illustrated by Figure 7.7. Now that we understand the concepts of consumer and producer surplus as well as the idea of deadweight loss, we can use these tools to quantify the negative impacts of price ceilings and price floors.

4.1 The Deadweight Loss from a Price Floor

Figure 7.6 shows how consumer and producer surplus are affected by the imposition of a price floor. Before the imposition of the price floor, the sum of consumer and producer surplus is given by the area of the triangle *ABC*, of which the area *BCD* denotes consumer surplus and the area *ACD* denotes producer surplus.

Now consider what happens to consumer surplus and producer surplus when a price floor is imposed. The impact on producer surplus is ambiguous. On the one hand, those producers who are fortunate enough to sell at a higher price will obtain more producer surplus. But because the quantity demanded is lower at the higher price, there will be a loss of producer surplus for those producers who previously were able to sell the good but now have no buyers. Producer surplus would be given by the area *AEFG*, which reflects an increase of *DEFI* (shown in the vertical striped area) and a decrease of *CGI* (shown in the shaded area) from the previous level of producer surplus. Consumer surplus is reduced unambiguously by the amount *CDEF* (shown in cross-hatched lines). Overall, when we add up the lost consumer and producer surplus and the gained producer surplus, a deadweight loss is equivalent to the area *CFG* in Figure 7.6.

FIGURE 7.5 Price and Quantity Effects of a Price Floor

If the price floor is set higher than the competitive market price, the quantity demanded by consumers decreases and the quantity supplied by firms increases, creating excess supply.

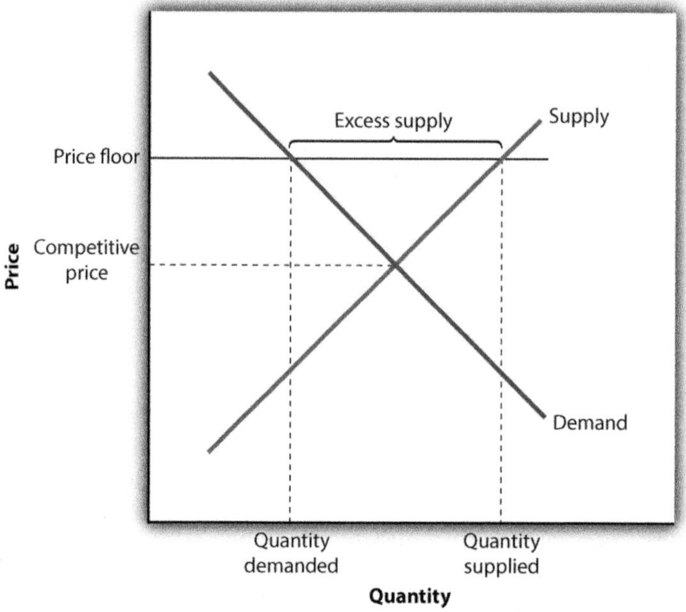

FIGURE 7.6 The Deadweight Loss from a Price Floor

The price floor creates an excess supply of goods at the new higher price. Consumers are unambiguously worse off. Producers may be better off or worse off depending on whether they are able to sell at the higher price. The sum of consumer and producer surplus is lower, indicating a deadweight loss associated with the floor.

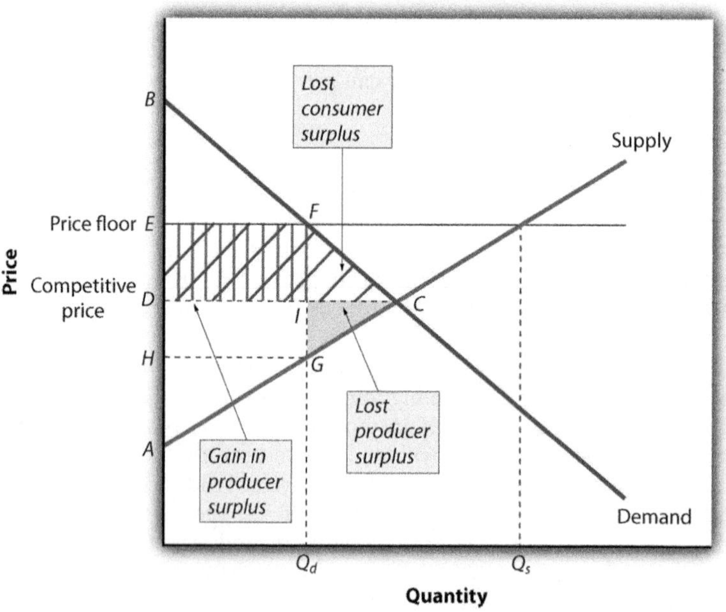

4.2 The Deadweight Loss from a Price Ceiling

Figure 7.8 shows how consumer and producer surplus are affected by the imposition of a price ceiling. As before, before the imposition of the price ceiling, the sum of consumer and producer surplus is given by the area of the triangle *ABC*, of which the area *BCD* denotes consumer surplus and the area *ACD* denotes producer surplus.

FIGURE 7.7 **Price and Quantity Effects of a Price Ceiling**

If the price ceiling is set below the competitive market price, the quantity demanded by consumers increases and the quantity supplied by firms decreases, creating excess demand.

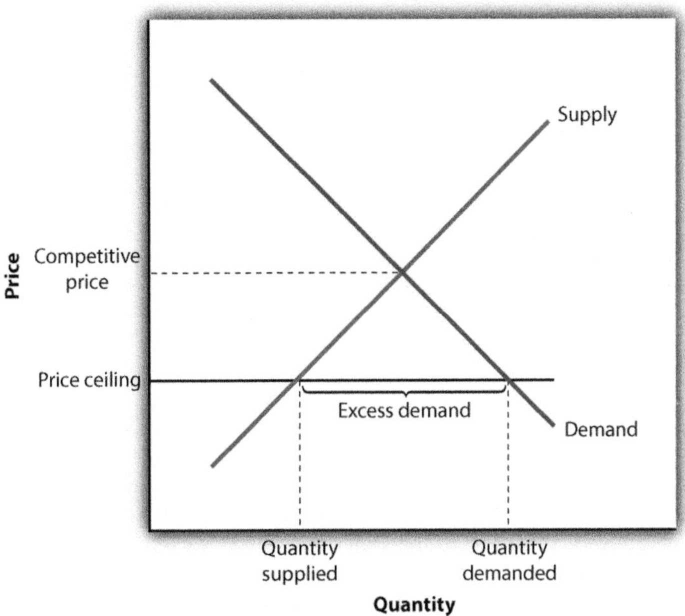

FIGURE 7.8 **The Deadweight Loss from a Price Ceiling**

The price ceiling creates an excess demand for goods at the new lower price. Producers are unambiguously worse off. Consumers may be better or worse off depending on whether they are able to buy at the lower price. The sum of consumer and producer surplus is lower, indicating a deadweight loss associated with the ceiling.

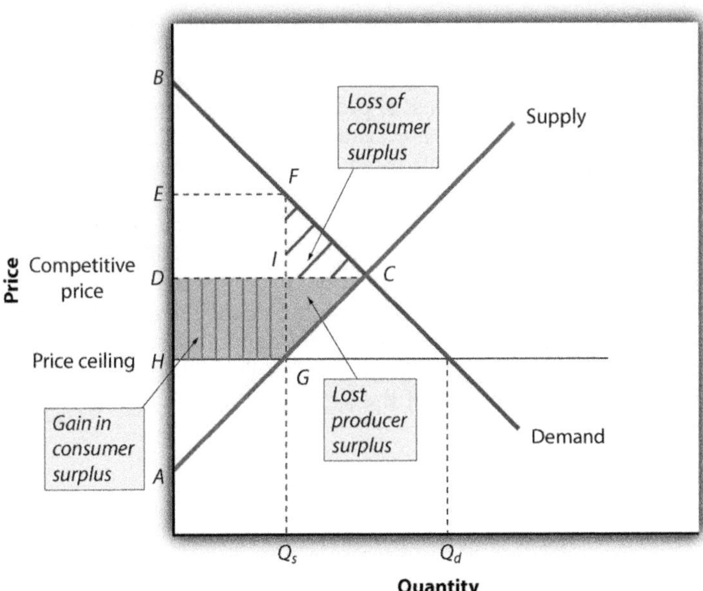

Now consider what happens to consumer surplus and producer surplus when a price ceiling is imposed. The impact on consumer surplus is ambiguous: Those consumers who are able to acquire the good at the lower price will obtain more consumer surplus. Because only a smaller quantity of goods is available for purchase, however, there will be a loss of consumer surplus for those who previously were able to buy the good but now cannot. Consumer surplus would be given by the area *BFGH*, which reflects an increase of *DHGI* (shown in the vertically striped area) and a decrease of *CFI* (shown in cross-hatched area) from the previous level of consumer surplus. Producer surplus is reduced unambiguously by the amount *CDHG* (shown by the shaded area). Overall, when we combine the lost consumer and producer surplus with the gained consumer surplus, a deadweight loss is equivalent to the area *CFG* in Figure 7.8.

REVIEW

- Both price floors and price ceilings bring about deadweight loss. Some parties clearly lose; other parties may gain, but overall, the losses exceed the gains.
- In the case of a price floor, consumers unambiguously lose because they buy fewer units at a higher price. Some producers gain because they are able to sell at a higher price than before. Others lose because they are no longer able to sell the good because the government does not allow them to lower the price to attract buyers.
- In the case of a price ceiling, producers unambiguously lose because they sell fewer units at a lower price. Some consumers gain because they are able to buy the good at a lower price than before. Others lose because they are no longer able to buy the good, even though they are willing to pay more, because the government does not allow firms to raise the price.

5. THE DEADWEIGHT LOSS FROM TAXATION

Another important application of deadweight loss is in estimating the impact of a tax. To see how, let's examine the impact of a tax on a good. We will see that the tax shifts the supply curve, leads to a reduction in the quantity produced, and reduces the sum of producer surplus plus consumer surplus.

Figure 7.9 shows a supply and demand diagram for a particular good. In the absence of the tax, the sum of producer and consumer surplus is given by the area of the triangle *ABC*, of which the area *BCD* denotes consumer surplus and the area *ACD* denotes producer surplus.

5.1 A Tax Paid by a Producer Shifts the Supply Curve

A tax on sales is a payment that must be made to the government by the seller of a product. The tax may be a percentage of the dollar value spent on the products sold, in which case it is called an ad valorem tax. A 6 percent state tax on retail purchases is an *ad valorem tax*. Or it may be proportional to the number of items sold, in which case the tax is called a *specific tax*. A tax on gasoline of $0.50 per gallon is an example of a specific tax.

Because the tax payment is made by the producer or the seller to the government, the immediate impact of the tax is to add to the marginal cost of producing the product. Hence, the immediate impact of the tax will be to shift the supply curve. For example, suppose each producer has to send a certain amount, say, $0.50 per gallon of gasoline produced and sold, to the government. Then $0.50 must be added to the marginal cost per gallon for each producer.

The resulting shift of the supply curve is shown in Figure 7.9. The vertical distance between the old and the new supply curves is the size of the sales tax in dollars. The supply curve shifts up by this amount because this is how much is added to the marginal costs of the producer. (Observe that this upward shift can just as accurately be called a leftward shift because the new supply curve is above and to the left of the old curve. Saying that the supply curve shifts up may seem confusing because when we say "up," we seem to mean "more supply." But the "up" is along the vertical axis, which has the price on it. The upward, or leftward, movement of the supply curve is in the direction of less supply, not more supply.)

FIGURE 7.9 Deadweight Loss from a Tax

In this graph, the lightly shaded triangle represents the deadweight loss and the shaded rectangle the amount of tax revenue that goes to the government. The sales tax, which is collected and paid to the government by the seller, adds to the marginal cost of each item the producer sells. Hence, the supply curve shifts up. The price rises, but by less than the tax increase.

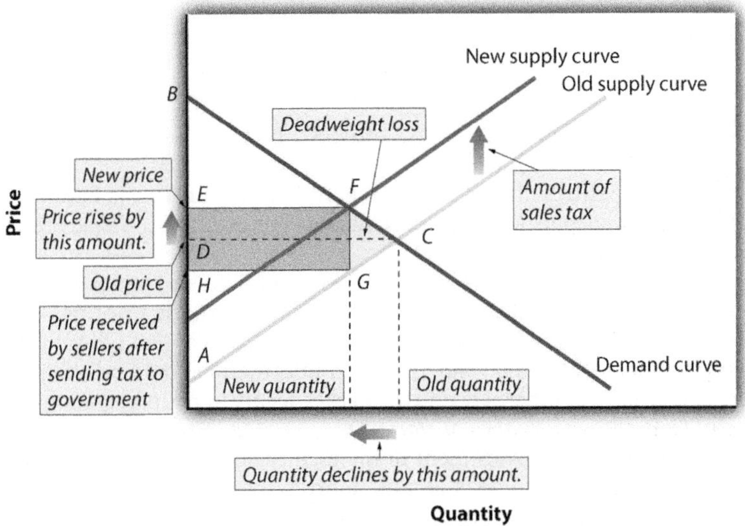

5.2 A New Equilibrium Price and Quantity

What does the competitive equilibrium model imply about the change in the price and the quantity produced? Observe the new intersection of the supply curve and the demand curve. Thus, the price rises to a new, higher level, and the quantity produced declines.

The price increase, as shown in Figure 7.9, is not as large as the increase in the tax. The vertical distance between the old and the new supply curves is the amount of the tax, but the price increases by less than this distance. Thus, the producers are not able to "pass on" the entire tax to the consumers in the form of higher prices. If the tax increase is \$0.50, then the price increase is less than \$0.50, perhaps \$0.40. The producers have been forced by the market—by the movement along the demand curve—to reduce their production, and by doing so they have absorbed some of the impact of the tax increase.

5.3 Deadweight Loss and Tax Revenue

Now consider what happens to consumer surplus and producer surplus with the sales tax. Because the total quantity produced is lower, there is a loss in consumer surplus and producer surplus. The right part of the triangle of consumer plus producer surplus, corresponding to the area *CFG*, has been cut off, and this is the deadweight loss to society, as shown in Figure 7.9.

Consumer surplus is now given by the triangle *BEF*, while producer surplus is given by the triangle *AGH* (keep in mind that producers do not receive the new price; they only get the new price less the tax). The tax generates revenue for the government that can be used to finance government activity. Some of what was producer surplus and consumer surplus thus goes to the government. If the tax is \$1 and 100 items are sold, the tax revenue is \$100. This amount is shown by the shaded rectangle *EFGH* on the diagram. Adding up consumer and producer surplus plus the government revenue gives us an area corresponding to *ABFG*, which differs from the original sum of consumer and producer surplus (*ABC*) by the magnitude of the deadweight loss (*CFG*). So even though taxes may be necessary to finance the government, they cause a deadweight loss to society in the form of lost consumer surplus and producer surplus that are no longer available to anyone in the economy.

REVIEW

- The impact of a tax on the economy can be analyzed using consumer surplus and producer surplus.
- Taxes are necessary to finance government expenditures, but they lower the production of the item being taxed.
- The loss to society from the decline in production is measured by the reduction in consumer surplus and producer surplus, the deadweight loss due to the tax.

6. INFORMATIONAL EFFICIENCY

We have shown that a competitive market works well in that the outcome is Pareto efficient. For every good, the sum of consumer surplus and producer surplus is maximized. These are important and attractive characteristics of a competitive market.

Another important and attractive characteristic of a competitive market is that the market processes information efficiently. For example, in a competitive market, the price reflects the marginal benefit for every buyer and the marginal cost for every seller. If a government official were asked to set the price in a real market, there would be no way that such information could be obtained, especially with millions of buyers and sellers. In other words, the market seems to be informationally efficient. Pareto efficiency is different from this *informational efficiency.*

In the 1930s and 1940s, as the government of the former Soviet Union tried to centrally plan production in the entire economy, economists became more interested in the informational efficiency of markets. One of the most outspoken critics of central planning, and a strong advocate of the market system, was Friedrich Hayek, who emphasized the importance of the informational efficiencies of the market. In Hayek's view, a major disadvantage of central planning—in which the government sets all the prices and all the quantities—is that it is informationally inefficient.

If you had all the information about all the buyers and sellers in the market, you could set the price to achieve a Pareto efficient outcome. To see Hayek's point, it is perhaps enough to observe that, without private information about every one of the millions of buyers and sellers, you or any government official would not know where to set the price. However, economists do not have results as neat as the first theorem of welfare economics to prove Hayek's point. In some situations, the market would be unwieldy, and it is difficult to describe these situations with any generality.

Difficulties arise in using a market system in situations in which prices will not bring about a sufficiently precise or speedy response. For example, if demand for furniture made out of mahogany timber rises, it is difficult for producers to meet that demand immediately, because it takes several dozen years for a mahogany tree to reach maturity. In such a situation, unscrupulous producers may chop down mahogany trees in a public forest to meet the demand. This result implies that we should not rely solely on the competitive market system to motivate producers to increase production in situations in which property rights are weak or communal resources need to be managed. Nevertheless, a competitive market system offers considerable informational advantages over other systems.

Coordination without a Market: Although prices provide a valuable coordination role in a market economy, some activities are better coordinated without the market. It would not be efficient to coordinate each of the hand and foot movements of these skydivers with prices.

Source: © Shutterstock, Inc.

REVIEW

- The market has the ability to process information efficiently. The lack of informational efficiency is a key reason why central planning does not work well in complex and changing environments.
- For some activities, however, the market has few informational advantages. A production process in situations in which property rights are weak or in which communal resources need to be managed will be poorly coordinated through prices.

7. END-OF-CHAPTER MATERIALS

7.1 Conclusion

Adam Smith's idea of the "invisible hand" is perhaps the most important discovery in economics: Individuals, by freely pursuing their own interests in a market economy, are led as if by an invisible hand to an outcome that is best overall. The first theorem of welfare economics is the modern statement of Adam Smith's famous principle; in tribute to Smith's seminal idea, we call it the "invisible hand theorem." Understanding why, and under what circumstances, the invisible hand theorem is true is an important part of thinking like an economist.

Understanding the theorem has required an investment in economic model building: The behavior of consumers and the behavior of firms were combined into a competitive equilibrium model describing how consumers and firms interact in markets. This model is an extension of the supply and demand model we used in Chapter 3 and Chapter 4.

Building the competitive equilibrium model has had payoffs beyond understanding this most important theorem in economics. We can use individual demand curves and individual firm supply curves to determine the actions of each individual consumer and each individual producer at the market equilibrium price. Armed with the ideas of consumer surplus and producer surplus, we can measure the costs of deviations from the competitive market equilibrium. Such measures are used by economists to assess the costs and benefits of government programs that interfere, for better or worse, with the market outcomes. Starting with Chapter 10, we will see that deviations from the competitive market equilibrium are caused by monopolies and other factors. But first, in Chapter 8 and Chapter 9, we will look more closely at how costs and production within individual firms and competitive industries change over time.

Key Points

1. Processing information and coordinating and motivating millions of consumption and production decisions is difficult, but the market is a device that can do the job remarkably well.
2. The interaction of producers and consumers in a market can be explained by the competitive equilibrium model, which is the supply and demand model with consumer and firm behavior made more explicit.
3. Using the competitive equilibrium model, we not only can find the equilibrium price and quantity, but also can use each individual's demand curve to find that individual's consumption decision and use each individual firm's supply curve to figure out its production decision.
4. An outcome is Pareto efficient if it is not possible to change production or consumption in a way that will make one person better off without hurting someone else.
5. Pareto efficiency requires three criteria to hold: Marginal benefit must equal marginal cost for the last item produced, all producers must have identical marginal costs, and all consumers must have identical marginal benefits.
6. A competitive market is Pareto efficient. In a competitive market, the sum of producer surplus and consumer surplus is maximized.
7. Efficiency is not the same thing as equality. An efficient outcome can coexist with an unequal outcome.
8. Attempts to remedy an unequal situation by the use of price ceilings or floors lead to inefficiencies in production and consumption. Using transfers to redistribute resources from the more affluent to the less well off may be better than imposing price or quantity controls.
9. Such transfers often need to be financed by tax revenue. The imposition of a tax that reduces the quantity produced creates deadweight loss for society. The competitive equilibrium model can be used to calculate the magnitude of this deadweight loss.
10. The market also has the ability to process information much more efficiently than a central planner could do. However, no general theorems prove the informational efficiency of the market.

QUESTIONS FOR REVIEW

1. What are the information-processing, coordination, and motivation functions that arise when buyers and sellers interact?
2. Why is it difficult for one person or group of persons to perform the functions listed in Question 1? How does the market perform these functions?
3. What is the relationship between the competitive equilibrium model and the supply and demand model?
4. How does the competitive equilibrium model explain the decisions of individual consumers and producers?
5. What is the meaning of Pareto efficiency?
6. What are the conditions that are needed for Pareto efficiency to hold? Why would the violation of any one of those conditions bring about a situation that is not Pareto efficient?
7. How does a competitive market satisfy the conditions that are needed for Pareto efficiency to hold?
8. Why is the sum of consumer surplus and producer surplus maximized in the competitive market?
9. How does the imposition of a price floor create deadweight loss for the economy?
10. How does the imposition of a tax create deadweight loss for the economy?

PROBLEMS

1. Suppose that in a competitive market for ukuleles, three buyers (Peter, Paul, and Mary) have the marginal benefit (*MB*) schedules below.

Quantity	*MB*—Peter	*MB*—Paul	*MB*—Mary
1	150	140	130
2	120	110	100
3	90	80	70
4	60	50	40
5	30	20	10

If the equilibrium price is $80, calculate the following:

a. The quantity purchased by each buyer.

b. The consumer surplus for each buyer.

c. The consumer surplus for the market as a whole.

2. In the same market, three sellers (John, George, and Ringo) have the marginal cost (*MC*) schedules shown below.

Quantity	*MC*—John	*MC*—George	*MC*—Ringo
1	30	20	10
2	60	50	40
3	90	80	70
4	120	110	100
5	150	140	130

If the equilibrium price is $80, calculate the following:

a. The quantity produced by each seller.

b. The producer surplus for each seller.

c. The producer surplus for the market as a whole.

3. Using the answers you provided above for Problems 1 and 2, verify that the three efficiency conditions are satisfied for the ukulele market.

4. Firm A and firm B both produce the same product with the following total costs:

Firm A		Firm B	
Quantity Produced	*Total Costs*	*Quantity Produced*	*Total Costs*
1	5	0	2
2	6	1	5
3	8	2	9
4	11	3	14
5	15	4	20

Consider a situation in which the market price is $3 and four units are produced in total: Firm A produces two units, and firm B produces two units.

a. Explain why this situation is not Pareto efficient.
b. Come up with two different production allocations for the two firms that allow the four items to be produced at a lower overall total cost.
c. Which of these two allocations would be the outcome in a competitive market in which both firms maximized profits?
d. How would the actions of the two firms be coordinated in a competitive market to achieve this outcome?

5. Suppose that in the ukulele market described in Problem 2, the government imposes a $40 sales tax, which causes the equilibrium price to go up to $100. Calculate the following:
   a. The quantity purchased by each buyer, the consumer surplus for each buyer, and the consumer surplus for the market as a whole.
   b. The quantity produced by each seller, the producer surplus for each seller, and the producer surplus for the market as a whole.
   c. The amount of revenue collected by the government.
   d. The deadweight loss for the economy resulting from the tax.
6. Consider the following supply and demand schedule for candy bars:

Price	Supply (millions of candy bars)	Demand (millions of candy bars)
$0.25	2	14
$0.50	6	12
$0.75	10	10
$1.00	14	8
$1.25	18	6
$1.50	22	4
$1.75	26	2

   a. Sketch the market supply and demand curves. Show the equilibrium quantity and price.
   b. Graphically show the producer surplus and consumer surplus in the market for candy bars.
   c. What would happen to the price of this product if a tax of $0.75 per candy bar sold were enacted by the government? Show your answer graphically.
   d. Show the deadweight loss due to the tax on your diagram.
7. Suppose that an unanticipated bout of good weather results in almost ideal growing conditions, leading to a substantial increase in the supply of wheat in the United States.
   a. Draw a supply and demand diagram to show what will happen to the equilibrium price and quantity of wheat in the United States, assuming that the demand curve does not shift.
   b. Suppose the U.S. government observes that the price of wheat is likely to fall rapidly and imposes a price floor equal to the original equilibrium price. What effect does the price floor have on the quantity supplied and demanded of wheat?
   c. How are consumer and producer surplus affected by the price floor?
   d. Graphically show the deadweight loss created by the price floor.
8. High international prices for soybeans in recent years led many Argentinean farmers to switch land that had been used as pasture to raise cattle to soybean production. This resulted in a shortfall in the supply of beef.
   a. Draw a supply and demand diagram to show what will happen to the equilibrium price and quantity of beef in Argentina, assuming that the demand curve does not shift.
   b. In March 2007, the Argentinean government, concerned about the rising price of beef, imposed a price ceiling on beef. Assuming that the price ceiling was equal to the original equilibrium price before the supply decreased, what effect does the price ceiling have on the quantity supplied and demanded of beef?
   c. How are consumer and producer surplus affected by the price ceiling?
   d. Graphically show the deadweight loss created by the price ceiling.

CHAPTER 8
Costs and the Changes at Firms Over Time

On a cold Saturday morning, a wrenching story appeared on the front page of a California newspaper. It began: The end came at precisely 11:46 A.M. Friday. After 82 years, after four generations of toil and take-home pay, with deep roots tapping into two centuries, the end came without frill or fanfare. . . . There were tears. There were handshakes. . . . "Listen. There's a silence. It's like a hush has fallen over the place," said Bob Armstrong, the superintendent of the plant.[1]

The story was an account of the Del Monte cannery in San Jose as it shut down production facilities forever. It sounds like something out of a Depression-era Steinbeck novel, but in fact this article was written in 1999, a year when the U.S. economy was enjoying an unprecedented boom. Even in a boom year, many firms, such as the Del Monte cannery, shut down. But many more firms start up each year in the United States—some 700,000—so that the number of firms in existence continues to increase year after year. Many of these firms are successful and will expand, but others may have to downsize and eventually shut down. The purpose of this chapter is to develop a model for analyzing the changes at firms over time. To do so, we will extend the model of firm behavior developed in Chapter 6.

Small businesses make up the largest share of businesses in the United States, employing, on average, half of all private sector employees. Nearly 23 million small businesses operate in the United States, and they open and close at a fairly steady rate. At least two thirds of small businesses survive the first two years; about 50 percent are still open after four years. Small businesses close for a variety of reasons, including lack of adequate capital, but some businesses simply run their course.

Source: © Shutterstock, Inc.

What we will find in this chapter is that costs are of vital importance to a firm's decision to start up or shut down. Some of the most successful new firms in the United States, as well as some of the most rapidly growing older firms, have prospered because of their ability to use innovative management techniques and new technologies that cut costs. For example, Jeffrey Bezos founded Amazon.com, which was able to become one of the largest bookstores in the world by conducting its entire business online on the Web, thus avoiding the "bricks and mortar" costs of building or renting space in which to sell books. Walmart—a firm that expanded rapidly in the past two decades—developed a system whereby sales clerks electronically scan a barcode on each item and automatically transmit the information back to the manufacturer, who then can begin producing more of that item. This process enabled Walmart to reduce costs by minimizing its need to hold lots of unsold goods in inventory.

In addition to determining which firms grow and which firms shrink, costs determine how large a firm should be. Differences in the costs of the equipment needed for manufacturing cement and the equipment needed to set up a hair salon, for example, mean that cement firms are usually large and hair salons are usually small.

Costs also determine where firms should expand. For example, firms take into account the costs of labor and transportation as well as the effects of government policy when they choose between expanding their manufacturing facilities in the United States or establishing facilities abroad. In recent years, many call centers—places that handle telephone calls and provide customer service—have relocated to India, where educated English-speaking workers can be hired for less money than in the U.S. Similarly, car manufacturers in Germany have set up plants in countries like Slovakia because the cost of hiring workers there is considerably cheaper than in Western Europe.

In this chapter, we will show how costs are a crucial determinant of firm behavior. You will learn how economists can capture the whole essence of a firm with a graph of its costs. By looking at such a graph, economists can determine the profitability of a firm and whether it should shut down or expand. This chapter shows how.

1. COSTS FOR AN INDIVIDUAL FIRM

In this section, we show how to find different types of cost measures for a hypothetical firm. These measures include total costs, average costs, fixed costs, variable costs, and marginal costs. It is important to have a clear and intuitive understanding of each of these concepts and how they relate to one another. We also will look at how the costs of a firm are related to the firm's production function. This will illuminate how changes in the technology used by firms to produce output affect the firm's cost function.

1.1 Total Costs, Fixed Costs, Variable Costs, and Marginal Cost

Total costs(*TC*) are the sum of all costs incurred by a firm in producing goods or services. The more that is produced, the larger the total costs. Recall from Chapter 6 that **fixed costs(*FC*)** and **variable costs(*VC*)** are the two key components of total costs.

Fixed costs are the part of total costs that do not vary with the amount produced in the short run; they include the cost of the factories, land, machines, and all other things that do not change when production changes in the short run. Variable costs are the part of total costs that vary in the short run as production changes. *Variable costs* include wage payments for workers, gasoline for trucks, fertilizer for crops, and all other things that change when the amount produced changes. By definition, total costs equal fixed costs plus variable costs; or, in symbols, $TC = FC + VC$.

Total costs

The sum of all costs incurred in producing goods or services.

fixed costs

Costs of production that do not depend on the quantity of production.

variable costs

Costs of production that vary with the quantity of production.

The Short Run and the Long Run

Distinguishing the short run from the long run is the key to distinguishing fixed costs from variable costs. The *short run* and the *long run* are two broad categories into which economists parcel time. The **short run** is the period of time during which it is not possible to change all the inputs to production; only some inputs, such as labor, can be changed in the short run. The short run is too short, for example, to build a new factory or apartment building, to lay a fiber-optic cable, to launch a new communications satellite, or to get out of a lease on a storefront. The **long run** is a period of time long enough that all inputs, including capital, can be changed. The cost of each of the items that cannot be changed in the short run—factories, buildings, satellites—can be changed in the long run.

short run

The period of time during which it is not possible to change all inputs to production; only some inputs, such as labor, can be changed.

long run

The minimum period of time during which all inputs to production can be changed.

Economists frequently use *capital* as an example of a factor that does not change in the short run and use labor as an example of a factor that can change in the short run. In the examples in this chapter, we refer to the cost of labor as the main variable cost and the cost of capital as the main fixed cost.

Figure 8.1 illustrates these definitions with cost data for a hypothetical firm called Melodic Movements. The firm, located in Houston, Texas, specializes in the strenuous but delicate job of moving pianos from one part of Houston to another. We use these hypothetical data rather than actual data to keep the example simple, but it is important to realize that the same analysis can be applied to data from any firm. Roadway Express, an actual moving firm that started in Houston with 16 trucks and has since gone nationwide, is a more complex example illustrating the same point. Figure 8.1 lists the total costs, fixed costs, and variable costs for different levels of output at Melodic Movements. Observe that, consistent with the definition, fixed costs do not change as output changes, but variable costs do increase with output.

FIGURE 8.1 Finding Average and Marginal Cost for Melodic Movements (costs measured in dollars per day)

Quantity (pianos moved per day) (Q)	Total Costs (*TC*)	Fixed Costs (*FC*)	Variable Costs (*VC*)	Marginal Cost (*MC*)	Average Total Cost (*ATC*)	Average Fixed Cost (*AFC*)	Average Variable Cost (*AVC*)
0	300	300	0	—	—	—	—
1	450	300	150	150	450	300	150
2	570	300	270	120	285	150	135
3	670	300	370	100	223	100	123
4	780	300	480	110	195	75	120
5	900	300	600	120	180	60	120
6	1,040	300	740	140	173	50	123
7	1,200	300	900	160	171	43	128
8	1,390	300	1,090	190	174	38	136
9	1,640	300	1,340	250	182	33	149
10	1,960	300	1,660	320	196	30	166
11	2,460	300	2,160	500	223	27	196
	$TC = FC + VC$			$\frac{\text{Change in } TC}{\text{Change in } Q}$	$ATC = \frac{TC}{Q}$	$AFC = \frac{FC}{Q}$	$AVC = \frac{VC}{Q}$

The pictographs in Figure 8.2 show that fixed costs do not change in the short run at Melodic Movements. Fixed costs, or the cost for four trucks and two terminals where the trucks are parked, are $300 per day regardless of how many pianos are moved during the day. Figure 8.2 also shows that variable costs increase with the amount produced.

FIGURE 8.2 Fixed Costs versus Variable Costs

Fixed costs remain constant as the output of the firm increases in the short run. In the example of Melodic Movements, fixed costs are the daily rental or interest costs for trucks and terminals under long-term lease or owned by the firm. Variable costs change with the level of output. In the case of MelodicMovements, more workers must be hired to move more pianos.

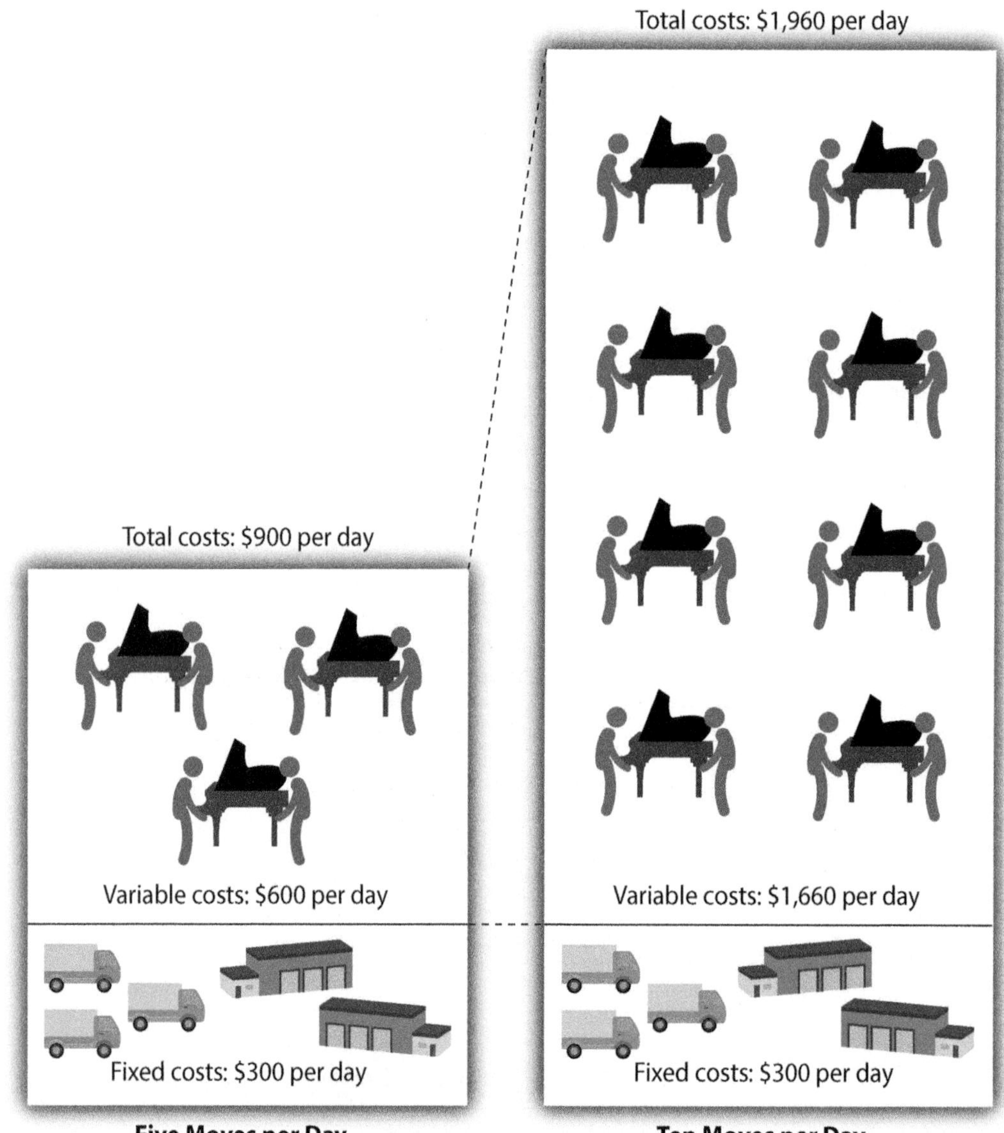

They increase from $600 to $1,660 as the number of pianos delivered per day rises from five to 10. Variable costs are shown in Figure 8.2 to rise because additional workers are hired to carry the goods and to drive and service the trucks. Thus, total costs rise from $900 to $1,960 as the number of pianos delivered rises from five to 10.

Figure 8.3 shows the same type of information as Figure 8.2 in graph form. Pairs of numbers on total costs and quantity from Figure 8.1 are plotted in Figure 8.3. Connecting these dots results in the total costs curve. You can see how the total costs of moving the pianos steadily increase with the number of pianos moved. Fixed costs are shown to be unchanged at all levels of output. Figure 8.3 shows variable costs by the distance between the total costs curve and the fixed costs curve.

FIGURE 8.3 Total Costs Minus Fixed Costs Equal Variable Costs

The two lines on the diagram show total costs and fixed costs for Melodic Movements. Variable costs are the difference between the two lines. Variable costs rise with production, but fixed costs are constant.

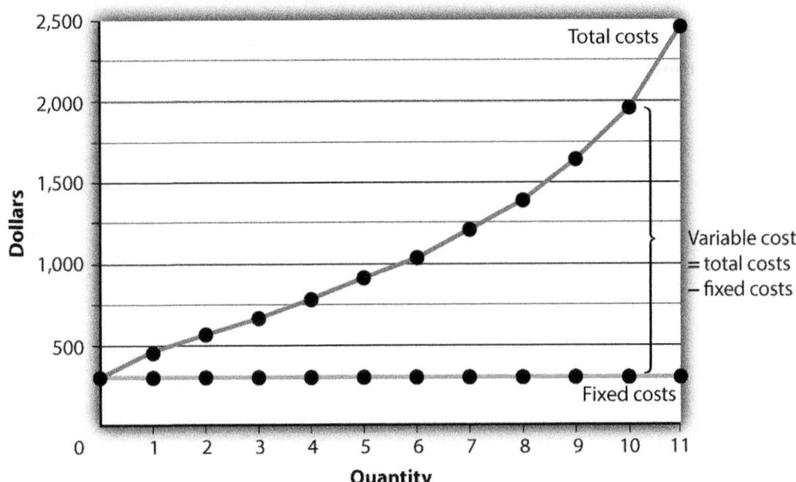

Marginal Cost

Figure 8.1 also shows how the **marginal cost** of Melodic Movements depends on the quantity of services produced (the number of pianos moved). Recall from Chapter 6 that marginal cost is the change in total costs resulting from a one-unit change in the quantity produced. For example, the marginal cost of increasing production from five piano moves to six piano moves a day is the change in total costs ($1,040 – $900 = $140) divided by the change in production (6 – 5 = 1). The fifth column of Figure 8.1 shows the marginal cost for each additional piano moved by Melodic Movements, from the first to the 11th piano.

marginal cost

The change in total costs resulting from a one-unit change in quantity produced.

Observe that in Figure 8.1, marginal cost declines at low levels of production and then begins to increase again. Marginal cost reaches a minimum of $100 when production increases from two to three units of output. Recall that in the examples in Chapter 6 (Table 6.4), marginal cost increased throughout the whole range of production. In the example of Melodic Movements, marginal cost declines over part of the range of production. We will explain the reason for the difference later in this chapter.

1.2 Average Cost

Average total cost (ATC) is defined as total costs (*TC*) of production divided by the quantity (*Q*) produced; in other words, it is the cost per unit of production. In symbols, $ATC = TC/Q$. For example, if the total costs of producing four items are $3,000, then the average total cost is $750 ($3,000/4). We also can define average cost for fixed and variable costs. Thus, **average variable cost (AVC)** is defined as variable costs divided by the quantity produced: $AVC = VC/Q$. **Average fixed cost (AFC)** is defined as fixed costs divided by the quantity produced: $AFC = FC/Q$. Of the three averages, we will use average total cost most frequently. However, the other two averages are important for knowing whether to shut down a firm or keep it open when it is losing money.

Average total cost (ATC)

Total costs of production divided by the quantity produced (also called cost per unit).

average variable cost (AVC)

Variable costs divided by the quantity produced.

Average fixed cost (AFC)

Fixed costs divided by the quantity produced.

Average total cost for Melodic Movements is shown in Figure 8.1. For example, total costs for two pianos moved ($Q = 2$) are $570; dividing $570 by two gives an average total cost of $285. For three pianos moved ($Q = 3$), total costs are $670; dividing by three gives $223 for average total cost. Notice that, in this example, average total cost initially declines as production increases from low levels. Then average total cost starts to increase once the output level reaches eight units. That average total cost first decreases and then increases as production rises is a common pattern for most firms.

Average variable cost is also illustrated in Figure 8.1. For two pianos moved ($Q = 2$), for example, average variable cost is $270 divided by two, or $135. You can see that average variable cost, in this example, first declines and then increases throughout the rest of the range of production. Finally, observe in Figure 8.1 that average fixed cost gets smaller as production rises. Because average fixed cost is calculated by dividing fixed costs (which are by definition fixed) by the quantity produced, average fixed cost must decline as the quantity produced rises.

1.3 The Relationship between a Firm's Costs and the Firm's Production Function

The cost information in Figure 8.1 is determined by how much input of labor and capital it takes to produce a given quantity of output and by the price of capital and labor. First consider some illustrative calculations of costs as the firm increases production. According to Figure 8.1, it costs Melodic Movements $300 a day for capital, which is four trucks and two terminals (suppose trucks cost $25 per day and a terminal costs $100 per day). If the trucks and terminals were leased for one year, then the fixed costs would include the rental payment on the lease. If the trucks and the terminals were purchased on credit by Melodic Movements, then the fixed costs would include interest payments on the loans. If the trucks and the terminals were bought outright, then the fixed costs would include the opportunity cost—the forgone interest payments—of the funds used to buy the trucks and the terminals. These fixed costs will be incurred even if zero pianos are moved.

Inputs and the Production Function: Labor (the two workers) and capital (the truck) are inputs to production (moving the piano).

Source: © Shutterstock, Inc.

To move pianos, however, Melodic Movements needs labor. To move one piano, it might be enough to have one driver, one mechanic to service the truck, and one worker to help carry and load the piano. As production increases from $Q = 0$ to $Q = 1$, variable costs increase from zero to $150 and total costs increase from $300 to $450. Thus, the marginal cost of moving one piano rather than zero pianos is $150. If wages are $10 an hour, this implies that 15 hours of work are needed collectively from the three employees to move that first piano.

To move to a higher level of production, Melodic Movements requires more hours of work. According to Figure 8.1, if production rises from one piano moved to two pianos moved, then total costs increase from $450 to $570; marginal cost is $120. With wages of $10 an hour, this marginal cost is the cost of 12 more hours of work. Notice that marginal cost declines as production increases from one to two units of output. Why? Because it takes less additional labor input to move from one piano move to two piano moves than it did to move from zero piano moves to one piano move. For instance, you may need to hire a second driver and a second loader, but the same mechanic may be able to service two trucks in less than twice the time it takes to service one truck. A full picture of how costs depend on the inputs to production becomes evident from the firm's production function.

The Production Function

production function

A relationship that shows the quantity of output for any given amount of input.

Table 8.1 shows the number of hours of work required to move different numbers of pianos at Melodic Movements. Melodic Movements' short-run **production function** shows how much output can be produced for each amount of labor input. You can calculate the variable costs at Melodic Movements, assuming a wage of $10 per hour, using the information in Table 8.1. To move one piano takes 15 hours of work; at $10 per hour, variable costs are $150. To move 10 pianos takes 166 hours of work; at $10 per hour, variable costs are $1,660. Similar calculations for all levels of output are shown in the third column of Table 8.1. Note that the variable costs in Table 8.1 are the same as those in Figure 8.1. Thus, we have shown explicitly how the firm's costs depend on its production function.

TABLE 8.1 Using the Production Function to Compute Variable Costs

Observe that increasing marginal product of labor exists at low levels of production; for example, it takes only 10 hours of labor to increase production [by one unit] from two to three units, whereas it takes 12 hours of labor to increase production [by one unit] from one to two units. At higher levels of production, decreasing marginal product of labor exists.

Quantity (pianos moved)	Hours of Work	Labor Costs at $10 Wage (variable costs)
0	0	0
1	15	150
2	27	270
3	37	370
4	48	480
5	60	600
6	74	740
7	90	900
8	109	1,090
9	134	1,340
10	166	1,660
11	216	2,160

Recall from Chapter 6 that the *marginal product of labor* is the change in production that can be obtained with an additional unit of labor. Decreasing marginal product of labor is called *diminishing returns to labor.* Increasing marginal product of labor is called *increasing returns to labor.* The marginal product of labor is illustrated in Figure 8.4, which shows a graph of the production function from Table 8.1. Be sure to distinguish between the marginal product of labor and the average product of labor. The **average product of labor** is the quantity produced, or *total product,* divided by the amount of labor input. Thus, the average product of labor is Q/L, where Q is total product and L is labor input. The marginal product of labor is $\Delta Q/\Delta L$, where ΔQ is the change in the quantity produced and ΔL is the change in labor input.

average product of labor
The quantity produced divided by the amount of labor input.

You can see in Figure 8.4 that, for low levels of labor input, the marginal product of labor increases as labor input increases. This relationship is akin to the previous example in which you needed one driver, one loader, and one mechanic to move that first piano, but you needed only another driver and another loader (but not a second mechanic) to increase production to two piano moves. But you also can see that, at high levels of labor input, the marginal product starts to decline as labor input increases: Diminishing returns set in. Adding a third loader or a third driver will not help the firm move more pianos unless it can expand its capital stock. In the short run, with a fixed capital stock, the marginal product while falling initially) is likely to rise as production increases.

FIGURE 8.4 Melodic Movements' Production Function

The curve shows the production function in which more labor input gives more output. Capital (trucks and terminals) is not changed. Observe that the marginal product of labor first increases and then decreases with more labor input.

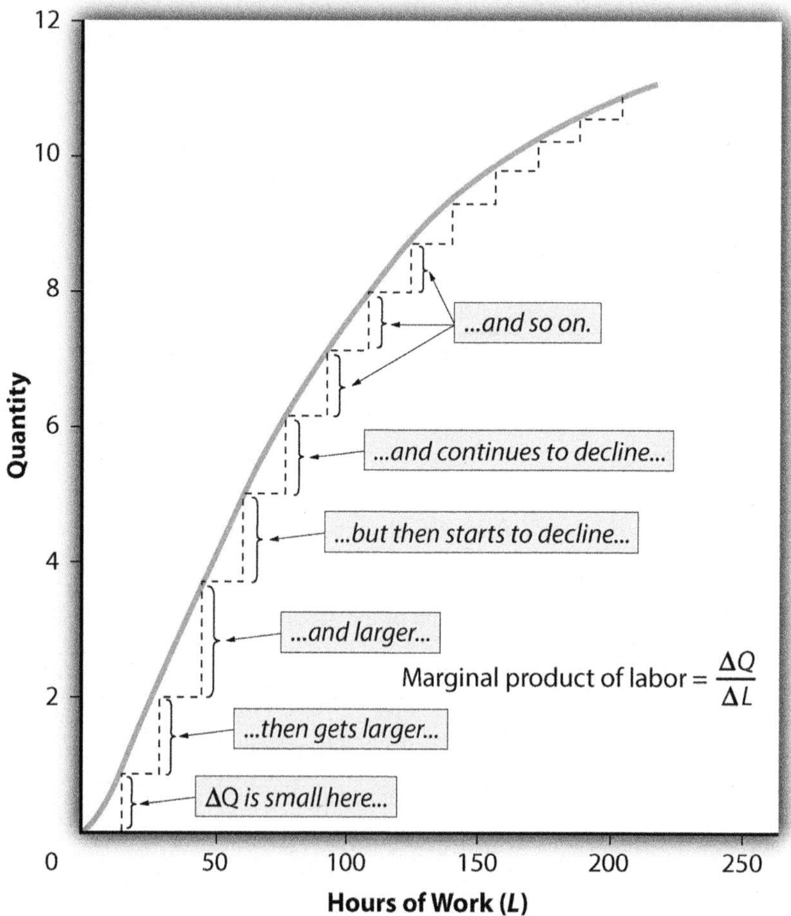

What this means is that initially, when the marginal product of labor is *increasing*, the marginal cost will be *decreasing*: Each additional unit of output requires fewer additional units of labor, and hence has a smaller additional cost. Subsequently, when the marginal product of labor is decreasing, the marginal cost will be increasing: Each additional unit of output requires more additional units of labor, and hence has a larger additional cost. To summarize:

Increasing marginal product of labor --> Decreasing marginal cost
Decreasing marginal product of labor --> Increasing marginal cost

REVIEW

- The short run is the period of time in which it is not possible to change all inputs to production; only some inputs, such as labor, can be changed.
- The long run is the period of time in which the firm can vary all inputs to production, including capital.
- Total costs are the sum of all costs incurred by the firm in producing goods and services. Total costs can be written as the sum of fixed costs plus variable costs. Fixed costs are constant in the short run for all levels of production. Variable costs increase as more is produced.
- The marginal cost is the change in total costs as a result of producing one more unit of output. Marginal cost may rise or fall as production increases.
- The total cost per unit produced is called the average total cost. It can be separated into two parts: average variable cost, defined as variable costs divided by quantity, and average fixed cost, defined as fixed costs divided by quantity.
- A firm's cost function depends on its production function. In the simple example we study, the firm's production function shows how many hours of labor are needed to produce a particular quantity of output, given a certain fixed level of capital.
- When the marginal product of labor is increasing, it takes fewer workers to produce an additional unit of output; hence the additional cost of producing that unit of output (marginal cost) is decreasing. Conversely, when the marginal product of labor is decreasing, it takes more workers to produce an additional unit of output; hence the additional cost of producing that unit of output (marginal cost) is increasing.

2. COST CURVES

A portion of Figure 8.1 can be turned into an informative graph, as shown in Figure 8.5. The vertical axis of Figure 8.5 shows the dollar cost, and the horizontal axis shows the quantity produced. The pairs of points from Figure 8.1 are plotted as dots in Figure 8.5, and the dots have been connected to help visualize the curves. The curves are called the *marginal cost curve*, the *average total cost curve*, and the *average variable cost curve*. We label the curves *MC*, *ATC*, and *AVC*, respectively.

It is clear from Figure 8.5 that marginal cost first decreases and then increases, as observed in Figure 8.1. We now know the reason: The marginal product of each additional worker increases at lower levels of production and then decreases at higher levels of production. Figure 8.5 also makes it clear that average total cost first declines and then increases. In other words, the average total cost curve is *U-shaped.*

FIGURE 8.5 **Average Cost and Marginal Cost from a Numerical Example**

Average total cost first declines and then increases as more is produced. Marginal cost is below average total cost when average total cost is falling and above average total cost when average total cost is rising. This relationship also holds between average variable cost and marginal cost. These cost curves are plotted from the data given in Figure 8.1.

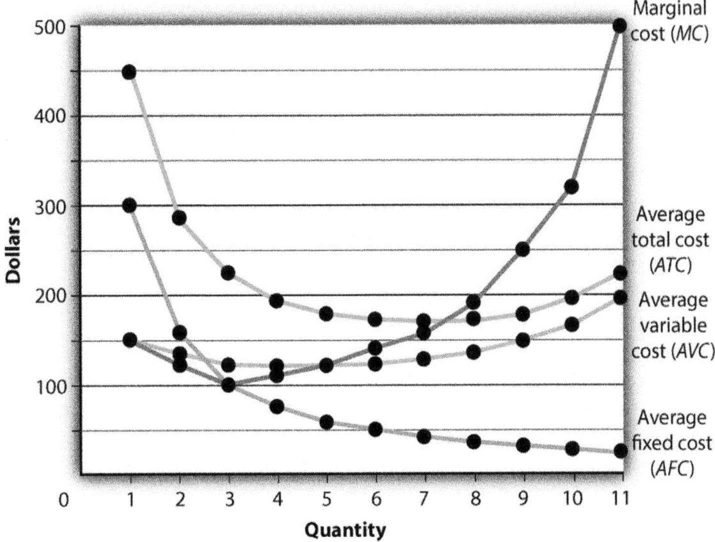

The relative positions of the average total cost curve and the marginal cost curve in Figure 8.5 are important and will come up repeatedly. Observe that whenever the marginal cost curve is below the average total cost curve, average total cost is declining. Whenever the marginal cost curve is above the average total cost curve, however, average total cost is increasing. This result also holds for average variable cost: If marginal cost is greater than average variable cost, then average variable cost is increasing; if marginal cost is less than average variable cost, then average variable cost is decreasing.

This relationship implies a general and important result: *Marginal cost intersects average total cost at the lowest point of the average total cost curve. This has to be the case because whenever marginal cost is less than average total cost (to the left of the intersection point), average total cost is falling. Whenever marginal cost is more than average total cost (to the right of the intersection point), average total cost is rising.*

The same result holds between marginal cost and average variable cost. These relationships between the two average cost curves and the marginal cost curve are essential to the analysis that follows.

2.1 Marginal versus Average in the Classroom

The reason for the relationship between marginal cost and average total cost or average variable cost can be seen with an analogy. Consider another example of averages, say, your average grades on the weekly homework assignments in your economics class. Suppose that the average grade you have received on your first two assignments is 75. Now suppose that you get a 100 on your third homework assignment. The 100 you received on the third assignment was greater than the average grade of 75 you had on the first two; in other words, your marginal grade of 100 is greater than your average grade of 75. What happens to your average homework grade? It will rise to 83.33. Now suppose that you had scored only a 60 on your third assignment. Then your marginal grade of 60 is less than the average grade of 75; hence, your average grade declines from 75 to 70.

This is a property of averaging, and it applies to grades, heights, weights, and so on, as well as to costs. When you add something into a group, an above-average contribution from the new addition increases the group average, whereas a below-average contribution decreases it.

2.2 Generic Cost Curves

The relationship between marginal and average allows us to sketch a *generic* cost curve diagram, the general properties of which characterize virtually all firms, not just Melodic Movements. Such a diagram is shown in Figure 8.6. Again, the vertical axis is the dollar cost and the horizontal axis is the quantity, but in a generic picture, we do not scale the axes because they apply to any firm, whether in textiles, moving, or electronics. Note that the marginal cost curve cuts both the average total cost curve and the average variable cost curve at the minimum point. If the marginal cost curve does not go through the lowest point of both the average total cost curve and the average variable cost curve, you have made an error in drawing a cost function.

Reminder: I t is helpful to use the following checklist when you draw this graph:

1. Ensure that the marginal cost curve cuts through the average total cost curve and the average variable cost curve at their minimum points, and understand the reason for this.
2. Ensure that the distance between average total cost and average variable cost gets smaller as you increase the amount of production.
3. Put a small dip on the left-hand side of the marginal cost curve before the upward slope begins. This allows for the possibility of decreasing marginal cost at very low levels of production.

Another important relationship is evident in Figure 8.6. The distance between the average total cost curve and the average variable cost curve gets smaller as production increases because fixed costs are an increasingly smaller proportion of total costs as production increases. Recall that fixed costs do not change as Q increases. The distance between the average total cost curve and the average variable cost curve is FC/Q, which declines as quantity increases. Hence, the distance between the *ATC* curve and the *AVC* curve grows smaller as you move to the right in the diagram. Any picture you draw should show this relationship.

Finally, observe that the marginal cost curve in the generic picture of Figure 8.6 has a region of declining marginal cost at low production levels. The graph allows for the possibility that at low production levels, the marginal product of labor increases and, therefore, marginal cost declines. This was true for Melodic Movements, which had increasing marginal product of labor initially, and we allow for it in the generic case.

For the cost curves for Melodic Movements in Figure 8.5, the marginal cost curve and the average variable cost curve touch at one unit of output. This occurs because the marginal cost of producing one rather than zero units of output must equal the variable cost of producing one unit, and hence the average variable cost of producing one unit, as shown in Figure 8.1. Thus, if the generic cost curve were drawn all the way over to one unit of output on the left of Figure 8.6 then the marginal cost curve and the average variable cost curve would start at the same point. Because we usually do not draw generic cost curves that go all the way over to the vertical axis, we do not show them starting at the same point.

FIGURE 8.6 Generic Sketch of Average Cost and Marginal Cost

Every firm can be described by cost curves of the type drawn here. Compare these generic curves with the specific curves in Figure 8.5. Check these curves against the checklist in the Reminder paragraph.

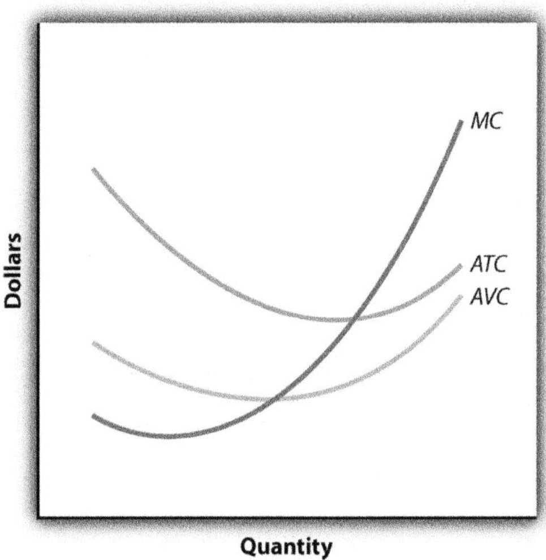

REVIEW

- The marginal cost curve, the average total cost curve, and the average variable cost curve are closely related. In the region in which the marginal cost is higher than the average total (or variable) cost, average total (or variable) cost is increasing, and vice versa.
- We can apply the lessons learned in the example of Melodic Movements to derive the generic shapes of a firm's cost curves. These curves should have the following attributes:
  - The marginal cost (*MC*) curve should cut through both the average total cost (*ATC*) curve and the average variable cost (*AVC*) curve at their lowest points.
  - The average fixed cost becomes very small as output increases. Therefore, the gap between average total cost and average variable cost gets smaller as more is produced.
  - The marginal cost curve typically slopes downward at very low levels of output before sloping upward. The marginal cost and the average variable cost are also identical at one unit of output.

3. THE PRODUCTION DECISION IN THE SHORT RUN

As we saw in Chapter 6, a competitive firm takes the market price as given. If it is maximizing profits, it will choose a quantity to produce in the short run such that its marginal cost equals the market price ($P = MC$). But when the firm produces this quantity, are its profits positive? Or is the firm running a loss? If it is running a loss, should it shut down in the short run? To answer these questions, we need to use the cost curves to find the firm's profits.

3.1 The Profit or Loss Rectangle

The level of production for a competitive firm with the cost curves in Figure 8.6 is shown in Figure 8.7. The quantity produced is determined by the intersection of the marginal cost (*MC*) curve and the market price line (*P*). We draw a dashed vertical line to mark the quantity (*Q*) produced. Because profits equal total revenue minus total costs, we need to represent total revenue and total costs on the average cost diagram.

FIGURE 8.7 Price Equals Marginal Cost

If a firm is maximizing profits, then it chooses a quantity (*Q*) such that price equals marginal cost. Thus, the quantity is determined by the intersection of the market price line and the marginal cost curve, as shown on the diagram. In this picture, the *ATC* and *AVC* curves are a sideshow, but they enter the main act in Figure 8.8, when we look at the firm's level of profits.

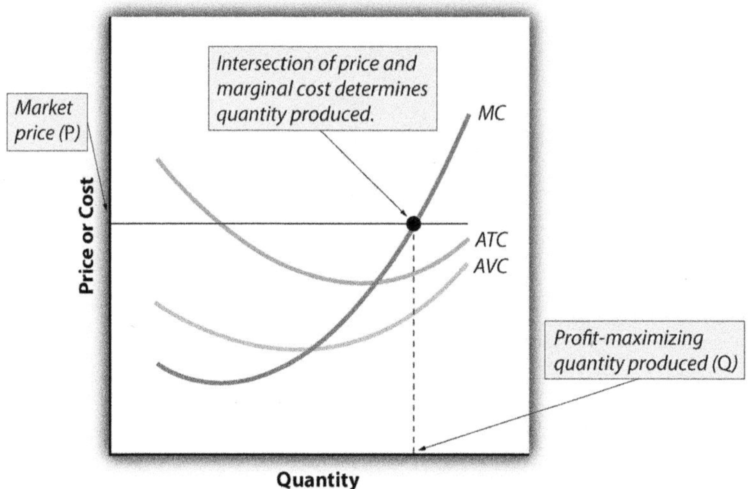

The Total Revenue Area

Figure 8.7 shows a particular market price *P* and the corresponding level of production *Q* chosen by the firm. The total revenue that the firm gets is price *P* times quantity *Q*. Figure 8.8 shows that this total revenue can be represented by the area of a rectangle with width *Q* and height *P*. The shaded area in Figure 8.8 illustrates this rectangle. The area of this rectangle, P × Q, is total revenue.

The Total Costs Area

Total costs also can be represented in Figure 8.8. First, observe the dashed vertical line in Figure 8.8 marking the profit-maximizing quantity produced. Next, observe the point at which the average total cost curve intersects this dashed vertical line. This point tells us what the firm's average total cost is when it produces the profit-maximizing quantity. The area of the rectangle with the hash marks shows the firm's total costs. Why? Remember that average total cost is defined as total costs divided by quantity. If we take average total cost and multiply by quantity, we get total costs: ATC × Q = TC. The quantity produced (*Q*) is the width of the rectangle, and average total cost (*ATC*) is the height of the rectangle. Hence, total costs are given by the area of the rectangle with the hash marks.

Profits or Losses

Because profits are total revenue less total costs, we compute profits by looking at the difference between the two rectangles. The difference is a rectangle, shown by the part of the revenue rectangle that rises above the total costs rectangle. *Profits are positive* in Figure 8.8 because total revenue is greater than total costs. But profits can also be negative, as shown in Figure 8.9.

Suppose that the market price is at a point at which the intersection of the marginal cost curve and the market price line gives a quantity of production for which average total cost is *above* the price. This situation is shown in Figure 8.9. At this lower price, we still have the necessary condition for profit maximization. The firm will produce the quantity that equates to price and marginal cost, as shown by the intersection of the price line and the marginal cost curve.

The amount of total revenue at this price is again price times quantity (P × Q), or the shaded rectangle. Total costs are average total cost times the quantity produced, that is, ATC × Q, or the area of the rectangle with the hash marks.

FIGURE 8.8 Showing Profits on the Cost Curve Diagram

The price and quantity produced are the same as those in Figure 8.7. The area of the shaded rectangle is total revenue. We use the *ATC* curve to find total costs to compute profits. First, we mark where the *ATC* curve intersects the dashed vertical line showing the quantity produced. The area of the rectangle with the hash marks is total costs because the total costs (*TC*) equal average total cost (*ATC*) times quantity produced, *TC* = *ATC* x *Q*. The part of the shaded rectangle rising above the hash-marked area is profits.

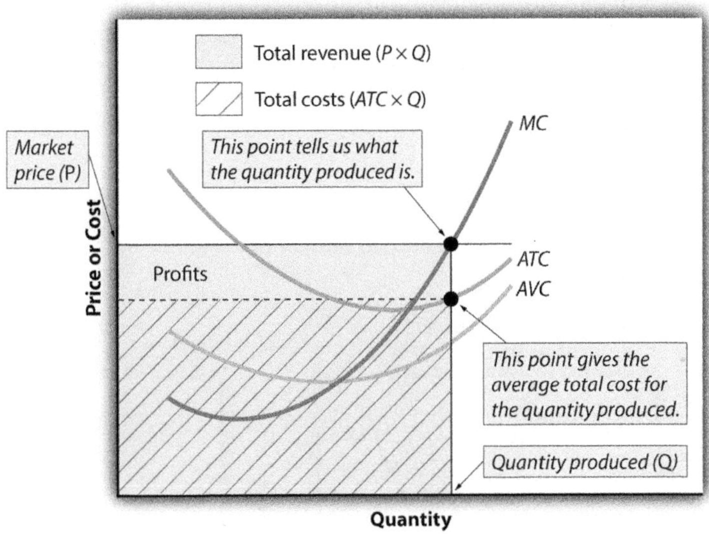

FIGURE 8.9 Showing a Loss on the Cost Curve Diagram

In this figure, the market price is lower than in Figure 8.8. The market price line intersects the marginal cost curve at a point below the average total cost curve. Thus, the area of the total costs rectangle is larger than the area of the total revenue rectangle. Profits are less than zero, and the loss is shown in the diagram.

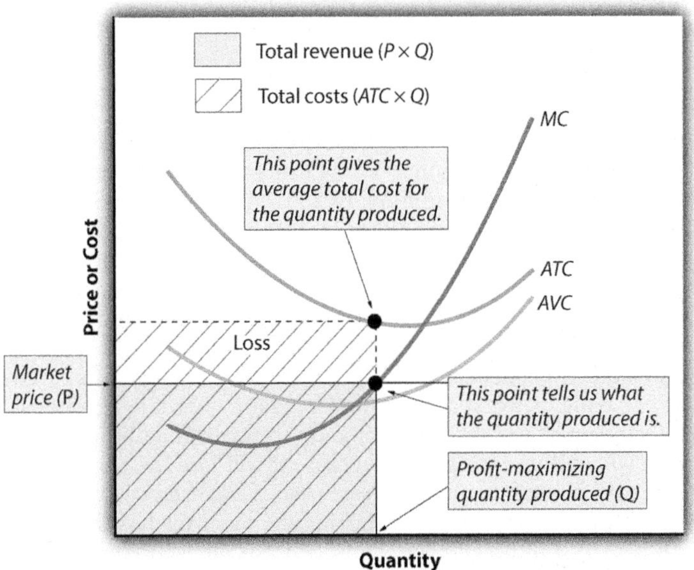

The difference between total revenue and total costs is profit, but in this case *profits are negative*, that is, at a loss. Total revenue is less than total costs, as shown by the cost rectangle's extending above the revenue rectangle. The extent of cost overhang is the loss.

3.2 The Breakeven Point

If the intersection of price and marginal cost is at a quantity at which price exceeds average total cost, the firm makes profits. If, on the other hand, the intersection of price and marginal cost is at a quantity at which price is less than the average total cost, the firm loses money. Therefore, if the intersection of price and marginal cost is at a quantity at which price is equal to average total cost, the firm is breaking even, neither making nor losing money.

breakeven point

The point at which price equals the minimum of average total cost.

Breaking even is shown in the middle panel of Figure 8.10. The market price is drawn through the point at which the marginal cost curve intersects the average total cost curve, which is the minimum point on the average total cost curve. At that price, average total cost equals the price, so that the total revenue rectangle and the total cost rectangle are exactly the same. Thus, the difference between their areas is zero. At $P =$ minimum ATC, the firm is at a **breakeven point** and economic profits are zero. The firm earns positive profits if the price is greater than the breakeven point ($P >$ minimum ATC), as shown in the left panel. The firm has negative profits (a loss) if the price is lower than the breakeven point ($P <$ minimum ATC), as shown in the right panel of Figure 8.10.

FIGURE 8.10 The Breakeven Point

When profits are zero, we are at the breakeven point, as shown in the middle panel. In this case, the market price line intersects the marginal cost curve exactly where it crosses the average total cost curve. The left panel shows a higher market price, and profits are greater than zero. The right panel shows a lower market price, and profits are less than zero—there is a loss. The cost curves are exactly the same in each diagram.

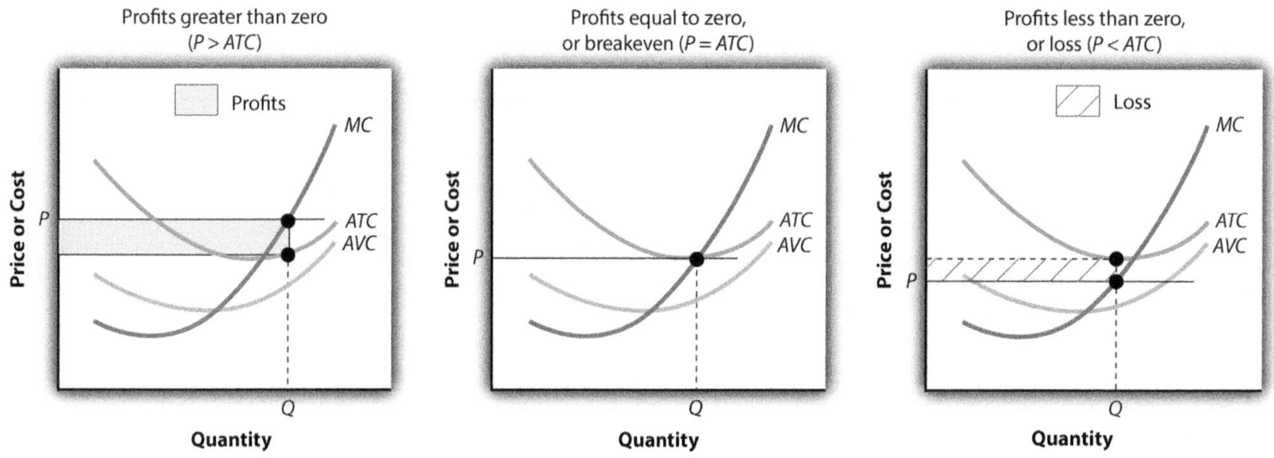

3.3 The Shutdown Point

The situation illustrated in the right panel of Figure 8.10 is not uncommon; every day we hear of businesses losing money. But many of these money-losing firms continue to stay in business. In 1993, Adidas, the running shoe company, lost $100 million. In 2001, Amazon.com lost more than $1 billion, but the money-losing firm did not shut down in either case. Why does a firm with negative profits stay in business? At what point does it decide to shut down? Let's examine this more carefully.

The key concept is that, in the short run, the fixed costs have to be paid even if the firm is shut down. So the firm should keep operating if it can minimize its losses by doing so, in other words, if the losses from shutting down exceed the losses from continuing to operate. Using our example of the piano-moving firm, Melodic Movements should keep producing as long as its revenue from moving pianos exceeds the cost of paying its workers to move the pianos, even if its revenue is insufficient to cover total costs, which include paying for the trucks and terminals in addition to paying the workers. If the firm shuts down, it will end up losing more because it will lose the entire fixed costs, whereas if it keeps operating, it will earn enough to cover at least part of the fixed costs. Conversely, if the price of moving pianos is so low that the revenue from moving the pianos is less than the workers are paid to move the pianos, it is best to shut down production and not move any pianos. The firm will lose the fixed costs for the trucks and the garage, but at least it will not lose any additional money.

We can make this analysis more formal by presenting it in terms of the cost curves shown in Figure 8.11. If the price is above minimum average variable cost ($P >$ minimum AVC), as shown in the left panel of Figure 8.11, the firm should not shut down, even if the price is below average total cost and profits are negative. Because total revenue is greater than variable costs, shutting down would eliminate this extra revenue. By continuing operations, the firm can minimize its losses, so it is better to keep producing in the short run. For example, Adidas did not shut down in 1993 because it had to pay fixed costs in the short run; with the price of running shoes greater than the average variable cost of producing them, the losses were less than if it had shut down.

FIGURE 8.11 The Shutdown Point

When price is above average variable cost, the firm should keep producing even if profits are negative. But if price is less than average variable cost, losses will be smaller if the firm shuts down and stops producing. Hence, the shutdown point is the point at which price equals average variable cost.

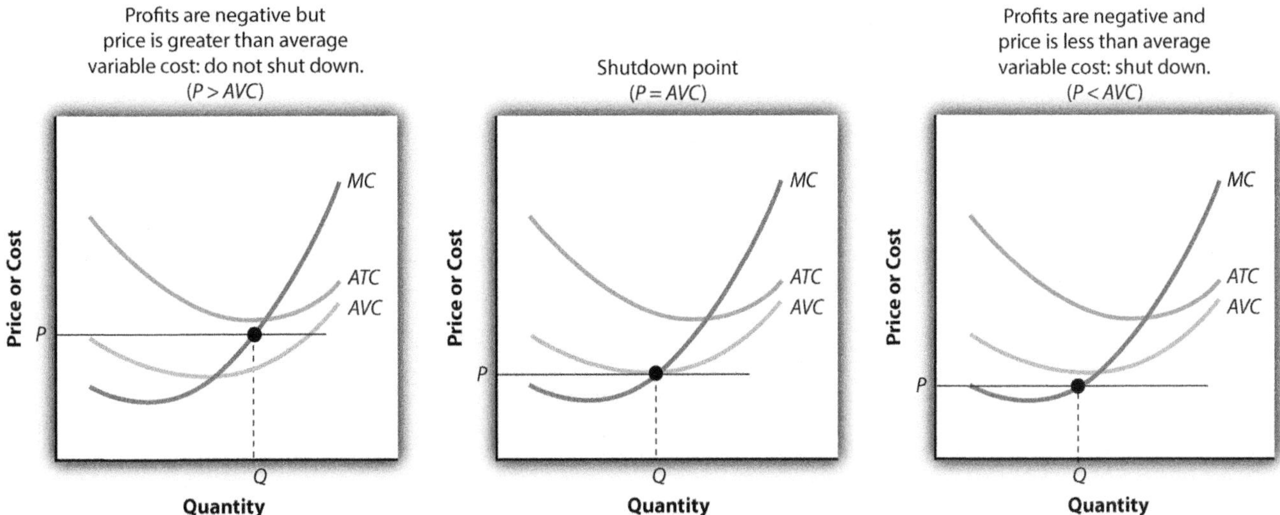

The firm should shut down if the price falls below minimum average variable cost ($P <$ minimum AVC) and is not expected to rise again, as shown in the right panel of Figure 8.11. Because total revenue is less than variable costs, shutting down would eliminate the extra costs. By shutting down, the firm will have to pay its fixed costs in the short run but will not have the burden of additional losses. Economists have developed the concept of sunk cost, which may help you understand and remember why a firm like Adidas would continue to operate in the short run even though it was reporting losses. A sunk cost is a cost that you have committed to pay and that you cannot recover. For example, if a firm signs a year's lease for factory space, it must make rental payments until the lease is up, whether the space is used or not. The important thing about a sunk cost is that once you commit to it, you cannot do anything about it, so you might as well ignore it in your decisions. The firm cannot recover these costs by shutting down. All Adidas could do in the short run was reduce its losses, and it did so by continuing to produce shoes (assuming that the revenue from each pair of shoes was greater than the variable cost of producing them).

Now, observe that the middle panel of Figure 8.11 shows the case in which price exactly equals the minimum point of the average variable cost curve ($P =$ minimum AVC). This is called the **shutdown point**: It is the price at which total revenue exactly equals the firm's variable costs. If the price falls below the shutdown point, the firm should shut down. If the price is above the shutdown point, the firm should continue producing.

shutdown point

The point at which price equals the minimum of average variable cost.

In thinking about the shutdown point, the time period is important. We are looking at the firm during the short run, when it is obligated to pay its fixed costs and cannot alter its capital. The question for Melodic Movements is what to do when it already has committed to paying for the trucks and terminals, but the price of moving pianos falls to such a low level that it does not cover variable costs. The shutdown rule says to stop producing in that situation. However, if profits are negative, but the price is greater than average variable cost, then it is best to keep producing.

The shutdown point can be incorporated into the firm's supply curve. Recall that the supply curve of a single firm tells us the quantity of a good that the firm will produce at different prices. As long as the price is above minimum average variable cost, the firm will produce a quantity such that marginal cost equals the price. Thus, for prices above minimum average variable cost, the marginal cost curve is the firm's supply curve, as shown in the marginal figure. If the price falls below minimum average variable cost, however, then the firm will shut down; in other words, the quantity produced will equal zero ($Q = 0$). Thus, for prices below minimum average variable cost, the supply curve jumps over to the vertical axis, where $Q = 0$, as shown in the marginal figure.

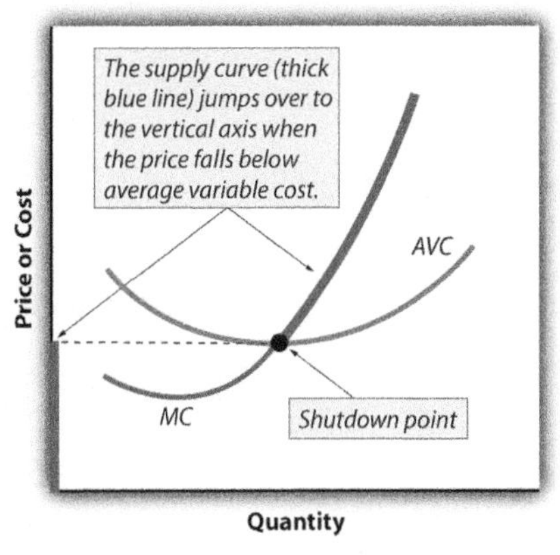

Ensure that you understand the difference between the shutdown point and the breakeven point. The shutdown point is the point at which price equals the minimum average variable cost (Figure 8.11). The breakeven point is the point at which price equals the minimum average total cost (Figure 8.10). If the price is between the minimum average total cost and the minimum average variable cost, then the firm is not breaking even; it is losing money. It does not make sense to shut down in the short run, however, unless the price falls below the shutdown point.

Two different points:

Shutdown point: P = minimum AVC

Breakeven point: P = minimum ATC

Reminder: *You can use some algebra to check the result that a firm should stop producing when the price is less than average variable cost:*

P < AVC

Note that Profits = total revenue – total costs

Because total costs equal variable costs plus fixed costs, we can replace total costs to get

Profits = P × Q – VC – FC

Now, since VC = AVC × Q,

we have

Profits = P × Q – AVC × Q – FC

Rearranging this gives

$$\text{Profits} = (P - AVC) \times Q - FC$$

If $P < AVC$, the first term in this expression is negative unless $Q = 0$. Thus, if $P < AVC$, the best your firm can do is set $Q = 0$. This eliminates the negative drain on profits in the first term in the last expression. You minimize your loss by setting $Q = 0$.

REVIEW

- Total revenue for a firm for a given price is represented by the area of the rectangle whose height is the price and whose width is the profit-maximizing quantity corresponding to that price. Total costs for a firm producing that quantity are represented by the area of the rectangle whose width is the quantity and whose height is the average total cost corresponding to that quantity.
- Profits also can be represented as a rectangle on the cost curve diagram. The profit or loss rectangle is the difference between the revenue rectangle and the loss rectangle.
- When P> minimum ATC, total revenue exceeds total costs, so the firm is making profits. When P< minimum ATC, total costs exceed total revenue, so the firm is losing money. When P= minimum ATC, the firm is making zero profits; this is called the breakeven point.
- A firm that is losing money may continue to operate, or it may choose to shut down. That decision depends on the relationship between price and average variable cost, keeping in mind that fixed costs already have been incurred in the short run.
- If P> minimum AVC, then the firm will continue to operate in the short run because it is earning enough to cover its variable costs and some, but not all, of its fixed costs. When P< minimum AVC, profits are maximized by shutting down because continuing to operate will result in the firm losing even more than its fixed costs.
- The point at which P= minimum AVC is called the shutdown point. When price is in between the breakeven point and the shutdown point, the firm is losing money, but it is minimizing its losses in the short run by continuing to operate.
- The shutdown point can be incorporated into the supply curve. Because the firm will choose to stay in business only when P> minimum AVC, the supply curve will be zero for prices below minimum AVC. Above minimum AVC, the marginal cost curve will be the supply curve.

4. COST AND PRODUCTION: THE LONG RUN

Thus far, we have focused our analysis on the short run. By definition, the short run is the period of time during which it is not possible for firms to adjust certain inputs to production. But what happens in the long run, when it *is* possible for firms to make such adjustments? For example, what happens to Melodic Movements when it opens new terminals or takes out a lease on a fleet of new trucks? To answer this question, we need to show how the firm can adjust its costs in the long run. All costs, fixed costs as well as variable costs, can be adjusted in the long run.

4.1 The Effect of Capital Expansion on Costs

First, consider what happens to fixed costs when the firm increases its capital. Suppose Melodic Movements increases the size of its fleet from four trucks to eight trucks and raises the number of terminals from two to four. Then its fixed costs would increase because more rent would have to be paid for four terminals and eight trucks than for two terminals and four trucks. To obtain the increase in fixed costs, we need to use the price of capital. Suppose trucks cost $25 per day and a terminal costs $100 per day. Then four trucks and two terminals would cost $300 and eight trucks and four terminals would cost $600. Fixed costs would rise from $300 to $600.

Second, consider what happens to variable costs when the firm increases its capital. An increase in capital increases the amount that each additional worker can produce. For example, according to Table 8.1, 166 worker-hours were required for Melodic Movements to move 10 pianos when it had four trucks and two terminals. With more capital (eight trucks and four terminals), it will take fewer hours of work to move the pianos. Assume, for example, that it takes only 120 worker-hours to deliver 10 pianos. In this scenario, with the wage equal to $10 per hour, the variable cost of moving 10 pianos falls from $1,660 to $1,200. In other words, variable costs decline as the firm expands its capital.

Now consider total costs. With fixed costs larger and variable costs smaller as a result of the increase in capital, what is the effect on total costs, which are the sum of fixed costs and variable costs? After the expansion, total costs will be higher at very low levels of output, in which case fixed costs dominate, but they will be lower at high levels of output, in which case variable costs dominate.

Figure 8.12 illustrates this using the total cost curve. Figure 8.12 is essentially the same as Figure 8.3 except that the curves show the old costs before the expansion of capital and the new costs with the additional capital. The diagram shows that the new fixed costs are higher and the new variable costs are lower. The new total cost curve (TC_2) is twisted relative to the old total cost curve (TC_1). The new total cost curve is above the old total cost curve at low levels of output and below the old total cost curve at high levels of output.

FIGURE 8.12 **Shifts in Total Costs as a Firm Increases Its Capital in the Long Run**

When a firm increases its capital, its fixed costs increase; as shown in the diagram, fixed costs rise from FC_1 to FC_2. Its variable costs decrease, however, which also is shown. Thus, the new total costs curve (TC_2) will be above the old total costs curve (TC_1) for low-level output and below the old total costs curve (TC_1) for high-level output.

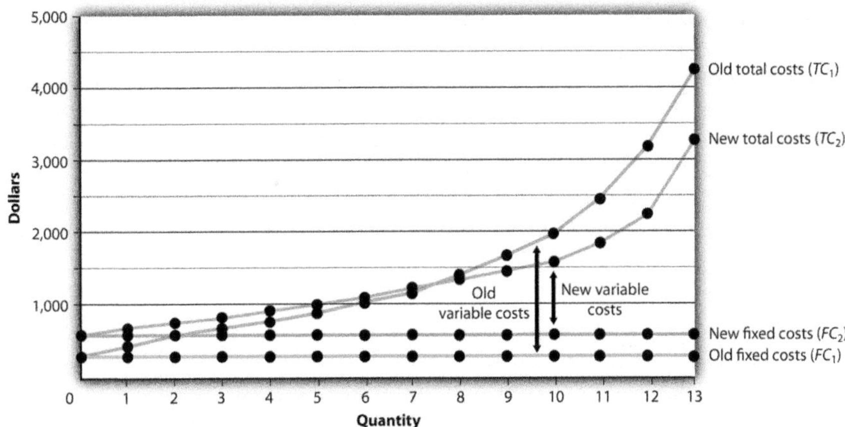

TABLE 8.2 Costs with More Capital

(Compared with the table in Figure 8.2, fixed costs are higher and variable costs are lower in this table because capital is higher than in Figure 8.2. Costs are measured in dollars.)

Quantity	Total Costs	Fixed Costs	Variable Costs	Average Total Cost
0	600	600	0	—
1	690	600	90	690
2	770	600	170	385
3	840	600	240	280
4	920	600	320	230
5	1,010	600	410	202
6	1,110	600	510	185
7	1,220	600	620	174
8	1,340	600	740	168
9	1,470	600	870	163
10	1,610	600	1,010	161
11	1,880	600	1,280	171
12	2,300	600	1,700	192

Table 8.2 provides the numerical information about the costs that appear in Figure 8.12. To see the effect of the firm's expansion on its costs, compare the fixed costs, variable costs, and total costs in Table 8.2 with those in Figure 8.1. Observe that fixed costs are higher: $600 rather than $300. Variable costs are lower throughout the range of production. As a result, total costs are higher in Table 8.2 than in Figure 8.1 for production of less than eight units, and total costs are lower in Table 8.2 than in Figure 8.1 for production of eight units or more.

Our analysis of the effects of the firm's capital expansion on total costs can be used to derive the effects on average total cost. Remember, average total cost (*ATC*) is total costs (*TC*) divided by the quantity (*Q*). Thus, if total costs increase at a given quantity of output, so too will average total cost. And if total costs decrease at a given level of output, so too will average total cost.

This scenario is illustrated in Figure 8.13. An average total cost curve, labeled ATC_1, corresponding to average total cost in Figure 8.1 is plotted. Another average total cost curve, labeled ATC_2, corresponding to average total cost in Table 8.2 also is plotted. The new average total cost curve (ATC_2) is above the old average total cost curve (ATC_1) at low levels of output and below the old average total cost curve (ATC_1) at higher levels of output. Average total cost is higher for production of less than eight units and lower for production of eight units or more. This is precisely what is shown for total costs in Figure 8.12.

4.2 The Long-Run *ATC* Curve

Now that we have seen what happens at Melodic Movements when capital is expanded by a certain amount, we can see what happens when capital increases by even larger amounts. For example, suppose Melodic Movements expands throughout Houston, and even beyond Houston, by expanding the size of its fleet of trucks and the number of terminals to park and service the trucks.

FIGURE 8.13 **Shifts in Average Total Cost Curves When a Firm Expands Its Capital**

The effects on average total cost follow directly from the effects on total costs in Figure 8.12. Here ATC_1 is the average total cost curve with a lower amount of capital, and ATC_2 is the average total cost curve with a higher amount of capital. To the left, at lower levels of output, higher fixed costs raise average total cost; to the right, at higher levels of output, lower variable costs tend to lower average total cost.

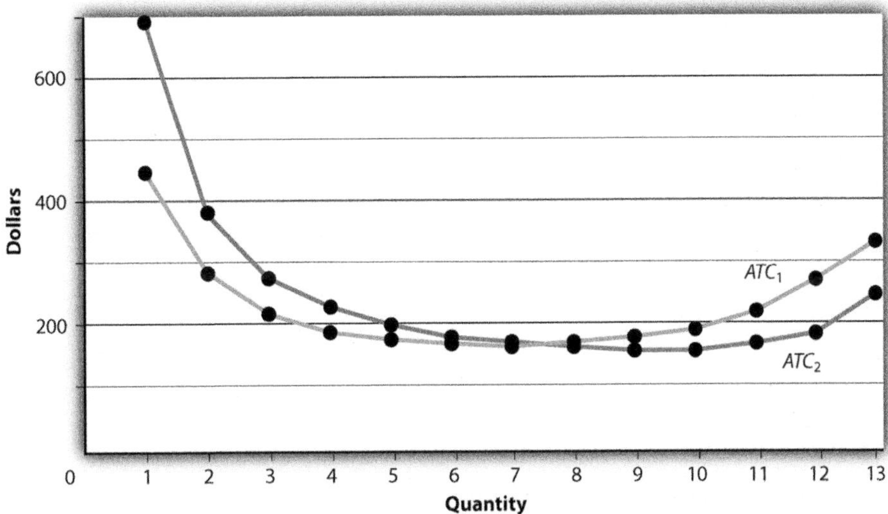

Figure 8.14 shows four different average total cost curves. Each of the average total cost curves corresponds to increased capital expansion at Melodic Movements. The first two of these, ATC_1 and ATC_2, are the average total cost curves from Figure 8.13. Note that the second curve (ATC_2) is above the first (ATC_1) at low levels of output and below the first at high levels of output. The third and fourth curves are for even more trucks and terminals. The third average total cost curve (ATC_3) is above the second (ATC_2) at lower levels of output and below the second (ATC_2) at higher levels of output. The same is true of the fourth curve compared with the third.

The thick light-orange curve tracing out the bottoms of the four average total cost curves gives the lowest average total cost at any quantity produced. This thick line tells us what average total cost is when the firm can expand (or contract) its capital; in other words, this is the average total cost curve for the long run. For this reason, we call the curve that traces out the points on the lowest average total cost curves the **long-run average total cost curve**. The other average total cost curve that we have been discussing is called the *short-run average total cost curve*, or simply the average total cost curve.

long-run average total cost curve

The curve that traces out the short-run average total cost curves, showing the lowest average total cost for each quantity produced as the firm expands in the long run.

The lack of smoothness in the long-run average total cost curve may seem strange. It occurs in Figure 8.14 because we have drawn only four short-run average total cost curves. If it is possible to expand capital in smaller amounts, then the curve will look smoother. For example, between the first and second short-run average total cost curves (ATC_1 and ATC_2) in Figure 8.14, there might be an average total cost curve for six trucks and three terminals. When we put in more and more short-run average total cost curves, the long-run average total cost curve gets smoother and smoother. But it simply traces out the points of lowest cost for each level of output.

FIGURE 8.14 Long-Run versus Short-Run Average Total Cost

In the short run, it is not possible to change certain inputs, like the size of the factory or the number of machines. In the long run, these inputs can be changed. For example, in the long run, Melodic Movements can build more terminals around town. This means that the *ATC* curve shifts. The diagram shows four different *ATC* curves for Melodic Movements; each new *ATC* curve represents more terminals, buildings, and machines than the *ATC* curve to its left. The long run average total cost curve is shown by the thicker orange line.

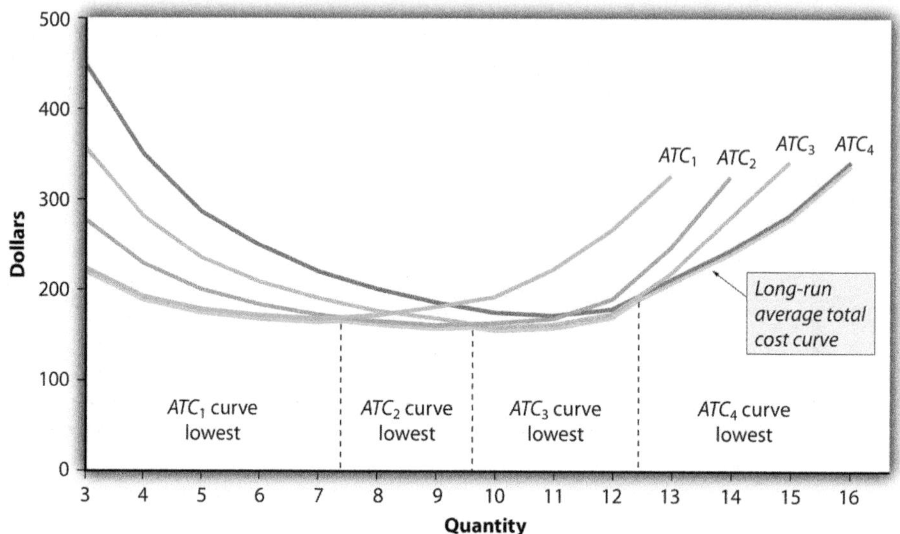

4.3 Capital Expansion and Production in the Long Run

How does a firm like Melodic Movements decide whether to expand or contract its capital in the long run? How much does it produce in the long run? The decision is similar to the short-run decision about whether to hire more workers to move more pianos. Again, the firm sets the quantity produced to maximize profits. But now the quantity produced and profits can be affected by changes in capital as well as labor. At any level of capital and labor input, we can compute profits.

If the firm can increase its profits by expanding its capital and its output, then we predict that it will do so. If we find that the firm can increase its profits by reducing its capital and its output, then we predict that it will do so. In other words, the firm adjusts the amount of capital to maximize profits.

Furthermore, in the long run, the firm adjusts both its capital and its labor. What determines the mix of labor and capital when both are variable? The relative price of labor compared with capital will be the deciding factor.

In deriving the cost curves for Melodic Movements, we assumed that the cost of labor was $10 per hour and that the cost of capital, consisting of trucks and terminals, was $25 a day for trucks and $100 a day for terminals. If the cost of labor was higher, say, $20 per hour, then Melodic Movements would have the incentive to rent more trucks rather than hire more workers, at least to the extent that this was feasible.

If the cost of capital rose relative to that of labor, however, then the firm would have the incentive to hire more workers. In general, the firm will use more capital relative to labor if the cost of capital declines relative to that of labor. Conversely, the firm will use less capital relative to labor if the cost of capital rises relative to that of labor.

REVIEW

- In the long run, the firm can expand by increasing its capital. Fixed costs increase and variable costs decline at each level of production as the firm expands its capital.
- Thus, total costs, and average total cost, are higher at low levels of production and lower at high levels of production.
- The average total cost in the long run can be found by tracing out the lowest points of the short-run average total cost curves.
- In the long run, the firm adjusts the amount of capital to maximize profits. It also will choose the mix of labor and capital that maximizes profits, so that when the price of labor rises relative to capital, the firm will switch away from labor toward capital, and vice versa.

5. ECONOMICS OF SCALE

The long-run average total cost curve is one way in which economists study the behavior of a firm over time. Whether the long-run average total cost curve slopes up or down, and over what range, is crucial for understanding the nature of a firm, the industry in which it operates, and the role of government.

The long-run average total cost curve describes a situation in which the firm can expand all its inputs. When all inputs increase, we say that the scale of the firm increases. For example, if the number of workers at the firm doubles, the number of trucks doubles, the number of terminals doubles, and so on, then we say that the scale of the firm doubles. Thus, the long-run average total cost curve describes what happens to a firm's average total cost when its scale increases. We use specialized terminology to describe different shapes of the long-run average total cost curve.

We say that there are **economies of scale**, or *increasing returns to scale*, if long run average total cost falls as the scale of the firm increases. We say that there are **diseconomies of scale**, or *decreasing returns to scale*, if long-run average total cost rises as the scale of the firm increases. The situation in the middle, in which case long run average total cost neither rises nor falls, is called **constant returns to scale**. Figure 8.15 illustrates these three possible shapes for the long-run average total cost curve.

economies of scale

A situation in which long-run average total cost declines as the output of a firm increases.

diseconomies of scale

A situation in which long-run average total cost increases as the output of a firm increases.

constant returns to scale

A situation in which long-run average total cost is constant as the output of a firm changes.

5.1 Determining Whether a Firm Has Economies or Diseconomies of Scale

Whether a firm has increasing, decreasing, or constant returns to scale depends on the type of firm and the type of product. Consider a firm like Melodic Movements. One can imagine that economies of scale would result as the firm expanded the number of terminals around the city of Houston; with more terminals, trucks could be serviced at many different locations and would not have to be driven so far at the end of the day or towed so far in the event of a breakdown. With a larger workforce, Melodic Movements could have workers who specialize in moving different types of pianos or who specialize in servicing different parts of the trucks. Some might specialize in moves to high-rise buildings. In other words, as the scale of a firm increases, the work can be divided into different tasks, and some members of the labor force can specialize in each task.

FIGURE 8.15 Economies and Diseconomies of Scale

If the long-run average total cost curve slopes downward, we say that there are economies of scale. If the long-run average total cost curve slopes upward, we say that there are diseconomies of scale. If the long-run average total cost curve is flat, we say that there are constant returns to scale, as shown in the middle panel.

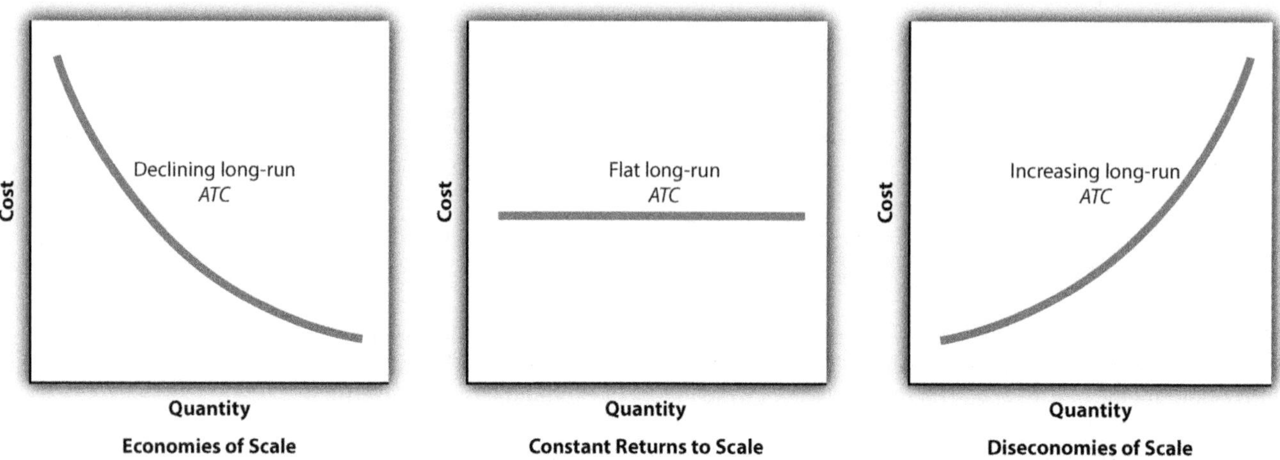

Is there a limit to economies of scale? What about expanding beyond Houston to Galveston, Dallas, Tulsa, Mexico City, or even Lima, Peru? In the case of piano moving, returns to scale probably would decline at some point. The extra administrative costs of organizing a large interstate or worldwide piano-moving firm probably would raise average total cost. Thus, one could imagine that the long-run average total cost curve for Melodic Movements would first decline and then increase as the firm grows in size.

minimum efficient scale

The smallest scale of production for which long-run average total cost is at a minimum.

Although no two firms are alike, the long-run average total cost curve for most firms probably declines at low levels of output, then remains flat, and finally begins to increase at high levels of output. As a firm gets very large, administrative expenses, as well as coordination and incentive problems, will begin to raise average total cost. The smallest scale of production for which long-run average total cost is at a minimum is called the **minimum efficient scale**. A typical long-run average cost curve and its minimum efficient scale are shown in Figure 8.16.

5.2 Mergers and Economies of Scope

An increase or decrease in the scale of a firm through capital expansion or contraction—as described in the previous two sections—is one kind of change in the firm over time. Firms can also change over time in other ways. They can grow through mergers between one firm and another firm. If the product lines of the two firms are similar, then such mergers may be a way to reduce costs, for example, by consolidating the number of executives or by reducing inefficient duplication of resources. That is one reason why large oil companies, such as Exxon and Mobil, merged in the 1990s.

Mergers are also a common way for firms to combine different skills or resources to develop new products. For example, America Online (AOL), an Internet firm, and Time Warner, a large firm producing movies, magazines, and compact discs, merged in 2001. By bringing together distribution resources with content resources, this merger was intended to widen the scope of both firms and help them develop new products. The results did not turn out as expected, however, and in 2003 Time Warner dropped AOL from its corporate name in an effort to demonstrate that the company still valued its "core" assets—magazines, books, cable channels (HBO, CNN), and movies. Combining different types of firms to reduce costs or create new products is sometimes called *economies of scope*. Table 8.3 lists some of the big mergers of recent years. Observe that most of the companies listed involve similar products.

FIGURE 8.16 Typical Shape of the Long-Run Average Total Cost Curve

For many types of firms, the long-run *ATC* curve slopes down at low levels of output, then reaches a flat area, and finally begins to slope up at high levels. The minimum efficient scale is shown.

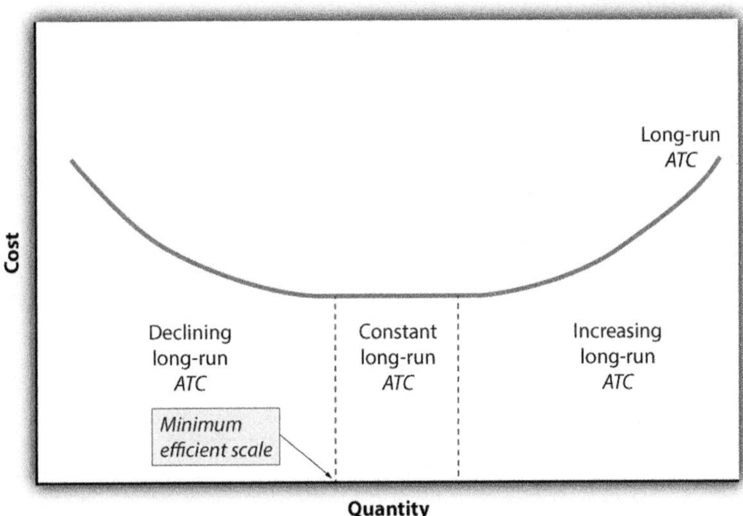

When two firms merge into one firm, each of the original firms may become a division within the new firm. A merger of one firm with another means that the coordination of production moves from the market to within the organization. For example, the merger of the U.S. firm Chrysler with the German firm Daimler-Benz meant that the different makes of cars were produced in two divisions of the same firm. As with the AOL–Time Warner merger, Daimler and Chrysler found out that the merger did not bring the anticipated gains; they parted ways in 2007.

Reminder: *Most of these mergers are in the same industry and illustrate economies of scale except for the last two mergers (America Online/Time Warner and Travelers/Citicorp), which may be the result of expected economies of scope.*

TABLE 8.3 Recent Big Mergers

Names before Merger		Name after Merger	Primary Industry
Exxon	Mobil	ExxonMobil	Oil
BP	Amoco	BP Amoco (now BP)	Oil
J.P. Morgan	Chase Manhattan	JP Morgan Chase	Banking
Bank of America	Fleet Boston Financial	Bank of America Corp.	Banking
Chrysler	Daimler-Benz	DaimlerChrysler	Motor Vehicles
WorldCom	MCI Communications	MCI WorldCom (now WorldCom)	Telecommunications
Walt Disney	Capital Cities/ABC	Walt Disney	Entertainment
Bank of America	Merrill Lynch	Bank of America	Banking
America Online	Time Warner	AOL Time Warner (now Time Warner)	Internet and Entertainment
Travelers	Citicorp	Citigroup	Financial Services

REVIEW

- Economies of scale are said to exist for a firm when the long-run average total cost curve declines as the scale of the firm increases. Economies of scale may occur because of the specialization that the division of labor in larger firms permits.
- Although economies of scale probably exist over some regions of production, the evidence indicates that as firms grow very large, diseconomies of scale set in.
- The smallest scale of production at which long-run average total cost is at a minimum is called the minimum efficient scale of the firm.
- Instead of changing by increasing the capital stock, firms sometimes change via mergers. Mergers between firms that produce similar products can result in lower costs and a higher minimum efficient scale of production.
- Mergers are also a common way for firms with different types of skills and expertise to combine that knowledge and widen the scope of what they jointly produce. Firms that have the ability to do this type of merger are said to have economies of scope.

6. END-OF-CHAPTER MATERIALS

6.1 Conclusion

In this chapter, we have developed a model for studying why firms shut down, expand, or contract. This analysis of changes at firms over time is an extension of the analysis of a firm's short-run behavior in Chapter 6.

A centerpiece of the model is a graph (Figure 8.6) that shows the firm's average total cost and average variable cost. Using this graph, we can determine whether a firm will shut down in the short run. Using additional average total cost curves corresponding to alternative levels of capital, we also can determine whether the firm will expand or contract.

We showed how this model can be used to find the firm's long-run total cost and average cost curves. By looking at a firm's long-run average total cost curve (Figure 8.16), we can tell whether a firm has economies of scale. We will use the long-run average total cost curve extensively in the next several chapters of this book.

Key Points

1. Firms start up, expand, contract, or shut down when conditions in the economy change.
2. The short run and the long run are two broad categories into which economists categorize time periods. The short run is the period of time during which it is not possible for the firm to change all the inputs to production; only some inputs, such as labor, can be changed. The long run is the minimum period of time in which the firm can vary all inputs to production, including capital.
3. Total costs are all the costs incurred by the firm in producing goods or services. Fixed costs are the portion of total costs that do not vary with the amount produced in the short run. Variable costs are the remaining portion of total costs that do vary as production changes.
4. Average total cost, or cost per unit, is widely used by economists, accountants, and investors to assess a firm's cost behavior. The profit made by the firm in the short run depends on the difference between the price and average total cost at the quantity corresponding to that price.
5. When the market price equals the minimum of average total cost, the firm breaks even. At higher prices, profits are positive. At lower prices, profits are negative.
6. The firm will keep producing, in some circumstances, even if profits are negative in the short run. This is because the fixed costs would have to be incurred regardless of whether or not any production is done. So if the price is enough to cover variable costs, the firm should keep producing to minimize its losses.
7. When the market price equals the minimum of average variable cost, the firm is just at the point of shutting down. If the price is below average variable cost, the firm should shut down.
8. The long-run average total cost curve describes how a firm's costs behave when the firm expands its capital.
9. If long-run average total cost declines, then there are economies of scale. For many firms, there is a range over which the long-run average total cost curve is flat, and we say that there are constant returns to scale over that range. When firms get very large, diseconomies of scale set in.
10. Firms can expand by merging with other firms. Such mergers can be motivated by either economies of scale or economies of scope.

QUESTIONS FOR REVIEW

1. What is the difference between total costs, fixed costs, and variable costs?
2. How is marginal cost related to total cost?
3. Why does the marginal cost curve cut through the average total cost curve exactly at the minimum of the average total cost curve?
4. Why does the marginal cost curve cut through the average variable cost curve exactly at the minimum of the average variable cost curve?
5. What rectangles in the cost curve diagram depict total revenue, total costs, and profits?
6. What is the difference between the breakeven point and the shutdown point?
7. How is the long-run average total cost curve derived?
8. What is the minimum efficient scale of a firm?
9. What is the relationship between the shape of the long-run total cost curve and economies of scale?
10. What are economies of scope? How are mergers related to economies of scale and scope

PROBLEMS

1. Consider the relationship between your average grade (your grade point average [GPA]) and your marginal grade. Suppose you have taken 12 courses so far, and your average GPA is 3.25. Suppose the marginal grade is the grade you get in this course.
   a. If the grade you get in this class is an A (4.0), which is above your average, what will happen to your average GPA?
   b. If the grade you get in this class is a B (3.0), which is below your average, what will happen to your average GPA?
   c. What does this illustrate about the relationship between marginal and average curves in general?
2. Consider the age of the people working in the firm that you are doing an internship with this summer. Suppose the first person you meet is 40 years old, and the second and third are 33 and 27 years old, respectively. Graph the average and marginal age of the three people in the firm, placing age on the vertical axis and quantity of people on the horizontal axis in the order in which you met them. What do you notice about the relationship between marginal and average age?
3. Fill out the entries in the table below.

Q	*TC*	*FC*	*VC*	*ATC*	*AVC*	*MC*
0	8					
1	12					
2	14					
3	20					
4	30					
5	50					

4. Fill out the entries in the table below.

Quantity	Total Cost	Fixed Cost	Variable Cost	Average Total Cost	Average Variable Cost	Marginal Cost
0						
1				$27.00		$9.00
2				$16.00		
3					$5.00	
4					$5.50	
5					$8.40	

5. Draw the typical average total cost, average variable cost, and marginal cost curves for a profit maximizing, price-taking firm. For the case in which price equals average total cost, show the rectangles that represent
   a. total costs and total revenue.
   b. fixed costs and variable costs.
   c. profits.
   d. In your diagram, show what happens to the size of the areas as the market price increases.
6. Consider the firm whose cost function was provided in Problem 3. Suppose that the firm is a price-taker, and that the market price is $15 per unit.
   a. What quantity will the firm produce?
   b. Will this firm be earning economic profits? If so, how much?
   c. What is the breakeven price?
   d. What is the shutdown price?

7. Consider the firm whose cost function was provided in Problem 4. Suppose that the firm is a price-taker, and that the market price is $13 per unit.
   a. What quantity will this firm produce? Why?
   b. At that quantity level, what profits or losses will this firm make?
   c. In the short run, at what price would this firm break even? Explain briefly.
   d. At what price would the firm shut down? Explain briefly.
8. Suppose the average total cost curves for a firm for three different amounts of capital are as follows in the table. Plot the three average total cost curves in the same diagram. Then determine the long-run average total cost curve and show it in the same diagram.

Quantity	ATC_1	ATC_2	ATC_3
1	40	50	60
2	30	35	40
3	20	25	30
4	30	15	25
5	40	30	20
6	50	40	30

9. Plot the following data on quantity of production and long-run average total cost for a firm. Show the areas of economies and diseconomies of scale and constant returns to scale. What is the minimum efficient scale?

Quantity	Long-Run ATC
1	33
2	27
3	25
4	25
5	30
6	38
7	50

10. Are there economies of scale to teaching an introductory economics course? What economies of scale are realized if class sizes increase? Is there a maximum class size beyond which diseconomies of scale are experienced?

7. APPENDIX TO CHAPTER 8: PRODUCER THEORY WITH ISOQUANTS

In this chapter, we looked at how firms adjust their labor and capital inputs when the cost of these inputs changes over time. Here we give a graphic illustration of a firm's choice between labor and capital. The graphs are similar to the budget lines and indifference curves used to describe consumer choice in the appendix to Chapter 5. We use these graphs to show exactly how a firm's choice between labor and capital depends on the relative price of labor and capital.

7.1 Combining Capital and Labor

Consider an example of a firm with two inputs to production: capital and labor. Table 8.4 shows the possible combinations of inputs available to the firm. For example, if the firm has two units of capital and uses 24 hours of labor, it can produce three units of output. The hypothetical numbers in Table 8.4 could represent a wide variety of firms producing different types of products, but observe that we have chosen the units in the table to be the same as those for the firm shown in Table 8.1. (To make a comparison between Table 8.4 and Table 8.1, you can think of a "unit" of capital as corresponding to four trucks and two terminals with a cost of $300; two units of capital is eight trucks and four terminals at a cost of $600.) Table 8.4 could refer to a firm with any type of capital (computers, machine tools, telephones, or pizza ovens). To allow for all these possibilities, we refer to capital as a "unit" of capital.

TABLE 8.4 Production with Four Levels of Capital

	Labor Input (hours)			
Quantity Produced	With One Unit of Capital	With Two Units of Capital	With Three Units of Capital	With Four Units of Capital
0	0	0	0	0
1	15	9	6	5
2	27	17	12	10
3	37	24	17	13
4	48	32	22	18
5	60	41	29	23
6	74	51	36	29
7	90	62	43	35
8	109	74	52	41
9	134	87	61	49
10	166	101	71	57
11	216	128	90	72
12	290	170	119	95
13	400	270	189	151
14	—	400	300	220
15	—	—	425	300
16	—	—	—	430

Note: The column showing labor input with one unit of capital corresponds to the production function for Melodic Movements discussed in Chapter 8 (see Table 8.2). The omitted entries in the table (—) represent quantities of production that cannot be achieved without more capital.

The information in Table 8.4 can be represented graphically, as shown in Figure 8.17. Each column is plotted with labor input on the horizontal axis and the quantity produced on the vertical axis. Each column represents the production function for a given level of capital. Note that higher levels of capital increase the amount that can be produced with a given amount of labor. In other words, as we add more capital, the relationship between labor and output shifts up.

FIGURE 8.17 The Production Function with Four Levels of Capital

As the amount of labor input increases, so too does the amount of output. Each curve corresponds to a different level of capital. Higher curves represent higher levels of capital. The points on these four curves are obtained from the four columns of Table 8.4.

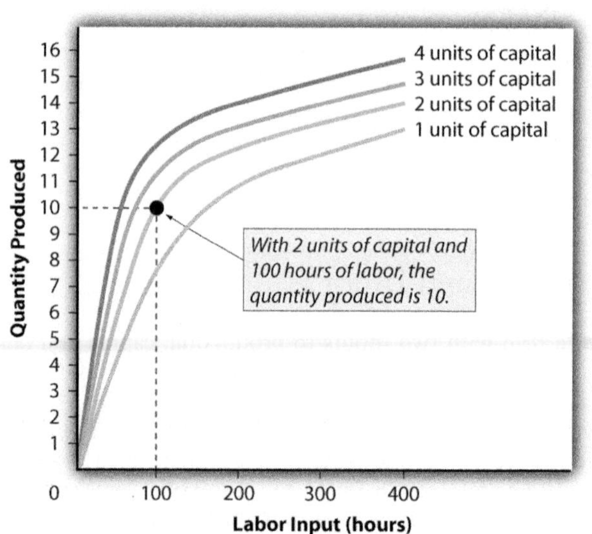

The information in Table 8.4 and Figure 8.17 can be displayed in another graph, Figure 8.18, which provides a visual picture of how labor and capital jointly help a firm produce its product. Figure 8.18 puts capital on the vertical axis and labor on the horizontal axis.We represent the quantity produced in Figure 8.18 by writing a number in a circle equal to the amount produced with each amount of labor and capital. For example, with one unit of capital and 60 hours of labor,the firm can produce five units of output, according to Table 8.4. Thus, we write the number 5 at the point in Figure 8.18 that represents labor input equal to 60 and capital input equal to one.

Isoquants

Observe in Figure 8.18 that the same amount of output can be produced using different combinations of capital and labor. We illustrate this in the figure by connecting the circles with the same quantity by a curved line. Each curve gives the combinations of labor and capital that produce the same quantity of output. The curves in Figure 8.18 are called isoquants, where iso means "the same" and quant stands for "quantity produced." Thus, an **isoquant** is a curve that shows all the possible combinations of labor and capital that result in the same quantity of production. Isoquants convey a lot of information visually. Higher isoquants—those up and to the right—represent higher levels of output. Each isoquant slopes down because ascapital input declines, labor input must increase if the quantity produced is to remain the same. The slope of the isoquants tells us how much labor must be substituted for capital (or vice versa) to leave production unchanged. Thus, the isoquants are good for studying how firms substitute one input for another when the prices of the inputs change. The slope of the isoquant is called the **rate of technical substitution**, because it tells us how much capital needs to be substituted for labor to give the same amount of production when labor is reduced by one unit.

isoquant

A curve that shows all the possible combinations of labor and capital that result in the same quantity of production.

rate of technical substitution

The rate at which one input must be substituted for another input to maintain the same production. The slope of the isoquant.

FIGURE 8.18 Isoquants

Each circled number gives the quantity produced for the amounts of labor and capital on the axes at that point. The lines connecting equal quantities are called isoquants.

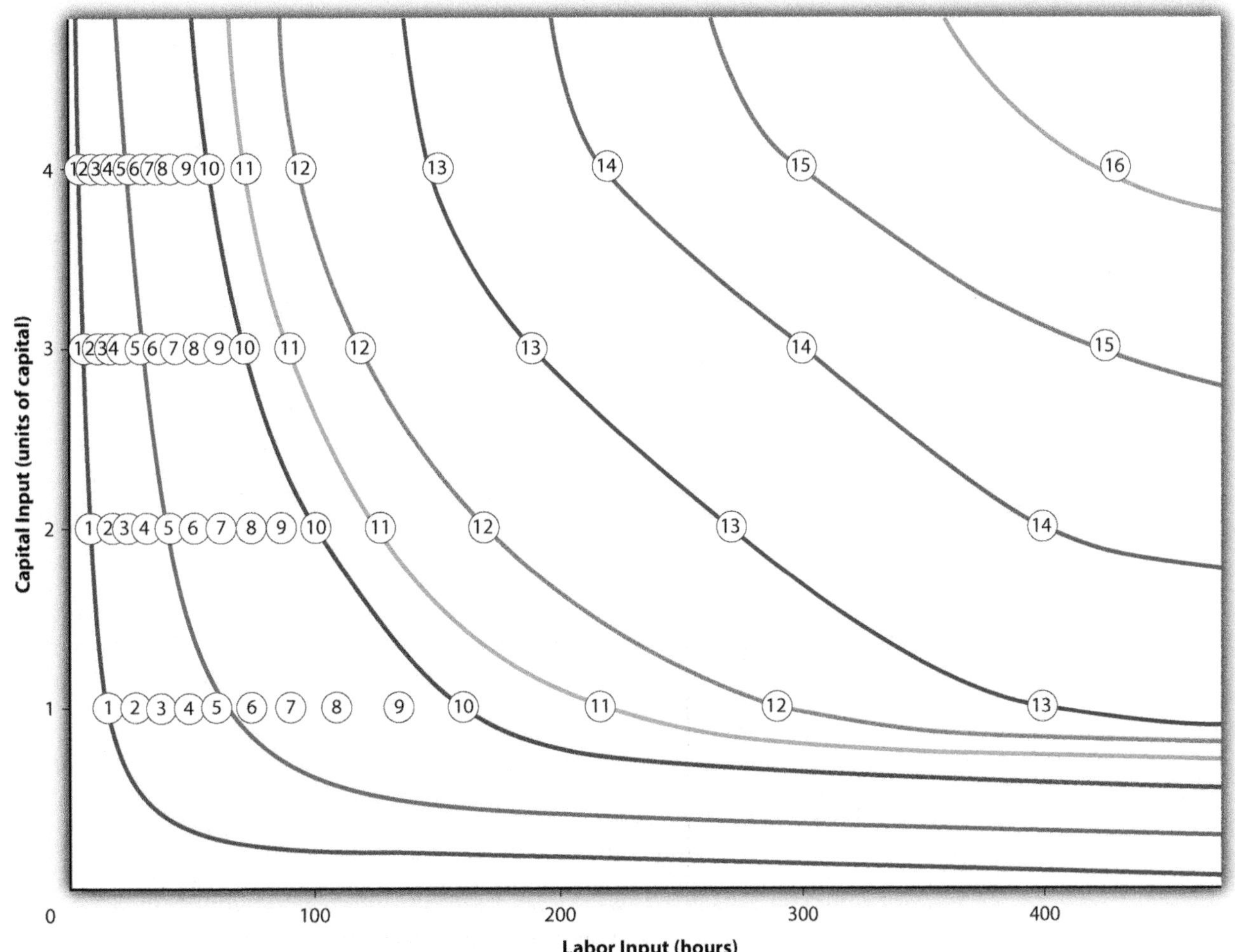

Remember that the points in Figure 8.18 do not display any information that is not in Table 8.4 or Figure 8.17. The same information appears in a different and convenient way.

Isocost Lines

A firm's total costs also can be shown on a diagram like Figure 8.18. In considering the choice between capital and labor, the firm needs to consider the price of both. Suppose that labor costs $10 per hour and capital costs $300 per unit. Then if the firm uses one unit of capital and 150 hours of labor, its total costs will be (1 × $300) + ($150 × $10) = $1,800. For the same total costs, the firm can pay for other combinations of labor and capital. For example, two units of capital and 120 hours of labor also cost $1,800. Other combinations are as follows:

Hours of Labor	Units of Capital	Total Costs
180	0	(180 x $10) + (0 x $300) = $1,800
150	1	(150 x $10) + (1 x $300) = $1,800
120	2	(120 x $10) + (2 x $300) = $1,800
90	3	(90 x $10) + (3 x $300) = $1,800
60	4	(60 x $10) + (4 x $300) = $1,800
30	5	(30 x $10) + (5 x $300) = $1,800
0	6	(0 x $10) + (6 x $300) = $1,800

In other words, the $1,800 can be spent on any of these combinations of labor and capital. With $1,800, the firm can use six units of capital, but that would not enable the firm to hire any workers.

FIGURE 8.19 An Isocost Line

Each isocost line shows all the combinations of labor and capital that give the same total costs. In this case, the price of capital is $300 per unit and the price of labor is $10 per hour. Total costs are $1,800. For example, if one unit of capital and 150 hours of labor are employed, total costs are $1,800 = (1 x $300) + (150 x $10).

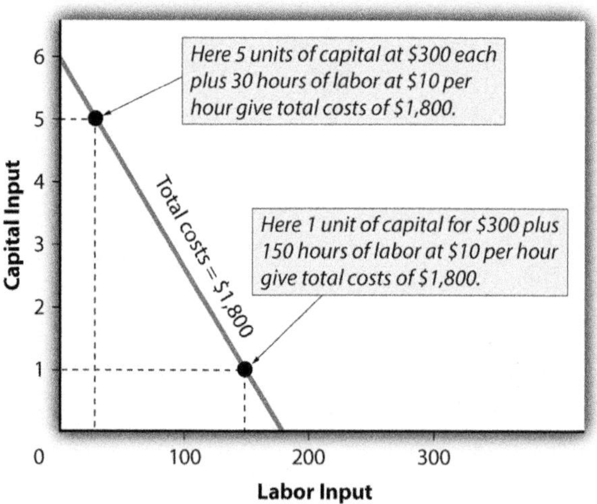

isocost line

A line that shows the combinations of capital and labor that have the same total costs.

These different combinations of labor and capital that have total costs of $1,800 are plotted in Figure 8.19. Each combination of labor and capital in the table is plotted, and the points are connected by a line. The line is called an **isocost line**. An isocost line shows the combinations of capital and labor that have the same total costs.

The position of the isocost line depends on the amount of total costs. Higher total costs are represented by higher isocost lines. This is shown in Figure 8.20. Observe that the isocost line for total costs of $2,100 is above the one for total costs of $1,800.

The slope of the isocost line depends on the ratio of the price of labor to the price of capital. In particular, the slope equals −1 times the ratio of the price of labor to the price of capital. This is illustrated in Figure 8.21 for the case in which total costs equal $1,800. If the price of labor falls from $10 to $6, then the isocost line gets flatter. Thus, if the hourly wage were $6 instead of $10, the firm would be able to pay for 250 hours of work and one unit of capital, compared with only 150 hours and one unit of capital, and still would have total costs of $1,800. Thus, as the price of labor (the wage) falls relative to the price of capital, the isocost line gets flatter.

FIGURE 8.20 Several Isocost Lines with Different Total Costs

Isocost lines with higher total costs are above and to the right of those with lower total costs. All the isocost lines in this diagram have a capital cost of $300 per unit and a labor cost of $10 per hour.

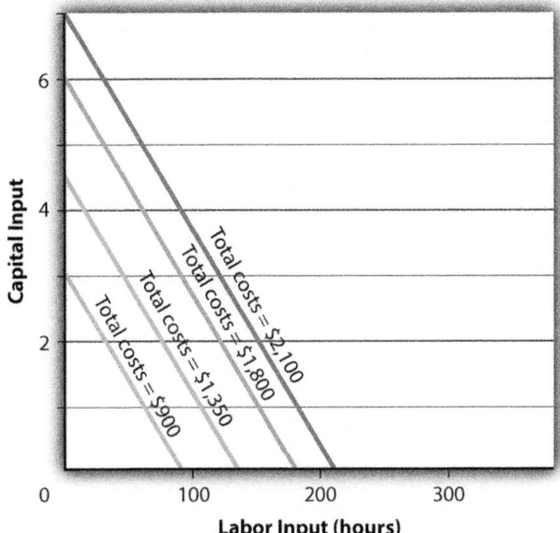

FIGURE 8.21 Effect of a Change in Relative Prices on the Isocost Line

When the price of labor falls relative to the price of capital, the isocost line gets flatter, as in this diagram. In this case, the price of labor falls from $10 per hour to $6 per hour while the price of capital remains at $300 per unit. Total costs remain equal to $1,800 in this case.

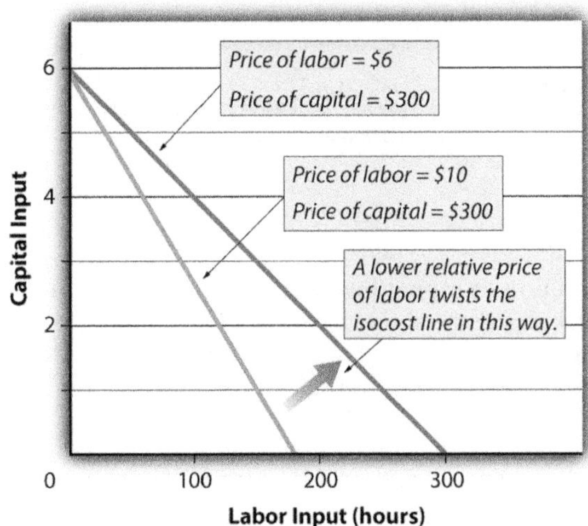

7.2 Minimizing Costs for a Given Quantity

The isoquant and isocost lines can be used to determine the least-cost combination of capital and labor for any given quantity of production. Figure 8.22 shows how. In Figure 8.22, we show three isocost lines, along with an isoquant representing 11 units of output. For the isocost lines, the price of labor is $10 and the price of capital is $300. The point at which the isocost line just touches the isoquant is a *tangency point.* It is labeled *A*.

Point *A* is the point at which the firm minimizes the cost of producing 11 units of output. To see this, suppose you are at point *A* and you move to the left and up along the same isoquant to point *B*

This means that the firm increases capital and decreases hours of labor, keeping the quantity produced constant at 11 units; that is, the firm substitutes capital for labor. But such a substitution increases the firm's costs, as shown in the figure. The payment for the extra capital will be greater than the saving from the reduced labor. Thus, moving along the isoquant from *A* to *B* would increase the total costs to the firm.

A similar reasoning applies to moving from point *A* to point *C*. The firm uses fewer labor hours and less capital at point *C*, so that total costs are lower than they are at point *A*. But at point *C*, the firm does not have enough inputs to produce 11 units of output. Thus, point *A* is the lowest-cost point at which the firm can produce 11 units of output. It is the point at which the lowest isocost line is touching the isoquant.

FIGURE 8.22 Choosing Capital and Labor to Minimize Total Costs

This diagram illustrates how a firm chooses a mix of labor and capital to minimize total costs for a given level of output. Here the given level of output is 11 units, as shown by the single isoquant. Total costs are minimized by choosing the combination of labor and capital given by the tangency (point *A*) between the isocost line and the isoquant. For any other point on the isoquant, the quantity would be the same, but total costs would be higher.

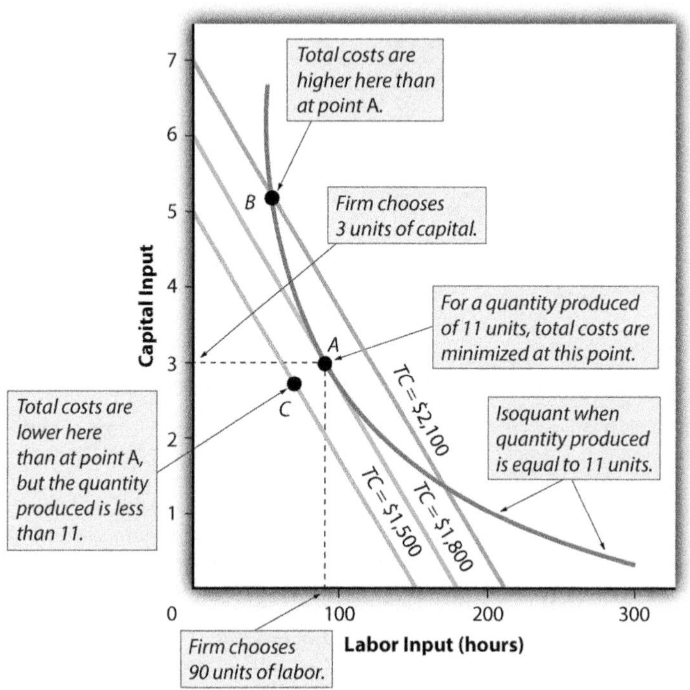

The Cost Minimization Rule

The rate of technical substitution of capital for labor and the ratio of the price of labor to the price of capital are equal at point *A*, because the slopes of the isoquant and of the isocost line are equal at point *A*. If the firm is minimizing its costs, then the rate of technical substitution must equal the input price ratio. The equality between the rate of technical substitution and the input price ratio is called the cost *minimization rule*.

Observe that isoquants are analogous to the indifference curves and the isocost lines are analogous to the budget line described in the appendix to Chapter 5. The cost minimization rule for a firm is much like the utility-maximizing rule for a consumer.

A Change in the Relative Price of Labor

Now we show how isoquants and isocost lines can be used to predict how a firm will adjust its mix of inputs when input prices change. For example, suppose that the hourly wage falls from $10 to $6 and the price of capital rises from $300 to $600. That is, labor becomes cheaper relative to capital. Originally, the ratio of the price of labor to the price of capital was 10/300 = 0.033; now it is 6/600 = 0.010. This is a big reduction, and we would expect the firm to adjust by changing capital and labor input. Figure 8.23 shows how the firm would adjust the mix of capital and labor for a given quantity of output. Figure 8.23 keeps the isoquant fixed but includes a new isocost line that reflects the lower relative price of labor and is tangent to the isoquant. Because the new isocost line is flatter, the point of tangency with the given isoquant no longer occurs at point *A*, at which three units of capital are combined with 90 hours of labor. Now tangency occurs at point *D*, at which two units of capital are combined with 130 hours of labor. In other words, the firm has substituted labor for capital when the relative price of labor fell. At the new point *D*, the firm would use one less unit of capital and 40 more hours of labor.

FIGURE 8.23 Effect of Lower Price of Labor Relative to Capital

The dark-orange isocost line has a lower price of labor relative to capital than the light-orange line. Hence, the amount of capital used by the firm decreases from three units to two units, and the amount of labor rises from 90 hours to 130 hours.

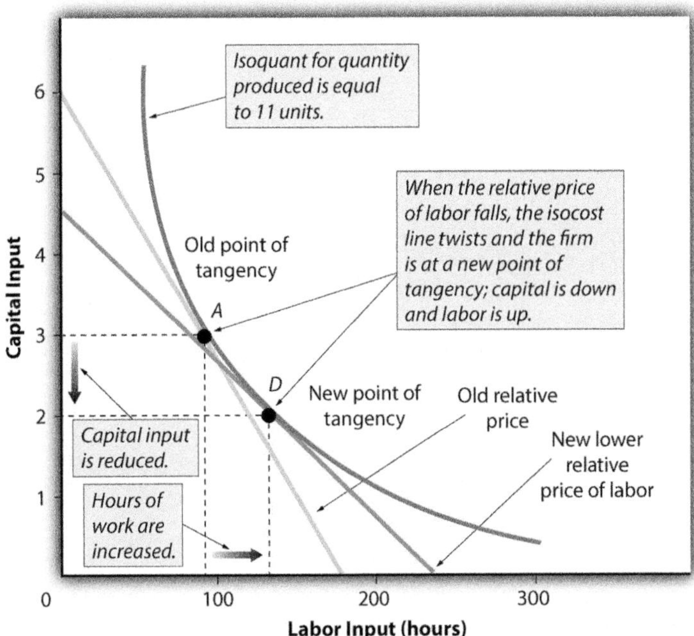

In summary, common sense tells us that the firm will hire more labor and use less capital when the price of labor falls relative to the price of capital. The isoquants and isocost lines confirm this and tell us by exactly how much.

QUESTIONS FOR REVIEW

1. Why does the isoquant slope downward?
2. Why does the isocost line slope downward?
3. What determines the slope of the isocost line?
4. Why does the firm minimize cost for a given level of output by choosing capital and labor at the point at which the isocost line is tangent to the isoquant?

PROBLEMS

1. Graph the isocost line associated with a wage of $10 per hour and a price of capital of $50 for total costs of $200, $240, and $300. Suppose the wage rises to $15 and the price of capital stays at $50. Show how the isocost line moves for the case in which total costs are $300.
2. Sketch a typical isocost line and isoquant for which the firm has chosen a combination of capital and labor that minimizes total costs for a given quantity of output. Now suppose the price of capital rises and the wage does not change. What must the firm do to maintain the same level of output as before the increase in the price of capital and still minimize costs? Will it substitute away from capital?
3. Draw a diagram with an isocost line and an isoquant next to a diagram with a budget line and an indifference curve from the appendix to Chapter 5. List the similarities and differences. How are the isocost and budget lines analogous? How are the isoquant and the indifference curve analogous? What is the importance of the tangency point in each case?

ENDNOTES

1. Geoffrey Tomb, "As the Final Harvest Ends, a Tech Torture Begins," San Jose Mercury News, December 18, 1999, p. 1.

CHAPTER 9
The Rise and Fall of Industries

Fred Smith's college term paper led to the birth of a new industry. In the paper, he described his idea for a new product: reliable overnight mail service. Although he got only a C on the paper, Fred Smith pursued his idea and became an entrepreneur. After graduating from college in 1973, he started a business firm that guaranteed next-day delivery of a letter or a package virtually anywhere in the United States. The firm, FedEx, was an extraordinary success; its sales reached $1 billion by 1982, $4 billion by 1988, $8 billion by 1992, $29 billion by 2005, and passed $50 billion for the first time in 2016.

FedEx trucks are a common sight on roads. Each day, they deliver millions of packages and documents to offices and residences across the country.

Source: © Antonio Gravante / Shutterstock.com

Seeing the high profits earned by FedEx, many other firms entered the express delivery industry. In the late 1970s, United Parcel Service (UPS) and DHL entered; in the early 1980s, the U.S. Postal Service entered; many small local firms you probably have never heard of also got into the act. The entire industry expanded along with FedEx.

The express delivery industry is an example of an industry that grew rapidly over time. Many other examples of fast-growing industries exist in the annals of economic history. Estee Lauder founded a cosmetics firm years ago; it grew along with the cosmetics industry as a whole. Kemmons Wilson started the motel franchising industry when he saw the potential demand for clean, reliable rooms for travelers and opened his first Holiday Inn in Memphis in 1952; by 1968, there were 1,000 Holiday Inns, and now the industry includes other motel firms, such as Days Inn and Motel 6.

Of course, industries do not always grow. The mainframe computer industry declined as the personal computer industry grew. The long-distance telephone industry declined when the use of cellular phones increased. The video rental store industry shrank as the DVD rental by mail industry and satellite and cable television companies became more widespread and taxi companies are struggling to deal with the entry of ride-sharing services like Uber and Lyft.

The causes of the rise and fall of industries can be traced to new ideas such as overnight delivery, to new cost-reducing technologies such as the Internet or DVDs, or to changes in consumer tastes. This latter shift, for example, is one reason behind the widespread popularity of low-carbohydrate diets, which favor reducing the intake of foods like bread and pasta in favor of high-protein foods like meat and cheese, providing an unexpected boost for meat producers. Some industries have recurring ups and downs. The oil tanker shipping industry, for example, regularly expands when oil demand increases and declines when oil demand falls.

In this chapter, we develop a model to explain the behavior of whole industries over time. We examine how economic forces cause industries to adjust to new technologies and to shifts in consumer tastes. Changes in the industry then occur as firms either enter or exit the industry. The initial forces causing an industry to rise or fall are described by shifts in a cost curve or a demand curve. Our analysis assumes that the firms are operating in competitive markets. The central task of this chapter is to show how an industry grows or contracts as firms enter or exit the industry. Do profits of individual firms fall or rise as a result? Do the prices consumers pay increase or decrease?

1. MARKETS AND INDUSTRIES

industry

A group of firms producing a similar product.

We begin this analysis by providing a brief definition of what an industry is and by giving some examples of different industry types. An **industry** is a group of firms producing a similar product. The cosmetics industry, for example, refers to the firms producing cosmetics. The term *market* sometimes is used instead of industry. For example, the phrases "the firms in the cosmetics industry" and "the firms in the cosmetics market" typically mean the same thing. But the term *market* also can refer to the consumers who buy the goods and to the interaction of the producers and the consumers. Both firms and consumers are in the cosmetics market, but only firms are in the cosmetics industry.

Firms in an industry can produce *services* such as overnight delivery or overnight accommodations as well as manufactured goods. Many industries are global. Firms in the United States compete with firms in Japan, Europe, and elsewhere. Reduced transportation and communication costs in recent years have made many industries global. Until competition from Europe and Japan intensified years ago, the automobile industry in the United States consisted mainly of three firms—General Motors, Ford, and Chrysler. Now the industry is truly global, with Honda, Toyota, Hyundai, and Nissan selling cars in the United States, and Ford and General Motors selling cars throughout the world.

2. THE LONG-RUN COMPETITIVE EQUILIBRIUM MODEL OF AN INDUSTRY

long-run competitive equilibrium model

A model of firms in an industry in which free entry and exit produce an equilibrium such that price equals the minimum of average total cost.

The model we develop to explain the behavior of industries assumes that firms in the industry maximize profits and that they are competitive. As in the competitive equilibrium model of Chapter 7, individual firms are price-takers; that is, they cannot affect the price. But to explain how the industry changes over time, in this chapter we add something new to the competitive equilibrium model. Over time, some firms will enter an industry and other firms will exit an industry. Because the entry and exit of firms takes time, we call this model the **long-run competitive equilibrium model**.

When we use the long-run competitive equilibrium model to explain the behavior of an actual industry, we do not necessarily expect that the industry conforms exactly to the assumptions of the model. A model is a means of explaining events in real-world industries; it is not the real world itself. In fact, some industries are competitive, and some are not competitive. But the model can work well as an approximation in many industries. In Chapter 10 and Chapter 11, we will develop alternative models of industry behavior that describe monopoly and the gray area between monopoly and competitive markets. For this chapter, however, we focus on the competitive model. This model was one of the first developed by economists to explain the dynamic behavior of an industry, and it has wide applicability and works well. Moreover, understanding the model will make it easier to understand the alternative models developed in later chapters.

2.1 Setting Up the Model with Graphs

Figure 9.1 illustrates the demand curve in a competitive market. The left graph views the market from the perspective of a single typical firm in an industry. The price is on the vertical axis, and the quantity produced by the single firm is on the horizontal axis. The assumption of a competitive firm implies that the firm faces a given price level, represented by a flat demand curve.

The market demand curve for the goods produced by the firms in the industry is shown in the right graph of Figure 9.1. The price is also on the vertical axis of the graph on the right, but the horizontal axis measures the *whole market or industry* production. Notice that even though the single firm takes the price as given, the market demand curve is downward sloping because it refers to the whole market. If the price in the market rises, then the quantity demanded of the product will fall. If the market price increases, then the quantity demanded will decline.

FIGURE 9.1 How a Competitive Firm Sees Demand in the Market

A competitive market is, by definition, one in which a single firm cannot affect the price. The firm takes the market price as given. Hence, the firm sees a flat demand curve, as shown in the graph on the left. Nevertheless, if all firms change production, the market price changes, as shown in the graph on the right. The two graphs are not alternatives. In a competitive market, they hold simultaneously. In the graph on the right, a given length along the horizontal axis represents a much greater quantity than the same length in the graph on the left.

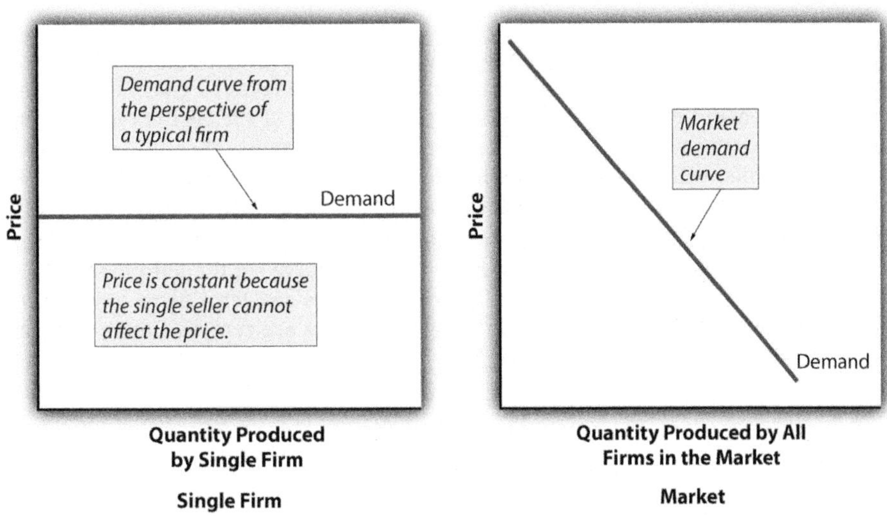

Entry and Exit

The new characteristic of competitive markets stressed in this chapter is the **free entry and exit** of firms in an industry. The question firms face is whether to *enter* an industry if they are not already in it or to *exit* from an industry they are in. The decisions are based on profits—total revenue less total costs. If profits are positive, firms have an incentive to enter the industry. If profits are negative, firms have an incentive to exit the industry. When profits are equal to zero, firms have no incentive for either entry or exit.

free entry and exit
Movement of firms into and out of an industry that is not blocked by regulation, other firms, or any other barriers.

When firms enter or exit an industry, the entire market or industry supply curve is affected. Recall that the market or industry supply curve is the sum of all the individual firms' supply curves. With more firms supplying goods, the total quantity of goods supplied increases at every price. Thus, more firms in the industry means that the market supply curve shifts to the right; fewer firms in the industry means that the market supply curve shifts to the left.

Long-Run Equilibrium

Figure 9.2 is a two-part diagram that shows the profit maximizing behavior of a typical firm along with the market supply and demand curves. This diagram is generic; it could be drawn to correspond to the numeric specifications of the grape industry or any other industry. The left graph shows the cost curves of the typical firm in the industry with their typical positions: Marginal cost cuts through the average total cost curve at its lowest point. We did not draw in the average variable cost curve to keep the diagram from getting too cluttered.

FIGURE 9.2 Long-Run Equilibrium in a Competitive Market

The left graph shows the typical firm's cost curves and the market price. The right graph shows the market supply and demand curves. The price is the same in both graphs because the market has a single price. The price is at a level at which profits are zero because price equals average total cost.

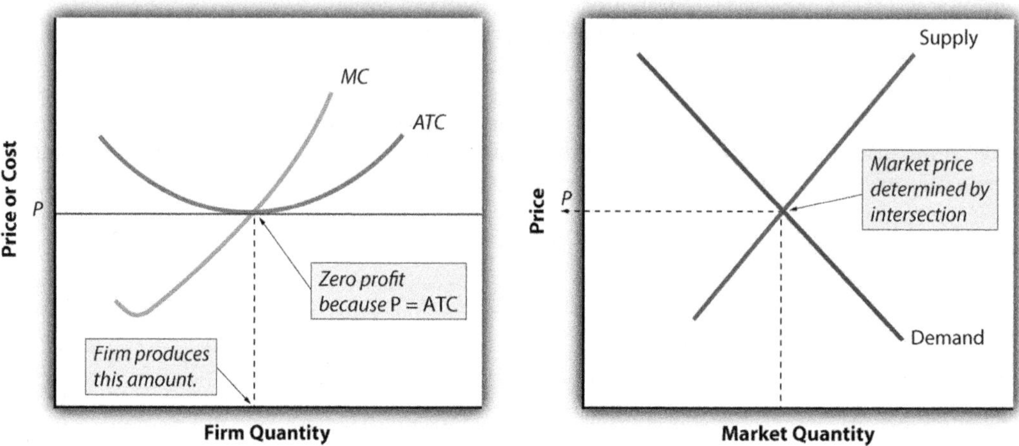

The left and right graphs of Figure 9.2 are drawn with the same market price, and this price links the two graphs together. This market price, which the individual firm takes as given, is determined by the market supply and demand curves, which are shown to the right of the cost curve diagram in Figure 9.2. As in Figure 9.1, even though the vertical axis on each graph shows the same price, the horizontal axes have different units, with an inch on the horizontal axis of the right-hand diagram representing much more production than an inch on the horizontal axis in the left-hand diagram.

long-run equilibrium

A situation in which entry into and exit from an industry are complete and economic profits are zero, with price (*P*) equal to average total cost (*ATC*).

The graphs are set up so that the price at the intersection of the market supply and demand curves is at a level that touches the bottom of the average total cost curve on the left graph. We know from Chapter 8 that profits are zero when $P = ATC$. Because profits are zero, firms have no incentive to either enter or exit the industry. This situation, in which profits are zero and there is no incentive to enter or exit, is called a **long-run equilibrium**.

2.2 An Increase in Demand

How does this long-run equilibrium come about? We can illustrate by examining what happens when demand shifts—for example, suppose the demand for grapes increases. We show this increase in demand in the top right graph of Figure 9.3; the market demand curve shifts out from *D* to *D'*.

Short-Run Effects

Focus first on the top part of Figure 9.3, representing the short run. As the demand curve shifts out, we move up along the supply curve to a new intersection of the market supply curve and the market demand curve at a higher price, *P'*.

The implications of the rise in the market price for the individual firm are shown in the top left graph, where the price line is moved up from *P* to *P'*. A profit-maximizing firm already in the industry will produce more because the market price is higher. This result is seen in the top left graph of Figure 9.3; the higher price intersects the marginal cost curve at a higher quantity of production. Note also—and this is crucial—that at this higher price and higher level of production, the typical firm is now earning profits, as shown by the shaded rectangle in the top left graph. Price is above average total cost, and so profits have risen above zero.

We have gone from a situation in which profits were zero for firms in the industry to a situation in which profits are positive. This shift has created a profit opportunity in the market, encouraging new firms to enter the industry. Thus, we have moved away from a long-run equilibrium (which was defined as a situation in which profits are zero and firms have no incentive to enter or exit) because of the disturbance that shifted the market demand curve.

Toward a New Long-Run Equilibrium

Now focus on the two graphs in the bottom part of Figure 9.3, representing what happens in this industry in the long run. In the lower right-hand graph, the supply curve for the whole industry or market shifts to the right from *S* to *S'*. Why? Because the market supply curve is the sum of the individual supply curves; as more firms, attracted by higher profits, enter the industry, they add to supply.

FIGURE 9.3 The Rise of an Industry after a Shift in Demand

The diagrams at the top show the short run. A shift in the demand curve to the right causes the price to rise from *P* to *P'*; each firm produces more, and profits rise. Higher profits cause firms to enter the industry. The diagrams at the bottom show the long run. As firms enter, the market supply curve shifts to the right, and the price falls back to *P*. New entry does not stop until profits return to zero in the long run.

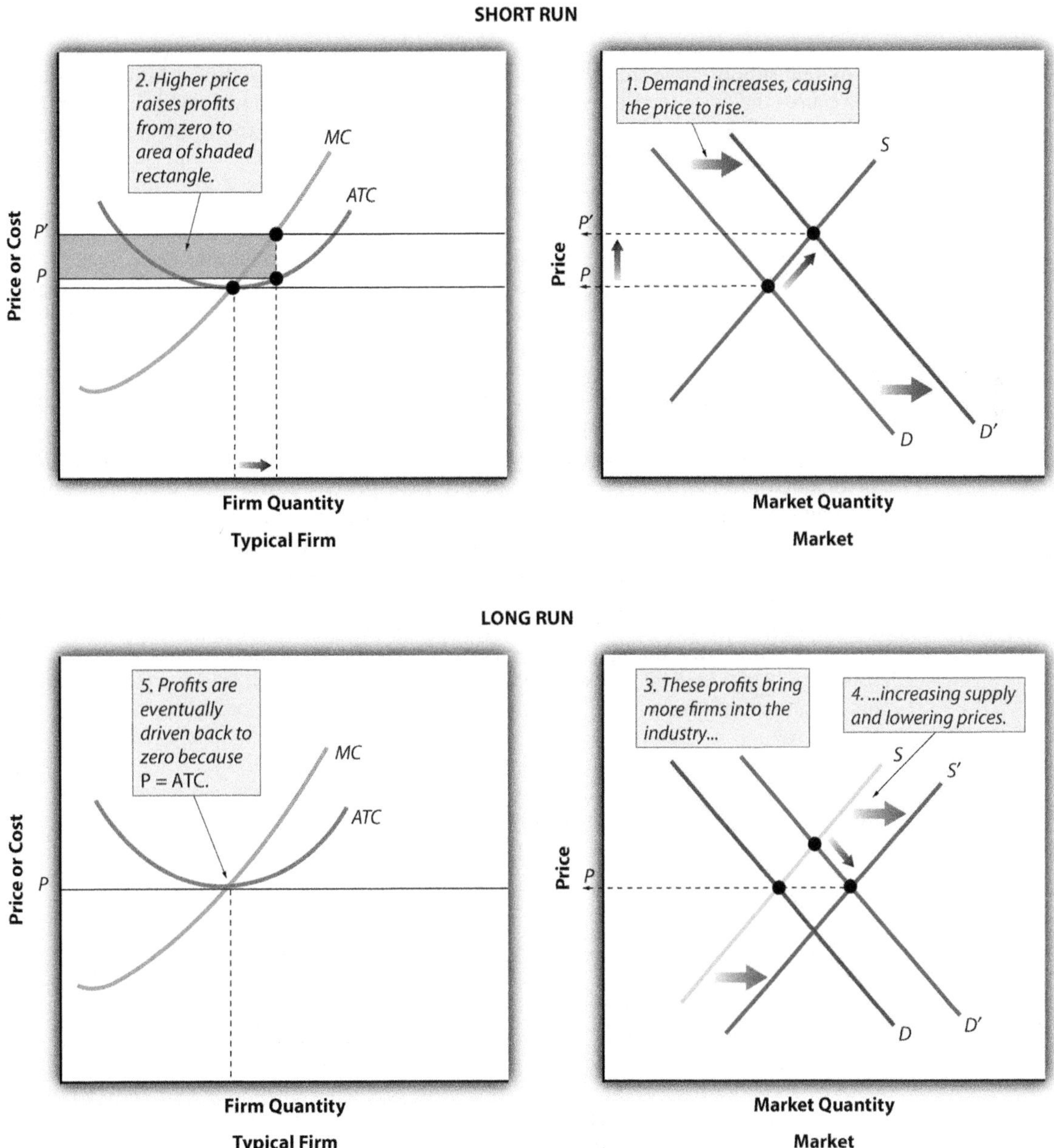

The rightward shift in the supply curve causes a reduction in the price below *P'*, where it was in the short run. The price will continue adjusting until the price line just touches the bottom of the average total cost curve, where average total cost equals marginal cost. At this point, profits will again be zero, no new firms have the incentive to enter, and the industry will be in long-run equilibrium. Of course, this adjustment to a new long-run equilibrium takes time. It takes time for firms to decide whether or not to go into business, and it takes time to set up a firm once a decision is made.

The new long-run equilibrium for the typical firm is shown in the lower left graph. It may take several years for an industry to move from the top of Figure 9.3 to the bottom. In fact, it would be more accurate to draw several rows of diagrams between the top and the bottom, showing how the process occurs gradually over time. These additional rows could show more and more firms entering the industry with the price falling until eventually profits are zero again and the incentive to enter the market disappears. The market supply curve will shift to the right until the price comes back to the point where average total cost is at a minimum, profits are zero, and no firms will enter or exit the industry.

2.3 A Decrease in Demand

The long-run competitive equilibrium model also can be used to explain the decline of an industry. Suppose the demand curve shifts from *D* to *D'*, as illustrated in the top right graph in Figure 9.4. This change in demand causes the market price to fall. The lower market price (*P'*) causes existing firms to cut back on production in the short run: At the new lower price, the individual firm depicted in the top left panel of Figure 9.4 is now running losses.

Over time, with profits less than zero, firms have an incentive to leave the industry. As they leave, the market supply curve shifts to the left from *S* to *S'*, as shown in the bottom right graph of Figure 9.4. This causes the price to rise again. The end of the process is a new long-run equilibrium, as shown in the bottom left graph of Figure 9.4. In the long run, fewer firms are in the industry, total production in the industry is lower, and profits are back to zero.

Economic Profits versus Accounting Profits

accounting profits

Total revenue minus total costs, where total costs exclude the implicit opportunity costs; this is the definition of profits usually reported by firms.

economic profits

Total revenue minus total costs, where total costs include opportunity costs, whether implicit or explicit.

It is important at this point to emphasize that the economist's definition of profits is different from an accountant's definition. When you read about the profits of Motorola in the newspaper, it is the accountant's definition that is being reported. Nothing is wrong with the accountant's definition of profits, but it is different from the economist's definition. When an accountant calculates profits for a firm, the total costs do not include the opportunity cost of the owner's time or the owner's funds. Such opportunity costs are *implicit*: The wage that the owner could get elsewhere and the interest that could be earned on the funds if they were invested elsewhere are not explicitly paid, and the accountant therefore ignores them. When computing **accounting profits**, such implicit opportunity costs are *not* included in total costs. When computing **economic profits**—the measure of profits economists use—implicit opportunity costs are included in total costs. Economic profits are equal to accounting profits less any opportunity costs that the accountants did not include when measuring total costs.

For example, suppose accounting profits for a movie rental store are $40,000 a year. Suppose the owner of the store could earn $35,000 a year running a bakery. Suppose also that the owner could sell the business for $50,000 and invest the money in a bank, where it would earn interest at 6 percent per year, or $3,000. Then the opportunity cost—which the accountant would not have included in total costs—is $38,000 ($35,000 plus $3,000). To get economic profits, we have to subtract this opportunity cost from accounting profits. Thus, economic profits would be only $2,000.

FIGURE 9.4 The Decline of an Industry after a Shift in Demand

In the short run, a reduction in demand lowers the price from *P* to *P′* and causes losses. Firms leave the industry, causing prices to rise back to *P*. In the long run, profits have returned to zero, the number of firms in the industry has declined, and the total quantity produced in the industry has fallen.

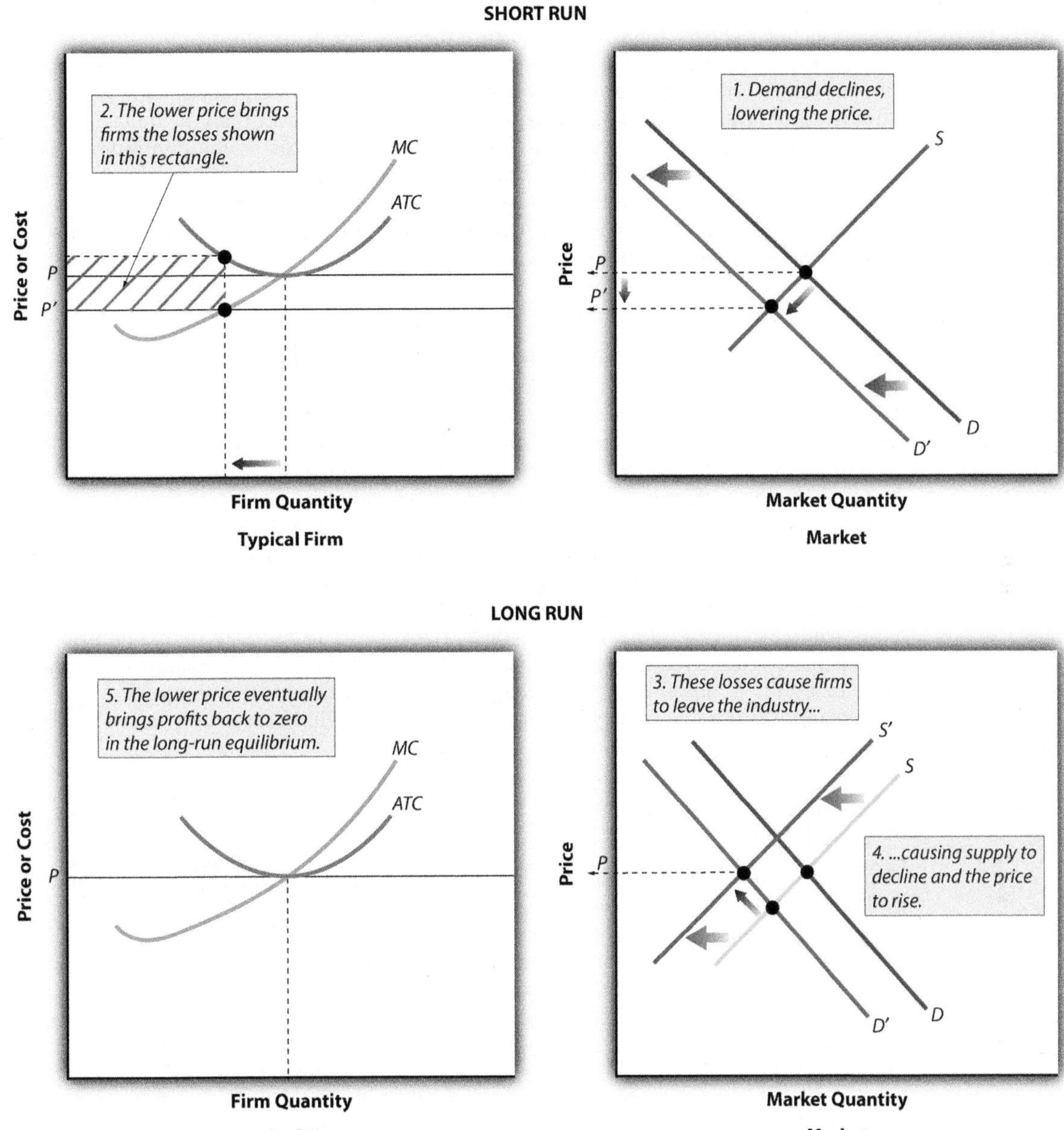

Economic profits are used by economists because these profits measure the incentive that the owner of the firm has to stay in business rather than do something else. In this case, with $2,000 in economic profits, the owner has an incentive to stay in the business. But if the owner could earn $39,000 running a bakery, then economic profits for the movie rental store would be –$2,000 ($40,000 – $39,000 – $3,000), and the owner would have an incentive to leave the movie rental store business, even though accounting profits at the store were $40,000. Thus, economic profits are a better measure of incentives than accounting profits. Because we are interested in the incentives that firms have to either enter or exit an industry, when we refer to profits in this book, we mean economic profits.

Observe that if the store owner could earn exactly $37,000 at the bakery, then economic profits at the movie rental store would be zero. Then the owner would be indifferent on economic considerations alone between staying in the movie rental business or going to work for the bakery. The term **normal profits** refers to the amount of accounting profits that exist when economic profits are equal to zero. In this last case, normal profits would be $40,000.

normal profits

The amount of accounting profits when economic profits are equal to zero.

The Equilibrium Number of Firms

The long-run equilibrium model predicts that a certain number of firms will be in the industry. The equilibrium number of firms will be such that there is no incentive for more firms to enter the industry or for others to leave. But how many firms is this? If the minimum point on the average cost curve of the typical firm represents production at a small scale, then the industry will have many firms. That is, many firms will each produce a small amount. If the minimum point represents production at a large scale, then the industry will have fewer firms; that is, a few firms will each produce a large amount.

To see this, consider the hypothetical case in which all firms are identical. For example, if the minimum point on the average total cost curve for each firm in the grape industry occurs at 10,000 tons and the equilibrium quantity in the whole market is 100,000 tons, then the model predicts that 10 firms will be in the industry. If the quantity at which average total cost is at a minimum 1,000 tons, then 100 firms will be in the industry. If the demand for grapes increases and brings about a new long-run equilibrium of 130,000 tons, then the number of firms in the industry will rise from 100 to 130 (in the case in which the minimum efficient scale was 1,000 tons) or from 10 to 13 (in the case in which the minimum efficient scale was 10,000 tons).

Entry or Exit Combined with Individual Firm Expansion or Contraction

Thus far, we have described the growth or decline of an industry in terms of the increase or decrease in the number of firms. Recall from Chapter 8 that, in the long run, a firm can expand its size by investing in new capital or reduce its size by getting rid of some of its capital. So the industry can grow or shrink as a result of changes in the size of existing firms.

In reality, industries usually grow by a combination of the expansion of existing firms and the entry of new firms. Similarly, industries can shrink either because of the exit of firms or because of a contraction in the size of existing firms. For example, when the expedited package express industry began to grow, it grew both because UPS and other firms entered and because FedEx expanded.

The expansion of an existing firm can occur under one of two conditions. First, the original size of the firm may be smaller than the minimum efficient scale, so the firm maybe able to lower its average costs while producing more units. Second, a change in technology or in the prices of inputs may change the cost function of the firm, pushing the minimum efficient scale to a larger number of units. Note that if the firm is already producing at the minimum long-run average total cost, then an increase in demand will not affect the size of the firm, and you will observe only entry of new firms into the industry.

2.4 Shifts in Cost Curves

Our analysis of the rise and fall of an industry thus far has centered around shifts in demand. But new technologies and ideas for new products that reduce costs also can cause an industry to change. The long-run competitive equilibrium model can be used to explain these changes, as shown in Figure 9.5.

The case of cost-reducing technologies—as when Walmart introduced checkout counter scanners—can be handled by shifting down the average total cost curve and the marginal cost curve, as shown in Figure 9.5. This will lead to a situation of positive profits because average total cost falls below the original market price *P*. If other firms already in the industry adopt similar cost-cutting strategies, the market price will fall to *P'*, but profits will still be positive, as shown in Figure 9.5. With positive profits, other firms will have incentives to enter the industry with similar technologies. As more firms enter the industry, the market supply curve shifts out. The price falls further to *P''*, and eventually competition brings economic profits back to zero.

If new entrants drive economic profits to zero in the long run, then what incentives do firms have to develop cost-cutting technologies? The answer is that the economic profits in the short run can be substantial. Walmart may have made hundreds of millions of dollars in economic profits before the competition eroded the profits away. Hence, Walmart benefited for a while from cost-cutting innovations. No idea will generate economic profits forever in a competitive market, but the short-run profits can provide plenty of incentive.

Average Total Cost is Minimized

In the long-run equilibrium, average total cost is as low as technology will permit. You can see this in Figure 9.2, Figure 9.3, Figure 9.4, and Figure 9.5. In each case, the typical firm produces a quantity at which average total cost is at the minimum point of the firm's average total cost curve. This amount of production must occur in the long-run equilibrium because profits are zero. For profits to be zero, price must equal average total cost ($P = ATC$). The only place where $P = MC$ and $P = ATC$ is at the lowest point on the ATC curve. At this point, costs per unit are at a minimum.

FIGURE 9.5 Effect of a Reduction in Costs

A new technology reduces costs and shifts the typical firm's *ATC* and *MC* curves down. The market supply curve shifts down by the same amount as the shift in marginal cost if other firms in the industry adopt the new technology right away. But because of the economic profits, new firms have incentives to enter the industry. As shown in the lower left graph, in the long run, profits return to zero.

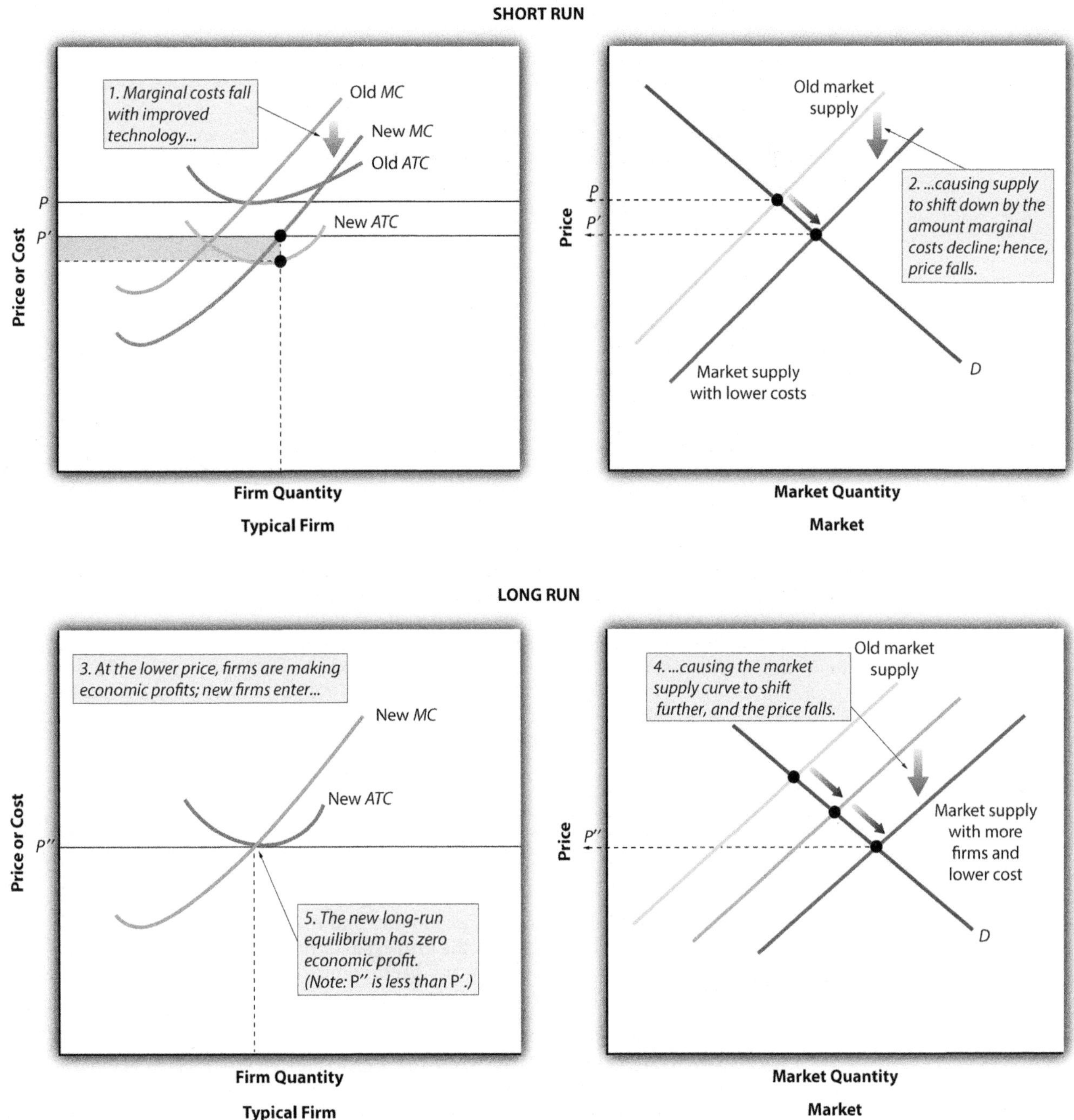

That average total cost is at a minimum is an attractive feature of a competitive market in which firms are free to enter and exit. It means that goods are produced at the lowest cost, with the price consumers pay being equal to that lowest cost. If firms could not enter and exit, this attractive feature would be lost.

Efficient Allocation of Capital among Industries

An efficient allocation of capital among industries also is achieved by entry and exit in competitive markets. Entry of firms into a booming industry, for example, means that more capital has gone into that industry, where it can better satisfy consumer tastes. In the case of a declining industry, capital moves out of the industry to other industries, where it is used more efficiently. Thus, the long-run competitive equilibrium has another attractive property: Capital is allocated to its most efficient use. Again, this property is due to the free entry and exit of firms. If entry and exit were limited or if the market were not competitive for some other reason, this advantage would be lost.

REVIEW

- Industries grow and shrink over time, with existing firms expanding or contracting in size, new firms entering the industry, and some existing firms going out of business. The long-run competitive equilibrium model explains how the entry and exit, expansion, and contraction patterns evolve.
- The decision to enter or exit an industry is determined by profit potential. Positive economic profits will attract new firms. Negative economic profits will cause firms to exit the industry. A long-run competitive equilibrium is a situation in which individual firms make zero profits ($P = ATC$) and no firms enter or exit an industry.
- If a demand increase causes market prices to rise, that increase in price will lead to positive profits for an individual firm in the short run because $P > ATC$. In response to the positive profit-making opportunity, new firms will enter, causing the market supply curve to shift to the right and causing price to come back down again until the profit-making opportunities have eroded, and the economy returns to long-run competitive equilibrium.
- If a demand decrease causes market prices to fall, that decrease in price will lead to negative profits for an individual firm in the short run because $P < ATC$. The negative profits increase the incentive for firms to leave the industry, causing the market supply curve to shift to the left. This raises price and reduces the losses incurred by individual firms until the economy returns to long-run competitive equilibrium.
- Similar adjustments take place if changes in technology bring about a shift of the cost curves of individual firms in the economy.
- How many firms are in an industry depends on the minimum efficient scale of the typical firm and the size of the industry. If firms are not operating at minimum efficient scale or if changes in technology make minimum efficient scale larger, then existing firms are likely to grow in size.
- When firms are allowed to freely enter and exit, another advantage is that average total cost is minimized. That goods are produced at the lowest possible cost is another advantage of competitive markets.
- Entry and exit also bring about an efficient allocation of capital. Booming industries will see entry of new firms and expansion of existing ones, which leads to more capital being allocated. Shrinking industries will see exit of firms and shrinking of firm size, which frees up capital for booming industries.
- Throughout this discussion, it is important to keep in mind that the profits being discussed are economic profits rather than accounting profits. Economic profits differ from accounting profits because they include the opportunity costs of the firm owners.

3. EXTERNAL ECONOMIES AND DISECONOMIES OF SCALE

In Chapter 8, we introduced the concept of economies and diseconomies of scale for a firm. A firm whose long-run average total cost declines as the firm expands has economies of scale. If long-run average total cost rises as the firm expands, there are diseconomies of scale. Economies and diseconomies of scale may exist for whole industries as well as for firms.

3.1 The Standard Assumption: A Flat Long-Run Industry Supply Curve

long-run industry supply curve

A curve traced out by the intersections of demand curves shifting to the right and the corresponding short-run supply curves.

Refer to the graphs in the lower right-hand panels of Figure 9.3 and Figure 9.4. You will see that the market price in the long-run equilibrium after the shift in demand is the same as that before the shift in demand. When demand increases, price rises, leading to higher profits for existing firms. The allure of positive profits brings new firms into the industry, pushing the supply curve out and lowering prices until profits are zero again. The intersections of the shifting demand and supply curves trace out the **long-run industry supply curve**, which, as you can see in Figure 9.6, is perfectly horizontal. The assumption of a flat long-run industry supply curve is the standard one economists use to study industries. Exceptions to this standard are examined below.

FIGURE 9.6 The Standard Assumption

As demand increases and price rises, more firms enter the industry, attracted by the prospect of higher profits. The increase in the number of firms pushes the supply curve out, lowering prices and reducing incentives for further entry. In the long run, the industry supply curve will be horizontal, at the price at which profits for this typical firm are zero.

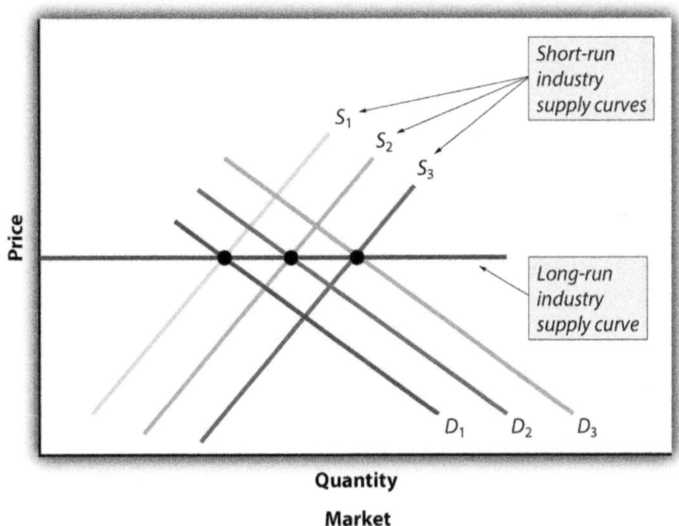

3.2 External Diseconomies of Scale

When the number of firms in the grape industry increases, the demand for water for irrigation in grape-growing regions also increases, and this may raise the price of water in these regions. Even though no single firm's decision affects the price of water for irrigation, the expansion of the industry does. If the price of water increases, then the cost of producing grapes increases for every firm. With the marginal cost of each grape producer increasing, the supply curve for each firm and for the industry or the market shifts up and to the left.

This is shown in the market supply and demand curves in Figure 9.7. Suppose the demand curve shifts from D_1 to D_2. As the industry expands, more firms enter the industry, and the supply curve shifts to the right from S_1 to S_2. Because the marginal cost at each firm rises as the industry expands, the supply curve does not shift to the right by as much as the demand curve shifts. Thus, the long-run equilibrium—the intersection of the demand curve D_2 and the supply curve S_2—occurs at a higher price than the intersection of S_1 and D_1.

We could consider a further shift in demand to D_3, leading to a shift in supply to S_3. This change in demand would result in yet another long-run equilibrium at a higher price because average total cost is higher. Observe that as successive market demand curves intersect successive market supply curves, the price rises and quantity rises; an upward-sloping long-run industry supply curve is traced out. We call the phenomenon of an upward-sloping long-run industry supply curve **external diseconomies of scale**. The word *external* indicates that cost increases are external to the firm, for example, because of a higher price for inputs (such as water) to production. In contrast, the diseconomies of scale considered in Chapter 8 were internal to the firm, for example, because of increased costs of managing a larger firm; they can be called *internal diseconomies of scale* to distinguish them from the external case.

external diseconomies of scale

A situation in which growth in an industry causes average total cost for the individual firm to rise because of some factor external to the firm; it corresponds to an upward-sloping long-run industry supply curve.

FIGURE 9.7 External Diseconomies of Scale

As demand increases and more firms enter the industry, each firm's costs increase, perhaps because the prices of inputs to production rise. The higher costs tend to limit the shift of the market supply curve to the right when new firms enter. The long-run industry supply curve slopes up, a phenomenon that is called external diseconomies of scale.

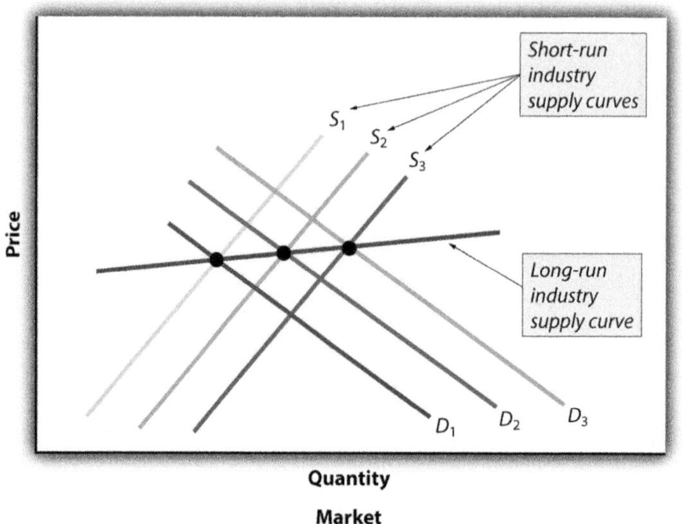

3.3 External Economies of Scale

External economies of scale

A situation in which growth in an industry causes average total cost for the individual firm to fall because of some factor external to the firm; it corresponds to a downward-sloping long-run industry supply curve.

External economies of scale also are possible. For example, an expansion of the domestic wine industry might make it worthwhile for students at agricultural schools to become specialists in wines made from domestic grapes. With a smaller industry, such specialization would not have been worthwhile. The expertise that comes from that specialization could reduce the cost of grape production by more than the cost of hiring the specialist. Then as the industry expands, both the average total cost and the marginal cost for individual firms may decline.

Another example is the expansion of the personal computer industry, which allowed many small specialized firms servicing personal computer manufacturers to emerge. With a smaller-scale industry, this would not have been possible.

The case of external economies of scale is shown in Figure 9.8. Again, suppose the demand curve shifts from D_1 to D_2. When the industry expands, the market supply curve shifts out from S_1 to S_2, or by *more* than the increase in demand, so that the price falls. The reason the market supply curve shifts more than the market demand curve is that marginal cost at each firm has declined as the number of firms in the industry has increased. This larger shift in supply compared with demand is shown in Figure 9.8. Thus, the price falls as the industry expands.

With additional shifts in demand from D_2 to D_3, the market demand curves intersect with successive market supply curves at lower prices, resulting in a long-run industry supply curve that is downward sloping. Again, the word *external* is used to distinguish these economies that occur outside the firm from those that are internal to the firm.

Note the difference between internal and external economies of scale. The expansion of a single firm can generate internal economies of scale with the number of firms in the industry fixed because individuals within the firm can specialize. The expansion of an industry can generate external economies of scale even if the size of each firm in the industry does not increase. As an industry expands, firms might even split up into several specialized firms, each concentrating on one part of the specialized work.

FIGURE 9.8 External Economies of Scale

As demand expands and more firms enter the industry, each firm's costs decline, which causes the supply curve to shift to the right by even more than it would as a result of the increase in the number of firms. The long-run industry supply curve thus is downward sloping, a phenomenon that is called external economies of scale

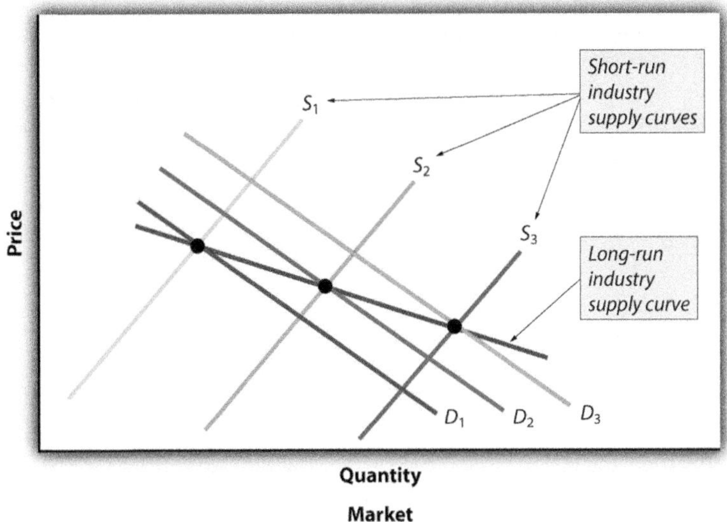

Reminder: *Internal economies or diseconomies of scale occur when a single firm expands (Chapter 8). External economies or diseconomies of scale occur when an industry expands (Chapter 9).*

3.4 External and Internal Economies of Scale Together

External Economies of Scale: As an industry expands in size, firms in other industries have incentives to develop new products to service the industry. These new products reduce average total cost in the industry, thereby giving rise to economies of scale, as illustrated by the development of special electronic scanners for use by the expanding express delivery service industry (left). The new ideas in turn may be used to reduce costs in other industries, as illustrated by the use of electronic scanners for self-service checkout in the retail industry (right).

Sources: © photocritical / Shutterstock, Inc.

In practice, it is possible for external and internal economies of scale to occur at the same time in one industry. When an industry grows in scale through the addition of new firms, it is common for the typical firm in the industry to expand its scale. FedEx has grown in size at the same time that more firms have entered the industry. Through its larger size, FedEx has achieved internal economies of scale (for example, by spreading the costs of its computer tracking system over more deliveries), and the larger industry as a whole has benefited from external economies of scale (as illustrated by the scanners shown in the photo).

REVIEW

- The long-run industry supply curve is horizontal for the typical industry. When demand increases, raising prices and profits for existing firms, new firms enter into the industry. This results in an increase in supply, pushing prices back down to the original level in the long run so that profits are zero again. The shifting demand and supply curves trace out a horizontal long-run industry supply curve.
- External diseconomies of scale occur when the expansion of an industry raises costs at individual firms, perhaps because of a rise in input prices. An increase in demand in such an industry will see a smaller shift out in supply because the marginal cost for each firm rises as the industry expands. This implies that the long-run industry supply curve is upward sloping.
- External economies of scale arise when expansion of an industry lowers costs at individual firms in the industry. Opportunities for specialization for individuals and firms serving the industry are one reason for external economies of scale. An increase in demand in such an industry will see a larger shift out in supply because the marginal cost for each firm falls as the industry expands, bringing with it opportunities for specialization. This implies that the long-run industry supply curve is downward-sloping.

4. END-OF-CHAPTER MATERIALS

4.1 Conclusion

In this chapter, we have developed a model that explains why whole industries rise or fall over time. As consumer tastes change and new ideas are discovered, such changes are an ever-present phenomenon in modern economies around the world.

The model we developed in this chapter to explain such changes extends the competitive equilibrium model we developed in Chapter 5 through Chapter 8 to allow for the entry or exit of firms into or out of an industry. Because such entry or exit usually takes time, we emphasize that this modification applies to the long run. Profits draw firms into the industry over time, whereas losses cause firms to leave. As firms enter, the industry expands. As firms leave, the industry declines. In the long-run equilibrium, profit opportunities have disappeared, and entry or exit stops.

In Chapter 10 and Chapter 11, we begin to leave the realm of the competitive market. We will develop models of the behavior of monopolies and other firms for which the assumption of a competitive market is not accurate. In the process, we will see that many of the results we have obtained with competitive markets in this chapter are no longer true.

However, many of the ideas and concepts developed in this and the previous few chapters on the competitive model will be used in these chapters. The cost curve diagram will reappear in the model of monopoly in Chapter 10; the idea of entry and exit will reappear in Chapter 11.

As we consider these new models and new results, we will use the models of this chapter as a basis of comparison. A central question will be: "How different are the results from those of the long-run competitive equilibrium model?" Keep that question in mind as you study the coming chapters.

Key Points

1. Economic history is filled with stories about the rise and fall of industries. Industries grow rapidly when cost-reducing technologies are discovered or demand increases. They decline when demand decreases or when technological advances render an industry's product obsolete.
2. The long-run competitive equilibrium model assumes that firms will enter or exit an industry until economic profits are driven to zero. This model can be used to explain many facts about the rise and fall of industries over time.
3. When demand increases, the market price rises, leading to positive profits for individual firms in the short run. New firms will enter, causing the market supply curve to shift to the right and causing price to come back down again until the profit-making opportunities are eroded.
4. When demand decreases, the market price falls, leading to losses for individual firms in the short run. Firms will exit the industry, causing the market supply curve to shift to the left, and causing price to rise until losses are eliminated and there is no further exit.
5. In discussing the condition of zero profits in long-run competitive equilibrium, you should keep in mind that it is economic profits (not accounting profits) that are being driven to zero. Economic profits are accounting profits less opportunity costs.
6. Entry and exit can take place if changes in technology bring about a shift of the cost curves of individual firms in the economy.
7. An industry can expand either because more firms enter the industry or because existing firms become larger. An industry can shrink either because existing firms leave the industry or because they become smaller in size.
8. The number of firms in an industry depends on its size and the minimum efficient scale of the typical firm in the industry.
9. In the long run, the competitive equilibrium model implies that after entry and exit have taken place, average total costs are minimized and capital is allocated efficiently among industries.
10. The typical assumption is that the long-run industry supply curve is horizontal. However, industries may exhibit either external economies of scale, when the long-run industry supply curve slopes down, or external diseconomies of scale, when the long-run industry supply curve slopes up.

QUESTIONS FOR REVIEW

1. What is the definition of an industry?
2. What are some possible sources of the rise of industries? Of the fall of industries?
3. What are the key characteristics of an economy that is in a long-run competitive equilibrium?
4. What happens to an industry in the long run when demand increases for the good produced by the industry?
5. What happens to an industry in the long run when demand decreases for the good produced by the industry?
6. What determines the number of firms in the economy?
7. When is it more likely for an increase in demand to lead to the entry of more firms in the economy rather than to existing firms becoming larger?
8. What is the difference between economic profits and accounting profits?
9. What are external economies of scale? How do they differ from internal economies of scale?
10. What are external diseconomies of scale? How do they differ from internal diseconomies of scale?

PROBLEMS

1. The data in the table are for a typical firm in a competitive industry (with identical firms). The firm can choose to have either one unit of capital or two units of capital in the long run. The two short-run average total cost curves (ATC_1 and ATC_2) and the two marginal cost curves (MC_1 and MC_2) are given in the table below.

	Costs with One Unit of Capital		Costs with Two Units of Capital	
Quantity	ATC_1	MC_1	ATC_2	MC_2
1	7.0	5	10.0	6
2	5.5	4	7.5	5
3	4.7	3	6.3	4
4	4.5	4	5.5	3
5	4.6	5	5.0	3
6	4.8	6	4.8	4
7	5.1	7	4.9	5
8	5.5	8	5.0	6
9	5.9	9	5.2	7
10	6.3	10	5.5	8
11	6.7	11	5.8	9
12	7.2	12	6.2	10

a. Suppose the firm currently is producing with two units of capital. If the current price is $9 per unit, how much will the firm produce? How much are its profits?

b. Suppose the price falls to $7 per unit. How much will the firm produce now? How much are its profits?

c. What is the long-run *ATC* of the firm? Will the firm contract its output when it is able to change its capital?

d. What is the long-run industry equilibrium price and quantity for the typical firm? If there is a market demand of 4,000 units at that price, how many of these identical firms will the industry have?

2. Consider a typical office-cleaning firm that currently faces $24 in fixed costs and an $8 hourly wage for workers. The price the firm gets for each office cleaned in a large office building is $56 at the present equilibrium. The production function of the firm is shown in the following table.

Number of Offices Cleaned	Hours of Work
0	0
1	5
2	9
3	15
4	22

a. Find marginal costs and average total costs for the typical firm.

b. How many offices are cleaned by the typical firm at the present equilibrium price of $56? What are the firm's profits at this equilibrium?

c. What is the long-run equilibrium price level, assuming that the office-cleaning market is competitive?

d. How many offices are cleaned by the typical firm in long-run equilibrium?

3. Suppose corn farming in the United States can be represented by a competitive industry. Describe how this industry, currently in long-run equilibrium, would adjust to an increase in demand for corn. Explain your answer graphically, showing the cost curves for the typical farmer as well as the market supply and demand curves. Distinguish between the short run and the long run.

4. Consider developments in the airline industry. The old large airline firms relied on hubs to move passengers; passengers were flown to a hub airport, where they changed planes to continue their journeys. Southwest Airlines pioneered a new model of airline transportation that involved point-to-point transportation (with no stop at a hub), reliance on a single type of aircraft, and more flexible job descriptions that enabled planes to return to the air more rapidly after landing. These innovations reduced the costs per mile of transporting passengers. Describe the impact of this new model on the airline industry in the short run and in the long run.

5. Consider developments in the newspaper industry, which has been hit hard by the growth of the Internet. Many people have given up the habit of reading a newspaper daily and instead get their news from other online sources. Explain what the impact of this change in people's preferences will be on the newspaper industry in the short run and in the long run.
6. Suppose the government imposes a sales tax on a good sold by firms in a competitive industry. Describe what happens to the price of the good in the short run and in the long run when firms are free to enter and exit. What happens to the number of firms in the industry and to total production in the industry?
7. Because there are zero profits in the long run for any firm in a competitive industry, what incentive does a firm have in a competitive industry to pursue cost-cutting measures?
8. List some external economies of scale that might be realized by a computer-manufacturing firm that locates in a high-technology industrial park. List some diseconomies of scale that might be realized by a computer-programming firm that locates in an area of India that is attracting dozens of other such firms in search of software programmers. How do these economies or diseconomies of scale affect the shape of the long-run industry supply curve?

CHAPTER 10
Monopoly

In 2005, a lawsuit was filed against Apple charging that the company's iTunes software was creating a monopoly in the market for digital music. The plaintiffs argued that iTunes was preventing users from playing digital music purchased from other sites on Apple iPod devices. Shortly afterwards, in early 2007, France and several other European countries announced that they intended to take steps to ensure that songs purchased from the iTunes website could be used on music players other than the iPod. According to news reports, Norwegian consumer advocate Erik Thon described this action as being needed because "It cannot be good for the music industry for [Apple] to lock music into one system."

In response to these legal actions, Apple also made the arguments that the restrictions on digital music was mostly encryption technology needed to prevent hackers from controlling users' iPod content. Steve Jobs, the chief executive officer of Apple, posted an item on Apple's website entitled "Thoughts on Music," in which he argued that most of the music that is played on iPods comes from CDs that users were free to put on any music player they wanted, meaning that consumers had plenty of choices in terms of music players. Furthermore, he argued that the restrictions that Apple had to impose on songs downloaded from iTunes were required by the companies that owned the rights to the music in the first place; these companies imposed such restrictions to prevent their songs from being copied and made available for free over the Internet.

What happened to these legal arguments? The European case was dropped in 2009 when Apple announced that it was lifting restrictions that limited songs purchased on Apple's iTunes store from being played on other devices. In 2015 Apple's arguments that it was justified in limiting the types of music that could be played on their own devices were vindicated in U.S. courts, when a federal jury ruled that these restrictions were not harmful to consumers.

The crux of Apple's argument was that any company that was able to come up with its own system for preventing illegal copying would be able to license and sell songs over the Internet. Apple simply had designed a successful system in iTunes, a product that had given consumers access to more choices in how to listen to music instead of restricting their choices.

The iTunes case involves a situation in which governments bring, or threaten to bring, action against a company because they believe that the company has effectively become a monopolist, a sole producer of a good. Monopolies operate differently from firms in competitive markets. The biggest difference is that monopolies have the power to set the price in their markets. Consumers suffer because the monopolist restricts their choices, charges them higher prices, and supplies fewer goods than a competitive market would. Among the most notable cases in the past few decades were the breakup of AT&T in the 1980s and the decision in the early 2000s to split Microsoft in two (a decision that the Justice Department decided against carrying out).

Source: © Twin Design / Shutterstock.com

The aim of this chapter is to develop a model of monopoly that can be used to understand how real world monopolies operate. The model explains how a monopoly decides what price to charge its customers and what quantity to sell. We also use the model to explain some puzzling pricing behavior, such as why some airlines charge a lower fare to travelers who stay over a Saturday night. Monopolies and the reasons for their existence raise important public policy questions about the role of government in the economy. The model we develop shows that monopolies cause a loss to society when compared with firms providing goods in competitive markets; the model also provides a way to measure that loss. This loss that monopolies cause to society creates a potential role for government to step in to try and reduce this loss.

Deciding when to, or whether to, intervene to break up a monopoly is an extremely complex task, however. As in the iTunes case or the Microsoft case, the Department of Justice often is faced with convincing arguments on both sides of the issue. Companies that are accused of being monopolists will argue that their products are simply superior to the competition and provide a service to consumers. Companies and governments will disagree on what the appropriate definition of the "market" is. For instance, Apple could argue that consumers buy music from a variety of sources and play it on a variety of different devices; hence, the iTunes-iPod combination, as popular as it is, hardly could be considered to be one that restricts consumer choice. In fact, even governments have a hard time agreeing with that notion. Shortly after the European action was announced, Thomas Barnett, a senior official in the Department of Justice's Antitrust Division, said in a speech that "consumers buy the expensive iPod device first, then have the option—not the obligation—to use the free iTunes software and buy the cheap iTunes songs."

Finally, it is important to keep in mind that in the twenty-first-century economy, monopolies frequently do not last long. The increased use of the Internet and the decreased use of software that resides on one's own computer greatly reduced concerns about Microsoft's monopoly; the rise of cellular phones made us less concerned about local phone monopolies; satellite television provided competition to your cable television company's local monopoly; the technological advances made by chip maker AMD eroded concerns about Intel's powerful role in the market for microprocessors. Similarly, as more music players and different music sales formats are introduced to the market, concerns about Apple may start to fade. Nevertheless, some monopolies do last a long time. De Beers is one of the most famous examples of a monopoly. It maintained its monopoly position from 1929 well into the 1980s, and even into the 2010s it controls about half of the diamond market (although the most recent surveys seem to suggest that millennials seem to have less of an attraction to the diamond as a symbol of lasting love and commitment).

1. A MODEL OF MONOPOLY

A **monopoly** occurs when only one firm in an industry is selling a product for which there are no close substitutes. Thus, implicit in the definition of monopoly are **barriers to entry**—other firms are not free to enter the industry. For example, De Beers created barriers to entry by maintaining exclusive rights to the diamonds in most of the world's diamond mines. Microsoft was accused of creating a barrier to entry in software production by bundling together its software with the Windows operating system that came preinstalled on computers. Sometimes the barriers to entry are artificially created by the government through systems of copyrights and patents that prevent other firms from duplicating a company's products. These patents and copyrights allow a company to earn revenue by licensing the right to produce the particular good that resulted from the company's innovation and creativity.

monopoly

One firm in an industry selling a product that does not have close substitutes.

barriers to entry

Anything that prevents firms from entering a market.

The economist's model of a monopoly assumes that the monopoly will choose a level of output that maximizes profits. In this respect, the model of a monopoly is like that of a competitive firm. If increasing production will increase a monopoly's profits, then the monopoly will raise production, just as a competitive firm would. If cutting production will increase a monopoly's profits, then the monopoly will cut its production, just as a competitive firm would.

The difference between a monopoly and a competitive firm is not what motivates the firm but rather how its actions affect the market price. The most important difference is that a monopoly has **market power**. That is, a monopoly has the power to set the price in the market, whereas a competitor does not. This is why a monopoly is called a **price-maker** rather than a *price-taker*, the term used to refer to a competitive firm.

market power

A firm's power to set its price without losing its entire share of the market.

price-maker

A firm that has the power to set its price, rather than taking the price set by the market.

1.1 Getting an Intuitive Feel for the Market Power of a Monopoly

We can demonstrate the monopoly's power to affect the price in the market by looking at either what happens when the monopoly changes its price or what happens when the monopoly changes the quantity it produces. We consider the price decision first.

No One Can Undercut the Monopolist's Price

When several sellers are competing with one another in a competitive market, one seller can try to sell at a higher price, but no one will buy at that price because another seller is always nearby who will undercut that price. If a seller charges a higher price, everyone will ignore that seller; there is no effect on the market price.

The monopoly's situation is quite different. Instead of several sellers, the market has only one seller. If the single seller sets a high price, it has no need to worry about being undercut by other sellers. There are no other sellers. Thus, the single seller—the monopoly—has the power to set a high price. True, the buyers probably will buy less at the higher price—that is, as the price rises, the quantity demanded declines—but because no other sellers offer that product or service, they probably will buy something from the lone seller.

The monopoly power of the salt industry has been illustrated throughout history. Salt monopolies have contributed to the rise of several state powers—from governments in ancient China to medieval Europe, where Venice's control of the salt monopoly helped finance its navy and allowed it to dominate world trade.

Source: © Shutterstock, Inc.

The Impact of Quantity Decisions on the Price

Another way to see this important difference between a monopoly and a competitor is to examine what happens to the price when a firm changes the quantity it produces. Suppose that 100 firms are competing in the bagel-baking market in a large city, each producing about the same quantity of bagels each day. Suppose that one of the firms—Bageloaf—decides to cut its production in half. Although this is a huge cut for one firm, it is a small cut compared with the whole market—only 0.5 percent. *Thus, the market price will rise very little.* Moreover, if this little price increase affects the behavior of the other 99 firms at all, it will motivate them to increase their production slightly. As they increase the quantity they supply, they partially offset the cut in supply by Bageloaf, and so the change in market price will be even smaller. Thus, by any measure, the overall impact on the price from the change in Bageloaf's production is negligible. Bageloaf essentially has no power to affect the price of bagels in the city.

But now suppose that Bageloaf and the 99 other firms are taken over by Bagelopoly, which then becomes the only bagel bakery in the city. Now, if Bagelopoly cuts production in half, the total quantity of bagels supplied to the whole market is cut in half, and *this will have a big effect on the price in the market.*

If Bagelopoly cut its production even further, the price would rise further. If Bagelopoly increased the quantity it produced, however, the price of bagels would fall. Thus, Bagelopoly has immense power to affect the price. Even if Bagelopoly does not know exactly what the price elasticity of demand for bagels is, it can adjust the quantity it will produce either up or down to change the price.

Showing Market Power with a Graph

Figure 10.1 contrasts the market power of a monopoly with that of a competitive firm. The right-hand graph shows that the competitive firm views the market price as essentially out of its control. The market price is shown by the flat line and is thus the same regardless of how much the firm produces. If the competitive firm tried to charge a higher price, nobody would buy because many competitors would be charging a lower price; so, effectively, the competitive firm cannot charge a higher price.

To a monopoly, on the other hand, things look quite different. Because the monopoly is the sole producer of the product, it represents the entire market. The monopoly—shown in the left-hand graph—sees a downward-sloping market demand curve for its product. *The downward-sloping demand curve seen by the monopoly is the same as the market demand curve.* If the monopoly charges a higher price, the quantity demanded declines along the demand curve. With a higher price, fewer people buy the item, but with no competitors to undercut that higher price, some demand still exists for the product. The difference in the market power of a monopoly and a competitive firm—illustrated by the slope of the demand curve each faces—causes the difference in the behavior of the two types of firms.

FIGURE 10.1 **How the Market Power of a Monopoly and a Competitive Firm Differ**

A monopoly is the only firm in the market. Thus, the market demand curve and the demand curve of the monopoly are the same. By raising the price, the monopoly sells less. In contrast, the competitive firm has no impact on the market price. If the competitive firm charges a higher price, its sales will drop to zero because many other sellers offer identical products.

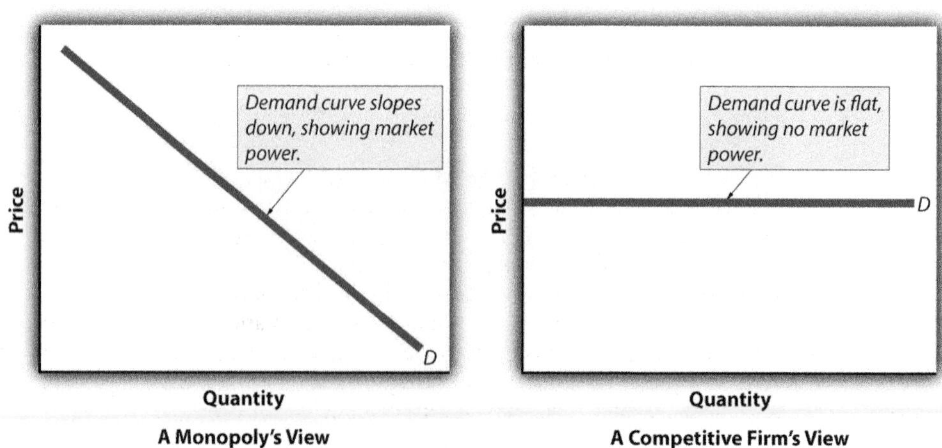

1.2 The Effects of a Monopoly's Decision on Revenues

Now that we have seen how the monopoly can affect the price in its market by changing the quantity it produces, let's see how its revenues are affected by the quantity it produces.

Figure 10.2 gives a specific numerical example of a monopoly. Depending on the units for measuring the quantity *Q*, the monopoly could be producing software, computer chips, or diamonds. The two columns on the left represent the market demand curve, showing a negative relationship between the price and the quantity sold: As the price falls from $130 to $120 per unit, for example, the quantity sold rises from three to four.

Total Revenue and Marginal Revenue

The third column of Figure 10.2 shows what happens to the monopoly's *total revenue*, or price times quantity, as the quantity of output increases. Observe that at the beginning, when the monopoly increases the quantity produced, total revenue rises: When zero units are sold, total revenue is clearly zero; when one unit is sold, total revenue is 1 × $150, or $150; when two units are sold, total revenue is 2 x $140, or $280; and so on. As the quantity sold increases, however, total revenue rises by smaller and smaller amounts and eventually starts to fall. In Figure 10.2, total revenue reaches a peak of $640 at eight units sold and then starts to decline.

FIGURE 10.2 **Revenue, Costs, and Profits for a Monopoly (price, revenue, and cost measured in dollars)**

Market Demand						
Quantity Produced and Sold (Q)	*Price (P)*	Total Revenue *(TR)*	Marginal Revenue *(MR)*	Total Costs *(TC)*	Marginal Cost *(MC)*	Profits
0	160	0	—	70	—	-70
1	150	150	150	79	9	71
2	140	280	130	84	5	196
3	130	390	110	94	10	296
4	120	480	90	114	20	366
5	110	550	70	148	34	402
6	100	600	50	196	48	404
7	90	630	30	261	65	369
8	80	640	10	351	90	289
9	70	630	−10	481	130	149
10	60	600	−30	656	175	-56
		$TR = P \times Q$	$\frac{\text{Change in } TR}{\text{Change in } Q}$		$\frac{\text{Change in } TC}{\text{Change in } Q}$	$TR - TC$

Marginal revenue, introduced in Chapter 6, is the change in total revenue from one more unit of that output sold. For example, if total revenue increases from $480 to $550 as output rises by one unit, marginal revenue is $70 ($550 - $480 = $70). Marginal revenue for the monopolist in Figure 10.2 is shown in the fourth column, next to total revenue. In addition, marginal revenue is plotted in the right-hand graph of Figure 10.3, where it is labeled *MR*.

The left-hand graph in Figure 10.3 shows how total revenue changes with the quantity of output for the example in Figure 10.2. It shows that total revenue increases by a smaller and smaller amount, reaches a maximum, and then begins to decline. In other words, *marginal revenue declines as the quantity of output rises and eventually becomes negative.* So, although a monopolist has the power to influence the price, this does not mean that it can get as high a level of total revenue as it wants.

Why does total revenue increase by smaller and smaller amounts and then decline as production increases? To sell more output, the monopolist must lower the price to get people to buy the increased output. As it raises output, it must lower the price more and more, and this causes the increase in total revenue to get smaller. As the price falls to very low levels, revenue actually declines.

FIGURE 10.3 Total Revenue, Marginal Revenue, and Demand

The graph on the left plots total revenue for each level of output in the table in Figure 10.2. Total revenue first rises and then declines as the quantity of output increases. Marginal revenue is the change in total revenue for each additional increase in the quantity of output and is shown by the bottom curve at the right. Observe that the marginal revenue curve lies below the demand curve at each level of output except $Q = 1$.

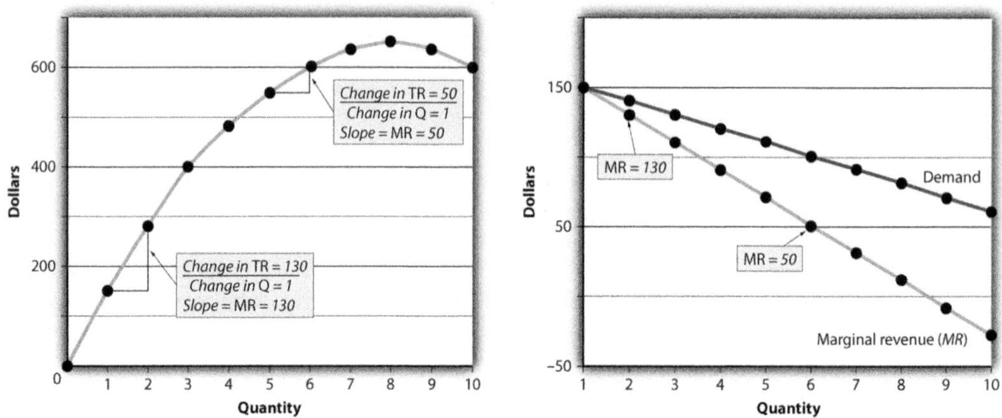

Marginal Revenue Is Less Than the Price

Another important relationship between marginal revenue and price is that for every level of output, *marginal revenue is less than the price* (except at the first unit of output, where it equals the price). To observe this, compare the price (*P*) and marginal revenue (*MR*) in Figure 10.2 or in the right-hand panel of Figure 10.3.

Graph Showing the Two Effects on Marginal Revenue. When the monopoly raises output from three units to four units, revenue increases; that is, marginal revenue is greater than zero. There is a positive effect (vertical rectangle) because one more item is sold and a negative effect (horizontal rectangle) because prices on the first three units fall. Here the positive effect of the sale of an extra unit at $120 (vertical rectangle) is greater than the negative effect of selling each of the first three units at a price that is $10 less than before (horizontal rectangle), so marginal revenue is $120 - $30 = $90.

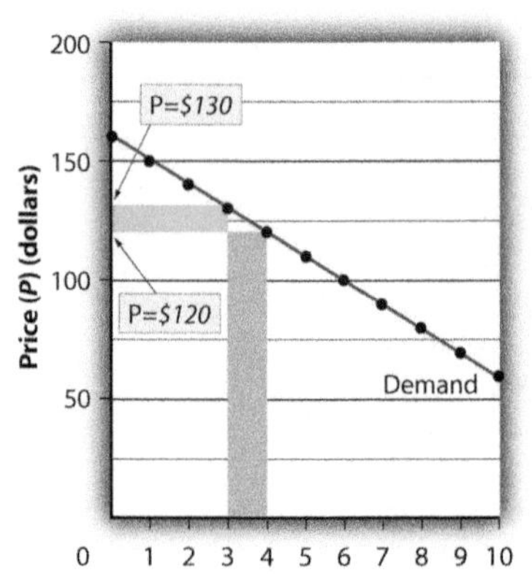

Note that the upper line in the right-hand graph in Figure 10.3 showing the price and the quantity of output demanded is simply the demand curve facing the monopolist. Thus, another way to say that marginal revenue is less than the price at a given level of output is to say that the *marginal revenue curve lies below the demand curve.*

Why is the marginal revenue curve below the demand curve? When the monopolist increases output by one unit, there are two effects on total revenue: (1) a positive effect, which equals the price *P* times the additional unit sold, and (2) a negative effect, which equals the reduction in the price on all items previously sold times the number of such items sold. For example, as the monopolist in Figure 10.2 increases production from four to five units and the price falls from $120 to $110, marginal revenue is $70. This $70 is equal to the increased revenue from the extra unit produced, or $110, less the decreased revenue from the reduction in the price, or $40 ($10 times the four units previously produced). Marginal revenue (*MR* = $70) is thus less than the price (*P* = $110). The two effects on marginal revenue are shown in the graph in the margin when quantity increases from 3 to 4. Because the second effect—the reduction in revenue due to the lower price on the items previously produced—is subtracted from the first, the price is always greater than the marginal revenue.

Marginal Revenue and Elasticity

Marginal revenue is negative when the price elasticity of demand is less than one. To see this, some algebra is helpful. Note from the examples in the table below that the following equation holds:

$$\text{Marginal Revenue} = (P \times \Delta Q) - (\Delta P \times Q)$$

If MR < 0 then

$$(P \times \Delta Q) < (\Delta P \times Q)$$

which implies that

$$\frac{\left(\frac{\Delta Q}{Q}\right)}{\left(\frac{\Delta P}{P}\right)} < 1$$

or, in words, that the price elasticity of demand is less than one. Because it would be crazy for a monopolist to produce so much that its marginal revenue was negative, we conclude that a monopoly would never produce a level of output for which the price elasticity of demand would be less than one.

Quantity Sold	Marginal Revenue (*MR*)		Price x (Change in Quantity) *P* x (Δ *Q*)	-	(Change in Price) x (Previous Quantity Sold) (Δ *P*) x (*Q*)
1	150	=	$150 x 1	-	$10 x 0
2	130	=	$140 x 1	-	$10 x 1
3	110	=	$130 x 1	-	$10 x 2
4	90	=	$120 x 1	-	$10 x 3
5	70	=	$110 x 1	-	$10 x 4
6	50	=	$100 x 1	-	$10 x 5
7	30	=	$90 x 1	-	$10 x 6
8	10	=	$80 x 1	-	$10 x 7
9	-10	=	$70 x 1	-	$10 x 8
10	-30	=	$60 x 1	-	$10 x 9

Average Revenue

We also can use average revenue to show that marginal revenue is less than the price. **Average revenue** is defined as total revenue divided by the quantity of output; that is, $AR = TR/Q$. Because total revenue (TR) equals price times quantity ($P \times Q$), we can write average revenue (AR) as $(P \times Q)/Q$ or, simply, the price P. In other words, the demand curve—which shows price at each level of output—also shows average revenue for each level of output.

Average revenue
Total revenue divided by quantity.

Now recall from Chapter 8 that when the average of anything (costs, grades, heights, or revenues) declines, the marginal must be less than the average. Thus, because average revenues (prices) decline (that is, the demand curve slopes down), the marginal revenue curve must lie below the demand curve.

1.3 Finding Output to Maximize Profits at the Monopoly

Now that we have seen how a monopoly's revenues depend on the quantity it produces, let's see how its profits depend on the quantity it produces. Once we identify the relationship between profit and the quantity the monopoly will produce, we can determine the level of output that maximizes the monopoly's profits. Revenues alone cannot determine how much a firm produces. For instance, we know that a monopolist will never produce a quantity for which marginal revenue is negative. But that does not mean that it will produce until marginal revenue is zero. Even if each additional unit brings in extra revenue, the firm will have to look at the costs of producing that extra unit as well.

The last three columns of Figure 10.2 show the costs and profits for the example monopoly. There are no new concepts to introduce about costs for a monopoly, so we can continue to use the cost measures we developed in Chapter 7 to Chapter 9. The most important features to note are that total costs increase as more is produced and that marginal cost also increases, at least for high levels of output.

Comparing Total Revenue and Total Costs

The difference between total revenue and total costs is profits. Observe in Figure 10.2 that as the quantity produced increases, both the total revenue from selling the product and the total costs of producing the product increase. At some level of production, however, total costs start to increase more than revenue increases, so that eventually profits must reach a maximum.

A quick glance at the profits column in Figure 10.2 shows that this maximum level of profits is $404 and is reached when the monopoly produces six units of output. The price the monopoly must charge so that people will buy six units of output is $100, according to the second column of Figure 10.2. To help you visualize how profits change with quantity produced and to find the maximum level of profits, Figure 10.4 plots total costs, total revenue, and profits from Figure 10.2. Profits are shown as the gap between total costs and total revenue. The gap reaches a maximum when output Q equals six.

Equating Marginal Cost and Marginal Revenue

Economists use an alternative, more intuitive approach to finding the level of production that maximizes a monopolist's profits. This approach looks at marginal revenue and marginal cost and employs a rule that economists use extensively.

Consider producing different levels of output, starting with one unit and then rising unit by unit. Compare the marginal revenue from selling each additional unit of output with the marginal cost of producing it. If the marginal revenue is greater than the marginal cost of the additional unit, then profits will increase if the unit is produced. Thus, the unit should be produced, because total revenue rises by more than total costs. For example, in Figure 10.2, the marginal revenue from producing one unit of output is $150 and the marginal cost is $9, so producing that unit increases profits by $141. Thus, at least one unit should be produced. What about two units? Then marginal revenue equals $130 and marginal cost equals $5, so that second unit adds $125 to profits, meaning that it makes sense to produce two units.

Continuing this way, the monopolist should increase its output as long as marginal revenue is greater than marginal cost. But because marginal revenue is decreasing, at some level of output, marginal revenue will drop below marginal cost. The monopolist should not produce at that level. For example, in Figure 10.2, the marginal revenue from selling seven units of output is less than the marginal cost of producing it. Thus, the monopolist should not produce seven units; instead, six units of production, with $MR = 50$ and $MC = 48$, is the profit-maximization level. This is the highest level of output for which marginal revenue is greater than marginal cost. Note that this level of output is exactly what we obtain by looking at the gap between total revenue and total costs.

Thus, the monopolist should produce up to the level of production at which marginal cost equals marginal revenue ($MC = MR$). If the level of production cannot be adjusted so exactly that marginal revenue is precisely equal to marginal cost, then the firm should produce at the highest level of output for which marginal revenue exceeds marginal cost, as in Figure 10.2. In most cases, the monopoly will be able to adjust its output by smaller fractional amounts (for example, pounds of diamonds rather than tons of diamonds), and therefore marginal revenue will equal marginal cost.

A picture of how this marginal revenue equals marginal cost rule works is shown in Figure 10.5. The marginal revenue curve is plotted, along with the marginal cost curve. As the quantity produced increases above very low levels, the marginal cost curve slopes up and the marginal revenue curve slopes down. Marginal revenue equals marginal cost at the level of output at which the two curves intersect.

FIGURE 10.4 **Finding a Quantity of Output to Maximize Profits**

Profits are shown as the gap between total revenue and total costs in the graph on the left and are plotted on the graph on the right. Profits are at a maximum when the quantity of output is six.

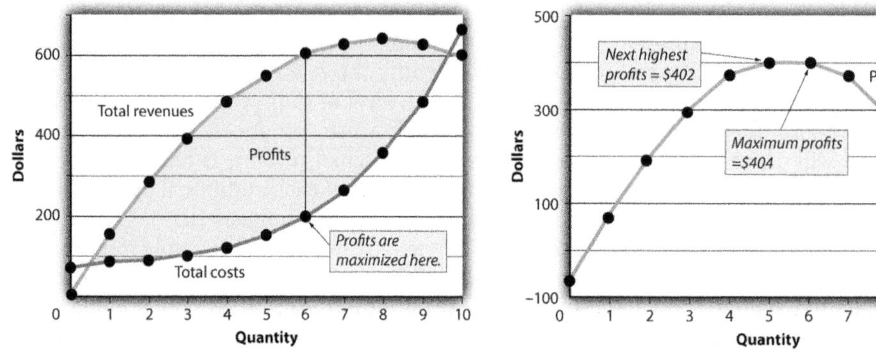

FIGURE 10.5 Marginal Revenue and Marginal Cost

The profit-maximizing monopoly will produce up to the point at which marginal revenue equals marginal cost, as shown in the diagram. If fractional units cannot be produced, then the monopoly will produce at the highest level of output for which marginal revenue is greater than marginal cost. These curves are drawn for the monopoly in the table in Figure 10.2.

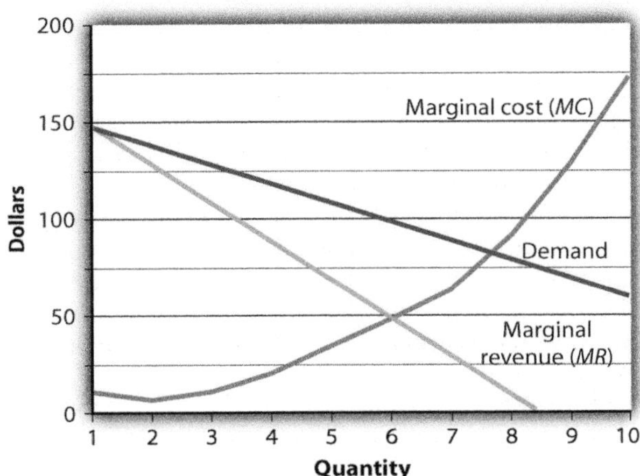

1.4 *MC* = *MR* at a Monopoly versus *MC* = *P* at a Competitive Firm

It is useful to compare the *MC* = *MR* rule for the monopolist with the *MC* = *P* rule for the competitive firm that we derived in Chapter 6.

Marginal Revenue Equals the Price for a Price-Taker

For a competitive firm, total revenue is equal to the quantity sold (*Q*) multiplied by the market price (*P*), but the competitive firm cannot affect the price. Thus, when the quantity sold is increased by one unit, revenue is increased by the price. In other words, for a competitive firm, marginal revenue equals the price; to say that a competitive firm sets its marginal cost equal to marginal revenue is to say that it sets its marginal cost equal to the price. Thus, the *MC* = *MR* rule applies to both monopolies and competitive firms that maximize profits.

A Visual Comparison

Figure 10.6 is a visual comparison of the two rules. A monopoly is shown on the right graph of Figure 10.6. We drew this kind of graph in Figure 10.4 except that it applies to any firm, so we do not show the units. A competitive firm is shown in the left graph of Figure 10.6. The scale on these two figures might be quite different; only the shapes are important for this comparison.

Look carefully at the shape of the total revenue curve for the monopoly and contrast it with the total revenue curve for the competitive firm. The total revenue curve for the monopoly starts to turn down at higher levels of output, whereas the total revenue curve for the competitive firm keeps rising in a straight line.

To illustrate the maximization of profits, we have put the same total costs curve on both graphs in Figure 10.6. Both types of firms maximize profits by setting production so that the gap between the total revenue curve and the total costs curve is as large as possible. That level of output, the profit-maximizing level, is shown for both firms. Higher or lower levels of output will reduce profits, as shown by the gaps between total revenue and total costs in the diagrams.

Observe that at the profit-maximizing level of output, the slope of the total costs curve is equal to the slope of the total revenue curve. Those of you who are mathematically inclined will notice that the slope of the total costs curve is how much total costs change when quantity is increased by one unit—that is, the marginal cost. Similarly, the slope of the total revenue curve is the marginal revenue—the increase in total revenue when output increases by one unit. Thus, we have another way of seeing that marginal revenue equals marginal cost for profit maximization.

For the competitive firm, marginal revenue is the price, which implies the condition of profit maximization at a competitive firm derived in Chapter 6: Marginal cost equals price. For the monopolist, however, marginal revenue and price are not the same thing.

FIGURE 10.6 **Profit Maximization for a Competitive Firm and a Monopoly**

Total revenue for a competitive firm rises steadily with the amount sold; total revenue for a monopoly first rises and then falls. However, both the monopolist and the competitor maximize profits by making the gap between the total costs curve and the total revenue curve as large as possible or by setting the slope of the total revenue curve equal to the slope of the total costs curve. Thus, marginal revenue equals marginal cost. For the competitive firm, marginal revenue equals the price.

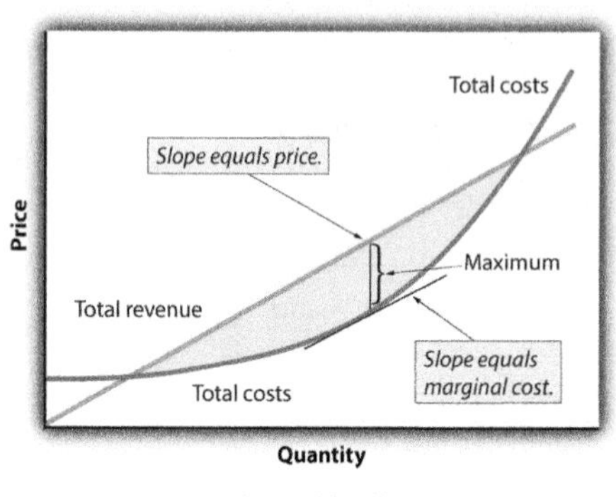

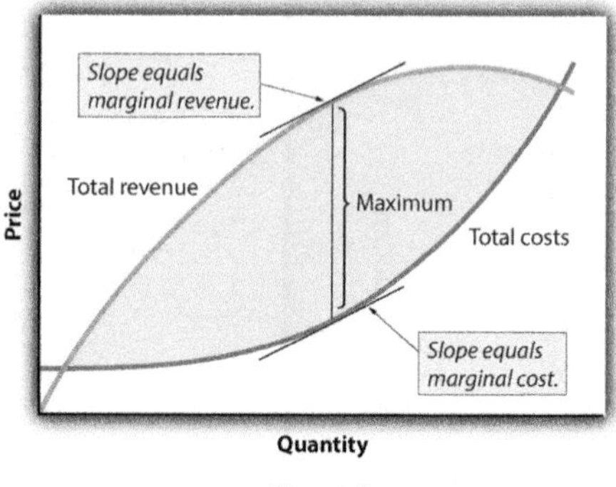

REVIEW

- When one firm is the sole producer of a product with no close substitutes, it is a monopoly. Most monopolies do not last forever. They come and go as technology changes. Barriers to the entry of new firms are needed to maintain a monopoly.
- Marginal revenue is the change in total revenue as output increases by one unit. Marginal revenue declines as quantity sold increases and may even become negative at some level of output.
- Marginal revenue is less than the price at each level of output (except the first). If we lower the price to increase the quantity sold by one unit, revenue increases by the amount of the sale price of the good, but revenue also decreases because the other units are now selling at a lower price.
- A monopolist will never produce at a quantity for which marginal revenue is negative. But it also will not produce until marginal revenue equals zero. Even if an additional unit brings in extra revenue, the firm's decision to produce depends on how much it costs to produce that extra unit.
- A monopoly is like a competitive firm in that it tries to maximize profits. But unlike a competitive firm, a monopoly has market power; it can affect the market price. The demand curve that the monopoly faces is the same as the market demand curve.
- The profit-maximizing quantity for a firm to produce is the quantity for which marginal revenue equals marginal cost ($MR = MC$). As long as $MR > MC$, the firm should keep producing, and if $MR < MC$, the firm should not produce that additional unit.
- For a competitive firm, marginal revenue equals price, because the firm cannot affect the price by increasing the quantity it sells. So marginal cost equals price, which in turn equals marginal revenue ($MR = MC = P$).
- For a monopoly, marginal revenue also equals marginal cost, but marginal revenue does not equal the price. Hence, for the monopolist, price is not necessarily equal to marginal cost.

2. THE GENERIC DIAGRAM OF A MONOPOLY AND ITS PROFITS

Look at Figure 10.7, which combines the monopoly's demand and marginal revenue curves with its average total cost curve and marginal cost curve. This diagram is the workhorse of the model of a monopoly, just as Figure 8.7 in Chapter 8 is the workhorse of the model of a competitive firm. As with the diagram for a competitive firm, you should be able to draw it in your sleep. It is a generic diagram that applies to any monopolist, not just the one in Table 10.1, so we do not put scales on the axes.

Observe that Figure 10.7 shows four curves: a downward-sloping demand curve (*D*), a marginal revenue curve (*MR*), an average total cost curve (*ATC*), and a marginal cost curve (*MC*). The position of these curves is important. First, the marginal cost curve cuts through the average total cost curve at the lowest point on the average total cost curve. Second, the marginal revenue curve is below the demand curve over the entire range of production (except at the vertical axis near one, where they are equal).

We already have given the reasons for these two relationships (in Chapter 8 and in the previous section of this chapter), but it would be a good idea for you to practice sketching your own diagram like Figure 10.7 to ensure that the positions of your curves meet these requirements.

2.1 Determining Monopoly Output and Price on the Diagram

In Figure 10.7 we show how to calculate the monopoly output and price. First, find the point of intersection of the marginal revenue curve and the marginal cost curve. Second, draw a dashed vertical line through this point and look down the dashed line at the horizontal axis to figure out the quantity produced. Producing a larger quantity would lower marginal revenue below marginal cost. Producing a smaller quantity would raise marginal revenue above marginal cost. The quantity shown is the profit-maximizing level. It is the amount the monopolist produces.

FIGURE 10.7 The Generic Diagram for a Monopoly

The marginal revenue and demand curves are superimposed on the monopoly's cost curves. The monopoly's production, price, and profits can be seen on the same diagram. Quantity is given by the intersection of the marginal revenue curve and the marginal cost curve. Price is given by the demand curve at the point corresponding to the quantity produced, and average total cost is given by the *ATC* curve at that quantity. Monopoly profits are given by the rectangle that is the difference between total revenue and total costs.

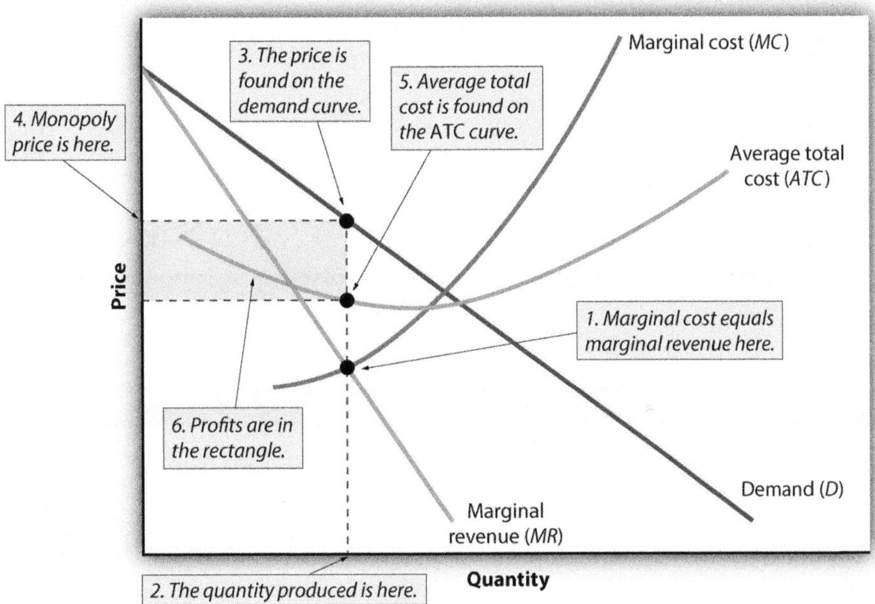

What price will the monopolist charge? We again use Figure 10.7, but be careful: Unlike the quantity, the monopolist's price is not determined by the intersection of the marginal revenue curve and the marginal cost curve. The price has to be such that the quantity demanded is equal to the quantity that the monopolist decides to produce. To find the price, we need to look at the demand curve in Figure 10.7. The demand curve gives the relationship between price and quantity demanded. It tells how much the monopolist will charge for its product to sell the amount produced.

To calculate the price, extend the dashed vertical line upward from the point of intersection of the marginal cost curve and the marginal revenue curve until it intersects the demand curve. At the intersection of the demand curve and the vertical line, we find the price that will generate a quantity demanded equal to the quantity produced. Now draw a horizontal line over to the left from the point of intersection to mark the price on the vertical axis. This is the monopoly's price, about which we will have more to say later.

Determining the Monopoly's Profits

Profits also can be shown on the diagram in Figure 10.7. Profits are given by the difference between the area of two rectangles, a total revenue rectangle and a total costs rectangle. Total revenue is price times quantity and thus is equal to the area of the rectangle with height equal to the monopoly price and length equal to the quantity produced. Total costs are average total cost times quantity and thus are equal to the area of the rectangle with height equal to *ATC* and length equal to the quantity produced. Profits are then equal to the shaded area that is the difference between these two rectangles.

It is possible for a monopoly to have negative profits, or losses, as shown in Figure 10.8. In this case, the price is below average total cost, and therefore total revenue is less than total costs. Like a competitive firm, a monopolist with negative profits will shut down if the price is less than average variable cost. It eventually will exit the market if negative profits persist.

FIGURE 10.8 **A Monopoly with Negative Profits**

If a monopoly finds that average total cost is greater than the price at which marginal revenue equals marginal cost, then it runs losses. If price is also less than average variable cost, then the monopoly should shut down, just like a competitive firm.

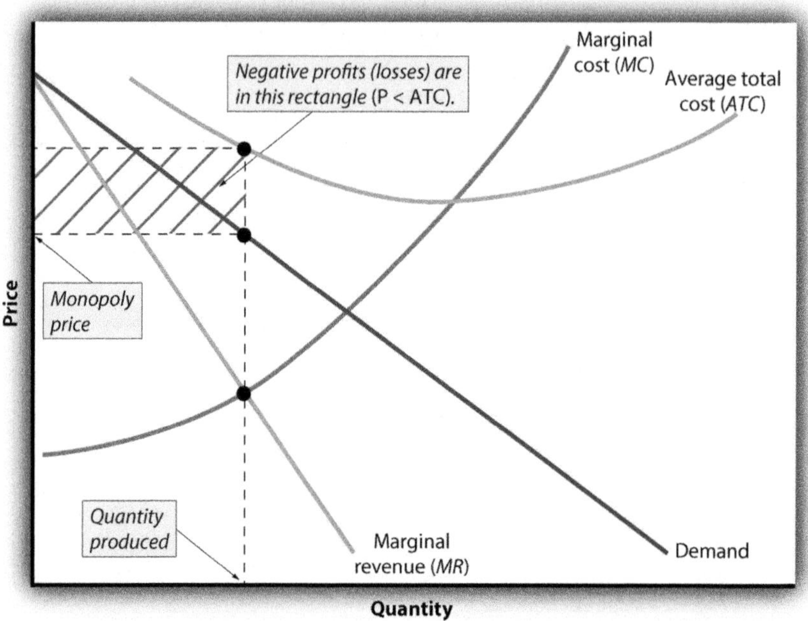

REVIEW

- A monopolist's profit-maximizing output and price can be determined graphically. The diagram shows four curves: the marginal revenue curve, the demand curve, the marginal cost curve, and the average total cost curve.
- The monopoly's production is determined at the point at which marginal revenue equals marginal cost.
- The monopoly's price is determined from the demand curve at the point at which the quantity produced equals the quantity demanded.
- The monopoly's profits are determined by subtracting the total costs rectangle from the total revenue rectangle. The total revenue rectangle is given by the price times the quantity produced. The total costs rectangle is given by the average total cost times the quantity produced.

3. COMPETITION, MONOPOLY, AND DEADWEIGHT LOSS

Are monopolies harmful to society? Do they reduce consumer surplus? Can we measure these effects? To answer these questions, economists compare the price and output of a monopoly with those of a competitive industry. First, observe in Figure 10.7 and Figure 10.8 that the monopoly does not operate at the minimum point on the average total cost curve even in the long run. Recall that firms in a competitive industry do operate at the lowest point on the average total cost curve in the long run. To go further in our comparison, we use Figure 10.9, which is a repeat of Figure 10.7, except that the average total cost curve is removed to reduce the clutter. All the other curves are the same.

3.1 Comparison with Competition

Suppose that instead of only one firm being in the market, it now includes many competitive firms. For example, suppose Bagelopoly—a single firm producing bagels in a large city—is broken down into 100 different bagel bakeries like Bageloaf. The production point for the monopolistic firm and its price before the breakup are marked as "monopoly quantity" and "monopoly price" in Figure 10.9. What are production and price after the breakup?

The market supply curve for the new competitive industry would be Bagelopoly's old marginal cost curve, because this is the sum of the marginal cost curves of all the newly created firms in the industry. Equilibrium in the competitive industry is the point at which this market supply curve crosses the market demand curve. The amount of production at that point is marked by "competitive quantity" in Figure 10.9. The price at that equilibrium is marked by "competitive price" on the vertical axis.

Compare the quantity and price for the monopolist and the competitive industry. It is clear that the quantity produced by the monopolist is less than the quantity produced by the competitive industry. It also is clear that the monopoly will charge a higher price than will emerge from a competitive industry. In sum, the monopoly produces less and charges a higher price than the competitive industry would.

FIGURE 10.9 **Deadweight Loss from Monopoly**

The monopolist's output and price are determined as in Figure 10.7. To get the competitive price, we imagine that competitive firms make up an industry supply curve that is the same as the monopolist's marginal cost curve. The competitive price and quantity are given by the intersection of the supply curve and the demand curve. The monopoly quantity is lower than the competitive quantity. The monopoly price is higher than the competitive price. The deadweight loss is the reduction in consumer plus producer surplus because of the lower level of production by the monopolist.

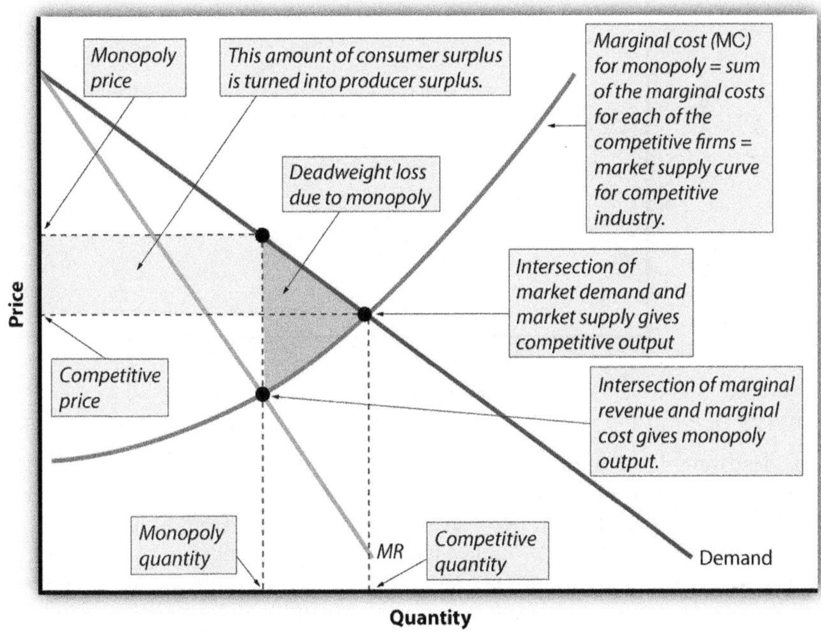

This is an important result. The monopoly exploits its market power by holding back on the quantity produced and causing the price to rise compared with the competitive equilibrium. This is always the case. Convince yourself by drawing different diagrams. For example, when De Beers exercises its market power, it holds back production of diamonds, thereby raising the price and earning economic profits.

Even though the monopoly has the power to do so, it does not increase its price without limit. When the price is set very high, marginal cost rises above marginal revenue. That behavior is not profit maximizing.

3.2 Deadweight Loss from Monopoly

The economic harm caused by a monopoly occurs because it produces less than a competitive industry would. How harmful, then, is a monopoly?

Consumer Surplus and Producer Surplus Again

Economists measure the harm caused by monopolies by the decline in the sum of consumer surplus plus producer surplus. Recall that *consumer surplus* is the area above the market price line and below the demand curve, the demand curve being a measure of consumers' marginal benefit from consuming the good. The *producer surplus* is the area above the marginal cost curve and below the market price line. Consumer surplus plus producer surplus is thus the area between the demand curve and the marginal cost curve. It measures the sum of the marginal benefits to consumers of the good less the sum of the marginal costs to the producers of the good. A competitive market will maximize the sum of consumer plus producer surplus.

With a lower quantity produced by a monopoly, however, the sum of consumer surplus and producer surplus is reduced, as shown in Figure 10.9. This reduction in consumer plus producer surplus is called the *deadweight loss due to monopoly*. It is a quantitative measure of the harm a monopoly causes the economy. A numerical example is given in Figure 10.10.

FIGURE 10.10 Numerical Example of Deadweight Loss Calculation

The monopoly shown in the diagram above produces only 12 items, but a competitive industry would produce 18 items. For the 13th through 17th items, which are not produced by the monopoly, the marginal benefit is greater than the marginal cost by the amounts \$5, \$4,\$3, \$2, and \$1, respectively, as shown by the areas between the demand curve and the supply curve for the competitive industry. Hence, the deadweight loss caused by the monopoly is the sum \$5 + \$4 + \$3 + \$2 + \$1 = \$15.

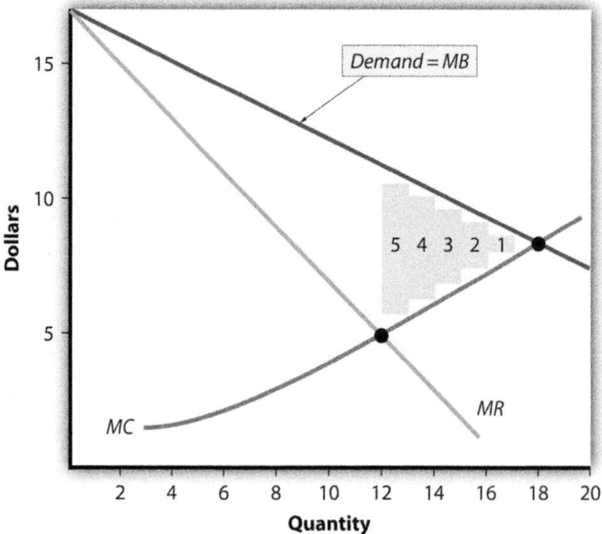

How large is the deadweight loss in the U.S. economy? Using the method illustrated in Figure 10.9, empirical economists estimate that the loss is between 0.5 and 2 percent of gross domestic product (GDP), or between \$60 billion and \$240 billion, per year. Of course, the deadweight loss is a larger percentage of production in industries in which monopolies have a greater presence.

Figure 10.9 also shows that the monopoly takes, in the form of producer surplus, some of the consumer surplus that would have gone to the consumers in competitive markets. Consumer surplus is now the area below the demand curve and above the monopoly price, which is higher than the competitive price. This transfer of consumer surplus to the monopoly is not a deadweight loss, however, because what the consumers lose, the monopoly gains. This transfer affects the distribution of income, but it is not a net loss to society.

Meaningful Comparisons

In any given application, we need to be careful that the comparison of monopoly and competition makes sense. Some industries cannot be broken up into many competitive firms without changing the cost structure of the industry. For instance, having 100 sewer companies laying down pipes to serve one local area would be costly. Therefore, transforming a monopolistic sewer industry into a competitive sewer industry is unlikely to lead to greater societal benefits. Instead, we should try to affect the monopoly's decisions by government actions.

We also should be careful about concluding that a competitive industry of one type is preferable to a monopolistic industry of another type. History provides many such examples. Western settlers in the United States during the nineteenth century had a larger consumer surplus from railroads—in spite of the railroad monopolists' profits—than they did from competitive wagon trains. Modern-day users of the information highway—computers and telecommunications—reap a larger consumer surplus from Microsoft's software and Intel's computer chips, even if they are produced monopolistically, than they would from a competitive pocket calculator industry.

3.3 The Monopoly Price Is Greater Than Marginal Cost

Another way to think about the loss to society from monopoly is to observe the difference between price and marginal cost. Figure 10.9, for example, shows that the monopoly price is well above the marginal cost at the quantity at which the monopoly produces.

Marginal Benefit Is More Than Marginal Cost

Because consumers will consume up to the point at which the marginal benefit of a good equals its price, the excessive price means that the marginal benefit of a good is greater than the marginal cost. This is inefficient because producing more of the good would increase benefits to consumers by more than the cost of producing it.

The size of the difference between price and marginal cost depends on the elasticity of the monopoly's demand curve. If the demand curve is highly elastic (close to a competitive firm's view as shown in Figure 10.1), then the difference between price and marginal cost is small.

The Price-Cost Margin

A common measure of the difference between price and marginal cost is the **price-cost margin**. It is defined as

$$\frac{\text{Price} - \text{marginal cost}}{\text{Price}}$$

price-cost margin

The difference between price and marginal cost divided by the price. This index is an indicator of market power, where an index of zero indicates no market power and a higher price-cost margin indicates greater market power.

For example, if the price is $4 and the marginal cost is $2, the price-cost margin is (4 - 2)/4 = 0.5. The price-cost margin for a competitive firm is zero because price equals marginal cost. Economists use a rule of thumb to show how the price-cost margin depends on the price elasticity of demand. The rule of thumb is shown in the equation below.

$$\text{Price-cost margin} = \frac{1}{\text{price elasticity of demand}}$$

For example, when the elasticity of demand is two, the price-cost margin is 0.5. The flat demand curve has an infinite elasticity, in which case the price-cost margin is zero; in other words, price equals marginal cost.

REVIEW

- A monopoly creates a deadweight loss because it restricts output below what the competitive market would produce. The cost is measured by the deadweight loss, which is the reduction in the sum of consumer plus producer surplus.
- Sometimes the comparison between monopoly and competition is only hypothetical because it would either be impossible or make no sense to break up the monopoly into competitive firms.
- Another way to measure the impact of a monopoly is by the difference between price and marginal cost. Monopolies always charge a price higher than marginal cost. The difference—summarized in the price-cost margin—depends inversely on the elasticity of demand.

4. WHY MONOPOLIES EXIST

Given this demonstration that monopolies lead to high prices and a deadweight loss to society, you may be wondering why monopolies exist. In this section, we consider three reasons for the existence of monopolies.

4.1 Natural Monopolies

The nature of production is a key factor in determining the number of firms in the industry. If big firms are needed to produce at low cost, it may be natural for a few firms or only one firm to exist. In particular, *economies of scale*—a declining long-run average total cost curve over some range of production—can lead to a monopoly. Recall from Chapter 8 that the *minimum efficient scale* of a firm is the minimum size of the firm for which average total costs are lowest. If the minimum efficient scale is only a small fraction of the size of the market, then the market will have many firms.

For example, suppose the minimum efficient scale for beauty salons in a city is a size that serves 30 customers a day at each salon. Suppose the quantity of hair stylings demanded in the city is 300 per day. We can then expect the city to have ten beauty salons (300/30 = 10). But if the minimum efficient scale is larger (for example, 60 customers per day), then the number of firms in the industry will be smaller (for example, 300/60 = 5 salons). At the extreme case, where the minimum efficient scale of the firm is as large as or larger than the size of the market (for example, 300 per day), there probably will be only one firm (300/300 = 1), which will be a monopoly.

natural monopolies

A single firm in an industry in which average total cost is declining over the entire range of production and the minimum efficient scale is larger than the size of the market.

A sewer company in a small town, for example, has a minimum efficient scale larger than the number of houses and businesses in the town. The fixed costs to lay pipe down the street are huge, but each house connection has a relatively low cost, so average total cost declines as more houses are connected. Other industries that usually have a very large minimum efficient scale are electricity and water service. In each of these industries, average total cost is lowest if one firm delivers the service. **Natural monopolies** exist when average total cost is declining and the minimum efficient scale is larger than the size of the market.

The government regulates the prices charged by many natural monopolies. The purpose of the regulation is to keep the price below the monopoly price and closer to the competitive price. Such regulation thereby can reduce the deadweight loss from the monopoly. Alternative methods of regulating natural monopolies are discussed in Chapter 12. The government regulates water companies and electric companies.

A change in technology that changes the minimum efficient scale of firms can radically alter the number of firms in the industry. For example, AT&T used to be viewed as a natural monopoly in long-distance telephone service. Because laying copper wire across the United States required a huge cost, it made little sense to have more than one firm. The U.S. government regulated the prices that AT&T charged its customers, attempting to keep the price of calls below the monopoly price and closer to the competitive price. But when the technology for transmitting signals by microwave developed, it became easier for other firms also to provide services. Thus, MCI and Sprint, as well as AT&T, could provide services at least as cheaply as one firm. Because of this technological change, the government decided to end the AT&T monopoly by allowing MCI and Sprint to compete with AT&T. Nationwide telephone service is no longer a monopoly because the technology of providing telephone service has changed—many companies now provide landline phone service through digital voice technology that uses the same broadband connections that bring internet services to your home.

4.2 Patents and Copyrights

Another way monopolies arise is through the granting of patents and copyrights by the government. Intel's patent was the source of its monopoly on its computer chips. The U.S. Constitution and the laws of many other countries require that governments grant patents to inventors. If a firm registers an invention with the U.S. government, it can be granted a monopoly in the production of that item for 20 years. In other words, the government prohibits other firms from producing the good without the permission of the patent holder. Patents are given for many inventions, including the discovery of new drugs. Pharmaceutical companies hold patents on many of their products, giving them a monopoly to produce and sell these products. Copyrights on computer software, chips, movies, and books also give firms the sole right to market the products. Thus, patents and copyrights can create monopolies.

The award of monopoly rights through patents and copyrights serves a useful purpose. It can stimulate innovation by rewarding the inventor. In other words, the chance to get a patent or copyright gives the inventor more incentive to devote time and resources to invent new products or to take a risk and try out new ideas. Pharmaceutical companies, for example, argue that their patents on drugs are a reward for inventing the drugs. The higher prices and deadweight loss caused by the patent can be viewed as the cost of the new ideas and products. By passing laws to control drug prices, the government could lower the prices of drugs to help people who currently are sick. This action would be popular, but doing so would reduce the incentive for the firms to invent new drugs. Society—and, in particular, people who get sick in future years—could suffer a loss. When patents expire, we usually see a major shift toward competition. In general, when assessing the deadweight loss resulting from a monopoly, one must consider the benefits of the research and the new products that monopoly profits may create.

As technology has advanced, patents and copyrights have had to become increasingly complex to prevent firms from getting around them. Nevertheless, patent and copyright protection does not always work in maintaining the monopoly. Many times, potential competing firms get around copyrights on computer software and chips by "reverse engineering," in which specialists look carefully at how each part of a product works, starting with the final output. Elaborate mechanisms have been developed, such as "clean rooms," in which one group of scientists and programmers tells another group what each subfunction of the invention does but does not tell them how it is done. The other group then tries to invent an alternative way to perform the task. Because they cannot see how it is done, they avoid violating the copyright.

4.3 Licenses

Sometimes the government creates a monopoly by giving or selling to one firm a license to produce a product. The U.S. Postal Service is a government-sponsored monopoly. A law makes it illegal to use a firm other than the U.S. Postal Service for first-class mail. However, even this monopoly is diminishing with competition from overnight mail services and electronic transmission of documents.

National parks sometimes grant or sell to single firms licenses to provide food and lodging services. The Curry Company, for example, was granted a monopoly to provide services in Yosemite National Park. For a long time the Pennsylvania Turnpike—a toll road running the width of the state—licensed a monopoly to Howard Johnson Company to provide food for travelers on the long stretches of the road. Seeing the advantage of competition, however, the turnpike authorities eventually allowed several different fast-food chains to get licenses.

4.4 Attempts to Monopolize and Erect Barriers to Entry

Adam Smith warned that firms would try to create monopolies to raise their prices. Smith favored free trade between countries because it would reduce the ability of firms in one country to form a monopoly. If a firm did form a monopoly and no restrictions on trade served as barriers to entry for firms in other countries, then foreign firms would break the monopoly.

History shows us many examples of firms attempting to monopolize an industry by merging with other firms and then erecting barriers to entry. De Beers is one example of such a strategy apparently being successful on a global level. In the last part of the nineteenth century, several large firms were viewed as monopolies. Standard Oil, started by John D. Rockefeller in the 1880s, is a well-known example. The firm had control of most of the oil-refining capacity in the United States. Thus, Standard Oil was close to having a monopoly in oil refining. However, the federal government forced Standard Oil to break up into smaller firms. We will consider other examples of the government's breaking up monopolies or preventing them from forming in Chapter 12.

Barriers to entry allow a monopoly to persist, so for a firm to maintain a monopoly, it needs barriers to entry. In addition to the ways mentioned earlier, barriers to entry also can be created by professional certification. For example, economists have argued that the medical and legal professions in the United States erect barriers to the entry of new doctors and lawyers by having tough standards for admittance to medical school or to the bar and by restricting the types of services that can be performed by nurses or paralegals. Doctors' and lawyers' fees might be lower if there were lower barriers to entry and, therefore, more competition.

Simply observing that a firm has no competitors is not enough to prove that barriers to entry exist. Sometimes the threat of potential entry into a market may be enough to get a monopolist to act like a competitive firm. For example, the possibility of a new bookstore's opening up off campus may put pressure on the campus bookstore to keep its prices low. When other firms, such as off-campus bookstores, can potentially and easily enter the market, they create what economists call a **contestable market**. In general, the threat of competition in contestable markets can induce monopolists to act like competitors.

contestable market

A market in which the threat of competition is enough to encourage firms to act like competitors.

REVIEW

- Economies of scale, patents, copyrights, and licenses are some of the reasons monopolies exist.
- Natural monopolies frequently are regulated by government.
- Many large monopolies in the United States, such as Standard Oil and AT&T, have been broken apart by government action.

5. PRICE DISCRIMINATION

price discrimination

A situation in which different groups of consumers are charged different prices for the same good.

In the model of monopoly we have studied in this chapter, the monopolists charge a single price for the good they sell. In some cases, however, firms charge different people different prices for the same item. This is called **price discrimination**. Price discrimination is common and is likely to become more common in the future as firms become more sophisticated in their price setting. Everyday examples include senior citizen discounts at movie theaters and discounts on airline tickets for Saturday-night stay overs.

Some price discrimination is less noticeable because it occurs in geographically separated markets. Charging different prices in foreign markets and domestic markets is common. For example, Japanese cameras are less expensive in the United States than in Japan. In contrast, the price of luxury German cars in the United States is frequently higher than in Germany. Volume or quantity discounts are another form of price discrimination. Higher prices are sometimes charged to customers who buy smaller amounts of an item. For example, electric utility firms sometimes charge more per kilowatt-hour to customers who use only a little electricity.

5.1 Consumers with Different Price Elasticities of Demand

What causes price discrimination? Figure 10.11 shows a diagram of a monopoly that gives one explanation. Suppose the good being sold is airline travel between two remote islands, and suppose only one airline operates between the two islands. The two graphs in Figure 10.11 represent demand curves with different elasticities. On the left is the demand for vacation air travel. Vacationers are frequently more price sensitive than business people. They can be more flexible with their time; they can take a boat rather than a plane; they can stay home and paint the house. Hence, for vacationers, the price elasticity of demand is high. Business travelers, however, do not have much choice. As shown in Figure 10.11, they are less sensitive to price. An important business meeting may require a flight to the other island with little advance notice. For business travel, the price elasticity of demand is low. Difference between price elasticities is a key reason for price discrimination.

In Figure 10.11, notice that both groups have downward-sloping demand curves and downward-sloping marginal revenue curves. For simplicity, marginal cost is constant and is shown with a straight line. Figure 10.11 predicts that business travelers will be charged a higher price than vacationers. Why? Marginal revenue equals marginal cost at a higher price for business travelers than for vacationers. The model of monopoly predicts that the firm will charge a higher price to those with a lower elasticity and a lower price to those with a higher elasticity.

FIGURE 10.11 Price Discrimination Targeted at Different Groups

The monopolist has two groups of potential buyers for its travel services. For convenience, we assume the marginal cost curve is flat. The group on the left has a high price elasticity of demand. The group on the right has a low price elasticity of demand. If the monopolist can discriminate between the buyers, then it is optimal to charge a lower price to the high-elasticity group and a higher price to the low-elasticity group.

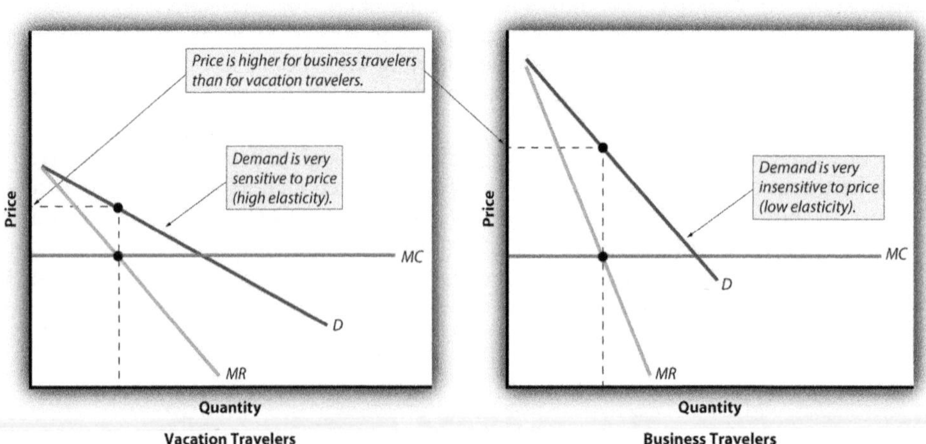

In fact, this is the type of price discrimination we see with airlines. But how can the airlines distinguish a business traveler from a vacation traveler? Clothing will not work: A business traveler easily could change from a suit to an aloha shirt and shorts to get the low fare. One device used by some airlines is the Saturday-night stay over. Business travelers prefer to work and travel during the week. They value being home with family or friends on a Saturday night. Vacationers frequently do not mind extending their travel by a day or two to include a Saturday night, and they may want to vacation over the weekend. Hence, a strong correlation exists between vacation travelers and those who do not mind staying over a Saturday night. A good way to price-discriminate, therefore, is to charge a lower price to people who stay at their destination on a Saturday night and to charge a higher price to those who are unwilling to do so.

Price discrimination based on different price elasticity of demand requires that the firm be able to prevent people who buy at a lower price from selling the item to other people. Thus, price discrimination is much more common in services than in manufactured goods.

5.2 Quantity Discounts

Another important form of price discrimination involves setting prices according to how much is purchased. If a business buys 1,000 units of a particular software package from a company, it probably has to pay a higher price per unit than if it purchases 10,000 units of that software. A software company can increase their profits by such a price scheme, as shown in Figure 10.12.

The single-price monopoly is shown in the bottom graph of Figure 10.12. Two ways in which the monopoly can make higher profits by charging different prices are shown in the top two panels. In both cases, there is no difference in the price elasticity of demand for different consumers. To make it easy, assume that all consumers are identical. The demand curve is the sum of the marginal benefits of all the consumers in the market.

On the upper left, the firm sets a higher price for the first few items a consumer buys and a lower price for the remaining items. Frequent flier miles on airlines are an example of this kind of pricing. If you fly more than a certain number of miles, you get a free ticket. Thus, the per-mile fare for 50,000 miles is less than the per-mile fare for 25,000 miles. As the diagram shows, profits for the firm are higher in such a situation. In the example on the left, the higher price is the fare without the discount.

On the upper right, we see how profits can be increased if the firm gives even deeper discounts to high-volume purchasers. As long as the high-volume purchasers cannot sell the product to the low-volume purchasers, extra profits can be made. This type of volume discount is common in software sales to companies, for example.

The upper right graph in Figure 10.12 illustrates an important benefit of price discrimination: It can reduce deadweight loss. With price discrimination, a monopoly actually produces more. For example, those who get a lower price because of frequent flier discounts actually may end up buying more. The result is that the airline has more flights. As noted, the deadweight loss from a monopolist occurs because production is too low. If price discrimination allows more production, then it reduces deadweight loss.

FIGURE 10.12 **Price Discrimination through Quantity Discounts or Premiums**

The standard single-price monopoly is shown at the bottom. If the monopoly can charge a higher price to customers who buy only a little, profits can increase, as shown on the upper left. If the monopoly can give a discount to people who purchase a lot, it also can increase profits, as shown on the upper right. In this case, production increases.

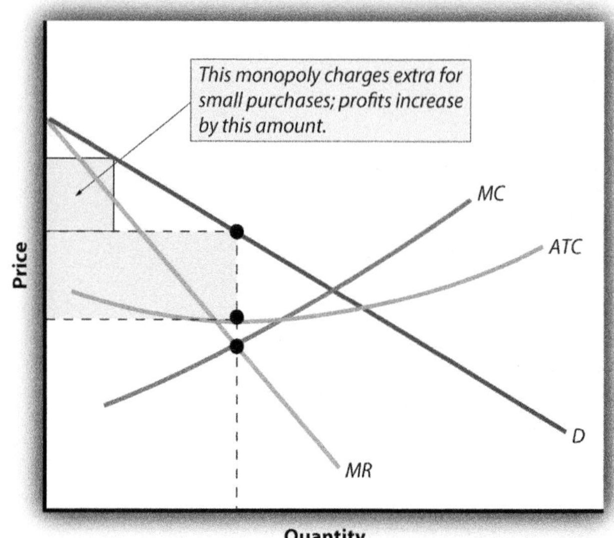

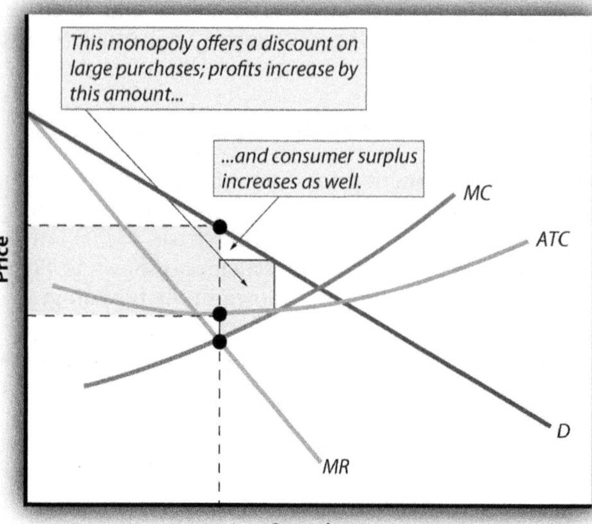

Two Examples of a Monopoly Charging Two Prices

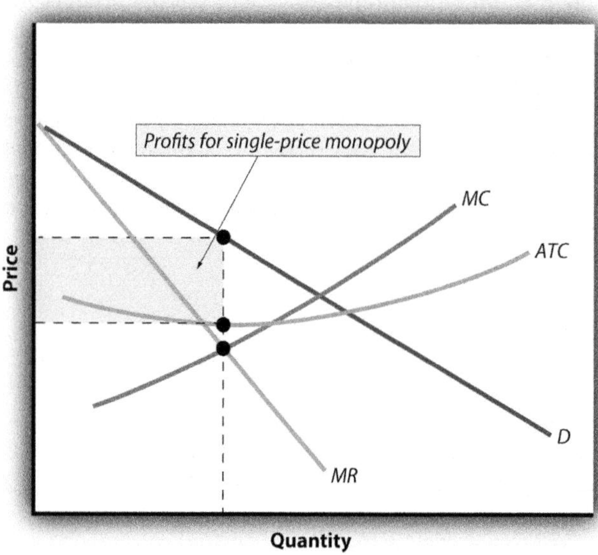

Single-Price Monopoly

REVIEW

- Because a monopolist has market power, it can charge different prices to different consumers as long as it can prevent the consumers from reselling the good.
- Price discrimination explains telephone pricing as well as the complicated airfares on airlines.
- Deadweight loss is reduced by price discrimination.

6. END-OF-CHAPTER MATERIALS

6.1 Conclusion

The model of a monopoly that we developed in this chapter centers on a key diagram: Figure 10.7. Learning how to work with this diagram of a monopoly is important. In fact, economists use this same diagram to describe any firm that has some market power, not just monopolies, as we show in Chapter 11. Before proceeding, it is a good idea to practice sketching this generic diagram of a monopoly and finding output, price, and profits for different positions of the curve.

From the point of view of economic efficiency, the economic performance of monopolies is not nearly as good as that of competitive industries. Output is too low, marginal benefits are not equal to marginal costs, and consumer surplus plus producer surplus is diminished. But when assessing these losses, the fact that the expectation of monopoly profits—even if temporary—is the inducement for firms to do research and develop new products also must be considered.

Nevertheless, the deadweight loss caused by monopolies provides a potential opportunity for government to intervene in the economy. In fact, the U.S. government actively intervenes in the economy either to prevent monopolies from forming or to regulate monopolies when it is not appropriate to break them apart. We look further into government prevention or regulation of monopolies in Chapter 12.

Key Points

1. A monopoly occurs when only one firm sells a product that does not have a close substitute. Many local markets for water, sewage, electricity, and cable television are monopolies.
2. A monopolist possesses market power in the sense that it can lower the market price by producing more or raise the market price by producing less.
3. A monopoly's total revenue increases, but at a decreasing rate, as it increases production. This implies that its marginal revenue initially is positive but gradually becomes smaller.
4. Marginal revenue for a monopolist is always less than price. Even though the firm can increase its revenue by producing and selling an additional unit, it earns lower revenues on previously produced units because it had to lower its price to increase its sales.
5. The model of a monopoly assumes that the monopoly tries to maximize profits. To maximize profits, a monopolist chooses a quantity such that marginal revenue equals marginal cost.
6. A monopoly produces a smaller quantity and charges a higher price than a competitive industry; the lower production causes a deadweight loss.
7. Monopolies exist because of economies of scale that make the minimum efficient size of the firm larger than the market, or because of barriers to entry, including government patents and licenses.
8. Even though they create monopolies, patents and copyrights are useful to society because they provide incentives for creators of innovative products and works.
9. Many monopolies are short lived; technological change can rapidly change a firm from a monopoly to a competitive firm, as exemplified by the long-distance telephone market.
10. A price-discriminating monopoly charges different prices to different customers depending on how elastic their demand is. If price discrimination leads a monopolist to increase its production, then it can help reduce deadweight loss.

QUESTIONS FOR REVIEW

1. What is a monopoly?
2. What market power does a monopoly have?
3. Why does marginal revenue decline as more is produced by a monopoly?
4. How does a monopoly choose its profit maximizing output and price?
5. Why is the marginal revenue curve below the demand curve for a monopoly but not for a competitive firm?
6. Why does a monopolist produce less than a competitive industry?
7. What forces tend to cause monopolies?
8. What is the deadweight loss from a monopoly?
9. What is price discrimination?
10. How does price discrimination reduce deadweight loss?

PROBLEMS

1. The following table gives the total cost and total revenue schedule for a monopolist.

Quantity	Total Cost (in dollars)	Total Revenue (in dollars)
0	144	0
1	160	90
2	170	160
3	194	210
4	222	240
5	260	250
6	315	240
7	375	210

   a. Calculate the marginal revenue and marginal cost.
   b. Determine the profit-maximizing price and quantity, and calculate the resulting profit.
   c. Sketch the demand curve, the marginal revenue curve, and the marginal cost curve, and show how to derive the profit-maximizing quantity graphically.

2. Fill in the missing data on a monopolist, with fixed costs of $10, in the following table:

Quantity of Output	Price	Total Revenue	Marginal Revenue	Marginal Cost	Average Total Cost
1	11				18.00
2	10				11.00
3	9				7.67
4	8				7.00
5	7				6.60
6	6				7.00
7	5				8.00

   a. At what quantity will the monopolist produce to maximize profits? What will be the price at this level of output? What will be the profits?
   b. What quantity maximizes total revenue? Why is this not the profit-maximizing quantity?
   c. Sketch the demand curve, the marginal revenue curve, the marginal cost curve, and the average total cost curve. Show how to derive the profit-maximizing quantity and the profits earned by the monopolist graphically.

3. Suppose you are an economic adviser to the president, and the president asks you to prepare an economic analysis of MonoTV, Inc., a firm that sells a patented device used in high-definition television sets. You have the following information about MonoTV, Inc.

Quantity (millions)	Price	Marginal Cost
1	10	4
2	9	5
3	8	6
4	7	7
5	6	8
6	5	9
7	4	10
8	3	11
9	2	12
10	1	13

a. Given the data in the table, graphically show all the elements necessary to represent the monopolist's profit maximization. Note: You do not need to draw the average total cost curve.

b. What level of output does MonoTV, Inc., produce? What price does it sell this output at?

c. Does MonoTV, Inc., produce at the socially optimal level? Why or why not? Show any inefficiency on your graph.

4. Consider the monopoly described in the following table.

Quantity	Price	Total Revenue	Marginal Revenue	Total Cost	Marginal Cost	Profit
0	320	0	--	140	--	-140
2	305	610	305	158	9	452
4	290	1,160	275	168	5	992
6	275	1,650	245	188	10	1,462
8	260	2,080	215	228	20	1,852
10	245	2,450	185	296	34	2,154
12	230	2,760	155	392	48	2,368
14	215	3,010	125	522	65	2,488
16	200	3,200	95	712	95	2,488
18	185	3,330	65	962	125	2,368
20	170	3,400	35	1,302	170	2,088
22	155	3,410	5	1,762	225	1,648
24	140	3,360	-25	2,322	280	1,038

a. What are the profit-maximizing quantity and price?

b. How much is the monopolist making in profits?

c. What would the equilibrium price and quantity have been if the market were competitive?

d. Calculate the deadweight loss caused by the monopolist.

5. Sketch the diagram for a monopoly with an upward-sloping marginal cost curve that is earning economic profits. Suppose the government imposes a tax on each item the monopoly sells. Draw the diagram corresponding to this situation. How does this tax affect the monopoly's production and price? Show what happens to the area of deadweight loss.

6. Why might a local electric company be a monopoly? Would your answer be the same for a local cable television company? How about your long-distance telephone company?

7. Under the Copyright Act of 1976, in the United States, authors and creators like Walt Disney were granted copyrights over their creations that would last for the life of the author plus 50 years. What are the trade-offs involved in granting monopoly rights to an author? In 1998, the U.S. Congress decided to allow companies to extend copyrights that were reaching the end of their 50-year protected period and would be expiring by an additional twenty years. What do you think about the merits and demerits of that decision?
8. The following table gives the round-trip airfares from Los Angeles to New York offered by United Airlines.

Price	Purchase Advance	Minimum Stay	Cancellation Policy
$418	14 days	Overnight on Saturday	100%
$683	3 days	Overnight on Saturday	100%
$1,900	None required	None required	None

   Explain why United might want to charge different prices for the same route. Why are there minimum-stay requirements and cancellation penalties?
9. Why do firms need market power to price-discriminate? What other circumstances are required for a firm to price-discriminate? Give an example of a firm or industry that price-discriminates and explain how it is possible in that case.
10. Children, students, and senior citizens frequently are eligible for discounted tickets to movies. Is this an example of price discrimination? Explain the conditions necessary for price discrimination to occur and draw the graphs to describe this situation.

CHAPTER 11
Product Differentiation, Monopolistic Competition, and Oligopoly

Source: By Jet Magazine (Jet Magazine) [Public domain], via Wikimedia Commons

When John Johnson launched his magazine business in 1942, he differentiated his products from existing products in a way that was valued by millions of African Americans. As a result, the new product lines, the magazines Ebony and Jet, were huge successes. Johnson became a multimillionaire, and his firm became the second-largest black-owned firm in the United States. Similarly, when Liz Claiborne started her new clothing firm in 1976, she differentiated her products from existing products in a way that was valued by millions of American women. She offered stylish yet affordable clothes for working women, and she too was successful: Thirty years later, Liz Claiborne, Inc., was one of the largest producers of women's clothing in the world. Such stories of people finding ways to differentiate their products from existing products are told thousands of times a year, although not everyone is as successful as John Johnson and Liz Claiborne.

John Johnson's magazines and Liz Claiborne's suits and dresses were different in a way that was valued by consumers. Because their products were different from the products made by the many other firms in their industries—magazine publishing and women's clothing, respectively—they each had market power in the sense that they could charge a higher price for their products and not lose all their customers. Thus, neither Johnson Publishing nor Liz Claiborne, Inc., was just another firm entering a competitive industry in which every firm sold the same product. But Johnson Publishing and Liz Claiborne, Inc., were not monopolies either; other firms were in their industries, and they could not prevent entry into the industries by even more firms. As is typical of many firms, they seemed to be hybrids between a competitive firm and a monopoly.

In this chapter, we develop a model that is widely used by economists to explain the behavior of such firms. It is called the *model of monopolistic competition.* **Monopolistic competition** occurs in an industry with many firms and free entry, where the product of each firm is slightly differentiated from the product of every other firm. We contrast the predictions of this model with those of the models of competition and monopoly developed in previous chapters.

Monopolistic competition

A market structure characterized by many firms selling differentiated products in an industry that has free entry and exit.

We also study another type of industry whose structure seems to fall between the models of monopoly and competition. In an **oligopoly**, very few firms are in the industry. Because the industry has very few firms, each firm has market power—the actions of any one firm can significantly affect the market price. In an oligopoly, each firm needs to anticipate what the others will do and develop a strategy to respond. Neither the model of a competitive

oligopoly

An industry characterized by few firms selling the same product with limited entry of other firms.

industry, in which case no one firm can affect the price, nor the model of monopoly, in which case one firm completely dominates the market, adequately describes such a situation. To develop a model of oligopoly, therefore, we need to extend our tools of economic analysis to deal with strategic behavior: How firms think about, anticipate, and react to other firms' moves.

Figure 11.1 compares the models of monopolistic competition, oligopoly, monopoly, and competition. Over time, an industry can change from being a monopoly to monopolistic competition, to oligopoly, to competition, and back again, as a result of changes in the number of firms or the degree of product differentiation.

To emphasize the distinction between the models of competition and monopolistic competition or between the models of monopoly and monopolistic competition, the terms *pure competition* and *pure monopoly* sometimes are used. In this book, we simply use the terms *competition* and *monopoly*.

FIGURE 11.1 **Four Types of Industries**

Monopoly and competition are at the extreme ends. Monopolistic competition and oligopoly are in between.

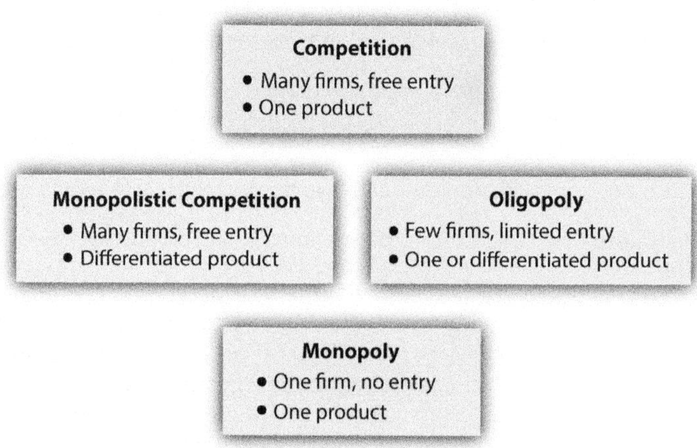

1. PRODUCT DIFFERENTIATION

product differentiation

The effort by firms to produce goods that are slightly different from other types of goods.

The effort by firms to fashion products that are different from other firms' products in ways that people value is called **product differentiation**. Product differentiation is pervasive in market economies. It leads to a great variety of consumer goods and capital goods. Goods that do not have product differentiation, such as aluminum ingots or gold bullion, are called *homogeneous products*, meaning that they are all exactly the same.

1.1 Variety of Goods in a Market Economy

Product differentiation is obvious from a casual examination of the wide variety of goods in a modern market economy. Table 11.1 gives an indication of this wide variety. If you like to run, you have a choice of 285 different types of running shoes. You can choose among 340 different types of cereals for breakfast and wear 70 different types of Levis' jeans.

The wide variety of products in a market economy contrasts starkly with the absence of such variety that existed in the centrally planned economies of Eastern Europe and the Soviet Union. Stores in Moscow or Warsaw typically would have only one type of each product—one type of wrench, for example—produced according to the specifications of the central planners. Even food and clothing had relatively little variety. One of the first results of market economic reform in these countries has been an increase in the variety of goods available.

Product differentiation is a major activity of both existing firms and potential firms. Business schools teach managers that product differentiation ranks with cost cutting as one of the two basic ways in which a firm can improve its performance. An entrepreneur can enter an existing industry either by finding a cheaper way to produce an existing product or by introducing a product that is differentiated from existing products in a way that will appeal to consumers.

TABLE 11.1 Variety: An Illustration of Product Differentiation

Item	Number of Different Types	Item	Number of Different Types
Automobile models	260	National soft drink brands	87
Automobile styles	1,212	Bottled water brands	50
SUV models	38	Milk types	19
SUV styles	192	Colgate toothpastes	17
Personal computer models	400	Mouthwashes	66
Movie releases	458	Dental flosses	64
Magazine titles	790	Over-the-counter pain relievers	141
New book titles	77,446	Levis' jeans styles	70
Amusement parks	1,174	Running shoe styles	285
TV screen sizes	15	Women's hosiery styles	90
Frito-Lay chip varieties	78	Contact lens types	36
Breakfast cereals	340		

Source: 1998 Annual Report, Federal Reserve Bank of Dallas.

Product differentiation usually means something less than inventing an entirely new product. Aspirin was an entirely new product when it was invented; wrapping aspirin in a special coating to make it easier to swallow is product differentiation. Coke, when it was invented in 1886, was a new product, whereas Pepsi, RC Cola, Jolt Cola, Yes Cola, and Mr. Cola, which followed over the years, are differentiated products.

Product differentiation also exists for capital goods—the machines and equipment used by firms to produce their products. The large earth moving equipment produced by Caterpillar is different from that produced by other firms, such as Komatsu of Japan. One difference is the extensive spare parts and repair service that go along with Caterpillar equipment. Bulldozers and road graders frequently break down and need quick repairs; by stationing parts distributorships and knowledgeable mechanics around the world, Caterpillar can offer quick repairs in the event of costly breakdowns. In other words, the products are differentiated on the basis of service and a worldwide network.

Product Differentiation versus Homogeneous Product. Even bottled water has become a highly differentiated product, more like breakfast cereal and soft drinks than like gold bullion, a homogeneous product that does not have product differentiation.

Source: © Shutterstock.com

1.2 Puzzles Explained by Product Differentiation

Product differentiation explains certain facts about a market economy that could be puzzling if all goods were homogeneous.

Intraindustry Trade

intraindustry trade

Trade between countries in goods from the same or similar industries.

interindustry trade

Trade between countries in goods from different industries.

Differentiated products lead to trade between countries of goods from the *same industry*, called **intraindustry trade**. Trade between countries of goods from *different industries*, called **interindustry trade**, can be explained by comparative advantage. Bananas are traded for wheat because one of these goods is grown better in warm climates and the other is grown better in cooler climates. But why should intraindustry trade take place? Why should the United States both buy beer from Canada and sell beer to Canada? Beer is produced in many different countries, but a beer company in one country will differentiate its beer from that of a beer company in another country. For people to benefit from the variety of beer, we might see beer produced in the United States (for example, Budweiser) being exported to Canada and, at the same time, see beer produced in Canada (for example, Molson) being exported to the United States. If all beer were exactly the same (a homogeneous commodity), such trade within the beer industry would make little sense, but it is easily understood when products are differentiated.

Advertising

Product differentiation also explains why firms use so much advertising—that is, the attempt by firms to tell consumers what is good about their products. If all products were homogeneous, then advertising would make little sense: A bar of gold bullion is a bar of gold bullion, no matter who sells it. But if a firm has a newly differentiated product in which it has invested millions of dollars, then it needs to advertise that product to prospective customers. You can have the greatest product in the world, but it will not sell if no one knows about it. Advertising is a way to provide information to consumers about how products differ.

Economists have debated the role of advertising in the economy for many years. Many have worried about the waste associated with advertising. For instance, the parent companies of Pepsi-Cola and Coca-Cola spend large sums of money on advertising for Aquafina and Dasani, their bottled water brands. It is hard to see how catchy phrases like "make your mouth water" and large advertising campaigns are providing useful information to consumers about a product that essentially is filtered tap water. One explanation is that the purpose of the advertising in these cases is to get people to try the product. If they like it, they will buy more; if they do not like it, they will not—but without the ad they might not ever try it. Whatever the reason, advertising will not sell an inferior product—at least, not for long. For example, despite heavy advertising, Federal Express failed miserably with Zapmail—a product that guaranteed delivery of high-quality faxes of documents around the country within hours—because of the superiority of inexpensive fax machines that even small businesses could buy. The Iridium satellite phone service was forced into bankruptcy in late 1999 because of the rapid spread of cell phone technology and networks all over the world.

Others say that advertising is wasteful partly because it is used to create a perception of product differentiation rather than genuine differences between products. For example, suppose Coke and Pepsi are homogeneous products (to some people's tastes, they are identical). Then advertising simply has the purpose of creating a perception in people's minds that the products are different. If this is the case, product differentiation may be providing a false benefit, and the advertising used to promote it is a waste of people's time and effort.

Consumer Information Services

The existence of magazines such as *Consumer Reports* is explained by product differentiation. These magazines would be of little use to consumers if all products were alike.

Such services also may help consumers sort through exaggerated claims in advertising or help them get a better perception of what the real differences between products are. It is hard to sell an expensive product that ends up last on a consumer-rating list, even with the most creative advertising.

1.3 How Are Products Differentiated?

Altering a product's *physical characteristics*—the sharpness of the knife, the calorie content of the sports drink, the mix of cotton and polyester in the shirt, and so on—is the most common method of product differentiation. JetBlue differentiated itself from other airlines by offering leather seats and satellite television on every seat on its airplanes. As the example of Caterpillar shows, products also can be differentiated on features other than the physical characteristics. Related features such as low installation costs, fast delivery, large inventory, and money-back guarantees also differentiate products.

Location is another important way in which products are differentiated. A CVS Pharmacy or a McDonald's down the block is a very different product for you from a CVS Pharmacy or a McDonald's 100 miles away. Yet only the location differentiates the product.

Time is yet another way to differentiate products. An airline service with only one daily departure from Chicago to Dallas is different from a service with 12 departures a day. Adding more flights of exactly the same type of air service is a way to differentiate the product. A 24-hour supermarket provides a different service from one that is open only during the day.

Convenience increasingly is being used by firms to differentiate products. How could peanut butter and jelly sandwiches, a standard for lunch, be more convenient? You can buy frozen peanut butter and jelly sandwiches on white bread. Prepackaged salads containing greens, dressing, and croutons; yogurt in a tube; single-serving microwaveable soup containers—these all are products that have become very popular in recent times as people's lives have become busier and more hectic. Similarly, a firm like Netflix has eliminated the need to make a trip to the video store by making it possible for consumers to get movie rentals delivered to their homes.

1.4 The Optimal Amount of Product Differentiation at a Firm

Product differentiation is costly. Developing a new variety of spot remover that will remove mustard from wool (no existing product is any good at this) would require chemical research, marketing research, and sales effort. Opening another Lenscrafters (the United States already has hundreds of stores) requires constructing a new store and equipping it with eyeglass equipment, trained personnel, and inventory.

But product differentiation can bring in additional revenue for a firm. The new spot remover will be valued by football fans who want to keep warm with woolen blankets or scarves but who also like mustard on their hot dogs. The people who live in the neighborhood where the new Lenscrafters opens will value it because they do not have to drive or walk as far.

The assumption of profit maximization implies that firms will undertake an activity if it increases profits. Thus, firms will attempt to differentiate their products if the additional revenue from product differentiation is greater than the additional costs. This is exactly the advice given to managers in business school courses. "Create the largest gap between buyer value ... and the cost of uniqueness" is the way Harvard Business School professor Michael Porter puts it in his book *Competitive Advantage*.[1] If the additional revenue is greater than the additional cost, then business firms will undertake a product-differentiation activity.

For a given firm, therefore, there is an *optimal* amount of product differentiation that balances out the additional revenue and the additional cost of the product differentiation. This is illustrated in Figure 11.2, which shows the amount of product differentiation chosen by a firm. For a company that owns and operates a haunted house, the horizontal axis is the amount of gore and scary features in the haunted house. The additional revenue from adding more gore and scary features to a haunted house is shown by the downward-sloping line. Although more gore and scary features attract additional customers, the additional revenue from increasing the amount of gore and scary features declines because only so many people would consider visiting a haunted house in a given area. It, therefore, is increasingly difficult to attract additional customers. The additional cost of adding more gore and scary features to a haunted house is shown by the upward sloping line. This additional cost increases because the cheapest effects that could be included for differentiation would be added first. The optimal amount of gore and scary features for a haunted-house operator is the point at which the additional revenue from more gore and scary features is just equal to the additional cost. Beyond that point, more gore and scary features would reduce profits, because the additional cost would exceed the additional revenue.

FIGURE 11.2 A Firm's Decision about Product Differentiation

A Firm's Decision about Product Differentiation. Determining how much product differentiation a firm should undertake is a matter of equating the additional revenue from and additional cost of another differentiated product. (Note that these "additional cost" and "additional revenue" curves are analogous to marginal cost and marginal revenue curves except that they depend on the amount of product differentiation rather than the quantity of a particular product.)

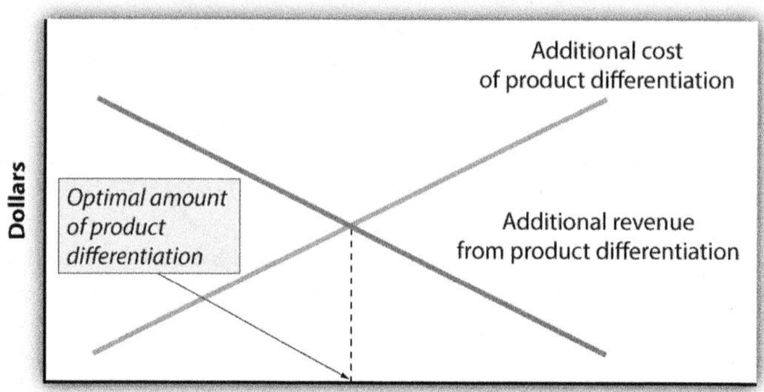

This analysis for haunted-house owners is far from trivial. Theme parks increasingly are interested in attracting Halloween traffic, and more gore and scary features attract more customers. In some theme parks, Halloween is the largest event all year.

Using this analysis in practice is difficult because the revenue gains from product differentiation depend on what other firms do. The amount of additional revenue generated by additional gore and scary features in a haunted house depends on how much gore and how many scary features are included in other nearby haunted houses. In the next section, we will look at more formal models of industries with differentiated products.

REVIEW

- Product differentiation is evident in the variety of products we see every day, in the absence of such variety in centrally planned economies, and in the proliferation of such variety after market reforms.
- Intraindustry trade, advertising, and consumer information are some of the facts that can be better explained by product differentiation.
- Products can be differentiated by physical characteristics, location, time, and convenience, among other features.
- Profit-maximizing firms will fashion a differentiated product if the additional revenue from doing so is greater than the additional cost.

2. MONOPOLISTIC COMPETITION

The model of monopolistic competition, first developed by Edward Chamberlin of Harvard University in the 1930s, is designed to describe the behavior of firms operating in differentiated product markets. Monopolistic competition gets its name from the fact that it is a hybrid of monopoly and competition. Recall that monopoly has one seller facing a downward-sloping market demand curve with barriers to the entry of other firms.

Competition has many sellers, each facing a horizontal demand curve with no barriers to entry and exit. Monopolistic competition, like competition, has many firms with free entry and exit, but, as in monopoly, each firm faces a downward-sloping demand curve for its product.

The monopolistically competitive firm's demand curve slopes downward because of product differentiation. When a monopolistically competitive firm raises its price, the quantity demanded of its product goes down but does not plummet to zero, as in the case of a competitive firm. For example, if Nike raises the price of its running shoes, it will lose some sales to Reebok, but it will still sell a considerable number of running shoes because some people prefer Nike shoes to other brands. Nike running shoes and Reebok running shoes are differentiated products to many consumers. On the other hand, a competitive firm selling a product like wheat, which is a much more homogeneous product, can expect to lose virtually all its customers to another firm if it raises its price above the market price.

As we will see, free entry and exit is an important property of monopolistic competition. Because of it, firms can come into the market if they can make a profit or leave the market if they are running losses.

2.1 A Typical Monopolistic Competitor

Figure 11.3 illustrates the key features of the model of monopolistic competition. Each graph in Figure 11.3 shows a typical monopolistically competitive firm. At first glance, the graphs look exactly like the graph for a monopoly, introduced in Chapter 10. They should, because both monopolistic and monopolistically competitive firms face downward-sloping demand curves. The demand curve facing a monopolistically competitive firm, however, has a different interpretation because other firms are in the industry. The demand curve is not the market demand curve; rather, it is the demand curve that is *specific* to a particular firm. When new firms enter the industry—for example, when Converse enters with Nike and Reebok—the demand curves specific to both Nike and Reebok shift to the left. When firms leave, the demand curves of the remaining firms shift to the right. The reason is that new firms take some of the quantity demanded away from existing firms, and when some firms exit, a greater quantity is demanded for the remaining firms.

FIGURE 11.3 Monopolistic Competition

Each graph shows a typical firm in a monopolistically competitive industry. Firms enter the industry if they can earn profits, as in graph (a). This will shift the demand and marginal revenue curves to the left for the typical firm because some buyers will switch to the new firms. Firms leave if they face losses, as in graph (b). This will shift the demand and marginal revenue curves to the right because the firms that stay in the industry get more buyers. In the long run, profits are driven to zero, as in graph (c).

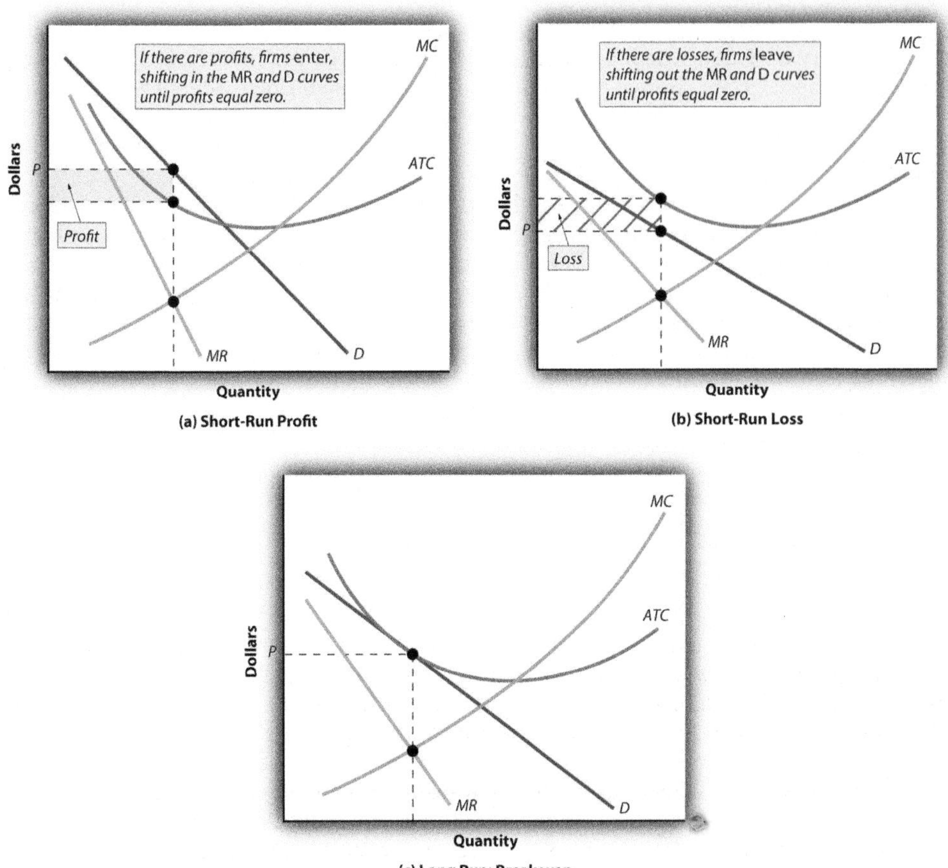

The difference between the graphs for a monopolist and a monopolistic competitor shows up when we move from the short run to the long run, that is, when firms enter and exit. This example is illustrated in Figure 11.3. Note that the three graphs in the figure have exactly the same average total cost curve. The graphs differ from one another in that the location of the demand and marginal revenue curves relative to the average total cost curve is different in each. Graphs (a) and (b) represent the short run. Graph (c) represents the long run, after the entry and exit of firms in the industry.

Observe that the demand curve in graph (c) is drawn so that it just touches the average total cost curve. At this point, the profit-maximizing price equals average total cost. Thus, total revenue is equal to total costs, and profits are zero. On the other hand, in graphs (a) and (b), the demand curve is drawn to show either a positive profit or a negative profit (loss) because price is either greater than or less than average total cost.

The Short Run: Just Like a Monopoly

Consider the short-run situation, before firms either enter or exit the industry. The monopolistic competitor's profit maximization decision is like that of the monopoly. To maximize profits, it sets its quantity to the point at which marginal revenue equals marginal cost. Because the monopolistically competitive firm faces a downward-sloping demand curve, its profit-maximizing price and quantity balance the increased revenue from a higher price with the lost customers brought on by the higher price. The marginal-revenue-equals-marginal-cost condition achieves this balance. The profit-maximizing quantity of production is shown by the dashed vertical lines in graphs (a) and (b) of Figure 11.3.

For example, For Eyes, Lenscrafters, and Pearle Vision are monopolistic competitors in many shopping areas in the United States. Each local eyeglass store has an optometrist, but each offers slightly different services. At a shopping area with several of these eyeglass stores, if one of them raises prices slightly, then fewer people will purchase glasses from that store. Some people will walk all the way to the other end of the mall to the store with the lower-priced glasses. Others, however, will be happy to stay with the store that raised its prices because they like the service and the location. These outlets are not monopolists, but the downward slope of their demand curves makes their pricing decision much like that of monopolists. The slope of the demand curve for a monopolistic competitor may be different from that for a monopolist, but the qualitative relationship between demand, revenue, and costs—and the firm's decisions in setting quantity and price—is the same.

Entry and Exit: Just Like Competition

Now consider entry and exit, which can take place over time. In the model of long-run competitive equilibrium in Chapter 9, we showed that if economic profits could be made, new firms would enter the industry. If firms were running losses, then firms would exit the industry. Only when economic profits were zero would the industry be in long-run equilibrium, with no tendency for firms either to enter or to exit.

In monopolistic competition, the entry and exit decisions are driven by the same considerations. If profits are positive, as in graph (a) of Figure 11.3, firms have an incentive to enter the industry. Consider the market for skin care products. Beginning in the 1980s, liquid soap products, especially soaps scented with natural oils, were introduced by a few manufacturers and quickly caught on with consumers. Soon, virtually every manufacturer of soap and shampoo products began to offer liquid soap products fortified with vitamins and flavored by aromatics. In contrast, if profits are negative, as shown in graph (b) of Figure 11.3, firms have an incentive to exit the industry. During the dotcom boom of the late 1990s, several companies entered the business of home delivery of groceries. Perhaps the best known of these firms, Webvan, tried to differentiate its product by offering to deliver groceries within a 30-minute delivery window requested by the consumer. Despite a promising start, most of these new entrants were unable to make profits and left the industry. Webvan, for example, foundered after the costs of building its own warehousing and distribution network turned out to be far greater than the revenue it could earn from grocery sales.

As we move from the short run to the long run, the entry and exit of competing firms will tend to shift the demand curve for each of the firms remaining in the industry to the point at which the demand curve and the average total cost curve are tangent—that is, the point at which the two curves just touch and have the same slope. Entry into the industry will shift the demand curve of each existing firm to the left because the existing firms will be sharing their sales with the new firms. If Suave sells a new brand of shampoo similar to Pantene shampoo, then some consumers who had been buying Pantene will instead buy Suave's similar new shampoo. The demand for Pantene and other shampoos therefore will decline because of the availability of Suave's new product. Thus, the existing firms will see their demand curves shift to the left—each one will find that it sells less at each price. The differences in the positions of the demand (and marginal revenue) curves in the short run and the long run illustrate this shift. The shift in the demand curve causes each firm's profits to decline, and profits eventually decline to zero. (Recall that these are economic profits, not accounting profits, and therefore are a good measure of the incentive for firms to enter the industry.)

The case of negative profits and exit is similar. If demand is such that firms are running a loss, then some firms will exit the industry, leaving their share of sales to the surviving firms. This action causes the demand curve facing the remaining firms to shift to the right until the losses (negative economic profits) are driven to zero. When Caribou Coffee closed in Ann Arbor, University of Michigan students bought coffee at other nearby coffee shops instead, increasing the demand for coffee at these nearby shops. This is illustrated by comparing graph (b) of Figure 11.3, which shows losses in the short run, with graph (c), which shows zero profits.

2.2 The Long-Run Monopolistically Competitive Equilibrium

Two differences are notable between monopolistically competitive firms and competitive firms in the long run. To see these differences, consider Figure 11.4, which replicates graph (c) of Figure 11.3, showing the position of the typical monopolistic competitor in long-run equilibrium, after entry and exit have taken place.

First, observe that the price is greater than marginal cost for a monopolistically competitive firm. This was also true for the monopoly; it means that the market is not as efficient as a competitive market. Production is too low because the marginal benefit of additional production is greater than the marginal cost. Because each firm has some market power, it restricts output slightly and gets a higher price. The sum of producer plus consumer surplus is reduced relative to that in a competitive market. In other words, the result is a loss of efficiency—a deadweight loss.

Second, as shown in Figure 11.4, the quantity produced is not at the minimum point on the average total cost curve, as it was for the competitive industry. That is, the quantity that the monopolistic competitor produces is at a higher-cost point than the quantity that the perfectly competitive firm would produce. Thus, monopolistically competitive firms operate in a situation of **excess costs**. If each firm expanded production and lowered its price, average total cost would decline. Each firm operates with some **excess capacity** in the sense that it could increase output and reduce average total cost. The firms choose not to do so because they have some market power to keep their prices a little higher and their output a little lower than that. Their market power comes from the downward-sloping demand curve that they face. For example, each coffee shop charges a little more and sells slightly fewer cups of coffee than it would in a perfectly competitive market.

excess costs

Costs of production that are higher than the minimum average total cost.

excess capacity

A situation in which a firm produces below the level that gives the minimum average total cost.

FIGURE 11.4 Excess Costs per Unit and Excess Capacity with Monopolistic Competition

In the long run, profits are zero for a monopolistically competitive firm, but the firm does not produce the quantity that minimizes average total cost. If the firm increases production, costs per unit will decline. In this sense, the firm operates at less than full capacity; it has excess capacity.

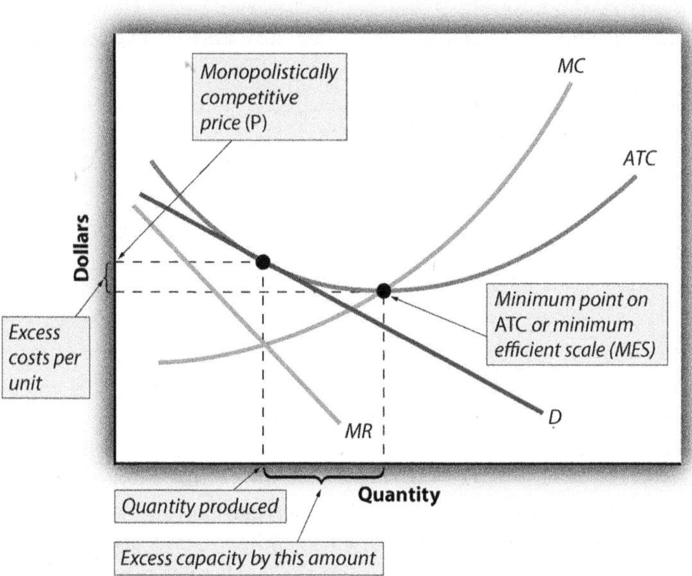

Comparing Monopoly, Competition, and Monopolistic Competition

Table 11.2 compares the different effects of competition, monopoly, and monopolistic competition.

A competitive firm will produce the quantity that equates price and marginal cost. A competitive market is efficient in that consumer surplus plus producer surplus is maximized and no deadweight loss results. Average total cost is minimized.

In a monopoly, price is greater than marginal cost. A monopoly is inefficient because consumer surplus plus producer surplus is not maximized, so a deadweight loss results. Moreover, average total cost is not minimized. Economic profits remain positive because firms cannot enter the market.

In monopolistic competition, price is also greater than marginal cost. Thus, consumer surplus plus producer surplus is not maximized, and deadweight loss results; average total cost is not minimized. Profits are zero in the long-run equilibrium, however, because of entry and exit. Monopolistic competition does not result in as efficient an outcome as competition. Monopolistic competition, as well as monopoly, is inefficient.

Product Variety versus Deadweight Loss

When comparing monopolistic competition with competition, we must recognize—as with the comparison of monopoly and competition in the last chapter—that replacing monopolistic competition with competition may be an impossibility or require a loss to society. Remember that product differentiation is the key reason for monopolistic competition. We showed in the previous section that consumers usually value the variety of products that comes from product differentiation. Some people like having both Pepsi and Coke. Roads and airports are better because of the different capabilities of earth moving equipment sold by Caterpillar and Komatsu. Thus, eliminating monopolistic competition by having a single competitive product, whether Coksi or Catematsu, even if it were possible, probably would reduce consumer surplus by more than the gain that would come from competition over monopolistic competition.

TABLE 11.2 A Comparison of Monopolistic Competition with Monopoly and Competition

Type of Model	Price	Deadweight Loss?	Average Total Cost Minimized?	Profit in Long Run?
Competition	$P = MC$	No	Yes	No
Monopolistic competition	$P > MC$	Yes	No	No
Monopoly	$P > MC$	Yes	No	Yes

More generally, product differentiation may be of sufficient value to consumers that it makes sense to have monopolistically competitive firms despite the deadweight loss. Or, to state it somewhat differently, the deadweight loss from monopolistic competition is part of the price consumers pay for the variety or the diversity of products.

REVIEW

- The model of monopolistic competition is a hybrid of competition and monopoly. Entry and exit are possible, as in competition, but firms see a downward-sloping demand curve, as in monopoly, although the market has many firms.
- The analysis of monopolistic competition in the short run is much like that of monopoly, but entry and exit lead to zero economic profits in the long run.
- Monopolistic competitors produce less than competitive firms and charge prices higher than marginal costs. Thus, a deadweight loss results from monopolistic competition. In the long run, monopolistic competition produces less than the quantity that would minimize average total cost.
- The deadweight loss and excess costs can be viewed as the price of product variety.

3. OLIGOPOLY

Thus far, we have seen two situations in which firms have market power: monopoly and monopolistic competition. But those are not the only two. When an industry has *very few* producers—a situation termed *oligopoly*—each firm can have an influence on the market price even if the goods are homogeneous. For example, if Saudi Arabia—one of the major producers of crude oil in the world and a member of the Organization of Petroleum Exporting Countries (OPEC)—decides to cut its production of crude oil, a relatively homogeneous commodity, it can have a significant effect on the world price of oil.The effect on the price, however, will depend on what other producers do. If the other producing countries—Iran, Kuwait, and so on—increase their production to offset the Saudi cuts, then the price will not change by much. Thus, Saudi Arabia, either through formal discussion with other oil-producing countries in OPEC or by guessing, must take account of what the other producers will do.

Such situations are not unusual. The managers of a firm in an industry with only a few other firms know that their firm has market power. But they also know that the other firms in the industry have market power too. If the managers of a firm make the right assessment about how other firms will react to any course of action they take, then their firm will profit. This awareness and consideration of the market power and the reactions of other firms in the industry is called **strategic behavior**. Strategic behavior also may exist when product differentiation exists, as in monopolistically competitive industries, but to study and explain strategic behavior, it is simpler to focus on oligopolies producing homogeneous products.

strategic behavior

Firm behavior that takes into account the market power and reactions of other firms in the industry.

A common approach to the study of strategic behavior of firms is the use of **game theory**, an area of applied mathematics that studies games of strategy like poker or chess. Game theory has many applications in economics and the other behavioral sciences. Because oligopoly behavior has many of the features of games of strategy, game theory provides a precise framework to better understand oligopolies.

game theory

A branch of applied mathematics with many uses in economics, including the analysis of the interaction of firms that take each other's actions into account.

3.1 An Overview of Game Theory

Game theory, like the basic economic theory of the firm and consumer (described in Chapter 5 and Chapter 6 of this book), makes the assumption that people make purposeful choices with limited resources. More precisely, game theory assumes that the players in a game try to maximize their payoffs—the amount they win or lose in the game. Depending on the application, a payoff might be measured by utility, if the player is a person, or by profits, if the player is a firm.

Game theory endeavors to go beyond basic economic theory in that each player takes explicit account of the actions of each and every other player. It asks questions like: "In a poker game, what should Mary do if Deborah sees her bet and raises her by $10?" The aims of game theory are to analyze the choices facing each player and to design utility-maximizing actions, or strategies, that respond to every action of the other players.

An important example in game theory is the game called the **prisoner's dilemma**, illustrated in Figure 11.5. The game is between Bonnie and Clyde, two prisoners who have been arrested for a crime that they committed. The **payoff matrix** shown in Figure 11.5 has two rows and two columns. The two columns for Bonnie show her options, which are labeled at the top "confess" and "remain silent." The two rows for Clyde show his options; these also are labeled "confess" and "remain silent." Inside the boxes, we see what happens to Bonnie and Clyde for each option, confess or remain silent. The top right of each box shows what happens to Bonnie. The bottom left of each box shows what happens to Clyde. Each year of prison sentence is considered to have a payoff equal to negative one. Both Bonnie and Clyde would like to maximize their payoff, which means they would prefer a shorter sentence of one year (with a payoff equal to negative one) to longer sentences of five years (with a payoff equal to negative five) or seven years (with a payoff equal to negative seven).

prisoner's dilemma

A game in which individual incentives lead to a nonoptimal (noncooperative) outcome. If the players credibly commit to cooperate, then they achieve the best (cooperative) outcome.

payoff matrix

A table containing strategies and payoffs for two players in a game.

The police already have enough information to get a conviction for a lesser crime, for which Bonnie and Clyde would each get a three-year jail sentence. Thus, if both Bonnie and Clyde remain silent, they are sent to jail for three years each, as shown in the lower right-hand corner of the table.

FIGURE 11.5 Two Prisoners Facing a Prisoner's Dilemma

Clyde and Bonnie are in separate jail cells, held for a crime they did commit. The payoff for each—with each year of prison having a payoff of -1—is given in the appropriate box and depends on whether they both confess or they both remain silent or one confesses while the other remains silent. The top right of each box shows Bonnie's payoff; the bottom left of each box shows Clyde's payoff.

Clyde \ Bonnie	Confess	Remain Silent
Confess	–5 (bottom left), –5 (top right)	–1 (bottom left), –7 (top right)
Remain Silent	–7 (bottom left), –1 (top right)	–3 (bottom left), –3 (top right)

But Bonnie and Clyde each have the option of confessing to the more serious crime that they committed. If Bonnie confesses and Clyde does not, she gets a reward. If Clyde confesses and Bonnie does not, he gets a reward. The reward is a reduced penalty: The jail sentence is only one year—not as severe as the three years it would be if the prosecutor had no confession. The penalty for being convicted of the more serious crime in the absence of a confession is seven years. Thus, if Bonnie confesses and Clyde does not, he gets a seven-year sentence. If both confess, they each get a five-year sentence.

What should Clyde and Bonnie do? The answer depends on their judgment about what the other person will do. And this is the point of the example. Bonnie can either confess or remain silent. The consequences of her action depend on what Clyde does. If Bonnie confesses and Clyde confesses, she gets five years. If Bonnie confesses and Clyde remains silent, Bonnie gets one year. If Bonnie remains silent and Clyde remains silent, she gets three years. Finally, if Bonnie remains silent and Clyde confesses, she gets seven years. Clyde is in the same situation as Bonnie.

Think about a strategy for Bonnie. Bonnie is better off confessing, regardless of what Clyde does. If Clyde confesses, then by confessing herself, Bonnie gets five years rather than the seven years she would get by remaining silent. If, on the other hand, Clyde remains silent, then Bonnie is still better off by confessing because she gets only one year rather than the three years she would get by remaining silent. Hence, Bonnie has a great incentive to confess because she gets a reduced sentence in either case.

Clyde is in the same situation. He can compare what his sentence would be whether Bonnie confesses or remains silent. In this case, Clyde also is better off confessing regardless of whether Bonnie confesses or remains silent.

What this reasoning suggests is that both Bonnie and Clyde will confess. If they both had remained silent, they would have gone to jail for only three years, but the apparently sensible strategy is to confess and go to jail for five years. This is the prisoner's dilemma. The case where both remain silent is called the **cooperative outcome** of the game because to achieve this, they would somehow have to agree in advance not to confess and then keep their word. The case in which both confess is called the **noncooperative outcome** of the game because Clyde and Bonnie follow an "everyone for himself or herself" strategy. Note that the cooperative outcome is preferred to the noncooperative outcome by both Clyde and Bonnie, yet both choose the option that results in the noncooperative outcome.

cooperative outcome

An equilibrium in a game in which the players agree to cooperate.

noncooperative outcome

An equilibrium in a game in which the players cannot agree to cooperate and instead follow their individual incentives.

The mathematician and Nobel laureate in economics John Nash defined the noncooperative equilibrium—which economists call a **Nash equilibrium**—as a set of strategies from which no player would like to deviate unilaterally—that is, no player would see an increase in his or her payoff by changing his or her strategy while the other players keep their strategies constant.

Nash equilibrium

A set of strategies from which no player would like to deviate unilaterally.

3.2 Applying Game Theory to Oligopolies

How do we apply game theory to determine the strategy of firms in an oligopoly? The easiest case is in an industry with only two firms. This is a particular type of oligopoly called *duopoly*. A prominent example of an industry characterized by a duopoly is the large commercial airplane manufacturing industry, where Boeing and Airbus have to plan their strategy taking the other's strategy into account. The competition between FedEx and UPS in the overnight package delivery business is another example. In a duopoly, market supply is determined by the output of the two firms, so in deciding how much more to produce of a good, the firm has to consider its own additional costs of production, the change in the market price when it increases production, and how the other firm's subsequent response in terms of increasing or decreasing its production will affect the market price. Economics and game theory predict that the outcome of the duopoly will be the Nash equilibrium of the game—that is, the quantity levels at which neither firm has an incentive to deviate.

Competition in Quantities versus Competition in Prices

The model of oligopoly in which firms compete by choosing what quantities to produce, given the other firm's production decision, is called *Cournot competition* in honor of the French economist Augustin Cournot, who created the original version of this model in 1838 (Cournot did not use game theory and the concept of Nash equilibrium, which was not invented until 1950). Instead of competing in quantities, oligopolists can also compete in prices; this is called *Bertrand competition* for the French mathematician who reworked Cournot's model in terms of prices in 1883. We do not analyze the Bertrand model in this book, but it predicts that with a homogeneous good, oligopolists will charge the same price and sell the same number of units as competitive firms would.

Comparison with Monopoly and Perfect Competition

How does the outcome for a duopoly compare with the outcomes for a perfectly competitive market and a monopoly? Suppose the market demand for giant pumpkins is Price = \$241 − \$2 × Quantity, where the quantity is the sum of what Jack and Jill independently and simultaneously bring to the market, and with a cost of \$1 for harvesting and transporting each pumpkin to market.

In a competitive market, price equals marginal cost. Since marginal cost equals a dollar, that means $P = \$1$ and we can solve for Quantity = 120. Profits will be zero.

Now suppose that Jack and Jill get together and behave like a monopolist. Further suppose that marginal revenue in this example can be found by the relationship Marginal revenue = \$241 – \$4 × Quantity. Setting marginal revenue equal to marginal cost (which is \$1) gives us a total quantity of 60 pumpkins. So if Jack and Jill between them bring sixty pumpkins to market, the price will be \$241 – 2 × (60) = \$121. Monopoly profits would equal \$121 × 60 – \$1 × 60 = \$7,200.

Now consider the duopoly case. To simplify our analysis, let's assume that Jack's and Jill's strategies are limited to three actions: They can bring either 30, 40, or 60 pumpkins to the market. The payoff matrix for Jack and Jill is shown in Figure 11.6. This is a three-by-three matrix with a total of nine blank boxes, one for each combination of Jack's and Jill's actions; the boxes are numbered for easy reference. Each of these boxes lists the profits that Jack and Jill obtain given their actions. For example, in box 1, both Jack and Jill choose to harvest and transport only 30 pumpkins to the market. In this case, Jack's payoff is \$3,600, which we write on the bottom left corner of the first box. The payoff for Jill is also \$3,600 (top right corner of the first box). The rest of the payoff matrix in Figure 11.6 can be interpreted in a similar way.

Jack and Jill are aware of the nine possible outcomes, and the question is how each of them is going to choose a quantity to deliver to the farmer's market. How many pumpkins each of them should harvest and bring to the market depends on how many the other person chooses to bring. So Jack and Jill engage in a mental exercise, each trying to figure out what the other will do.

Put yourself in Jill's shoes. She can easily see that her maximum payoff of \$4,000 happens when she sends 40 pumpkins to the market while Jack sends only 30. If Jill sells 40 pumpkins, however, then Jack can increase his payoff from \$3,000 to \$3,200 by selling 40 instead of 30 pumpkins. So box 2 cannot be a solution to Jill's and Jack's problem. Similarly, Jack's maximum payoff of \$4,000 happens when he sends 40 pumpkins to the market while Jill sends only 30. But were he to do so, then Jill would be able to increase her payoff by selling 40 pumpkins instead of 30. So box 4 cannot be a solution.

At this point you can guess that we are looking for a combination of strategies from which neither player would like to deviate unilaterally—that is, a Nash equilibrium. By carefully exploring all the boxes and checking to see whether either player has an incentive to deviate from that particular combination, we find that the only Nash equilibrium in this example is in box 5, where Jack and Jill sell 40 pumpkins each, for a payoff of \$3,200 each. At that level, neither Jack nor Jill wants to produce more or less pumpkins, given the production of their competitor. The duopoly solution will have a total of 80 pumpkins supplied to the market (40 by Jack and 40 by Jill). The market price will be \$241 – \$2 * 80 = \$81 and profits for each producer will be \$3,200.

Figure 11.7 shows the demand and marginal cost curves for pumpkins in the case study involving the pumpkin duopoly. The intersection of demand and marginal cost represents the competitive equilibrium, in which case Jack and Jill each supply sixty pumpkins at a price of \$1 and obtain zero profits. The maximum combined payoff is the monopoly solution, which occurs when each farmer sells thirty pumpkins at a price of \$121 per pumpkin. The duopoly solution lies between the monopoly and competitive equilibria in terms of price, quantity, and profit.

FIGURE 11.6 Payoff Matrix for Jack and Jill

The payoff matrix contains the profits for Jack and Jill for every possible combination of their actions. For example, in box 6, Jack sends 40 pumpkins to the market, while Jill delivers 60; Jack's payoff is $1,600. Jill has a payoff of $2,400.

		Jill		
		30 pumpkins	40 pumpkins	60 pumpkins
Jack	30 pumpkins	1 $3,600 $3,600	2 $4,000 $3,000	3 $3,600 $1,800
	40 pumpkins	4 $3,000 $4,000	5 $3,200 $3,200	6 $2,400 $1,600
	60 pumpkins	7 $1,800 $3,600	8 $1,600 $2,400	9 $0 $0

FIGURE 11.7 Comparison of Monopoly, Duopoly, and Competitive Equilibria

Prices and quantities for a Cournot duopoly lie between the equilibria for a monopoly and a competitive market.

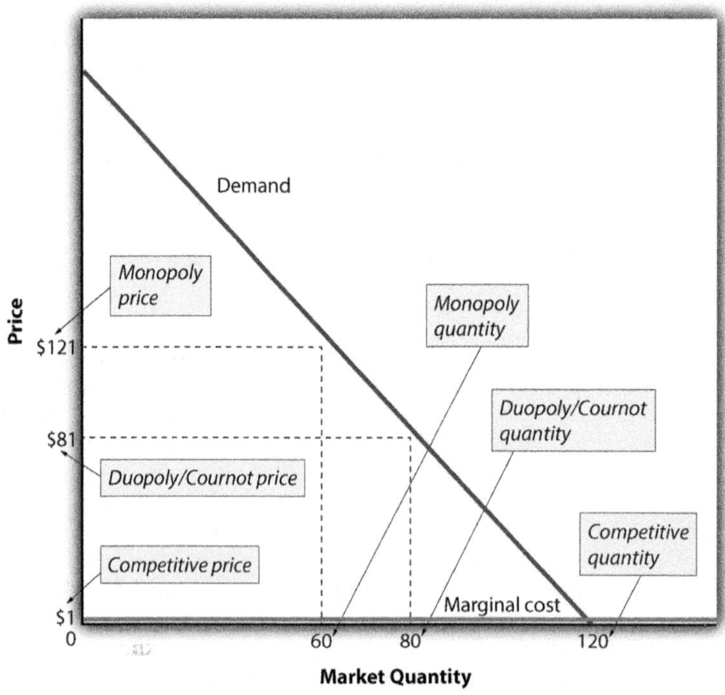

Collusion

Firms in an oligopoly know that their combined profits can be maximized if they act together as a monopolist. Firms might act together in three ways. The first is by **explicit collusion**, in which the managers communicate with each other and agree to fix prices or cut back on production. Although explicit collusion is illegal, it still happens. In the 1980s and 1990s, several firms in Florida and Texas were found guilty of agreeing to fix prices for milk sold to schools. In 1990, the Justice Department charged that several Ivy League universities colluded to offer similar financial aid packages to admitted students, thus depriving these students of the more generous aid packages that would have resulted from the schools competing with one another for the best students. The governments of many countries that produce oil routinely collude to cut back production and raise prices. A group of producers that coordinates its pricing and production decisions is called a **cartel**.

Second, in **tacit collusion** no explicit communication occurs between firms, but firms keep prices high by regularly following the behavior of one firm in the industry. The dominant firm is sometimes called a **price leader**. Third, the firms could merge and form a single entity.

explicit collusion

Open cooperation by firms to make mutually beneficial pricing or production decisions.

cartel

A group of producers in the same industry who coordinate pricing and production decisions.

tacit collusion

Implicit or unstated cooperation of firms to make mutually beneficial pricing or production decisions.

price leader

The price-setting firm in a collusive industry in which other firms follow the leader.

Incentives to Defect

In oligopoly, game theory predicts that unless there is a way to bind each firm to cooperation, there is a tendency to defect. Because the defection results in a lower than monopoly price, consumers gain from the defection, and deadweight loss is reduced.

3.3 Incentives to Cooperate: Repeated Games

Although the prisoner's dilemma and the Cournot duopoly suggest a tendency toward the noncooperative outcome, a difference exists between the situation of the prisoners Bonnie and Clyde and the farmers Jack and Jill: Pumpkinville's farmer's market probably will be open for many years, allowing Jack and Jill to interact with each other in the future. Firms that interact with each other repeatedly may behave quite differently from firms that interact only once. If the same game is to be played year after year—a repeated game—then the firms might be able to build up a reputation for not defecting.

Experimental economists have conducted experiments in which two people play the same prisoner's dilemma game over and over again. (The people in the experiments are given small monetary rewards rather than jail penalties.) These experiments indicate that people frequently end up using strategies that lead to a cooperative outcome. A typical strategy that people use is called "tit-for-tat." Using a tit-for-tat strategy, one player regularly matches, *in the next game*, the actions of the other player *in the current game*. For example, Clyde's tit-for-tat strategy would be to confess the next time the game is played if Bonnie confesses in the current game, and not to confess the next time the game is played if Bonnie does not confess in the current game. A tit-for-tat strategy gives the other player an incentive to follow the cooperative action—not confess—and thereby leads to a cooperative outcome. Players can use several other strategies to support a specific outcome in a repeated game.

Secret Defections

Even though reputational consequences may help firms better sustain a cooperative outcome, firms still have incentives to defect. The incentives for a firm to defect from an agreement will be greater if it is difficult for other firms to detect the defection. In the pumpkin example, it is impossible for Jack to increase his production without Jill's knowing it. This makes defection less likely. If one firm can secretly increase production or cut prices, enforcing the agreement will be more difficult. But it may be possible for a member of OPEC to sell oil to China under a secret agreement, or for a member of the world coffee cartel to ship coffee without being detected, at least for a while. The impact of such secret defections is much like the situation in boxes 2 and 4 in Figure 11.6. Profits to the defector increase, and profits to the other producers decrease. Consumers are better off because the quantity supplied to the market increases, helping to lower the price.

For a long time, Japanese construction firms operated a now well-known collusion scheme called *dango*. Firms took turns offering a slightly lower bid, while all the other firms submitted high-priced bids to the government. This collusion ensured that each construction firm would get periodic contracts that were lucrative, without worrying about being undercut by its competitors. Ironically, and unfortunately for consumers, making the bids public made it harder for any firm to defect because firms in the agreement would know at once which firm had lowered its prices.

REVIEW

- Game theory provides a framework to study strategic behavior in an oligopoly. A game theory setting typically describes how the outcomes that a player can achieve by pursuing a particular strategy vary depending on the strategies pursued by the other players.
- A game theory setting can have a cooperative outcome, in which the players agree to cooperate, or a noncooperative outcome, which results when players follow their individual incentives.
- The concept of a Nash equilibrium—a set of strategies from which no player wishes to unilaterally deviate—is used to identify the noncooperative solution.
- The prisoner's dilemma is a widely known example in which the two parties will not be able to achieve the superior cooperative equilibrium. Instead, they have to settle for the inferior noncooperative equilibrium.
- Firms can compete with one another on the basis of quantity (Cournot) or price (Bertrand). The examples we look at in this chapter are for Cournot competition.
- Game theoretic concepts can illustrate why firms in an oligopoly will be tempted to defect from any agreement and not act like a monopolist. Because a market has only a few producers, however, the outcome will not be the same as in the case of perfect competition. Prices and quantities for an oligopoly lie in between the solutions for a monopolist and for a competitive market.
- To the extent that a firm colludes, either explicitly or tacitly, it acts more like a monopolist and reduces economic efficiency by raising price above marginal cost.
- Repeated interactions among firms and the inability to defect secretly from an agreement make it more likely that collusive behavior among a group of firms is sustainable.

4. END-OF-CHAPTER MATERIALS

4.1 Conclusion

In this chapter, we have explored two different types of models—monopolistic competition and oligopoly—that lie in the complex terrain between competition and monopoly. The models were motivated by the need to explain how real-world firms—Johnson Publications, Liz Claiborne, Nike, and PepsiCo—and the members of OPEC operate in markets with differentiated products or with a small number of other firms or countries.

In the models introduced in this chapter, firms have market power in that they can affect the price of the good in their market. Market power enables a firm to charge a price higher than marginal cost. It is a source of deadweight loss. Observations of the behavior of actual firms show a wide variation in market power among firms.

Economists in government and businesses use the ideas about monopolistic competition and oligopoly discussed in this chapter. Economists working in the U.S. Department of Justice use them to determine whether the government should intervene in certain industries, as we will explore in Chapter 12. Consultants to business use them to help firms decide how to differentiate their products from those of other firms.

Having concluded our discussion of the four basic types of models of markets in this chapter, it is useful to remember the important distinction between models and the facts that the models endeavor to explain or predict. None of the assumptions of these models—such as homogeneous products or free entry—hold exactly in reality. For example, when contrasted with the monopolistic competition model of this chapter, the model of competition (with its assumption of homogeneous goods) might seem not to apply to many markets. Few goods are exactly homogeneous. But when economists apply their models, they realize that these models are approximations of reality. How close an approximation comes to reality heavily depends on the application. The model of competition can be helpful in explaining the behavior of firms in industries that are approximately competitive, just as the model of monopoly can be helpful in explaining the behavior of firms in industries that are approximately monopolistic. We now have a richer set of models that apply to situations far removed from competition or monopoly.

Key Points

1. Firms that can differentiate their product and act strategically are in industries that fall between competition and monopoly.
2. Product differentiation—the effort by firms to create different products of value to consumers—is pervasive in a modern market economy. It helps explain intraindustry trade, advertising, and information services.
3. Monopolistic competition arises because of product differentiation. With monopolistic competition, firms have market power, but exit from and entry into the industry lead to a situation of zero profits in the long run.
4. With monopolistic competition, the firm sets the quantity produced so that price exceeds marginal cost. A deadweight loss results, and average total cost is not minimized.
5. The deadweight loss and excess costs of monopolistic competition are part of the price paid for product variety.
6. Strategic behavior occurs in industries with a small number of firms because each firm has market power to affect the price, and each firm cannot ignore the response of other firms to its own actions.
7. The tools of game theory, such as the Nash equilibrium, help us identify the cooperative and noncooperative outcomes of strategic interaction by firms competing on the basis of quantity or price.
8. The price, quantity, and deadweight loss outcomes from an oligopoly fall in between the outcomes from a monopoly and a competitive market.
9. Game theory suggests that collusive behavior frequently will break down, making noncooperative outcomes more likely.
10. Collusion is more likely when firms interact repeatedly in a market and secret defections can be prevented.

QUESTIONS FOR REVIEW

1. What is product differentiation?
2. What factors are relevant to the determination of optimal product differentiation?
3. Why is product differentiation an important reason for monopolistic competition?
4. What are two key differences between monopolistic competition and monopoly?
5. Why don't monopolistic competitors keep their average total cost at a minimum?
6. Why is the noncooperative outcome of a prisoner's dilemma game likely?
7. Why is duopoly like a prisoner's dilemma?
8. How does the market outcome for an oligopoly compare with the outcome for a monopoly? To the outcome for a competitive market?
9. What is the difference between explicit and tacit collusion?
10. Why are secret defections a problem for cartels?

PROBLEMS

1. Match the following characteristics with the appropriate models of firm behavior and explain the long-run efficiency (or inefficiency) of each.
   a. Many firms, differentiated product, free entry
   b. One firm, patents, licenses, or barriers to entry
   c. Many firms, homogeneous product, free entry
   d. Few firms, strategic behavior
2. You are traveling by taxi in a South American city. When the taxi stops at a stoplight, you observe several people walking among the stopped cars offering apples for sale. Your taxi driver rolls down the window and purchases an apple from one of the vendors. You ask the taxi driver, "Why did you buy the apple from that vendor?" The driver replies, "I often buy from that vendor because the apple is always of excellent quality." In what market structure are the vendors operating at that site? Why?
3. Consider Al's gasoline station, which sells Texaco at a busy intersection along with three other stations selling Shell, Conoco, and Chevron.
   a. Draw the marginal cost, average total cost, demand, and marginal revenue curves for Al's station, assuming that the profit-maximizing price is greater than average total cost.
   b. Show Al's profits on the diagram.
   c. Explain what would happen in this situation to bring about a long-run equilibrium. Would more stations open, or would some leave?
4. Compare the long-run equilibrium of a competitive firm with that of a monopolistically competitive firm with the same cost structure. Why is the long-run price different in these two models? Which type of firm operates at a minimum cost? Draw a diagram and explain.
5. Suppose 10 monopolistically competitive restaurants operate in your town with identical costs. Given the following information, calculate the short-run price and quantity produced by each of the firms.

Each Firm's Demand		Each Firm's Costs	
Quantity	Price	Average Total Cost	Marginal Cost
1	$10	12	—
2	$ 8	9	6
3	$ 6	8	6
4	$ 4	9	12
5	$ 2	10	14

   a. Would the price rise or fall at the typical firm in the long run? Explain.
   b. What would be the level of production if this industry were a competitive industry?
   c. If free entry and exit is an option in both monopolistic competition and competition, explain the difference in the quantity the typical firm produces.

6. Suppose the government places a sales tax on firms in a monopolistically competitive industry. Draw a diagram showing the short-run impact and the adjustment to the new long-run industry equilibrium. What happens to the equilibrium price and number of firms in the industry?
7. Which of the following conditions will tend to induce collusion among sellers in a market?
   a. The transactions are publicly announced.
   b. The market has few sellers.
   c. Some sellers have lower costs than other sellers.
   d. The market is open for only one year.
   e. The sellers cannot meet one another
8. How can firms in an oligopoly ensure that their industry earns the largest possible profit? Why is it likely that this outcome will not be reached? If this outcome is not reached, will the deadweight loss in the market be larger or smaller?
9. Two firms, Faster and Quicker, are the only two producers of sports cars on an island that has no contact with the outside world. The firms collude and agree to share the market equally. If neither firm cheats on the agreement, each firm makes $3 million in economic profits. If only one firm cheats, the cheater can increase its economic profit to $4.5 million, while the firm that abides by the agreement incurs an economic loss of $1 million. If both firms cheat, they earn zero economic profit. Neither firm has any way of policing the actions of the other.
   a. What is the payoff matrix of the game if it is played just once?
   b. What is the equilibrium if the game is played only once? Explain.
   c. What do you think will happen if the game can be played many times? Why?
   d. What do you think will happen if a third firm comes into the market? Will it be harder or easier to achieve cooperation among the three firms? Why?
10. Store A and Store B are the only two flower shops in a small town. The demand for a dozen roses is $P = 25 = Q$. Neither Store A nor Store B has any fixed costs, whereas the marginal cost of Store A is constant at $3, and the marginal cost of Store B is constant at $5. Each seller can sell either five dozen or 10 dozen roses, and they meet only once in this market.
    a. Create the payoff matrix. Show your calculations and explain verbally as necessary.
    b. Find the Nash equilibrium or equilibria. Explain verbally.
    c. If multiple equilibria exist, which equilibrium do you think is most likely to occur and why?

ENDNOTES

1. Michael Porter, *Competitive Advantage* (New York: Free Press, 1985), p. 153.

CHAPTER 12

Antitrust Policy and Regulation

It was the biggest breakup that never happened. In April 2000, a federal judge issued a ruling that software giant Microsoft should be broken up into two entities—one that sold operating systems and the other that sold its web browser, Internet Explorer, and the company's flagship Microsoft Office software. In issuing this ruling, the court concluded that "Microsoft maintained its monopoly power by anticompetitive means and attempted to monopolize the Web browser market, both in violation of [Section] 2 [of the Sherman Antitrust Act]." Subsequently, an appeals court overturned the ruling that Microsoft be broken up because certain actions of the judge who had issued the ruling had called his impartiality into question. The appeals court, however, did uphold the legal finding that Microsoft had a monopoly in the market for operating systems and was sustaining that monopoly by anticompetitive actions.

Source: © Paul Brady Photography / Shutterstock, Inc.

The U.S. government has been involved in many cases in which it intervened to prevent a restriction of competition in an industry. When two office superstores, Staples and Office Depot, wanted to merge in 1997, the U.S. Federal Trade Commission (FTC) objected and eventually succeeded in stopping the merger. Two decades later, the two firms tried to merge again but the FTC blocked the merger again in 2016. When DIRECTV and Echostar, two competing satellite television providers, wanted to unite to form a single company, the Federal Communications Commission (FCC)—the federal agency that regulates the telecommunications industry—rejected the merger on the grounds that this would create a monopoly that would raise prices for satellite television customers. More recently, reports that the FTC may block a merger between two drugstore chains—RiteAid and Walgreens—sent the stock of both companies down sharply.

The intent of the government in these cases was to promote competition, which we know is an essential ingredient of market efficiency. The models of monopoly and monopolistic competition that you studied in Chapter 10 and Chapter 11 showed that when firms have market power, they raise prices above marginal cost, reduce the quantity produced, and create a deadweight loss to society. In such cases, the government may be able to reduce the deadweight loss and increase economic efficiency by taking actions that can lead to increased competition.

In this chapter, you will learn about some of the different ways the government can promote competition and regulate firms with market power. We consider two broad types of policy: (1) antitrust policy, which is concerned with preventing anticompetitive practices like price fixing and with limiting firms' market power by preventing mergers or breaking up existing firms; and (2) regulatory policy, in which the government requires firms that have a natural monopoly to set prices at prescribed levels. We also will talk about the limits and difficulties of government intervention. The government may step in and regulate markets even when a clear indication of anticompetitive behavior is lacking. In fact, because government agencies are susceptible to external influences, sometimes the regulators may end up limiting competition through their interventions. The ability to understand and appreciate the problems associated with both market failure and government failure is an important skill for an economist to possess.

1. ANTITRUST POLICY

Antitrust policy

Government actions designed to promote competition among firms in the economy; also called competition policy or antimonopoly policy.

Antitrust policy refers to the actions the government takes to promote competition among firms in the economy. Antitrust policy includes challenging and breaking up existing firms with significant market power, preventing mergers that would increase monopoly power significantly, prohibiting price fixing, and limiting anticompetitive arrangements between firms and their suppliers.

1.1 Attacking Existing Monopoly Power

Antitrust policy began in the United States more than 100 years ago in response to a massive wave of mergers and consolidations. Similar merger movements occurred in Europe at about the same time. These mergers were made possible by rapid innovations in transportation, communication, and management techniques. Railroads and telegraph lines expanded across the country, allowing large firms to place manufacturing facilities and sales offices in many different population centers. It was during this period that the Standard Oil Company grew rapidly, acquiring about 100 firms and gaining about 90 percent of U.S. oil refinery capacity. Similarly, the United States Steel Corporation was formed in 1901 by merging many smaller steel companies. It captured about 65 percent of the steel ingot market. These large firms were called *trusts.*

Sherman Antitrust Act

A law passed in 1890 in the United States to reduce anticompetitive behavior; Section 1 makes price fixing illegal, and Section 2 makes attempts to monopolize illegal.

The **Sherman Antitrust Act** of 1890 was passed in an effort to prevent these large companies from using their monopoly power. Section 2 of the act focused on the large existing firms. It stated, "Every person who shall monopolize, or attempt to monopolize...any part of the trade or commerce among the several states, or with foreign nations, shall be deemed guilty of a felony."

A Brief History: From Standard Oil to Microsoft

It was on the basis of the Sherman Antitrust Act that Theodore Roosevelt's administration took action to break apart Standard Oil. After 10 years of litigation, the Supreme Court ruled in 1911 that Standard Oil monopolized the oil-refining industry illegally. To remedy the problem, the courts ordered that Standard Oil be broken into a number of separate entities. Standard Oil of New York became Mobil; Standard Oil of California became Chevron; Standard Oil of Indiana became Amoco; Standard Oil of New Jersey became Exxon. Competition among these companies was slow to develop, because John D. Rockefeller still controlled their shares. But as the shares were distributed to heirs and then sold, the companies began to compete against each other. Now the oil-refining companies have much less monopoly power. In fact, with the greater degree of competition, the Clinton administration allowed some of these firms to merge, although not into one single oil refining firm. For example, on November 30, 1999, Exxon and Mobil merged to form a new firm called ExxonMobil.

rule of reason

An evolving standard by which antitrust cases are decided, requiring not only the existence of monopoly power but also the intent to restrict trade.

Soon after its success in splitting apart Standard Oil, the U.S. government took successful action under the Sherman Act against the tobacco trust, splitting up the American Tobacco Company into sixteen different companies. It also broke up several monopolies in railroads, food processing, and chemicals. The government was not successful, however, in using the Sherman Act against United States Steel. As part of the Standard Oil decision, the Supreme Court developed a **rule of reason** that required not only that a firm have monopoly power but also that it intends to use that power against other firms in a way that would restrict competition. Monopoly per se, in and of itself, was not enough, according to the Supreme Court in 1911. Because most competitors and customers of United States Steel said that the company's actions did not restrain competition, the Supreme Court, applying its rule of reason, decided in 1920 that United States Steel was not guilty under the Sherman Act.

Twenty-five years later, a 1945 Supreme Court decision that found Alcoa Aluminum guilty of monopolization refined the rule of reason to make it easier to prove guilt. Although a monopoly per se still was not enough, the intent to willingly acquire and maintain a monopoly—easier to prove than an intent to restrict competition—was enough to establish guilt.

In 1969, the U.S. government brought antitrust action against IBM because of its dominance in the mainframe computer market. After a number of years of litigation, the government dropped the case, in part because of the rapid change in the computer market. Mainframes were facing competition from smaller computers. Firms such as Digital Equipment and Apple Computer were competing with IBM by 1982, when the government withdrew its case. Looking at the competition picture more broadly and recognizing that it already had spent millions, the government decided that antitrust action was no longer warranted.

The U.S. government took action against AT&T in the 1970s. It argued thatAT&T, as the only significant supplier of telephone service in the nation, was restraining trade. As a result of that antitrust action, AT&T was broken apart and had to compete with MCI and Sprint to provide long-distance telephone service nationwide. This increase in competition lowered the cost of long-distance calls.

In the 1990s, attention switched to the computer industry. After several antitrust-related investigations, negotiations, and lawsuits in the 1990s, a federal judge found that Microsoft had monopoly power and used it to harm its competitors and consumers, and ordered the firm's breakup in June 2000. That order was reversed in 2001, however, and the federal government reached an agreement whereby the U.S. Department of Justice proposed that Microsoft should instead permit computer manufacturers to install software from Microsoft's competitors and that Microsoft should make enough information about its operating system available so that other companies could write software that worked well with Microsoft's operating systems.

One of the more important cases to be filed recently was the one filed in December 2010 against American Express, MasterCard, and Visa. This suit argued that these companies, the three largest issuers of credit cards in the United States, were preventing stores from "offering their customers a discount or benefit for using a network credit card that is less costly to the merchant. Merchants cannot reward their customers based on the customer's card choice. Merchants cannot even suggest that their customers use a less costly alternative card by posting a sign stating 'we prefer' another card or by disclosing a card's acceptance fee."

The U.S. Department of Justice estimated that more than $1.6 trillion in economic transactions were done using these three major credit cards and thus lowering transaction fees could save stores (and the customers to whom a portion of the charges get passed on to) tens of billions of dollars a year.

The Staples/Office Depot case is also interesting because in 1997 the FTC objected to the merger arguing that it would reduce competition and increase the cost of office supplies for consumers, individual-owned businesses and small businesses. By 2017, the rise of retailers like Amazon meant that the merger of brick and mortar office supply stores was not as much of a concern but the objection of the FTC was based on a complaint that the merger would adversely impact competition in the market supplying office supplies to large businesses.

Predatory Pricing

Attempts by firms to monopolize by predatory pricing also have been challenged by the government and by other firms, though breakup usually is not the intended remedy. **Predatory pricing** refers to an attempt by a firm to charge a price below its shutdown point to drive its competitors out of business, after which it then forms a monopoly.

Predatory pricing

Action on the part of one firm to set a price below its shutdown point to drive its competitors out of business.

A 1986 Supreme Court decision, *Matsushita v. Zenith*, made predatory pricing harder to prove. Matsushita and several other Japanese companies were accused by Zenith of predatory pricing of televisions in the U.S. market. After five years of litigation and appeals, the Court decided that evidence was insufficient to determine predatory pricing. The Court argued that the Japanese firms' share of the U.S. market was too small compared with Zenith's share to make monopolization plausible. Moreover, the low price of the Japanese televisions seemed to be based on low production costs. Thus, the Court's majority opinion stated that this predatory pricing case appeared to make "no economic sense."

Predatory pricing is difficult to distinguish from vigorous competition, which is essential to a well-functioning market economy. For example, Walmart has been accused of predatory pricing by smaller retailers, who find it hard to compete with Walmart's low prices. Yet, in many of these cases, it is likely that Walmart is more efficient. Its lower prices are due to lower costs. In 1993, Northwest Airlines sued American Airlines for predatory pricing in Texas but lost. Although American Airlines was charging prices below its shutdown point, the jury decided that it was not attempting to monopolize the market. In 2016, a cab firm in San Francisco filed a complaint in federal court charging that the ride-share firm Uber was engaged in predatory pricing—using the many millions of venture capital funds to bankroll a strategy of driving fares so low as to put local taxi companies out of business as Uber sought to expand and consolidate in many cities across the world.

1.2 Merger Policy

The frequency of government-forced breakups has declined in recent years, perhaps due to greater international competition or due to the effectiveness of merger policy, which we now consider. For firms to occupy a huge share of the market, they must either grow internally or merge with other firms. If the government can implement a merger policy that manages to prevent the formation of firms with substantial market power, then the need to break up firms because they have gained too much market power will be lower.

Clayton Antitrust Act

A law passed in 1914 in the United States aimed at preventing monopolies from forming through mergers.

Federal Trade Commission (FTC)

The government agency established to help enforce antitrust legislation in the United States; it shares this responsibility with the Antitrust Division of the Justice Department.

Antitrust Division of the Justice Department

The division of the U.S. Justice Department that enforces antitrust legislation, along with the Federal Trade Commission.

Herfindahl-Hirschman Index (HHI)

An index ranging in value from 0 to 10,000 indicating the concentration in an industry; it is calculated by summing the squares of the market shares of all the firms in the industry.

contestable market

A market in which the threat of competition is enough to encourage firms to act like competitors.

The Sherman Antitrust Act dealt with monopolies that were already in existence. The **Clayton Antitrust Act** of 1914 aimed to prevent the creation of monopolies and now provides the legal basis for preventing mergers that would reduce competition significantly. The **Federal Trade Commission (FTC)** was set up in 1914 to help enforce these acts along with the Justice Department.

To this day, the **Antitrust Division of the Justice Department** and the FTC have dual responsibility for competition policy in the United States. The U.S. Department of Justice has more investigative power and can bring criminal charges, but for the most part, the agencies share a dual responsibility.

How does the government decide whether a merger by firms reduces competition in the market? The economists and lawyers in the U.S. Department of Justice and the FTC provide much of the analysis. They focus on the market power of the firm. The more concentrated the firms are in an industry, the more likely it is that the firms have significant market power.

The "Herf"

Concentration usually is measured by the **Herfindahl-Hirschman Index (HHI)**. This index is used so frequently to analyze the impact of mergers on the competitive structure of an industry that it has a nickname: the "Herf." The HHI is defined as the sum of the squares of the market shares of all the firms in the industry. The more concentrated the industry, the larger the shares and, therefore, the larger the HHI. For example, if one firm controls the entire market, the HHI is $(100)^2 = 10{,}000$, the maximum value it can attain. If two firms each have a 50 percent share, the HHI is $(50)^2 + (50)^2 = 5{,}000$. If 10 firms have equal shares, the HHI is 1,000. Values of the HHI for several hypothetical examples of firm shares in particular industries are listed in Table 12.1.

Observe that the HHI is not merely a measure of the number of firms that exist within an industry. The HHI tends to be lower when an industry has more firms, but it also tends to be lower when all the firms' shares are more equal. Even when the number of firms in the industry is very large, the HHI can be large if one or two firms have a large share. For example, an industry with 20 firms in which one firm has 81 percent of the market and the others each have 1 percent has a very large HHI of 6,580, even greater than that of a two-firm industry with equal shares.

According to the *merger guidelines* put forth by the U.S. Justice Department and the FTC, mergers in industries with a post-merger HHI *above 1,800* are likely to be challenged if the HHI rises by 50 points or more. When the HHI is *below 1,000*, a challenge is unlikely. *Between 1,000 and 1,800*, a challenge is likely to occur if the HHI rises by 100 points or more.

Some examples are found in Table 12.1. Suppose that the two smallest firms in industry C in Table 12.1 merge, and the industry thereby takes the form of industry B. Then the HHI rises by 32, from 3,376 to 3,408. It is unlikely that the government would challenge this merger. In contrast, suppose that the two smallest firms in industry B merge. Then the HHI increases by 192, from 3,408 to 3,600, and the government would be likely to challenge the merger.

TABLE 12.1 Examples of the HHI in Different Industries

Industry Example	Number of Firms	Shares (percent)	HHI
A	3	40, 40, 20	3,600
B	4	40, 40, 12, 8	3,408
C	5	40, 40, 12, 4, 4	3,376

The HHI is used because it indicates how likely it is that firms in the industry after the merger will have enough market power to raise prices well above marginal cost, reduce the quantity produced, and cause economic inefficiency. For example, when the FTC blocked the merger of Office Depot and Staples in 1997, it stated that the "post-merger HHIs average over 3000" and that "increases in HHIs are on average over 800 points."[1]

The FTC or the U.S. Justice Department looks at other things in addition to concentration measures. Ease of entry of new firms into the industry is an important factor, as is the potential contestability of the market by other firms. Recall the idea of **contestable markets** discussed in Chapter 10: Even if firms are highly concentrated in an industry, potential entry by other firms provides competitive pressure on the industry. Thus, an industry with a high degree of concentration, in fact, may be acting competitively because of the threat of new firms coming into the business.

Price-Cost Margins

Another way to measure market power is the**price-cost margin**. The greater the price (P) is above the marginal cost (MC), the more market power firms have. Table 12.2 gives some estimates of the price-cost margin [$(P - MC)/P$] for firms in several different industries. The higher the price-cost margin, the more market power firms in the industry have. Observe in Table 12.2 that the price-cost margin is very small for coffee roasting, rubber, textiles, retail gasoline, and standard automobiles. The firms in these markets apparently have little market power. In contrast, the price-cost margin is very high for food processing and tobacco.

An interesting example is Anheuser-Busch, the producer of Budweiser beer. Before the introduction of Lite Beer by Miller, Anheuser-Busch had considerable market power; the price-cost margin was 0.3. After Lite Beer was introduced, the firm lost market power. The price-cost margin dropped to 0.03. Evidently Lite Beer made Miller a more visible player in the beer market, thus increasing competition in the market, and Anheuser-Busch's market power declined.

price-cost margin

The difference between price and marginal cost divided by the price. This index is an indicator of market power, where an index of zero indicates no market power and a higher price-cost margin indicates greater market power.

TABLE 12.2 Price-Cost Margins in Several Industries

Industry	Price-Cost Margin
Food processing	0.50
Coffee roasting	0.04
Rubber	0.05
Textiles	0.07
Electrical machinery	0.20
Tobacco	0.65
Retail gasoline	0.10
Standard automobiles	0.10
Luxury automobiles	0.34

Source: T. F. Bresnahan, "Empirical Studies of Industries with Market Power," Handbook of Industrial Organization, Vol. II, ed. R. Schmalensee and R. D. Willig (Amsterdam: Elsevier Science Publishers, 1989).

Market Definition

When measuring concentration in a market, the market definition is very important. A **market definition** is a demarcation of a geographic region and a category of goods and services in which firms compete. Table 12.3 shows the range of possibilities for market definitions when considering the merger of soft drink producers. Should the market definition be narrow (carbonated soft drinks) or broad (all nonalcoholic beverages)? The market definition makes a big difference for concentration measures. In 1986, the FTC blocked a merger between Coca-Cola and Dr. Pepper that would have increased the HHI by 341 in the carbonated soft drink market. The HHI would have increased by only 74, however, if bottled water, powdered soft drinks, tea, juices, and coffee also were included in the market, along with carbonated soft drinks.

Defining the geographic area of a market is also a key aspect of defining the market for a good or service. In an integrated world economy, a significant amount of competition comes from firms in other countries. For example, the automobile industry in the United States has featured only three major producers. Although this industry is highly concentrated, intense competition coming from Japanese, Korean, German, and other automobile companies increases the amount of competition. The rationale for challenging a merger is mitigated substantially by international competition.

market definition

Demarcation of a geographic region and a category of goods or services in which firms compete.

Horizontal versus Vertical Mergers

Merger policy also distinguishes between **horizontal mergers**, in which two firms selling the same good or the same type of good merge, and **vertical mergers**, in which a firm merges with its supplier—for example, when a clothing manufacturer merges with a retail clothing store chain. The merger guidelines refer to horizontal mergers. Virtually all economists agree that horizontal mergers have the potential to increase market power, all else being the same.

horizontal mergers

A combining of two firms that sell the same good or the same type of good.

vertical mergers

A combining of two firms, one of which supplies goods to the other.

TABLE 12.3 Different Market Definitions in the Beverage Industry

						Milk
					Tea	Tea
				Coffee	Coffee	Coffee
			Juice drinks	Juice drinks	Juice drinks	Juice drinks
		Bottled water	Bottled water	Bottled water	Bottled water	Bottled water
	Powdered soft drinks	Powdered soft drinks	Powdered soft drinks	Powdered soft drinks	Powdered soft drinks	Powdered soft drinks
Carbonated soft drinks	Carbonated soft drinks	Carbonated soft drinks	Carbonated soft drinks	Carbonated soft drinks	Carbonated soft drinks	Carbonated soft drinks
Narrow Market Definition			**Medium Market Definition**			**Broad Market Definition**

Economists disagree considerably about the effects of vertical mergers, however. A vertical merger seldom will reduce competition if firms are competing at each level of production. However, some feel that a vertical merger may aid in reducing competition at the retail store level.

1.3 Price Fixing

Price fixing

The situation in which firms conspire to set prices for goods sold in the same market.

treble damages

Penalties awarded to the injured party equal to three times the value of the injury.

In addition to breaking up firms and preventing firms with a great amount of market power from merging, antitrust policy prevents firms from conspiring to restrict competition. For example, when two or more firms conspire to fix prices, they engage in an illegal anticompetitive practice. **Price fixing** is a serious offense that is deemed to be illegal per se by Section 1 of the Sherman Antitrust Act.

Laws against price fixing are enforced by bringing lawsuits against the alleged price fixers. Suits can be brought both directly by the U.S. Department of Justice and by individual firms that are harmed by price fixing; typically, the number of private suits greatly exceeds the number of government suits. Individual firms can collect **treble damages** (a provision included in the Clayton Act)—three times the actual damages. The treble damage penalty aims to deter price fixing.

One of the most famous price-fixing cases in U.S. history occurred in the 1950s and involved Westinghouse and General Electric. Through an elaborate system of secret codes and secret meeting places, the executives of these two firms agreed to set the price of electrical generators and other equipment that they were selling in the same market. Through this agreement, they set the price well above competitive levels, but they were discovered and found guilty of price fixing. Treble damages amounting to about $500 million were awarded, and criminal sentences were handed down; some executives went to prison.

A more recent price-fixing case involved the production of computer memory chips. Several firms, including the leading chipmaker Samsung, were fined $300 million for fixing prices for computer memory chips. Newspapers reported at the time that the fine was the second largest in U.S. history. Other notable cases included the 1996 suit filed by the U.S. Department of Justice against the large agricultural firm Archer-Daniels-Midland (ADM) for fixing prices of animal feed and the 2001 settlement of a lawsuit brought against the legendary auction houses Sotheby's and Christie's by clients who had bought or sold items at auction. Both cases resulted in large fines: ADM paid more than $100 million in fines, while Sotheby's and Christie's each paid more than $250 million in fines.

1.4 Vertical Restraints

The price-fixing arrangements just described are an effort to restrict trade in one horizontal market, such as the electrical machinery market or the market for computer memory chips. Such restraints of trade clearly raise prices, reduce the quantity produced, and cause deadweight loss. But firms also attempt to restrain trade vertically by limiting the number of sellers of a particular product in a market. Trade in a product can be restrained vertically in several ways. For example, **exclusive territories** occur when a manufacturer of a product gives certain retailers or wholesalers exclusive rights to sell that product in a given area. This practice is common in soft drink and beer distribution. **Exclusive dealing** is the practice by which a manufacturer does not allow a retailer to sell goods made by a competitor. **Resale price maintenance** is the practice of a manufacturer's setting a list price for a good and then forbidding the retailer to offer a discount.

exclusive territories

The regions over which a manufacturer limits the distribution or selling of its products to one retailer or wholesaler.

Exclusive dealing

A condition of a contract by which a manufacturer does not allow a retailer to sell goods made by a competing manufacturer.

Resale price maintenance

The situation in which a producer sets a list price and does not allow the retailer to offer a discount to consumers.

Do vertical restraints reduce economic efficiency? Economists agree that manufacturers cannot increase their own market power by placing restraints on the firms to which they supply goods. A manufacturer's requirement that a retailer take a certain action with respect to the manufacturer's product does not give the manufacturer a greater ability to raise prices over competitors without losing sales. In addition, in some circumstances, such restraints actually may increase economic efficiency.

Consider resale price maintenance, for example. Suppose that low-price, low-service discount stores compete with high-price retail stores that provide lots of useful services to customers. If a discount store could offer the same product with little or no service, then people could go to the high-price store, look the product over, get some useful advice from knowledgeable salespeople, and then buy at the discount store. In such a world, the high-service stores would disappear. Resale price maintenance thus can be viewed as a means to preserve stores that offer such service by preventing the discount store from charging a lower price.

Sometimes stores are able to maintain this high level of service by other means: High-end wedding dress stores often will remove the labels from wedding dresses so that prospective brides will not be able to try on dozens of dresses using the time and expertise of a knowledgeable store assistant, choose the perfect dress, and then go buy it for a much lower price from a discount store that provides no such service. But for most goods, resale price maintenance will ensure that more stores are selling the product, with some providing a high level of service for those who value that attribute over a lower price, and others offering a low level of service for those customers who value lower prices more than service. In 2007, the Supreme Court ruled that minimum resale price maintenance would no longer be illegal *per se* under the Sherman Antitrust Act. Instead such agreements would have to be examined on a case-by-case basis to determine whether they were being used to reduce competition.

Similar arguments can be made for exclusive territories and for exclusive dealing. If McDonald's wants to allow only two franchises to serve a particular town, nothing prevents Wendy's or Burger King from opening franchises in that town to cater to potential customers. If a producer wants to limit stores that carry its product from selling competitors' products, it would be no different from the case in which a producer and a retailer are vertically integrated into one firm. For example, the Gap sells only its own products in its retail outlets. Why should a producer like Levi Strauss be treated differently and not be permitted to dictate that stores sell only Levis, were it to want to impose such a limitation?

Some argue, however, that resale price maintenance is a way to reduce competition at the retail level. They see retailers having competitive pressure to keep prices low as more important than the possible loss of some retail customer services. In sum, controversy among economists is greater about the effect of vertical restraints than about horizontal restraints.

REVIEW

- Breaking up monopolies, preventing mergers that would create too much market power, and enforcing laws against price fixing are the main government actions that constitute antitrust policy.
- These actions are backed by several important laws. Section 1 of the Sherman Antitrust Act outlaws price fixing, while Section 2 of the Sherman Antitrust Act allows the government to break up firms with monopoly power. The Clayton Antitrust Act provides the legal basis for merger policy.
- All these policies aim to increase competition and thus improve the efficiency of a market economy.
- The U.S. government has broken up several monopolies since the Sherman Act was passed, including Standard Oil, American Tobacco, and AT&T. In recent years the number of breakups of firms has decreased.
- The U.S. government also takes action to prevent mergers that can create too much market power. It uses tools like the HHI to gauge how competitive an industry is. The HHI tends to be lower, indicating more competition, when the market shares of firms are more equal and the market has more such equal firms.
- Both the U.S. government and private entities that have been harmed by higher prices can bring lawsuits against firms that conspire to fix prices. In recent years, several firms have been found guilty of price fixing and have been fined hundreds of millions of dollars.
- Mergers and price restraints are differentiated into two types: vertical (suppliers, producers, manufacturers, and retailers of a particular product) and horizontal (firms selling the same product). Vertical mergers and vertical restraints on making markets are considered less likely to make markets anticompetitive than are horizontal mergers and horizontal restraints.

2. REGULATING NATURAL MONOPOLIES

The goal of antitrust policy is to increase competition and improve the efficiency of markets. Under some circumstances, however, using antitrust policy to break up a monopoly into several competing firms is not necessarily in the interest of efficiency. For example, to provide its services, a water company must dig up the streets, lay the water pipes, and maintain them. It would be inefficient to have two companies supply water because that would require two sets of pipes and would be a duplication of resources. Another example is electricity. It makes no sense to have two electric utility firms supply the same neighborhood with two sets of wires. A single supplier of electricity is more efficient.

natural monopolies

A single firm in an industry in which average total cost is declining over the entire range of production and the minimum efficient scale is larger than the size of the market.

Water and electricity are examples of **natural monopolies**—industries in which one firm can supply the entire market at a lower cost than two firms can. Recall from the discussion in Chapter 10 that the key characteristic of a natural monopoly is that the minimum efficient scale is larger than the size of the market; the average total cost curve is declining over the entire range of production. Average total cost declines as more is produced because fixed costs are very large compared with variable costs. Once the main line is laid for the water supply, it is relatively easy to hook up another house. Similarly, with electricity, once the main lines are installed, it is relatively easy to run wires into a house. A large initial outlay is necessary to lay the main water pipes or main electrical lines, but thereafter the cost is relatively low. The greater the number of houses that are hooked up, the lower the average total cost.

Figure 12.1 shows graphically why one firm always can produce more cheaply than two or more firms when the average total cost curve is downward-sloping. The figure shows quantity produced on the horizontal axis and dollars on the vertical axis; a downward-sloping average total cost curve is plotted. If two firms divide up the market (for example, if two water companies supply water to the neighborhood), then the average total cost is higher than if one firm produces for the entire market. In the case of a declining average total cost curve, it is more costly for two or more firms to produce a given quantity than for one firm.

FIGURE 12.1 Natural Monopoly: Declining Average Total Cost

If two firms supply the market, dividing total production between them, costs are higher than if one firm supplies the market. The costs would be even greater if more than two firms split up the market.

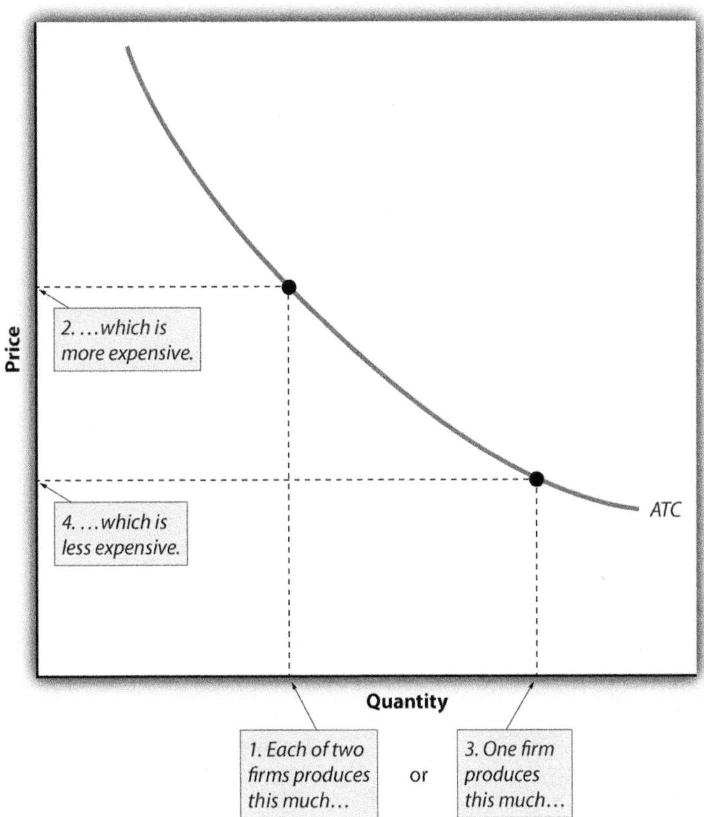

2.1 Methods of Regulating a Natural Monopoly

What is the best government policy toward a natural monopoly? On the one hand, having one firm in an industry will result in a lower average cost of production, but inefficiencies will be associated with a monopoly: Price will be higher than marginal cost, and there will be a deadweight loss. On the other hand, breaking up the monopoly into two firms will result in more competition, but each firm will be saddled with a higher average cost of production and it will be inefficient to have both firms incur the high fixed costs. To get both the advantages of one firm producing at a lower average cost *and* a lower price, the government can regulate the firm.

The monopoly price and quantity of a natural monopoly with declining average total cost are illustrated in Figure 12.2. The monopoly quantity occurs when marginal revenue equals marginal cost, the profit-maximizing point for the monopolist. The monopoly price is above marginal cost. If the firm's price is regulated, then the government can require the firm to set a lower price, thereby raising output and eliminating some of the deadweight loss associated with the monopoly. The government can regulate price in three ways: marginal cost pricing, average total cost pricing, and incentive regulation. We discuss each in turn.

Marginal Cost Pricing

We know that there is no deadweight loss with competition because firms choose a quantity of output such that marginal cost is equal to price. One possibility to create competition is for the government to require the monopoly to set its price equal to marginal cost. This method is called **marginal cost pricing**. However, with declining average total cost, the marginal cost is lower than average total cost. This is shown in Figure 12.2 for the case in which marginal cost is constant. Thus, if price were equal to marginal cost, *the price would be less than average total cost*, and the monopoly's profits would be negative (a loss). Firms would not have an incentive to enter the market.

marginal cost pricing

A regulatory method that stipulates that the firm charge a price that equals marginal cost.

FIGURE 12.2 Monopoly Price versus Alternative Regulatory Schemes

Two alternatives, marginal cost pricing and average total cost pricing, are compared with the monopoly price. Marginal cost pricing gives the greatest quantity supplied, but because price is less than average total cost, the firm earns negative profits. Average total cost pricing results in a larger quantity supplied, and the firm earns zero economic profits.

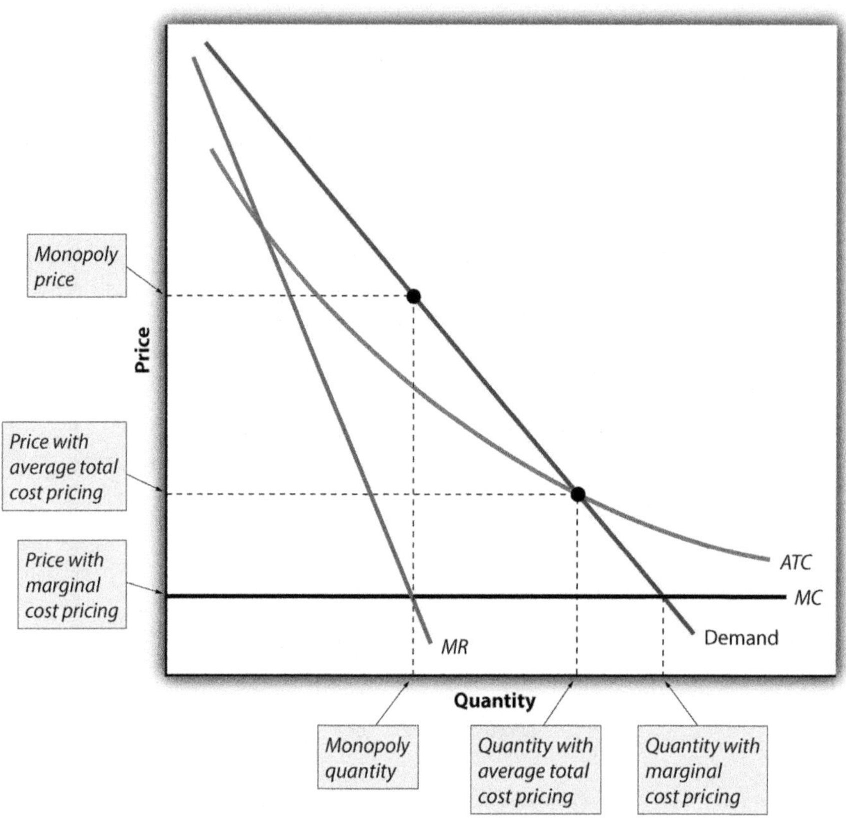

For example, if the regulators of an electrical utility use a pricing rule with price equal to marginal cost, the electrical utility would not have an incentive to build a plant or produce electricity. Although the idea of mimicking a competitive firm by setting price equal to marginal cost might sound reasonable, it fails to work in practice.

Average Total Cost Pricing

average total cost pricing

A regulatory method that stipulates that the firm charge a price that equals average total cost.

Another method of regulation requires the firm to set the price equal to average total cost. This method is called **average total cost pricing** or, sometimes, cost-of-service pricing. It also is illustrated in Figure 12.2. When price is equal to average total cost, we know that economic profits will be equal to zero. With the economic profits equal to zero, there will be enough to pay the managers and the investors in the firm their opportunity costs. Although price is still above marginal cost, it is less than the monopoly price. The deadweight loss will be smaller, and more electricity will be produced compared with the monopoly.

But average total cost pricing has serious problems. Suppose the firm knows that whatever its average total cost is, it will be allowed to charge a price equal to average total cost. In that situation, firms do not have an incentive to reduce costs. Sloppy work or less innovative management could increase costs. With the regulatory scheme in which the price equals average total cost, the price would rise to cover any increase in cost. Inefficiencies could occur with no penalty whatsoever. This approach provides neither an incentive to reduce costs nor a penalty for increasing costs at the regulated firm.

Incentive Regulation

The third regulation method endeavors to deal with the problem that average total cost pricing provides too little incentive to keep costs low. The method is called **incentive regulation**. It is a relatively new idea, but it is spreading quickly, and most economists predict that it is the way of the future. The method projects a regulated price out over a number of years. That price can be established on the basis of an estimate of average total cost. The regulated firm is told that the projected price will not be revised upward or downward for a number of years. If the regulated firm achieves an average total cost that is lower than the price, it will be able to keep the profits, or perhaps pass on some of the profits to a worker who came up with the idea for the innovation. Similarly, if sloppy management causes average total cost to rise, then profits will fall because the regulatory agency will not revise the price.

incentive regulation

A regulatory method that sets prices for several years ahead and then allows the firm to keep any additional profits or suffer any losses over that period of time.

Thus, under incentive regulation, the regulated price is only imperfectly related to average total cost. The firm has a profit incentive to reduce costs. If a firm does poorly, it pays the penalty in terms of lower profits or losses.

Under incentive regulation, the incentives can be adjusted. For example, the California Public Utility Commission (the regulator of utility firms in California) has incentive schemes by which electrical utility firms and their customers share equally in the benefits of reduced costs and in the penalties from increased costs. This reduces the firm's incentive to lower costs in comparison to the case in which the benefits and penalties are not shared.

Incentive regulation is sometimes made difficult by *asymmetric information*—that is, when one of the parties has access to more or better information. In this case, the regulated firm has more information than the regulator about its equipment, technology, and workers. Thus, the firm can mislead the regulator and say that its average total cost is higher than it actually is to get a higher price, as shown in Figure 12.3.

FIGURE 12.3 Asymmetric Information and Regulation

If a regulator uses average total cost pricing but does not have complete information about costs at the firm, the firm could give misleading information about its costs to get a higher price from the regulator. In an extreme case, shown in this figure, the firm could say its costs were so high that it could get the monopoly price.

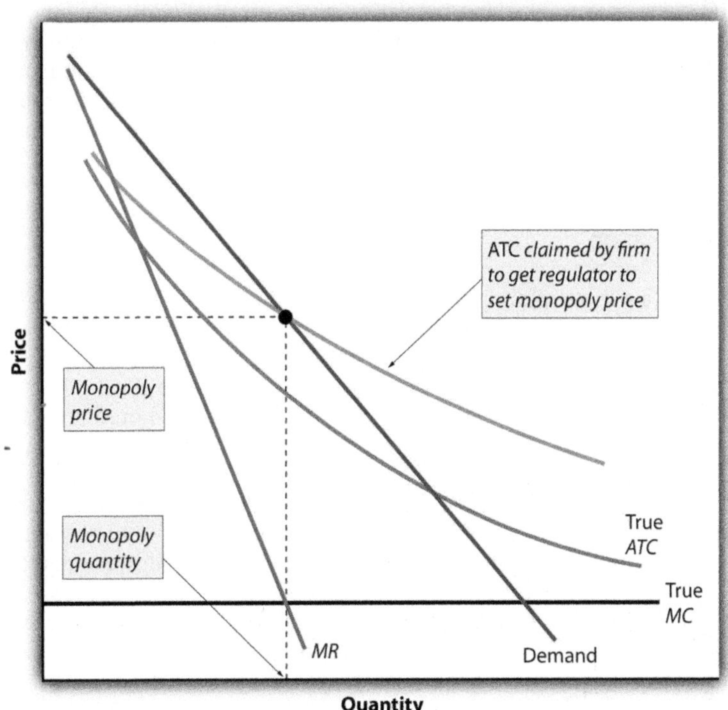

REVIEW

- A natural monopoly is said to exist when the minimum efficient scale is larger than the size of the market, implying that one firm can produce at a lower average total cost than two or more firms.
- A government may not want to allow a natural monopoly to exist unhindered, even though the single firm is producing at the lowest average total cost, because a monopoly creates deadweight loss. Conversely, breaking up the natural monopoly can reduce deadweight loss but also will lead to inefficiently high costs of production.
- The solution is to allow a single firm to produce the output to take advantage of the declining average total cost, but regulate the firm so that it charges a price less than the monopoly price. The government has several alternatives, including marginal cost pricing, average total cost pricing, and incentive regulation.
- If the government regulates the monopoly by setting a price equal to marginal cost, the firm will run losses because, for natural monopolies, average total cost tends to exceed marginal cost given the high level of fixed costs.
- If the government regulates the monopoly by setting a price equal to average total cost, it encourages firms to incur high costs because the price they are allowed to charge increases with costs.
- Incentive regulation is becoming the preferred method of regulation. By allowing firms to charge a price that is not revised up or down for a number of years, firms are encouraged to pursue strategies to lower costs and increase profits.

3. TO REGULATE OR NOT TO REGULATE

Our analysis thus far suggests that the government should regulate firms' prices in situations in which natural monopolies exist. In practice, this requires deciding when a natural monopoly exists, which is frequently difficult.

U.S. history includes many examples of government regulation of a firm's prices even when it is far-fetched to think of the firm as a natural monopoly. For example, for a long time, trucking was regulated by the federal government. Trucking regulation grew out of railroad regulation, which originally was justified when railroads were the only rapid form of transportation and thus were natural monopolies. Under trucking regulation, the federal government controlled which companies had permits to ship goods across state lines and also set uniform rates that the trucking firms could charge. Federal regulation of trucking was disbanded in the early 1980s. Studies have shown that trucking rates fell as a result.

3.1 Borderline Cases

Clearly, trucking is not a natural monopoly. The trucking industry is at the opposite end of the spectrum from water or electrical utility companies, which almost always are regulated.

But many borderline cases are more controversial. Many of these arise in high technology industries such as telecommunications and computing. An important example is cable television. In 1992, there was considerable debate about whether the federal government should regulate cable television. At first glance, it may appear that cable television is no different from electricity or water. Once a cable television company lays down the cable in a neighborhood, the cost is fairly small to connect each individual house to it. On the other hand, consumers have alternatives to cable television for many homes. For example, over-the-air television channels do provide some competition to cable television. If one lives in an area with few over-the-air channels, competition is low. If, however, an area has six, seven, or eight over-the-air channels, then competition is higher.

Until 1992, the FCC measured competition by the number of over-the-air channels. At first, the commission decided that three over-the-air channels represented effective competition. It did not regulate cable television companies in areas that had more than three over-the-air channels. Later on, when it noticed that prices of cable television were rising and consumers were complaining, the FCC raised the limit to six over-the-air channels. In 1992, Congress passed a law saying that it did not matter how many channels there were; the law required the FCC to regulate cable television firms in any case.

Over-the-air channels are not the only competition for cable television. People can use satellite dishes, which provide access to numerous channels at a price competitive with cable. The rise of broadband internet and its use for providing telephone services has allowed companies like Verizon, which used to provide only landline telephone services, to now provide mobile phone service, home telephone service, and also compete with the cable television companies to provide cable television.

Because high-tech industries change quickly, it is difficult for government regulators to keep up with the changes. Inflexible regulatory rules could slow innovation, but inadequate regulation could stifle competition. In 2002, the FCC ruled that neither phone nor cable companies would be required to share their broadband connections with competitors like America Online. The FCC argued that such restrictions discouraged phone and cable companies from investing in high-speed Internet service. Critics of the FCC decision argued that this would reduce competition in the broadband market and limit high-speed Internet access. Both critics and supporters of the FCC decision argued that the action was needed to ensure that the United States did not fall behind in broadband access compared with countries like South Korea.

Competition for Cable. Satellites provide customers in remote areas with access to television broadcasts. In more densely populated areas, satellites provide competition to cable companies and help keep cable prices lower than they would be otherwise.

Source: © Shutterstock, Inc.

More recently, the FCC has had to make decisions involving technologies that were barely in existence a few years ago, and that will change and evolve rapidly in the years immediately ahead. Recent examples include Net Neutrality, a proposal to ensure that broadband providers would not be able to charge different rates to certain types of websites, especially ones that provide telephone services or video and audio content. In 2014, the FCC announced a policy decision on Net Neutrality that was built on former chairman Michael Powell's Four Freedoms: (1) that Internet users had the right to use the software they desired to access the internet, (2) that they could access their desired content, (3) that they could use whatever devices they wanted to access that content, and (4) that they could obtain accurate information about what they received from their online provider for the price they pay. This ruling did leave open the possibility that consumers could be charged different amounts for different tiers of Internet usage; however, providers were not allowed to favor their content through creating "high-speed lanes" for their own content and for the content of firms who were willing to pay a higher price to use those lanes while leaving a slower internet for other firms.

In 2017, the newly appointed chairman of the FCC, Ajit Pai announced that the FCC was reversing the previous decision because the additional limits it placed on broadband companies reduced incentives for large companies to invest in their networks and made it more challenging for smaller companies to provide services to rural customers. In May of 2017, the FCC will vote on the revised regulations and then go through the process of inviting and responding to public and industry comments, followed by possible legal challenges.

3.2 Regulators as Captives of Industry

Government and government agencies are run by people who have their own motivations, such as being reelected or increasing their power, wealth, and influence, which may differ from doing what's best for society. Thus, despite the economic advice about what government regulatory agencies should do, the agencies may end up doing something else.

The railroad industry is an example of how regulators sometimes have helped the industry at the expense of the consumer. Originally, railroads were considered to be a natural monopoly for moving goods across the country, and regulation was intended to reduce prices below the monopoly price. But as competition to the railroads from trucks and eventually airlines increased, the industry continued to be regulated. Eventually, the regulators were helping the industry; they kept prices from falling to prevent railroad firms from failing. Furthermore, to keep trucking firms from competing with the railroads, government authorities regulated trucking prices as well to keep them at a high level. The Teamsters Union, which represents truck drivers, was one of the strongest supporters of regulation because it knew that the regulations were keeping trucking prices high. In a sense, the regulators became captives of both the firms and the workers in the industry.

An economist, George Stigler, won the Nobel Prize for showing how regulatory agencies can become captive to an industry and thwart competition. The concern that regulators will become captives is one reason some economists worry about allowing the government to regulate a new industry, like broadband Internet. Eventually, the government may try to protect the broadband Internet operators to prevent them from failing. The government might limit competition in the future from DSL (digital subscriber line) service or from fiber-optic lines laid by the telephone company or from wireless Internet providers.

3.3 The Deregulation Movement

deregulation movement

Begun in the late 1970s, the drive to reduce the government regulations controlling prices and entry in many industries.

Starting in the late 1970s under Jimmy Carter and continuing in the 1980s under Ronald Reagan, the **deregulation movement**—the lifting of price regulations—radically changed several key industries. The list of initiatives that constitute this deregulation movement is impressive. For example, air cargo was deregulated in 1977, air travel was deregulated in 1978, satellite transmissions were deregulated in 1979, trucking was deregulated in 1980, cable television was deregulated in 1980 (although regulation was reimposed in 1992), crude oil prices and refined petroleum products were deregulated in 1981, and radio was deregulated in 1981. Price deregulation also occurred in the financial industry. Before the 1980s, the price—that is, the interest rate on deposits—was controlled by the financial regulators. Regulation of brokerage fees also was eliminated. This deregulation of prices reduced deadweight loss. Airline prices have declined for many travelers, it is now cheaper to ship goods by truck or by rail, and both satellite television and satellite radio options are available for consumers.

But deregulation has its critics. Deregulation of the airline industry led to widespread fears that large airlines would dominate the industry because of their market power at the hubs. However, the large airlines are now so cost heavy that smaller regional airlines have made significant headway in attracting even business travelers with their low-cost flights. Boston-based business travelers, for example, might be willing to suffer the inconvenience of traveling to Providence to take a cheaper Southwest Airlines flight rather than fly out of Boston on one of the large carriers. Also when price regulations are lifted, firms may figure out ways to price-discriminate. Price discrimination can be welfare-enhancing if it allows the firm to sell to a larger customer base, but clearly some groups will be unhappy. For instance, business travelers complain that they now have to pay more for air travel, although vacation travelers can pay less.

REVIEW

- In many cases, determining whether or not a natural monopoly exists (and thus that price regulation is needed) is a challenge.
- There frequently has been price regulation even when there is no natural monopoly, as in trucking. Continuing to regulate an industry long after it has ceased to be a natural monopoly will keep prices artificially high.
- With certain industries, such as cable television or broadband Internet access, it is much more difficult to definitively determine whether the industry is a natural monopoly. Fast-changing technology and the need to balance incentives for innovation with effective competition make the task of a regulator a challenging one.
- Regulators can become captives of the industries they are assigned to regulate. If individuals are motivated more by personal gain than by societal benefit, they may use their regulatory power to protect the interests of the firms they regulate by thwarting competition rather than to protect the interests of consumers by enhancing competition.
- In response to economic analysis that showed that it is harmful to regulate the prices of firms that are not natural monopolies, many industries were deregulated in the 1970s and the 1980s. Trucking, airline, and railroad transportation prices are lower as a result of this deregulation.
- As with most economic changes, not everyone benefited, and not everyone agreed that all industries saw enhanced competition. Some industries, like cable television, were reregulated in the 1990s.

4. END-OF-CHAPTER MATERIALS

4.1 Conclusion

This chapter analyzed a key role of government in a market economy: maintaining competitive markets through antitrust policy or the regulation of firms. By reducing the deadweight loss caused by monopoly, the government can reduce market failure and improve people's access to services and affordable goods.

This analysis must be placed in the context of what really motivates government policy makers. The example of regulators becoming captives of industry reminds us that analyzing what should be done is different from getting it done. Government failure is a problem that must be confronted just like market failure. Reducing government failure requires designing government institutions that give decision makers the proper incentives.

Key Points

1. The government has an important role to play in maintaining competition in a market economy.
2. Part of antitrust policy is breaking apart firms with significant market power, although this technique is now used infrequently. Section 2 of the Sherman Antitrust Act provides the legal authority for challenging existing monopolies.
3. A more frequently used part of antitrust policy is preventing mergers that would cause significant market power. In the United States, the government must approve mergers.
4. Concentration measures such as the HHI are used to decide whether a merger should take place.
5. Price fixing is a serious antitrust offense in the United States, and the laws against it are enforced by allowing private firms to sue, providing for treble damages, and allowing the government to ask for criminal penalties.
6. In the case of natural monopolies, the government can either run the firm or regulate a private firm. In the United States, the latter route usually is taken.
7. A natural monopoly can be regulated by using marginal cost pricing, average total cost pricing, or incentive regulation. Marginal cost pricing will discourage firms from making the investments needed to provide services, and average total cost pricing discourages firms from producing in a cost-efficient manner, so regulatory agencies have been using incentive regulation more frequently to give firms incentives to hold costs down.
8. Determining whether regulation is needed is a challenging task, especially in industries in which technology changes rapidly.
9. Even when regulation is needed, the regulator is vulnerable to regulatory capture—acting to protect the interests of the firms being regulated by thwarting competition instead of acting to protect the interests of consumers by enhancing competition.
10. In response to economic research showing that several industries were no longer natural monopolies and regulatory capture had taken place, many industries were deregulated in the 1970s and 1980s, including trucking and airlines.

QUESTIONS FOR REVIEW

1. What historical development gave the impetus to the original antitrust legislation in the United States?
2. What are the key laws that govern antitrust policy in the United States?
3. What are the different ways in which the government intervenes to promote competition in the economy?
4. What does the HHI measure? Under what type of market structure would the HHI be highest? When would it be lowest?
5. Why does the government allow firms affected by price fixing to file lawsuits and collect treble damages if they win?
6. Why are vertical mergers and price restraints considered less likely to be anticompetitive than horizontal mergers and price restraints?
7. Why would a government prefer a regulated natural monopoly to an unregulated natural monopoly or to breaking up the natural monopoly firm into several competing firms?
8. What are the different ways in which the government can regulate the price of a natural monopoly? Which of these methods is an improvement on the others?
9. What is regulatory capture? Why is it damaging for the economy?
10. Why is controversy greater about regulating industries in which technology changes rapidly?

PROBLEMS

1. Which legislation—Section 1 of the Sherman Act, Section 2 of the Sherman Act, or the Clayton Act—gives the government the authority to take action in each of the following areas: prosecuting price fixing, preventing proposed mergers, breaking up existing monopolies, and suing for predatory pricing?
2. Consider an industry with 10 firms whose market shares are given in the frequency table here:

Market Share	Number of Firms
5 percent	2
10 percent	7
20 percent	1

   a. Calculate the HHI for this industry.
   b. Suppose one of the firms with a 5 percent market share announces a plan to buy the other firm with a 5 percent market share. Is the U.S. Department of Justice likely to challenge the merger? Why or why not?
   c. Suppose the firm with the 20 percent market share announces a plan to buy one of the firms with a 5 percent market share. Is the U.S. Department of Justice likely to challenge the merger? Why or why not?
   d. Suppose one of the firms with a 10 percent market share announces a plan to buy the firm with the 20 percent market share. Is the U.S. Department of Justice likely to challenge the merger? Why or why not?
3. The table here shows the market share of firms in three different industries.

Industry	Number of Firms	Shares	HHI
1	100	Each firm with 1 percent	
2	15	10 firms with 5 percent	
		5 firms with 10 percent	
3	3	1 firm with 60 percent	
		2 firms with 20 percent	

   a. Complete the above table by calculating the Herfindahl-Hirschman Index.
   b. Will the FTC try to prevent a significant merger in Industry 2? In Industry 3? Why?
4. Compare the following two hypothetical cases of price fixing. Which is more likely to raise prices and cause a deadweight loss? Explain.
   a. General Motors, Ford, and Chrysler are found to be coordinating their prices for Chevy Blazers, Ford Broncos, and Jeep Cherokees.
   b. General Motors is coordinating with Chevy dealers around the country to set the price for Chevy Blazers.
5. In 2007, the European Union sued Apple under its antitrust laws. Apple has established country-specific websites for European customers of iTunes. The music inventory and prices vary among the different country-specific sites, and customers are prohibited from purchasing music from an iTunes site outside their country of residence. The European Union claims that this is an unlawful territorial sales restriction. Do you think Apple should be permitted to engage in this practice?
6. Why is it better to break up monopolies that are not natural monopolies than to regulate them, even if it is possible to regulate them?
7. Sketch a graph of a natural monopoly with declining average total cost and constant marginal cost.
   a. Show how the monopoly causes a deadweight loss.
   b. Describe the pros and cons of three alternative ways to regulate the monopoly and reduce deadweight loss: marginal cost pricing, average total cost pricing, and incentive regulation.

8. The demand schedule and total costs for a natural monopoly are given in the following table.

Price	Quantity	Total Costs
16	6	82
15	7	87
14	8	92
13	9	97
12	10	102
11	11	107
10	12	112
9	13	117
8	14	122
7	15	127
6	16	132
5	17	137
4	18	142

a. Why is this firm a natural monopoly? What will the monopoly price be? Calculate profits.
b. Suppose the government sees that this is a natural monopoly and decides to regulate it. If the regulators use average total cost pricing, what will the price and quantity be? What should profits be when the regulators are using average total cost pricing?
c. If the regulators use marginal cost pricing, what will the price and quantity be? What are profits in this situation? Why is this policy difficult for regulators to pursue in practice?
d. Why might the government want to use incentive regulation?

9. Before 1982, AT&T had a monopoly on local telephone service throughout most of the United States. It also provided long-distance telephone service and did not give other companies access to its local telephone lines. As a result of the development of satellites, fiber-optic cable, and other technological advances, it became possible for other companies to provide long-distance service, but their lack of access to local lines seriously inhibited the development of this service. The U.S. Department of Justice sued AT&T under the antitrust laws, and a 1982 settlement required AT&T to sell its local operating companies. In the years after 1982, the local operating companies gradually merged, and by 2006, almost all the local operating companies had merged and rejoined with AT&T long distance. The U.S. Department of Justice did not challenge the re-creation of the 1982 AT&T structure. What changes occurred between 1982 and 2006 that led to this lack of action by the U.S. Department of Justice?
10. In reflecting on a recent term of service, a former head of the Antitrust Division of the U.S. Department of Justice said, "I was convinced that a little bit of efficiency outweighs a whole lot of market power." Evaluate this statement by considering two sources of efficiency: decreasing average total cost and research and development. Describe how these should be balanced against the deadweight loss from market power.

ENDNOTES

1. Public Brief to D.C. District Court on FTC v. Staples and Office Depot, April 7, 1997.

CHAPTER 13
Labor Markets

The labor market touches more people than any other market, and it is by far the most important market in people's lives. Odds are that you will be asking questions about the labor market long after you finish this course. In your twenties, you may have to make a decision about moving to work in a new location or about leaving work temporarily to pursue graduate work or to raise a family. In your thirties, you may have to worry about hitting a ceiling in your career progress or about whether it is too late to make a career switch. In your forties, you may worry about earning enough money to pay for your kid's college or your own retirement. In your fifties, you may worry about your ability to find a comparable job at your age were you to lose your job, and about how you would cope without health insurance. In your sixties, you will try to figure out how long to keep working and how to coordinate retirement decisions with your spouse. Understanding how labor markets work is even more important than learning how the stock market works.

Source: © Shutterstock, Inc.

The importance of labor markets is not confined to one's own experiences. Many important economic policy issues relate to labor markets. What is the effect of the minimum wage? What impact do labor unions have on wages and unemployment? Why do certain vital occupations, such as nursing, firefighting, or teaching, pay less than other occupations that seem to have less of a beneficial social impact?

In this chapter, we show that the standard supply and demand model can be applied to the labor market. Many people are surprised to hear that the same model used to explain changes in the price and quantity of oil helps us understand wage and employment trends. Although we have to adapt the basic model to the labor market, it still is based on the central idea that people make purposeful choices with limited resources and interact with other people when they make these choices.

1. THE MEASUREMENT OF WAGES

We begin our discussion of labor markets by defining what exactly is meant by "the wage" and showing how it is measured. We also will look at recent wage trends in the United States to see whether wages

have been increasing, and if they have been increasing, whether they have been increasing more rapidly or more slowly than in the recent past.

1.1 Measuring Workers' Pay

When examining data on workers' pay, we must be specific about (1) what is included in the measure of pay, and (2) whether inflation may be distorting that measure.

Pay Includes Fringe Benefits

fringe benefits

Compensation that a worker receives excluding direct money payments for time worked: insurance, retirement benefits, vacation time, and maternity and sick leave.

Pay for work includes not only the direct payment to a worker—whether in the form of a payroll check, currency in a pay envelope, or a direct deposit into the worker's bank account—but also **fringe benefits**. Fringe benefits may include many of the following: health or life insurance, such as employer provided partial or full insurance; retirement benefits, such as employer-funded retirement plans; paid time off, such as vacations and sick or maternity leave; and discounts on company products.

Fringe benefits are a large share of total compensation in the United States and many other countries. In recent years in the United States, fringe benefits have accounted for about 30 percent of total pay. For example, in 2011, the average cost per hour to employ a worker was $29.72, of which $9.02 came in the form of fringe benefits.

wage

The price of labor defined over a period of time worked.

The term wage sometimes refers to the part of the payment for work that excludes fringe benefits. But in most economics textbooks, the term **wage** refers to the *total* amount a firm pays workers, *including* fringe benefits. This book uses the usual textbook terminology. Thus, the wage is the total price of labor.

Adjusting for Inflation: Real Wages versus Nominal Wages

real wage

The way or price of labor adjusted for inflation; in contrast, the nominal wage has not been adjusted for inflation.

When comparing wages in different years, it is necessary to adjust for inflation, that is, the general increase in prices over time. The term *nominal wage* is used to emphasize that a wage has not been corrected for inflation. The **real wage** is a measure of the wage that has been adjusted for changes in inflation. The real wage is computed by dividing the stated wage by a measure of the price of the goods and services. The most commonly used measure of the price for this purpose is the consumer price index (CPI), which gives the price of a fixed collection, or market basket, of goods and services each year compared with some base year. For example, the CPI increased from 1 in the 1983 base year to 1.70 in 2000; it rose further to 2.40 in 2016. This increase means that the same goods and services that cost $100 in 1983 would cost $170 in 2000 and $240 in 2016.

Suppose the hourly wage for a truck driver increased from $20 to $30 between 2000 and 2016. The nominal wage increase would be 50 percent. The real wage is found by dividing this hourly wage by the CPI. Thus, the real wage would have changed from $11.76 (= $20/1.70) to $12.50 (=$30/2.40), which would only be a 6.25 percent increase. Because of the increase in prices, the real wage for the truck driver rose much less than the stated wage increase. The real wage is the best way to compare wages in different years.

1.2 Wage Trends

Having described how to measure wage trends, let's now look at wages in the United States. Figure 13.1 shows average real hourly wages in the United States over the past quarter century. In 2016, the average real wage was about $34.90 per hour (in year 2016 dollars) including about $11.00 per hour in real fringe benefits.

What is most noticeable in Figure 13.1 is that the real wage (including fringe benefits) did not change very much over this period, rising from $29.00 in 1991 to $34.90 in 2016, an increase of less than 1% per year. If we had shown the same figure in nominal terms, the increase would look more impressive, more than doubling from $16.45 per hour in 1991 to $34.90 per hour in 2016.

Figure 13.1 shows the change in the average wage over time for all workers. What about differences across workers? Table 13.1 shows the differences for major occupation categories of workers at private firms as well as at state and local governments. Jobs requiring higher skills, such as teaching or management, pay more than jobs with lower skills, such as service workers. A more detailed breakdown would show much larger differences between the wages of different people. Top athletes, entertainment celebrities, and corporate executives at large firms are paid many times the average wage in the United States.

The distribution of wages across workers also has changed substantially in recent years. One development that has received much attention from economists is that the pay gap between skilled and less skilled workers has increased. In the mid-1970s, college graduates earned about 45 percent more than high school graduates. In the 1990s, this was up to about 65 percent. Another change is in the wage difference between women and men, which, although still wide, has been narrowing in recent years. In the mid-1970s, women on average earned less than $0.60 for each $1 men earned. By the late 1990s, the gap had closed to around $0.76.

FIGURE 13.1 Average Hourly Real Wage Since 1991

In the last 25 years, the average hourly wage, including fringe benefits, has more than doubled, increasing from about $16.45 per hour in 2001 to about $34.90 per hour in 2016, an increase of around 3% per year. Note, however, that in real terms, the average real wage has changed considerable less, rising from around $29.00 (in 2016 dollars) in 1991 to around $34.90 (in 2016 dollars), an increase of 0.75% per year.

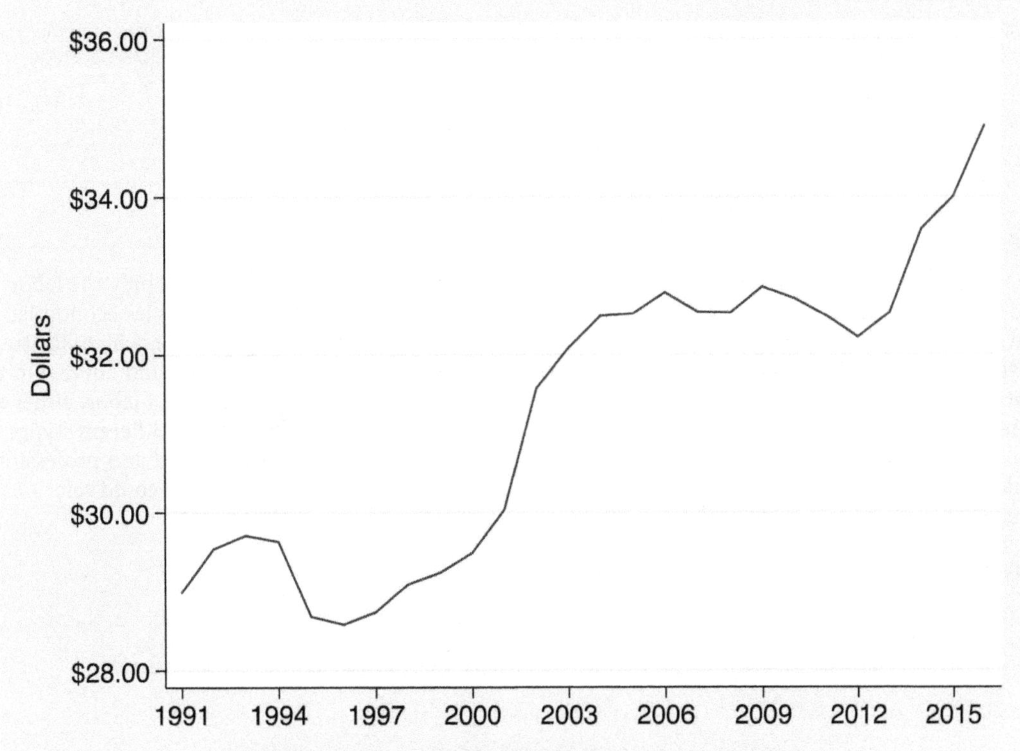

Source: U.S. Bureau of Labor Statistics, Employer costs for employee compensation per hour worked.

TABLE 13.1 Average Hourly Wages of Workers in the United States (dollars)

All workers (excluding federal)		**34.90**
Management, professional	58.00	
Sales and office	25.05	
Service	17.77	
Workers at private firms		**32.76**
Management, professional	58.14	
Sales and office	24.35	
Service	15.18	
Construction	34.81	
Production, transportation	27.45	
Workers at state and local governments		**47.85**
Management, professional	57.60	
Teachers	63.56	
Sales and office	33.00	
Service	34.42	

Source: "Employer Costs of Employee Compensation" (Bureau of Labor Statistics, March 9, 2011).

What causes these changes? Can the economists' model of labor markets explain them? After developing the model in the next section, we will endeavor to answer these questions.

REVIEW

- Workers' pay includes the direct payments plus fringe benefits, which are about 30 percent of workers' pay in the United States.
- When you talk about wages, you should be clear as to whether it is about wages including benefits or wages without benefits and whether it is about the real wage or the nominal wage.
- Real hourly wages have grown at a slow rate in the past 25 years.
- Discussions about the average real wage in the economy must be accompanied by an understanding of how wages are dispersed by skill, gender, industry, occupation, size of firm, part-time or full-time status, and geographic region.
- In recent times, the dispersion of wages between skilled and unskilled workers has increased, with college-educated workers gaining over those without a college education. The difference between the average wage of women and men is substantial, although it has narrowed in recent years.

2. THE LABOR MARKET

labor market

The market in which individuals supply their labor time to firms in exchange for wages and salaries.

The **labor market** consists of firms that have a demand for labor and people who supply the labor. In analyzing labor markets, economists stress their similarity to other markets; this enables economists to use the standard supply and demand model. To see the analogy, consider Figure 13.2, which illustrates a typical *labor market.* It shows a typical labor supply curve and a typical labor demand curve. On the vertical axis is the price of labor, or the wage. On the horizontal axis is the quantity of labor, either the number of workers or the number of hours worked. People work at many different types of jobs—physical therapists, accountants, mechanics, teachers, Web developers, judges, and professional athletes—and each type has a labor market. The labor market diagram in Figure 13.2 could refer to any one of these particular types of labor.

FIGURE 13.2 Labor Demand Curve and Labor Supply Curve

The basic economic approach to the labor market is to make an analogy with other markets. Labor is what is bought or sold on the labor market. The demand curve shows how much labor firms are willing to buy at a particular wage. The supply curve shows how much labor workers are willing to sell at a particular wage.

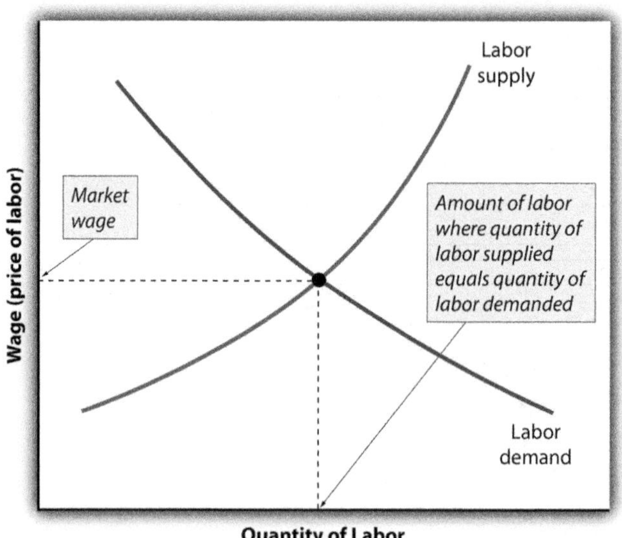

The first thing to remember about the labor demand curve and the labor supply curve is that firms demand labor and people supply it. Firms demand labor—like other factors of production—because it can be used to produce goods and services. The labor demand curve tells us the quantity of labor demanded by firms at each wage; the labor supply curve tells us the quantity of labor supplied by workers at each wage.

Note that the labor demand curve slopes downward and the labor supply curve slopes upward, just like other demand and supply curves. Thus, a higher wage reduces the quantity of labor demanded by firms, and a higher wage increases the quantity of labor supplied by people. Note also that the curves intersect at a particular wage and a particular quantity of labor. As with any other market, this intersection predicts the quantity of something (in this case, labor) and its price (in this case, the wage). Having defined the basics of the labor supply and demand model, we will more closely study how these curves are derived.

3. LABOR DEMAND

In this section, we look at **labor demand**, the relationship between the quantity of labor demanded by firms and the wage. In the next section, we look at **labor supply**, the relationship between the quantity of labor supplied by people and the wage. We start with a single firm's demand for labor and then sum up all the firms that are in the labor market to get the market demand for labor.

In deriving a firm's labor demand, economists assume that the firm's decision about how many workers to employ, like its decision about how much of a good or service to produce, is based on profit maximization. The demand for labor is a **derived demand**; that is, it is derived from the firm's decision about how many goods or services it can produce with the labor. The firm sells these goods and services to consumers in product markets, which are distinct from the labor market. Labor and other factors of production are not directly demanded by consumers; the firm's demand for labor is derived from consumers' demand for the firm's goods and services.

labor demand

The relationship between the quantity of labor demanded by firms and the wage.

labor supply

The relationship between the quantity of labor supplied by individuals and the wage.

derived demand

Demand for an input derived from the demand for the product produced with that input.

3.1 A Firm's Employment Decision

Recall how the idea of profit maximization was applied to a firm's decision about the optimal quantity to produce: If producing another ton of steel will increase a steel firm's profits—that is, if the marginal revenue from producing a ton is greater than the marginal cost of producing that ton—then the firm will produce that ton of output. However, if producing another ton of steel reduces the firm's profits, then the firm will not produce that ton.

The idea of profit maximization is applied in a similar way to a firm's decision about how many workers to employ: If employing another worker increases the firm's profits, then the firm will employ that worker. If employing another worker reduces the firm's profits, then the firm will not employ the worker.

We have already seen that a firm produces a quantity that equates marginal revenue to marginal cost ($MR = MC$). The firm satisfies an analogous condition in deciding how much labor to employ, as we discuss next.

From Marginal Product to Marginal Revenue Product

To determine a firm's demand curve for labor, we must examine how the firm uses labor to produce its output of goods and services. We start by assuming that the firm sells its output in a *competitive market*; that is, the firm is a *price-taker.* We also assume that the firm takes the wage as given in the labor market; in other words, the firm is hiring such a small proportion of the workers in the labor market that it cannot affect the market wage for those workers. Figure 13.3 gives an example of such a competitive firm. It shows the weekly production and labor input of a firm called Getajob, which produces professional-looking job resumes in a college town. To produce a resume, workers at Getajob talk to each of their clients (usually college seniors), give advice on what should go into the resume, and then produce the resume.

FIGURE 13.3 Labor Input and Marginal Revenue Product at a Competitive Firm

Workers Employed Each Week (*L*)	Quantity Produced (*Q*)	Marginal Product of Labor (*MP*)	Price of Output (dollars) (*P*)	Total Revenue (dollars) (*TR*)	Marginal Revenue Product of Labor (dollars) (*MRP*)
0	0	—	100	0	—
1	17	17	100	1,700	1,700
2	31	14	100	3,100	1,400
3	42	11	100	4,200	1,100
4	51	9	100	5,100	900
5	58	7	100	5,800	700
6	63	5	100	6,300	500
7	66	3	100	6,600	300
8	68	2	100	6,800	200
9	69	1	100	6,900	100
		Change in *Q* / Change in *L*	*P* does not depend on *Q*	*P* × *Q*	Change in *TR* / Change in *L* or *P* × *MP*

marginal product (*MP*) of labor

The change in production due to a one-unit increase in labor input, holding other inputs fixed.

The first two columns of Figure 13.3 show how Getajob can increase its production of resume's each week by employing more workers. This is the *production function* for the firm; it assumes that the firm has a certain amount of capital—word-processing equipment, a small office near the campus, and so on. We assume that labor is the only variable input to production in the short run, so that the cost of increasing the production of resumes depends only on the additional cost of employing more workers. Observe that the **marginal product (*MP*) of labor**—which we defined in Chapter 6 as the change in the quantity produced when one additional unit of labor is employed, holding other inputs fixed—declines as more workers are employed. In other words, there is a diminishing marginal product of labor, or diminishing return to labor: As more workers are hired, with office space and equipment fixed, each additional worker adds less and less to production. For example, the first worker employed can produce 17 resumes a week, but if Getajob already employed eight workers, hiring a ninth worker will increase production by only one resume.

Suppose that the market price for producing this type of resume service is $100 per resume, as shown in the fourth column of Figure 13.3. Because Getajob is assumed to be a *competitive firm*, it cannot affect this price. Then, the total revenue of the firm for each amount of labor employed can be computed by multiplying the price (*P*) times the quantity produced (*Q*) with each amount of labor (*L*). This calculation is shown in the next-to-last column. For example, total revenue with $L = 3$ workers employed is $P = \$100$ times $Q = 42$, or $4,200.

marginal revenue product (*MRP*) of labor

The change in total revenue due to a one-unit increase in labor input, holding other inputs fixed.

The last column of Figure 13.3 shows the **marginal revenue product (*MRP*) of labor**. *The marginal revenue product of labor is defined as the change in total revenue when one additional unit of labor is employed, holding all other inputs fixed.* For example, the marginal revenue product of labor from hiring a third worker is the total revenue with three workers ($4,200) minus the total revenue with two workers ($3,100), or $4,200 – $3,100 = $1,100. The marginal revenue product of labor is used to find the demand curve for labor, as we will soon see.

What is the difference between the marginal product (*MP*) and the marginal revenue product (*MRP*)? The marginal product is the increase in the quantity produced when labor is increased by one unit, holding other inputs fixed. The marginal revenue product is the increase in total revenue when labor is increased by one unit, holding other inputs fixed. For a competitive firm taking the market price as given, the marginal revenue product (*MRP*) can be calculated by multiplying the marginal product (*MP*) by the price of output (*P*). For example, the marginal product when the third worker is hired is 11 resumes; thus, the additional revenue that the third worker will generate for the firm is $100 per resume times 11, or $1,100.

Observe in Figure 13.3 that the marginal revenue product of labor declines as more workers are employed. This result occurs because the marginal product of labor declines.

Reminder - *Wait: Before you read any further, make sure you can explain the difference between marginal product (MP) and marginal revenue product (MRP).*

The Marginal Revenue Product of Labor Equals the Wage ($MRP = W$)

Now we are almost ready to derive the firm's demand curve for labor. Suppose first that the wage for workers with the type of skills Getajob needs to produce resumes is $600 per week (for example, $15 per hour for 40 hours). Then, hiring one worker certainly makes sense because the marginal revenue product of labor is $1,700, or much greater than the $600 wage cost of hiring the worker. How about two workers? The marginal revenue product from employing a second worker is $1,400, still greater than $600, so it makes sense to hire a second worker. Continuing this way, we see that *the firm will hire a total of five workers when the wage is $600 per week*, because hiring a sixth worker would result in a marginal revenue product of only $500, less than the $600 per week wage.

Thus, if a firm maximizes profits, it will hire the largest number of workers for which the marginal revenue product of labor is greater than the wage; if fractional units of labor input (for example, hours rather than weeks of work) are possible, then the firm will keep hiring workers until the marginal revenue product of labor exactly equals the wage. Thus, we have derived a key rule of profit maximization: Firms will hire workers up to the point at which *the marginal revenue product of labor equals the wage.* The rule that the marginal revenue product of labor equals the wage can be written in symbols as $MRP = W$.

Looking for Work. Day workers who are job hunting for construction cleanup work will signal their availability by showing up at a specified location; labor contractors will come by and hire the number of workers they need that day.

Source: © Shutterstock, Inc.

3.2 The Firm's Derived Demand for Labor

Now, to find the demand curve for labor, we need to determine how many workers the firm will hire at *different* wages. We know that Getajob will hire five workers if the wage is $600 per week. What if the wage is $800 per week? Then the firm will hire only four workers; the marginal revenue product of the fifth worker ($700) is now less than the wage ($800), so the firm will not be maximizing its profits if it hires five workers. Thus, we have shown that a higher wage reduces the quantity of labor demanded by the firm. What if the wage is lower than $600? Suppose the wage is $250 a week, for example. Then the firm will hire seven workers. Thus, a lower wage increases the quantity of labor demanded by the firm.

Figure 13.4 shows how to determine the entire demand curve for labor. It shows the wage on the vertical axis and the quantity of labor on the horizontal axis. The plotted points are the marginal revenue products from Figure 13.3. To find the demand curve, we ask how much labor the firm would employ at each wage. Starting with a high wage, we reduce the wage gradually, asking at each wage how much labor the firm would employ. At a weekly wage of $2,000, the marginal revenue product is less than the wage, so it does not make sense to hire any workers. Therefore, the quantity demanded is zero at wages more than $2,000. At a weekly wage of $1,500, it makes sense to hire one worker, and so on. As the wage is lowered gradually, the quantity of labor demanded rises, as shown by the vertical lines in Figure 13.4. The step-like downward-sloping curve is the labor demand curve. There would be more black dots and the curve would be smooth if we measured work in fractions of a week rather than in whole weeks.

FIGURE 13.4 Determining a Firm's Demand Curve for Labor

The black dots are exactly the same as the marginal revenue product of labor in the table in Figure 13.3. The vertical lines indicates the quantity of labor demanded at each wage.

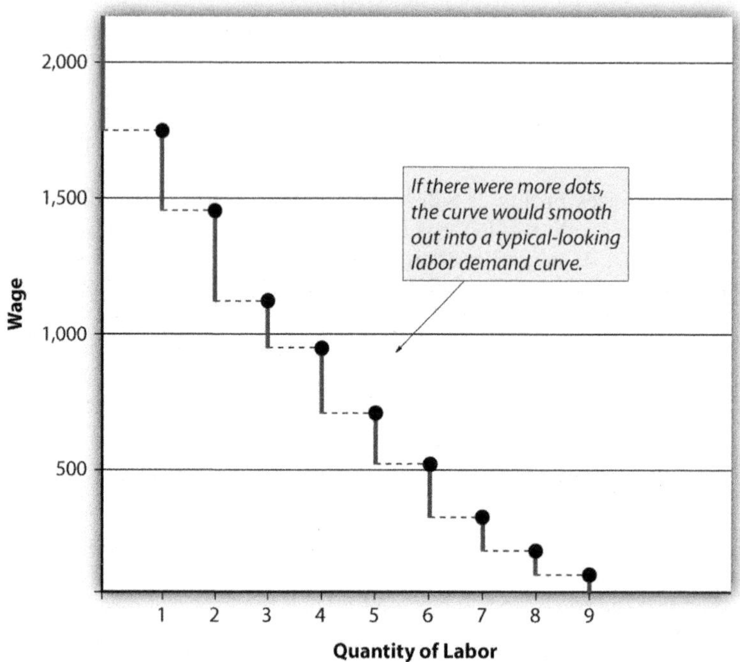

Observe in Figure 13.4 that a firm's demand curve for labor is completely determined by the firm's marginal revenue product of labor. We have shown that the demand curve for labor is downward sloping because the marginal revenue product of labor curve is downward sloping. A higher wage will reduce the quantity of labor demanded, and a lower wage will increase the quantity of labor demanded, because workers with a marginal revenue product that is lower than the wage will not be hired. Changes in the quantity of labor demanded that result from changes in the wage are *movements along* the downward-sloping labor demand curve.

We also can explain why a firm's labor demand curve would *shift*. For example, if the price (*P*) of the good (resumes) rises—perhaps because the demand curve for resumes shifts outward—then the marginal revenue product of labor ($MRP = P \text{ X } MP$) will rise and the firm will be willing to employ more workers at any given wage level. This result implies that the demand curve for labor will shift outward. Similarly, a rise in the marginal product of labor (*MP*) also will lead the firm to increase the quantity demanded of labor at each wage level, shifting the labor demand curve outward. On the other hand, a decline in the price (*P*) or a decline in the marginal product (*MP*) will shift the labor demand curve to the left.

What if the Firm Has Market Power?

This approach to deriving the demand curve for labor works equally well for the case of a firm that is not a price-taker but instead is a monopoly or a monopolistic competitor. Figure 13.5 shows an example of such a firm. The key difference between the firm in Figure 13.3 and this firm is in the column for the price. Rather than facing a constant price for its output and thus a horizontal demand curve, this firm faces a downward-sloping demand curve: It can increase the quantity of resumes demanded by lowering its price. For example, if Getajob's resumes are differentiated slightly from those of other resume producers in town, then the demand curve that Getajob faces when selling resumes may be downward sloping.

Once we observe that the price and output are inversely related, we can continue just as we did with the competitive firm. Again, total revenue is equal to the price times the quantity, and marginal revenue product is the change in total revenue as one more worker is hired. Again, the marginal revenue product declines as more workers are hired, as shown in the last column of Figure 13.5. However, now the marginal revenue product declines more sharply as more workers are employed, and it even turns negative. It turns negative as more workers are hired and more output is produced and sold, because the price of output must fall. This cuts into revenue because all units, not just the last unit, are sold at the lower price. But the principle of labor demand is the same: Firms hire up to the point at which the marginal revenue product of labor equals the wage. The marginal revenue product determines the labor demand curve.

In the case of a firm with market power, the simple relationship $MRP = P \text{X} MP$ no longer holds, however, because the firm does not take the market price as given. Instead, we replace the price (P) by the more general marginal revenue (MR) in that relationship. Marginal revenue product is now equal to the marginal revenue (MR) times the marginal product (MP). The relationship $MRP = MR \text{X} MP$ holds for all firms, whether they have market power or not. Only for a competitive firm is $MR = P$.

FIGURE 13.5 Labor Input and Marginal Revenue Product for a Firm with Power to Affect the Market Price

Workers Employed Each Week (*L*)	Quantity Produced (*Q*)	Marginal Product of Labor (*MP*)	Price of Output (dollars) (*P*)	Total Revenue (dollars) (*TR*)	Marginal Revenue Product of Labor (dollars) (*MRP*)
0	0	—	100	0	—
1	17	17	92	1,564	1,564
2	31	14	85	2,635	1,071
3	42	11	79	3,318	683
4	51	9	75	3,825	507
5	58	7	71	4,118	293
6	63	5	69	4,347	229
7	66	3	67	4,422	75
8	68	2	66	4,488	66
9	69	1	65	4,485	-3
		Change in Q / Change in L	P declines with Q	P×Q	Change in TR / Change in L

Market Demand for Labor

To get the demand for labor in the market as a whole, we must add up the labor demand curves for all the firms demanding workers in the labor market. At each wage, we sum the total quantity of labor demanded by all firms in the market; this is illustrated in Figure 13.6 for the case of two firms producing resumes. The two curves on the left are the labor demand curves for two resume-producing firms, Getajob and Careerpro. (The curves are smoothed out compared with that in Figure 13.4 so that they are easier to see.) The process of summing individual firms' demands for labor to get the market demand is analogous to summing individual demand curves for goods to get the market demand curve for goods. At each wage, we sum the labor demand at all the firms to get the market demand.

3.3 A Comparison of $MRP = W$ with $MC = P$

A firm's decision to employ workers is closely tied to its decision about how much to produce. We have emphasized the former decision in this chapter and the latter decision in earlier chapters. To draw attention to this connection, Figure 13.7 shows the marginal cost when the wage is $600. Marginal cost is equal to the change in variable costs divided by the change in quantity produced. Variable costs are the wage times the amount of labor employed.

Now, consider the quantity of output the firm would produce if it compared price and marginal cost as discussed in earlier chapters. If the price of output is $100, the firm will produce 58 resumes, the highest level of output for which price is greater than marginal cost. This is exactly what we found using the $MRP = W$ rule, because 58 units of output require five workers. Recall that employing five workers is the profit-maximizing labor choice when the wage is $600.

FIGURE 13.6 **Summing Firms' Demands to Get the Labor Market Demand Curve**

The labor demand curve in the market is obtained by summing the quantities of labor demanded by all the firms at each wage.

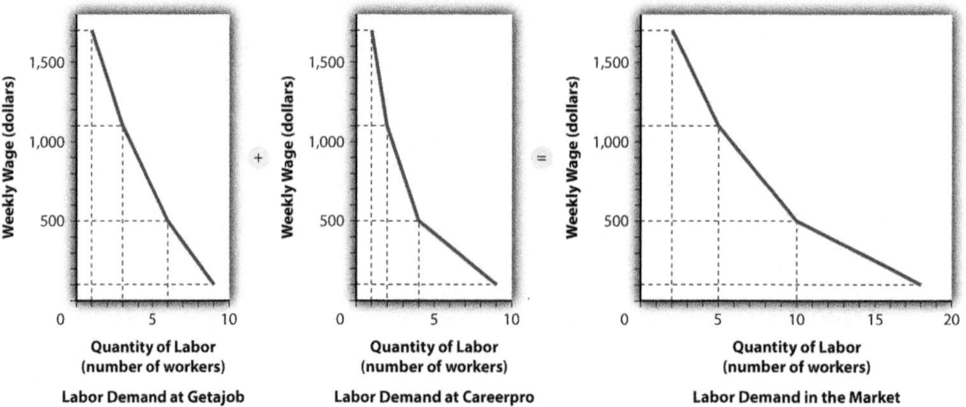

FIGURE 13.7 **Marginal Cost and the Production Decision at Getajob**

Workers Employed Each Week (*L*)	Quantity Produced (*Q*)	Variable Costs (dollars) (*VC*)	Marginal Cost (dollars) (*MC*)
0	0	0	0
1	17	600	35
2	31	1,200	43
3	42	1,800	55
4	51	2,400	67
5	58	3,000	86
6	63	3,600	120
7	66	4,200	200
8	68	4,800	300
9	69	5,400	600

$600 wage × *L*

$\frac{\text{Change in } VC}{\text{Change in } Q}$

If the profit-maximizing firm could produce fractional units, then it would set marginal cost exactly equal to price ($MC = P$). The resulting production decision would be exactly the same as that implied by the rule that the marginal revenue product of labor equals the wage.

REVIEW

- The demand for labor is a relationship between the quantity of labor a firm will employ and the wage, which is the price of labor.
- The demand for labor is a derived demand because it is derived from the goods and services produced by labor.
- If the marginal revenue product of an additional worker exceeds the wage, the firm should employ that worker. If the marginal revenue product of an additional worker is less than the wage, the firm should not employ that worker.
- Accordingly, a profit-maximizing firm will hire workers until the marginal revenue product of labor equals the wage.
- When the wage rises, the quantity of labor demanded by firms declines. When the wage falls, the quantity of labor demanded increases. These are movements along the labor demand curve.
- When the marginal revenue product of labor rises, the demand curve for that type of labor shifts outward. The marginal revenue product of labor can increase if either the marginal product of labor rises or the price of the good produced using labor rises.
- The market demand for labor is obtained by adding up the labor demand curves of all firms looking for workers in the labor market.

4. LABOR SUPPLY

We now focus on *labor supply*. An individual's labor supply curve is derived from that person's decision about whether to work and how much to work, at different wage rates. The market labor supply curve is the sum of many people's individual labor supply curves. The decision about whether to work and how much to work depends very much on individual circumstances, so we begin by examining the individual's decision.

4.1 Work versus Two Alternatives: Home Work and Leisure

Consider a person deciding how much to work—either how many hours a week or how many weeks a year. As with any economic decision, we need to consider the alternative to work. Economists traditionally have called the alternative *leisure*, although many of the activities that make up the alternative to work are not normally thought of as leisure. These activities include "home work," like painting the house or caring for children at home, as well as pure leisure time, such as simply talking to friends on the telephone, going bowling, or hiking in the country. The price of leisure is the opportunity cost of not working, that is, the wage. If a person's marginal benefit from more leisure is greater than the wage, then the person will choose more leisure. The decision to consume more leisure is thus like the decision to consume more of any other good. This analogy may seem strange, but it works quite well in practice.

Effects of Wage Changes: Income and Substitution Effects

Like the decision to consume a commodity, the decision to work can be analyzed with the concepts of the *substitution effect* and the *income effect*.

Recall that the *substitution effect* says that a higher price for a good will make that good less attractive to purchase relative to alternatives. In the case of the labor market, because the wage is the price of leisure (or home work), the higher the wage, the less attractive leisure (or home work) will seem relative to work. In other words, a higher wage makes work more rewarding compared with the alternatives. So even if you really enjoy your nonwork activities, including sleeping, watching movies, playing video games, or even studying, if the wage paid for part-time student employment triples from $10 an hour to $30 an hour, you would be more likely to sacrifice these nonwork activities and work an extra hour each day. The sacrifice—less time to study, sleep, watch television, and so on—will be worth the higher wage. Therefore, the quantity of labor supplied tends to increase when the wage rises because of the substitution effect.

Recall also that the *income effect* reflects the fact that changes in the price of a good either reduce (if a price increase) or expand (if a price decrease) your ability to buy all goods, even ones whose prices have not changed, by changing your real income. In the case of the labor market, a higher wage will increase the real income of an individual and enable that individual to buy more of all goods, including leisure. For example, if you were working 10 hours a week at a wage of $10 an hour, you might decide that at a wage of $30 an hour, you would be happier working five hours a week and enjoying five more hours of leisure. In this case, even after working fewer hours, you have more money to buy other goods. The income effect works in the opposite direction from the substitution effect: The quantity of labor supplied tends to decrease, rather than increase, when the wage rises because of the income effect.

The Shape of Supply Curves

Because the substitution effect and the income effect work in opposite directions, the labor supply curve can slope either upward or downward. The supply curve slopes upward if the substitution effect dominates—that is, as the wage rises, individuals work more because the price of leisure (the opportunity cost of not working) rises. The labor supply curve slopes downward if the income effect dominates—as the wage rises, individuals choose to work less because they can earn as much if not more money by working fewer hours. Several possibilities for the shape of a labor supply curve are illustrated in Figure 13.8.

backward-bending labor supply curve

The situation in which the income effect outweighs the substitution effect of an increase in the wage at higher levels of income, causing the labor supply curve to bend back and take on a negative slope.

Moreover, the same supply curve may slope upward for some range of wages and downward for another range. For example, at high wage levels—when people earn enough to take long vacations—the income effect may dominate. At lower wages, the substitution effect may be dominant, which then would result in a **backward-bending labor supply curve**, as shown in Figure 13.9.

This derivation of the labor supply curve may seem unrealistic. After all, the work week is forty hours for many jobs; you may not have much choice about the number of hours you work per week. In fact, the sensitivity of the quantity of labor supplied to the wage is probably small for many workers. But economists have shown that the effect is large for some workers, and therefore it is useful to distinguish one worker's supply curve from another's.

In a family with two adults and children, for example, one of the adults already may have a job and the other may be choosing between working at home and working outside the home. This decision may be sensitive to the wage and perhaps the cost of childcare or of consuming more prepared meals. In fact, the increased number of women working outside the home may be the result of increased opportunities and wages for women. The increase in the wage induces workers to work more in the labor market. Economists have observed a fairly strong wage effect on the amount women work.

FIGURE 13.8 Three Labor Supply Curves

The three curves differ in the relative strength of the income and substitution effects. The labor supply curve on the left slopes upward because the substitution effect is stronger than the income effect. For the curve on the right, the income effect is stronger than the substitution effect. For the vertical curve in the middle, the two effects are the same.

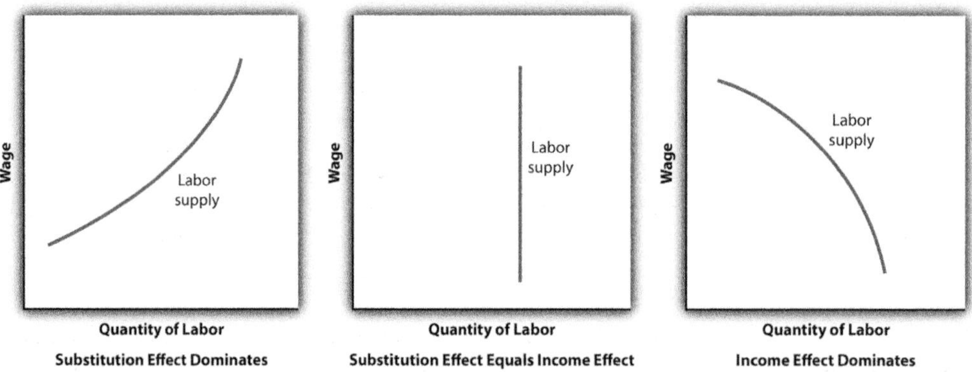

One also needs to distinguish between the effects of a temporary change in the wage and those of a more permanent change. Empirical studies show that the quantity of labor supplied rises more in response to a temporary increase in the wage than to a permanent increase. What's the explanation? Consider an example. If you have a special one-time opportunity tomorrow to earn $100 an hour rather than your usual $6 an hour, you are likely to put off some leisure for one day; the substitution effect dominates. But if you are lucky enough to land a lifetime job at $100 an hour rather than $6 an hour, you may decide to work fewer hours and have more leisure time; the income effect dominates.

This difference between temporary and permanent changes helps explain the dramatic decline in the average hours worked per week as wages have risen over the last century. These are more permanent changes, for which the income effect dominates.

FIGURE 13.9 Backward-Bending Labor Supply Curve

A person may have a labor supply curve that is positively sloped for a low wage, is steeper for a higher wage, and then bends backward for a still higher wage.

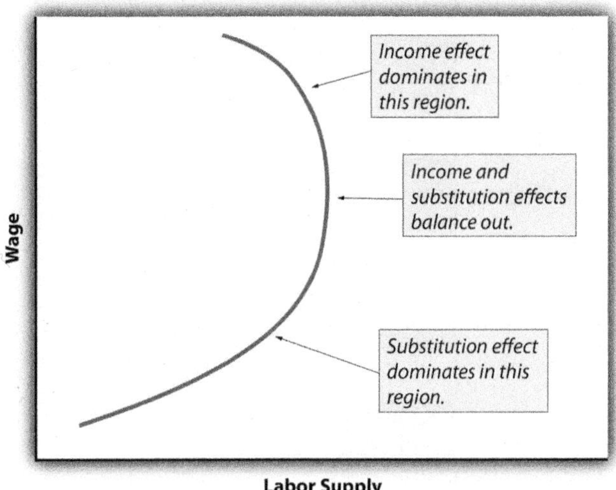

4.2 Work vs. Another Alternative: Getting Human Capital

The skills of a worker depend in part on how much schooling and training the worker has had. The decision to obtain these skills—to finish high school and attend a community college or obtain a four-year college degree—is much like the choice between work and leisure. In fact, an important decision for many young people is whether to go to work or to finish high school; if they have finished high school, the choice is whether to go to work or to go to college.

Economists view the education and training that raise skills and productivity as a form of *investment*, a decision to spend funds or time on something now because it pays off in the future. Continuing the analogy, an investment in a college education raises the amount of **human capital**—a person's knowledge and skills—in the same way that the investment in a factory or machine by a business firm raises physical capital. Figure 13.10 demonstrates the kind of difference this investment can make.

human capital

A person's accumulated knowledge and skills.

The decision to invest in human capital can be approached like any other economic choice. Suppose the decision is whether Angela should go to college or get a job. If she does not go to college, she saves on tuition and can begin earning an income right away. If she goes to college, she pays tuition and forgoes the opportunity to earn income at a full-time job. However, if Angela is like most people, college will improve her skills and land her a better job at higher pay. The returns on college education are the extra pay. Angela ought to go to college—invest in human capital—if the returns are greater than the cost.

People can increase their skills at work as well as in school. In fact, **on-the-job training** is one of the most important ways in which workers' productivity increases. On-the-job training can be either *firm specific*, in which case the skills are useful only at one firm, or *general purpose*, in which case the skills are transferable to other jobs.

on-the-job training

The building of the skills of a firm's employees while they work for the firm.

FIGURE 13.10 **Higher Education and Economic Success**

According to this chart, education pays off in terms of earnings, with doctorate degree holders earning the most, followed by workers with professional and master's degrees. The data shown are for 2016.

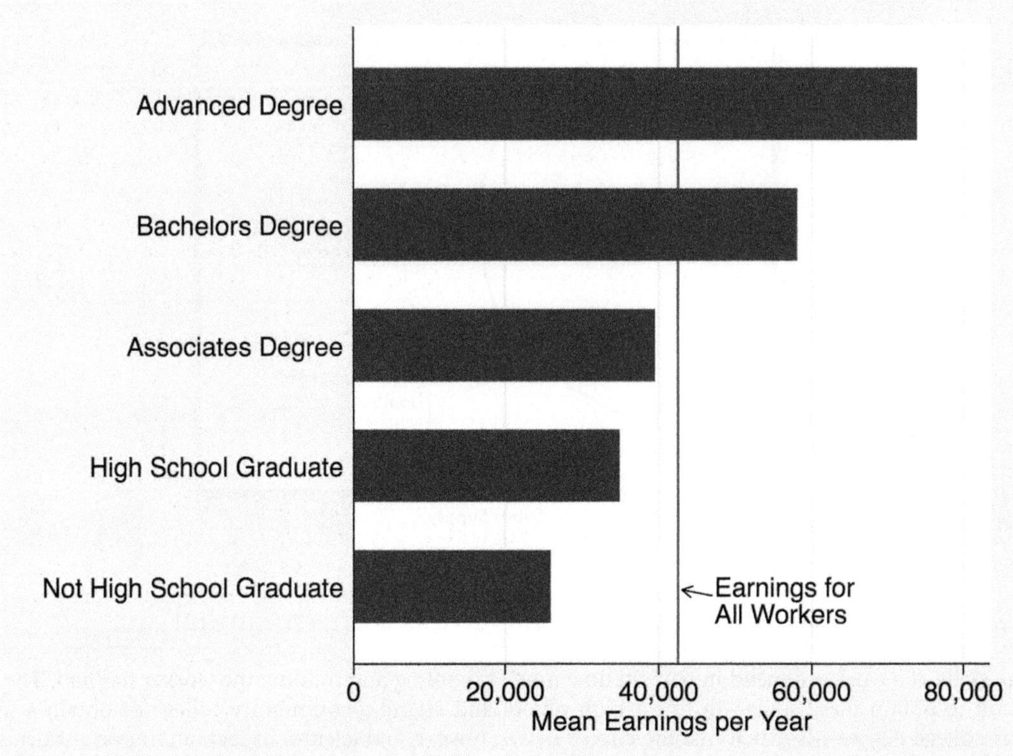

Source: Bureau of Labor Statistics, Current Population Survey (weekly earnings figure multiplied by 50).

REVIEW

- An individual's labor supply curve can be viewed as the outcome of the choice between work and some other activity, whether home work or leisure.
- Wages can be thought of as the price of that alternative activity, whether home work or leisure. This is because the opportunity cost of allocating an hour to that activity is the forgone wage that could have been earned from work.
- Changes in wages have both a substitution effect and an income effect on the labor supply. The substitution effect is that as wages rise, the cost of not working rises—the attractiveness of work increases relative to its alternatives. The income effect is that a rise in the wage increases the real income of an individual and enables that individual to enjoy more of all goods, including leisure.
- The income effect will tend to lower the incentive to work as the wage rises, while the substitution effect will increase the incentive to work. In some situations, the substitution effect dominates, leading to an increase in the quantity of labor supplied as the wage rises—an upward-sloping labor curve. In other situations, the income effect dominates, leading to a decrease in the quantity of labor supplied as the wage rises—a downward-sloping labor curve.
- Individuals also have to make decisions between working and acquiring human capital through education and training. Then the cost of acquiring human capital is the forgone wages, whereas the benefit of human capital is the extra wages one can earn using the knowledge and skills accumulated from going to school or receiving on-the-job training. If the returns are greater than the costs, then individuals should continue with their education.

5. EXPLAINING WAGE TRENDS AND DIFFERENCES

5.1 Labor Productivity

When we combine the labor demand and labor supply curves derived in the previous two sections, we get the model of the labor market summarized in Figure 13.2. The model predicts that the wage in the labor market will be at the intersection of the supply and demand curves. The point of intersection, where the quantity of labor supplied equals the quantity of labor demanded, is the **labor market equilibrium**.

labor market equilibrium

The situation in which the quantity of labor supplied equals the quantity of labor demanded.

The model also predicts that the equilibrium wage equals the marginal revenue product. If the marginal product of labor employed at a firm increases, then the model predicts that the firm's labor demand curve will shift to the right, as the firm will be willing to hire more workers at any given wage. Suppose the marginal product of labor rises for the economy as a whole; then the labor demand curve for the economy should shift to the right and both the equilibrium quantity of labor and the equilibrium wage should also rise. Is this what occurs in reality?

The Relationship between Real Wages and Labor Productivity

The lines in Figure 13.11 show the relationship between output per hour of work and the real wage. Output per hour of work is called **labor productivity** and is a good indication of trends in the marginal product of labor on average in the United States. Labor productivity growth in the United States was robust in the decade from the mid-1990s to the mid-2000s; it has slowed down somewhat since then. The labor market model predicts that wages in the United States should increase when labor productivity increases. Do they?

labor productivity

Output per hour of work.

Figure 13.11 shows a strong correlation between labor productivity and the real wage. As labor productivity declined in the 1970s and 1980s, so did real wages and when labor productivity rebounded in the late 1990s, so did real wages. Note that the empirical association between wages and labor productivity was less pronounced in the period leading up to the 2008/09 recession. Nevertheless, the data series shown in this chart suggests that labor productivity is a key explanation of changes in real wages over time.

FIGURE 13.11 Labor Productivity Growth and Real Wage Growth

As the figure shows, real wages and labor productivity are correlated. The relationship is not perfect though, in the 1980s and 1990s, real wage growth was consistently lower than labor productivity growth even though the two series seemed to move in concert to each other.

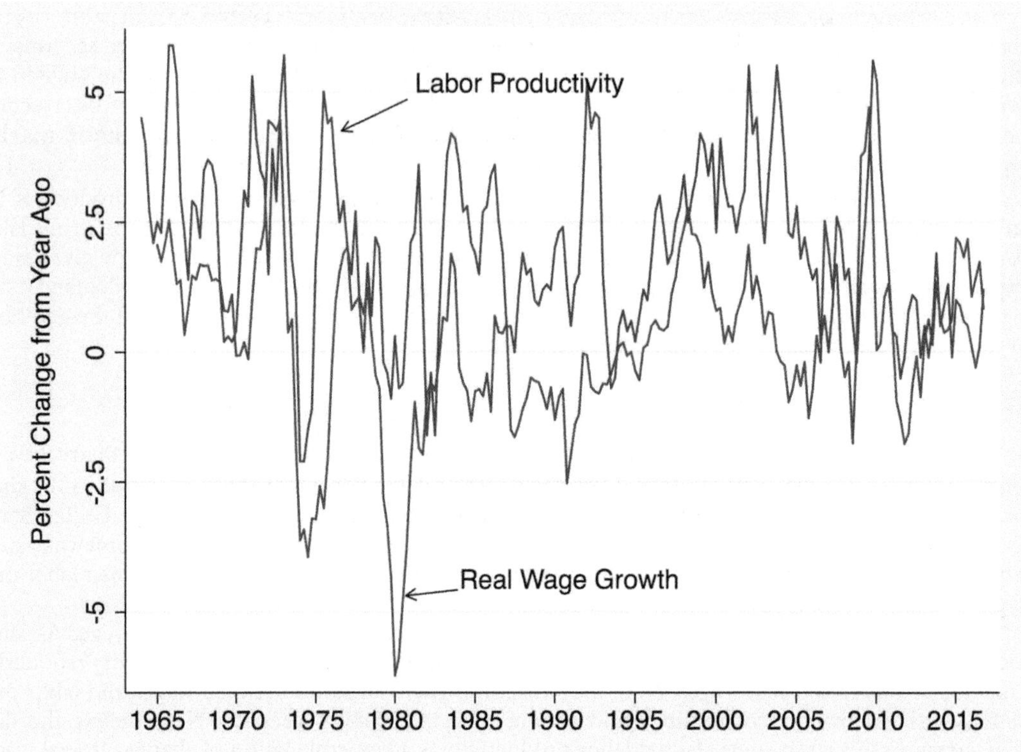

Source: Author's calculation following a data exercise suggested by the St. Louis Fed Economics blog of 8/29/2016, at https://fredblog.stlouisfed.org/2016/08/testing-theory-marginal-product-and-wages/.

5.2 Wage Dispersion and Productivity

Can labor productivity also explain wage differences between groups of people? As we saw earlier in this chapter, real wages vary across workers depending on their occupation, the industry they work in, full- or part-time status, union status, and education, among other reasons. For instance, if the marginal product of labor increases with additional skills from investment in human capital, then, on average, wages for people with a college education should be higher than those for people without a college education. Hence, productivity differences are an explanation for the wage gap between workers who do not receive education beyond high school and those who are college educated.

Although human capital differences undoubtedly explain some of the dispersion of wages, some people have argued that the greater productivity of college-educated workers is due not to the skills learned in college, but to the fact that colleges screen applicants. For example, people who are not highly motivated or who have difficulty communicating have trouble getting into college. Hence, college graduates would earn higher wages even if they learned nothing in college. If this is so, a college degree signals to employers that the graduate is likely to be a productive worker.

Unfortunately, it is difficult to distinguish the skill-enhancing from the signaling effects of college. Certainly your grades and your major in college affect the kind of job you get and how much you earn, suggesting that more than signaling is important to employers. In reality, signaling and human capital both probably have a role to play in explaining the higher wages of college graduates.

Whether it is signaling or human capital that explains the higher wages of college graduates, labor productivity differences still are the underlying explanation for the wage differences. Labor productivity, however, does not explain everything about wages. Consider now some other factors.

Compensating Wage Differentials

Not all jobs that require workers with the same level of skill and productivity are alike. Some jobs are more pleasant, less stressful, or safer than other jobs. For example, the skills necessary to be a deep-sea salvage diver and a lifeguard are similar—good at swimming, good judgment, and good health. But the risks—such as decompression sickness—for a deep-sea diver are greater and the opportunity for social interaction is less. If the pay for both jobs were the same, say, $10 per hour, most people would prefer the lifeguard job.

But this situation could not last. With many lifeguard applicants, the beach authorities would be unlikely to raise the wage above $10 and might even try to cut the wage if they faced budget cuts. With few applicants, the deep-sea salvage companies would have to raise the wage. After a while, it would not be surprising to see the equilibrium wage for lifeguards at $9 per hour and the equilibrium wage for deep-sea divers at $18 per hour. Thus, we would be in a situation in which the skills of the workers were identical, but their wages were much different. The higher-risk job pays a higher wage than the lower-risk job.

Situations in which wages differ because of the characteristics of the job are widespread. Hazardous duty pay is common in the military. Wage data show that night-shift workers in manufacturing plants are paid wages that are about 3 percent higher on average than those of daytime workers, presumably to compensate for the inconvenience.

High Wages for High Work: Compensating wage differentials are illustrated by the relatively high wages paid to someone for performing risky jobs such as window washing on a skyscraper.

Source: © Shutterstock, Inc.

Such differences in wages are called **compensating wage differentials**. They are an important source of differences in wages that are not based on marginal product. With compensating differentials, workers may seek out riskier jobs to be paid more.

compensating wage differentials

A difference in wages for people with similar skills based on some characteristic of the job, such as riskiness, discomfort, or inconvenience of the work schedule.

Discrimination

As noted, a gap in earnings exists between women and men, even though that gap has been narrowing in recent years. Women now make close to 80 percent of the wages of men, whereas 50 years ago, women earned only about 50 percent of the wages of men. The gap between the wages of blacks and whites is also closing, although not quite as quickly. In the 1950s, the ratio of the wages of blacks to those of whites was about 60 percent; it has narrowed to about 70 percent since then. Wage differences between white and minority workers and between men and women are indications of discrimination if the wage differences cannot be explained by differences in marginal product or other factors unrelated to race or gender.

Some, but not all, of these differences may be attributed to differences in human capital. The wage gaps between blacks and whites and between men and women with comparable education and job experience are smaller than the ratios in the preceding paragraph. But a gap still exists.

Discrimination on the basis of race or gender prejudice can explain such differences. This is shown in Figure 13.12. *Discrimination* can be defined in the supply and demand model as not hiring women or minority workers even though their marginal product is just as high as that of other workers, or paying a lower wage to such workers even though their marginal product is equal to that of other workers. Either way, discrimination can be interpreted as a leftward shift of the labor demand curve for women or minority workers. As shown in Figure 13.12, this reduces the wages and employment for those discriminated against.

FIGURE 13.12 Discrimination in the Labor Market

Firms that discriminate against women pay them a wage that is less than their marginal product. But this gives other firms an opportunity to recruit workers from prejudiced firms by paying higher wages.

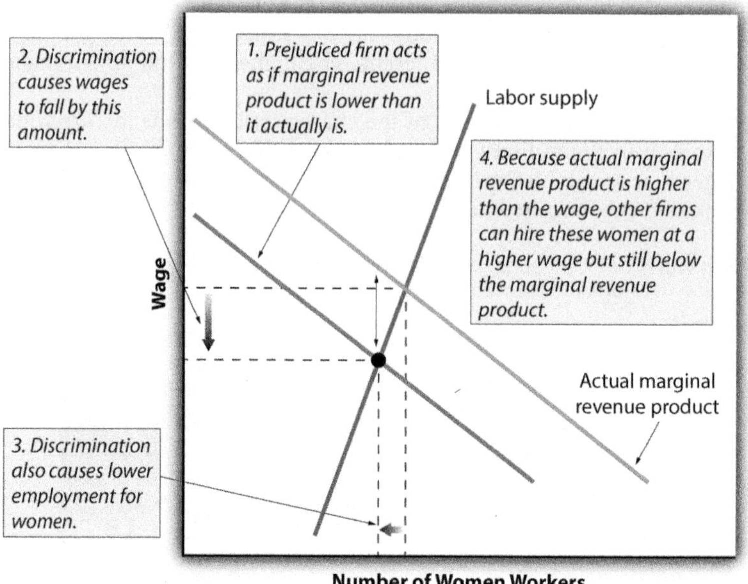

An important implication of this supply and demand interpretation of the effects of discrimination is that competition among firms may reduce it. Why might competition reduce discrimination? Remember that a firm will increase profits if the wage is less than the marginal revenue product. If markets are competitive, then firms that discriminate against women or minorities will pay them a wage lower than their marginal revenue product, as shown in Figure 13.12. In this situation, any profit-maximizing firm will see that it can raise its profits by paying these workers a little more—but still less than their marginal revenue product—and hiring them away from firms that discriminate. Thus, firms in competitive markets that discriminate will lose out to firms that do not. Much like firms that do not keep their costs as low as other firms, they eventually will be driven out of the industry. This advantage of competitive markets should be added to the advantages mentioned thus far. Furthermore, competition for workers will raise wages until the wages eventually are equal to the marginal products of labor.

This description of events relies on a market's being competitive. If firms have monopoly power or entry is limited, so that economic profits are not driven to zero, then discrimination can continue to exist. That discrimination effects on wages do persist may be a sign of market power and barriers to entry. In any case, laws against discrimination give those who are discriminated against for race, gender, or other reasons the right to sue those who are discriminating.

FIGURE 13.13 Effects of a Minimum Wage

If government restrictions on wages hold them above the labor market equilibrium, then a surplus (unemployment) will arise. Unemployment is more likely for unskilled workers because the equilibrium wage is lower.

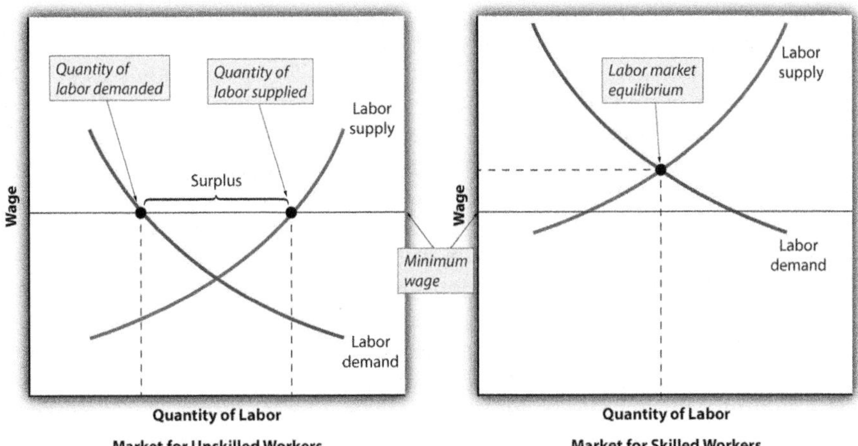

Some laws have been proposed requiring that employers pay the same wage to workers with comparable skills. Such proposals are called *comparable worth proposals.* The intent of such proposals is to align the wages of different groups. However, such laws might force wages to be the same in situations in which wages are different for reasons other than discrimination, such as compensating wage differentials. This law would lead to shortages or surpluses, much as price ceilings or price floors in any market do. In the lifeguard/deep-sea diver example, a law requiring employers to pay lifeguards and deep-sea divers the same wage would cause a surplus of lifeguards and a shortage of deep-sea divers. For example, suppose that with comparable worth legislation, the wage for both lifeguards and deep-sea divers was $10 per hour. Because the labor market equilibrium wage for lifeguards, $9 per hour, is less than $10 per hour, there would be a surplus of lifeguards: More people would be willing to be lifeguards than employers would be willing to hire. And because the labor market equilibrium wage for deep-sea divers, $18 per hour, is greater than $10, there would be a shortage of deep-sea divers: Firms would be willing to hire more deep-sea divers than the number of deep-sea divers willing to dive for the $10 per hour wage.

Minimum Wage Laws

Another example in which the wages received by a worker may not be connected to the worker's marginal product is seen when the government stipulates a wage floor, or a *minimum wage,* which must be paid to workers. Because wages differ due to skills, the impact of the minimum wage depends on the skills of the workers. Figure 13.13 shows what the supply and demand model predicts about the impact of the minimum wage on skilled and unskilled workers. A labor market for unskilled workers is shown on the left; the minimum wage is shown to be above the labor market equilibrium wage. Thus, a surplus arises, or unemployment: The quantity of labor demanded by firms at the minimum wage is less than the quantity of labor that workers are willing to supply at that wage. A labor market for skilled workers is shown on the right: The minimum wage is shown to be below the market equilibrium wage for skilled workers. Thus, a minimum wage at the level shown in the graph would not cause unemployment among skilled workers.

Therefore, the labor supply and demand model predicts that the minimum wage is a cause of unemployment among less skilled or less experienced workers, and thereby ends up hurting some of the least well off in society. This unintended result is why many economists are concerned about the impact of minimum wage legislation.

In interpreting this result, remember that the supply and demand model is a *model* of reality, not reality itself. Although the model explains much about wages, its predictions about minimum wage laws should be verified like the predictions of any other economic model. In fact, labor economists have been trying to check the predictions of the model for the minimum wage for many years. Some economists, such as David Card of the University of California at Berkeley and Alan Krueger of Princeton University, have examined the effects of different minimum wage laws in different states on low skilled fast-food workers and have not found evidence of the predicted impact on unemployment. Others, like David Neumark of Michigan State University and William Wascher of the Federal Reserve, have disputed Card's and Krueger's data and have found that the minimum wage enacted in those same states did have a negative effect on employment.

Fixed Wage Contracts

The agreement to buy or sell labor is frequently a long-term one. Job-specific training and the difficulty of changing jobs make quick turnover costly for both firms and workers. Most workers would prefer a certain wage to an uncertain one; such workers will prefer a fixed wage that does not change every time the marginal revenue product changes. Long-term arrangements of this kind are quite common. A worker—a person working at Getajob, for example—is hired at a given weekly wage. If marginal revenue product declines because of a week of stormy winter weather with frequent power outages, Getajob will not reduce the weekly wage. On the other hand, when college graduation season arrives in May, the Getajob workers will have to work harder—their marginal revenue product will rise—but they will not be paid a higher wage. Thus, the weekly wage does not change with the actual week-to-week changes in the marginal revenue product of the worker. The wage reflects marginal revenue product over a longer period. Most workers in the United States are paid in this way.

piece-rate system

A system by which workers are paid a specific amount per unit they produce.

An alternative wage payment arrangement endeavors to match productivity with the wage much more closely. Such contracts are used when the weekly or hourly wage does not provide sufficient *incentive* or in cases in which the manager cannot observe the worker carefully. Under a **piece-rate system**, the specific amount that workers are paid depends on how much they produce. Thus, if their marginal product drops off, for whatever reason, they are paid less. Piece rates are common in the apparel and agriculture industries.

Consider California lettuce growers, for example. The growers hire crews of workers to cut and pack the lettuce. A typical crew consists of two cutters and one packer, who split their earnings equally. The crew is paid a piece rate, about $1.20 for a box of lettuce that might contain two dozen heads of lettuce. A three-person crew can pick and pack about 75 boxes an hour. Thus, each worker can earn about $30 an hour. But if they slack off, their wages decline rapidly.

On the same lettuce farms, the truck drivers, the workers who carry the boxes to the trucks, and the workers who wash the lettuce may be paid by the hour. Why the difference? Piece rates are used when it is difficult to monitor the quantity of a worker's effort. If you pay crews of lettuce workers in the field by the hour, then some of them will put in less effort and generate less output. Paying them according to the quantity of lettuce they pick ensures that those with the highest marginal revenue product earn the highest wages. This system would not work with the workers washing lettuce at the main building or the workers carrying the boxes to the trucks. The quality of their work (whether the lettuce was damaged by rough handling, whether all the dirt was properly washed out) cannot be measured as easily as with the lettuce pickers. These workers might sacrifice quality for speed under a piece-rate system.

Deferred Wage Payments

deferred payment contracts

An agreement between a worker and an employer whereby the worker is paid less than the marginal revenue product when young, and subsequently paid more than the marginal revenue product when old.

Yet another payment arrangement occurs when a firm pays workers less than their marginal revenue product when they are young and more than their marginal revenue product at a later time as a reward for working hard. Lawyers and accountants frequently work hard at their firms when they are young; if they do well, they make partner and then are paid much more than their marginal revenue product when they are older. Such contracts are called **deferred payment contracts**. Generous retirement plans are another form of deferred payment contract. A reward for staying at the firm and working hard is a nice retirement package.

REVIEW

- The labor supply and demand model predicts that economywide increases in marginal product should lead to an increase in the real wage.
- Using labor productivity as a measure of marginal product for an economy, we can see that the growth rate of labor productivity is positively correlated with the growth rate of real wages. The relationship was especially strong in the mid-1990s.
- Differences in labor productivity also provide an explanation for some of the differences in wages across groups, especially the differences between workers with different levels of education.
- Other factors bring about a disconnect between labor productivity and real wages. These include compensating wage differentials, discrimination, minimum wage laws, fixed wage contracts, and deferred wage payments.
- Compensating wage differentials occur because some jobs are more attractive than others. Workers with the same level of productivity will earn more in the sector that is less desirable to work in.
- Discrimination reduces the wages of those who are discriminated against below their marginal revenue product. Competition can be a force against the effects of discrimination because other firms can step in and hire the workers who are being discriminated against, offering to pay them a wage that is higher than what they currently are getting but still less than their marginal revenue product.
- Minimum wage laws also can lead to workers being paid a wage higher than their marginal revenue product. If the government imposes a minimum wage that is higher than the marginal revenue product of unskilled workers, it will cause some of these workers to lose their jobs, while the lucky ones earn a wage that is higher than what their marginal revenue product will indicate.
- Many labor market transactions are long term. Most employees receive a fixed hourly or weekly wage, even though their marginal revenue product fluctuates.
- In certain types of jobs, piece-rate contracts adjust the payment directly according to actual marginal product; they are a way to increase incentives to be more productive.
- Deferred compensation is another form of payment that aims at improving incentives and worker motivation.

6. LABOR UNIONS

The model of labor supply and demand also can help us understand the impact of labor unions. **Labor unions** such as the United Auto Workers or the United Farm Workers are organizations with the stated aim of improving the wages and working conditions of their members. There are two types of unions: **Industrial unions** represent most of the workers in an industry—such as the rubber workers, farm workers, or steelworkers—regardless of their occupation; **craft unions** represent workers in a single occupation or group of occupations, such as printers or dockworkers. In the 1930s and 1940s, disputes arose between those organizing craft unions and industrial unions. John L. Lewis, a labor union leader, argued that craft unions were not suitable for large numbers of unskilled workers. Hence, he and other union leaders split in 1936 from the American Federation of Labor (AFL), a group representing many labor unions, and formed the Congress of Industrial Organizations(CIO). It was not until 1955 that the AFL and the CIO resolved their disputes and merged; one reason behind their reconciliation was that union membership was beginning to decline.

Labor unions

A coalition of workers, organized to improve the wages and working conditions of the members.

Industrial unions

A union organized within a given industry, whose members come from a variety of occupations.

craft unions

A union organized to represent a single occupation, whose members come from a variety of industries.

But the decline continued. In 2005, a split occurred within the AFL-CIO. Three large unions representing service workers, truck drivers, and food and commercial workers withdrew from the AFL-CIO, expressing their unhappiness over the decline of union membership. About 12.5 percent of the U.S. labor force currently is unionized, down from about 25 percent in the mid-1950s. The fraction is much higher in other countries.

Unions negotiate with firms on behalf of their members in a collective bargaining process. Federal law, including the National Labor Relations Act (1935), gives workers the right to organize into unions and bargain with employers. The National Labor Relations Board has been set up to ensure that firms do not illegally prevent workers from organizing and to monitor union elections of leaders.

In studying unions, it is important to distinguish between the union leaders who speak for the union members and the union members themselves. Like politicians, union leaders must be elected, and as with politicians, we sometimes can better understand the actions of union leaders by assuming that they are motivated by the desire to be elected or reelected.

6.1 Union-Nonunion Wage Differentials

Studies of the wages of union workers and nonunion workers have shown that union wages are about 15 percent higher than nonunion wages, even when workers' skills are the same. Two different theories explain how unions raise wages.

The Restricted Supply Explanation

One theory is that unions raise wages by restricting supply. By restricting membership, for example, they shift the labor supply curve to the left, raising wages, just as a monopolist raises the price of the good it sells by restricting supply. But when a union restricts supply, workers outside the union in another industry get paid less.

This effect of unions is illustrated in Figure 13.14. The graph on the right is one industry; the graph on the left is another industry. Suppose both industries require workers of the same skill level. Imagine the situation before the union is formed. Then the wages for the workers on the left and on the right in Figure 13.14 would be the same.

Now suppose a union organizes the industry on the left. Wages rise in the industry on the left, but the quantity of labor demanded in the industry falls. The workers in the industry on the left who become unemployed probably will move to the industry on the right. As they do so, the labor supply curve in the right-hand graph of Figure 13.14 shifts and the wage in that industry declines. Thus, a wage gap between the similarly skilled union and nonunion workers is created.

The Increased Productivity Explanation

Another theory, which was developed extensively in the book *What Do Unions Do?* by Richard Freeman and James Medoff of Harvard University, is that labor unions raise the wages of workers by increasing their marginal product. They do this by providing a channel of communication with management, motivating workers, and providing a democratic means of resolving disputes.

FIGURE 13.14 The Effect of Unions on Wages

According to one view of labor unions, the union wage is increased relative to nonunion wages as a result of restricting the supply of workers. The supply in the union sector is reduced, but the supply in the nonunion sector is increased.

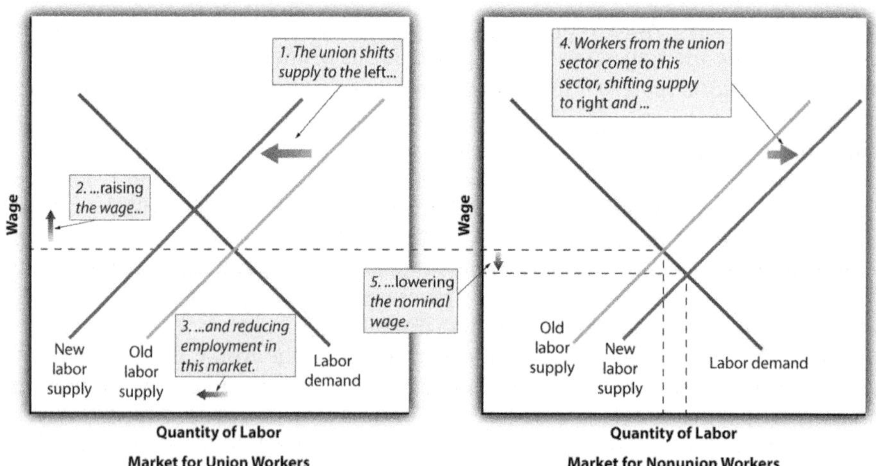

A worker who has a dispute with the management of a firm or who sees the opportunity to get a higher wage at another firm, in principle, could move. But such moves can have huge costs: The firm may have invested in job-specific training, and the worker might like the area where the firm is located. In situations in which exit from a firm is costly, people find other ways to improve their situation without exiting. The economist Albert Hirschman, in a famous book called *Exit, Voice, and Loyalty*, has called this alternative "voice." Rather than exit or quit, the worker may try to show the firm that a raise is deserved. Or the worker can discuss with the employer how conditions can be changed. The choice between exit and voice arises in many contexts: Should you transfer to a new college or tell the dean how the teaching might be improved? Should parents send their children to a private school or work to improve the local public school?

In many situations, exercising your voice requires collective action. If you alone complain to the dean, nothing much will happen, but if you organize a "students against lousy teaching" group, you may see some changes. Those who emphasize this collective-voice role of labor unions argue that unions provide a means through which workers improve their productivity. This collective-voice approach explains why the wages of union workers are higher than those of nonunion workers with the same skills and training.

6.2 Monopsony and Bilateral Monopoly

The analysis of labor unions in Figure 13.14 stresses the market power of unions as *sellers* of their members' labor in the labor market: By restricting supply, the union can raise the price of its members' wages, much as a monopolist or a group of oligopolists with market power can raise the price of the goods they sell.

However, the *buyers* in the labor market—that is, the firms that purchase the labor—also may have market power to affect the wage, contrary to the assumption we have made throughout this chapter that firms do not have such market power in the labor market. **Monopsony** is a situation in which only one buyer exists. By reducing its demand for the good (in this case, labor), a monopsony can reduce the price in the market (in this case, the wage). In fact, few examples of monopsony exist; most types of workers—such as sales clerks, accountants, or engineers—typically have many potential employers. Exceptions are found in small towns, for example, that have only one auto repair shop. Then, if auto mechanics do not want to move, the auto repair shop is effectively the only employer. Another exception is found in professional sports leagues, where team owners form agreements with one another restricting workers' (that is, the players') mobility between teams.

Monopsony

A situation in which there is a single buyer of a particular good or service in a given market.

The situation in which a market has only one seller (a monopoly) and one buyer (a monopsony) is called a **bilateral monopoly**. A labor market with one labor union deciding the labor supply (the monopolist) and one firm deciding the labor demand (the monopsonist) is an example of a bilateral monopoly. Even though we typically associate a monopolist with the creation of deadweight loss, the outcome of a bilateral monopoly is difficult to predict. Compared with a situation in which a monopsony faces competitive sellers, however, the bilateral monopoly can lead to a more efficient outcome.

bilateral monopoly

The situation in which there is one buyer and one seller in a market.

For instance, a firm with monopsony power over the labor market would choose to hire fewer workers, to drive down the wage, than would a group of competitive firms. By banding together in a labor union, the workers can confront this monopsony power with their own monopoly power. For example, they could refuse to work for less than the competitive wage. If their refusal is credible, they could take away the incentive for the monopsony to reduce labor demand because doing so would not reduce the wage. An example is in the arena of professional sports, in which powerful players' unions have helped reduce the effects of the teams' monopsony power and led to players' salaries rising dramatically in recent years. The players were aided in their cause by the erosion of teams' monopsony power through rulings that allowed for things like free agency in major league baseball.

REVIEW

- In the twenty-first century, less than 15 percent of U.S. workers belong to labor unions, a significant decline from the mid-1950s, when about a quarter of workers belonged to unions.
- Workers who belong to unions are paid about 15 percent more on average than workers with the same skills who are not in unions.
- One explanation for this difference is that labor unions improve productivity by improving worker motivation and providing workers with a collective voice.
- Another view is that labor unions raise productivity by restricting supply, much as a monopolist would, rather than by increasing productivity.
- In certain situations in which a single firm, a monopsonist, has market power in hiring workers, the creation of a labor union as a monopoly provider of labor services actually can increase the efficiency of the resulting market outcome.

7. END-OF-CHAPTER MATERIALS

7.1 Conclusion

In this chapter, we have shown that the labor supply and demand model is a powerful tool with many applications. In fact, the model may apply to you, so consider carefully what it implies.

First, increasing your own labor productivity is a good way to increase your earnings. Many of the large differences in wages across individuals and across time are due to differences in productivity. Productivity is enhanced by increases in human capital, whether obtained in school or on the job. Such human capital also will prove useful if your firm shuts down and you need to find another job.

Second, if you are choosing between two occupations that you like equally well, choose the one that is less popular with other students of your generation and for which it looks like demand will be increasing. Both the supply and the demand for labor affect the wage, and if the supply is expected to grow more rapidly than the demand in the occupation for which you are training, wages will not be as high as in the occupation for which labor is in relatively short supply.

Third, be sure to think about the wage you receive or the raises you get in real terms, not nominal terms, and make sure you are aware of fringe benefits offered or not offered. Fourth, think about your job in a long-term perspective. Partly for incentive reasons, some jobs pay little at the start, with the promise of higher payments later.

Key Points

1. When measuring workers' pay, it is important to consider fringe benefits and to adjust for inflation before comparing wages at different points in time.
2. Wage growth in the United States, which is defined by the real hourly average pay (including fringe benefits), began increasing at a faster rate in the mid-1990s but has flattened out somewhat more recently. Wage dispersion also has increased.
3. The supply and demand framework can be applied to the labor market to gain insight into labor market trends. The demand for labor is a derived demand that comes from the profit-maximizing decisions of firms. Firms adjust their employment until the marginal revenue product of labor becomes equal to the wage.
4. The supply curve for labor can be explained by looking at the choices of individuals or households. A person will work more hours if the wage is greater than the marginal benefit of more leisure.
5. An increase in the wage will have both an income effect (real income rises, so the worker does not have to work as many hours as before to afford other goods and services) and a substitution effect (the opportunity cost of engaging in leisure or home work activities instead of working rises, increasing the incentive to work).
6. The substitution effect and the income effect work in opposite directions, so that the labor supply curve can be upward sloping, vertical, downward sloping, or backward bending.
7. Long-term trends in wages are correlated closely with changes in labor productivity.
8. Labor productivity differences also explain some of the differences in wages paid to different people. However, differences in marginal productivity do not explain everything. Compensating wage differentials, discrimination, minimum wages, long-term contracts, and deferred compensation are all examples of why workers may not be paid a wage equivalent to their marginal revenue product.
9. The number of union workers in the United States has been declining, but union workers still earn more than nonunion workers who have the same skills. This occurs either because unions increase labor productivity or because they restrict the supply of workers in an industry.
10. Even though unions act like monopolists or oligopolists in the labor market in terms of selling the services of their members, they are not always associated with inefficient economic outcomes. In cases of bilateral monopoly, a monopoly seller of labor (such as a union) can counter a monopsony buyer of labor services and bring about more efficient economic outcomes.

QUESTIONS FOR REVIEW

1. What are fringe benefits? How significant a part of average pay are they in the United States?
2. Why is it important to distinguish between real wages and nominal wages? What about between hourly wages and weekly wages?
3. Why do we say that the demand for labor is a derived demand?
4. How does the relationship between marginal revenue product and the wage determine how many workers the firm should hire?
5. Why is the demand for labor downward sloping?
6. Provide an intuitive explanation of the income and substitution effects. Then explain why the substitution effect and the income effect of a wage increase work in opposite directions on labor supply.
7. What is the empirical relationship between labor productivity and the real wage in the United States since 1990?
8. What factors can lead to workers being paid a wage that differs from their marginal revenue product of labor?
9. What are the two main views of labor unions?
10. Explain when a labor union will reduce economic efficiency. When could it increase economic efficiency?

PROBLEMS

1. Marcelo farms corn on 500 acres in a competitive industry, receiving $3 per bushel. The relationship between the number of workers Marcelo hires and his production of corn is shown below.

Number of Workers	Production (bushels per year)
1	30,000
2	43,000
3	51,000
4	55,000
5	57,000
6	58,000

   a. Calculate the marginal product and marginal revenue product of labor for Marcelo's farm.
   b. If the wage for farm workers is $8,000 per year, how many workers will Marcelo hire? Explain.
   c. Suppose the yearly wage for farm workers is $8,000, the fixed rent is $600 per acre per year, and there are no other costs. Calculate Marcelo's profits or losses.
   d. Will there be entry into or exit from this industry?

2. Suppose a firm with some market power faces a downward-sloping demand curve for the product it produces. Using the information on demand given in the table below, complete the table and draw the resulting demand curve for labor. If the hourly wage is $30, how many workers will this firm hire?

Quantity of Labor	Quantity of Output	Marginal Product of Labor	Price of Output	Total Revenue	Marginal Revenue	Marginal Revenue Product of Labor
10	100		9			
20	180		8			
30	240		7			
40	280		6			
50	300		5			
60	310		4			

3. Recently, demand has increased for corn-based ethanol to substitute for gasoline in the United States. How will this affect the marginal product, marginal revenue product, and wages of farm workers on corn farms?

4. Use the definition of the demand for labor as the marginal revenue product to argue that the increasing wage dispersion between skilled and unskilled workers could come from (a) increases in the relative productivity of skilled workers and (b) increases in the demand for the products produced by skilled workers.
5. Since 1950, Americans have greatly reduced their home cooking in favor of eating at restaurants.
   a. What is the explanation for this?
   b. Do you expect it to continue in the next half century?
6. Analyze the labor supply schedules for Joshua and Scott below.

Wage	Hours Worked by Scott	Hours Worked by Joshua
$5	5	0
$8	10	8
$12	20	15
$15	30	25
$18	40	35
$20	45	33
$25	50	30

   a. Draw the labor supply schedules for Joshua and Scott.
   b. How does Scott's marginal benefit from more leisure compare with Joshua's?
   c. At what point does the income effect begin to outweigh the substitution effect for Joshua? Explain.
7. College professors frequently are paid less than others with equivalent skills working outside academia. Use the idea of compensating differentials to explain why professors' wages are relatively low.
8. The government of Egalitariania wants to favor firms, and it is considering implementing a maximum wage. As an economic adviser to the government of Egalitariania, explain (verbally and graphically) the consequences of the maximum wage in the competitive labor market. Ensure that your explanation includes the gains or losses to firms, workers, and the people of Egalitariania as a whole.
9. Draw a typical supply and demand for labor diagram to represent a labor market. Now suppose you are asked to modify this diagram to depict the market for doctors. To practice medicine in the United States, your medical education has to be certified, and you have to obtain a state license after completing a residency program.
   a. What impact does this restriction have on the wage rate for doctors in the economy?
   b. Will there be a shortage or a surplus of doctors at that wage rate?
   c. Should the government intervene and reduce these requirements to increase the supply of doctors?
   d. Would your answer change if the market (and the licensing requirement) were for lawyers?
   e. What about economists?
10. A toy manufacturing company is considering hiring sales representatives to market its new toys to retail stores. Under what circumstances should it pay a commission for every order of toys promoted by its sales representatives, and under what circumstances should it pay the sales representatives an hourly wage?

CHAPTER 14
Taxes, Transfers, and Income Distribution

In 1996 one of the most significant and controversial pieces of legislation affecting government transfers and taxes was enacted. Called "welfare reform," this legislation allowed state governments to limit the period of time during which people with low incomes could receive transfers—welfare payments—without working. As a result of the legislation, millions of people left the welfare rolls and the percentage of the federal budget going to this form of public assistance was reduced. The legislation was popular because it removed people from the welfare rolls and placed many in jobs. It also reduced the amount of taxes needed to pay for welfare. But it was severely criticized as being unfair and too harsh on families with low incomes.

In 2010, another significant and controversial piece of legislation was enacted—health care reform, which also affected taxes and transfers. This legislation expanded government assistance by increasing the income level below which people could qualify for Medicaid—the major health care program for the poor in the United States—and by providing subsidies to people at higher income levels to buy private health insurance. The act will increase the number of people receiving public assistance for health care expenses. In contrast to the 2006 legislation, it would increase the amount of taxes needed to pay for public assistance.

As the reactions to these two major pieces of legislation illustrate, individual opinion ranges widely about income inequality and what the government should do about it. Many feel compassion and amoral obligation to help the poor. Others feel it is unfair that some people make more in one day than others do in an entire year. Some see nothing unfair about an unequal income distribution as long as opportunities are equal. Others worry that government programs will reduce incentives to work, increase dependency on government, and lower incomes further. Still others worry that a very unequal distribution of income can cause social unrest and deter a society from achieving other goals, including a growing economy.

Source: © Shutterstock, Inc.

The purpose of this chapter is to provide an economic analysis of these issues. We begin the chapter with an analysis of the tax system, which is used to pay not only for transfer payments to the poor but also for government spending of all types—military, police, road building, and schools. We then consider transfers, such as welfare and health care payments to the poor and social security payments to the elderly. After we examine how various features of the tax and transfer system affect incentives, we examine the actual distribution of income and discuss how it has been affected by the tax and transfer system in the United States.

1. THE TAX SYSTEM

We begin by considering the tax system. The first part of our analysis is descriptive, looking at the different types of taxes used in the United States. Then we move into a more analytical mode, and review the efficiency and distributional implications of the tax system. Finally, we draw on these analytical findings to look at some policy proposals for reforming the tax system and discuss their merits.

The major types of taxes that exist in the United States are the *personal income tax* on people's total income, the *payroll tax* on wage and salary income, the *corporate income tax* on corporate profit income, *excise/sales taxes* on goods and services purchased, estate and *gift taxes* on inheritances and gifts from one person to another, and *tariffs*, which are taxes on goods imported into the country. In addition, many local governments raise revenue through *property taxes.*

As shown in Figure 14.1, the personal income tax and the payroll tax are by far the largest sources of tax revenue for the federal government. Together they account for about 80 percent of federal tax revenue. Hence, we focus most of our attention on these two taxes in the following discussion.

FIGURE 14.1 **Taxes Paid to the Federal Government in 2016**

More than 80 percent of federal taxes comes from the personal income tax and the payroll tax.

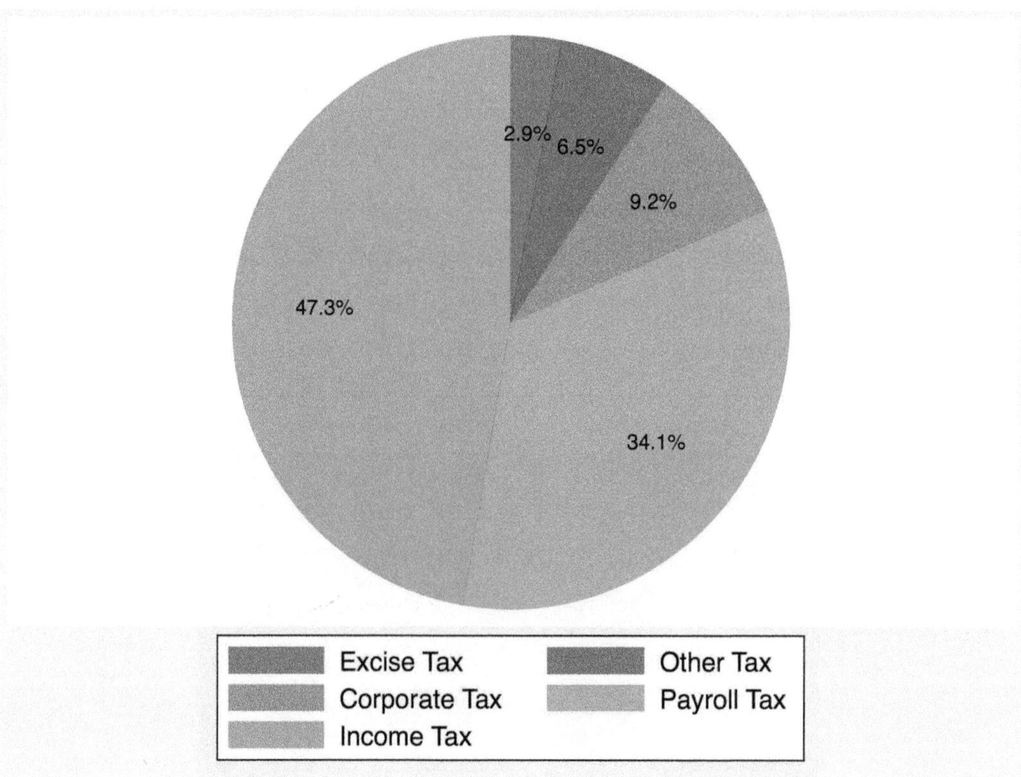

Source: Congressional Budget Office

1.1 The Personal Income Tax

The **personal income tax** is a tax on all the income an individual or household receives, including wage and salary income, interest and dividend income, income from a small business, rents on property, royalties, and capital gains. (A *capital gain* is the increase in the value of an asset like a corporate stock. When the asset is sold, the capital gain—equal to the difference between the original purchase price and the selling price of the asset—is treated as income and is taxed.) The personal income tax was introduced in 1917 in the United States, soon after the ratification of the Sixteenth Amendment to the U.S. Constitution, which authorized income taxes. Most states have now followed the federal government and have enacted a personal income tax at the state level; we focus our attention on the personal income tax collected by the federal government.

personal income tax
A tax on all forms of income an individual or household receives.

Computing the Personal Income Tax

To explain the economic effects of the personal income tax, we must examine how the amount of tax a household owes is determined. The amount of tax owed by a household depends on the tax rate and the amount of taxable income. **Taxable income** is defined as a household's income minus certain exemptions and deductions. An *exemption* is a dollar amount that can be subtracted from income for each person in the household. *Deductions* are other expenditure items actually incurred—such as interest payments on a home mortgage, charitable contributions, and moving expenses—that can be subtracted from income before taxes are assessed.

Taxable income
A household's income minus exemptions and deductions.

Consider, for example, the Lee family, which has four members: a wife, a husband, and two children. Suppose the Lees can subtract $4,050 as a personal exemption for each of the four people in the family, for a total of $16,200, and are entitled to a deduction of $11,300. Thus, they can subtract a total of $27,500 ($16,200 + $11,300) from their income. Suppose that the husband and wife together earn a total income of $80,000. Then their taxable income is $52,500 ($80,000 - $27,500).

FIGURE 14.2 Two Tax Rate Schedules from the 1040 Form for 2016

The tables show how to compute the tax for each amount of taxable income. Observe how the marginal rates rise from one tax bracket to the next.

ABBREVIATED 1040 FORM
Line 37 Taxable income ______
Line 38 Tax ______

Schedule X—Use if your filing status is **Single**

If your taxable income is: Over—	But not over—	The tax is:		of the amount over—
$0	$9,275	-----	10%	$0
9,275	37,650	$927.50	+ 15%	9,275
37,650	91,150	5,183.75	+ 25%	37,650
91,150	190,150	18,558.75	+ 28%	91,150
190,150	413,350	46,278.75	+ 33%	190,150
413,350	415,050	119,934.75	+ 35%	413,350
415,050	-----	120,529.75	+ 39.6%	415,050

Schedule Y-1—If your filing status is **Married filing jointly** or **Qualifying widow(er)**

If your taxable income is: Over—	But not over—	The tax is:		of the amount over—
$0	$18,550	-----	10%	$0
18,550	75,300	$1,855.00	+ 15%	18,550
73,300	151,900	10,367.50	+ 25%	75,300
151,900	231,450	29,517.50	+ 28%	151,900
231,450	413,350	51,791.50	+ 33%	231,450
413,350	466,950	111,818.50	+ 35%	413,350
466,950	-----	130,578.50	+ 39.6%	466,950

Taxable income

Marginal tax rates

Now let us see how we combine taxable income with the tax rate to compute the tax. Figure 14.2 shows two different tax rate schedules from the IRS 1040 form (throughout this chapter, the examples use the tax law as of 2016). The tax rate schedule labeled "Schedule X" in the figure is for a taxpayer who is single; the tax rate schedule labeled "Schedule Y-1" is for two married taxpayers who are paying their taxes together. The first two columns give a range for taxable income, or the "amount on Form 1040, line 37." The next two columns tell how to compute the tax. The percentages in the tax rate schedule are the tax rates.

tax bracket

A range of taxable income that is taxed at the same rate.

Look first at Schedule Y-1: The 10 percent tax rate in the schedule applies to all taxable income up to $18,550, at which point any additional income up to $75,300 is taxed at 15 percent. Any additional income over $75,300 but less than $151,900 is taxed at 25 percent, and so on for tax rates of 28 percent, 33 percent, 35 percent and 39.6 percent. Each of the rows in these schedules corresponds to a different tax rate; the range of taxable income in each row is called a **tax bracket**.

As an example, let us compute the Lees' tax. Recall that their taxable income is $52,500. They are married and filing jointly, so we look at Schedule Y-1. We go to the second line because $52,500 is between $18,550 and $75,300. In other words, the Lees are in the 15 percent tax bracket. We find that they must pay $1,855 plus 15 percent of the amount their income is over $18,550—that is, $1,855 + 0.15 x ($52,500 - $18,550) = $5,092.50. Thus, the amount of tax they must pay is $1,855 + $5,092.50 = $6,947.50.

The Marginal Tax Rate

Now consider what happens when the Lees' income changes. Suppose that one of the Lees decides to earn more income by working more hours and the Lees' income rises by $5,000. Thus, their taxable income rises from $52,500 to $57,500. Now what is their tax? Again looking at Schedule Y-1, we see that the tax is $1,855 + 0.15 X ($57,500 - $18,550) = $1,855 + $5,842.50 = $7,697.50. Thus, the Lees' tax has increased from $6,947.50 to $7,697.50, or by $750, as their income rose by $5,000. Observe that the tax rose by exactly 15 percent of the increase in income.

marginal tax rate

The change in total tax divided by the change in income.

The amount by which taxes change when an individual's income changes is the **marginal tax rate**. It is defined as the change in taxes divided by the change in income. In examining how the Lees compute their tax, we have discovered that their marginal tax rate is 15 percent. In other words, when their income increased, their taxes rose by 15 percent of the increase in income. As long as they stay within the 15 percent tax bracket, their marginal tax rate is 15 percent.

Observe that the marginal tax rate depends on one's income. The marginal rate varies from 10 percent for low incomes up to 35 percent for very high incomes. Suppose that one of the Lees did not work and that their taxable income was $15,000 rather than $52,500. Then they would be in the 10 percent bracket, and their marginal tax rate would be 10 percent.

average tax rate

The total tax paid divided by the total taxable income.

In contrast to the marginal tax rate, the **average tax rate** is the total tax paid divided by the total taxable income. For example, the Lees' average tax rate before we considered changes in their income was (6,947.5/52,500) = 0.1323, or 13.23 percent, which is lower than the 15 percent marginal tax rate. In other words, the Lees pay 13.23 percent of their total taxable income in taxes but must pay 15 percent of any additional income in taxes. The average tax rate is less than the marginal tax rate because the Lees pay only 10 percent on the first $18,550 of taxable income.

Economists feel that the marginal rate is important for assessing the effects of taxes on individual behavior. Their reasoning can be illustrated with the Lees again. Suppose that the Lees' marginal tax rate was 10 percent rather than 15 percent. Then, if one of the Lees decided to work an additional half day a week, the family would be able to keep $0.90 of each extra dollar earned, sending $0.10 to the government. But with a marginal tax rate of 15 percent, the Lees could keep only $0.85 on the dollar. If the marginal tax rate for the Lees was 35 percent, then they could keep only $0.65 of each dollar earned. To take the example to an even greater extreme, suppose the marginal rate was 91 percent, which was the highest marginal rate before President Kennedy proposed reducing tax rates. Then, for each extra dollar earned, one could keep only $0.09. Clearly, the marginal tax rate is going to influence people's choices about how much to work if they have a choice. The marginal tax rate has a significant effect on what people gain from working additional hours. This is why economists stress the marginal tax rate rather than the average tax rate when they look at the impact of the personal income tax on people's behavior.

Figure 14.3 provides a visual perspective on marginal tax rates. It plots the marginal tax rate from IRS Schedule Y-1 in Figure 14.2; the marginal tax rate is on the vertical axis, and the taxable income is on the horizontal axis. Observe how the marginal tax rate rises with income.

A tax is **progressive** *if the amount of the tax as a percentage of income rises as income increases.* If the marginal tax rate rises with income—in which case people with higher incomes pay a larger percentage of their income in taxes—then the tax is progressive. *A tax is* **regressive** *if the amount of the tax as a percentage of income falls as income rises.* An income tax would be regressive if the marginal tax rate declined as income rose, or if people with high incomes could use deductions or other schemes to reduce the tax they paid to a smaller percentage of income than people with lower incomes paid. *A tax is* **proportional** *if the amount of the tax as a percentage of income is constant as income rises.*

progressive

A tax for which the amount of an individual's taxes rises as a proportion of income as the person's income increases.

regressive

A tax for which the amount of an individual's taxes falls as a proportion of income as the person's income increases.

proportional

A tax for which the amount of an individual's taxes as a percentage of income is constant as the person's income rises.

Zero Tax on Low Incomes

In assessing how progressive the income tax is, remember that the taxes are based on taxable income, which is less than the income a household actually receives. Taxable income can be zero even if a household's income is greater than zero. For example, if the Lee family earned only $26,000 for the year, then their taxable income would be zero, because $26,000 equals the sum of their exemptions and deductions. In general, the personal income tax is zero for household incomes up to the sum of the exemptions and deductions.

FIGURE 14.3 Marginal Tax Rates

As an example, the marginal tax rates from the IRS tax rate Schedule Y-1 are plotted. The marginal tax rate is the change in the amount of tax paid for an extra dollar earned. The marginal tax rate increases with income. Each step takes the tax payer to a higher tax bracket. Thus, higher-income people have a higher marginal tax rate than lower-income people. Under a flat tax, the marginal tax rate would be constant for all taxable income levels.

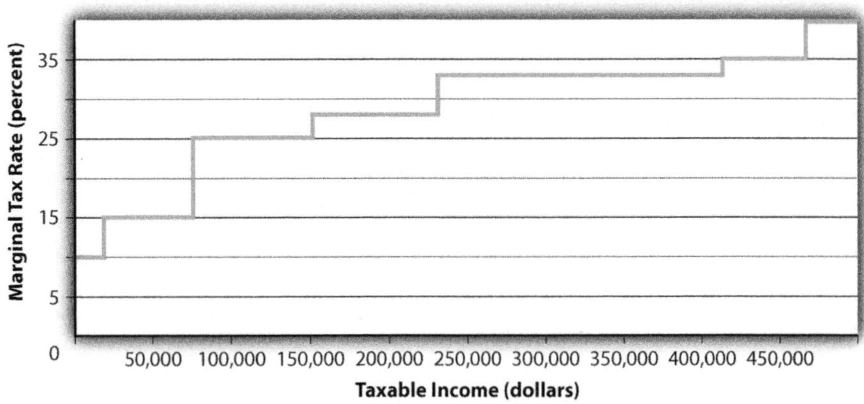

A **flat tax** occurs when the marginal tax rates are constant for all levels of taxable income, in which case the line in Figure 14.3 would become flat. Even a flat rate tax system would have a degree of progressivity: The tax paid would rise as a percentage of income from zero (for workers below the sum of exemptions and deductions) to a positive amount as income rises.

flat tax

A tax system in which a marginal tax rate for all levels of taxable income is constant.

1.2 The Payroll Tax

The **payroll tax** is a tax on the wages and salaries of individuals; the payroll tax goes to finance social security benefits, Medicare, and unemployment insurance. Employers submit payroll taxes to the government. For example, the Lees' employers must submit 15.3 percent of the Lees' wage and salary income to the federal government. Thus, the payroll tax on the Lees' wage and salary income of $80,000 would be $12,240 (that is, 0.153 x $80,000), more than 50 percent higher than the total that the Lees would pay in personal income taxes.

payroll tax

A tax on the wages and salaries of individuals.

The tax law says that half of the 15.3 percent payroll tax is to be paid by the worker and half is to be paid by the employer. Thus, the Lees would be notified of only half of the payroll tax, or $6,120, even though their employer sent $12,240 to the government. If a person is self-employed—a business consultant, say, or a freelance editor—then the person pays the full 15.3 percent, because a self-employed person is both the employee and the employer. One of the most important things to understand about the payroll tax is that, as we will soon prove, its economic effects do not depend on who is legally required to pay what share of the tax; only the total 15.3 percent matters.

1.3 Other Taxes

Corporate income taxes

A tax on the accounting profits of corporations.

Excise taxes

A tax paid on the value of goods at the time of purchase.

sales tax

A type of excise tax that applies to total expenditures on a broad group of goods.

property taxes

A tax on the value of property owned.

All other federal taxes together amount to a little over one-fifth of total revenue. **Corporate income taxes** are taxes on the accounting profits of corporations. As of 2011, the corporate tax rate ranges from 15 percent to 38 percent, depending on the level of earnings.

Excise taxes are taxes on goods that are paid when the goods are purchased. The federal government taxes several specific items, including gasoline, tobacco, beer, wine, and hard liquor. A **sales tax** is a type of excise tax that applies to total expenditures on a broad group of goods. For example, if your expenditures on many different goods at a retail store total $100 and the sales tax rate is 5 percent, then you pay $5 in sales tax. There is no national sales tax in the United States, but sales taxes are a major source of revenue for many state and local governments.

The federal government also raises revenue by imposing tariffs on goods as they enter the United States. Until the Sixteenth Amendment was ratified and the personal income tax was introduced, tariffs were the major source of revenue for the U.S. government. Now revenue from tariffs is a minor portion of total revenue.

Local governments rely heavily on **property taxes**—taxes on residential homes and business real estate—to raise revenue. Recall that income taxes—both personal and corporate—are used at the state level to raise revenue for state governments.

1.4 The Effect of Taxes

The purpose of most of these taxes is to raise revenue, but taxes can have significant effects on people's behavior. To examine these effects, let us start with a tax we looked at before in Chapter 7: a tax on a good or service.

The Effect of Tax on a Good

Recall that a tax on a good adds the amount of the tax to the marginal cost of the seller of the good. For example, a tax of $1 on a gallon of gasoline will shift the supply curve up by the amount of the tax, a result shown in Figure 7.9. Once the supply curve shifts as a result of the tax, equilibrium price and quantity also will change. The ultimate impact on price and quantity will depend on the price elasticities of supply and demand.

The four panels of Figure 14.4 are designed to enable us to show how the price elasticity of demand and the price elasticity of supply determine the impact of the tax. In each of the figure's four panels, the supply curve shifts up because of a tax of the same amount, shown by the arrow to the left of each vertical axis. As a result of the tax, in each of the four panels, the equilibrium price rises and the equilibrium quantity falls. The decline in the equilibrium quantity creates a loss of consumer surplus plus producer surplus, which we call the deadweight loss from the tax. The size of the deadweight loss and the relative size of the impact on the price and the quantity are different in each panel of Figure 14.4 because the supply curve and the demand curve have different price elasticities.

FIGURE 14.4 How Elasticities Determine the Effects of Taxes

(1) Deadweight loss effects: When price elasticities are low, as in the left graphs, the deadweight loss is small and the change in equilibrium quantity is small. When price elasticities are high, as in the right graphs, the deadweight loss is large and the change in equilibrium quantity is large. (2) Tax incidence and price effects: When the price elasticity of demand is low or the price elasticity of supply is high, the tax is largely passed on to the consumer in the form of higher prices. In contrast, when the price elasticity of demand is high or the price elasticity of supply is low, the burden of the tax falls on the producer because the price changes little.

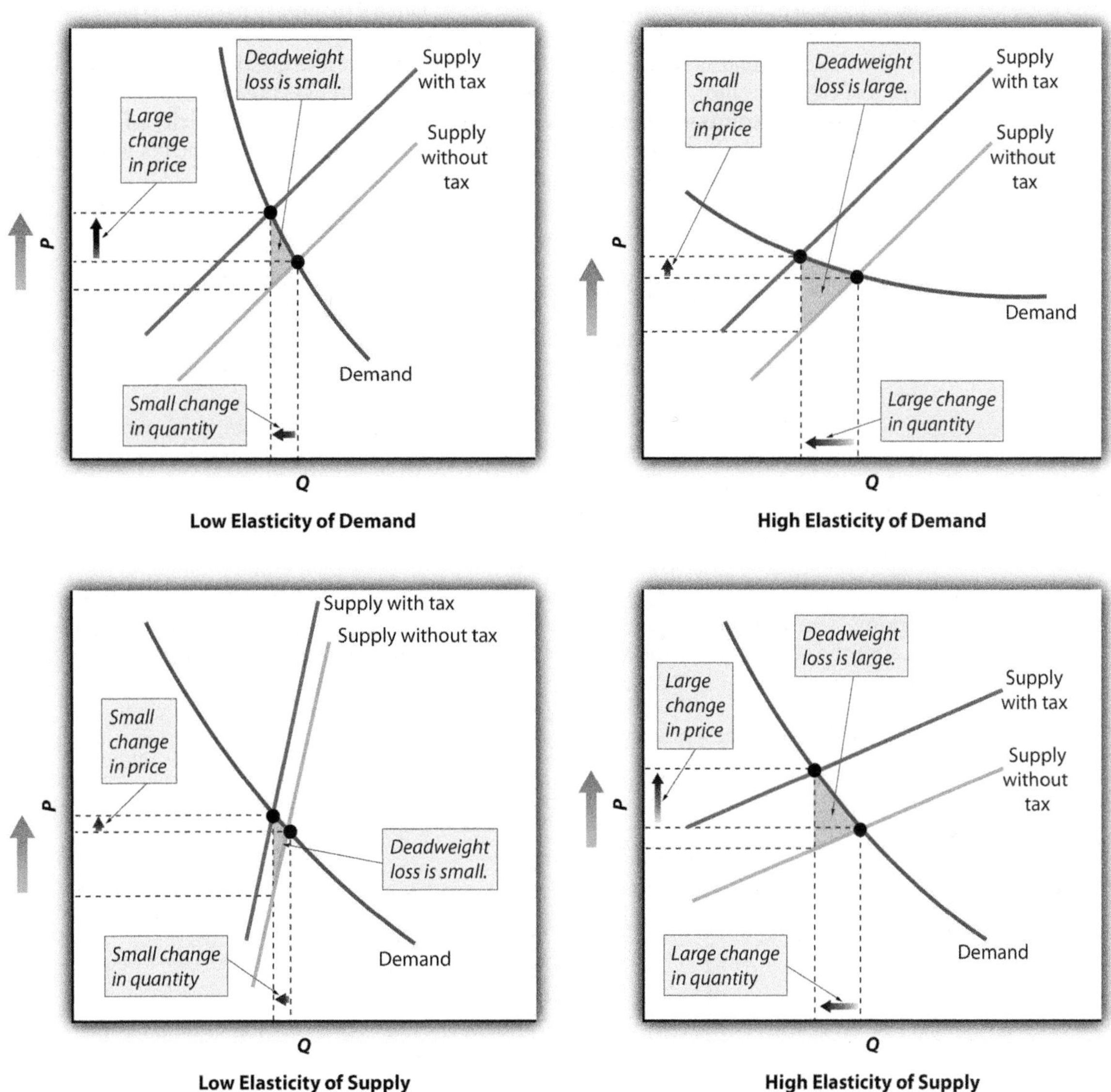

A key point illustrated in Figure 14.4 is that *when the price elasticity of demand or the price elasticity of supply is very low, the deadweight loss from the tax is small.* This deadweight loss is shown in the two graphs in the left part of Figure 14.4, which have either a low elasticity of demand (top left) or a low elasticity of supply (bottom left). In either case, the deadweight loss is small compared with that in the graphs at the right, which have higher elasticities.

The intuitive reason why low elasticities result in small deadweight losses is that the quantity of the good does not change very much when the price changes. Recall that a low price elasticity of demand means that quantity demanded is not very sensitive to a change in the price, as, for example, in the case of a good like salt, which has few substitutes. A low elasticity of supply means that only a small change occurs in the quantity supplied when the price changes. Thus, in the case of low elasticities, only a small difference exists between the efficient quantity of production and the quantity of production with the tax. There is little loss of efficiency. On the other hand, *when the price elasticity of demand or the price elasticity of supply is very high, the deadweight loss from the tax will be relatively large.* In this case, changes in price have big effects on either the quantity demanded or the quantity supplied, and the deadweight loss is large.

Tax incidence

The allocation of the burden of the tax between buyer and seller.

The price elasticities of supply and demand also affect how much the price changes in response to a tax. If the price rises by a large amount, then the tax is passed on to buyers in the form of higher prices, and the burden of the tax falls more on buyers. If the price rises little or not at all, then the seller absorbs the burden of the tax, and most of the tax is not passed on to buyers. **Tax incidence** refers to who actually bears the burden of the tax, the buyers or the sellers.

The graphs in Figure 14.4 suggest the general principle that *the smaller the price elasticity of demand and the larger the price elasticity of supply, the greater the rise in the price.* The opposite will be true if the elasticity of demand is large and the elasticity of supply is small—that is, the impact of the tax will raise the price by only a little.

This tells us that taxing a good like cigarettes, with a low elasticity of demand, will result in the buyers of cigarettes bearing the tax. The seller will be able to pass the tax on to the buyers in the form of higher prices. In contrast, taxing a good like land, which has a low elasticity of supply, will not affect the price very much. The supplier of the land will not be able to pass on the tax to the consumers in the form of higher prices and will bear the burden of the tax.

Effects of the Personal Income Tax

We can apply the results of this analysis to the personal income tax. The personal income tax is a tax on *labor* income (wages and salaries) as well as on *capital* income (interest, dividends, small business profits). Labor income, however, is by far the larger share of most people's income: For all 1040 forms filed, wages and salaries account for more than 75 percent of total income. Thus, we model the personal income tax as a tax on labor income.

The analysis of the personal income tax is illustrated in Figure 14.5. Because the personal income tax is a tax on labor income, we need a model of the labor market to examine the effects of the tax. Figure 14.5 shows a labor demand curve and a labor supply curve. The wage paid to the worker is on the vertical axis, and the quantity of labor is on the horizontal axis. Figure 14.5 shows that the personal income tax shifts the labor supply curve up. The size of the upward shift depends on the marginal tax rate because the income received from work would be reduced by the marginal tax. If the person was in the 15 percent bracket, the income received from working would be $0.85 for each extra dollar earned working. Thus, to supply exactly the same quantity as without the tax, people require a higher wage. Because the wage paid to the worker is on the vertical axis, the labor supply curve shifts up to show this.

FIGURE 14.5 **Effects of a Higher Income Tax on Labor Supply**

An income tax shifts the labor supply curve up by the amount of the tax on each extra hour of work because the worker must pay part of wage income to the government and thus receives less for each hour of work. Thus, the quantity of labor supplied declines. The decline in hours worked would be small if the supply curve had a low elasticity.

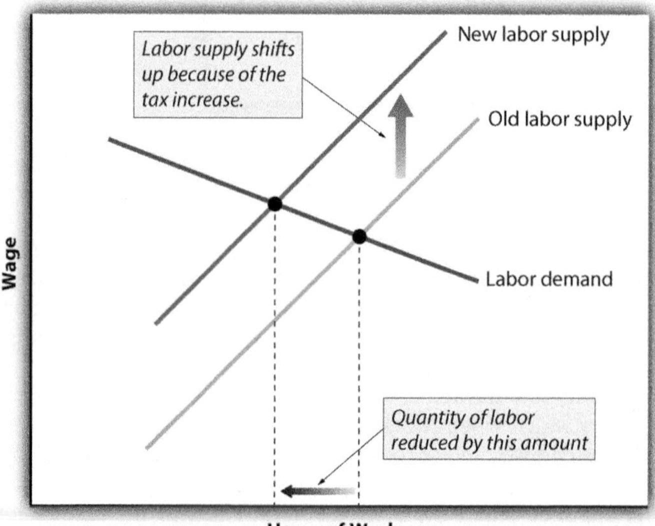

As the labor supply curve shifts up, the equilibrium quantity of labor declines. Thus, we predict that an income tax will reduce the amount of work. The reduced amount of work will cause a deadweight loss just like that caused by the tax on a commodity. The size of the decline in hours of work will depend on the labor supply and labor demand elasticities. The higher the labor supply elasticity, the greater the reduction in the quantity of labor supplied in response to the personal income tax.

Economists disagree about the size of the labor supply elasticity. One thing that is certain is that the elasticity is different for different people. For example, the labor supply elasticity appears to be quite high for second earners in a two-earner family such as the Lees. If elasticity is high, a high marginal tax rate can reduce hours of work and thereby income. But if the labor supply curve has a low elasticity, it has little effect on hours of work.

The Effect of a Payroll Tax

We can use the same type of labor market diagram to analyze a payroll tax, as shown in Figure 14.6. Clearly, the payroll tax is a tax on labor in that it applies to wages and salaries. In the case of the payroll tax, however, we need to consider that both the employer and the employee pay this tax, as required by law. Figure 14.6 handles the two cases.

Suppose that the wage before the tax is $10 per hour and that the payroll tax is 10 percent, or $1 per hour. The case in which the employee pays the tax is shown on the right of Figure 14.6. This picture looks much like Figure 14.5. The labor supply curve shifts up by the amount of the tax ($1) because the worker now has to pay a tax to the government for each hour worked. In other words, the worker will supply the same amount of work when the wage is $11 and the tax is $1 as when the wage is $10 and the tax is zero.

When the labor supply curve shifts up, the equilibrium quantity of labor employed declines (see the right-hand panel of Figure 14.6). Observe that, because of the lower supply of labor, the wage paid by the employer rises. The after-tax wage—that is, the wage less the tax—declines, however, because the increase in the wage is less than the tax increase.

The case in which the employer pays the tax is shown in the left graph of Figure 14.6. In this case, the labor demand curve shifts down by the amount of the tax ($1) because the firm has to pay an additional $1 for each hour of work. When the labor demand curve shifts down, the equilibrium quantity of labor employed declines and the wage falls. Observe that the impact of the payroll tax is the same in both cases: A new equilibrium emerges in the labor market with a lower wage and a lower quantity of labor.

Thus, a payroll tax has both an employment-reduction effect and a wage-reduction effect. As with any tax, the size of the quantity change and the price (wage) change depends on the supply and demand elasticities. If we apply the results from Figure 14.4, we know that when the labor supply elasticity is low and the labor demand elasticity is high, the reduction in employment will be small, but the wage will fall by a large amount. If the labor supply elasticity is high and the labor demand elasticity is low, however, the employment effect will be large, but the wage effect will be small.

FIGURE 14.6 The Effect of a Payroll Tax

If a payroll tax is paid by the employer, the labor demand curve shifts down by the amount of the tax because the firm's labor costs increase by the amount of the tax. Thus, the quantity of labor employed declines, as does the wage paid to the worker (shown on the left). A payroll tax paid by the employee (shown on the right) causes the labor supply curve to rise by the amount of the tax, but the effects on after-tax wages received by the worker and the quantity of work are the same as when the employer pays.

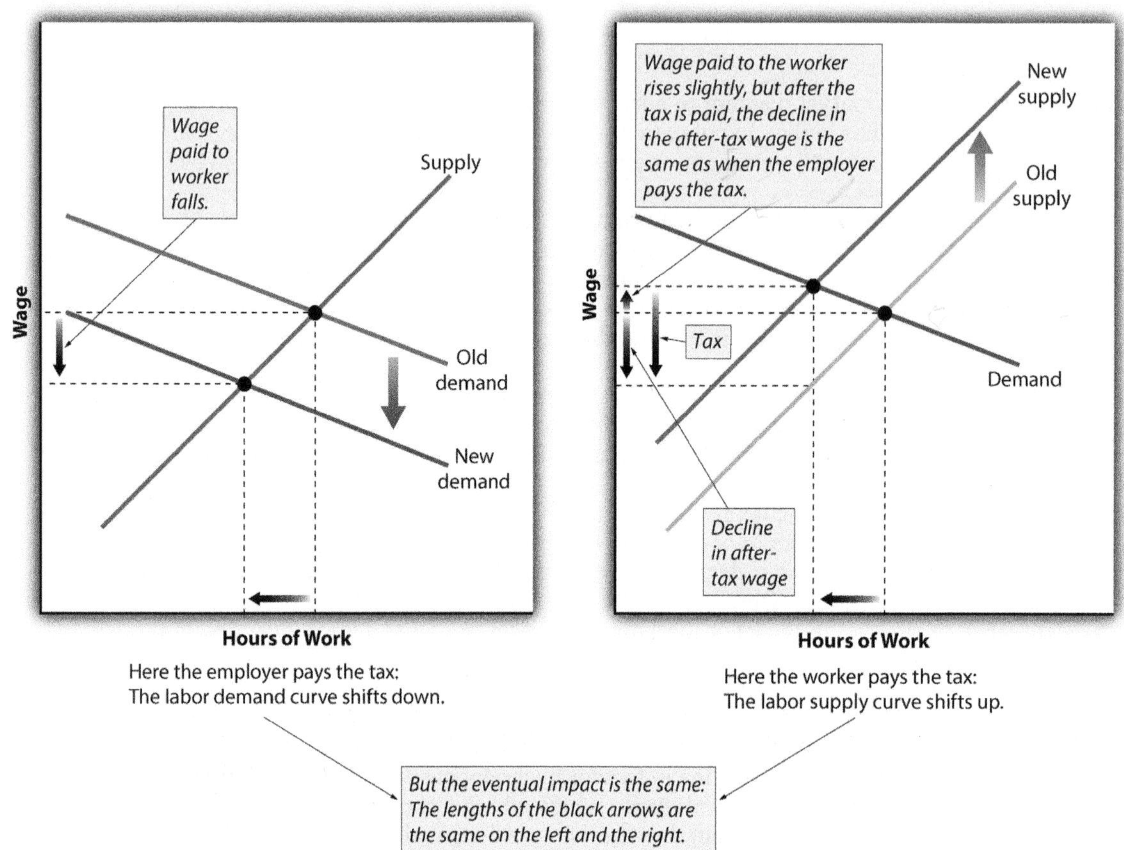

TABLE 14.1 Tax Rates and Tax Revenue: An Example

Tax Rate	Wage	Hours Worked	Tax Revenues
0.50	$10/hour	2,000	$10,000
0.75	$10/hour	1,500	$11,250
0.90	$10/hour	500	$4,500

The Possibility of a Perverse Effect on Tax Revenue

Tax revenue

The tax rate times the amount subject to tax.

Tax revenue received by the government is equal to the tax rate times the amount that is subject to the tax. For example, in the case of a gasoline tax, the tax revenue is the tax per gallon times the number of gallons sold. As the tax rate increases, the amount subject to the tax will fall because the higher price resulting from the tax reduces the quantity demanded. If the quantity demanded falls sharply enough, then tax revenue actually could fall when the tax rate is increased.

The same possibility arises in the case of taxes on labor, either the payroll tax or the personal income tax. In the case of the payroll tax or the personal income tax for a worker, tax revenue is equal to the tax rate times the wage and salary income. As the tax rate rises, the amount of income subject to tax may fall if labor supply declines. Thus, in principle, it is possible that a higher tax rate could result in reduced tax revenue. For example, consider the high marginal tax rates shown in Table 14.1: 50 percent, 75 percent, and 90 percent. If labor supply declines with a higher tax rate, as assumed in the table, then tax revenue first increases as the tax rate goes from 50 to 75 percent but then declines as the tax rate goes from 75 to 90 percent.

The general relationship between tax rates and tax revenue is illustrated in Figure 14.7. As in the example of Table 14.1, tax revenue first rises and then falls as the tax rate increases. Figure 14.7 can apply to any tax on anything. At the two extremes of zero percent tax rate and 100 percent tax rate, tax revenue is zero. What happens between these two extremes depends on the elasticities. This relationship between the tax rate and tax revenue, frequently called the Laffer curve after the economist Arthur Laffer, who made it popular in the 1980s, has long been known to economists. It implies that if the tax rate is so high that we are on the downward-sloping part of the curve, then reducing the tax rate may increase tax revenue. Economists debate greatly, however, about the tax rate at which the curve bends around. Few economists believe that the curve bends at the current top marginal rate in the United States, which is 39.6 percent.

FIGURE 14.7 The Tax Rate and Tax Revenue

As the tax rate increases from low levels, tax revenue rises. At some point, however, the high tax rate reduces the quantity of the item that is taxed and encourages so much tax avoidance that the amount of tax revenue declines. This curve is frequently called the Laffer curve.The particular tax rate at which the curve bends depends on the price elasticity of the item being taxed and is a subject of great debate among economists.

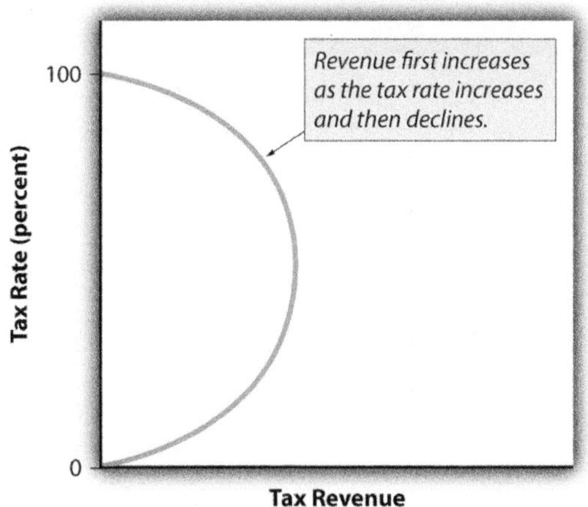

Other factors that influence tax revenue, especially when marginal tax rates get very high, are tax avoidance and tax evasion. *Tax avoidance* means finding legal ways to reduce taxes, such as buying a home rather than renting, to have a deduction for interest payments on a mortgage. Tax evasion is an illegal means of reducing one's tax. For example, at high tax rates, people have incentives to evade the tax by not reporting income. Workers are tempted not to report tips. Or people resort to barter, which is difficult for the government to track down. For example, an employer may "pay" a little extra to a truck driver by allowing free use of the truck on weekends for fishing trips.

1.5 Tax Policy and the Trade-off between Efficiency and Equality

We have observed in our analysis of each tax that the equilibrium quantity of the item taxed declines when the tax rate rises. This is where the inefficiency of the tax comes from. If the tax rate is very high, or the elasticities are very high, the inefficiency can be so severe that it could thwart one of the purposes of raising the taxes: that is, to provide income support to increase the well-being of the least well-off in the society. This is because a reduction in the quantity of labor supplied or goods produced could be so great that society would have less total income, and thus less support would go to the poor even if they received a larger share of total income. In other words, a *trade-off exists between equality and efficiency.* If one raises taxes too high for the purpose of making the income distribution more equal, the total amount of income may decline. In that event, there will be less available to redistribute.

Given these considerations, how should the tax system—the combination of all the taxes in society—be designed or improved? First, to reduce deadweight loss to a minimum, the ideal tax system should tax items with small price elasticities of supply and demand rather than items with large elasticities. We know that the deadweight loss is small when elasticities are small. The optimal tax system would inversely relate tax rates to the elasticities.

Second, the ideal tax system would try to keep the marginal tax rates low and the amount that is subject to tax high. For example, we saw that deductions reduce the amount subject to personal income tax by lowering taxable income. Some deductions are put in the tax system to encourage certain activities: A deduction for research expenses may encourage firms to fund research, for example. The more deductions there are, however, the higher the tax rate has to be to get the same tax revenue. Economists use the term *broadening the tax base* to describe an increase in the amount of income subject to taxation by limiting or eliminating deductions and exemptions. With a broader tax base, a lower marginal tax rate can generate the same amount of revenue; the lower marginal tax rate has the additional advantage of reducing the inefficiency of the tax. Most tax reform efforts have involved trying to broaden the tax base while lowering marginal tax rates. This was the idea behind the tax reform efforts in the 1960s under President Kennedy and in the 1980s under President Reagan. In the early 2000s, the marginal tax rates on all taxpayers were reduced substantially. Because many new deductions, exemptions, and credits also were introduced, however, the tax base was not broadened.

ability-to-pay principle

The view that those with greater income should pay more in taxes than those with less income.

Third, the ideal tax system should be as simple and as fair as possible. If a tax system is not simple, then valuable resources—people's time, computers, and so on—must be devoted to paying and processing taxes. A tax system is seen as unfair if it is regressive. Another view of fairness frequently used is the **ability-to-pay principle**; this view is that those with greater income should pay more in taxes than those with less income. The tax system also is viewed as unfair if people with the same incomes are taxed at different rates. For example, in the U.S. tax system, a married couple with each making $80,000 a year pays a higher tax than an unmarried couple with exactly the same income. Some view this system as unfair.

REVIEW

- Taxes are a vital source of revenue for the government. In the United States, the personal income tax and the payroll tax are the largest sources of tax revenue for the government. Other sources of tax revenue include corporate income taxes, excise taxes, and gift taxes.
- In analyzing how a tax system works, key variables to pay attention to include deductions and exemptions, tax brackets and the associated marginal tax rates, and how progressive the tax code is.
- Taxes cause inefficiencies in the form of reduced economic activity and deadweight loss. The deadweight loss associated with a tax is high when the price elasticities of supply and demand are high.
- Tax incidence identifies who bears the burden of paying the tax. When the elasticity of demand is low and the elasticity of supply is high, the burden of paying the tax falls largely on the consumer. Conversely, in situations in which the elasticity of demand is high and the elasticity of supply is low, the burden of paying the tax is largely borne by the seller.
- The impact of higher taxes on tax revenue depends on the impact of equilibrium quantity. If the equilibrium quantity falls by a sufficiently large amount, then tax revenue actually could decline.
- A trade-off exists between efficiency and equality in designing tax policy; raising taxes to reduce inequality may increase economic inefficiency and thereby reduce the amount of total income and tax revenue.
- To minimize the inefficiencies, items with low elasticities should be taxed more than items with high elasticities. Other methods of eliminating inefficiencies include policies that broaden the tax base while lowering the marginal tax rate, and keeping the tax system simple and fair to avoid creating incentives for tax evasion and tax avoidance.
- The criterion of "fairness" also is used to evaluate how ideal a tax system is. Principles of fairness include progressivity and treating people who have the same income identically—regardless of marital status, for example.

2. TRANSFER PAYMENTS

Transfer payments

A grant or funds from the government to an individual.

means-tested transfers

A transfer payment that depends on the income of the recipient.

social insurance transfers

A transfer payment, such as social security, that does not depend on the income of the recipient.

Transfer payments, payments made by the government to an individual that are not in exchange for goods or services, have important implications for the alleviation of poverty and the distribution of income in the United States. Transfer payments can be either in cash or in kind, such as vouchers that can be used to buy food or housing.

The United States has two types of government transfer payments: **means-tested transfers**, which depend on the income (the means) of the recipient and focus on helping poor people, and **social insurance transfers**, which do not depend on the income of the recipient.

2.1 Means-Tested Transfer Programs

Means-tested transfer payments are made to millions of people in the United States each year. The major programs are listed in Table 14.2.

TABLE 14.2 Means-Tested Transfer Programs in the United States (Each of these federal programs requires that the recipient's income or assets be below a certain amount to receive payment.)

Temporary Assistance to Needy Families (TANF)	Payments to poor families with children as determined by each state
Medicaid	Health insurance primarily for welfare recipients
Supplemental Security Income (SSI)	Payments to poor people who are old, disabled, or blind
Food Stamp Program	Coupons allowing low-income people to buy food
Head Start	Preschool education for low-income children
Housing Assistance	Rental subsidies and aid for construction

The 1996 federal welfare law (called the Personal Responsibility and Work Opportunity Reconciliation Act, or PRWORA) created the **Temporary Assistance to Needy Families (TANF) program**, replacing the Aid to Families with Dependent Children (AFDC) program, which was what people typically referred to as "welfare" in the United States. TANF is a transfer program that provides cash payments to eligible poor families with children. The federal government provides grants to the states, which then decide which poor families are eligible. Unlike AFDC, TANF assistance is limited in duration (the program has a five-year lifetime limit) and requires that recipients work a certain number of hours per week.

Temporary Assistance to Needy Families (TANF) program

Transfer program through which the federal government makes grants to states to give cash to certain low-income families.

Medicaid is a health insurance program that is designed primarily to pay for health care for people with low incomes. Once income increases to a certain level, Medicaid support stops, so that the family must find another means of obtaining health insurance. **Supplemental security income (SSI)** is designed to help the neediest elderly as well as poor people who are disabled or blind. About 6.6 million people receive SSI assistance, including 4.6 million disabled and 2 million elderly people.

Medicaid

A health insurance program designed primarily for families with low incomes.

Supplemental security income (SSI)

A means-tested transfer program designed primarily to help the poor who are disabled or blind.

The **food stamp program** is a major means-tested transfer program; it makes payments to about 17 million people each year. Like Medicaid, food stamps are an in-kind payment. People are not supposed to use the coupons to buy anything but food. This program is popular because the intent of the money is to provide nutrition and because the program is fairly inexpensive to run. The National School Lunch Program is similar to food stamps in that it aims to provide food to lower-income children. It provides school lunches for about 29 million children.

food stamp program

A government program that provides people with low incomes with coupons (food stamps) that they can use to buy food.

Head Start, another in-kind program, provides for preschool assistance to poor children to help them get a good start in school. It also is a popular program because evidence indicates that it improves the performance, at least temporarily, of preschool children as they enter elementary school.

Head Start

A government transfer program that provides day care and nursery school training for poor children.

Housing assistance programs provide rental subsidies to people who cannot afford to buy a home. The programs sometimes provide aid to business firms that construct low-income housing. Those that oppose the programs complain about waste and poor incentives in the housing programs and argue that these programs are in need of reform.

Housing assistance programs

Government programs that provide subsidies either to low-income families to rent housing or to contractors to build low-income housing.

The **Earned Income Tax Credit (EITC)** program is a means-tested transfer payment program received by about 20 million working poor families. The EITC actually is part of the personal income tax, and the form to obtain the transfer payment is sent to people by the IRS along with the 1040 form. Working people whose income is below a certain level, either because their wage is very low or because they work part time, get a refundable credit that raises their take-home pay. For example, consider the four-person Lee family again. We know that if the Lees earn less than $27,500, they pay no income tax. However, if the Lees earn between $0 and $14,040 in wages and salary and have no other income, then the EITC will pay $0.40 for each dollar they earn up to a maximum of $5,616 per year. To ensure that the EITC does not make payments to high-income people, the payments decline if the Lees make more than $23,930. For each dollar they earn above $23,930, they lose $0.21 of their $5,616 until the benefits run out, when their income reaches $50,597.

Earned Income Tax Credit (EITC)

A part of the personal income tax through which people with low income who work receive a payment from the government or a rebate on their taxes.

Observe that the EITC raises the incentive to work for incomes up to $14,040 and reduces the incentive to work for incomes greater than $23,930 and less than $50,597. With the EITC, the marginal tax rate is effectively *negative* 40 percent for income below $5,036; that is, you *get* $0.40 rather than *pay* $0.40 for each dollar you earn. But the EITC adds 21 percent to the marginal tax rate for incomes between $23,930 and $50,597.

2.2 Incentive Effects

The previous section describes a variety of government programs that aim to transfer funds to the poor. As we will see, evidence suggests that these programs do have an impact on reducing income inequality. Some people feel that the programs may create a disincentive to work, however, because welfare payments are reduced when income from work rises.

The top panel of Figure 14.8 illustrates the first disincentive problem. The total income of an individual is plotted against the number of hours worked. Total income consists of wage income from work plus a welfare payment. The more steeply sloped solid black line shows the individual's wage income from work: The more hours worked, the more wage income the individual receives. This line intercepts the horizontal axis at zero income, so if the person does not have work and does not receive welfare or charity, the person is in a state of extreme poverty.

FIGURE 14.8 Welfare Reform to Improve Work Incentives

The top graph shows how welfare reduces the marginal earnings from working more hours because welfare payments are phased out. The two basic approaches to reform are (1) phasing out the payments more slowly (as in the middle graph) or (2) lowering the welfare payment (as in the lower graph). Both approaches have advantages and disadvantages.

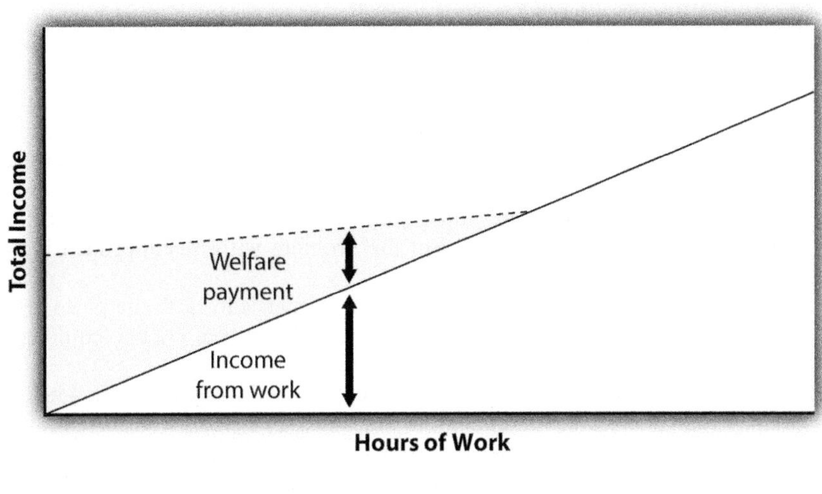

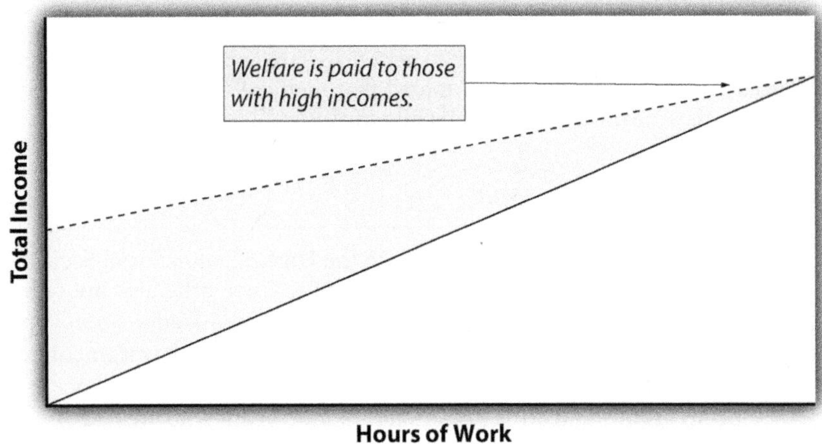

Reform by phasing out payments more slowly

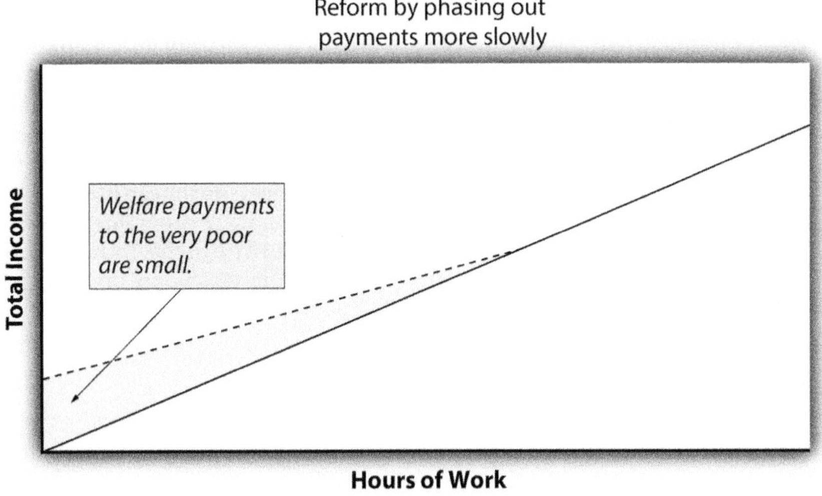

Reform by paying less welfare

The individual's total income is shown by the less steeply sloped dashed line in the top graph of Figure 14.8. This line intercepts the vertical axis at an amount equal to the welfare payment the individual gets when he or she is not working at all. As the individual begins to work, the need for welfare declines, and so the welfare payment declines. Observe that the amount of the welfare payment, which is represented by the shaded gap between the steep line and the less steep line, diminishes as the hours of work increase, and finally, after a certain number of hours worked, the welfare payment disappears.

Because the welfare payment is reduced when the individual's income from work rises, it creates a disincentive. The flatter the dashed line, the greater the disincentive. For example, if someone decides to work 10 hours a week for a total of $50 per week, but the welfare payment is reduced by $30 per week, then effectively the marginal tax rate is 60 percent, which is high enough to discourage work.

Welfare reform seeks to change the welfare system to reduce this disincentive. Looking at Figure 14.8, there are two ways to make the dashed line steeper and thereby provide more incentive to work. One way is to reduce the amount of welfare paid at the zero income amount. Graphically, this is shown in the lower graph of Figure 14.8. This reduction twists the dashed line because the intercept on the vertical axis is lower, but the intersection of the dashed line and the solid line appears at the same number of hours of work as in the top graph. This will increase the slope of the dashed line and therefore provide more incentive to work. But the problem with this approach is that poor people receive less welfare: The poverty rate could rise.

A second way to make the dashed line steeper is to raise the place at which it intersects the black solid line, as in the middle graph of Figure 14.8. But that change could result in making welfare payments to people who do not need them at all.

The welfare reform act signed into law by President Clinton in 1996 left the decision as to which welfare reform approach to take up to the states. The states went off in different directions; some chose to cut welfare benefits for those who were not working, while others raised the amount that can be earned before welfare is reduced. Some states require adult welfare recipients to go to work immediately. Twenty-four states require that people work after two years on welfare. Other states require that a single parent finish high school to receive the full welfare payment. These proposals are aimed at increasing the incentive to get off welfare and go to work. In fact, welfare rolls have been reduced dramatically, but critics contend that many of these people do not have adequate support services, such as health insurance and child care.

2.3 Social Insurance Programs

Social Security

The system through which individuals make payments to the government when they work and receive payments from the government when they retire or become disabled.

Medicare

A government health insurance program for the elderly.

Unemployment insurance

A program that makes payments to people who lose their jobs.

The largest transfer payment programs in the United States, Social Security, Medicare, and unemployment insurance, are not means-tested programs. These programs are called *social insurance* programs because they make payments to anyone—rich or poor—under certain specific circumstances. **Social Security** is the system through which payments from the government are made to individuals when they retire or become disabled. **Medicare** is a health insurance program for older people. **Unemployment insurance** pays money to individuals who are laid off from work.

These programs have effects on income distribution because they transfer income between different groups. Social Security and Medicare payments are financed by payroll taxes from workers. But the payroll taxes paid by a currently working individual are related only loosely to the funds paid out to the same individual after he or she retires. In reality, each year, the funds paid in by current workers are paid out to current retirees. In other words, Social Security and Medicare are, in effect, transfer programs from young people to older people.

Because the social insurance programs are not means-tested, they can end up transferring income from the current working poor to middle-income and even wealthy retirees. In other words, these programs are not well targeted at the low-income groups. For this reason, many people have suggested that these programs be means-tested. The arguments for means-testing have become stronger as the aging of the U.S. population increases the strain on these programs, especially on Medicare. In fact, recent legislation has effectively reduced Social Security benefits to high-income older people by requiring that a major part of the benefits be included in taxable income; Social Security benefits formerly were excluded from taxable income.

2.4 Mandated Benefits

Mandated benefits

Benefits that a firm is required by law to provide to its employees.

Mandated benefits occur when a firm is required by the government to provide a benefit for its workers. For example, a federal law requires firms to give unpaid leave to employees to care for a newborn baby or a sick relative. Such benefits are a cost to the firm (for example, the cost of finding and training replacements or providing health insurance to the workers on leave). But, of course, they are a benefit to the workers.

We can analyze the effects of mandated benefits using the supply and demand for labor diagram, much as we analyzed the effects of a payroll tax. As shown in Figure 14.9, the labor demand curve shifts down, as it did in Figure 14.6 for the employer-paid payroll tax—to hire a given quantity of labor, the wage that the firm will be willing to pay is lower because it also has to pay the mandated benefits. But the mandated benefits also shift the labor supply curve down—workers will be willing to work for a lower wage because they receive the mandated benefits by working. The labor supply curve probably will not shift down as much as the labor demand curve does because the workers probably will not value the benefit quite as much as the benefit costs the firm.

FIGURE 14.9 Effect of a Mandated Benefit

A mandated benefit is a cost to the firm; it shifts down the demand curve for labor just as a payroll tax does. But in the case of a mandated benefit, the labor supply curve shifts down too. Hence, the wage paid to the worker falls, as does employment.

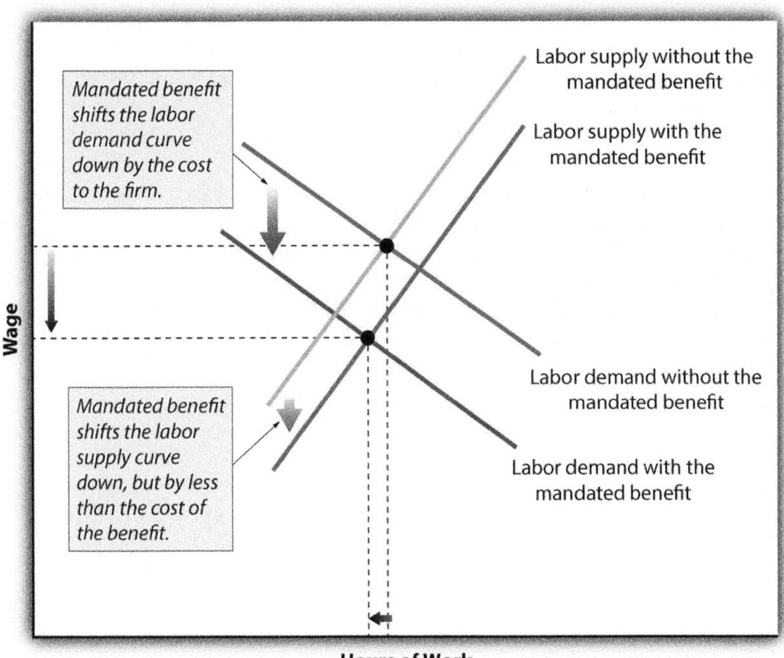

The new equilibrium in Figure 14.9 shows that the wage paid to the workers will fall as a result of the creation of the mandated benefit. In other words, despite the fact that the employer is the one supposedly "paying" for the mandated benefit, both the employer and the employee end up paying the benefit. Employment also will be reduced. If the workers value the benefit exactly as much as it costs the firm, then the wage will fall by the full amount of the benefit. In this case, employment will not fall at all.

REVIEW

- The two major types of transfer payments are means-tested programs, which depend on the income of the recipient, and social insurance programs, which do not depend on the income of the recipient.
- The major means-tested transfer programs in the United States include the following: the TANF program, Medicaid, and the EITC program. These transfer programs all target their benefits to the poor and reduce benefits as the income levels of individuals rise
- As a result, means-tested transfer payments create disincentives for work. The loss of assistance from means-tested programs as one's labor income rises implies that these programs act as a tax on labor income.
- The purpose of welfare reform is to reduce those disincentives for the TANF program by imposing work requirements and time limits on payment of benefits to welfare recipients. The EITC program also is designed to create an incentive for the very poor to work because their benefits initially rise with labor income.
- Social insurance programs like Social Security and Medicare are the largest transfer programs in the United States. These programs are not means- tested, which means that they transfer income from current workers to current retirees regardless of how poor the current worker is and how wealthy the current retiree is.
- As the number of elderly Americans rises and the cost of these transfer programs increases, economists and policy makers have advocated turning social insurance programs into means-tested programs.
- Another way that the government can transfer money to individuals is through mandated benefits, such as family leave. If individuals do not value the benefit as much as it costs firms to provide the benefit, then the workers' wages will fall by an amount less than the increase in the benefit. If the workers value the benefit at exactly the level that it costs the firm to provide it, then the wage will fall by the full amount of the benefit. In either case, the costs of the benefit are borne by both the firm and the worker, even if the firm technically pays for the benefit.

3. THE DISTRIBUTION OF INCOME IN THE UNITED STATES

Now that we have understood some important details about the tax and transfer system in the United States, we can take a closer look at how these have affected the distribution of income in the United States. We begin by examining what the distribution of income in the United States actually looks like, and how that distribution compares to the distribution in other countries. We then ask what changes in income distribution have occurred over time, and how those changes are related to the tax and transfer policies adopted by the government.

3.1 The Personal Distribution of Income

Current Population Survey

A monthly survey of a sample of U.S. households done by the U.S. Census Bureau; it measures employment, unemployment, the labor force, and other characteristics of the U.S. population.

To answer questions about income distribution in the United States, we first need to know what kinds of data are available and how we can construct a quantitative measure of income distribution using those data. Data about people's income in the United States are collected by the U.S. Census Bureau in a monthly survey of about 60,000 households called the **Current Population Survey**.

Economists and statisticians usually study the income distribution of families or households rather than individuals. A *family* is defined by the Census Bureau as a group of two or more people related by birth, marriage, or adoption who live in the same housing unit. A *household* consists of all related family members and unrelated individuals who live in the same housing unit. Because the members of a family or a household typically share their income, it usually is more sensible to consider families or households rather than individuals. One would not say that a young child who earns nothing is poor if the child's mother or father earns $100,000 a year. In a family in which one spouse works and the other remains at home, one would not say that the working spouse is rich and the nonworking spouse is poor.

quintiles

Divisions or groupings of one-fifth of a population ordered by income, wealth, or some other statistic.

Because the population comprises so many people, it is necessary to have a simple way to summarize the income data. One way to do this is to arrange the population into a small number of groups ranging from the poorest to the richest. Most typically, the population is divided into fifths, called **quintiles**, with the same percentage of families or households in each quintile. For example, in Table 14.3, the 77 million families in the United States are divided into five quintiles, with 15.4 million families in each quintile. The first row shows the poorest 20 percent—the bottom quintile. The next several rows show the higher-income quintiles, with the last row showing the 20 percent with the highest incomes.

The second and third columns of Table 14.3 show how much income is earned by families in each of the five groups. The bottom 20 percent of families have incomes below $20,453, the families in the next quintile have incomes greater than $20,453 but less than $38,550, and so on. Note that the lower limit for families in the top 20 percent is $100,000. The lower limit for the top 5 percent (not shown in the table) is $173,640.

Inequality can be better measured by considering the total income in each quintile as a percentage of the total income in the country. Table 14.4 provides this information. The second column in Table 14.4 shows the income received by families in each quintile as a percentage of total income in the United States.

A quick look at Table 14.4 shows that the distribution of income is far from equal. Those in the lower 20 percent earn only 3.4 percent of total income. On the other hand, those in the top 20 percent earn 50.2 percent of total income. Thus, the amount of income earned by the richest quartile is over 15 times the amount of income earned by the poorest quartile.

3.2 The Lorenz Curve and the Gini Coefficient

The third column of Table 14.4 shows the cumulative portion of income earned by the different segments of the distribution in the year 2009 (the last year for which coverage is available in the Statistical Abstract of the United States). The bottom 20 percent earned 3.4 percent of the income, the bottom 40 percent earned 12.0 percent of the income, the bottom 60 percent earned 26.6 percent of the income, and the bottom 80 percent earned just under 50 percent of the income. The top 5 percent, not shown in Table 14.4, earned 21.7 percent of the aggregate income.

TABLE 14.3 Range of Annual Family Incomes (in 2009 dollars) for Five Quintiles

Quintile	Income Greater Than	Income Less Than
Bottom 20 percent	0	$20,453
Second 20 percent	$20,453	$38,550
Third 20 percent	$38,550	$61,801
Fourth 20 percent	$61,801	$100,000
Top 20 percent	$100,000	--

Source: Statistical Abstract of the United States (Washington, DC: U.S. Census Bureau, 2012), table 696.

TABLE 14.4 Distribution of Family Income by Quintile

Quintile	Percentage of Income	Cumulative Percentage of Income
Bottom 20 percent	3.4	3.4
Second 20 percent	8.6	12.0
Third 20 percent	14.6	26.6
Fourth 20 percent	23.2	49.8
Top 20 percent	50.2	100.0

Source: Statistical Abstract of the United States (Washington, DC: U.S. Census Bureau, 2012), table 694.

These data can be presented in a useful graphic form. Figure 14.10 shows the cumulative percentage of income from the third column of Table 14.4 on the vertical axis and the percentage representing each quintile from the first column on the horizontal axis. The five dots in the figure are the five pairs of observations from the table. For example, point *A* at the lower left corresponds to the 4 percent of income earned by the lowest 20 percent of people. Point *B* corresponds to the 13.6 percent of income earned by the lowest 40 percent of people. The other points are plotted the same way. The uppermost point occurs where 100 percent of the income is earned by 100 percent of the people.

If we connect these five points, we get a curve that is bowed out. This curve is called the **Lorenz curve**. To measure how bowed out the curve is, we draw the solid black 45-degree line. The 45-degree line is a line of perfect equality. On that line, the lowest 20 percent earn exactly 20 percent of the income, the lowest 40 percent earn exactly 40 percent of the income, and so on. Every household earns exactly the same amount.

Lorenz curve

A curve showing the relation between the cumulative percentage of the population and the proportion of total income earned by each cumulative percentage. It measures income inequality.

FIGURE 14.10 The Lorenz Curve for the United States

Each point on the Lorenz curve gives the percentage of income received by a percentage of households. The plotted points are for the United States. Point *A* shows that 3.4 percent of income is received by the lowest 20 percent of families. Point *B* shows that 12.0 percent of income is received by the lowest 40 percent of families. These two points and the others in the figure come from Table 14.4. In addition, the 45-degree line shows perfect equality, and the solid lines along the horizontal and right-hand vertical axes show perfect inequality. The shaded area between the 45-degree line and the Lorenz curve is a measure of inequality. The ratio of this area to the area of the triangle below the 45-degree line is the Gini coefficient. The Gini coefficient for 2012 is 0.433.

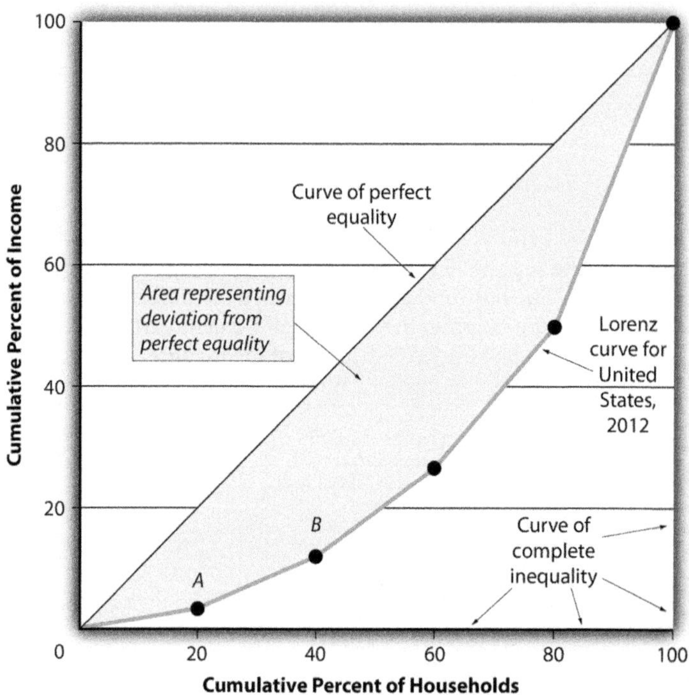

The degree to which the Lorenz curve is bowed out from the 45-degree line provides a visual gauge of the inequality of income. The more bowed out the line is, the more unequal the income distribution. The most unequal distribution possible would occur when only one person earns all the income. In that case, the curve could be so bowed out from the 45-degree line that it would consist of a straight line on the horizontal axis up to 100 and then a vertical line. For example, 99.9 percent of the households would earn 0 percent of the income. Only when the richest person is included do we get 100 percent of the income.

FIGURE 14.11 Changes in Income Inequality: The U.S. Gini Coefficient

The Gini coefficient is large when inequality is greater, as measured by the Lorenz curve in Figure 14-10. Thus, by this measure, inequality fell in the United States from 1950 to 1970 but increased from 1970 to 2004.

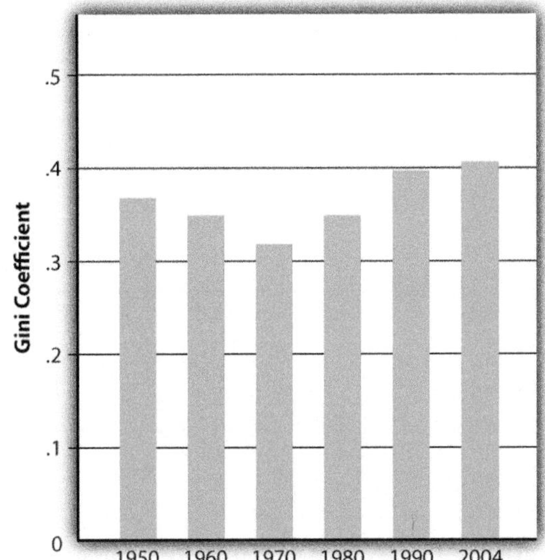

The **Gini coefficient** is a useful numerical measure of how bowed out the Lorenz curve is. It is defined as the ratio of the area of the gap between the 45-degree line and the Lorenz curve to the area between the lines of perfect equality and perfect inequality. The Gini coefficient can range between zero and one. It has a value of one if the area between the diagonal line and the Lorenz curve is one. Thus, when the Gini coefficient is zero, we have perfect equality. The Gini coefficient would be one if only one person earned all the income in the economy.

Gini coefficient

An index of income inequality ranging between zero (for perfect equality) and one (for absolute inequality); it is defined as the ratio of the area between the Lorenz curve and the perfect equality line to the area between the lines of perfect equality and perfect inequality.

Figure 14.11 shows how the Gini coefficient has changed in the United States over the last 50 years. The Gini coefficient has varied within a narrow range, from 0.3 to slightly more than 0.4. The most notable feature of the trend in the Gini coefficient in Figure 14.11 is the decline after World War II until around 1970 and the subsequent increase. It is clear that income inequality has increased in recent years. Higher earnings of skilled and educated workers relative to the less skilled and less educated may partly explain this change in income distribution. But the reason for these changes in income inequality remains a major unsettled question for economists.

An increase in income inequality, as in Figure 14.11, does not necessarily mean that the rich got richer and the poor got poorer. For example, if one looks at average income in each quintile, one finds an increase for all groups from 1970 to 2004, even after adjusting for inflation. However, average income, in the top quintile increased by a larger percentage amount than average income in the bottom quintile.

Comparison with Other Countries

Lorenz curves and Gini coefficients can be calculated for different countries or groups of countries. For most European countries, the Lorenz curve is closer to equality than it is for the United States. Canada, Australia, and the United Kingdom have Lorenz curves similar to that of the United States. Income distribution, however, varies much more when we look beyond the industrial countries. As Figure 14.12 shows, Bangladesh, an extremely poor country, has a more equal income distribution than the United States. Brazil, a middle-income country also much poorer than the United States, has a much less equal income distribution. Among individual countries, Bangladesh and Brazil are close to the extremes: 60 percent of the population receives 40 percent of the income in Bangladesh, 19 percent of the income in Brazil, and 29 percent in the United States.

FIGURE 14.12 Income Distribution around the World

Income distributions vary widely around the world. Bangladesh and Brazil are on either side of the United States. When we look at the world as a whole, income inequality is highest because we combine the very poor of Sub-Saharan Africa with the very rich of the member countries of the Organisation for Economic Co-operation and Development (OECD).

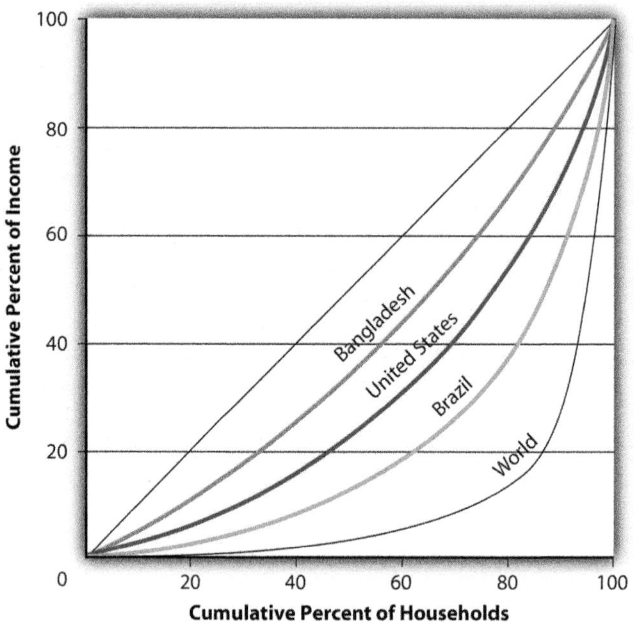

Note: World curve computed from population data for low-, lower-middle-, upper-middle-, and high income countries.

Income distribution for the world as a whole is far more unequal than that for any one country because the very poor in some countries are combined with the very rich in other countries. For example, when West Germany united with East Germany to form one country, the income distribution became more unequal for the unified country as a whole than it had been for either country before unification. The Lorenz curve for the world as a whole—as illustrated in Figure 14.12—shows far greater inequality than the curve for any one country: 60 percent of the world's population receives only 5 percent of the income.

Income Mobility

In interpreting income distribution statistics, it is important to recognize that the quintiles do not refer to the same people as years pass. In its 2003 *Survey of Income and Program Participation*, the U.S. Census Bureau reported that 38 percent of those households in the lowest-income quintile in 1996 were in a higher-income quintile in 1999. People who are in the top quintile in one year may be in the bottom quintile the next year (perhaps because they retired, or because they temporarily left the labor force). And people who are in the bottom quintile one year may be in the top quintile the next year (because they completed their MBA degree or because they reentered the work force after a short absence).

How significant is income mobility? Economic research on the United States shows that about two-thirds of the people in any one quintile move to another over a 10-year period. About half of those in the top quintile move to a lower quintile, and about half of those in the bottom quintile move to a higher quintile. Some recent studies have shown, however, that the persistence of income inequality across generations is higher in the United States than in other OECD countries, like Germany.

Long-Term Income Inequality

Distinguishing between income in any one year and income over several years is also important. In a typical life span, people usually earn less when they are young than when they are middle aged. As they grow older and become more experienced, their wages and salaries increase. When people retire, their income usually declines again. Thus, even if everyone had the exact same lifetime income, one would see inequality in the income distribution every year. Middle-aged people would be relatively rich, whereas young and old people would be relatively poor.

Changing Composition of Households

The formation or splitting up of households also can affect the distribution of income. For example, if two individuals who were living separately form a household, the household income doubles. Households splitting apart can alter the income distribution drastically. If one adult leaves the family, perhaps because of divorce or desertion, and the other one stays home with the children, the income of the household declines substantially. It appears that the splitting apart of households has had an impact on income distribution in the United States. According to some estimates, if household composition had not changed in the United States in the last 20 years, the increase in inequality as measured by the Gini coefficient would have been only half as great.

Distribution of Income versus Distribution of Wealth

Another factor to keep in mind when interpreting data on the income distribution is the distinction between *income* and *wealth.* Your annual income is what you earn each year. Your wealth, or your net worth, is all you own minus what you owe others. Wealth changes over a person's lifetime even more than income does as people save for retirement. For example, a young person who has just graduated and gotten a high-paying job may have a high income but little wealth or, with a college loan still to pay off, may even have negative net worth. Conversely, a diligent saver who has just retired will have little income, but may have a sizable retirement fund, and thus be relatively wealthy.

According to most recent surveys, the top 10 percent of households have two-thirds of the wealth in the United States and the top 1 percent hold one-third of the wealth. Although such surveys are not as accurate as the regular monthly surveys of 60,000 households on which our information about income distribution is based, it is clear that the distribution of wealth is less equal than the distribution of income.

3.3 Poverty and Measurement

Poverty can be observed virtually everywhere. The poor are visible in the blighted sections of cities and in remote rural areas. Almost everyone has seen the serious problems of the homeless in cities of the United States. CNN has brought the agony of poverty from faraway countries like Somalia and from nearby cities like New Orleans closer to us through our television screens.

As with inequality, economists have developed quantitative measures of poverty. The **poverty rate** is the percentage of people who live in poverty. To calculate the poverty rate, one needs to define what it means to live in poverty. In the United States, poverty usually is defined quantitatively by a **poverty line,** an estimate of the minimal amount of annual income a family needs to avoid severe economic hardship. The poverty line in the United States is based on a survey showing that families spend, on average, one-third of their income on food. The poverty line is thus obtained by multiplying by three the U.S. Department of Agriculture's estimate of the amount of money needed to purchase a low-cost nutritionally adequate amount of food. In addition, adjustments are made for the size of the family. Table 14.5 shows the poverty line for several different family sizes. Since the 1960s, when it was first developed, the poverty line has been increased to adjust for inflation.

poverty rate
The percentage of people living below the poverty line.

poverty line
An estimate of the minimum amount of annual income required for a family to avoid severe economic hardship.

TABLE 14.5 **The Poverty Line in the United States, 2011**

Persons in Family or Household	Poverty Line
1	$12,060
2	$16,240
3	$20,420
4	$24,600
5	$28,780

Source: U.S. Census Bureau.

Using the poverty line and data on the income distribution, one can determine the number of people who live in poverty and the poverty rate. The overall poverty rates in the United States have varied over the last 50 years. The overall poverty rate declined sharply from 22 percent in 1960 to 11.1 percent in 1973, but it has risen since then. In 2015, the poverty rate was 13.5 percent, or 43.1 million people.

Important trends in poverty emerge among different groups in the U.S. population. For example, the percentage of children who live in poverty rose in the 1970s, 1980s, and early 1990s. During the same time period, the poverty rate for the elderly declined, and this held down the overall poverty rate. In 1993, when child poverty was at a peak, 22.7 percent of children were living in poverty; at the same time, the poverty rate for the elderly was 12.2 percent. In 2015, 19.7 percent of children and 8.8 percent of the elderly were living in poverty. The dramatic decline in the poverty rate for the elderly since the 1970s (from 24.6 percent in 1970) is largely attributed to the change in Social Security benefits and other retirement benefits.

The increase in poverty for children is troublesome, and it is difficult to explain. Some of it may have to do with the increase in single-headed households with children, which are usually poorer than two-adult households. Poverty rates in households with a single head and at least one child have ranged between 35 and 40 percent in the last 20 years—three times the overall poverty rate. Between 1993 and 2000, the poverty rate for children declined from 22.7 percent to 16.2 percent. Since the 2008/09 recession, it has risen, reaching a rate of 19.7 percent in 2015.

3.4 Effects of Taxes and Transfers on Income Distribution and Poverty

Many believe that the main purpose of government redistribution of income through taxes and transfers is to help the poor. For this reason, the term *social safety net* sometimes is used for an income redistribution system. These programs try to prevent those who were born into poverty, or who have become poor, from falling too far down in income and therefore in nutrition, health, and general well-being.

How successful has this redistribution effort been? Estimates by the U.S. Census Bureau indicate that the tax and transfer system reduces the poverty rate by about 10 percentage points: These estimates ignore any of the incentive effects mentioned earlier, such as the reduced work incentives that might result from the tax and transfer system. And they ignore any possible response of private efforts to redistribute income—such as charities—that might occur as a result of changes in the government's role.

REVIEW

- The distribution of income can be measured by the percentage of income earned by quintiles of households or families. In the United States in 2004, the bottom quintile earned about 4 percent of the income, whereas the top quintile earned about 48 percent.
- The Lorenz curve provides a graphic summary of the relationship between the cumulative quintiles (ordered from poorest to richest) and cumulative income. If income inequality is not pronounced, the Lorenz curve will lie closer to the 45-degree "line of perfect equality."
- The Gini coefficient is a numerical measure of inequality—it captures how bowed out the Lorenz curve is from the 45-degree line. The higher the Gini coefficient, the more unequal the distribution of income is.
- Income inequality has risen in the United States since 1970. Part of the explanation may be the materialization of higher returns to educated and skilled workers in recent times, but this by no means is the only explanation.
- Before we worry about the magnitude of the Gini coefficient, we should recognize the possibility that (1) people may be mobile across quintiles, (2) long-term income inequality may paint a different picture from that provided by a study done at one point in time, (3) aging populations and changing compositions of households can affect income inequality measures without any changes in the earning patterns of different groups in the economy, and (4) the distribution of wealth is also an important measure of inequality.
- Taxes and transfers are used widely to combat poverty and reduce income inequality in the United States. Evaluating the success of these programs requires an understanding of how poverty is defined and measured.
- The poverty rate is a quantitative measure of the amount of poverty in the United States; it is defined as the percentage of people living below a poverty line. The poverty line for the United States is an estimate of how much money a family needs to avoid severe economic hardship.
- Over the last three decades in the United States, the poverty rate among children has increased and the poverty rate for the elderly has declined. Estimates indicate that the tax and transfer system currently makes the poverty rate lower than it otherwise would be. Nevertheless, the increase in poverty among children has raised serious concerns about the tax and transfer system in the United States.

4. END-OF-CHAPTER MATERIALS

4.1 Conclusion

In a democracy, the people and their representatives determine the amount of government redistribution of income. A majority seems to want some redistribution of income, but debate continues about how much the government should do. Why doesn't a democracy lead to much more redistribution? After all, 60 percent of the people, according to Table 14.4, receive only 26.6 percent of the income. Because 60 percent of the voting population is enough to win an election, this 60 percent could vote to redistribute income much further. Why hasn't it?

This probably has not happened for a number of reasons. The first reason is the trade-off that exists between equality and efficiency. People realize that taking away incentives to work will reduce the size of the pie for everyone. Another reason is that most of us believe that people should be rewarded for their work. Just as we can think of a fair income distribution, we can think about a fair reward system. If some students want to work hard in high school so that they can attend college, why shouldn't they earn the additional income that comes from that hard work?

The second reason is the connection between personal freedom and economic freedom. Government involvement in income distribution means government involvement in people's lives. Those who cherish the idea of personal freedom worry about a system that takes a large amount of income from people who work.

The third reason is that much income redistribution occurs through the private sector—private charities and churches. The distribution of food and the provision of health care have long been supported by nongovernment organizations. In times of floods or earthquakes, it is common for people to volunteer to help those in distress. Private charity has certain advantages over government. Individuals become more personally involved if they perform a public service, whether volunteering at a soup kitchen or tutoring at an elementary school.

In recent years, the United States has experienced a rise in income inequality, which has raised concerns about the adequacy of the existing transfer and tax policies. Expanding the EITC program, means-testing social insurance programs, and changing the progressivity of the income tax system all have been proposed to deal with the fact that the incomes of the poor have been growing much more slowly than have the incomes of the rich. Similar concerns have been raised about poverty, including the increase in poverty among children and the rising number of people without adequate health insurance programs, who could suffer a serious hit to their net worth if they were to fall ill. If income inequality continues to rise, and more people begin to worry about its potential to have detrimental effects on the economy, the democratic system should bring about policies and policy makers who take a keen interest in the issues discussed in this chapter.

Key Points

1. In modern democracies, the government plays a major role in trying to help the poor and in providing a more equal income distribution through the use of taxes and transfers.
2. Taxes are needed to pay for transfers and other government spending. In the United States, the personal income tax and the payroll tax are by far the most significant sources of tax revenue at the federal level. Sales taxes and property taxes play a significant role at the local level.
3. Taxes cause inefficiencies, as measured by deadweight loss, because taxes reduce the amount of the economic activity being taxed—whether it is the production of a good or the labor of workers.
4. The incidence of a tax depends on the price elasticity of supply and demand. The deadweight loss from taxes on goods with low price elasticities is relatively small.
5. Transfer payments are classified into means-tested programs—such as welfare and food stamps—and social insurance programs—such as Social Security and unemployment insurance.
6. Transfer payments can cause inefficiency as a result of disincentives to work or the incentive for families to split up.
7. A trade-off exists between equality and efficiency. Tax reform and welfare reform try to improve incentives and reduce inefficiency.
8. The distribution of income has grown more unequal in recent years.
9. Poverty among children has increased, while poverty among the elderly has declined in recent years.
10. The tax and transfer system has reduced income inequality and lowered poverty rates, but much room exists for improvement and reform.

QUESTIONS FOR REVIEW

1. Provide simple definitions of the following: tax bracket, marginal tax rate, average tax rate, deductions, and exemptions.
2. Why does a deadweight loss result from the personal income tax? What factors can lead to the deadweight loss being large or small?
3. What do economists mean when they talk about "tax incidence"? How is the incidence of taxes related to the elasticities of demand and supply?
4. What are the impacts of an increase in the income tax on the labor market?
5. Intuitively explain why the effects of a payroll tax are the same whether the employer or the worker pays it.
6. What is the relationship between the tax rate and tax revenue? Explain under what circumstances a Laffer curve would emerge.
7. What are the major types of transfer programs in the United States? Provide examples of specific programs that fall under each type.
8. How do these transfer programs affect the incentives to work? Describe both positive and negative effects.
9. How is the distribution of income measured by the Lorenz curve and the Gini coefficient?
10. Why are income mobility and lifetime income important to consider in interpreting Gini coefficients and other income distribution statistics?

PROBLEMS

1. Consider the following 2016 personal income tax schedule obtained from the IRS website. It applies to a taxpayer who is not married (single).

If Taxable Income Is Over	But Not Over	The Tax Is
$0	$9,275	10% of the amount over $0
$9,275	$37,650	$927.50 plus 15% of the amount over $9,275
$37,650	$91,150	$5,183.75 plus 25% of the amount over $37,650

   a. What is the tax due on a taxable income of $25,000?
   b. What is the tax due on a taxable income of $50,000?
   c. Why does the tax more than double when the income doubles?
   d. Is this tax system progressive?

2. Consider the following 2016 personal income tax schedule obtained from the IRS website. It applies to a married couple that is combining their incomes and filing jointly.

If Taxable Income Is Over	But Not Over	The Tax Is
$0	$18,550	10% of the amount over $0
$18,550	$75,300	$1,855 plus 15% of the amount over $18,550
$75,300	$151,900	$10,367.50 plus 25% of the amount over $75,300

   a. What is the tax due for a couple if each spouse has a taxable income of $25,000?
   b. Use the results from the preceding question to compare the tax the couple would have paid if they were not married (and filed as single persons) to the amount of tax they pay as a married couple (filing jointly).
   c. What is the tax due for a couple if one spouse has a taxable income of $50,000 and the other spouse has no taxable income?
   d. Does the tax system treat households making the same amount of income in an identical manner? Can it do so while remaining a progressive system?

3. Two popular programs for helping workers with very low incomes are to raise the minimum wage and to raise the EITC. Why do economists tend to favor the EITC?
4. California tried to impose a "snack" tax—one that applied only to what the legislators thought was junk food. Suppose snack food has a higher elasticity of demand than non-snack food. Draw a supply and demand diagram to explain which tax—on snack food or on non-snack food—will cause the price to rise more. Which will produce a greater deadweight loss?
5. Suppose the government decides to increase the payroll tax paid by employers. If the labor supply curve has a low elasticity, what will happen to the workers' wages? Who actually bears the burden of the tax, the workers or the firms? Would it be different if the labor supply had a high elasticity?
6. Suppose that the labor demand curve is perfectly flat. What is the impact on a typical worker's hourly wage if the government increases the payroll tax paid by employers by 10 percent of the wage? Show what happens in a labor supply and labor demand graph. Why does the slope of the labor supply curve not affect your answer?
7. The Family Leave Act is a federal law that requires employers to give employees unpaid leave to care for a newborn or a sick relative. Show how the Family Leave Act affects the supply and demand for labor. According to this model, what will happen to wages and employment compared with the situation before the law was passed?
8. The following table gives hours worked and the welfare payment received.

Hours Worked	Wage Payment	Welfare Payment	Total Income
0		$10,000	
500		$8,000	
1,000		$6,000	
1,500		$4,000	
2,000		$2,000	

   a. Calculate the missing data in the table, given that the hourly wage is $5 and total income is the sum of the wage payment and the welfare payment.
   b. Draw a graph that shows how much total income a worker earns with and without this welfare program. Put the number of hours worked on the horizontal axis and total income on the vertical axis.
   c. What is the increase in total income for each additional hour worked without any welfare program? Compare it with the increase in total income for each additional hour worked under the welfare program.
   d. How could the welfare program be changed to increase the incentive to work without reducing total income for a full-time worker (40 hours per week, 50 weeks per year, $5 per hour) below $12,000, which is already below the poverty line for a family of four?
9. The following table gives the income distribution in Brazil and in Australia. Draw the Lorenz curve for each. Which country has the larger Gini coefficient?

Quintile	Percent of Income in Brazil	Percent of Income in Australia
Bottom 20 percent	2.4	4.4
Second 20 percent	5.7	11.1
Third 20 percent	10.7	17.5
Fourth 20 percent	18.6	24.8
Top 20 percent	62.6	42.2

10. Analyze the distribution of income, using the household incomes in the following table. Rank the families by income. Compute the percentage of total income going to the poorest 20 percent of the families, the second 20 percent, and the richest 20 percent. Draw a Lorenz curve for the income distribution of these 10 families. Is their distribution more equal or less equal than that of the U.S. population as a whole?

Family	Income
Jones	$12,000
Pavlov	$100,000
Cohen	$24,000
Baker	$87,000
Dixon	$66,000
Sun	$72,000
Tanaka	$18,000
Bernardo	$45,000
Smith	$28,000
Lopez	$33,000

CHAPTER 15
Public Goods, Externalities, and Government Behavior

When asked what it was like to work on the President's Council of Economic Advisers, Nobel Laureate Robert Solow answered:

> *On any given day in the executive branch, there are more meetings than Heinz has varieties. At a very large proportion of these meetings, the representative of some agency or some interest will be trying to sell a hare-brained economic proposal. I am exaggerating a little. Not every one of these ideas is crazy. Most of them are just bad: either impractical, inefficient, excessively costly, likely to be accompanied by undesirable side effects, or just misguided—unlikely to accomplish their stated purpose. Someone has to knock those proposals down. . . . That is where the Council's comparative advantage lies. . . . [But that] does not mean that we won all the battles; we lost at least as many as we won. The race is not always won by the best arguments, not in political life anyway. But we always felt we had a chance and we kept trying.*

The purpose of this chapter is to examine two of the most basic economic principles—public goods and externalities—that economists on the president's Council and elsewhere use to determine whether proposals for government intervention are crazy, just bad, or actually good. We also show how cost-benefit analysis can help make decisions about particular government programs. Finally, we examine models of government behavior to understand why "in political life," as Solow puts it, the best economic arguments do not always win. We will see that politicians are influenced by incentives as much as anyone else.

Source: © cdrin / Shutterstock, Inc.

1. PUBLIC GOODS

Table 15.1 shows the range of goods and services produced by all levels of government in the United States: The federal government, the 50 state governments, and more than 85,000 local governments (counties, cities, towns, and school districts). According to data from the U.S. Census Bureau, in terms of employment, the largest sector of government production in the United States is education at all levels, from elementary school to graduate school. Education is followed by health and hospital services, police, national defense, the postal service, corrections (prisons), and highways. (The figures for national defense include only civilian workers; if Table 15.1 included those serving in the armed forces, national defense would be second on the list.) The other categories, ranging from the judicial and legal system (federal, state, and county courts) to parks and recreation, each are significant but small relative to the total.

TABLE 15.1 Types of Goods and Services Produced by Government in the United States

Type of Good or Service	Employment as a Percent of Total Government
Education	49.8
Health and hospitals	8.6
Police protection	5.4
National defense (civilian)	3.6
Corrections (prisons)	3.4
Postal Service	2.7
Highways	2.4
Judicial and legal	2.2
Parks and recreation	1.9
Fire protection	1.9
All other	18.1

Source: Bureau of Census, 2012 Census of Governments: Employment Summary Report

Observe also the types of goods and services that are not on the list because they are produced by the private sector. Manufacturing, mining, retail trade, wholesale trade, hotel services, and motion picture production are some of the items that are largely left to the private sector. Note also that for all the goods and services on the list in Table 15.1, the private sector provides at least some of the production. The private health care sector has 60 millions workers, for example, compared with 2 million in government health care. The private sector also is involved in mail delivery, education, garbage collection, and even fire protection (volunteer fire departments).

Why is the government involved in the production of police services and education services but not in the production of automobiles? Why are education and health services provided by both the private sector and the government sector, whereas judicial services and national defense services are provided only by the government? In more general terms, why is it necessary for governments to produce *any* goods and services? The concept of a public good helps us answer the question.

1.1 Nonrivalry and Nonexcludability

public good

A good or service that has two characteristics: nonrivalry in consumption and nonexcludability.

Nonrivalry

The situation in which increased consumption of a good by one person does not decrease the amount available for consumption by others.

Nonexcludability

The situation in which no one can be excluded from consuming a good.

A **public good** is a good or service that has two characteristics: *nonrivalry in consumption* and *nonexcludability*. **Nonrivalry** in consumption means that more consumption of a good by one person does not imply less consumption of it by another person. Clean air and national defense are examples of goods with nonrivalry. For example, if you were to take a walk outside and bask in the warm sunshine and breathe more clean air, you are not depriving another person of the opportunity to enjoy the sunshine or to breathe the clean air. Similarly, the sense of security that you get from a country's national defense—the military personnel, the strategic alliances, the missile defense system—is not reduced by the fact that your neighbor enjoys the same benefits of a national defense system.

In contrast, for most goods, there is rivalry in consumption. For example, if you purchase a ripe apple from the supermarket and eat it, then no one else can consume that apple. When you sit in the library and read this economics textbook, no one else can read this particular copy of the textbook. But for a good with nonrivalry in consumption, everybody can consume more if they want to. The good has a collective aspect, and the total benefit is the sum of the benefits to every person.

Nonexcludability means that one cannot exclude people from consuming the good. For example, the supermarket will not let you eat the apple unless you pay for it. The library will not let you check out the copy of the textbook unless you have a valid student ID card. These are excludable goods. On the other hand, no one can stop you from going outside, basking in the sunshine, and breathing clean air. The security provided by national defense is available to you, and no one can prevent you from benefiting from that security. A good or service that has nonrivalry in consumption and nonexcludability is a *public good.* In contrast, a *privategood* has excludability and *rivalry.*

1.2 Free Riders: A Difficulty for the Private Sector

People can enjoy the consumption of a nonexcludable good or service without having to pay for it. Furthermore, if that good is also a nonrival good, then its use by nonpaying consumers does not reduce the ability of paying consumers to enjoy that good. Hence, instead of people clamoring to deny the use of a good to nonpaying consumers, you would see previously paying consumers also turn into nonpaying consumers. Pretty soon, the only consumers of the nonrival, nonexcludable good will be nonpaying ones, and hence no one will have the incentive to provide that public good to the marketplace. We describe this situation as a **free-rider problem** associated with public goods: People who do not contribute to the costs of providing the good end up benefiting from the good because they cannot be excluded.

free-rider problem

A problem arising in the case of public goods because those who do not contribute to the costs of providing the public good cannot be excluded from the benefits of the good.

To better understand this concept, imagine that you bought a huge bus for the purpose of transporting students around the college town and collecting a little money for your service. But suppose the bus had a broken rear door that allowed people to get on and off without paying and without interfering with other people's travel. In that situation, you soon would find that all your riders would be nonpaying ones. If you could not fix the door or do something else to exclude the free riders, you would not be in the transportation business long, because without fares, you would have losses.

National defense is like the huge bus with the broken rear door. You cannot exclude people from enjoying it, even if they do not pay—for instance, if an enemy aircraft is intent on dropping bombs on a city, then shooting down that plane protects everyone's house, not just those of the people who paid for the antiaircraft missile. It is clear, then, that a private firm will have difficulty producing and selling national defense to the people of a country, because everyone will be hoping that someone else will pay for the antiaircraft missile that protects his or her house. Given the free-rider problem, the public good would have to be provided by the government. For instance, the government will be willing to provide national defense. Similar actions are taken with other public goods such as police protection, fire protection, and the judicial system. The government can broadly fund its provision of these public goods by assessing taxes on households.

In the wake of Hurricane Katrina. A Chinook helicopter drops sand bags to plug a canal levee break in the Gentilly neighborhood of New Orleans, Louisiana, on September 11, 2005. Levees are a public good, having characteristics of both nonrivalry and nonexcludability.

Source: © Shutterstock, Inc.

Certain types of information also have the features of a public good. Everyone can benefit from information that a hurricane is on the way; there is no rivalry in consuming this information. Excluding people from consuming that information also would be difficult, because the most effective ways of notifying people quickly would involve radio and television broadcasts that are accessible to all. The U.S. Weather Service therefore will collect and distribute information about hurricanes and other adverse weather events. But you should keep in mind that not all information is nonexcludable. For example, if you want to analyze broad trends in the U.S. economy, you will find that much of the information you need is freely available through the Department of Commerce. If you want to analyze detailed information about companies trading on the New York Stock Exchange, however, you will have to pay a fee to a company before you can gain access to that information. We focus on the type of information that has a public good feature associated with it.

1.3 Avoiding Free-Rider Problems

Even though we define public goods as being goods and services that are nonrival and nonexcludable, few goods are completely nonexcludable. Sometimes the private sector is able to find ways of making a good excludable to a degree sufficient to overcome the free-rider problem. A classic example used by economists to explore the nature of public goods is the lighthouse that warns ships of nearby rocks and prevents them from running aground. A lighthouse has the feature of nonrivalry. If one ship enjoys the benefit of the light and goes safely by, this does not mean that another ship cannot go by. Similarly, it is impossible to exclude ships from using the lighthouse because any ship can benefit from the light it projects.

Lighthouse services, however, are not always provided by the government. Early lighthouses were built by associations of shippers, who charged fees to the ships in nearby ports. This system worked well because the fees could be collected from most shippers as they entered nearby ports. So even if not every ship that used the lighthouse's services could be charged individually for that service (for instance, a ship that did not come into port but sailed by, using the lighthouse to gauge where land was, would not be charged for lighthouse services), many of those who benefited from the good were charged fees, thus alleviating the free-rider problem without government involvement.

The Classic Lighthouse Example: How can the free-rider problem be avoided without government providing the service?

Source: © Shutterstock, Inc.

Another example is over-the-air radio or television broadcasts. Such broadcasts have both characteristics of a public good. They are nonexcludable because anyone can tune into the broadcast, regardless of whether they have paid to see or hear that particular show. They are nonrival because the use of an antenna or an aerial to capture a television or radio signal does not prevent anyone else from doing the same. Despite the public good characteristics of radio and television services, however, private firms always have provided the vast majority of such services in the United States. They are able to do so by using advertising to pay for the provision of the broadcast service, thus avoiding the free-rider problem.

Sometimes governments are able to charge people for the use of particular services that have a certain amount of excludability. This charge is called a **user fee**. In recent years, user fees have become more common in many government-provided services, including the national parks. The aim is to target the payments more closely to the users of the goods and services.

user fee

A fee charged for the use of a good normally provided by the government.

Some public goods and services have closely associated supplements that are provided privately. For instance, even though police services almost always are provided by a local government, businesses and wealthier families in a town may choose to avail themselves of security services provided by private firms to supplement the police services. In these cases, no free-rider problem arises because the private security service is excludable; it is targeted at a particular group, which will be charged for the use of that service.

1.4 Changes in Technology and Excludability

Modern technology is constantly changing the degree to which certain goods are nonexcludable. A good example is the changing public good features of television. Cable television and the ability to scramble signals for those who use satellites to obtain their television signals have reduced the problem of nonexcludability. If one does not pay a cable television bill, the service can be turned off. If one does not pay the satellite fee, the signals can be scrambled so that reception is impossible. Thus, it is now common to see cable television stations like HBO and Showtime delivering specialized programming to small audiences that pay extra for the special service. Such broadcasts may have the luxury of being free of advertising because users can be charged directly for the services.

1.5 The Production of Goods by the Government

If we look at the types of goods produced by government in Table 15.1, we see many public goods, such as national defense, police protection, and the judicial and legal system. Other goods in the list, however, do not have features of public goods. Postal delivery, for example, is a service that has rivalry both in consumption and excludability. If you do not put a stamp on your letter, it is not delivered, and a postal delivery worker's time certainly has rivalry. In principle, education also is characterized by rivalry in consumption and excludability. For a given-size school, an additional student may reduce the education of other students, and it is technologically feasible to exclude a student who does not pay school fees or meet certain admissions criteria.

The mere production of a good by the government does not make that good a public good. In centrally planned economies, the government produces virtually everything, private goods as well as public goods. The economist's definition of a public good is specific and is useful for determining when the government should produce something and when it is better left to the market. If a good or service being produced by the government is not a public good, then it is important to find out the other reasons why the government is involved in the production of that good or service.

1.6 Cost-Benefit Analysis

cost-benefit analysis

An appraisal of a project based on the costs and benefits derived from it.

Suppose the government decides that a particular good or service is a public good and that because of free-rider problems, the private sector will not get involved in the production of that good. Should the good be produced by the government? If so, how much of the good should be produced? Such decisions ultimately are made by voters and elected officials after much political debate. Economic analysis of the costs and benefits of providing the goods and services is critical if the participants in this debate are to make informed decisions. Balancing the costs and benefits of providing a good or service before making a decision is called **cost-benefit analysis**.

Marginal Cost and Marginal Benefit

To determine the quantity of a government-provided service that should be produced, the marginal cost and marginal benefit of the service should be considered. In the case of police services, for example, a decision about whether to increase the size of the police force should consider both the marginal benefit to the people in the city—the reduction in the loss of life and property caused by crime, the increased enjoyment from a secure environment, and safer schools—and the marginal cost—the increased payroll for the police. If the marginal benefit of having more police is greater than the marginal cost of providing more police, then the police force should be increased. The optimal size of the police force should be such that the marginal cost of providing more police is equal to the marginal benefit of having more police.

Measuring the costs of producing government-provided services is not difficult because government workers' wages and materials used in production have explicit dollar values. But measuring the benefits of government-provided services is much more difficult. How do we measure how much people value greater security in their community? How do we value a reduction in violence at schools or a reduced murder rate? Public opinion polls in which people are asked how much they would be willing to pay are a possibility. For example, people can be asked in surveys how much they would be willing to pay for more police in an area. Such estimates of willingness to pay are called **contingent valuations** because they give the value contingent on the public good's existing and the person's having to pay for it. Some economists think that contingent valuation is not reliable if people actually do not have to pay for the good or service. People may not give a good estimate of their true willingness to pay.

contingent valuations

An estimation of the willingness to pay for a project on the part of consumers who may benefit from the project.

REVIEW

- Public goods have two characteristics: nonrivalry, which means that more consumption of the good by one person does not mean that less of the good would be available for someone else, and nonexcludability, which means that it is not possible to exclude those who do not pay for the good from consuming the good.
- These two characteristics lead public goods to have a free-rider problem—people who do not pay for the good can use it without interfering with the ability of those who paid for the good to use it. Instead of objecting to nonpayers' use of the good, the paying customers will soon stop paying. This means that private producers have little incentive to produce this good; thus, government production is frequently necessary.
- If the goods are not completely nonexcludable, the private sector may be able to come up with ways to charge at least some users of the good, enabling it to deal with the free-rider problem and produce goods in the market. Changes in technology also can help make previously nonexcludable goods and services at least partially excludable. Sometimes, even the government may levy user fees on users of some public goods that the government provides.
- In deciding how much of a public good should be provided, cost-benefit analysis can be used. The optimal quantity of the public good or service is the quantity at which the marginal benefit of the good or service equals its marginal cost.
- Even though the marginal cost of providing a public good can be fairly easily calculated, the marginal benefit is harder to calculate. Estimates of willingness to pay, known as contingent valuations, are a somewhat controversial measure of the marginal benefit of a public good.

2. EXTERNALITIES: FROM THE ENVIRONMENT TO EDUCATION

externality

The situation in which the costs of producing or the benefits of consuming a good spill over onto those who are not producing or consuming the good.

negative externalities

The situation in which costs spill over onto someone who is not involved in producing or consuming the good.

positive externality

The situation in which benefits spill over onto someone who is not involved in producing or consuming the good.

We have seen that the existence of public goods provides an economic rationale for government involvement in the production of certain goods and services. Another rationale for government involvement in production is a market failure known as an externality. An **externality** occurs when the costs of producing a good or the benefits from consuming a good spill over onto individuals who are not producing or consuming the good. The production of goods that cause pollution is the classic example of an externality. For example, when a coal-fired electric utility plant produces energy, it emits smoke that contains carbon dioxide, sulfur dioxide, and other pollutants into the air. These pollutants can make life miserable for people breathing the air and can cause serious health concerns. Similarly, people who smoke cigarettes pass on the health risks associated with secondhand smoke to those in their vicinity and reduce the quality of life for people who have negative reactions to the smell of cigarette smoke. These are examples of **negative externalities** because they have a negative effect—a cost—on the well-being of others. A **positive externality** occurs when a positive effect—a benefit—from producing or consuming a good spills over onto others. For example, you might benefit if your neighbor plants a beautiful garden that is visible from your house or apartment. Similarly, if you decide to get a flu shot, then you not only are protected against the flu, but also will not pass on the flu to others with whom you come into contact. We first will look at the effects of negative externalities and then consider positive externalities.

Oil Spill: A Negative Externality. The BP oil spill that lasted three months beginning in April, 2010 is an example of a negative externality: The production of goods or services (oil for fuel) raises costs and/or reduces benefits to the livelihood of people living in and around the Gulf of Mexico who work in the fishing and tourism industries.

Source: © Cheryl Casey/Shutterstock, Inc.

2.1 Negative Externalities

In the case of negative externalities, a competitive market produces a quantity that exceeds the efficient amount of production. For example, companies may be too inclined to use air-polluting fossil fuels to generate energy instead of using a nonpolluting source of energy like solar power. The reason is that producers do not take into account the external costs when they calculate their costs of production. If they did take these costs into account, they would produce less.

marginal private cost

The marginal cost of production as viewed by the private firm or individual.

marginal social cost

The marginal cost of production as viewed by society as a whole.

The reason why competitive markets are not efficient in the case of negative externalities can be illustrated using the supply and demand curves. For example, consider an example of a negative externality resulting from pollution caused by the production of electricity. This negative externality occurs because the production of electricity raises pollution costs to other firms and to individuals. The actual cost of producing electric power is greater than the costs perceived by the electrical utility. In other words, because of the externality, the marginal cost as perceived by the private firm, which we now call the **marginal private cost**, is less than the true marginal cost that is incurred by society, which we call the **marginal social cost**. Marginal social cost is the sum of the firm's marginal private cost and the marginal external cost, that is, the increase in external costs to society as more is produced.

$$\text{Marginal social cost} = \text{marginal private cost} + \text{marginal external cost}$$

We illustrate this equation in Figure 15.1 by drawing a marginal private cost curve below the marginal social cost curve. We use the term *marginal private cost* to refer to what we have thus far called marginal cost to distinguish it from marginal social cost. Recall that adding up all the marginal (private) cost curves for the firms in a market gives the market supply curve, as labeled in the diagram.

FIGURE 15.1 Illustration of a Typical Negative Externality

Because production of the good creates costs external to the firm, the marginal social cost is greater than the marginal private cost to the firm. Thus, the equilibrium quantity that emerges from a competitive market is too large: Marginal benefit is less than marginal social cost.

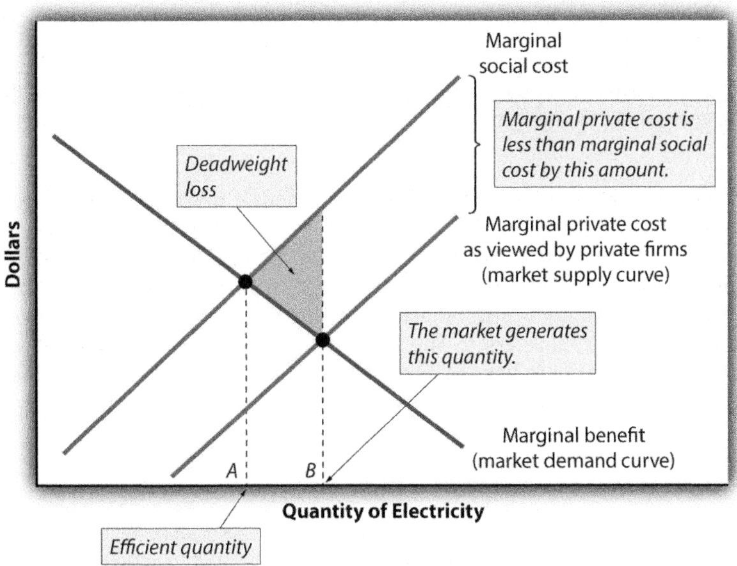

Figure 15.1 also shows the marginal benefit to consumers from using the product, in this case, electrical energy. This is the market demand curve for electricity. According to the supply and demand model, the interaction of firms and consumers in the market will result in a situation in which the marginal cost of production—the marginal private cost—equals marginal benefit. This situation occurs at the market equilibrium, the point at which the quantity supplied equals the quantity demanded. The resulting quantity produced is indicated by point *B* in Figure 15.1.

At this amount of production, however, the marginal benefit of production is less than the *marginal social cost* of production. Marginal benefit equals marginal private cost but is less than marginal social cost. Only at point *A* in the figure is marginal benefit equal to marginal social cost. Thus, point *A* represents the efficient level of production. Because of the externality, too much is produced. Firms produce too much because they do not incur the external costs.

Recall that we calculated how well off an economy is as a result of a particular outcome by adding up the values of consumer surplus and producer surplus. The sum of consumer and producer surplus is the area between the market supply curve and the market demand curve over the range of output produced. Another way to think about it is as the difference between marginal benefit (demand) and marginal cost (supply) over the range of output produced.

In the presence of a negative externality, how well off an economy is really should be measured as the difference between marginal benefit and the *marginal social cost* of production. For each additional unit that is produced above point *A* and below point *B*, the marginal benefit is *less* than the marginal social cost. Hence, the production of each additional unit is a net loss to society, and the overall deadweight loss from producing at the market equilibrium quantity of *B* is indicated by the shaded triangle in Figure 15.1.

2.2 Positive Externalities

A positive externality occurs when the activity of one person makes another person better off, either by reducing costs or by increasing benefits. For example, an individual who acquires additional education will obtain private benefits in the form of increased earnings. But the education also benefits society. Going to school and learning to read, write, and think makes people better citizens who will be able to teach their kids how to read and write, who will be able to pass on knowledge about discoveries they make to others, and who will be able to read about proper hygiene and health practices and thus reduce the burden on the public health system.

Another example of a good with a positive externality is research. Firms that engage in research get some of the benefits of that research through the products that they can sell—for instance, a new pharmaceutical to treat a particular disease. But the benefits from the research expenditures often go well beyond the individual or the company undertaking the research. The research spreads, and other people take advantage of it as well. An example is military research into global positioning systems (GPS), which spilled over into the private sector and found its way into devices such as navigation systems for automobiles.

marginal private benefit

The marginal benefit from consumption of a good as viewed by a private individual.

marginal social benefit

The marginal benefit from consumption of a good from the viewpoint of society as a whole.

Let us examine what happens when a positive externality raises social benefits above private benefits. To show how positive externalities affect the quantity produced in a competitive market, we need to look at the supply and demand curves. The externality makes the marginal benefit as perceived by the consumer, which we now call the **marginal private benefit**, less than the true benefit to society, which we call the **marginal social benefit**. With a positive externality, the marginal social benefit is greater than the marginal private benefit because a marginal external benefit results from more consumption. That is,

Marginal social benefit = marginal private benefit + marginal external benefit

We illustrate this equation in Figure 15.2 by drawing a marginal private benefit curve that lies below the marginal social benefit curve. We use the term *marginal private benefit* curve to refer to what we have thus far called marginal benefit or the market demand curve to distinguish it from marginal social benefit. Suppose that Figure 15.2 refers to the market for education. The market equilibrium is the point at which the marginal private benefit curve (the market demand curve) intersects the marginal cost curve (the market supply curve). The resulting quantity produced is indicated by point *C* in Figure 15.2.

FIGURE 15.2 **Illustration of a Typical Positive Externality**

Because consumption of the good gives benefits to others, the marginal social benefit is greater than the marginal private benefit. Hence, the equilibrium quantity that emerges from a competitive market is too low.

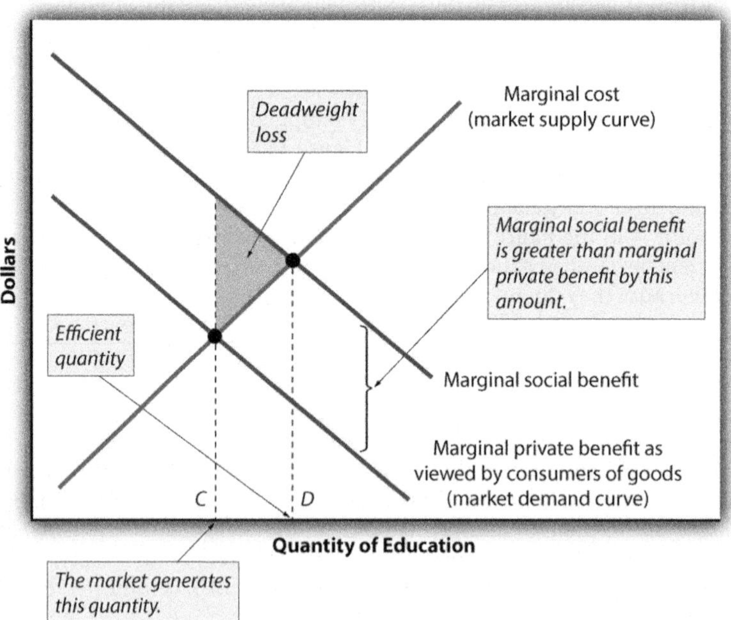

At this amount of production, however, the marginal social benefit of production exceeds the marginal cost of production. Only at point *D* in the figure is marginal social benefit equal to marginal cost. Thus, point *D* represents the efficient level of production. Because of the positive externality, too little is produced. Firms do not have the incentive to produce more because they do not gain directly from the benefits that are spilling over onto others.

In the presence of a positive externality, the sum of consumer and producer surplus really should be measured as the difference between the *marginal social benefit* and marginal cost. You can see that each additional unit that is not produced above point *C* and below point *D* results in forgone net benefit to society because the marginal social benefit exceeds the marginal cost of production. By not increasing production from point *C* to point *D*, we incur a deadweight loss that is indicated by the shaded triangle in Figure 15.2.

Externalities Spread across Borders

Externalities are by no means limited in their geographic impact. Sulfur dioxide emissions from electrical utility plants are an externality with international effects. The sulfur dioxide travels high into the air and then is dispersed by winds across long distances. Rainfall then brings the sulfur dioxide back to Earth in the form of acid rain, which lands on forests and lakes hundreds of miles away. In some cases, the acid rain occurs in countries different from the country in which the sulfur dioxide was first emitted. In North America, acid rain that results from burning fuel in the Midwest industrial centers may fall in Canada or upstate New York.

Global warming is another example of an externality with international dimensions. When too much carbon dioxide accumulates in the Earth's atmosphere, it prevents the sun's warmth from escaping out of the atmosphere, causing a greenhouse effect. Global warming is caused by the emission of carbon dioxide by firms and individuals but has effects around the world.

The ease and prevalence of modern air travel also leads to negative spillover effects on other countries from a poor health care system in one country. For instance, if patients in one country fall victim to an infection like the avian flu but go untreated, they very easily can spread that disease to many other countries as the people they come into contact with travel the world.

REVIEW

- Externalities occur when the benefits or costs of producing and consuming spill over onto others. The spillovers can be negative, as in the case of air pollution, or positive, as in the case of vaccinations.
- Externalities are a cause of market failure. For goods with negative externalities, more than the efficient amount is produced because the marginal social cost exceeds the marginal private cost. Private firms produce until the marginal benefit equals the marginal private cost, even though the optimal level is lower—the point at which the marginal benefit equals the marginal social cost.
- For goods with positive externalities, less than the efficient amount is produced because the marginal social benefit exceeds the marginal private benefit. Private firms will produce only until the marginal private benefit equals the marginal cost, even though the optimal level is higher—the point at which the marginal social benefit equals the marginal cost.
- Both positive and negative externalities result in deadweight loss. In the case of negative externalities, this loss occurs because too many goods are being produced; these additional goods have a marginal social cost that exceeds the marginal benefit. In the case of positive externalities, this loss occurs because too few goods are being produced; the forgone goods have a marginal social benefit that exceeds the marginal cost.
- Externalities are not necessarily local in their impact. Air pollution and global warming are examples of externalities whose effects are not hemmed in by borders. Changes in technology also are increasingly making the impact of one country's policy on, say, public health issues have a spillover effect on other countries.

3. REMEDIES FOR EXTERNALITIES

As the previous section shows, competitive markets do not generate an efficient level of production when externalities exist. What are some of the ways in which a society can alleviate problems caused by these externalities? In some cases involving positive externalities, the solution has been for the government to produce the good or service because the private sector will produce less than the socially efficient level of output. For instance, elementary education is provided by governments around the world with requirements that children attend school through a certain age. But in most cases in which externalities are present, production is left to the private sector, and the government endeavors to influence the quantity produced.

How can production in the private sector be influenced by government to lead to a more efficient level of production of goods and services in the economy? We will see that the answer involves changing behavior so that the externalities are taken into account internally by firms and consumers. In other words, the challenge is to **internalize** the externalities.

internalize
The process of providing incentives so that externalities are taken into account internally by firms or consumers.

Four alternative ways can bring about a more efficient level of production in the case of externalities. The first method we discuss, private remedies, does not require direct government intervention. The other three—command and control, taxes or subsidies, and tradable permits—do.

3.1 Private Remedies: Agreements between the Affected Parties

private remedies

A procedure that eliminates or internalizes externalities without government action other than defining property rights.

In some cases, through **private remedies**, people can eliminate externalities without government assistance. A Nobel Prize winner in economics, Ronald Coase of the University of Chicago, pointed out this possibility in a famous paper published in 1960.

Consider the following simple example. Suppose that the externality relates to the production of two products: health care and candy. Suppose that a hospital is built next door to a large candy factory. Making candy requires noisy pounding and vibrating machinery. Unfortunately, the walls of the new hospital are thin. The loud candy machinery can be heard in the hospital. Thus, we might call this noise pollution an externality. It has a cost. It makes the hospital less effective; for example, it is difficult for the doctors to hear their patients' hearts through the stethoscopes.

What can be done? The city mayor could adopt a rule prohibiting loud noise near the hospital, but that would severely impinge on candy production in the city. Or, because the hospital was built after the candy factory, the mayor could say, "Too bad, doctors; candy is important too" and tell the hospital to relocate somewhere where the noise is not too great. Alternatively, it might be better for the candy workers and doctors to work this externality out on their own. The supervisor of the candy workers could negotiate with the doctors. Perhaps the candy workers could agree to use the loud machines only at designated hours during the afternoon, during which time the doctors would avoid scheduling procedures that are sensitive to noise. Or perhaps the hospital would be willing to pay for a more insulated wall between the candy company and the hospital so that the noise is dampened, especially because that option would be cheaper than relocation. Or perhaps the candy company will be willing to pay for newer, less noisy machinery because it is preferable to the risk of having to shut down because of the noise pollution.

Thus, it is possible to resolve the externality by negotiation between the two parties affected. The privately negotiated alternatives seem more efficient than the mayor's rulings because the production of both candy and health care continues. Note that, in these alternatives, both parties alter their behavior. For example, the doctors change their scheduling of noise-sensitive procedures, and the candy factory limits loud noise to the afternoon. Thus, the parties find a solution in which the polluter does not make all the adjustments, as would be the case if the mayor adopted a "no loud noise" rule.

The Importance of Assigning Property Rights

property rights

Rights over the use, sale, and proceeds from a good or resource.

For a negotiation like this to work, however, it is essential that property rights be well defined. **Property rights** determine who has the right to pollute or infringe on whom. Who, for example, is being infringed on in the case of the noise pollution? Does the candy factory have the right to use loud machinery, or does the hospital have the right to peace and quiet? The mayor's ruling could establish who has the property right, but it is more likely that the case would be taken to a court and the court would decide. After many such cases, precedent would establish who has the property rights in future cases.

Coase theorem

The idea that private negotiations between people will lead to an efficient resolution of externalities regardless of who has the property rights as long as the property rights are defined.

The property rights will determine who actually pays for the adjustment that remedies the externality. If the candy factory has the right, then the workers can demand some compensation (perhaps free health care services) from the hospital for limiting their noise in the afternoon, or the candy company can demand that the hospital bear some of the cost of the new machinery. If the hospital has the right, then perhaps the hospital staff and patients can get compensated with free candy, or the hospital can ask the candy company to pay for some of the cost of building a thicker wall. The **Coase theorem** states that no matter who is assigned the property rights, the negotiations will lead to an efficient outcome as described in the candy–health care example. The assignment of the property rights determines who makes the compensation.

Transaction Costs

Transaction costs

The costs of buying or selling in a market, including search, bargaining, and writing contracts.

Even if property rights are well defined, for a private agreement like this to occur, transaction costs associated with the agreement must be small compared with the costs of the externality itself. **Transaction costs** are the time and effort needed to reach an agreement. As Coase put it,

> *in order to carry out a market transaction, it is necessary to discover who it is that one wishes to deal with, to inform people that one wishes to deal and on what terms, to conduct negotiations leading up to a bargain, to draw up the contract, to undertake the inspection needed to make sure that the terms of the contract are being observed, and so on. These operations are often extremely costly.*[1]

Real-world negotiations are clearly time-consuming, requiring skilled and expensive lawyers in many cases. If these negotiation costs are large, then the private parties may not be able to reach an agreement. If the negotiation in the health care–candy example took many years and had to be repeated many times, then it might be better to adopt a simple "no loud noise" rule or an "existing firms get precedence over new arrivals" rule.

The Free-Rider Problem Again

Free-rider problems also can prevent a private agreement from taking place. For example, a free-rider problem might occur if the hospital was very large, say, 400 doctors. Suppose that the candy workers have the right to noise pollute, so that they require a payment in the form of health care. The hospital would need contributions from the doctors to provide the care. Thus, if each doctor worked in the hospital an extra day a year, this might be sufficient.

Any one of those 400 doctors, however, could refuse to work the extra day. Some of the doctors could say that they have other job opportunities that do not require them to work an extra day. In other words, doctors who did not pay could free-ride: They could work at the hospital and still benefit from the agreement. Because of this free-rider problem, the hospital might find it hard to provide health care to the candy workers, and a private settlement might be impossible.

Thus, in the case in which the transaction costs are high or free-rider problems exist, a private remedy may not be feasible. Then the role of government comes into play, much as it did in the case of public goods, in which case the free-rider problem was significant. Again, as Coase put it, "Instead of instituting a legal system of rights which can be modified by transactions on the market, the government may impose regulations which state what people must or must not do and which have to be obeyed."[2]

3.2 Command and Control Remedies

When private remedies for externalities are not feasible, either because transaction costs are too high or because of free-rider problems, the government has a role for intervention. One form of government intervention to solve the problem of externalities is the placement of restrictions or regulations on individuals or firms, often referred to as **command and control**. Firms that do not heed these restrictions and regulations are fined for their violations. Command and control methods are used widely by agencies such as the U.S. Environmental Protection Agency (EPA), which is responsible for federal environmental policy in the United States. For example, in the United States, the corporate average fleet efficiency (CAFE) standards require that the fleet of cars produced by an automobile manufacturer each year achieve a stated number of miles per gallon on the average. Another example is a government requirement that electrical utilities put "scrubbers" in their smokestacks to remove certain pollutants from the smoke they emit. Through *commands*, the government *controls* what the private sector does. The government's actions, in principle, make the externalities internal to the firm by requiring that the firm act as if it was taking the external costs into account.

Big Brother Is Watching Your Car! Closed circuit television cameras loom above traffic in central London to monitor the license plates of the estimated 250,000 cars entering the city each day. Drivers pay a "congestion charge" to drive in central London, making it more expensive to drive in that area of the city, with the ultimate goal of reducing traffic backups.

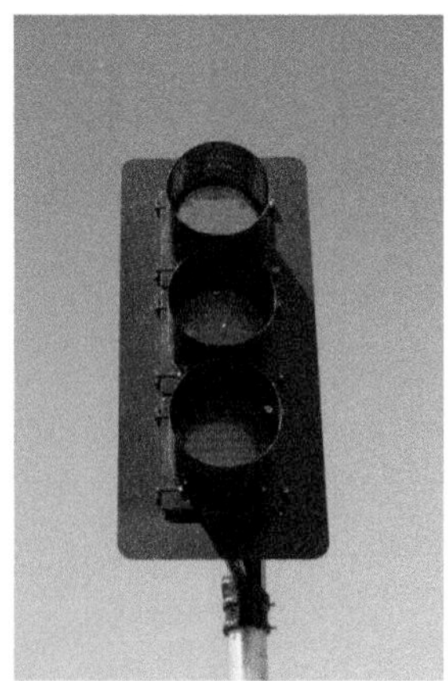

Source: © Shutterstock, Inc.

The use of command and control to reduce externalities has many disadvantages, especially in the environmental area. The most significant disadvantage is that command and control does not allow firms to find other, cheaper ways to reduce pollution. For example, under command and control, electrical utilities have to install a scrubber to remove pollutants; they do not have the incentive to discover a cheaper alternative technology that might be more effective at reducing pollution. Similarly, CAFE standards can lead to inefficient production decisions—because firms have to produce smaller, more fuel-efficient cars that they did not want to produce simply to offset the production of the less fuel-efficient SUVs—or to more gasoline consumption because people find that the per-mile cost of driving has fallen because of the higher fuel efficiency, and hence they drive more.

3.3 Taxes and Subsidies

command and control

The regulations and restrictions that the government uses to correct market imperfections.

Because of the disadvantages associated with command and control, economists recommend alternative techniques to reduce the inefficiencies that result from externalities. The use of taxes and subsidies often is recommended by economists, with goods and services that have negative externalities being taxed while goods and services that have positive externalities are subsidized.

For example, consider the negative externalities that are imposed by drivers. When a city has many drivers, roads become congested, leading to traffic backups and delays. Each driver contributes to the congestion, imposing external costs on the other drivers. In 2003, a new tax, called a congestion charge, was imposed on vehicles that drive in central London during the day. Drivers can pay £8 before they travel or £10 the day after they travel; cameras mounted above the roads check vehicle registration numbers to ensure that the taxes are paid. The idea was to internalize the externality of congestion in central London during rush hour by making drivers pay for the external congestion costs through the tax. If the demand for days of driving in central London is downward sloping, the tax will bring about a cutback in driving in central London, lower the external costs imposed on drivers by reducing congestion, and create government revenue. In fact, the evidence suggests that traffic in central London fell by one-third.

The way that taxes can be used to reduce negative externalities is illustrated graphically in Figure 15.3, which uses the same curves as Figure 15.1. Recall that the marginal social cost of production is greater than the marginal private cost, as viewed from the private firm, because of the negative externality, resulting in the equilibrium quantity produced by the market exceeding the efficient quantity. We know that taxes raise the marginal cost to the individual firm. They thereby shift up the market supply curve. If the tax is chosen to exactly equal the difference between the marginal social cost and the marginal private cost, then the quantity produced by the market will decline from the inefficient quantity shown at point *B* to the efficient quantity shown at point *A* in Figure 15.3.

Many examples illustrate the use of taxes in part to reduce pollution. Gasoline taxes reduce gasoline consumption and thus pollution. In the United States, a federal tax is levied of $0.184 per gallon and a variety of state taxes are assessed averaging an additional $0.236 per gallon. The big advantage of taxes or subsidies compared with command and control is that the market is used. Instead of restricting the ratio of SUVs to small, fuel-efficient cars that a producer can manufacture, the government simply raises the relative cost of driving an SUV versus driving a subcompact car by increasing the gasoline tax. If users of SUVs respond by switching over to smaller cars, then the car manufacturer has an incentive to produce smaller cars that consumers actually want to buy, or to research more fuel-efficient SUV engines.

FIGURE 15.3 **Using Taxes in the Case of a Negative Externality**

A tax equal to the difference between the marginal private cost and the marginal social cost in Figure 15.1 shifts the supply curve up. This reduces the equilibrium quantity produced to the lower, more efficient level.

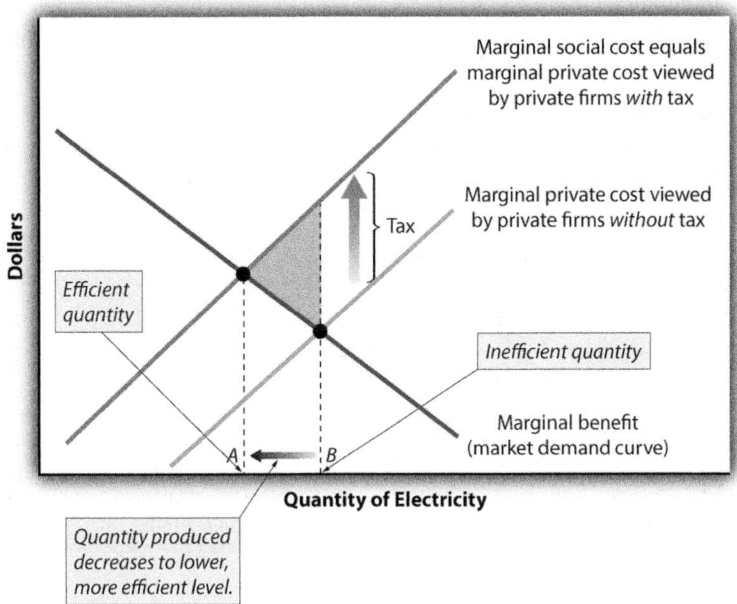

Next, we consider the use of subsidies for goods that have positive externalities. Recall that when a good has a positive externality, too little of it is produced in a competitive economy; a subsidy can be used to increase production and consumption of the good. The Vaccines for Children (VFC) program provides free vaccines for children who are poor and do not have access to health insurance. This program was implemented following an outbreak of measles that killed hundreds of children in the late 1980s. Vaccinations not only protect the child directly, but also produce a positive externality for others who will no longer risk being infected by that child. Government intervention to effectively drive the price of vaccinations to zero through the use of a subsidy will enable more children to be vaccinated and allow parents to internalize the positive externality of having their children vaccinated.

In Figure 15.4, which uses the same curves as Figure 15.2, we demonstrate how a subsidy can be used to encourage the production and consumption of a good with a positive externality. In this case, a subsidy to the user will raise the demand for the good. If the subsidy is chosen to be exactly the difference between the marginal private benefit and the marginal social benefit, then the quantity of the good that is produced and consumed will rise from the inefficient level (*C*) to the efficient level (*D*), as illustrated in Figure 15.4.

FIGURE 15.4 Using Subsidies in the Case of a Positive Externality

A subsidy equal to the difference between the marginal social benefit and the marginal private benefit of education or research shifts the demand curve up. This increases the equilibrium quantity produced to the higher, more efficient level and eliminates the deadweight loss resulting from the externality.

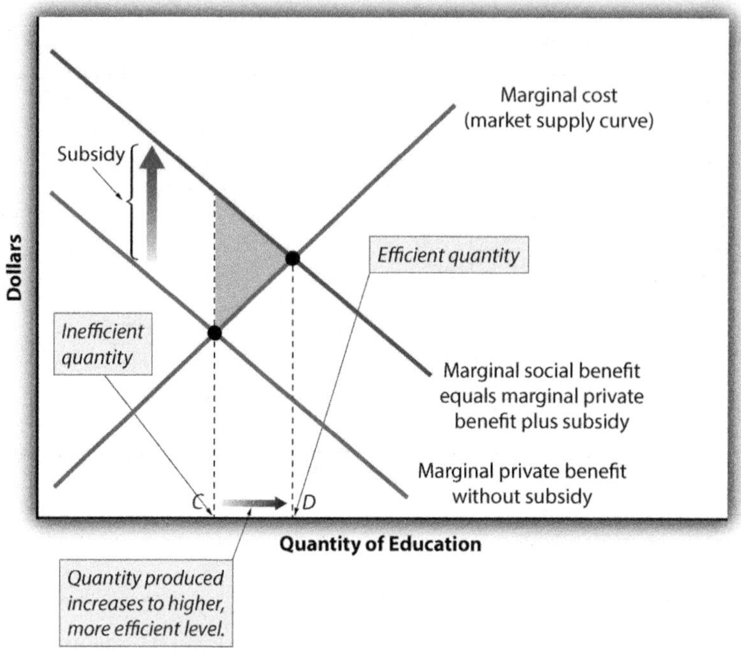

Another example of subsidizing positive externalities is the government's funding of research by providing grants to private firms and individuals. The National Science Foundation supports basic research, and the National Institutes of Health support medical research. In supporting research with a limited budget, it is important for the government to place more emphasis on research that has large positive externalities. Many view basic research as having larger positive externalities than applied research. The ideas in basic research, such as that on the structure of the atom, affect many parts of the economy. Applied research, such as that on a new lightweight metal for a bike, has more limited spillover effects, and the products developed through applied research usually can be sold by the creator for profit. In fact, the U.S. federal government does spend more to subsidize basic research than applied research.

Emission Taxes

emission taxes

A charge made to firms that pollute the environment based on the quantity of pollution that they emit.

A more direct way to use taxes to deal with pollution externalities is to tax the firm based on the amount of pollution emitted rather than on the quantity of the potentially polluting good that is produced or consumed. For example, an electrical utility could be charged fees depending on how many particles of sulfur dioxide it emits, rather than on how much electricity it produces. Such charges are called **emission taxes**. These taxes are much like those levied on the amount of the product sold, but they focus directly on the amount of pollution.

Emission taxes have an advantage over taxes on production in that the firm can use technology to change the amount of pollution associated with its production. Thus, rather than producing less electricity, the firm can reduce the amount of pollution associated with a given amount of electricity, if it can find a cheaper way to do so. Emission taxes have an even greater advantage over command and control than a tax on the product has.

Why Is Command and Control Used More Than Taxes?

Many people like one feature of command and control: The total amount of pollution can be better controlled than with a tax. This perceived advantage may explain why command and control is used more than taxes. Suppose, for example, that a tax is used to equate marginal social cost with marginal benefit, as in Figure 15.3. Now suppose that the private cost of producing electricity suddenly reduces. The private marginal cost curve will shift down, and, with the tax unchanged, production (and pollution) will increase. A regulation that stipulates a certain quantity to produce would not have this problem. The total amount of pollution would be fixed. Fortunately, in recent years, a new idea in pollution control has emerged that has both this advantage of command and control and the flexibility of the market. This new idea is tradable permits.

3.4 Tradable Permits

Tradable permits use the market to help achieve the standards set by the government. The way these permits work is as follows. The government decides what limit it wants to impose on the overall level of a particular pollutant. The government then issues a number of permits specifying permissible amounts of pollution. The total amount of pollution in the economy is equal to the total amount specified in the permits issued. If a firm plans to emit more pollutants than it has permits for, it will have to acquire additional permits from other firms. On the other hand, if a firm has more permits than the pollutants it plans to emit, it can sell its permits to another firm that wants them.

Tradable permits

A governmentally granted license to pollute that can be bought and sold.

Firms now have an incentive to lower their emissions because they can sell the permits if they do not use them. Firms that can lower their emissions cheaply will choose to do so and benefit by selling their permits to other firms for which reducing the pollution is more costly. Tradable permits not only allow the market system to work, but also give firms an incentive to find the least costly form of pollution control. Rather than forcing individual firms to limit the quantity of the pollutant that they can release, tradable permits enable those firms that can reduce the emissions in the most cost-efficient manner to do the bulk of the emissions reduction. Firms that face a high cost of reducing pollution will cut back less on their pollution, but they will have to internalize their pollution costs because of the need to buy permits. Those firms also will have an incentive to adopt technologies that eventually will emit fewer pollutants.

Tradable permits illustrate how important property rights are for resolving externalities. The role of government in this case is to create a market by defining certain rights to pollute and then allowing firms to buy and sell these rights. Once rights are assigned, the market can work and achieve efficiency.

Perhaps the best-known use of tradable permits in the United States has been to reduce emissions of sulfur dioxide. Tradable permits also can work in combating global warming. The amount of global warming depends on the total amount of carbon dioxide emissions in the world's atmosphere. It does not matter whether a firm in Los Angeles or in Shanghai emits the carbon dioxide. Tradable permits could control the total amount of pollution. The permits would let firms or individuals decide on the most cost-effective way to reduce their total amount of pollution.

3.5 Balancing the Costs and Benefits of Reducing Externalities

As with public goods, it is important to use cost-benefit analysis when considering how best to intervene in the economy to fix problems caused by externalities. Clear benefits can accrue from reducing pollution, but associated costs can result in the form of lower production, lost jobs, administrative expenses, and so on. These costs should be compared with the associated benefits on a case-by-case basis before deciding on the appropriate intervention method.

For example, the EPA introduced a new rule for stricter standards on the amount of sulfur allowed in diesel fuel in 2000. Environmentalists saw a clear benefit from these new standards because they were concerned that diesel exhaust was causing accelerated cancer rates. On the other hand, trucking companies that use diesel fuel saw a clear cost because the effect of the stricter standards was to raise the price of the fuel needed to run their trucks. The EPA estimated that the new, stricter standards would prevent 8,300 deaths and 360,000 asthma attacks, while increasing the price of diesel fuel by $0.04 to $0.05 per gallon. The oil industry reported that implementation of the stricter standards would cost $8 billion. Policy makers would have to do a cost-benefit analysis to determine whether the additional benefits coming from a stricter standard on sulfur justified the additional costs.

As the following two examples illustrate, policy makers sometimes rule that the benefits justify the costs, whereas at other times they conclude that the costs outweigh the benefits. The first example was the regulation of carbon dioxide emissions, a policy that President George W. Bush had advocated during his 2000 campaign for the presidency. In 2001, President Bush changed his mind about regulating carbon dioxide emissions. A study by the Energy Department showed that this regulation would result in nearly a quadrupling of the cost of producing electricity from coal, causing large price increases for both electricity and natural gas. President Bush stated that the impact on utility prices made the cost of regulating carbon dioxide emissions too high.

The second example relates to stricter standards on the level of arsenic allowed in drinking water that President Clinton imposed shortly before leaving office. In March 2001, the EPA rescinded the new, stricter standard and debated its merits. Scientific studies showed that higher levels of arsenic in drinking water lead to higher risks of fatal cancer, heart disease, and diabetes. The cost of the stricter standard for arsenic in drinking water was estimated at billions of dollars because arsenic is a byproduct in mining, is used as a wood preservative for lumber, and occurs naturally in water in some areas. After examining the evidence, the Bush administration decided to impose the stricter standard, convinced that the health benefits were worth the cost.

Some people object to the use of cost-benefit analysis for deciding whether environmental regulations should be implemented. They argue that environmental regulations can benefit rather than cost the economy, because requiring individuals to reduce pollution creates a demand for pollution-reducing devices and creates jobs in the pollution reducing industry. But unless the pollution-reducing equipment is creating a benefit to society greater than the benefits of other goods, shifting more resources to pollution abatement will not be an efficient allocation of society's resources.

In recent years, there has been significant concern about rising pollution levels in other parts of the world, especially in very fast-growing economies like China, India, and Brazil. As more factories start producing goods and services, more forests are cleared to meet the space needs of expanding cities, more power generation is needed to meet the demands of newly electrified homes, more vehicles enter the streets as people spend their rising incomes, and air- and water-pollution problems in these countries become magnified. This poses a dilemma for policy makers because asking these countries to cut back on their rates of economic growth to reduce pollution clearly does not seem like a feasible plan. In fact, many people argue that the surest way to reduce pollution around the world is to ensure that the less-developed economies of the world increase their level of income. This will give them more resources to spend on pollution control.

Environmental economists and policy makers will continue to study these vexing cost-benefit analyses of how to reduce pollution at both local and global levels. What you have learned in this chapter about externalities, public goods, taxes, regulations, tradable permits, and private remedies will play an important role in their deliberations.

REVIEW

- There are four basic ways to improve the efficiency of markets in the presence of externalities: private remedies, command and control, taxes and subsidies, and tradable permits. In each of these approaches, the goal is to get firms to internalize the externality—to change their behavior to take into account the impact their actions have on others.
- Private remedies do not require direct government intervention. The affected parties can negotiate among themselves and efficiently resolve the externalities. The Coase theorem states that as long as property rights are defined clearly, parties will come to an agreement. This approach also requires that transaction costs not be too high and that free-rider problems associated with the settlement be minimized.
- Command and control refers to direct rules and regulations imposed by the government to limit market imperfections. Examples include the imposition of fuel-efficiency standards on auto manufacturers and requirements that coal-burning utilities install scrubbers.
- Taxes and subsidies are considered by economists to be superior to command and control techniques because they use the market to internalize the externality. Taxes of an appropriate magnitude can help reduce the output of goods with negative externalities to the socially efficient level. Similarly, subsidies at an appropriate level can help increase the consumption and production of goods with positive externalities to the socially efficient level.
- Tradable permits are a method of internalizing externalities that economists typically favor. The government can set strict limits on the production of a negative externality, such as a pollutant, by issuing a limited number of permits. By allowing the permits to be traded, however, the reduction in the pollutant can be done efficiently by allowing firms that are able to reduce it at the lowest cost to do the bulk of the reductions. Firms also have incentives to come up with new ways to reduce the externality because they can sell their permits to less efficient producers.
- Regardless of which method is used to eliminate the impact of an externality, policy makers still have to do a cost-benefit analysis of the proposed intervention.

4. MODELS OF GOVERNMENT BEHAVIOR

The previous two sections outlined what government should do to correct market failure caused by public goods and externalities. Regardless of the reason that market failure occurs, the outcome is similar: Production may be too little or too much, and producer surplus plus consumer surplus is not maximized, resulting in deadweight loss. The role of government is to intervene in the economy to reduce this deadweight loss.

Using economics to explain the role of government in this way is considered a *normative* analysis of government policy. Normative economics is the study of what *should be* done. But another way to look at government policy falls into the area of *positive* economics and looks at what governments *actually do* rather than what they should do.

One of the reasons for studying what governments actually do is that governments sometimes fail because the normative recommendations are ignored or poorly implemented. **Government failure** occurs when the government intervention fails to improve on the market or even makes things worse. One objective of positive analysis of government is to understand why success occurs in some situations and failure results in others.

government failure
The situation in which the government fails to improve on the market or even makes things worse.

4.1 Public Choice Models

People run the government. Government behavior depends on the actions of voters, members of political parties, elected politicians, civil servants, and political appointees from judges to cabinet officials. The work of government also depends on the large number of people who lobby and who participate in grassroots campaigns, from letter writing to e-mail messages to political protests. What motivates the behavior of all these people?

The motivations of politicians and government workers are complex and varied. Many people enter politics for genuine patriotic reasons and are motivated by a desire to improve the well-being of people in their city, state, or country, or even the world. Their motivations may be deeper than watching out for their own best interests, narrowly defined.

For example, Alexander Hamilton, the first secretary of the U.S. Department of Treasury, worked hard to put the newly formed country on a firm economic foundation by having the federal government assume the debts of the states after the Revolutionary War. But to get the votes of the Virginia and Maryland representatives for the federal government to assume the debts of the states, Hamilton had to agree to vote to place the capital of the new country along the banks of the Potomac River between the two states, instead of selecting New York City, which was his home base.

At the same time, many other politicians are motivated by their own self-interest. The central idea of economics that people make purposeful choices with limited resources should apply to politics and government, as well as to consumers and firms. Economic models of government behavior are called **public choice models**. They start from the premise that politicians are motivated by increasing their chances of getting themselves or the members of their party elected or reelected. And without explicit incentives to the contrary, government workers are presumed to be motivated by increasing their power or prestige by increasing the size of their department or by getting promoted. By understanding this self-interest, we can learn much about government, including the reasons for government failure and the reasons for government success.

public choice models
Models of government behavior that assume that those in government take actions to maximize their own well-being, such as getting reelected.

4.2 The Voting Paradox

Let us first examine how voting is used to make economic policy decisions in a political environment. We will use the assumption of public choice models: that getting elected is the primary motivation of politicians.

Unanimity

Let us start with the easiest case: Only one economic policy decision can be made, and all the voters agree on what that decision should be. For example, suppose that the issue is spending on national defense, a public good for which the government has a key role to play according to the normative economic analysis. Suppose the specific issue is how much to spend on national defense. Some alternatives are shown in Table 15.2.

TABLE 15.2 Alternative Levels of National Defense Spending

National Defense as a Share of Gross Domestic Product	
1 percent	Japan's maximum
2 percent	U.S. in 1940
4 percent	U.S. in 2000
6 percent	U.S. in 2010
10 percent	U.S. in 1960
39 percent	U.S. in 1944

Suppose that everyone agrees that a level of national defense spending of around 4 percent of gross domestic product (GDP) in the United States is appropriate, in the absence of major world political changes such as the events of September 11, 2001. In reality, of course, opinions differ greatly about the appropriate level of spending. But suppose that after looking at history or making international comparisons or listening to experts on defense and world politics, everyone agrees that 4 percent of GDP is the right amount to spend.

Under these circumstances, when all voters agree on only one issue, voting will lead to the action that everyone prefers, that is, 4 percent, even if politicians are motivated by nothing other than getting elected. Suppose that one politician or political party runs for election on a plank of 39 percent defense spending and that the other argues in favor of 2 percent. Clearly, the party with 2 percent will win because it is much closer to the people's views. But then the other politician or party will see the need to move toward the consensus and will run on a 5 percent spending platform. Thus, if the other party stays at 2 percent, then the higher-spending party will win. But clearly the other party then will try to get closer to 4 percent, and eventually 4 percent will be the winner.

This example shows that the political system yields the preferred outcome. Of course, after being elected, the politician might break the promise made during the campaign. But if such a change cannot be justified on the basis of a change in circumstances, that politician may have difficulty getting reelected.

The Median Voter Theorem

What if people have different views? Suppose there is no unanimity about a 4 percent share of GDP for defense. Instead, the country consists of people with many different opinions. Some want more than 4 percent; some want less than 4 percent. Suppose that about half of the people want more than 4 percent and half want less than 4 percent; in other words, 4 percent is the desire of the *median* voter.

If only one issue is on the ballot, the positions of the politicians or the parties will converge toward the median voter's belief. For example, if one party or politician calls for 7 percent spending and the other party calls for 4 percent, then the party calling for 4 percent will attract more voters. The **median voter theorem** predicts that the politicians who run on what the median voter wants will be elected. The views of the people at the extremes will not matter at all.

Convergence of Positions in a Two-Party System

convergence of positions

The concentration of the stances of political parties around the center of citizens' opinions.

An interesting corollary to the median voter theorem is that political parties or politicians will gravitate toward the center of opinion—toward the median voter. For example, in the case of national defense, it makes no sense for any politician to run on a 39 percent recommendation. The parties will gravitate toward the median voter. This **convergence of positions** may explain the tendency for Democrats and Republicans to take similar positions on many issues.

Voting Paradoxes

voting paradox

A situation in which voting patterns will not consistently reflect citizens' preferences because of multiple issues on which people vote.

When many different issues are on the ballot—defense, taxes, welfare, health care reform—and people have different opinions and views about each of those issues, the outcome of voting becomes more complicated. Certain decision-making problems arise. The example of the **voting paradox** illustrates some of these problems.

Suppose three voters have different preferences on three different economic policy options—A, B, and C. Ali likes A best, B second best, and C the least; Betty likes B best, C second best, and A the least; and Camilla likes C best, A second best, and B the least. The three policy options could be three different levels of defense spending (high, medium, and low) or three different pollution control plans (emission taxes, tradable permits, and command and control). Table 15.3 shows the three voters and their different preferences on each option.

TABLE 15.3 Preferences That Generate a Voting Paradox

Note the paradox: A wins over B and B wins over C, yet C wins over A.

Ranking	Ali	Betty	Camilla
First	A	B	C
Second	B	C	A
Third	C	A	B
In voting on one option versus another, we get:			
On A versus B: A wins 2 to 1			
On B versus C: B wins 2 to 1			
On A versus C: C wins 2 to 1			

Consider three different elections held at different points in time, each with one issue paired up against another. First, an election is held on A versus B, then on B versus C, and then on C versus A. The voting is by simple majority: The issue with the most votes wins. When the vote is on the alternatives A versus B, we see that A wins two to one. That is, both Ali and Camilla like A better than B and vote for it, whereas only Betty likes B better than A and votes for B. When the vote is on B versus C, we see that B wins two to one. Finally (this vote might be called for by a frustrated Camilla, who sees an opportunity), a vote is taken on C versus A, and we see that now C wins two to one. Although it looked like A was a winner over C—because A was preferred to B and B was preferred to C—we see that in the third vote, C is preferred to A: This is the paradox.

The voting paradox suggests the possibility of instability in economic policies. Depending on how the votes were put together, the policy could shift from high defense to medium defense to low defense, or from one pollution control system to another, then to another, and then back again. Or taxes could be cut, then raised, and then raised again. All these changes could happen with nothing else in the world having changed. We even could imagine shifting between different economic systems involving different amounts of government intervention—from Communism to Capitalism to Socialism to Communism and back again.

This particular voting paradox has been known for 200 years, but only relatively recently have we come to know that the problem is not unique to this example. Kenneth Arrow showed that this type of paradox is common to any voting scheme. That no democratic voting scheme can avoid inefficiencies of the type described in the voting paradox is called the **Arrow impossibility theorem.**

Arrow impossibility theorem

A theorem that says that no democratic voting scheme can avoid a voting paradox.

The voting paradox suggests a certain inherent degree of instability in decisions made by government. Clearly, shifting frequently between different tax systems is a source of uncertainty and inefficiency. The voting paradox may be a reason for government failure in cases in which the government takes on some activity such as correcting a market failure.

4.3 Special Interest Groups

The voting paradox is one reason for government failure. Special interest groups are another. It is not unusual for special interest groups to spend time and financial resources to influence legislation. They want policies that are good for them, even if those policies are not necessarily good for the country as a whole. For example, the farming industry has a history of being able to successfully lobby for government intervention in the form of subsidies. If you look back at the reasons for government intervention—income distribution, public goods, and externalities—you will see that they do not apply to the farm sector. Food does not fit the definition of a public good, farming does not have positive externalities, and many farmers who benefit from the intervention have higher incomes than other people in the society who do not benefit from such intervention. One can thus view the government regulation of agricultural markets as a form of government failure.

Concentrated Benefits and Diffuse Costs

One explanation for government failure in such situations is that special interest groups can have powerful effects on legislation that harms or benefits a small group of people a great deal but affects almost everyone else only a little. For example, the federal subsidy to the sugar growers in the United States costs taxpayers and consumers somewhere between $800 million and $2.5 billion per year, or about $3.20 to $10 per consumer per year. The gain from the subsidy, however, amounts to about $136,000 per sugar grower. When a proposal to repeal the subsidy comes before Congress, almost no consumers are going to expend the resources to travel to Washington and support the legislation or even to call up their representatives to encourage them to vote for the repeal; the $3 to $10 benefit is just not worth the time. However, the prospect of losing $136,000 is certainly worth the sugar growers' time and effort. These growers will travel to Washington, lobby representatives vigorously, and contribute to some political campaigns. Because the process of obtaining funds for election or getting support from the powerful interest groups is critical for politicians' reelection chances, these elected officials will be much more likely to listen to those interest groups that have the incentive to lobby and work hard for the policy even if the majority of voters oppose it.

Wasteful Lobbying

Another economic harm results from special interest lobbying. It is the waste of time and resources that the lobbying entails. Lobbyists are usually highly talented and skilled people, and millions of dollars in resources are spent on lobbying for legislation or other government actions. In many less-developed countries—where special interest lobbying is more prevalent than in the United States—such activity consumes a significant amount of scarce resources.

4.4 Incentive Problems in Government

In any large government, many of the services are provided by civil servants rather than by politicians and political appointees. In fact, it was to avoid the scandals of the spoils system—in which politicians would reward those who helped in a political campaign with jobs—that the civil service system set rules to protect workers against firing and established examinations and other criteria to qualify workers for jobs.

But what motivates government managers and workers? Profit maximization as in the case of business firms is not a factor. Perhaps increasing the size of the agency or the department of government, rather than an efficient delivery of services, is the goal of managers. Profit motives and competition with other firms also give private firms an incentive to keep costs down and look for innovative production techniques and new products. These incentives do not automatically arise in government; thus, it is likely that a government service, whether a public good or a regulation, will not be provided as efficiently as a good provided by the private sector.

In recent years, economists have suggested incentives to improve the efficiency of government by using market-like incentives, such as more competition. Vouchers—including food stamps, housing vouchers, school vouchers, college tuition grants, and elementary school grants—have been suggested by economists as a way to add competition and improve government efficiency. The successes of these policies often are hotly debated, with both opponents and proponents being able to point to specific cases that bolster their side's arguments.

REVIEW

- Public choice models of government behavior assume that politicians and government workers endeavor to improve their own well-being, much as models of firms and consumer behavior assume that firms and consumers do.
- In cases in which voters have consensus, voting will bring about the consensus government policy. When voters do not have consensus, the median voter theorem shows that the center of opinion is what matters for decisions. In more complex decisions with many options, however, the voting paradox points out that the decisions can be unstable, leading to government failure.
- Other causes for government failure include special interest groups, especially in cases in which policies whose costs are greater but widely distributed while benefits are smaller but more narrowly concentrated are involved. By the use of campaign contributions and lobbying, special interest groups are able to influence politicians to implement policies that are inefficient and run contrary to the wishes of a majority of voters.
- Poor incentives in government also lead to government failure. Government employees may be more interested in enhancing their own power and influence than in carrying out policies that increase societal well-being.
- Economic models of government behavior suggest ways to reduce the likelihood of government failure and increase government efficiency through the use of incentives and competition. The success of these policies remains a hotly debated topic.

5. END-OF-CHAPTER MATERIALS

5.1 Conclusion

In this chapter, we have explored market failure resulting from public goods and externalities. A competitive market provides too little in the way of public goods, such as national defense, and too little in the way of goods for which positive externalities result, such as education and research. A competitive market results in too much production of goods for which negative externalities arise, such as goods that pollute the environment.

Most of the remedies for market failure involve the action of government. The provision of public goods by the government should require a careful cost-benefit analysis to ensure that the benefits are greater than the cost of producing a public good. Even though private parties can work out externalities by themselves, their ability to do so may be limited by transaction costs and free-rider problems. In that case, the government can intervene by using command and control policies, taxes and subsidies, or tradable permits. In these cases, the main role of the government is to ensure that firms internalize the externalities.

In addition to reaching normative conclusions about government intervention, it is important to consider a positive analysis of government intervention. Doing so requires developing models of government behavior and recognizing the possibility of government failure. In reality, political considerations enter into the production of public goods. To be reelected, a member of Congress from one part of the country might push for a public works project in his or her local district. Moreover, the externality argument emphasized in this chapter is frequently abused as a political device, providing justification for wasteful expenditures. Thus, finding ways to improve decision making in government, such as through market-based incentives, is needed if government is to play its role in providing remedies for market failures.

Key Points

1. Public goods are defined by two key characteristics: nonrivalry and nonexcludability. Nonrival goods are goods for which increased use of the good by one person does not result in decreased use by another. Nonexcludable goods are goods whose use cannot be restricted to only those who have paid for them.
2. The nonexcludable and nonrival aspects of public goods result in the existence of free riders, people who use the good without paying for it. Free riding can explain why the private sector typically will not provide, or will underprovide, public goods. This creates a role for government intervention in the form of government supply of public goods like defense services.
3. Cost-benefit analysis is a technique for deciding how much of a public good should be produced. Measuring benefits is often difficult in the case of public goods. Furthermore, not all goods produced by the government are public goods. Examples in the United States include the postal service and education.
4. Externalities occur when the costs or benefits of a good spill over onto other parts of the economy. They create another potential role for government intervention because the private sector will supply less than the socially efficient quantity of goods with positive externalities, and more than the socially efficient quantity of goods with negative externalities.
5. To move the economy to the socially efficient outcome, producers and consumers of goods with externalities have to be made to internalize those externalities. This can be accomplished in certain cases by private agreements between the affected parties. In other cases, it will require government intervention in the form of regulations and restrictions, taxes and subsidies, or tradable permits.
6. Command and control, or regulations and restrictions imposed by the government on the economy, is the least flexible method of reducing externalities.
7. Taxes on goods with negative externalities and subsidies for goods with positive externalities can either restrict or expand output from the level provided by the market to the socially efficient level.
8. Tradable permits are favored by economists for reducing negative externalities because they allow the government to maintain a tight control on the quantity of the externality-causing good, while allowing the market to play a major role. Firms that can reduce pollution most effectively will do so, and they will be rewarded for their actions by being able to sell permits to firms with a high cost of reducing pollution.
9. Even though public goods and externalities provide a normative theory for government intervention, you also should consider the positive theory of government intervention. Models of government behavior are based on the economic assumption that people try to improve their well-being. They can be used to explain why government failure occurs.
10. The voting paradox, the prominent role of special interest groups, and poor incentives for government employees are some of the other reasons for government failure. Market-like incentives and competition are ways suggested by economists to reduce government failure.

QUESTIONS FOR REVIEW

1. What types of goods are produced or supplied by the government at the federal, state, and local levels?
2. Define the concepts of nonexcludability and nonrivalry, and provide examples of goods that are nonexcludable, nonrival, neither, and both.
3. Define the concept of free riding. How is it related to public goods?
4. What is the use of cost-benefit analysis for governments in deciding whether to supply public goods?
5. What is an externality? What is the difference between a positive externality and a negative externality?
6. What is the Coase theorem? How is it related to externalities?
7. What is the advantage of a system of taxes over command and control as a method of reducing the production of a good with a negative externality?
8. What are the advantages of using a system of tradable permits to reduce pollution?
9. What is government failure? How similar is it to market failure?
10. What are some explanations for why government failure occurs?

PROBLEMS

1. Suppose there is a neighborhood crime watch in which people volunteer to patrol the street where you live. If you do not participate in the patrol, but your neighborhood is safer because of the crime watch, are you a free rider? Why? What can your neighbors do to eliminate the free-rider problem?
2. The following table shows the marginal benefit per year (in dollars) to all the households in a small community from the hiring of additional firefighters. The table also shows the marginal cost per year (in dollars) of hiring additional firefighters.

Number of Firefighters	Marginal Benefit for the Community	Marginal Cost
1	1,000,000	34,000
2	500,000	35,000
3	300,000	36,000
4	100,000	37,000
5	70,000	38,000
6	50,000	39,000
7	40,000	40,000
8	30,000	41,000
9	20,000	42,000
10	10,000	44,000

a. Is the service provided by the additional firefighters a public good?
b. Plot the marginal benefit and the marginal cost in a graph, placing the number of firefighters on the horizontal axis.
c. What is the optimal amount of this public good (in terms of the number of firefighters)? Illustrate your answer on the graph in part (b).
d. Is this marginal benefit schedule the same as the town's demand curve for firefighters?

3. Suppose that there are only three households in the town in Problem 2. Each household's marginal benefit (in dollars) from additional firefighters is described in the following table:

Number of Firefighters	Household A	Household B	Household C
1	500,000	300,000	200,000
2	300,000	100,000	100,000
3	200,000	50,000	50,000
4	50,000	30,000	20,000
5	36,000	20,000	14,000
6	25,000	15,000	10,000
7	20,000	14,000	6,000
8	15,000	13,000	2,000
9	10,000	9,000	1,000
10	5,000	4,500	500

a. Plot each of the three marginal benefit schedules and the marginal benefit schedule for the whole town on the same graph, with the number of firefighters on the horizontal axis. (You will need a big vertical scale.) What is the relationship between the three household curves and the curve for the whole town?

b. Consider a system in which the town chooses the optimal amount of the public good and decides to pay for it by taxing each household the identical dollar amount. Which of the households would rather free-ride than pay the taxes, if it were possible to evade paying taxes?

4. Suppose that people value the continued existence of dolphins in the Pacific Ocean, but that tuna-fishing fleets kill large numbers of these mammals. Draw a graph showing the externality. Describe two alternative approaches to remedy the externality.

5. Is public education a public good? Does it have positive externalities? Explain what the implications are for whether public education should be provided by the government. Could the same outcomes be achieved if private education were subsidized by the government?

6. Consider two college roommates, one who smokes and one who does not. The smoker wishes to smoke in the room, and the nonsmoker dislikes smoking in the room. Suppose the smoker would be willing to pay $500 to be allowed to smoke in the room during the semester, and the nonsmoker would be willing to pay $600 to keep the room smoke-free.

a. What would be the socially optimal outcome? Why is it optimal?

b. How might this outcome be achieved by an agreement between the two roommates? What theorem does this illustrate?

c. Suppose that the most the nonsmoker would be willing to pay was $200. Would this change the socially optimal outcome? Why or why not?

7. After the September 11 terrorist attacks, the media paid closer attention to the potential use of shipped cargo containers to smuggle weapons and terrorists into the United States.

a. Discuss why a negative externality may be associated with the use of shipping containers.

b. Graphically show the market for ship transportation of cargo. Make sure you include all the relevant aspects of this market, given your answer to part (a). Explain verbally as necessary.

c. Graphically show any deadweight loss that occurs in this market.

d. Discuss potential ways of reducing or eliminating deadweight loss in this market and the advantages and disadvantages of these remedies, including their impact on other markets.

8. The world's oceans are in trouble. Recently, experts have noted that stocks of fish are declining as the seas' resources are overused. Governments increasingly are becoming interested in ways of preserving fish stocks by limiting the catch. Consider the following four ways of doing so:
   - Assign property rights so that each shipping vessel is assigned a specific patch of ocean to catch fish in.
   - Tax fishing vessels heavily to reduce the number of such vessels that go out into the ocean.
   - Impose strict quotas on the amount of each species that a fishing vessel can catch.
   - Issue tradable permits to all fishing vessels such that the sum of the catch allowed by the permits is the desired catch limit.

   a. Which of these do you think is the best way to accomplish the conservation of the resource (fish in the ocean) efficiently? Explain.
9. Use the set of preferences for Ali, Betty, and Camilla shown in the following table to show that the paradox of voting does not always occur.

	Ali	Betty	Camilla
First	A	B	C
Second	B	A	A
Third	C	C	B

10. In recent years, we have heard much about the rise of extremely ideologically rigid attachment of segments of the population to particular political parties. Suppose that 25 percent of the population remains attached to Republicans, no matter what the party does, and a similar fraction stays attached to Democrats, no matter what the party does.
    a. Should this be a cause for concern in that the preferences of these voters will start driving public policy in the United States toward the fringes? Explain.
    b. Would your answer change if you were told that less than half of the U.S. population regularly votes in national elections and that the more ideologically attached voters have a higher likelihood of voting?

ENDNOTES

1. Ronald Coase, "The Problem of Social Cost," *Journal of Law and Economics* 3 (October 1960): 15.
2. Ronald Coase, "The Problem of Social Cost," *Journal of Law and Economics* 3 (October 1960): 17.

CHAPTER 16

Capital and Financial Markets

In this chapter we extend our analysis of markets to *financial markets*, such as the stock market and the bond market, as well as to markets in physical capital, such as housing, office buildings, and factories. These markets have a profound impact on people's lives, especially during times of economic and financial crisis when prices fluctuate wildly.

Source: Shutterstock.com

Figure 16.1 shows why. Each bar in the figure shows how much $1 invested in the stock market back at the beginning of 1987 would have given back to the buyer if sold at the beginning of subsequent years. For example, $1 invested in the stock market in 1987 would have given back $5.35 at the beginning of 2009. That sounds good, but if you had sold the stocks one year before, prior to the huge drop in the stock market in 2008, you would have gotten much more, $8.25. And if you held on after the 2008 crash, you would have gotten back up to $13.62 in early 2016. As Figure 16.1 makes clear, although the long-term trend in the stock market investments is positive, the market experienced short-term setbacks in 2008 and in other years such as 2001–2003. This volatility is what makes investing in the stock market risky, especially over shorter periods of time. Figure 16.1 shows the return on an average of 500 stocks. The returns on individual stocks can be even more volatile. For example, the price of the stock of the financial firm JP Morgan Chase & Co. fell from $53 in April 2007 to a low of $16 in March 2008 and then bounced back to $92 in March of 2017.

Markets in physical capital also can be volatile, as illustrated in Figure 16.2, which shows the median price of a house in the United States during the same period of time as Figure 16.1. Note that housing prices were stable through most of the 1990s, but they rose rapidly from 2000 to 2006 before coming back down rapidly. By the end of 2008, housing prices had returned to the levels of early 2004. As with the individual stock price, the prices of different houses rise or fall at rates different from the averages, depending on individual and local demand and supply factors. Prices in Michigan did not rise much during the national housing boom, whereas prices rose more rapidly than average in California and Florida. The bust in housing prices in California and Florida was also sharp.

We begin by defining physical and financial capital and describing how firms use them. We then consider the specific markets for financial capital, stocks, and bonds, while developing new tools to handle risk and uncertainty.

FIGURE 16.1 Returns from Investing in the Stock Market

Although the trend is up over several decades, the volatility over shorter periods of time can be dramatic and risky.

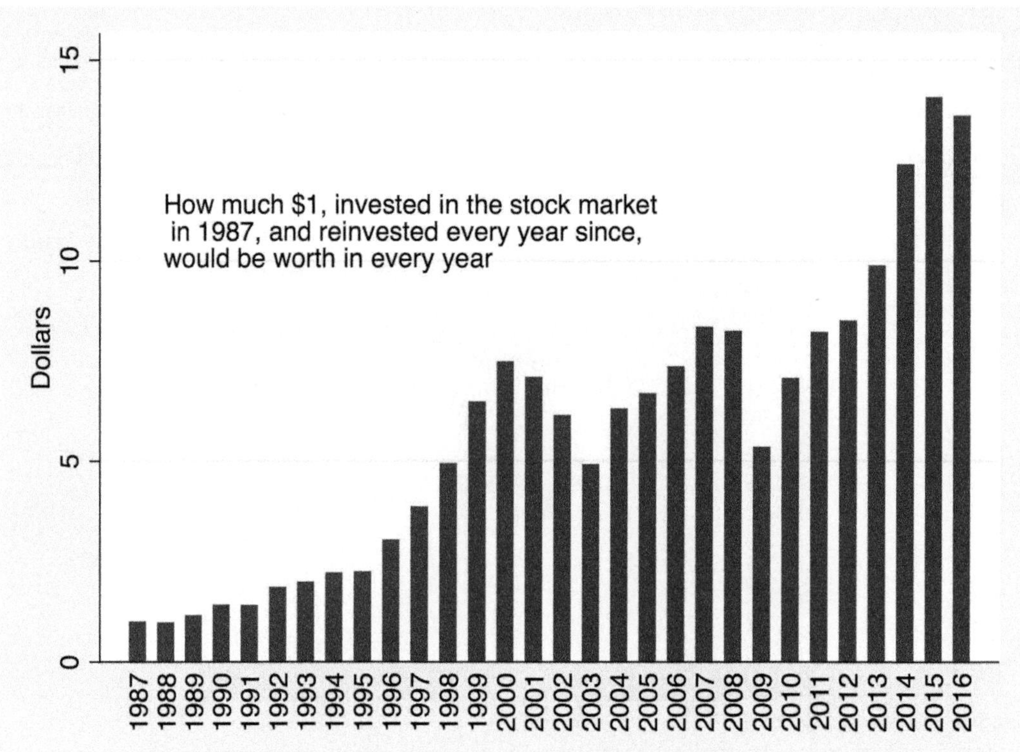

Source: Computed from S&P 500 data available to the public on the website of Prof. Robert Shiller (http://www.econ.yale.edu/~shiller/data.htm)

FIGURE 16.2 Housing Boom and Bust

House prices rose rapidly—a boom—until 2006, then fell rapidly—a bust—illustrating how prices in physical capital markets can be as volatile as financial markets. The recovery in the housing market did not happen until 2013

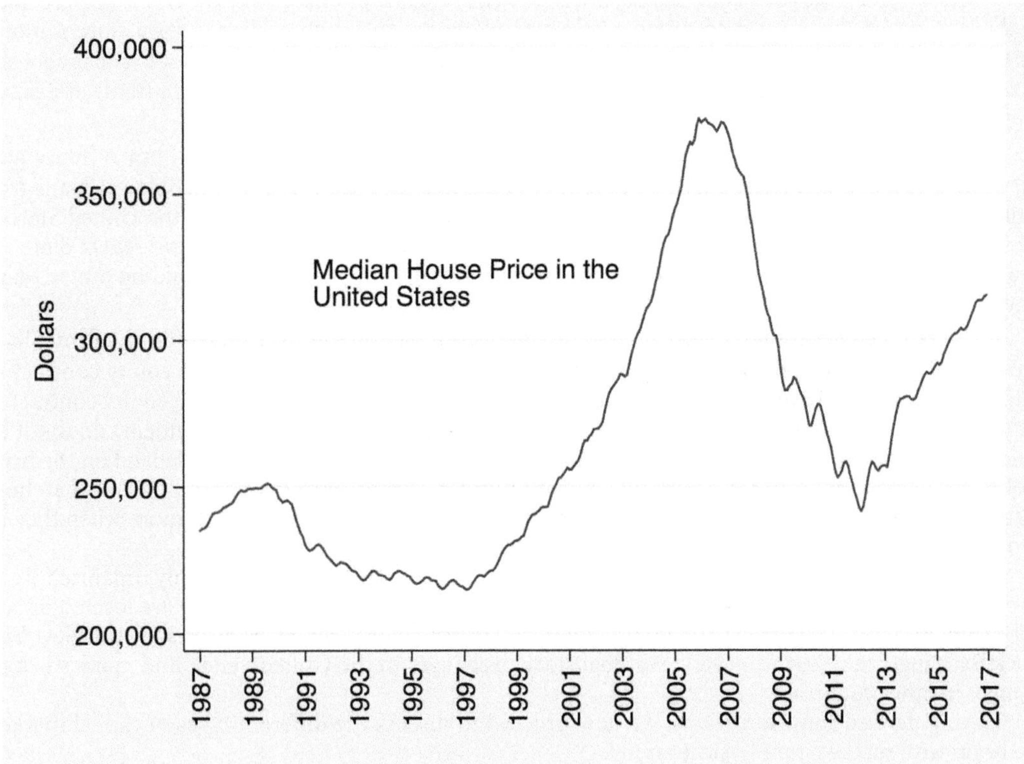

Source: Computed from the Case-Shiller Price Index using the median price of a U.S. house in the year 2015.

1. THE DISTINCTION BETWEEN PHYSICAL CAPITAL AND FINANCIAL CAPITAL

Some basic terminology about physical and financial capital is useful in studying capital markets. *Physical capital* refers to all the machines, factories, oil tankers, office buildings, and other physical resources used in the production of goods or services. In previous chapters on the behavior of firms, we simply used the term *capital* when referring to"physical capital" because we were not contrasting it with financial capital. Firms combine physical capital with labor inputs to produce goods and services. They obtain physical capital by either building it, buying it, or renting it. For example, McDonald's might hire a construction firm to build a new facility near a highway, a local school district might purchase several hundred computers for use in classrooms, and a real estate developer might rent a construction crane for a year to help move building materials onto the site of a large apartment building project.

An important characteristic of physical capital is that it provides productive services for a number of years. Residential housing—single-family homes, apartments, and trailers—also is a form of physical capital. It provides productive services in the form of living space that people can enjoy year after year. Government-owned roads, schools, and military equipment also are physical capital. It is useful to think of government capital as helping to produce services, whether transportation services, education services, or national security.

Another important characteristic of physical capital is that it does not remain in new condition permanently. The gradual decline in the productive usefulness of capital is called **depreciation**. Trucks, trailers, roads, machines, and even buildings wear out and eventually must be either replaced or refurbished.

depreciation

The decrease in an asset's value over time; for capital, it is the amount by which physical capital wears out over a given period of time.

To purchase, rent, or build capital, a firm needs to obtain funds. These funds are an example of financial capital. Firms can obtain *financial capital* in two different ways: by issuing debt (borrowing) and by issuing equity (selling an ownership stake in the firm).

debt contract

A contract in which a lender agrees to provide funds today in exchange for a promise from the borrower, who will repay that amount plus interest at some point in the future.

mortgage

A loan to purchase a house.

equity contract

Shares of ownership in a firm; payments to the owners of the shares depend on the firm's profits.

When a firm takes out a loan, it agrees to pay back the amount it borrowed plus interest at a future date. The amount of interest is determined by the *interest rate.* If the amount borrowed is $10,000 and is due in one year and the interest rate is 10 percent per year, then the borrower pays the lender $11,000 at the end of the year. The $11,000 includes the *principal* on the loan ($10,000) plus the *interest payment* ($1,000 = 0.1 times $10,000). Larger firms also can issue *corporate bonds.* A bond is an agreement by the issuer to make a specified number of payments in the future in exchange for a sum of money today. Both loans and bonds are a type of contract called a **debt contract** in which the lender agrees to provide funds today in exchange for a promise that the borrower will pay back the funds at a future date with interest.

Firms are not the only entities that take out debt contracts. Most people who buy a house get a **mortgage**, which is a loan of funds to purchase real estate. In addition, many people get loans from banks to buy cars and consumer appliances. The biggest single issuer of bonds in the United States is the federal government. The federal government borrows funds by selling *government bonds.* State and local governments also issue bonds to finance physical capital investments like building a new public school, fixing a highway, or building a tunnel.

Firms also can obtain financial capital by issuing *stock,* or shares of ownership in the firm. Shares of ownership are a type of contract called an **equity contract**. The purchaser of an equity contract acquires an ownership share in the firm that typically is proportional to the size of the equity contract. In contrast to a debt contract, in which case the payment by the firm (the interest payment) does not depend on the profits of the firm, in an equity contract the payment by the firm does depend on the firm's profits. Firms that make lots of profits will pay out more in *dividends* to their shareholders. Shareholders also can benefit if the firm increases in value because their shares will be worth more when they are sold.

Once bonds or stocks have been issued, they can be exchanged or traded. Highly organized financial markets trade stocks and bonds. The government and corporate bond markets are located in New York City, London, Tokyo, and other large financial centers. The stock markets include the New York Stock Exchange, the Nasdaq, several regional stock exchanges in the United States, and many stock exchanges in other countries.

Having defined some key terms, we now proceed to discuss the different types of capital markets. We begin with markets for physical capital.

REVIEW

- Physical capital and financial capital are distinct but closely related. Physical capital refers to the machines, buildings, and physical resources needed to produce output. To expand their physical capital, firms need to raise funds in some way. These funds are known as financial capital.
- Firms can buy, build, or rent physical capital. They can acquire financial capital by means of debt contracts or equity contracts.
- Debt contracts, such as bonds or loans, allow borrowers access to a sum of money today in exchange for a promise to repay that sum of money plus interest in the future. Equity contracts allow firms to obtain money today in exchange for handing over an ownership stake in the firm.
- The bonds or stocks that firms issue can be traded. Organized markets for trading bonds and stocks are found in all the world's financial centers.

2. MARKETS FOR PHYSICAL CAPITAL

The demand for physical capital is a relationship between the quantity of capital demanded by firms and the price of this capital. The demand for capital is a *derived demand* in the same sense that the demand for labor is a derived demand; that is, the demand for capital derives from the goods and services that firms produce with capital. In this section we show that just as the quantity of labor that the firm employs depends on the marginal revenue product of labor, the quantity of capital that the firm employs depends on the marginal revenue product of capital.

2.1 Rental Markets

The firm's capital decision is best understood if we first assume that the firm rents capital in a competitive rental market. In fact, it is common for firms to rent capital; many types of equipment have a rental market in which many rental firms specialize in renting the equipment to other firms. For example, a construction firm can rent a dump truck; a clothing store can rent a storefront at a mall; an airline can lease an airplane. The price in the rental market is called the **rental price of capital**. It is the amount that a rental firm charges for the use of capital equipment for a specified period of time, such as a month.

rental price of capital
The amount that a rental company charges for the use of capital equipment for a specified period of time.

Consider a hypothetical construction company, called Lofts-R-Us, deciding whether to rent a dump truck from a rental company called Acme Truck Rental. To show how much capital a firm like Lofts-R-Us would rent, we need to consider the effect of this capital on the firm's profits. The marginal revenue product of capital can be used to assess this effect on profits. The **marginal revenue product of capital** is defined as the change in total revenue as the firm increases its capital by one unit. We assume that the marginal revenue product of capital declines as more capital is employed at the firm. For example, suppose the marginal revenue product of capital is $3,000 as capital rises from zero trucks to one truck, $1,500 as capital rises from one truck to two trucks, and $500 as capital rises from two trucks to three trucks.

marginal revenue product of capital
The change in total revenue because of a one-unit increase in capital.

Suppose the rental price of a dump truck is $1,000 a month. This price is what Acme Truck Rental charges, and all other rental firms in the area charge essentially the same price. Because the rental market is competitive, neither Acme Truck Rental nor Lofts-R-Us has enough market power to affect the rental price. How many dump trucks would Lofts-R-Us use? With the marginal revenue product of capital from one dump truck equal to $3,000 a month, the firm will employ at least one dump truck. In other words, if the firm's total revenue increases by $3,000 and the rental price for the truck is $1,000, then it makes sense to rent the dump truck. With the marginal revenue product of capital from a second dump truck equal to $1,500, the firm will employ a second dump truck; by doing so, it can increase its profits by $500. With the marginal revenue product of capital from a third dump truck equal to only $500, however, the firm will lower its profits if it rents a third dump truck. Thus, if the rental price of the dump truck is $1,000, the firm will employ exactly two dump trucks. The firm rents the largest amount of capital for which the marginal revenue product of capital is greater than the rental price; if fractional units of capital were possible, then the firm would keep renting more capital until *the marginal revenue product of capital was exactly equal to the rental price.*

The Demand Curve for Capital

To derive the demand curve for capital, we must determine the quantity of capital demanded by the firm as the rental price of capital changes. For example, if the rental price of dump trucks declines to $400, then the quantity of dump trucks demanded by the firm will increase; a third dump truck will be rented because the price is now below the marginal revenue product of capital. In other words, as the rental price of capital falls, the quantity of capital demanded increases. Similarly, as the rental price of capital rises, the quantity of capital demanded decreases.

Figure 16.3 illustrates this general principle. It shows the marginal revenue product of capital for any firm. As more capital is employed, the marginal revenue product declines. For profit maximization, the firm will rent capital to the point at which the marginal revenue product of capital equals the rental price. Thus, as we lower the rental price, the quantity of capital demanded increases. In other words, the demand curve for capital is downward sloping.

FIGURE 16.3 Demand for Physical Capital by One Firm

A profit-maximizing firm chooses a quantity of capital that gives a marginal revenue product of capital equal to the rental price. Because the marginal revenue product of capital declines as more capital is used, a lower rental price of capital results in a larger quantity of capital demanded.

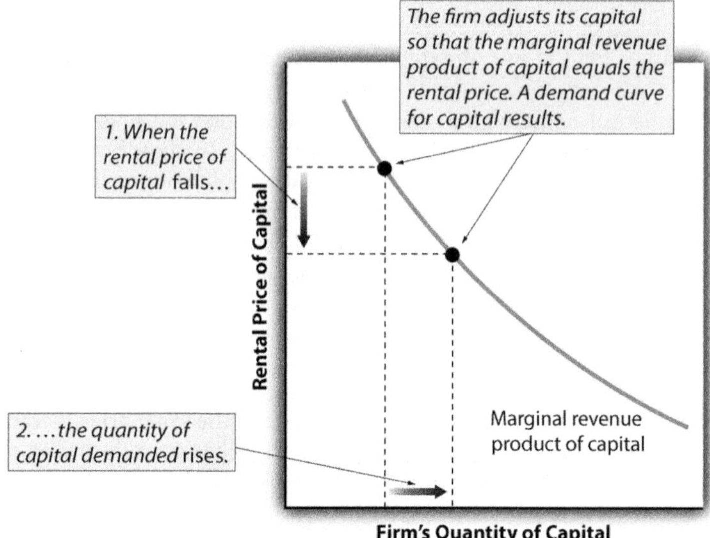

The demand curve for capital is determined by the marginal revenue product of capital. If the marginal revenue product changes, the demand curve for capital will shift. For example, if the marginal product of dump trucks rises, the demand for dump trucks by Lofts-R-Us will shift outward.

Demand for Factors of Production in General

Observe that the marginal revenue product of capital equals the rental price. This same principle applies to any factor of production for which the market in that factor is competitive. *For any input to production, a profit-maximizing firm will choose a quantity of that input such that the marginal revenue product equals the price of that input.*

The Market Demand and Supply

The market demand for physical capital is found by adding up the demand for physical capital by many firms. Figure 16.4 shows such a market demand curve.

On the same diagram, we show the market supply curve. It is the sum of the supply curves for all the firms in the industry providing capital for rent, such as Acme Truck Rental. The higher the rental price of capital, the more likely Acme Truck Rental is to buy new dump trucks and offer them as rentals to firms like Lofts-R-Us. If other rental firms behave the way that Acme Truck Rental does, then the market supply of rental capital will be increasing with rental prices.

FIGURE 16.4 Market Supply and Demand for Physical Capital

The market demand for capital is the sum of the demands of the individual firms that use the equipment. The market supply is the sum of the supplies at the individual firms that provide the equipment. Market equilibrium occurs in cases in which the quantity of capital demanded equals the quantity of capital supplied.

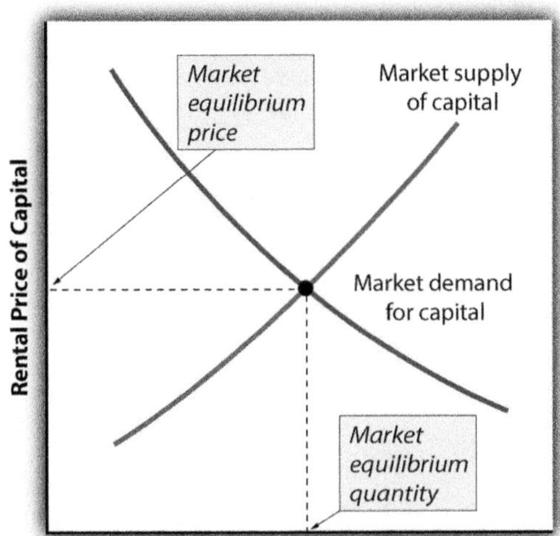

The equilibrium rental price and the equilibrium quantity of capital rented are shown in the diagram. The supply and demand model for capital illustrated in Figure 16.4 then can be used to predict the effects of tax changes or other changes in the capital market in much the same way as any other supply and demand model. For example, if the government places a tax on construction firms like Lofts-R-Us proportional to the quantity of trucks they rent, perhaps because the heavy trucks damage city roads more than cars do, then the marginal revenue product of capital will decline and the demand curve for capital will shift down, or to the left. This shift in demand will lower the equilibrium rental price received by Acme and reduce the quantity of capital rented. Alternatively, if the city government is eager to have new apartment buildings in the city, it may offer a subsidy on the rental of capital by construction firms. This would shift the demand curve for capital up, or to the right, and increase the quantity of capital rented.

The Case of Fixed Supply: Economic Rents

An important special case of a market for physical capital occurs when the supply of physical capital is completely fixed. Alfred Marshall gave the following famous example of physical capital with a completely fixed supply: "Let us suppose that a meteoric shower of a few thousand largest ones harder than diamonds fell all in one place, so that they were all picked up at once, and no amount of search could find any more. These stones, able to cut every material, would revolutionize many branches of industry."[1]

The important thing about Marshall's stones is that their supply cannot be increased or decreased regardless of the price of the stones. In other words, the supply curve for Marshall's stones is perfectly vertical, or perfectly inelastic, as shown in Figure 16.5.

FIGURE 16.5 The Case of a Fixed Supply of Capital

When the supply of capital is perfectly inelastic, a shift in demand changes the rental price but not the quantity supplied. Marshall's stones are a hypothetical example of capital with a perfectly inelastic supply.

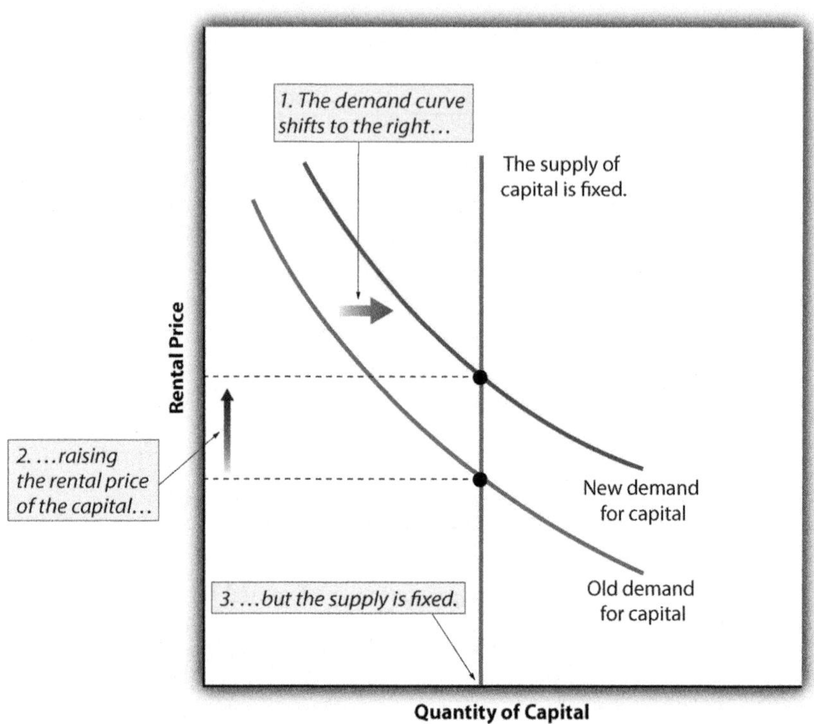

Figure 16.5 shows what happens when the demand for capital that is in fixed supply shifts, such as Marshall's stones. A change in demand will change the price, but it will not change the quantity. Demand completely determines the price in this case because the quantity supplied cannot change.

economic rent

The price of something that has a fixed supply.

Economists have a special terminology for the price in this circumstance: **Economic rent** is the price of anything that has a fixed supply. Economic rent is also sometimes called *pure rent.* Economic rent is a significant concept in economics precisely because the quantity supplied does not depend on the price. Thus, a tax on economic rents would not change the amount supplied; it would not affect economic efficiency or cause a dead weight loss. For example, if the government passed a tax (even a 99.9 percent tax) on the rental payments charged by the lucky owners of Marshall's stones, the quantity of stones supplied would not change.

Marshall's stones are of course a hypothetical example. In practice, certain types of land may come close to being an item in fixed supply, but it is always possible to improve land or clear land and thereby change its supply to some degree. The perfectly inelastic supply of Marshall's stones or the near perfectly inelastic supply of certain types of land is in sharp contrast to the higher elasticity of supply of most capital goods. The supply of dump trucks, apartment buildings, and other types of capital is sensitive to changes in the price. Increases in the price provide an incentive to increase the quantity supplied, and decreases in the price provide an incentive to decrease the quantity supplied. In reality, therefore, taxes on capital would be expected to change the quantity of capital supplied.

2.2 The Ownership of Physical Capital

Rental markets for capital are common, but they are not the only way in which firms obtain capital. The same construction firm that rents dump trucks might choose to purchase and own a dump truck rather than rent one, especially if it expects to continually be engaged in projects for which a truck is required. The firm also may own the warehouse where it stores its building materials and the office where it keeps its books and meets prospective customers. Although legal and tax differences exist between renting and ownership, the economic principles are similar. In fact, even though owners of physical capital do not pay a rental price, economic considerations indicate that they pay an *implicit* rental price.

When a firm buys equipment, it must either borrow funds to pay for the equipment or use its own funds, funds that it could have put in an interest-earning account at a bank. If it borrows the funds, the monthly interest payment on the loan is like a rental payment. If it uses its own funds, the interest it would have received at the bank is an opportunity cost and is considered to be similar to a rental payment. In addition to these payments, the firm that owns the equipment must factor in the wear and tear, or depreciation, on the equipment. The amount by which the firm's equipment deteriorates is also a cost.

In sum, for a firm that chooses to purchase and own capital, the **implicit rental price** of capital for a year equals the interest payments for the year plus the amount of depreciation during the year. For example, suppose the interest rate is 10 percent, the purchase price of a dump truck is $40,000, and the dump truck depreciates $8,000 per year. Then the implicit rental price is $12,000 per year (0.10 times $40,000, plus $8,000), or $1,000 a month, the same as the rental price in our dump truck example. The implicit rental price depends on the interest rate. The higher the interest rate, the higher the interest payments during the year, and thus the higher the implicit rental price. When the interest rate rises, the implicit rental price rises. When the interest rate falls, the implicit rental price falls.

implicit rental price

The cost of the funds used to buy the capital plus the depreciation of the capital over a given period of time.

The concept of the implicit rental price makes the firm's decision to buy a dump truck, or any other piece of capital, analogous to the decision to rent. The demand curve looks the same as that in Figure 16.3, except that it is the implicit rental price rather than the actual rental price that is on the vertical axis.

2.3 The Housing Market

The model of the demand and supply of physical capital can be applied to the demand and supply for residential houses, which for many people is the largest capital item they rent or own. The application of the model to housing is straightforward because many people have had the experience of renting a house or an apartment.

Let's start with a market for rental housing. The rental price of a house is simply the rent on the house for a period of time, such as $500 per month. Rather than the marginal revenue product of a truck to a firm, think of the marginal benefit of a house to an individual. Then, applying the same reasoning, we conclude that an individual will rent a house if the rental price is less than the marginal benefit of the house to the individual. Because few people rent more than one house, we assume that marginal benefit decreases with the size of the house rather than with the number of houses. Thus, an individual will consume housing up until the marginal benefit of the housing is equal to the rental price. The implication is that the *quantity of housing demanded is related negatively to the rental price of housing.*

Finally, by adding up all the individual demand curves, we get a market demand for housing. In the housing market as a whole, the higher the rental price on houses, the lower the quantity of houses demanded. Hence, *the demand curve for housing is sloped negatively.* The supply curve of housing is analogous to the supply curve for other kinds of capital. Rather than the Acme Truck Rental company, we might have the Acme Student Apartment Rental company. The concepts are similar.

To move from markets in which people rent their homes to markets in which people own their homes, we can use the implicit rental price concept. For a house owned by an individual or a family, the *implicit rental price* will equal the interest rate on the mortgage (the loan on the house) plus the amount of depreciation on the house during the year. The quantity of housing demanded depends negatively on the implicit rental price. Hence, we have a demand for housing that looks just like the demand curve in Figure 16.4.

Observe that because the quantity of housing demanded depends negatively on the implicit rental price, it also depends negatively on the mortgage interest rate. Hence, if mortgage interest rates decline, we would predict an increase in the demand for housing. Indeed, many experts think a major reason for the housing boom during the years leading up to the housing bust in 2006 was that mortgage interest rates were low. The theory thus explains important trends in housing markets.

REVIEW

- The demand for physical capital at a firm is a derived demand. What firms are willing to pay for capital depends on the value of the goods and services they can produce with that capital.
- Firms that rent capital will choose to rent capital up to the point at which the marginal revenue product of capital equals the rental price of capital.
- The marginal revenue product of capital decreases as the quantity of capital used by the firm increases. So when the rental price goes down, the firm will want to add extra machines until the marginal revenue product of capital equals the rental price.
- If capital is purchased rather than rented, the firm still faces an implicit rental price.
- The demand curve for purchased capital, then, looks similar to the demand curve for rental capital; the demand curve is downward sloping in the (implicit) rental price.
- The theory also implies a demand curve for housing and offers an explanation for the housing boom in 2002–2006.

3. MARKETS FOR FINANCIAL CAPITAL

Having seen how markets for physical capital work, let us turn to the examination of markets for financial capital. As we discussed, firms that want to acquire physical capital need to obtain financial capital. They can obtain financial capital by issuing stocks and bonds. Stocks and bonds are traded on financial markets. Their prices are determined by the actions of buyers and sellers, like prices in any other market. Understanding what drives the prices of stocks and bonds is important for determining firms' ability to acquire financial capital. It is also important for investors who buy stocks and bonds as a way to save for their future retirement or simply as a way to make money.

3.1 Stock Prices and Rates of Return

return

The income received from the ownership of an asset; for a stock, the return is the dividend plus the capital gain.

capital gain

The increase in the value of an asset through an increase in its price.

capital loss

The decrease in the value of an asset through a decrease in its price.

dividend yield

The dividend stated as a percentage of the price of the stock.

rate of return

The return on an asset stated as a percentage of the price of the asset.

Prices of the stocks of most large firms can be found in daily newspapers. Investors are interested in buying those stocks whose prices are likely to rise and that are more likely to pay back their profits to shareholders in the form of dividends. We can define the annual **return** from holding a stock as the *dividend* plus the *capital gain* during the year. The **capital gain** during the year is the increase in the price of the stock during the year. A **capital loss** is a negative capital gain: a decrease in the price. When comparing dividends across companies, we typically look at the **dividend yield**, that is, the dividend stated as a percentage of the price. Similarly, in comparing returns across companies, we typically look at the **rate of return**, that is, the return stated as a percentage of the price of the stock.

A simple example can illustrate these terms. For example, suppose you had purchased a share of stock in the giant communications technology company Verizon at the end of 2015 and held the stock for one year. The cost of a share of Verizon stock at the end of 2015 was $46.22. The dividend for Verizon in 2016 was $2.27 per year. At the purchase price of $46.22, the dividend yield was 4.91 percent. During 2016, the price of Verizon stock rose from $46.22 to $53.38, a capital gain of $7.16. Combined with the dividend, the total return was $9.43, a rate of return of 20.4 percent on the original $46.22 purchase price. In this example, the capital gain is a much bigger portion of the rate of return than the dividend.

Check the result. *The dividend was $0.32. The closing price was $41.19. Dividing 0.32 by 41.19 gives 0.008, or 0.8 percent.*

But stock market returns are not always as good as in this example. Consider what happened to Verizon's stock price in 2008, when it fell from $43.69 to $33.90 per share during 2008, a *negative* capital gain or a capital loss of $9.79. Including the $1.67 in dividends it paid during the year, Verizon's total return was negative $8.12, which would represent a rate of return of negative 18.5 percent for someone who purchased the share at the end of 2007. 2008 was not a good year for stocks. The stock price of Caterpillar, the famous maker of large-scale construction equipment, fell from $72.56 to $44.67 during the year. Including a $1.56 dividend payout, its return was negative 36.3 percent. Indeed, the average stock price of all the 500 major U.S. companies—as measured by the Standard and Poor's (S&P) 500 Index—fell by 38.5 percent during 2008, which substantially cut into gains made in the previous two decades, as shown in Figure 16.1.

You can figure out which firms are the most profitable, and hence more likely to generate a high rate of return for their shareholders, by looking at firms' accounting profits, also known as **earnings**. Firms pay out some of their profits as dividends; the rest of the profits are retained and invested in physical capital or research. Stock tables list the **price-earnings ratio**: the price of the stock divided by the annual earnings per share. The price-earnings ratio for Verizon in 2016 was 12.77. With the year-end price of the stock at $53.38, this means that earnings for the year were $4.1801 per share ($53.38/ $4.1801 = 12.77). A firm's earnings ultimately influence the return on the firm's stock, so the price-earnings ratio is watched closely.

earnings

The accounting profits of a firm.

price-earnings ratio

The price of a stock divided by its annual earnings per share.

3.2 Bond Prices and Rates of Return

Bond prices for both corporate and government bonds also can be found in the financial pages of the newspaper. A bond has four key characteristics: *coupon, maturity date, face value,* and *yield.* The **coupon** is the fixed amount that the borrower agrees to pay the bondholder each year. The **maturity date** is the time when the coupon payments end and the principal is paid back. The **face value** is the amount of principal that will be paid back when the bond matures. Consider a $1,000 face value bond that has a maturity date of February 2037 and a coupon equal to 4.75 percent of the face value of the bond. That is, the bond will pay 4.75 percent of the $1,000 face value, or $47.50, a year, until 2037, and in February 2037, the $1,000 face value will be paid back.

coupon

The fixed amount that a borrower agrees to pay to the bondholder each year.

maturity date

The date when the principal on a loan is to be paid back.

face value

The principal that will be paid back when a bond matures.

Once the government has issued bonds, they can be sold or bought in the bond market. In the bond market, bond traders make a living buying and selling bonds. The bond traders will *bid* a certain price at which they will buy, and they will *ask* a certain price at which they will sell. The bid price is slightly lower than the ask price, which enables the bond traders to earn a profit by buying at a price that is slightly lower than the price at which they sell.

The **yield**, or yield to maturity, is defined as the annual rate of return on the bond if the bond were bought at the current price and held to maturity. When people refer to the current interest rate on bonds, they are referring to the yield on the bond.

yield

The annual rate of return on a bond if the bond were held to maturity.

Are bond yields the same as the coupon rate? An inverse, or negative, relationship exists between the yield and the price. They have an inverse relationship because the payments of the bond are fixed—the borrower (bond issuer) agrees to pay back the lender (bondholder) the principal on the maturity date and make coupon payments in the interim—regardless of what the buyer paid for the bond. The higher the price you pay today to get this fixed stream of interest and principal payments in the future, the lower the rate of return (yield) you earn. So unlike the coupon rate, which stays fixed, the yield will fluctuate with price. Furthermore, as the price rises, the yield will fall, and vice versa.

Here is a typical quote on bond yields: "*The price of the 30-year Treasury bond rose less than 1/8 point, or less than $1.25 for a bond with $1,000 face value, to 84 4/32. Its yield, which moves in the opposite direction of its price, dropped to 7.60 percent from 7.61 percent on Thursday.*"

Why do bond yields fluctuate? Consider a simple example. Suppose you just bought a one-year bond for $100 that says that the government will pay 5 percent of the face value, or $5, plus $100 at the end of the one-year period. Now suppose that just after you bought the bond, interest rates on bank deposits suddenly jumped to 10 percent. Your bond says that you earn 5 percent per year, so if you hold it for the entire year, your rate of return is less than you could get on a bank deposit. Suddenly the bond looks much less attractive. You probably would want to sell it, but everyone else knows the bond is less attractive, also. You would not be able to get $100 for the bond. The price would decline until the rate of return on the bond was close to the interest rate at the bank. For example, if the price fell to $95.45, then the payment of $105 at the end of the year would result in a 10 percent rate of return [that is, 0.10 = (105 – 95.45)/95.45]. In other words, the yield on the bond would rise until it reached a value closer to 10 percent than to 5 percent.

If you look at a table listing the yields of government bonds, you will notice bonds maturing in 2017 with very high coupon rates: for example there is a U.K. government bond maturing in 2017 that has a coupon rate of 8.75 percent. This bond must have been issued at a time when market interest rates were closer to 8.75 percent. As interest rates in the United Kingdom fell, people found that holding the bond was a more attractive proposition than keeping money in the bank, so they bid up the price of the bond, driving down the yield until it approached the new market interest rates in the United Kingdom. This implies that periods of falling interest rates are good for bond holders and bond issuers because the prices of their bonds rise, while periods of rising interest rates are bad for both bond holders and bond issuers.

On the basis of these considerations, we can use a formula to calculate the relationship between the price and the yield for bonds of any maturity. Let P be the price of the bond. Let R be the coupon. Let F be the face value. Let i be the yield. The formula relating to the price and the yield in the case of a one-year bond is indicated in the first row of Table 16.1.

TABLE 16.1 Bond Price Formula

One-year maturity:	$P = \frac{R}{(1+i)} + \frac{F}{(1+i)}$
Two-year maturity:	$P = \frac{R}{(1+i)} + \frac{R}{(1+i)^2} + \frac{F}{(1+i)^2}$
Three-year maturity:	$P = \frac{R}{(1+i)} + \frac{R}{(1+i)^2} + \frac{R}{(1+i)^3} + \frac{F}{(1+i)^3}$
For very long term:	$P = \frac{R}{i}$

P = price of bond; R = coupon; F = face value; i = yield

For a one-year bond, a coupon payment of R is paid at the end of one year together with the face value of the bond. The price P is what you would be willing to pay *now, in the present,* for these future payments. It is the *present discounted value* of the coupon payment plus the face value at the end of the year. By looking at the formula in the first row of Table 16.1, you can see the negative relationship between the price (P) of the bond and the yield (i) on the bond. The higher the yield, the lower the price; and conversely, the lower the yield, the higher the price.

A two-year-maturity bond is similar. You get R at the end of the first year and R plus the face value at the end of the second year. Now you want to divide the first-year payment by $1 + i$ and the second-year payment by $(1 + i)^2$. The formula still shows the inverse relationship between the yield and the price. A bond with a three-year or longer maturity is similar. Computers do the calculation for the news reports, so even 30-year bond yields can easily be found from their price.

We can use a convenient and simple approximation method to determine the price or yield on bonds with very long maturity dates. It says that the price is equal to the coupon divided by the yield: $P = R/i$. This formula is the easiest way to remember the inverse relationship between the price and the yield. It is a close approximation for long term bonds like the 30-year bond.

REVIEW

- Firms that want to purchase physical capital need financial capital to do so. They obtain financial capital by issuing stocks and bonds. Stocks and bonds are traded on financial markets.
- The return from holding stock is the dividend plus the change in the price. The rate of return is equal to the return measured as a percentage of the price of the stock.
- The return from holding bonds to maturity is the yield of the bond. Bond yields and bond prices move in opposite directions.
- Periods of falling interest rates are good for bond holders and bond issuers because the prices of bonds rise, while periods of rising interest rates are bad for both bond holders and bond issuers.

4. THE TRADE-OFF BETWEEN RISK AND RETURNS

One of the hallmarks of financial markets is volatility. The prices of individual stocks and bonds rise and fall over time. Over the long run, stock prices show a positive trend, but there are periods of significant decline from time to time, and the prices of individual stocks traded in the financial markets are volatile. Similarly, even though you always can earn a rate of return equivalent to the yield by holding a bond issued by the U.S. government to maturity, in the interim, the price of the bond will vary.

If you had bought stock in United Airlines in the summer of 2007 you would have paid around $45 a share. By the following summer, however, shares in United Airlines were trading around $4 a share, so you would have lost almost 90 percent of your investment. On the other hand, if you had held on to the stock, 7 years later the price would have been over $75 a share an 18-fold increase from the depths it had sunk to in 2007. Because of such variability, buying stocks is a risky activity. Even the broad S&P 500 Index fell by 38.5 percent in 2008. The price of bonds can also change by a large amount. For example, from mid-1996 to mid-1997, the price of government bonds rose by nearly 20 percent, but from mid-1993 to mid-1994, the price of government bonds *fell* by nearly 20 percent. Thus, government bonds are also a risky investment.

In this section, we show that the riskiness of stocks and bonds affects the decision of people to trade in financial markets. To do so, we first examine how individuals behave when they face risk.

4.1 Behavior under Uncertainty

Most people do not like uncertainty. They are *risk averse* in most of their activities. Given a choice between two jobs that pay the same wage, most people will be averse to choosing the riskier job where there is a good chance of being laid off. Similarly, given a choice between two investments that pay the same return, people will choose the less risky one.

Let us examine this idea of risk aversion further. To be more precise, suppose that Melissa has a choice between the two alternatives shown in Table 16.2. She must decide what to do with her life savings of $10,000 for the next year. At the end of the year, she plans to buy a house, and she will need some money for a down payment. She can put her $10,000 in a bank account, where the interest rate is 5 percent, or she can buy $10,000 worth of a stock that pays a dividend of 5 percent and will incur either a capital gain or a capital loss. In the bank, the value of her savings is safe, but if she buys the stock, she has a 50 percent chance that the price of the stock will fall by 30 percent and a 50 percent chance that the price of the stock will rise by 30 percent. In other words, the risky stock will leave Melissa with the possibility of a return of negative $2,500 (a loss) or a return of $3,500 (a gain). The bank account leaves her with a guaranteed $500 return.

TABLE 16.2 Two Options: Different Risks, Same Expected Return

Low-Risk Option	High-Risk Option
A bank deposit with	*A corporate stock with either*
5 percent interest (return = $500)	a. A 5 percent dividend and a 30 percent price decline ($500 - $3,000 = $2,500)
	b. A 5 percent dividend and a 30 percent price increase ($500 + $3,000 = $3,500)

expected return
The return on an uncertain investment calculated by weighting the gains or losses by the probability that they will occur.

Both of the options in Table 16.2 have the same **expected return**. The expected return on an investment weights the different gains or losses according to how probable they are. In the case of the safe bank account, there is a 100 percent chance that the return is $500, so the expected return is $500. In the case of the stock, the expected return would be negative $2,500 times the probability of this loss (1/2) plus $3,500 times the probability of this gain (also 1/2). Thus, the expected return is $500 (-2,500/2 + 3,500/2 = -1,250 + 1,750 = 500), the same as the return on the bank account.

The expected return is one way to measure how attractive an investment is. The word *expected* may appear misleading, because in the risky option $500 is not "expected" in the everyday use of the word. You do not expect $500; you expect either a loss of $2,500 or a gain of $3,500. If the term is confusing, think of the expected return as the average return that Melissa would get if she could take the second option year after year for many years. The losses of $2,500 and gains of $3,500 would average out to $500 per year after many years. (The term *expected return* has been carried over by economists and investment analysts from probability and statistics, in which case the term *expected value* is used to describe the mean, or the average, of a random variable.)

Given that the expected returns are the same, if Melissa is a risk-averse person (that is, if she would dread a capital loss more than she would cherish a capital gain of a similar magnitude), she will choose the less risky of these two options. Although it is clear that Melissa would choose the less risky of the two options in Table 16.2, perhaps Melissa would accept some compensation to offset her risk aversion. Although most people are averse to risk, they are willing to take on some risk if they are compensated for it. In the case of a risky financial investment, the compensation for higher risk could take the form of a higher expected return.

How could we make Melissa's expected return higher in the risky investment? Suppose Melissa had the choice between the same safe option as in Table 16.2 and a high risk stock that paid a dividend of 20 percent. This new choice is shown in Table 16.3; the difference is that the risky stock now offers a dividend of 20 percent, much greater than the 5 percent in the first example and much greater than the 5 percent on the bank account. With the greater chance of a higher return on the stock, Melissa might be willing to buy the stock. Even in the worst situation, she loses just $1,000, which may still leave her with enough for the down payment on her new house. The expected return for the high-risk option is now $2,000, much greater than the $500 for the bank account (-1,000/2 + 5,000/2 = -500 + 2,500 = 2,000)

TABLE 16.3 Two Options: Different Risks, Different Expected Returns

Low-Risk Option	High-Risk Option
A bank deposit with	*A corporate stock with either*
5 percent interest (return = $500)	a. A 20 percent dividend and a 30 percent price decline ($2,000 - $3,000 = -$1,000)
	b. A 20 percent dividend and a 30 percent price increase ($2,000 + $3,000 = $5,000)

In other words, Melissa probably would be willing to take on the risky investment. And if the 20 percent dividend in the example is not enough for her, some higher dividend (25 percent? 30 percent?) would be. This example illustrates the general point that risk-averse people are willing to take risks if they are paid for it.

Playing It Safe? Most people are risk-averse when it comes to large sums, but many are risk lovers when the stakes are low or when they can limit their potential losses—such as at casinos where people can choose to gamble a set amount or combine gambling with entertainment.

Source: Shutterstock.com

Before we develop the implication of our analysis of individual behavior under uncertainty, we should pause to ask about the possibility that some people might be risk lovers rather than risk avoiders. The billions of dollars that are bet in state lotteries in the United States and in private gambling casinos in Las Vegas, Atlantic City, and Monte Carlo indicate that some people enjoy risk. With few exceptions, however, most of the gambling on lotteries, slot machines, and even roulette wheels represents a small portion of the income or wealth of the gambler. Thus, you might be willing to spend $0.50 or even $5 on lottery tickets or a slot machine for the chance of winning big, even if the odds are against you. Many people get enjoyment out of such wagers; but if the stakes are large compared with one's income or wealth, then few people want to play. For small sums, some people are risk lovers, but for large sums, virtually everybody becomes a risk avoider to some degree or another.

Risk and Rates of Return in Reality

What are the implications of our conclusion that investors will be willing to take risks if they are compensated with a higher return on the stock or bond? In the stock market, the prices of individual stocks are determined by the bidding of buyers and sellers. Suppose a stock, AOK, had a price that gave it the same expected rate of return as a bank account. Now AOK, being a common stock, clearly has more risk than a bank account because its price can change. Hence, no risk averse investor will want to buy AOK. Just as Melissa will prefer to put her funds in a bank account in the example in Table 16.2, rather than into the risky option, investors will put their funds in a bank rather than buy AOK. People who own shares of AOK will sell and put their funds into a bank. With everybody wanting to sell AOK and no one wanting to buy it, the price of AOK will start to fall.

Now, the price and the expected rate of return are inversely related—recall that for a stock, the rate of return is the return divided by the price. Thus, if the price falls and the dividend does not change, the rate of return will rise. This fall in the price will drive up the expected rate of return on AOK. As the expected rate of return increases, it eventually will reach a point at which it is high enough to compensate risk-averse investors. In other words, when the expected rate of return rises far enough above the bank account rate to compensate people for the risk, the price fall will stop. We will have an equilibrium, at which point the expected rate of return on the stock is higher than the interest rate on the safe bank account. The higher rate of return will be associated with the higher risk.

Now some stocks are more risky than others. For example, the risk on the stocks of small firms tends to be higher than the risk on the stocks of larger firms, because small firms tend to be those that are just starting up. Not having yet proved themselves, small firms have a higher risk. People like Melissa will sell the more risky stocks of smaller companies until the expected rate of return on those stocks is high enough compared with the less risky stocks of larger companies.

In equilibrium, we therefore expect to see a positive relationship between risk and the expected rate of return on securities. Securities with higher risks will have higher returns than securities with lower risks. Figure 16.6 shows the resulting **equilibrium risk-return relationship**.

equilibrium risk-return relationship

The positive relationship between the risk and the expected rate of return on an asset, derived from the fact that, on average, risk-averse investors who take on more risk must be compensated with a higher return.

There is probably no more important lesson about capital markets than this relationship. Individual investors should know it well. It says that to get a higher rate of return *on average over the long run,* you have to accept a higher risk. Again, the market forces at work are the same as the ones that led to the compensating wage differentials in the labor market. In the labor market, the higher wage in some jobs is the price that workers accept to take on the greater risk, or, more generally, the less pleasant aspects of the job.

FIGURE 16.6 The Equilibrium Relationship between Return and Risk

More risky securities tend to have higher returns on average over the long term. For example, bank deposits are low risk and have a low expected return. Corporate stocks are higher risk—their price fluctuates—but on average over the long term have a higher return. The higher return is like a compensating wage differential in the labor market. It compensates those who take on more risk.

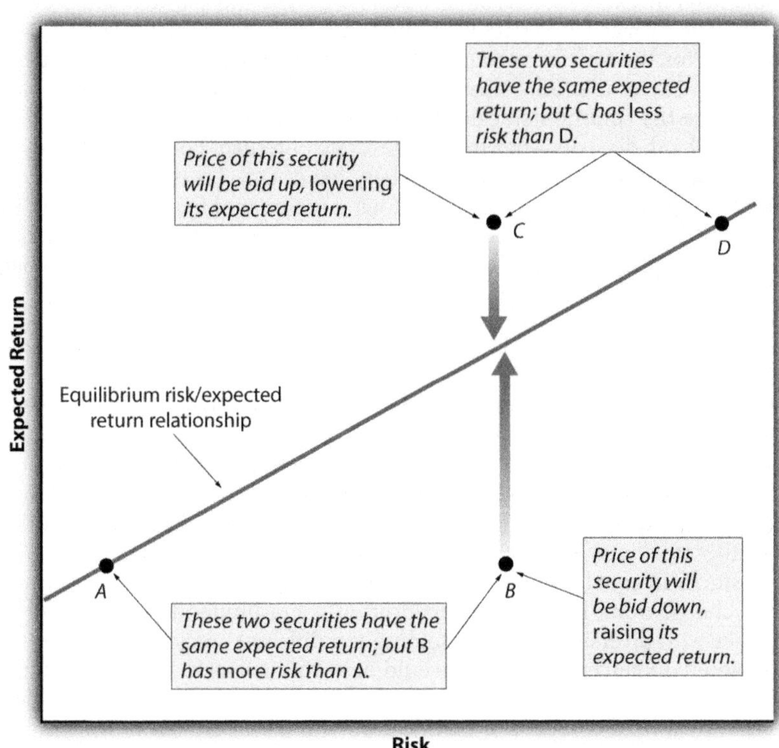

TABLE 16.4 Average Rates of Return for Different Risks

	Average Rate of Return per Year (percent)	Risk (average size of price fluctuations)
U.S. Treasury bills	3.7	3.1
Long-term government bonds	5.9	9.5
Large-company stocks	11.9	20.4
Small-company stocks	16.7	32.6

Data Source: © 2011 Morningstar, Inc. All Rights Reserved. Reproduced with permission. The information contained herein: (1) is proprietary to Morningstar and/or its content providers; (2) may not be copied or distributed; (3) does not constitute investment advice offered by Morningstar; and (4) is not warranted to be accurate, complete or timely. Neither Morningstar nor its content providers are responsible for any damages or losses arising from any use of this information. Past performance is no guarantee of future results. Use of information from Morningstar does not necessarily constitute agreement by Morningstar, Inc. of any investment philosophy or strategy presented in this publication. Note: These rates of return are for 1926-2010 and are not adjusted for inflation. The average rate of inflation was 3.1 percent, which can be subtracted from each of the average returns to get the real return. The risk is the "standard deviation," a measure of volatility commonly used in probability and statistics.

Risk and Rates of Return in Theory

In reality, this theoretical relationship works very well. A tremendous amount of data over long periods of time on the financial markets support this relationship. The most widely cited evidence was compiled by Roger Ibbotson of Yale University who tabulated data, shown in Table 16.4, on the average return over many years for the four important types of securities we have mentioned in the theoretical discussion. The most risky of the four—the stocks of small firms—has the highest rate of return. The next highest in risk are the common stocks of large firms. The least risky—short-term U.S. Treasury bills that are as safe as bank deposits—has the smallest rate of return. Long-term bonds, for which price changes can be large, have a rate of return greater than that of U.S. Treasury bills. Although the relative risks of these four types of securities may seem obvious, a measure of the differences in the sizes of their price volatility is shown in the second column and confirms the intuitive risk rankings. In general, Table 16.4 is a striking confirmation of this fundamental result of financial markets that higher expected rates of return are associated with higher risk.

Diversification Reduces Risk

portfolio diversification

Spreading the collection of assets owned to limit exposure to risk.

The familiar saying "Don't put all your eggs in one basket" is particularly relevant to stock markets. Rather than a basket of eggs, you have a portfolio of stocks. A portfolio is a collection of stocks. Putting your funds into a portfolio of two or more stocks, whose prices do not always move in the same direction, rather than one stock is called **portfolio diversification**. The risks from holding a single stock can be reduced significantly by putting half your funds in one stock and half in another. If one stock falls in price, the other stock may fall less, may not fall at all, or may even rise.

Holding two stocks in equal amounts is the most elementary form of diversification. With thousands of stocks to choose from, however, diversification is not limited to two. Figure 16.7 shows how sharply risk declines with diversification. By holding ten different stocks rather than one, you can reduce your risk to about 30 percent of what it would be with one stock. If you hold some international stocks, whose behavior will be even more different from that of any one U.S. stock, you can reduce the risk even further. Mutual fund companies provide a way for an investor with only limited funds to diversify by holding 500 or even 5,000 stocks along with other investors. Some mutual funds—called *index funds*—consist of all the stocks in an index like the S&P 500 Index.

FIGURE 16.7 Risk Declines Sharply with Diversification

By holding more than one stock, risk can be reduced. By holding 10 U.S. securities, the risk is reduced to 30 percent of the risk of holding one security. Diversifying internationally permits one to reduce risk further. (The risk is measured by the standard deviation.)

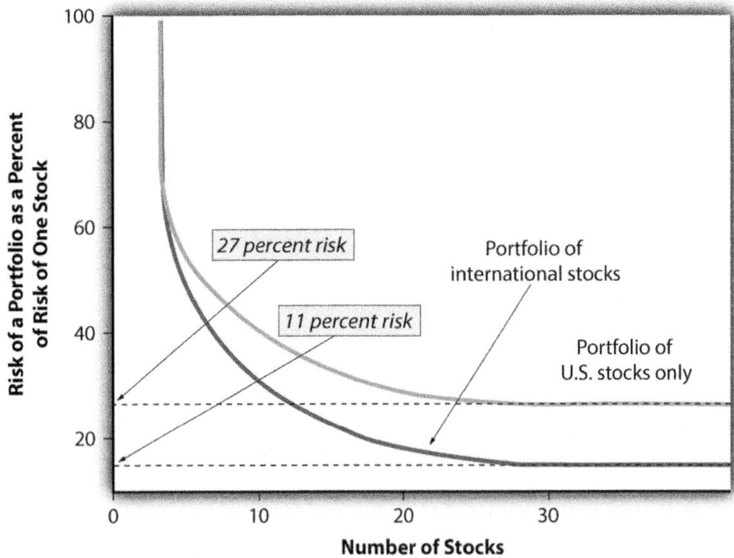

Efficient Market Theory

The shares of firms' stock on the market can be traded quickly at any time of day. For most large and medium-size companies, some people are always willing to buy and sell. If people hear that Intel has made a discovery that is expected to raise its profits, they rush to buy Intel stock. If people suddenly learn about a decline in a company's profits or about losses, then people rush to sell that company's stock. This rush to buy and sell changes prices instantaneously, so that the price adjusts rapidly to good news or bad news. The rapid adjustment means that unexploited profit opportunities are rare for regular investors without inside information or a special ability to anticipate news, whether good or bad. The **efficient market hypothesis** states that profit opportunities are eliminated in financial markets as stock prices adjust quickly to new information. Rates of return greater than those resulting from the price of risk disappear soon after any good news about a stock appears.

efficient market hypothesis
The idea that markets adjust rapidly enough to eliminate profit opportunities immediately.

Many tests over the years have found the efficient market hypothesis to be a close approximation of security price determination. It has led to the growth in popularity of index funds, for which investors do not pay advisers to tell them when to buy and sell stock. They simply invest in a fund that includes a large number of stocks.

REVIEW

- Financial markets are volatile; both stock prices and bond prices tend to rise and fall over time. The riskiness of bonds and stocks affects the willingness of people to buy and sell these financial assets, and hence, affects their return.
- We can calculate the expected return of a risky asset by weighting the possible gains and losses by the probability that these gains or losses will occur. Given the choice between a risky asset and a safe asset that have the same expected return, an individual who is risk averse always will choose the safe asset.
- Risk-averse investors will hold risky assets only if they are compensated in the form of a higher expected return. Thus, when buyers and sellers trade stocks or bonds in the market, a relationship between return and risk emerges: Higher risk is associated with higher returns.
- Investors can reduce risk by diversifying their portfolio, that is, by holding many different stocks. Mutual funds and index funds offer diversification opportunities even to investors who have little money to put into the stock market.
- Earning stock returns in excess of those justified by the greater level of associated risk is difficult. The efficient market hypothesis predicts that stock prices adjust quickly to eliminate such lucrative return opportunities.

5. CORPORATE GOVERNANCE PROBLEMS

When corporations issue stock to buy physical capital or to start up operations, a separation between the owners of the corporation—the stockholders—and the managers of the corporation is created. This separation leads to incentive problems—the manager might not act in the interest of the shareholder. Here we show how these problems can be analyzed with a theory called *asymmetric information theory.*

5.1 Asymmetric Information: Moral Hazard and Adverse Selection

asymetric information

Different levels of information available to different people in an economic interaction or exchange.

moral hazard

In insurance markets, a situation in which a person buys insurance against some risk and subsequently takes actions that increase the risk; analogous situations arise when other markets have asymetric information.

adverse selection

In insurance markets, a situation in which the people who choose to buy insurance will be the riskiest group in the population; analagous situations apply in other markets.

Consider a start-up firm. When an entrepreneur at a start-up firm obtains financial capital by issuing stock, a special relationship is formed. Those who supplied the financial capital by buying the stock become owners or at least part owners of the company. If the entrepreneur does well and the company is successful, they reap large returns. But shareholders of a firm have less information than the managers about the firm. This difference in information, called **asymetric information**, can cause several problems. First, the manager might not act in the interest of the owners. Taking unnecessary business trips on the company's aircraft to exotic places or not working hard to find the right employees is harmful to the shareholders' interests. This is sometimes called **moral hazard**, a term borrowed from research on the insurance industry, for which asymmetric information is also a problem. Moral hazard in insurance occurs when people are less careful about trying to prevent fires after they get fire insurance. In the case of the firm, the manager may be less careful about the firm after the shareholders' or investors' funds have been obtained.

Another problem is that those entrepreneurs who have more risky projects would seek equity financing—for which dividend payments to shareholders would be optional—rather than debt financing, for which interest payments are required. This is called **adverse selection**, yet another term borrowed from insurance. In insurance, adverse selection occurs, for example, when people who are unhealthy select health insurance while healthy people do not. In this case, managers who have more risky projects elect equity financing more often than those who have less risky projects. This makes potential shareholders or investors less willing to supply funds to equity markets.

5.2 Incentives to Overcome Adverse Selection and Moral Hazard Problems

profit-sharing

Programs in which managers and employees receive a share of profits earned by the firm.

One way in which problems of moral hazard and adverse selection can be limited is through the use of **profit-sharing** agreements, whereby managers are given a share of the profits earned by the firm. That way, the managers of the firms have a financial stake in the firm's success, and hence, their interests are aligned with the shareholders' interests—agents gain when the principal gains and agents lose when the principal loses.

A Shareholder Meeting: Principals, Agents, and Asymmetric Information. Theories of corporate governance view a firm's shareholders (shown in the crowd) as the principals and the managers (shown on the stage) as the agents. Management incentive plans such as profit sharing are seen as ways to foster good management performance when the principals have little information about what the *agents* actually do—a situation called *asymmetric information*.

Source: Shutterstock.com

Another way to overcome the problems caused by moral hazard and adverse selection is for shareholders to get together and take over the company so that the problematic management team can be replaced. The mere threat of such a takeover can be an incentive for management to act in shareholders' interest rather than their own. *Private equity* firms like the Blackstone Group specialize in buying shares of a public company and taking it private, so that they can replace the existing management with managers who presumably can improve the firm's performance.

Such takeovers also have been criticized. Some say that the threat of being bought out by a hostile takeover firm or a private equity firm leads management to adopt a more shortsighted attitude toward the operation of the company's affairs than is ideal. Companies also expend considerable resources constructing "takeover defenses," which attempt to make it more difficult for outsiders to use a hostile takeover to take control of the firm.

REVIEW

- Managers of a firm usually know more about the firm than the shareholders. This asymmetric information causes moral hazard—in which the firm's managers may run the firm less efficiently than the shareholders would want.
- Profit sharing—in which the managers share in the profits of the firm or in the returns to holding the stock—is a way to prevent moral hazard.

6. THE ROLE OF GOVERNMENT IN FINANCIAL MARKETS

Government policy has a role to play in financial markets. Poor governance which takes the extreme form of outright fraud is illegal under U.S. law. Indeed, managers who commit fraud against their shareholders are prosecuted and sent to jail if they are caught; the Federal Bureau of Investigation has a whole division on the lookout for such crimes.

One common type of fraud in financial markets—securities fraud—occurs when managers lie or misreport facts about the firm's financial statements or the firm's profitability to entice investors to buy or hold their stock. The Securities and Exchange Commission(SEC) has responsibilities for such securities violations. It also regulates certain investment management firms, such as mutual funds, under the Investment Act of 1940 to promote accurate financial reporting.

One glaring example of fraud arose in the case of Bernard Madoff, who ran an investment company with responsibility for managing billions of dollars of his clients'money. His fraudulent scheme cost his investors a reported $50 billion. It was called a *Ponzi scheme*, in which his existing investors' returns were paid using his new investors'funds rather than from legitimate investments in the stock or bond markets. Madoff was sentenced to prison for 150 years in June 2009. Some accused the SEC for failing in its responsibility to detect this fraud long before it became so big.

6.1 Examples from a Financial Crisis

Many examples of mismanagement and fraudulent action can be found during the financial crisis in 2007 and 2008. Indeed, some analysts think that such actions were in part responsible for the crisis. For example, mortgage loans were offered to high-risk individual homeowners who were unlikely to make the interest payments. The resulting high risk mortgages were then sold to other financial institutions, whose managers apparently were unaware of the risks. When the homeowners with these mortgages stopped making their payments, the financial institutions found the mortgages were nearly worthless. In the meantime, the originators were far from the scene and no longer accountable. As a result, the risk at these financial institutions rose; they were reluctant to make more loans or they charged much higher interest rates on the loans, which added to the crisis.

Another possible role for government is to intervene to prevent the failure of large financial institutions and thereby prevent instability in the financial markets. Indeed, during 2008, the federal government intervened in several ways by loaning or investing funds to help some of these financial institutions. The expectation of such intervention can cause its own form of moral hazard, however, if investors expect the government always to rescue them. This expectation will reduce the incentives they have to manage risks themselves. Moreover, government intervention can cause uncertainty and perhaps make matters worse, an example of government failure.

Consider the financial panic of 2008. Although the financial crisis had been going on for more than a year, it suddenly worsened into a full-fledged sell-off in the fall of 2008. The S&P 500 Index fell from 1,255 on September 19 to 899 on October 10, a decline of 28 percent in three weeks, a staggering loss for many people.

Many argued that the panic was caused by the U.S. government's decision not to intervene to prevent the bankruptcy of a financial institution, Lehman Brothers, which then led to expectations of more failures and instability. An examination of the timing of stock price movements, however, shows that the answer is more complicated. Figure 16.8 focuses on a few key dates and events, including the panic itself, which is marked with the brackets.

Monday, September 15, is the day that Lehman declared bankruptcy after learning over the previous weekend that the government would not provide funds to pay its creditors and keep it open. You can see that the stock market moved down a bit, but it then bounced back up on September 16. By the end of the week, the S&P 500 was virtually the same as it was one week earlier, so the decision to let Lehman Brothers go bankrupt apparently was not what caused the panic. But if not, then what was the cause?

On Friday of that same week, the U.S. Treasury announced that it was going to propose a large rescue package for the entire U.S. banking system, although the size and details were not determined. During the weekend, the package was put together; on Tuesday, September 23, Federal Reserve Board Chairman Ben Bernanke and Treasury Secretary Henry Paulson testified in the Senate about the package, which they called the Troubled Assets Relief Program(TARP). They said it would be enormous, $700 billion, yet provided few details and made no mention of oversight or restrictions on the use. They were questioned intensely and the reaction was quite negative. Members of Congress received a large volume of critical mail.

As shown in Figure 16.8, following this poorly received testimony, the crisis seriously deepened, as measured by the sharp fall in the stock market for the next three weeks. It is plausible that events around September 23 increased risks and drove the markets down, including the realization by the public that the intervention plan had not been fully thought through and that conditions were much worse than many had been led to believe. A great deal of uncertainty about what the government would do to aid financial institutions, and under what circumstances, was revealed. Such uncertainty would have driven up risk and thereby driven down the market. Clarity about the TARP improved on October 13 when the government announced it would buy shares in banks with the TARP money. The panic ended at that time.

FIGURE 16.8 Stock Prices during the Panic

The S&P 500 Index fell by nearly 30 percent, but was it the result of the Lehman bankruptcy or the government actions?

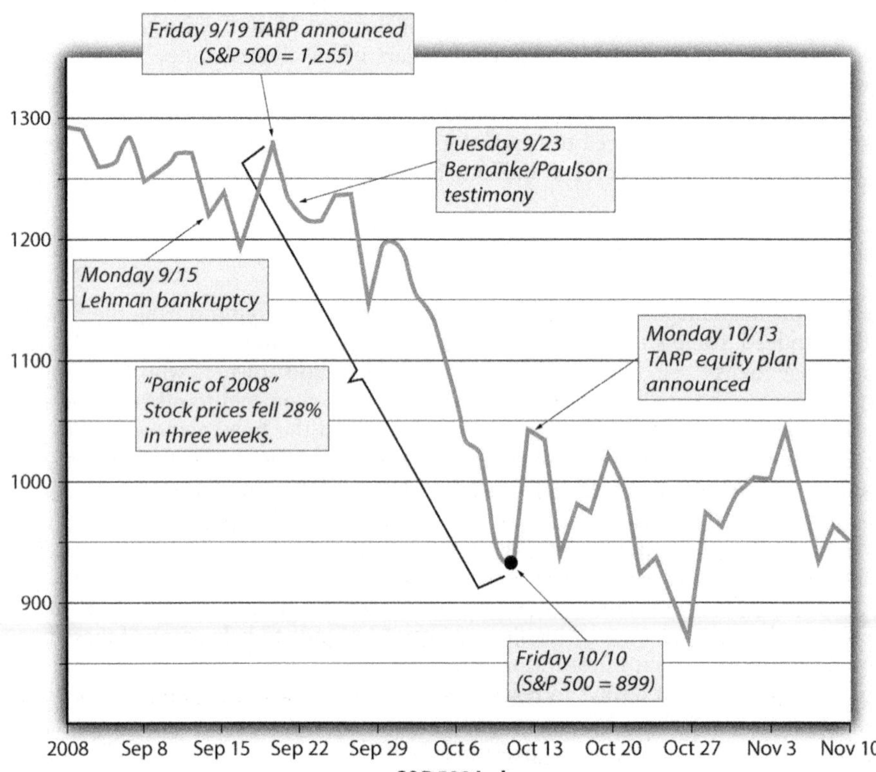

6.2 Government Regulation of Financial Institutions

Financial institutions—especially banks—are the most heavily regulated firms in the United States. The main rationale for the federal government to regulate banks is that the federal government guarantees the deposits that people hold at the banks. If the bank takes on too much risk and fails as a result, then the deposit holders will be paid off, subject to certain limits, by the government. Because taxpayer money is at risk, the government has responsibility for ensuring that the banks do not put too much risk on the taxpayers.

The government does this by issuing regulations that require that the banks' capital, including the dollar amount of shares held by shareholders, to be above a certain fraction of the bank's loans and other investments. This ensures that the shareholders will pay before the government in the case of large loan losses. The government also supervises the banks to ensure that the loans they hold do not exceed certain risk levels.

In the United States, the banks are regulated by the Office of the Comptroller of the Currency, the Federal Reserve System, and in some cases the state governments. It is now clear that many banks—including the large Citicorp, headquartered in New York City—took on too much risk in the years leading up to the financial crisis, and this has raised questions about the effectiveness of the regulation and supervision. People ask why hundreds of government regulators on the premises of banks like Citicorp did not see or report such risks or take actions to limit the risks. Because of these concerns, many of the regulations were changed in legislation passed in 2010 after the financial crisis. But economists and others debate whether the new legislation actually will improve the effectiveness of the regulation and supervision.

One concern is that the operations of the financial institutions are too complex for government regulators to monitor. Another concern is that government supervisors are too close to the management of the banks, a form of regulatory capture in which the regulators are "captured" by the banks and tend to overlook certain risky activities.

Indeed, a book published in 2011 by Gretchen Morgenson and Joshua Rosner, *Reckless Endangerment: How Outsized Ambition, Greed, and Corruption Led to Economic Armageddon*, argues that such cozy relationships were responsible for the risks taken leading up to the financial crisis. The authors give many examples of cases in which government officials took actions that benefited banks and other financial institutions and showed that these individuals in turn helped the government officials. This mutual support system thwarted good economic policies and encouraged reckless ones. It thereby brought on the crisis, sending the economy into a deep recession.

REVIEW

- The government has a role to play in the financial markets, including enforcing the law against securities fraud.
- The government also has a role to play in regulating and supervising financial firms that can cause a risk to taxpayers or the economy.
- In considering the role of government in financial markets, however, the possibility of government failure also must be considered.

7. END-OF-CHAPTER MATERIAL

7.1 Conclusion

This chapter has used some basic economic tools to analyze capital and financial markets. In reviewing the chapter, it is helpful to see how the key results apply to you personally.

First, by diversifying a portfolio of stocks, you can reduce risk substantially. Conversely, by holding an undiversified portfolio, you are needlessly incurring risk.

Second, remember the efficient market hypothesis that profit opportunity disappears quickly in financial markets. Instead of buying and selling securities frequently, you may be better off investing in a mutual fund.

Third, if you do try to pick your own portfolio rather than use a mutual fund, concentrate on areas with which you are familiar. If you go into a medical career, you may know more than even the best investors about the promise of a new medical device or drug.

Fourth, over the short run, holding corporate stocks is more risky than putting your funds in a bank account, but over the long term, the higher rate of return on stocks outweighs the risks for most people. If you need money in the short term—to pay next year's tuition, for example—stocks may not be worth the risk. Years like 2008 during which stocks fall by as much as 38 percent are a reminder of these risks.

Key Points

1. Physical capital refers to the physical resources used to produce goods and services.
2. Financial capital, which includes stocks and bonds, is used by firms to obtain funds to invest in physical capital.
3. A firm's demand for physical capital is a derived demand. A firm will use capital up to the point at which the marginal revenue product of capital equals the rental price.
4. The supply and demand for capital determines the rental price or the implicit rental price. Tax and subsidy policies that affect the demand for capital goods will affect both the equilibrium rental price of capital and the equilibrium quantity of capital used by firms.
5. Firms raise money for investing in physical capital by issuing stocks and bonds. Once issued, the stocks and bonds trade on financial markets.
6. The rate of return on stocks is equal to the dividend plus the change in the price as a percentage of the price. The rate of return on bonds held to maturity is the yield of the bond.
7. The rate of return on stocks tends to rise when firms have higher earnings, which are either paid out in the form of dividends or reinvested in the company. The rate of return on bonds tends to rise in periods during which market interest rates are falling.
8. Stock markets and bond markets tend to be extremely volatile. To understand how the riskiness of these assets affects their return, we need to understand how investors behave. Risk-averse investors will buy more risky stocks or bonds only if the expected rate of return is higher.
9. In market equilibrium, a positive relationship exists between risk and rate of return. If you want to get a higher rate of return, you have to accept higher risk.
10. Diversification helps reduce risk. Even individuals with limited resources can diversify their portfolios by investing in mutual funds.

QUESTIONS FOR REVIEW

1. What is the difference between physical capital and financial capital?
2. How is the relationship between the marginal revenue product of capital and the rental price related to the firm's decision to rent additional units of physical capital?
3. Why is the quantity of physical capital demanded negatively related to the rental price of capital?
4. How does the implicit rental price of capital depend on the interest rate and depreciation?
5. What is the difference between a stock and a bond?
6. What determines the rate of return on stocks? On bonds?
7. What does it mean for an individual to be risk averse?
8. How do the actions of risk-averse individuals influence the relationship between risk and return in financial markets?
9. What is diversification? How does it affect risk?
10. What do economists mean when they say that financial markets are efficient?

PROBLEMS

1. Which of the following are physical capital, and which are financial capital?
   a. A Toyota Camry at Avis Car Rental.
   b. A loan you take out to start a newspaper business.
   c. New desktop publishing equipment.
   d. A bond issued by the U.S. government.
   e. A pizza oven at Pizza Hut.
2. Suppose that Marshall's stones were dropped all over the earth and finding them was difficult.
   a. Would the supply curve for capital still be perfectly inelastic?
   b. Would there be economic rent?
3. Suppose a company owns a computer that costs $5,000 and depreciates $1,000 per year.
   a. If the interest rate is 5 percent, what is the implicit rental price of the computer?
   b. Explain why the implicit rental price depends on the interest rate.
4. The U.S. government issues a one-year bond with a face value of $1,000 and a zero coupon.
   a. If the yield is 10 percent, what will the market price of the bond be?
   b. Now suppose you observe that the bond price falls by 5 percent What happens to its yield?
5. Suppose a two-year bond has a 5 percent coupon and a $1,000 face value, and the current market interest rate is 5 percent.
   a. What is the price of the bond?
   b. Now suppose that you believe that the interest rate will remain 5 percent this year, but next year will fall to 3 percent. How much are you willing to pay for the two-year bond today? Why?
6. Consider the following possibilities for your stock market investment portfolio.

	Good Market	Bad Market	Disastrous Market
Probability	0.50	0.30	0.20
Rate of return	0.25	0.10	-025

   a. What is the expected return of this stock market investment portfolio?
   b. Would you choose this expected return or take a safe return of 7 percent from a savings deposit in your bank? Why?
   c. Suppose your teacher chooses the safe return from the bank. Is your teacher risk averse? How can you tell?
7. You are considering the purchase of stocks of two firms: a biotechnology corporation and a supermarket chain. Because of the uncertainty in the biotechnology industry, you estimate that there is a 50–50 chance of your either earning an 80 percent return on your investment or losing 80 percent of your investment within a year. The food industry is more stable, so you estimate that you have a 50–50 chance of either earning 10 percent or losing 10 percent.
   a. Which stock would you buy if you were a risk-averse individual? Why?
   b. What do you think other investors (most of whom are risk averse) would do?
   c. What would be the effect of these actions on the relative prices of the two stocks?

8. Graph the data on risk and expected return (in percent) for the following securities.

Asset	Expected Rate of Return	Risk
Bank deposit	3	0
U.S. Treasury bills	4	3
Goodcorp bonds	9	10
ABC stock	11	24
XYZ	13	24
Riskyco stock	16	39

Draw an equilibrium risk-return line through the points.

a. Which two assets should have changes in their prices in the near future?
b. In which direction will their prices change?

9. Suppose a study indicated that stock prices usually were lower during the holiday season than during the rest of the year. What would be the likely reaction of the market?
10. Suppose you have $10,000 and must choose between investing in your own human capital or investing in physical or financial capital.
    a. What factors will enter into your decision-making process?
    b. How much risk will be involved with each investment?
    c. What would you do? Why?

8. APPENDIX: PRESENT DISCOUNTED VALUE

A dollar in the future is worth less than a dollar today. This principle underlies all economic decisions involving actions over time. Whether you put some dollars under the mattress to be spent next summer, borrow money from a friend or family member to be paid back next year, or are a sophisticated investor in stocks, bonds, or real estate, that same principle is essential to making good decisions. Here we explain why the principle is essential and derive a formula for determining exactly *how much* less a dollar in the future is worth than a dollar today. The formula is called the *present discounted value formula.*

8.1 Discounting the Future

First let's answer the question, why is the value of a dollar in the future less than the value of a dollar today? The simplest answer is that a dollar can earn interest over time. Suppose a person you trust completely to pay off a debt gives you an IOU promising to pay you $100 in one year: How much is that IOU worth to you today? How much would you be willing to pay for the IOU today? It would be less than $100, because you could put an amount less than $100 in a bank and get $100 at the end of a year. The exact amount depends on the interest rate. If the interest rate is 10 percent, the $100 should be worth $90.91. If you put $90.91 in a bank earning 10 percent per year, at the end of the year you will have exactly $100. That is, $90.91 plus interest payments of $9.09 ($90.91 times 0.1 rounded to the nearest penny) equals $100.

The process of translating a future payment into a value in the present is called **discounting**. The value in the present of a future payment is called the **present discounted value**. The interest rate used to do the discounting is called the **discount rate**. In the preceding example, a future payment of $100 has a present discounted value of $90.91, and the discount rate is 10 percent. If the discount rate were 20 percent, the present discounted value would be $83.33 (because if you put $83.33 in a bank for a year at a 20 percent interest rate, you would have, rounding to the nearest penny, $100 at the end of the year). The term *discount* is used because the value in the present is less than the future payment; in other words, the payment is "discounted," much as a $100 bicycle on sale might be "discounted" to $83.33.

discounting

The process of translating a future payment into a value in the present.

present discounted value

The value in the present of future payments.

discount rate

An interest rate used to discount a future payment when computing present discounted value.

8.2 Finding the Present Discounted Value

The previous examples suggest that a formula can calculate present value, and indeed it can. Let

the present discounted value be *PDV*

the discount rate be i

the future payment be F

The symbol *i* is measured as a decimal, but we speak of the discount rate in percentage terms; thus, we would say, "the discount rate is 10 percent" and write, $i = 0.1$.

Now, the present discounted value *PDV* is the amount for which, if you put it in a bank today at an interest rate *i*, you would get an amount in the future equal to the future payment *F*. For example, if the future date is one year from now, then if you put the amount *PDV* in a bank for one year, you would get *PDV* times $(1 + i)$ at the end of the year. Thus, the *PDV* should be such that

$$(\text{PDV})(1 + \text{i}) = \text{F}$$

Now divide both sides $(1 + i)$; you get

$$\text{PDV} = \frac{\text{F}}{1+\text{i}}$$

which is the formula for the present discounted value in the case of a payment made one year in the future. That is,

$$\text{Present discounted value} = \frac{\text{payment in one year}}{1 + \text{discount rate}}$$

For example, if the payment in one year is $100 and the discount rate $i = 0.1$, then the present discounted value is $90.91 [$100/(1 + 0.1)], just as we reasoned previously.

To obtain the formula for the case for which the payment is made more than one year in the future, we must recognize that the amount in the present can be put in a bank and earn interest at the discount rate for more than one year. For example, if the interest rate is 10 percent, we could get $100 at the end of two years by investing $82.64 today. That is, putting $82.64 in the bank would give $82.64 times (1.1) at the end of one year; keeping all this in the bank for another year would give $82.64 times (1.1) times (1.1), or $82.64 times 1.21, or $100, again rounding off. Thus, in the case of a future payment in two years, we would have

$$\text{PDV} = \frac{\text{F}}{(1+\text{i})^2}$$

Analogous reasoning implies that the present discounted value of a payment made *N* years in the future would be

$$\text{PDV} = \frac{\text{F}}{(1+\text{i})^n}$$

For example, the present discounted value of a $100 payment to be made 20 years in the future is $14.86 if the discount rate is 10 percent. In other words, if you put $14.86 in the bank today at an interest rate of 10 percent, you would have about $100 at the end of 20 years. What is the present discounted value of a $100 payment to be made 100 years in the future? The above formula tells us that the *PDV* is only $0.00726, less than a penny. All of these examples indicate that the higher the discount rate or the further in the future the payment is to be received, the lower the present discounted value of a future payment.

In many cases, we need to find the present discounted value of a *series* of payments made in several different years. We can do this by combining the previous formulas. The present discounted value of payments F_1 made in one year and F_2 made in two years would be

$$\text{PDV} = \frac{F_1}{(1+i)} + \frac{F_2}{(1+i)^2}$$

For example, the present discounted value of $100 paid in one year and $100 paid in two years would be $90.91 plus $82.64, or $173.55. In general, the present discounted value of a series of future payments F_1, F_2, …, F_N over N years is

$$\text{PDV} = \frac{F_1}{(1+i)} + \frac{F_2}{(1+i)^2} + \cdots + \frac{F_N}{(1+i)^N}$$

Key Points

1. A dollar to be paid in the future is worth less than a dollar today.
2. The present discounted value of a future payment is the amount you would have to put in a bank today to get that same payment in the future.
3. The higher the discount rate, the lower the present discounted value of a future payment.

QUESTIONS FOR REVIEW

1. Why is the present discounted value of a future payment of $1 less than $1?
2. What is the relationship between the discount rate and the interest rate?
3. What happens to the present discounted value of a future payment as the payment date stretches into the future?
4. Why is discounting important for decisions involving actions at different dates?

PROBLEMS

1. Find the present discounted value of
   a. $100 to be paid at the end of three years.
   b. $1,000 to be paid at the end of one year plus $1,000 to be paid at the end of two years.
   c. $10 to be paid at the end of one year, $10 at the end of two years, and $100 at the end of three years.
2. Suppose you win $1 million in a lottery and your winnings are scheduled to be paid as follows: $300,000 at the end of one year, $300,000 at the end of two years, and $400,000 at the end of three years. If the interest rate is 10 percent, what is the present discounted value of your winnings?
3. You are considering two job offers. You expect to work for the employer for five years. For simplicity, we assume that you will be paid at the end of each year. The two offers are summarized in the following table.

Year	Offer 1	Offer 2
1	$30,000	$40,000
2	$33,000	$30,000
3	$36,000	$33,000
4	$39,000	$36,000
5	$42,000	$39,000

The primary difference between the two offers is a signing bonus of $10,000 paid under Offer 2. The annual salary paid in years two through five is higher under Offer 1 than under Offer 2. If the interest rate is 5 percent, which is the better offer? If the interest rate is 10 percent, which is better?

ENDNOTES

1. Alfred Marshall, *Principles of Economics*, 8th ed. (New York: Macmillan, 1920), 415.

CHAPTER 17

Macroeconomics: The Big Picture

The most recent decade, the period from 2007 to 2016, was a time of remarkable macroeconomic developments. It was an fascinating time to be a student of macroeconomics but that fascination was tempered by the fact that the economic changes being studied were ones that had brought about upheaval in the lives of millions of people. At the end of 2006, the U.S. economy had been basking in the glow of a period known as "the Great Moderation." During the quarter century that followed the serious economic downturn of 1981–1982, the economy only experienced two minor recessions (in 1990–1991 and in 2001), both of which were much milder than previous recessions. The Great Moderation saw almost continuous economic growth, accompanied by declining rates of inflation and unemployment, as well as greater stability—the economy was less likely to experience significant ups and downs—over this period. This growth was in sharp contrast to the turbulent decade of the 1970s, leading up to the 1981–1982 recession, when double-digit inflation, high unemployment, and economic volatility were the norm.

This period of prosperous tranquility was shaken by tremors in various parts of the economy during 2007, culminating in the dramatic upheaval that began in December of that year. The U.S. economy suffered through an 18-month long downturn that economists now refer to as "the Great Recession." The headlines told a dismal tale: "U.S. GDP fall at record rate," "U.S. stocks suffer worst year since Great Depression," "Rise in U.S. unemployment tipped to be biggest for 60 years," "New home sales set record low last year." This was, in many ways, the worst shock to hit the U.S. economy since the Great Depression. In response, policymakers embarked on policy responses that were also more ambitious than anything that had been since the Great Depression. The outgoing Bush administration and the incoming Obama administration worked with Congress to provide two substantial stimulus packages worth hundreds of billions of dollars in tax cuts and increased government expenditures. The Obama administration worked with Congress on another multi-billion dollar plan to help the troubled banking system. The Federal Reserve lowered interest rates to as low a level as they could possibly go and then embarked on an even more ambitious program to provide credit to the economy, sustaining the program for many years after the recession officially had been declared over in June of 2009.

By the end of 2016, seven and a half years had passed since the recession had been officially declared over. Many economic measures suggested that the economy had improved dramatically over those 90 months. The number of unemployed Americans had doubled, from 7.5 million to 15 million during the Great Recession but the number had returned to the pre-recession levels by the end of 2016. The Labor Department reported that in 2016 alone more than 2 million jobs had been created in the U.S. economy and that the economy had experienced 75 consecutive months in which the number of jobs in the economy increased. Various indices that capture the value of the U.S. stock market reached all-time record highs by the end of 2016. The Federal Reserve continued the task of gradually unwinding some of the extraordinary policies that had been put in place to deal with the disruption caused by the Great Recession.

In spite of the progress that had been made since the end of the recession, the Presidential Election of 2016 showed that anxiety and concern about the economy remained a potent issue. Many Americans who had lost their jobs in the Great Recession had not been able to find comparable work, some had returned to work in different industries but others, particularly older men, had stopped looking for work. So even though the economy was growing and the number of new jobs being created was increasing, the benefits of that economic recovery were not necessarily being enjoyed by those who had borne the brunt of the economic pain caused by the recession. In addition other long-term concerns about the U.S. economy lingered, and in some cases became more important, over the decade. Some examples of these issues include rising government debt, widening economic inequality, caring for an aging population with rising health bills and dwindling savings, dilapidated infrastructure and U.S. children falling further behind in education outcomes.

The turmoil and upheaval of the 2007–2016 decade was a global phenomenon, not just a U.S one. The Great Recession affected most industrial nations, including the United Kingdom, Japan, and the countries in the Eurozone; emerging market economies like the Republic of Korea, the Russian Federation, and Brazil; poor countries that rely on exports to rich countries; and even the highest flyers, China and India. Many of the emerging market economies and the export-oriented economies have recovered, but the industrial world still faces major economic challenges. The Eurozone has experienced repeated episodes of crisis that have threatened to break up the ties that bind these 19 nations together in a common currency area. Greece has been the most prominent of the troubled Eurozone countries but at various points, Ireland, Italy, Spain, and Portugal have had to embark on large adjustment programs to either rescue banks from failure or to impose fiscal austerity in which the government has to cut spending drastically and raise taxes to reduce the path of budget deficits and government debt. In 2011 , Japan was hit by a triple shock of an earthquake, a tsunami, and potential nuclear catastrophe while the United Kingdom set of tremors of a different kind through the global economy in 2016 when its voters indicated that they wanted to leave the European Union in what became knows as the decision to "Brexit". Even good news such as the fact that oil prices fell by almost 50% in the latter part of the decade was bad news for resource-exporting nations like Russia and Brazil.

It is important, however, not to let gloomy stories about the economy obscure the happier stories about economic progress over a longer term. The period since 1980 is filled with remarkable economic developments, none more remarkable than the rapid economic growth of developing economies, such as China. According to data collected by the International Monetary Fund's *World Economic Outlook*, production per person in China in 2015 was thirty times as large as it had been in 1980. China's economy has faced its own challenges in the last few years but these concerns have been offset somewhat by the rapid growth of the economy of the second most populous nation in the world, India. Production per person in India in 2015 was almost twelve times as large as it had been in 1980. Such rapid rates of economic growth in China, India, and several other countries mean a better quality of life for hundreds of millions of people. The World Bank calculated that the number of people living on an income of less than $1 a day fell by almost 200 million even as the world population increased by more than a billion people over this period. We should be delighted that the progress made by China and India has given so many of their people a brighter future. Sub-Saharan African countries like Sierra Leone, Togo, and

Niger—economies that essentially are producing as much output per person in the twenty-first century as they produced in 1980—can benefit from a better understanding of why China and India grew so fast, so that they, too, can achieve even moderate rates of growth. An increase in economic growth over the next decade or two is vital for improving the living conditions of the world's poorest.

Skyline of Mumbai, the financial capital of India

Source: Shutterstock.com

Macroeconomics is an exciting field of study that helps you better understand these types of changes going on in the world around you. More formally, macroeconomics refers to the study of the whole market economy. Like other parts of economics, macroeconomics uses the central idea that people make purposeful decisions with scarce resources. However, instead of focusing on the workings of one market— whether the market for peanuts or the market for bicycles—macroeconomics focuses on the economy as a whole. Macroeconomics looks at the big picture: Economic growth, recessions, unemployment, and inflation are among its subject matter. You should accordingly put on your "big picture glasses" when you study macroeconomics.

By studying macroeconomics, you can better understand the changes that are taking place in your country and in the global economy. You can become a better citizen, one who understands the role of good economic policies in driving economic growth and reducing unemployment, and can help support the election of leaders who support such policies. Hopefully, you will be inspired by the study of macroeconomics to do your part to bring about strong economic growth, which in turn can help alleviate poverty, free up resources to improve the environment, and lead to a brighter future for your generation.

In terms of the organization of the macroeconomics section of the book, this introductory chapter summarizes the overall workings of the economy and provides a brief preview of the macroeconomic theory designed to explain these facts. The theory will be developed in later chapters.

1. MEASURING THE "SIZE" OF AN ECONOMY

To understand why some economies have done so much better than others, we first need to understand how macroeconomists measure the size of an economy. Gross domestic product (GDP) is the economic variable that is of most interest to macroeconomists. GDP is the total value of all new goods and services produced in the economy during a specified period of time, usually a year or a quarter. The total value of goods and services can change either because the quantities of goods and services are changing or because their prices are changing. As a result, economists often prefer to use **real gross domestic product (real GDP)** as the measure of production; the adjective *real* means that we adjust the measure of production to account for changes in prices over time. Real GDP, also called *output* or *production,* is the most comprehensive measure of how well the economy is doing.

real gross domestic product (real GDP)

A measure of the value of all the goods and services newly produced in a country during some period of time, adjusted for changes in prices over time.

economic growth

An upward trend in real GDP, reflecting expansion in the economy over time.

economic fluctuations

Swings in real GDP that lead to deviations of the economy from its long-term growth trend.

Figure 17.1 shows the changes in real GDP in recent years in the United States. When you look at real GDP over time, as in Figure 17.1, you notice two simultaneous patterns emerging. Over the long term, increases in real GDP demonstrate an upward trend, which economists call long-term **economic growth**. In the short term, you notice more transient increases or decreases in real GDP, called **economic fluctuations**. These short-term fluctuations in real GDP also are called *business cycles.* The difference between the long-term economic growth trend and the economic fluctuations can be better seen by drawing a relatively smooth line between the observations on real GDP. Such a smooth trend line is shown in Figure 17.1. Sometimes real GDP fluctuates above the trend line, and sometimes it fluctuates below the trend line. In this section, we look more closely at these two patterns: economic growth and economic fluctuations.

1.1 Economic Growth: The Relentless Uphill Climb

The large increase in real GDP shown in Figure 17.1 means that people in the United States now produce a much greater amount of goods and services each year than they did 50 years ago. Improvements in the economic well-being of individuals in any society cannot occur without such an increase in real GDP. To get a better measure of how individuals benefit from increases in real GDP, we consider average production per person, or *real GDP per capita.* Real GDP per capita is real GDP divided by the number of people in the economy. It is the total production of all food, clothes, cars, houses, compact discs, concerts, education, computers, and so on per person. When real GDP per capita is increasing, then the well-being—or the standard of living—of individuals in the economy, at least on average, is improving.

FIGURE 17.1 Economic Growth and Fluctuations

Real GDP has grown by more than $12 trillion during the last 50 years. The trend in growth is shown by the line labeled "Long-Term Growth Trend." At the same time, the economy has fluctuated up and down as it has grown, with eight recessions—marked by the vertical shaded bars—and eight subsequent expansions (the most recent expansion was ongoing at the end of 2016).

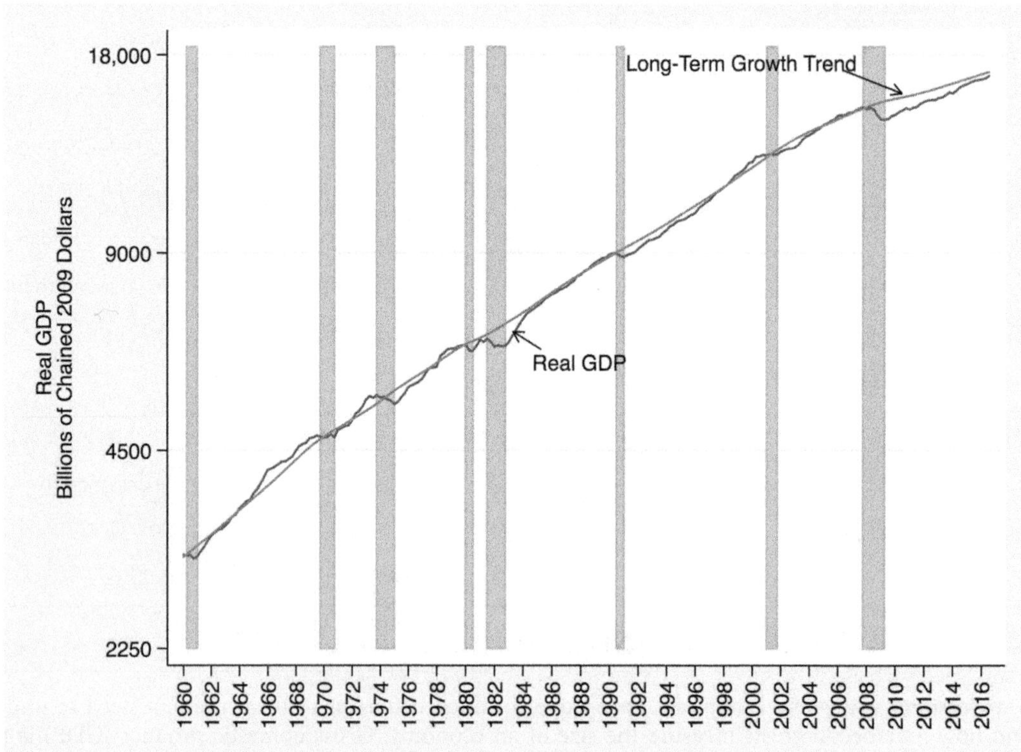

Source: Bureau of Economic Analysis, "National Income and Product Accounts"

How much economic growth has occurred during the last 50 years in the United States? The annual *economic growth rate*—the percentage increase in real GDP each year—provides a good measure. On average, for the last 50 years, the annual economic growth rate has been a little under 3 percent per year. This growth may not sound like much, but it means that real GDP has quadrupled. The increase in production in the United States over the past 50 years is larger than what Japan and Germany together now produce. It is as if all the production of Japan and Germany—what is made by all the workers, machines, and technology in these countries—were annexed to the U.S. economy, as illustrated in Figure 17.2.

How much did real GDP *per capita* increase during this period? Because the U.S. population grew by more than 120 million people during this period, the increase in real GDP per capita has been less dramatic than the increase in real GDP, but it is impressive nonetheless. The annual growth rate of real GDP per capita is the percentage increase in real GDP per capita each year. It has averaged around 1.8 percent per year. Again, this might not sound like much, but it has meant that real GDP per capita more than doubled, from about $21,000 per person in 1965 to about $51,000 per person in 2015. That extra $30,000 per person represents increased opportunities for travel, televisions, housing, washing machines, aerobics classes, health care, antipollution devices for cars, and so on.

FIGURE 17.2 Visualizing Economic Growth

Over the last 50 years, production in the U.S. economy has increased by more than the total current production of the Japanese and German economies combined. It is as if the United States had annexed Germany and Japan.

Over long time spans, small differences in economic growth—even less than 1 percent per year—can transform societies. For example, economic growth in the southern states was only a fraction of a percent greater than that in the North in the 100 years after the Civil War. Yet this enabled the South to rise from a real income per capita about half that of the North after the Civil War to one about the same as that of the North in the twenty-first century. Economic growth is the reason that fast-growing countries like Korea can catch up with and even surpass slow-growing countries like Mexico. Data from the International Monetary Fund show that in 1980, Korea had a real GDP per capita that was about 60 percent of Mexico's real GDP per capita, but by 2005, Korea's real GDP per capita was almost twice as large as Mexico's real GDP. Economic growth is also key to improvements in the less-developed countries in Sub-Saharan Africa, South Asia, and Latin America. Because economic growth has been lagging in many of these countries, their real GDP per capita is considerably less than that of the United States.

1.2 Economic Fluctuations: Temporary Setbacks and Recoveries

Clearly, real GDP grows over time, but every now and then real GDP stops growing, falls, and then starts increasing rapidly again. These ups and downs in the economy—that is, economic fluctuations or business cycles—can be seen in Figure 17.1.

One of these business cycles, the one in 2008–2009, is blown up for closer examination in Figure 17.3. No two business cycles are alike. Certain phases are common to all business cycles, however. These common phases are shown in the bar graph. In the United States, the "official designator" of business cycles is the National Bureau of Economic Research (NBER)'s Business Cycle Dating Committee. Economists on this committee try to identify key turning points in overall economic activity to identify, and designate as, recessions and expansions. In the definitions that follow, economic activity is usually, but not always, synonymous with real GDP.

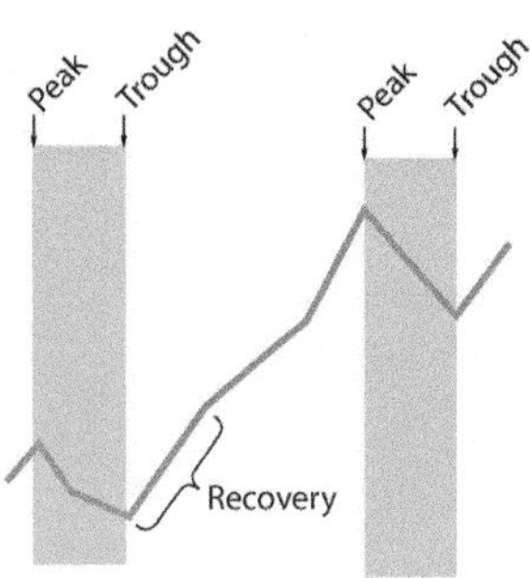

FIGURE 17.3 The Phases of Business Cycles

Although no two business cycles are alike, they have common features, including the *peak, recession,* and *trough,* shown here for the 2008–2009 recession.

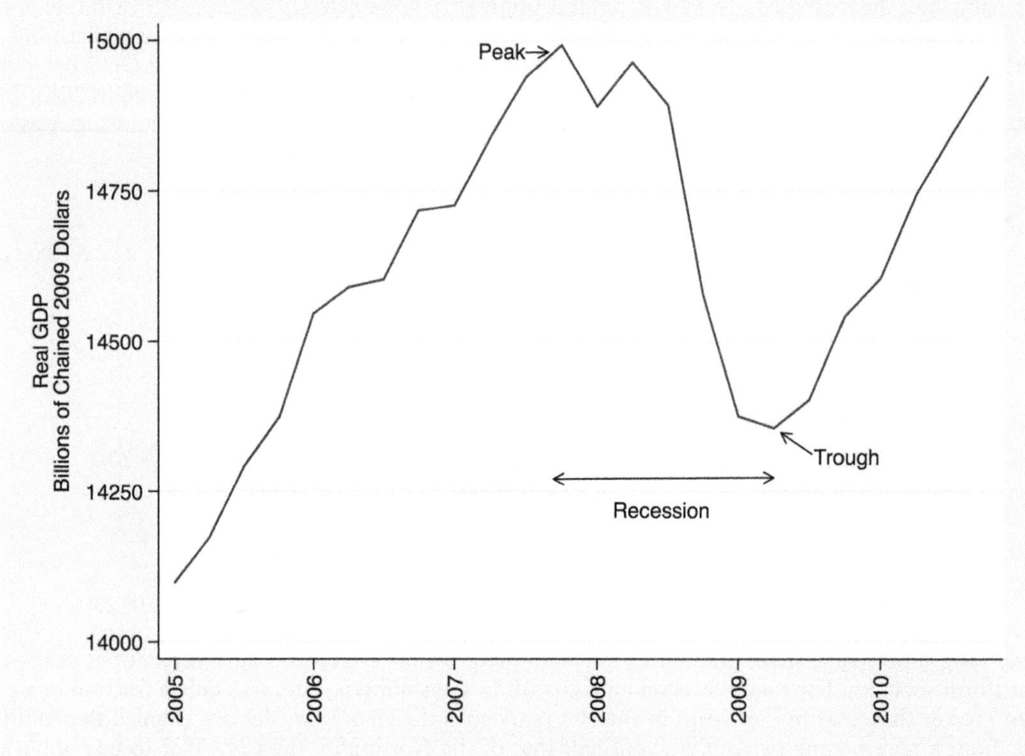

recession

A decline in economic activity that lasts for at least six months.

peak

The highest point in economic activity before a recession.

trough

The lowest point of economic activity at the end of a recession.

expansion

The period between the trough of a recession and the next peak, consisting of a general rise in output and employment.

recovery

The early part of an economic expansion, immediately after the trough of the recession.

When economic activity falls, economists call this a **recession**; a rule of thumb says that the fall must last for a half year or more before the decline is considered a recession. The highest point in economic activity before the start of a recession is called the **peak**. The lowest point in economic activity at the end of a recession is called the **trough**, a term that may cause you to imagine water accumulating at the bottom of one of the dips. The period between recessions—from the trough to the next peak—is called an **expansion**, as shown for a typical fluctuation in the bar graph in this section. The early part of an expansion usually is called a **recovery** because the economy is just recovering from the recession.

The peaks and troughs of the eight recessions since the mid-1960s are shown by vertical bars in Figure 17.1. The shaded areas represent the recessions. The areas between the shaded bars show the expansions. The dates of all peaks and troughs back to 1920 are shown in Table 17.1. The average length of each business cycle from peak to peak is slightly more than five years, but it is clear from Table 17.1 that business cycles are not regularly occurring ups and downs, like sunup and sundown. Recessions occur irregularly. There were only 12 months between the back-to-back recessions of the early 1980s, while 58 months of uninterrupted growth occurred between the 1973–1975 recession and the 1980 recession. The recession phases of business cycles also vary in duration and depth. The 1990–1991 recession, for example, was not nearly as long or as deep as the 1973–1975 recession.

Table 17.1 illustrates how much less volatile the U.S. economy had been in recent times, at least until the most recent recession. The 1990–1991 recession and the 2001 recession were among the shortest recessions in U.S. history, each lasting about eight months. Both of these recessions were preceded by long economic expansions lasting between seven and ten years. The economic expansion that began after the 2001 recession lasted almost six years before the economy went into recession at the end of 2007. That recession lasted 18 months (exceeding the 1990–1991 and 2001 recessions in duration), ending in the middle of 2009.

TABLE 17.1 Comparison of Recessions

Recession		Duration of Recession (months from peak to trough)	Decline in Real GDP (percent from peak to trough)	Duration of Next Expansion (months from trough to peak)
Peak	Trough			
Jan 1920-Jul 1921		18	8.7	22
May 1923-Jul 1924		14	4.1	27
Oct 1926-Nov 1927		13	2.0	21
Aug 1929-Mar 1933		43	32.6	50
May 1937-Jun 1938		13	18.2	80
Feb 1945-Oct 1945		8	11.0	37
Nov 1948-Oct 1949		11	1.5	45
Jul 1953-May 1954		10	3.2	39
Aug 1957-Apr 1958		8	3.3	24
Apr 1960-Feb 1961		10	1.2	106
Dec 1969-Nov 1970		11	1.0	36
Nov 1973-Mar 1975		16	4.9	58
Jan 1980-Jul 1980		6	2.5	12
Jul 1981-Nov 1982		16	3.0	92
Jul 1990-Mar 1991		8	1.4	120
Mar 2001-Nov 2001		8	0.0	72
Dec 2007-June 2009		18	4.1	90*

**As of December 2016. Source: Columns 1, 2, and 4, National Bureau of Economic Research.*

Amid the euphoria of the Great Moderation, economists debated whether economic policies were responsible for the length of the recent expansions and the brevity of the recent recessions. Was this "Great Moderation" the result of better policy making by the Federal Reserve and by our elected leaders? Or was it because we benefited from technological advances like more effective pharmaceuticals, the invention of the personal computer, or the creation of the Internet? Or was it simply the result of "good luck" in terms of the economy being hit by less disruptive shocks than in the 1970s? As you can see from the table here, the current economic expansion has lasted over 90 months but, as you will see later, the economy has not grown very rapidly during this expansion. In recent years, economists have been engaged in a spirited public debate about whether slow economic growth even during expansions will become the "new normal" for the U.S. economy.

When the economy is in the midst of a serious recession, economists have focused on understanding the factors that caused the recession. The most recent recession was associated with a number of factors, including the dramatic fall in house prices and sales, rising foreclosures of homes, a banking crisis that made it difficult for firms and consumers to obtain credit, and dramatic increases in fuel prices during the early part of 2008. Economists do not always agree on what the factors causing a recession were. The factors to which the 2001 recession has been ascribed include a fall in spending on equipment and buildings by firms and a sharp decline in the stock market. The first month of the 1990–1991 recession occurred just after Iraq invaded Kuwait, causing a disruption in the oil fields and a jump in world oil prices, so some argue that this jump in oil prices was a factor in the recession.

A Recession's Aftermath

After a recession, the economy usually takes several years to return to its prerecession state. Thus, a period of bad economic times always follows a recession while the economy recovers. Technically, economists define recessions as periods in which real GDP is declining, and recoveries as periods in which real GDP is rising again. However, despite this technical distinction between bad economic times when things are getting worse (recession) and bad economic times when things are improving (recovery), many people still associate the word *recession* with bad economic times in general.

Furthermore, not all economic indicators move in lockstep with real GDP. For example, although the 2008–2009 recession ended in June of 2009, the unemployment rate kept rising for five more months and did not fall below the levels reached at the end of the recession until another year had passed. Technically speaking, though, the recession was over in June 2009 when economic activity (including real GDP) began to pick up again—long before the effects of an improving economy were felt by most people. Conversely, when this recession began in December 2007, real GDP kept rising for another six months even though other indicators of economic activity showed a downturn much earlier.

Recessions versus Depressions

Fortunately, we have not experienced a depression in the United States for a long time, and we all hope that it stays that way. Figure 17.4 shows the history of real GDP for about 100 years. The most noticeable decline in real GDP occurred in the 1929–1933 recession. Real GDP fell by 32.6 percent in this period. This decline in real GDP was so large that it was given its own designation by economists and historians—the Great Depression.

FIGURE 17.4 Growth and Fluctuations Since the Early Twentieth Century

Economic growth has been steady in the United States from the beginning of the twentieth century. The frequency and size of economic fluctuations, however, has diminished remarkably since the end of World War II. The most recent economic downturn was one of the more severe recessions that the economy had seen in the postwar period but still remained small in comparison with the Great Depression.

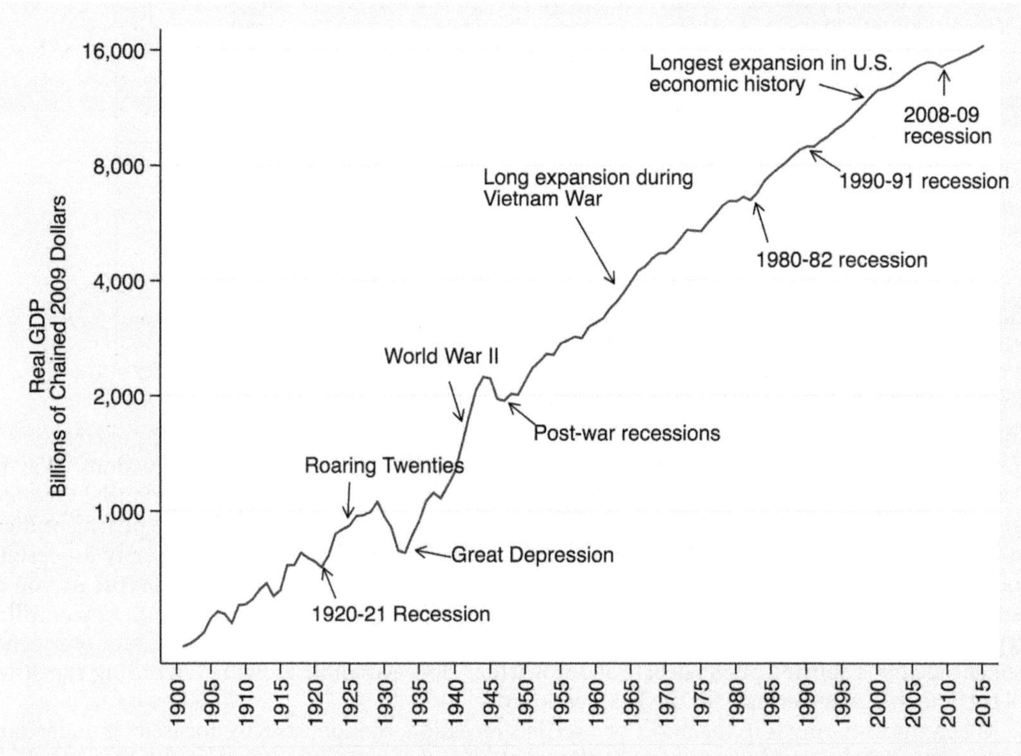

Table 17.1 shows how much real GDP fell in each of the 17 recessions since the 1920s. The 1920–1921 recession and the 1937–1938 recession were big enough to be classified as depressions, but both were small compared with the Great Depression. Real GDP also declined substantially after World War II, when war production declined.

The postwar recessions are not remotely comparable in severity to the Great Depression or the other huge recessions of the 1920s and 1930s. The 2008–2009 recession, sometimes referred to as the Great Recession, was a significant slowdown in comparison to postwar recessions, both in terms of severity and length. But it had only one-eighth the decline in real GDP that occurred during the Great Depression, which was a downturn of a more significant scale. But because any recession focuses attention on people's hardship and suffering, the tendency always is to view a current recession as being worse than most previous recessions.

REVIEW

- The behavior of real GDP in the United States is characterized by a long-term upward trend (economic growth) and more transient increases and decreases around that trend (economic fluctuations).
- Economic growth provides lasting improvements in the well-being of people. Small differences in economic growth, sustained over long time spans, can transform societies.
- Periodically, economic activity stops increasing and begins to decline. A decline in economic activity that lasts for at least six months is known as a recession. Recessions vary in length and intensity, but have become less severe since the 1980s.
- A recession that is very severe is called a depression. The Great Depression of the 1930s was about eight times more severe than the 2008–2009 recession when measured by the decline in real GDP.

2. UNEMPLOYMENT, INFLATION, AND INTEREST RATES

As real GDP changes over time, so do other economic variables, such as unemployment, inflation, and interest rates. Looking at these other economic variables gives us a better understanding of the human story behind the changes in real GDP. They also provide additional information about the economy's performance—just as a person's pulse rate or cholesterol level gives information different from the body temperature. No one variable is sufficient.

2.1 Unemployment during Recessions

Unemployment fluctuates just as real GDP fluctuates. The **unemployment rate** is the number of unemployed people as a percentage of the labor force; the labor force consists of those who either are working or looking for work. Every time the economy goes into a recession, the unemployment rate rises because people are laid off and new jobs are difficult to find. The individual stories behind the unemployment numbers frequently represent frustration and distress.

unemployment rate

The percentage of the labor force that is unemployed.

Figure 17.5 shows what happens to the unemployment rate as the economy goes through recessions and recoveries. The increase in the unemployment rate during a recession eventually is followed by a decline in unemployment during the recovery. Note, for example, how rapidly unemployment rose as the economy moved into recession in 2008, with the unemployment rate rising by more than 2.5 percentage points in 2008. Similar sharp increases in unemployment were seen during the recessions of 1973–1975 and 1981–1982.

FIGURE 17.5 The Unemployment Rate

The number of unemployed workers as a percentage of the labor force—the unemployment rate—increases during recessions because people are laid off and it is difficult to find work. Sometimes the unemployment rate continues to increase for a while after the recession is over, as in 1991 and 2001. But eventually unemployment declines during the economic recovery.

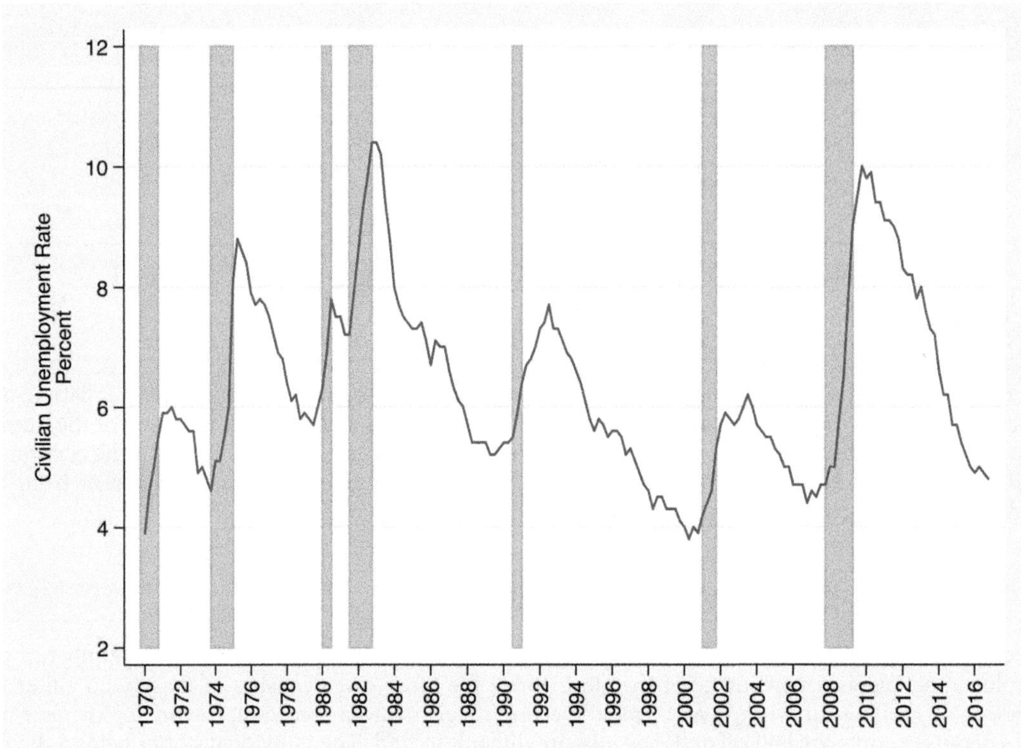

Source: Bureau of Labor Statistics, "Unemployment Rate—Civilian Labor Force."

Figure 17.6 shows how high the unemployment rate got during the Great Depression. It rose to nearly 25 percent; one in four workers was out of work. Fortunately, recent increases in unemployment during recessions have been much smaller. The unemployment rate reached 10.4 percent in the early 1980s, the highest level since World War II.

FIGURE 17.6 Unemployment during the Great Depression

The increase in unemployment in the United States during the Great Depression was huge compared with the increases in unemployment during milder downturns in the economy. Almost one in four workers was unemployed during the Great Depression.

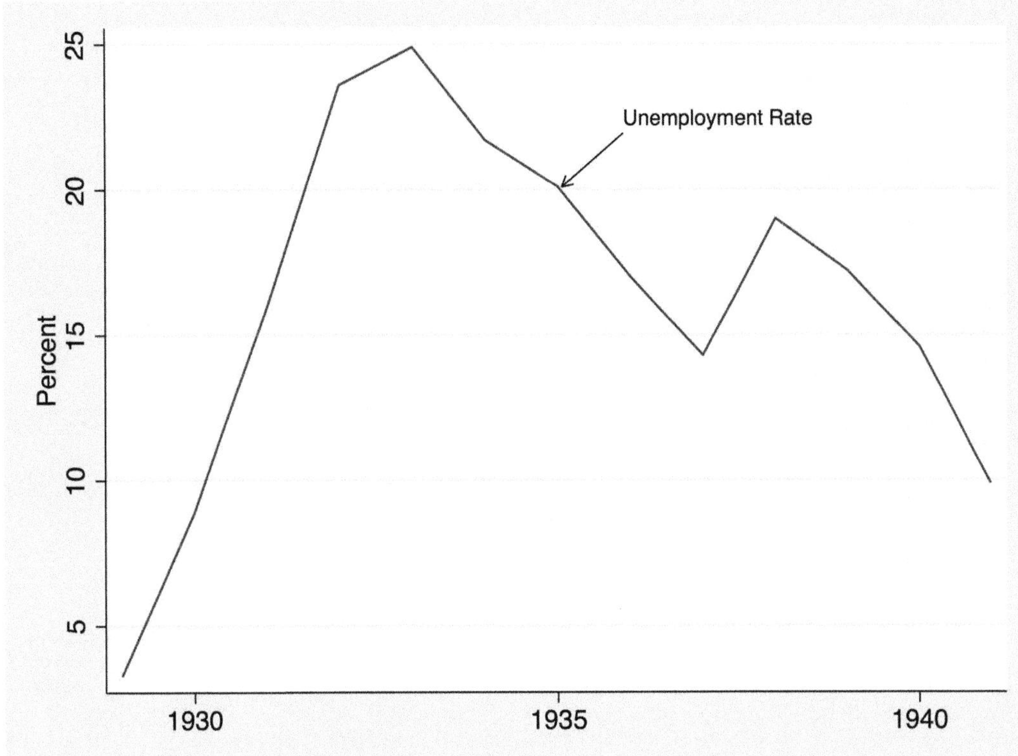

Source: Robert Van Giezen and Albert E. Schwenk, "Compensation from before World War I Through the Great Depression" (Bureau of Labor Statistics).

The highest unemployment level reached in the most recent recession was 10.1 percent in October 2008, a figure that pales in comparison to the levels reached in the Great Depression. It also is slightly lower than the peak levels reached in the 1982 recession. However, unemployment was much lower in the period leading into the recent recession (around 5 percent) than it was in the period leading up to the 1982 recession (7.5 percent). The extremely rapid rise in the unemployment rate clearly shows that this is a downturn whose impact will be felt for years to come. Figure 17.7 illustrates how rapidly unemployment rose during the calendar years of 2008 and 2009. During these two years, the unemployment rate increased from 4.9 percent to 9.9 percent. To put this number in more human terms, the number of unemployed workers across the country doubled from 7.6 million to 15.2 million.

FIGURE 17.7 **The Rapid Rise of Unemployment in 2008/09**

When the economy moves from expansion into recession, unemployment can climb rapidly over a period of a few months, as we saw during the most recent recession.

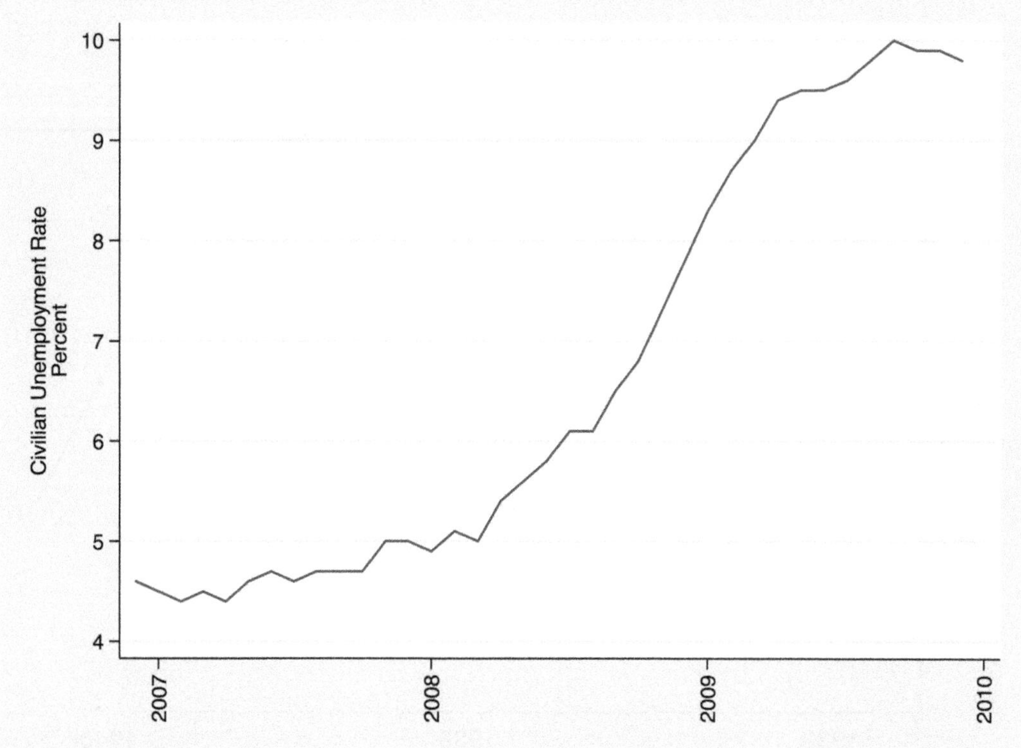

Source: Bureau of Labor Statistics.

2.2 Inflation

inflation rate

The percentage increase in the overall price level over a given period of time, usually one year.

Just as output and unemployment have fluctuated over time, so too has inflation. The **inflation rate** is the percentage increase in the average price of all goods and services from one year to the next. Figure 17.8 shows the inflation rate for the same 40-year period we have focused on in our examination of real GDP and unemployment. Clearly, a low and stable inflation rate has not been a feature of the United States during this period. We can note several useful facts about the behavior of inflation.

First, inflation is closely correlated with the ups and downs in real GDP and employment: Inflation increased before every recession in the last 40 years and then subsided during and after every recession. We will want to explore whether this close correlation between the ups and downs in inflation and the ups and downs in the economy explains economic fluctuations.

FIGURE 17.8 The Ups and Downs in Inflation

Inflation has increased before each recession and then declined during and immediately after each recession. In addition, a longer-term upward trend in inflation reached a peak in 1980. Since 1981, America has experienced a disinflation—a decline in the rate of inflation.

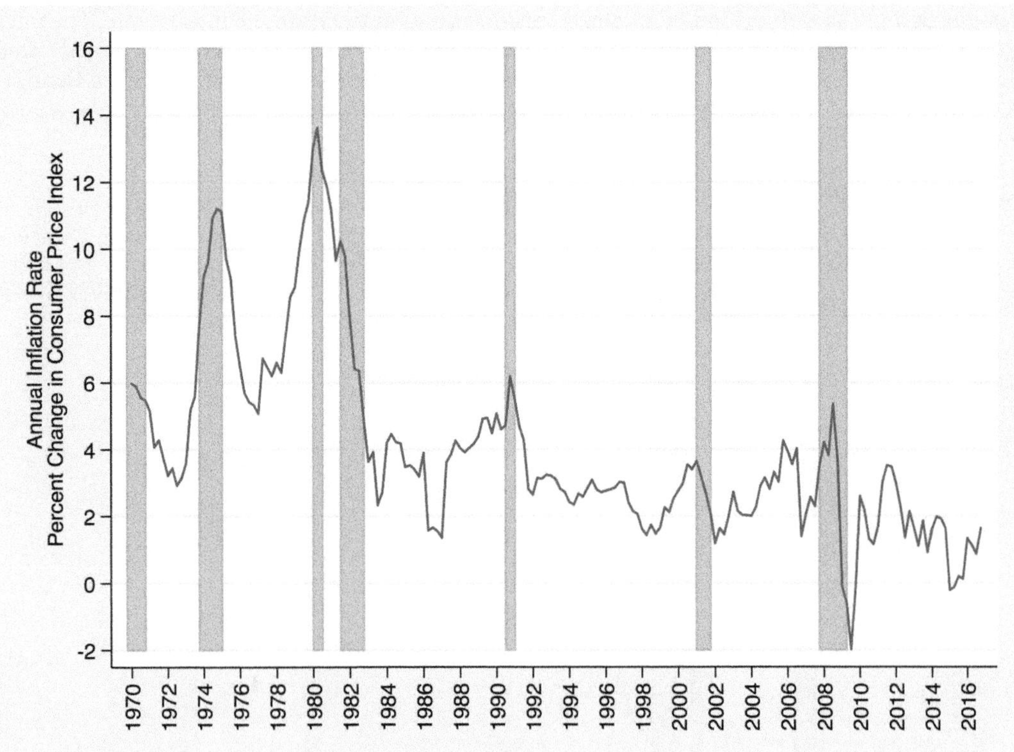

Source: Bureau of Labor Statistics, "Percent Change in CPI for All Urban Consumers."

Second, there are long-term trends in inflation. For example, inflation rose from a low point during the 1970s to a high point of double-digit inflation in 1980. This period of persistently high inflation until 1980 is called the Great Inflation. The Great Inflation ended in the early 1980s, when the inflation rate declined substantially. Such a decline in inflation is called disinflation. A much rarer occurrence is what economists call deflation, a period during which inflation is negative and the average price level falls. The U.S. economy experienced deflation at the end of 2009; this was the first time in 50 years that deflation from one year to the next had occurred in the U.S. economy. Even after the recession ended, inflation in the United States has remained low, below the 2 percent value that the Federal Reserve considers as being a long-term objective goal for the economy.

Third, judging by history, we have no reason to expect the inflation rate to be zero, even on average. The inflation rate has averaged a little over 2.25 percent in the United States since 1990.

Why does inflation increase before recessions? Why does inflation fall during and after recessions? What caused the Great Inflation? Why did the economy move into deflation for the first time in 50 years? Why is inflation not equal to zero even in more normal times, when the economy is neither in recession nor in a boom? What can economic policy do to keep inflation low and stable? These are some of the questions and policy issues about inflation addressed by macroeconomics.

2.3 Interest Rates

The **interest rate** is the amount that lenders charge when they lend money, expressed as a percentage of the amount loaned. For example, if you borrow $100 for a year from a friend and the interest rate on the loan is 6 percent, then at the end of the year you must pay your friend back $6 in interest in addition to the $100 you borrowed. The interest rate is another key economic variable that is related to the growth and change in real GDP over time.

interest rate

The amount received per dollar loaned per year, usually expressed as a percentage (for example, 6 percent) of the loan.

Different Types of Interest Rates and Their Behavior

The economy includes many different interest rates: The *mortgage interest rate* is the rate on loans to buy a house; the *savings deposit interest rate* is the rate people get on their savings deposits at banks; the *Treasury bill rate* is the interest rate the government pays when it borrows money from people for a year or less; the *federal funds rate* is the interest rate banks charge each other on short-term loans.

Interest rates influence people's economic behavior. When interest rates rise, for example, it is more expensive to borrow funds to buy a house or a car, so many people postpone such purchases.

Figure 17.9 shows the behavior of a typical interest rate, the federal funds rate, during the last 40 years. First, note how closely the ups and downs in the interest rate are correlated with the ups and downs in the economy. Interest rates rise before each recession and then decline during and after each recession. Second, as with the inflation rate, there are long-term trends in the interest rate. The interest rate rose in the 1970s and early 1980s. Each fluctuation in interest rates during this period brought forth a higher peak in interest rates. Then, in the 1980s, the interest rate began a downward trend; each peak was lower than the previous peak. During the most recent recession, the federal funds rate fell to close to 0 percent, which is the lowest it can go.

FIGURE 17.9 **The Ups and Downs in Interest Rates**

Interest rates generally rise just before a recession and then decline during and just after the recession. There was also a longer-term trend upward in interest rates in the 1970s and a downward trend after the 1980s. The nominal interest rate fell to unprecedented low levels in the aftermath of the 2008–09 recession. (The interest rate shown here is the federal funds interest rate.)

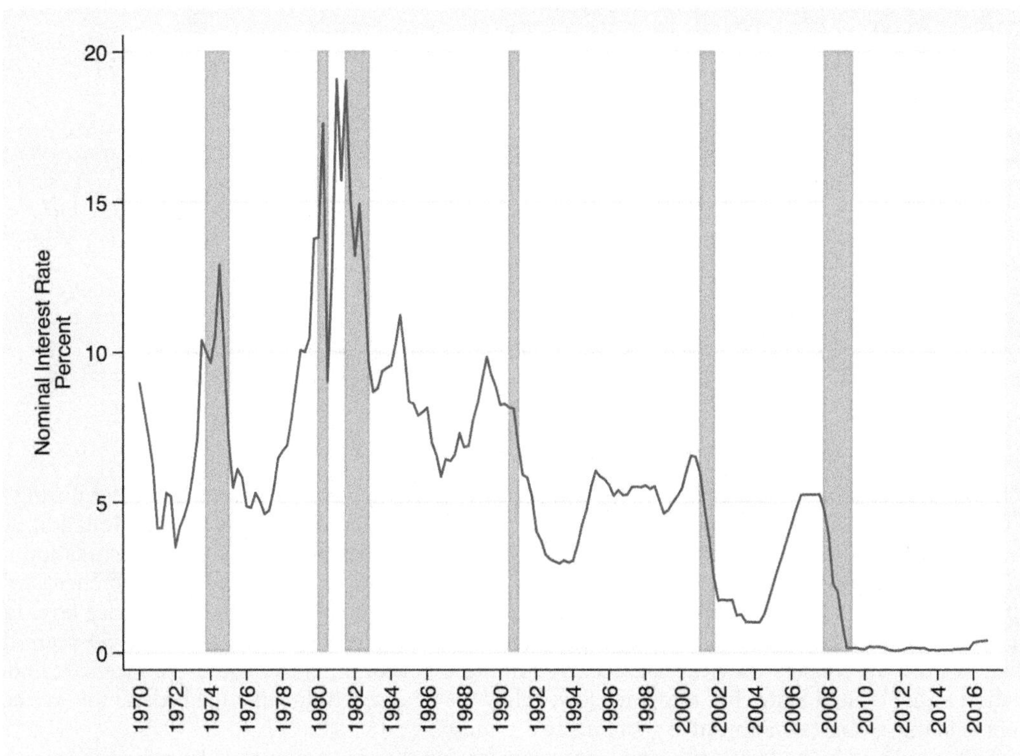

Source: Board of Governors of the Federal Reserve, "Selected Interest Rates—Federal Funds Rate."

The Concept of the Real Interest Rate

real interest rate

The interest rate minus the expected rate of inflation; it adjusts the nominal interest rate for inflation.

nominal interest rate

The interest rate uncorrected for inflation.

As we will see, the trends and fluctuations in interest rates are intimately connected with the trends and fluctuations in inflation and real GDP. In fact, the long-term rise in interest rates in the 1960s and 1970s was partly due to the rise in the rate of inflation. When inflation rises, people who lend money will be paid back in funds that are worth less because the average price of goods rises more quickly. To compensate for this decline in the value of funds, lenders require a higher interest rate. For example, if the inflation rate is 20 percent and you lend someone $100 for a year at 6 percent, then you get back $106 at the end of the year. However, the *average* price of the goods you can buy with your $106 is now 20 percent higher. Thus, your 6 percent gain in interest has been offset by a 20 percent loss. It is as if you receive *negative* 14 percent interest: 6 percent interest less 20 percent inflation. The difference between the stated interest rate and the inflation rate is thus a better measure of the real interest rate. Economists define the **real interest rate** as the interest rate less the inflation rate that people expect. The term **nominal interest rate** is used to refer to the interest rate on a loan, making no adjustment for inflation. For example, the real interest rate is 2 percent if the nominal interest rate is 5 percent and inflation is expected to be 3 percent (5 - 3 = 2). To keep the real interest rate from changing by a large amount as inflation rises, the nominal interest rate has to increase with inflation. Thus, the concept of the real interest rate helps us understand why inflation and interest rates have moved together. We will make much more use of the real interest rate in later chapters.

REVIEW

- The unemployment rate rises during recessions and falls during recoveries.
- Inflation and interest rates rise before recessions and then fall during and just after recessions.
- There was a long-term increase in interest rates and inflation in the 1970s. Interest rates and inflation were lower in the 1990s and into the 2000s.
- Two unusual features of the U.S. economy in recent times have been the negative rate of inflation, also known as deflation, and the nominal interest rate falling to a level of zero, which is the lowest it can go.

3. MACROECONOMIC THEORY AND POLICY

Because strong economic growth raises the living standards of people in an economy, and because increases in unemployment during recessions cause hardship, two key goals of economic policy are to raise long-term growth and to reduce the size of short-term economic fluctuations. However, the facts—summarized above—about economic growth and fluctuations do not give economists a basis for making recommendations about economic policy. Before one can be confident about recommending a policy, one needs a coherent theory to explain the facts.

Macroeconomic theory is divided into two branches. *Economic growth theory* aims to explain the long-term upward rise of real GDP over time. *Economic fluctuations theory* tries to explain the short-term fluctuations in real GDP. Economic growth theory and economic fluctuations theory combine to form *macroeconomic theory*, which explains why the economy both grows and fluctuates over time.

3.1 The Theory of Long-Term Economic Growth

Economic growth theory starts by distinguishing the longer-term economic growth trend from the short-term fluctuations in the economy. This distinction is not as easy to make as it may seem because the long-term growth trend itself may change.

It will be useful to give a name to the upward trend line in real GDP shown in Figure 17.1. We will call it **potential GDP**. Potential GDP represents the long-run tendency of the economy to grow. Real GDP fluctuates around potential GDP. No one knows exactly where potential GDP lies and exactly what its growth rate is, but any trend line that has the same long-term increase as real GDP and intersects real GDP in several places is probably a good estimate.

potential GDP
The economy's long-term growth trend to real GDP, determined by the availability of capital, labor, and technology. Real GDP fluctuates above and below potential GDP.

Potential GDP as defined here and as used by most macroeconomists is not the maximum amount of real GDP. As Figure 17.1 shows, real GDP sometimes goes above potential GDP. Thus, potential GDP is more like the average or trend level of real GDP.

aggregate supply

The total value of all goods and services produced in the economy by the available supply of capital, labor, and technology (also called potential gross domestic product [GDP]).

labor

The number of hours people are available to work in producing goods and services.

capital

The factories, improvements to cultivated land, machinery and other tools, equipment, and structures used to produce goods and services.

technology

Anything that raises the amount of output that can be produced with a given amount of labor and capital.

Economic growth theory postulates that the potential GDP of an economy is given by its **aggregate supply**. *Aggregate* means total. Aggregate supply is all goods and services produced by all the firms in the economy using the available labor, capital, and technology. **Labor** is the total number of hours workers are available to work in producing real GDP. **Capital** is the total number of factories, cultivated plots of land, machines, computers, and other tools available for the workers to use to produce real GDP. **Technology** is all the available know-how—from organizational schemes to improved telecommunications to better computer programming skills—that workers and firms can use when they produce real GDP. Labor, capital, and technology jointly determine aggregate supply.

The theory of economic growth is based on the production function, which is a model of how labor, capital, and technology jointly determine the aggregate supply of output in the economy. In these photos, the workers at the automobile plant are part of the economy's labor (left), the tools that the workers are using to assemble the cars are the economy's capital (middle), and computer programming skills are part of the economy's technology (right), which raises the value of output for a given amount of labor and capital.

Aggregate Supply and the Production Function

Source: Shutterstock.com

The Production Function

We can summarize the relationship between the three determinants and the aggregate supply of real GDP as

$$\text{Real GDP} = F\,(\text{labor},\ \text{capital},\ \text{technology})$$

production function

The relationship that describes output as a function of labor, capital, and technology.

which we say in words as "real GDP is a function, *F*, of labor, capital, and technology." The function *F* means that some general relationship exists between these variables. For this relationship, we assume that higher capital, higher labor, and higher technology all mean higher real GDP; and lower capital, lower labor, and lower technology all mean less real GDP. We call this relationship the **production function** because it tells us how much production (real GDP) of goods and services can be obtained from a certain amount of labor, capital, and technology inputs. A higher long-term economic growth rate for the economy requires a higher growth rate for one or more of these three determinants. A lower long-term economic growth rate may be due to a slower growth rate for one or more of these three determinants.

The production function applies to the entire economy, but we also have production functions for individual firms in the economy. For example, consider the production of cars. The car factory and the machines in the factory are the capital. The workers who work in the factory are the labor. The assembly-line production method is the technology. The cars coming out of the factory are the output. The production function for the economy as a whole has real GDP as output, not just cars, and all available labor, capital, and technology as inputs, not just those producing cars.

3.2 Government Policy and Economic Growth

Most governments have been interested in finding ways to increase economic growth. Economic policies that aim to increase long-term economic growth are sometimes called *supply-side policies* because they concentrate on increasing the growth of potential GDP, which is the aggregate supply of the economy.

Fiscal Policy

Our preview of growth theory already tells us that policies to increase growth should focus on increasing the available supply of labor, capital, and technology. The growth rate of capital depends on how much businesses invest in new capital each year. The amount that businesses choose to invest depends in part on the incentives they have to invest. We will see that the incentive to invest depends on the amount of taxing, spending, and borrowing by government. Hence, government policy can affect the incentive to invest and thereby stimulate long-term economic growth. Government policy concerning taxing, spending, and borrowing is called *fiscal policy*.

Labor supply also depends on incentives. In the case of labor, it is the incentive for firms to hire workers, for people to work harder or longer, for workers who are not in the labor force to come into the labor force, or for people to retire later in life. Again, government policy toward taxing, spending, and borrowing affects these incentives.

Finally, technology growth also can be affected by government policy if the government gives incentives for researchers to invent new technologies or provides funds for education so that workers can improve their skills and know-how.

Monetary Policy

Keeping inflation low and stable is another part of government policy to stimulate long-term economic growth. We will see that the government has an important role to play in determining the inflation rate, especially over the long term, because the inflation rate in the long term depends on the growth rate of the money supply, which can be controlled by the government. Government policy concerning the money supply and the control of inflation is called *monetary policy*. The government institution assigned to conduct monetary policy is the central bank. In the United States, the central bank is the Federal Reserve System.

Why should low and stable inflation be part of an economic growth policy? An examination of inflation and economic growth in a number of countries indicates that inflation is negatively correlated with long-term economic growth. The reason for this negative correlation over the long term may be that inflation raises uncertainty and thereby reduces incentives to invest in capital or improve technology. The theory of economic growth tells us that lower capital growth and lower technological growth reduce economic growth.

3.3 The Theory of Economic Fluctuations

Our review of the performance of the economy showed some of the hardships that come from economic fluctuations, especially recessions and unemployment. Can government economic policy improve economic performance by reducing the size of these fluctuations? To answer these questions, we need a theory to interpret the facts of economic fluctuations.

Aggregate Demand and Economic Fluctuations

The theory of economic fluctuations emphasizes fluctuations in the demand for goods and services as the reason for the ups and downs in the economy. Because the focus is on the sum of the demand for all goods and services in the economy—not just the demand for peanuts or bicycles—we use the term *aggregate demand*. More precisely, **aggregate demand** is the sum of the demands from the four groups that contribute to demand in the whole economy: consumers, business firms, government, and foreigners.

aggregate demand
The total demand for goods and services by consumers, businesses, government, and foreigners.

According to this theory, the declines in real GDP below potential GDP during recessions are caused by declines in aggregate demand, and the increases in real GDP above potential GDP are caused by increases in aggregate demand. For example, the decrease in real GDP in the recession that began in 2008 was driven by lower spending by consumers who were affected adversely by the collapse in the housing market, the dramatic declines in the stock market, and the rapidly rising gasoline prices in the early part of 2008, and by firms that were affected adversely by the lack of access to credit following the turmoil in the banking sector.

Thus, a key assumption of the theory of economic fluctuations is that real GDP fluctuates around potential GDP. Why is this a good assumption? How do we know that the fluctuations in the economy are not due solely to fluctuations in potential GDP, that is, in the economy's aggregate supply? The rationale for the assumption is that most of the determinants of potential GDP usually change rather smoothly. Clearly, population grows relatively smoothly. We do not have a sudden drop in the U.S. population every few years, nor do huge numbers of people migrate from the United States during recessions. The same is true with factories and equipment in the economy. Unless we have a major war at home, we do not suddenly lose equipment or factories in the economy on a massive scale. Even such disasters as the 1994 earthquake in California, the terrorist attacks of September 11, 2001, or the deadly Gulf Coast hurricanes of 2005 (Katrina and Rita), although devastating for affected individuals, take only a tiny fraction out of the potential GDP of the entire U.S. economy. Finally, technological know-how does not suddenly decline; we do not suddenly forget how to produce things. The steady upward movement of potential GDP thus represents gradual accumulations—growth of population, growth of capital, and growth of technology. Although many economists place greater emphasis on the role of aggregate demand in short-run economic fluctuations than on fluctuations in potential GDP, it is too extreme to insist that there are absolutely no fluctuations in potential GDP.

3.4 Macroeconomic Policy and Economic Fluctuations

Macroeconomic policy can have substantial effects on economic fluctuations. Many governments would like to implement policies that either help to avoid recessions or minimize the impact of recessions when they do occur. Monetary policy makers typically prefer to implement policies that minimize fluctuations in GDP. Policies used to influence economic fluctuations are sometimes called *demand-side policies* because they aim to influence aggregate demand in the economy.

Fiscal Policy

On the fiscal side, the primary tools that the government uses to influence demand are government purchases and taxes. If the economy shows signs of entering a recession, the government can try to increase demand by implementing tax cuts or spending increases. Examples include the stimulus packages of 2008 and 2009, which were enacted to help bring the economy out of recession. These policies often are intended to mitigate the negative impact on aggregate demand of other factors, such as a fall in consumer or investor confidence or a fall in exports because of a recession in one of the countries among major U.S. trading partners. Economists debate the effectiveness of such policies.

Monetary Policy

To keep inflation low and stable, the Federal Reserve also will implement policies that influence demand. The primary tools that the Federal Reserve uses to influence demand are changes in interest rates and the money supply. If signs indicate that inflation is on the rise because aggregate demand is growing faster than potential output, the Federal Reserve may step in and raise interest rates, which will slow down spending, as you will soon learn in Chapter 19. In addition to keeping inflation low and stable, the Federal Reserve also is concerned with minimizing the adverse impact of recessions. When the economy goes into recession, the Federal Reserve will try to increase demand by lowering interest rates. Again, 2008 was a good example of this type of behavior, as the Federal Reserve lowered interest rates dramatically—going from an interest rate of 4.25 percent to an interest rate of zero percent.

REVIEW

- Economic growth theory concentrates on explaining the long-term upward path of the economy.
- Economic growth depends on three factors: the growth of capital, labor, and technology.
- Government policy can influence long-term economic growth by affecting these three factors. To raise long-term economic growth, government policies can provide incentives for investment in capital, for research and development of new technologies, for education, and for increased labor supply. A monetary policy of low and stable inflation can have a positive effect on economic growth.
- Economic fluctuations theory assumes that fluctuations in GDP are due to fluctuations in aggregate demand.
- Monetary policy and fiscal policy can reduce the fluctuations in real GDP. Finding good policies is a major task of macroeconomics.

4. END-OF-CHAPTER MATERIAL

4.1 Conclusion

This chapter started with a brief review of the facts of economic growth and fluctuations. The key facts are that economic growth provides impressive gains in the well-being of individuals over the long term, that economic growth is temporarily interrupted by recessions, that unemployment rises in recessions, and that inflation and interest rates rise before recessions and decline during and after recessions. These are the facts on which macroeconomic theory is based and about which macroeconomic policy is concerned. Remembering these facts helps you understand theory and make judgments about government policy.

After showing how we measure real GDP and inflation in Chapter 18, we will look at explanations for the facts and proposals for macroeconomic policies in Chapter 19 through Chapter 27.

Key Points

1. Macroeconomics is concerned with economic growth and fluctuations in the whole economy.
2. China, India, the Republic of Korea, and many other economies have grown dramatically in recent years.
3. Economic growth occurs because of increases in labor, capital, and technological know-how.
4. Economic policies that provide incentives to increase capital and resources devoted to improving technology can increase growth rates.
5. Economic fluctuations consist of recessions (when economic activity falls) followed by recoveries (when economic activity picks up again).
6. Recent recessions have been much less severe than the Great Depression of the 1930s, when real GDP fell by more than 30 percent.
7. Inflation and interest rates rise before recession and fall in the aftermath.
8. The most popular theory of economic fluctuations is that they occur because of fluctuations in aggregate demand.
9. Macroeconomic policies include monetary and fiscal policies that are aimed at keeping business cycles small and inflation low.
10. Economic growth theory and economic fluctuations theory combine to form macroeconomic theory, which explains why the economy grows and fluctuates over time.

QUESTIONS FOR REVIEW

1. What are the two broad branches of macroeconomic theory?
2. What is the difference between economic growth and economic fluctuations?
3. What is the difference between a recession period and a recovery period?
4. How do unemployment, inflation, and interest rates behave during recessions?
5. How many recessions have there been since the Great Depression?
6. How do the two most recent recessions compare to past recessions?
7. What is potential gross domestic product (GDP)?
8. What is aggregate demand?
9. What are the primary determinants of economic growth?
10. Describe how monetary policy and fiscal policy can affect economic growth and economic fluctuations.

PROBLEMS

1. The following graph shows a period of back-to-back recessions that occurred in the United States in the 1980s. Show the peaks, recessions, troughs, and recovery phases of this unusual period.

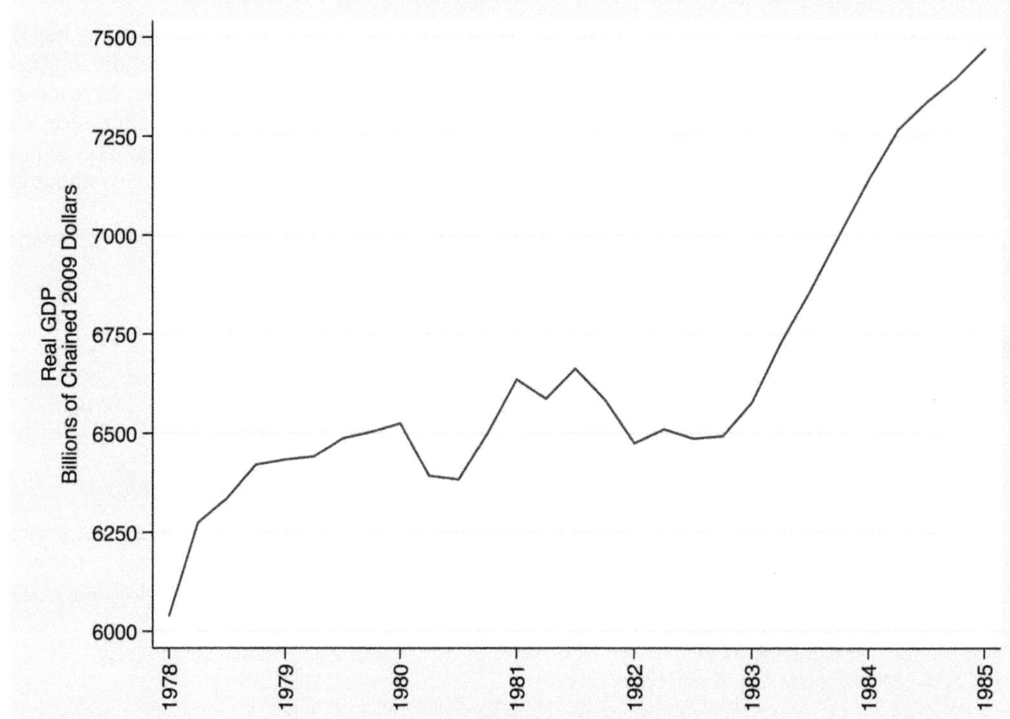

2. What determines potential GDP? What factors could cause the growth rate of potential GDP to slow down? What economic policies can the government use to affect potential GDP?
3. Suppose the U.S. economy is at the trough of a business cycle.
   a. What is the relationship between real and potential GDP?
   b. Is it likely that real GDP will stay in this position relative to potential GDP for a long period of time (say, 10 years)? Explain briefly.
4. Suppose people start retiring at a later age because of improved medical technology.
   a. How will this affect the economy's potential GDP?
   b. Why might the government want to encourage later retirement?

5. Using the data from Canada and Britain shown in the following table, plot the unemployment rate on the vertical axis. How do these unemployment rates compare with the U.S. rate shown in Figure 17.5?

Year	Canada	Britain
1990	7.7	6.9
1991	9.8	8.8
1992	10.6	10.1
1993	10.8	10.5
1994	9.5	9.6
1995	8.6	8.7
1996	8.8	8.1
1997	8.4	7.0
1998	7.7	6.3
1999	7.0	6.0
2000	6.1	5.5

6. Compare Figure 17.5, showing unemployment, with Figure 17.8, showing the inflation rate for the same period in the United States. Describe how unemployment and inflation are correlated over the long term and over the short term.
7. Suppose that you had savings deposited in an account at an interest rate of 5 percent and your father told you that he earned 10 percent interest 20 years ago.
   a. Which of you was getting the better return?
   b. How would your answer change if you were told that the inflation rate in the United States was 12 percent 20 years ago and is 3 percent now?
8. Suppose you have $1,000, which you can put in two different types of accounts at a bank. One account pays interest of 8 percent per year; the other pays interest of 2 percent per year plus the rate of inflation.
   a. Calculate the real return you will receive after one year if the inflation rate is 5 percent.
   b. Which account will you choose if you expect the rate of inflation to be 8 percent? Why?

5. APPENDIX: THE MIRACLE OF COMPOUND GROWTH

Compound growth explains why small differences in the annual economic growth rate make such huge differences in real gross domestic product (GDP) over time. Here we explain this compounding effect, show how to compute growth rates, and discuss alternative ways to plot growing variables over time.

5.1 How Compound Growth Works

Compound growth works just like compound interest on a savings account. Compound interest is defined as the "interest on the interest" you earned in earlier periods. For example, suppose you have a savings account in a bank that pays 6 percent per year in interest. That is, if you put $100 in the account, then after one year you will get $100 times 0.06, or $6 in interest. If you leave the original $100 plus the $6—that is, $106—in the bank for a second year, then at the end of the second year you will get $106 times 0.06, or $6.36 in interest. The $0.36 is the "interest on the interest," that is, $6 times 0.06.

At the end of the second year, you have $100 + $6 + $6.36 = $112.36. If you leave that in the bank for a third year, you will get $6.74 in interest, of which $0.74 is "interest on the interest" earned in the first two years. Note how the "interest on the interest" rises from $0.36 in the second year to $0.74 in the third year. Following the same calculations, the "interest on the interest" in the fourth year would be $1.15. After 13 years, the "interest on the interest" is greater than the $6 interest on the original $100. As a result of this compound interest, the size of your account grows rapidly. At the end of 20 years, it is $320.71; after 40 years, your $100 has grown to $1,028.57.

compound growth

Applying the growth rate to growth from the previous period; similar to compound interest.

Compound growth applies the idea of compound interest to the economy. Consider, for example, a country in which real GDP is $100 billion and the growth rate is 6 percent per year. After one year, real GDP would increase by $100 billion times 0.06, or by $6 billion. Real GDP rises from $100 billion to $106 billion. In the second year, real GDP increases by $106 billion times 0.06, or by $6.36 billion. Real GDP rises from $106 billion to $112.36 billion. Table 17.2 shows how, continuing this way, real GDP grows, rounding to the nearest $0.1 billion.

TABLE 17.2 Example of Compound Growth

	Real GDP (billions)		Real GDP (billions)
Year 0	$100.0	Year 20	$320.7
Year 1	$106.0	Year 30	$574.3
Year 2	$112.4	Year 40	$1,028.6
Year 3	$119.1	Year 50	$1,842.0
Year 4	$126.2	Year 60	$3,298.8
Year 5	$133.3	Year 70	$5,907.6
Year 10	$179.1		

Thus, in one person's lifetime, real GDP would increase by about 60 times.

5.2 Exponential Effects

A convenient way to compute these changes is to multiply the initial level by 1.06 year after year. For example, the level of real GDP after one year is $100 billion times 0.06 plus $100 billion, or $100 billion times 1.06. After two years, it is $106 billion times 1.06, or $100 billion times $(1.06)^2$. Thus, for n years, we have:

$$\text{(Initial level)} \times (1.06)^{n} = \text{level at end of n years}$$

where the initial level could be $100 in a bank, the $100 billion level of real GDP, or anything else. For example, real GDP at the end of 70 years in Table 17.2 is $100 billion times $(1.06)^n$ = $100 billion times 59.076 = $5,907.6 billion, with $n = 70$. Here the growth rate (or the interest rate) is 6 percent. In general, we have:

$$\text{(Initial level)} \times (1 + g)^{n} = \text{level at end of n years}$$

where g is the annual growth rate, stated as a decimal; that is, 6 percent is 0.06. If you have a hand calculator with a key that does y^x, it is fairly easy to make these calculations, and if you try it you will see the power of compound growth. The term *exponential growth* is sometimes used because the number of years (n) appears as an exponent in the above expression.

When economists refer to average annual growth over time, they include this compounding effect. The growth rate is found by solving for g. That is, the growth rate, stated as a decimal fraction, between some initial level and a level n years later is given by

$$g = \left(\frac{\text{level at end of n years}}{\text{initial level}}\right)^{\frac{1}{n}} - 1$$

For example, the average annual growth rate from year zero to year 20 in the table is

$$\begin{aligned} g &= \left(\frac{320.7}{100}\right)^{\frac{1}{20}} - 1 \\ &= (1.06) - 1 \\ &= 0.06 \end{aligned}$$

or 6 percent. Again, if your calculator has a key for y^x you can make these calculations easily.

To get the annual growth rate for one year, you simply divide the level in the second year by the level in the first year and subtract one to get the growth rate.

5.3 Rule of 72

You also can find how long it takes something to increase by a certain percentage. For example, to calculate how many years it takes something that grows at rate g to double, you solve $(1 + g)^n = 2$ for n. The answer is approximately $n = 0.72/g$. In other words, if you divide 72 by the growth rate in percent, you get the number of years it takes to double the amount. This is called the *rule of 72*. If your bank account pays 6 percent interest, it will double in 12 years.

5.4 Plotting Growing Variables

You may have noticed that some time-series charts have vertical scales where the magnitudes represented by two equidistant points on the vertical axis increase. Look, for example, at the scale in Figure 17.1, where real GDP increases from \$2.25 billion to \$4.5 billion to \$9 billion are represented by three equal-sized steps. In contrast, in Figure 17.3 real GDP increases from \$14 billion to \$14.25 billion to \$14.5 billion are represented by three equal-sized steps. Financial analysts and economists use the type of scale shown in Figure 17.1, which is called a *ratio scale* (or sometimes a proportional scale or logarithmic scale), to present variables that grow over time. The purpose of a ratio scale is to make equal percentage changes in the variable have the same vertical distance.

FIGURE 17.10 Comparison of Two Different Scales: Regular versus Ratio

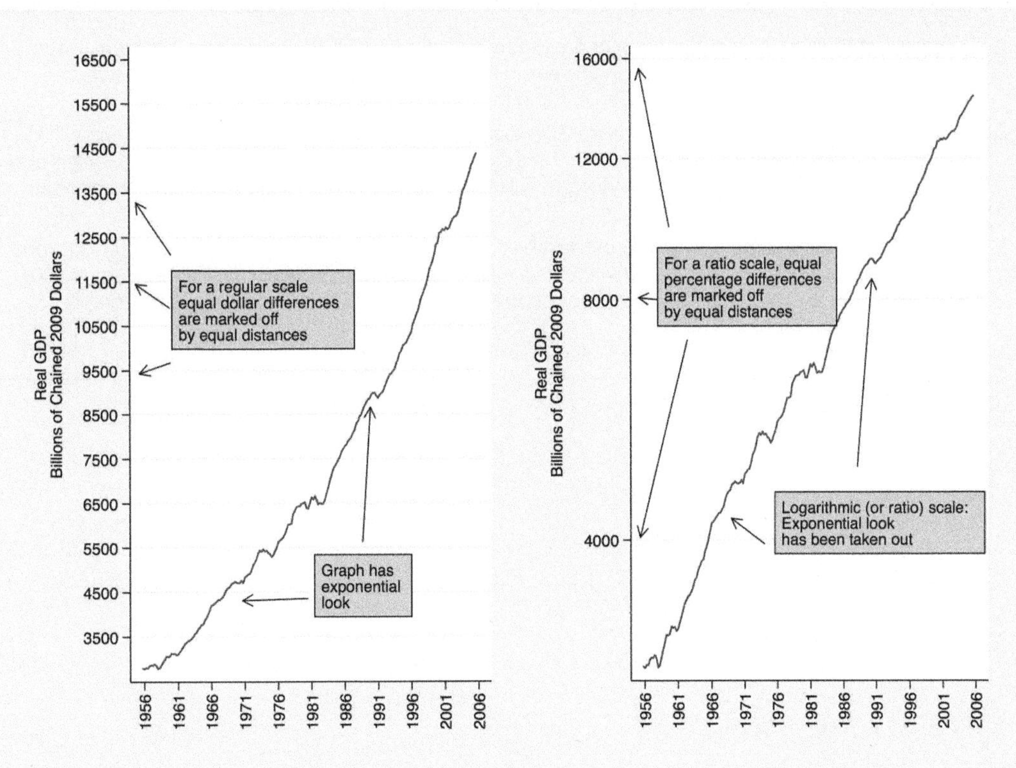

If you plot a variable that grows at a constant rate on a ratio scale, it looks like a straight line, even though it would look as if it were exploding on a standard scale. To show what ratio scales do, real GDP for the past 50 years is plotted in Figure 17.10 using a regular scale and a ratio scale. Note how the fluctuations in real GDP in the 1960s look smaller on a regular scale compared with the ratio scale, and how the ratio scale tends to take out the exponential look. This difference is one reason to look carefully at the scales of graphs. (The reason that ratio scales sometimes are called logarithmic scales is that plotting the logarithm of a variable is the same as plotting the variable on a ratio scale.)

Key Points

1. Compound growth is similar to compound interest. Rather than applying the interest rate to the interest from earlier periods, one applies the growth rate to the growth from the previous period.
2. With compound growth, seemingly small differences in growth rates result in huge differences in real GDP.
3. When you see a diagram with the scale shrunk for the higher values, it is a logarithmic or ratio scale.
4. A ratio or logarithmic scale is more useful than a regular scale when a variable is growing over time.

QUESTIONS FOR REVIEW

1. What is the rule of 72?
2. What is a ratio scale?

PROBLEMS

1. Suppose that the annual rate of growth of gross domestic product (GDP) per capita is 2 percent. How much will real GDP per capita increase in 10 years? How much will it increase in 50 years? Answer the same questions for a growth rate of 1 percent and for a growth rate of 4 percent.
2. According to recent data, China's per capita GDP is growing at about 9 percent a year. How long will it take for China's per capita GDP to double? If China can grow at 9 percent a year for the next 16 years and at 6 percent a year for the following 24 years, how large will China's per capita GDP in 40 years be relative to its per capita GDP today?
3. Plot the data for the example economy in the table in this appendix on a graph at 10-year intervals from year 20 to year 60 on a regular scale. Now create a new graph with a ratio scale by first marking off 300, 600, 1,200, 2,400, and 4,800 at equal distances on the vertical axis. Plot the same data on this graph. Compare the two graphs.

CHAPTER 18
Measuring the Production, Income, and Spending of Nations

Imagine, if you will, that you were one of a small group of subsistence farmers eking out a living on a small island where the only thing that grew was coconut trees. If you were asked to calculate the production of this economy, all you would have to do was count the number of coconuts that the people living on the island plucked from the trees. But suppose the island also had an abundance of banana plants. Then calculating the production of the economy would require that you count both coconuts and bananas. Understanding whether production had increased over time would be a challenge—would the 500 pounds of bananas and 1,000 coconuts produced this year be considered an increase in production compared with last year's crop of 750 pounds of bananas and 750 coconuts? You would have to figure out how to compare bananas to coconuts—perhaps not as impossible a task as comparing apples to oranges, but a challenge nonetheless.

Now imagine, if you will, being asked to calculate the production of the economy of the United States. You would have to add up not just apples and oranges, but millions of other goods. You also would have to think about how to measure the output of doctors, lawyers, teachers, and economists. Some of the goods being produced in the economy would be shipped to other countries. Other goods that people were buying had been shipped to the United States from abroad. Some goods, like bicycle tires, were being used as inputs into the production of other goods, like bicycles. Measuring the production of a nation is indeed a challenge.

In the United States, that challenge has been assigned to the Bureau of Economic Analysis (BEA), an agency of the U.S. Department of Commerce. The BEA states its mission as being to promote "a better understanding of the U.S. economy by providing the most timely, relevant, and accurate economic accounts data in an objective and cost-effective manner." Every quarter, the BEA releases the official government statistics on real gross domestic product (GDP), the most widely used measure of production in the U.S. economy. BEA releases are eagerly awaited throughout the economy. Top officials at the White House (including the president) find these data so important that they ensure that they get them the night before they are released to the public. Because measuring the economy in a timely and accurate manner is essential for people in financial markets and other lines of business, bond and stock traders in New York, Tokyo, London, and everywhere else keep their eyes glued to their computer terminals when a new government statistic measuring the course of the economy is about to be released. By buying or selling quickly in response to the new information, they can make millions or avoid losing millions.

Source: Shutterstock.com

To economists, measurement of the economy is interesting in its own right, involving clever solutions to intriguing problems. One of the first Nobel Prizes in economics was given to Simon Kuznets for solving some of these measurement problems. As economics students, you cannot help but learn a little about how the economy works when you study how to measure it, just as geology students cannot help but learn a little about earthquakes when they study how the Richter scale measures them. Understanding economic problems, designing possible policy solutions to these problems, and understanding whether the policy solutions did in fact work all require access to reliable data.

The purpose of this chapter is not to train you to work in the BEA. Instead, the goals are to give you a general understanding of what measures the BEA uses, to help you better grasp the strengths and weaknesses of these measures, and to make you more familiar with some key macroeconomic relationships that exist in the economy.

1. MEASURING GDP

To use GDP as a measure of production, we must be precise about *what* is included in production, *where* production takes place, and *when* production takes place.

1.1 A Precise Definition of GDP

GDP is a measure of the value of all the newly produced goods and services in a country during some period of time. Let us dissect this definition to determine what is in GDP and what is not, as well as where and when GDP is produced.

- *What?* Both *goods*—such as automobiles and new houses—and *services*—such as bus rides or a college education—are included in GDP. However, only *newly produced* goods and services are included. A ten-year-old baby carriage that is being sold at a garage sale is not included in this year's GDP; it was included in GDP ten years ago, when it was produced.
- *Where?* Only goods and services produced *within the borders* of a country are included in that country's GDP. Goods produced by Americans working in another country are not part of U.S. GDP; they are part of the other country's GDP. Goods and services produced by foreigners working in the United States are part of U.S. GDP.
- *When?* Only goods and services produced during some specified period of time are included in GDP. We always need to specify the period during which we are measuring GDP. For example, GDP in 2015 is the production between January 1st and December 31st of 2015. GDP for the third quarter of 2015 is the production between July 1 and September 30 of 2015. Rounded off to the nearest billion, GDP, or total production, was $18,037 billion in the United States in 2015. That is an average production of about $50 billion worth of goods and services a day for each of the 365 days of the year.

Prices Determine the Importance of Goods and Services in GDP

GDP is a single number, but it measures the production of many different things, from apples to oranges, from car insurance to life insurance, from movie tickets to concert seats. How can we add up such different products? Is a movie ticket more important than a concert ticket? Does a coconut count more toward GDP than a banana?

Each good is given a weight when we compute GDP, and that weight is its *price.* If the price of a milkshake is greater than that of a smoothie, then the milkshake will count more in GDP. To see this, imagine that production consists entirely of milkshakes and smoothies. If a smoothie costs $6 and a milkshake costs $5, then producing five smoothies will add $30 to GDP, and producing three milkshakes will add $15 to GDP. Thus, producing five smoothies plus three milkshakes adds $45 to GDP, as shown in Figure 18.1.

Although this method of weighting by price might not appeal to you personally—you might like milkshakes more than smoothies—it is hard to imagine anything more workable. In a market system, prices tend to reflect the cost and value of the goods and services produced. One of the great problems of measuring GDP in centrally planned economies such as the former Soviet Union was that the price of goods was set by the government; thus, the weight given each item may have had little to do with either its cost or its value to individuals. Without market prices, measuring GDP in the Soviet Union was difficult.

Intermediate Goods versus Final Goods

When measuring GDP, it is important not to count the same item more than once. Consider bicycle tires. When you buy a $150 bicycle, the tires are considered part of the bicycle. Suppose the tires are worth $20. It would be a mistake to count both the $20 value of the tires and the $150 value of the bicycle, for a total value of $170. That would count the tires twice, which is called double counting. When a tire is part of a new bicycle, it is an example of an **intermediate good**. Intermediate goods are part of **final goods**, which by definition are goods that undergo no further processing—in this case, the bicycle. *To avoid double counting, we never count intermediate goods; only final goods are part of the GDP.* If in a few years you buy a new $25 bicycle tire, then the tire will be a final good.

intermediate good

A good that undergoes further processing before it is sold to consumers.

final good

A new good that undergoes no further processing before it is sold to consumers.

FIGURE 18.1 Adding Up Unlike Products: Smoothies and Milkshakes

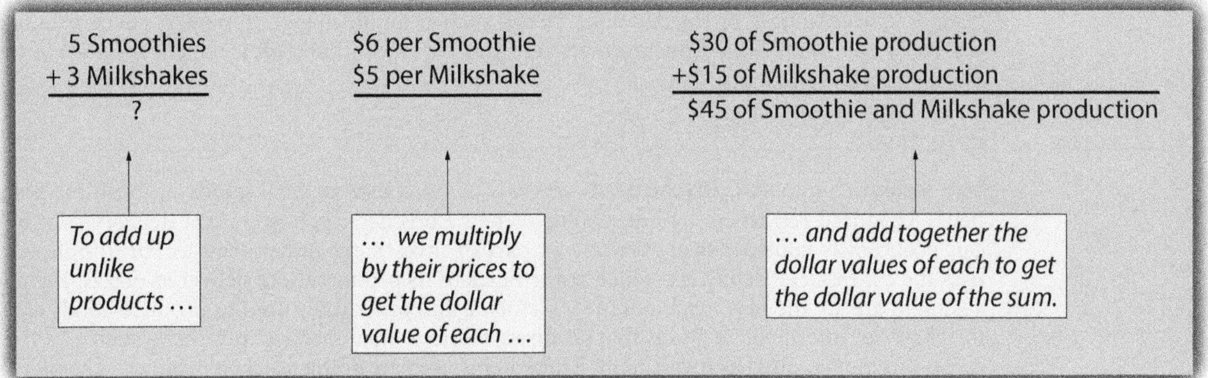

Stocks versus Flows

The distinction between *stocks* and *flows* is one of the most useful concepts in economics, and it is especially important in understanding GDP. GDP is a measure of the flow of new goods and services—it measures the value of all the newly produced goods and services in the economy. GDP is not a measure of the stock of goods and services in the economy—it does not tell us the value of all the goods and services that exist in the economy.

For example, the number of new cars produced in the United States during a given time period is a flow measure, while the number of cars in the United States is a stock measure. Therefore, only the former will count toward GDP. Similarly, U.S. GDP for 2015 will count the value of new houses built in the United States in 2015 (a flow measure), but it will not count the value of all homes in the United States as of 2015 (a stock measure).

The economist's distinction between stocks and flows can be illustrated by picturing water flowing into a bathtub from a tap. The water coming from the tap is a flow measure, while the water that is in the bathtub is a stock measure. GDP in essence is measuring the flow from the tap (the new goods and services added to the economy) and not the water in the tub (all the goods and services that already exist).

Three Ways to Measure GDP

Economists measure GDP in three ways. All three give the same answer, but they refer to conceptually different activities in the economy and provide different ways to think about GDP. All three are reported in the national income and product accounts, the official U.S. government tabulation of GDP put together by economists and statisticians at the U.S. Department of Commerce's BEA.

The first way measures the total amount that people *spend* on goods and services made in the United States. This is the *spending* approach. The second way measures the total income that is earned by all the workers and businesses that produce American goods and services. This is the *income* approach. In this approach, your income is a measure of what you produce. The third way measures the total of all the goods and services as they are *produced,* or as they are shipped out of the factory. This is the *production* approach. Note that each of the approaches considers the whole economy, and thus we frequently refer to them as aggregate spending, aggregate income, and aggregate production, in which case the word *aggregate* means total. Let us consider each of the three approaches in turn.

1.2 The Spending Approach

Typically, total spending in the economy is divided into four components: *consumption, investment, government purchases,* and *net exports,* which equal exports minus imports. Each of the four components corresponds closely to one of four groups into which the economy is divided: consumers, businesses, governments, and foreigners. Before considering each component, look at Table 18.1, which shows how the $18,037 billion of GDP in the United States in 2015 was divided into the four categories.

Consumption

consumption

Purchases of final goods and services by individuals.

The first component, **consumption**, is purchases of final goods and services by individuals. Government statisticians, who collect the data in most countries, survey department stores, discount stores, car dealers, and other sellers to see how much consumers purchase each year ($12,284 billion in 2015, as given in Table 18.1). They count anything purchased by consumers as consumption. Consumption does not include spending by business or government. Consumer purchases may be big-ticket items such as a new convertible, an operation to remove a cancerous tumor, a new stereo, a weekend vacation, or college tuition, or smaller-ticket items, such as an oil change, a medical checkup, a bus ride, or a driver's education class. Consumption accounts for a whopping 68.1 percent of GDP in the United States (see Figure 18.2).

Investment

investment

Purchases of final goods by firms plus purchases of newly produced residences by households.

The second component, **investment**, consists of purchases of final goods by business firms and of newly produced residences by households. When a business such as a pizza delivery firm buys a new car, economists consider that purchase as part of investment rather than as consumption. The firm uses the car to make deliveries, which contributes to its production of delivered pizzas. Included in investment are all the new machines, new factories, and other tools used to produce goods and services. Purchases of intermediate goods that go directly into a manufactured product—such as a tire on a bicycle—are not counted as investment. These items are part of the finished product—the bicycle, in this case—purchased by consumers. We do not want to count such items twice.

TABLE 18.1 Components of Spending in 2015 (billions of dollars)

Gross domestic product (GDP)	$18,037
Consumption	12,284
Investment	3,057
Government purchases	3,218
Net exports	-522

Source: U.S. Department of Commerce, Bureau of Economic Analysis.

The new machines, factories, and other tools that are part of investment in any year are sometimes called *business fixed investment;* this amounted to $3,057 billion in 2015. Government statisticians include two other items as part of investment: inventory investment and residential investment.

Inventory investment is defined as the change in *inventories,* which are the goods on store shelves, on showroom floors, or in warehouses that have not yet been sold or assembled into a final form for sale. For example, cars on the lot of a car dealer are part of inventories. When inventory investment is positive, then inventories are rising. When inventory investment is negative, then inventories are falling.

For example, if a car dealer had an inventory of 50 cars on December 31, 2014, got 35 new cars shipped from the factory during 2015, and sold 20 cars to consumers during the year, then the dealer's inventory will be 65 cars on December 31, 2015. The contribution of the car dealer to inventory investment for the year 2015 is positive 15 cars (inventory investment=+15 cars) because the dealer's inventory rose from 50 cars to 65 cars.

If, instead, the dealer had an inventory of 50 cars on December 31, 2014, got 35 new cars shipped from the factory during 2015, and sold 45 cars to consumers during the year, then the dealer's inventory will be 40 cars on December 31, 2015. The contribution of the car dealer to inventory investment for the year 2015 is negative 10 cars (inventory investment=-10 cars) because the dealer's inventory fell from 50 cars to 40 cars.

Inventory investment is included as a spending item when we compute GDP because we want an accurate measure of production. Consider the first car example again. If we looked only at consumption, then we would have concluded that only 20 cars were produced in the economy in 2015, even though 35 cars actually were produced. We need to add the 15 cars of inventory investment to the 20 cars of consumption to get an accurate measure of production for that year.

FIGURE 18.2 Consumption as a Share of GDP

Consumption was 68.1 percent of GDP in the United States in 2015.

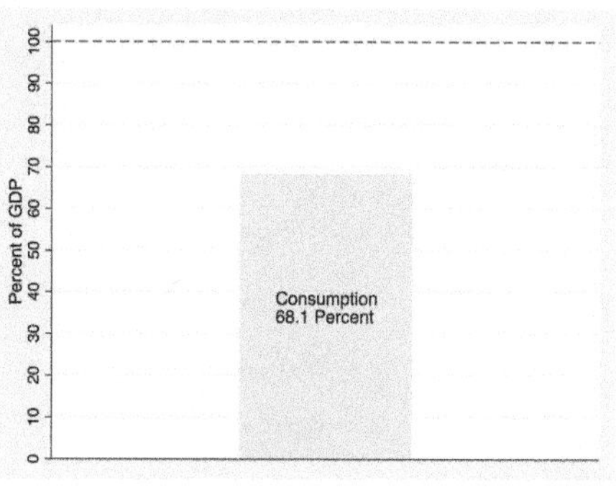

What happens when consumers eventually purchase the cars that the dealer has in inventory? Suppose, in 2016, consumers buy 25 of the cars that were in the dealer's inventory. For 2016, consumption will rise by 25 cars, whereas inventory investment will be negative 25 cars, reflecting the fall in the dealer's inventory. Adding 25 cars of consumption to negative 25 cars of inventory investment gives zero cars added to overall GDP in 2016, which is just what we want because none of these cars were produced in 2016; we already had counted them as production for 2015.

In 2015, inventory investment throughout the economy was $93.4 billion. Some firms reduced inventories, but others added a greater amount. Inventory investment tends to fluctuate up and down and therefore plays a big role in the business cycle.

The other part of investment that is not business fixed investment is *residential investment,* the purchase of new houses and apartment buildings. About $652 billion worth of housing and apartments were constructed in 2015. This was a dramatic increase from the $340 billion worth constructed at the beginning of the recovery in 2010. That number in turn represented a sharp decline from the $757 billion worth of housing and apartments that were constructed in 2006 at the height of the housing boom before house prices collapsed and drove the U.S. economy into recession. Although much of this new housing was purchased by consumers rather than businesses, it is included in investment because it produces services: shelter and, in some cases, a place to relax and enjoy life.

FIGURE 18.3 Investment and Consumption as a Share of GDP in 2015

Investment is a much smaller share of GDP than is consumption. In 2015, investment was 16.9 percent of GDP.

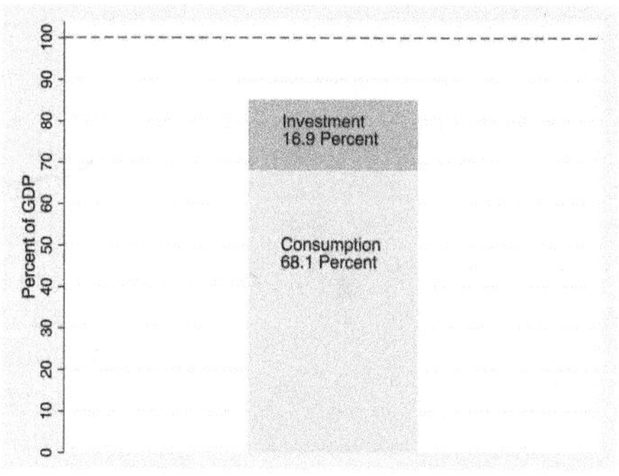

Combining the three parts of investment, we find that investment was $3,057 billion in 2015: $2,311 billion of business fixed investment, $652 billion of residential investment, and $93 billion of inventory investment. Investment was about 16.9 percent of GDP in 2015 (see Figure 18.3).

FIGURE 18.4 Government Purchases, Investment, and Consumption as a Share of GDP in 2015

Government purchases as a share of GDP were around 17.8 percent in 2015, comparable in magnitude to investment but much less than consumption. In 2015, When the stacked bar goes above the 100 percent line, negative net exports result (a trade deficit), as shown here. If the stacked bar stops below the 100 percent line, a trade surplus results.

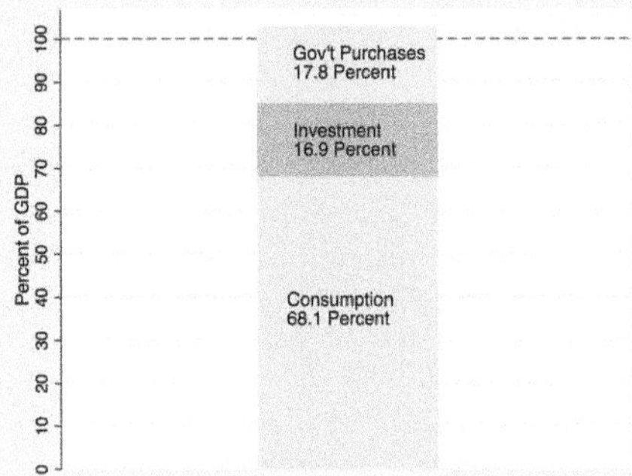

Note the special way the term *investment* is used in this discussion. To an economist, investment means the purchase of new factories, houses, or equipment. In everyday language, however, investment usually refers to an individual's putting away some funds for the future, perhaps in the stock market, such as "I'll invest in the stock market." Be sure to stay aware of this distinction.

Government Purchases

The third component of spending, **government purchases**, is spending by federal, state, and local governments on new goods and services. Most U.S. government purchases are for the military. At the state and local levels, education, roads, and police dominate government purchases. Government purchases of goods and services were equal to $3,218 billion in 2015 (see Figure 18.4).

Not all government outlays are included in GDP. A government welfare payment or retirement payment to an individual is not a purchase of a good or service; it is a *transfer payment* of income from the government to an individual. Transfer payments do not represent new production of anything, unlike the purchase of a weapon or a new road or a new building. Because GDP measures the production of new goods and services, government outlays on transfer payments like social security, unemployment compensation, and welfare payments are excluded. Only purchases are counted because only these items represent something produced. Government *outlays* are purchases plus transfer payments.

Net Exports

government purchases

Purchases by federal, state, and local governments of new goods and services.

net exports

The value of exports minus the value of imports.

exports

The total value of the goods and services that people in one country sell to people in other countries.

imports

The total value of the goods and services that people in one country buy from people in other countries.

trade balance

The value of exports minus the value of imports.

The final spending component is **net exports**, the difference between exports and imports. American **exports** are what Americans sell to foreigners, whether pharmaceuticals, computers, grain, or a vacation in Florida. American **imports** are what Americans buy from foreigners, whether cars, plasma televisions, shirts, or a vacation in France. Net exports are defined as exports minus imports. Net exports are a measure of how much more we sell to foreigners than we buy from foreigners. Another term for net exports is the **trade balance**. If net exports are positive, we have a trade surplus. If net exports are negative, we have a trade deficit. The United States had a trade deficit in 2015: $2,264 billion in exports and $2,786 billion in imports. Hence, net exports were a negative $522 billion, and appear in Table 18.1 as –$522 billion.

Net exports are added in when computing GDP by the spending approach for two reasons. First, we included foreign goods in consumption and investment spending. For example, an imported Toyota purchased at a car dealer in the United States is included in consumption even though it is not produced in the United States. To measure what is produced in the United States, that Toyota must be deducted. Thus, imports must be subtracted to get a measure of total production in the economy. The second reason is that the exports that Americans sell abroad are produced in the United States, but they are not counted in consumption or investment or government purchases in the United States. Thus, exports need to be added in to get a measure of production. Because, by definition, net exports are exports minus imports, adding net exports to spending is the same as adding in exports and subtracting out imports. Adding net exports to total spending kills two birds with one stone.

In 2015, the United States imported more than it exported, so the sum of consumption plus investment plus government purchases overstated what was produced in America. The sum of these three items exceeds GDP, as shown in Figure 18.4. In other words, GDP was $522 billion less than the sum of consumption plus investment plus government purchases.

Algebraic Summary

The notion that we can measure production by adding up consumption, investment, government purchases, and net exports is important enough to herald with some algebra.

Let the symbol C stand for consumption, I for investment, G for government spending, and X for net exports. Let Y stand for GDP because we use G for government purchases. We will use these symbols many times again. The idea that production equals spending can then be written as

$$Y = C + I + G + X$$

This equation states, using algebraic symbols, that production, Y, equals spending: consumption, C, plus investment, I, plus government purchases, G, plus net exports, X (meaning exports minus imports). In 2015, the values of these items (in billions of dollars) were as follows:

$$18{,}036.6 = 12{,}283.7 + 3{,}056.6 + 3{,}218.3 + (-522.0)$$

This simple algebraic relationship plays a key role in later chapters.

1.3 The Income Approach

The income that people earn producing GDP in a country provides another measure of GDP. To see why, first consider a simple example of a single business firm.

Suppose you start a wedding planning business. Your production and sales of wedding planning services in your first year is $50,000; this is the amount you are paid in total by 50 people for the $1,000 service. To produce these services, you pay a catering consultant and a florist consultant $20,000 each, or a total of $40,000, which is your total cost. Your profits are defined as the difference between sales and costs, or $50,000 – $40,000 = $10,000. Now, if you add the total amount of income earned in the production of your wedding planning service—the amount earned by the two consultants plus the profits you earn—you get $20,000 + $20,000 + $10,000. This sum of incomes is exactly equal to $50,000, which is the same as the amount produced. Thus, by adding up the income of the people who produce the output of the firm, you get a measure of the output. The same idea is true for the country as a whole, which consists of many such businesses and workers.

TABLE 18.2 Aggregate Income and GDP in 2015 (billions of dollars)

Aggregate income	
Labor income (wages, salaries, fringe benefits)	$9,693.1
Capital income (profits, interest, rents)	4,648.6
Depreciation	2,830.8
Taxes, subsidies, and transfers	1,323.6
Net income of foreigners	-205.7
Statistical discrepancy	-253.8
Equals GDP	18,036.6

Source: U.S. Department of Commerce.

To show how this works, we look at each of the income items in Table 18.2. We first describe each of these items and then show that when we add the items up, we get GDP.

Labor Income

Economists classify wages, salaries, and fringe benefits paid to workers as **labor income**, or payments to people for their labor. *Wages* refers to payments to workers paid by the hour; *salaries* refers to payments to workers paid by the month or year; and *fringe benefits* refers to retirement, health, and other benefits paid by firms on behalf of workers. As shown in Table 18.2, labor income was $9,693.1 billion in 2015, around 54 percent of GDP.

labor income

The sum of wages, salaries, and fringe benefits paid to workers.

Capital Income

Economists classify profits, rental payments, and interest payments as **capital income**. *Profits* include the profits of large corporations like General Motors or Exxon and also the income of small businesses and farms. The royalties that an independent screenwriter receives from selling a movie script also are part of profits. *Rental payments* are income to persons who own buildings and rent them out. The rents they receive from their tenants are rental payments. *Interest payments* are income received from lending to business firms. Interest payments are included in capital income because they represent part of the income generated by the firms' production. Because many individuals pay interest (on mortgages, car loans, and so on) as well as receive interest (on deposits at a bank and so on), interest payments are defined as the difference between receipts and payments. Table 18.2 shows that capital income was $4,648.6 billion in 2015. Capital income was around 26 percent of GDP, about half of what labor income's share of GDP was.

capital income

The sum of profits, rental payments, and interest payments.

Depreciation

depreciation

The decrease in an asset's value over time; for capital, it is the amount by which physical capital wears out over a given period of time.

Depreciation is the amount by which factories and machines wear out each year. A remarkably large part of the investment that is part of GDP each year goes to replace worn-out factories and machines. Businesses need to replace depreciated equipment with investment in new equipment just to maintain productive capacity—the number of factories and machines available for use. In 2015, depreciation was $2,830.8 billion.

The difference between investment, the purchases of final goods by firms, and depreciation is called *net investment,* a measure of how much increase there has been in the stock of physical capital. Net investment was $225.8 billion ($3,056.6 billion – $2,830.8 billion) in 2015. This implies that even though firms in the U.S. economy spent over 3 trillion dollars in purchases of new goods and services in 2015, the stock of physical capital rose only by around 7 percent of that 3 trillion in new expenditures. The rest of the expenditures were filling in what was lost through the wear and tear of existing capital. Sometimes the $3,056.6 billion of new investment is called gross investment because it does not account for what is being lost from the existing stock of capital. The reason for the term *gross* in gross domestic product is that it includes gross investment, not just net investment.

When profits and the other parts of capital income are reported to government statisticians, depreciation has been subtracted out. But depreciation must be included as part of GDP because the new equipment that replaces old equipment must be produced by someone. Thus, when we use the income approach, it is necessary to add in depreciation if we are to have an accurate measure of GDP.

Taxes, Subsidies, and Transfers

When you buy a good, you often will pay a sales tax in addition to the price of the good; sales taxes are collected by businesses and sent directly to the government, either local, state, or federal. For example, the price of gasoline at the pump includes a tax that people who buy gasoline pay as part of the price and that the gasoline station sends to the government. When we tabulate total production by adding up the value of what people spend, we use the prices that businesses charge for a specific good—such as gasoline. That price includes the sales tax that is sent to the government. When we tabulate production by adding up income of consumers and profits of firms, however, the sales tax is not included in firms' profits. Thus, capital income does not include the sales taxes paid by businesses to the government. But those taxes are part of the income generated in producing GDP; the income happens to go to the government. We therefore must add such taxes to capital and labor income. Similarly, some subsidies from the government to firms are included in profits but do not represent income generated in producing GDP. Subsidies need to be subtracted. Similarly, transfer payments, which are payments between parties that do not involve goods or services being exchanged (for example, a charitable contribution to a museum by a corporation), also need to be removed from calculations because they do not represent income generated in producing GDP. Transfers and subsidies are considerably smaller in magnitude than taxes.

Net Income of Foreigners

Foreigners produce part of the GDP in the United States. Their income, however, is not included in labor income or capital income. For example, the salary of a Canadian hockey player who plays for the Pittsburgh Penguins and keeps his official residence as Canada would not be included in U.S. labor income. But that income represents payment for services produced in the United States and so is part of U.S. GDP. We must add such income payments to foreigners for production in the United States because that production is part of GDP. Moreover, some of the U.S. labor and capital income is earned producing GDP in other countries, and to get a measure of income generated in producing U.S. GDP, we must subtract that amount. For example, the salary of a U.S. baseball player who plays for the Toronto Blue Jays and keeps his official residence as the United States represents payment for services produced in Canada and so is not part of U.S. GDP. We must exclude such income payments for production in other countries. To account for both of these effects, we must add *net* income earned by foreigners in the United States—that is, the income earned by foreigners in the United States less what Americans earned abroad—to get GDP. [In 2015, Americans earned more abroad ($813.1 billion) than foreigners earned in the United States ($607.4 billion); hence, in 2010, *net* income of foreigners was –$205.7 billion, as shown in Table 18.2.]

Table 18.2 shows the effects of adding up these five items. The sum is close but not quite equal to GDP. The discrepancy reflects errors made in collecting data on income or spending. This discrepancy has a formal name: the *statistical discrepancy.* In percentage terms the amount is small, around 1 percent of GDP, considering the different ways the data on income and spending are collected. If we add in the statistical discrepancy, then we have a measure of *aggregate income* that equals GDP. From now on we can use the same symbol (Y) to refer to GDP and to aggregate income, because GDP and aggregate income amount to the same thing.

The circular flow diagram in Figure 18.5 illustrates the link between aggregate income and aggregate spending. People earn income from producing goods and services, and they spend this income (Y) to buy goods and services (C, I, G, and X).

1.4 The Production Approach

The third measure of GDP adds up the production of each firm or industry in the economy. To make this method work, we must avoid the "double counting" problem discussed earlier. For example, if you try to compute GDP by adding new automobiles to new steel to new tires, you will count the steel and the tires that go into producing the new automobiles twice. Thus, when we measure GDP by production, it is necessary to count only the **value added** by each manufacturer. Value added is the value of a firm's production less the value of the intermediate goods used in production. In other words, it is the value the firm adds to the intermediate inputs to get the final output. An automobile manufacturer buys steel, tires, and other inputs and adds value by assembling the car. When we measure GDP by production, we count only the value added at each level of production. Figure 18.6 shows how adding up the value added for each firm involved in producing a cup of espresso in the economy will automatically avoid double counting and give a measure of the final value of the cup of espresso when it is purchased at a coffeehouse or cafe. The same is true for the economy as a whole.

value added

The value of a firm's production minus the value of the intermediate goods used in production.

FIGURE 18.5 The Circular Flow of Income and Expenditure

This figure illustrates how aggregate expenditures equal aggregate income. Starting at the bottom right part of the figure, consumption (C) is joined by government purchases (G), investment (I), and net exports (X) to sum to aggregate expenditures ($C + I + G + X$) on the left. At the top of the figure, this aggregate spending is received by firms that produce the goods, and they pay out aggregate income (Y) to households in the form of wages and salaries as well as rents, interest, and profits. The government takes in taxes and makes transfer payments and government purchases.

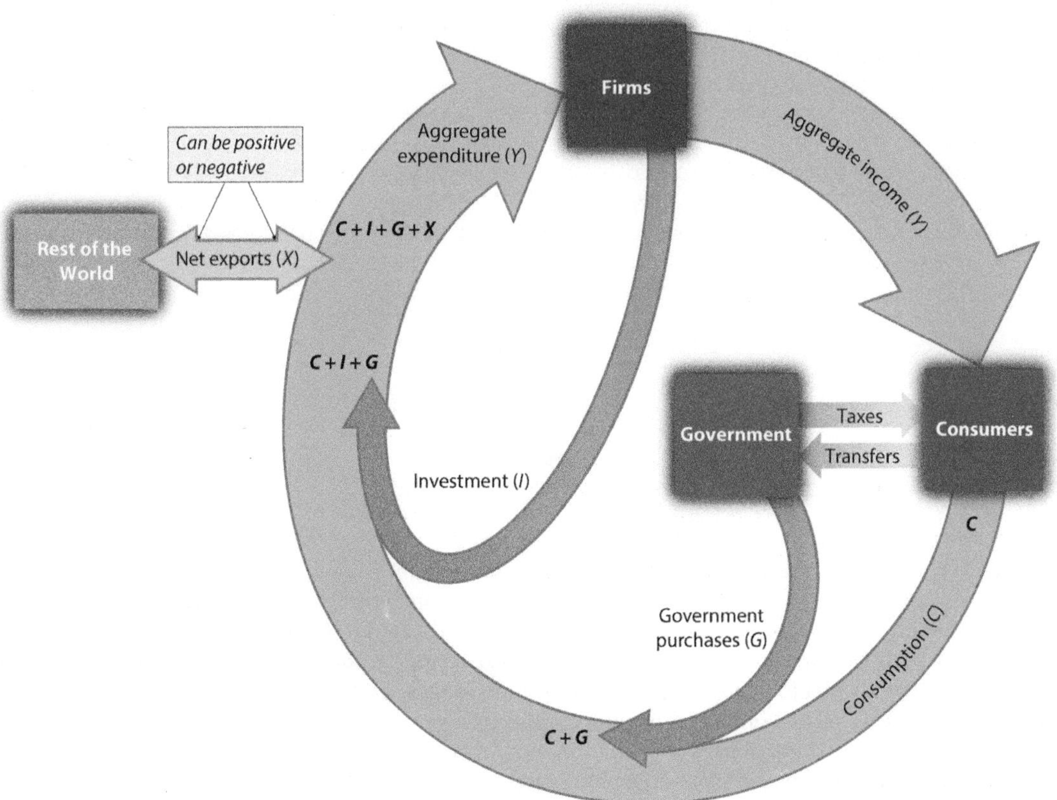

FIGURE 18.6 Value Added in Coffee: From Beans to Espresso

By adding up the value added at each stage of production, from coffee bean growing to espresso making, we get a measure of the value of a cup of espresso. Double counting is avoided. Using the same procedure for the whole economy permits us to compute GDP by adding up production.

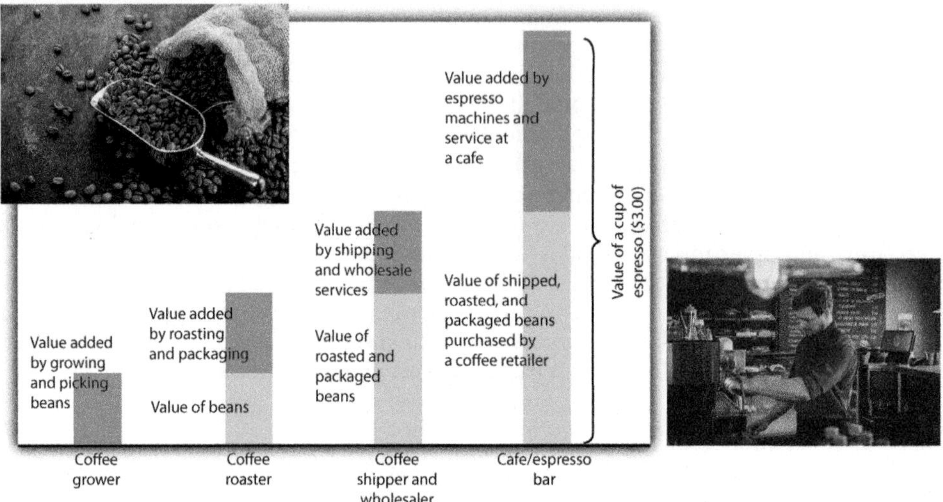

REVIEW

- GDP is a measure of all the goods and services newly produced in the economy during some period of time. GDP is a flow measure—how many new goods and services are being produced in the economy. It is not a stock measure—how many goods and services exist in the economy.
- GDP can be measured in three ways: by adding up all the spending in the economy, by adding up all the income in the economy, and by adding up all the production in the economy. All three give the same answer.
- Spending in the economy can be placed in one of four categories—consumption, investment, government purchases, and net exports.
- The sum of labor income; capital income; depreciation; taxes, subsidies, and transfers; and net income paid to foreigners gives another way to measure GDP.
- GDP also can be measured by adding up production, but with this method we must be careful not to double count. By adding up only the value added by each firm or industry, we automatically prevent double counting. Value added is the difference between a firm's sales and its payments for intermediate inputs to production.

2. SAVING

total amount of saving

A measure of the amount of resources that a country has for investment, either in its own country or abroad.

Another important macroeconomic measure is the total amount of saving undertaken by an economy. Investment and saving have an important symbiotic relationship. To see why this is, consider what would happen if you wanted to build a factory that makes shoes. To build the factory, you would have to either use your own (or a friend or family member's) saving or borrow money from a bank. But the money that a bank lends to you will be some other individual's saving. Therefore the **total amount of saving** is a measure of the amount of resources the country has available for investment, either in its own country or abroad. Similarly, the total amount of investment depends on how much saving is available from that country and from other countries.

Countries with a high level of saving have a greater ability to undertake investment projects than countries with a low level of saving. A country with a low level of saving, however, can increase investment if people and firms in other nations are willing to lend to or invest their own saving in that country. The U.S. economy in recent years has been able to sustain a high level of investment even when U.S. saving was low. In this section, we will define the concept of national saving and show how it is calculated.

2.1 Individual Saving

For an individual, saving is defined as income less taxes and consumption. If you earn $25,000 in income during the year and pay taxes of $5,000 while spending $18,000 on consumption—food, rent, and movies, for example—by definition, your saving for the year is $2,000 ($25,000 – $5,000 – $18,000). But if you instead spend $23,000 on food, rent, and movies for the year, then your saving is –$3,000; you will have to either take $3,000 out of the bank or borrow $3,000.

2.2 National Saving

For a country, saving is defined in a similar manner: by subtracting from a country's economy what is consumed. We subtract government purchases of goods and services in addition to consumer purchases. **National saving**, the sum of all saving in the economy, is defined as income less consumption and government purchases. That is,

national saving
Aggregate income minus consumption minus government purchases.

$$\text{National Saving} = \text{Income} - \text{Consumption} - \text{Government Purchases}$$

Using the symbol *S* for national saving and the symbols already introduced for income (*Y*), consumption (*C*), and government purchases (*G*), we define national saving as follows:

$$S = Y - C - G$$

Algebraic definition of national saving.

Using the numbers from Table 18.1, national saving in 2015 was $2,534.6 billion ($18,036.6 billion – $12,283.7 billion – $3,218.3 billion).

The major component of national saving is private saving: the sum of all savings by individuals in the economy. Some people save a lot, some do not save at all, and some are *dissaving*—that is, they have negative saving. For example, when people retire, they usually consume a lot more than their income—they are dissaving. When people are middle aged, their income is usually greater than their consumption—they are saving. Most young people either save very little or, if they are able to borrow, dissave. We define private saving using the symbol *T* for taxes, as follows:

$$\text{Private Saving} = Y - C - T$$

A country, however, also has a government, and so we need to include government saving in our calculation of national saving. What do we mean by saving by the government? The difference between the government's receipts from taxes and the government's expenditures, the budget balance, is called government saving. When the balance is positive, a budget surplus results—that is, the government is saving. When the balance is negative, a budget deficit results—that is, the government is dissaving. Algebraically, we define government saving as follows:

$$\text{Government Saving} = T - G$$

Combining private and government saving, we see that

$$\text{Private Saving} + \text{Government Saving} = (Y - C - T) + (T - G) = (Y - C - G)$$

$$\text{Private Saving} + \text{Government Saving} = \text{National Saving}$$

REVIEW

- National saving is an important macroeconomic variable because it is a measure of the resources that a country has available for investment, either in its own economy or abroad.
- A country with a high level of national saving can have a high level of investment if it desires. A country with a low level of national saving can have a high level of investment only if people in other countries are willing to lend their savings to or invest them in the low-saving country.
- National saving is defined as income minus consumption minus government purchases. It can be decomposed into the sum of private saving and government saving.
- Private saving equals income minus consumption minus taxes. Government saving is the difference between government tax receipts and government expenditures, also known as the budget balance.

3. MEASURING REAL GDP

Economists also are interested in assessing how the economy is changing over time. For example, they might want to know how rapidly the production of goods and services in India has grown over the last decade, and how that increase compares with the change in China's economy. However, the value of goods and services in an economy, as measured by GDP, is determined by both the quantity of goods and services produced and the price of these goods and services. Thus, an increase in the prices of all goods and services will make measured GDP grow, even if the amount of production in the economy does not increase.

Suppose, for example, that the prices of all goods in the economy double and that the number of items produced of every good remains the same. The dollar value of these items then will double even though physical production does not change. A $10,000 car will become a $20,000 car, a $10 book will become a $20 book, and so on. Thus, GDP will double as well. Clearly, GDP is not useful for comparing production at different dates when all prices increase. Although the example of doubling all prices is extreme, we do know from Chapter 17 that prices on the average tend to rise over time—a tendency that we have called inflation. Thus, when inflation exists, GDP becomes an unreliable measure of the changes in production over time.

3.1 Adjusting GDP for Inflation

real GDP

A measure of the value of all the goods and services newly produced in a country during some period of time, adjusted for changes in prices over time.

nominal GDP

Gross domestic product without any correction for inflation; the same as GDP; the value of all the goods and services newly produced in a country during some period of time, usually a year.

Real GDP is a measure of production that corrects for inflation. To emphasize the difference between GDP and real GDP, we will use the term **nominal GDP** to refer to what previously has been defined as GDP.

Calculating Real GDP Growth

To see how real GDP is calculated, consider an example. Suppose that total production consists entirely of the production of books and smoothies and that we want to compare total production in two different years: 2014 and 2015.

	2014		2015	
	Price	*Quantity*	*Price*	*Quantity*
Books	$15	1,000	$20	1,200
Smoothies	$10	2,000	$15	2,200

Notice that the number of books produced increases by 20 percent and the number of smoothies produced increases by 10 percent from 2014 to 2015. Notice also that the price of books is greater than the price of smoothies, but both increase between the two years. Nominal GDP is equal to the dollar amount spent on books plus the dollar amount spent on smoothies, which is $35,000 in 2014 and $57,000 in 2015, a substantial 63 percent increase.

$$\text{Nominal GDP in 2014} = \$15 \times 1000 + \$10 \times 2000 = \$35{,}000$$
$$\text{Nominal GDP in 2015} = \$20 \times 1200 + \$15 \times 2200 = \$57{,}000$$

Clearly, nominal GDP is not a good measure of the increase in production: Nominal GDP increases by 63 percent, a much greater increase than the increase in either the production of books (20 percent) or the production of smoothies (10 percent). Thus, failing to correct for changes in the price of a good gives a misleading estimate.

To calculate real GDP, we must use the *same* price for both years. That is, the number of books and smoothies produced in the two years must be evaluated at the same prices. For example, production could be calculated in both years using 2014 prices. That is,

$$\text{Using 2014 prices, production in 2014} = \$\,15 \times 1000 + \$\,10 \times 2000 = \$\,35{,}000$$
$$\text{Using 2014 prices, production in 2015} = \$\,15 \times 1200 + \$\,10 \times 2200 = \$\,40{,}000$$

Keeping prices constant at 2014 levels, we see that the increase in production is from $35,000 in 2014 to $40,000 in 2015, an increase of 14.3 percent.

Production, however, also can be calculated in both years using 2015 prices. That is,

Using 2015 prices, production in 2014 = $ 20 × 1000 + $ 15 × 2000 = $ 50,000
Using 2015 prices, production in 2015 = $ 20 × 1200 + $ 15 × 2200 = $ 57,000

Keeping prices constant at 2015 levels, we see that the increase in production is from $50,000 in 2014 to $57,000 in 2015, an increase of 14.0 percent.

Observe that the percentage increase in production varies (14.3 percent versus 14 percent) depending on whether 2014 or 2015 prices are used. Such differences are inevitable, because we have no reason to prefer the prices in one year to those of another year when controlling for inflation. Economists arrive at a single percentage by simply *averaging* the two percentages.[1] In this example, they would conclude that the *increase in real GDP from 2014 to 2015 is 14.15 percent,* the average of 14.3 percent and 14 percent.

This 14.15 percent increase in real GDP is much lower than the 63 percent increase in nominal GDP and much closer to the actual increase in the number of books and smoothies produced. By adjusting for inflation in this way, real GDP gives a better picture of the increase in actual production in the economy.

A Year-to-Year Chain

This example shows how the growth rate of real GDP between the two years 2014 and 2015 is calculated in the case of two goods. The same approach is used for any other two years and more than two goods. To correct for inflation across more than two years, economists simply do a series of these two-year corrections and then "chain" them together. Each year is a link in the chain. For example, if the growth rate from 2013 to 2014 was 12.15 percent, then chaining this together with the 14.15 percent from 2014 to 2015 would imply an average annual growth rate of 13.15 percent for the two years from 2013 to 2015. That is,

Observe that 12.15 percent and 14.15 percent are chained together to get a 13.15 percent average for two years.

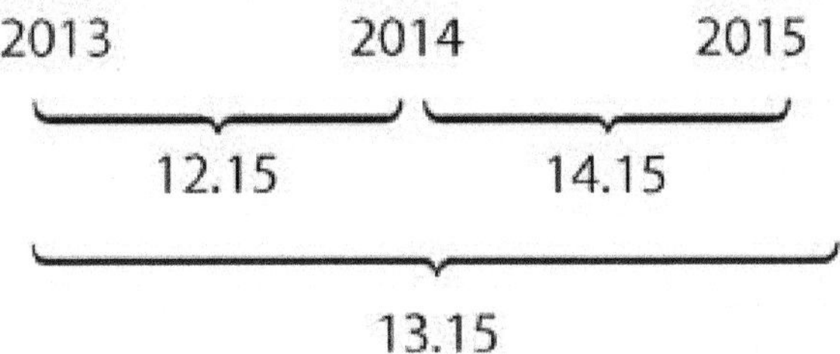

By chaining other years together, link by link, the chain can be made as long as we want.

Obtaining the Values of Real GDP

To obtain real GDP in any one year, we start with a *base year* and then use the growth rates to compute GDP in another year. The base year is a year in which real GDP is equal to nominal GDP because GDP is valued using that year's price. Currently, 2009 is the base year for government statistical calculations of GDP in the United States. Thus, real GDP in 2009 and nominal GDP in 2009 are the same: $14,418.7 billion.

To get real GDP in other years, economists start with the base year and use the real GDP growth rates to find GDP in any other year. Consider 2010. The growth rate of real GDP in 2010—calculated using the methods just described for the entire economy—was 3.78 percent. Thus, real GDP in 2010 was $14,964.4 billion, or 3.78 percent greater than $14,418.7 billion. The $14,964.4 billion is 2010 real GDP measured in 2009 dollars. To emphasize that this number is calculated by chaining years together with growth rates, government statisticians say that real GDP is measured in "chained 2009 dollars."

Real GDP versus Nominal GDP over Time

Figure 18.7 compares real and nominal GDP from 1990 to 2010. Observe that for the 2009 base year, real GDP and nominal GDP are equal. However, by 2015, nominal GDP had reached about $18 trillion, whereas real GDP was at $16.4 trillion. Thus, just as in the example, real GDP increased less than nominal GDP. For the years prior to 2009, real GDP is more than nominal GDP because 2009 prices were higher than prices in earlier years. From Figure 18.7 we can see that nominal GDP would give a misleading picture of the U.S. economy.

FIGURE 18.7 **Real GDP versus Nominal GDP**

Real GDP increases less than nominal GDP because real GDP takes out the effect of rising prices. The chart shows that for the 2009 base year, real GDP and nominal GDP are equal. Nominal GDP is below real GDP in earlier years because prices were generally lower before 2009.

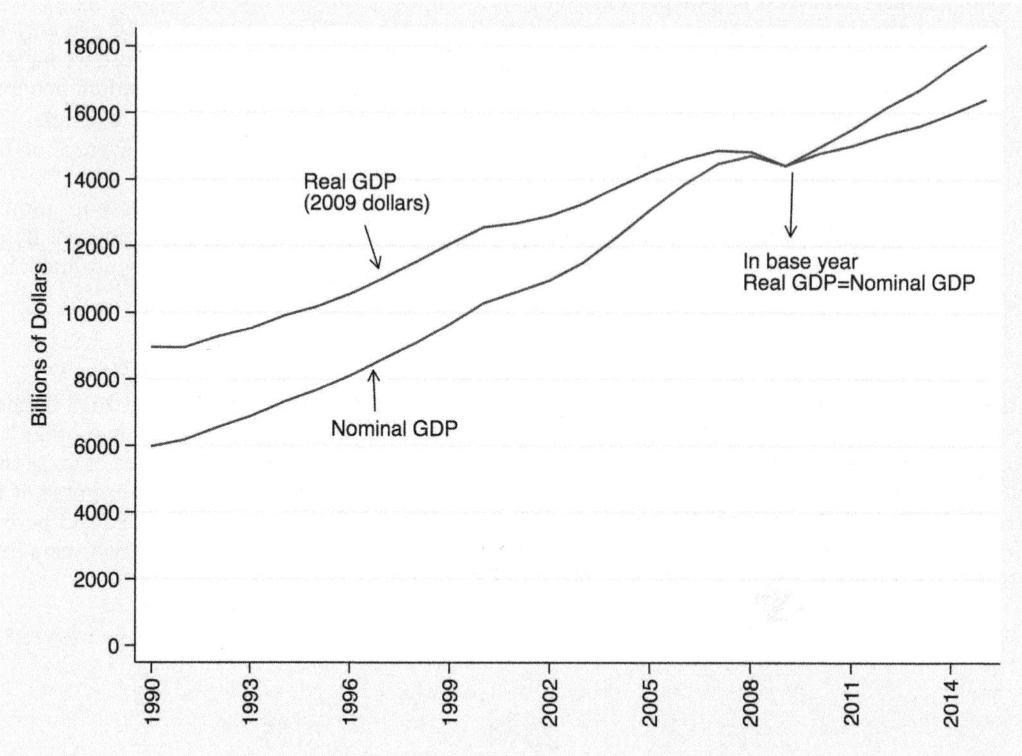

3.2 The GDP Deflator

Nominal GDP grows faster than real GDP because of inflation. The greater the difference between nominal GDP growth and real GDP growth, the greater the rate of inflation. In the case of deflation, with prices falling, nominal GDP would increase less than real GDP. Hence, a by-product of computing real GDP is a measure of the rate of inflation.

More precisely, if we divide nominal GDP by real GDP, we get the **GDP deflator**, a measure of the **price level**, which is the level of all the prices of the items in real GDP. That is,

GDP deflator

Nominal GDP divided by real GDP; it measures the level of prices of goods and services included in real GDP relative to a given base year.

price level

The average level of prices in the economy.

$$\text{GDP Deflator} = \frac{\text{Nominal GDP}}{\text{Real GDP}}$$

Here the GDP deflator is defined so that its value in the base year, such as 2005, is 1.00. (Sometimes it is scaled to equal 100 in the base year by multiplying by 100.)

The reason for the term *deflator* is that to get real GDP, we can deflate nominal GDP by dividing it by the GDP deflator. That is,

$$\text{Real GDP} = \frac{\text{Nominal GDP}}{\text{GDP Deflator}}$$

The percentage change in the GDP deflator from one year to the next is a measure of the rate of inflation.

3.3 Alternative Inflation Measures

The percentage change in the GDP deflator is not the most widely used measure of inflation. A much more frequently cited measure of inflation is based on the percentage change in the **consumer price index (CPI)**, which is the price of a fixed collection—a "market basket"—of consumer goods and services in a given year divided by the price of the same collection in some base year. For example, if the market basket consists of one book and two smoothies, then the CPI for 2015 compared with the base year 2014 in the previous example would be

consumer price index (CPI)
A price index equivalent that calculates current price of a fixed market basket of consumer goods and services relative to a base year.

$$\frac{(\$\,20 \times 1 + \$\,15 \times 2)}{(\$\,15 \times 1 + \$\,10 \times 2)} = \frac{\$\,50}{\$\,35} = 1.43$$

The CPI inflation rate is the percent change in the CPI; it measures how fast the prices of the items in the basket increase. What are the differences between inflation measured using the CPI and inflation measured using the GDP deflator? The first difference is that the GDP deflator is measuring the price level of all domestically produced goods and services. This includes goods that affect the day-to-day life of consumers, such as the price of milk, the price of orange juice, and the cost of airplane tickets, but it also includes goods that individuals never purchase directly, such as the price of heavy machinery and the price of truck engines. Thus the CPI, as its name suggests, may be a more relevant measure of the price level that consumers care about.

The second difference is that CPI measures the price of a fixed collection of goods and services—the price of the basket—whereas the goods and services that make up GDP, and hence are measured by the GDP deflator, change from year to year. The use of a fixed collection of goods and services in the CPI is one of the reasons economists think the CPI overstates inflation. When the price of goods rises, the quantity demanded should decline; when the price falls, the quantity demanded should rise. Thus, by not allowing the quantities to change when the price changes, the CPI puts too much weight on items with rising prices and too little weight on items with declining prices. The result is an overstatement of inflation; in other words, by assuming that people buy no less of the goods and services that have increased in price and buy no more of the goods and services that have decreased in price, the CPI tends to indicate that prices have gone up by more than they really have. During the 1990s, a group of economists appointed by the U.S. Senate and chaired by Michael Boskin of Stanford University found that the government, by adjusting expenditures according to this overstated CPI, was spending billions of dollars more than it would with a correct CPI. Hence, getting the economic statistics right makes a big difference.

The third difference between the CPI and the GDP deflator is that the CPI market basket can include goods and services that are produced in other countries, whereas the GDP deflator, by definition, will measure the price of domestically produced goods and services. In countries where imported goods lack good domestic substitutes, inflation measured using the CPI may be a better measure of the difficulties that both people and businesses in the economy face.

Figure 18.8 shows how measures of inflation using the GDP deflator and the CPI compare. The general inflation movements are similar, but the CPI is more volatile. The GDP deflator and the CPI each have strengths and weaknesses relative to the other. So you should think of them as alternative ways of measuring price levels and inflation rates, rather than as competing measurements.

Yet another measure of inflation is the producer price index (PPI), which measures the prices of raw materials and intermediate goods as well as the prices of final goods sold by producers. Prices of raw materials—oil, wheat, and copper—sometimes are watched carefully because they give early warning signs of increases in inflation.

FIGURE 18.8 **Comparison of Measures of Inflation**

Measuring inflation with either the CPI or the GDP deflator shows the rise in inflation in the 1960s and 1970s and the lower inflation in the 1980s and 1990s. The CPI is more volatile: It bounces around more. (The inflation rate is based on yearly percent changes in the stated variable.)

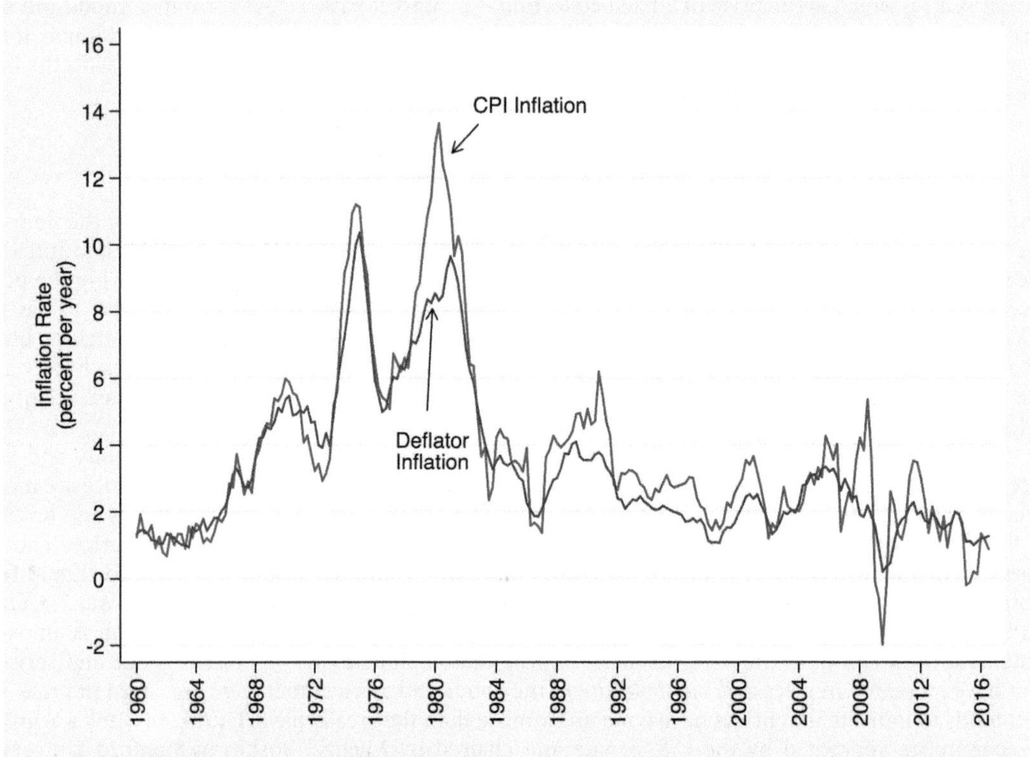

REVIEW

- Nominal GDP changes when either the quantity of Nominal GDP changes, check the quantity of goods and services changes, or the prices of those goods and services changes. Therefore the change in nominal GDP is not a good measure of how the physical amount of production in the economy is changing over time.
- Economists use real GDP when they want to compare production over time. Real GDP corrects nominal GDP for inflation by measuring the production of goods and services in the dollars of a given base year, such as 2005.
- The GDP deflator is a measure of the price level in the economy. It is defined as the ratio of nominal GDP to real GDP. The percentage change in the GDP deflator from year to year is a measure of the inflation rate.
- The CPI is the most widely used measure of the price level in the economy. It is defined as the price of a representative market basket of goods and services, relative to the price of that basket in a base year. The percentage change in the CPI from year to year is the most widely used measure of the inflation rate.
- Some important differences exist between the CPI and the GDP deflator. Each has strengths and weaknesses compared with the other. You should think of them as alternative ways of measuring price levels and inflation rates.

4. SHORTCOMINGS OF THE GDP MEASURE

Although nominal GDP is the best measure of overall production that we have, it is deficient in several ways. You need to understand what these limitations are, so that you can make informed judgments about what is really happening in the economy. Nominal GDP has three main types of limitations: (1) revisions to GDP can change the assessment of the economy; (2) some types of production are omitted from GDP; and (3) the production of goods and services is only part of what affects the quality of life. When you compare two countries, the one with a higher level of GDP is not necessarily better off than the one with a lower level of GDP.

4.1 Revisions to GDP

Government statisticians obtain data on GDP from surveys of stores and businesses, and even from income tax data from the Internal Revenue Service. Not all of these data are collected quickly. Data on sales at stores and large firms come in within a month; however, data on exports and imports take several months. Some income tax data are reported only once a year. Information about small firms comes in even more slowly.

For this reason, the statistics on GDP frequently are revised as new data come in. For those who use the GDP data to make decisions, either in business or in government, faulty data on GDP, which are apparent only when the data are revised, can lead to mistakes. Revisions of GDP are inevitable and occur in all countries. These revisions can be quite large in magnitude. For example, in January 2006, the first estimate for GDP for the fourth quarter of 2005 was given as $12.735 trillion. In March 2006, the "final revision" of that number was given as $12.766 trillion, a difference of around $30 billion.

4.2 Omissions from GDP

Given the description of how GDP is calculated, you will hardly be surprised to hear that production that does not occur in a formal market is difficult for government statisticians to measure. Examples include work done in the home and illegal commerce. The other principal difficulty in calculating GDP is how to deal with quality improvements in goods. Both of these problems are explained in more detail.

Home Work and Production

Much of the production that people do at home—making dinner or a sweater, changing the car oil or a baby's diapers, cutting the grass or the kids' hair—is productive activity, but it is not included in GDP because the transactions are not recorded in the markets in which statisticians measure spending. Such production would be included in GDP if people hired and paid someone else to do any of these things. So if you look after your young siblings after school while your parents are at work, that typically will not count toward GDP, whereas if your parents were to take your siblings to a day-care center and pay for child-care services, that would count toward GDP. Some home production is included in GDP. If you run a mail order or telemarketing business out of your home and pay taxes on your income, for example, then this production likely will be counted in GDP.

Leisure Activity

Much leisure activity is not included in GDP even though it may be enjoyable. Going to the beach or hiking in the mountains more often and working less might be something you decide to do as your income increases. If people start taking Friday afternoons off, GDP will go down, but the level of well-being may increase. The consumption of leisure is omitted from GDP unless it involves a purchase in the market, such as a ticket to a movie or a ballgame.

The Underground Economy

A large amount of production is not counted in GDP because it is purposely hidden from the view of the government. Illegal activity—growing marijuana in the California coastal range, selling pharmaceuticals not yet approved by the Food and Drug Administration—is excluded from GDP because no one wants to report this activity to the government. People who get cash payments—perhaps in the form of tips at hotels or restaurants, or babysitting money from a neighbor—may not report this income, perhaps to avoid taxes, and thus it also is not counted. If people do not report interest on a loan to a friend or relative, this, too, is omitted from GDP.

The sum of all the missing items is referred to as the *underground economy*. Estimates of the size of the underground economy are understandably uncertain. They range from about 10 percent of GDP in the United States to about 25 percent in Italy to more than 40 percent in Peru.

The underground economy makes GDP a less useful measure of the size of an economy, and we should be aware of this fact when we use GDP. But the underground economy does not render GDP useless. It is unlikely that the underground economy grows much more or much less rapidly than the rest of the economy. Changes in laws can increase or decrease the incentives to produce outside the legal market economy, but these changes are unlikely to be large enough to affect the estimated growth rates of GDP by much.

Quality Improvements

Our measure of GDP sometimes misses improvements in the quality of goods and services. For example, a $1,000 notebook computer purchased in 2015 may be of substantially better quality than a

$2,000 notebook computer purchased in 2010. So the price of the notebook computer not only has fallen by 50 percent, but in fact the quality-adjusted price also has fallen by even more. Government statisticians, especially in industrial countries like the United States, have developed sophisticated techniques to measure the quality-adjusted price change of a good accurately. These techniques, however, do not always work perfectly, especially when the improvements are in hard-to-measure attributes. So, for example, the government statisticians can look at the amount of memory, the speed of the processor, and the storage capacity of the hard drive to gauge how much the quality of the notebook computer has improved; however, they may not be able to gauge as effectively the quality improvements that make a new model car more comfortable and better able to absorb shocks than the old model.

4.3 Other Measures of Well-Being

Even if real GDP did include the underground economy and all the improvements in goods and services, it would not serve as the only measure of well-being. The well-being of an individual has many other important aspects, including, for example, a long and healthy life expectancy; a clean environment; and a small chance of war, crime, or the death of a child. The production of goods and services in a country can affect these other things, and indeed be affected by them, but it is not a measure of them.

Consider what has happened to some other measures of well-being as real GDP per capita has grown. Life expectancy in the United States has increased from about 69 years in the 1950s to 78 years in 2004. This compares with a life expectancy of only 47 years in the early part of the last century. Infant mortality also has declined, from about 26 infant deaths per 1,000 live births in the mid-1950s to 6.9 in 2000. In the early part of the twentieth century, infant mortality in the United States was 10 deaths for every 100 live births. The fraction of women who die in childbirth also has declined. So by some of these important measures, the quality of life has improved along with real GDP per capita.

But serious problems and room for gains still remain; as death rates from car accidents, heart disease, and stroke have decreased, death rates among young people from AIDS, suicide, and murder have been rising. Also of serious concern is the increasing percentage of children who live in poverty. Thus, the impressive gain in real GDP per capita has been correlated with both gains and losses in other measures of well-being.

A clean and safe environment is also a factor in the quality of life. But GDP itself does not provide an indication of whether pollution or many of the other measures of the quality of life are improving or getting worse. If a factory produces a lot of output while also putting out a considerable amount of airborne and waterborne pollutants, its production of goods is all that counts toward GDP. No mechanism is being used to subtract the damage to the environment.

REVIEW

- Real GDP per capita is not without its shortcomings as an indicator of well-being in a society. Certain items are omitted—home production, leisure, the underground economy, and some quality improvements.
- Other indicators of the quality of life, including vital statistics on mortality and the environment, can be affected by GDP per capita, but these indicators are conceptually distinct and independently useful.

5. END-OF-CHAPTER MATERIAL

5.1 Conclusion

In this chapter, we have shown how to measure the size of an economy in terms of its GDP. In the process, we have explained that income, spending, and production in a country are all equal and that GDP can be adjusted to make comparisons over time.

It is important to recall that aggregate income (or production or spending), the subject of our study, tells us much about the quality of life of the people in a country, but it does not tell us everything. As the economist-philosopher John Stuart Mill said in his *Principles of Political Economy,* first published in 1848: "All know that it is one thing to be rich, another to be enlightened, brave or humane ... those things, indeed, are all indirectly connected, and react upon one another."[2]

Key Points

1. Gross domestic product (GDP), also known as nominal GDP, is the total production of new goods and services in an economy during a particular period.
2. GDP can be measured in three ways: by adding all spending on new goods and services in the economy, by adding all income earned in the domestic economy, and by adding all the value of goods and services produced in the economy.
3. The spending method of calculating GDP requires adding up expenditures on consumption goods, investment goods (machines, factories, housing, and inventories), government purchases, and net exports (exports–imports).
4. In the income method, GDP is calculated by adding labor income; capital income; depreciation; taxes, subsidies, and transfers; and net income of foreigners. Except for a small statistical discrepancy, the income approach gives us the same answer as the spending approach.
5. Value added is used to calculate GDP under the production method. Value added is defined as the difference between the value of the production sold and the cost of inputs to production.
6. Real GDP is a measure of production adjusted for inflation. It is the best overall measure of changes in the production of goods and services over time.
7. The GDP deflator, or the ratio of nominal GDP to real GDP, is a measure of the price level in the economy. The percentage change in the GDP deflator is a measure of inflation.
8. An alternative measure of the price level is the consumer price index (CPI), which is a measure of the price of a basket of representative goods and services in a particular year relative to the price of that basket in a base year. The change in the CPI is an alternative measure of inflation in the economy.
9. National saving is defined as income less consumption less government purchases. Countries that have a high level of national saving have more resources to use for investment in their own economy or abroad. Countries with low levels of national saving need other countries to be willing to lend to or invest their savings in those countries if they are to sustain high levels of investment.
10. GDP is not without its shortcomings. It does not include production in the underground economy or much work done in the home. And it is only one of many measures of well-being.

QUESTIONS FOR REVIEW

1. Why do we add up total spending to compute GDP when GDP is supposed to be a measure of production?
2. Approximately what are the percentages of consumption, investment, government purchases, and net exports in GDP in the United States?
3. What is the significance of value added, and how does one measure it for a single item?
4. Why is the sum of all income equal to GDP?
5. Why is the purchase of a used car not included in GDP? Should it be?
6. Why do we add inventory investment to spending when computing GDP?
7. Why are increases in nominal GDP not a good measure of economic growth?
8. What is national saving?
9. Why does national saving equal the sum of private and government saving?
10. Why is the production of meals in the home not included in GDP? Should it be?

PROBLEMS

1. Determine whether each of the following would be included in GDP, and explain why or why not.
   a. You buy a used CD from a friend.
   b. You purchase a song from an online music provider like iTunes.
   c. You cook a romantic dinner for two on Valentine's Day.
   d. You buy a nice bottle of French wine to serve with dinner.
   e. You take your mom out to brunch on Mother's Day.
   f. The restaurant where you intend to go for brunch purchases strawberries, which it intends to serve at the brunch, from a local vendor.
2. Determine whether each of the following is consumption, investment, or neither. Explain your answer.
   a. A landscaping company buys a new four-wheel-drive vehicle to carry fertilizer and flowers.
   b. A doctor buys a new four-wheel-drive vehicle to use on vacation.
   c. A family puts a new kitchen in their house.
   d. The campus bookstore increases its inventory of textbooks.
   e. Your parents purchase their dream home, newly built to their specification by a local contractor.
   f. Your parents buy a vacation home from a friend who had owned that home for years.
3. A phenomenon of the twentieth-century U.S. economy was the replacement of home production by production purchased through markets.
   a. Give an example of a food item that was widely produced by family members in 1915 and that was widely purchased from businesses by 2015.
   b. Give an example of a clothing item that was widely produced by family members in 1915 and that was widely purchased from businesses by 2015.
   c. Give an example of a service that was widely produced by family members in 1915 and that was widely purchased from businesses by 2015.
   d. How does the replacement of home production with production purchased through markets affect real GDP? How does it affect the usefulness of comparisons of real GDP per capita today with the same measure a hundred years ago?
   e. The economies of some countries in the twenty-first century are more similar to the U.S. economy in 1915 than they are to the U.S. economy in 2015. How useful are comparisons between real GDP in the United States and in these economies?
4. Recognizing that both positive and negative effects may occur, how will GDP be affected by
   a. The legalization of drugs
   b. A law making the standard workweek 35 hours
   c. The replacement of checks by online banking
   d. A program granting legal status to previously undocumented immigrants working in the United States

5. Suppose the economy has only the following three goods:

Year	Good	Price	Quantity
2014	Ice cream cones	$2.50	1,000
	Hot dogs	$1.25	500
	Surfboards	$100.00	10
2015	Ice cream cones	$3.50	800
	Hot dogs	$2.25	400
	Surfboards	$100.00	14

a. Calculate nominal GDP for 2014 and 2015.
b. Calculate the percentage change in GDP from 2014 to 2015, first using 2014 prices and then using 2015 prices.
c. Calculate the percentage change in real GDP from 2014 to 2015, using your answers from part (b).
d. What is the GDP deflator for 2015 if it equals 1.0 in 2014?

6. Given the information in the following table for three consecutive years in the U.S. economy, calculate the missing data.

Year	Nominal GDP (in billions of U.S. dollars)	Real GDP (in billions of 2005 dollars)	GDP Deflator (2005=100)	Inflation (percent change in GDP deflator)	Real GDP per Capita (in 2005 dollars)	Population (in millions)
2005	12,623		100.0	3.3		297.4
2006		12,959		3.2		300.3
2007			106.2		45,542	303.3

7. Look at two scenarios, details of which are provided below, for monthly inventories and sales for a company producing cereal. In both scenarios, the company's sales are the same.
a. Calculate the inventory investment during each month and the resulting stock of inventory at the beginning of the following month for both scenarios.
b. Does maintaining constant production lead to greater or lesser fluctuations in the stock of inventory? Explain.

Scenario A				
Month	Start-of-the-Month Inventory Stock	Production	Sales	Inventory Investment
Jan.	50	50	45	
Feb.		50	55	
Mar.		50	80	
Apr.		50	50	
May		50	40	

Scenario B				
Month	Start-of-the-Month Inventory Stock	Production	Sales	Inventory Investment
Jan.	50	45	45	
Feb.		55	55	
Mar.		80	80	
Apr.		50	50	
May		40	40	

8. Suppose General Motors buys $50 million worth of tires from Goodyear in November of 2014 for use in its Chevrolet line of cars. Of these tires, $20 million are put into cars that are sold to consumers in December of 2014, and $10 million are put into cars that are produced in December but will not be sold to consumers until February of 2015. The remaining $20 million will be put into cars manufactured and sold in 2015. Describe how each of these tire-related transactions enters into inventory investment calculations in 2014 and 2015.
9. Use the following data for a South Dakota wheat farm.

Revenue	$1,000
Costs	
Wages and salaries	$700
Rent on land	$50
Rental fee for tractor	$100
Seed, fertilizer	$100
Pesticides, irrigation	$50

   a. Calculate the value added by this farm.
   b. Profits are revenue minus costs. Capital income consists of profits, rents, and interest. Show that value added equals capital income plus labor income paid by the farm.
   c. Suppose that, because of flooding in Kansas, wheat prices increase suddenly and revenues rise to $1,100, but the prices of intermediate inputs do not change. What happens to value added and profits in this case?
10. Suppose the data in the following table describe the economic activity in a country. Given these data, calculate the following:
   a. Inventory investment
   b. Net exports
   c. Gross domestic product
   d. Statistical discrepancy
   e. National saving

   Verify that national saving equals investment plus net exports.

Components of Spending	Value (billions of dollars)
Consumption	$140
Business fixed and residential investment	$27
Inventory stock at the end of prior year	$10
Inventory stock at the end of current year	$5
Depreciation	$12
Government outlays	$80
Government purchases	$65
Exports	$21
Imports	$17
Labor income	$126
Capital income	$70
Net income of foreigners	$5
Taxes, subsidies, and transfers	$28

ENDNOTES

1. A "geometric" average is used. The geometric average of two numbers is the square root of the product of the two numbers.
2. John Stuart Mill, *Principles of Political Economy* (New York: Bookseller, 1965), pp. 1–2.

CHAPTER 19

The Spending Allocation Model

George Osborne, Former Chancellor of the Exchequer

Source: Twocoms / Shutterstock.com

On June 23, 2016 voters in the United Kingdom surprised observers all over the world when a majority of them voted for the U.K. to leave the European Union. The economic ramifications of this decision were hotly debated but the immediate political ramifications were clear. Prime Minister David Cameron resigned, and was replaced by Theresa May as the leader of the Conservative Party. Soon after taking office, Prime Minister May announced that she was replacing George Osborne the chancellor of the exchequer (the British equivalent of the secretary of treasury) bringing a sudden, and unexpected end to Mr. Osborne's five year stint as the chancellor. The new chancellor, Phillip Hammond, announced that he was ending Mr. Osborne's signature economic program, one that had deeply divided expert opinion in the United Kingdom during Mr. Osborne's tenure.

When he was first appointed as chancellor, Mr. Osborne was not even forty years old, the youngest man to hold that office since the early twentieth century. Mr. Osborne immediately captured everyone's attention with his first budget, which proposed a drastic series of cuts to government expenditures and increases to taxes to reduce the United Kingdom's budget deficit. In his speech to the House of Commons, Mr. Osborne said,

> *This Budget is needed to deal with our country's debts. This Budget is needed to give confidence to our economy. This is the unavoidable Budget. I am not going to hide hard choices from the British people or bury them in the small print of the Budget documents. You're going to hear them straight from me, here in this speech. Our policy is to raise from the ruins of an economy built on debt a new, balanced economy where we save, invest and export. An economy where the state does not take almost half of all our national income, crowding out private endeavour. An economy not overly reliant on the success of one industry, financial services—important as they are—but where all industries grow. An economy where prosperity is shared among all sections of society and all parts of the country.*

The vision of the British economy that Mr. Osborne laid out was one where increases in government spending and higher budget deficits would result in less investment and less accumulation of capital in the economy. By cutting government spending and raising taxes, the government would have more fiscal resources coming in and less going out, enabling it to borrow less, which in turn would allow private investors to invest and help grow the economy. In this section, we develop an economic model that will help you better understand how lowering budget deficits and decreasing the share of government purchases in gross domestic product (GDP) would result in lower interest rates, and, in turn, how lower interest rates would raise the share of investment in GDP.

The model we develop is called the *spending allocation model* because of its use in determining how GDP is allocated among the major components of spending: consumption, investment, government purchases, and net exports. Because each share of spending must compete for the scarce resources in GDP, an increase in the share of one of the components will lead to a reduction in the share of another component. Our model shows that real interest rates are a key factor that both influences and is influenced by spending. By explaining how real interest rates are determined in the long run, our model helps us predict how much of GDP in the long run goes to each of the four components.

The spending allocation model has some useful applications. You can use it to understand why the aging of the population of the United States, coupled with the increases in spending that will be required for programs like Medicare and Social Security, poses a threat to U.S. citizens. The increased costs of these programs makes it difficult to invest and grow in the decades ahead.

As you study the spending allocation model, it is imperative that you keep in mind that this model applies more to the long run than to the short run. Therefore, it is most useful in thinking about economic developments that occur over a period of years instead of months. For example, Mr. Osborne kept announcing that the target for seeing the benefit of his reforms was the 2020s, almost a decade after the program began. In the end that long-horizon may have been responsible for Mr. Osborne's departure. Dealing with the immediate aftermath of the events of "Brexit" had taken precedence over the long-run plan. As Mr. Hammond said, announcing the end of Mr. Osborne's program, "But when times change, we must change with them"

1. THE SPENDING SHARES

We know that GDP is divided into four components: consumption, investment, government purchases, and net exports. Symbolically,

$$Y = C + I + G + X$$

where Y equals GDP, C equals consumption, I equals investment, G equals government purchases, and X equals net exports. This equation is the starting point for determining how large a share of GDP is allocated to each spending component.

1.1 Defining the Spending Shares

We define the spending shares by looking at how GDP is allocated among its various components. The **consumption share** of GDP is the proportion of GDP that is used for consumption. The consumption share of GDP is defined as consumption (C) divided by GDP, or C/Y. For example, if C= $6 trillion and Y= $10 trillion, then the consumption share is C/Y= 0.6, or 60 percent. We can define the other shares of GDP analogously: I/Y is the **investment share**, X/Y is the **net exports share**, and G/Y is the **government purchases share**. Sometimes the investment share is called the *investment rate*.

We can establish a simple relationship between the shares of spending in GDP by taking the equation $Y = C + I + G + X$ and dividing both sides by Y. This simple division gives us a relationship that says that the sum of the shares of spending in GDP must equal one. Writing that algebraically yields the following:

$$1 = \frac{C}{Y} + \frac{I}{Y} + \frac{G}{Y} + \frac{X}{Y}$$

If we use the shares that existed in 2015 (see Table 18.1 in Chapter 18), we get

$$\begin{aligned} 1 &= \frac{12{,}284}{18{,}037} + \frac{3{,}057}{18{,}037} + \frac{3{,}218}{18{,}037} + \frac{-522}{18{,}037} \\ &= 0.6810 + 0.1695 + 0.1784 + (-0.0289) \end{aligned}$$

In other words, consumption accounted for around 68.1 percent of GDP, investment for around 16.9 percent of GDP, government purchases for around 17.8 percent of GDP, and net exports, in deficit at negative $522 billion, for negative 2.9 percent of GDP. The negative share for net exports occurs because Americans imported more than they exported in 2015. In this example, the sum of the four shares on the right equals one, or, in percentage terms, 100 percent. And, of course, this must be true for any year.

Figure 19.1 shows the four shares of spending in GDP for the last 75 or so years in the United States. A huge temporary fluctuation in the shares of spending in GDP occurred in World War II, when government spending on the military rose sharply. Government purchases reached almost 50 percent of GDP, and the other three shares declined. Since World War II, the shares have been much steadier, but the movements in government spending as a share of GDP seem to be related to the movements in the investment share of GDP. Between 1990 and 2000, the government purchases share decreased from about 20 percent to 17.5 percent, while the investment share increased from 14.8 percent to 17.7 percent. Between 2000 and 2010, however, the government purchases share of GDP increased from 17.5 percent to 20.5 percent, while the investment share decreased from 17.7 percent to 12.4 percent. The other two shares have shown more sustained patterns: The consumption share generally has been rising during the 30-year period 1980–2010, while the net exports share has been negative over that period, as the United States ran trade deficits that got progressively larger in the period leading up to the 2009 recession. (Recall that when net exports are negative, there is a trade deficit.)

consumption share

The proportion of GDP that is used for consumption; equals consumption divided by GDP, or C/Y.

investment share

The proportion of GDP that is used for investment; equals investment divided by GDP, or I/Y. Sometimes called investment rate.

net exports share

The proportion of GDP that is used for net exports; equals net exports divided by GDP, or X/Y.

government purchases share

The proportion of GDP that is used for government purchases; equals government purchases divided by GDP, or G/Y.

FIGURE 19.1 History of Spending Shares in GDP

The government purchases share rose sharply during World War II, and the other three shares declined. The government purchases share fell in the late 1990s through the early 2000s before rising after the 2008/09 recession and then falling again in recent years.

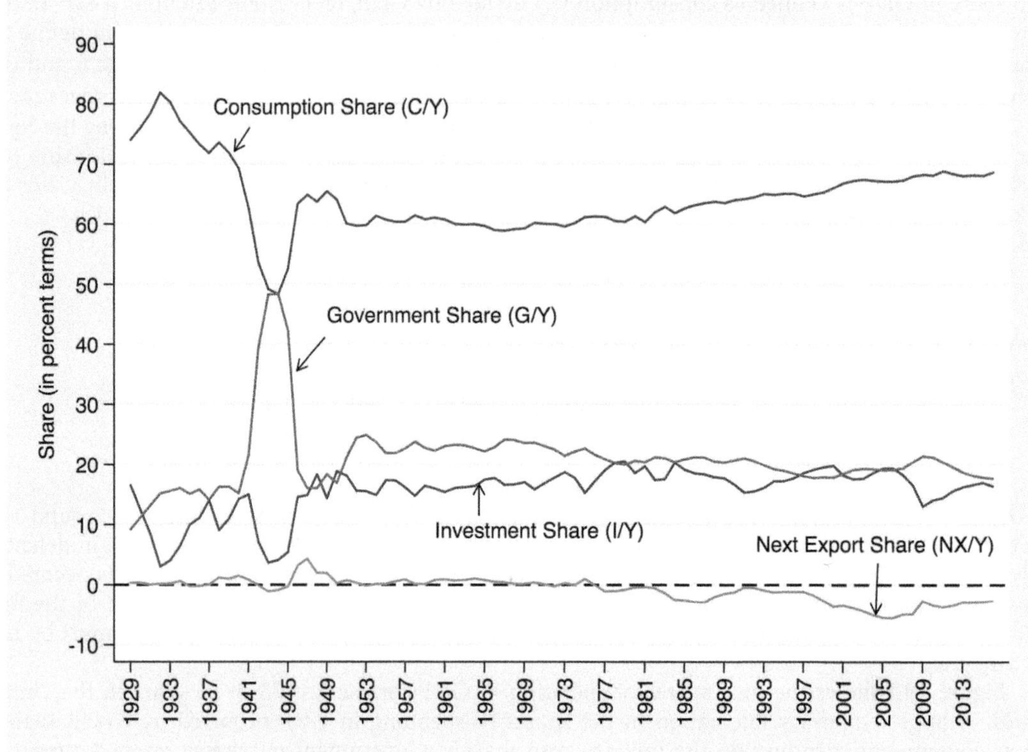

1.2 If One Share Goes Up, Another Must Go Down

The shares of spending equation demonstrates a simple but important point: A change in one of the shares implies a change in one or more of the other shares. That the shares must sum to one means that an increase in any of the shares must entail a reduction in one of the other shares. For example, an increase in the share of spending going to government purchases must result in a decrease in the share going to one or more of the other components of spending. Similarly, a decrease in the government purchases share must result in an increase in some other share, such as the investment share. One cannot have an increase in government purchases as a share of GDP (going from, say, 20 percent to 25 percent) without a decline in the share of either consumption or investment or net exports.

What determines how the shares of GDP are allocated? What is the mechanism through which a change in one share—such as the government share of GDP—brings about a change in one of the other shares? Is it only the investment share that changes in response to a rise in the government share of GDP? Or do the consumption and net exports shares change as well? Which share would change by more as a result of the increase in the government share? To answer these questions, we develop the spending allocation model. At the heart of the spending model lies the real interest rate, which plays an important role in relating changes in one share to changes in another. We begin the derivation of the spending allocation model by taking a closer look at how real interest rates influence the various shares of GDP.

Before beginning this derivation of the spending allocation model, it is important to remember that the spending allocation model relates changes in one spending share to changes in the other spending shares *in the long run*. Recall from Chapter 17 that potential GDP is the economy's long-term trend level of GDP. We will refer to potential GDP as Y^*, to distinguish it from GDP. In the short run, actual GDP can (and does) fluctuate around potential GDP, but in the long run, we know that GDP is equal to potential GDP ($Y = Y^*$).

We will modify the equation that relates the shares to one another to represent a long-run relationship among the values of the spending shares. Because $Y = Y^*$ in the long run, this relationship can easily be written as follows:

$$1 = \frac{C}{Y^*} + \frac{I}{Y^*} + \frac{G}{Y^*} + \frac{X}{Y^*}$$

The intuition is unchanged—an increase in the long-run share of one of the components of GDP implies a decrease in the long-run share of one or more of the other components.

REVIEW

- GDP is divided into four components: consumption, investment, government purchases, and net exports. Expressing each as a share of GDP is a convenient way to describe how spending is allocated among the components.
- Simple arithmetic tells us that the sum of all the shares of spending in GDP must equal one. Thus, an increase in the share of GDP going to government purchases, for example, must be accompanied by a reduction in one or more of the other three shares—consumption, investment, or net exports.
- Several interesting patterns emerge when we look at data on these shares for the past 75 years. The government share of GDP rose sharply during World War II, resulting in substantial falls in the other three shares.
- Changes in the government share of GDP seem to be inversely related to changes in the investment share of GDP over the last 25 years. During that period, the consumption share of GDP has been rising, while the net exports share of GDP has remained negative.
- The real interest rate plays a critical role in how changes in one share affect the other shares in the economy over the long run. To develop this relationship further, we redefine the spending shares in terms of potential GDP, because we know that in the long run, GDP will equal potential GDP.

2. THE EFFECT OF INTEREST RATES ON SPENDING SHARES

In this section, we show that the interest rate affects the three shares of spending by the private sector: consumption, investment, and net exports. Each private-sector spending component competes for a share of GDP along with government purchases, and the interest rate is a key factor in determining how the spending is allocated.

2.1 Consumption

In the long run, the value of the consumption share of GDP (C/Y^*) depends on people's decisions to consume, which are like any other choice with scarce resources, as defined in Chapter 1. If people decide to consume a larger fraction of their income, then the consumption share of GDP will increase. Conversely, if people decide to lower the fraction of income that they consume, then the consumption share of GDP will decrease.

Consumption and the Real Interest Rate

Keep in mind that people's decisions to consume more or less of their income today have implications for their consumption decisions tomorrow. Individuals who consume *more* today save *less*, and therefore have less to consume tomorrow. On the other hand, individuals who consume *less* today save *more*, and therefore have more to consume tomorrow. A person's choice between consuming today and consuming tomorrow depends on a relative price, just like any other economic decision. The price of consumption today relative to the price of consumption tomorrow is the real interest rate.

Why is the real interest rate the relative price of current consumption? If the real interest rate is high, then any saving you do today will deliver more funds in the future, which then can be used for future consumption (a larger home or more college education, for example). Conversely, when the real interest rate is high, increasing current consumption will reduce your saving and result in your passing up opportunities for future consumption.

FIGURE 19.2 The Consumption Share and the Real Interest Rate

A higher real interest rate discourages consumption and encourages saving. Therefore, the share of GDP allocated to consumption will decrease in the long run.

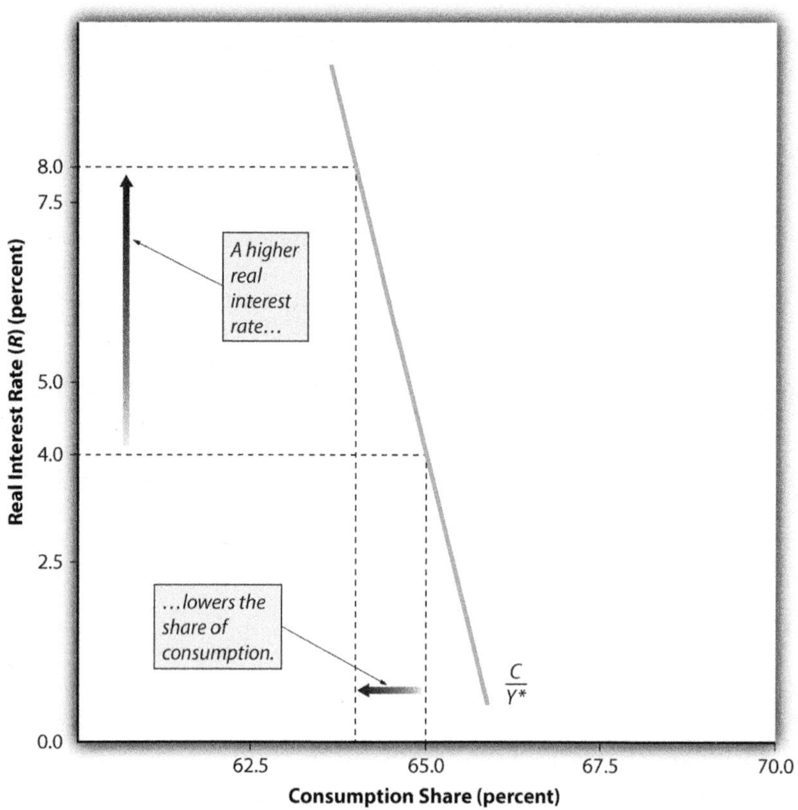

We can better illustrate this link between the real interest rate and consumption with a numerical example. Suppose you earned enough to buy $1,000 worth of goods, but you were buying only $900 worth of goods and saving the remainder. If the real interest rate was 2 percent, your saving plus the interest you earned would allow you to consume $102 worth of goods next year. In other words, by consuming $100 less in goods today, you get to consume $102 more in goods tomorrow. But if the real interest rate instead were 6 percent, you would be able to consume $106 worth of goods in a year by consuming $100 less in goods today. The increase in the real interest rate from 2 percent to 6 percent raises the price of consuming $100 worth of goods today by $4 worth of goods in the future.

Even though this may seem like a small amount, keep in mind that small differences in interest rates can add up when you consider saving large sums of money to finance a college education or to save for retirement. So a higher real interest rate gives people more incentive to consume less and save for the future, whereas a lower real interest rate gives people more incentive to consume today instead of saving for the future. We therefore can conclude that consumption is negatively related to the real interest rate.

What is true for individuals on average also will be true for the economy as a whole. Figure 19.2 describes an economy in which the consumption share is negatively related to the real interest rate. For this example, when the real interest rate is 4 percent, the share of consumption in GDP will be about 65 percent. If the real interest rate increases to 8 percent, then the share declines to 64 percent. Alternatively, if the real interest rate declines, the consumption share increases.

Movements Along versus Shifts of the Consumption Share Line

Observe that the relationship between the real interest rate and consumption as a share of GDP in Figure 19.2 looks like a demand curve. Like a demand curve, it is downward sloping. And like a demand curve, it shows the quantity that consumers are willing to consume at each price, where the price is the real interest rate. A higher price—that is, a higher real interest rate—reduces the amount of goods and services that people will consume, and a lower price—that is, a lower real interest rate—increases the amount that they will consume. As with demand curves, when a change in the price (in this case, the real interest rate) leads to a change in the quantity demanded (in this case, the consumption share), we see a *movement along* the consumption share line, as shown in Figure 19.2.

As with a demand curve, it is also important to distinguish such movements along the consumption share line from *shifts of* the consumption share line. The real interest rate is not the only thing that affects consumption as a share of GDP. When a factor other than the real interest rate changes the consumption share of GDP, the consumption share line in Figure 19.2 shifts. For example, an increase in taxes on consumption—such as a national sales tax—would reduce the quantity of goods people would consume relative to their income. In other words, an increase in taxes on consumption would shift the consumption share line in Figure 19.2 to the left: Less would be consumed relative to GDP at every interest rate. Conversely, a decrease in taxes on consumption would shift the consumption share line in Figure 19.2 to the right.

2.2 Investment

A similar inverse, or negative, relationship exists between investment and the real interest rate. When businesses decide to invest, by buying new machines and equipment or by building a new factory, they need funds. Typically, they acquire these funds by borrowing. Higher real interest rates raise the cost of borrowing—the firm would need to produce enough additional output to pay back the loan plus interest, which implies that it would be willing to borrow only if it were confident about the success of the investment project. Another way of stating this is that investment projects undertaken at lower real interest rates may be postponed or canceled when interest rates rise because of the higher costs of borrowing.

Therefore, when real interest rates rise, firms are less likely to spend on investment, fewer new equipment purchases will be made, and fewer new factories will be built. Conversely, when real interest rates fall, firms are encouraged to spend more on investment, more equipment will be purchased, and more new factories will be built. This relationship holds even if firms use their own funds to finance their investment projects. Higher real interest rates increase the opportunity cost of using their own funds for investment: Firms are tempted to leave their money in the bank earning the higher interest rate, instead of putting those funds into investment projects.

FIGURE 19.3 The Investment Share and the Real Interest Rate

A higher real interest rate lowers the share of investment. The sensitivity of investment to the interest rate is greater than that of consumption to the interest rate, as shown in Figure 7.2.

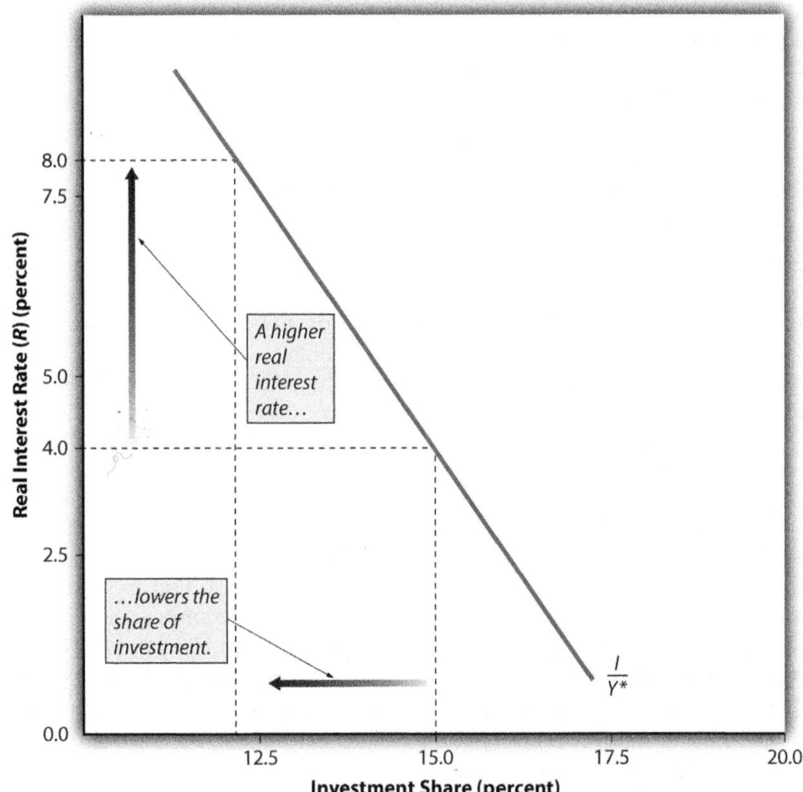

Recall that investment also includes the purchases of new houses by individuals. Most people need to take out loans (mortgages) to purchase houses. When the real interest rate on mortgages rises, people purchase fewer or smaller houses because they would have to give up too much consumption to repay their mortgage plus interest; when the real interest rate falls, people purchase more or larger houses because they are more easily able to repay their mortgage plus interest. The story would be similar even if individuals used their savings to pay for their new home. A higher real interest rate increases the opportunity cost of taking the money out of the bank account and using it to buy a house.

Combining the behavior of firms that borrow or use their own funds to finance investment projects with that of individuals who take out mortgages or use their own funds to buy houses, the negative relationship between investment as a share of GDP and the interest rate that has been observed in the economy for many years makes sense: A higher real interest rate discourages investment, and a lower real interest rate encourages investment. Figure 19.3 shows this negative relationship between the interest rate and the investment share. For this example, when the interest rate rises from 4 percent to 8 percent, the investment share decreases from 15 percent to 12 percent. Economists have observed that investment is more sensitive to interest rates than consumption. Therefore, the line for I/Y^* in Figure 19.3 is flatter than the line for C/Y^* in Figure 19.2. As before, when a change in the real interest rate leads to a change in the investment share, this is reflected as a *movement along* the consumption share line. An example is shown in Figure 19.3.

Other factors besides the interest rate also affect investment; when these factors change, the investment share line in Figure 19.3 will *shift.* For example, an investment tax credit, which lowers a firm's taxes if the firm buys new equipment, would increase the amount that firms would invest at each interest rate. An investment tax credit would shift the investment share line in Figure 19.3 to the right: The investment that firms are willing to make as a share of GDP at a given interest rate would rise. A change in firms' expectations of the future also could shift the investment share line: If firms feel that new computing or telecommunications equipment will lower their costs in the future, they will purchase the equipment, thereby increasing their investment at a given interest rate; the investment share line will shift to the right. Conversely, pessimism on the part of firms about the benefits of investment could shift the line to the left.

2.3 Net Exports

exchange rate

The price of one currency in terms of another in the foreign exchange market. We express the exchange rate as the number of units of foreign currency that can be purchased with one unit of domestic currency.

Net exports also are negatively related to the real interest rate. The explanation behind this relationship is somewhat more involved than that for investment or for consumption. The **exchange rate**—the rate at which one country's currency can be exchanged for another—plays an integral role in this relationship. This explanation has three parts. First, we need to understand the relationship between the real interest rate and the exchange rate. Second, we need to understand the relationship between the exchange rate and exports and imports. Third, we will combine these two parts to obtain a relationship between the real interest rate and net exports.

The Interest Rate and the Exchange Rate

Let us start with the relationship between the interest rate and the *exchange rate.* We will express the exchange rate in terms of the number of units of foreign currency that are needed to purchase one unit of domestic currency, or, in other words, as the price of a unit of domestic currency in terms of foreign currency. Thus, the exchange rates for the dollar for various international currencies will be expressed in the form of euros per dollar, yen per dollar, pounds per dollar, and so on.

A substantial influence on exchange rates is exerted by international investors, who must decide whether to put their funds in assets denominated in dollars—such as an account at a U.S. bank in New York City—or in assets denominated in foreign currencies—such as an account at a Japanese bank in Tokyo. If real interest rates rise in the United States, but not elsewhere, then international investors will put more funds in dollar-denominated assets because they can earn more by doing so. As international investors shift their funds from London, Frankfurt, Tokyo, and other financial centers to New York to take advantage of the higher interest rate in the United States, the demand for dollars will rise. This increased demand puts upward pressure on the dollar exchange rate, so that more units of foreign currency will be needed to buy $1 in the foreign exchange market. For example, an increase in the interest rate in the United States might cause the U.S. dollar to increase from 100 yen per dollar to 120 yen per dollar. Conversely, a lower interest rate in the United States brings about a lower exchange rate for the dollar. Thus, the interest rate and the exchange rate are positively related.

The Exchange Rate and Net Exports

The next part of the relationship deals with how the exchange rate affects net exports. When the dollar becomes more valuable—that is, the dollar exchange rate becomes higher—foreign goods imported into the United States become more attractive to U.S. consumers because they are less expensive. For example, at the end of 2015, the dollar exchange rate against the euro was 0.90 euro (€) per dollar compared with the exchange rate at the end of 2005, which was €0.80 per dollar. In 2005, an American consumer could have bought a German-made Audi costing €40,000 for $50,000 (40,000/0.8). In 2015, when the exchange rate was €0.90 per dollar, the Audi would be cheaper; it would cost around $44,444 (40,000/0.90). Thus, a higher exchange rate increases the quantity demanded of imported goods.

Conversely, the higher exchange rate makes U.S. exports less attractive to foreign consumers. For example, a $20,000 Jeep Grand Cherokee would have cost a German consumer €16,000 in 2005 but would cost €18,000 in 2015. Thus, a higher exchange rate decreases U.S. exports. We have shown that a higher exchange rate will lower exports and raise imports. Because net exports is the difference between exports and imports, a higher exchange rate must mean a decrease in net exports. Conversely, a lower exchange rate will mean an increase in net exports.

Combining the Two Relationships

Finally, we can combine these two relationships—one that relates the real interest rate to the exchange rate, and the other that relates the exchange rate to net exports—to obtain the desired relationship between the real interest rate and net exports:

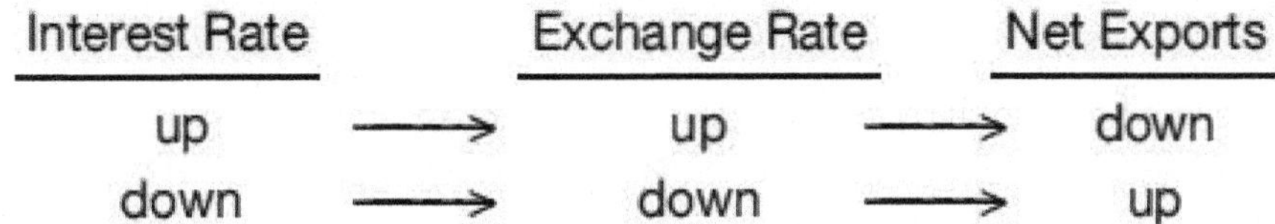

Interest Rate		Exchange Rate		Net Exports
up	→	up	→	down
down	→	down	→	up

FIGURE 19.4 The Net Exports Share and the Real Interest Rate

A higher real interest rate lowers the share of net exports because it tends to raise the exchange rate. The higher exchange rate lowers exports and raises imports, thereby lowering net exports. When net exports are negative, there is a trade deficit. When net exports are positive, there is a trade surplus.

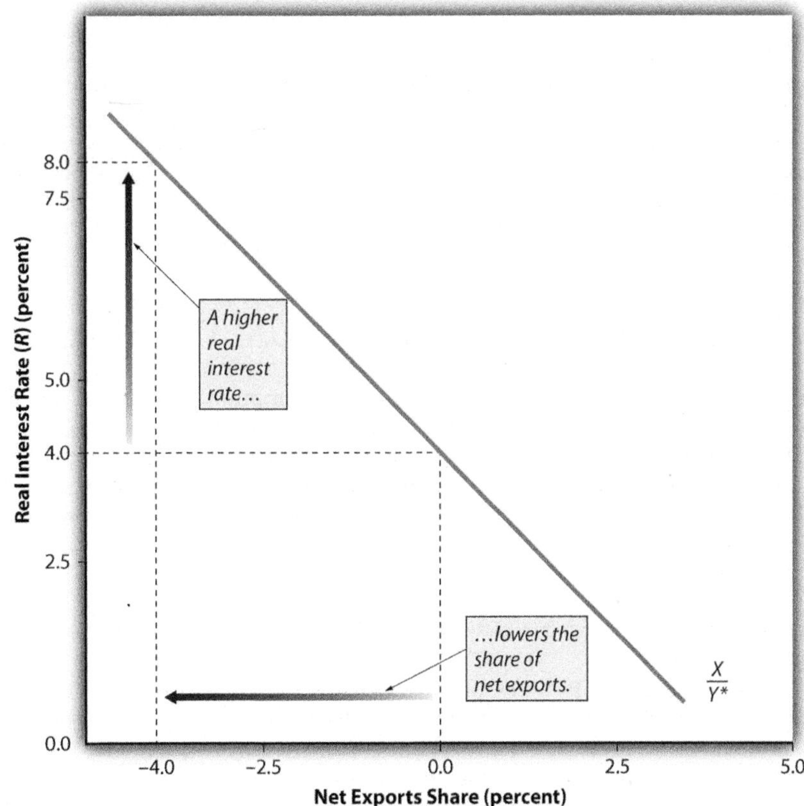

If the interest rate goes up, then net exports go down. The link is the exchange rate. The dollar increases in value (the exchange rate rises) as a result of the higher interest rate, which, in turn, makes net exports fall. Of course, all of this works in reverse, too. If the interest rate goes down, then the dollar decreases in value (the exchange rate goes down) and net exports go up.

The relationship between net exports as a share of GDP and the interest rate is shown in Figure 19.4. Like the consumption share line and the investment share line, the net exports share line is downward sloping. For this example, when the interest rate goes up from 4 percent to 8 percent, net exports go from zero to about –4 percent of GDP. Remember that when net exports are negative, there is a trade deficit. Changes in the interest rate lead to movements along the net exports line in Figure 19.4. Changes in other factors—such as a shift in foreign demand for U.S. products—may cause the line to shift.

2.4 Putting the Three Shares Together

We have shown that the consumption, investment, and net exports shares are all negatively related to the interest rate. The three diagrams—Figure 19.2, Figure 19.3, and Figure 19.4—summarize this key idea. Our next task is to determine the interest rate, which then will enable us to determine the particular value of each share.

REVIEW

- Consumption, investment, and net exports are all negatively related to the real interest rate.
- The real interest rate is the price of consumption this year relative to next year. When the real interest rate rises, consumers will be more inclined to forgo current consumption and save so that they can consume more in the future. Accordingly, the share of consumption will rise when the real interest rate falls and will fall when the real interest rate rises.
- Changes in the real interest rate affect investment because they change the borrowing costs (and also the opportunity cost of using one's own money) for firms looking to invest in machines and factories and for individuals looking to buy and build homes. Business firms and individuals will spend less on investment when the real interest rate rises. Accordingly, the share of investment will rise when the real interest rate falls and will fall when the real interest rate rises.
- Changes in the real interest rate affect net exports through their effects on the exchange rate. A higher real interest rate raises the value of the domestic currency (a higher exchange rate) and thereby discourages exports and encourages imports, while a lower real interest rate results in a fall in the value of the domestic currency (a lower exchange rate), which encourages exports and discourages imports. Accordingly, the share of net exports will rise when the real interest rate falls and fall when the real interest rate rises.
- A downward-sloping relationship exists between the real interest rate and each of these three shares. Changes in the real interest rate are reflected as movements along these curves. Other factors besides the interest rate may also affect consumption, investment, and net exports. When one of these factors changes, the relationship between the interest rate and consumption, investment, or net exports shifts.

3. DETERMINING THE EQUILIBRIUM INTEREST RATE

Because the interest rate affects each of the three shares (consumption, investment, and net exports), it also affects the sum of the three shares. We will refer to the sum of the three shares as the non government share of GDP, or NG/Y, because the fourth component of GDP is the government share. The collective impact is shown by the downward sloping line in diagram (d) of Figure 19.5. As before, we are focusing on the shares in the long run, so the diagram shows the sum of consumption, investment, and net exports as a share of potential output (NG/Y^*).

3.1 The Nongovernment Share of GDP

Note carefully how Figure 19.5 is put together and how the downward-sloping line in diagram (d) is derived. We have taken the graphs from Figure 19.2, Figure 19.3, Figure 19.4 and assembled them horizontally in diagrams (a), (b), and (c) of Figure 19.5. The downward-sloping line in diagram (d) is the sum of the three downward-sloping lines in diagrams (a), (b), and (c). For example, when the interest rate is 4 percent, the line in diagram (d) shows that the nongovernment share—the sum of investment, consumption, and net exports as a share of GDP—is 80 percent; this is the sum of 65 percent for the consumption share, 15 percent for the investment share, and 0 percent for the net exports share. Similarly, the other points in diagram (d) are obtained by adding up the three shares at other interest rate levels. For example, at an interest rate of 5 percent, we see that the sum of the shares of consumption, investment, and net exports is down to about 78 percent.

FIGURE 19.5 Summing Up Consumption, Investment, and Net Exports Shares

Diagrams (a), (b), and (c) are reproductions of Figures 7.2, 7.3, and 7.4. For each interest rate, the three shares are added together to get the sum of shares shown in diagram (d). For example, when the real interest rate is 4 percent, we get 65 percent for consumption share, 15 percent for investment share, and 0 percent for net exports, summing to 80 percent. The sum of the three nongovernment shares is negatively related to the real interest rate (*R*).

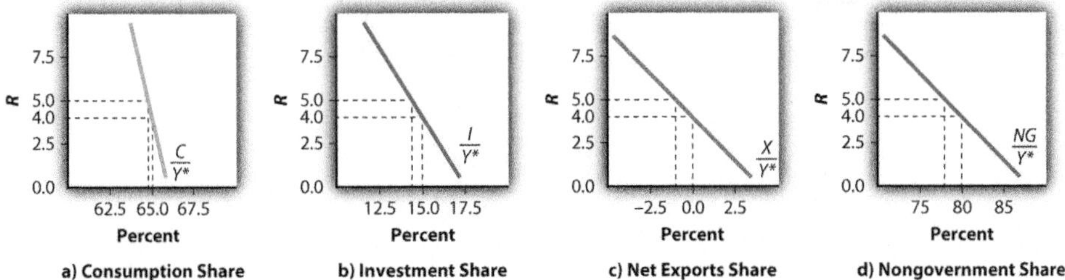

3.2 The Government's Share of GDP and the Share of GDP Available for Nongovernment Use

We have determined that the real interest rate has a negative effect on the consumption, investment, and net exports shares of GDP. What about the impact of real interest rates on government purchases? We will assume that government purchases do not depend on the real interest rate; instead, they likely will be affected by the decisions made by elected representatives on behalf of the voters who elected them to office. So the share of government purchases (G/Y) will not be affected by fluctuations in interest rates. For example, if the decisions made by elected officials result in a government purchases share that is 22 percent of GDP, then that share will not be affected by changes in the real interest rate. This is shown by the vertical line in diagram (a) of Figure 19.6.

The government share determines how much is available for nongovernment use, that is, for either consumption, investment, or net exports. The share available for nongovernment use is easily defined as follows:

$$\text{Share available for nongovernment use} = 1 - \frac{G}{Y}$$

FIGURE 19.6 Finding the Share Available for Nongovernment Use

If the government share of GDP is known, then the remaining share of GDP is what is available for nongovernment use. In this example, a 22 percent share of government purchases means that 78 percent of GDP is available for nongovernment use. Because the share G/Y^* is not dependent on R, the share available for nongovernment use is also a vertical line, not dependent on R.

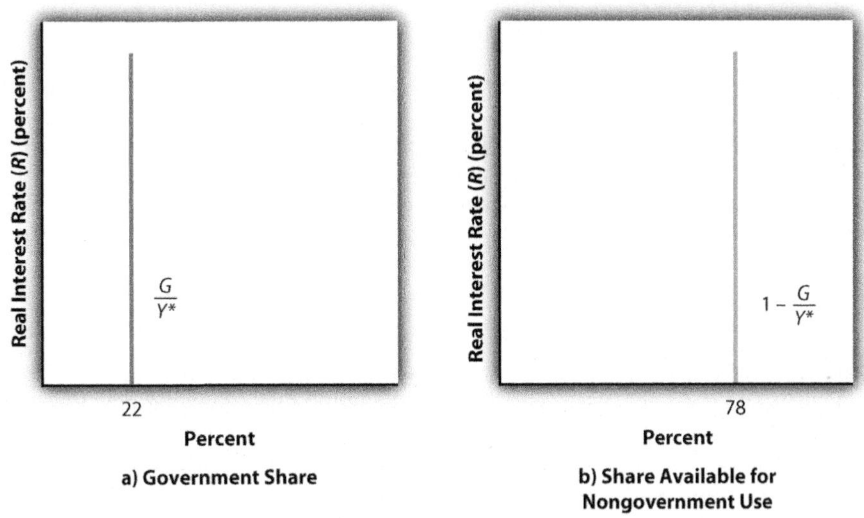

If the government share is not affected by changes in the real interest rate, the share that is available for nongovernment use also will not be affected. For the case shown in diagram (a) of Figure 19.6, with a

share of government purchases of 22 percent, the share available for nongovernment use must equal 78 percent. The share of GDP available for nongovernment use is shown in diagram (b) of Figure 19.6. As always, we are looking at the long run, so the diagram shows the share of potential output available for nongovernment use.

3.3 Finding the Equilibrium Interest Rate

In equilibrium, the nongovernment share of GDP should equal the share of GDP available for nongovernment use. In mathematical terms, we can describe this equilibrium relationship in the long run as follows:

$$\frac{NG}{Y*} = 1 - \frac{G}{Y*}$$

equilibrium interest rate

The interest rate that equates the sum of the consumption, investment, and net exports shares to the share of GDP available for nongovernment use.

What brings this equality about is the real interest rate, which is the key to the spending allocation model. Figure 19.7 illustrates how the interest rate brings about this equality. Look first at diagram (d). In diagram (d), the share available for nongovernment use ($1 - G/Y^*$) is indicated by the vertical line at 78 percent. The nongovernment share of GDP (NG/Y^*), which is the sum of the consumption, investment, and net export shares, is shown by the downward-sloping line in Figure 19.7(d). This is the same line we derived in Figure 19.5(d). The equilibrium is the point at which the nongovernment share equals the share available for nongovernment use. Graphically, this is the intersection of the downward-sloping line and the vertical line. We see in diagram (d) of Figure 19.7 that the point of intersection for that economy occurs when the interest rate is 5 percent. This is the **equilibrium interest rate**, that is, the interest rate that makes the nongovernment share equal to the share available for nongovernment use.

FIGURE 19.7 Determining the Equilibrium Real Interest Rate and the Shares of Spending

In this case, government purchases are assumed to be 22 percent of GDP. Mark the implied share available for nongovernment uses, 78 percent, in diagram (d). The equilibrium real interest rate is determined at the intersection of the two lines in diagram (d). Given this real interest rate, we can compute the consumption, investment, and net exports shares of spending in GDP using diagrams (a), (b), and (c).

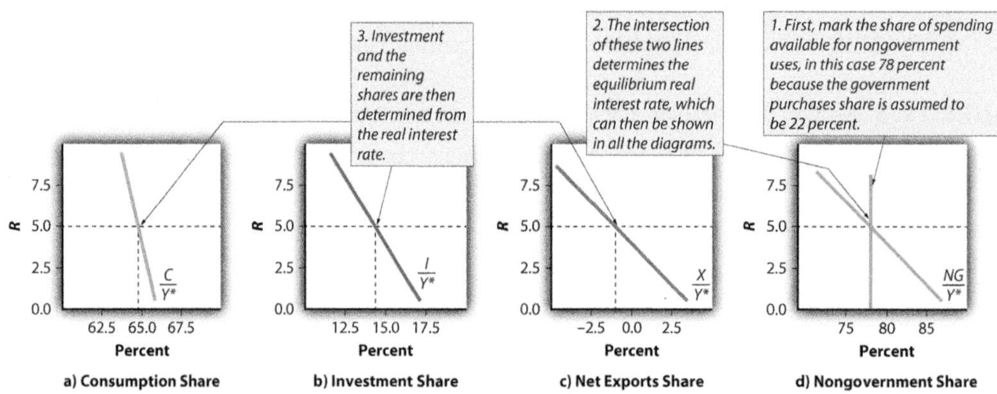

Once we determine the equilibrium interest rate, we can find the investment, consumption, and net exports shares. Each of these shares depends on the interest rate, as shown in diagrams (a), (b), and (c) of Figure 19.7. To determine each of the shares, simply draw a line across the three diagrams at the equilibrium interest rate. Then in diagram (a) we find the consumption share, in diagram (b) the investment share, and in diagram (c) the net exports share.

Analogy with Supply and Demand

Observe that the intersection of the two lines in diagram (d) of Figure 19.7 is much like the intersection of a demand curve and a supply curve. The downward-sloping line—showing how the sum of investment, consumption, and net exports is negatively related to the interest rate—looks just like a demand curve. The vertical line—showing the share of GDP available for consumption, investment, and net exports—looks like a vertical supply curve. The intersection of the two curves determines the equilibrium price—in this case, the equilibrium interest rate of the economy as a whole.

The Real Interest Rate in the Long Run

Having determined the equilibrium interest rate, it is important to mention once more two key features of this model. First, this analysis applies to the *long run*—perhaps three years or more—rather than to short-run economic fluctuations. Moreover, the interest rate in the analysis is the *real* interest rate, which, as defined in Chapter 17, is the nominal interest rate less the expected inflation rate. If the inflation rate is low, there is little difference between the real interest rate and the nominal interest rate; but if inflation is high, there is a big difference, and the real interest rate is a much better measure of the incentives affecting consumers and firms. An interest rate of 50 percent would seem high but actually would be quite low—2 percent in real terms—if people expected inflation to be 48 percent.

3.4 Using the Spending Allocation Model to Analyze the Long-Run Implications of a Shift in Government Purchases

What happens if the share of government purchases increases? Then the share available for nongovernment use will fall, which will be reflected in a leftward shift of the vertical line indicating the share available for nongovernment use. This causes the equilibrium interest rate in the economy to increase. Conversely, if the share of government purchases decreases, then the share available for nongovernment use will rise, which will be reflected in a rightward shift of the vertical line that indicates the share available for nongovernment use. This causes the equilibrium interest rate in the economy to decrease.

Suppose that the government share of GDP decreases by 2 percent, as happened in the 1990s as a result of a decrease in defense spending and other budget cuts. The effects of this change are shown in Figure 19.8. If government purchases as a share of GDP decrease by 2 percent, then we know that the share available for nongovernment use must increase by 2 percent. Thus, in diagram (d) of Figure 19.8, we shift the vertical line marking the available nongovernment share to the right by 2 percentage points. As Figure 19.8(d) shows, there is now a new intersection of the two lines and a new, lower equilibrium real interest rate. The new real interest rate is 4 percent rather than 5 percent, a decrease of 1 percentage point. The decrease in the real interest rate is the market mechanism that brings about an increase in the shares of consumption plus investment plus net exports. To see the effect on the consumption, investment, and net exports shares, we draw a horizontal line at a real interest rate of 4 percent, as shown in Figure 19.8, and read off the implied shares. According to the diagram, the share of consumption increases, the share of investment increases, and the share of net exports increases.

FIGURE 19.8 Analyzing the Impact of a Decrease in the Share of Government Purchases

If the government purchases of GDP falls, then the share available for nongovernment use must rise by the same amount. This causes a fall in real interest rates, which increases the consumptions, investment, and net exports share.

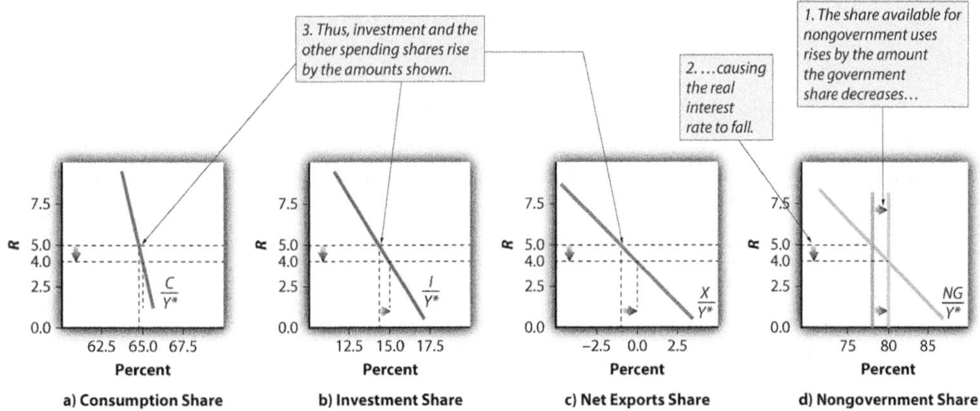

The lessons from this case study can also help you understand the statements made by the chancellor of the exchequer George Osborne that were described in this chapter's introduction.

REVIEW

- The sum of the consumption, investment, and net exports shares of GDP is called the nongovernment share of GDP. It is negatively related to the interest rate because each of the individual components is negatively related to the interest rate.
- The government share of GDP is assumed to be unaffected by the real interest rate, being determined by the preferences of voters expressed through their elected representatives. The share of GDP available for nongovernment use then can be defined as one minus the government share of GDP. This, too, is unaffected by the real interest rate.
- The equilibrium interest rate is determined by the condition that the nongovernment share equals the share available for nongovernment use. Graphically, this is the interest rate at the intersection of the downward-sloping nongovernment share of GDP line and the vertical share of GDP available for nongovernment use line.
- Once we find the equilibrium interest rate, we can then find the shares of consumption, investment, and net exports by looking at the graphs of those relationships.
- We also can use the model to analyze what would happen to the equilibrium interest rate when there is a change in the government share or in one of the three nongovernment shares.
- Once we know the equilibrium interest rate, we also can find out how exactly the other shares in the economy respond to a change in one of the shares. This is helpful in understanding how a change in government purchases affects investment, for example.

4. THE RELATIONSHIP BETWEEN SAVING AND INVESTMENT

By now you should be able to use the spending allocation model to illustrate how changes in the share of spending in one component of GDP affect the other components. In particular, we were able to use it to show how an increase in the consumption share of GDP or an increase in the government purchases share of GDP leads to a decrease in the investment share of GDP. In this section, we derive a similar relationship between the changes in the shares of GDP that are being saved and the share that is being invested. This alternative viewpoint is important to complete your understanding of how one sector of the economy can affect the others. For instance, we will show that the investment share of GDP will decrease when the government's budget deficit as a percentage of GDP rises, all else equal. The rise in the government budget deficit can be caused either by an increase in government spending or by a decrease in tax revenue. The latter effect is much better understood by looking at the economy from the saving side rather than the spending side.

In Chapter 18, we defined national saving (*S*) as GDP minus consumption minus government purchases, or

$$S = Y - C - G$$

national saving

The proportion of GDP that is saved, neither consumed nor spent on government purchases, equals national savings (*S*) divided by GDP, or *S/Y*.

The ratio of national saving to GDP, or *S*/ *Y*, is the national saving rate. For example, in 2015, **national saving** was \$2,535 billion and GDP was \$18,037 billion, so the national saving rate was 2,535/18,037 = 0.141 or 14.1 percent. If we divide each term in the definition of national saving by *Y*, we can write the national saving rate as one minus the shares of consumption and government purchases in GDP. That is,

National saving rate = 1 − consumption share − government purchases share,

or

$$\frac{S}{Y} = 1 - \frac{C}{Y} - \frac{G}{Y}$$

This equation tells us that a change in the economy will affect the national saving rate through its effect on the consumption share and the government purchases share. We once again will express everything in the long run, so the national saving rate in the long run is

$$\frac{S}{Y^*} = 1 - \frac{C}{Y^*} - \frac{G}{Y^*}$$

Note also that the equations tell us that the national saving rate depends on the interest rate. Because the consumption share of GDP is negatively related to the real interest rate and the government share of GDP is unrelated to the real interest rate, you easily can show that the national saving rate is positively related to the real interest rate. When the real interest rate rises, the consumption share of GDP falls, implying that the national saving rate rises. On the other hand, when the real interest rate falls, the consumption share of GDP rises, implying that the national saving rate falls.

FIGURE 19.9 **Determining the Interest Rate Using the Saving Rate Relationship**

The saving rate (nearly vertical line) depends positively on the real interest rate. The sum (nearly horizontal line) of the investment share and the net exports share depends negatively on the real interest rate. The equilibrium interest rate is determined at the point at which national saving equals investment plus net exports, or the intersection of the two lines.

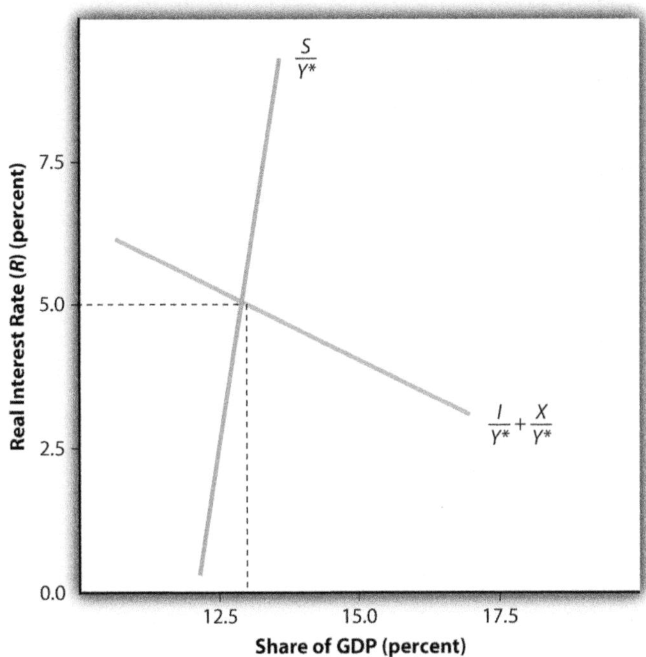

Because we know that

$$1 = \frac{C}{Y^*} + \frac{I}{Y^*} + \frac{G}{Y^*} + \frac{X}{Y^*}$$

we can use the above definition of the national saving rate in the long run to write

$$\frac{S}{Y^*} = \frac{I}{Y^*} + \frac{NX}{Y^*}$$

or, in other words, the national saving rate equals the investment share plus the net exports share. Both sides of this equation depend on the interest rate, as shown in Figure 19.9. The upward-sloping line in Figure 19.9 shows the national saving rate. An increase in the real interest rate causes the saving rate to rise. The downward-sloping line shows the sum of the investment and net exports shares; this sum is negatively related to the real interest rate because both the investment share and the net exports share are negatively related to the real interest rate.

The intersection of the two lines in Figure 19.9 determines the equilibrium interest rate. The interest rate is exactly the same as that in Figure 19.7. The only difference is that we are looking at the economy from a government and individual saving perspective rather than from a spending perspective.

Consider the same increase in the consumption share considered in the case study. An upward shift in the consumption share is equivalent to a downward shift in the saving rate. Thus, we shift the interest rate–saving rate relationship to the left in Figure 19.10, representing a downshift in the national saving rate. As shown in the figure, this leads to a higher interest rate and lower shares for investment and net exports. Similarly, an increase in the government expenditure share is also equivalent to a downward shift in the saving rate. This will lead to a shift in the interest rate–saving rate relationship to the left in Figure 19.10, resulting in a higher interest rate and lower shares for investment and net exports.

FIGURE 19.10 The Effect of a Downward Shift in the Saving Rate

The lower national saving rate raises real interest rates and lowers the investment share and the net exports share.

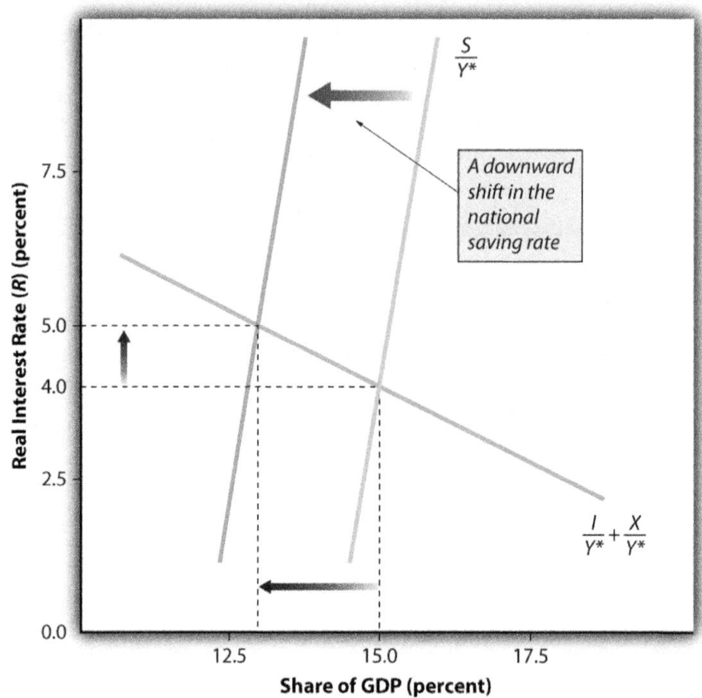

Obviously, we would not want to derive this alternative way of looking at the economy merely to replicate predictions that we were already able to make. We can make this model adaptable to more situations if we go back to another relationship we derived in Chapter 18, namely, that

$$S = (Y - C - T) + (T - G)$$

where T denotes taxes. This relationship states that national saving is equal to the sum of private and government saving. Therefore, the national saving rate will be the sum of the private saving rate and the government saving rate. The government saving rate is simply the budget balance as a percentage of GDP; when there is a budget deficit, this will be negative. We can express the relationship between saving, investment, and net exports in the economy in more detail then as

$$\text{Private saving rate+government saving rate} = \frac{I}{Y^*} + \frac{NX}{Y^*}$$

This equation has powerful implications for the economy. If the government budget deficit increases (the government saving rate decreases), then the investment share of GDP will fall, assuming that the private saving rate or the net exports share of GDP does not change. If the economy is to keep its investment share unchanged in the face of rising budget deficits, then either private saving will have to increase to offset the fall in government saving, or the share of net exports will have to decrease. Practically speaking, if the rising demands of an aging society cause budget deficits as a percentage of GDP in the United States to increase (thus reducing the government saving rate), then one or more of the following outcomes will occur:

1. The private saving rate will have to increase, meaning that consumers most likely will have to cut back on spending.
2. The investment rate will decrease, which means less capital accumulation and the likelihood for slower economic growth in the future.
3. The trade balance will worsen, and we will buy more foreign goods while foreigners will buy fewer U.S. goods.

REVIEW

- We can apply the concepts used to derive the spending allocation model to examine how changes in saving behavior by consumers and the government affect other sectors of the economy.
- Because national saving is defined as $Y-C-G$, we can show that national saving is equal to the sum of investment and net exports. Expressing this relationship as shares of GDP in the long run, we can show that the national saving rate equals the sum of the investment share and the net exports share of GDP.
- The national saving rate is positively related to the interest rate, whereas the sum of the investment share and the net exports share of GDP is negatively related to the interest rate. The equilibrium real interest rate can be found as the rate that equates the national saving rate and the sum of the investment and net exports shares.
- An increase in the consumption share or the government share is equivalent to a downward shift in the national saving rate. This will result in a higher interest rate and will lower the shares of investment and net exports.
- We can disaggregate the national saving rate into the sum of the private saving rate and the government saving rate. This allows us to illustrate that the impact of rising budget deficits will be to create some combination of a lower investment share of GDP, a higher private saving rate, or a worsening of the trade balance.

5. END-OF-CHAPTER MATERIAL

5.1 Conclusion

In this chapter, we have developed a model that determines the equilibrium interest rate and explains how the shares of spending are allocated in the whole economy. The model can be used to analyze the impact of a change in government purchases or a shift in consumption or saving behavior.

The model has introduced an important macroeconomic factor to consider when assessing the appropriate size of government. Private investment is affected by the size of government in the economy. Private investment is greater when government purchases are less, even though government spending is needed to provide the roads, education, and legal system that help produce economic growth. What the model shows is that even when government spending does these good things, it reduces the share of GDP available for private investment.

The model also has strong predictions about the appropriate budget policy for the government to follow. In the long run, private investment is affected by the size of government saving in the economy. Private investment is greater when the government saving rate is high. So once the government figures out the appropriate amount of spending for the roads, education, and legal system that help produce economic growth, it needs to ensure that it sets the tax rates appropriate for collecting the revenue needed to pay for that expenditure.

To the extent that consumption and net exports also shrink as government purchases increase, the effect on private investment of an increase in the share of government purchases is smaller. This also can be stated as to the extent that private savings increase and net exports shrink (the trade balance worsens), the effect on private investment of a decrease in the government saving rate is smaller.

Thus, there is a need for balance between government purchases and private investment. The mix ultimately will be determined in the political debate. This chapter provides some economic analysis that is useful in that debate.

Key Points

1. Over the long term, consumption, investment, net exports, and government purchases compete for a share of gross domestic product (GDP). The four spending shares must sum to one.
2. Higher real interest rates raise the price of consumption and lead to a reduction of consumption as a share of GDP.
3. Higher real interest rates also reduce investment by raising the cost of borrowing and by raising the opportunity cost of using one's own funds.
4. Higher real interest rates lower the share of net exports by causing the exchange rate to rise, which reduces exports and raises imports.
5. The combined effect is a downward-sloping relationship between the real interest rate and the nongovernment share of GDP.
6. The government share of GDP is not dependent on the real interest rate. Accordingly, the share of GDP available for nongovernment use, which is one minus the government share of GDP, is not dependent on the real interest rate and is shown as a vertical line.
7. The equilibrium interest rate is found by equating the nongovernment share of GDP—the sum of the consumption, investment, and net exports shares—to the share of GDP available for nongovernment use.
8. An increase in the share of government purchases crowds out the investment share of GDP by raising interest rates. The consumption and net exports shares also fall, crowding out the investment less severely. A decrease in the share of government purchases will lead to a lower real interest rate and an increase in all the other shares of spending.
9. The national saving rate is equal to the sum of the investment and net exports shares of GDP. The national saving rate, which equals the sum of private and government saving, is positively related to the real interest rate, while the sum of the investment and net exports shares of GDP is negatively related to the real interest rate.
10. An increase in consumption (a decrease in private saving) or an increase in government purchases (a decrease in government saving) will reduce national saving and shift the national saving curve inward. This will raise the equilibrium real interest rate and lower the investment share of GDP or lower the net exports share of GDP (worsen the trade balance).

QUESTIONS FOR REVIEW

1. Why does an increase in the share of one component of gross domestic product (GDP) require a decrease in some other share?
2. What is the relationship between the consumption share and the real interest rate?
3. What is the relationship between the investment share and the real interest rate?
4. Explain carefully all the steps that relate the share of net exports to the real interest rate.
5. How do we indicate that the model in this chapter applies much more to the long run than to the short run?
6. Describe the following five relationships: (a) the government share of GDP and the real interest rate, (b) the government share of GDP and the share of GDP available for nongovernment use, (c) the real interest rate and the share of GDP available for nongovernment use, (d) the real interest rate and the nongovernment share of GDP, and (e) the share of GDP available for nongovernment use and the nongovernment share of GDP.
7. What determines the equilibrium interest rate?
8. What is crowding out? Graphically illustrate how it works, using the spending allocation model.
9. Describe the relationships that exist among the following: the national saving rate, the private saving rate, the government saving rate, the net exports share of GDP, and the investment share of GDP.
10. What are the long-term implications of a rise in the government budget deficit as a percentage of GDP (also known as a fall in the government saving rate)?

PROBLEMS

1. Suppose $C = 700$, $I = 200$, $G = 100$, and $X = 0$.
   a. What is gross domestic product (GDP)? Calculate each component's share of GDP.
   b. Suppose government spending increases to 150, but the other components of GDP do not change. What is government spending's share of GDP now? What is the new nongovernment share?
   c. Suppose that the level of potential GDP (Y^*) is 1,000 and is unaffected by the increase in government spending described previously. Without doing any calculations, explain in general terms what happens to C/Y^*, X/Y^*, and I/Y^* after the government spending increase in (b).
   d. Describe the mechanism by which each of these changes happens.
2. Suppose the following equations describe the relationship between the long-run shares of spending in GDP and the interest rate (R), measured in decimal fractions (that is, $R = 0.05$ means that the interest rate is 5 percent).
   a. Use algebra to determine the values of the interest rate and the long-run shares of spending in GDP.
   b. Do the calculations again for a long-run government share of 17 percent rather than 20 percent (that is, $G/Y^* = 0.17$).
   c. Suppose that the share of government purchases changes from 20 percent to 17 percent. Describe, in words, the mechanism by which each of the other shares changes.

$$\frac{C}{Y^*} = 0.7 - 0.2(R - 0.05) \text{ and } \frac{I}{Y^*} = 0.2 - 0.8(R - 0.05)$$

$$\frac{NX}{Y^*} = 0.0 - 0.95(R - 0.05) \text{ and } \frac{G}{Y^*} = 0.2$$

3. Graph the relationships defined in Problem 2 to scale in a four-part diagram like Figure 19.7. Use the diagram to analyze each of the following situations:
   a. Suppose an increase in the foreign demand for U.S. goods changes the coefficient in the net exports share equation from 0 to 0.05. What happens to the interest rate and the consumption, investment, net exports, and government purchases shares in the United States in the long run?
   b. Determine how an increase in taxes that reduces the coefficient in the consumption share equation from 0.7 to 0.68 would affect the interest rate and the consumption, investment, net exports, and government purchases shares in the long run.
   c. Suppose firms are willing to invest 30 percent rather than 20 percent of GDP at an interest rate of 5 percent. How would this affect the interest rate and the shares of spending in GDP in the long run?
4. Using the diagram at the end of this section, find the equilibrium interest rate when the share of government purchases in the long run is 20 percent. Show what happens to all the variables if there is an increase in investment because of a new tax policy that encourages investment.
5. Describe the long-run impact of a decline in defense spending by 1 percent of GDP on interest rates and on consumption, investment, and net exports as a share of GDP. Consider two different cases:
   a. No other changes in policy accompany the defense cut.
   b. The funds saved from the defense cut are used to increase government expenditures on roads and bridges.
6. Suppose personal income tax rates are cut and government spending is increased. Using a diagram, show what will happen to real interest rates. What will happen to the spending shares of GDP in the long run?
7. Draw two sets of diagrams like Figure 19.7 to depict two situations. In one set, draw investment and net exports as sensitive to interest rates—that is, the I/Y and X/Y curves are very flat. In the other set, draw investment and net exports as insensitive to interest rates—that is, the I/Y and X/Y curves are nearly vertical. For the same increase in government's share of GDP, in which set of diagrams will interest rates rise more? Why?
8. If China increases the value of its currency relative to the dollar, what will happen to interest rates in the United States? Explain your answer.
9. Many people believe that the U.S. saving rate is too low. Suppose all private citizens save at a higher rate. Show what happens to investment in this case, using the saving and investment diagram, where the S/Y^* curve shifts. Now show what happens to investment in the same situation using the spending share diagrams.
10. Suppose that the government imposes a consumption tax to discourage consumption and increase saving. Suppose that the impact of the consumption tax is a leftward shift in the C/Y^* line over time. Describe graphically how this affects each of the shares of GDP, using a saving and investment diagram. How would your answer change if the government used the tax money to increase its spending?

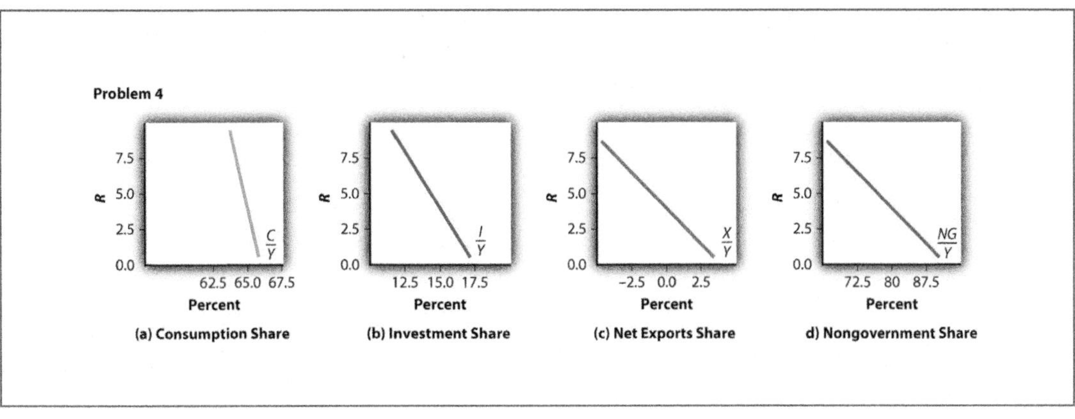

(a) Consumption Share (b) Investment Share (c) Net Exports Share d) Nongovernment Share

CHAPTER 20

Unemployment and Employment

The first Friday of every month, the Bureau of Labor Statistics releases its summary of the Employment Situation of the economy, a report eagerly awaited by those who study the economy closely for a living. Commenting on the report that came out in December of 2016, Jason Furman, the Chairman of the President's Council of Economic Advisers (CEA) noted that the economy had added 178,000 new jobs in November and that this increase represented the longest streak of months with job growth that the U.S. economy had recorded (74 months and counting, a period of over 6 years). The unemployment rate had fallen to 4.6 percent, while the number of unemployed workers had fallen to 1.4 unemployed workers per job opening. The result of a strong labor market was reflected in the fact that the earnings of workers in the private sector had increased by 2.7 percent over the past year. The news summarized in the 2016 report also provided an opportunity to reflect on how much the economy had improved from the depths of the 2008/09 recession. During that recession the economy had LOST around 400,000 jobs per month, the unemployment rate had risen to 9.9 percent and at one point the economy was creating so few jobs, and there were so many unemployed workers, that there were 6.6 unemployed workers per job opening.

Source: Shutterstock.com

Unemployment is the macroeconomic variable that affects people most personally. When the economy is booming and unemployment is low, it is easier for individuals to find jobs that are satisfying to them and that pay well. In contrast, when the economy is in recession and unemployment is high, jobs are harder to find, and people will settle for jobs that do not closely match their skills and do not pay very much money. Unemployment has painful economic consequences. Those who are unemployed experience the obvious hardships of income loss, loss of self-esteem, and an increasing toll on family life. Young people who live in a world of persistent unemployment fail to acquire job skills that will help them become productive citizens in the future. Beyond these individual and family hardships, unemployment has macroeconomic consequences as well. When more workers are unemployed, the production of goods and services is lower than it would be if more of those workers were employed. In other words, the economy is underutilizing its productive resources.

Even though college students are less likely than the general population to feel the immediate economic impact of a layoff, those students who graduated in the 2009–2011 period faced considerable challenges, in comparison to those graduating in 2016. Poor labor market conditions make it more difficult for new college graduates to find a job in which they could put their knowledge and learning to use. They may have to move hundreds of miles to cities that offer more plentiful job opportunities, taking them far from friends and family. Some start making plans to head to graduate school, hoping to acquire more skills, and to delay their entry into the labor market. Day-to-day interactions among friends become a real challenge when some of them have found good jobs and others wonder whether they will ever be employed.

Unemployment rates can, and do, vary among groups of individuals of different gender, age, race, and education, with the unemployment rate for college graduates being much lower than it is for the general population. They also vary dramatically across countries, even to the extent that the United States in a recession may have a lower unemployment rate than other economies that are booming. For instance, the 9.9 percent unemployment rate that the United States experienced during the worst point of the 2008/09 recession pales in comparison to the unemployment rate of 26 percent that Greece is currently experiencing as it struggles to extricate itself from the Eurozone crisis. Young people in Greece have it even worse—economists have estimated that unemployment rates for youth had reached levels close to 55 percent. The entire economic future of a nation is at risk if only one out of every two young people can find a job, buy a house, develop their skills and earn the money needed to provide for their needs and to start a family.

It is essential for aspiring macroeconomists to learn more about unemployment and how to reduce it. This chapter examines the nature and causes of unemployment and teaches you how to use a simple model that will help answer such questions as the following: Why does unemployment rise in a recession? Why do people become unemployed, and how long do they remain unemployed? Why does the unemployment rate remain high even after the recession has ended? Why do unemployment rates differ so much among countries? Is it because of differences in education levels? Is it because of differences in attitudes toward work? Or, is it because of differences in the economic policies implemented by the different countries' governments?

1. UNEMPLOYMENT AND OTHER LABOR MARKET INDICATORS

In this section, we show how unemployment is defined and measured, and we discuss the various causes of unemployment.

1.1 How Is Unemployment Measured?

To understand what the data on unemployment mean, one must understand how unemployment is measured. Each month, the U.S. Census Bureau surveys a sample of about 60,000 households in the United States. This survey is called the **Current Population Survey**. By asking the people in the survey a number of questions, the U.S. Census Bureau determines whether each person 16 years of age or over is employed or unemployed.

Current Population Survey

A monthly survey of a sample of U.S. households done by the U.S. Census Bureau; it measures employment, unemployment, the labor force, and other characteristics of the U.S. population.

Who Is Employed and Who Is Unemployed?

To be counted as **unemployed**, a person must be looking for work but not have a job. To be counted as employed, a person must have a job, either a job outside the home—as in the case of a teaching job at a high school or a welding job at a factory—or a paid job inside the home—as in the case of a freelance editor or a telemarketer who works for pay at home. A person who has an *unpaid* job at home—for example, caring for children or working on the house—is not counted as employed.

unemployed

An individual who does not have a job and is looking for work.

The **labor force** consists of all people 16 years of age and older who are either employed or unemployed. If a person is not counted as either unemployed or employed, then that person is not in the labor force. For example, a person who is working at home without pay and who is not looking for a paid job is considered not in the labor force.

labor force

All those 16 years of age and older who are either employed or unemployed.

Figure 20.1 illustrates the definitions of employment, unemployment, and the labor force. Using December 2016 as an example, it shows that out of a **working-age population** of 254.7 million, 152.1 million were employed and 7.5 million were unemployed. The remaining 95.1 million were of working age but were not in the labor force.

working-age population

Persons over 16 years of age who are not in an institution, such as a jail or a hospital.

The Labor Force and Discouraged Workers

It is difficult to judge who should be counted as being in the labor force and who should not be counted. For example, consider two retired people. One decided to retire at age 65 and is now enjoying retirement in Florida. The other was laid off from a job at age 55 and, after looking for a job for two years, got discouraged and stopped looking, feeling forced into retirement. You may feel that the second person, but not the first, should be counted as unemployed. According to the official statistics, however, neither is unemployed; they are not in the labor force because they are not looking for work. In general, workers, such as the second retired worker, who have left the labor force after not being able to find a job are called *discouraged workers*.

Defining and measuring the labor force is the most difficult part of measuring the amount of unemployment. When a change was made in the way the questions in the *Current Population Survey* were phrased, it revealed that many women who were working at home without pay actually were looking for a paid job; as a result of the change in the question, these women are now counted as unemployed rather than as out of the labor force.

Part-Time Work

A person is counted as employed in the *Current Population Survey* if he or she has worked at all during the week of the survey. Thus, part-time workers are counted as employed. The official definition of a part-time worker is one who works between one and 34 hours per week. About 26 percent of U.S. workers are employed part-time. Because of part-time work, the average number of hours of work per worker each week is about 38.6 hours, less than the typical 40 hours a week.

A big difference exists between the percentage of men who work part-time and the percentage of women who work part-time. In 2015, about 32 percent of employed women worked part-time, while only about 19 percent of employed men did so. Women give personal choice rather than unavailability of full-time jobs as a reason for part-time work more frequently than men do.

FIGURE 20.1 How to Find Labor Market Indicators

As shown at the top of this diagram, the working-age population (16 years of age and older) is divided into three groups: employed, unemployed, and not in the labor force. Three key labor market indicators are then computed from these categories. For example, the unemployment rate is the number of people unemployed divided by the number of people in the labor force. (The numbers in parentheses are in millions and are the statistics for December 2016.)

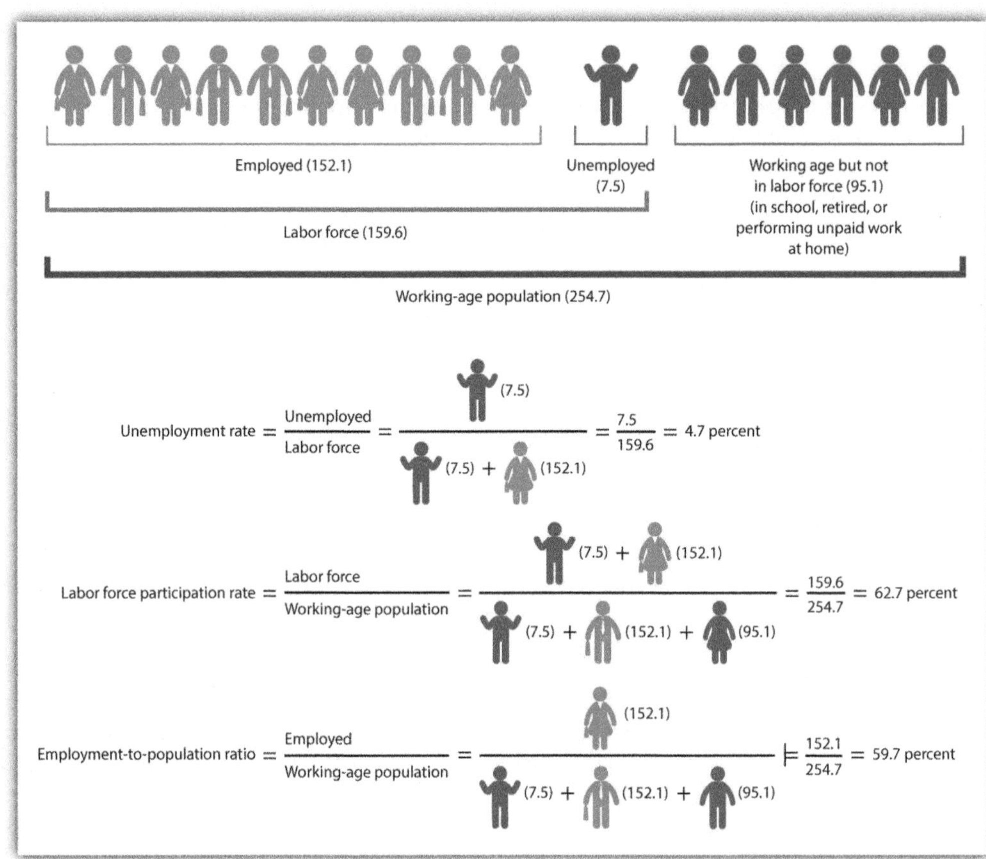

Source: Bureau of Labor Statistics

Comparing Three Key Indicators

Now let us examine the three key indicators of conditions in the labor market. These are

1. The **unemployment rate,** the percentage of the labor force that is unemployed.
2. The **labor force participation rate**, the ratio of people in the labor force to the working-age population.
3. The **employment-to-population ratio**, the ratio of employed workers to the working-age population.

unemployment rate

The percentage of the labor force that is unemployed.

labor force participation rate

The ratio (usually expressed as a percentage) of people in the labor force to the working-age population.

employment-to-population ratio

The ratio (usually expressed as a percentage) of employed workers to the working-age population.

Figure 20.1 gives an example of how each indicator is calculated. Both the unemployment rate and the labor force participation rate depend on the labor force, and therefore they have the same measurement difficulties that the labor force does. Only the employment-to-population ratio does not depend on the labor force. The labor force participation rate and the employment-to-population ratio both have had important long-term upward trends. For example, the employment-to-population ratio increased from about 57 percent in 1950 to more than 64 percent in 2000, but after the 2008/09 recession, this number fell back to about 58 percent. This indicates that the 2008/09 economic downturn erased almost 50 years of gains in the fraction of the employed among the working-age population. In the years since the recession ended, labor force participation has increased only slightly, rising to 59.7 percent at the end of 2016.

Participation in the labor force has also changed over the decades, as shown in Figure 20.2. This increase is mainly due to more women entering the labor force, a trend that has been going on since the 1950s. In 1950, about 34 percent of women were in the labor force, but in 2015, 65 years later, about 57 percent of women are in the labor force. Possible explanations for this trend include reduced discrimination, increased opportunities and pay for women, the favorable experience of many women working for pay during World War II, and the women's movement, which emphasized the attractiveness of paid work outside the home. In recent years, this number has not grown by very much—in fact over the quarter century from 1990 to 2015, the labor force participation rate of women was essentially unchanged.

FIGURE 20.2 Employment-to-Population Ratio for Men, Women, and Everyone

The percentage of working-age women who are employed has increased steadily since the 1950s. The percentage of working-age men who are employed declined until the late 1970s. After the mid-1990s, both series leveled off before declining during the 2008/09 recession.

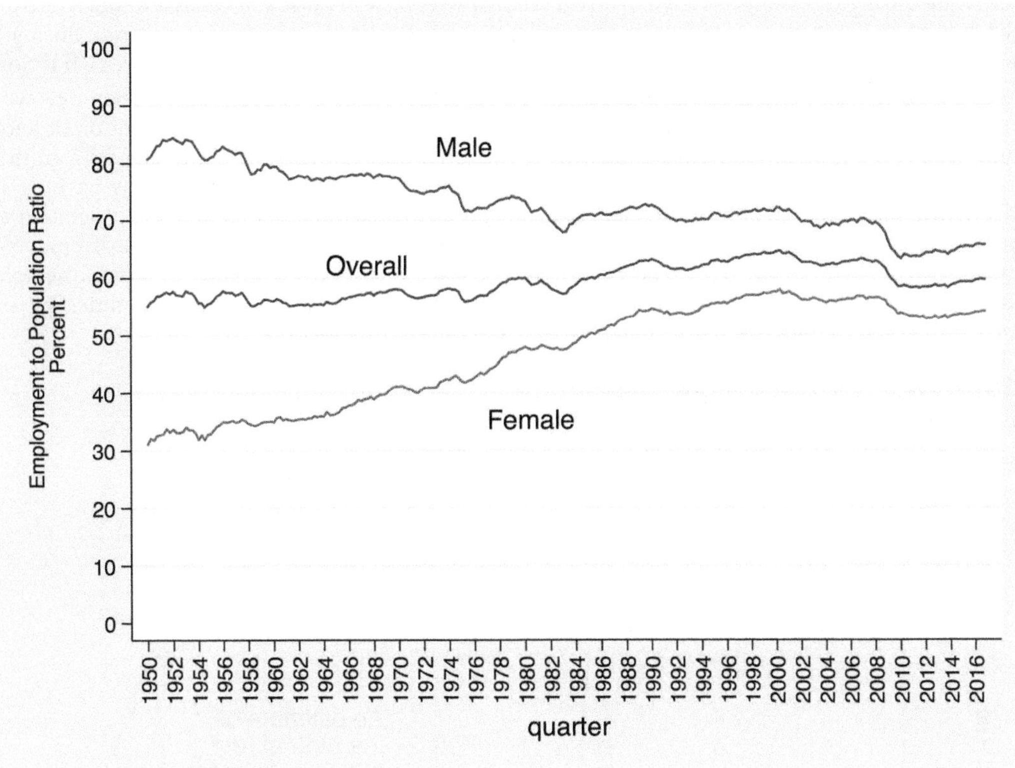

Aggregate Hours of Labor Input

As we have seen, some people work part time, others work full time, and some work overtime. For these reasons, the number of people employed is not a good measure of the labor input to production in the economy. For example, consider two bank tellers who both work half-time: One works four hours in the morning, the other works four hours in the afternoon, and both work five days a week. Even though they are two workers, together they work only as much as one full-time bank teller. So to count the labor input of these two part-time tellers as being twice as much as the labor input of one full-time teller would be an obvious mistake. Instead of the number of employed people, economists use hours worked to measure labor input. In the example of the bank tellers, the combined labor input of the two part-time tellers is the same as that of the one full-time teller: 40 hours a week.

Thus, the most comprehensive measure of labor input to the production of real gross domestic product (GDP) is the total number of hours worked by all workers, or **aggregate hours**. The number of aggregate hours of labor input depends on the number of hours of work for each person and the number of people working.

aggregate hours
The total number of hours worked by all workers in the economy in a given period of time.

The growth of aggregate labor hours in the United States is slowing down. It grew by about 1.7 percent per year in the two decades between 1975 and 1995, but it increased by only 1 percent a year between 1995 and 2005 and only around 0.6 percent per year between 2005 and 2015. This slowdown can be attributed to a reduction in the growth of the working-age population.

Cyclical, Frictional, and Structural Unemployment

The unemployment rate fluctuates over time, sometimes fairly dramatically. Recall from Chapter 17 that the unemployment rate rises when the economy goes into a recession and falls when the economy expands. For example, as shown in Figure 20.3, when the economy expanded rapidly in the mid- to late 1990s, the unemployment rate was cut in half, falling from a peak of 7.8 percent in mid-1992 to a value of 3.9 percent by the end of 2000. When the U.S. economy went into recession in 2001, the unemployment rate rose back to above 6 percent. As the economy expanded again, the unemployment rate fell back down, reaching 4.5 percent by the end of 2006. The recession that began at the end of 2007 brought a dramatic increase in unemployment, peaking at 10 percent in October of 2009, and declining back down to 4.7 percent in 2016, close to pre-recession levels.

Because the unemployment rate fluctuates so much depending on whether the economy is in a recession or a boom, economists always are interested in understanding what the unemployment rate would have been in the absence of these economic fluctuations. Economists use the term **natural unemployment rate** to refer to the unemployment rate that exists when the economy is not in a recession or a boom and real GDP is equal to potential GDP. The increase in unemployment above the natural rate during recessions is called **cyclical unemployment** because it is related to the short-term cyclical fluctuations in the economy. For example, the increase in the unemployment rate during the last recession was cyclical. The natural unemployment rate is caused by a combination of **frictional unemployment** and **structural unemployment**. Frictional unemployment occurs when new workers enter the labor force and must look for work, or when workers change jobs for one reason or another and need some time to find another job. Most frictional unemployment is short-lived. In contrast, some workers are unemployed for a long time, six months or more. These workers may have trouble finding work because they have insufficient skills or because their skills are no longer in demand as a result of a technological change or a shift in people's tastes toward new products. Such unemployment is called structural unemployment. The amount of frictional unemployment and structural unemployment in the economy is not constant, so the natural unemployment rate changes over time. But such changes are gradual and are not related to short-term economic fluctuations.

natural unemployment rate

The unemployment rate that exists when the economy is not in a recession or a boom and real GDP is equal to potential GDP.

cyclical unemployment

Unemployment resulting from a recession, when the rate of unemployment is above the natural rate of unemployment.

frictional unemployment

Unemployment arising from normal turnover in the labor market, such as when people change occupations or locations, or are new entrants.

structural unemployment

Unemployment resulting from structural problems, such as poor skills, long-term changes in demand, or insufficient work incentives.

FIGURE 20.3 The Unemployment Rate

The unemployment rate fluctuates around the natural unemployment rate, rising during recessions and falling when the economy grows rapidly during expansions.

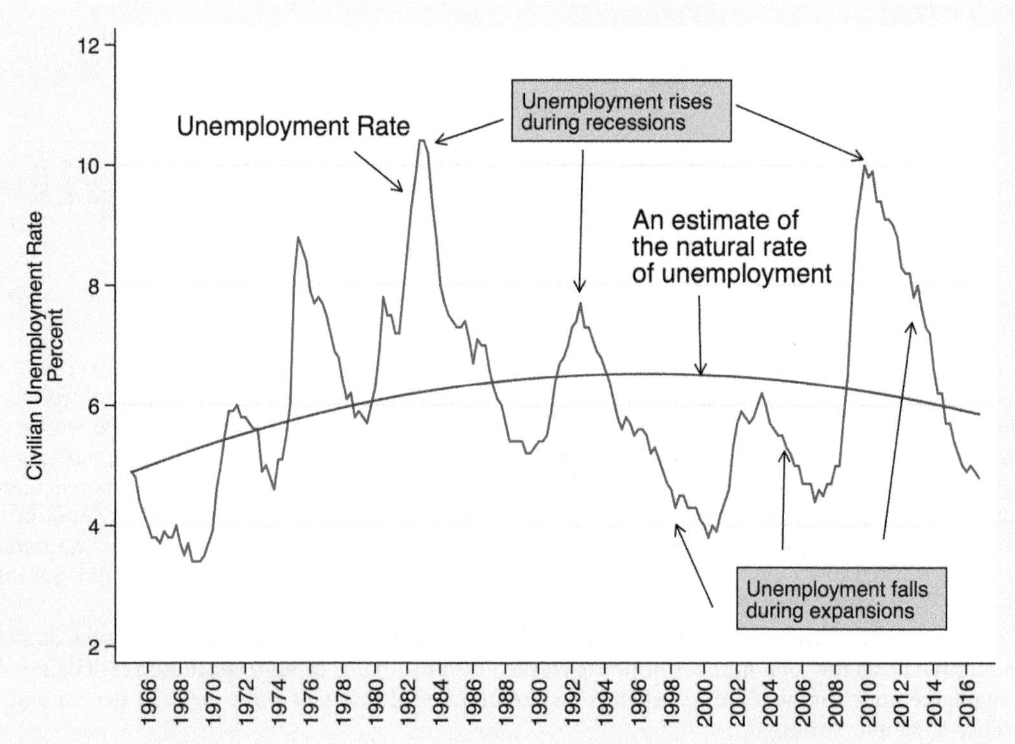

Source: Bureau of Labor Statistics (unemployment rate); authors' calculation (natural rate).

An estimate of the natural unemployment rate is shown in Figure 20.3. The natural rate of unemployment increased in the 1970s. One possible reason for the increase was the influx of young baby-boom workers into the labor force in the 1970s. Young people tend to have higher unemployment rates than older people. The natural unemployment rate declined in the 1990s as the labor force aged. The natural unemployment rate is not a constant and economists do not know its value precisely.

When economists use the term *natural unemployment rate*, they do not mean to say that this is "okay" or "just fine." They simply mean that whenever the operation of the overall macroeconomy is close to normal in the sense that real GDP is near potential GDP, the unemployment rate hovers around this natural rate. All else equal, having a low natural rate of unemployment is preferable because it means that, in normal times, fewer workers who are looking for work are unable to find it.

REVIEW

- Unemployment and employment in the United States are measured by the Current Population Survey.
- An unemployed individual is someone who does not have a job but is looking for work. An employed individual is someone who has a paid job. The labor force consists of all those who are either employed or unemployed.
- Because not all workers work full time, economists consider the aggregate number of hours worked to be the most comprehensive measure of labor input.
- The unemployment rate is the percentage of the labor force that is unemployed. The unemployment rate in the United States fluctuates cyclically, rising in times of recession and falling in times of expansion.
- The unemployment rate in the absence of cyclical increases or decreases is called the natural rate of unemployment. The natural rate of unemployment is caused by a combination of frictional unemployment (people changing jobs or occupations) and structural unemployment (unemployment caused by poor skills or changes in the types of goods produced in the economy).
- Two other important measures are the labor force participation rate (what fraction of the working-age population is in the labor force) and the employment-to-population ratio (what fraction of the working-age population has a job). Both ratios rose in the period from the 1960s to the 1990s because of more women entering the labor force.

2. THE NATURE OF UNEMPLOYMENT

Having examined the aggregate data, let us now look at the circumstances of people who are unemployed. People become unemployed for many reasons, and people's experiences with unemployment vary widely.

2.1 Reasons People Are Unemployed

We can divide the many reasons people become unemployed into four broad categories. People are unemployed because they have either lost their previous job (*job losers*), quit their previous job (*job leavers*), entered the labor force to look for work for the first time (*new entrants*), or re-entered the labor force after being out of it for a while (*re-entrants*). Figure 20.4 shows how the 4.7 percent unemployment rate in December 2016 was divided into these four categories.

Job Losers

Among the people who lost their jobs in a typical recent year was a vice president of a large bank in Chicago. When the vice president's financial services marketing department was eliminated, she lost her job. After three months of unemployment, which she spent searching for work and waiting for responses to her letters and telephone calls, the former vice president took a freelance job, using her expertise to advise clients on financial planning matters. Within a year, she was making three times her former salary.

The vice president's unemployment experience, although surely trying for her at the time, had a happy ending. In fact, you might say that the labor market worked pretty well. At least judging by her salary, she is more productive in her new job. Although one job was destroyed, another one—a better one, in this case—was created.

FIGURE 20.4 Job Losers, Job Leavers, New Entrants, and Re-entrants (December 2016)

A significant part of the unemployment rate consists of people who lost their jobs. The rest consists of people who left their jobs to look for another job or who have just entered or reentered the labor force.

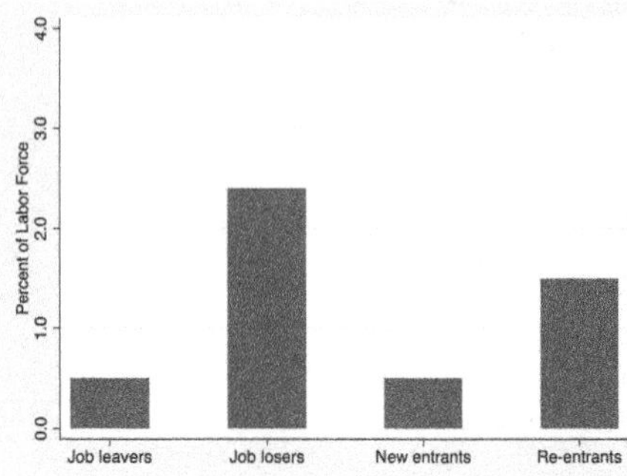

Source: Bureau of Labor Statistics

This transition from one job to another is part of the dynamism of any free market economy. The economist Joseph Schumpeter called this dynamism creative destruction, referring to the loss of whole business firms as well as jobs when new ideas and techniques replace the old. Creative destruction means that something better is created as something else is destroyed. In this case, a better job was created when one job was destroyed. The labor market in the United States is extremely fluid, with a large number of jobs being created and destroyed every month. In October of 2016 alone, 3.7 million new jobs were created and 3.5 million jobs ceased to exist.

In an economy with growing employment, more jobs are created than are destroyed. In times of recession, however, when employment is likely to fall, more jobs are destroyed than are created. So the bank manager was lucky to have lost her job during a period when finding a comparable job was relatively easy, but many people who lose their jobs are not as lucky as the woman in our story.

On average, about half of all unemployed workers are unemployed because they lost their jobs for one reason or another. This number typically will rise in a recession. People may lose their jobs even when the economy is not in a recession. The economy is always in a state of flux, with some firms going out of business or shrinking and other firms starting up or expanding. Tastes change, new discoveries are made, and competition improves productivity and changes the relative fortunes of firms and workers.

Among the unemployed in the last recession were real estate agents let go by realtors who were seeing drastic slumps in new home sales; construction workers unable to find jobs in the formerly booming housing markets of Nevada, Florida, Arizona, and California; managers laid off by banks that had been acquired by other banks because of financial difficulties; and workers in service sector firms who were struggling to survive turbulent times. Finding a comparable job was difficult for such workers: Most other firms at which they could have worked also were facing financial difficulties and therefore were laying off workers instead of hiring them, or they were undergoing the same type of structural changes that led to the workers being laid off from their previous firms.

People are unemployed for different reasons: Some lost their job and are looking for another job (left), others quit their previous job and still are looking for a new job (middle), and yet others just entered or re-entered the labor force and are unemployed while looking for work (right).

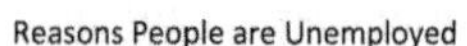

Reasons People are Unemployed

Source: Hadrian / Shutterstock.com

The loss of a job not only has disastrous effects on income, but also can have psychological effects. It may mean that a worker's children cannot go to college or that the worker must sell his or her house. Unemployment compensation provides some relief—perhaps about $200 a week until it runs out. In many cases, however, this is well below what these workers were earning. Until they find a new job, they are part of the millions of unemployed. Some may wait until a comparable job comes along; others may accept a lower-paying job. For example, a laid-off software programmer may take a job as a community college instructor for a much lower salary.

job vacancies

Positions that firms are trying to fill, but for which they have yet to find suitable workers.

At the same time that unemployed workers are looking for jobs, many firms have jobs that have not been filled; these are called **job vacancies**. Job vacancies and unemployment exist simultaneously. You might think that these two should not coexist because the unemployed workers should be able to take the unfilled jobs, but unfortunately, that is not always possible. Many job vacancies require different skills from those of unemployed workers, are located in another part of the country, or offer lower wages than these workers' former salaries.

Job Leavers

On average, American workers change jobs every three or four years. Many of these job changes occur when people are young: Young workers are finding out what they are good at or what they enjoy or are rapidly accumulating skills that give them greater opportunities. A small part of unemployment—less than one-fourth—consists of people who quit their previous job to look for another job. While they are looking for work, they are counted as unemployed. Unemployment increases very little as a result of quits during recessions. In a recession, when unemployment is high, fewer workers quit their jobs because they fear being unemployed for a long period of time.

New Entrants and Re-entrants

Figure 20.4 also shows that a large number of the unemployed workers have just entered the workforce. If a college student does not have a job lined up before she graduates, then she will be counted as an unemployed worker for the period of time while she looks for work. In fact, unemployment increases significantly each June as millions of students enter the labor force for the first time. This is called seasonal unemployment because it occurs each graduation "season." In contrast, unemployment is relatively low around the holiday season, when many businesses hire extra employees. Government statisticians smooth out this seasonal unemployment to identify other trends in unemployment, so newspaper reports on the unemployment rate rarely mention this phenomenon.

Some unemployed workers are re-entering the labor force. For example, a young person may decide to go back to school to improve her skills and then re-enter the labor force afterward. Others might drop out of the labor force for several years to take care of small children at home—a job that is not counted in the unemployment statistics.

Some new entrants and some re-entrants into the labor force find it difficult to get a job and therefore remain unemployed for long periods of time. In fact, although the hardships of people who lose their jobs are severe, the hardships for many young people, especially for those who dropped out of high school and who seem to be endlessly looking for work, also are severe. Similarly, re-entrants who have been away from the labor market for a long time, perhaps for as long as a couple of decades to raise children, will not find it easy to find work in a labor market that is quite different from the one in which they were last employed.

2.2 The Duration of Unemployment

The hardships associated with unemployment depend on its duration. Figure 20.5 show show the unemployment rate is divided according to how long the unemployed workers have been unemployed. A significant fraction of unemployment is short term. A market economy with millions of people exercising free choice could not possibly function without some short-term unemployment as people changed jobs or looked for new opportunities.

As of December 2016, 24 percent of unemployed workers (a little over 1 percent of the labor force) had been unemployed for more than six months—the truly long-term unemployed. This represented a dramatic improvement, five years ago that number was around 44 percent. Although the number of short-term unemployed does not vary much over the business cycle, the number of long-term unemployed increases dramatically in recessions.

FIGURE 20.5 Unemployment by Duration (December 2016)

The overall unemployment rate was 4.7 percent in December 2016. Around a quarter of the unemployed can be classified as being long term unemployed—more than 26 weeks looking for but unable to find work.

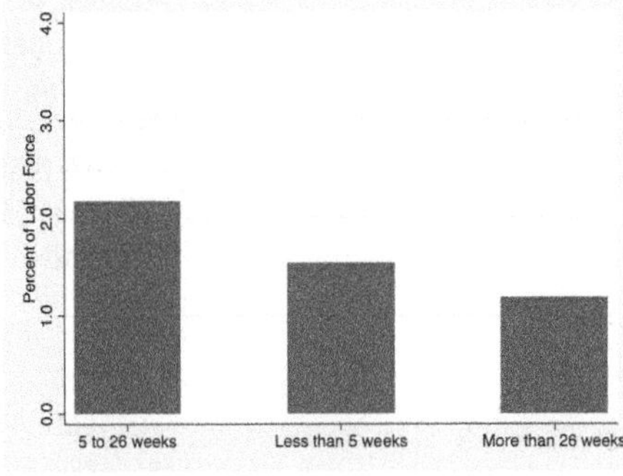

Source: Current Employment Survey (Washington, DC: Bureau of Labor Statistics).

2.3 Unemployment for Different Groups

Regardless of how one interprets the numbers, certain groups of workers experience very long spells of unemployment and suffer great hardships as a result of the difficulty they have in finding work. Table 20.1 shows the unemployment rates for several different demographic groups in the United States in four time periods: 1998, 2004, 2010, and 2016. During all three of these time periods, the economy was a couple of years into the beginning of economic recovery from a recession.

Unemployment is lowest for adult men and women. But unemployment is quite high for teenagers. To some extent this is due to more frequent job changes and the time it takes to find work after graduating from school. But many teenagers who are looking for work have dropped out of school and therefore are unskilled and have little or no experience. Their unemployment rates are extremely high, especially those for young minorities. Thus, even when the news is good about the overall unemployment rate, the news may remain bleak for those with low skills and little experience. The overall unemployment rate does not capture the long-term hardships experienced by certain groups.

TABLE 20.1 **Unemployment Rates for Different Demographic Groups (percent of labor force for each group)**

	1998	2004	2010	2016
All persons	4.4	5.4	9.3	4.7
All females	4.4	5.1	8.5	4.6
All males	4.3	5.5	10.0	4.8
All whites	3.8	4.5	8.5	4.3
All blacks	7.7	10.7	15.5	7.8
All Hispanics	7.7	6.6	12.9	5.9
All females 20 years and older	3.9	4.6	8.0	4.3
All males 20 years and older	3.6	4.8	9.4	4.4
All teens 16-19	13.5	17.6	25.3	14.7

Source: Bureau of Labor Statistics. All numbers are for the month of December of the respective year.

REVIEW

- People become unemployed when they lose their job, quit their job, or decide to enter or re-enter the labor force to look for a job.
- Being a new entrant is the least likely reason for a person to be unemployed. Losing a job and looking for work after some time out of the labor force are more likely reasons to be unemployed.
- In a large, dynamic economy like that of the United States, millions of jobs are created and lost during each month. In times of recession, more jobs are lost than are created.
- Many unemployed people are able to find a job fairly quickly. On average, only about one-sixth of unemployed people have been unemployed for six months or more. These workers often lack appropriate skills or were employed in industries that are undergoing fundamental structural changes.
- At the same time that unemployed workers are looking for jobs, firms with job vacancies are looking for workers. Because of skill differences and geographic mismatches, it is not easy to fill vacant jobs with unemployed workers.
- Unemployment rates vary across different groups. Teenagers and minorities in the United States have very high unemployment rates, even in boom years, and often are the first to suffer in times of recession.

3. MODELING THE LABOR MARKET

Thus far in this chapter, we have introduced key labor market variables, like the unemployment rate and the labor force participation rate; looked at data on both the current values and past trends of these variables; and discussed why people become (and stay) unemployed. In this section, we change our focus from data and definitions to theory, and discuss how to construct a model of the labor market. If we are able to come up with a model that provides a good explanation of the labor market trends we discussed earlier, then we can use this model to identify policy changes, as well as other economic changes, that can help reduce the rate of unemployment in the economy. Lowering the rate of unemployment, especially the natural rate of unemployment, will give individuals the opportunity to earn a living and allow a country to make full use of its labor resources.

3.1 Labor Demand and Labor Supply

We begin with the basic supply and demand framework developed in Chapter 3. Figure 20.6 shows a labor demand curve and a labor supply curve. On the vertical axis is the price of labor (wage), and on the horizontal axis is the quantity of labor supplied or demanded. In a labor market, the **labor demand curve** describes the behavior of firms, indicating how much labor they would demand at a given wage. The **labor supply curve** describes the behavior of workers, showing how much labor they would supply at a given wage. The wage, usually measured in dollars per hour of work, is the price of labor. To explain employment in the whole economy, it is best to think of the wage relative to the average price of goods. In other words, the wage on the vertical axis is the **real wage**, which we define as follows:

$$\text{Real wage} = \frac{\text{wage}}{\text{price level}}$$

Firms consider the wages they must pay their workers in comparison with the price of the products they sell. The workers consider the wage in comparison with the price of the goods they buy. Thus, in the whole economy, it is the real wage that affects the quantity of labor supplied and demanded.

The labor demand curve slopes downward because a lower real wage implies that the wage that the firm has to pay to hire a worker is falling relative to the price of the goods that the firm is selling. This reduced wage gives firms an incentive to hire more workers and pay existing workers to work more hours—the now-familiar result that the quantity demanded of labor rises as the price of labor (the real wage) falls. The labor supply curve slopes upward, because a higher real wage implies that the wage that the worker receives is rising compared with the price of the goods that the worker buys. This increased wage gives people greater incentive to work and gives those who are working an incentive to work more hours—another familiar result that the quantity of supplied labor rises as the price of labor (the real wage) rises.

As in any market, we would predict that the equilibrium quantity (hours of work) and the equilibrium price (the real wage) should occur at the intersection of the labor demand curve and the labor supply curve, as shown in Figure 20.6.

labor demand curve

A downward-sloping relationship showing the quantity of labor firms are willing to hire at each wage.

labor supply curve

Upward sloping relationship showing the quantity of labor workers are willing to supply at each wage.

real wage

The wage or price of labor adjusted for inflation; in contrast, the nominal wage has not been adjusted for inflation.

FIGURE 20.6 Labor Supply, Labor Demand, and Equilibrium Employment

The intersection of the labor supply curve and the labor demand curve determines equilibrium employment and the real wage.

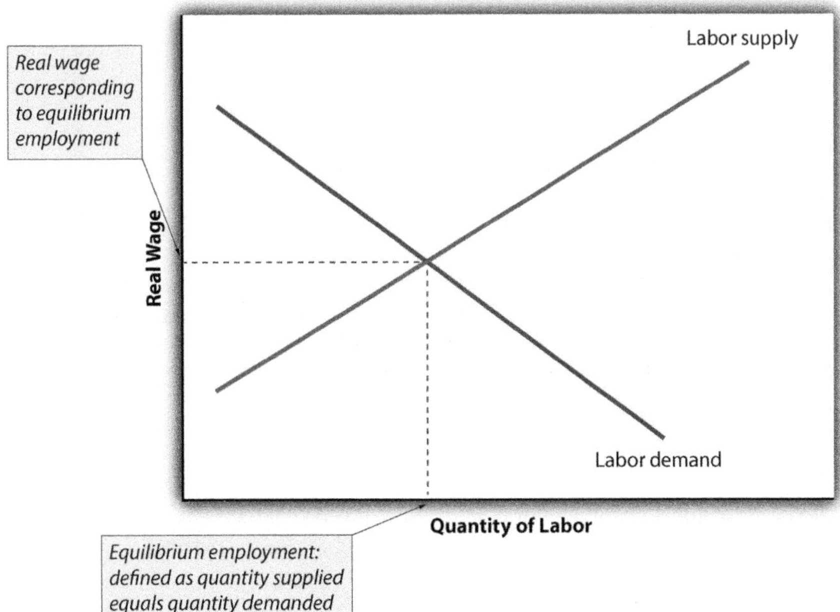

3.2 Explaining Labor Market Trends

Let's use this basic supply and demand framework to analyze labor market behavior. Suppose the economy enters a boom period during which firms are facing an increasing demand from consumers for the goods and services they produce. Firms will be eager to hire more workers to produce the goods and services that their consumers are clamoring for, resulting in an increase in the demand for labor. As the labor demand curve shifts to the right, as shown in Figure 20.7, both the equilibrium price and the equilibrium quantity of labor will rise. In other words, during an economic expansion, the model predicts an increase in the real wage and an increase in employment. Suppose instead that the economy had tumbled into a recession, during which time firms were cutting back on their production and did not need to hire as many workers. Then the demand for labor would shift to the left, and the real wage and employment would decrease.

The prediction of the model that wages and employment should rise in expansions and fall in recessions seems intuitive. The simple model as depicted in Figure 20.7 however, has a glaring weakness. Notice that the economy is at the intersection of the supply curve and the demand curve, regardless of whether it is in an expansion or a recession. In other words, the real wage always adjusts so that the quantity of labor demanded is equal to the quantity of labor supplied. Given the definition of an unemployed worker as someone who is looking for work but unable to find a job, the model implies that unemployment is always zero, no matter what state the economy is in. The simple model, which predicts that the economy will be at the intersection of the supply and demand curves, is inconsistent with the facts. We need to modify the model before we can use it for analysis.

3.3 Why Is the Unemployment Rate Always Greater Than Zero?

job rationing

A reason for unemployment in which the quantity of labor supplied is greater than the quantity demanded because the real wage is too high.

job search

A reason for unemployment in which uncertainty in the labor market and workers' limited information require people to spend time searching for a job.

Economists have developed two different explanations that adapt the standard labor supply and demand analysis to account for unemployment. Although quite different, the explanations are complementary. In fact, it is essential for us to use both simultaneously if we are to understand unemployment. We will refer to the two explanations as **job rationing** and **job search**.

FIGURE 20.7 **Modeling the Labor Market during an Economic Expansion**

When the economy enters an expansion period, firms produce more output and thus need more workers. The demand for labor increases, shifting the demand curve to the right. Equilibrium real wages and equilibrium employment rise.

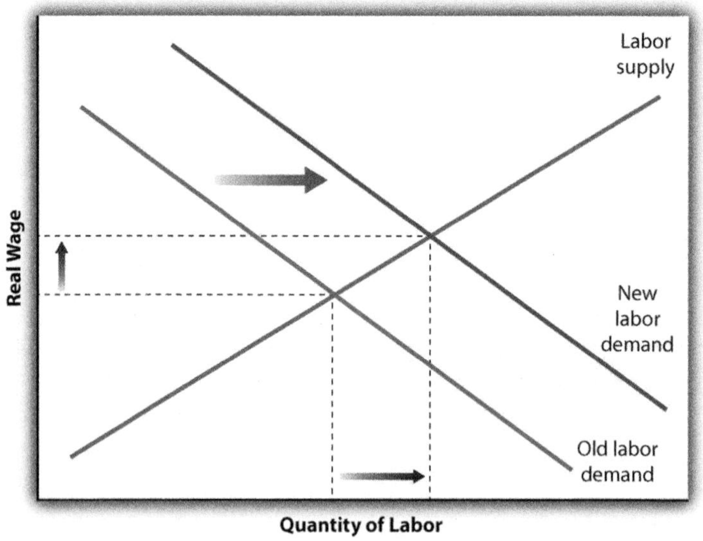

Job Rationing

The job-rationing story has two parts. One is an assumption that *the wage is higher than what would equate the quantity of labor supplied with the quantity of labor demanded.* This assumption may be true for several reasons, but first consider the consequences for the labor supply and demand diagram. Figure 20.8 shows the same labor supply and demand curves as Figure 20.6. In Figure 20.8, however, the wage is higher than the wage that would equate the quantity of labor supplied with the quantity of labor demanded. At this wage, the number of workers demanded by firms is smaller than the number of workers willing to supply their labor.

The other part of the job-rationing story tells us how to determine the number of workers who are unemployed. This part of the story assumes that the number of workers employed equals the quantity of labor demanded by business firms. When the wage is too high, firms hire a smaller number of workers, and workers supply whatever the firms demand. Figure 20.8 shows the resulting amount of employment at the given wage as point A on the labor demand curve. With employment equal to the number of workers demanded, we see that the number of workers willing to supply their labor is greater than the number of workers employed; the excess supply therefore results in unemployment. In the diagram, the amount of unemployment is measured in the horizontal direction.

This is a situation in which workers would be willing to take a job at the wage that firms are paying, but the job offers at that wage are insufficient. In effect, the available jobs are rationed—for example, by a first-come-first-served rule or by seniority. When enough workers have been hired, the firms essentially close their hiring offices, and the remaining workers stay unemployed. If the wage were lower, then the firms would hire more workers, but the wage is not lower.

FIGURE 20.8 Excess Supply of Labor and Unemployment

The supply and demand curves are exactly as in Figure 8.6, except that the horizontal axis is interpreted as employment here. However, the real wage is too high to bring the quantity supplied into equality with the quantity demanded. The number of workers employed is given by point A on the demand curve, at which point the real wage is above the equilibrium wage. At this higher real wage, the quantity supplied is greater than the quantity demanded—a situation that we think of as unemployment.

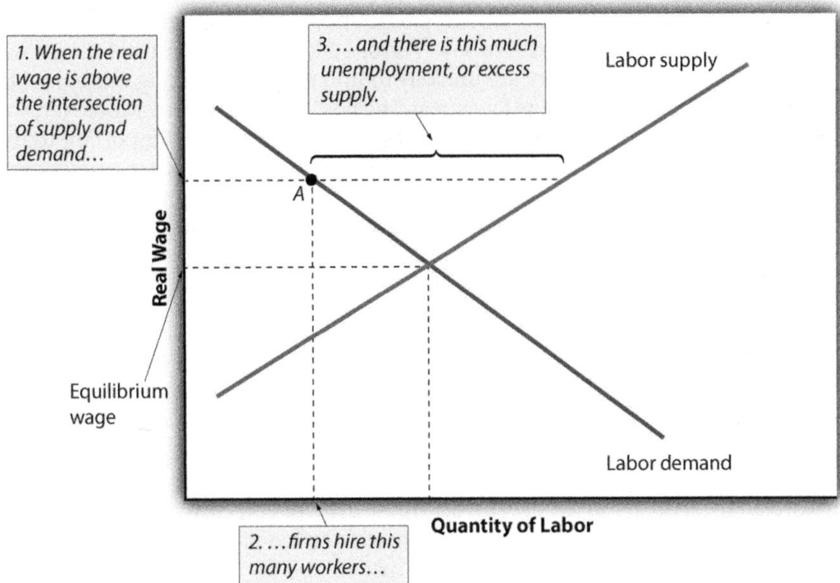

In most markets, a situation of excess supply brings about a reduction in the price—in this case, the wage. Thus, if this explanation of unemployment is to work in practice, a force has to be at work that prevents the wage from falling. If the theory is to be helpful in explaining unemployment, then the force has to be permanently at work, not just in a recession. Why doesn't the wage fall when there is an excess supply of workers? Three reasons explain why the wage always might be too high to bring the quantity of labor demanded into balance with the quantity of labor supplied.

minimum wage

A wage per hour below which it is illegal to pay workers.

insiders

A person who already works for a firm and has some influence over wage and hiring policy.

outsiders

Someone who is not working for a particular firm, making it difficult for him or her to get a job with that firm even though he or she is willing to work for a lower wage.

efficiency wage

A wage higher than that which would equate quantity supplied and quantity demanded, set by employers to incr ease worker efficiency-for example, by decreasing shirking by workers.

1. *Minimum wages.* Most countries have a legal **minimum wage**, or lowest possible wage, that employers can pay their employees. A minimum wage can cause unemployment to be higher than it otherwise would be, as shown on the diagram in Figure 20.8: Employers would move down and to the right along their labor demand curve and hire more workers if the wage were lower. One of the reasons teenage unemployment is high (as shown in Table 20.1) may be related to the minimum wage. Because many teenagers are unskilled, the wage that firms would be willing to pay them is low. A minimum wage, therefore, may price them out of the market and cause them to be unemployed
2. *Insiders versus outsiders.* Sometimes groups of workers—**insiders**, who have jobs—can prevent the wage from declining. If these workers have developed skills that are unique to the job, or if legislation prevents their being fired without significant legal costs, then they have some power to keep wages up. Labor unions may help these workers keep the wage higher than it otherwise would be. One consequence of the higher wage is to prevent the firm from hiring unemployed workers—the **outsiders**—who would be willing to work at a lower wage. This is a common explanation for the very high unemployment in Europe, and the theory has been developed and applied to Europe by the Swedish economist Assar Lindbeck and the American economist Dennis Snower.
3. *Efficiency wages.* Firms may choose to pay workers an **efficiency wage**—an extra amount to encourage them to be more efficient. Workers' efficiency or productivity might increase with the wage for many reasons. Turnover will be lower with a higher wage because workers will have less reason to look for another job: They are unlikely to find a position paying more than their current wage. Lower turnover means lower training costs for employers. Moreover, workers might not avoid work as much with a higher wage. This is particularly important to the firm when jobs are difficult to monitor. With efficiency wages, workers who are working are paid more than the wage that equates the quantity supplied with the quantity demanded. When workers are paid efficiency wages, unemployment will be greater than zero. Unemployed workers are eager to work at the prevailing wage, but they may be unable to obtain those jobs because existing workers value the high-paying jobs and are loath to give them up.

Job Search

We now turn to the second explanation that modifies the standard labor supply and demand analysis. The labor market is constantly in a state of flux, with jobs being created and destroyed and people moving from one job to another. The demand for one type of work falls, and the demand for another type of work increases. Labor supply curves also shift.

In other words, the labor market is never truly in the state of rest conveyed by the fixed supply and demand curves shown in Figure 20.6. But how can we change the picture? Imagine labor demand and labor supply curves that constantly bounce around. The demand for labor, the supply of labor, and the wage will be different during every period. Figure 20.6 will be in perpetual motion. Mathematicians use the adjective stochastic to describe this constant bouncing around. Economists apply the term stochastic to models of the labor market that are in perpetual motion. Rather than a fixed equilibrium of quantity and a fixed wage, a *stochastic equilibrium* exists. This stochastic equilibrium in the labor market characterizes the constant job creation and job destruction that exist in the economy. People enter the workforce, move from one job to another, lose their jobs, or drop out of the labor force. Wages change, inducing people to enter or reenter the market. Figure 20.9 is a schematic representation of the flows of workers into and out of the labor market.

In a stochastic equilibrium, at any point in time people will be searching for a job. Many who do so will be unemployed for some time. They lost their job, quit their job, or came back to the job market after an absence from work. One of the reasons they remain unemployed for a while is that they find it to their advantage not to accept the first job that comes along. Rather, they wait for a possibly higher-paying job. While they wait, they are unemployed.

FIGURE 20.9 Labor Market Flows

The labor market is constantly in a state of flux, as people lose jobs, quit jobs, find jobs, and move into and out of the labor force. Most people pass through the unemployment box for a short period, but among the unemployed, some have not held jobs for a long time.

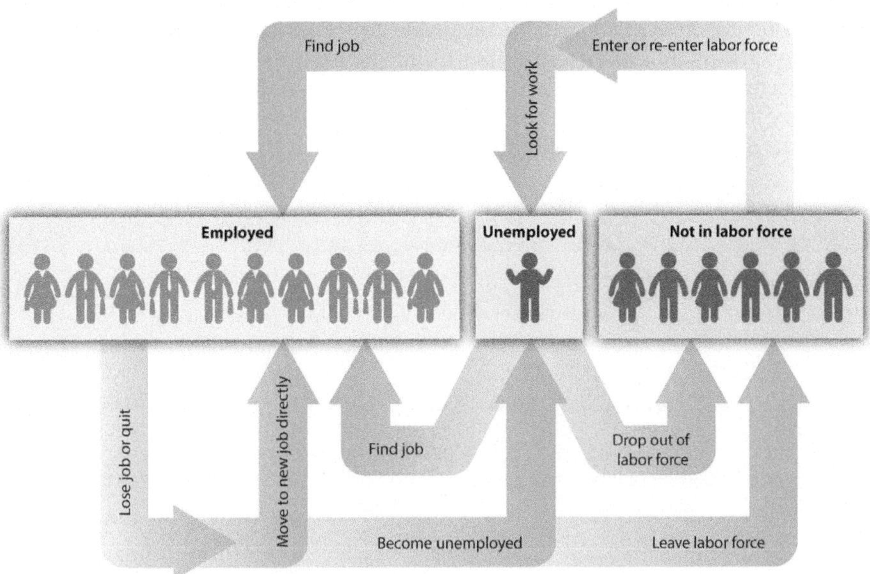

Policies to Reduce Unemployment

Both the job-rationing model and the job-search model have implications for how public policy can reduce both the rate of unemployment and the natural rate of unemployment. The job-rationing model predicts that high minimum wages, rigid insider-outsider arrangements, and a greater need to pay efficiency wages can lead to more unemployment. This implies that public policies that reduce minimum wages or encourage more flexible union-employer relationships can reduce unemployment. Similarly, economic changes and policy changes that make it easier for firms to monitor shirking workers and cheaper to train new workers will enable firms to hire more workers at a reduced efficiency wage. As with any case of rationing, those who are lucky enough to have access to the commodity (in this case, jobs) are better off as a result of the restriction. Policies that remove the constraint and allow the market to reach equilibrium benefit those who now are able to obtain jobs while hurting those who previously had jobs but now earn a lower wage.

The job-search model implies that improved job-placement programs, retraining of unemployed workers, increasing the incentives of unemployed workers to look for work, and decreasing the costs of hiring new workers all will help reduce unemployment. In an economy in which unemployment compensation—money paid to workers who have been laid off from their job—is high, workers are likely to spend more time looking for a job or to hold out for a higher-paying job. Reducing unemployment compensation will provide more incentives for workers to look for work and increases the likelihood that they will find a good job match. Here too, you have to consider the trade-offs before implementing a policy change. Unemployment compensation mitigates the hardships associated with unemployment and allows people more time to search. But the more generous unemployment compensation is, the less incentive a worker has to actually take a job. If workers continue a perfunctory search for jobs, unemployment will remain high. The challenge is to design an unemployment compensation system that supports workers who lose their jobs without increasing unemployment by a lot.

What about the natural rate of unemployment? If you take a closer look at the labor market flows in Figure 20.9, you will see that the rate of unemployment that usually prevails in an economy will depend on two things: (1) how great the flows into the group of employed workers are (these flows come from those who were unemployed and those who were already employed), and (2) how great the flows into the group of unemployed workers are (these flows come from both previously employed workers and those who previously were out of the labor force). Economies in which the flows into employment are relatively low or the flows into unemployment are relatively high (or both) will have a high natural rate of unemployment. Similarly, economies in which the flows into employment are high or the flows into unemployment are low (or both) will have a low natural rate of unemployment.

In the United States, lots of workers lose their jobs in a given month, but many of them are able to find new jobs easily, because firms face relatively few restrictions in their ability to hire workers. In addition, unemployment compensation in most of the United States typically runs out after 26 weeks; the evidence shows that many people stop searching and take a job just when their unemployment compensation runs out. Furthermore, new entrants to the labor market, like college students, typically are not eligible for unemployment compensation; these young workers are likely to find a job quickly, even if it is a lower-paying position than they ideally would like to have.

In contrast, in an economy like Spain's, workers who lose their jobs may find it difficult to move to another job because stronger unions restrict the quantity of labor demanded by firms or because generous long-term unemployment benefits, available to those without much work experience, discourage unemployed workers and new entrants from intensively searching for work. As a result, the natural rate for unemployment in Spain is likely to be higher than the natural rate in the United States. Furthermore, this can explain why a U.S. college student would be much more likely to find a job after graduation than the graduate's Spanish counterpart.

REVIEW

- The supply and demand for labor is the starting point for modeling the labor market. The quantity demanded of labor falls as the real wage rises, whereas the quantity supplied of labor rises. The intersection of the labor supply and demand curves determines the amount of employment and the equilibrium real wage.
- The basic supply and demand framework predicts that employment and wages will rise during economic expansions and fall during recessions. Because the economy is always at the intersection of the supply and demand curves, the model seems to predict that unemployment is zero—the quantity of labor supplied is always equal to the quantity of labor demanded, and no one is looking for but unable to find work.
- The basic supply and demand theory needs to be modified to account for unemployment. Economists use two approaches, job rationing and job search, to explain why unemployment occurs.
- Job rationing occurs when the wage is too high. Unemployment can be interpreted as the difference between the quantity supplied and the quantity demanded at that high wage. Wages can be too high because of minimum-wage laws, insiders, or efficiency wages.
- Job search is another reason for unemployment. It takes time to find a job, and people have an incentive to wait for a good job.
- Policies that reduce the amount of rationing or lower the cost of job search can reduce unemployment.

4. END-OF-CHAPTER MATERIAL

4.1 Conclusion

This chapter provided two important lessons about labor markets. The first lesson introduced key concepts, such as the unemployment rate and the labor force participation rate. Understanding who the unemployed are, how long they stay unemployed, and how unemployment rates vary across time and across countries is a critical prerequisite for designing policies that can reduce unemployment.

The second lesson constructed a model of the labor market that would replicate the patterns observed in the labor market. That model then could be used to come up with policy recommendations that could help workers obtain jobs and help economies make better use of one of their most important productive resources. We showed that the simple supply and demand model could not realistically describe the labor market, but that augmenting that model to take into account job rationing and job search provides insight into possible policy interventions. Lower minimum wages, less rigid unions, better job training, and less generous unemployment benefits all can increase the rate at which people who are either unemployed or out of the labor force move into employment, as well as decrease the rate at which employed workers or workers who are out of the labor force move into the ranks of the unemployed. The challenge for policy makers is how to carry out these reforms to balance the benefits to currently unemployed workers with the costs to currently employed workers.

Key Points

1. Unemployment and employment data are collected by the Bureau of Labor Statistics and are made available in the monthly *Current Population Survey*.
2. A person is unemployed if he or she is old enough to work and is looking for work, but does not have a job. The unemployment rate is the number of unemployed as a percentage of the labor force, which consists of all the employed and unemployed in the economy.
3. Two other widely used measures of the labor market are the employment-to-population ratio (the number of people employed as a percentage of the working-age population) and the labor force participation rate (the labor force as a percentage of the working-age population). Both of these indicators rose in the United States following the end of World War II as more women entered the workforce.
4. Not all workers work full time; many work part-time, or fewer than 35 hours a week. This part-time work is especially common among women with young children. Because of part-time work, economists use aggregate hours worked, rather than aggregate employment, to measure the quantity of labor engaged in production.
5. The unemployment rate tends to rise during recessions and fall during expansion. The unemployment rate when the economy is neither in recession nor in an expansion is called the natural rate of unemployment.
6. People are unemployed for four reasons: They have lost their job, they have quit their job, they have entered the labor force for the first time, or they have re-entered the labor force.
7. The simple labor supply and demand model can predict some aspects of the behavior of labor markets but cannot explain the existence of unemployment in the economy.
8. To explain the behavior of unemployment, the simple model needs to be modified to take into account both job rationing, in which the wage is too high to equate supply and demand, and job search, in which unemployed people look for work but are unable to find work if an appropriate job opportunity does not come along.
9. Countries that have low natural rates of unemployment tend to be the ones in which it is relatively easy for the unemployed or those out of the labor force to find jobs and/or relatively more unlikely that people who do lose their job will be unable to find another job.
10. Economic policies such as exemptions for teenagers from the minimum-wage laws, time limits on unemployment compensation, or the provision of information about job openings to reduce job-search time can reduce the natural unemployment rate.

QUESTIONS FOR REVIEW

1. How do economists define unemployment, and how do they measure how many people are unemployed?
2. How is the working-age population defined?
3. What is the definition of the labor force?
4. What has happened to the employment-to-population ratio for men and women since the 1950s?
5. What is the difference between frictional and structural unemployment?
6. Why isn't the unemployment rate equal to zero?
7. What is the difference between unemployment resulting from job rationing and unemployment resulting from job search?
8. What economic policies would reduce the natural rate of unemployment?

PROBLEMS

1. Which of the following people would be unemployed according to official statistics? Which ones would you define as unemployed? Why?
   a. A person who is home painting the house while seeking a permanent position as an electrician.
   b. A full-time student.
   c. A recent graduate who is looking for a job.
   d. A parent who decides to stay home taking care of children full time.
   e. A worker who quits his job because he thinks the pay is insufficient.
   f. A teenager who gets discouraged looking for work and stops looking.
2. The table below contains some information about employment, labor force, and population levels in the United States at the turn of each decade.
   a. Using the data, fill in the table.
   b. Suppose the projection for the working-age population in the year 2020 for the United States is 265 million. If the unemployment rate and the labor force participation rate are the same in 2020 as they were in 2000, how much employment will there be?
   c. Using the same projection of 265 million for the working-age population in 2020, calculate employment with an unemployment rate of 5 percent and a labor force participation rate of 60 percent.
   d. Calculate the same for a labor force participation rate of 70 percent. Which of these estimates do you think is more realistic? Why?

Year	Total Employment (millions)	Unemployment Rate (percent)	Labor Force Participation Rate (percent)	Working-Age Population (millions)
1980		7.2	63.6	168.9
1990		6.3	66.4	190.0
2000		3.9	67.0	213.7
2010	138.4		64.8	236.8

Source: U.S. Department of Labor.

3. What effect would a decline in part-time employment have on average weekly hours per worker in the United States? If the employment-to-population ratio increases, what will happen to total hours of work in the United States?
4. Job search and advertising now are available on the Internet. Using e-mail, job applicants can submit resumes to prospective employers. One popular website of this kind is www.monster.com.
   a. How should this service affect the unemployment rate?
   b. Suppose everybody in the working-age population has access to www.monster.com. Would you expect unemployment to be eliminated? Explain.
5. The age distribution of the population changes over time—in the United States, better health care (longer lives) and lower fertility (fewer kids) in recent years means that the proportion of people over age 16 is increasingly larger. At the same time, the labor force participation rate is likely to decline as baby boomers retire. Using the same method as in the previous problem, calculate total employment and the employment-to-population ratio based on the scenario in the table below.
   a. Describe what happens to total employment and the employment-to-population ratio in this scenario.
   b. Is it possible that labor force participation would fall so much that total employment would fall? How low would the labor force participation rate have to be in 2020 for total employment to be lower than in 2000?

Year	Unemployment Rate (percent)	Labor Force Participation Rate (percent)	Working-Age Population (millions)	Total Employment (millions)	Employment-to-Working-Age-Population Ratio
2000	3.9	67.0	214		
2010	9.8	64.8	237		
2020	5.0	62.0	260		

Source: U.S. Department of Labor.

6. The table below shows the demand for and supply of skilled labor at different hourly wages.
    a. Draw the supply and demand curves for labor.
    b. What are the wage and quantity of labor at equilibrium?
    c. Suppose a law is passed forbidding employers to pay wages less than $20 per hour. What will the new quantity of labor in the market be? Who gains and who loses from this law?

Demand for Labor		Supply of Labor	
Wage/Hour	*Quantity*	*Wage/Hour*	*Quantity*
$12	75	$12	47
14	68	14	54
16	61	16	61
18	54	18	68
20	47	20	75
22	40	22	82

7. Use a supply and demand diagram to show the possible reduction in teenage unemployment from a lower minimum "training" wage for workers younger than 20 years old. For what reasons might older unskilled workers complain about such a policy?
8. Use the theories of job rationing and job search to explain why the natural rate of unemployment in the United States is lower than that in France. What can the French government do to try to remedy this situation? Might these remedies be politically unpopular?
9. Why do young workers have higher unemployment rates than older workers? Is labor productivity different? Why?
10. Why do some firms pay efficiency wages? What would you expect to be true in regions or industries for which the payment of efficiency wages is widespread?

CHAPTER 21
Productivity and Economic Growth

For most of human history, there was no economic growth. True, kings and queens amassed vast quantities of wealth through conquest and exploitation; millions of slaves constructed coliseums, pyramids, and great walls; and talented individuals on all continents produced great works of art. But output per hour of work—the productive power of labor that determines the well-being of most people—hardly grew for thousands of years. Except for the ruling classes, people lived in extreme poverty.

productivity
Output per hour of work.

This situation changed dramatically around the eighteenth century. Figure 21.1 shows the growth rates of *output per hour of work*, or **productivity**, for different periods during the last three centuries. Observe that almost no growth in output per hour of work occurred for most of the 1700s, much as in the thousands of years before. Then, in the late 1700s and early 1800s—the period historians call the Industrial Revolution—economic growth began to pick up, first in Europe and then in the United States. Productivity growth accelerated in the early 1800s and then rose to historically unprecedented levels in the twentieth century. And, as productivity rose, people's incomes also rose and poverty declined.

FIGURE 21.1 Productivity Growth during the Past 300 Years
Productivity is defined as output per hour of work. Productivity *growth* is defined as the percentage increase in productivity from one year to the next. The bars indicate the average productivity growth during the years stated. The data are collected from Europe and the United States.

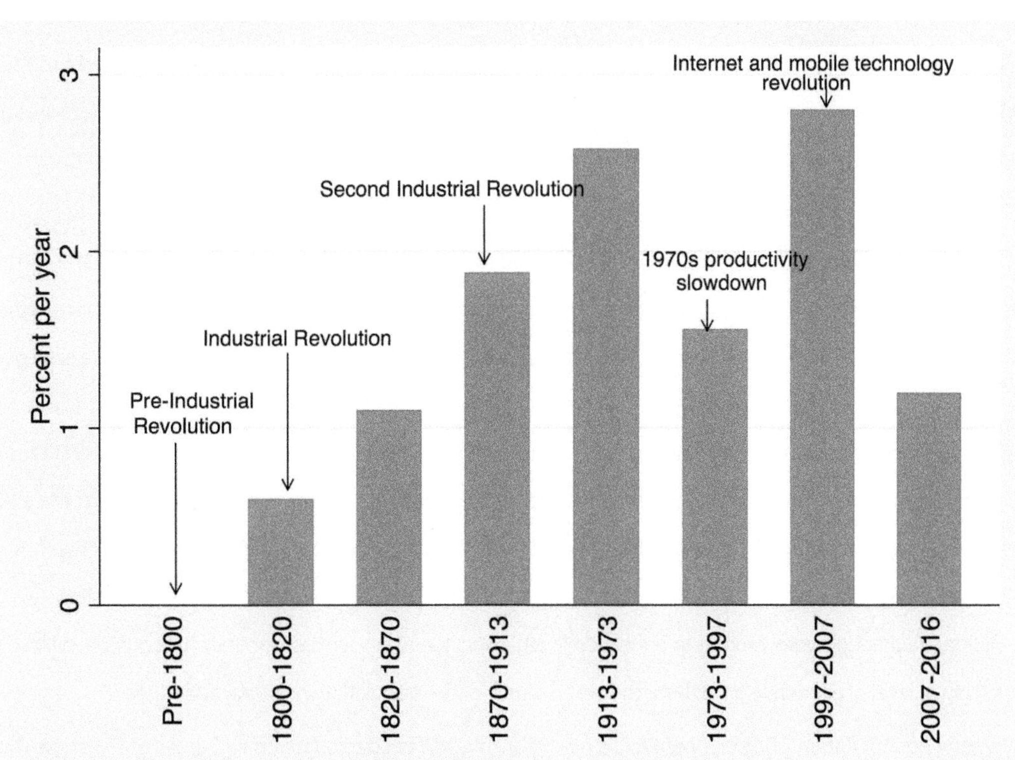

Angus Maddison (1997), Nicholas Crafts (1985) and Bureau of Labor Statistics

Just as productivity growth raised standards of living and reduced poverty in Europe and the United States in the 200 years since the Industrial Revolution, in the twenty-first century it is spreading around the world to China, India, and many other countries. In fact, differences in productivity growth among countries explain why some countries are poor and some are rich. Simply put, if productivity in a country is high, then that country is rich; if productivity in a country is low, then that country is poor. If you want to reduce the number of poor countries, then you have no choice but to increase productivity in poor countries. The ticket out of poverty is higher productivity.

Source: Shutterstock.com

Why did the growth of real gross domestic product (GDP) per hour of work begin to increase and then take off in the eighteenth century? Why is productivity growth high in some countries and low in other countries? The purpose of this chapter is to develop a theory of economic growth that helps answer these and many other questions. The theory of economic growth tells us that increases in hours worked can increase the growth of real GDP, but not the growth of real GDP per hour of work. To explain the growth of productivity, we must focus on the two other factors: capital and technology. Capital raises real GDP per hour of work by giving workers more tools and equipment to work with. As we will show in this chapter, however, capital alone is not sufficient to achieve the growth we have seen over the past 200 years. Technology—the knowledge and methods that underlie the production process—also has played a big role.

Recent work by the economist Robert Gordon has added a twist to this tale. He argues that, just as the 18th century acceleration in productivity came from the Industrial Revolution and its discoveries such as steam engines and railroads, an even larger acceleration in productivity came from a second industrial revolution in the early part of the 20th century thanks to discoveries such as electricity, the internal combustion engine, and infrastructure to provide sanitation and access to clean water for households. But, he argues, as the gains from that second industrial revolution began diminishing in the 1970s and 1980s, the hope that this decline would be reversed by the late 20th century and early 21st century innovations like personal computers, the internet, and mobile phone technology have been hitherto unfounded. Instead, Gordon argues that a series of what he terms "headwinds"—aging population, stagnating improvements in education levels, rising inequality, environmental challenges—will lead to a much lower level of economic growth for the vast majority of the population in the decades ahead.

Whether or not Robert Gordon is right in his pessimism, we will need to come up with policies to reverse this decline in growth and overcome the headwinds. Understanding the role of capital and technology will enable economists to better evaluate the advantages and disadvantages of various economic policies to improve economic growth. For example, should economic policies designed to stimulate economic growth focus more on capital or more on technology? What role will technological advances have in overcoming the environmental challenges posed by fossil-fuel emissions? How will technological advances like driverless cars or industrial robots affect the future of work?

1. LABOR AND CAPITAL WITHOUT TECHNOLOGY

To better understand the important role played by technology in driving economic growth, we begin with a simplified theory in which economic growth depends only on labor and then consider a theory in which it depends on labor and capital.

1.1 Labor Alone and Capital without Technology

Suppose real GDP depends only on labor. That is, the amount of output in the economy can be described by the production function $Y = F(L)$, where Y is real GDP and L is labor input. When labor input increases, real GDP increases.

To understand this production function for the whole economy, it helps to consider the production of a single good. Imagine workers on a one-acre vineyard planting, maintaining, and harvesting grapes, and suppose that the only input that can be varied is labor. With more workers, the vineyard can produce more grapes, but according to the simple story that output depends only on labor, the vineyard cannot increase capital because there is no capital. For example, the vineyard cannot buy wagons or wheel barrows to haul fertilizer around. The only way the vineyard can increase output is by hiring more workers to haul the fertilizer.

Now, suppose all this is true for the economy as a whole. The firms in the economy can produce more output by hiring more workers, but they cannot increase capital. The situation is shown for the entire economy in Figure 21.2. On the vertical axis is output. On the horizontal axis is labor input. The curve shows that more labor can produce more output. The curve is a graphical plot of the aggregate production function $Y = F(L)$ for the whole economy.

Diminishing Returns to Labor

The shape of the curve in Figure 21.2 is important. The flattening out of the curve shows **diminishing returns** to labor: The greater the number of workers used in producing output, the less the additional output that comes from each additional worker. Consider production of a single good again, such as grapes at the vineyard. Increasing employment at the one-acre vineyard from one to two workers raises production more than increasing employment from 1,001 to 1,002 workers. A second worker could take charge of irrigation or inspect the vines for insects while the first worker harvested grapes. But with 1,001 workers on the vineyard, the 1,002nd worker could find little to do to raise production. Diminishing returns to labor exist because labor is the only input to production that we are changing. As more workers are employed on the same one-acre plot, the contribution that each additional worker makes goes down. Adding one worker when only one worker is employed can increase production by a large amount. But adding one worker when 1,001 already are working on the one-acre plot cannot add as much. For the same reasons, diminishing returns to labor exist for the whole economy.

diminishing returns

A situation in which successive increases in the use of an input, holding other inputs constant, eventually will cause a decline in the additional production derived from one more unit of that input.

FIGURE 21.2 Only Changes in Labor Can Change Output

The curve shows the production function $Y = F(L)$, where Y is output and L is labor input (hours of work). In this theory, capital and technology are out of the picture. With more labor working on a fixed supply of land, there are diminishing returns, as shown by the curvature of the production function.

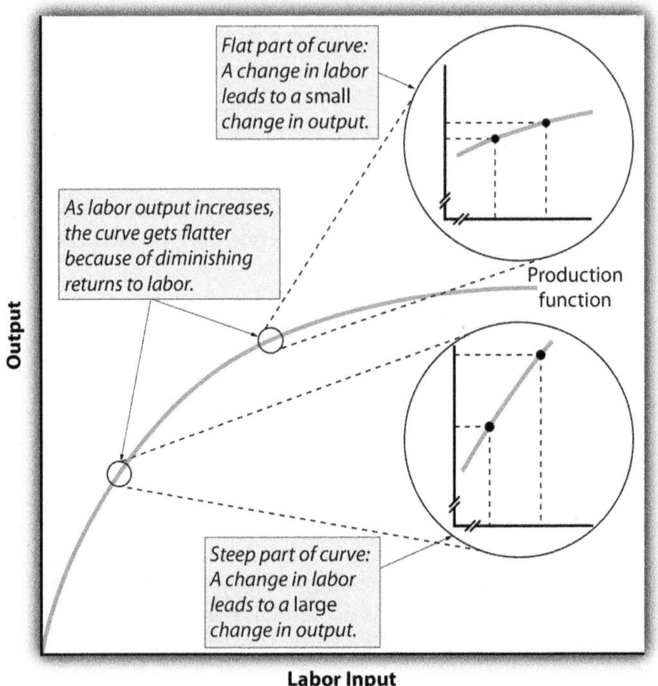

1.2 Adding Capital

Now let us add capital to the production function. The total amount of capital in the economy increases each year by the amount of net investment during the year. More precisely,

Capital at the end of this year = net investment this year + capital at the end of last year

Recall that net investment is equal to gross investment less depreciation. Depreciation is the amount of capital that wears out each year.

For example, if $10,000 billion is the value of all capital in the economy at the end of last year, then $100 billion of net investment during this year would raise the capital stock to $10,100 billion by the end of this year. This is a 1 percent increase in the capital stock.

With capital as an input to production, the production function becomes $Y = F(L, K)$, where K stands for capital. Output can be increased by using more capital, even if the amount of labor is not increased. Consider the vineyard example again. If a wheelbarrow is bought to haul the fertilizer around the vineyard, the vineyard can produce more grapes with the same number of workers. More capital at the vineyard increases output. The same is true for the economy as a whole. By increasing the amount of capital in the economy, more real GDP can be produced with the same number of workers.

Figure 21.3 illustrates how more capital raises output. The axes are the same as those in Figure 21.2, and the curve again shows that more output can be produced by more labor. But, in addition, Figure 21.3 shows that if we add capital to the economy—by investing a certain amount each year—the relationship between output and labor shifts up: More capital provides more output at any level of labor input. To see this, pick a point on the horizontal axis, say, Point A, to designate a certain amount of labor input. Then draw a vertical line up from this point, such as the dashed line shown in Figure 21.3. The vertical distance between the curve marked "Less capital"and the curve marked "More capital" shows that additional capital raises production.

FIGURE 21.3 Capital Is Also a Factor of Production

The axes in this figure are just like those in Figure 9.2, but now if more capital is added to production, more output can be produced with the same labor input. For example, when labor input is at Point *A*, more output can be produced with more capital.

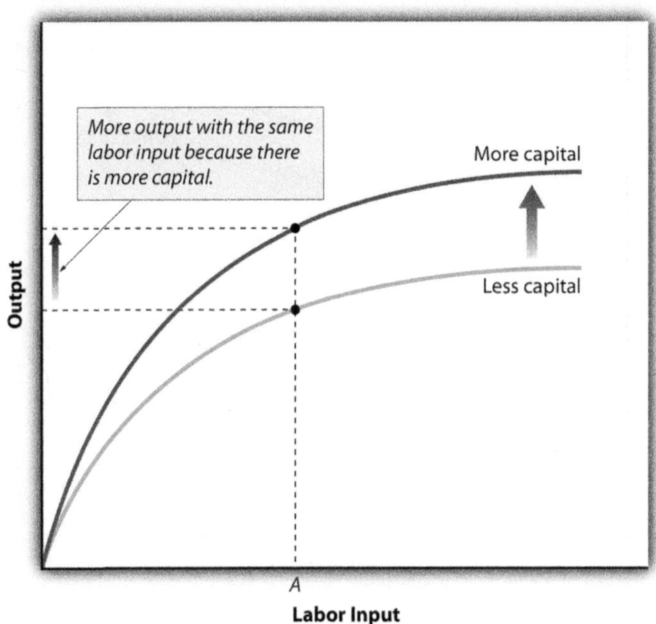

Diminishing Returns to Capital

Figure 21.4 also shows *diminishing returns to capital*. Each additional amount of capital—another wheelbarrow or another hoe—results in a smaller addition to output. Hence, the gaps between the several production functions in Figure 21.4 get smaller and smaller as more capital is added. As more capital is added, the ability to increase output per worker reduces. Compare adding one wheelbarrow to the vineyard without any wheelbarrows with adding one wheelbarrow to the vineyard that already has 50 wheelbarrows. Clearly, the 51st wheelbarrow would increase farm output by only a minuscule amount, certainly much less than the first wheelbarrow. A one-acre vineyard would not even have much room for the 51st wheelbarrow.

Diminishing returns to capital also occur for the economy as a whole. Thus, adding more capital per worker cannot raise real GDP per worker above some limit, and even getting close to that limit will require an enormous amount of capital. Eventually, growth in output per hour of work will stop.

Thus, labor and capital alone cannot explain the phenomenal growth in real GDP during the last 200 years.

FIGURE 21.4 Capital Has Diminishing Returns Also

As capital per worker increases, each additional unit of capital produces less output. Thus, there is a limit to how much growth per worker additional capital per worker can bring.

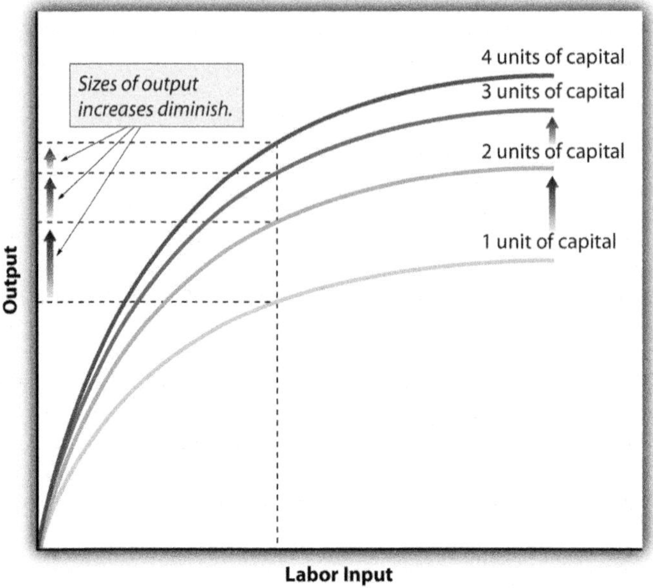

REVIEW

- Both labor and capital have diminishing returns. A graph of the production function for the economy shows these diminishing returns.
- An economic growth theory with labor and capital alone cannot account for the sustained increase in real GDP per hour of work that began in the late 1700s and continues in the twenty-first century.

2. TECHNOLOGY: THE ENGINE OF GROWTH

We have seen that growth driven by increases in capital and labor, although important, is not sustainable. Diminishing returns imply that the additional output obtained by increasing these inputs becomes smaller and smaller, eventually leading to no further economic growth. For output to grow over the very long run, we need not just to *increase* inputs, but also to get more output from *existing* inputs. Technology is what enables us to get more output from a given quantity of inputs.

2.1 What Is Technology?

technology

Anything that raises the amount of output that can be produced with a given amount of labor and capital.

Technology is difficult to define, envision, and measure. A broad definition of **technology** is that it is anything that raises the amount of output that can be produced with a given amount of inputs (labor and capital). In essence, technology is the stock of knowledge or ideas that exist in an economy: the ideas that help produce goods and services such as baby clothes, wine, and television shows; the ideas that help save lives, such as penicillin, vaccines, and heart transplants; and the ideas that help us communicate around the world, such as cell phones and the Internet.

When we add technology to capital and labor, we have the modern theory of economic growth. The theory can be summarized by the now familiar aggregate production function

$$Y = F(L, K, T)$$

technological change

Improvement in technology over time.

where *T* stands for technology. Increases in technology therefore will increase output. Such increases in technology are termed *technological progress.* We sometimes use the term **technological change** instead of technological progress.

Invention, Innovation, and Diffusion

Technological change occurs when new ideas are developed into new products that increase production, such as the steel plow, the harvester, the combine, the automobile, radar, the telephone, the computer, the airplane, lasers, and fiber-optic cable. Economists distinguish between an **invention**, which is the discovery of new knowledge or a new principle, such as electricity, and **innovation**, in which the new knowledge is brought into application with a new product, such as the electric light bulb. Economists also distinguish between the innovation itself and the **diffusion** of the innovation throughout the economy, a process that involves advertising, marketing, and spreading the innovation to new uses, such as the use of the electric light bulb to create night shifts in factories.

invention

A discovery of new knowledge.

innovation

Application of new knowledge in a way that creates new products or significantly changes old ones.

diffusion

The spreading of an innovation throughout the economy.

The sewing machine is a good illustration of invention, innovation, and diffusion. By 1847, inventors had built 17 different machines capable of mechanically forming a stitch. But only one of these, Elias Howe's sewing machine, developed into a commercially successful innovation. As Howe tried to sell his invention to consumers, he discovered how to modify it to make it more useful and attractive. Soon the invention turned into a popular innovation that was used widely. Wide diffusion of the innovation occurred as others produced household versions of the sewing machine, like the one marketed by the Singer Company. This example also illustrates that innovation and diffusion require the work of an entrepreneur who recognizes the potential of the invention.

Technology depends in part on scientific knowledge, and many people feel that science will become more and more important in driving future technological change. But technology is much more than scientific knowledge. The discovery of DNA did not improve technology until it was applied to genetic engineering. The knowledge of mathematics made the invention and development of computers possible, a technology that obviously has improved productivity.

Organization and Specialization

Technology also includes the way firms are organized. Better organization schemes can mean a smaller bureaucracy and more output per hour of work without the addition of capital. More efficient organization can improve the flow of information within a firm and thereby affect labor productivity. Better incentive programs that encourage workers to communicate their ideas to management, for example, increase productivity.

Henry Ford's idea of the assembly line greatly increased the productivity of workers. The assembly line enabled the car to come to the worker rather than having the worker go to the car. Thus, each worker could specialize in a certain type of activity; through specialization, productivity increased. The assembly line alone is estimated to have reduced the time it took a group of workers to produce a car from 12.5 hours to 0.5 hours. Productivity increased, and so too did wages.

New technology can affect how labor and capital are used at a firm. Economists distinguish between *labor-saving* and *capital-saving* technological change. *Labor-saving technological change* means that fewer workers are needed to produce the same amount of output; *capital-saving technological change* means that fewer machines are needed to produce the same amount of output. An example of a labor-saving technological change would be a steam-powered tractor replacing a horse-drawn plow, and later gasoline power replacing steam power, enabling the same worker to plow many more acres. An example of a capital-saving technological change is the night shift. Adding two crews of workers—one working in a steel mill from 4 P.M. to midnight and another working from midnight to 8 A.M.—makes the same steel-making furnaces three times as productive as when the working hours are only from 8 A.M. to 4 P.M.

Specialization of workers at a firm adds to productivity. Adam Smith emphasized the importance of specialization in his *Wealth of Nations*; his term *division of labor* refers to the way a manufacturing task could be divided among a group of workers, each of whom would specialize in a part of the job.

Because specialization permits workers to repeat the same task many times, their productivity increases, as in the old adage "practice makes perfect." Each time the task is repeated, the worker becomes more proficient—a phenomenon that economists call **learning by doing**. The commonsense principle of learning by doing is that the more one does something, the more one learns about how to do it. For example, as the number of airplanes produced of a particular type—say, a Boeing 777—increases, the workers become more and more skilled at producing that type of airplane. Careful studies of aircraft production have shown that productivity increases by 20 percent for each 100 percent increase in output of a particular type of plane. This relationship between learning and the amount of production is commonly called the "learning curve." Learning is a type of technological progress.

learning by doing

A situation in which workers become more proficient by doing a particular task many times.

Human Capital

Many firms provide training courses for workers to increase their skills and their productivity. *On-the-job training* is a catchall term for any education, training, or skills a worker receives while at work.

Most workers receive much of their education and training before they begin working, whether in grade school, high school, college, or professional schools. Because increases in education and training can raise workers' productivity, such increases are considered another source of technological change.

human capital

A person's accumulated knowledge and skills.

The education and training of workers, called **human capital** by economists, is similar to physical capital—factories and equipment. To accumulate human capital—to become more educated or better trained—people must devote time and resources, much as a firm must devote resources to investment if physical capital is to increase.

The decision to invest in human capital is influenced by considerations similar to those that motivate a firm to invest in physical capital: the cost of the investment versus the expected return. For example, investing in a college education may require that one borrow the money for tuition; if the interest rate on the loan rises, then people will be less likely to invest in a college education. Thus, investment in education may be negatively related to the interest rate, much as physical investment is. Thus, to encourage more education and thereby increase economic growth and productivity, the U.S. government provides low-interest loans to college students, making an investment in college more attractive. We will return to the government's role in education as part of its broader policy to increase economic growth later in the chapter.

2.2 The Production of Technology: The Invention Factory

Technology sometimes is discovered by chance by a lone inventor and sometimes by trial and error by an individual worker. A secretary who experiments with several different filing systems to reduce search time or with different locations for the computer, the printer, the telephone, and the photocopier is engaged in improving technology around the office. Frequently, technological progress is a continuous process in which a small adjustment here and a small adjustment there add up to major improvements over time.

But more and more technological change is the result of huge expenditures of research and development funds by industry and government. Thomas Edison's "invention factory" in Menlo Park, New Jersey, was one of the first examples of a large industrial laboratory devoted to the production of technology. It in turn influenced the development of many other labs, such as the David Sarnoff research lab of RCA. Merck & Co., a drug company, spends nearly $1 billion per year on research and development for the production of new technology.

Edison's Menlo Park laboratory had about 25 technicians working in three or four different buildings. In the six years from 1876 to 1882, the laboratory invented the light bulb, the phonograph, the telephone transmitter, and electrical generators. Each of these inventions turned out to be a successful innovation that was diffused widely. For each innovation, the Federal government granted a patent. A patent indicates that the invention is original and gives the inventor the exclusive right to use it until the patent expires. To obtain a patent on the rights to an invention, an inventor must apply to the Patent and Trademark Office of the Federal government. Patents give inventors an inducement to invent. The number of patents granted is an indicator of how much technological progress is going on. Edison obtained patents at a pace of about 67 a year at his lab.

Edison's invention factory required both labor and capital input, much like factories producing other commodities. The workers in such laboratories are highly skilled, with knowledge obtained through formal schooling or on-the-job training—human capital. A highly trained workforce is an important prerequisite to the production of technology.

The supply of technology—the output of Edison's invention factory, for example—depends on the cost of producing the new technology, which must include the great risk that little or nothing will be invented, and the benefits from the new technology: how much Edison can charge for the rights to use his techniques for making light bulbs. Inventive activity often has changed as a result of shifts in the economy that change the costs and benefits. For example, increases in textile workers' wages stimulated the invention of textile machines, because such machines yielded greater profits by enabling the production of more output with fewer workers.

2.3 Special Features of Technology

Technology has two special qualities. The first is *nonrivalry*. This means that one person's use of the technology does not reduce the amount that another person can use. If one university uses the same student registration system as another university, that does not reduce the quality of the first university's system. In contrast, most goods are rivals in consumption: If you drink a bottle of Coke, one fewer bottle of Coke is available for other people to drink.

The second feature of technology is *nonexcludability*. This occurs when the inventor or the owner of the technology cannot exclude other people from using it. For example, the system software for Apple computers shows a series of logos and pull-down menus that can be moved around the screen with a mouse. The idea easily could be adapted for use in other software programs by other companies. In fact, the Windows program of Microsoft has features similar to those of the Apple software, but according to the court that ruled on Apple's complaint that Microsoft was illegally copying, the features were not so similar that Microsoft could not use them. If the court had ruled in favor of Apple, then Apple could have excluded Microsoft from using the Apple features.

As the example of Apple and Microsoft shows, the legal system determines in part the degree of nonexcludability. Trademarks, copyrights, and patents help inventors exclude others from using their inventions without compensation. But it is impossible to exclude others from using such technology.

Thus, technology may *spill over* from one activity to another. If your economics teacher invents a new way to teach economics on a computer, it might spill over to your chemistry teacher, who sees how the technology can be applied to a different subject. Spillovers sometimes occur because research personnel move from one firm to another. Henry Ford knew Thomas Edison and was motivated to experiment on internal combustion engines by Edison. Hence, Edison's research spilled over to another industry, but Edison would have found it difficult to receive compensation from Henry Ford even if he had wanted to.

Because inventors cannot be fully compensated for the benefits their ideas provide to others, they may produce too little technology. The private incentives to invent are less than the gain to society from the inventions. If the incentives were higher—say, through government subsidies to research and development—more inventions might be produced. Thus, the government has a potential role to play in providing funds for research and development, both in industry and at universities.

REVIEW

- Technological change has a broad definition. It is anything that increases production for a given level of labor and capital. Technological change has been an essential ingredient for the increase in the growth of real GDP per hour of work in the last 200 years.
- Technology can be improved by the education and training of workers—investment in human capital. Technology also can be improved through inventions produced in industrial research laboratories, as well as by trial and error. In any case, the level of technology is determined by market forces.
- But technology exhibits nonrivalry in consumption and a high degree of nonexcludability. These are precisely the conditions in which an underproduction of technology will occur.

3. FUNDAMENTAL CAUSES OF ECONOMIC GROWTH

Thus far we have seen the roles that labor, capital, and technology play in the production function of the economy, and thus in driving economic growth. In his recent treatise *Introduction to Modern Economic Growth*, the MIT Economist Daron Acemoglu poses the question "If [labor, capital and technology] are so important in generating cross-country income differences and causing the takeoff into modern economic growth, why do certain societies fail to improve their technologies, invest more in physical capital, and accumulate more human capital?" to argue that it is too limiting to focus only on what he calls the proximate causes of economic growth, the things that directly lead to increased output from the production function. Instead, Acemoglu asks students of economic growth to dig deeper and find out the fundamental causes of economic growth, the factors that led different economies to acquire different levels of labor, capital, and technology. As Acemoglu puts it eloquently in his book,

> *If physical capital accumulation is so important, why did Nigeria fail to invest more in physical capital? If education is so important, why are education levels in Nigeria still so low, and why is existing human capital not being used more effectively? The answer to these questions is related to the fundamental causes of economic growth—the factors potentially affecting why societies make different technology and accumulation choices.*

What are some of the fundamental causes of economic growth? One possible candidate, that Acemoglu himself has studied extensively, is the role played by institutions. Institutions are systems that the people in the country have created or adopted to govern themselves. Institutions include the legal system, the political system, and the regulatory system, for example. Institutions can lend themselves to more labor, capital, and technology accumulation in a variety of ways. For instance, a system of strong property rights is an institution that encourages people to make investments and use resources wisely. Without property rights, slash-and-burn agriculture, overexploitation of natural resources, and urban shantytowns with no access to clean water, sewer or electricity services are common. Good governance is a key institution because corruption and red tape can prohibit the ability of entrepreneurs to engage in economic activity. A functioning legal system that protects the sanctity of contracts encourages more economic activity among firms and individuals, and allows the creation of credit markets that investors can tap into. Protection of patents and copyrights in the legal system can encourage innovative activity within the country. Democracy can be an important political institution because, without the right to vote, the existing elite will be able to run the country for their own welfare as the examples of Mobutu in Zaire, Marcos in the Philippines, and Duvalier in Haiti have shown.

Geography is another fundamental cause of economic growth. Two of the best known public advocates of the importance of geography are the anthropologist Jared Diamond and the economist Jeffrey Sachs. Both have written compellingly about the importance of diseases that thrive in tropical but not temperate regions and the role these diseases can play in shaping the destiny of those regions. Diamond argues that the shape of a continent can influence its destiny—because agricultural crops vary by latitude, technological advances in one area of the extremely wide Eurasian or North American continents could be adopted by other areas in those continents far more easily than a similar adaptation could occur in the more elongated continents of Africa and South America. Similarly, whether or not a country is landlocked, whether or not it has navigable rivers, and how vulnerable it is to natural disasters all are geography-related explanations for why countries could end up with different endowments of capital, labor, and technology.

A third fundamental cause of economic growth is the willingness of a country to be open to interactions with the rest of the world. Openness can affect the pool of labor that is available in the economy through immigration policies that can address shortfalls of either skilled or unskilled labor. These policies have played an enormous role in the economic fortunes of countries like the United States, Australia, Brazil, and South Africa. Openness also can help an economy expand its access to capital because domestic investment does not have to be constrained by the availability of domestic saving. In an open economy, foreign investors can provide us with access to capital for investment projects. We also can look at the links between openness and technology. The development of new ideas is a difficult task: Creating the right environment requires financial resources for research, skilled scientists and engineers, and a strong system of intellectual property rights that allows incentives for firms who develop new technologies. Many developing countries will find it difficult to develop these new technologies by themselves mostly because they lack scientists and engineers or the resources to devote to research. Through economic, education, and scientific interactions with other countries, these developing countries can have access to a base of ideas and knowledge that is far greater than what they would have been able to access on their own.

REVIEW

- Labor, capital, and technology are proximate factors that help an economy directly produce more output. Students interested in better understanding the process of economic growth also may be interested in the fundamental causes, that is, the factors that led the economy to adopt a certain level of capital, labor, or technology.
- Institutions such as a well-functioning legal system or a strong system of property rights or intellectual property rights can encourage people to make long-term investments, engage in the costly process of innovation, and encourage more labor, capital, and technology accumulation.
- Fundamental causes could result from nature rather than the actions of man. Geography is one such example. The local disease climate, access to waterways, and vulnerability to natural disasters are all factors that can influence how much labor, capital, or technology an economy has.

4. MEASURING TECHNOLOGY

growth accounting formula

An equation stating that the growth rate of productivity equals the growth rate of technology plus capital's share of income times the growth rate of capital per hour of work.

Both technology and capital cause productivity—real GDP per hour of work—to grow. Perhaps surprisingly, it is possible to determine how much productivity growth is due to technology, as distinct from capital. Robert Solow of MIT first showed how to do this and won the Nobel Prize for his innovation. In 1957 he published a paper that contained a simple mathematical formula. It is this formula—called the **growth accounting formula**—that enables economists to estimate the relative contributions of capital and technology.

4.1 The Formula

The growth accounting formula is remarkably simple. It can be written as follows:

$$\text{Growth rate of productivity} = \text{Growth rate of technology} + \left(\frac{1}{3}\right)\text{Growth rate of capital per hour of work}$$

It is important to know why the growth rate of capital per hour of work is multiplied by a coefficient that is less than one, or only one-third in the formula. The reason is that economists view the production function for the economy as one in which output rises by only one-third of the percentage by which capital increases. For example, a vineyard owner can estimate by what percent grape output will rise if the workers have more wheelbarrows. If the number of wheelbarrows at the vineyard is increased by 100 percent and if the one-third coefficient applies to the vineyard, then grape production per hour of work will increase by 33 percent. In other words, this growth rate is a property of the grape production function. Statistical studies suggest that the one-third coefficient seems to apply to the production function for the economy as a whole.

We should not give the impression, however, that economists know the coefficient on capital growth in the growth accounting formula with much precision. Uncertainty exists about its size. It could be one-fourth or even five-twelfths. In any case, the growth accounting formula is a rule of thumb to help policy makers decide what emphasis to place on capital versus technology when developing programs to stimulate economic growth.[1]

4.2 Using the Formula

Here is how the formula works. The growth rates of productivity and capital per hour of work are readily determined from available data sources in most countries. Using the formula, we can express the growth rate of technology.

$$\text{Growth rate of technology} = \text{Growth rate of productivity} - \left(\frac{1}{3}\right)\text{Growth rate of capital per hour of work}$$

Thus, the growth rate of technology can be determined by subtracting one-third times the growth rate of capital per hour of work from the growth rate of real GDP per hour of work.

Consider an example. Suppose the growth rate of real GDP per hour of work is 2 percent per year. Suppose also that the growth rate of capital per hour of work is 3 percent per year. Then the growth rate of technology must be 1 percent per year: 2 – (1/3 x 3) = 1. Thus, one-half of the growth of productivity is due to technological change, and one-half is due to growth of capital per hour of work.

REVIEW

- The growth accounting formula shows explicitly how productivity growth depends on the growth of capital per hour of work and on the growth of technology.
- Using the growth accounting formula along with data on productivity and capital, one can calculate the contribution of technology to economic growth.

5. TECHNOLOGY POLICY

The growth accounting formula tells us that if economic policy is to help maintain or increase productivity growth, it must provide incentives for, or remove disincentives to, technological progress. What policies might improve technological progress?

5.1 Policy to Encourage Investment in Human Capital

One policy to encourage investment in human capital is to improve education. A more highly trained workforce is more productive. Better-educated workers are more able to make technological improvements. Hence, education reform (higher standards, incentives for good teaching) and increased funding would be ways to increase technological change. Some studies have shown that the U.S. education system is falling behind other countries, especially in mathematics and science in the kindergarten through 12th grade schools; hence, additional support seems warranted to increase economic growth.

5.2 Policy to Encourage Research and Innovation

In the twenty-first century, the United States and other industrial countries spend huge amounts of money on *research and development (R&D)*. Some of the research supports pure science, but much of it is applied research in engineering and medical technology. About 2.6 percent of U.S. GDP goes to R&D. The government provides much of its R&D funds through research grants and contracts to private firms and universities through the National Science Foundation and the National Institutes of Health and through its own research labs. Private firms, however, use most of the research funds.

The United States spends less on R&D as a share of GDP than other countries, but more in total. Total spending on research is a better measure of the usefulness of the spending than spending as a share of GDP if the benefits spill over to the whole economy.

Increased government support for R&D regardless of industry can be achieved through tax credits. A *tax credit for research* allows firms to deduct a certain fraction of their research expenditures from their taxes to reduce their tax bill. This increases the incentive to engage in R&D. Another way to increase the incentive for inventors and innovators is to give them a more certain claim to the property rights from their inventions. The government has a role to play in defining and enforcing property rights through patent laws, trademarks, and copyrights.

5.3 Technology Embodied in New Capital

Although we have emphasized that capital and technology have two distinct effects on the growth rate of productivity, it is not always possible to separate them in practice. To take advantage of a new technology, it may be necessary to invest in new capital. Consider the Thompson Bagel Machine, invented by Dan Thompson, which automatically can roll and shape bagels. Before the machine was invented, bakers rolled and shaped the bagels by hand. According to Dan Thompson, who in 1993 was running the Thompson Bagel Machine Manufacturing Corporation, headquartered in Los Angeles, "You used to have two guys hand shaping and boiling and baking who could turnout maybe 120 bagels an hour. With the machine and now the new ovens, I have one baker putting out 400 bagels an hour."[2] That is a productivity increase of more than 500 percent. But the new technology is inseparable from the capital. To take advantage of the technology, bagel producers have to buy the machine and the new ovens to go with it.

Economists call this *embodied technological change* because it is embodied in the capital. An example of *disembodied technological change* would be the discovery of a new way to forecast the demand for bagels at the shop each morning so that fewer people would be disappointed when bagels run out on popular days and fewer bagels would be wasted on slack days. Taking advantage of this technology might not require any new capital.

The relationship between capital and technology has implications for technology policies. For example, policies that provide incentives for firms to invest might indirectly improve technology as they encourage investment in new, more productive equipment.

5.4 Is Government Intervention Appropriate?

Any time a question arises about whether government should intervene in the economy, such as with the technology policies just discussed, the operation of the private market should be examined carefully. For example, we noted that incentives for technology production may be too low without government intervention. Certainly, some of the research a business firm undertakes can be kept secret from others. In such cases, the firm may have sufficient incentive to do the research. But many research results are hard to keep secret. In that case, government intervention has a role to play in subsidizing the research. In general, policies to increase economic growth should be given the test for whether government intervention in the economy is necessary: Is the private market providing the right incentives? If not, can the government do better without a large risk of government failure? If the answers are "no" and "yes," respectively, then government intervention is appropriate.

REVIEW

- Policy proposals to increase productivity growth by providing incentives to increase technology include educational reform, tax credits for research, increased funding for research, moving government support toward areas that have significant spillovers, and improving intellectual property laws to better define the property rights of inventors and extend them globally.
- Many technologies are embodied in new capital. Hence, policies to stimulate capital formation could also increase technology.

6. END-OF-CHAPTER MATERIAL

6.1 Conclusion: The Importance of Productivity Growth

No concept in economics is more important to people's economic well-being than productivity growth, and economists widely agree about this essential principle. For example, William Baumol and his colleagues at New York University wrote in *Productivity and American Leadership*: "It can be said without exaggeration that in the long run probably nothing is as important for economic welfare as the rate of productivity growth."

Paul Krugman, the Nobel Prize–winning economist and columnist for the *New York Times*, wrote in his *Age of Diminished Expectations*: "Compared with the problem of slow productivity growth, all our other long-term economic concerns—foreign competition, the industrial base, lagging technology, deteriorating infrastructure and so on—are minor issues."

And Edward Lazear, chair of President Bush's Council of Economic Advisers, said, "Productivity growth is important and it's key, because it means that firms can pay workers higher wages. Indeed, real wage growth over any significant period of time is directly linked to productivity growth. For that reason, we must keep productivity growth strong."

In this chapter, we defined productivity growth and discussed how capital and technology are its essential determinants. We also pointed out that capital, like labor, is subject to diminishing returns, so that technological progress must be an essential part of productivity growth in the long run. Even though labor, capital, and technology are what proximately determine an economy's ability to produce goods and services, we also discussed the need to look at the fundamental causes of economic growth, such as a country's institutions, geography, and culture of openness. These causes provide us with important insight about why some countries have an easier time accumulating capital, labor, or technology.

If economic policy makers want to increase people's income and reduce poverty—whether in the United States or in other countries—they must focus on increasing and maintaining productivity growth. Economists differ about the best way to accomplish this goal. For example, they debate whether policy should focus more on stimulating technology by subsidizing research or on increasing incentives for investment by keeping taxes on investment low. The growth accounting formula helps resolve some of these differences by determining the relative importance of capital and technology. In recent years in the United States, technology and capital both have contributed substantially to productivity growth, suggesting that policy should not focus solely on one determinant at the expense of the other.

Key Points

1. The productivity growth rate—the percentage increase in output per hour of work—determines the economic well-being of people in the long run.
2. Along with labor and capital, technology determines economic growth. Technological progress explains much of the productivity growth wave that started in the late 1700s and enabled industrial countries to get rich.
3. Technology as defined by economists is much broader than high-technology products or inventions. Technology includes such things as better organizational structure for a firm and better education for workers as well as innovations like fiber-optic cables.
4. As a commodity, technology has the special features of nonexcludability and nonrivalry. Patent laws attempt to make technology more excludable and thereby increase the incentives to invest.
5. In studying economic growth, we should not just focus on the proximate factors, such as labor, capital, and technology, which directly determine an economy's ability to produce goods and services. We also should look to more fundamental causes of economic growth for important insights about how difficult it is to add more capital, labor, or technology.
6. Examples of fundamental causes could include a country's institutions, geography, and culture of openness—all of which can play an important role in driving economic growth.
7. The growth accounting formula is a great invention that has enabled economists to better understand the role of technology in the economy.
8. Technology policy has the goal of offsetting disincentives to invest and innovate that exist in the private market.
9. Policy proposals to increase technology include education reform, tax credits for research, increased funding for research, and improving intellectual property laws.
10. Government support for education and research is a key part of a modern technology policy.

QUESTIONS FOR REVIEW

1. What is the essential difference between economic growth in the last 200 years and in the 2,000 years before that?
2. Why do capital and labor have diminishing returns?
3. Why are economists so sure that technology played a big role in economic growth during the last 200 years?
4. Why does technology include different ways to organize a business firm?
5. How is technology produced?
6. What is the importance of nonrivalry and nonexcludability for technology?
7. Of what practical use is the growth accounting formula?
8. What is wrong with a growth policy that focuses on capital formation but not on technology?
9. What do patents have to do with economic growth?
10. What is the rationale for government intervention in the production of technology?

PROBLEMS

1. The table here shows how output (those cells not bolded) depends on capital and labor.
   a. Using the table, draw the production function $Y = F(L)$ when the capital stock (K) is 50. What do you observe about the shape of the production function?
   b. Now draw three similar curves that correspond to a capital stock of 100, 150, and 200. What happens to the production function?
   c. Using the diagrams you drew above, indicate the diminishing returns to labor and to capital.

	Labor				
Capital	**50**	**100**	**150**	**200**	**250**
50	200	324	432	528	618
100	246	400	532	650	760
150	278	452	600	734	858
200	304	492	654	800	936
250	324	526	700	856	1,000

2. Name one way in which use of the following technologies has made you more productive:
   a. ATM machine
   b. Cell phone
   c. The Internet
   d. Laptop computer
3. Identify each of the following as either a capital saving or a labor-saving technological change:
   a. A public library installs an electronic machine that can automatically scan books for library patrons.
   b. A university upgrades its email system to be accessible by users with smartphones.
   c. A university reorganizes its departments to cut back on administrative costs.
4. Consider a country in which capital per hour of work from 1950 to 1973 grew by 3 percent per year and output per hour of work grew by about 3 percent per year. Suppose that from 1973 to 1991, capital per hour of work did not grow at all and output per hour of work grew by about 1 percent per year. How much of the slowdown in productivity (output per hour of work) growth was due to technological change? Explain. (Assume that the coefficient on capital in the growth accounting formula is one-third.)
5. If we estimate the share of capital in income incorrectly, it can affect our estimation of how large technological growth has been. Rework Problem 4 assuming that capital's share is one-fourth. Explain intuitively the difference in the importance of technology.
6. According to Chapter 19, a decrease in government spending results in, among other things, an increase in investment in the long run. Suppose the capital stock is \$1 trillion and a fall in government spending causes a \$50 billion rise in investment. Determine the effect of the change in government purchases on long-run per capita output growth, using the growth accounting formula. (Assume that the coefficient on capital in the growth accounting formula is one-third.)
   a. Suppose that a country has no growth in technology, and that capital and labor hours are growing at the same rate. What is the growth rate of real GDP per hour of work? Explain.
   b. Suppose that capital in the country described in part (a) continues to grow at its previous rate and technology growth is still zero, but growth in labor hours falls to half its previous rate. What happens to growth in real GDP per hour of work?
7. Which of the following types of government spending are likely to help economic growth? Why?
   a. Military spending on advertising for recruits
   b. Military spending on laser research
   c. Funding for a nationwide computer network
   d. Subsidies for a national opera company
   e. Extra funding for education programs

8. Many U.S. companies in the software, music, and movie industries have been asking the Chinese government to better enforce intellectual property rights. Discuss the impact of this enforcement on
    a. Chinese firms
    b. U.S. firms
    c. Chinese consumers
9. Suppose that Lesotho, an extremely poor African country, announces that it will ignore patents held by companies in the Western Hemisphere on HIV/AIDS-related pharmaceuticals and instead will buy copies of the drugs produced by Indian firms.
    a. Would you support such a decision? Why?
    b. Would your answer change if, instead of Lesotho, it was a richer country like Thailand or Brazil that was threatening to break the patent? Why?

7. APPENDIX: DERIVING THE GROWTH ACCOUNTING FORMULA

The growth accounting formula states that

$$\text{Growth rate of productivity} = \text{Growth rate of technology} + \left(\frac{1}{3}\right)\text{Growth rate of capital per hour of work}$$

To derive the formula, we start with the relationship between productivity (Y/L) and capital per hour of work (K/L) shown in Figure 21.5. Because of diminishing returns to capital, the line is curved: As capital per hour of work increases, the increased productivity that comes from the additional capital per hour diminishes.

The curve in Figure 21.5 is called a **productivity curve**; it can be represented in symbols as $(Y/L) = f(K/L)$, or productivity is a function of capital per hour of work.

FIGURE 21.5 Productivity Curve

Productivity, or output per hour of work, is shown to increase with the amount of capital that workers have, as measured by capital per hour of work. The productivity curve gets flatter as output per hour of work increases because of diminishing returns to capital.

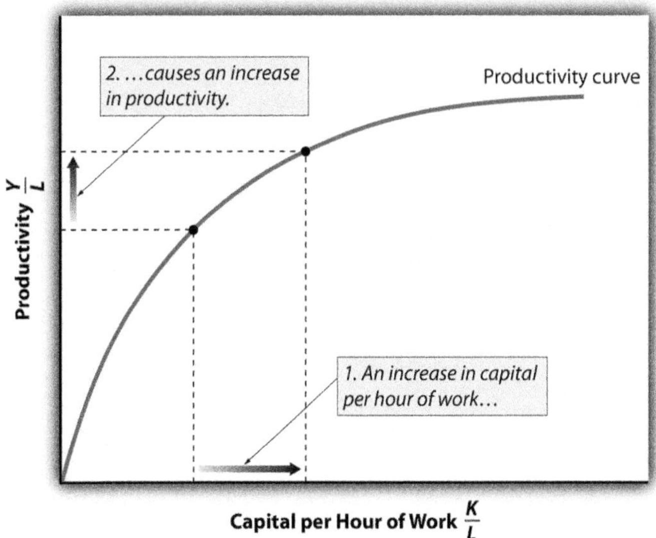

An upward shift in the productivity curve due to an increase in technological change is shown in Figure 21.6. For example, with capital per hour constant at Point A in the figure, more technology leads to more productivity.

FIGURE 21.6 A Shift in the Productivity Curve Due to Technology

An increase in technology permits an increase in productivity even if capital per hour of work does not change. For example, if capital per hour of work stays at *A*, productivity increases when the productivity curve shifts up.

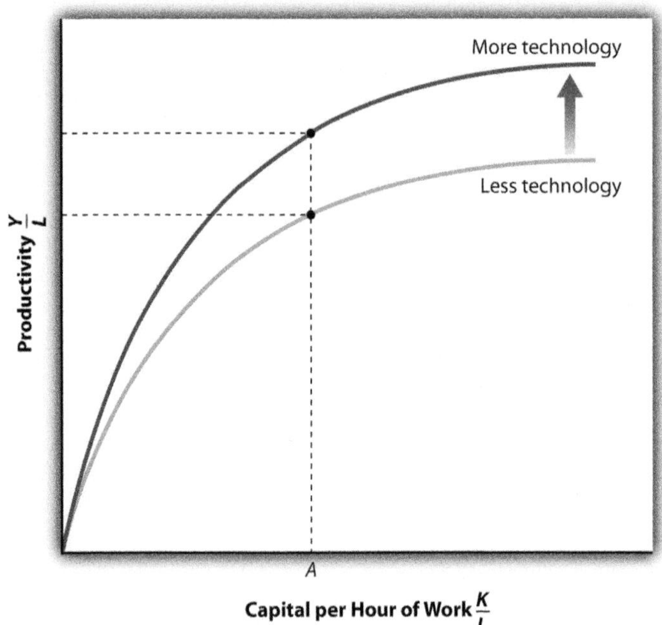

Productivity increases in the economy are due to a combination of *movements along* the productivity curve because of more capital per hour and *shifts of* the productivity curve because of technological change. The growth accounting formula is derived by translating the *movements along* and the *shifts of* the curve into two algebraic terms.

In Figure 21.7, productivity and capital per hour in two different years (year one and year two) are shown. These could be 2003 and 2004 or any other two years. In this example, the growth rate of productivity is given by the increase in productivity ($C - A$) divided by the initial level of productivity (A), or $(C - A)/A$. (The definition of the growth rate of a variable is the change divided by the initial level.)

FIGURE 21.7 **Growth Accounting with Capital per Hour and Technology Increasing**

Here a shift in the productivity curve and a movement along the productivity curve due to more capital per hour of work are combined. Productivity increases. The part of the increase due to capital and the part due to technological change are shown in the diagram.

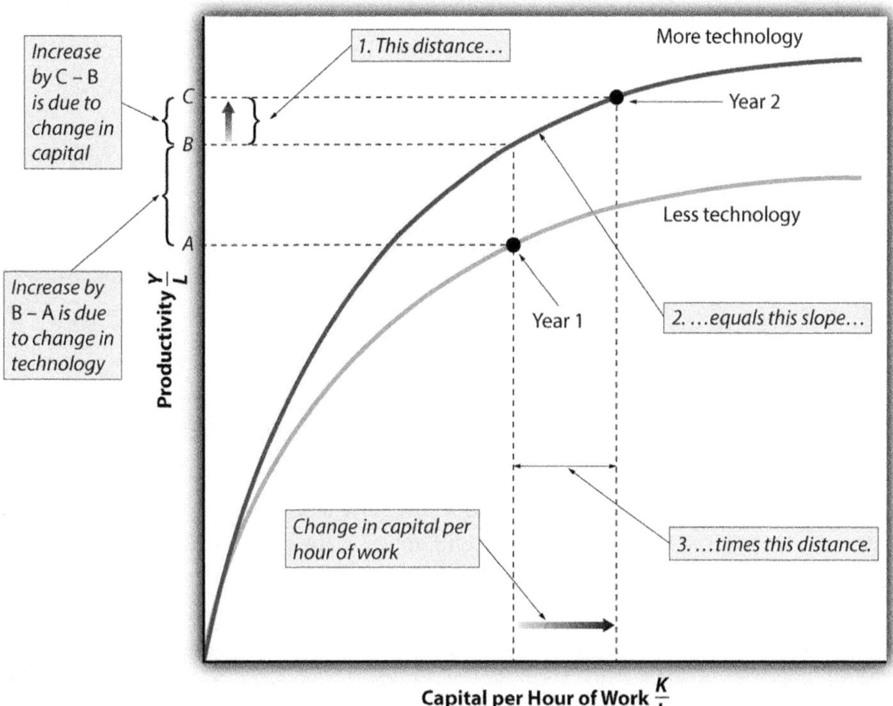

Observe in Figure 21.7 how the increase in productivity can be divided into the part resulting from higher capital per hour of work ($C-B$) and the part resulting from technology ($B-A$). Thus, we have

$$\underbrace{(C-A)/A}_{\text{Growth rate of productivity}} = \underbrace{(C-B)/A}_{\text{term related to capital per hour}} + \underbrace{(B-A)/A}_{\text{growth rate of technology}}$$

To finish the derivation, we need to examine the first term on the right. How does this term relate to capital per hour of work? The numbered boxes in Figure 21.7 show that $C-B$ equals the change in capital per hour of work $\Delta(K/L)$ times the slope of the productivity curve. (The slope times the change along the horizontal axis gives the changes along the vertical axis.) Let the symbol r be the slope, which measures how much additional capital increases output. Thus, $(C-B)/A$ is given by

$$\frac{\Delta(K/L)r}{Y/L} = \frac{\Delta(K/L)r(K/Y)}{(Y/L)(K/Y)} = \frac{\Delta(K/L)r(K/Y)}{(K/L)}$$

The expression on the right is obtained by multiplying the numerator and the denominator of the expression on the left by (K/Y). Now the term on the right is simply the growth rate of capital per hour times $r\,(K/Y)$. The amount of income paid to capital is r times K if capital is paid according to how much additional capital increases output. Aggregate income is given by Y. Thus, the term $r\,(K/Y)$ is the share of capital income in aggregate income. This share is approximately one-third. Thus, the expression $(C - B)/A$ is the growth rate of capital per hour of work times one third. Thus, the growth accounting formula is derived.

Key Points

1. The productivity curve describes how more capital per hour of work increases productivity, or output per hour of work.
2. The productivity curve shifts up if technology increases.
3. The growth accounting formula is derived by dividing an increase in productivity into (1) a shift in the productivity curve resulting from more technology and (2) a movement along the productivity curve resulting from more capital per worker.

QUESTIONS FOR REVIEW

1. What is the difference between the productivity curve and the production function?
2. What is the difference between a shift of the productivity curve and a movement along the curve?
3. Why does the share of capital income in total income appear in the growth accounting formula?

PROBLEMS

1. Consider the following relation between productivity and capital per hour for the economy.

Capital per Hour of Work (K/L)	Output per Hour of Work (Y/L)
\$20	\$40
\$40	\$80
\$60	\$110
\$80	\$130
\$100	\$140

   a. Plot the productivity curve.
   b. Suppose that in Year 1, $K/L = 40$ and $Y/L = 80$, but in Year 2, $K/L = 60$ and $Y/L = 110$. How much has technology contributed to the increase in productivity between the two years?
   c. Suppose that between Year 2 and Year 3, the productivity curve shifts up by \$20 at each level of capital per hour of work. If $K/L = 80$ and $Y/L = 150$ in Year 3, how many dollars did capital contribute to productivity growth between Year 2 and Year 3? How much was the contribution as a fraction of the growth rate of capital per worker?
2. Suppose the production function $Y = F(K, L)$ is such that Y equals the square root of the product (K times L). Plot the production function with Y on the vertical axis and L on the horizontal axis for the case in which K = 100. Plot the productivity curve with Y/L on the vertical axis and K/L on the horizontal axis.

ENDNOTES

1. A graphic derivation of the growth accounting formula is found in the appendix to this chapter.
2. New York Times, April 25, 1993.

CHAPTER 22
Money and Inflation

Money provides an essential foundation for the economy, so if you want to understand how the economy works, you have to learn about money. Historians trace the origins of money to the very origins of civilization. As Babylon, Ur, and other ancient cities of Mesopotamia were being built 5,000 years ago, primitive forms of money, such as silver rings or even scraps of silver, were used to buy and sell in the street markets thousands of different goods—mortar, bricks, sandals for workers—that were needed for construction. The term shekel, which meant one-third of an ounce of silver, came into use at that time. Years later, images of kings or goddesses would be impressed on round pieces of silver, giving coins the look they still have in the twenty-first century. Without money, it is doubtful that these first large-scale civilizations could have arisen.

Source: Shutterstock.com

If the economy is working smoothly, you hardly notice the importance of money. Of course, you can see money being exchanged at the market—just as the Mesopotamians did—but this is hardly worth a comment. But occasionally the monetary foundation of an economy breaks down, and then you really notice the importance of money. After World War I, the government of Germany printed way too much money, and the price of everything rose by millions of percent, causing havoc in the economy and helping sow the seeds for World War II. In the 1970s, the U.S. government also created too much money. Although less pronounced than in Germany, inflation rose for more than a decade, and the U.S. economy went through one of its roughest periods, with one recession after another. Through much of the 1980s and 1990s, money was managed much better in the United States; inflation was low, and economic growth far steadier. In the aftermath of the 2008/09 recession, the money supply in the United States increased sharply as actions were taken to deal with first the financial crisis and then the slow recovery. This sharp increase initially raised concerns in some people's minds about whether inflation would start to rise but the primary concern in the aftermath of the recession was that inflation was too low, rather than being too high.

Sometimes government control of money completely breaks down. In 2001, 12 different provinces of Argentina started printing their own monies, causing great confusion. In Iraq under Saddam Hussein, the northern provinces used a different money from the southern provinces. After Saddam Hussein fell from power in 2003, a new currency had to be printed and flown into the country to prevent a financial collapse. This was no minor undertaking, as twenty-seven 747 planeloads of new currency were shipped into the country—a noticeable reminder of the importance of money. In Zimbabwe, the government of Robert Mugabe engaged in a desperate, but failing, race to print money faster than prices were rising to pay for all the government's expenditures. The economist Steve Hanke calculated that inflation in Zimbabwe had reached 89.7 sextillion percent (89.7×10^{21}) in later 2008. By early 2009, the people of Zimbabwe had abandoned the Zimbabwe dollar and were using the U.S. dollar to conduct economic transactions.

The purpose of this chapter is to examine the role of money in the economy. After defining money, we show that commercial banks play a key role in providing money in a modern economy. We then examine how central banks—such as the Fed (the Federal Reserve) in the United States or the ECB (European Central Bank) in Europe—can control the supply of money. We also show why excessive increases in the supply of money cause inflation—one of the most important principles of macroeconomics.

1. WHAT IS MONEY?

money

That part of a person's wealth that can be used readily for transactions; money also serves as a store of value and a unit of account.

In a broad sense, money performs three functions in the economy: It can serve as a medium of exchange, a unit of account, and a store of value. More details about the three functions are given in the following sections. Economists emphasize the medium of exchange dimension in defining money. They define **money** as the part of a person's wealth that can be used readily for transactions, such as buying a sandwich or a bicycle. This definition differs from the more typical usage, in which the term is used to describe someone's wealth or income—as when we say, "she makes a lot of money" or "he has a lot of money." To an economist, money does not include what a person earns in a year or the total assets that she has, but it does include the portion of that person's wealth—such as the notes and coins in her purse—that can be used easily for transactions.

1.1 Three Functions of Money

Medium of Exchange

medium of exchange

Something that generally is accepted as a means of payment.

Money is a **medium of exchange** in that it is an item that people are willing to accept as payment for what they are selling because they in turn can use it to pay for something else they want. For example, in ancient times, people received coins for their agricultural produce, such as grain, and then used these coins to buy clothing.

The use of coins was a great technological improvement over *barter*, in which goods are exchanged only for other goods. A barter system does not have a single medium of exchange. Thus, under a barter system, if you make shoes and want to buy apples, you have to find an apple seller who needs new shoes. The disadvantage of a barter system is that it requires a rare *coincidence of wants* in which the person who wants to consume what you want to sell (shoes, for example) has exactly what you want to consume (apples, for example).

Store of Value

Money also is a **store of value** from one period to another. For example, in ancient times, people could sell their produce in September for gold coins and then use the coins to buy staples in January. In other words, they could store their purchasing power from one season to another.

store of value

Something that will allow purchasing power to be carried from one period to the next.

Coins are not the only thing that can serve as a store of value. For example, rice and corn also can be stored from one season to the next; therefore, they also can serve as a store of value. But if you are not a farmer with a large storage bin, coins are much more likely to be used as money.

Unit of Account

Money also has a third function: providing a **unit of account**. The prices of goods usually are stated in units of money. For example, prices of shoes or apples in ancient Greece were stated in a certain number of tetradrachmas—silver coins that had the goddess Athena on one side and her sacred animal, the owl, on the other—because people using these coins were familiar with that unit. Originally, units of money were determined by the weight of the metal. The British pound, for example, was originally a pound of silver. That terminology stuck even though, as we will see, modern money is unrelated to silver or any other metal.

unit of account

A standard unit in which prices can be quoted and values of goods can be compared.

To better understand the difference between the unit of account and the medium of exchange, it is helpful to find examples in which they are based on different monies. For example, when inflation got very high in Argentina in the early 1990s, the prices of many goods were quoted in U.S. dollars rather than Argentine pesos, but people usually exchanged pesos when they bought or sold goods. Thus, the U.S. dollar was the unit of account, while the medium of exchange was still the peso. But such cases are the exception; the unit of account and the medium of exchange are usually the same money.

1.2 Commodity Money

Many items have been used for money throughout history: Salt, cattle, furs, tobacco, shells, and arrowheads. Traces of their former use still can be found in our vocabulary. The word *salary* comes from the Latin word for salt, and the word *pecuniary* comes from the Latin word for cattle. In World War II prisoner-of-war camps, cigarettes were used for money. On the island of Yap in the Pacific Ocean, huge stones weighing several tons were used for money.

Traditional Stone Money of Yap Island, Micronesia

Source: Shutterstock.com

Throughout history, the most common form of money has been metallic coins, usually made of gold, silver, or bronze. Gold coins were used as early as the seventh century B.C. in Lydia (now western Turkey); the Chinese were issuing bronze coins with a hole in the middle in the fifth century B.C.; and, in the fourth century, the Greeks issued the tetradrachmas. All these examples of money are commodities and therefore are called *commodity money.* Metals proved to be the most common form of commodity money because they could be divided easily into smaller units, are durable, and could be carried around.

When gold, silver, and other commodities were used as money, changes in the supply of these commodities would change their price relative to all other goods. An increase in the supply of gold, all else equal, would increase the number of gold coins that people were willing to pay to purchase other goods and services. In other words, the price of all other goods in the economy would rise relative to that of gold. Such an increase in the price of all goods in the economy is called inflation, as you may recall from the definitions of key economic concepts given in Chapter 18. Thus, increases in the supply of gold or any other commodity used as money would cause inflation. Whenever huge gold discoveries were made, the price of gold fell and inflation increased in countries that used gold as money. Thus, inflation was determined largely by the supply of precious metals. This relationship between the supply of money and inflation, which seems so clear in the case of commodity money, has persisted into modern times, even though now we use many other forms of money.

Ancient Roman gold coin of Emperor Honorius

Source: Shutterstock.com

1.3 From Coins to Paper Money to Deposits

Although coins and other commodity monies are improvements over barter, other forms of money are more efficient. Starting in the late eighteenth and early nineteenth centuries, *paper money* began to be used widely and supplemented or replaced coins as a form of money. Although in a few examples paper money was used earlier, at this time paper money generally was recognized as easier to use and it could save greatly on the use of precious metals.

currency

Money in its physical form: coin and paper money.

Originally, the amount of paper currency was linked by law or convention to the supply of commodities. One reason for this link was the recognition that more money would cause inflation and that limiting the amount of paper money to the amount of some commodity like gold would limit the amount of paper money. Irving Fisher of Yale University, perhaps the most prolific and influential American economist of the early twentieth century, argued for linking paper money to commodities for precisely this reason. Many countries of the world linked their paper money to gold in the nineteenth and early twentieth centuries. They were on a *gold standard*, which meant that the price of gold in terms of paper money was fixed by the government. The government fixed the price by agreeing to buy and sell gold at that price. In the twenty-first century, the United States and other countries have severed all links between their money and gold. They are no longer on the gold standard and apparently have no intention of returning. Governments now supply virtually all the coin and paper money—the two together are called **currency**.

checking deposits

An account at a financial institution on which checks can be written; also called a checkable deposit.

Although paper money was much easier to make and to use than coins, it too has been surpassed by a more efficient form of money. Many people now have **checking deposits** at banks or other financial institutions. These are deposits of funds on which an individual can write a check to make payment for goods and services. The deposits serve as money because people can write checks on them or use a debit card linked to that checking account. For example, when a student pays $100 for books with a debit card or a check, the student's checking deposit at the bank goes down by $100, and the bookstore's checking deposit at the bank goes up by $100. Checking deposits are used in much the same way as when a student pays with a $100 bill, which then is placed in the store's cash register. The student's holding of money goes down by $100, and the store's goes up by $100.

1.4 Measures of the Money Supply

money supply

The sum of currency (coin and paper money) and deposits at banks.

In the twenty-first century, economists define the **money supply** as the sum of currency (coin and paper money) and deposits at banks. But opinions vary about what types of deposits should be included.

The narrowest measure of the money supply is called *M1*. The M1 measure consists mainly of currency plus checking deposits (travelers checks are also part of M1 but constitute less than 1 percent of total M1). The items in M1 have a great degree of *liquidity*, which means that they can be quickly and easily used to purchase goods and services.

Many things that people would consider money, however, are not included in M1. For example, if you had no cash but you wanted to buy a birthday gift for a relative, you could withdraw cash from your savings deposit. A *savings deposit* is a deposit that pays interest and from which funds normally can be withdrawn at any time. In other words, a savings deposit is also liquid, but not quite as liquid as a checking deposit. Similarly, *time deposits*—which require the depositor to keep the money at the bank for a certain amount of time or else lose interest—are not as liquid as checking deposits, but it is possible to withdraw funds from them. Economists have created a broader measure of the money supply, called *M2*, that includes everything that is in M1 plus savings deposits, time deposits, and certain accounts on which check writing is limited. Still broader concepts of the money supply can be defined, but M1 and M2 are the most important ones. Table 22.1 shows the total amounts of different definitions of the money supply for the whole U.S. economy at 4 points in time - June 2007 (before the recession), June 2010 (a year after the recession had officially ended), June 2013 (four years into the recovery) and June 2016 (more recent value). All three measures of the money supply grew rapidly during the downturn that began in 2008 and the ensuing recovery.

TABLE 22.1 **Measures of Money in the United States, 2007-2016 (billions of dollars)**

	June 2007	June 2010	June 2013	June 2016
Currency	756	884	1,125	1,385
M1	1,366	1,729	2,530	3,246
M2	7,245	8,578	10,651	12,811
Note: M1 is currency plus checking deposits, while M2 is M1 plus savings deposits, time deposits and other deposits on which check writing is limited or not allowed.				

Source: Federal Reserve Board

Less than one-half of the M1 definition of the money supply is currency, and only about one-tenth of the M2 definition is currency. Economists disagree as to whether the more narrowly defined M1 or the more broadly defined M2 or something else is the best definition of the money supply. There is probably no best definition for all times and all purposes. For simplicity, in the rest of this chapter, we make no distinction between the M1 and M2 but simply refer to the money supply, M, as currency plus deposits.

REVIEW

- Commodity money—usually gold, silver, or bronze coins—originally served as the main type of money in most societies. Increases in the supply of these commodities would reduce their price relative to those of all other commodities and thereby cause inflation.
- Later, paper currency and deposits at banks became forms of money.
- Money has three roles: a medium of exchange, a store of value, and a unit of account.

2. THE FED, THE BANKS, AND THE LINK FROM RESERVES TO DEPOSITS

We have seen that increases in the supply of commodity money such as gold would increase inflation. So would the excessive printing of paper money (currency) by governments. But in the twenty-first century, money consists of both currency and deposits. Nevertheless, it is possible for governments—usually through a central bank—to control the supply of money. In the United States, the central bank is the **Federal Reserve System**, nicknamed the "Fed." To understand how the Fed can control the supply of money, we must first look at how the Fed can control the amount of deposits at banks.

Federal Reserve System

The central bank of the United States, which oversees the creation of money in the United States.

A **bank**—such as Bank of America or Citibank—is a firm that channels funds from savers to investors by accepting deposits and making loans. Figure 22.1 illustrates this function of banks. Banks are a type of *financial intermediary* because they "intermediate" between savers and investors. Other examples of financial intermediaries are credit unions and savings and loan institutions. Banks are sometimes called *commercial banks* because many of their loans are to business firms engaged in commerce. Banks accept deposits from people who have funds and who want to earn interest and then lend the funds to other individuals who want to borrow and who are willing to pay interest. A bank earns profits by charging a higher interest rate to the borrowers than it pays to the depositors.

bank

A firm that channels funds from savers to investors by accepting deposits and making loans.

FIGURE 22.1 Channeling Funds from Savers to Investors

Savers, those whose income is greater than their consumption, can supply funds to investors in two ways: through banks (and other types of financial intermediaries) or by making direct loans, perhaps by buying bonds issued by a business firm. The banks earn profits by charging a higher interest rate on their loans than they pay on their deposits.

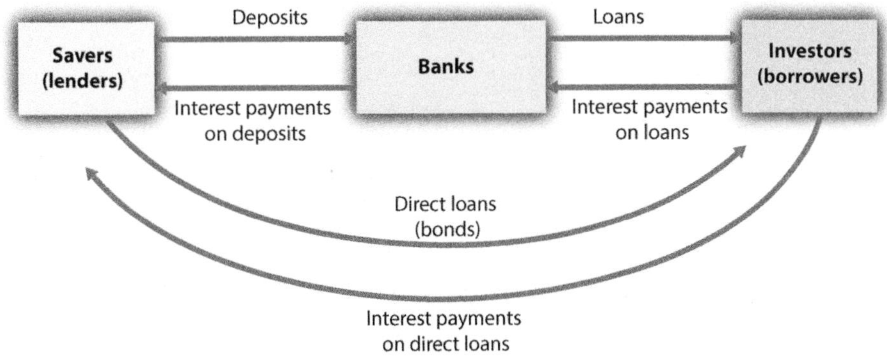

2.1 The Fed

The *central bank* of a country serves as a bank to other banks. In other words, commercial banks deposit funds at the central bank, and the central bank in turn makes loans to other commercial banks. We will see that the deposits of the commercial banks at the central bank are important for controlling the money supply. The Fed was established as the central bank for the United States in 1913 and now has more than 25,000 employees spread across the country.

Board of Governors

At the core of the Fed is the *Federal Reserve Board*, or Board of Governors, consisting of seven people appointed to nonrenewable fourteen-year terms by the president of the United States and confirmed by the Senate. The Federal Reserve Board is located in Washington, D.C.

One of the governors is appointed by the president as chairman of the board; this appointment also requires Senate confirmation and can be renewed for additional terms. Alan Greenspan was first appointed chairman by President Reagan in 1987 and served until 2006. In 2006, Ben Bernanke was appointed by President George W. Bush. Chairman Bernanke's term was renewed by President Obama in 2010 so he served as the chair until 2014. In 2014, President Obama appointed Janet Yellen as the new chair, the first woman to hold the position. Yellen's term as chair will end in 2018 at which point President Trump will have to decide whether to renew her term, as President Obama had done with Ben Bernanke, or to appoint a new chair.

The District Federal Reserve Banks

The Federal Reserve System includes not only the Federal Reserve Board in Washington but also twelve Federal Reserve Banks in different districts around the country (see Figure 22.2).

The term *Fed* refers to the whole Federal Reserve System, including the Board of Governors in Washington and the twelve district banks. Each district bank is headed by a president, who is chosen by commercial bankers and other people in the district and approved by the Board of Governors.

The Federal Open Market Committee

Federal Open Market Committee (FOMC)

The committee, consisting of the seven members of the Board of Governors and the twelve presidents of the Fed district banks, that meets about eight times per year and makes decisions about the supply of money; only five of the presidents vote at any one time.

The Fed makes decisions about the supply of money through a committee called the **Federal Open Market Committee (FOMC)**. The members of the FOMC are the seven governors and the twelve district bank presidents, but only five of the presidents vote at any one time. Thus, the FOMC has twelve voting members at any one time. The FOMC meets in Washington, D.C., about eight times a year to decide how to implement monetary policy. Figure 22.3 shows the relationship between the FOMC, the Board of Governors, and the district banks.

Even though the chair of the Fed has only one of the twelve votes on the FOMC, the position has considerably more power than this one vote might indicate. The chair also has executive authority over the operations of the whole Federal Reserve, sets the agenda at FOMC meetings, and represents the Fed in testimony before Congress. When journalists in the popular press write about the Fed, they usually talk as if the chair has almost complete power over Fed decisions. Now that we have described the Fed, let us examine the operation of banks and how they, along with the Fed, create money.

FIGURE 22.2 **The Twelve Districts of the Fed**

The country is divided into 12 districts, each with a district Federal Reserve Bank. Each district bank is headed by a president, who sits on the Federal Open Market Committee. Alaska and Hawaii are in District 12.

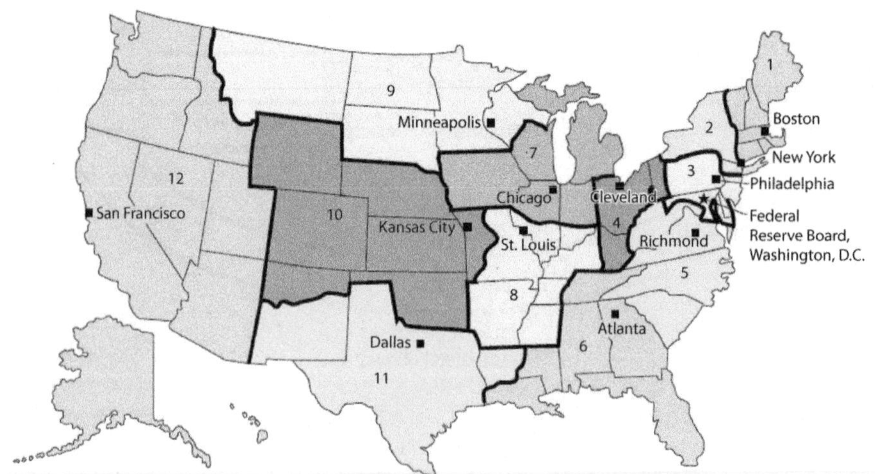

FIGURE 22.3 The Structure of the Fed

Decisions about monetary policy are made by the FOMC, which consists of the Fed governors and district Fed presidents.

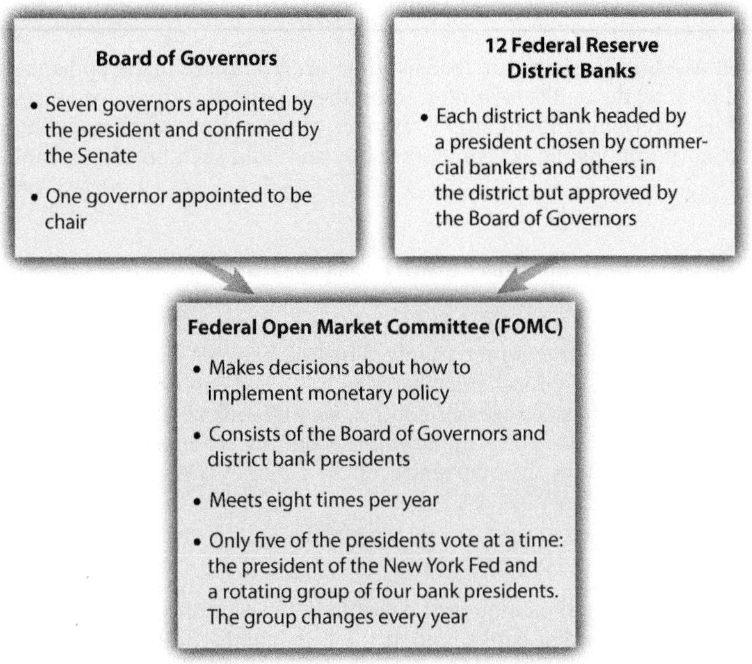

Board of Governors

- Seven governors appointed by the president and confirmed by the Senate
- One governor appointed to be chair

12 Federal Reserve District Banks

- Each district bank headed by a president chosen by commercial bankers and others in the district but approved by the Board of Governors

Federal Open Market Committee (FOMC)

- Makes decisions about how to implement monetary policy
- Consists of the Board of Governors and district bank presidents
- Meets eight times per year
- Only five of the presidents vote at a time: the president of the New York Fed and a rotating group of four bank presidents. The group changes every year

2.2 The Banks

A commercial bank accepts deposits from individuals and makes loans to others. To understand how a bank functions, it is necessary to look at its balance sheet, which shows these deposits and loans. Table 22.2 is an example of a balance sheet for a bank, called BankOne.

TABLE 22.2 Balance Sheet of BankOne (millions of dollars)

Assets		Liabilities	
Loans	70	Deposits	100
Bonds	20		
Reserves	10		

This table shows the initial situation. The ratio of reserves to deposits is 0.1.

The different items are divided into *assets* and *liabilities*. An **asset** is something of value owned by a person or a firm. A **liability** is something of value that a person or a firm owes, such as a debt, to someone else. Thus a bank's assets are anything the bank owns and any sum owed to the bank by someone else. A bank's liabilities are anything the bank owes to someone else. People's *deposits* at banks are the main liability of banks, as shown in Table 22.2. Certain assets, such as the bank's building and furniture, are not shown in this balance sheet because they do not change when the money supply changes. Also, when a bank starts up, the owners must put in some funds, called the bank's capital stock, that can be used if the bank needs cash in an emergency. This asset also is not shown in the balance sheet.

asset

Something of value owned by a person or a firm.

liability

Something of value that a person or a firm owes to someone else.

Consider each of the assets shown in the balance sheet in Table 22.2. **Reserves** are deposits that commercial banks hold at the Fed, much as people hold deposits at commercial banks. Remember, the Fed is the bank for the commercial banks. Just as you can hold a deposit at a commercial bank, a commercial bank can hold a deposit at the Fed. Reserves are simply a name for these deposits by commercial banks at the Fed.

reserves

Deposits that commercial banks hold at the Fed.

required reserve ratio

The fraction of a bank's deposits that it is required to hold at the Fed.

Under U.S. law, a commercial bank is required to hold reserves at the Fed equal to a fraction of the deposits people hold at the commercial bank; this fraction is called the **required reserve ratio**. Banks may choose to hold a greater fraction of their deposits in the form of reserves at the Fed than required. In reality, then, the ratio of reserves to deposits, known as the *reserve ratio*, may differ from the required reserve ratio: It can be larger, but it cannot be smaller. In the following example, we will assume that the required reserve ratio is 10 percent. We will then consider what happens when the reserve ratio changes.

The two other assets of the bank are loans and bonds. *Loans* are made by banks to individuals or firms for a period of time; the banks earn interest on these loans. Bonds are promises of a firm or government to pay back a certain amount after a number of years. Bonds are issued by the U.S. government and by large corporations. Banks sometimes buy and hold such bonds, as BankOne has done in Table 22.2.

2.3 The Link between Reserves and Deposits

Because deposits at banks are a form of money, the Fed must be able to control the total amount of these deposits if it is to control the money supply. The link between the deposits at banks and the reserves at the Fed provides the key mechanism by which the Fed can exert control over the amount of deposits at the commercial banks. To see this control, we first look at some examples to show how this link between reserves and deposits works in the whole economy. To make the story simpler, we assume that everyone uses deposits rather than currency for their money. (We will take up currency again in the next section.)

A Formula Linking Reserves to Deposits

To see how the Fed can change the amount of deposits in the economy, let us assume that the Fed increases the amount of reserves that banks hold at the Fed. The Fed can cause such an increase in reserves simply by buying something from a bank and paying for it by increasing that bank's reserves at the Fed. The Fed typically has purchased bonds when it wants to increase reserves. So we will start there.

open market operation

The buying or selling of bonds by the central bank.

When the Fed buys bonds, it has to pay for them with something. It pays for them with bank reserves—the deposits banks have with the Fed. For example, if the Fed wants to buy bonds held by Citibank, it says, "We want $10 million worth of bonds, and we will pay for them by increasing Citibank's account with us by $10 million." This purchase is an electronic transaction. Citibank's deposits at the Fed (reserves) have increased by $10 million, and the Fed gets the bonds. It has exchanged bank reserves for the bonds. The buying or selling of bonds by the Federal Reserve is called an **open market operation**.

So next assume that the Fed buys $10 million of bonds from BankOne and pays for the bonds by increasing BankOne's reserves by $10 million. Thus, reserves rise at banks in the economy. Now, with the reserve ratio the same (in this example, equal to 0.1) for each bank in the economy, a formula links reserves and deposits for the whole economy. It is given by

$$\text{Reserves} = (\text{reserve ratio}) \times \text{deposits}$$

where reserves and deposits refer to the amounts in the whole economy. If we divide both sides of this expression by the reserve ratio, we get

$$\text{Deposits} = \left(\frac{1}{\text{reserve ratio}}\right) \times \text{reserves}$$

Thus, any increase in reserves is multiplied by the inverse of the reserve ratio to get the increase in deposits. For example, if the $10 million change in reserves is multiplied by (1/0.1) = 10, we get $100 million change in deposits.

One could have started the example by assuming that the Fed bought $10 million in bonds from some person other than a bank. That person would deposit the check from the Fed in a bank, and in the end, the answer would be exactly the same: A $10 million increase in reserves leads to a $100 million increase in deposits.

One also could analyze the effects of a decrease in reserves using the same formula linking reserves and deposits. A decrease in reserves occurs when the Fed sells bonds. For example, a decrease in reserves of $10 million would lead to a decrease in deposits of $100 million.

Bank-by-Bank Deposit Expansion

Now let's look at the details of what is going on in the banks. In our example, when the Fed buys bonds, BankOne's holdings of bonds decline by $10 million, from $20 million to $10 million, and BankOne's reserves at the Fed increase by $10 million, from $10 million to $20 million. The balance sheet would then look like Table 22.3, a change from Table 22.2. The key point is that now $10 million more reserves are in the economy than before the Fed purchased the bonds from BankOne. The reserves are held by BankOne, but they will not be held for long.

Recall that in this example we are assuming that banks hold reserves equal to 10 percent of their deposits. But now, after the Fed's actions, BankOne has 20 percent of its deposits as reserves, or more than the 10 percent. Because banks can earn more by making loans or buying bonds than by holding reserves, the bank will have an incentive to reduce its reserves and make more loans or buy more bonds.

Suppose BankOne decreases its reserves by making more loans; with the reserve ratio of 0.1, the bank can loan $10 million. Suppose the bank loans $10 million to UNO, a small oil company, which uses the funds to buy an oil tanker from DOS, a ship building firm. UNO pays DOS with a check from BankOne, and DOS deposits the check in its checking account at its own bank, BankTwo. Now BankTwo must ask BankOne for payment; BankOne will make the payment by lowering its reserve account at the Fed and increasing BankTwo's reserve account at the Fed by $10 million. BankOne's balance sheet at the end of these transactions is shown in Table 22.4.

Hence, after BankOne makes the loan and transfers its reserves to BankTwo, its reserves are back to 10 percent of its deposits. The story ends here for BankOne, but not for the economy as a whole because BankTwo now has $10 million more in reserves, and this addition will affect BankTwo's decisions. Let us see how.

TABLE 22.3 Balance Sheet of BankOne after Reserves Increase (millions of dollars)

Assets		Liabilities	
Loans	70	Deposits	100
Bonds	10		
Reserves	20		

Note the effect of the Fed's purchase of bonds: Compared with Table 10.2, bonds are lower and reserves are higher in Table 10.3. The ratio of reserves to deposits is 0.2.

TABLE 22.4 Balance Sheet of BankOne after It Makes Loans (millions of dollars)

Assets		Liabilities	
Loans	80	Deposits	100
Bonds	10		
Reserves	10		

By making more loans, the bank reduces the ratio of reserves to deposits back to 0.1.

Now BankTwo finds itself with $10 million in additional deposits and $10 million in additional reserves at the Fed. (Remember that deposits are a liability to BankTwo and the reserves are an asset; thus, assets and liabilities each have risen by $10 million.) Continuing with the 10 percent reserve ratio assumption, however, BankTwo needs to hold only $1 million in reserves for the additional $10 million in deposits. Thus, BankTwo will want to make more loans until its reserves equal 10 percent of its deposits. It will lend to other people an amount equal to 90 percent of the $10 million, or $9 million. The first row of Table 22.5 shows the increase in deposits, loans, and reserves at BankTwo. The story ends here for BankTwo, but not for the economy as a whole.

The people who get loans from BankTwo will use these loans to pay others. Thus, the funds probably will end up in yet another bank, called BankThree. Then, BankThree will find it has $9 million in additional deposits and $9 million in additional reserves. BankThree then will lend 90 percent of the $9 million, or $8.1 million, as shown in the second row of Table 22.5. This process will continue from bank to bank. We begin to see that the initial increase in reserves is leading to a much bigger expansion of deposits. The whole process is shown in Table 22.5. Each row shows what happens at one of the banks. The sums of the columns show the change for the whole economy. If we sum the columns through the end of the process, we will see that deposits, and thus the money supply, increase by $100 million as a result of the $10 million increase in reserves. The increase in deposits is 10 times the actual increase in reserves—exactly what the formula predicted. Usually, the whole process takes a short period of time (days rather than weeks) because banks quickly adjust their loans and reserves.

TABLE 22.5 Deposit Expansion (millions of dollars)

	Deposits	Loans	Reserves
BankTwo	10.00	9.00	1.000
BankThree	9.00	8.10	0.900
BankFour	8.10	7.29	0.810
BankFive	7.29	6.56	0.729
BankSix	6.56	5.90	0.656
BankSeven	5.90	5.31	0.590
BankEight	5.31	4.78	0.531
BankNine	4.78	4.30	0.478
BankTen	4.30	3.87	0.430
-	-	-	-
-	-	-	-
-	-	-	-
Final sum	100.00	90.00	10.000

The numbers in each column get smaller and smaller; if we add up the numbers for all the banks, even those beyond BankTen, we get the sum at the bottom.

2.4 The Explosion of Reserves and the Reserve Ratio in the Aftermath of the 2008/09 Recession

Banks sometimes hold more than the required amount of reserves at the Fed, and the reserve ratio can rise above the required reserve ratio. In our examples so far, we have assumed that the reserve ratio is constant. In this section, we explain what can happen when the reserve ratio changes. We focus on a particularly interesting real-world example.

In the fall of 2008, reserves at the Fed started increasing at a rapid rate. As in our examples in the previous section, the Fed increased reserves by purchasing bonds and paying for them by creating deposits. In this case, however, the Fed purchased large amounts of bonds and other securities issued by private firms rather than the federal government as it usually does. It also made *loans* to private financial firms to contain the financial crisis. The Fed reasoned that by buying the bonds it could drive the interest rate on those bonds down, which would ease the financial crisis, and that making loans to certain financial firms would help those firms avoid bankruptcy and reduce risks to the financial system.

When the Fed purchased these bonds and made the loans, it paid for them by creating reserves—crediting banks with deposits at the Fed. The increase in reserves was unprecedented. Figure 22.4 shows how large, sudden, and unusual the increase was. After remaining relatively steady, reserves exploded in the fall of 2008. They increased from $44 billion in August 2008 to $858 billion in January 2009, almost a 20-fold increase.

FIGURE 22.4 **The Great Expansion of Reserves and Deposits in the Aftermath of the 2008/09 Recession**

This chart shows bank reserves (deposits of banks at the Fed) and demand deposits at banks. The explosion of reserves occurred beginning in the fall of 2008. Reserves increased as the Fed bought bonds and made loans, in an attempt to contain the fallout from the financial crisis, and paid for them by crediting banks with deposits at the Fed.

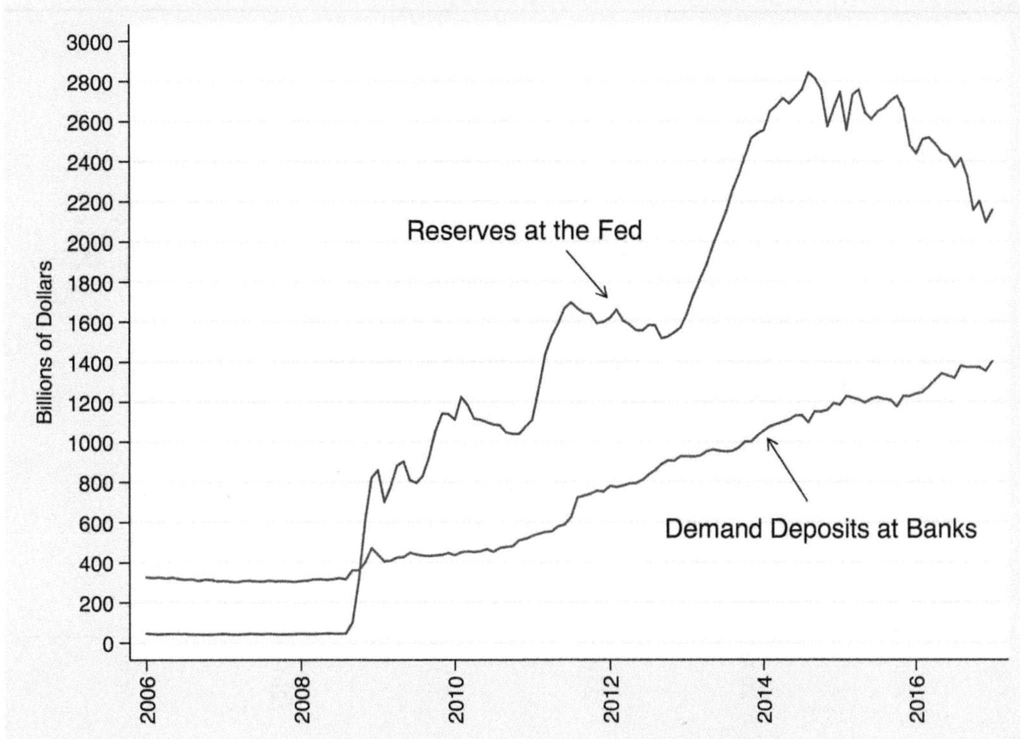

Demand deposits at banks also increased as a result of this increase in reserves, which is not surprising, given the connection between deposits and reserves explained in the previous section. The increase in demand deposits at banks also is shown in Figure 22.4. Note that the increase in demand deposits was not as large as one would expect if the reserve ratio were constant. In fact, as shown in Figure 22.5, the reserve ratio was not constant. It was nearly constant for a number of years, but then it increased sharply in the fall of 2008 as banks held some of the large increase in reserves as **excess reserves** over the amount they were required to hold. In other words, they did not lend out all the reserves. Banks did not lend out all the reserves because demand was insufficient for loans and because they were concerned about risks.

excess reserves

The amount of reserves over and above required reserves.

FIGURE 22.5 The Great Increase in the Reserve Ratio

The reserve ratio jumped beginning in the fall of 2008 as the Fed increased the supply of reserves to the banking system. Since the recession ended the reserve ratio has been extremely volatile but seems to be on a downward trend in 2016.

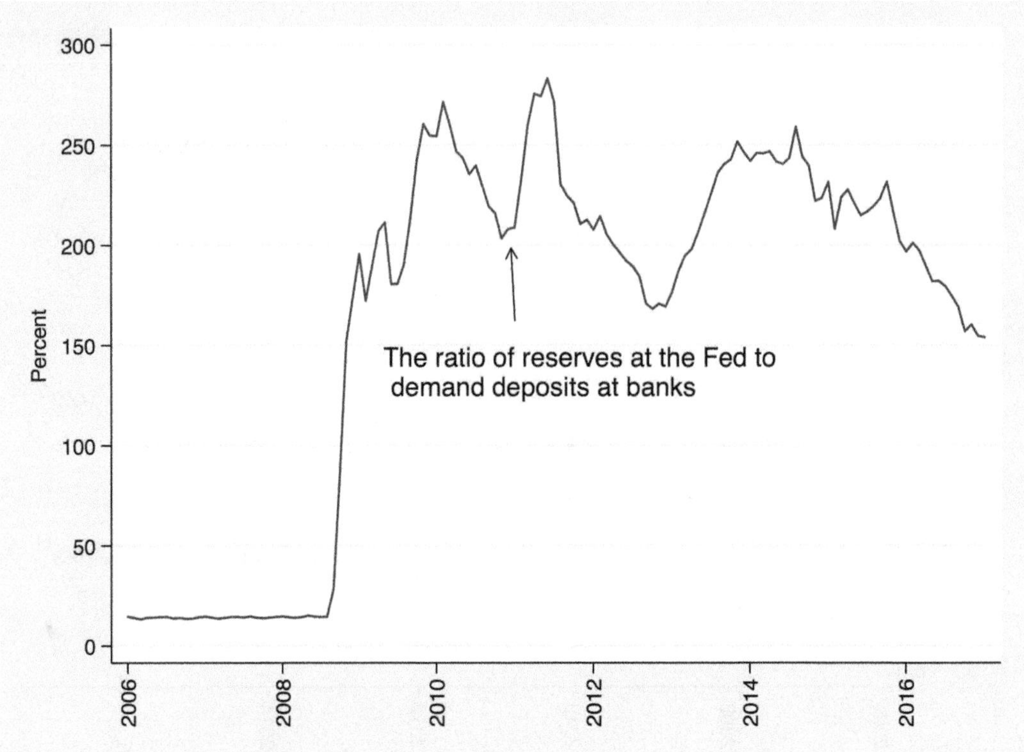

The increase in demand deposits, in turn, increased the money supply, because demand deposits are part of the money supply. Recalling earlier periods of high money growth, some people became concerned that the increase in the money supply would cause inflation, and they criticized the Fed for increasing the money supply by such a large amount. The Fed, however, indicated that it did not see inflation as a problem. Policy officials were more concerned about the financial crisis. These officials indicated that if inflation picked up, they would be able to reduce the amount of reserves and reduce deposits and the money supply. In fact, inflation remained low in this period even though demand deposits increased sharply, for reasons we will explore later in this chapter.

2.5 How the Fed Controls the Money Supply: Currency plus Deposits

We now have seen how an increase in reserves will increase the amount of deposits or a decrease in reserves will reduce the amount of deposits. But the money supply includes currency as well as deposits. With currency in the picture, the Fed must keep track of whether people want to hold more currency or less currency compared with deposits.

Although currency and deposits are both part of the money supply, they have different characteristics. For some purposes, people prefer currency to checking deposits, and vice versa. These preferences determine the amount of currency and checking deposits in the economy. If you want to hold more currency in your wallet because you find it is more convenient than a checking deposit, you just go to the bank and reduce your checking deposit and carry around more currency. If you are worried about crime and do not want to have much currency in your wallet, then you go to the bank and deposit a larger amount in your checking account. Thus, people decide on the amount of currency versus deposits in the economy. In Japan, where crime is less prevalent than in many other countries, people use much more currency compared with checking accounts than in other countries. Even Japanese business executives who earn the equivalent of $120,000 a year frequently are paid monthly with the equivalent of $10,000 in cash.

As long as the Fed keeps track of the amount of currency versus deposits that people want to hold, it can control the money supply—the sum of currency plus demands. For example, if it observes a decline in deposits compared with currency, it can increase reserves, thereby increasing deposits and preventing the money supply from declining.

2.6 How a Credit Crunch Affects Deposit Expansion

Earlier, we saw how the Fed can influence the money supply in the economy through an increase in reserves, which is transformed into a much larger increase in deposits by way of the banking sector. Occasionally, the economy suffers from a **credit crunch**, a period during which banks become cautious about making new loans. A credit crunch greatly reduces the amount by which deposits respond to an increase in reserves initiated by the Fed. An extreme version of this can be demonstrated using the balance sheet for Bank-One, shown in Table 22.3. Once the Fed increases BankOne's reserves by $10 million through an open market operation, if BankOne holds onto $20 million in reserves (even though they are required to hold only $10 million), or if they buy $10 million worth of safe U.S. government bonds instead of making $10 million worth of new loans, then no further expansion of deposits will occur through the banking sector.

credit crunch
A period when banks become cautious in making new loans.

Why might banks become more cautious about making loans? One possibility is that they perceive an increased risk of lending to all of their clients. For example, in late 2008, with house prices falling and many borrowers defaulting on their mortgages, banks may have become extremely cautious about the creditworthiness of clients. Another possibility is that bank balance sheets have suffered because an existing asset has lost value. For example, if some of the bonds that BankOne was holding in Table 22.3 were mortgage-linked bonds whose value declined sharply in 2008, then BankOne may decide to use the expanded reserves to fortify their other assets instead of to make new loans. To overcome the credit crunch, the central bank may have to dramatically increase the amount of new reserves to increase the money supply by the desired amount.

REVIEW

- Banks serve two important functions: They channel funds from savers to investors, and their deposits can be used as money.
- Commercial banks hold deposits, called reserves, at the Fed.
- The Fed increases reserves by buying bonds and reduces reserves by selling bonds.
- The deposits at banks expand by a multiple of any increase in reserves. Thus, a connection exists between reserves and deposits in the overall economy. The reserve ratio is not a constant, however, as observed in 2008.
- By keeping track of currency, the Fed can control the total money supply, which is the sum of currency and deposits.

3. MONEY GROWTH AND INFLATION

Early in this chapter, in the section "Commodity Money," we showed that when gold, silver, or other commodities were the primary form of money, increases in the supply of money would cause inflation. Even though paper currency and deposits are now the main forms of money, the same principle holds in the twenty-first century. That is, *all other things being equal*, an increase in the supply of money will cause inflation. In this section, we examine this principle by looking at some important episodes of inflation during the twentieth century. Before we do so, we introduce a famous equation that can help us test the principle that an increase in the supply of money eventually causes inflation.

Consider first a simple example. Suppose that all of your transactions are in a video game arcade with food-vending machines and video game machines. You will need money in your pocket to carry out your transactions each day. If you use the vending and video game machines 10 times a day, you will need 10 times more money in your pocket than if you use the machines once a day. Hence, 10 times more transactions means 10 times more money. If the prices for vending machine items and minutes on a video game machine double, then you will need twice as much money for each day's activities, assuming that the higher price does not cure your habit. Hence, whether the value of transactions increases because the number of items purchased increases or because the price of each item increases, the amount of money used for transactions will rise.

What is true for you and the machines is true for the whole population and the whole economy. For the whole economy, real gross domestic product (GDP) is like the number of transactions with the machines, and the GDP deflator (a measure of the average price in the economy) is like the average price of the vending and game machines. Just as the amount of money you use for transactions in the game arcade is related to the number of transactions and the price of each transaction, so too is the supply of money in the economy related to real GDP and the GDP deflator.

3.1 The Quantity Equation of Money

quantity equation of money

The equation relating the price level and real GDP to the quantity of money and the velocity of money: The quantity of money times its velocity equals the price level times real GDP.

This relationship between money, real GDP, and the GDP deflator can be summarized by the **quantity equation of money**, which is written

$$\text{Money supply} \times \text{velocity} = \text{GDP deflator} \times \text{real GDP}$$

or

$$MV = PY$$

where V is velocity, P is the GDP deflator, and Y is real GDP. For example, if the money supply was $1,000 billion, real GDP was $8,000 billion, and the GDP deflator was 1.1, then a value of 8.8 for velocity would satisfy the quantity equation (1,000 x 8.8 = 1.1 x 8,000).

velocity

A measure of how frequently money is turned over in the economy.

The term **velocity** measures how frequently money is turned over. It is the number of times a dollar is used on average each period to make purchases. To see this, suppose an automatic teller machine (ATM) is installed in the room with the vending machines and video games from the preceding example. Each morning, you withdraw cash from the ATM for your morning games, and each day at midday, an employee takes the cash from the vending and game machines and restocks the ATM. You then replenish your cash from the ATM to pay for your afternoon use of the games and vending machines; you now need to carry only half as much currency in your pocket as before the ATM was installed, when you had to bring enough cash to last all day. From your perspective, therefore, the velocity of money doubles. Money turns over twice as fast. As this example shows, velocity in the economy depends on technology and, in particular, on how efficient we are at using money.

Now, let's use the quantity equation to show how an increase in the money supply is related to inflation. If you look carefully at the quantity equation of money, you can see that if velocity and real GDP are not affected by a change in money, then an increase in the money supply will increase the GDP deflator (the average level of prices in the economy). A higher percentage increase in money—that is, *higher money growth*—will lead to a higher percentage increase in prices—that is, *higher inflation.* Thus, the quantity equation of money shows that higher rates of money growth lead to higher inflation, just as in the case of commodity money early in the chapter.

A restatement of the quantity equation using growth rates leads to a convenient relationship between money growth, inflation, real GDP growth, and velocity growth. In particular,

$$\text{Money growth} + \text{velocity growth} = \text{inflation} + \text{real GDP growth}$$

For example, if the money supply growth is 5 percent per year, velocity growth is 0 percent per year, and real GDP growth is 3 percent per year, then this equation says that inflation is 2 percent per year. (This growth rate form of the quantity equation follows directly from the quantity equation itself; in general, the rate of growth of a product of two terms is approximately equal to the sum of the growth rates of the two terms. Thus, the growth rate of M times V equals the growth rate of M plus the growth rate of V, and the growth rate of P times Y equals the growth rate of P plus the growth rate of Y.)

According to the quantity equation, along a long-run economic growth path in which real GDP growth is equal to potential GDP growth, an increase in money growth by a certain number of percentage points in the long run will result in an increase in inflation of the same number of percentage points unless velocity growth changes. Thus, higher money growth will lead to higher inflation in the long run. If velocity growth remains at zero, as in the previous example, and real GDP growth remains at 3 percent per year, then an increase in money growth by 10 percentage points, from 5 to 15 percent, will increase inflation by 10 percentage points, from 2 to 12 percent.

3.2 Evidence

What evidence do we have that higher money growth leads to more inflation? The quantity equation tells us that we should look for evidence during periods when changes in real GDP and velocity were small compared with changes in money growth and inflation. During such periods, the change in money growth and inflation will be the dominant terms in the quantity equation.

Worldwide Inflation in the 1970s and 1980s

Figure 22.6 shows such a period: the years from 1973 to 1991, when many economies had big inflations, some much bigger than others. Money growth is plotted on the vertical axis, and inflation on the horizontal axis. In Figure 22.6, each point represents a country. For countries with higher money growth, inflation was higher. Hence, the quantity equation works well during this period. During the 1990s, inflation was low in all these countries, so the difference was insufficient to test how well the equation works. This period of high inflation is sometimes called the Great Inflation.

FIGURE 22.6 **The Relation between Money Growth and Inflation**

As the data for these several countries show, higher money growth is associated with higher inflation. The data pertain to the period 1973–1991, when inflation differed greatly among the countries. Inflation and money growth are now lower in all these countries.

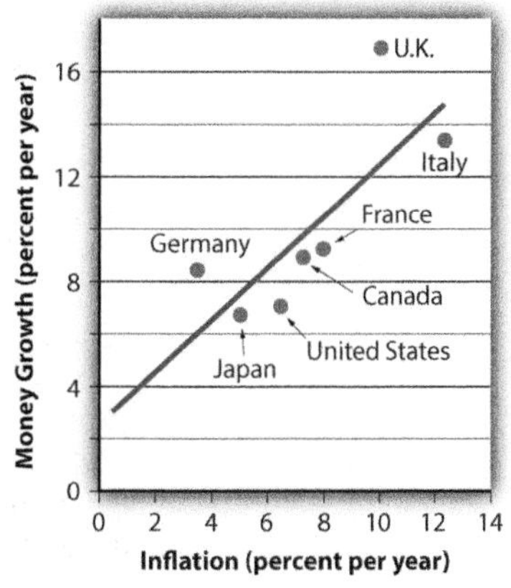

Hyperinflations

An even more dramatic type of evidence showing that high money growth can cause inflation is hyperinflation. A hyperinflation is simply a period of very high inflation. The inflation in Germany in 1923 is one of the most famous examples of a hyperinflation. The German government had incurred huge expenses during World War I, and huge demands for war reparations from the victors in World War I compounded the problem. Because the government could not raise enough taxes to pay its expenses, it started printing huge amounts of money, which caused the hyperinflation of 1923. Figure 22.7 shows the *weekly* increase in German prices.

The German hyperinflation of 1923 was not a unique historic episode, and hyperinflation is not necessarily linked to war. Until recently, hyperinflations were common in Latin America. The size of the Latin American inflations is hard to imagine. The inflation rate in Brazil averaged 43.6 percent per year from 1912 to 1996. A Brazilian good that cost one dollar in 1912 would cost a quadrillion dollars (1,000 trillion) in the 1990s. Inflation in Chile was also very high—about 90 percent throughout the 1970s.

Figure 22.8 shows the price level in Brazil and Chile as well as the money supply in both countries. Clearly, money and prices are closely related. Fortunately, inflation in Chile has been much lower since the 1990s, and inflation in Brazil also has been declining. Not surprisingly, money growth is much lower now too. Money growth has been the cause of all hyperinflations. The most recent hyperinflation occurred in Zimbabwe starting in February 2007 when inflation exceeded 50 percent per month. By late 2009 the inflation rate was 98 percent a day. Prices doubled overnight and the currency became worthless. The Zimbabwean inflation was the second worst in history after Hungary in 1946.

FIGURE 22.7 **German Hyperinflation of 1923**

The chart shows the weekly percent change in the price level in Germany in 1923. Inflation rose to truly astronomical levels for several months.

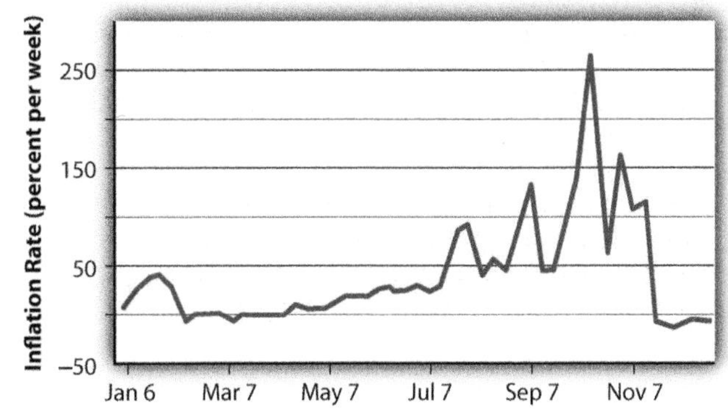

FIGURE 22.8 Money and Prices in Brazil and Chile during the Twentieth Century

The close relationship between money and the price level is obvious during this period of very high inflation. So far in the twenty-first century, inflation and money growth have been much lower in both countries.

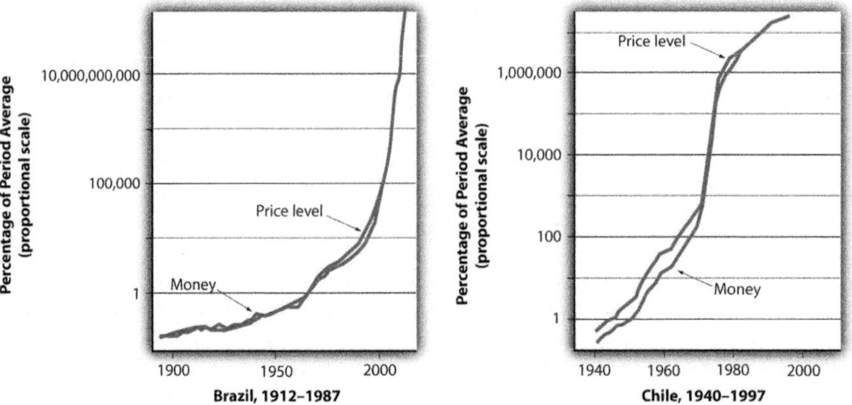

Source: Gerald Dwyer and Rik Hafer, "Are Money Growth and Inflation Still Related?" (Federal Reserve Bank of Atlanta, *Economic Review*, Second Quarter 1999).

REVIEW

- The quantity equation of money says that the money supply times velocity equals real GDP times the GDP deflator.
- Higher rates of money growth eventually will lead to higher inflation.
- Evidence of the relation between money growth and inflation is found in the 1970s and 1980s in the United States and other large economies, as well as in hyperinflations in Germany in the 1920s, Brazil and Chile in the twentieth century, and Zimbabwe in the twenty-first century.

4. END-OF-CHAPTER MATERIAL

4.1 Conclusion

Money has fascinated economists for centuries. The famous quantity equation introduced in this chapter predates Adam Smith and was used by the economist philosopher David Hume in the eighteenth century. Adam Smith placed money second in importance only to the division of labor in the first chapters of the *Wealth of Nations*.

Although the role of money appears mysterious and has caused some great debates in economics and politics, the ideas presented in this chapter are not controversial. The three functions of money, the deposit expansion process, the technical ability of the central bank to control the money supply, and the fact that money is the cause of inflation in the long run, are things many economists now agree on.

Many of the controversies about money pertain to the short-run fluctuations in the economy and revolve around the effects the Fed has on real GDP in the short run. After considering the reasons why real GDP may depart from potential GDP in the short run in Chapter 23 and Chapter 24, we will return to the effects the Fed has on short-run fluctuations in the economy.

Key Points

1. Money has three roles: a medium of exchange, a store of value, and a unit of account.
2. Commodity money, ranging from salt to gold coins, has been used in place of barter for many centuries. Now paper money and deposits are also part of money.
3. Commercial banks are financial intermediaries; their deposits are part of the money supply.
4. Commercial banks hold reserves at the central bank.
5. The central bank changes reserves by buying and selling bonds.
6. The central bank can control the money supply by buying and selling bonds.
7. The central bank in the United States is the Federal Reserve System (the Fed).
8. When stated in terms of growth rates, the quantity equation of money describes the relationship between money growth, real GDP growth, and inflation.
9. Higher money growth eventually leads to higher inflation.

QUESTIONS FOR REVIEW

1. What are the differences between the medium of exchange, store of value, and unit of account roles of money?
2. What are some examples of commodity money?
3. Why is currency a part of money even though an expensive purse to put the currency in is not?
4. What is a bank?
5. What is the Fed, and how is the FOMC organized?
6. What happens to bank reserves when the Fed buys bonds?
7. Why does higher money growth cause inflation?
8. What is the quantity equation of money?

PROBLEMS

1. Which of the following are money and which are not?
   a. A credit card
   b. A debit card
   c. A check in your checkbook
   d. A dollar bill
   e. A necklace containing 8 ounces of gold
2. Cigarettes were a popular form of currency in prisoner-of-war (POW) camps in World War II, and still are a valuable form of currency in prisons in many countries. Why would cigarettes be likely to serve as currency in such settings?
3. Who are the current members of the Board of Governors of the Federal Reserve? What positions did they hold previously that made them well suited for a position on the board?
4. State whether each of the following statements is true or false. Explain your answers in one or two sentences.
   a. When commodity money is the only type of money, a decrease in the price of the commodity serving as money is inflation.
   b. The same money is always used as both a unit of account and a medium of exchange at any one time in any one country.
   c. The smaller the reserve ratio at banks, the larger the money multiplier.
   d. The Federal Reserve reduces reserves by buying government bonds.
5. Assume that required reserves are 7 percent of deposits and that people hold no currency—all money is held in the form of checking deposits.
   a. Suppose that the Federal Reserve purchases $30,000 worth of government bonds from Ellen (a private citizen), and that Ellen deposits all of the proceeds from the sale into her checking account at Z Bank. Construct a balance sheet, with assets on the left and liabilities on the right, to show how Ellen's deposit creates new assets and liabilities for Z Bank.
   b. How much of this new deposit can Z Bank lend out? Assume that it lends this amount to George, who then deposits the entire amount into his account at Y Bank. Show this on Y Bank's balance sheet.
   c. How much of this new deposit can Y Bank lend out? Suppose Joe takes out a loan for this amount from Y Bank and deposits the money into his account at X Bank. Show this on X Bank's balance sheet.
   d. The process of lending and relending creates money throughout the banking system. As a result of Ellen's deposit, how much money, in the form of deposits, has been created so far? If this process resulting from Ellen's deposit continues forever, how much money will be created?
6. Why are credit cards not included in the money supply even though they can be used easily for transactions? (*Hint:* What do you think happens when you use a credit card to purchase an item at a store?)
7. According to the quantity equation, changes in the money supply will lead directly to changes in the price level if velocity and real GDP are unaffected by the change in the money supply. Will velocity change over time? What factors might lead to changes in velocity? Are those changes related to changes in the money supply?
8. Consider the following table:

Year	Quantity of Money (billions of $)	Velocity	Real GDP (billions of 2009 $)	GDP Deflator
2006	$1,369	10.274	$14,717	
2009	$1,684	8.650		1.002
2012	$2,434	6.696	$15,384	

   a. Fill in the missing data, using the quantity equation of money.
   b. Why might velocity change in this way?
   c. Calculate the average inflation rate between 2006 and 2009 and between 2009 and 2012.
   d. If velocity had remained at the 2006 level, what would the deflator have been in 2009 and 2012, assuming real GDP and money are as in the table?

CHAPTER 23
The Nature and Causes of Economic Fluctuations

Studying economic fluctuations is important because recessions bring unemployment and hardship to many people. Although the importance of long-run economic growth cannot be overstated, fluctuations around the growth trend affect the livelihood of millions of people. As John Maynard Keynes put it, "Economists set themselves too easy, too useless a task if in tempestuous seasons they can only tell us that when the storm is long past the ocean is flat again." Hence, the study of economic fluctuations is vital to understanding economics.

Source: Shutterstock.com

The 2008/09 recession is one of many economic fluctuations that the United States and other economies have experienced over the years. In this chapter, we take a closer look at economic fluctuations, which are defined as departures of the economy from its long-term growth trend. These departures include recessions, which are periods in which gross domestic product (GDP) declines sharply, moving the economy below its long-term trend. Another type of departure occurs when GDP rises rapidly, moving the economy above its long-term trend.

Economic fluctuations have been common for at least 200 years, but they have changed over time. One notable change was that recessions diminished in frequency and moderated in severity in the United States, and many other countries, during the 25-year period from 1982 to 2007, a phenomenon that many economists call the Great Moderation. The only recession that occurred in the United States during this period was the 2001 recession, which lasted only eight months, starting in March 2001 and ending in November 2001. Between 2001 and 2007 the economy then grew and 7.1 million jobs were created until the peak in December 2007. A key purpose of studying economic fluctuations is to explain why this Great Moderation occurred and to determine whether economic policies were responsible for it.

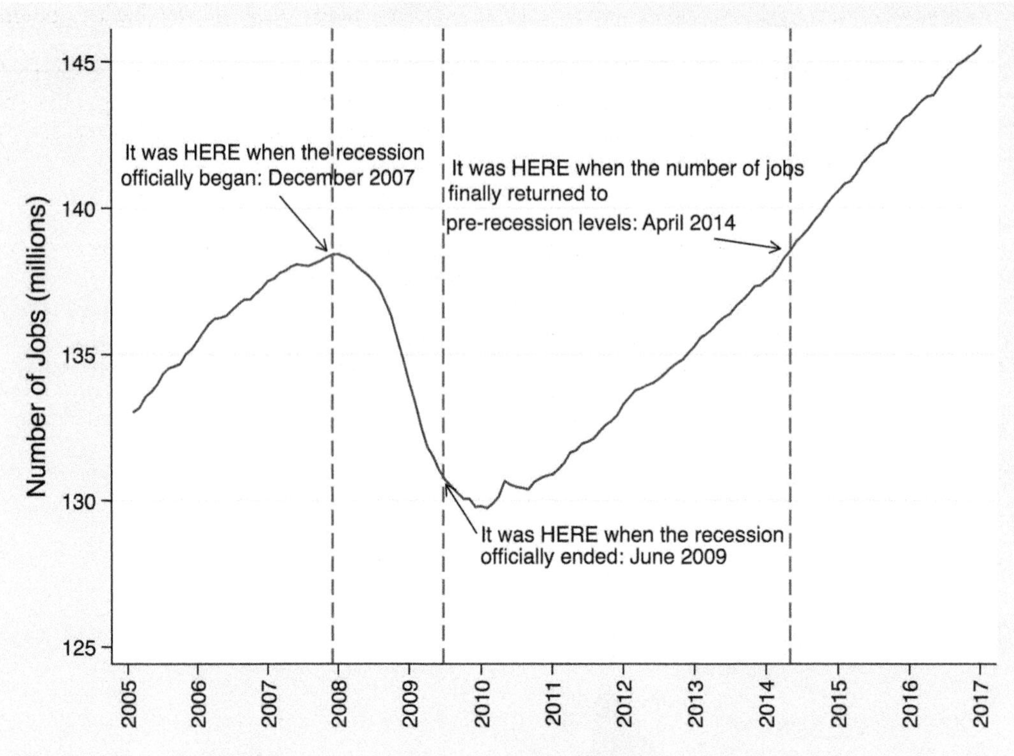

In December 2007, this period of Great Moderation came to an end when the economy entered a severe recession. Employment steadily declined all through 2008 as the recession worsened because of panic in the financial markets in the fall of 2008. By the time the recession officially ended in June of 2009, 7.8 million jobs in the U.S. economy had been lost. Recessions cause obvious harm to individuals who lose their job, and they make it much more difficult to find a job if you are looking for one. A person who entered the labor force in the summer of 2008 had a much greater difficulty finding a job than a person who entered the labor force in the summer of 2007 when the economy was near a peak. Understanding why the most recent recession was so severe in comparison with the 2001 recession will be an important first step in devising policies that could prevent millions of people from experiencing the hardship caused by job loss.

Even after the economy began growing again, employment continued to decline with almost 1 million more jobs being lost until the number of jobs finally started growing again in early 2010. It took until April of 2014, almost five years after the recession had ended, for the number of jobs to reach pre-recession levels. Another key purpose of studying economic fluctuations is to understand why the recovery from the 2008/09 recession was so slow and how economic policy, both in terms of policies actually implemented and policies that could have been (but were not) implemented, could have been responsible for the slow recovery.

1. CHANGES IN AGGREGATE DEMAND LEAD TO CHANGES IN PRODUCTION

Figure 23.1 illustrates the nature of economic fluctuations with particular reference to the 2008/09 recession. As shown in the upper portion of Figure 23.1, after the 2001 recession, real GDP clearly returned to potential GDP by 2005, and the economy stayed at or above potential output until the recession began in December 2007. Real GDP fell sharply below potential GDP, and it continued to decline until the recession officially ended in June 2009. Since then real GDP has grown, but the initial decline was so dramatic that even seven years later, real GDP has not made it all the way back to potential GDP.

Economic fluctuations occur simultaneously with long-term growth, as shown by the longer history in the lower panel of Figure 23.1. Real GDP has fluctuated around what otherwise might have been a steady upward-moving trend. Although no two economic fluctuations are alike—some are long, some are short; some are deep, some are shallow—they do have common features. Perhaps the most important one is that after a departure of real GDP from potential GDP, the economy eventually returns to a more normal long-run growth path.

We begin by looking at the first steps the economy takes as it moves away from potential GDP. In other words, we examine the initial, or short-run, increase or decrease of real GDP above or below potential GDP as in 2001 and 2008. We will show that the first steps of real GDP away from potential GDP are caused by changes in aggregate demand. Aggregate demand is the total amount that consumers, businesses, government, and foreigners are willing to spend on all goods and services in the economy. In contrast, the growth of potential GDP is caused by increases in the available supply of inputs to production: labor, capital, and technology.

FIGURE 23.1 Narrowing the Focus on Economic Fluctuations

The magnified economic fluctuation centers on the recession that began in December 2007.

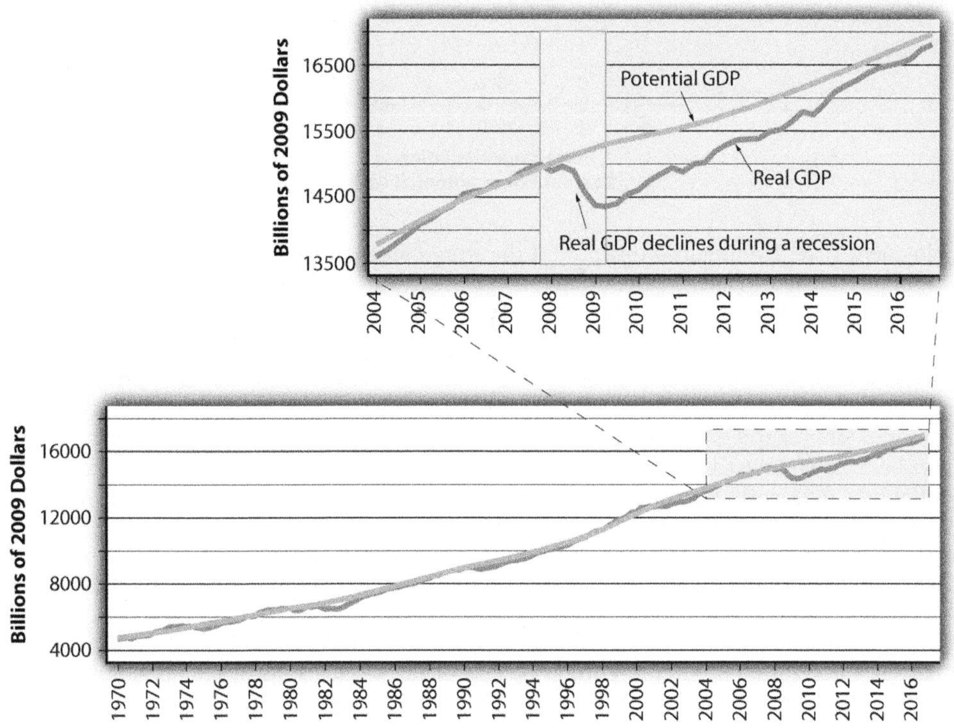

Figure 23.2 illustrates the essential idea used to explain economic fluctuations: Increases or decreases in real GDP to levels above or below potential GDP occur largely because of increases or decreases in aggregate demand in the economy. Changes in aggregate demand occur when consumers, business firms, government, or foreigners expand or cut back their spending. Potential GDP in three years is represented by points *a*, *b*, and *c* in Figure 23.2. These three values of potential GDP are part of the long-term steady increase in potential GDP over time resulting from increases in the supply of labor and capital and improvements in technology. Potential GDP represents what firms would want to produce in "normal times," when the economy is not in a recession. In normal times, real GDP is equal to potential GDP. Years 1 and 2 in Figure 23.2 are assumed to be normal years. Year 3, however, is not a normal year. Point *d* in the left panel of the figure shows a recession because real GDP has declined from Point *b*. Real GDP is below potential GDP at Point *d*. Firms produce less and lay off workers.

FIGURE 23.2 The First Step of an Economic Fluctuation

Potential GDP is shown by the black upward-sloping line in both diagrams. Points *a*, *b*, and *c* represent three different levels of potential GDP in three years. A downward departure of real GDP (shown in orange) from potential GDP is illustrated by point *d* on the left. Because real GDP falls, this is a recession. An upward departure of real GDP from potential GDP is illustrated by point *e* on the right. The departures are explained by changes in aggregate demand. The line at the bottom shows the percent deviation of real GDP from potential GDP.

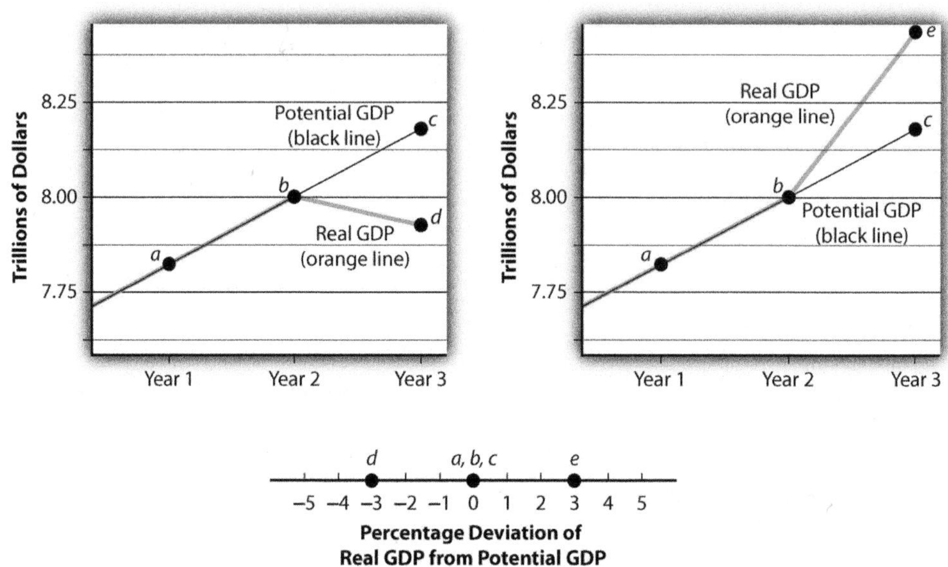

Unemployment rises. Eventually—this part of the story comes in later chapters—if demand stays low, firms begin to cut their prices, and real GDP moves back toward potential GDP. Thus, in recessions, changes in aggregate demand cause fluctuations in real GDP.

potential GDP

The economy's long-term growth trend for real GDP, determined by the available supply of capital, labor, and technology. Real GDP fluctuates above and below potential GDP.

Point *e* in the right panel represents another departure of real GDP from **potential GDP.** In this case, real GDP rises above potential GDP. Firms produce more in response to the increase in aggregate demand; they employ more workers, and unemployment declines. Eventually—again, this part of the story comes in later chapters—if demand for their product stays high, firms raise their prices, and real GDP goes back down toward potential GDP.

Economists frequently measure the departures of real GDP from potential GDP in percentages rather than in dollar amounts. For example, if potential GDP is $8 trillion and real GDP is $8.4 trillion, then the percentage departure of real GDP from potential GDP is 5 percent: (8.4 – 8.0)/8.0 = 0.05. If real GDP were $7.6 trillion and potential GDP remained at $8 trillion, then the percentage departure would be -5 percent: (7.6 – 8.0)/8.0 = –0.05. Percentages make it easier to compare economic fluctuations in different countries that have different sizes of real GDP. At the bottom of the two panels in Figure 23.2 is a horizontal line representing the size of the fluctuations in real GDP around potential GDP in percentage terms for Year 1, Year 2, and Year 3. Points *d* and *e* in Figure 23.2 represent the first steps of an economic fluctuation.

1.1 Production and Demand at Individual Firms

Why do firms produce more—bringing real GDP above *potential* GDP—when the demand for their products rises? Why do firms produce less—bringing real GDP below potential GDP—when the demand for their products falls? These questions probably have occupied more of economists' time than any other question in macroeconomics. Although more work still needs to be done, substantial improvements in economists'understanding of the issues have been made in the last 20 years.

The Unemployment Rate and the Deviations of Real GDP from Potential GDP

First consider some simple facts about how firms operate. In normal times, when real GDP is equal to potential GDP, most firms operate with some excess capacity so that they can expand production without major bottlenecks. Small retail service businesses from taxi companies to dry cleaners usually can increase production when customer demand increases. Another taxi is added to a busy route and one of the drivers is asked to work overtime. One of the dry cleaning employees who has been working part time is happy to work full time. The same is true for large manufacturing firms. When asked what percent of capacity their production is in normal times, manufacturing firms typically answer about 80 percent. Thus, firms normally have room to expand production: Capacity utilization sometimes goes up to 90 percent or higher. If firms need more labor to expand production, they can ask workers to work overtime, call workers back from previous layoffs, or hire additional workers. *The unemployment rate drops below the natural unemployment rate when real GDP rises above potential GDP.*

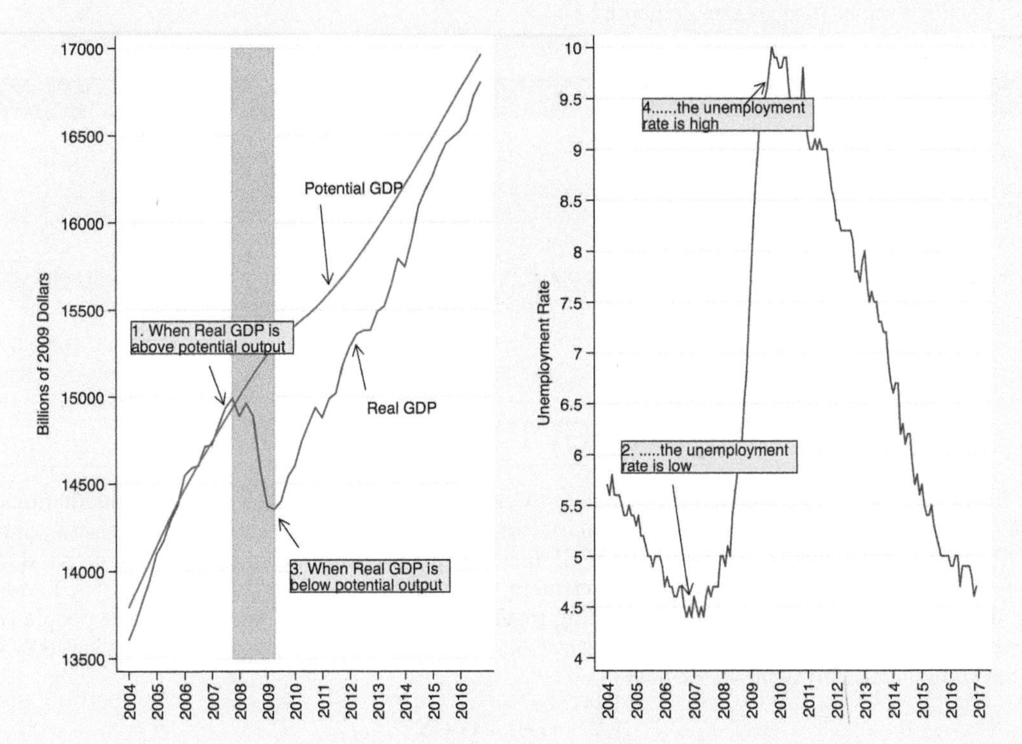

In recessions, when demand declines, these same firms clearly have the capability to reduce production, and they do. In recessions, capacity utilization goes down to 70 percent or lower. Firms ask workers to stop working overtime, they move some workers to part time, or they lay off some workers. Some firms institute hiring freezes to ensure that the personnel office does not keep hiring workers. *The unemployment rate rises above the natural unemployment rate when real GDP falls below potential GDP.* For example, the unemployment rate rose to almost 10 percent when the 2008/09 recession brought real GDP below potential GDP. The relationship between the unemployment rate and the movements of real GDP relative to potential GDP is illustrated at right.

1.2 Could Economic Fluctuations Also Be Due to Changes in Potential GDP?

Reminder: Recall from Chapter 17 that potential GDP depends on the economy's aggregate supply, which is determined by the available capital, labor, and technology. A drought or a flood would reduce aggregate supply.

Our discussion thus far of the production decisions of individual firms has shown why it is natural to identify fluctuations in real GDP with fluctuations in aggregate demand. To be sure, economic fluctuations also occur because of changes in potential GDP. For example, when agriculture was a much larger fraction of real GDP, droughts and floods had more noticeable effects on real GDP. Although agriculture currently accounts for a very small fraction of total production, the possibility that increases or decreases in potential GDP may still play a large role in economic fluctuations currently is being examined by economists. Economic theories that emphasize changes in potential GDP as a source of economic fluctuations are called **real business cycle theories**. Most frequently, changes in technology are assumed to be the reason for changes in potential GDP in real business cycle theories.

real business cycle theories

A theory of macroeconomics that stresses that shifts in potential GDP are a primary cause of fluctuations in real GDP; the shifts in potential GDP usually are assumed to be caused by changes in technology.

The factors that underlie potential GDP growth—population, capital, technological know-how—tend to evolve relatively smoothly. Population growth, for example, is much steadier than real GDP growth. We do not have a drop in the population every few years and a sudden spurt the next year. Slowdowns in population growth occur gradually over time as birth rates and death rates change. Similarly, although individual factories or machines may be lost in a hurricane or flood, such losses do not happen in such a massive way across the whole country that they would show up as a recession or a boom in the whole economy. Thus, the amount of capital changes slowly over time. Even technological change does not seem capable of explaining most fluctuations. It is true that some inventions and innovations raise productivity substantially in certain sectors of the economy over short periods of time. The impact on the whole economy is more spread out and gradual, however. Moreover, people do not suddenly forget how to use a technology. Technological know-how does not seem to decrease suddenly. For these reasons, potential GDP usually tends to grow relatively smoothly over time, compared with the fluctuations in aggregate demand.

REVIEW

- Economic fluctuations are largely a result of fluctuations in aggregate demand.
- When aggregate demand decreases, firms produce less; real GDP falls below potential GDP. Unemployment rises. When aggregate demand increases, firms first produce more; real GDP rises above potential GDP. Firms also hire more workers, and the unemployment rate falls.
- Short-run fluctuations in potential GDP also occur, but in reality, most of the larger fluctuations in real GDP seem to be due to fluctuations of real GDP around a more steadily growing potential GDP.

2. FORECASTING REAL GDP

To illustrate how we use the idea that changes in aggregate demand lead to short-run fluctuations in real GDP, we will focus on an important macroeconomic task: short-term economic forecasting of real GDP about one year ahead. To *forecast* real GDP, economic forecasters divide aggregate demand into its four key components: consumption, investment, government purchases, and net exports. Remember that real GDP can be measured by adding together the four types of spending: what people *consume*, what firms *invest*, what *governments purchase*, and what *foreigners purchase* net of what they sell in the United States. In symbols, we have

$$Y = C + I + G + X$$

In other words, real GDP (Y) is the sum of consumption (C), investment (I), government purchases (G), and net exports (X).

2.1 A Forecast for Next Year

Suppose that it is December 2016 and a forecast of real GDP (Y) is being prepared for the year 2017. Using the preceding equation, a reasonable way to proceed would be to forecast consumption for the next year, then forecast investment, then forecast government purchases, and, finally, forecast net exports. When forecasting each item, the forecaster would consider a range of issues: Consumer confidence might affect consumption; business confidence might be a factor in investment; the electoral prospects of the political party controlling Congress might be a factor in government purchases; and developments in foreign countries might affect the forecast for net exports. In any case, adding these four spending items together would give a forecast for real GDP for the year 2017. For example, one economist may forecast that $C =$ \$11,500 billion, $I =$ \$3,250 billion, $X =$ –\$500 billion, and $G =$ \$2,750 billion. Then, that economist's forecast for real GDP is \$17,000 billion. Forecasts typically are expressed as growth rates of real GDP from one year to the next. If real GDP in 2016 is \$16,700 billion then the forecast would be for about 1.8 percent growth for the year 2017.

2.2 Impact of a Change in Government Purchases

The preceding forecast is prepared by making one's best assumption about what is likely for government purchases and the other three components of spending. Another type of forecast—called a *conditional forecast*—describes what real GDP will be under alternative assumptions about the components of spending. For example, the U.S. president or Congress might want an estimate of the effect of a proposal to change government purchases on the economy in 2016. A conditional forecast would be a forecast of real GDP conditional on this change in government purchases.

Suppose the proposal is to raise federal government purchases by \$250 billion in real terms in one year. What is the effect of such a change in government purchases on aggregate demand in the short run? If the government demands \$250 billion more, then firms will produce \$250 billion more. A forecast conditional on a \$250 billion spending increase would be \$250 billion more for real GDP, or \$17,250 billion. Again, we just add up \$11,500 billion, \$3,250 billion, –\$500 billion, and now \$3,000 billion. Real GDP growth for the year is now forecast to be 3.3 percent, conditional on the policy proposal.

The forecast is based on the equation $Y = C + I = G + X$ and the idea that changes in aggregate demand cause real GDP fluctuations. Although simple, it is specific and substantive. According to this method of forecasting, changes in aggregate demand are responsible for most of the short-run ups and downs in the economy. It is this explanation that most economic forecasters use when they forecast real GDP for one year ahead.

REVIEW

- The four components of spending can be added to make a forecast for real GDP. Making such a forecast is an important application of macroeconomics.
- Forecasts may be conditional on a particular event, such as a change in government purchases or a change in taxes.

3. THE RESPONSE OF CONSUMPTION TO INCOME

In the forecasting example, we assumed that none of the other components—consumption, investment, or net exports—change in response to the increase in government purchases. For example, consumption (C) was unchanged at $11,500 billion when we altered G in our conditional forecast. But these components of spending are likely to change. Thus, something important is missing from the procedure for forecasting real GDP. To improve the forecast, we must describe how the other components of aggregate demand—consumption, investment, and net exports—might change in response to other developments in the economy. We eventually will consider the response of consumption, investment, and net exports to many factors, including interest rates, exchange rates, and income. Bringing all these factors into consideration at once is complicated, however, and we must start with a simplifying assumption. Here the *simplifying assumption* is that consumption is the only component of expenditures that responds to income and that income is the only influence on consumption. Consumption is a good place to begin because it is by far the largest component of real GDP. Before we finish developing a complete theory of economic fluctuations, we will consider the other components and the other influences. Let us begin by examining why consumption may be affected by income.

3.1 The Consumption Function

The **consumption function** describes how consumption depends on income. The notion of a consumption function originated with John Maynard Keynes, who wrote about it during the 1930s. Research on the consumption function has been intense ever since. For each individual, the consumption function says that the more income one has, the more one consumes. For the national economy as a whole, it says that the more income Americans have, the more Americans consume. For the world economy as a whole, it says that the more income the world has, the more the people in the world consume. Table 23.1 gives a simple example of how consumption depends on income in the U.S. economy.

consumption function
The positive relationship between consumption and income.

TABLE 23.1 An Example of the Consumption Function (billions of dollars)

Consumption	Income
4,400	5,000
5,000	6,000
5,600	7,000
6,200	8,000
6,800	9,000
7,400	10,000
8,000	11,000
8,600	12,000
9,200	13,000
9,800	14,000
10,400	15,000
11,000	16,000
11,600	17,000
12,200	18,000

As you can see from the table, as income increases from $5,000 billion to $6,000 billion, consumption increases as well, from $4,400 billion to $5,000 billion, and as income increases from $8,000 billion to $9,000 billion, consumption increases from $6,200 billion to $6,800 billion. More income means more consumption, but the consumption function also tells us *how much* consumption increases when income increases. Each change in income of $1,000 billion causes an increase in consumption of $600 billion. The changes in consumption are smaller than the changes in income. Notice that, in this example, at very low levels of income, consumption is greater than income. If consumption were greater than income for a particular individual, that individual would have to borrow. At higher levels of income, when consumption is less than income, the individual would be able to save.

The consumption function is supposed to describe the behavior of individuals because the economy is made up of individuals. Consequently, it summarizes the behavior of all people in the economy with respect to consumption. The simple consumption function is not meant to be the complete explanation of consumption. Recall that it is based on a simplifying assumption.

The Marginal Propensity to Consume

marginal propensity to consume (MPC)

The slope of the consumption function, showing the change in consumption that is due to a given change in income.

A concept related to the consumption function is the **marginal propensity to consume (MPC)**. The MPC measures how much consumption changes for a given change in income. The term marginal refers to the additional amount of consumption that is due to a change in income. The term propensity refers to the inclination to consume. By definition,

$$\text{Marginal Propensity to Consume (MPC)} = \frac{\text{change in consumption}}{\text{change in income}}$$

What is the MPC for the consumption function in Table 23.1? Observe that the change in consumption from row to row is 600. The change in income from row to row is 1,000; thus, the MPC = 600/1,000 = 0.6. Although this is only a simple example, the MPC for the U.S. economy is around that magnitude.

Figure 23.3 graphs the consumption function by putting income on the horizontal axis and consumption on the vertical axis. We get the upward-sloping line by plotting the pairs of observations on consumption and income in Table 23.1 and connecting them with a line. This line, which demonstrates that consumption rises with income, is the consumption function. Its slope is equal to the MPC. For this example, the MPC = 0.6. The graph shows that at low levels of income, consumption is greater than income, but at high levels of income, consumption is less than income.

FIGURE 23.3 **The Consumption Function**

For the economy as a whole, more income leads to more consumption, as shown by the example of an upward-sloping consumption function in the figure. This represents the sum of all the individuals in the economy, many of whom consume more when their income rises. The graph is based on the numbers in Table 11.1.

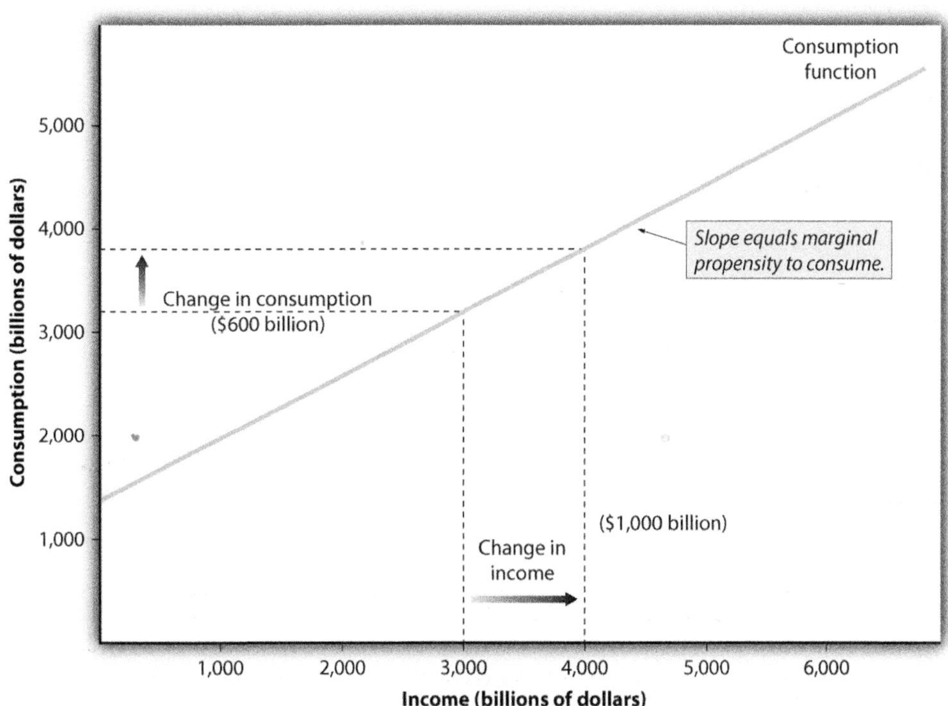

Which Measure of Income

The consumption function is a straight-line relationship between consumption and income. Income in the relationship is sometimes measured by *aggregate income* (Y), which also is equal to real GDP, and sometimes by disposable income. *Disposable income* is the income that households receive in wages, dividends, and interest payments plus transfers they may receive from the government minus any taxes they pay to the government. Disposable income is the preferred measure of income when one is interested in household consumption because this is what households have available to spend. But the consumption function for the whole economy for aggregate income and that for disposable income look similar because aggregate income and disposable income fluctuate and grow together. In the United States and most other countries, taxes and transfers are nearly proportional to aggregate income.

For the rest of this chapter, we will use aggregate income, or real GDP, as the measure of income in the consumption function. We put real GDP, or income (we drop the word *aggregate* in *aggregate income*), on the horizontal axis of the consumption function diagram, because real GDP and income always are equal. Figure 23.4 shows the actual relationship between consumption and income, or real GDP. Note, however, that when we consider an explicit change in taxes, we must take into account the difference between disposable income and income.

FIGURE 23.4 **Consumption versus Aggregate Income**

The graph shows the close relationship between consumption and aggregate income, or real GDP, in the U.S. economy. The points fall close to the straight line drawn in the diagram.

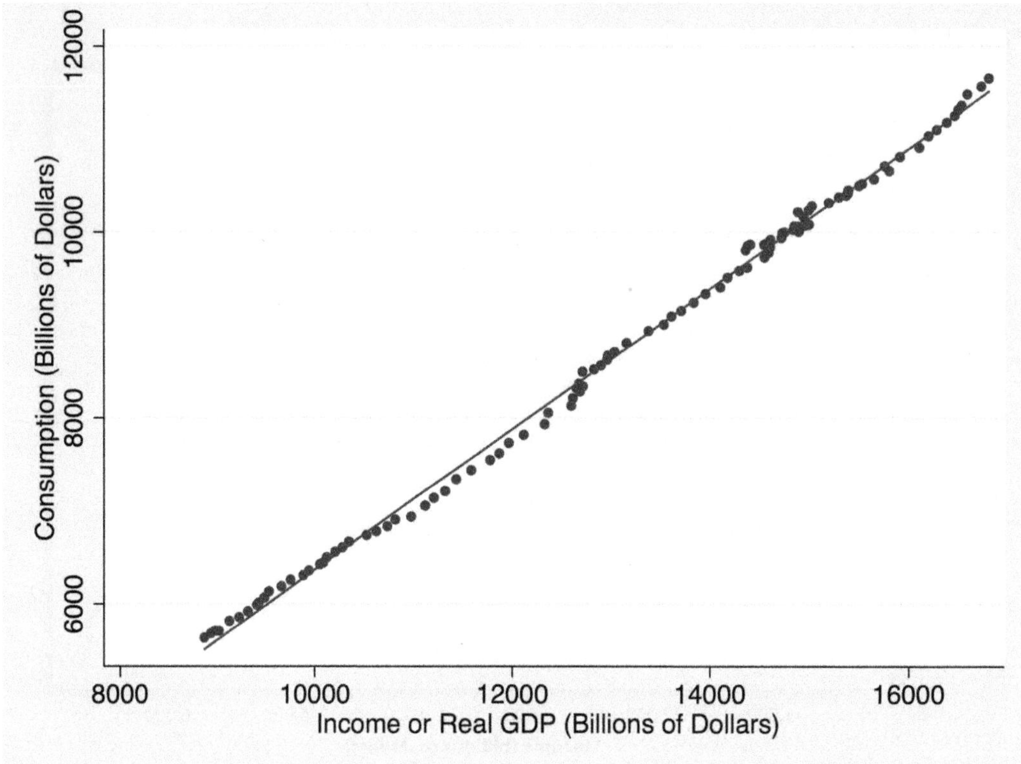

3.2 What about Interest Rates and Other Influences on Consumption?

Other factors besides income affect consumption. For example, you may recall from Chapter 19 that people's consumption is affected by the interest rate. Also, people's wealth—including their savings in a bank and their house—may affect their consumption. A person with a large amount of savings in a bank might consume a considerable amount even if the person's income in any one year is very low. Why have we not brought the interest rate or wealth into the picture here?

The answer is simple. To keep the analysis manageable at the start, we are putting the interest rate and other influences aside. We eventually return to consider the effects of interest rates and other factors on consumption. But during economic fluctuations, the effects of changes in income on consumption are most important, and we focus on these now.

REVIEW

- The consumption function describes the response of consumption to changes in income. The elementary consumption function ignores the effects of interest rates and wealth on consumption.
- The MPC tells us how much consumption changes in response to a change in income.
- For the economy as a whole, the consumption function can be expressed in terms of aggregate income or disposable income. Aggregate income is always equal to real GDP.

4. FINDING REAL GDP WHEN CONSUMPTION AND INCOME MOVE TOGETHER

Now let us use the consumption function to get a better prediction of what happens to real GDP in the short run when government purchases change. In other words, we want to improve the conditional forecast of real GDP when government purchases change by taking the consumption function into account. Again, as in the earlier example of forecasting, let us assume that government spending will increase by $250 billion next year. Our goal is to find out what happens to real GDP in the short run.

Our first attempt at forecasting proposed that an increase in government spending would increase real GDP. But now we see that something else must happen, because consumption depends on income, and real GDP is equal to income. An increase in government spending will increase income. The consumption function tells us that an increase in income must increase consumption, which further increases GDP.

Here is the chain of logic in brief:

1. An increase in government spending increases real GDP.
2. Real GDP equals income; thus income increases.
3. Consumption depends on income; thus consumption increases.
4. An increase in consumption further increase real GDP.

In sum, consumption will increase when we raise government spending.

For example, when the government increases spending on new highway construction, the firms that produce materials and services for highway construction find demand rising and produce more. Existing workers work more hours and new workers find jobs working on highway construction. Therefore, they will receive a higher income than before. In addition, the profits at the construction firms will increase; thus, the income of the owners of the firms will rise as well. With more income, the workers and the owners will spend more; that is, their consumption will rise. This is the connection between government spending and consumption about which we are concerned: The increase in government purchases raises construction workers' income, which results in more consumption.

The process can work in reverse as well. This type of logic was applied by economists to estimate the impact of closing Fort Ord, the military base near Monterey Bay in California, on the Monterey economy. When the estimates were made, the base employed 3,000 civilians and 14,000 military personnel. Payroll was $558 million. Thus, closing the base would reduce incomes by as much as $558 million as these workers were laid off or retired. Although some workers might quickly find jobs elsewhere, the decline in income would result in a reduction in consumption by those workers. Using an MPC of 0.6, consumption would decline by $335 million (0.6 times 558) if income was reduced by $558 million. This reduced income would tend to throw others in the Monterey area out of work as spending in retail and service stores declined. This would further reduce consumption, and so on. Although this case study refers to a small region of the entire country, the same logic applies to the economy as a whole.

4.1 The 45-Degree Line

We can use a convenient graph to calculate how much income and consumption change in the whole economy and thereby project what will happen to real GDP. A line in Figure 23.5 shows graphically that income in the economy is equal to spending. In Figure 23.5, income is on the horizontal axis and spending is on the vertical axis. All the points at which spending equals income are on the upward-sloping line in Figure 23.5. The line has a slope of 1, or an angle of 45 degrees with the horizontal axis, because the distances from any point on the line to the horizontal axis and the vertical axis are equal. Along that line—which is called the **45-degree line**—spending and income are equal.

45-degree line

The line showing that expenditure equals aggregate income.

4.2 The Expenditure Line

Figure 23.6 shows another relationship called the **expenditure line**. As in Figure 23.5, income, or real GDP, is on the horizontal axis, and spending is on the vertical axis. The top line in Figure 23.6 is the expenditure line. It is called the expenditure line because it shows how expenditure, or spending, depends on income. The four components that make up the expenditure line are consumption, investment, government purchases, and net exports. The expenditure line, however, shows how these four components depend on income. It is this dependency of spending on income that is the defining characteristic of the expenditure line. The next paragraph explains how the expenditure line is derived.

expenditure line

The relation between the sum of the four components of spending ($C+I+G+X$) and aggregate income.

FIGURE 23.5 The 45-Degree Line

This simple line is a graphical representation of the income equals spending identity. The pairs of points on the 45-degree line have the same level of spending and income. For example, the level of spending at *A* is the same dollar amount as the level of income at *A*. Moreover, because income equals real GDP, we can put either income or real GDP on the horizontal axis.

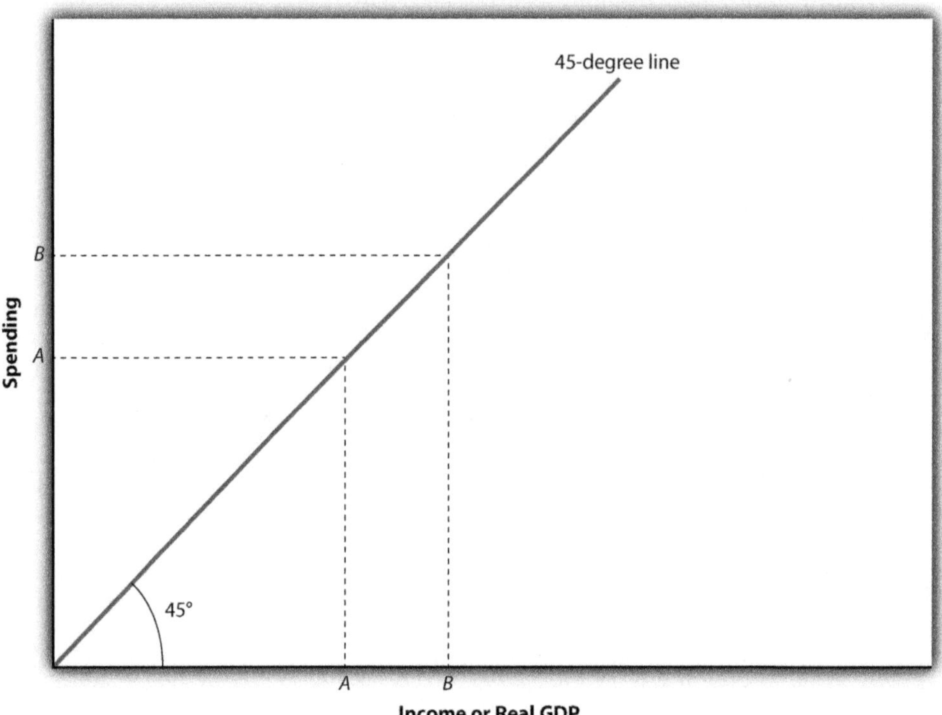

The consumption function is shown as the lowest line in Figure 23.6. It is the consumption function from Figure 23.3, which says that the higher income is, the more people want to consume. The next line above the consumption function in Figure 23.6 is parallel to the consumption function. This line represents the addition of investment to consumption at each level of income. It says that investment is so many billions of dollars in the U.S. economy, and the distance between the lines is this amount of investment. For example, if investment equals $800 billion, the distance between the consumption function and this next line is $800 billion.

FIGURE 23.6 The Expenditure Line

By adding investment (I), government purchases (G), and net exports (X) to the consumption function, we build the expenditure line.

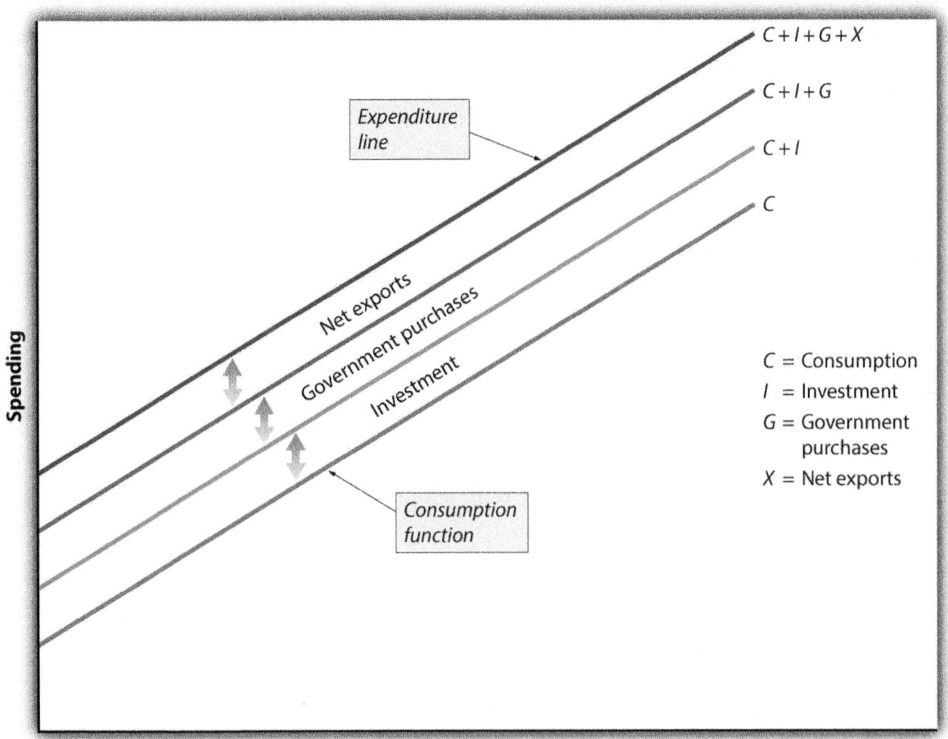

The reason the line is parallel to the consumption line is that we are starting our explanation by saying that investment does not depend on income. This simplifying assumption means that investment is a constant number, and the distance between the lines is the same regardless of income. We just add the same amount at each point.

The next line in Figure 23.6 adds in a constant level of government purchases. This line is also parallel to the other lines because the increase at every level of income is the same. The distance between the lines represents a fixed level of government purchases, say, $2,500 billion, at every level of income.

Finally, to get the top line in Figure 23.6, we add in net exports. For simplicity, we assume that net exports do not depend on income, an assumption that we will change soon. Thus, the top line is parallel to all the other lines. The top line is the sum of $C + I + G + X$. It is the expenditure line. The most important thing to remember about the expenditure line is that it shows how the sum of the four components depends on income. Before we can use the expenditure line, we must know what determines its slope and what causes it to shift.

The Slope of the Expenditure Line

Observe in Figure 23.6 that the expenditure line is parallel to the consumption function. Therefore, the slope of the expenditure line is the same as the slope of the consumption function. We already know that the slope of the consumption function is the MPC. Hence, the slope of the expenditure line also is equal to the MPC.

Because the MPC is less than 1, the aggregate expenditure line is flatter (the slope is smaller) than the 45-degree line, which has a slope of exactly 1. This fact will soon be used to find real GDP.

Shifts in the Expenditure Line

The expenditure line can shift for several reasons. Consider first what happens to the expenditure line if government purchases fall because of a cut in defense spending. As shown in Figure 23.7, the expenditure line shifts downward in a parallel fashion. The expenditure line is simply the sum $C + I + G + X$. Because G is less at all income levels, the line shifts down. The expenditure line is lowered because the distance between the consumption function and the other lines declines (see Figure 23.6). The reverse of this, an increase in government purchases, will cause the expenditure line to shift up.

FIGURE 23.7 Shifts in the Expenditure Line

The expenditure line shifts down if (1) government purchases (*G*) fall, (2) investment (*I*) falls, (3) taxes (*T*) increase, or (4) net exports (*X*) fall. The expenditure line shifts up if (1) government purchases rise, (2) investment rises, (3) taxes are cut, or (4) net exports rise.

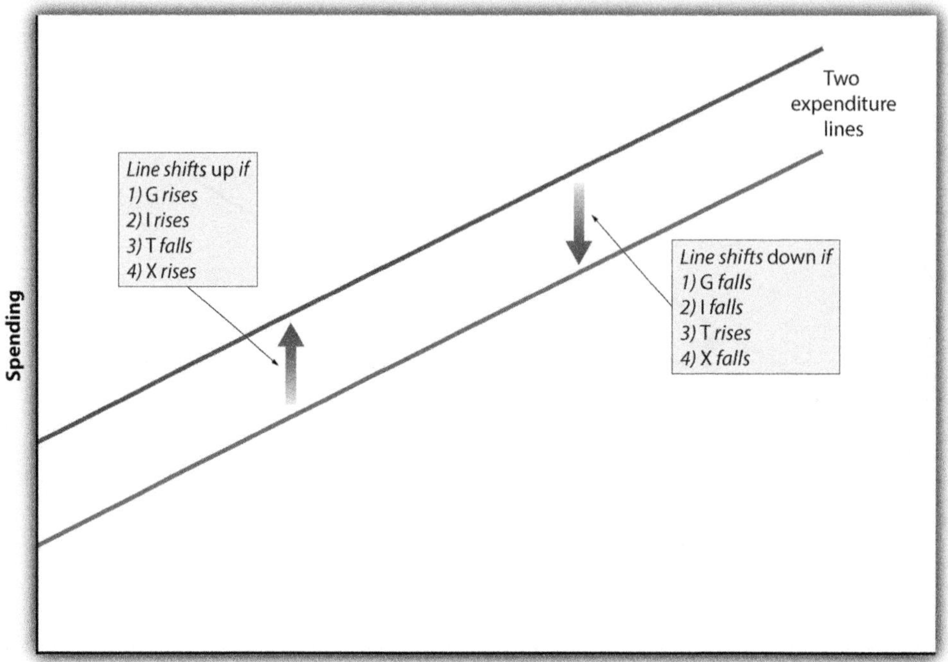

What happens to the expenditure line if investment falls? Investment, remember, is the gap between the first and second lines in Figure 23.6. If investment declines (as might happen if businesses become pessimistic about the future and invest less), then the expenditure line shifts downward. With less investment, the gap between the lines shrinks. The reverse of this, an increase in investment, will cause the expenditure line to shift up, as shown in Figure 23.7.

A change in net exports, perhaps because of a change in the demand for U.S. exports to other countries, also will shift the expenditure line. A downward shift in net exports lowers the expenditure line, and an upward shift in net exports raises the expenditure line.

Finally, the expenditure line also can be shifted by changes in taxes. At any given level of income, an increase in taxes means that people have less to spend, and this will cause people to consume less. Hence, the expenditure line shifts down when taxes rise. The reverse of this, a cut in taxes, causes the expenditure line to shift up. We will use the symbol *T* to refer to taxes. For example, if *T* = $2,000 billion, then people pay and the government receives $2,000 billion in taxes.

4.3 Determining Real GDP through Spending Balance

Having derived the expenditure line and the 45-degree line, we can combine the two to find real GDP. Figure 23.8 shows the expenditure line and the 45-degree line combined in one diagram. Observe that the two lines intersect. They must intersect because they have different slopes. Real GDP is found at the point of intersection of these two lines. Why?

FIGURE 23.8 Spending Balance

Spending balance occurs when two relations are satisfied simultaneously: (1) income equals spending, and (2) spending equals consumption, which is a function of income, plus investment plus government purchases plus net exports. Only one level of income gives spending balance. That level of income is determined by the intersection of the 45-degree line and the expenditure line.

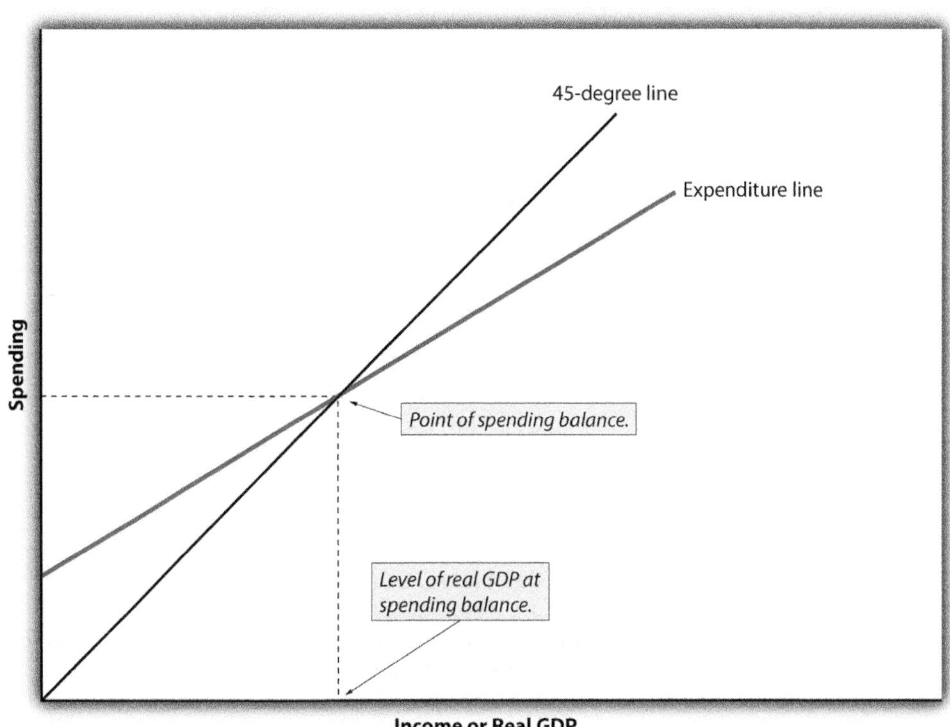

Income and spending always are equal, and the 45-degree line is drawn to represent this equality. Therefore, at any point on the 45-degree line, income equals spending. Moreover, income and spending must be on the expenditure line, because only at points on that line do people consume according to the consumption function.

If both relationships hold—that is, income and spending are the same (we are on the 45-degree line) and people's consumption is described by the consumption function (we are on the expenditure line)—then, logically, we must be at the intersection of these two lines. We call that point of intersection **spending balance**. The level of income determined by that point is just the right level to cause people to purchase an amount of consumption that—when added to investment, government purchases, and net exports—gives exactly the same level of income. We would not have spending balance at either a higher or a lower level of income. The diagram in Figure 23.8 showing that the 45-degree line and the expenditure line cross is sometimes called the "Keynesian Cross" after John Maynard Keynes.

spending balance

The level of income or real GDP at which the 45-degree line and the expenditure line cross; also called equilibrium income.

Table 23.2 provides an alternative way to determine spending balance. It uses a numerical tabulation of the consumption function rather than graphs. Total expenditure is obtained by adding the four columns on the right of Table 23.2. Consumption is shown to depend on income according to the same consumption function as in Table 23.1. Observe that income equals total expenditure in only one row. That row is where spending balance occurs. The row is shaded and corresponds to the point of intersection of the 45-degree line and the expenditure line in Figure 23.8.

Because the point of spending balance is at the intersection of two lines, we can think of it as an equilibrium, much as the intersection of a demand curve and a supply curve for wheat is an equilibrium. Because real GDP is not necessarily equal to potential GDP at this intersection, however, in a sense, the equilibrium is temporary; real GDP eventually will move back to potential GDP, as we will show in later chapters.

The point of spending balance is also an equilibrium in the sense that economic forces cause real GDP to be at that intersection. To see this, consider Table 23.2. As we noted, the shaded row corresponds to the intersection of the 45-degree line and the expenditure line: Income or real GDP equals expenditure. Suppose that income or real GDP were less than expenditure, as in one of the rows above the bolded row in Table 23.2. This would not be an equilibrium because firms would not be producing enough goods and services (real GDP) to satisfy people's expenditure on goods and services. Firms would increase their production, and real GDP would rise until it equaled expenditure. Similarly, if real

GDP were greater than expenditure, as in one of the rows below the shaded row in Table 23.2, firms would be producing more than people would be buying. Hence, firms would reduce their production, and real GDP would fall until it equaled expenditure.

TABLE 23.2 A Numerical Example of Spending Balance (billions of dollars)

Income or Real GDP	Total Expenditure	Consumption	Investment	Government Purchases	Net Exports
14,000	15,200	9,700	3,250	2,750	-500
15,000	15,800	10,300	3,250	2,750	-500
16,000	16,400	10,900	3,250	2,750	-500
17,000	**17,000**	**11,500**	**3,250**	**2,750**	**-500**
18,000	17,600	12,100	3,250	2,750	-500
19,000	18,200	12,700	3,250	2,750	-500
20,000	18,800	13,300	3,250	2,750	-500
21,000	19,400	13,900	3,250	2,750	-500
22,000	20,000	14,500	3,250	2,750	-500

4.4 A Better Forecast of Real GDP

Now let us return to forecasting real GDP using these new tools. Recall the example of making a forecast of real GDP for the year 2017 (from the vantage point of December 2016), conditional on a proposed increase in government purchases of $250 billion. Our new tools will enable us to take into account the effect of this increase on consumption, which we ignored in the simple forecast.

Figure 23.9 shows two expenditure lines. The bottom expenditure line is without the change in government purchases. In this case, $G =$ $2,750 billion, $C =$ $11,500 billion, $I =$ $3,250 billion, and $X =$ –$500 billion, yielding income, or real GDP, of $17,000 billion. For the conditional forecast, we assume that G is increased by $250 billion, to $3,000 billion. In Figure 23.9, that causes the expenditure line to shift up to the "new"line. Observe that the expenditure line shifts up by $250 billion—a parallel shift. This new expenditure line cuts the 45-degree line at a higher point.

Logic tells us that the economy will now operate at a different point of spending balance, the point at which the expenditure line and the 45-degree line now intersect. Thus, we move from one intersection to a new intersection as a result of the increase in the expenditure line. The new point of spending balance is at a higher level of GDP.

We now have a prediction that real GDP will rise if government spending increases. Observe in Figure 23.9 that the increase in real GDP is larger than the $250 billion increase in government purchases and, therefore, larger than the $250 billion increase in real GDP in the simple forecast. In addition to the increase in government purchases, consumption has risen because income has increased. The initial $250 billion is *multiplied* to create a larger than $250 billion change in real GDP because of the induced change in consumption. This multiplier phenomenon, which makes the change in real GDP larger than the change in government purchases, is called the *Keynesian multiplier* and applies to increases as well as to decreases in government purchases. In Figure 23.9, the multiplier looks quite large; the horizontal arrow is at least twice as large as the vertical arrow. It is certainly large enough to influence the government's decision to reduce government purchases. The example and the application illustrate that it is not just for fun that we have derived the expenditure line. It is an essential tool of the practicing macroeconomist.

FIGURE 23.9 From One Point of Spending Balance to Another

The expenditure line shifts up because of an increase in government purchases. This shifts up the forecast for real GDP. A forecast of real GDP conditional on the increase in government purchases therefore would be higher.

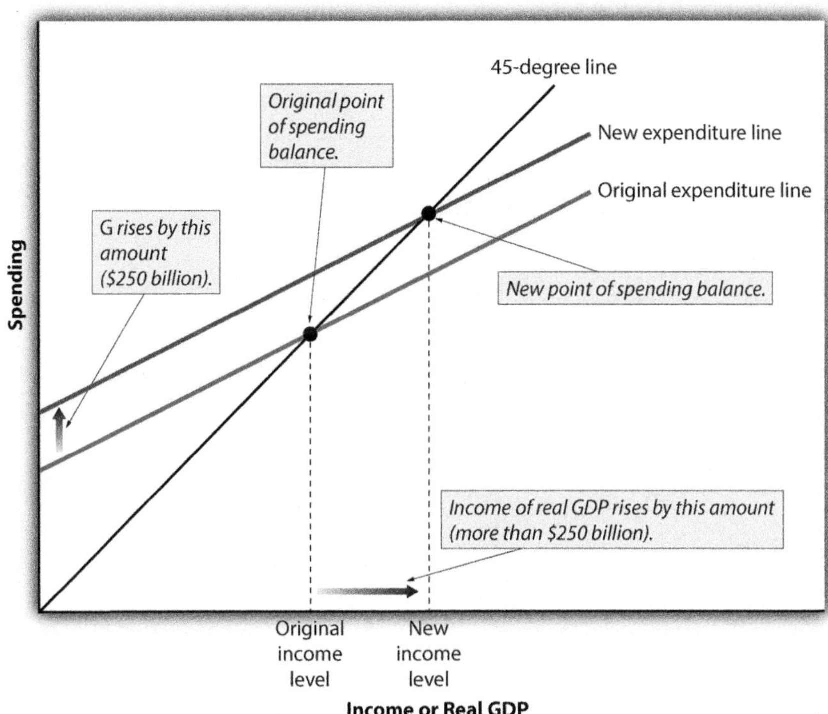

REVIEW

- Spending balance occurs when the identity $Y = C + I + G + X$ and the consumption function relating C to Y hold simultaneously.
- Spending balance can be shown on a graph with the 45-degree line and the expenditure line. The intersection of the two lines determines a level of income, or real GDP, that gives spending balance.
- A shift in the expenditure line brings about a new level of spending balance.

5. SPENDING BALANCE AND DEPARTURES OF REAL GDP FROM POTENTIAL GDP

We have shown how to compute a level of real GDP for the purpose of making short-term forecasts. This level of real GDP is determined by aggregate demand—consumption, investment, government purchases, and net exports. It is not necessarily equal to potential GDP, which depends on the supply of labor, capital, and technology. Thus, we can have real GDP departing from potential GDP, as it does in recessions. Let's now show this graphically.

5.1 Stepping Away from Potential GDP

Figure 23.10 illustrates how the departures of real GDP from potential GDP can be explained by shifts in the expenditure line. The left panel of the figure shows three different expenditure lines. Each line corresponds to a different level of government purchases or a different level of net exports or investment. The right panel of Figure 23.10—which is much like Figure 23.2—shows real GDP and potential GDP during a three-year period. A close connection exists between the left and right panels of Figure 23.10. The vertical axes are identical, and the points *c*, *d*, and *e* represent the same level of spending in both panels.

Observe how the three expenditure lines intersect the 45-degree line at three different levels of real GDP. Let us suppose that the middle expenditure line intersects the 45-degree line at a level of real GDP that is the same as potential GDP in Year 3. This is Point *c*. The lower expenditure line represents a recession; real GDP at the intersection of this expenditure line and the 45-degree line (Point *d*) is at a level below potential GDP and also below the level of real GDP in Year 2. Thus, real GDP would decline from Year 2 to Year 3 with this expenditure line. On the other hand, the higher expenditure line corresponds to the case in which real GDP is above potential GDP in Year 3.

FIGURE 23.10 **Spending Balance and Departures of Real GDP from Potential GDP**

This figure shows how the levels of real GDP found through spending balance can explain the first steps of a recession or boom. The left panel shows spending balance for three expenditure curves; one (*c*) gives real GDP equal to potential GDP, a second (*e*) gives real GDP above potential GDP, and a third (*d*) gives real GDP below potential GDP. As shown in the right panel, two of these entail departures of real GDP from potential GDP.

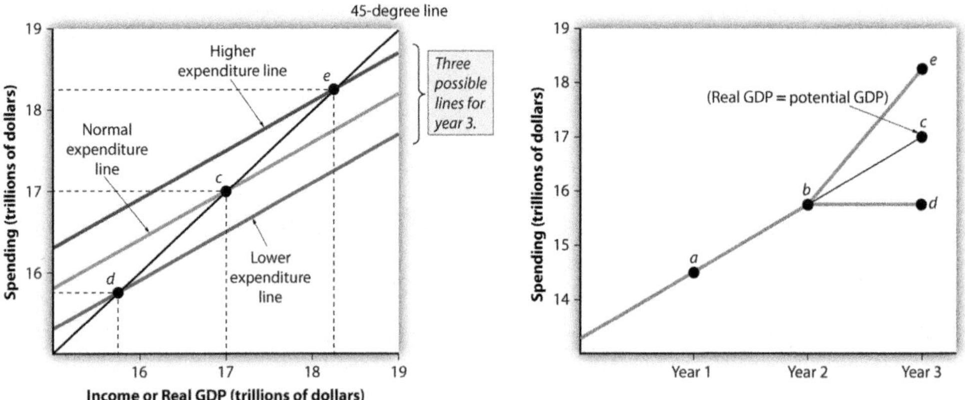

By referring to these values of real GDP as the *first* steps, we are emphasizing that they are not the end of the story. We will see that forces in the economy tend to bring real GDP back toward potential GDP. This calculation of real GDP gives only the short-run impact of changes in government spending, investment, net exports, or taxes.

REVIEW

- Shifts in the expenditure line can explain the departures of real GDP from potential GDP.
- When the expenditure line shifts down, real GDP declines, and, if it was previously equal to potential GDP, it will fall below potential GDP. Upward shifts in the expenditure line will bring real GDP above potential GDP.
- The expenditure line can shift for many reasons. Changes in taxes, government purchases, investment, and net exports will cause the expenditure line to shift.

6. END-OF-CHAPTER MATERIAL

6.1 Conclusion

With this chapter, we have begun to develop a theory of economic fluctuations. We have shown how economists explain departures of real GDP from potential GDP, using the idea that these fluctuations are due to changes in aggregate demand. A recession occurs when aggregate demand falls, bringing real GDP below potential GDP. We used this explanation to make short-term forecasts of real GDP. The expenditure line—showing how the demand for consumption, investment, and net exports depends on income—and the 45-degree line are key parts of the forecasting process. Thus far, however, our analysis has made several simplifying assumptions. For example, we assumed that the only thing people's consumption decisions respond to is a change in income.

In the next chapter, we show that consumption—as well as investment and net exports—responds to interest rates and inflation. The responses to interest rates and inflation will explain why real GDP returns to potential GDP in the long run.

Key Points

1. Economic fluctuations are temporary deviations of real GDP from potential GDP.
2. Employment and unemployment fluctuate with real GDP. Unemployment increases in recessions and decreases in booms.
3. The fluctuations in real GDP and potential GDP are mainly due to fluctuations in aggregate demand.
4. The idea that fluctuations in real GDP are mainly due to aggregate demand is used to find real GDP when making a short-term forecast.
5. Real GDP can be predicted on the basis of forecasts of consumption, investment, net exports, and government purchases. But these items depend on income and, thus, on the forecast of real GDP itself.
6. The consumption function describes how consumption responds to income.
7. The expenditure line is built up from the consumption function.
8. The 45-degree line tells us that expenditures equal income.
9. Combining the expenditure line and the 45-degree line in a diagram enables us to determine the level of income, or real GDP.
10. The level of real GDP that gives spending balance changes when government spending changes. Real GDP will decline in the short run when government purchases are cut.

QUESTIONS FOR REVIEW

1. Why do theories of economic fluctuations focus on aggregate demand rather than potential GDP as the main source of short-run economic fluctuations?
2. Why do theories of economic growth focus on potential GDP (with its three determinants) rather than aggregate demand as the main source of economic growth?
3. Why does the unemployment rate rise when real GDP falls below potential GDP?
4. What is the normal rate of capacity utilization in manufacturing firms? What is the significance of this normal rate for explaining economic fluctuations?
5. What accounting identity does the 45-degree line represent?
6. Why does the expenditure line have a slope less than 1?
7. Why do economic forecasters have to take into account the consumption function?
8. Why is real GDP given by the intersection of the 45-degree line and the expenditure line?

PROBLEMS

1. In the latter part of 2008, the U.S. economy was hit by a sudden plunge in stock markets, accompanied by a slowdown in consumer and investor spending. Explain why these events would move real GDP below potential GDP.
2. Recall that aggregate demand is made up of consumption, investment, government purchases, and net exports. How would the terrorist attacks on September 11, 2001, affect the components of aggregate demand in the three-month period that immediately followed?
3. Suppose the information in the following table described the economic situation in the United States at the end of 2016.

Year	Real GDP (billions of 2009 dollars)	Potential GDP (billions of 2009 dollars)
2014	16,200	16,400
2015	16,500	16,700
2016	16,800	16,960
2017 (pessimistic forecast)	17,000	17,250
2017 (optimistic forecast)	17,500	17,250

   a. Graph real GDP over time, placing the year on the horizontal axis. Calculate the growth rate of real GDP between 2014 and 2015, and between 2015 and 2016.
   b. The optimistic forecast for the year 2017 is based on the possibility that businesses are optimistic about the economy. What will the growth rate of real GDP be if the optimistic forecast is true?
   c. The pessimistic forecast is based on the possibility that businesses will be pessimistic about the economy. What will the growth rate of real GDP be if this forecast is correct?
   d. What is the deviation (in terms of dollars and as a percentage) of real GDP from potential GDP in 2017 if the optimistic forecast is correct? What is the deviation (in terms of dollars and as a percentage) from potential GDP in 2017 if the pessimistic forecast is correct?
4. When a war begins, what happens to the relationship between GDP and potential GDP? Does your answer depend on the size of the war or its duration?
5. Sketch a diagram with a 45-degree line and an expenditure line that describes macroeconomic spending balance. What factors determine how steep the expenditure line is? Show on the diagram that, when government purchases increase, U.S. income increases by more than the upward shift in government purchases.
6. Suppose government purchases will increase by $100 billion, and a forecasting firm predicts that real GDP will rise in the short run by $100 billion as a result. Would you say that that forecast is accurate? Why? If you were running a business and you subscribed to that forecasting service, what questions would you ask about the forecast?
7. Suppose that business executives are very optimistic, and they raise their investment spending. What happens to the expenditure line? How will this affect real GDP? Sketch a diagram to demonstrate your answer.
8. Suppose that U.S. goods suddenly become unpopular in Europe. What happens to net exports? How will this shift the expenditure line? What happens to real GDP? Demonstrate this in a diagram.

9. The following table shows the relationship between income and consumption in an economy.

Income (Y) (in billions of dollars)	Consumption (C) (in billions of dollars)
0	5
10	11
20	17
30	23
40	29
50	35
60	41
70	47
80	53
90	59
100	65

Assume that the investment (I) is $5 billion, government purchases (G) are $4 billion, and net exports (X) are $2 billion.

a. What is the numerical value of the MPC?
b. Construct a table that is analogous to Table 23.2 for this economy. What is the level of income at the point of spending balance?
c. For this level of income, calculate national saving. Is national saving equal to investment plus net exports?
d. Sketch a diagram with a 45-degree line and an expenditure curve that describes the preceding relationships. Show graphically what happens to income when the government lowers taxes.

10. In 2005, the Department of Defense announced its Base Realignment and Closure (BRAC) plan outlining which military bases were going to be shut down. This plan immediately caused great concern among the congressional representatives in whose districts the bases designated for closure were located. Suppose that a military base that employs 10,000 people was closed down. Describe the different sectors of the local economy that would be affected by the shutdown.

7. APPENDIX: DERIVING THE FORMULA FOR THE KEYNESIAN MULTIPLIER AND THE FORWARD-LOOKING CONSUMPTION MODEL

7.1 The Keynesian Multiplier

Here we derive a formula for the **Keynesian multiplier**, which gives the *short-run* impact on real gross domestic product (GDP) of things such as cuts in military purchases or a new federal program for road and bridge construction. We show how the multiplier depends on the marginal propensity to consume and on the marginal propensity to import.

Keynesian multiplier

The ratio of the change in real GDP to the shift in the expenditure line; the formula is 1/(1 − MPC), where MPC is the marginal propensity to consume.

A Graphical Review

Figure 23.11 is a diagram like the one derived in Figure 23.6, with income or real GDP on the horizontal axis and spending on the vertical axis. The 45-degree line equates spending and income. Figure 23.11 has two expenditure lines. The "new" expenditure line is $250 billion higher than the "old" expenditure line, representing an upward shift resulting from an increase in government purchases, for example. Both expenditure lines show that expenditure in the economy—the sum of consumption plus investment plus government purchases plus net exports, or $C + I + G + X$—rises with income. We assume that the marginal propensity to consume (MPC) is equal to 0.6. Thus, the slope of both expenditure lines is 0.6.

Note that the "new" expenditure line intersects the 45-degree line at a different point from the "old" expenditure line. At this new intersection, the level of income, or real GDP, is higher than at the old intersection. On the horizontal axis, the arrow pointing to the right shows this shift to a higher level of real GDP. Look carefully at the diagram to note the size of the change in real GDP along the horizontal axis and compare it with the change in the expenditure line. Observe that the horizontal change is *larger* than the vertical change. This is due to the *multiplier*. In fact, the term multiplier is used because the change in real GDP is a multiple of the shift in the aggregate expenditure line.

FIGURE 23.11 Graphical Calculation of the Multiplier

An upward shift in the expenditure line raises real GDP in the short run by a multiple of the shift in the expenditure line. The multiplier can be found graphically. It is the ratio of the length of the horizontal arrow to the length of the vertical arrow.

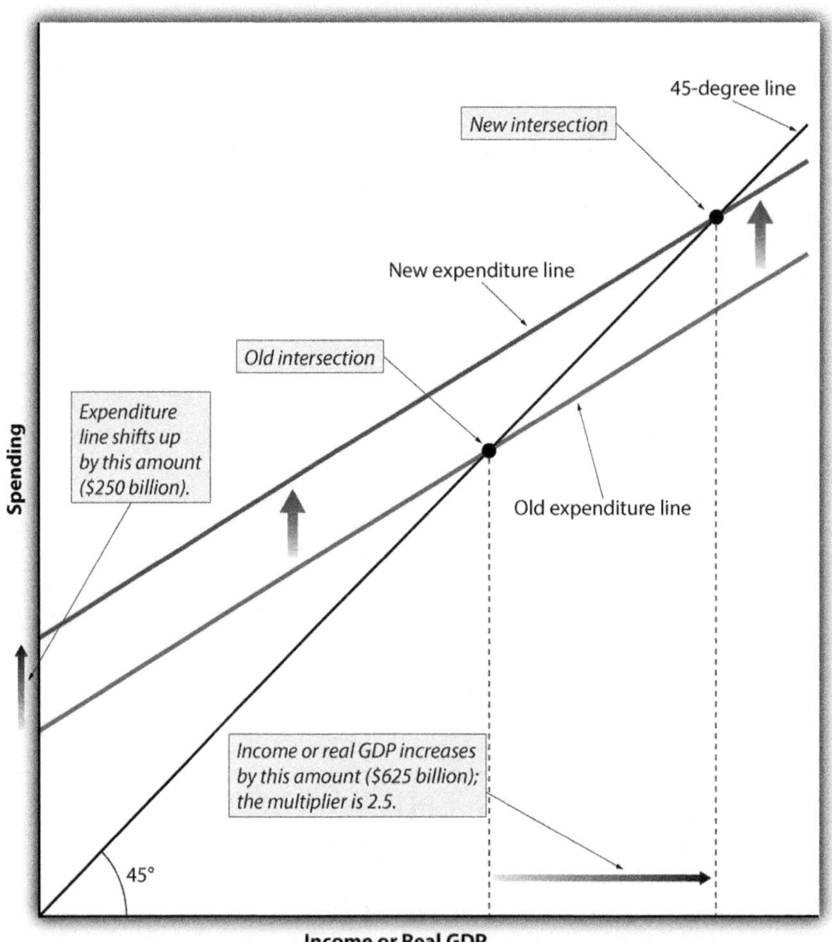

The multiplier is the ratio of the change in real GDP to the shift in the expenditure line, regardless of the reason for the shift in the expenditure line (whether it is due to a change in government purchases, a change in taxes, a change in investment, or a change in foreign demand). Thus, the multiplier is equal to the ratio of the length of the arrow along the horizontal axis to the length of the arrow along the vertical axis in Figure 23.11. You can find the multiplier by measuring these lengths. If you do so, you will find that for the expenditure line with a slope of 0.6 in Figure 23.11, the multiplier is 2.5.

The multiplier applies to anything that shifts the expenditure line. For example, an increase in government purchases of $250 billion would shift the expenditure line up by $250 billion. This would increase real GDP by $625 billion if the multiplier for government purchases is 2.5.

The Algebraic Derivation

We now want to derive a formula for the multiplier using algebra. Let us focus first on the case where the MPC is 0.6. To be specific, let us suppose that the particular reason for a change in the aggregate expenditure line is an increase in government purchases. Then the multiplier is the ratio of the change in real GDP to the change in government purchases.

The identity that income or real GDP (*Y*) equals consumption (*C*) plus investment (*I*) plus government purchases (*G*) plus net exports (*X*) can be written algebraically as

$$Y = C + I + G + X$$

To find the multiplier, we want to determine the impact of a *change* in government purchases on real GDP. That is, we want to find the change in *Y* that occurs when *G* changes. Any change in *Y* must come either directly from a change in *G* or indirectly from a change in *C*, *I*, or *X*, according to the preceding identity. Denote the change in any of these items by the Greek letter Δ. Then we can write the identity in terms of changes:

$$\Delta Y = \Delta C + \Delta I + \Delta G + \Delta X$$

That is, the *change* in real GDP is equal to the *change* in consumption plus the *change* in investment plus the change in government purchases plus the *change* in net exports. Now consider each of the four terms.

The change in government purchases (ΔG) equals $250 billion. For convenience, we continue to assume that investment and net exports do not change. In other words, we assume that neither responds to changes in income. This is expressed in symbols as $\Delta I = 0$ and $\Delta X = 0$.

But we cannot assume that $\Delta C = 0$. The *consumption function* tells us that consumption changes when income changes. The consumption function we use for the algebraic calculation has an MPC of 0.6. Using algebra, we write $\Delta C = 0.6 \times \Delta Y$. That is, the change in consumption equals 0.6 times the change in income; for example, if the change in income ΔY = $10 billion, then the change in consumption ΔC = $6 billion if the MPC is 0.6.

Now let us take our ingredients:

1. $\Delta Y = \Delta C + \Delta I + \Delta G + \Delta X$
2. The changes in investment and net exports are zero ($\Delta I = \Delta X = 0$)
3. The change in consumption is 0.6 times the change in income ($\Delta C = 0.6\Delta Y$)

Replacing ΔI with zero and ΔX with zero removes ΔI and ΔX from the right-hand side of the identity. Replacing ΔC with 0.6ΔY in the same identity results in

$$\Delta Y = 0.6\Delta Y + \Delta G$$

Note that the term ΔY appears on both sides of this equation. Gathering terms in ΔY on the left-hand side of the equation gives

$$(1 - 0.6)\Delta Y = \Delta G$$

Dividing both sides by ΔG and by (1 – 0.6) results in

$$\begin{aligned} \frac{\Delta Y}{\Delta G} &= \frac{1}{1-0.6} \\ &= \frac{1}{0.4} \\ &= 2.5 \end{aligned}$$

Thus, the change in income, or real GDP, that occurs when government purchases change, according to this calculation, is 2.5 times the change in government purchases. That is, $\Delta Y = 2.5 \times \Delta G$. The number 2.5 is the multiplier. The algebraic calculation agrees with the graphical calculation.

You can perform this same calculation for *any value* of the MPC, not just 0.6. To see this, note that the change in consumption equals the MPC times the change in income, where the MPC is any number. Using the same approach as in the case of MPC = 0.6, we obtain a *formula for the multiplier*, which is

$$\frac{\Delta Y}{\Delta G} = \frac{1}{1 - MPC}$$

The derivation of this formula is summarized in Table 23.3.

Following the Multiplier through the Economy

To get a more complete understanding of the formula for the multiplier, it is useful to examine what happens as a change in government purchases winds its way through the economy.

Assume that the government increases its purchases, perhaps to build new highways. In this example, the government increases purchases of highway construction services and equipment at construction firms. The immediate impact of the change in government purchases is an increase in the production of this equipment. With an increase in demand, construction firms produce more, and real GDP rises. The initial increase in real GDP from an increase in government purchases of $250 billion is that same $250 billion. If the government is purchasing more equipment, the production of equipment increases. We call this initial increase in real GDP the *first-round effect*, which includes only the initial change in government purchases.

TABLE 23.3 Derivation of a Formula for the Keynesian Multiplier

Start with the identity	$Y = C + I + G = X$
and convert it to change form:	$\Delta Y = \Delta C + \Delta I + \Delta G + \Delta X$
Substitute $\Delta I = 0$, $\Delta X = 0$, and $\Delta C = MPC \times \Delta Y$	
into the change form of the identity to get	$\Delta Y = MPC \times \Delta Y + \Delta G$
Gather terms involving ΔY **to get**	$(1 - MPC) \times \Delta Y = \Delta G$
Divide both sides by ΔG **and by 1 - MPC to get**	$\frac{\Delta Y}{\Delta G} = \frac{1}{1 - MPC}$

The first round is not the end of the story. A further increase in real GDP occurs when the workers employed in highway construction start working more hours and new workers are hired. As a result, the workers' income rises, and the profits made by the firms increase. With both wage income and profit income rising, income in the economy as a whole rises by $250 billion. According to the consumption function, people will consume more. How much more? The consumption function tells us that 0.6 times the change in income, or $150 billion, will be the additional increase in consumption by the workers and owners of the construction firms. Real GDP rises by $150 billion, the increased production of the goods the workers and owners consume. This $150 billion increase in real GDP is the *second-round effect.* It is hard for anyone to know what the workers in the construction industry or the owners of the construction firms will start purchasing; presumably it will be an array of goods: clothes, movies, and restaurant meals. But with an MPC of 0.6, we do know that they will purchase $150 billion more of these goods. The increase in production spreads throughout the economy. After this second round, real GDP has increased by $400 billion, the sum of $250 billion on the first round and $150 billion on the second round. This is shown in the first and second rows of Table 23.4.

TABLE 23.4 A Numerical Illustration of the Multiplier at Work (billions of dollars)

Round	Changes in Real GDP	Cumulative Change in Real GDP
First round	250.00	250.00
Second round	150.00	400.00
Third round	90.00	490.00
Fourth round	54.00	544.00
Fifth round	32.4	576.4
-	-	-
-	-	-
-	-	-
After an infinite number of rounds	0.00	625.00

The story continues. The workers who make the clothes and other goods and services for which there is $150 billion more in spending also have an increase in their income. Either they are no longer unemployed or they work more hours. Similarly, the profits of the owners of those firms increase. As a result, they consume more. How much more? According to the consumption function, 0.6 times the increase in their income. The increase in income outside of construction was $150 billion, so the increase in consumption must now be 0.6 times that, or a $90 billion increase. This increase is the *third-round effect.* As the increase permeates the economy, it is impossible to say what particular goods will increase in production, but we know that total production continues to increase. After three rounds, real GDP has increased by $490 billion, as shown in the third row of Table 23.4.

The increase does not stop there. Another $90 billion more in consumption means that people somewhere in the economy have $90 billion more in income. This increases consumption further, by

0.6 times the $90 billion, or $54 billion. According to the column on the right of Table 23.4, the cumulative effect on real GDP is now up to $544 billion after four rounds. Observe that each new entry in the first column is added to the previous total to get the cumulative effect on real GDP.

The story is now getting repetitive. We multiply 0.6 times $54 billion to get $32.4 billion. The total effect on real GDP is now $576.4 billion at the fifth round. In fact, we are already close to $625 billion. If we kept on going for more and more rounds, we would get closer and closer to the $625 billion amount obtained from the graphs and the formula for the multiplier.

What if Net Exports Depend on Income?

Thus far, we have made the simplifying assumption that net exports do not respond to income. When net exports do respond to income, the formula for the multiplier is a bit different. We now incorporate this response into our analysis.

We first need to consider how net exports respond to income. Recall that net exports are exports minus imports. To examine the effect of income on net exports, we look first at exports and then at imports.

Exports are goods and services that we sell to other countries, such as aircraft, pharmaceuticals, and telephones. Do U.S. exports depend on income in the United States? No, not much. If Americans earn a little more or a little less, the demand for U.S. exports is not going to increase or decrease. What is likely to make the demand for U.S. exports increase or decrease is a change in income abroad—changes in income in Japan, Europe, or Latin America will affect demand for U.S. exports. U.S. exports will not be affected even if the United States has a recession. Of course, if Japan or Europe has a recession, that is another story. In any case, we conclude that U.S. exports are unresponsive to the changes in U.S. income.

Imports are goods and services that people in the United States purchase from abroad, such as automobiles, sweaters, and vacations. Does the amount purchased of these goods and services change when our incomes change? Yes, because imports are part of consumption. Just as we argued that consumption responds to income, so must imports respond to income. Higher income will lead to higher consumption of both goods purchased in the United States and goods purchased abroad. That reasoning leads us to hypothesize that imports are related positively to income. The hypothesis is accurate when we look at observations on income and imports.

The **marginal propensity to import (MPI)** is the amount that imports change when income changes. Suppose the MPI is 0.2. The MPI is smaller than the MPC because most of the goods we consume when income rises are not imported.

marginal propensity to import (MPI)
The change in imports because of a given change in income.

If exports are unrelated to income and imports are positively related to income, then net exports—exports less imports—must be related negatively to income.

Algebraically, we have

$$\Delta X = -\text{MPI} \times \Delta Y$$

Using this expression for ΔX, we can now follow the same algebraic steps we followed earlier to derive a formula for the multiplier. The multiplier now depends on the MPI along with the MPC. The derivation is summarized in Table 23.5. The formula for the multiplier is

$$\frac{\Delta Y}{\Delta G} = \frac{1}{1 - \text{MPC} + \text{MPI}}$$

For example, if MPC = 0.6 and MPI = 0.2, the multiplier is 1.7.

7.2 The Forward-Looking Consumption Model

Although the consumption function introduced in Chapter 23 gives a good prediction of people's behavior in many situations, it sometimes works very poorly. For example, the MPC turned out to be quite small when taxes were cut in 1975; people saved almost the entire increase in disposable income that resulted from the tax cut. The MPC turned out to be quite large, however, for the tax cuts in 1982, only seven years later; in that case, people saved very little of the increase in disposable income. The forward-looking consumption model was designed to explain such changes in the MPC.

TABLE 23.5 Derivation of a Formula for the Keynesian Multiplier with Both the MPC and the MPI

Start with	$\Delta Y = \Delta C + \Delta I + \Delta G + \Delta X$
Assume that	$\Delta I = 0$
and that	$\Delta C = MPC \times \Delta Y$
and that	$\Delta X = -MPI \times \Delta Y$
Putting the above expressions together, we get	$\Delta Y = MPC \times \Delta Y + \Delta G - MPI \times \Delta Y$
and solving for the change in *Y*, we get	$\frac{\Delta Y}{\Delta G} = \frac{1}{1 - MPC + MPI}$

forward-looking consumption model

A model that explains consumer behavior by assuming that people anticipate future income when deciding on consumption spending today.

permanent income model

A type of forward-looking consumption model that assumes that people distinguish between temporary changes in their income and permanent changes in their income; the permanent changes have a larger effect on consumption.

life-cycle model

A type of forward-looking consumption model that assumes that people base their consumption decisions on their expected lifetime income rather than on their current income.

consumption smoothing

The idea that although their incomes fluctuate, people try to stabilize consumption spending from year to year.

The **forward-looking consumption model** assumes that people anticipate their future income when making consumption decisions. The forward-looking consumption model was developed independently and in different ways by two Nobel Prize–winning economists, Milton Friedman and Franco Modigliani. Friedman's version is called the **permanent income model**, and Modigliani's version is called the **life-cycle model**. Both models improved on the idea that consumption depends only on current income.

Forward-Looking People

The forward-looking model starts with the idea that people attempt to look ahead to the future. They do not simply consider their current income. For example, if a young medical doctor decides to take a year off from a high-paying suburban medical practice to do community service at little or no pay, that doctor's income will fall below the poverty line for a year. But the doctor is unlikely to cut consumption to a fraction of the poverty level of income. Even if the doctor were young enough to have little savings, borrowing would be a way to keep consumption high and even to buy an occasional luxury item. The doctor is basing consumption decisions on expected income for several years in the future—making an assessment of a more permanent income, or a life-cycle income—not just for one year.

We have many other examples of this model. Farmers in poor rural areas of Asia try to save something in good years so that they will be able to maintain their consumption in bad years. They try not to consume a fixed fraction of their income. In many cases, the saving is in storable farm goods like rice.

As these examples indicate, instead of allowing their consumption to vary with their income, which may be quite erratic, most people engage in **consumption smoothing** from year to year. Once people estimate their future income prospects, they try to maintain their consumption around the same level from year to year. If their income temporarily falls, they do not cut their consumption by much; the *MPC is very small—maybe about 0.05—in the case of a temporary change in income.* But if they find out that their income will increase permanently, they will increase their consumption a lot; *the MPC is very large—maybe 0.95—in the case of a permanent change in income.* For example, if a new fertilizer doubles the rice yield of a rice farmer's land permanently, we can expect that the farmer's consumption of other goods will about double because of higher permanent income.

The difference between the forward-looking consumption model and the simple consumption function in which consumption depends only on current income is illustrated in Figure 23.12. In the right panel of Figure 23.12, income is expected to follow a typical life-cycle pattern: lower when young, higher when middle-aged, and very low when retired. Consumption, however, does not follow these ups and downs; it is flat. The left panel shows the opposite extreme: the standard consumption function with a fixed MPC. In this case, people consume a lot when they are middle-aged, but they consume very little when they are young or old.

FIGURE 23.12 Two Extreme Forms of Consumption Behavior

The right panel shows the future outlook of a young person or family described by the forward-looking model of consumption. The left panel shows the outlook of a young family with a constant MPC. The path of income is the same in both cases.

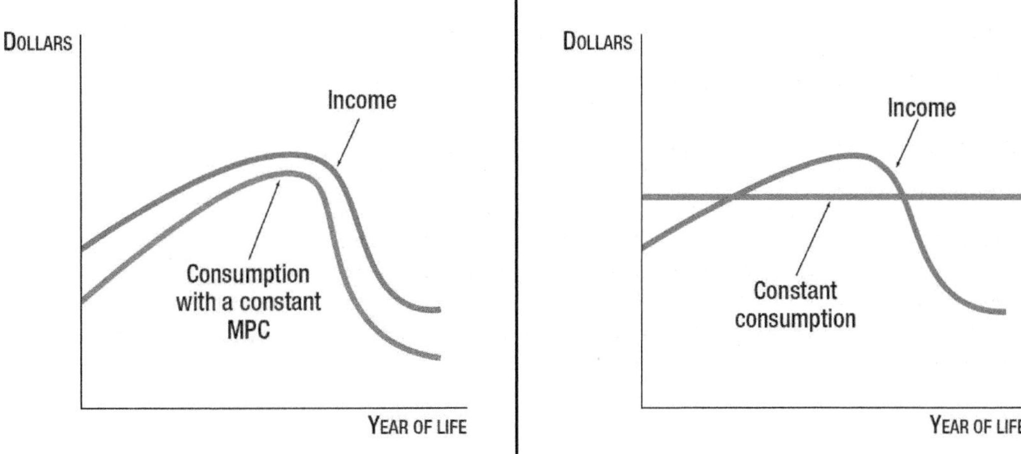

Occasionally, some people are prevented from completely smoothing their income because they have a **liquidity constraint**; that is, they cannot get a loan, and so they cannot consume more than their income. Such liquidity constraints do not appear to be important enough in the economy as a whole to negate the forward-looking model completely. Of course, not all people try to smooth their income; some people like to go on binges, spending everything, even if the binge is followed by a long lull.

liquidity constraint
The situation in which people cannot borrow to smooth their consumption spending when their income is low.

Tests and Applications of the Forward-Looking Model

Observations on consumption and income for the economy as a whole indicate that the forward-looking model significantly improves our understanding of observed changes in the MPC. For example, economists have demonstrated that the measured MPC for the economy as a whole is lower for the temporary changes in income that occur during recessions and booms than for the more permanent increases in income that occur as potential GDP grows over time. Studies of thousands of individual families over time show that the individual MPC for temporary changes in income is about one-third of the MPC for permanent changes in income.

Permanent versus Temporary Tax Cuts

The forward-looking model is also the most promising explanation for the low MPC during the tax cut of 2008. That tax cut was explicitly temporary—a one time tax rebate, good for only one year. Figure 23.13 shows that the impact was hard to notice in the data.

FIGURE 23.13 **Some Evidence from the 2008 Stimulus Act in Favor of the Permanent Income Hypothesis**

Temporary rebate payments in May through August 2008 increased disposable personal income but had no noticeable effect on consumption.

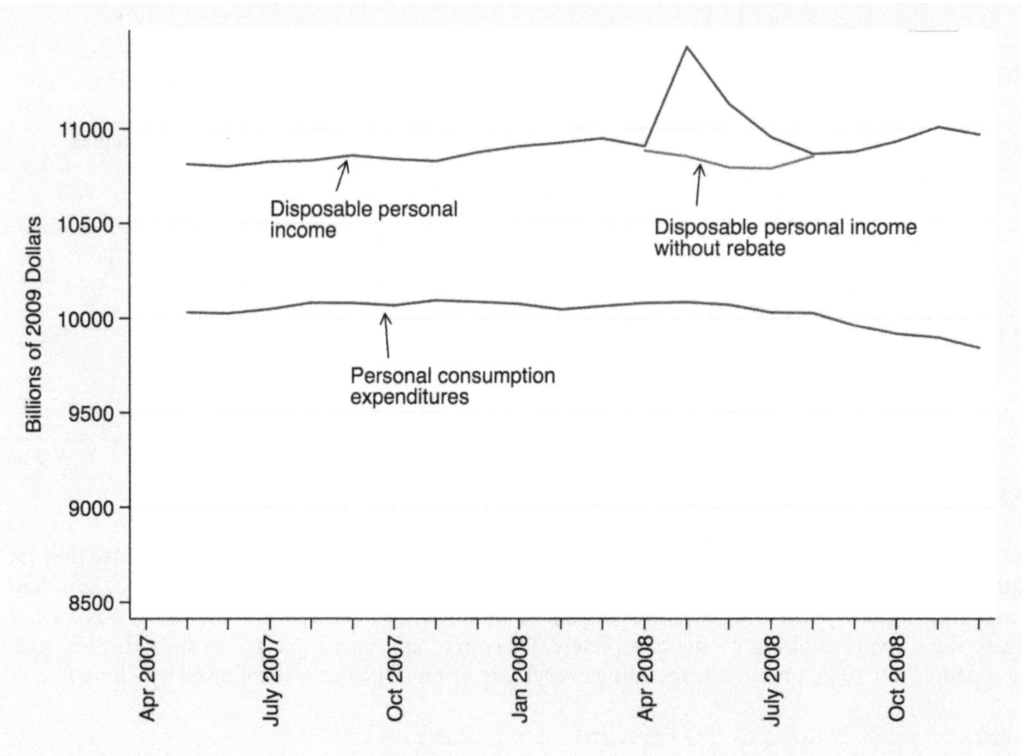

With a permanent tax cut, the MPC is high, so it has a big impact on real GDP. For a temporary tax cut, the MPC is low, so it has only a small impact on GDP. In estimating the effects of various tax proposals on the economy, economic forecasters try to take these changes in the MPC into account.

Anticipating Future Tax Cuts or Increases

The forward-looking model changes our estimate of the impact of changes in taxes that are expected to occur in the future. For example, if people are certain of tax cuts in the future, they may begin to increase their consumption right away, before the tax decreases. In this case, the MPC is technically huge, because consumption increases with little or no observed change in current income. Conversely, people may reduce their consumption in anticipation of a tax increase.

It is difficult to know how large these effects are because we do not observe people's expectations of the future. Estimates based on the assumption that people forecast the future no better and no worse than economic forecasters—this is the *rational expectations assumption*—suggest that the effects are large and significant.

In situations in which the expectations effects are obvious, we do see an impact. For example, in December 1992, after the 1992 presidential election, when a tax increase became more likely, it was evident that many people who could do so shifted their reported income for tax purposes from 1993 to 1992. But whether people held back their consumption in anticipation of future tax increases is difficult to say. In any case, because people's behavior is affected by their expectations of the future, attempts to estimate the impact of a policy proposal like a change in taxes need to take these expectations into account.

Key Points

1. The multiplier can be found with graphs and with algebra. The algebraic approach results in a convenient formula.
2. The formula for the multiplier is 1/(1 – MPC) when net exports do not depend on income.
3. If net exports are negatively related to income, then the formula for the multiplier is 1/(1 –MPC + MPI).
4. The forward-looking consumption model explains why the MPC is low in some cases and high in others. It helps economists deal with the uncertainty in the multiplier.
5. The forward-looking consumption model also implies that anticipated changes in taxes affect consumption and are another reason for uncertainty about the MPC. Although such effects have been observed, it is difficult to estimate their size in advance.
6. The rational expectations assumption, which suggests that people forecast the future no better and no worse than economic forecasters, is one basis for making such estimates. With this assumption, the effects of anticipated tax changes on consumption are quite high.

QUESTIONS FOR REVIEW

1. Why is the size of the multiplier positively related to the MPC?
2. Why is the size of the multiplier negatively related to the marginal propensity to import (MPI)?
3. How does the forward-looking consumption model differ from the consumption function with a fixed MPC?
4. Why is the MPC for a temporary tax cut less than the MPC for a permanent tax cut? What examples, if any, prove the point?
5. What is consumption smoothing?
6. Why do changes in future taxes that are anticipated in advance affect consumption?

PROBLEMS

1. Are the following statements true or false? Show using algebra.
   a. The multiplier is greater than one and rises if the marginal MPC rises.
   b. The multiplier for an economy in which net exports respond to income is smaller than the multiplier for an economy in which net exports do not respond to income.
2. The following table shows real GDP and imports (in billions of dollars) for an economy.

Real GDP or Income	Imports
2,000	400
3,000	500
4,000	600
5,000	700
6,000	800
7,000	900

Suppose that exports are equal to $700 billion.

   a. Construct a graph showing how imports depend on income.
   b. Construct a graph showing how net exports depend on income.
   c. If the level of real GDP that occurs at spending balance is $6,000 billion, will a trade surplus or a trade deficit result? What type of policy regarding government purchases would bring the trade deficit or trade surplus closer to zero?
   d. If the MPC is 0.6, what is the size of the multiplier?
3. a. Suppose Joe spends every additional dollar of income that he receives. What is Joe's MPC? What does his consumption function look like?
   b. Suppose that Jane spends half of each additional dollar of income that she receives. What is Jane's MPC? What does her consumption function look like?
   c. What differences in Joe's and Jane's incomes or jobs might explain the differences in their MPCs?
4. Suppose Uncle George sent you a check for $500 tomorrow because he is proud of your excellent grades and feels that you are a credit to the family. What would you do with the largest part of the money? Would you spend it, would you save it, or would you pay down your credit card debt (technically a form of saving)? Why? If Uncle George said that he would send you $500 every month while you are in college, would you allocate the funds among spending, saving, and debt reduction any differently? Why or why not?
5. Each month, a certain fraction of employees' pay is withheld and sent to the government as part of what is owed for personal income taxes. If the taxes owed for the year are less than the amount withheld, then a refund is sent early in the following year. If the taxes owed for the year exceed the amount withheld, then additional taxes must be paid by April 15. In 1992, the amount of income tax withheld was lowered by about $10 billion to increase consumption and real GDP and thereby speed recovery from the 1990–1991 recession. However, the amount of taxes owed was not changed. Discuss why the impact of this change would be smaller than that of an actual cut in taxes of $10 billion during that year.

CHAPTER 24
The Economic Fluctuations Model

On February 17, 2009, the then newly elected President Barack Obama signed into law a $787 billion stimulus package that he claimed would "begin making the immediate investments necessary to put people back to work doing the work America needs done." The bill represented one of the most significant fiscal interventions in the history of the United States, yet it was enacted only 17 days after being proposed. Democrats and Republicans were bitterly divided on the bill, with Democratic leaders in Congress arguing that the bill would create millions of jobs, rebuild the nation's infrastructure, and give the economy a much-needed shot in the arm. On the other hand, not a single Republican member of the House and only three Republican senators voted for the bill. The Republican opponents argued that the bill was wasteful and would have little stimulative impact on the economy.

President Barack Obama delivers remarks on the economic benefits of the Recovery Act after touring the Fairfax County Parkway Extension bridge construction site in Fairfax, Virginia in October of 2009.

Source: Lawrence Jacksonn (P101409LJ-0067) [Public domain], via Wikimedia Commons

Eighteen months later, in the run up to the 2012 midterm Congressional elections, the debate raged on. The Council of Economic Advisers issued a report evaluating the American Recovery and Reinvestment Act (ARRA, the official name of the stimulus package) in which it concluded that the package had "raised the level of GDP [gross domestic product] as of the third quarter of 2010, relative to what it otherwise would have been, by 2.7 percent" and that "as of the third quarter of 2010, the ARRA has raised employment relative to what it otherwise would have been by between 2.7 and 3.7 million." Other economists disagreed with this assessment. In an article in the *Wall Street Journal*, the economists John Cogan and John Taylor (one of the authors of this text) argued that the stimulus package did not have much of an impact because it did not lead to an increase in the purchase of goods and services. They concluded that "[t]he bottom-line is the federal government borrowed funds from the public, transferred these funds to state and local governments, who then used the funds mainly to reduce borrowing from the public. The net impact on aggregate economic activity is zero."

Bitter political debates over economic issues, such as the 2009 stimulus bill, are a common sight in U.S. politics as well as in many other political systems around the world. The debate over the stimulus package illustrates the primary reason for this debate—we only got to see what the employment and output outcomes were in the United States economy with the $787 stimulus bill enacted, we never go to see what the outcome would have been in an alternative world where the stimulus bill was not enacted. In order to overcome this challenge economists use a combination of economic models—which allow them to simulate what the economy would have looked like with and without a stimulus package—and data analysis that tries to find real-world examples where they can get an idea of what the outcomes would have been with and without the stimulus policy. One such attempt by the Dartmouth economists Jim Feyrer and Bruce Sacerdote, evaluated the stimulus package by looking at the impact on employment across states that received a lot of funding from the stimulus package and states that received relatively less funding. They also look at different types of stimulus funding, comparing the economic impact of funds for state and local governments to fund activities such as paying police officers or teachers to the economic impact of funds to assist low-income families through expansions of food stamps. They find evidence to support arguments made on both sides of the debate—the economic assistance to low-income households seems to have led to a substantial impact on spending and economic activity whereas the funds to local governments seems to have merely substituted for funds that local and state governments would have borrowed and spent anyway resulting in little net economic activity.

As an observer of this debate, you should try to independently evaluate the validity of the underlying economic arguments made by the opposing parties and come to your own informed conclusion as to who has the more tenable position. This evaluation requires that you have a framework for understanding the fascinating, dynamic process through which a recession ends and a new expansion begins, and for deciding which government actions, if any, can cut the length of a recession or speed up the expansion. This chapter presents just such a framework in the form of a model of economic fluctuations—a simplified description of how the economy adjusts over time when it moves away from potential GDP, as in a recession.

Economic fluctuations models are used to make decisions about monetary policy at the Fed and at other central banks around the world. Private business analysts use the ideas to track the economy and predict central bank decisions. This model is much newer than the supply and demand model, which has been around for more than 100 years. It combines Keynes's idea, developed 75 years ago, that aggregate demand causes the departure of real GDP from potential GDP, with newer ideas, developed in the 1980s and 1990s, about how expectations and inflation adjust over time. Although newer, the economic fluctuations model is analogous to the supply and demand model (Chapter 3). Just as we presented the supply and demand model in a graph consisting of three elements:

- a demand curve
- a supply curve, and
- an equilibrium at the intersection of the two curves.

We present the economic fluctuations model in a graph consisting of three elements:

- an aggregate demand (*AD*) curve,
- an inflation adjustment (*IA*) line, and
- an equilibrium at the intersection of the curve and the line.

We use the economic fluctuations model to explain fluctuations in real GDP and inflation in much the same way that we used supply and demand curves to explain quantity and price in the market for peanuts or other microeconomic markets. In the microeconomic supply and demand model, the intersection of the demand curve and the supply curve gives us a prediction of price and quantity. In the economic fluctuations model, the intersection of the aggregate demand (*AD*) curve and the inflation adjustment (*IA*) line gives us a prediction of real GDP and inflation.

We start our construction of the economic fluctuations model by deriving the aggregate demand curve and then the inflation adjustment line. We then will show how their intersection determines real GDP and inflation.

1. THE AGGREGATE DEMAND CURVE

The **aggregate demand (*AD*) curve** is a relationship between two economic variables: real GDP and the inflation rate. The inflation rate usually is measured as the annual percentage change in the overall price level from year to year. Figure 24.1 shows an aggregate demand curve for the United States. Observe that inflation is measured on the vertical axis, that real GDP is measured on the horizontal axis, and that we have drawn a vertical dashed line to mark the point at which real GDP equals potential GDP. The aggregate demand curve shows different combinations of real GDP and inflation. It is downward sloping from left to right because real GDP is related negatively to inflation along the curve. The term *aggregate demand* is used because the movements of real GDP away from potential GDP are due to fluctuations in the sum (aggregate) of the demand for consumption, investment, net exports, and government purchases.

aggregate demand (*AD*) curve

A line showing a negative relationship between inflation and the aggregate quantity of goods and services demanded at that inflation rate.

FIGURE 24.1 The Aggregate Demand Curve

The aggregate demand curve shows that higher inflation and real GDP are negatively related.

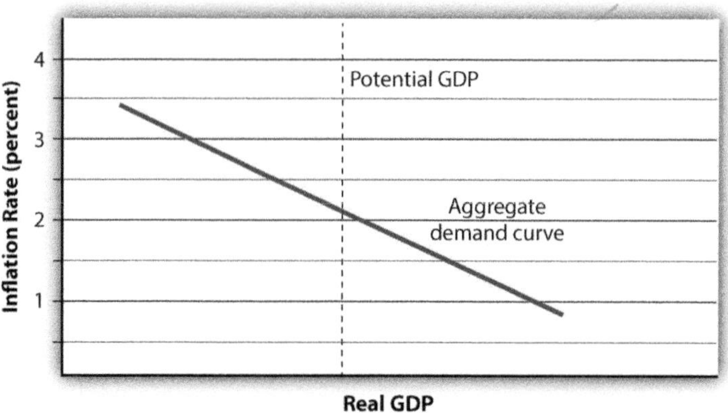

Why does the aggregate demand curve slope downward? We will answer this question and derive the curve in three stages. First, we show that a negative relationship exists between the real interest rate and real GDP. Second, we show that a positive relationship exists between inflation and the real interest rate. Third, we show that these two relationships are simply a negative relationship between real GDP and inflation, and that that relationship is the aggregate demand curve. The following schematic chart shows how the three stages fit together.

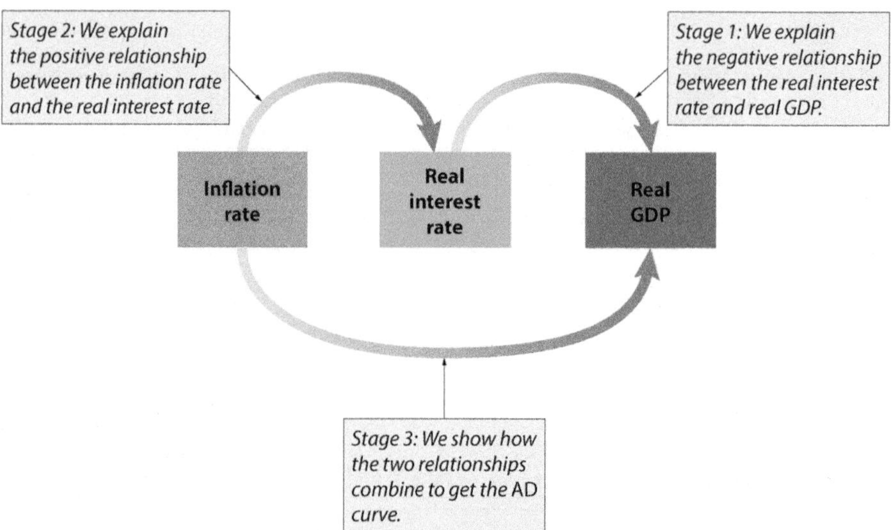

1.1 Interest Rates and Real GDP

Consumption, investment, and net exports each are related negatively to the interest rate. Combining these components provides an explanation of the negative relationship between real GDP and the interest rate. Keep in mind that the real interest rate is a better measure of the effects of interest rates on investment, consumption, and net exports because it corrects for inflation. Recall from Chapter 17 that the real interest rate equals the stated, or nominal, interest rate minus the inflation rate. The negative effect of the real interest rate on consumption, investment, and net exports is no different from that discussed in Chapter 19. If you already have studied that chapter, the next few pages will review that information.

Investment

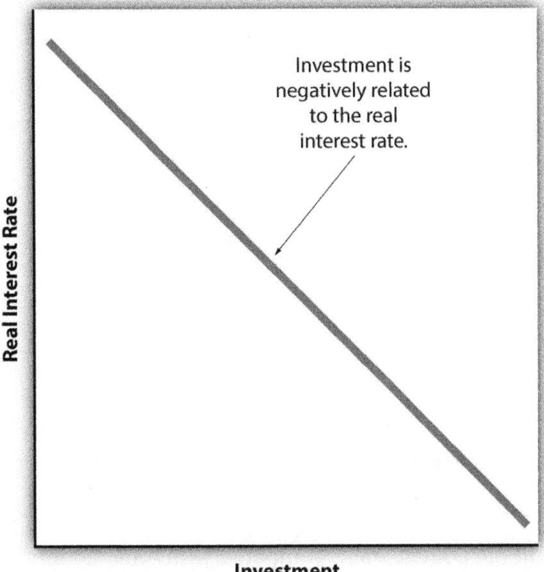

Investment is the component of expenditure that is probably most sensitive to the real interest rate. Recall that part of investment is the purchase of new equipment or a new factory by a business firm. Many firms must borrow funds to pay for such investments. Higher real interest rates make such borrowing more costly. The additional profits the firm might expect to earn from purchasing a photocopier or a truck are more likely to be lower than the interest costs on the loan if the real interest rate is high. Hence, businesses that are thinking about buying a new machine and need to borrow funds will be less inclined to purchase such an investment good if real interest rates are higher, and so higher real interest rates reduce investment spending by businesses. Also, remember that part of investment is the purchase of new houses. Most people need to take out a mortgage to buy a house. Like any loan, the mortgage has an interest rate, and higher interest rates make mortgages more costly. Hence, with higher real interest rates, fewer people take out mortgages and buy new houses. Spending for new housing declines.

The same reasoning works to show why lower real interest rates will increase investment spending: Lower real interest rates reduce the cost of borrowing and make investment more attractive to firms and households.

To summarize, both business investment and housing investment decline when the real interest rate rises, and they increase when the real interest rate falls. At any given time some firms or households are deciding whether to buy a new machine or a new house, and they are going to be less inclined to buy such things when the interest rate is higher.

Net Exports

The negative relationship between net exports and the real interest rate requires a somewhat more involved explanation than the relationship between the real interest rate and investment. The relationship exists because higher real interest rates in the United States tend to lead to a higher dollar exchange rate and, in turn, a higher exchange rate reduces net exports.

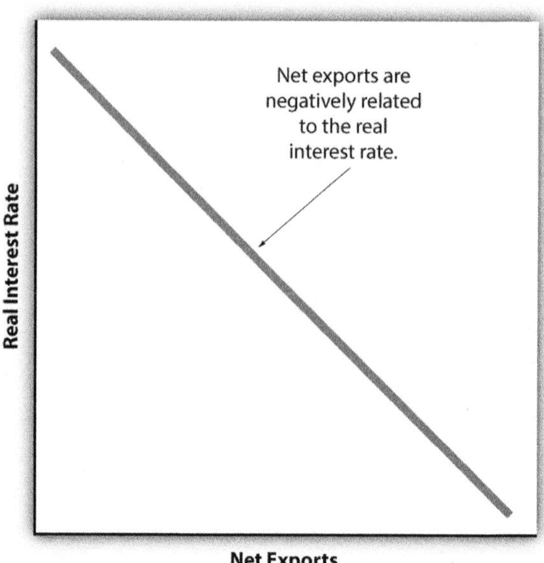

A higher real interest rate in the United States compared with other countries increases the demand for U.S. dollar bank accounts and other assets that pay interest. That increased demand bids up the price of dollars; hence, the exchange rate—the price of dollars—rises. Now, with a higher exchange rate, net exports will be lower because U.S.-produced exports become more expensive to foreigners, who must pay a higher price for dollars, and imported foreign goods become cheaper for Americans, who can get more foreign goods for higher-priced dollars. With exports falling and imports rising, net exports—exports less imports—must fall. In sum, higher real interest rates reduce net exports.

The same reasoning works for lower real interest rates as well. If the real interest rate falls in the United States, then U.S. dollar bank accounts are less attractive compared with bank accounts in other currencies, such as those of Germany or Japan. This falling interest rate bids down the price of dollars, and the exchange rate falls. Now, with a lower exchange rate, net exports will be higher because U.S.-produced exports are less expensive to foreigners and imported foreign goods are more expensive for Americans. With exports rising and imports falling, net exports must rise. Thus, lower real interest rates increase net exports. To summarize, a negative relationship exists between the interest rate and the net exports that works through the exchange rate, as shown below.

Interest Rate		Value of the Domestic Currency		Net Exports
up	→	up	→	down
down	→	down	→	up

Reminder: Finished with Stage 1: Real GDP is related negatively to the real interest rate. Why?

- *Consumption (C) is negatively related to the real interest rate.*
- *Investment (I) is negatively related to the real interest rate.*
- *Net exports (X) are negatively related to the real interest rate.*

If the interest rate goes up, then the value of the domestic currency goes up, causing net exports to go down. If the interest rate goes down, then the value of the domestic currency goes down, causing net exports to go up.

Consumption

We have shown that two of the components of expenditure—investment and net exports—are sensitive to the real interest rate. What about consumption?

Although consumption probably is less sensitive to the real interest rate than the other components, some evidence indicates that higher real interest rates encourage people to save a larger fraction of their income. Higher real interest rates encourage people to save because they earn more on their savings. Because more saving means less consumption, this implies that consumption is related negatively to the interest rate. Most economists, however, feel that the effect of interest rates on consumption is much less than on investment and net exports.

The Overall Effect

To summarize the discussion thus far, investment, net exports, and consumption all are related negatively to the real interest rate. The overall effect of a change in real interest rates on real GDP can now be assessed.

Figure 24.2 shows the 45-degree line and two different expenditure lines corresponding to two different interest rates. Higher interest rates shift the expenditure line down because a higher interest rate lowers investment, net exports, and consumption, which all are part of expenditure.

FIGURE 24.2 The Interest Rate, Spending Balance, and Real GDP

A higher real interest rate shifts the expenditure line down because consumption, investment, and net exports depend negatively on the real interest rate. Thus, real GDP declines with a higher real interest rate. Conversely, a lower real interest rate raises real GDP.

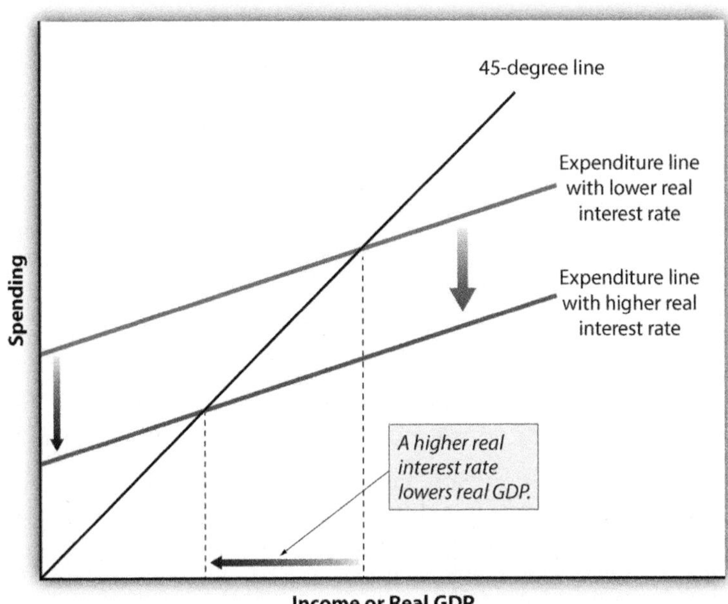

Observe how the downward shift of the expenditure line leads to a new point of spending balance. The intersection of the expenditure line with the 45-degree line occurs at a lower level of real GDP. Note that real GDP is lower not only because the higher real interest rate lowers investment, net exports, and consumption, but also because a decline in income will lower consumption further. Real GDP declines by the amount shown on the horizontal axis, which is larger than the downward shift in the expenditure line. *Thus, an increase in the real interest rate lowers real GDP.*

What about a decline in the real interest rate? A lower real interest rate will raise the expenditure line. In that case, when the expenditure line shifts up, the point of spending balance at the intersection with the 45-degree line will be at a higher level of real GDP. *Thus, a decrease in the real interest rate raises real GDP.* In sum, we have shown that a negative relationship exists between the real interest rate and real GDP.

1.2 Interest Rates and Inflation

Now that we have seen why interest rates affect real GDP, let us proceed to the second stage in our analysis. We want to show why a rise in inflation will increase the real interest rate and thereby lower real GDP, or why a decline in inflation will decrease the real interest rate and thereby raise real GDP.

Central Bank Interest Rate Policy

The easiest way to see why the real interest rate rises when the inflation rate increases is to examine the behavior of the Fed. The Fed and central banks in other countries typically follow policies in which they respond to an increase in the inflation rate by raising the nominal interest rate. By far the most widely followed and analyzed decision by the Fed is its nominal interest rate decision.

Why do central banks raise the nominal interest rate when they think the inflation rate is rising? The inflation rate is ultimately the responsibility of the Fed, and the goal of controlling inflation requires that the central bank raise the nominal interest rate so that the real interest rate rises when the inflation rate rises. If the central bank raises the real interest rate successfully, then the higher real interest rate will reduce investment, consumption, and net exports. The reduced demand will then reduce inflationary pressures and bring inflation back down again.

The goal of controlling inflation also requires that the central bank lower the real interest rate when inflation falls. Suppose that the inflation rate starts to fall. If the central bank lowers the nominal interest rate so that the real interest rate falls, then the lower real interest rate will increase investment, consumption, and net exports. The increase in demand will put upward pressure on inflation.

Table 24.1 illustrates these actions of the Fed using a hypothetical example. For each inflation rate, a nominal interest rate decision by the Fed is shown. For example, when inflation is 2 percent, the nominal interest rate decision is 4 percent. When inflation rises to 4 percent, the nominal interest rate decision by the Fed is 7 percent. Thus, when inflation rises, the central bank raises the nominal interest rate, and when inflation falls, the central bank lowers the nominal interest rate.

TABLE 24.1 A Numerical Example of Central Bank Interest Rate Policy

(a) Inflation Rate	(b) Nominal Interest Rate Decision (made by the central bank)	Resulting Real Interest Rate (b) - (a)
0.0	1.0	1.0
1.0	2.5	1.5
2.0	4.0	2.0
3.0	5.5	2.5
4.0	7.0	3.0
5.0	8.5	3.5
6.0	10.0	4.0
7.0	11.5	4.5
8.0	13.0	5.0

monetary policy rule

A description of how much the interest rate or other instruments of monetary policy respond to inflation or other measures of the state of the economy.

Note that the nominal interest rate rises more than inflation rises in Table 24.1. The reason is that for an increase in the nominal interest rate to reduce demand, the real interest rate must rise because investment, consumption, and net exports depend negatively on the real interest rate, as described in the previous section. The nominal interest rate has to rise by more than the inflation rate for the real interest rate to rise and demand to decline. If, instead, the nominal interest rate rose by less than the increase in the inflation rate, then the real interest rate would not rise; rather, it would fall. The behavior of the central bank illustrated in the third column of Table 24.1 is called a **monetary policy rule** because it describes the systematic response of the real interest rate to inflation as decided by the central bank.

How the Fed Changes the Interest Rate

federal funds rate

The interest rate on overnight loans between banks that the Federal Reserve influences by changing the supply of funds (bank reserves) in the market.

Keep in mind that the central bank does not set interest rates by decree or by direct control. Governments sometimes do control the price of goods; for example, some city governments control the rents on apartments. The central bank does not apply such controls to the interest rate. Rather, it enters the market in which short-term interest rates are determined by the usual forces of supply and demand. In the United States, the short-term interest rate the Fed focuses on is the interest rate on overnight loans between banks. This is called the **federal funds rate**, and the overnight loan market is called the federal funds market because reserves at the Fed are what are loaned or borrowed in this market. When the Fed wants to lower this interest rate, it supplies more reserves to this market. When it wants to raise the interest rate, it reduces reserves. Recall from Chapter 22 that the Fed can change the amount of reserves in the banking system through *open market operations*—that is, by buying and selling government bonds. If the Fed wants to increase reserves and thereby lower the federal funds rate, it buys government bonds. If the Fed wants to decrease reserves and thereby increase the federal funds rate, it sells government bonds.

Reminder: **Actions the Fed takes**: *To reduce the federal funds rate, the Fed increases the supply of reserves by buying bonds. To raise the federal funds rate, the Fed decreases the supply of reserves by selling bonds. The buying and selling of bonds are called open market operations.*

A Graph of the Response of the Interest Rate to Inflation

Figure 24.3 represents the monetary policy rule graphically, using the information in Table 24.1. When the inflation rate rises, the nominal interest rate rises along the top upward sloping line. When the inflation rate declines, the nominal interest rate declines. The nominal interest rate must rise by *more* than the inflation rate if the *real* interest rate is to rise when inflation rises; this requires that the slope of the monetary policy rule in Figure 24.3 be greater than 1. For example, if the slope is 1.5, then when the inflation rate increases by 1 percentage point, the interest rate rises by 1.5 percentage points, as in Table 24.1. In other words, the nominal interest rate rises by 0.5 percentage point *more* than the inflation rate rises, causing the *real* interest rate to rise by 0.5 percentage point. The resulting real interest rate decision of the Fed is indicated by the bottom line: The real interest rate changes by 0.5 percentage point when the inflation rate changes by 1 percentage point. The real interest rate policy rule is shown in Figure 24.4.

FIGURE 24.3 **A Monetary Policy Rule**

The monetary policy rule shows that the Fed raises the real interest rate when inflation rises and lowers the real interest rate when inflation falls. To accomplish this, the Fed has to move the nominal interest rate by more than 1 percentage point when the rate of inflation changes by 1 percentage point.

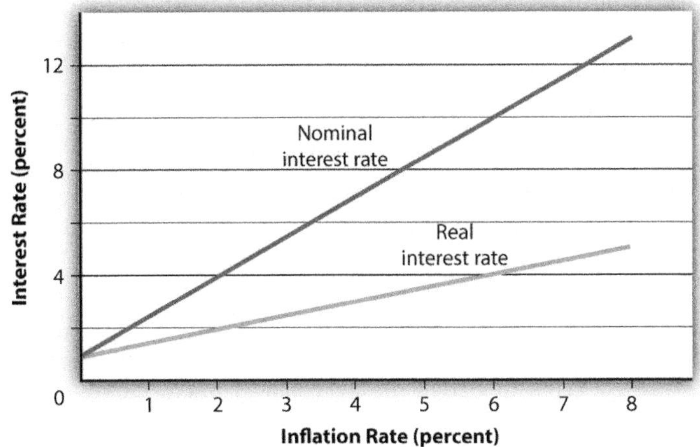

FIGURE 24.4 **The Real Interest Rate is Positively Related to Inflation**

From now on, the monetary policy rule of the Fed will be presented as a relationship between the inflation rate and the real interest rate. When inflation rises, the Fed raises the real interest rate (through a more than proportional increase in the nominal interest rate), whereas when inflation falls, the Fed lowers the real interest rate (by decreasing the nominal rate in a more than proportional manner).

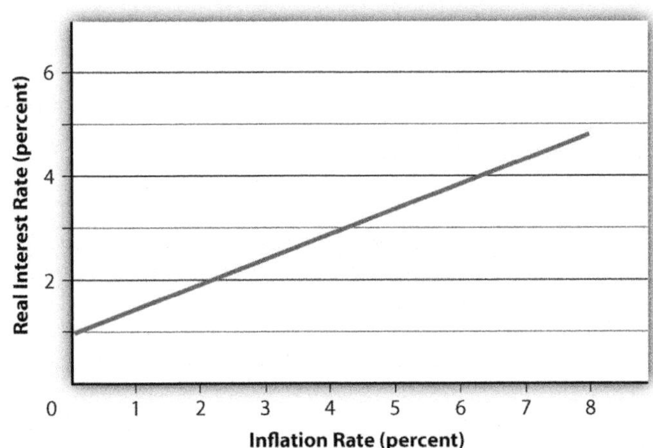

Most central banks have a **target inflation rate**, the inflation rate that the central bank tries to maintain on average over the long run. Because of various shocks to the economy, the central bank cannot control the inflation rate perfectly; sometimes the inflation rate will rise above the target inflation rate, and sometimes the inflation rate will fall below the target inflation rate. By reacting to these movements in inflation according to a monetary policy rule—that is, by increasing the interest rate when inflation rises and cutting the interest rate when inflation falls—the central bank will cause the actual inflation rate to move back toward the target inflation rate over time. Some central banks, such as the Bank of England and the Reserve Bank of New Zealand, have explicit inflation targets. Other central banks, like

target inflation rate

The central bank's goal for the average rate of inflation over the long run.

the Fed, have implicit inflation targets that are not announced explicitly, but that can be assessed by observing central bank decisions overtime. The target inflation rate for many central banks is about 2 percent. For the economy described in Figure 24.3, at the target inflation rate of 2 percent, the central bank sets real interest rates at 2 percent by choosing a nominal rate of 4 percent.

Reminder: **Finished with Stage 2: The interest rate is related positively to inflation.** *The Fed and other central banks tend to*

- *Raise the real interest rate when inflation rises.*
- *Lower the real interest rate when inflation falls.*

This is the behavioral description of the people at the Fed, much as a demand curve is a behavioral description of consumers. This response is called a monetary policy rule.

A Good Simplifying Assumption

The behavior of the central bank described in this section provides the easiest explanation of the response of interest rates to inflation, but it is not the only possible explanation. Economists have found that the general upward-sloping relationship in Figure 24.4, which we call the monetary policy rule, is common to many different types of monetary policies, including policies in which the central bank focuses on money growth. Although the position and shape of the monetary policy rule will differ for these different types of policies, the overall response of interest rates to inflation will be similar. We use this particular derivation because it is the easiest to explain and describes the actual behavior of the Fed and other central banks.

1.3 Derivation of the Aggregate Demand Curve

Thus far, we have shown that the level of real GDP is related negatively to the real interest rate and that the real interest rate is related positively to the inflation rate through the central bank's policy rule. We now combine these two concepts to derive the aggregate demand curve—the inverse relationship between the inflation rate and real GDP.

The chain of reasoning that brings about the aggregate demand curve can be explained by considering what would happen if the inflation rate rose. First, the interest rate would rise because the Fed would raise the real interest rate in response to the higher inflation rate. Next, the higher real interest rate would mean less investment spending, a decline in net exports, and a decline in consumption. Lower investment spending would occur because investment would be made more costly by the high real interest rate. U.S. goods would become more expensive, and foreign goods would become cheaper. Thus, net exports—exports minus imports—would decline.

The opposite chain of events would occur if inflation fell. First, the Fed would lower the real interest rate according to the monetary policy rule. The lower real interest rate, in turn, would cause investment, net exports, and consumption to rise. Hence, real GDP would rise.

Thus, we see that when the inflation rate rises, real GDP decreases, and when the inflation rate falls, real GDP increases. In other words, a negative relationship exists between inflation and real GDP. When we graph this relationship in a diagram with real GDP on the horizontal axis and inflation on the vertical axis, we get a downward-sloping curve like the one shown in Figure 24.1; this curve is the aggregate demand curve, which we have thus derived.

If you want to review the derivation, seeing all the paragraphs together on the same page, a self-guided graphic overview is provided in Figure 24.5. If you read the explanatory boxes in numerical order, you will be able to trace the chain of events following an increase in inflation, including the Fed's real interest rate increase according to its policy rule and the decline in real GDP.

FIGURE 24.5 A Self-Guided Graphic Overview

Follow the numbers to see an overview of the derivation of the aggregate demand curve. The black dots represent the situation before we increase the inflation rate. The red dots represent the situation after we increase the inflation rate. When inflation rises, the central bank raises the real interest rate, and this lowers real GDP. Hence, we have the aggregate demand curve.

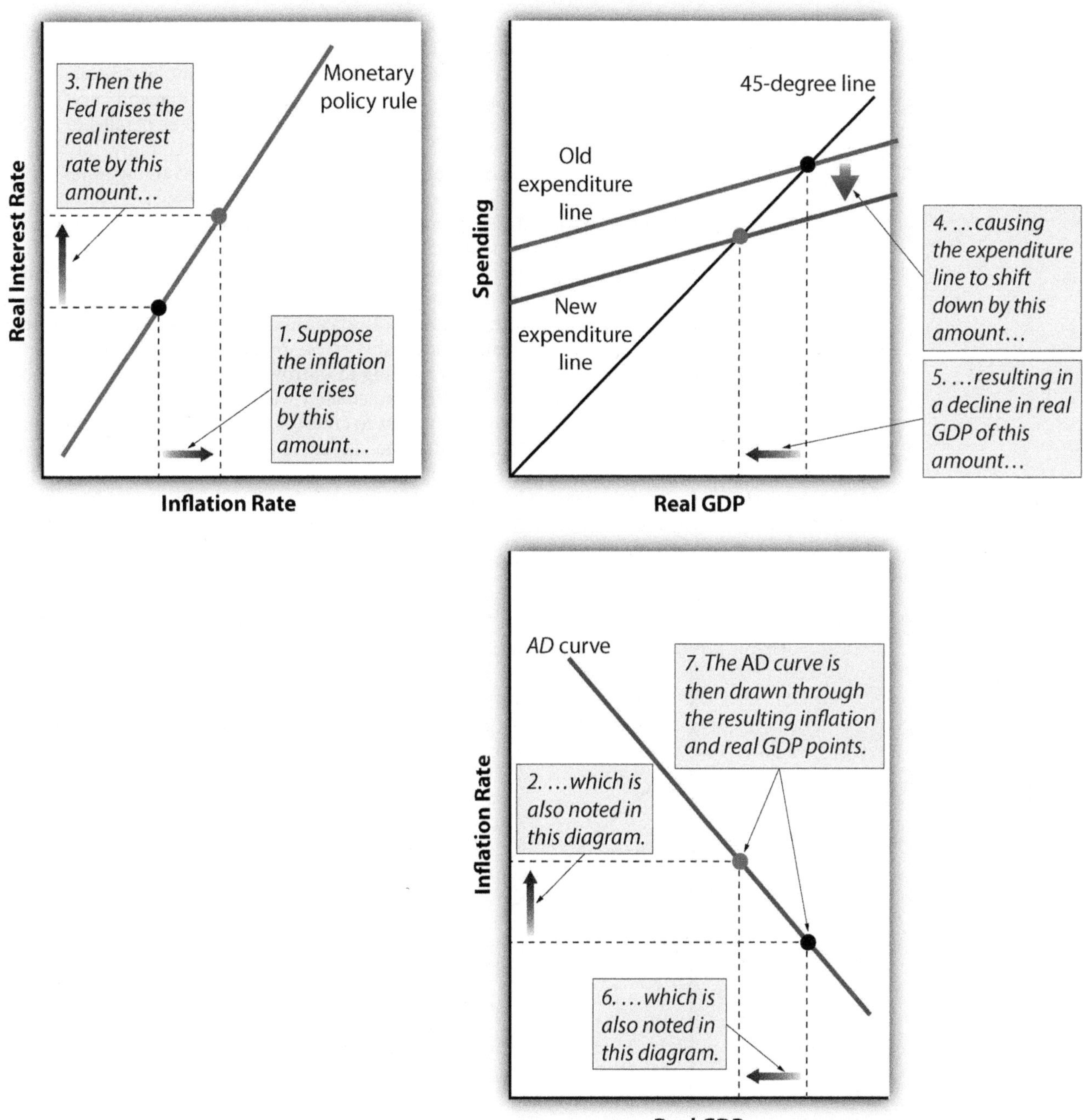

Movements along the Aggregate Demand Curve

Thus far, we have explained why the aggregate demand curve has a negative slope—that is, why higher inflation means a lower real GDP. A change in real GDP due to a change in inflation is thus a *movement along* the aggregate demand curve. In microeconomics, a similar movement along the demand curve occurs when a *change in the price* leads to a *change in quantity demanded.* When inflation rises, causing the Fed to raise the interest rate, and real GDP declines, a movement occurs up and to the left along the aggregate demand curve. When inflation declines and the Fed lowers the interest rate, causing GDP to rise, a movement occurs down and to the right along the aggregate demand curve.

Shifts of the Aggregate Demand Curve

Now, the inflation rate is not the only thing that affects aggregate demand. Changes in government purchases, shifts in monetary policy, shifts in foreign demand for U.S. exports, changes in taxes, and changes in consumer confidence, among other things, affect aggregate demand. When any one of these factors changes aggregate demand, we call it a *shift* in the aggregate demand curve. Let us briefly consider some of those sources of shifts in the aggregate demand curve.

Government Purchases Imagine that government purchases rise. We know from our analysis of spending balance in Chapter 23 that an increase in government purchases will increase real GDP in the short run. This increase in real GDP occurs at any inflation rate: at 2 percent, at 4 percent, or at any other level. Now, if real GDP increases at a given inflation rate, the aggregate demand curve will shift to the right. This is shown in Figure 24.6. The new aggregate demand curve will be parallel to the original aggregate demand curve because no matter what the inflation rate is in the economy, the shift in government purchases is going to have the same effect on real GDP. The same reasoning implies that a decline in government spending shifts the aggregate demand curve to the left.

Changes in the Target Inflation Rate Suppose the Fed has an inflation target of 2 percent. Consider what happens when the Fed shifts its policy objectives. Suppose, for instance, that the Fed chair decides that a somewhat higher inflation rate, say, 3 percent, would be tolerable to achieve some other objective. One example of such a change would be if the Fed was concerned about credit market conditions because firms were curtailing investment, or because consumers were cutting back on spending because of the difficulty in obtaining loans at affordable rates—or because the Fed believed that the banking sector was in trouble with more banks needing to borrow money from one another to meet their obligations to depositors. In that case, the Fed immediately will try to increase spending by lowering the real interest rate. This move will enhance access to credit, stimulate greater spending, and affect real GDP regardless of the current inflation rate: The *AD* curve will shift to the right, as shown in Figure 24.7.

FIGURE 24.6 How Government Purchases Shift the Aggregate Demand Curve

An increase in government purchases shifts the *AD* curve to the right. Real GDP rises by the same amount at every level of inflation.

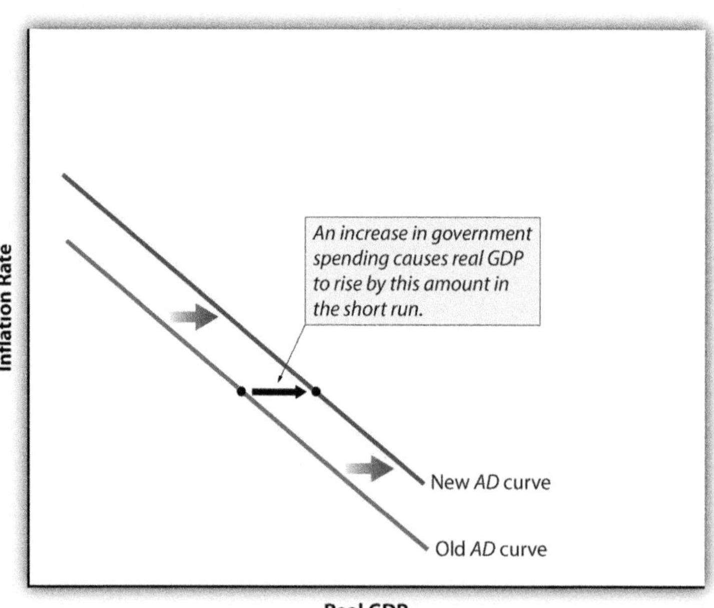

This type of action also could work in reverse—the Fed could decide that the current inflation target is too high and that it needs to act to lower the targeted rate of inflation. To get inflation to fall, the Fed immediately will try to lower spending by raising the real interest rate: The *AD* curve will shift to the left. In practice, such a shift to a lower targeted rate of inflation could happen for a variety of reasons, including changes in the preferences of policymakers. For instance, when Paul Volcker took over as chairman of the Federal Reserve, it was clear that he had a much greater dislike of inflation than his predecessors. Therefore, it was not a surprise when he raised interest rates substantially, shortly after taking office.

FIGURE 24.7 A Shift in the Monetary Policy Rule

A shift in the policy rule to higher inflation implies a decline in the real interest rate. The lower real interest rate increases real GDP in the short run. As a result, at a given inflation rate, the *AD* curve shifts to the right.

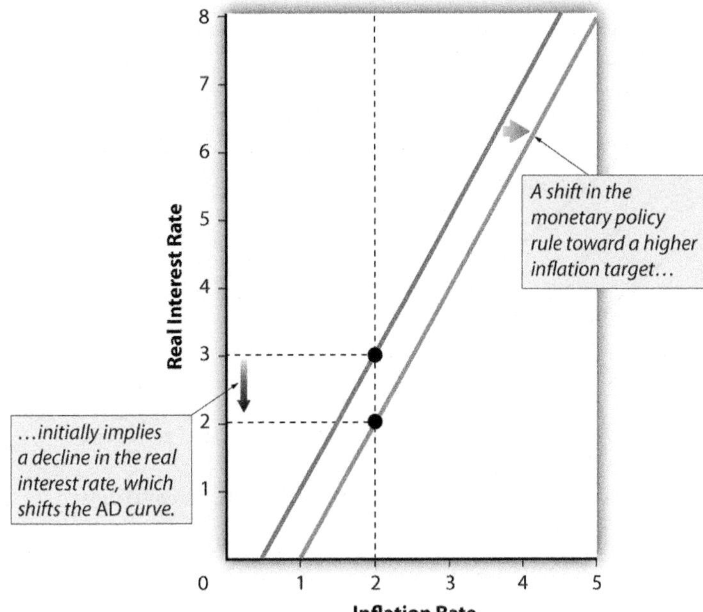

Other Changes Many other changes in the economy (other than a change in the inflation rate, which is a movement along the *AD* curve) will shift the *AD* curve. We considered many such possibilities in Chapter 23; their effects on the aggregate demand curve are listed in Figure 24.8. For example, an increase in the foreign demand for U.S. products will increase net exports, raise real GDP, and shift the aggregate demand curve to the right. A drop in consumer confidence that reduces the amount of consumption at every level of income will shift the aggregate demand curve to the left. Finally, an increase in taxes shifts the aggregate demand curve to the left, whereas a decrease in taxes shifts the aggregate demand curve to the right.

FIGURE 24.8 A List of Possible Shifts in the Aggregate Demand Curve

Many things shift the *AD* curve. An increase in government purchases shifts the *AD* curve to the right. A change in the monetary policy rule toward a higher inflation target shifts the *AD* curve to the right. A decline in government purchases and a change in the monetary policy rule toward a lower inflation target shift the curve to the left.

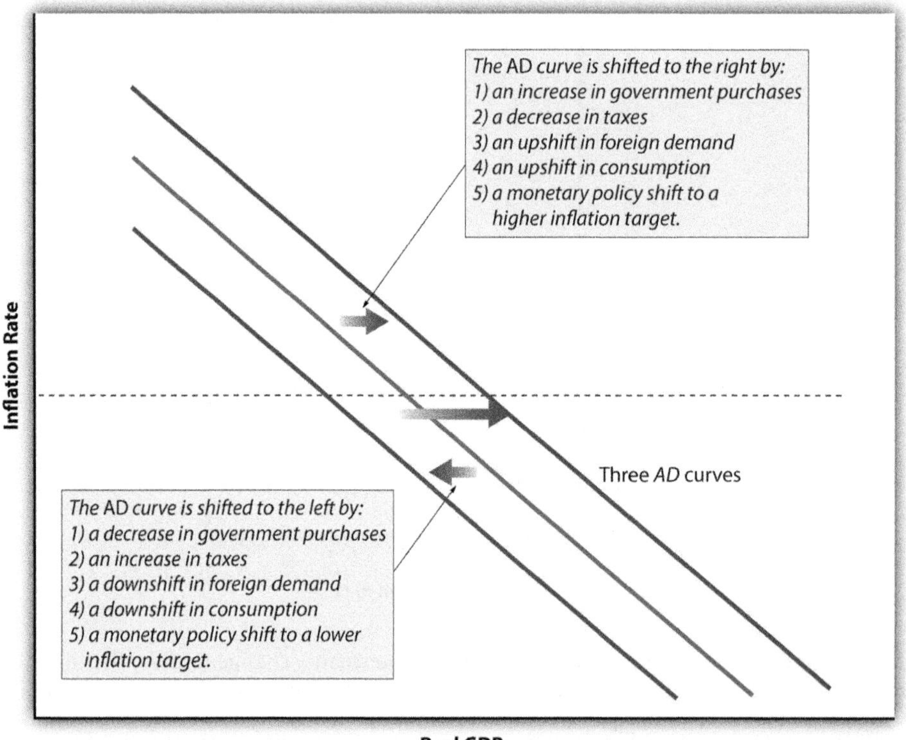

REVIEW

- The aggregate demand curve is an inverse relationship between inflation and real GDP.
- Investment, net exports, and consumption are negatively related to the real interest rate. Hence, real GDP falls when the real interest rate rises, and vice versa.
- When inflation increases, the central bank raises the real interest rate, and this lowers real GDP. Conversely, when inflation falls, the central bank lowers the real interest rate, and this raises real GDP. It does so by moving nominal interest rates by more than 1 percentage point when inflation changes by 1 percentage point. These are movements along the aggregate demand curve.
- The aggregate demand curve shifts to the right when the central bank changes its monetary policy rule toward more inflation and shifts to the left when the central bank changes its policy rule toward less inflation.
- Higher government purchases shift the aggregate demand curve to the right. Lower government purchases shift the aggregate demand curve to the left.

2. THE INFLATION ADJUSTMENT LINE

inflation adjustment (*IA*) line

A flat line showing the level of inflation in the economy at any point in time.

Having derived the aggregate demand curve and studied its properties, let us now look at the inflation adjustment line, the second element of the economic fluctuations model. The **inflation adjustment (*IA*) line** is a flat line showing the level of inflation in the economy at any point in time. Figure 24.9 shows an example of the inflation adjustment line in a diagram with inflation on the vertical axis and real GDP on the horizontal axis. For example, if the line touches 4 percent on the vertical axis, it tells us that inflation is 4 percent.

The inflation adjustment line describes the economic behavior of firms and workers setting prices and wages in the economy. Next, we discuss several important features about the slope and position of the inflation adjustment line.

2.1 The Inflation Adjustment Line Is Flat

That the inflation adjustment line is flat indicates that firms and workers adjust their prices and wages in such a way that the inflation rate remains steady in the short run as real GDP changes. Only over time does inflation change significantly and the line move. In the short run, inflation stays at 4 percent, or wherever the line happens to be when real GDP changes.

In interpreting the inflation adjustment line, it is helpful to remember that it is part of a *model* of the overall economy and thus is an approximation of reality. In fact, inflation does not remain *perfectly* steady, and the inflation adjustment line can have a small upward slope. But it is a good approximation to assume that the inflation adjustment line is flat.

Inflation does not change very much in the short run even if real GDP and the demand for firms' products changes for two good reasons: (1) expectations of continuing inflation and (2) staggered wage and price setting at different firms throughout the economy.

Expectations of Continuing Inflation

Expectations about the price and wage decisions of other firms throughout the economy influence a firm's price and wage decisions. For example, if the overall inflation rate in the economy has been hovering around 4 percent year after year, then a firm can expect that its competitors' prices probably will increase by about 4 percent per year, unless circumstances change. To keep prices near those of the competition, this firm will need to increase its price by about 4 percent each year. Thus, the inflation rate stays steady at 4 percent per year.

Wage adjustments also are influenced by expectations. If firms and workers expect that workers at other firms will be getting large wage increases, then meeting the competition will require similar large wage increases. A smaller wage increase would reduce the wage of the firm's workers relative to that received by other workers. Many firms base their wage decisions on the wages paid by other firms. If they see the wages at other firms rising, they will be more willing to increase wages.

Firms and workers also look to expectations of inflation when deciding on wage increases. In an economy with 4 percent inflation, wages will have to increase by 4 percent for workers just to keep up with the cost of living. Lower wage increases would result in a decline in workers' real wages.

Staggered Price and Wage Setting

Not all wages and prices are changed at the same time throughout the economy. Rather, price setting and wage setting are staggered over months and even years. For example, autoworkers might negotiate three-year wage contracts in 1996, 1999, 2002, and so on. Dockworkers might negotiate three year contracts in 1997, 2000, 2003, and so on. Bus companies and train companies do not adjust their prices at the same time, even though they may be competing for the same riders. On any given day, we can be sure that a wage or price is adjusting somewhere in the economy, but the vast majority of wages and prices do not change.

Staggered price and wage setting slows down the adjustment of prices in the economy. When considering what wage increases are likely in the next year, firms and workers know about the most recent wage increases. For example, an agreement made by another firm to increase wages by 4 percent per year for three years into the future will affect the expectations of wages paid to competing workers in the future. This wage agreement will not change unless the firm is on the edge of bankruptcy, and perhaps not even then. Hence, workers and firms deciding on wage increases tend to match the wage increases recently made at other firms. Thus, price and wage decisions made today are directly influenced by price and wage decisions made yesterday.

As with many things in life, when today's decisions are influenced by yesterday's decisions, inertia sets in. The staggering of the decisions makes it difficult to break the inertia. Unless policy makers have a reason to make a change—such as a persistent decline in demand or a change in expectations of inflation—the price increases or wage increases continue from year to year. The flat inflation adjustment line describes this inertia.

2.2 The Inflation Adjustment Line Shifts Gradually When Real GDP Departs from Potential GDP

The inflation adjustment line does not always stay put; rather, it may shift up or down from year to year. If real GDP stays above potential GDP, then inflation starts to rise. Firms see that the demand for their products is remaining high, and they begin adjusting their prices. If the inflation rate is 4 percent, then the firms will have to raise their prices by more than 4 percent if they want their relative prices to increase. Hence, inflation starts to rise. The inflation adjustment line is shifted upward to illustrate this rise in inflation; it will keep shifting upward as long as real GDP is above potential GDP.

If real GDP is below potential GDP, however, then firms will see that the demand for their products is falling off, and they will adjust their prices. If inflation is 4 percent, the firms will raise their prices by less than 4 percent—perhaps by 2 percent—if they want the relative price of their goods to fall. Hence, inflation will fall. The inflation adjustment line is shifted down to illustrate this fall in inflation. Figure 24.9 shows the direction of these shifts.

If real GDP stays at potential GDP, neither to the left nor to the right of the vertical potential GDP line in Figure 24.9, then inflation remains unchanged. This steady inflation is represented by an unmoving inflation adjustment line year after year.

Reminder: **The Following is a brief summary of the inflation adjustment in the economy as a whole:**

- *If real GDP = potential GDP, then the inflation rate does not change (IA line does not shift).*
- *If real GDP > potential GDP, then the inflation rate increases (IA line shifts up).*
- *If real GDP < potential GDP, then the inflation rate decreases (IA line shifts down).*

2.3 Changes in Expectations or Commodity Prices Shift the Inflation Adjustment Line

Even if real GDP is at potential GDP, some special events in the economy can cause the inflation adjustment line to shift up or down. One important example is *shifts in expectations* of inflation. If firms and workers expect inflation to rise, they are likely to raise wages and prices by a large amount to keep pace with the expected inflation. Thus, an increase in expectations of inflation will cause the inflation adjustment line to shift up to a higher inflation rate. And a decrease in expectations of inflation will cause the inflation adjustment line to shift down.

FIGURE 24.9 **Inflation Adjustment and Changes in Inflation**

In the top panel, real GDP is above potential GDP and inflation is rising; the inflation adjustment line shifts up. In the bottom panel, real GDP is below potential GDP and inflation is falling; thus, the inflation adjustment line shifts down.

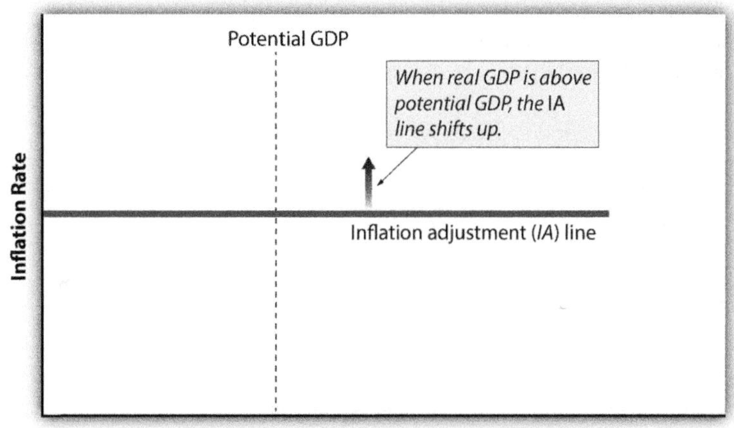

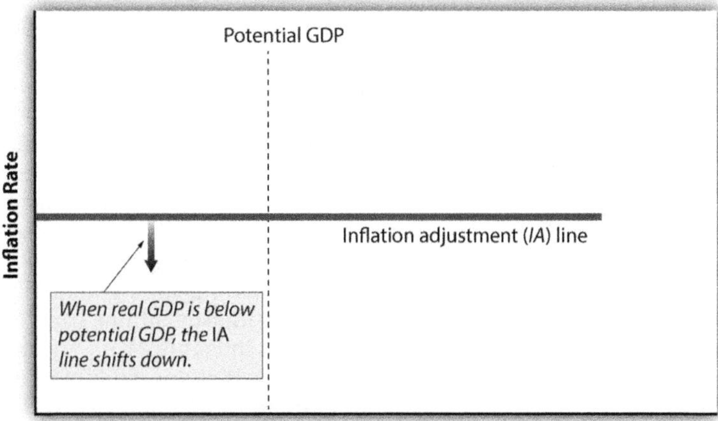

Another example is a change in commodity prices that affects firms' costs of production. For example, we will examine the effects on inflation of an oil price increase in Chapter 25. By raising firms' costs, such an oil price increase would lead firms to charge higher prices, and the inflation adjustment line would rise, at least temporarily.

2.4 Does the Inflation Adjustment Line Fit the Facts?

Are these assumptions about the inflation adjustment line accurate? Does inflation rise when real GDP is above potential GDP and fall when real GDP is below potential GDP? Although there are exceptions, the answer is generally yes. Look back at Figure 17.8 in Chapter 17 for evidence.

One of the biggest declines in inflation occurred in the recession of 1982, when real GDP was far below potential GDP. Inflation also fell during the recessions of 1990–1991, 2001, and 2008 when real GDP fell below potential GDP. In 1998 and 1999, real GDP rose above potential GDP, but inflation did not immediately start to rise. This delay led some commentators to think that the inflation adjustment relationship was changing, but by late 1999 and 2000, inflation rose as predicted by the theory.

REVIEW

- The inflation adjustment (*IA*) line, the second element of the economic fluctuations model, is a flat line showing the level of inflation in the economy at any point in time. The inflation adjustment line describes the economic behavior of firms and workers setting prices and wages in the economy.
- Firms do not change their prices instantaneously when the demand for their product changes. Thus, when aggregate demand changes and real GDP departs from potential GDP, the inflation rate does not change immediately; the inflation adjustment line does not shift in response to such changes in the short run.
- Staggered wage and price setting tends to slow down the adjustment of inflation in the economy as a whole.
- Over time, inflation does respond to departures of real GDP from potential GDP. This response can be described by upward and downward shifts in the inflation adjustment line over time.

3. COMBINING THE AGGREGATE DEMAND CURVE AND THE INFLATION ADJUSTMENT LINE

We have now derived two relationships—the aggregate demand curve and the inflation adjustment line—that describe real GDP and inflation in the economy as a whole. The two relationships can be combined to make predictions about real GDP and inflation.

Along the aggregate demand curve in Figure 24.1, real GDP and inflation are negatively related. This curve describes the behavior of firms and consumers as they respond to a higher real interest rate caused by the Fed's response to higher inflation. They respond by lowering consumption, investment, and net exports. This line presents a range of possible values of real GDP and inflation.

The inflation adjustment line in Figure 24.9, on the other hand, tells us what the inflation rate is at any point in time. Thus, we can use the inflation adjustment line to determine exactly what inflation rate applies to the aggregate demand curve. For example, if the inflation adjustment line tells us that the inflation rate for 2007 is 3 percent, then we can go right to the aggregate demand curve to determine what the level of real GDP will be at that 3 percent inflation rate. The inflation adjustment line tells us the current location of inflation—and therefore real GDP—on the aggregate demand curve.

Figure 24.10 illustrates the determination of real GDP and inflation graphically. It combines the aggregate demand curve from Figure 24.1 with the inflation adjustment line from Figure 24.9. At any point in time, the inflation adjustment line is given, as shown in Figure 24.10. The inflation adjustment line intersects the aggregate demand curve at a single point. It is at this point of intersection that inflation and real GDP are determined. The intersection gives an *equilibrium* level of real GDP and inflation. At that point, we can look down to the horizontal axis of the diagram to determine the level of real GDP corresponding to that level of inflation. For example, the point of intersection in the left panel of Figure 24.10 might be when inflation is 5 percent and real GDP is 2 percent below potential GDP. The point of intersection in the right panel is at a lower inflation rate when real GDP is above potential GDP. The point of intersection in the middle panel of Figure 24.10 has real GDP equal to potential GDP.

As Figure 24.10 makes clear, the intersection of the inflation adjustment line and the aggregate demand curve may give values of real GDP that are either above or below potential GDP. But if real GDP is not equal to potential GDP, then the economy has not fully recovered from a recession, as on the left of Figure 24.10, or returned to potential GDP after being above it, as on the right. To describe dynamic movements of inflation and real GDP, we must consider how the inflation adjustment line and the aggregate demand curve shift over time. That is the subject of Chapter 25.

FIGURE 24.10 **Determining Real GDP and Inflation**

Real GDP is determined at the intersection of the AD curve and the IA line. All three panels have the same AD curve and the same vertical line marking potential GDP. Three different levels of the IA line give three different levels of real GDP: less than, equal to, and greater than potential GDP.

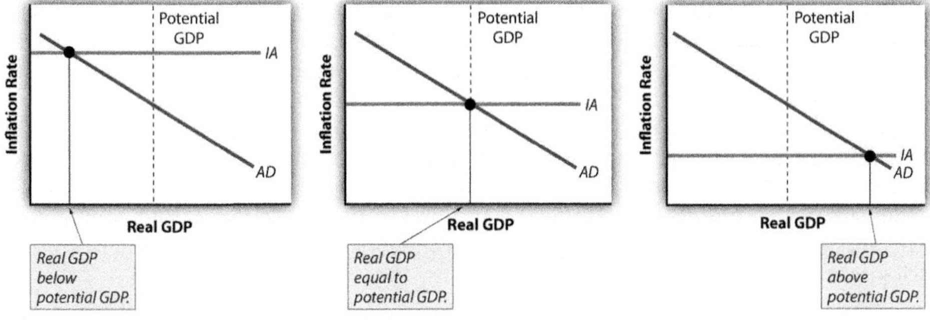

REVIEW

- In any year, the inflation adjustment line tells what the inflation rate is. Using the aggregate demand curve, we can then make a prediction about what real GDP is.
- The intersection of the aggregate demand curve and the inflation adjustment line gives a pair of observations on real GDP and inflation at any point in time.

4. END-OF-CHAPTER MATERIAL

4.1 Conclusion

With the three essential elements of the economic fluctuations model—the aggregate demand curve, the inflation adjustment line, and their intersection—put together, we now are ready to use the model to explain the fluctuations of real GDP and inflation. In reviewing the model, it is useful to consider the scissors analogy mentioned in our discussion of the supply and demand model in Chapter 3.

The aggregate demand curve is like one blade of the scissors. The inflation adjustment line is the other blade. Either blade alone is insufficient to explain economic fluctuations. Either blade alone is an incomplete story. But when the two blades of the scissors are put together to form a pair of scissors, they become a practical tool to explain the ups and downs in the economy. And compared with the complexity and vastness of the whole economy with millions of firms and consumers, this particular pair of scissors is amazingly simple.

Key Points

1. Investment, net exports, and consumption depend negatively on the real interest rate. Hence, real gross domestic product (GDP), which includes investment, net exports, and consumption, depends negatively on the real interest rate.
2. Central banks' actions to adjust the nominal interest rate to maintain low inflation result in a relationship between the real interest rate and inflation. When inflation rises, the real interest rate rises. When inflation falls, the real interest rate falls.
3. The combined behavior of (1) the real interest rate response to inflation and (2) the private sector adjusting spending in response to the interest rate generates an inverse relationship between real GDP and inflation—the aggregate demand curve.
4. Movements along the aggregate demand curve occur when inflation rises, causing the real interest rate to rise and real GDP to fall. Such movements along the curve also occur when inflation falls, the interest rate declines, and real GDP rises.
5. The aggregate demand curve shifts for many reasons, including a change in government purchases and a change in monetary policy toward a higher inflation target.
6. When adjusting prices, firms respond slowly to changes in demand and take into account expectations of inflation. So do workers when wages are being adjusted. As a result, inflation tends to increase when real GDP is above potential GDP and tends to decrease when real GDP is below potential GDP.
7. The staggering of price and wage decisions tends to slow the adjustment of prices in the economy as a whole.
8. When combined with the aggregate demand curve, the inflation adjustment line provides us with a way to determine real GDP and inflation.

QUESTIONS FOR REVIEW

1. Why are investment, net exports, and consumption inversely related to the real interest rate?
2. Why is real GDP inversely related to the real interest rate in the short run?
3. Why does the real interest rate rise when inflation begins to rise?
4. Why is real GDP inversely related to inflation in the short run? What is this relationship called?
5. What are examples of movements along the aggregate demand curve?
6. Why does a change in government purchases shift the aggregate demand curve to the right or left?
7. Why does a shift in monetary policy shift the aggregate demand curve to the right or left?
8. Why does inflation increase when real GDP is above potential GDP?
9. What is the significance of expectations of inflation for inflation adjustment?
10. Why does staggered price setting slow down price adjustment in the economy?

PROBLEMS

1. Compare and contrast the graphs used in the microeconomic supply and demand model with those used in the economic fluctuations model.
2. Which of the following statements are true, and which are false? Explain your answers in one or two sentences.
   a. An increase in the U.S. real interest rate will cause the dollar exchange rate to decline.
   b. The central bank typically raises the real interest rate when inflation rises.
   c. A higher real interest rate leads to greater net exports because the higher interest rate raises the value of the dollar.
3. Suppose the Fed is considering two different policy rules, shown in the following table. Graph the policy rules.

Inflation	Policy Rule 1 Interest Rate	Policy Rule 2 Interest Rate
0	1	3
2	3	5
4	5	7
6	7	9
8	9	11

   If the Fed currently is following Policy Rule 1 and then shifts to Policy Rule 2, which way will the aggregate demand curve shift? What reasons might the Fed have for changing its policy?
4. Suppose you have the following information on the Fed's and the European Central Bank's (ECB) policy rules:

$$\text{Fed real interest rate} = 0.5\ (\text{inflation rate} - 2)$$

$$\text{ECB real interest rate} = 0.2 \times (\text{inflation rate} - 2) + 1$$

   a. Graph these policy rules. If the inflation rate is 2 percent in each, what will be the real interest rate in the U.S. and the ECB area?
   b. Some argue that Europe has a much lower tolerance for inflation than the United States. Can you tell—either from the diagram or from the equations—whether this is true?
5. The table below gives a numerical example of an aggregate demand curve.
   a. Sketch the curve in a graph.
   b. What is the average rate of inflation in the long run?
   c. Suppose that the central bank shifts policy so that the average rate of inflation in the long run is 2 percentage points higher than in (b). Sketch a new aggregate demand curve corresponding to the higher inflation rate.

Real GDP (percent deviation from potential GDP)	Inflation (percent per year)
3.0	1.0
2.0	1.5
1.0	2.0
0.0	3.0
-1.0	4.0
-2.0	6.0
-3.0	9.0

6. State which of the following changes cause a shift in the aggregate demand curve and which ones are a movement along it. Also provide the direction of the change.
   a. A cut in government purchases.
   b. A crash in the U.S. stock market.
   c. A shift to a lower inflation target in the monetary policy rule.
   d. Being thrifty now becoming fashionable.
   e. An increase in the European interest rate.
7. The following table gives an example of an inflation adjustment line.

Real GDP (percent deviation from potential GDP)	Inflation (percent per year)
3.0	2.0
2.0	2.0
1.0	2.0
0.0	2.0
-1.0	2.0
-2.0	2.0
-3.0	2.0

   a. Sketch the line in a graph.
   b. If real GDP is above potential GDP, will the inflation adjustment line shift up or down? Explain.
   c. In the same graph as part (a), sketch in the aggregate demand curve given in Problem 5. Find the equilibrium level of real GDP and inflation.
   d. Show what happens to the inflation adjustment line if inflation expectations suddenly increase.
8. Suppose that a decline in unionization reduces the amount of wage contracts that are being signed and also brings about a reduction in the length of the typical wage contract that is signed. What would the impact on the *IA* line for that economy be? Explain.
9. Give three examples of goods and services that you buy whose prices change only periodically and therefore contribute to staggered pricing in the economy.
10. Suppose potential GDP is $5,000 billion. Use the data below to graph the aggregate demand curve.

Inflation (percent)	Real GDP (billions of dollars)
5	4,800
4	4,900
3	5,000
2	5,100
1	5,200

   a. Suppose the current inflation rate is 2 percent. Draw the inflation adjustment line. What is the current value of real GDP?
   b. In the long run, what will the inflation rate be if economic policy does not change? Explain how this adjustment takes place.

CHAPTER 25
Using The Economic Fluctuations Model

For students and teachers of macroeconomics, the seven years 2008–2014 had a Dickensian feel to them. "It was the best of times, it was the worst of times, it was the age of wisdom, it was the age of foolishness." [1] On the one hand, it was the worst of times: to live in what then-President Barack Obama termed "the worst economic crisis since the Great Depression," consoling friends and family who had lost their jobs, studying at universities forced to make budget cuts and raise tuition, and facing a future with dwindling job prospects of one's own. Even after the recession officially ended in June 2009, the subsequent recovery was one of the most anemic recoveries the U.S. economy has experienced. Unemployment remained above 7 percent until the end of 2013 and it was not until the end of 2015 that unemployment returned to pre-recession levels. An exact accounting of the costs of a recession is a challenging exercise—one such attempt by three economists at the Federal Reserve Bank of Dallas calculated that the cost of the recession was the equivalent of $50,000 to $120,000 for every U.S. household.[2]

Source: Shutterstock.com

On the other hand, it was the best of times to be studying macroeconomics, trying to understand how what began as a slowdown in housing prices in the United States ended up as a global economic recession that seemed to spare no country in its wake, and trying to understand the challenges that monetary and fiscal policy makers faced in getting the economy back on track in a world in which uncertainty was rife, government budgets already were stretched to the limit, and central bankers had used up most of their conventional policy tools. The concept that the Federal Reserve could not lower the nominal interest rates beyond zero moved from being an interesting academic exercise that instructors dreamt up to challenge students on midterm exams to being a central plank of policy for the Federal Reserve for almost seven years. And when the Federal Reserve finally began to raise interest rates from zero to what were still historically unprecedented low levels, some economists were extremely critical that the Federal Reserve was moving too soon!

The goal of this chapter is to show you how you can use the economic fluctuations model to develop a good understanding of what causes recessions, expansions, and other vital developments in a modern dynamic economy. Indeed, economists around the world use such a model to study events in their own countries. The model also is extremely useful in determining the appropriate choices of economic policy—how a tax cut, a new spending program, or an interest rate cut is needed to stimulate the economy.

We begin by using the model in a general way to determine the path the economy takes after a shift in aggregate demand, whether that shift is due to a big change in government purchases, a shift in monetary policy, or some other factor. We trace the path of real gross domestic product (GDP) from the time of its initial departure from potential GDP—as in a recession—to its recovery. We explain why a recovery occurs and how long it takes. We also look at the effect of price shocks on the economy.

After we cover these general applications, we demonstrate the usefulness, and power, of the economic fluctuations model by applying it to understand the most recent recession experienced by the United States. Economists can provide invaluable contributions to society if they can use models like the economic fluctuations model to better understand economic developments and to formulate policies that can help the economy recover from a crisis or prevent such a serious crisis from occurring in the first place.

1. CHANGES IN GOVERNMENT PURCHASES

We first use the economic fluctuations model to examine the forces leading to the return of real GDP to potential GDP. To do so, we focus on a particular example, a change in government purchases. In Chapter 23, we showed how a change in government purchases could push real GDP away from potential GDP in the short run. Now let's see the complete story.

1.1 Real GDP and Inflation over Time

Suppose the government cuts military purchases permanently. We want to examine the effects of this decrease in government purchases on the economy in the short run (about one year), the medium run (two to three years), and the long run (four to five years and beyond). The three lengths of time given in the parentheses are approximations; in reality, the times will not be exactly these lengths, but rather they will be somewhat longer or shorter. We use the term *short run* to refer to the initial departure of real GDP from potential GDP, *medium run* to refer to the recovery period, and *long run* to refer to the time at which real GDP is nearly back to potential GDP.

Figure 25.1 shows the aggregate demand curve and the inflation adjustment line on the same diagram. The intersection of the aggregate demand curve and the inflation adjustment line determines a level of inflation and real GDP. Let us assume that we began with real GDP equal to potential GDP. Thus, the initial intersection of the aggregate demand curve and the inflation adjustment line occurs at a level of real GDP equal to potential GDP.

Now, recall from Chapter 24 that a change in government purchases shifts the aggregate demand curve; in particular, a decline in government purchases shifts the aggregate demand curve to the left. Because the inflation adjustment line is flat, and because it does not move in the short run, a change in government purchases—shown by the shift from the "old" to the "new" aggregate demand curve in Figure 25.1—leads to a change in real GDP of the same amount as the shift in the aggregate demand curve. This is the short-run effect. The decrease in government purchases initially moves the aggregate demand curve to the left, and real GDP falls to the point indicated by the intersection of the inflation adjustment line and the new aggregate demand curve. At the new intersection, real GDP is below potential GDP.

As real GDP falls below potential GDP, employment falls because the decline in demand forces firms to cut back on production and lay off workers. The model predicts that unemployment rises, just as it does during actual declines in real GDP.

Now consider what happens over time. The tendency for inflation to adjust over time is represented by upward or downward shifts of the inflation adjustment line. Only in the short run does the inflation adjustment line stay put. What is likely to happen over time when real GDP is below potential

GDP? Inflation should begin to decline, because firms will increase their prices by smaller amounts. We represent a decline in inflation by shifting the inflation adjustment line down, as shown in Figure 25.2. The initial impact of the change in government spending took us to the point we label *SR*, for short run, in Figure 25.2. At that point, real GDP is lower than potential GDP. Hence, inflation will fall and the inflation adjustment line shifts down, as shown in the diagram. Now we have a new point of intersection; we label that point *MR*, for medium run.

FIGURE 25.1 Short-Run Effects of a Reduction in Government Purchases

In the short run, the *IA* line does not move. Thus, in the short run, real GDP declines by the amount of the shift in the *AD* curve, as noted on the horizontal axis.

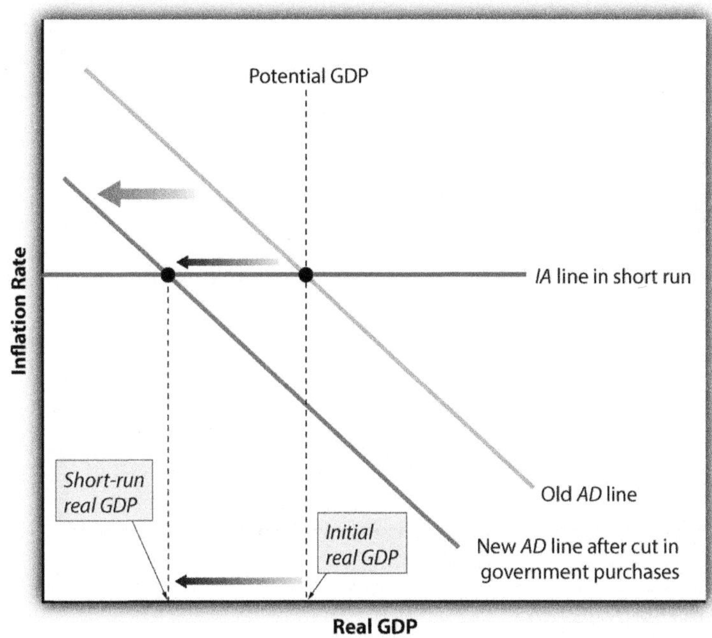

Note that real GDP has started to recover. At the point labeled *MR* in the diagram, real GDP is still below potential GDP, but it is higher than at the low (*SR*) point in the downturn. The reason real GDP starts to rise is that the lower inflation rate causes the central bank to lower the real interest rate. The lower real interest rate increases investment spending and causes net exports to rise. As a result, real GDP rises, and as it does, firms start to call back workers who were laid off. As more workers are employed, unemployment begins to fall.

Because real GDP is still below potential GDP, the tendency is for inflation to fall. Thus, the inflation adjustment line continues to shift downward until real GDP returns to potential GDP. Figure 25.2 shows a third intersection at the point marked *LR*, for long run, the point at which production has increased all the way back to potential GDP. At this point, real GDP has reached long-run equilibrium in the sense that real GDP equals potential GDP. With real GDP equal to potential GDP, the inflation adjustment line stops shifting down. Inflation is at a new lower level than before the decline in government purchases, but at the final point of intersection in the diagram, it is no longer falling. Thus, real GDP remains equal to potential GDP.

Note how successive downward shifts of the inflation adjustment line with intersections along the aggregate demand curve trace out values for real GDP and inflation as the economy first goes into recession and then recovers. In the short run, a decline in production comes about because of the decrease in government spending; that decline is followed by successive years of reversal as the economy recovers and real GDP returns to potential GDP. This behavior is shown in the sketch in the lower part of Figure 25.2. Thus, we have achieved one of the major goals of this chapter: showing how real GDP returns to potential GDP after an initial departure because of a shift in aggregate demand. In the case in which the shift in aggregate demand is large enough to cause real GDP to decline, as in a recession, we have shown how recessions end and recoveries take the economy back to normal.

FIGURE 25.2 **Dynamic Adjustment after a Reduction in Government Purchases**

Initially, the reduction in government purchases shifts the *AD* curve to the left. This reduces real GDP to the point labeled *SR*, or the short run. Then the *IA* line begins to shift down because real GDP is less than potential GDP. The *IA* line keeps shifting down until real GDP is back to potential GDP.

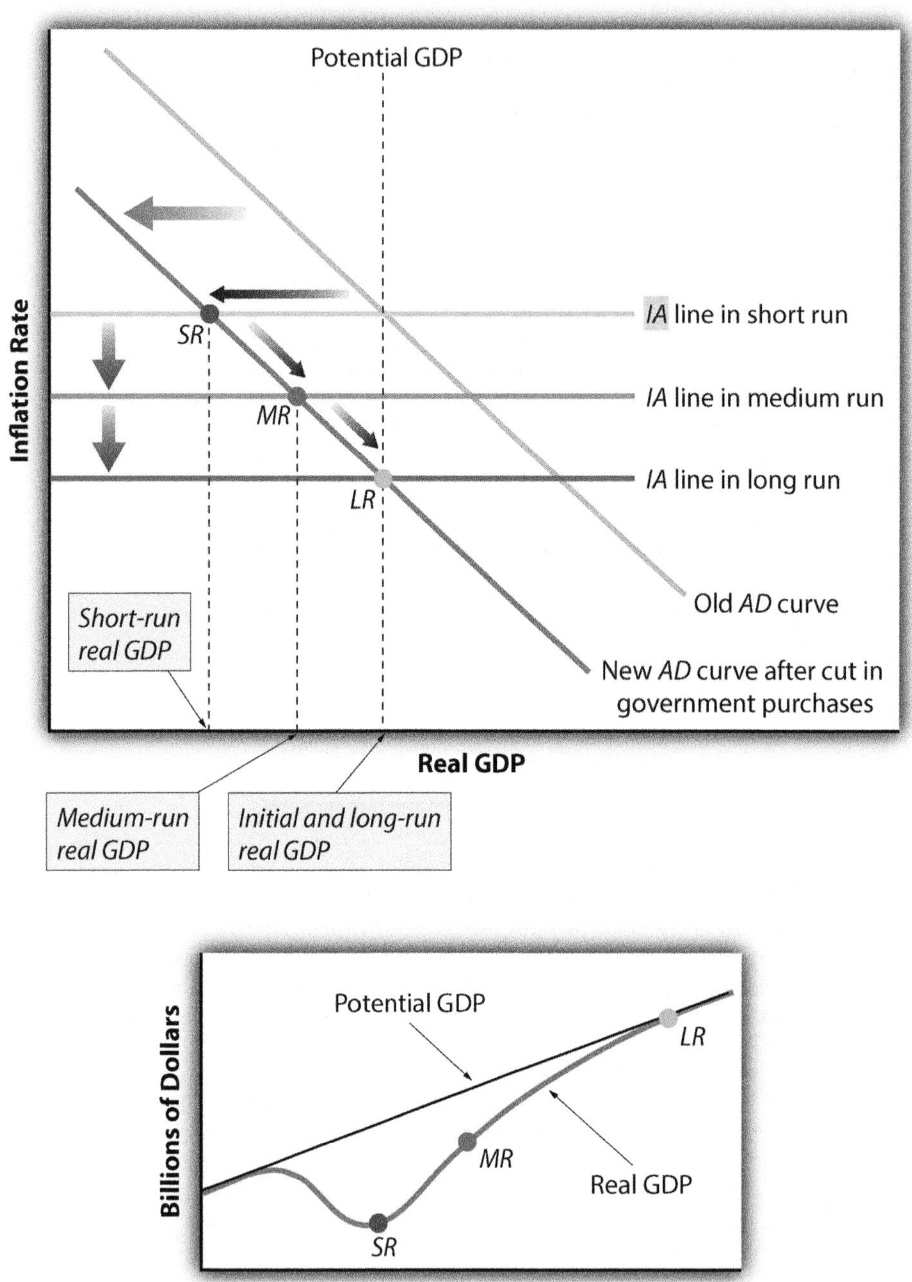

1.2 Details on the Components of Spending

It is possible to give a more detailed description of what happens to consumption, net exports, and investment during this temporary departure from, and return to, potential GDP.

Let's focus first on the short run and then on the long run. Figure 25.3 summarizes how each component of real GDP changes in the short run and the long run. The arrows in the table indicate what happens compared with what would have happened in the absence of the change in government purchases. The path of the economy in the absence of the hypothetical change is called the *baseline*. The term *baseline* is commonly used in public policy discussions to refer to what would happen if a contemplated policy action were not taken; the arrows in the table tell whether a variable is up or down relative to the baseline. In this case, the *baseline* for real GDP is potential GDP. Thus, a downward-pointing arrow in the real GDP column means that real GDP is below potential GDP; the sideways arrows indicate that real GDP is equal to the baseline or potential GDP; an upward-pointing arrow would mean that real GDP is above potential GDP.

Short Run

The decline in government spending gets things started, lowering aggregate demand and the level of real GDP. With lower real GDP, income is down, and so people consume less, as explained by the consumption function in Chapter 23. In the short run, investment does not change because interest rates have not yet changed. Net exports rise, however, because the lower level of income in the United States means that people will import less from abroad. Recall that *net exports is defined as exports minus imports.* Thus, if imports fall, then net exports must rise.

These short-run effects are shown in the first row in the table. Real GDP and consumption are down *relative to the baseline.* Net exports are up *relative to the baseline.*

Long Run

Now consider the long run, approximately four to five years. By this time, real GDP has returned to potential GDP. Government spending is still lower than it was originally because we have assumed that this is a permanent decline in military spending. Because real GDP is equal to potential GDP, aggregate income in the economy—which equals real GDP—is back to normal. Because income is back to normal, the effects of income on consumption and net exports are just what they would have been in the absence of the change in government purchases.

What about interest rates and their effect on consumption, investment, and net exports? We know that the real interest rate would be lowered by the monetary policy maker when inflation declined. With a lower real interest rate, more real GDP will go to investment, net exports, and consumption to make up for the decline in the amount of real GDP going to the government. The diagram in Figure 25.3 shows that consumption, investment, and net exports are higher in the long run. We would expect the consumption effects to be small, however, because consumption is not sensitive to interest rates. Most of the long-run impact of the decline in government purchases is to raise investment and net exports.

FIGURE 25.3 More Detailed Analysis of a Reduction in Government Purchases

The arrows in the diagram keep track of the changes in the major variables relative to the baseline.

	Y	C	I	X	G
SR	↓	↓	↔	↑	↓
LR	↔	↑	↑	↑	↓

A Higher Growth Path after a Recession

To summarize, a decrease in government purchases has negative effects on the economy in the short run. Real GDP declines. Workers are laid off. Unemployment rises. In the long run, the economy is back to potential GDP, and consumption, investment, and net exports have gone up. Workers are called back, and unemployment declines to the point at which it was before the recession. In the long run, the decrease in government purchases permits greater private investment and more net exports. The increase in investment benefits long-run economic growth, as we know from Chapter 19; hence, the path of potential GDP over time has risen, and now real GDP is growing more quickly, as shown in Figure 25.4.

FIGURE 25.4 **Increase in the Long-Term Growth after a Recession Caused by a Decrease in Government Purchases**

The higher investment share of real GDP that results from the decline in government purchases leads to more capital and a higher growth of potential GDP. After the recession, real GDP will grow along, or fluctuate around, this higher growth path.

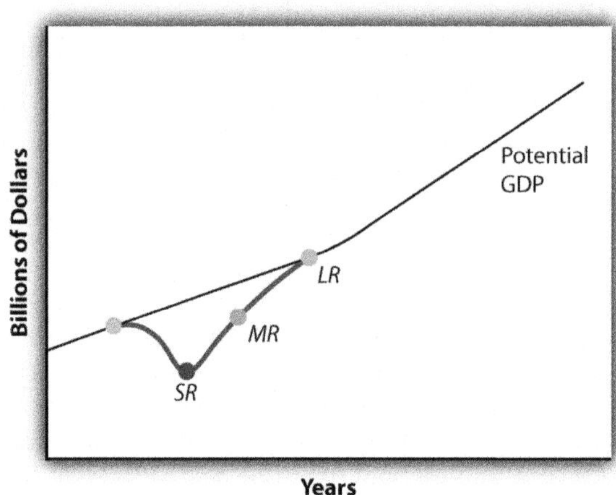

Observe also that the rate of inflation is lower in the long run than it was before the temporary decline in real GDP. Inflation declined during the period when real GDP was lower than potential GDP, and it did not increase again. This lower inflation rate means that the Fed implicitly has allowed the *target* rate of inflation—the average level of inflation over the long run—to drift down. If the Fed had wanted to keep the target rate of inflation from falling, it would have had to lower interest rates before the inflation rate started to fall. This decline in the interest rate would have pushed the aggregate demand curve back to the right and thereby kept the inflation rate from falling.

A good example occurred in the mid-1990s when government purchases were cut in an effort to reduce the federal budget deficit. Economists argued that the Fed should cut interest rates by an extra amount. They recognized that such action would cause the aggregate demand curve to shift to the right and prevent real GDP from declining in the short run while at the same time keeping the inflation rate from falling in the long run.

The Return to Potential GDP after an Increase in Government Spending

What if real GDP rises above potential GDP? Surprisingly, the adjustment of real GDP back to potential GDP can be explained using the same theory. For example, suppose an increase in real GDP above potential GDP is caused by an increase in government purchases for new highway construction. Starting from potential GDP, the aggregate demand curve would shift to the right. Real GDP would increase above potential GDP in the short run.

With real GDP above potential GDP, however, firms start to raise their prices more rapidly; inflation begins to rise. We would represent that as an upward shift in the inflation adjustment line. In the medium run, real GDP still would be above potential GDP, and inflation would continue to rise. Eventually, real GDP would go back to potential GDP. Thus, we predict that real GDP goes back to potential GDP. In this case, however, because government purchases have risen, the new long-run equilibrium will have a higher interest rate, and the sum of consumption, investment, and net exports will be lower.

REVIEW

- Using the inflation adjustment line and the aggregate demand curve, we now can explain both the initial steps of real GDP away from potential GDP and the return to potential GDP.
- In the short run, a decline in government purchases shifts the aggregate demand curve to the left and causes real GDP to fall below potential GDP.
- In the medium run, when the interest rate starts to fall, real GDP begins to increase again. Investment and net exports start to rise and partly offset the decline in government purchases.
- In the long run, real GDP returns to potential GDP. Interest rates are lower, and consumption plus investment plus net exports has risen.

2. CHANGES IN MONETARY POLICY

A large change in government spending, of course, is not the only thing that temporarily can push real GDP away from potential GDP. Changes in taxes, consumer confidence, or foreign demand also can cause recessions. But a particularly important factor is a change in monetary policy.

Consider, for example, a change in monetary policy that aims to lower the rate of inflation. Suppose that the inflation rate is too high, say 10 percent, as it was in the late 1970s, and the Fed decides to reduce the inflation rate to 3 percent. In effect, the central bank changes the target inflation rate from 10 percent to 3 percent. A reduction in the inflation rate is called **disinflation**. Declining prices, or a negative inflation rate is **deflation**, which is different from a declining inflation rate. The aim of the policy in this example is disinflation, not deflation.

disinflation

A reduction in the inflation rate.

deflation

A decrease in the overall price level, or a negative inflation rate.

Figure 25.5 shows the short-run, medium-run, and long-run impact of such a shift in monetary policy. Recall from Chapter 24 (see Figure 24.7 and Figure 24.8) that a change in monetary policy will shift the aggregate demand curve. A change in monetary policy toward higher inflation will shift the *AD* curve to the right, and a change in monetary policy toward lower inflation will shift the *AD* curve to the left. In this case, we are examining a change in monetary policy that aims to lower the inflation rate, so the change shifts the aggregate demand curve to the left. This shift occurs because the Fed raises interest rates to curtail demand and thereby lower inflationary pressures.

One effect of the increase in the interest rate is to lower investment. In addition, the higher interest rate causes the dollar to appreciate, and this tends to reduce net exports. Because inflation is slow to adjust, we do not move the inflation adjustment line yet. Thus, inflation remains at 10 percent in the short run. At this time, things seem grim. The short-run effect of the change to a new monetary policy is to cause real GDP to fall below potential GDP. If the disinflation is large enough, this might mean a decline in real GDP, or a recession. If the disinflation is small and gradual, then the decline in real GDP could result in a *temporary growth slowdown.* In a temporary growth slowdown, real GDP growth does not turn negative, as it does in a recession.

FIGURE 25.5 Disinflation: A Transition to Lower Inflation

The figure shows how a change in monetary policy to a lower target for inflation affects real GDP over time. In the end, inflation is lower and real GDP is back to potential GDP.

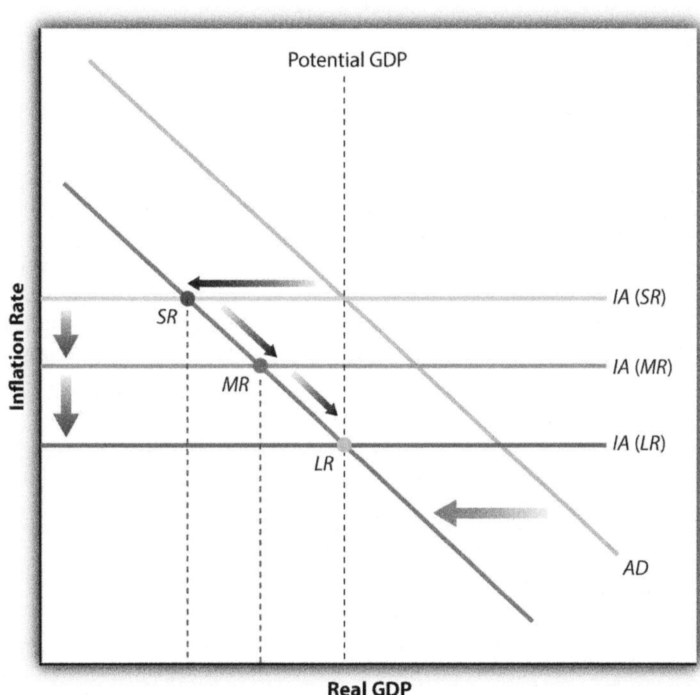

In any case, with real GDP below potential GDP, inflation will begin to decline. We show this in the diagram in Figure 25.5 by moving the inflation adjustment line down. The lower inflation adjustment line, labeled *MR* for medium run, intersects the aggregate demand curve at a higher level of real GDP. Thus, the economy has begun to recover. The recovery starts because as inflation comes down, the Fed begins to lower the interest rate. As the interest rate declines, investment and net exports begin to rise again, and we move back along the aggregate demand curve.

At this medium-run situation, however, real GDP is still below potential GDP, so the inflation rate continues to decline. We show this in the diagram by shifting the inflation adjustment line down again. To make a long story short, we show the inflation adjustment line shifting all the way down to where it intersects the aggregate demand curve at potential GDP. Thus, in the long-run equilibrium, the economy has fully recovered, and the inflation rate is at its new lower target. The long-run equilibrium has consumption, investment, and net exports back to normal.

The overall dynamic impacts of this change in monetary policy are important. The initial impact of a monetary policy change is on real GDP. It is only later that the change shows up in inflation. Thus, the effect of monetary policy on inflation has a long lag.

Lower inflation, for example, 3 percent rather than 10 percent in this case, is likely to make potential GDP grow faster, perhaps because uncertainty is lower and productivity rises faster. If this is so, the return of real GDP to potential GDP will mean that real GDP is higher, and the long-run benefits of the disinflation to people in the economy may be great over the years. But such changes in the growth of real GDP will appear small in the span of years during which a disinflation takes place and will not change the basic story that a reduction in the rate of inflation, unless it is gradual, usually results in a recession.

2.1 The Volcker Disinflation

The scenario we just described is similar to the disinflation in the United States in the early 1980s under Paul Volcker, the head of the Fed from 1979 to 1987. First, interest rates skyrocketed as the disinflation began. The federal funds rate went to more than 20 percent. By any measure, real GDP fell well below potential GDP in the early 1980s. Workers were laid off, the unemployment rate rose to 10.8 percent, investment declined, and net exports fell. Eventually, pricing decisions began to adjust and inflation began to come down. As inflation came down, the Fed began to lower the interest rate. The economy eventually recovered: In 1982, the recovery was under way, and by 1985, the economy had returned to near its potential. The good news was that inflation was down from over 10 percent to about 4 percent.

2.2 Reinflation and the Great Inflation

reinflation

An increase in the inflation rate caused by a change in monetary policy.

The opposite of disinflation might be called **reinflation**, an increase in the inflation rate caused by a shift in monetary policy. This could be analyzed with our theory simply by reversing the preceding process, starting with a change in monetary policy to a higher inflation rate target. This higher target would cause the aggregate demand curve to shift right. Real GDP would rise above potential GDP, and unemployment would decline. But eventually inflation would rise and real GDP would return to potential.

Although it would be unusual for central bankers to explicitly admit they were raising the target inflation rate, there could be political pressures that would lead to less concern about inflation. In such a case, the target for inflation would rise implicitly.

Reinflation is one way to interpret the Great Inflation in the United States and other countries in the 1970s. In the late 1960s and 1970s, the Fed and other central banks around the world let the inflation rate increase. Other things were going on at that time, including a quadrupling of oil prices, but without the inflationary monetary policy, the decade-long inflation would not have been sustained for so long.

REVIEW

- Disinflation is a reduction in inflation. It occurs when the central bank shifts monetary policy in the direction of a lower inflation target.
- According to the theory of economic fluctuations, disinflation has either a temporary slowing of real GDP growth or a recession as a by-product. A higher interest rate at the start of a disinflation lowers investment spending and net exports. This lower spending causes real GDP to fall below potential GDP. Eventually the economy recovers. Inflation comes down, and so does the interest rate.
- The large disinflation in the early 1980s in the United States was accompanied by a recession, as predicted by the theory.

3. PRICE SHOCKS

Shifts in the aggregate demand curve are called **demand shocks**. The change in government purchases and the shift in monetary policy described in the previous two sections of this chapter are examples of demand shocks. However, shifts in the aggregate demand curve are not the only things that can push real GDP away from potential GDP. In particular, the inflation adjustment line can shift.

demand shocks

A shift in one of the components of aggregate demand that leads to a shift in the aggregate demand curve.

3.1 What Is a Price Shock?

Shifts in the inflation adjustment line are called **price shocks.** A price shock usually occurs when a temporary shortage of a key commodity, or group of commodities, drives up prices by such a large amount that it has a noticeable effect on the rate of inflation. Oil price shocks have been common in the last 35 years. For example, oil prices rose sharply in 1974, in 1979, in 1990, in 2005, in 2007–2008 and then again in 2011. After many of these shocks, but not all, real GDP usually has declined and unemployment has increased. Hence, such shocks appear to move real GDP significantly, though temporarily, away from potential GDP.

Price shocks sometimes are called *supply shocks* to distinguish them from demand shocks resulting from changes in government spending or monetary policy. However, a shift in potential GDP—rather than a shift in the inflation adjustment line—is more appropriately called a supply shock. Shifts in potential GDP—such as a sudden spurt in productivity growth because of new inventions—can, of course, cause real GDP to fluctuate. Recall that **real business cycle theory** places great emphasis on shifts in potential GDP. Although a price shock might be accompanied by a shift in potential GDP, it need not be. In this case, we are looking at departures of real GDP from potential GDP and thus focusing on price shocks.

price shock

A change in the price of a key commodity such as oil, usually because of a shortage, that causes a shift in the inflation adjustment line; also sometimes called a supply shock.

real business cycle theory

A theory of macroeconomics that stresses that shifts in potential GDP are a primary cause of fluctuations in real GDP; the shifts in potential GDP usually are assumed to be caused by changes in technology.

3.2 The Effect of Price Shocks

How does our theory of economic fluctuations allow us to predict the effect of price shocks? The impact of a price shock can be illustrated graphically, as shown in Figure 25.6. In the case of a large increase in oil prices, for example, the inflation adjustment line will shift up to a higher level of inflation. A large increase in oil prices at first will lead to an increase in the price of everything that uses oil in production: heating homes, gasoline, airplane fuel, airfares, plastic toys, and many other things. The overall inflation rate is affected. When the inflation rate rises, the inflation adjustment line must shift up.

FIGURE 25.6 A Price Shock

Initially, inflation and the *IA* line rise because of a shock to oil or agricultural prices. This causes real GDP to fall. With real GDP below potential GDP, inflation begins to decline. As inflation declines, real GDP returns to potential GDP.

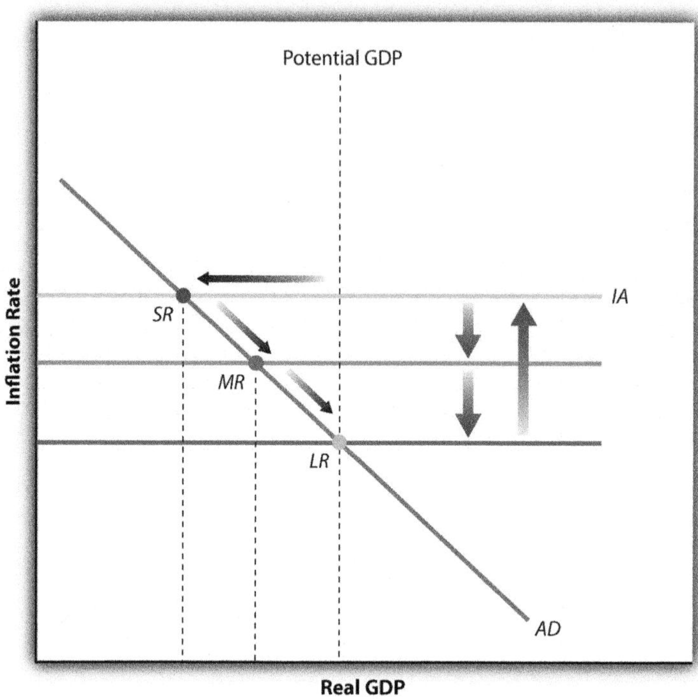

The immediate impact of the shock is to lower real GDP, as the intersection of the inflation adjustment line with the aggregate demand curve moves to the left. This result occurs because the higher inflation rate causes the central bank to raise interest rates, reducing investment spending and net exports.

With real GDP below potential GDP, however, the reduction in spending will put pressure on firms to adjust their prices. The lower price increases bring about a lower rate of inflation. Thus, in the period following the rise of inflation, we begin to see a reversal. Inflation starts to decline. As inflation falls, interest rates begin to decline, and the economy starts to recover again. The rate of inflation will return to where it was before the price shock.

Temporary Shifts in the Inflation Adjustment Line

In this analysis of the price shock, the central bank raises interest rates, and the resulting decline in real GDP exerts a countervailing force to reduce inflation. It is possible for some price shocks to have only a temporary effect on inflation. Such a temporary effect can be shown graphically as a rise followed by a quick fall in the inflation adjustment line. In such a situation—in which case the price shock would be expected to automatically reverse itself—it would be wise for the central bank to delay raising the interest rate. Then if the price shock has only a temporary effect on inflation, the decline in real GDP can be avoided. In reality, whenever a price shock occurs, a great debate results about whether it will have a temporary or a permanent effect on inflation. The debate is rarely settled until after the fact.

Price shocks also can occur when commodity prices fall. In this case, the inflation adjustment line would shift downward—just the opposite of the case of an increase in commodity prices—and this would cause real GDP to rise as the Fed lowered interest rates. For example, in the later part of 2008, oil prices declined. This resulted in a temporary decrease in inflation and a rise in real GDP—exactly what would be predicted by the theory of economic fluctuations.

Stagflation

An important difference between price shocks and demand shocks is that, in the case of a price shock, output declines while inflation rises. With demand shocks, inflation and output are positively related over the period of recession and recovery. The situation in which inflation is up and real GDP is down is called **stagflation**. As we have shown, price shocks can lead to stagflation.

stagflation

The situation in which high inflation and high unemployment occur simultaneously.

REVIEW

- A price shock is a large change in the price of some key commodity like oil. Such shocks can push real GDP below potential GDP.
- In the aftermath of a price shock, the interest rate rises. Eventually, with real GDP below potential GDP, inflation begins to come down, and the economy recovers.

4. USING THE ECONOMIC FLUCTUATIONS MODEL TO UNDERSTAND THE RECENT RECESSION

By now you should be comfortable with using the economic fluctuations model in a general setting to examine the impact of particular economic events—changes in fiscal policy, monetary policy, consumer behavior, or price shocks—in isolation. What the economic fluctuations model is most useful for, however, is to understand actual economic developments in which many things change, often simultaneously, in the economy. In this section, we show how the model can explain what brought about the recession that began in late 2007. We also can show how the model could be used to understand the policies that were implemented to help the recovery phase that began when the recession ended in June 2009.

4.1 What Caused the Recession?

Historically, economists do not always agree on what factors triggered a particular recession; a good example is the recession that began at the end of 2007 and especially its subsequent worsening in 2008. Some of the factors mentioned include the following:

1. *Collapse of the Housing Bubble.* A long period of rapidly rising housing prices came to an end. The slowdown and a subsequent sharp fall in housing sales, starts, and prices led to rising foreclosures, lower consumer spending, and large-scale layoffs in housing and construction-related jobs.
2. *Financial Crisis.* Sharp falls in the value of mortgage loans had a negative impact on the financial health of banks, investment banks, and mortgage lenders, leading to the collapse of several leading financial institutions.
3. *Credit Crunch.* Substantial cutbacks in lending as the remaining banks and financial institutions became extremely cautious about making new loans to nongovernmental entities, leading to a sharp curtailment of economic activity because of the lack of credit.
4. *Commodity Price Inflation.* Substantial increases in commodity prices and, especially, the price of gasoline in 2007 and the early part of 2008 eating into consumer expenditure.
5. *Stock Market Collapse.* Sharp decreases in stock markets in the United States and worldwide, on the order of 30–50 percent in 2008, substantially eroding wealth and retirement portfolios of consumers.
6. *Greater Uncertainty.* A substantial rise in uncertainty, as consumers worried about their job security, retirement income, and ability to afford mortgage payments on their homes began to cut back on their purchases; firms concerned about access to credit, deteriorating sales conditions, and concerns about the sharp decline in stock prices cut back on investment projects; and state and local governments operating under balanced budget requirements faced shortfalls in tax revenue and rising demand for income support programs for the needy.

If we are to accurately understand the causes of the recession, we need to look at the period leading up to the onset of the recession to understand what might have precipitated these events. The classic explanation of financial crises, going back hundreds of years, is that they are caused by excesses—frequently monetary excesses—which lead to a boom and an inevitable bust. In the recent crisis, then, it was monetary excesses that created the conditions for the housing boom (although much of the responsibility of the subsequent spillover of that boom into the financial industry has to be shared with the decision makers at the firms that collapsed or suffered in the subsequent bust). In terms of the federal funds interest rate, from 2000 to 2006, the Federal Reserve lowered its inflation target in a manner that was inconsistent with the type of policy that it had followed fairly regularly during the previous 20-year period of good economic performance.

FIGURE 25.7 Explaining the Onset of the Recession

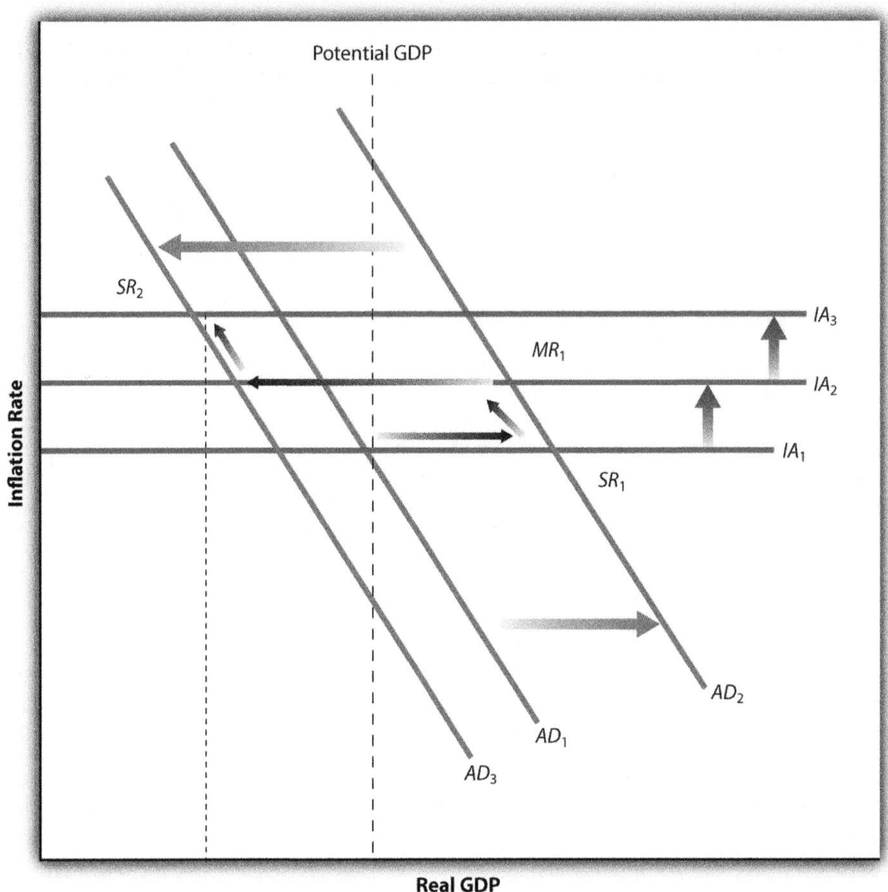

Figure 25.7 provides a graphic analysis of how these factors can be represented using the economic fluctuations model. The boom in spending can be modeled as a rightward shift of the *AD* curve from AD_1 to AD_2. This shift first causes real GDP to rise above potential GDP, then leads to rising inflation as the *IA* line shifts up gradually. Two intersections of the *AD* curve and the *IA* line, labeled SR_1 and MR_1, show this movement. This is the period leading up to the onset of recession, when the U.S. economy still seemed to be doing well, with the main concern being signs of rising inflation.

Figure 25.7 then shows a shift in the *AD* curve to the left as the housing bubble collapses and consumers and firms cut back on their spending in the face of dwindling wealth, greater uncertainty, and lack of access to credit. The rise in commodity prices causes the *IA* line to shift up as well. The combination of these shifts causes a recession, with real GDP falling well below potential GDP, and this is shown on the diagram as SR_2.

The time-series sketches in the lower part of the figure show the movement in real GDP that is traced out by the combination of these shifts. If you compare these fluctuations in real GDP with what actually happened, you will see a close resemblance.

4.2 How to Recover from the Recession

The basic analysis we have done with the economic fluctuations model shows us that when an economy goes into recession, it eventually will recover on its own as inflation falls gradually over time and the Federal Reserve lowers real interest rates to facilitate the recovery. The recovery will be further aided if some of the factors that precipitated the initial downturn, such as a rise in commodity prices or cutbacks in consumer and firm spending driven by uncertainty, reverse themselves.

It is very likely, however, that policy makers would like to take steps to speed up this recovery process further, leading to substantial changes in fiscal and monetary policy designed to boost aggregate demand in the economy. This was indeed the case in the 2008–2009 recession, with the Fed lowering interest rates rapidly until the nominal interest rate reached zero, and the government implementing a $152 billion and a $787 billion stimulus package of spending increases and tax cuts in 2008 and 2009, respectively. In addition, the price of commodities decreased drastically in the fall of 2008, and the Fed, in conjunction with the U.S. Treasury Department, created a package to ease the woes of the banking sector and enable more credit to flow to support economic activity.

We can use the economic fluctuations model to show how a combination of lower commodity prices, increases in government spending and tax cuts, and a decision by the Federal Reserve to lower interest rates preemptively—that is, to tolerate a higher inflation target if it meant that the lack of credit in the economy would be eased by the lower interest rates—could help the economy return to potential output.

FIGURE 25.8 Recovering from the Recession

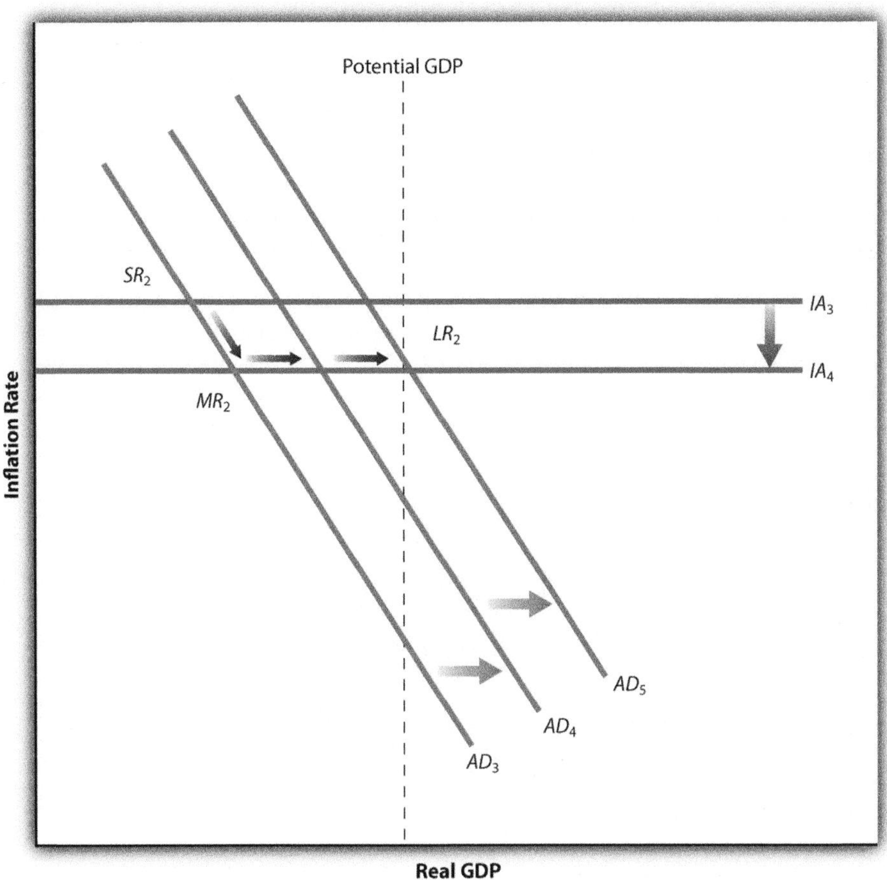

Figure 25.8 provides a graphic analysis of how these factors can be represented using the economic fluctuations model. The combination of falling commodity prices and the gradual fall in inflation over time as a result of the economy being below potential output will move the *IA* line down from the intersection of the *AD* curve and the *IA* line, labeled SR_2 (where the analysis in Figure 25.7 left off) to the new intersection shown as MR_2. The figure then shows two shifts out of the *AD* curve to the right as the Fed resorts to a large preemptive cut of interest rates and the government implements a stimulus package. The combination of these shifts moves real GDP back to potential GDP, shown on the diagram as LR_2.

The portrait of recovery laid out in Figure 25.8 does not actually match the experience of the U.S. economy, which was below potential output even at the end of 2016, over half a decade since the recession ended. This sluggish recovery can be attributed to the complexity of the macroeconomic challenges that the United States economy faced. Some of these complexities include the constraints imposed by the fact that nominal interest rates could not drop below zero, the doubts about the speed or extent of the economic impact of the nearly $1 trillion stimulus package, the fiscal constraints imposed by the contractionary policies that the Federal government adopted in 2013 because of political disagreements about the appropriate future path of U.S. fiscal policy or the complexities of rescuing the banking sector without rewarding the bad behavior that led to the crisis in the first place. Others factors include the rise of commodity prices in 2011/12, that the problems in the banking sector and the housing market needed time to sort themselves out because large numbers of homes were foreclosed on and remained unsold as property of the banks until three or four years after the recession had ended and because the workers who were in the sectors that bore the brunt of the recession in 2008/09 were not necessarily the same workers who benefited from the economic recovery. A 2016 study by the Council of Economic Advisers estimated that 10 million men had gone "missing" from the labor force because they had lost their jobs and were no longer looking for work presumably because the type of jobs that were available were not a good match for the skill and experience they had obtained in sectors of the economy that had lost jobs in the recession.

The disconnect between the description in Figure 25.8 and the experience of reality is a good reminder that being a good student of economics requires that one understand both the value and the limitations of a simplified model of the economy. A clear understanding of how the process *should* have worked is what enables us to better understand what the key factors were that impeded the recovery. This can help policymakers better deal with those more nuanced challenges in future recessions.

5. END-OF-CHAPTER MATERIAL

5.1 Conclusion

Using a diagram with the aggregate demand curve and the inflation adjustment line, we can explain not only the first steps toward recessions but also the economy's recovery. The model works well in explaining actual economic fluctuations and thus is useful for analyzing macroeconomic policy, as we do in Chapter 26 and Chapter 27.

This model implies that real GDP returns toward potential GDP in the long run, which is an attractive feature of the model because, in reality, all recessions have ended. Real GDP appears to fluctuate around potential GDP rather than getting stuck forever in a recession. The tendency for real GDP to return toward potential GDP allows us to use the theory of long-run growth when discussing long-run trends in the economy. As the economy fluctuates, potential GDP gradually increases over time.

Key Points

1. Using the economic fluctuations model is much like using the supply and demand model in microeconomics. You need to understand whether a particular line, as well as the direction in which the respective curves shift.
2. An increase in government purchases temporarily causes real GDP to rise, but eventually real GDP returns to potential GDP.
3. A decline in government purchases temporarily reduces real GDP, but over time, the economy recovers.
4. Shifts in monetary policy, including explicit attempts to disinflate or reinflate, cause real GDP to depart from potential GDP temporarily. Eventually, real GDP returns to potential GDP and only the inflation rate is changed.
5. Price shocks can cause recessions. A price shock that raises the inflation rate will cause the interest rate to rise and real GDP to fall.
6. If the Fed sets interest rates according to a monetary policy rule, then it will raise interest rates following a rise in inflation and eventually inflation will come back down.
7. If a price shock is clearly temporary, then the Fed should not change the interest rate.
8. Shifts of the aggregate demand curve and the inflation adjustment line trace out actual observations fairly closely. Thus, the economic fluctuations model works well, but, like most models in economics and elsewhere, it is not perfect.

QUESTIONS FOR REVIEW

1. What causes the economy to recover after a recession?
2. What is the difference between the long-run and short-run effects of a change in government spending?
3. What is disinflation, and how does the central bank bring it about?
4. What is reinflation, and what impact does it have on real GDP in the short run and the long run?
5. What is a price shock, and why have price shocks frequently been followed by increases in unemployment?
6. What is the difference between a price shock and a supply shock?
7. Why do monetary policy errors lead to economic fluctuations?
8. In what way is the economic fluctuations model discussed in this chapter consistent with real-world observations?

PROBLEMS

1. Using the aggregate demand curve and the inflation adjustment line, describe what would happen to real GDP and inflation in the short run, in the medium run, and in the long run if the government increased spending permanently. Assume that the economy was initially at potential output before the increase. Be sure to provide an economic explanation for your results.
2. Consider an economy that is at potential output. Using the aggregate demand curve and the inflation adjustment line, describe what would happen to real GDP and inflation in the short run, in the medium run, and in the long run if the government cut spending on defense. Be sure to provide an economic explanation for your results.
3. For each of the scenarios in Problems 1 and 2, describe what would happen to consumption, investment, and net exports in the short run and in the long run.
4. Suppose that an increase in government spending had the long-run effects that you described in Problem 1. If the central bank wants to return to the original inflation rate that existed before the increase, how can it achieve its objective? Describe the proposed change in policy and its short-run, medium-run, and long-run effects on real GDP and inflation.
5. Suppose gasoline prices increase sharply when the time comes for you to graduate. Use the economic fluctuations model to explain why you might have difficulty in finding a job in the six months after you graduate.
6. The economy begins at potential GDP with an inflation rate of 2 percent. Suppose a price shock pushes inflation up to 6 percent in the short run, but the Fed views the effect on inflation as temporary. It expects the inflation adjustment line to shift back down to 2 percent the next year, and in fact, the inflation adjustment line does shift back down.
   a. If the Fed follows its usual policy rule, where will real GDP be in the short run? How does the economy adjust back to potential?
   b. Now suppose that because the Fed is sure that this inflationary shock is only temporary, it decides not to follow its typical policy rule, but instead maintains the interest rate at its previous level. What happens to real GDP? Why? What will the long-run adjustment be in this case? Do you agree with the Fed's handling of the situation?
7. Suppose that two countries are similar except that one has a central bank with a higher target inflation rate. The two countries have identical potential GDP and are both at their long-run equilibrium. Explain this situation by using two diagrams with an aggregate demand curve and an inflation adjustment line. Explain how these different equilibrium levels of inflation are possible.
8. If U.S. productivity increases, what will happen to potential GDP? What will happen to the inflation rate?
9. Would an increase in government spending lead to a higher rate of inflation in the long run? Show that the answer depends on where the economy was, relative to potential GDP, before the increase.
10. China's economy has seen dramatic increases in investment, consumer spending, government expenditure on infrastructure, and exports to the United States and to Europe. Inflation in China, however, has remained fairly moderate. Explain why this may be the case using the aggregate demand curve and the inflation adjustment line.

ENDNOTES

1. Charles Dickens, *A Tale of Two Cities*.
2. http://dallasfed.org/assets/documents/research/staff/staff1301.pdf

CHAPTER 26

Fiscal Policy

Soon after Donald Trump's election, economic analysts began to use variations on the theme that his election signaled a change in economic policy. Some wrote about President Trump's proposals for a large infrastructure package; others wrote about proposals for tax cuts. Many articles pointed out that concerns about rising debt level in the aftermath of the 2008/09 recession in the United States and in Europe. Many had observed that much of the task of driving the recovery forward had been placed with monetary policy. Central banks all over the world had sharply lowered interest rates and in some cases, engaged in other unconventional practices after interest rates had gone as low as they could go. After so many years of monetary policy activism, the argument went, it was time for other types of policy to do their part.

However, the situations at the start of the Trump administration were very different from the challenges that the previous two administrations had faced a decade earlier. In response to the recession that began in December 2007 and ended in June 2009, Presidents George W. Bush and Barack Obama both proposed and Congress enacted countercyclical fiscal policy legislation with the express purpose of stimulating the economy. In February 2008 President Bush signed the $152 billion Economic Stimulus Act, which included direct payments to individuals and families so that they would increase consumption and thereby jump-start the economy. A year later President Barack Obama signed the much larger $787 billion American Recovery and Reinvestment Act of 2009, which included not only payments to individuals and families but also grants to the state and local governments to finance increased infrastructure and other spending.

Protesters rally against government tax and spending policies at the U.S. Capitol on September 12, 2009.

Source: Rena Schild / Shutterstock.com

Even though ostensibly aimed at helping the economy recover from recession, these fiscal policy packages generated substantial policy disagreements and controversy. Critics of the 2008 stimulus bill argued that people used at best a small fraction of the stimulus funds to increase consumption. Critics of the 2009 stimulus argued that the funds sent to the states were not used to increase infrastructure spending and thereby did not jump-start government purchases of goods and services. Proponents of the legislation argued that the recession would have been much worse without the fiscal policy actions.

Soon after these short-run stimulus packages were passed another fiscal policy issue took center stage: the large government budget deficits and growing federal debt. In part, because the payments to individuals or the grants to the states were financed by issuing more debt, the growing debt was caused by the stimulus packages. But the debt began before the recession when legislation was passed that implied increased spending in the future. Disagreements over debt reduction measures led to the 2013 budget sequester, whereby across-the-board spending cuts were adopted until and unless the Administration and Congress was able to resolve their disagreements and come up with a more sustainable policy moving forward. The across-the-board cuts were not what the economy needed in 2013, a time when unemployment was still high, the economy was still in the midst of a slow recovery, and more sustainable fiscal and monetary policies were called for.

The economic situation that the Trump administration faced in early 2017 was very different from the economic situation that the Obama administration faced in early 2009. How should that difference impact the types of fiscal policies that the Trump Administration should adopt? How does that difference affect the macroeconomic impact that these fiscal policies will have on the economy? How should an administration weigh the short-term impacts of fiscal policy against the longer-term impact on debt? In this chapter, we examine the economic theories and facts that bear on the controversies over short term countercyclical fiscal policy and the problem of long-term debt. We begin by reviewing how federal government decisions are made whether about spending, tax revenues, the deficit, or the debt.

1. THE GOVERNMENT BUDGET

federal budget

A summary of the federal government's proposals for spending, taxes, and the deficit.

The **federal budget** is the major document describing fiscal policy in the United States. The budget includes the estimates of the surplus or deficit that gets so much attention as well as proposals for taxes and spending. Let's look at how the federal budget in the United States is put together.

1.1 Setting the Annual Budget

In the United States, the president submits a new budget to Congress each year for the following fiscal year. The fiscal year runs from October to October. For example, *The Budget of the United States: Fiscal Year 2017* applies to spending and taxes from October 1, 2016, through September 30, 2017. It was submitted to Congress by the president in February 2016. The president typically devotes part of the State of the Union address to describing the budget and fiscal policy. Also at the start of each year, the Council of Economic Advisers (CEA) prepares and releases the *Economic Report of the President*, providing the economic forecasts underlying the budget. The Congressional Budget Office (CBO) makes its own economic forecasts.

In putting together the federal budget, the president proposes specific spending programs that fit into an overall philosophy of what the government should be doing. In any one year, however, most of the spending in the budget is determined by ongoing programs, which the president usually can do little to change. For example, payments of social security benefits to retired people are a large item in the budget, but the amount of spending on social security depends on how many people are eligible. As more people retire, spending automatically goes up unless the social security law is changed. Thus, in reality, the president can change only a small part of the budget each year, unless new legislation is passed.

A Balanced Budget versus a Deficit or Surplus

Taxes to pay for the spending programs also are included in the budget. As part of the budget, the president may propose an increase or a decrease in taxes. *Tax revenues* are the total dollar amount the government receives from taxpayers each year. When tax revenues are exactly equal to spending, there is a **balanced budget**. When tax revenues are greater than spending, there is a **budget surplus**. When spending is greater than tax revenues, there is a **budget deficit**, and the government must borrow to pay the difference.

balanced budget

A budget in which tax revenues equal spending.

budget surplus

The amount by which tax revenues exceed government spending.

budget deficit

The amount by which government spending exceeds tax revenues.

Budget Deficit	Budget Balance	Budget Surplus
Tax revenues < spending	Tax revenues = spending	Tax revenues > spending

The Proposed Budget versus the Actual Budget

Keep in mind that the budget the president submits is only a *proposal*. The actual amounts of tax revenues and spending during the fiscal year are quite different from what is proposed. There are two main reasons for this difference.

First, Congress usually modifies the president's budget, adding programs and deleting others. Congress deliberates on the specific items in the president's budget proposal for months before the fiscal year actually starts. After the president's budget has been debated and modified, it is passed by Congress. Only when the president signs the legislation is the budget enacted into law. Because of this congressional modification, the enacted budget is always different from the proposed budget. Figure 26.1 shows the budget moving from a proposal to completion. The same budget cycle occurs every year, but it does not always progress smoothly. In many years the president and Congress do not settle on a budget until well into the fiscal year.

Second, because of changes in the economy and other unanticipated events such as wars and natural disasters, the actual amounts of spending and taxes will be different from what is enacted. After the fiscal year has begun and the budget has been enacted, various *supplementals* are proposed and passed. A supplemental is a change in a spending program or a change in the tax law that affects the budget in the current fiscal year.

Reminder: Note the difference between tax rate and tax revenues. For the income tax, if the average tax rate is 20 percent and income is $3,000 billion, then tax revenues are $600 billion.

FIGURE 26.1 A Typical Budget Cycle

The budget cycle begins well before the fiscal year begins. After considering various spending and tax options, the president submits a budget proposal to the Congress in February. The cycle is not complete until the end of the fiscal year. By then, a new budget is being enacted.

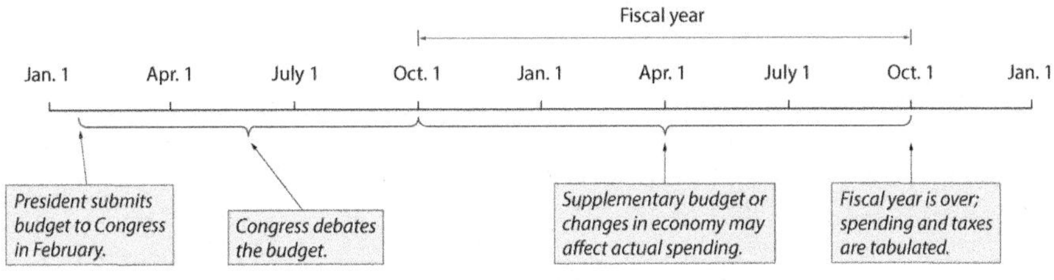

1.2 A Look at the Federal Budget

Table 26.1 contains a summary of tax revenues and expenditure for the federal budget for fiscal year 2017.

The Deficit

Table 26.1 shows more expenditures than tax revenues, so there is a deficit. Budget deficits have been common in the United States for many years, although 1998 to 2001 were years of surplus. Deficits are projected to continue in the future unless government programs change. Figure 26.2 shows the deficit in recent years and projections into the future. It also shows tax revenue and spending.

Taxes and Spending

Sources of tax revenue include *personal income taxes* paid by individuals on their total income, *corporate income taxes* paid by businesses on their profits, and *payroll taxes*, a percentage of wages paid by workers and their employers that supports government programs such as social security. Payroll taxes provide a large amount of revenues, nearly as much as personal income tax revenues.

On the expenditure side of the budget, one must distinguish between *purchases* of goods and services (such as defense), *transfer payments* (such as social security and Medicare and Medicaid), and *interest payments*. Only purchases are included in the symbol *G* that we have been using in the text. Purchases represent *new* production, whether of computers, federal courthouses, or food for military troops.

TABLE 26.1 FY 2017 Federal Tax Revenues and Expenditures (billions of dollars)

Tax revenues	3,644	
Personal income		1,788
Corporate income		419
Payroll		1,081
Other		356
Expenditures	4,147	
Social security		967
Medicare		598
Medicaid		386
Defense		608
Interest		303
Other		1,285
Deficit	503	

Source: Office of Management and Budget.

Interest payments are what the federal government pays every year on its debt. The government pays interest on its borrowings just like anyone else. Total interest payments equal the interest rate multiplied by the amount of government debt outstanding. For example, if the interest rate on government debt is 5 percent and total outstanding debt held by the public is $5,000 billion, then interest payments would be $250 billion (0.05 x $5,000).

FIGURE 26.2 **Federal Tax Revenues, Expenditures, and the Surplus or Deficit 2000–2016**

The surplus turned to deficit in 2002 as tax revenues fell while spending continued to increase. After nearly reaching a surplus in 2007, the deficit then grew larger as spending rose and tax revenues fell in the 2007–2009 recession. Since the recession ended, the gap between expenditures and revenue has closed somewhat.

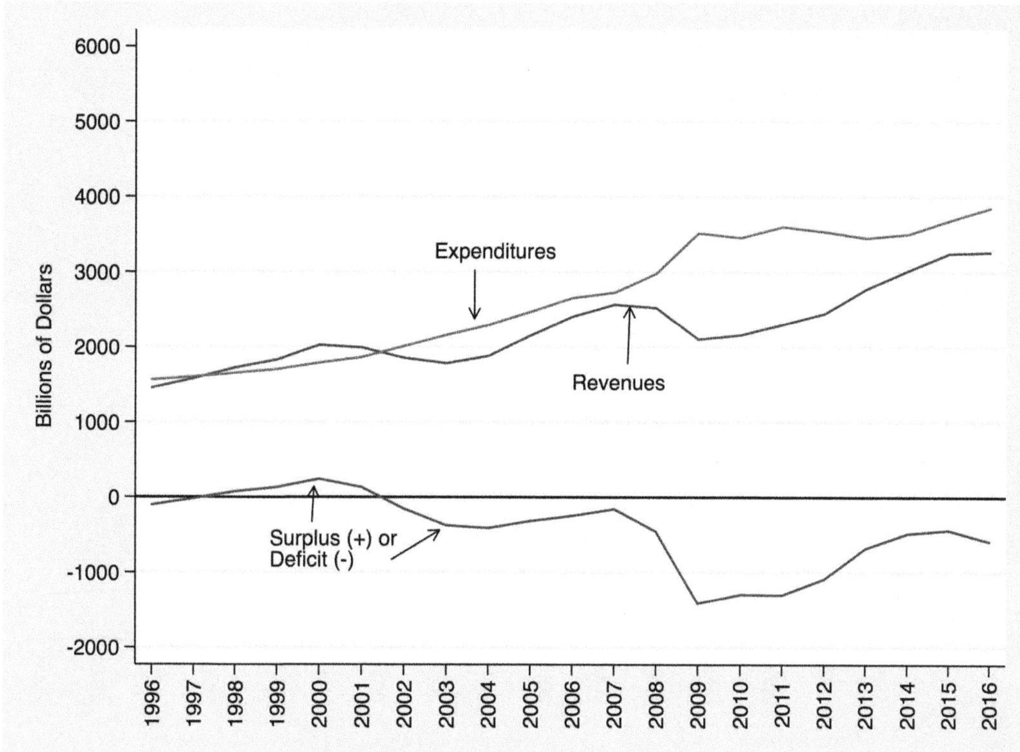

A significant part of the budget—nearly 50 percent—consists of social security, Medicare, and Medicaid. Social security and Medicare provide income and health care for the elderly, and Medicaid provides health care for people and families with very low incomes. Under current law, federal spending is projected to grow rapidly because of the increase in spending on these programs as the baby boomers retire and then live longer, and spending on health care increases. If Congress and the president do not change the law to either reduce the growth of spending or increase tax revenue, then the federal deficit will grow much larger in the future.

1.3 The Federal Debt

The **federal debt** is the total amount of outstanding loans that the federal government owes. If the government runs a surplus, the debt comes down by the amount of the surplus. If the government has a deficit, the debt goes up by the amount of the deficit.

federal debt

The total amount of outstanding loans owed by the federal government.

Consider an example involving thousands of dollars rather than trillions of dollars. Think of a student, Sam, who graduates from college with a $14,000 outstanding loan. In other words, he has a debt of $14,000. Suppose that the first year he works, his income is $30,000, but he spends $35,000. Sam's deficit for that year is $5,000, and his debt rises to $19,000. Assume that in his second year of work, he has an income of $35,000 and spends $38,000; his deficit is $3,000, and his debt rises to $22,000. Each year his debt rises by the amount of his deficit. In the third year, Sam earns $40,000 and spends $33,000; he has a surplus of $7,000. This would reduce his debt to $15,000.

The laws of accounting that we apply to Sam also apply to Uncle Sam. A federal government deficit of $1 trillion means that the outstanding government debt increases by $1 trillion. Figure 26.3 shows the debt along with the deficit in the United States for three decades. The first two decades are history as tabulated by federal government economists. The years from 2017 to 2026 are forecasts made by government economists in 2016.

FIGURE 26.3 The Government Debt and Deficit

When there is a deficit, the debt increases. When there is a surplus, the debt falls. After a brief period in which government debt fell in the early 2000s, debt has grown steadily in the past 15 years.

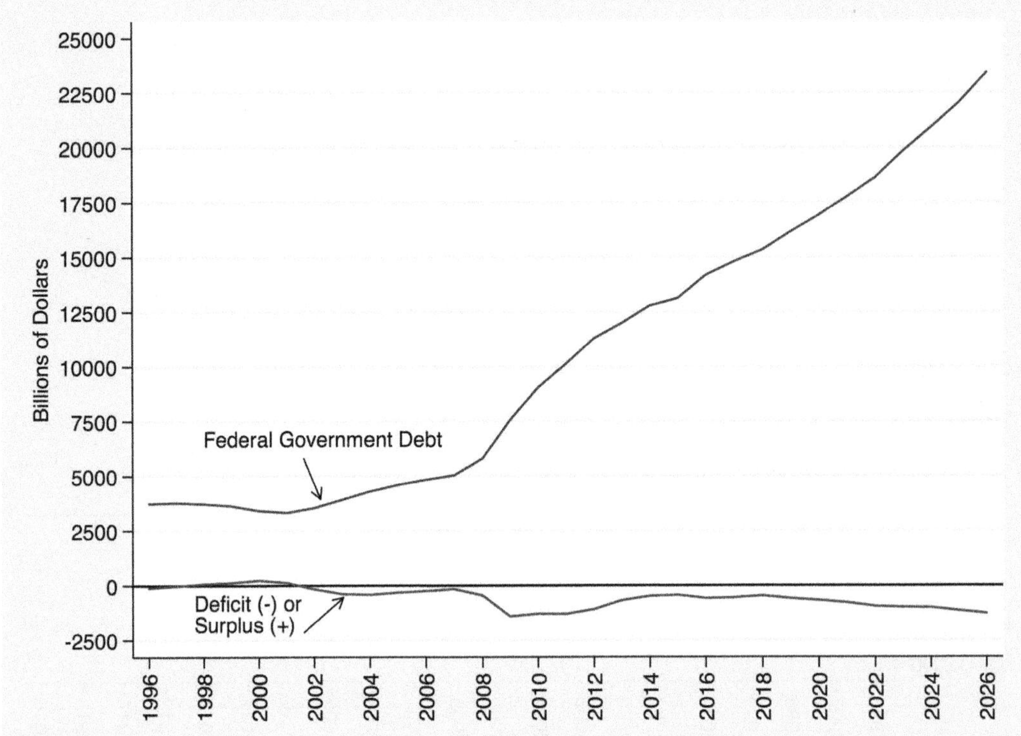

For most of these years the debt increases because there are deficits. Observe, however, that the debt declined in 2000 and 2001 when there was a surplus. The debt then started increasing again. It rose particularly sharply during the 2007–2009 recession, but it has continued to rise after the recession ended and is projected to continue increasing in the future.

If Congress and the president do not change the law to either reduce the growth of spending or increase tax revenue, then the federal deficit will remain and the debt will continue to grow rapidly. As the debt grows, interest payments on the debt also will grow and absorb an ever larger share of the spending, leaving a smaller share for government to provide public goods and a social safety net.

As the government debt increases other problems occur. History shows that governments with high debt are prone to financial crises, which has been evident in Greece in recent years as many Americans have noticed. In fact, excessive debt in Greece, Ireland, Portugal, and Spain put the whole of Europe into a financial crisis. One concern is that holders of the debt lose confidence and refuse to continue financing the deficit. From the time of the first U.S. secretary of the treasury, Alexander Hamilton, the United States has established a strong reputation for paying its debts, but that credibility could decline if actions are not taken to control the growth of the debt. In addition, because foreign governments hold nearly one-half of the federal debt, people are concerned that they suddenly might sell the debt and cause an international crisis. Because of these concerns, interest has been renewed in dealing with the problem and politicians in Washington have begun to look for solutions.

The Debt-to-GDP Ratio

debt-to-GDP ratio

The total amount of outstanding loans the federal government owes divided by nominal GDP.

When looking at the debt and the deficit over time, it is important to consider the size of the economy. For example, a $3 trillion debt may not be much of a problem for an economy with a gross domestic product (GDP) of $10 trillion but could be overwhelming for an economy with a GDP of $1 trillion. An easy way to compare the debt to the size of the economy is to measure the debt as a percentage of GDP—the **debt-to-GDP ratio**. It is appropriate to consider the ratio of debt to nominal GDP rather than real GDP because the debt is stated in current dollars, just as nominal GDP is.

FIGURE 26.4 Debt as a Percentage of GDP

The debt history since the founding of the United States is shown along with future projections by the CBO. Debt as a percentage of GDP normally has increased in major war periods, such as World War II, but then declined as the deficit is reduced and GDP grows. The projection is made under the assumption that the federal law for Medicare, social security, and taxes as of 2016 does not change.

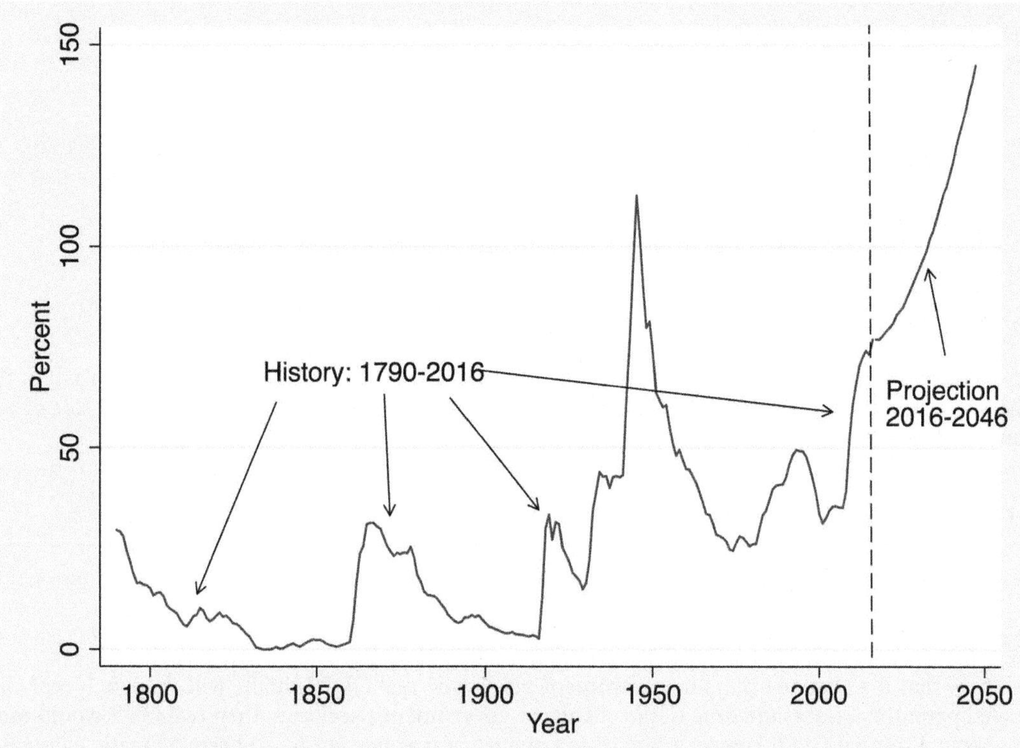

Figure 26.4 shows the history of the debt as a percentage of GDP in the United States since 1795 and projections by the CBO into the future. Note that the debt was a high percentage of GDP at the end of World War II because the U.S. government had borrowed large amounts to finance its military expenditures during the war. The debt-to-GDP ratio rose in the 1980s and then leveled off and fell in the 1990s, but it began to increase again when deficits returned, particularly in the years surrounding the 2008/09 recession. Unless budget reforms are put in place, the debt will explode in the future.

1.4 State and Local Government Budgets

Much of the government spending and taxation in the United States occurs outside of the federal government, in state and local governments. Although fiscal policy usually refers to the plans of the federal government, it is the combined action of federal, state, and local governments that has an impact on the overall economy. For example, during the 2008–2009 recession, many states cut back on spending, which would tend to reduce real GDP in the short run, just as reduced spending at the federal level would. The 2009 stimulus bill included hundreds of billions in assistance to state or local governments intended to ward off cuts. Taken as a whole, state and local governments are a large force in the economy. In 2016 state and local government expenditures were about two-thirds of federal government expenditures.

Most of the state and local government expenditures are for public schools, local police, fire services, and roads. Observe that state and local government purchases of goods and services are larger than federal government purchases, especially when national defense is excluded.

Like the federal government, the state and local governments, on average, have been running deficits after a few years of surpluses in the late 1990s. These deficits worsened dramatically during the 2008 recession.

REVIEW

- In the United States, the president submits a budget to Congress giving proposals for spending, for taxes, and for the deficit or surplus. The actual budget is different from the proposed budget because of congressional modifications and unforeseen events like unusually fast or slow economic growth.
- A budget surplus occurs when spending is less than tax revenues. Deficits occur when spending exceeds revenues.
- When a government or individual runs a deficit, the debt increases. Surpluses reduce the debt.
- It is appropriate to consider the debt in relation to the size of the economy by measuring it as a percentage of GDP.
- Federal government expenditures are larger than state or local government expenditures, but state and local government purchases are larger than federal government purchases.

2. COUNTERCYCLICAL FISCAL POLICY

Government spending and taxes are called the *instruments* of fiscal policy. They are the variables that affect the economy. Now let's see how changes in the instruments of fiscal policy affect the size of economic fluctuations.

2.1 Impacts of the Instruments of Fiscal Policy

We first consider a change in government purchases and then go on to consider a change in taxes.

Changes in Government Purchases

We know that if a change occurs in government purchases, real GDP initially will change. If real GDP equaled potential GDP at the time of the change in government purchases, then real GDP would move away from potential GDP. Hence, a first lesson about fiscal policy is "do no harm." Erratic changes in government purchases can lead to fluctuations of real GDP away from potential GDP.

But suppose real GDP was already away from potential GDP. Then the change in government purchases could move real GDP closer to potential GDP. This is shown in Figure 26.5. In the top panel, real GDP starts out below potential GDP. An increase in government purchases shifts the aggregate demand curve to the right and moves real GDP back toward potential GDP. In the bottom panel, real GDP is above potential GDP, and a decrease in government purchases shifts the aggregate demand curve to the left, bringing real GDP back toward potential GDP. The important point is that a change in government purchases shifts the aggregate demand curve from wherever it happens to be at the time of the change.

Remember that these government purchases will make a difference for real GDP only in the short term. Had the government not intervened, prices eventually would have adjusted; consumption, investment, and net exports would have changed; and real GDP would have returned to potential GDP, albeit with a lower inflation rate in the top panel of Figure 26.5, and a higher inflation rate in the bottom panel. The short-term effect, however, may have partially offset a temporary decline in aggregate demand in a recession. So the short-run impacts of government purchases provide fiscal policy with the potential power to reduce the size of economic fluctuations.

FIGURE 26.5 Effect of a Change in Government Purchases

If real GDP is below potential GDP, as in the top panel, an increase in government purchases, which shifts the *AD* curve to the right, will move real GDP toward potential GDP. If real GDP is above potential GDP, as in the bottom panel, a decrease in government purchases will move real GDP toward potential GDP. These are short-run effects.

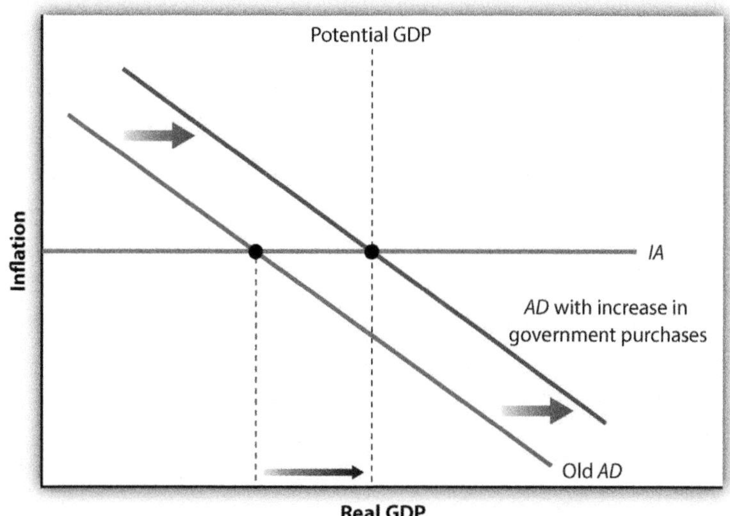

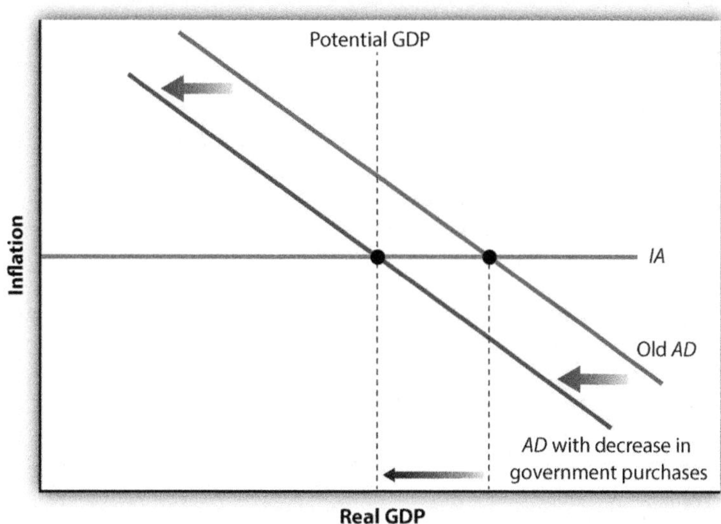

An increase in government purchases on roads and bridges is one example of how changes in government spending could affect investment and therefore impact potential GDP in the long run. But, for now, we focus on how the government can move the economy closer to potential GDP, rather than on how it can move potential GDP through fiscal policy changes.

Changes in Taxes

A change in taxes also affects real GDP in the short run. At any given level of real GDP, people will consume less if taxes increase because they have less income to spend after taxes. They will consume more if taxes are cut. In either case, the aggregate demand curve will shift. The top panel of Figure 26.6 shows how a tax cut will shift the aggregate demand curve to the right and push real GDP closer to potential GDP if it is below potential GDP. The bottom panel shows a tax increase reducing real GDP from a position above potential GDP. Again, these are short-term effects. Prices eventually will adjust and real GDP will return to potential GDP.

Both increases and decreases in taxes also can affect potential GDP. For example, if an increase in tax rates causes some people to work less, then the labor supply will not be as large and potential GDP will be lower. Again, our focus here is on the departures of real GDP from potential GDP.

2.2 Countercyclical Fiscal Policy

countercyclical policy

A policy designed to offset the fluctuations in the business cycle.

As the analysis in Figure 26.5 and Figure 26.6 shows, fiscal policy, in principle, can offset the impact of shocks that push real GDP away from potential GDP because government spending and taxes affect real GDP in the short run. Such use of fiscal policy is called **countercyclical policy**, because the cyclical movements in the economy are being "countered," or offset, by changes in government spending or taxes. Recessions can be countered by cuts in taxes or increases in spending. The stimulus package of 2009 was a good example of a countercyclical fiscal policy—a $787 billion package of government spending increases and tax cuts that aimed to help the U.S. economy recover from a deep recession by increasing real GDP and moving the economy closer to potential output.

FIGURE 26.6 **Effects of a Change in Taxes**

A decrease in taxes shifts the *AD* curve to the right and can move real GDP toward potential GDP, as in the top panel. An increase in taxes moves real GDP toward potential GDP in the lower panel.

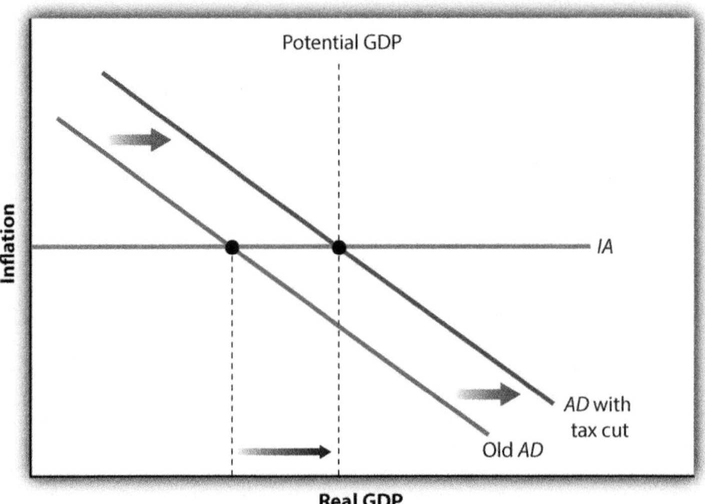

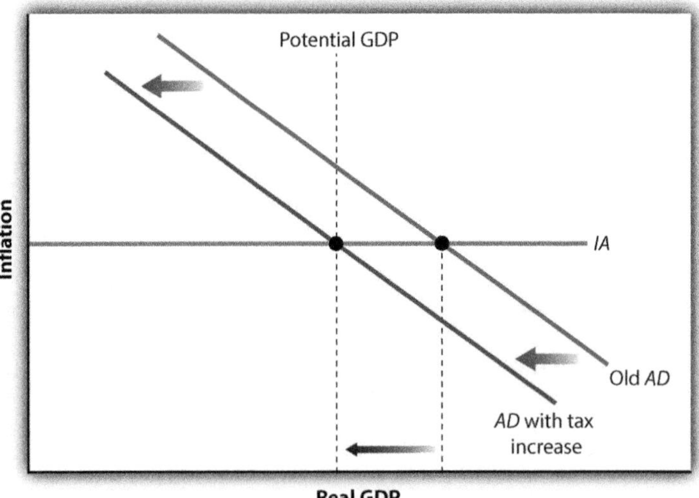

But why would such an intervention be controversial? Clearly, Republicans and Democrats disagreed strongly about the 2009 stimulus package with only three Republican senators and no Republican members of the House of Representatives voting in favor of the bill. Similar vigorous debates were conducted among economists through newspaper op-ed columns, blog posts, and television appearances. Well-known economists like Paul Krugman were strongly in support of the plan as being exactly what the ailing economy needed, while equally well-known economists like Eugene Fama and Robert Barro were just as confident that the bill would do little for the economy compared with the long-term budgetary costs it would impose on the United States.

Clearly, then, our analysis needs to be more sophisticated than what was presented in Figure 26.5 and Figure 26.6, or else we would have no tools with which to evaluate the arguments made by the proponents and opponents of the stimulus package. The analysis presented in Figure 26.7 through Figure 26.9 provides the detail needed to understand the arguments on both sides, given the economic circumstances that prevailed at the time the stimulus package was being debated in 2009.

Figure 26.7 shows what a stimulus policy ideally would do. A deep recession in 2009 is shown. Without any change in government purchases or taxes, the economy would have eventually recovered, as shown in the figure, even though the recovery may have taken several years. But suppose the government implemented the $787 billion stimulus plan with its mix of spending on infrastructure, aid to state governments so they can provide money to the poor to purchase food and utilities, and tax cuts that increase consumer spending. If these policies were put into place immediately, they would have raised real GDP, as shown in the figure, and hastened the return to potential GDP.

FIGURE 26.7 **Effects of a Well-Timed Countercyclical Fiscal Policy**

The figure shows a likely path of recovery from a recession caused by a decline in demand for U.S. products. A well-timed cut in taxes or increase in government purchases can reduce the size of the recession and bring real GDP back to potential GDP more quickly. The size of the economic fluctuation is smaller. The analysis is shown in Figure 14.8.

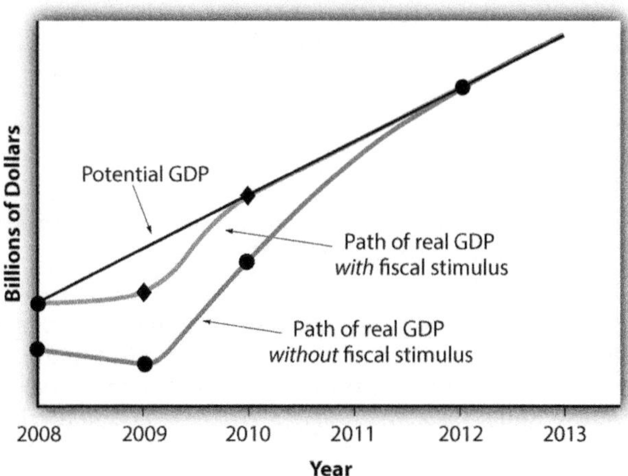

FIGURE 26.8 Analysis of a Well-Timed Countercyclical Fiscal Policy

A decline in demand shifts the *AD* curve to the left. Without a countercyclical fiscal policy, real GDP recovers back to potential GDP, but a timely cut in taxes or an increase in government purchases can offset the drop in demand and bring real GDP back to potential GDP more quickly.

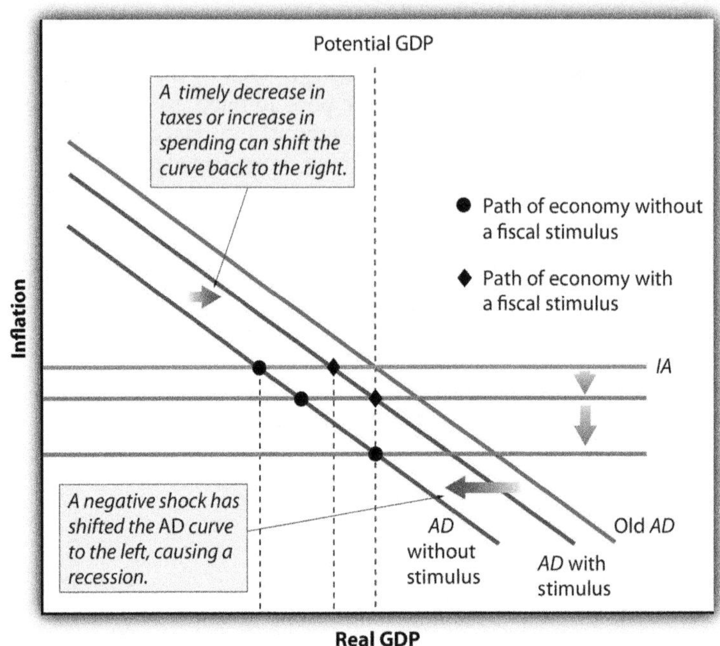

How would this work when prices are adjusting and when the inflation rate is changing as well? Figure 26.8 provides the analysis. The recession is caused by the leftward shift in the aggregate demand curve. But the cut in taxes or increase in spending shifts the aggregate demand curve in the opposite direction. The aggregate demand curve shifts back to the right. If these countercyclical measures are timely enough and if they are of the appropriate magnitude—both big ifs—then the recession may be small and short-lived. The example shows real GDP falling only slightly below potential GDP.

Figure 26.9 shows two less ideal cases that reflects the arguments of some of the critics. Some critics argued that too few of the projects targeted by the stimulus bill were ready to be implemented immediately, so it took a year or two before they were enacted. Furthermore, the critics argued that consumers will be reluctant to increase spending even if they receive tax cuts either because the cuts are temporary or because consumers are concerned about what will happen to their taxes in the future when the government has to repay the money it borrowed to implement the stimulus bill. If government purchases are increased, but the response is too late, and if consumer spending does not respond immediately to the tax cuts, the outcome in terms of real GDP may not be much better than in the absence of stimulus, as shown in Figure 26.9. Given the substantial budgetary cost, this would imply that the stimulus was a worse option than doing nothing at all in terms of countercyclical fiscal policy. It also is possible that if the bulk of the spending projects in the stimulus package kick in after the economy has begun to recover on its own, the excessive growth in aggregate demand will cause inflation to increase.

Other critics argued that the stimulus bill was insufficient both in terms of its initial magnitude (some economists had called for a trillion dollar fiscal stimulus) but also in terms of how long it lasted—the bulk of the stimulus package was enacted in the first couple of years after the recession. Because spending in the rest of the economy was slow to recover from the recession, in hindsight it seems like a fiscal policy that was better targeted, longer-lasting and of greater magnitude could have helped boost the recovery. However, it is always easier to make these assessments with the benefit of hindsight. As the previous case shows, a fiscal policy could just as easily have lasted too long and caused inflation instead of lasting too short to be effective. Furthermore, providing the economy with more tax cuts that consumers are reluctant to spend and increasing government spending in ways that raise consumer fears about rising government debt would not help but in fact hurt the economy.

Disagreements about the usefulness of fiscal policy boil down to an assessment of whether the scenario in Figure 26.7 or in Figure 26.9 is more likely. Let's first consider some examples from recent history that may guide us in assessing which path is more likely.

Discretionary Change in the Instruments of Fiscal Policy

Discretionary fiscal policy refers to specific changes in laws or administrative procedures, such as a change in an existing program to speed up spending, the creation of a new program (such as a new welfare program), or a change in the tax system (such as lower tax rates). These changes in the law are discretionary changes because they require action on the part of the Congress or the president.

discretionary fiscal policy

Changes in tax or spending policy requiring legislative or administrative action by the president or Congress.

FIGURE 26.9 Effects of a Poorly Timed Fiscal Policy

Here, in contrast to Figure 14.7, the fiscal stimulus comes too late, when the economy is already recovering, possibly leading to an increase in inflation or it was insufficient, delaying the economy's return to potential GDP.

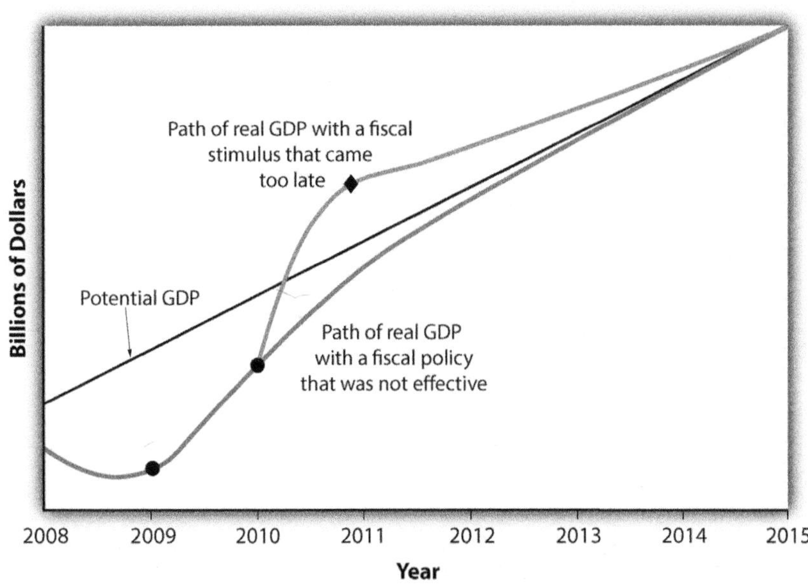

One of the most significant post–World War II discretionary fiscal policy actions was the tax cut proposed by President John F. Kennedy in 1963 and enacted after his death when Lyndon Johnson was president. The early 1960s were a period when real GDP was below potential GDP, and this large discretionary tax cut was a factor in speeding the economic recovery. This cut in taxes probably also stimulated the growth of potential GDP and therefore was good for the long run.

More recent examples of discretionary fiscal policies include the Economic Growth and Tax Relief Reconciliation Act, enacted by Congress in June 2001. One part of the plan was a $300 ($600 for couples) rebate check that the government mailed to eligible taxpayers in the summer of 2001. Some economists argue that the tax cut was helpful in raising spending during the recession, although, because of its temporary nature, the extent to which it helped is the source of some debate among economists.

The tax component of the 2009 stimulus package signed into law by President Obama is similar to the tax cut–based stimulus bill signed into law early in 2008 by President Bush. As Figure 26.10 suggests, these temporary increases in disposable income did little or nothing to stimulate consumption demand, and thereby aggregate demand, or the economy.

Figure 26.10 illustrates the economic impact of the temporary payments in 2008 and in 2009. The upper line shows U.S. disposable personal income, which is income after taxes and government transfers; it therefore includes the temporary payments from the government. Notice the sharp increase in disposable personal income in May 2008, when checks were mailed or deposited in people's bank accounts. Disposable personal income then started to come down in June and July as total payments declined and by August had returned to the trend that was prevailing in April.

The lower line in Figure 26.10 is personal consumption expenditures over the same period. Observe that consumption shows no noticeable increase at the time of the rebate. As the picture illustrates, the temporary rebate apparently did little to stimulate consumption demand, and thereby aggregate demand, or the economy.

FIGURE 26.10 Income and Consumption during the Two Discretionary Stimulus Programs

The 2008 and 2009 stimulus programs raised disposable personal income as checks were sent to people. The purpose was to jump-start consumption and stimulate aggregate demand. According to the data shown in this chart, consumption did not show an obvious increase as a result of these programs. Economists who view the programs as effective argue that consumption would have declined more without the programs. The Cash for Clunkers program was a program offered in the summer of 2009 that offered subsidies from $3,500 to $4,500 to people who purchased new cars if they agreed to trade in their old gas-guzzling clunker.

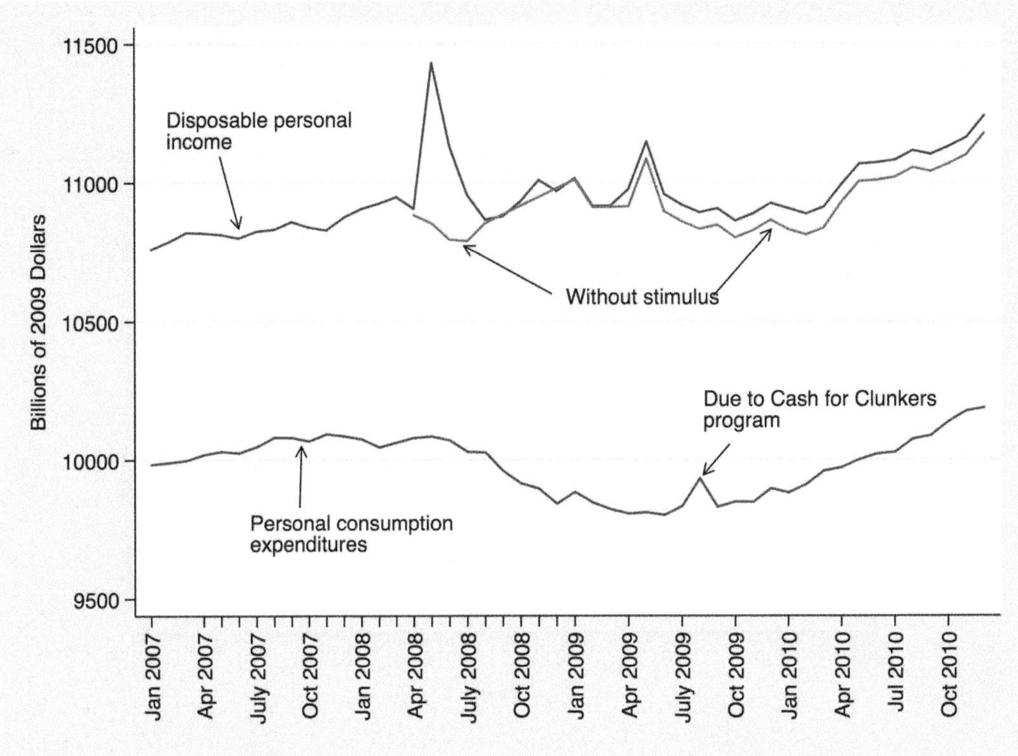

What could explain this discrepancy between what was predicted by our model and the empirical reality? One possibility—though difficult to prove—is simply that consumption would have fallen further without the program. The permanent income model of consumption is a more likely explanation. It implies that consumers respond less to changes in income that are temporary compared with more lasting changes. If so, the magnitude of the outward shift of the *AD* curve in response to a tax cut depends very much on whether the tax cut is permanent or temporary. Temporary tax rebates would have little impact on consumer spending.

Figure 26.10 also casts some doubt on the success of the temporary tax and transfer provisions of the 2009 stimulus bill. Although the increase in disposable income was smaller, it was spread out over more time. Still, it is difficult to see an effect on consumption. Again we can't rule out the possibility that consumption would have fallen further if not for the tax cuts and transfer payments associated with the program.

Automatic Changes in the Instruments of Fiscal Policy

Discretionary actions by the government are not the only way in which taxes and spending can be changed. In fact, many of the very large changes in taxes and spending are automatic. Income tax revenues expand when people are making more and fall when people are making less. Thus, tax revenues respond automatically to the economy. Tax payments rise when the economy is in a boom and more people are working. Tax revenues fall when the economy is in a slump and unemployment rises.

These changes in tax revenues are even larger with a progressive income tax. With a *progressive tax system*, individual tax payments *rise* as a proportion of income as income increases. With a progressive tax, a person earning $100,000 per year pays proportionately more in taxes than a person earning $20,000 per year. Because of this progressive tax system, as people earn more, they pay a higher tax rate, and when they earn less, they pay a lower tax rate.

Parts of government spending also change automatically. Unemployment compensation, through which the government makes payments to individuals who are unemployed, rises during a recession. When unemployment rises, so do payments to unemployed workers. Social security payments also increase in a recession because people may retire earlier if job prospects are bad. Welfare payments rise in a recession because people who are unemployed for a long period of time may qualify for welfare. As poverty rates rise in recessions, welfare payments increase.

These automatic tax and spending changes are called automatic stabilizers because they tend to stabilize the fluctuations of real GDP. How significant are these **automatic stabilizers**? Consider the 2001 recession, when discretionary fiscal stimulus was quite small. Real GDP in 1999 and 2000 was above potential GDP. But by late 2001 and 2002, real GDP was dropping below potential GDP. As this happened, government spending went up and taxes went down.

automatic stabilizers

Automatic tax and spending changes that occur over the course of the business cycle that tend to stabilize the fluctuations in real GDP.

The magnitude of these effects was quite large. The difference between proposed and actual taxes and spending in the 2002 budget provides an estimate of the effect of the recession on taxes and spending. Tax revenue was $336 billion less than had been proposed before the recession. Thus, taxes were reduced automatically by this amount. Spending, however, was $50 billion more than had been proposed before the recession. Thus, spending rose by $50 billion in response to the recession. The combined effect of a $336 billion reduction in taxes and a $50 billion increase in spending was vital in keeping the recovery going. Because tax receipts went down in the recession and transfer payments went up, people's consumption was at a higher level than it otherwise would have been. These automatic changes in tax revenues and government spending tended to stabilize the economy and probably made the recession less severe than it otherwise would have been. These changes did not completely offset other factors, however, because there still was a recession.

2.3 The Discretion versus Rules Debate for Fiscal Policy

For many years, economists have debated the usefulness of discretionary and automatic fiscal policy. Automatic fiscal policy is an example of a fiscal policy rule describing how the instruments of fiscal policy respond to the state of the economy. Thus, the debate is sometimes called the "discretion versus rules" debate.

Proponents of discretionary fiscal policy argue that the automatic stabilizers will not be large enough or well timed enough to bring the economy out of a recession quickly. Critics of the discretionary policy emphasize that the effect of policy is uncertain and that the impact of policy has long lags. By the time spending increases and taxes are cut, a recession could be over; if so, the policy would only lead to an overshooting of potential GDP and an increase in inflation. Three types of lags are particularly problematic for discretionary fiscal policy: a recognition lag, the time between the need for the policy and the recognition of the need; an implementation lag, the time between the recognition of the need for the policy and its implementation; and an impact lag, the time between the implementation of the policy and its impact on real GDP.

Although lags and uncertainty continue to contribute to the discretion versus rules debate, other issues have become central. Many economists feel that policy rules are desirable because of their stability and reliability. A fiscal policy rule emphasizing the automatic stabilizers might make government plans to reduce the deficit more believable. Countercyclical fiscal policy raises the deficit or reduces the surplus during recessions. With discretionary policy, nothing guarantees that the surplus will return or increase after the recession. With an automatic policy rule, the expectation is that the deficit will decline after the recession is over.

REVIEW

- Countercyclical fiscal policy is undertaken by governments to reduce economic fluctuations. The aim is to keep real GDP closer to potential GDP.
- Two types of countercyclical fiscal policy are (1) discretionary policy, such as the 2008 and the 2009 stimulus bills, and (2) automatic stabilizers, such as changes in unemployment payments, social security payments, and tax revenues resulting from changes in people's incomes.

3. THE STRUCTURAL VERSUS THE CYCLICAL SURPLUS

We noted earlier that taxes and spending change automatically in recessions and recoveries. These automatic changes affect the budget, so to analyze the budget, it is important to separate out these automatic effects. The structural, or full-employment, surplus was designed for this purpose. The **structural surplus** is what the surplus would be if real GDP equaled potential GDP.

Figure 26.11 introduces a graph to explain the structural surplus. On the horizontal axis is real GDP. On the vertical axis is the budget surplus: tax revenues less expenditures. The budget is balanced when the surplus is zero, which is marked by a horizontal line in the diagram. The region below zero represents a situation in which taxes are less than spending and the government has a deficit. The region above zero is a situation in which the government budget has a surplus. On the horizontal axis, *A*, *B*, and *C* represent three different levels of real GDP.

FIGURE 26.11 The Effect of Real GDP on the Budget

When real GDP falls, the budget moves toward deficit because spending rises and tax receipts fall. When real GDP is at point *A*, there is a deficit; at point *B*, the budget is balanced; and at point *C*, there is a budget surplus.

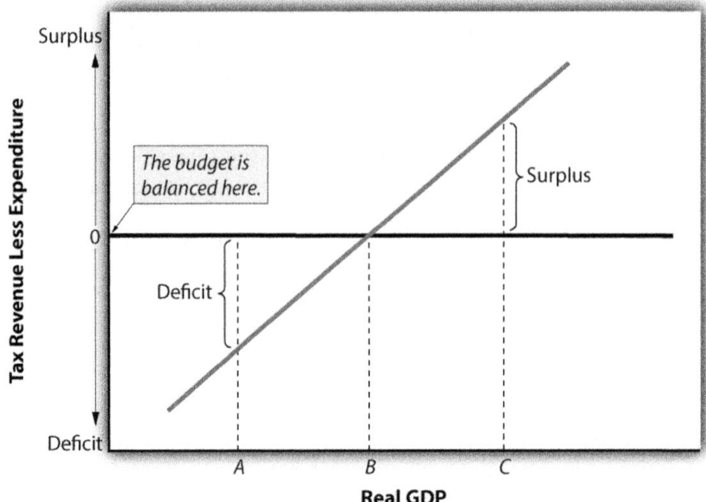

The upward-sloping line in Figure 26.11 indicates that as real GDP rises, the budget surplus gets larger. Why? The automatic stabilizers are the reason. When real GDP rises, tax revenues rise and spending on transfer programs falls. Because the surplus is the difference between tax revenues and spending, the surplus gets larger. Conversely, when real GDP falls, tax receipts decline and spending on transfer programs increases, so the surplus falls. The upward-sloping line in Figure 26.11 pertains to a particular set of government programs and tax laws. A change in these programs or laws would shift the line. For example, a decrease in tax rates would shift the line down.

FIGURE 26.12 The Structural Surplus versus the Actual Surplus in a Recession Year

The surplus that occurs when real GDP is equal to potential GDP is called the structural surplus, as shown in the figure. The actual surplus falls below the structural surplus when real GDP falls below potential GDP. If the recession is big, an actual deficit could result even with a structural surplus.

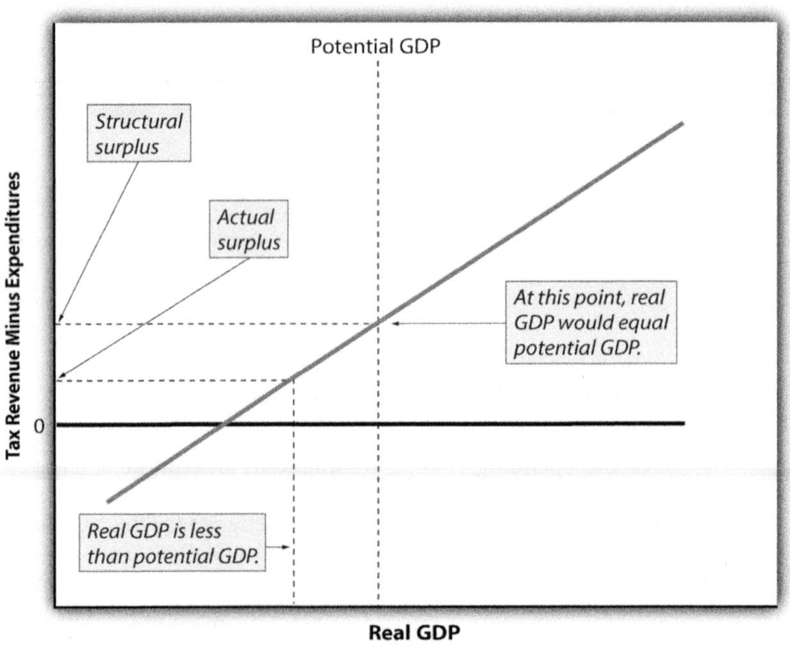

Figure 26.12, a similar diagram, shows potential GDP and real GDP in a year when real GDP is below potential GDP. Imagine raising real GDP up to potential GDP. We would predict that the surplus would go up, because tax receipts would rise as the economy grew and transfer payments would go down because fewer people would be unemployed, fewer people would be retiring, and fewer people would be on welfare. As we move to the right in the diagram, the surplus gets larger. The structural surplus occurs when real GDP equals potential GDP. The structural surplus provides a way to separate out cyclical changes in the budget caused by cyclical changes in the economy.

REVIEW

- Because tax revenues and spending fluctuate as the economy fluctuates, the surplus, or deficit, is cyclical. Deficits frequently arise or get bigger in recessions.
- The structural surplus adjusts the actual surplus for these cyclical changes in the economy.

4. END-OF-CHAPTER MATERIAL

4.1 Conclusion

Because the government is such a large player in the economy, its fiscal actions (spending, taxing, and borrowing) exert a powerful influence on real GDP and employment. Such actions can cause real GDP to depart from potential GDP and can alter the long-term growth rate of potential GDP.

A first principle of fiscal policy, therefore, is that the government should not take actions that would harm the economy. Avoiding erratic changes in fiscal policy and ensuring that taxes are not increased during recessions are part of this first principle.

A second principle is that fiscal policy in principle can smooth the fluctuations in the economy. Tax cuts and spending increases during recessions can help offset the declines in demand. Economists debate about whether the government is capable of taking discretionary actions that will have these effects. Policy lags and uncertainty make discretionary fiscal policy difficult.

Economists disagree little, however, about the importance of automatic stabilizers, under which tax and spending actions occur automatically without legislation. Automatic stabilizers cause the deficit to rise in recessions and fall during better times.

Another part of government policy that has powerful effects on the economy is monetary policy. We take up monetary policy in Chapter 27.

Key Points

1. Fiscal policy consists of the government's plans for spending and taxes.
2. The government's budget is the primary document of fiscal policy. It gives the priorities for spending and taxes. In the United States, the president must submit a budget proposal to Congress.
3. The United States has had large federal budget deficits in recent years. These are increasing the debt and raising risks to the economy.
4. Because Congress modifies the proposals and because of unanticipated events, the actual budget differs considerably from the proposed budget.
5. Changes in spending and taxes can move real GDP away from potential GDP in the short run. But in the long run, real GDP returns to potential GDP.
6. Changes in taxes and spending can offset shocks to real GDP.
7. Lags and uncertainty make discretionary fiscal policy difficult.
8. Automatic stabilizers are an important part of fiscal policy. Tax revenues automatically decline in recessions. Transfer payments move in the reverse direction.

QUESTIONS FOR REVIEW

1. Why are actual expenditures and revenues always different from the president's proposals?
2. How is the government's debt affected by the government's budget surplus?
3. Why would a tax cut in a recession reduce the size of the recession?
4. Why might a proposal to cut taxes in a recession do little to mitigate the recession?
5. What is meant by the discretion versus rules debate?
6. What are automatic stabilizers, and how do they help mitigate economic fluctuations?
7. What is the difference between the structural surplus and the actual surplus?
8. What would happen to the actual surplus in a recession?

PROBLEMS

1. Suppose you have the following data on projected and actual figures for the U.S. budget for a given year (in billions of dollars).

	Projected Budget	Actual Budget
Taxes	2,286	2,407
Expenditures	2,709	2,655

   a. What was the projected budget surplus or deficit? What was the actual budget surplus or deficit? Why might this happen?
   b. If the government debt was $4,592 billion at the start of the year, what was the debt at the end of the year?
   c. If real GDP was $12,300 billion, what is the debt-to-GDP ratio?

2. Examine the hypothetical budget data, shown below, for calendar years 2013–2016 (in billions of dollars).

Year	Budget Surplus	Government Debt as of January 1	GDP
2013	-150	1,000	4,000
2014	-100	1,150	4,200
2015	100		4,800
2016	200		5,400

   a. Fill in the missing values in the table.
   b. What is the percentage change in debt and GDP from 2013 to 2014?
   c. Calculate the debt-to-GDP ratio for each year. How does this ratio change over time? Why?

3. Suppose you are in charge of deciding the appropriate fiscal policy for an economy in which real GDP is less than potential GDP. One of your economic advisers recommends a reduction in government spending. Using an *AD-IA* diagram, indicate the short-run, medium-run, and long-run effects of this plan. Did you receive good advice from your economic adviser?
4. Suppose the economy is currently $100 billion above potential GDP, and the government wants to pursue discretionary fiscal policy to cool off the economy. Show this situation using an *AD-IA* diagram.
5. Suppose Congress is considering a balanced budget amendment to the Constitution that requires that the budget be balanced every fiscal year. Explain how this law could make the economy more unstable.
6. Do you think that a zero national debt would be best for the country? Why or why not? Do you think that a zero level of debt would be best for you? Why or why not?
7. Suppose you get a summer job working in Congress and a recession begins while you are there. Write a memo to your boss, who is a member of Congress, on the pros and cons of a big highway and bridge-building program to combat the recession.
8. Will projects such as Alaska's proposed "bridge to nowhere," a $300 million bridge that would connect two remote Alaskan communities, help the national economy avoid a recession? How would you reconcile this with your answer to Problem 7?
9. Suppose that real GDP has just fallen below potential GDP in a recession and the Council of Economic Advisers is trying to forecast the recovery from the recession. They are uncertain about whether Congress will pass the president's proposed tax cut right away or will delay it a year. Trace out two possible scenarios with an *AD-IA* diagram that describes the impact of the uncertainty.
10. Suppose the government surplus is 3 percent of real GDP, but economists say that the structural surplus is 2 percent. Is real GDP currently above or below potential GDP? Why? Draw the diagram showing this situation.

CHAPTER 27
Monetary Policy

In a speech she delivered in early March 2017[1], Federal Reserve Chair Janet Yellen assessed the role that the Federal Reserve had played over the past decade. She dissected this decade into two distinct periods. The first was the period between 2007 and 2014, when the Fed, under her predecessor Ben Bernanke, took several unprecedented policy steps with three goals in mind: to help the economy out of the recession, to stabilize the financial and banking systems and to sustain the recovery. The second was the period after 2014 when the Fed began steps to unwind some of these extraordinary measures and try to return to a more normal stance of policy.

Federal Reserve Building, Washington DC

Source: Shutterstock.com

The Federal Reserve's decisions during these two periods have attracted both praise and criticism from observers and economic analysts. We saw in earlier chapters that the Fed normally works by changing the interest rate. For example, when inflation starts to rise, the Fed typically increases the interest rate in order to bring inflation back down. When inflation starts to fall, the Fed typically lowers the interest rate in order to keep inflation from falling further and to prevent a deflation. These actions by the Federal Reserve are part of the mechanism whereby the economy recovers after a demand or supply shock. We also saw how monetary policy occasionally has led to inflation or instability, such as when the Fed kept interest rates too low in the 1970s, which likely led to the Great Inflation, or when it kept interest rates very low from 2003 to 2005, which may have accelerated the housing price boom and the resulting housing bust, which was a factor in the financial crisis of 2007 and 2008. In this chapter, we delve deeper into the operations of monetary policy to better understand the decisions that the Fed made, and will be making, as it seeks to return to a more normal monetary policy stance.

We consider six key policy issues. First, we look at how the Federal Reserve responded to the financial crisis by expanding the size of its balance sheet. Second, we examine the demand for money in terms of the interest rate, and consider what happens when the interest rate hits its lower bound of zero, as also occurred during the recent financial crisis. Third, we look at how the Fed can take steps to reduce the size of its balance sheet and return interest rates and balance sheets to levels more consistent with historical norms. Fourth, we study how the Fed can avoid getting into such situations by responding in a systematic way to both inflation and to real gross domestic product (GDP). Fifth, we consider the rationale for central bank independence, and finally, we look at the international role of monetary policy in affecting the exchange rate.

The topics you learn in this chapter will help you develop a better understanding of the description that Janet Yellen provides in her speech about how the Federal Reserve began the process of unwinding or reversing those extraordinary policy measures after 2014, with a particular focus on some of the challenges it faced during the period.

1. THE FEDERAL RESERVE'S BALANCE SHEET

At the time of the financial crisis in early 2009, the Fed released a statement saying that it planned to "stimulate the economy through open market operations and other measures that are likely to keep the size of the Federal Reserve's balance sheet at a high level." We already know what open market operations are from Chapter 22, but what are these "other measures" and what does it mean to keep "the size of the Federal Reserve's balance sheet at a high level"? To answer these questions we first need to take a look at the Federal Reserve's balance sheet.

1.1 The Federal Reserve's Assets and Liabilities

Table 27.1 shows the basic form of the balance sheet of the Fed or other central banks. As with any balance sheet, we put assets on the left and liabilities on the right. The most important thing about a balance sheet is that any change in assets implies an equal change in liabilities.

Consider first the liability side of the Fed's balance sheet. The first item is *currency*, which is the amount of dollar bills and coins of various denominations in circulation. Recall that currency held by the public is part of the money supply.

The second item is *reserves*, which are deposits that banks hold at the Fed. When the Fed purchases bonds in an open market operation, it pays for the bonds by crediting banks with a deposit on itself. In Chapter 22, we showed that these reserves are an asset on the banks' balance sheets. From the perspective of the balance sheet of the Fed, we see that they are a liability.

Now consider the asset side of the balance sheet. This side has four major items: government securities, private securities, loans to banks, and loans to other financial institutions.

Government securities are mainly U.S. Treasury bonds with maturities over a year and U.S. Treasury bills with maturities less than a year. Buying and selling these securities is a traditional role of central banks as they go about doing open market operations. If the Fed buys $10 billion in government securities, then the left-hand asset side of the Fed's balance sheet increases by $10 billion. What adjusts on the right-hand liability side? If the Fed pays for the government securities by crediting the banks' deposit accounts, then reserves increase by $10 billion. So we see the basic principle at work: Changes in assets must always equal changes in liabilities. The balance sheet is a convenient way to keep track of the traditional open market operations.

Next consider *private securities*, which are bonds issued by firms. What types of securities are in this category? One example is commercial paper, which is a type of bond with a short-term maturity issued by a financial or nonfinancial firm. Another example is a mortgage-backed security (MBS), which is a collection of mortgages bunched together into one bond. These collections were put together by financial firms and government sponsored enterprises, such as Fannie Mae and Freddie Mac, to make the mortgages more attractive to investors. Other examples in the private securities category are securities backed by student loans, automobile loans, or credit card debt.

TABLE 27.1 **Major Items on the Balance Sheet of the Fed**

Assets	Liabilities
Government Securities	Currency
Private Securities	Reserves
Loans to Banks	
Loans to Other Financial Institutions	

During the financial crisis, the Fed bought these securities to prevent the financial crisis from worsening. For example, in March 2008, the Fed was concerned that Bear Stearns would fail and that this would cause other firms who had lent money to Bear Stearns to fail, harming the whole financial system and the economy. So it bought some of Bear Stearns's assets and arranged the sale of the rest of Bear Stearns to another financial firm, JP Morgan. Similarly, it bought some of the assets of AIG to prevent it from failing in September 2008. By the end of 2008, the Fed was buying MBS to reduce mortgage interest rates and thereby help stop the bust in housing markets. It bought commercial paper because few investors were buying it, and the Fed was concerned that the lack of credit availability would harm the economy.

The last two items on the asset side of the balance sheet are loans. Making *loans to banks* is one of the traditional roles of the Fed. It is part of the Fed's *lender of last resort* function. The Fed originally made loans to banks that take deposits from the public to prevent runs on the banks. A run occurs when many people simultaneously withdraw their deposits from the bank. In the nineteenth century and in the Great Depression of the 1930s, people would lose confidence in banks and withdraw their deposits. But simple rumors could cause such runs and ruin banks that otherwise were solvent. By acting as the lender of last resort, ready to lend in such circumstances, the Fed could prevent these runs and preserve financial stability. When the Fed makes loans to banks it charges an interest rate called the **discount rate**. During the financial crisis, many banks borrowed large amounts from the Fed, and the Fed made it easier by creating a special term auction facility (TAF) for which the interest rate could be less than the discount rate.

discount rate
The interest rate that the Fed charges commercial banks when they borrow from the Fed.

The final category on the Fed's balance sheet consists of loans to other financial institutions that are not banks. These other financial institutions include insurance companies, such as AIG. The Fed might lend to these institutions for reasons that are similar to its reason for buying private securities: It might be concerned that, without these loans, the firms would fail and that the failure would ripple through the economy.

Purchasing private securities and making loans to financial institutions other than banks are quite unusual actions for central banks. Economists debate about whether such actions have the intended effects, although the Fed has argued that they are effective. Economists also debate about the legality and appropriateness of the Fed taking on these responsibilities, which certainly are not in the traditional set of monetary policy tools. Economists generally agree, however, that the Fed eventually should revert to its traditional role after the effects of the crisis dissipate.

1.2 The Size of the Balance Sheet

What does the Fed mean by the size of the balance sheet? It simply means the sum of all the assets on the balance sheet or equivalently the sum of all the liabilities. When the Fed purchases assets, the size of the balance sheet increases.

Think about the size of the Fed's balance sheet using the liability side—currency plus reserves. Economists have another term for the sum of currency plus reserves. They call it the **monetary base**. Figure 27.1 shows how the Fed's balance sheet exploded at the time of the financial crisis and afterwards.

monetary base
Currency plus reserves.

FIGURE 27.1 The Monetary Base and the Size of the Fed's Balance Sheet

The monetary base—currency plus reserves—is a measure of the size of the Fed's balance sheet. The monetary base increased substantially during three bouts of quantitative easing: the first during the financial crisis at the end of 2008, the second in late 2010 and 2011, and the third in September of 2012. These are labeled QE1, QE2, and QE3 in the diagram.

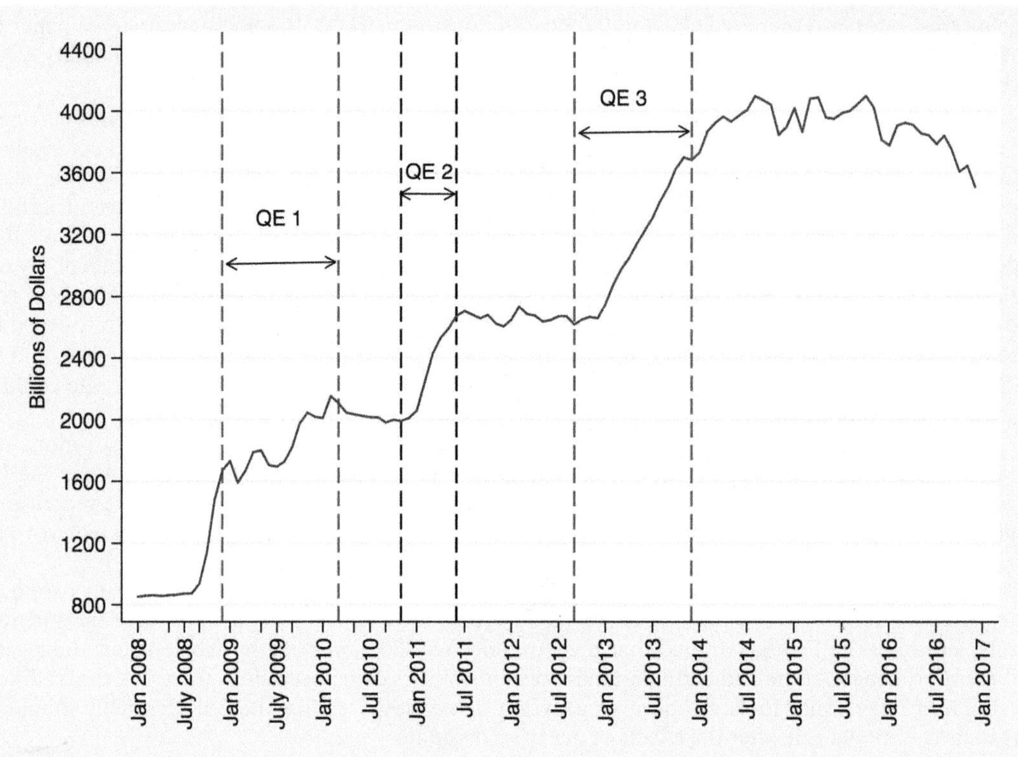

REVIEW

- The size of the Fed's balance sheet is the sum of all the assets, or all the liabilities. The size of the balance sheet has expanded by a large amount during the financial crisis.
- The major items on the asset side of the Fed's balance sheet are securities and loans. The major items on the liability side are currency and reserves.
- Securities consist of government securities and private securities. Purchases and sales of government securities, commonly called open market operations, are a traditional role of monetary policy.
- Purchasing private securities is an unusual action taken to lessen the severity of financial crises.
- Loans consist of loans to banks and loans to other firms. Loans to banks are part of the traditional lender of last resort function of the Fed.
- Loans to other firms are also unusual. They are undertaken to prevent the firms from failing, which the Fed worries would disrupt the financial system.

2. MONEY DEMAND AND ZERO INTEREST RATE

Now that we have examined the balance sheet of the Fed and shown how changes in the Fed's purchases lead to changes in reserves, let us examine how changes in reserves affect the interest rate. We will show that (1) decreases in the money supply caused by decreases in reserves will increase the interest rate; (2) increases in the money supply created by increases in reserves will lower the interest rate; and (3) the interest rate cannot go below zero, so at some point increases in reserves will stop lowering the interest rate.

2.1 The Money Demand Curve

Money demand is defined as a relationship between the interest rate and the quantity of money people are willing to hold at any given interest rate. As shown in Figure 27.2, the amount of money demanded is related negatively to the nominal interest rate. One reason people hold money is to carry out transactions: to buy and sell goods and services. People will hold less money if the nominal interest rate is high. That is, a higher interest rate reduces the amount of money people want to carry around in their wallets or hold in their checking accounts. Conversely, a lower nominal interest rate will increase the amount of money people want to hold. Why is money demand negatively related to the nominal interest rate?

money demand

A relationship between the nominal interest rate and the quantity of money that people are willing to hold at any given nominal interest rate.

Money (currency plus checking deposits) is only part of the wealth of most individuals. People also hold some of their wealth in financial assets that pay interest. For example, some people have time deposits at banks. Others hold securities, such as Treasury bills. Holding money is different from holding time deposits or Treasury bills because currency does not pay interest and checking deposits pay low, or no, interest. If you hold all your money in the form of cash in your wallet, clearly you do not earn any interest. Thus, an individual's decision to hold money is best viewed as an alternative to holding some other financial asset, such as a Treasury bill. If you hold money, you get little or no interest; if you hold one of the alternatives, you earn interest.

The interest rate on the vertical axis in Figure 27.2 is the average nominal interest rate on these other interest-bearing assets that people hold as alternatives to money. Now, if the interest rate on these alternatives rises, people want to put more funds in the alternatives and hold less as money. If they hold the funds as currency, they get no interest on the funds. If they hold the funds in a checking account, they may get a small amount of interest, but certainly less than they would get from other financial assets. The quantity of money demanded is lower at higher interest rates because putting the funds in interest-bearing assets becomes more attractive compared with keeping the funds in a wallet.

FIGURE 27.2 The Demand for Money

The interest rate is the opportunity cost of holding money. A higher interest rate on U.S. Treasury bills or other interest-bearing assets raises the opportunity cost of holding money and lowers the quantity of money demanded.

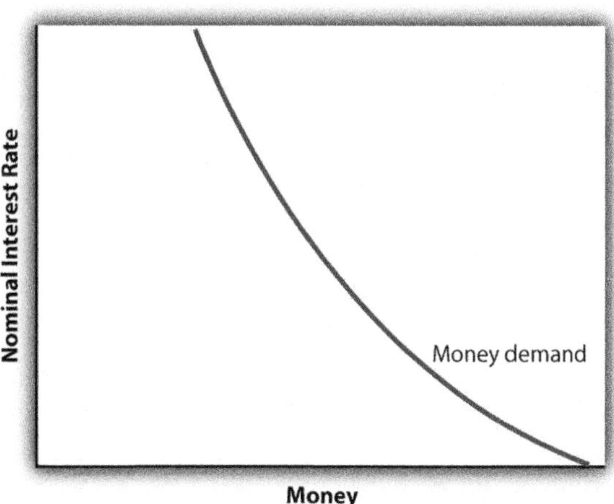

The interest rate on the alternatives to holding money is the *opportunity cost* of holding money. When the opportunity cost increases, people hold less money. When the opportunity cost decreases, people hold more money.

Figure 27.2 represents money demand in the economy as a whole. The curve is obtained by adding up the money demanded by all the individuals in the economy at each interest rate. The money held by businesses—in cash registers or in checking accounts—also should be added in.

The Interest Rate and the Quantity of Money

Using the money demand curve, it is possible to find the quantity of money in the economy that will be associated with any given nominal interest rate decision by the Fed. First, note that close correlation exists between the federal funds rate set by the Fed and interest rates on short-term Treasury bills and other interest-bearing assets that people can hold as an alternative to holding money. This close correlation is shown in Figure 27.3. Thus, when the Fed changes the federal funds rate, other interest rates tend to change in the same direction.

Now, for any given interest rate, one can use the money demand curve to find the quantity of money in the economy. This is illustrated in Figure 27.4. If the Fed lowers the federal funds rate, then the lower interest rate increases the quantity of money demanded and, as shown in the left graph, the quantity of money in the economy rises. Or, if the Fed raises the interest rate, the quantity of money in the economy decreases, as shown in the right graph of Figure 27.4.

What about Focusing on the Money *Supply*?

One question you might ask about Figure 27.4 is, "Where is the money *supply*?" Recall from Chapter 22 that the Fed affects the quantity of money supplied in the economy by open market operations. Does the quantity of money supplied equal the quantity of money demanded? Yes, of course it does. The demand and supply of money is no different from any other demand and supply model. As monetary policy now works in the United States and most other countries, the central bank adjusts the money supply so that it intersects the money demand curve at the nominal interest rate chosen by the central bank. For example, as the interest rate falls in the left graph of Figure 27.4, the money supply must be increased so that the intersection of money demand and money supply moves as shown. Figure 27.5 shows how the money supply shifts in both cases shown in Figure 27.4.

FIGURE 27.3 Short-Term Interest Rates

The federal funds rate is the interest rate set by the Fed. Other short-term interest rates, such as the three month Treasury bill rate, move up and down with the federal funds rate. Note how the interest rates reached zero in late 2008 and stayed there for the next seven years!

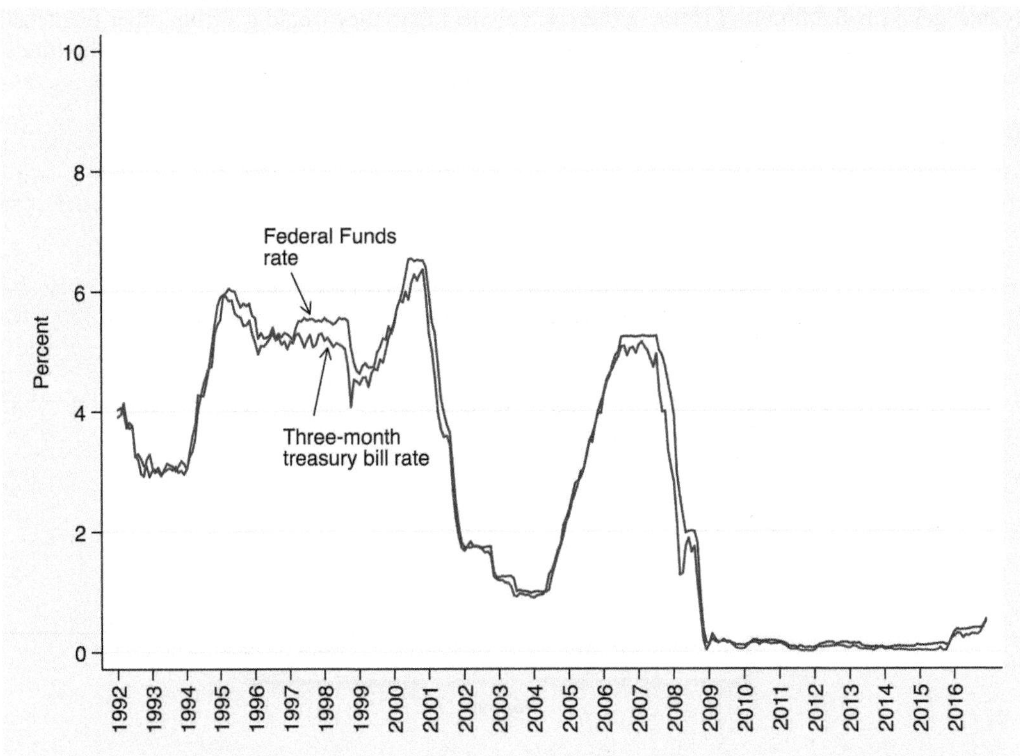

FIGURE 27.4 **When the Fed Changes the Interest Rate, the Quantity of Money Changes**

When the Fed lowers the interest rate, people want to hold more money. When the Fed raises the interest rate, people want to hold less money.

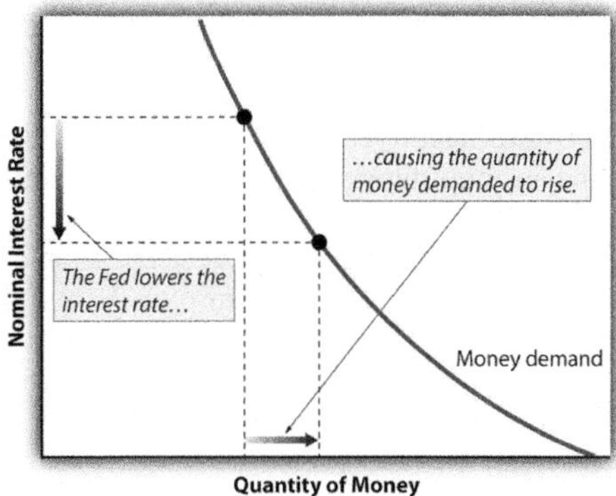

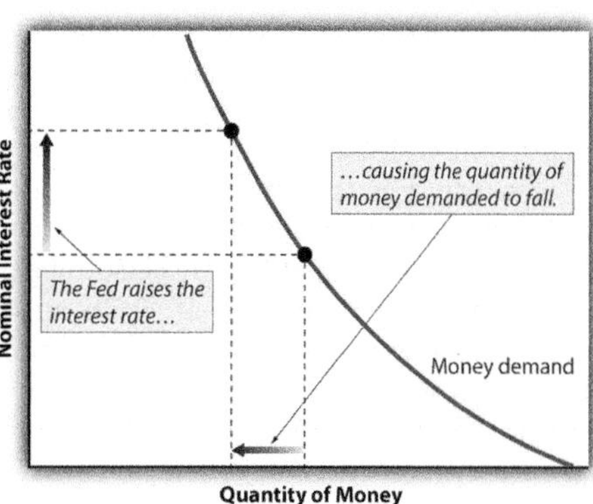

Such movements in the money supply occur as the Fed makes open market purchases or sales to change the interest rate. When the Fed decides to lower the interest rate, for example, it must increase reserves. And we know from Chapter 22 that when the Fed increases reserves, the money supply increases. Thus, the increase in the money supply in the left graph of Figure 27.5 is exactly what the analysis in Chapter 22 tells us will happen when the central bank increases reserves. Whether you focus on the interest rate or the money supply, the story is the same.

Then why doesn't the Fed simply focus on the money supply? Because the money demand curve tends to shift around a lot; if the Fed simply kept the money supply constant, the interest rate would fluctuate as money demand shifted back and forth. These fluctuations in the interest rate would cause fluctuations in real GDP—perhaps large enough to cause a recession—and thus would not be good policy.

Some economists, such as Milton Friedman, have argued that the Fed should simply hold the growth of the money supply constant, a policy that is called a constant money growth rule. Central banks, however, now feel that money demand shifts around too much for a constant money growth rule to work well. As we saw in Chapter 22, however, throughout history large increases in money growth cause large increases in inflation.

Those who object to the constant money growth rule do not object to keeping inflation low. They feel that a constant money growth rule will lead to more and larger fluctuations in real GDP and inflation than other policies would. That is why they recommend that the Fed and other central banks focus more on interest rates.

FIGURE 27.5 **Money Supply Changes Implied by Interest Rate Changes**

When the Fed decides to lower or raise the interest rate, the money supply must change. Increases in reserves raise the money supply and lower the interest rate. Decreases in reserves will lower the money supply and raise the interest rate.

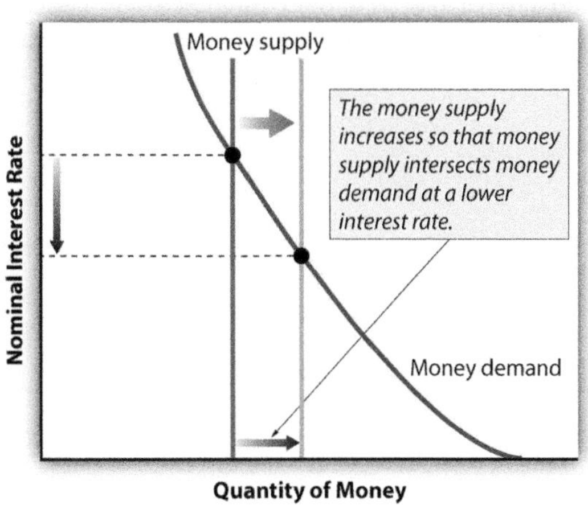

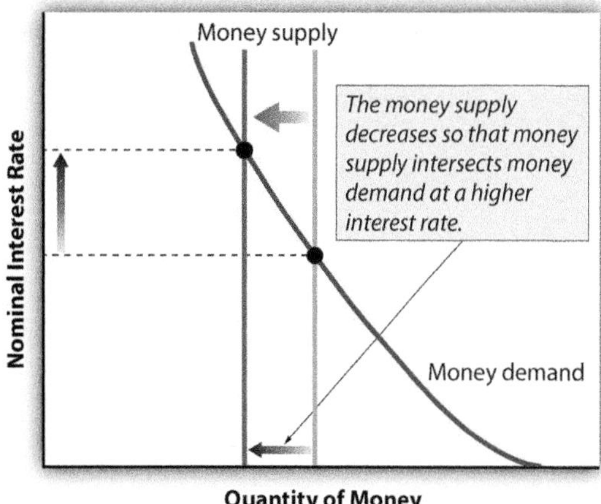

3. WHEN THE INTEREST RATE HITS ZERO

If you look carefully at Figure 27.4 and Figure 27.5, you will notice that the money demand curve flattens out as it approaches the horizontal axis, which represents the zero interest rate. The curve does not cross the horizontal axis because the nominal interest rate cannot go negative. Why? Because a negative interest rate means that you would have to pay interest to people for loaning them your money instead of having them pay you. Rather than pay someone, you could simply hold onto your money in dollar bills, which would at least pay a zero interest rate, better than negative. So the interest rate does not go into zero territory. For this reason, we have drawn the money demand curve so that it flattens out rather than crosses the horizontal axis.

In recent years, there have been periodic examples of countries where interest rates have become negative—Japan at -0.1%, Sweden at -0.5% and Switzerland at -0.75%—as examples. While these are interesting cases, they are not really a refutation of the claim that interest rates have a lower bound of zero. Technically, the central bank can charge what amounts to a storage fee for very large sums of money; but the option that money can be stored outside the banking system in the form of currency that earns zero interest will always limit how negative interest rates can be.

liquidity trap

A situation in which increases in the money supply (liquidity) do not lower the interest rate any further; the interest rate is at or near zero.

Now suppose that the Fed continued increasing the money supply beyond the amount shown in Figure 27.5. For example, in Figure 27.6, we show in more detail how the money demand curve flattens out as the interest rate approaches zero. When the interest rate gets to zero, we have reached what is called the **liquidity trap**, a situation in which increases in the money supply (liquidity) will not lower the interest rate any further.

FIGURE 27.6 The Liquidity Trap

Increases in the money supply result in smaller reductions in the interest rate until the interest rate approaches zero.

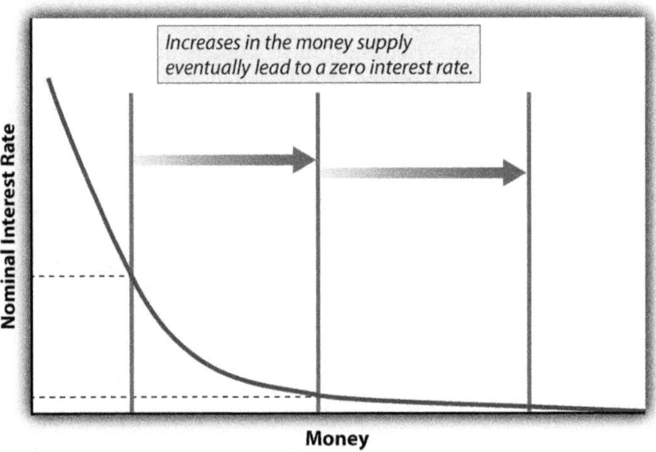

As you can see in Figure 27.7, the interest rate did effectively reach zero in the United States in December 2008. The Federal Open Market Committee announced that its target for the federal funds rate would be in the range of 0 to 0.25 percent. Figure 27.7 shows how the interest rate fell from 2 to about 0 as reserves at the Fed increased.

FIGURE 27.7 Toward the Zero Interest Rate

As the Fed increased reserves sharply in 2008, the federal funds interest rate declined toward zero. This result is what would be expected from the theory of the money demand curve, because the increase in reserves increased the money supply to some extent.

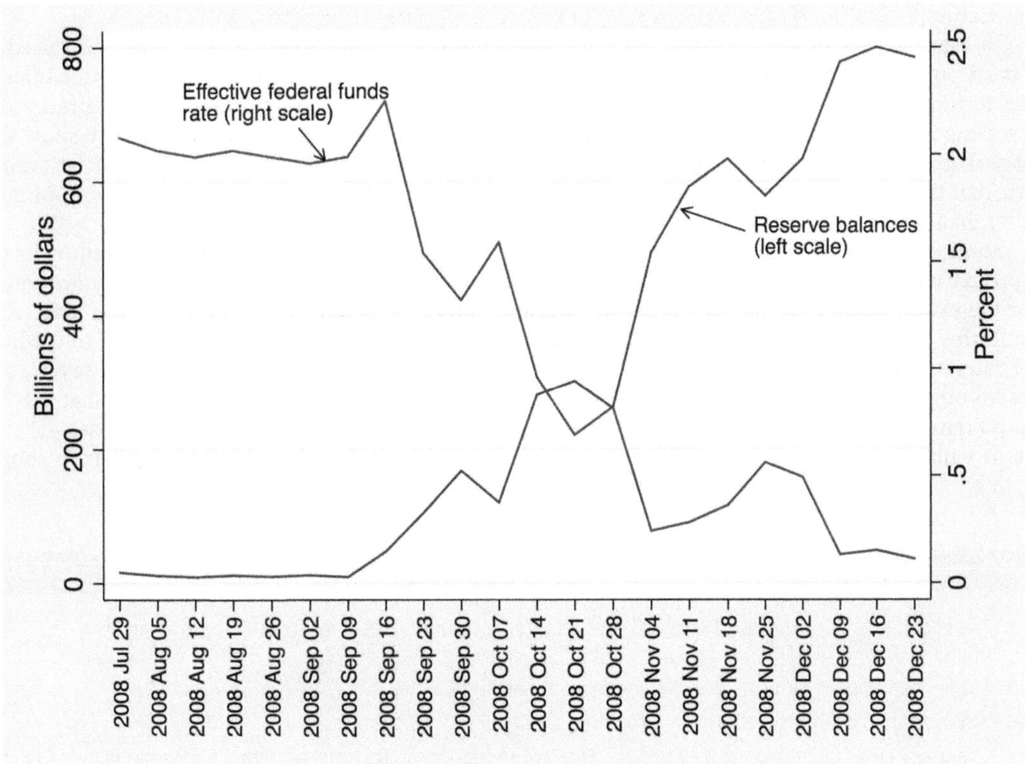

3.1 Quantitative Easing

What should central banks do when the interest rate hits zero? As shown in Figure 27.6 they can continue to increase the money supply by increasing reserves; even though that will not lower the interest rate, it can stimulate the economy. This is called *quantitative easing* because the emphasis is on increasing the quantity of reserves or money rather than reducing the interest rate.

In the United States, following the 2008/09 recession the Federal Reserve embarked on three separate episodes of quantitative easing. In 2009, the Federal Reserve purchased more than a trillion dollars worth of mortgage-backed securities and treasury bonds, a program that later came to be known as QE1.[2] In late 2010, after the recession had officially ended but with the recovery being slow to get going, the Fed announced a program to buy $600 billion worth of long-term Treasury securities, a program that soon acquired the catchy nickname of QE2.[3] Then, in late 2012, more than three years after the recession had ended the Federal Reserve, citing concerns about slow growth in the United States and other nations, embarked on QE3, an open ended purchase of $85 billion worth of mortgage-backed securities and long-term Treasury securities.[4]

How do QE programs impact the economy? Some economists argued that people might use the larger amount of reserves or money to purchase goods and services directly and thereby stimulate the economy. Others argued that more reserves or money will lower the interest rates on a range of securities. For example, by choosing to focus the quantitative easing program on purchases of mortgage-backed securities and longer-term Treasury securities, the Federal Reserve sought to bring down interest rates on other type of loans in the economy. Lower interest rates in turn would boost borrowing and spending in the economy.

3.2 Unwinding Quantitative Easing

By 2014, the Fed began to see signs that the economy was finally returning to health as unemployment fell to below 6 percent and inflation rose from near deflation levels to around 1.5 percent, both figures more consistent with historical norms than what had been experienced in the aftermath of the 2008/09 recession. The Fed announced that its first steps towards restoring policy normalcy would be to gradually cut back on asset purchases, a policy that became popularly known as the "taper."[5]

The next step would have been to raise interest rates from their lower bound and then gradually reduce the size of the balance sheet by either selling off the securities or by not repurchasing new securities when existing securities reached their maturity date and made their final payments. But the Fed became very cautious in 2015 because they were worried that the inflation rate was too low in the economy. This idea that the economy has to be "just right—not too hot or not too cold" is discussed in the next section.

In December of 2015, the Federal Reserve finally announced that interest rates would be raised by 25 basis points (a quarter of a percentage point), seven years after the initial decision to lower interest rates to zero had gone into effect. Since then the Fed has continued to be cautious in raising rates only increasing it by another 25 basis points in 2016. Internal deliberations at the Federal Reserve show that this was not the pace at which the Fed had hoped to return to policy normalcy, the expectation had been that the key interest rate would have been raised by 2 full percentage points by the end of 2016 rather than by the half a percentage point it actually was increased by.

Some economists have been critical of the pace at which the Fed has gone about unwinding its extraordinary policies. In Congressional testimony, one of the authors of this text, John Taylor, argued that the extra low interest rates and unconventional monetary policy had gone on for too long. As a result, this unconventional policy had widened the gap between the rich (who had access to credit at low rates and benefited from stock market appreciation) and the poor, adversely affected savers, and created other imbalances and distortions in the economy. The overall policy conclusion—that the Fed should return to a systematic rules-based monetary policy like the one that worked in the past—is consistent with the Fed's stated goals. The disagreements are about the pace at which the return should happen.

REVIEW

- The Fed affects the short-term nominal interest rate by changing reserves through open market operations.
- Money demand depends negatively on the nominal interest rate.
- When the Fed changes the interest rate, the quantity of money changes.
- Changes in the quantity of money supplied lead to reductions in the interest rate. Changes in reserves lead to changes in the money supply.
- At some point, the interest rate hits zero. Then the central bank uses quantitative easing or credit easing.

4. THE ECONOMIC FLUCTUATIONS MODEL

The best way to avoid the problems of the zero interest bound is to run monetary policy in a way that avoids hitting the bound in the first place. This means avoiding booms and busts, which cause crises.

4.1 Aggregate Demand: Just Right, Too Hot, or Too Cold?

First consider Figure 27.8, which illustrates the problem monetary policy faces in trying to avoid booms and busts by keeping real GDP near to potential GDP. The three graphs in Figure 27.8 each illustrate a different situation.

The Goldilocks Economy: Just Right

In the middle graph, the aggregate demand curve intersects the inflation adjustment line at the point at which real GDP equals potential GDP and the inflation rate is equal to the target inflation rate. Because real GDP is equal to potential GDP, inflation does not have the tendency to rise or to fall. Thus, this graph represents an ideal point: The inflation rate is equal to the target inflation rate, and real GDP is equal to potential GDP. The aggregate demand curve is in the correct place, because it intersects the inflation adjustment line at the point at which real GDP equals potential GDP *and* at which the inflation rate equals the target inflation rate. Financial market analysts refer to this situation as a "Goldilocks economy": not too hot, not too cold, just right.

Misalignment: Aggregate Demand Is Too High

In contrast to the middle graph in Figure 27.8, the other two graphs represent misalignments of real GDP and potential GDP. In the right graph aggregate demand has increased too much—perhaps because of an expansionary shift in consumption, investment, or net exports. At this position, inflationary forces are in place that soon will cause the inflation adjustment line to rise. Unlike the short-run position in Figure 27.9 (the gain-then-pain scenario, in which the central bank intentionally has shifted monetary policy), the situation in the right graph of Figure 27.8 is unintentional. The task of monetary policy is to prevent such misalignments and to correct them once they occur.

How would the central bank correct this type of misalignment? It would raise the real interest rate above the level it would choose in the middle graph. The higher real interest rate would reduce aggregate demand and bring the *AD* curve back to a point at which it intersected the inflation adjustment line at potential GDP. Financial market analysts would say that the Fed was trying to "cool off the economy" by raising the interest rate in this way.

Another Type of Misalignment: Aggregate Demand Is Too Low

The left graph of Figure 27.8 represents the opposite, but no less undesirable, type of misalignment of real GDP and potential GDP. In this case, aggregate demand has gotten too low—perhaps because of a contractionary shift in consumption, investment, or net exports. With real GDP less than potential GDP, the inflation adjustment line soon will fall below the target inflation rate. Moreover, with real GDP below potential GDP, unemployment has increased. Monetary policy should try to prevent or correct this type of misalignment, too.

To correct such a misalignment, the central bank would lower the real interest rate below the level it would choose in the middle graph. The lower real interest rate would increase consumption, investment, and net exports and bring the *AD* curve back to the right.

FIGURE 27.8 Aligning the Aggregate Demand Curve

The aggregate demand curve is lined up correctly when real GDP equals potential GDP and the inflation rate is on target, as in the middle graph. Otherwise, aggregate demand is too high, and the Fed must raise the interest rate; or aggregate demand is too low, and the Fed must lower the interest rate.

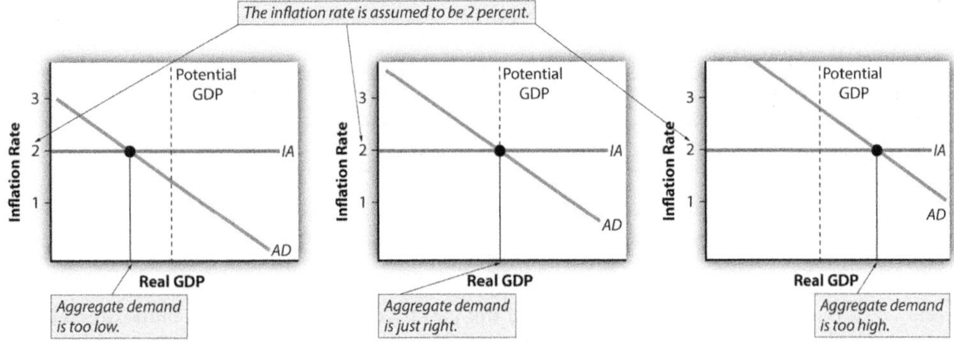

4.2 The Inherent Uncertainty in Monetary Policy

This example also illustrates that, in practice, it is not easy for the Fed to keep real GDP near potential GDP by varying the interest rate. Although the Fed increased interest rates to rein in aggregate demand, economists were concerned that real GDP would not respond as quickly as in the past. At the time, it appeared that investment and consumption might be more responsive to the increase in the interest rate than the Fed thought they would be.

In general, how long it takes for a change in the interest rate to affect aggregate demand is uncertain. Other things affect aggregate demand, too, and some of those things might work in the opposite direction to the change in interest rates.

Moreover, potential GDP is difficult to estimate. Recall that potential GDP is determined by the underlying supply of labor, capital, and technological change. In many situations, central banks do not know for sure whether real GDP is or is not equal to potential GDP. Uncertainty about potential GDP is particularly high during periods when technology seems to be changing rapidly and the path of potential GDP is changing.

4.3 Increased Transparency and Predictability

To bring real GDP into alignment with potential GDP, the Fed reacts to the *gap*, or the *difference*, between real GDP and potential GDP. That is, it raised the real interest rate when real GDP rose above potential GDP. Similarly, if real GDP were to fall below potential GDP, as shown in the furthest left graph of Figure 27.8, the Fed would lower the real interest rate.

This type of interest rate reaction to the gap between real GDP and potential GDP is typical of the Fed and many other central banks. Just as responding promptly and by enough to an increase in inflation represents a good policy, so too does moving the aggregate demand curve in a way that brings real GDP back into equality with potential GDP.

Central banks have endeavored to be more transparent and predictable in their responses to inflation and real GDP. Some have formally announced a target for inflation. The increased predictability can be described using the concept of a monetary policy rule, as we discussed in Chapter 24. In fact, it is possible to combine the reaction to inflation and the reaction to the gap into one monetary policy rule, and thereby obtain a more accurate description of central bank behavior. Remember that a monetary policy rule is a description of a central bank's behavior in the same sense that a microeconomic demand curve is a description of a person's consumption behavior. Just as a person's purchase decisions may depend on two variables, (1) price and (2) income, so too may the central bank's real interest rate decisions depend on two variables, (1) the inflation rate and (2) the gap between real GDP and potential GDP.

Table 27.2 shows a numerical example of this type of policy rule. On the left is the inflation rate. On the top is the gap between real GDP and potential GDP. The entries in the shaded part of the table show the real interest rate. For example, the bold entry shows that when inflation is 2 percent and real GDP is equal to potential GDP (the percent gap between real GDP and potential GDP is zero), the real interest rate is 2 percent. When inflation rises to 4 percent, the real interest rate rises to 3 percent. Each column of Table 24.1 tells the same story: When inflation rises, the central bank raises the real interest rate. To raise the real interest rate, the nominal interest rate has to rise by more than inflation rises.

TABLE 27.2 **Real Interest Rate Reaction to Inflation and to the Gap between Real GDP and Potential GDP (compare with Table 12-1)**

		Percent Gap between Real GDP and Potential GDP		
		-2	*0*	*2*
Inflation Rate (percent)	0	*0*	1	2
	2	1	**2**	3
	4	2	3	4
	6	3	4	5
	8	4	5	6

Note: The entries in italics show the real interest rate for each inflation rate and the gap between real GDP and potential GDP.

Now observe in Table 27.2 that the central bank's response also depends on what happens to real GDP. When real GDP rises above potential GDP—and the gap increases—the central bank raises the real interest rate. And when real GDP falls below potential GDP, the central bank lowers the real interest rate.

The monetary policy rule in Table 27.2 is a more accurate description of monetary policy than the rule in Chapter 24, Table 24.1, because central banks do react to the gap between real GDP and potential GDP, as the discussion of Fed policy makes clear. Hence, financial market analysts use monetary policy rules like this one to predict interest rate changes in many different countries.

REVIEW

- Monetary policy is a constant struggle to avoid booms and busts. The Fed carries out this policy by trying to keep the aggregate demand curve in a position at which real GDP is equal to potential GDP and the inflation rate is equal to the target inflation rate.
- The Fed and other central banks increase the real interest rate when real GDP grows above potential GDP and lower the real interest rate when real GDP falls below potential GDP.
- The response of the real interest rate to the gap between real GDP and potential GDP can be combined with the response to inflation to get a monetary policy rule that accurately describes central bank behavior.

5. CENTRAL BANK INDEPENDENCE

Fed officials are appointed to long terms that may span several different presidents; the four-year term of the chair of the Fed does not necessarily coincide with the term of any president. For example, Paul Volcker served through most of the Reagan years, even though he was appointed by President Carter.

Alan Greenspan, originally appointed by President Reagan, served throughout the eight years of the Clinton presidency. Therefore, like Supreme Court justices in the United States, Fed officials develop an independence from government influence.

The Federal Reserve Board has had six chairs during the past 60 years. Inflation was low during most of Martin's term but rose in the late 1960s and even more in the 1970s under Burns and Miller. Inflation fell dramatically under Volcker and remained low under Greenspan. Bernanke began his term with inflation pressures rising, but three years later, in early 2009, deflation seemed to be more of a problem.

William McChesney Martin 1951–1970

Arthur Burns 1970–1978

G. William Miller 1978–1979

Paul Volcker 1979–1987

Alan Greenspan 1987–2006

Ben Bernanke 2006–2014

Janet Yellen 2014–

Seven Decades of Fed Chairs

Sources: By Federalreserve (00564) [Public domain], via Wikimedia Commons; By Oscar Porter, U.S. Army Photograph [Public domain], via Wikimedia Commons; By Federalreserve (00478) [Public domain], via Wikimedia Commons; By Kenneth C. Zirkel (Own work) [CC BY-SA 3.0 (http://creativecommons.org/licenses/by-sa/3.0)], via Wikimedia Commons; Rob Crandall / Shutterstock.com; By United States Federal Reserve (Obtained via email from Federal Reserve OPA.) [Public domain], via Wikimedia Commons; By United States Federal Reserve [Public domain], via Wikimedia Commons

The unprecedented actions by the Fed during the financial crisis have raised questions about its independence. Some say that distinctions between the actions of the Fed and what usually would be done by other government agencies are getting fuzzier. For example, providing loans to individuals or firms usually is not done by independent agencies of government. Such loans are made by agencies like the Department of Housing and Urban Development or the Department of Commerce. These agencies must have their loans authorized by Congress; the cabinet members who head the departments are in no way independent of the president of the United States. They do not have fixed terms. To assess these challenges to **central bank independence**, one needs to understand the rationale for central bank independence. The main rationale is that an independent central bank can prevent the government in power from using monetary policy in ways that appear beneficial in the short run but that can harm the economy in the long run.

central bank independence

A description of the legal authority of central banks to make decisions on monetary policy with little interference by the government in power.

5.1 The Gain-Then-Pain Scenario

We showed in Chapter 25 that a shift in monetary policy toward a higher inflation target will temporarily raise real GDP above potential GDP, but that only inflation will be higher in the long run. Such a change in monetary policy would first entail a reduction in interest rates and would shift the aggregate demand (*AD*) curve to the right, as shown in Figure 27.9. Real GDP would rise along with investment, consumption, and net exports; unemployment would fall. In the short run, this change in GDP does not have an effect on inflation because of the slowness of firms to change their price decisions. The economic gain from the reduction in unemployment without an increase in inflation might help in a reelection campaign, or it might enable the government to push legislation for new programs through the political system. The economic pain—higher inflation in the long run, also shown in Figure 27.9—would not be seen until after the election or after the legislation is passed.

Thus, the political system has a natural tendency toward higher inflation. If the government in power had complete control over the decisions of the central bank, it could take actions to make the economy look good in the short run for political purposes and not worry that the economy might look bad in the long run. Removing the central bank from the direct control of the government reduces this politically induced bias toward higher inflation because then it is more difficult for the government to get the central bank to take such actions.

The Phillips Curve

Observe that during the period of time when the *IA* line is shifting up in the gain-then-pain scenario, real GDP is above potential GDP, and the inflation rate is higher than at the start of the scenario. For example, inflation is higher and real GDP is higher at the point labeled *MR* in Figure 27.9 than they are at the starting point. And during this period, the unemployment rate is lower because the unemployment rate falls when real GDP rises. In sum, during the period of time between the initial shift of the *AD* curve and the end of the scenario, the unemployment rate is *down* and the inflation rate is up. Thus, unemployment and inflation have a negative correlation.

In fact, a negative correlation between unemployment and inflation has been observed for many years in the real world, because of such shifts in the *AD* curve. This negative correlation between inflation and unemployment is called the *Phillips curve*, after A. W. Phillips, the economist who first showed that such correlations existed in British data from 1861 to 1957. A replica of the original Phillips curve is shown in Figure 27.10.

The Phillips curve was used in the 1960s and 1970s to justify a monetary policy that included higher inflation. People argued that higher inflation would lead to lower unemployment. In other words, they argued that a long-run trade-off existed between inflation and unemployment.

FIGURE 27.9 **The Gain-Then-Pain Scenario**

The Fed can temporarily stimulate the economy in the short run—real GDP rises above potential GDP. But soon inflation starts to rise. In the long run, the inflation rate is higher and real GDP is back to potential GDP.

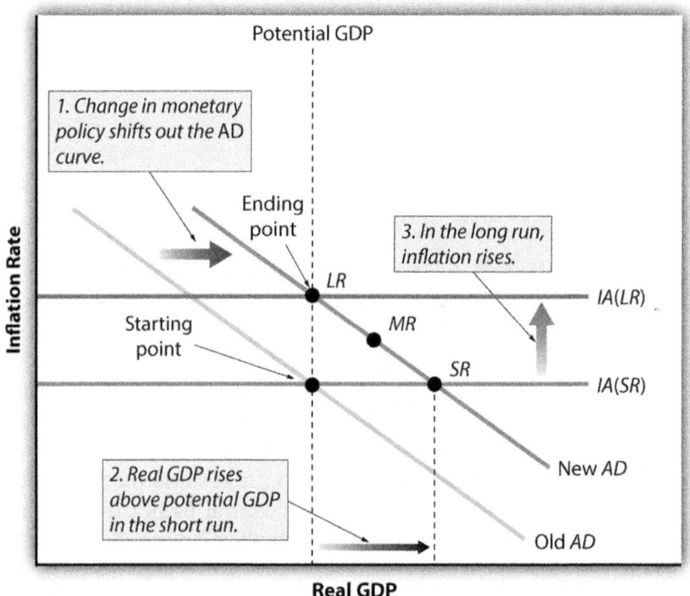

FIGURE 27.10 The Original Phillips Curve (1861-1957)

This graph shows the data originally presented by A. W. Phillips. Each point represents one year. The negatively sloped curve drawn through the scatter of points had enormous influence and led some to argue, mistakenly, that a long-run trade-off existed between inflation and unemployment.

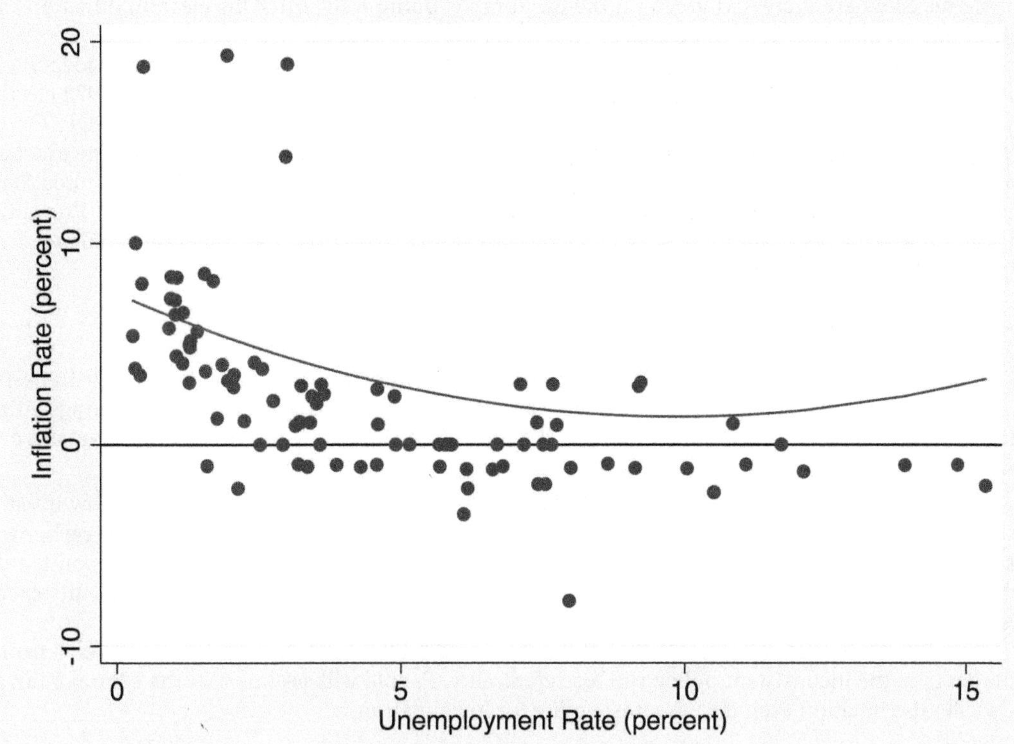

Source: Authors' graph using public data provided by the Journal of Applied Econometrics for Jushan Bai and Pierre Perron, "Computation and Analysis of Multiple Structural Change Models", Journal of Applied Econometrics, Vol. 18, No. 1, 2003, pp. 1-22.

How did they use the Phillips curve to support this view? Look at the Phillips curve in Figure 27.10. You might think that a monetary policy that aimed for higher inflation could lead to a lower unemployment rate in the long run. That is what the curve seems to suggest. But the theory in the *AD-IA* diagram and, in particular, the gain-then-pain scenario shows that no such trade-off exists in the long run. If monetary policy raised inflation, real GDP eventually would return to potential GDP, the unemployment rate would return to the natural rate, and we would be left with only higher inflation, not lower unemployment.

It has become a basic principle of modern macroeconomics—implied by the *AD-IA* diagram—that no long-run trade-off exists between inflation and unemployment. The facts are consistent with the principle: In the 1950s and early 1960s, inflation was low; in the late 1960s and 1970s, inflation was high; and in the 1980s and 1990s, inflation was low again. But the average unemployment rate during these periods was roughly the same, around 5 or 6 percent. Furthermore, the lower unemployment rate in the late 1990s did not result in much higher inflation. Any tendency for unemployment and inflation to be correlated negatively will disappear in the long run. This does not mean that a higher-inflation monetary policy will not produce a short-run gain. It does mean, however, that it will result in long-run pain.

Check your thinking about the implications of the gain-then-pain scenario for the relationship between unemployment and inflation. In the short run, between the start and the end of the scenario:

Inflation ↑

Real GDP > potential GDP

Unemployment rate < natural rate

So a negative correlation exists between inflation and unemployment, a Phillips curve. In the long run:

Inflation ↑

Real GDP = potential GDP

Unemployment rate = natural rate

So, a long-run trade-off does not exist between inflation and unemployment.

The Political Business Cycle

political business cycle

A business cycle caused by politicians' use of economic policy to overstimulate the economy just before an election.

The **political business cycle** is the tendency of governments to use economic policy to cause real GDP to rise and unemployment to fall just before an election and then let the economy slow down right after the election. Many economic and political studies have shown that an incumbent's chances of being reelected are increased greatly if the economy is doing well. After the election, inflation may rise and cause a bust, but that would occur long before the next election.

Research in the 1970s by William Nordhaus of Yale University uncovered some evidence of a political business cycle in the United States. For example, the strong economy before the 1972 election may have been due to a monetary policy change that pushed real GDP above potential GDP. On the other hand, the U.S. economy was in a recession just before the 1980 and 1992 elections—the exact opposite of a political business cycle. Thus, the evidence for a political business cycle in the United States is no longer strong. In either case, political business cycles are harmful to the economy. Preventing political business cycles is another reason for having a central bank that has some independence from the politicians that are in power.

Time Inconsistency

It is difficult for governments to resist the temptation to use monetary policy for short-run gain despite the long-run pain. Even governments whose sole aim is to improve the well-being of the average citizen will say that they want low inflation but then will stimulate the economy to lower unemployment, even though they are fully aware of the inflationary consequences down the road.

time inconsistency

The situation in which policy makers have the incentive to announce one economic policy but then change that policy after citizens have acted on the initial, stated policy.

This situation is known as **time inconsistency** because governments say they want low inflation but are later inconsistent by following policies that lead to higher inflation. They act like a teacher who tells the class that they will have to take an exam just to get the students to study, but then, on the day of the exam, announces that it is canceled. The students are happy to miss the exam, and the teacher does not have to grade it. Everyone appears better off in the short run.

Just as the teacher who cancels the exam will lose credibility with future classes, however, a central bank that tries the inconsistent policy will lose credibility. People will assume that the central bank actually will raise inflation even if it says it is aiming for low inflation.

5.2 Potential Disadvantages of Central Bank Independence

Central bank independence is no guarantee against monetary policy mistakes, however, and it could even lead to more mistakes. In principle, an independent central bank could cause more inflation than a central bank under government control. For example, those in charge of the central bank—after they are appointed—could succumb to arguments that high inflation is not so harmful after all. Or, at the other extreme, those in charge of the central bank become so focused on inflation that they are blinded to the effects of monetary policy on real GDP and employment and thus either cause a recession or make an existing recession deeper or longer. Therefore, a disadvantage of central bank independence is that it can be taken too far.

Whether independent or not, central banks need to be held *accountable* for their actions. If those in charge of the central bank do not perform their job well, it is appropriate that they not be reappointed. When the central bank of New Zealand was given greater independence in the 1980s, its accountability was formalized explicitly: If the head of the central bank does not achieve low inflation goals agreed to in advance, the head is fired. But the central bank has independence in determining how to achieve these goals.

Is there any evidence that independence has led to better inflation performance without any increase in the severity or frequency of recessions? If you look at Figure 27.11, you will see that central banks that have more independence have had lower inflation. This lower inflation has not been associated with more or longer recessions. The figure shows New Zealand *before* the central bank was given more independence; since then, it has moved down and to the right, toward lower inflation.

FIGURE 27.11 Central Bank Independence and Inflation

The scatter plot shows that the more independent a central bank is, the lower the average inflation rate. The independence of the central bank is calculated by studying the laws of each country, including the length of the term of office of the head of the central bank (a longer term means more independence) and restrictions on the central bank lending to the government.

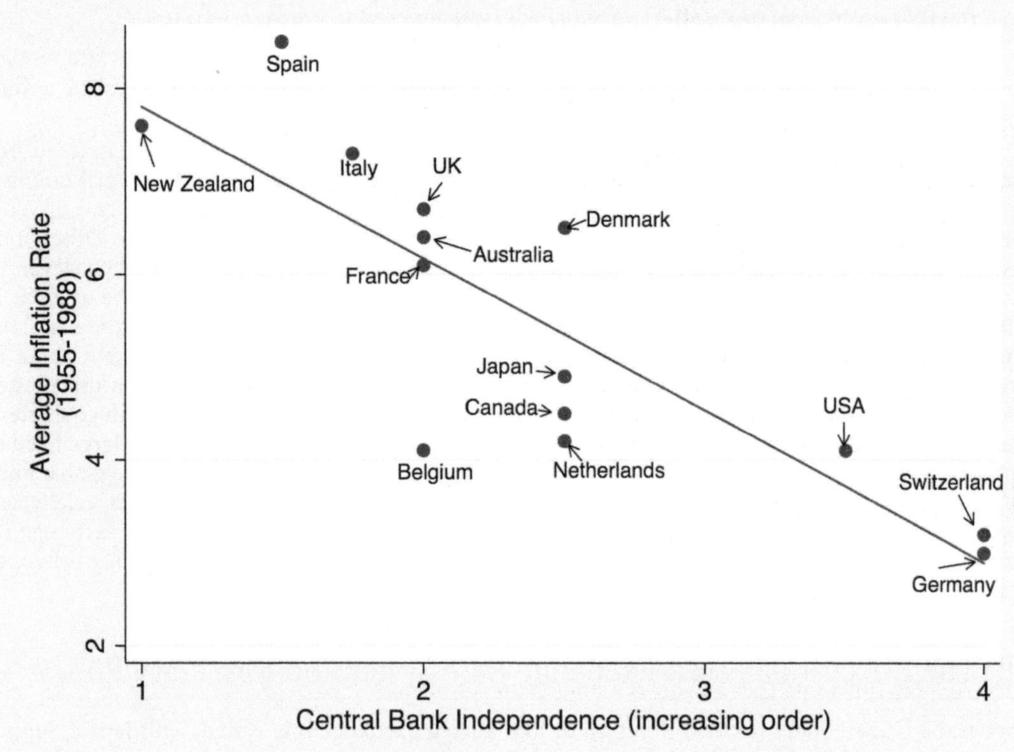

REVIEW

- Unprecedented actions by the Fed during the crisis have raised questions about its independence.
- Central bank independence insulates the central bank from short-run political pressures to overstimulate the economy, which ultimately would raise inflation.
- The gain-then-pain scenario shows that a central bank can lower unemployment below the natural unemployment rate in the short run, but by doing so, it will raise inflation in the long run.
- The Phillips curve is a negative correlation between inflation and unemployment. However, no long run trade-off exists between inflation and unemployment.
- Countries with more independent central banks have tended to have lower inflation than countries with less independent central banks.

6. THE EXCHANGE RATE

Thus far in this chapter we have focused on the interest rate as the main consideration in conducting monetary policy. But the exchange rate is affected by changes in interest rates and also must be considered carefully in a full assessment. When the Fed cuts the interest rate, the value of the dollar declines because the lower interest rate makes dollar assets less attractive. And the lower value of the dollar makes exports cheaper and imports more expensive, which will add to the stimulus of the economy.

flexible exchange rate policy

A policy in which exchange rates are determined in foreign exchange markets and governments do not agree to fix them.

fixed exchange rate policy

A policy in which a country maintains a fixed value of its currency in terms of other currencies.

Some economists argue that the exchange rate is even more important when the interest rate hits zero, as in the recent crisis, because it can continue to fall, stimulating the economy by increasing exports and reducing imports. When much of the global economy is in recession or crisis, however, a depreciation of the dollar could make the recession worse in other countries by reducing those country's exports. Such changes in exchange rates are an essential part of the impact of monetary policy in the economic fluctuations model explained in Chapter 24 and Chapter 25, because the United States follows a **flexible exchange rate policy**, allowing the exchange rate to fluctuate in this way.

But what if the Fed did not want the exchange rate to change? Or what if the U.S. government and another country, such as Japan, agreed to fix the exchange rate? Such a policy is called a **fixed exchange rate policy**. How would that policy affect monetary policy?

Such questions are not simply hypothetical. Throughout history, governments have decided from time to time to adopt fixed exchange rate policies. The United States and most industrial countries were part of a fixed exchange rate system—called the Bretton Woods system—from the end of World War II until the early 1970s. Until 2005, China fixed its exchange rate to the U.S. dollar. Other countries, like Ecuador and El Salvador, have adopted the U.S. dollar as their currency. In 1999, eleven nations formed the European Economic and Monetary Union (the EMU or Eurozone), gave up their individual currencies and adopted a common currency known as the Euro. The Eurozone has subsequently expanded to 19 member countries. Initially, there was a great deal of excitement about the Eurozone and people began to speculate about the possibility that the other countries in the Western Hemisphere join with the United States in a permanently fixed exchange rate system, with countries in Asia joining a fixed exchange rate system with Japan. This scenario would result in three large fixed exchange rate systems in the world—centered around the dollar, the euro, and the yen. The global financial crisis and the subsequent travails of the Eurozone beginning with Ireland, but especially with Greece, have put an end to such speculation. Understanding the implications of a fixed exchange rate or a common currency area for monetary policy makers is essential for understanding what is happening in different countries in the twenty-first century.

6.1 The Effects of a Fixed Exchange Rate System on Monetary Policy

Suppose the United States decided to set up or join a fixed exchange rate system with Japan. Suppose also that after the United States joins the system, inflation starts to rise in the United States, and monetary policy makers want to raise the interest rate. Such an increase in the interest rate will tend to raise the value of the dollar relative to the Japanese currency. But if the dollar were fixed in value, as it would be with a fixed exchange rate policy, such a rise in the dollar would not be possible. Hence, if exchange rates were fixed, the Fed could not raise the interest rate in the United States relative to the interest rate in Japan. The fixed exchange rate would impose a serious restriction on U.S. monetary policy because interest rates in the United States could not be changed.

In general, if two countries have a fixed exchange rate and people are free to move funds back and forth between the two countries, then the interest rates in the two countries must move together. If, in the example of the United States and Japan, the Fed wanted to raise interest rates, then the Bank of Japan would have to raise interest rates by the same amount. But that might not be in the best interests of Japan, especially if the Japanese economy was in a recession. Like the two steering wheels of a driver's training car, which move in tandem, interest rates in any two countries with a fixed exchange rate must move together.

The euro is the single currency used in the European Monetary Union. On January 1, 2002, euro notes and coins came into circulation in 12 European countries, replacing the national currencies of each of the countries, including Germany, where the European Central Bank (shown at right) is located. The seven banknote denominations have a common design in all the countries. In 2010, people began to worry that the euro would break apart because of the debt crisis in Greece and Ireland.

A Single European Currency and a Single Central Bank

Source: ilolab / Shutterstock.com

The connection between interest rates in different countries is visible to people in smaller countries that fix their currencies to the dollar, as Argentina painfully found out in 2001 and 2002. In 1991, Argentina chose to fix the value of the peso to the dollar, thus forcing its central bank to give up an independent monetary policy. When interest rates in the United States fell in the mid-1990s, this was beneficial to Argentina, as its interest rates fell as well. When U.S. rates rose rapidly in 2000 as the Fed battled inflation, however, Argentina was forced to raise its interest rates as well, pushing the weakened economy into a recession that lasted almost four years.

Ever since the Eurozone countries adopted a common currency, effectively permanently fixing their exchange rates with each other, there effectively has been only one overnight interest rate in Europe. The central banks of Germany, France, Italy, Spain, and other countries in the Eurozone banded together into a new European Central Bank. The overnight interest rates in France, Germany, Italy, and the other countries move together, so in reality, the central bank makes decisions about only one interest rate. With the Eurozone, Germany and Greece cannot have separate monetary policies. They have only one monetary policy. If real GDP fell below potential GDP in Greece, and remained equal to potential GDP in all the other countries, then a reduction in the interest rate by the European Central Bank, which would be right for Greece, would be wrong for Europe as a whole. In such a circumstance, it might be necessary to use countercyclical fiscal policy in Greece—spending increases or tax cuts, as described in the previous chapter—because monetary policy could not be changed. The fact that Greece has had to struggle with rising debt levels that have forced them to adopt contractionary fiscal policies—spending cuts and tax increases—has resulted in one of the deepest recessions ever to hit a developed nation since the Great Depression.

Conversely, if Germany experienced an economic boom while the rest of the Eurozone was at or below potential output then the European Central Bank will not raise rates even though the Bundesbank, Germany's central bank, would have done so if it had the authority to set monetary policy for Germany. If inflation were to rise in Germany, the German government would have to use contractionary fiscal policy to keep the economy from overheating.

Another historical real-life example of the effect of fixed exchange rates on monetary policy arose in Britain in 1992. At that time, interest rates were rising in Germany, because the German inflation rate was rising. But policy makers in Britain, which was facing hard economic times, did not want British interest rates to rise. The British faced a decision: Either they could raise their interest rates to keep them near Germany's, or they could let their interest rates fall below Germany's rate. In the latter case, their exchange rate would depreciate. For much of 1991 and 1992, the British kept their exchange rate stable, and this necessitated a rise in British interest rates. But by the end of 1992, increasingly poor economic conditions in Britain forced the British to give up the fixed exchange rate. Then interest rates in Britain could fall.

Interventions in the Exchange Market

exchange market intervention

Purchases and sales of foreign currency by a government in exchange markets with the intention to affect the exchange rate.

Why wasn't it possible for the British government to go into the exchange market and buy and sell foreign exchange and thereby prevent these changes in the exchange rate? For example, if the British government purchases British pounds, this increases the demand for pounds and thereby raises the pound exchange rate. Thus, if the high interest rates in Germany were reducing the value of the British pound, why couldn't the British government buy pounds to offset these pressures? Such buying and selling of foreign currency by governments is called **exchange market intervention**. Such intervention does occur, and it can affect the exchange rate for short periods of time. The world currency markets are so huge and fast moving, however, that even governments do not have the funds to affect the exchange rate for long by buying and selling foreign exchange.

If one currency has a substantial interest rate advantage, funds will flow into that currency, driving up its value; exchange market intervention by governments cannot do much about this. Empirical studies have shown that exchange market intervention—if it is not matched by a change in interest rates by the central bank—can have only small effects on the exchange rate.

Another possibility is to prevent funds from flowing between the countries. If a law restricted the flow of funds into and out of a country, then that country could have both a fixed exchange rate and a separate interest rate policy. Such controls on the flow of capital were discussed intensely after the collapse of fixed exchange rates in Asia in 1997, and Malaysia did institute some restrictions on financial capital flows. Such restrictions have disadvantages, however. They are difficult to enforce, and they can reduce the amount of foreign capital a country needs for development.

6.2 The Rationale for Fixed Exchange Rates

If fixed exchange rates lead to the loss of a separate monetary policy, then why do countries form fixed exchange rate systems? One reason to adopt a fixed exchange rate is that exchange rate volatility can interfere with trade, which certainly is one of the reasons the European countries established the European Monetary Union. Firms may not develop long-term relationships and contacts with other countries if they are worried about big changes in the exchange rate.

Another, perhaps more important, reason to form a fixed exchange rate system is that some countries have had a history of poor monetary policies. For example, Italy had high inflation before it decided to join with the other countries of Europe in a monetary union. And Argentina had many years of hyperinflation before it fixed its exchange rate with the United States and abandoned its own monetary policy.

The goal of fixing the exchange rate in these cases is to adopt the good monetary policy of a country whose central bank has a history of good policy: the Fed in the case of Argentina, and the central banks of Germany and France in the case of Italy. In these cases, the benefits of a fixed exchange rate system may outweigh the loss of a separate monetary policy. The evidence, however, is mixed. In the case of Italy, the policy seems to have worked: Inflation has been in single digits for many years. Conversely, in Argentina, where the policy seemed to work well initially in bringing down inflation, restricting the hand of monetary policy makers seemed to make it tough for the country to recover from its recession of the late 1990s.

REVIEW

- Interest rates must move together in countries with fixed exchange rates and with a free flow of funds between the countries.
- With a fixed exchange rate, each country cannot have a separate monetary policy.
- By permanently fixing exchange rates, a country can adopt the monetary policy of another country.

7. END-OF-CHAPTER MATERIAL

7.1 Conclusion

Monetary policy making is a powerful, but difficult, job. It is especially difficult during a financial crisis, as this chapter has shown. Central bankers like to say that the job is like driving a car by looking only through the rear-view mirror. They have to take actions that greatly affect the economy without knowing where the economy is going, only where it has been.

In this chapter, we have seen exactly why the job is difficult. During an unprecedented financial crisis, it may be necessary to use unprecedented and untested tools. It is difficult to resist political pressure for short-term benefits at the expense of long-term costs. And even in normal times, it is difficult to keep aggregate demand in line with potential GDP in a world where potential GDP is hard to estimate and policy effects on aggregate demand are uncertain.

We also have learned that while monetary policy has a powerful effect, it cannot do everything. It cannot lower unemployment permanently, and trying to do so will only raise inflation. And a country cannot have both a fixed exchange rate and the ability to adjust interest rates to control inflation and prevent recessions.

All these ideas are useful for understanding the frequent headlines and news stories about the Fed. And they help take some of the mystique out of what many people feel is the most mysterious institution in the world.

Key Points

1. The Fed's balance sheet shows the key actions of the Fed during the crisis and in normal times.
2. The Fed introduced credit easing during the financial crisis.
3. Central bank independence is a way to avoid political business cycles and the temptation to raise inflation for short-term gain.
4. The gain-then-pain scenario illustrates that a monetary policy shift to high inflation has short-run benefits but long-run costs.
5. An important task of monetary policy is to manage aggregate demand so that real GDP equals potential GDP.
6. A good monetary policy rule is responsive to real GDP as well as to inflation.
7. The demand for money is negatively related to the interest rate.
8. The Fed changes the quantity of money when it changes the interest rate.
9. Reserve requirements are rarely changed. The Fed also can increase the money supply by lowering the discount rate. This typically, but not always, is done in conjunction with lowering the federal funds rate.
10. Fixed exchange rates restrict monetary policy.

QUESTIONS FOR REVIEW

1. What is the size of the Fed's balance sheet?
2. What is credit easing?
3. What are some "other measures" taken by the Fed in the financial crisis?
4. What is the zero lower bound on the interest rate?
5. What are the advantages and disadvantages of central bank independence?
6. What is an example of a political business cycle?
7. Why would the Fed raise real interest rates if real GDP were above potential GDP?
8. What is the Phillips curve?
9. Why is the demand for money inversely related to the interest rate?
10. What is the opportunity cost of holding money?
11. Why is there a loss of monetary policy independence with fixed exchange rates?
12. Why would a country adopt a fixed exchange rate policy?

PROBLEMS

1. Why is an independent central bank more likely to put emphasis on price stability rather than on keeping unemployment low, compared with a central bank that is not independent?
2. The original Federal Reserve Act of 1913 allowed the secretary of the U.S. Treasury to be a member of the Federal Reserve Board, but a later amendment prohibited this. How would allowing the secretary of the U.S. Treasury to be a member affect the conduct of monetary policy?
3. What is the discount rate? How does it differ from the federal funds rate? Describe how the Fed affects each of these interest rates.
4. Banks can borrow from each other on the federal funds market or borrow from the Fed. Banks borrow far more on the federal funds market than from the Fed. You can borrow from your friends or from your parents. From whom are you more likely to borrow? Why do you think banks prefer to borrow from each other?
5. During the early 1990s, Japan experienced deflation and real GDP was below potential GDP. Draw a diagram showing the situation in Japan. Suppose the Japanese central bank decided that it had to reinflate and set a target inflation rate of 2 percent. How would it accomplish this? Show the short-run, medium-run, and long-run effects.
6. Using the aggregate demand curve and the inflation adjustment line, show what the Fed should do if real GDP is below potential GDP and the current inflation rate is equal to the target inflation rate, which is the ideal inflation rate from the Fed's perspective.
7. The Taylor Rule states that the central bank should set the short-term nominal interest rate (i) based on the inflation gap [the difference between inflation (π) and desired inflation (π^*)] and the output gap [the percentage difference between real GDP (Y) and potential GDP (Y^*)]. An example of a Taylor Rule would be the formula

$$i - \pi = 1.5 + 0.5(\pi - \pi^*) + 0.5\left(\frac{Y - Y^*}{Y^*}\right)$$

The term on the left-hand side is the real interest rate. Consider the following table

	Base Scenario	Scenario B	Scenario C
Inflation rate (π), %	2.0	4.0	2.0
Target inflation rate (π^*), %	2.0	2.0	2.0
Output gap, %	0.0	0.0	2.0
Real interest rate			
Nominal interest rate			

   a. Fill in the real and nominal interest rates chosen by the policy maker in the base scenario.
   b. How does scenario B differ from the base scenario in terms of the inflation and output gaps? Calculate the real interest rate. Has the real interest rate moved in the direction that would move the inflation rate toward its target?
   c. How does scenario C differ from the base scenario in terms of the inflation and output gaps? Calculate the real interest rate. Has the real interest rate moved in the direction that would move output toward the potential level?
   d. Suppose a new chair of the central bank is appointed and she switches to a new policy rule of the form given in the next equation. Recalculate the real and nominal interest rates for the three scenarios. What has been the effect of the change in weights?

$$i - \pi = 1.5 + 0.75(\pi - \pi^*) + 0.25\left(\frac{Y - Y^*}{Y^*}\right)$$

8. Suppose two countries are identical except for the fact that the central bank of one country lets interest rates rise sharply when real GDP rises above potential GDP and the other does not. Draw the aggregate demand curve for each country. What are the benefits and drawbacks of each country's policy?
9. Sweden and the United Kingdom chose not to join the European Monetary Union (EMU). Explain what a decision to join the EMU would imply for the monetary policy-making abilities of the central banks of these two countries.
10. Explain why restricting flows of funds into or out of a country can give that country's central bank the ability to conduct monetary policy even with a fixed exchange rate. What are some of the disadvantages of such a restriction?

ENDNOTES

1. https://www.federalreserve.gov/newsevents/speech/yellen20170303a.htm
2. https://www.federalreserve.gov/newsevents/press/monetary/20090318a.htm
3. https://www.federalreserve.gov/newsevents/press/monetary/20101103a.htm
4. https://www.federalreserve.gov/newsevents/press/monetary/20121212a.htm
5. https://www.federalreserve.gov/newsevents/press/monetary/20131218a.htm

CHAPTER 28

Economic Growth Around the World

In 2000, many countries in the world signed on to challenge of achieving the United Nations Millennium Development Goals (MDGs), quantitative targets related to reducing poverty around the world by 2015. The first of the MDGs was to reduce the proportion of the world population living in extreme poverty, defined then as income of less than $1 a day, by half. Periodically, this number has been updated to reflect changing measure of prices—to $1.25 a day in 2005 and most recently to $1.90 a day in 2011—but the idea is the same, to come up with a simple method for assessing how much progress had been made to improve the lives of those living in absolute poverty in some of the poorest places on earth.

In 2015, the United Nations released a report on how much progress the world actually made in striving towards reaching those goals.[1] On the first MDG, the United Nations assessed that the world had indeed made significant progress. The fraction of the world population living in extreme poverty had declined from 47 percent in 1990 to 14 percent in 2015, reflecting a decline greater than the 50% envisaged in the MDGs. In terms of numbers this was a substantial improvement in the lives of people around the world—more than 1 billion people had been lifted from extreme poverty since 1990, with much of the progress being achieved after the MDGs were signed at the turn of the century.

Source: Shutterstock.com

These disparities reflect fundamental differences in economic growth across countries. Much of the progress in reducing extreme poverty in the world has come from the sustained economic growth achieved by China. Much of the progress that the world will make in the next decade will depend on whether India can sustain high rates of economic growth and on whether other populous nations in Africa and Asia, like Bangladesh, Vietnam and Nigeria can follow suit. In earlier chapters of this text we examined what economic growth theory teaches us about how technology and capital have provided people with the means to raise their productivity. However, when we compare living standards, it is clear that people in some countries are much better off than people in other countries. This chapter will look at what the theory of economic growth has to say about why some countries have been able to grow faster than others. Why has access to capital been so difficult for some poor countries who have spent decades stuck in poverty and not growing at all? Why hasn't the spread of technological information allowed poor countries to grow faster? These are some of the important questions that you will be more informed about from reading this chapter.

1. CATCHING UP (OR NOT?)

growth accounting formula

Productivity growth rate = (1/3) (growth rate of capital per hour of work) + (growth rate of technology).

If technological advances can spread easily, as seems reasonable with modern communications, then poorer regions with low productivity and low income per capita will tend to catch up to richer regions by growing more rapidly. Why? If the spread of new technology is not difficult, then regions with lower productivity can adopt the more advanced technology of other regions to raise their productivity. Recall from the **growth accounting formula** that an increase in the growth of technology leads to an increase in productivity growth.

Investment in new capital also would tend to cause poor regions to catch up to the rich. Consider a relatively poor region in which both capital per worker and output per worker are low. Imagine several hundred workers constructing a road with only a little capital—perhaps only a few picks and shovels, not even a jackhammer. With such low levels of capital, the returns to increasing the amount of capital would be very high. The addition of a few trucks and some earth moving equipment to the construction project would bring huge returns in higher output. Regions with relatively low levels of capital per worker therefore would attract a greater amount of investment, and capital would grow rapidly. The growth accounting formula tells us that productivity grows rapidly when capital per worker grows rapidly. Thus, productivity would grow rapidly in poorer regions where capital per worker is low.

A rich region in which the capital per worker is high, however, would gain relatively little from additional capital. Such a region would attract little investment, and the growth rate of capital would be lower; therefore, the growth of productivity also would be lower.

In summary, economic growth theory predicts that regions with low productivity will grow relatively more rapidly than regions with high productivity. Regions with low productivity will tend to catch up to the more advanced regions by adopting existing technology and attracting capital.

catch-up line

The downward-sloping relation between the level of productivity and the growth of productivity predicted by growth theory.

Figure 28.1 illustrates this catch-up phenomenon. It shows the level of productivity on the horizontal axis and the growth rate of productivity on the vertical axis. The downward-sloping line is the **catch-up line**. A country or region on the upper left-hand part of the line is poor—with low productivity and, therefore, low income per capita—but growing rapidly. A country on the lower right-hand part of the line is rich—with high productivity and, therefore, high income per capita—but its growth is relatively less rapid. That the catch-up line exists and is downward sloping is a prediction of growth theory.

1.1 Catch-up within the United States

Let us first see how the catch-up line works when the regions are the states within the United States. Figure 28.2 presents the data on real income per capita and the growth rate of real income per capita for each of the states. Because productivity and real income per capita move closely together, we can examine the accuracy of the catch-up line using the real income per capita data. (Again, the adjective real means that the income data are adjusted for inflation.) Real income per capita in 1880 is on the horizontal axis, and the growth rate of real income per capita from 1880 to 1980 is on the vertical axis. Each point on the scatter diagram represents a state, and a few of the states are labeled. If you pick a state (observe Nevada, for example, down and to the right), you can read its growth rate by looking over to the left scale, and you can read its 1880 income per capita level by looking down to the horizontal scale.

FIGURE 28.1 The Catch-up Line

Growth theory with spreading technology and diminishing returns to capital and labor predicts that regions with lower productivity will have higher growth rates of productivity. The catch-up line illustrates this prediction. Because productivity is so closely related to income per capita, the catch-up line also can describe a relationship between income per capita and the growth rate of income per capita.

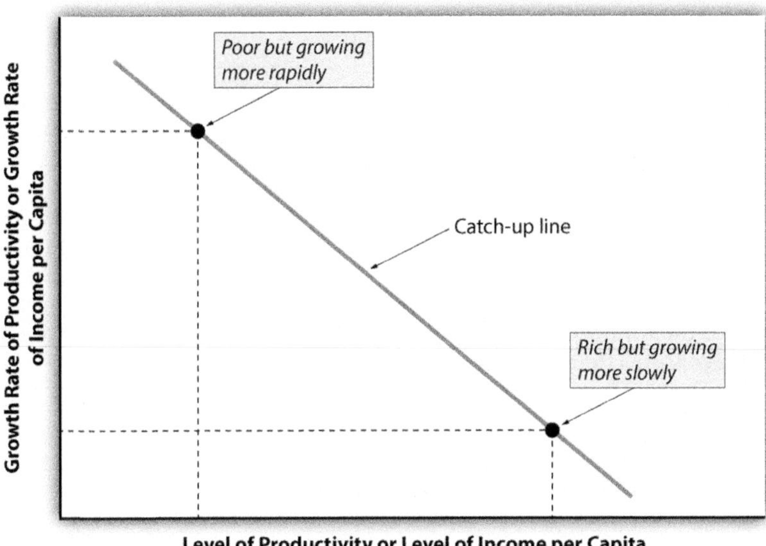

FIGURE 28.2 Evidence of Catch-up within the United States, 1880–2015

In the United States, those states that had low real income per capita in 1880 grew relatively rapidly compared to states that had high income per capita. The poor states tended to catch up to the richer states. A catch-up line is drawn through the dots.

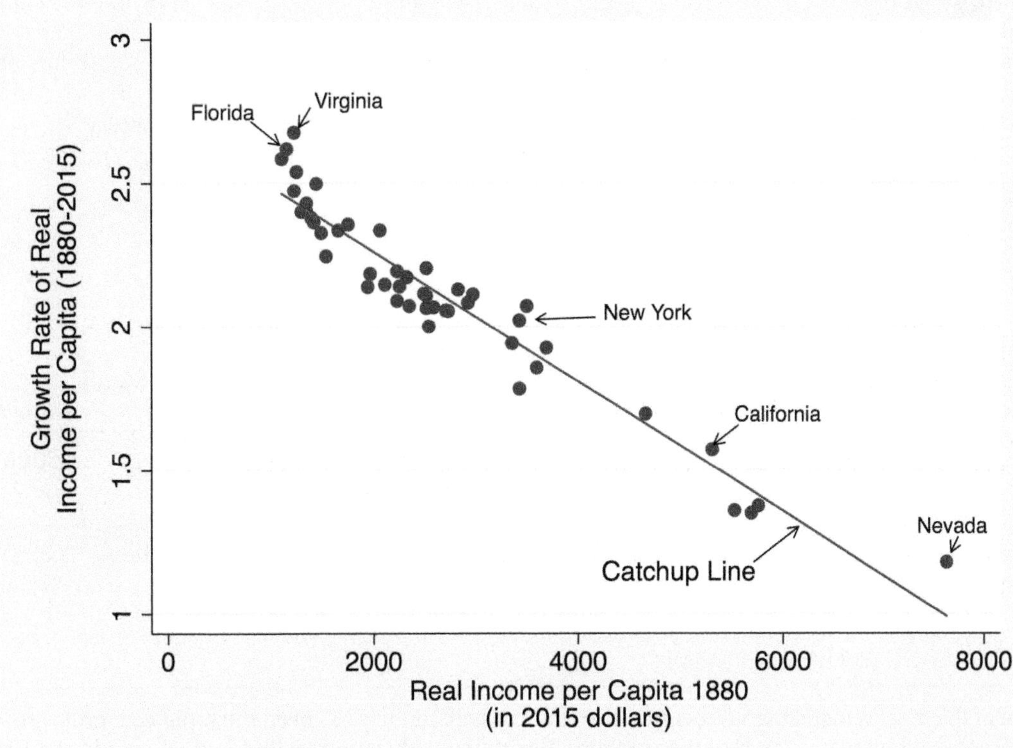

Source: Authors' calculations using data from Bureau of Economic Analysis, Bureau of Labor Statistics, and Richard A. Easterlin (1960) "Interregional Differences in Per Capita Income, Population, and Total Income"

The diagram clearly shows a tendency for states with low real income per capita in 1880 to have had high growth rates since then. The state observations fall remarkably near a catch-up line. Southern states like Florida and Texas are in the high-growth group. On the other hand, in states that had a relatively high income per capita in 1880, income per capita grew relatively slowly. This group includes California and Nevada.

Thus, the theory of growth works quite well in explaining the relative differences in growth rates in the U.S. states. The tendency is for relatively poor regions to grow more rapidly than relatively rich regions.

1.2 Catch-up in the Industrial Countries

What if we apply the same thinking to different countries? After all, communication is now global. Figure 28.3 is another scatter diagram with growth rate and income per capita combinations. It is like Figure 28.2 except that it plots real gross domestic product(GDP) per capita in 1960 against growth in real GDP per capita from 1960 to 2005 for several industrial countries.

Observe in Figure 28.3 that the richer countries, such as the United States and Switzerland grew less rapidly. In contrast, relatively less rich countries, such as Japan, Korea, and Spain, grew more rapidly. Canada and France are somewhere in between. These countries tend to display the catch-up behavior predicted by growth theory. Apparently, technological advances are spreading and capital-labor ratios are rising more rapidly in countries where they are low and returns to capital are high. So far, our look at the evidence confirms the predictions of growth theory.

FIGURE 28.3 **Evidence of Catch-up in Industrial Countries, 1960–2005**

For the industrial countries shown in the diagram, GDP per capita growth has been more rapid for those that started from a lower level of GDP per capita. Thus, there has been catching up, as shown by the catch-up line drawn through the points.

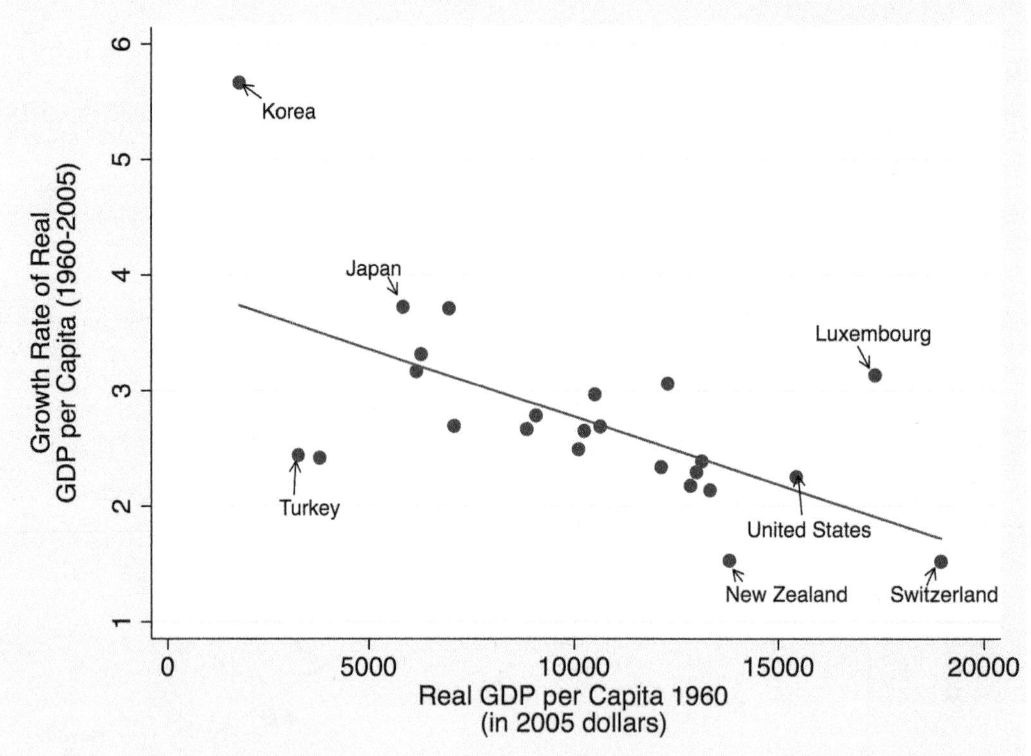

Source: Authors' calculations using data from the IMF's World Economic Outlook

1.3 Catch-up in East Asia

One of the most remarkable success stories of the last half-century has been the rapid economic growth rates achieved by many East Asian economies. Beginning with countries like South Korea in the 1960s and picked up by countries like China in the 1980s, the East Asian economies have grown extremely rapidly, resulting in a dramatic transformation of their economies and of the living standards of their people. Figure 28.4 shows what the growth experience of East Asian economies has been over the last few decades. As you can see, many economies grew extremely rapidly, with China and South Korea being the most striking examples.

FIGURE 28.4 Evidence of Catch-up in East Asia, 1980–2005

Since 1980, many East Asian economies have grown extremely rapidly. As a result, they have experienced dramatic improvements in per capita GDP and closed the gap between themselves and richer economies like the United States.

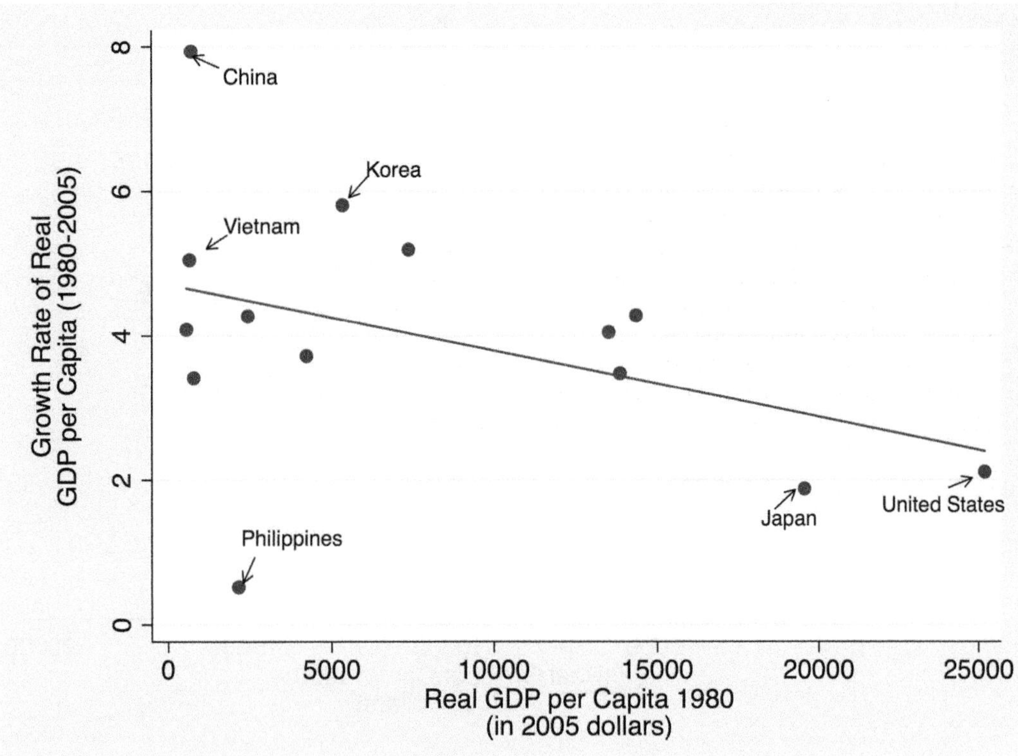

Source: Authors' calculations using data from the IMF's World Economic Outlook

1.4 Catch-up in the Whole World

However, so far we have not looked at whether the poorest economies also are experiencing catch-up. Figure 28.5 shows a broader group of countries that includes not only the industrial countries in Figure 28.3 and the East Asian economies in Figure 28.4 but also a broader set of developing countries. It is apparent that this larger group of countries has little tendency to fall along a catch-up line.

The countries with very low growth rates, such as Bangladesh and Ethiopia, are also the countries with very low GDP per capita. On the other hand, many countries with higher growth rates had a much higher GDP per capita. The United States and Singapore had higher growth rates than Zimbabwe and Congo even though their GDP per capita was above that of these countries.

FIGURE 28.5 Lack of Catch-up for Developing Countries,1960–2005

Unlike the U.S. states or the industrial countries, there has been little tendency for poor countries to grow more rapidly than rich countries. The gap between rich and poor has not closed.

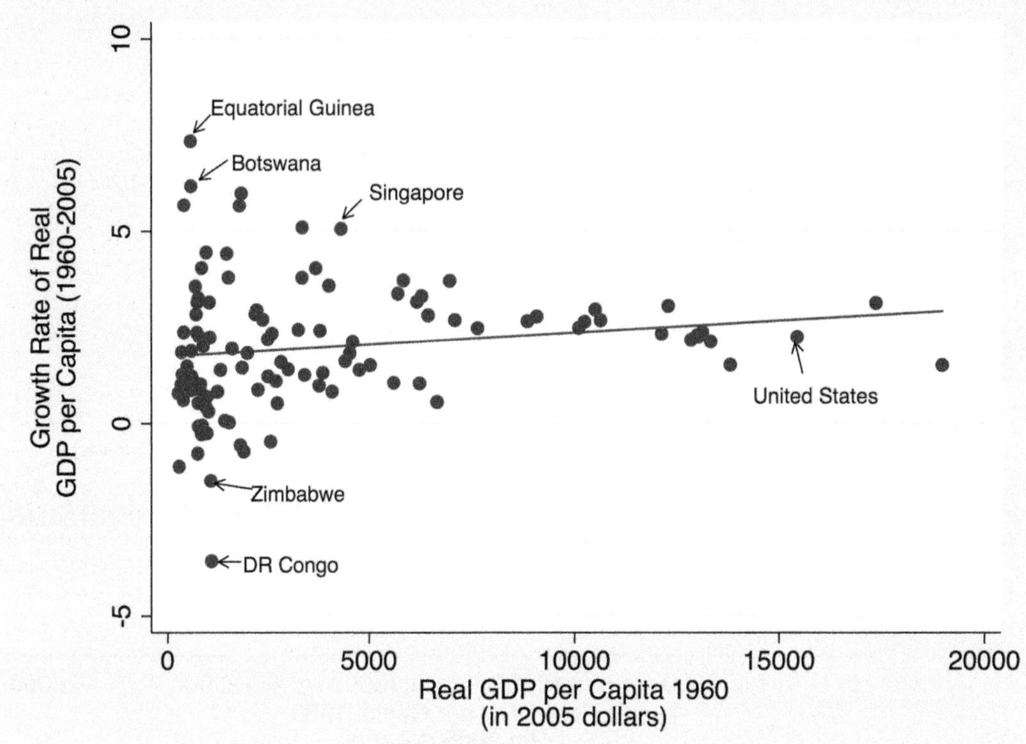

Source: Authors' calculations using data from the IMF's World Economic Outlook

Comparing countries like Indonesia and South Korea with countries like Bangladesh and Nigeria is striking. South Korea and Indonesia had about the same real GDP per capita as Nigeria and Bangladesh in 1960, but South Korea and Indonesia surged ahead with a more rapid growth rate over the next 45 years, leaving Bangladesh and Nigeria behind. And this is not the exception. Contrary to the predictions of economic growth theory, which says that technological advances should spread and capital per hour of work should rise from low levels, Figure 28.5 shows little tendency for relatively poor countries to grow relatively rapidly. It appears that something has been preventing either the spread and the adoption of new technology or the increase in investment needed to raise capital-labor ratios. We examine possible explanations as this chapter proceeds.

REVIEW

- Economic growth theory predicts that poorer regions will tend to catch up to richer ones. The flow of technology around the world and investment in new capital will bring this about.
- Data for the U.S. states and for the advanced countries show that such catch-up exists and is quite strong.
- However, little evidence indicates catch-up in the world as a whole. Many of the poor countries have fallen even further behind the industrial countries, whereas other poor countries, in particular those in East Asia, have grown rapidly.

2. ECONOMIC DEVELOPMENT

As well as raising questions about economic growth theory, the lack of catch-up evidenced in Figure 28.5 presents a disturbing situation. The substantial disparities in income distribution around the world has resulted in billions of people in low-income countries lacking the necessities that those in high-income countries frequently take for granted. **Economic development** is the branch of economics that attempts to explain why poor countries do not develop faster and to find policies that do help them develop faster. Economists who specialize in economic development frequently are experts on the problems experienced by particular countries—such as a poor education system, political repression, droughts, or poor distribution of food. The term **developing country** describes those countries that are relatively poor. In contrast, the term *industrial country* or *advanced economy* describes relatively well-off countries. Sometimes the term *less-developed country (LDC)* is used rather than developing country. Other terms also distinguish between different developing countries. For example, *emerging-market countries* such as Chile and Malaysia are countries that once were poor but have since grown rapidly and moved to a stage of economic development during which they are closer to advanced economies than most other developing economies.

economic development

The process of growth by which countries raise incomes per capita and become industrialized; also refers to the branch of economics that studies this process.

developing country

A country that is poor by world standards in terms of real GDP per capita.

Table 28.1 shows the shares of world GDP produced by advanced economies and developing countries. Thus, this table looks at aggregate income (which equals GDP) rather than at income per capita. More than 50 percent of world GDP comes from industrial countries. As the table shows, China is now the largest economy in the world and a major force in the world economy even though its per capita income is fairly low. China's GDP is already almost four times as large as that of the third-largest economy, Japan. If you take out China, Japan, and India, the remaining 29 countries in Asia only produce about 7.4 percent of world GDP, a number that would be even less if we removed industrialized Asian countries like Korea, Singapore, Taiwan, and Hong Kong from the group. Even more striking is the fact that all 45 countries in Sub-Saharan Africa produce only about 3 percent of world GDP. As we soon will see, the distribution of the world population does not look like the distribution of world GDP because the majority of the world's people live in China, India and other developing economies.

TABLE 28.1 Shares of World GDP Produced by Different Countries

	Number of Countries	Percent of World GDP
Advanced Economies	**39**	**42.4**
Major Industrial Countries:	***7***	***31.5***
United States		15.8
Japan		4.2
Germany		3.4
United Kingdom		2.4
France		2.3
Italy		1.9
Canada		1.4
Rest of Euro area	**16**	**4.4**
Other Industrialized	**16**	**6.6**
Developing Countries	***152***	***57.6***
China		17.3
India		7.0
Rest of Developing Asia	29	7.4
Sub-Saharan Africa	45	3.1
Middle East/North Africa	20	6.7
Latin America/Caribbean	32	8.2
Central and Eastern Europe	24	7.9

Source: Data from IMF's World Economic Outlook October 2016

2.1 Geographic Patterns

Figure 28.6 shows the location of the relatively rich and the relatively poor countries around the world. Notice that the higher-income countries tend to be in the northern part of the world. Exceptions to this rule are Australia and New Zealand, with relatively high income per capita. Aside from these exceptions, income disparity appears to have a geographic pattern—the North is relatively rich and the South is relatively poor. Often people use the term *North-South problem* to describe world income disparities.

But whether it is North versus South or not, many rich or many poor countries appear to be located together in large contiguous regions. The original increase in economic growth that occurred at the time of the Industrial Revolution started in northwestern Europe—England, France, and Germany. It then spread to America, which industrialized rapidly in the nineteenth and twentieth centuries. It also spread to Japan during the late-nineteenth-century Meiji Restoration, one of the main purposes of which was to import Western technology into the Japanese economy.

FIGURE 28.6 **Rich and Poor Countries around the World**

The highest-income regions tend to be located in North America, Europe, Japan, Australia, and the Middle East.

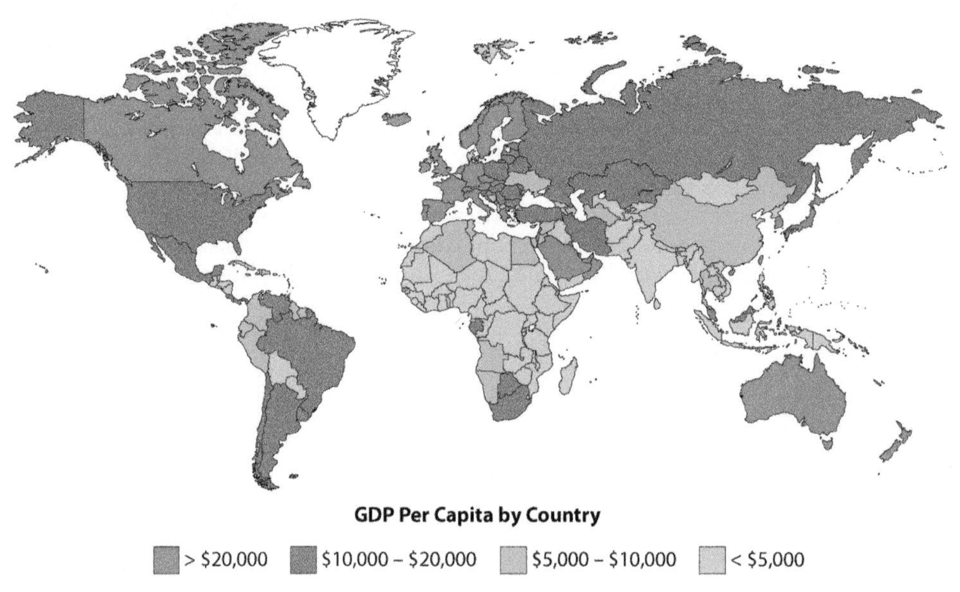

2.2 Billions Still in Poverty

The richest countries in the world, with more than $30,000 in GDP per capita (adjusted for differences in purchasing power across countries), account for about a billion people. The United States, with more than 300 million people, is among the richest, along with Japan and most of Western Europe. This group of countries, which accounted for more than 50 percent of world GDP, accounts for about one-sixth of the world's population.

Close to a billion people also live in emerging-market economies with a per capita GDP of between $15,000 and $30,000, many of them in the large economies of Brazil, Mexico, Turkey, and South Africa as well as in other Latin American and Eastern European economies. Another 1.7 billion people (400 million of them outside of China) live in countries that have an income per capita between $5,000 and $15,000. But the rest of the world's people—about 45 percent—live in countries with an income per capita of less than $5,000 per year. This amount is below the poverty level in advanced countries. Income per capita in China, Brazil, and South Africa is about one-quarter of that in the United States. Income per capita for the poorest Sub-Saharan African countries like Ethiopia, Uganda, and Zimbabwe is a mere 3 percent to 5 percent of that in the United States.

The economists Shaohua Chen and Martin Ravallion calculated that, in 2005, about 900 million people lived on less than US$1.00 a day and that close to 2.5 billion people—close to half the human race—lived on less than US$2.00 per day. The consequences of this poverty are staggering. Every year, some 3 million people die for lack of immunization, 1 million die from malaria, 3 million die from water-related diseases, and 2 million die from exposure to stove smoke inside their own homes. In addition, HIV/AIDS has ravaged the populations of developing nations, particularly in Africa. More than 1 billion people do not have safe water to drink, 2 billion have no electricity, and 2 billion lack adequate sanitation. Low income per capita is a serious economic problem, but the implications go well beyond economics. Large differences in income per capita and extensive poverty can lead to war, revolution, or regional conflicts.

2.3 Hope for the Future

We have plenty of reasons, however, to be optimistic about the future. One of the most encouraging developments of the last few decades has been the dramatic economic growth rates experienced by China and India, home to more than one-third of the world population. As Figure 28.7 shows, China grew extremely rapidly beginning in the 1980s and India began to grow more rapidly about a decade later. Economic growth in these two economies has lifted hundreds of millions of people out of a life of dire poverty. Chen and Ravallion's calculations indicate that in the quarter century between 1980 and 2005, the number of people living on less than US$1 a day was cut in half, a reduction of nearly 700 million people living in dire poverty with almost all of that reduction occurring in China. Even though the reduction in India was minuscule by comparison, the fact that the number of poor people held stable was an encouraging sign for a country whose population increased by several hundred million people over this period.

FIGURE 28.7 Rapid Growth in China and India

China and India are the two most populous nations in the world, home to more than 2.5 billion people. Rapid growth in these two economies has been one of the great success stories of the last quarter century for the world economy.

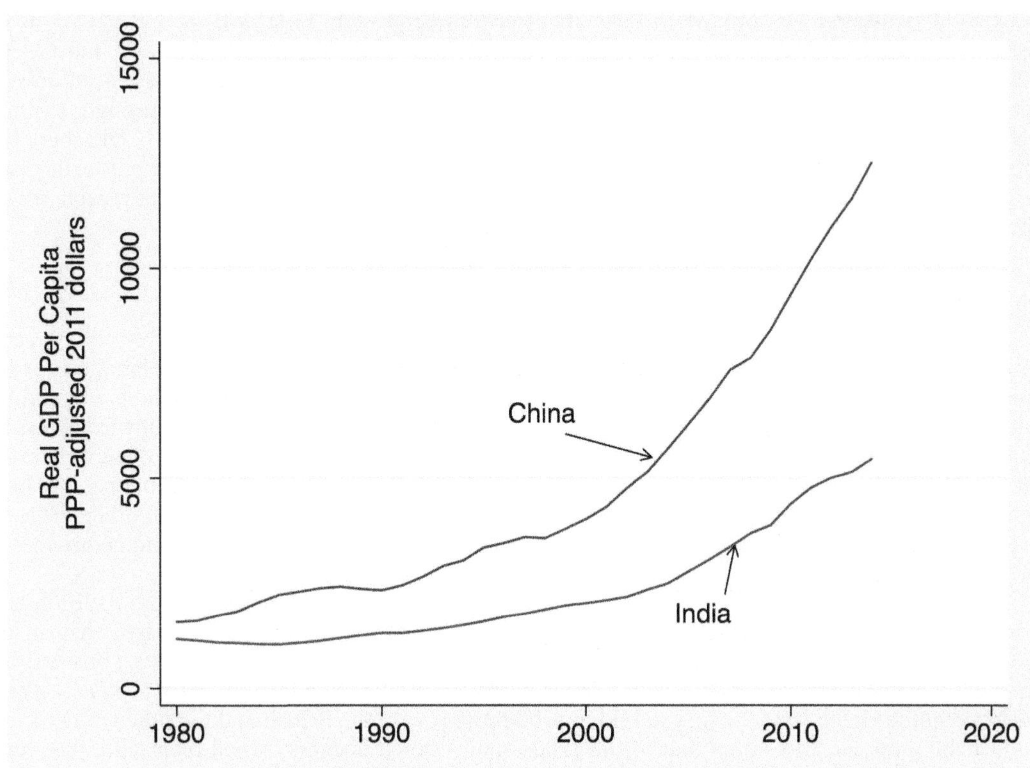

Source: Authors' calculations using data from Penn World Tables

Further signs of encouragement recently have emerged in parts of Sub-Saharan Africa, a region that has long produced a steady stream of news stories about poverty, conflict, and human suffering. Such stories remain the norm from countries like Somalia, Sudan, Zimbabwe, and the Congo; however, for the first time in many decades, more than a handful of countries in the region seem to provide cause for genuine optimism. The economist Steven Radelet has been one of the most prominent chroniclers of this new "Emerging Africa," writing about how countries like Ghana, South Africa, Tanzania, and Zambia have demonstrated more than a decade-long trend of improved economic performance, thus lowering poverty and providing better prospects and more hope for the youth of the region.

Will these improvements persist? Is the lack of catch-up that has left so many behind finally a thing of the past? We next examine the reasons why some countries or regions have been unable to catch up to the rich countries in the way that the East Asian economies or China seems to have been able to do. Our examination will consider the two key determinants of increasing productivity—improvements in technology and higher capital per worker. We consider technology in the next section and then consider capital in the following section.

REVIEW

- The lack of catch-up experienced by poor countries has resulted in considerable income inequality around the world. The vast majority of the people in the world do not live in the rich industrial nations.
- With a few exceptions, most of the rich countries are in the northern regions of the globe and most of the poor countries are in the southern regions.
- Low income per capita is a serious economic problem for well-being. Millions of people die in poor countries from a lack of access to basic amenities like childhood immunization, clean water, lack of sanitation, and environmental hazards.
- Economic growth in China and India has improved the lives of hundreds of millions of people and provided cause for optimism. More recent indicators suggest that some parts of Sub-Saharan Africa finally are beginning to experience economic development.
- More work needs to be done to understand why only a subset of the LDCs seem to have been able to catch up with the wealthier economies.

3. THE SPREAD AND USE OF TECHNOLOGY

You should remember two important facts about economic growth. First, a large and persistent increase in economic growth began during the Industrial Revolution about 200 years ago, and this increase in economic growth raised income per capita in some countries to levels experienced only by royalty throughout most of human history. Second, economic growth did not spread throughout much of the world, leaving people in many countries hardly better off than their ancestors. Could these two facts be linked? Could they have the same explanation? A number of ideas have been put forth to explain the increase in economic growth in the late 1700s, and some of these ideas may explain why growth has not accelerated in many developing countries.

3.1 Entrepreneurs in the Industrial Nations

Some economists and historians have pointed to developments in science as the explanation for the rapid increase in economic growth in Europe in the 1700s. But if that is the explanation, why did the Industrial Revolution not begin in China or in the Islamic nations, where scientific knowledge was far more advanced than in Europe? Others note the importance of natural resources, but these were available in many other countries that did not have an Industrial Revolution; also, growth in Japan has been high since the mid-nineteenth century, yet Japan has almost no natural resources. Still others have focused on exploitation, slavery, colonialism, and imperialism, but these evils existed long before the Industrial Revolution.

What, then, is the reason for this increase in economic growth that we associate with the Industrial Revolution? Historians of capitalist development from Karl Marx onward have stressed that, in the 1700s, for the first time in human history, entrepreneurs were gaining the freedom to start business enterprises. Economic historian Angus Maddison shows in an influential book, *Phases of Capitalist Development*, that the Dutch were the first to lead in productivity, with the British and then the United States soon catching up. He also shows that in the 1700s, many Dutch farmers owned their land, the feudal nobility was small and weak, and the potential power was in the hands of entrepreneurs. Hence, people had greater freedom to produce and sell manufactured and agricultural products. By the late 1700s and early 1800s, similar conditions existed in the United Kingdom and the United States. Firms could ship their products to market and hire workers without political restrictions.

Moreover, these firms were able to earn as much as they could by selling whatever they wanted at whatever price the market determined. They began to invent and develop products that were most beneficial to individuals. The business enterprises could keep the profits. Profits were no longer confiscated by nobles or kings. Individual property rights—including the right to earn and keep profits—were being established and recognized in the courts.

Karl Marx—although known more for his critique of capitalism—saw earlier than others that the unleashing of business enterprises and entrepreneurs was the key to economic growth. He credited the business and entrepreneurial class—what he called the bourgeois class—with the creation of more wealth than previously had been created throughout all of history.

The sudden increase in technology and productivity may have occurred when it did because of the increased freedom that entrepreneurs had to start businesses, to invent and apply new ideas, and to develop products for the mass of humanity in areas where the large markets existed.

Knitting cooperatives in Ecuador open up a market for women who traditionally knitted at home for their families. The freedom to start businesses and to produce and sell manufactured products without restriction is a critical piece of the economic growth puzzle for many developing countries.

Source: Shutterstock.com

3.2 Remaining Problems in Developing Countries

If true, the idea that an economic growth surge follows the removal of restrictions on business enterprises may have lessons for economic development. Many developing countries, which have yet to experience rapid growth and catch-up, place restrictions on entrepreneurial activity and have weak enforcement of individual property rights.

Regulation and Legal Rights

Good examples of these restrictions have been documented in the research of economist Hernando de Soto on the economy of Peru. De Soto showed that developing countries have a tremendous amount of regulation. This regulation has been so costly that a huge informal economy has emerged. The **informal economy** consists of large numbers of illegal businesses that can avoid the regulations. Remarkably, de Soto found that 61 percent of employment in Peru was in the informal, unregulated, illegal sector of the economy. In the city of Lima, around 33 percent of the houses were built by this informal sector. About 71,000 illegal vendors dominated retail trade, and 93 percent of urban transportation was in the informal sector.

informal economy

The portion of an economy characterized by illegal, unregulated businesses.

This large informal sector exists because the costs of setting up a legal business are high. It takes 32 months—filling out forms, waiting for approval, getting permission from several agencies—for a person to start a retail business. It takes six years and 11 months to start a housing construction firm. Hence, it is essentially impossible for someone to try to start a small business in the legal sector. Therefore, the informal sector grows.

Why does it matter if the informal sector is large? How does this impede development? Precisely because the sector is informal, it lacks basic legal rights such as the enforcement of the laws of property rights and contracts. These laws cannot been forced on a sector that is outside the law. Bringing new inventions to market requires the security of private property so that the inventor can capture the benefits from taking the risks. Without this, the earnings from the innovation might be taken away by the government or by firms that copy the idea illegally. For example, if a business in the informal sector finds that another firm has reneged on a contract to deliver a product, that business has no right to use the courts to enforce the contract because the business itself is illegal.

The explanation given earlier for why the Industrial Revolution occurred in Western Hemisphere countries seems to point to this as a reason. In Europe in the 1700s, a new freedom for businesses to operate in the emerging-market economy led to new products and technology. Laws to prevent theft or fraud gave people more certainty about reaping the returns from their entrepreneurship.

Lack of Human Captial

For existing technology to be adopted—whether in the form of innovative organizational structures of firms or as new products—it is necessary to have well-trained and highly skilled workers. For example, it is hard to make use of sophisticated computers to increase productivity when few skilled computer programmers are available.

Recall that human capital refers to the education and training of workers. Low investment in human capital is a serious obstacle to increasing productivity because it hampers the ability of countries that are behind to use new technology.

In fact, economists have found that differences in human capital in different countries can explain why some countries have been more successful at catching up than others. The developing countries that have been catching up most rapidly—in particular, the newly industrialized countries like South Korea, Hong Kong, Taiwan, and Singapore—have strong education systems in grade school and high school. This result demonstrates the enormous importance of human capital for raising productivity.

REVIEW

- The removal of restrictions on private enterprise and enforcement of individual property rights may have been the key factors unleashing the growth of productivity at the time of the Industrial Revolution.
- In more recent times, both China and India saw dramatic economic transformations after policies that were designed to suppress private enterprise and create obstacles to entrepreneurship were lifted.
- Similar restrictions may explain why other developing countries have not been able to experience the kind of rapid economic growth that China and India have experienced in recent years.
- An educated workforce is needed to adopt technology. Better-educated and more highly skilled workers—those with human capital—also can use available capital more efficiently.

4. INCREASING CAPITAL PER WORKER

In addition to obstacles to the spread and adoption of new technology, obstacles to the increase in capital per worker can prevent poor countries from catching up.

4.1 Population Growth

For the capital-to-labor ratio to increase, it is necessary to invest in new capital. The amount of investment in new capital, however, must be larger than the increase in labor, or capital will increase by less than labor and the ratio of capital to labor—the factor influencing productivity—will fall. Thus, high population growth raises the amount of investment needed to increase, or even maintain, the level of capital per worker. High population growth rates, therefore, can slow down the increase in capital per worker.

Population growth rates have declined substantially in locations where income per capita has risen to high levels, such as Europe, Japan, and the United States. Economic analysis of the determinants of population indicates that the high income per capita and resulting greater life expectancy may be the reason for the decline in population growth. When countries reach a level of income per capita at which people can survive into their old age without the support of many children, or at which the chance is greater of children reaching working age, people choose to have fewer children.

Population growth rates also have declined in the fast-growing East Asian economies and in China and India. Fertility rates in India were cut in half during the latter part of the twentieth century and the decline in China may have been even more dramatic as a result of the controversial "one-child" policy. Other poor nations in the twenty-first century probably could follow the example of these countries and raise income per capita by lowering their rates of population growth.

4.2 National Saving

Capital accumulation requires investment, which requires saving. From our national income accounting equation, $Y = C + I + G + X$, we get the equation $Y - C - G = I + X$, which states that national saving is equal to the sum of investment plus net exports. Recall that national saving is the sum of private saving and government saving. In some developing countries where income per capita is barely above subsistence levels, the level of private saving—people's income less their consumption—is low. Government saving—tax receipts less expenditures—also is low, perhaps because there is little income to tax and because governments have trouble controlling expenditures. Saving rates in Africa are low compared with the higher saving rates in advanced economies and in Asia. This could explain why capital accumulation is low in these nations that have not experienced catch-up.

On the other hand, some of the economies that did experience catch-up, such as China or the East Asian economies, increased saving quite dramatically, which in turn meant that they had more resources that they could invest into the domestic economy. For many poor countries, however, it is natural for national saving to be less than investment and thus for imports to be greater than exports (net exports less than zero). In other words, a poor country naturally looks to investment from abroad as a source of capital formation for economic growth.

National saving = investment + net exports

$S = I + X$

4.3 Foreign Investment from the Advanced Economies

Investment from abroad can come in the form of **foreign direct investment (FDI)**, such as when the U.S. firm Gap Inc. opens a store in Mexico. Technically, when a foreign firm invests in more than 10 percent of the ownership of a business in another country, that investment is defined as direct investment.

foreign direct investment (FDI)

Investment by a foreign entity in at least a 10 percent direct ownership share in a firm.

Foreign investment also occurs when foreigners buy smaller percentages (less than 10 percent) of firms in developing economies. For example, foreign investment in Mexico takes place when a German buys newly offered common stock in a Mexican firm. In that case, the foreign investment from abroad is defined as **portfolio investment**, that is, less than 10 percent of ownership in a company.

As you may have read about in the newspapers, FDI has played a substantial role in the rapid catch-up demonstrated by China over the last few years. China has leveraged the substantial amount of unskilled resources and manufacturing-friendly policies and regulations to become the "manufacturer to the world" in recent years. India has been just as successful in attracting FDI in areas related to the provision of services as China has been in attracting FDI related to the production of manufactured goods. Indian call centers, software programmers, and information technology firms have attracted substantial foreign resources seeking to take advantage of the skilled English-speaking workforce that India is able to offer.

Another way investment can flow in from abroad is through borrowing. Firms in developing economies or their governments can borrow from commercial banks, such as Bank of America, Mizuho, or Credit Lyonnais. Sometimes the governments of developing economies obtain loans directly from the governments of industrial economies. Borrowing from government-sponsored international financial institutions, such as the IMF and the World Bank, also can occur. Many emerging market economies have expanded and improved their banking sectors and their financial markets to attract foreign investors. Although these liberalizations have greatly expanded access to capital for domestic firms, recent history suggests that a country can face negative effects from too much unregulated money entering, and then rapidly departing, the domestic economy.

Activists such as U2 star Bono have been effective proponents of efforts to improve the effectiveness of foreign aid. By working with the governments of the United States, the United Kingdom, and others, activists have helped improve and increase foreign aid through such programs as the MCC and 100 percent debt cancellation of World Bank loans to the poorest countries.

Source: JStone / Shutterstock.com

portfolio investment

Investment by a foreign entity in less than a 10 percent ownership share in a firm.

4.4 Borrowing from International Agencies

World Bank

An international agency, established after World War II, designed to promote the economic development of poorer countries through lending channeled from industrial countries.

International Monetary Fund (IMF)

An international agency, established after World War II, designed to help countries with balance of payments problems and to ensure the smooth functioning of the international monetary system.

The **World Bank** and the **International Monetary Fund (IMF)** were established after World War II as part of a major reform of the international monetary system. Both institutions make loans to developing countries. They serve as intermediaries, channeling funds from the industrial countries to the developing countries.

Many of the World Bank's loans are for specific projects—such as building a $100 million dam for irrigation in Brazil and a $153 million highway in Poland. Although these project loans have been helpful, they are much smaller in total than private investment in these countries.

In recent years, the IMF has tried to use its loans to encourage countries to implement difficult economic reforms. Frequently, it tries to induce countries to make these reforms by making the loans conditional on the reforms; this is the idea of conditionality. Under conditionality, the IMF gives loans to countries only if the countries undertake economic reform—such as eliminating price controls or privatizing firms. This conditionality is viewed as a way to encourage reforms that are difficult to put into effect because of the various vested interests in each country.

The IMF has been criticized heavily in recent years for going too far with its conditions and actually giving bad economic advice to developing countries. For example, during the financial crisis in East Asia in 1997 and 1998, the IMF insisted that the countries in crisis implement politically controversial reforms before it would agree to make loans to deal with the crisis.

REVIEW

- High rates of population growth and low national saving rates are two of the obstacles to raising capital per worker in developing economies. Many of the economies that experienced catch-up were able to lower their population growth rates and increase national saving.
- Poor economies that are open can increase domestic investment by attracting FDI and portfolio investment. These policies can help raise capital per worker in the poor economies even in cases in which they are unable to save more. Both China and India have been successful at attracting FDI inflows in recent years.
- Poor countries can accumulate capital per worker by borrowing money from international organizations. The IMF makes loans to developing countries that frequently are conditional on an economic reform program, a practice that came under heavy criticism in the Asian financial crisis of the 1990s. The World Bank makes loans mainly for specific projects.

5. END-OF-CHAPTER MATERIAL

5.1 Conclusion

In this chapter, we documented fundamental differences in economic growth across countries and demonstrated that these differences do not have a broad-based tendency to go away over time. The consequence of this lack of catch-up is that people in the industrial nations are much better off on average than the people in developing nations. Some developing countries have managed to catch up over the past half-century, most noticeably countries in East Asia, such as South Korea and Malaysia. These countries have either become industrial nations (for example, South Korea) or have been categorized as emerging market economies (for example, Brazil, Russia, or China), closer in spirit to the industrial economies than to their poorer counterparts.

Over the past three decades, the most remarkable improvements in economic growth have come from China, and more recently from India. The consequence of this economic growth has been a remarkable reduction in poverty, especially in China. But many other countries have not been able to replicate the experiences of South Korea, China, and India and have spent decades stuck in poverty without any growth. This has been particularly true for countries in Africa, although a few African nations recently have shown some promising signs of growth.

How can we explain the lack of catch-up in the global economy? Among the possible explanations for the lack of catch-up are obstacles to the spread of technology, such as government restrictions on entrepreneurs and a shortage of human capital, and obstacles to higher capital per worker, such as low saving rates and low foreign investment. The removal of similar obstacles in Western Europe in the eighteenth century may have been the cause of the Industrial Revolution. Their removal in China and India set the stage for the now almost three-decades-long boom in economic growth that has transformed the lives of people living in the two most populous nations of the world. Similar reforms in the other nations, yet to experience catch-up, may result in another great growth wave in the developing economies. If real GDP in all the other countries of the world grows at a rate that is even half of what a country like China has achieved, then the economic landscape of the world will be transformed in the rest of this century. These countries face many obstacles to such a transformation. One threat comes from the rise of terrorism and military conflicts that divide nations, disrupt progress, and divert resources from more productive uses. The increasing tendency for economic fluctuations, such as the recent U.S. recession, to be synchronized into a global economic slowdown may lead to a backlash in the form of increased protectionism and a more vocal antiglobalization movement. It is hardly an exaggeration to say that the progress of humankind in the twenty-first century may depend critically on whether increased globalization is a force for, or an obstacle to, global economic growth.

Key Points

1. Economic growth theory pinpoints capital accumulation and technological change as the two key ingredients of productivity growth. In a world without obstacles to the spread of technology or to investment in new capital, growth theory predicts that poor regions will catch up to rich regions.
2. Catch-up has occurred in the U.S. states, among the industrial countries, and among some economies in East Asia but is distressingly absent from many developing countries.
3. Low incomes and poverty have persisted for the vast majority of the world's population while other countries have become richer.
4. Some countries may have poor growth performance because of restrictions on markets and a lack of property rights. The lifting of those restrictions in Europe in the 1700s was a cause of the economic growth associated with the Industrial Revolution.
5. Similarly, the removal of such restrictions was a key factor to the increased productivity and economic development in India and China and is likely to have a similar result for any other developing country that hopes to break free of economic stagnation and to catch up with the industrial nations.
6. In many countries in the twenty-first century, especially in Latin America and Asia, the potential for higher economic growth is great, as the market system is being encouraged and restrictions on entrepreneurs are being removed.
7. High rates of population growth and low national saving rates are two of the obstacles to raising capital per worker in developing economies.
8. Poor economies can increase capital per worker by attracting foreign direct investment (FDI) and portfolio investment. Both China and India have been successful at attracting FDI inflows in recent years.

QUESTIONS FOR REVIEW

1. Why does economic growth theory predict that productivity and real income per capita will grow relatively more rapidly in poor countries?
2. In what way does the catch-up line describe more rapid growth in poor countries?
3. Why is catch-up observed among the industrial economies but not for the whole world?
4. How did the removal of government restrictions on entrepreneurs lead to more economic growth, both historically in the industrial nations as well as in modern times in countries like China and India that experienced catch-up?
5. What role does human capital play in the adoption and spread of technology?
6. Why is the identity that investment plus net exports equals saving important for understanding the flow of capital around the world?
7. How did countries like China and India benefit from the flows of capital in a globalized world?
8. What is the difference between foreign direct investment and portfolio investment?
9. What role do international organizations like the International Monetary Fund and the World Bank play in promoting economic growth and economic development?
10. Why do we say that increased globalization occasionally can harm an economy as well as help the economy catch up?

PROBLEMS

1. Plot on a scatter diagram the data for the Asian countries that appear below. Does a catch-up line appear in the scatter diagram?

Country	Per Capita Real GDP in 1960 (2000 U.S. dollars)	Average Annual Rate of Growth from 1960 to 2000 (%)
Thailand	1,051	4.6
Pakistan	526	2.9
Philippines	1,581	1.3
China	746	4.3
Malaysia	1,918	3.9
Indonesia	403	3.4

2. The rule of 72 gives the approximate doubling time of a variable if you know its rate of growth. For example, if the population of a country is 200 million and the rate of growth of its population is 2 percent per year, then it will take approximately 36 years for the country's population to reach 400 million. Assume that per capita income in 2006 is $40,000 in the United States and $5,000 in China. If the per capita growth rate in China is 9 percent a year, how long will it take for China to reach a per capita income level that is equivalent to the United States' 2006 per capita income level?
3. Which of the following will increase the likelihood of poor countries catching up to rich countries, and which will decrease the likelihood? Explain.
    a. Industrial countries do not allow their technology to be bought or leased by firms in developing countries.
    b. Worldwide saving rates shift up.
    c. The legal system in developing countries is improved to protect property rights.
    d. Governments in developing countries make use of their international aid to buy armaments from developed countries.
    e. Investment in human capital increases in the developing countries.
4. The U.S. states have moved toward one another in real income per capita over the past 100 years, but the countries of the world have not. What differences between state borders and country borders might explain this problem?
5. Figure 28.2 shows that California and Nevada had very high levels of per capita income in 1880. What was the source of their high income? Identify some countries in the world that currently have relatively high per capita income for a similar reason.
6. Figure 28.6 identifies the countries with the highest GDP per capita in the world. What characteristics of the labor forces in these countries provide part of the explanation for their higher incomes?
7. Suppose a developing country does not allow foreign investment to flow into the country and, at the same time, has a very low saving rate. Use the fact that saving equals investment plus net exports and the growth accounting formula to explain why this country will have difficulty catching up with the industrial countries. What can the country do to improve its productivity if it does not allow capital in from outside the country?
8. Most developing countries have low saving rates and governments that run budget deficits. What will be required for such countries to have large increases in their capital stocks? What will happen if industrial countries' saving rates decline as well? How does this affect the developing countries' prospects for catching up?

ENDNOTES

1. http://www.un.org/millenniumgoals/news.shtml

CHAPTER 29

International Trade

The topic of international trade featured prominently in the 2016 presidential election. Even though the candidates remained bitterly divided on many issues, they both seemed to agree that the Trans-Pacific Partnership (TPP), a trade agreement between the United States, Japan, Canada, Mexico, Australia and several Pacific Rim nations that had been agreed to but not yet ratified, was harmful to American workers.

Throughout the campaign, Donald Trump, the Republican presidential nominee, argued that the trade agreements that the United States had entered into over the past few decades, such as the North-American Free Trade Agreement (NAFTA) had weakened the U.S. economy and made the life of American workers worse. He argued that the United States government needed to take more actions to defend U.S. interests in the World Trade Organization (WTO), the international organization whose rules govern nearly all of the world's trade between countries.

Bagmane Tech Park, known as India's Silicon Valley, is a software technology park in Bangalore, India.

Source: Shutterstock.com

The election results showed that this message seemed to resonate with the public. The election was significantly impacted by voters in Midwestern states like Ohio, Wisconsin, Michigan and Pennsylvania who felt that their lives had been adversely impacted by international trade. Over the last few decades, many small towns in these states had suffered as a result of the only large employer in town, typically a large manufacturing firm, either closing up their factory and moving production overseas or shutting down in the face of increased competition from foreign producers. These workers seemed to long for a change in international trade policy that would help restore these factories to their communities, even though most economists were very skeptical that those same jobs would ever return.

One of the first actions that President Trump took in office was to withdraw the United States from the TPP. Analysts pointed to the potential for conflict between pre-trade and anti-trade factions in the country and in particular to disagreements between the Administration and the Republican majority in Congress, many of whom favored the trade agreements and had voted to provide the president with "trade promotion authority" in which the Administration could negotiate trade deals that Congress could then approve or deny but not hold up or change.

In other parts of the world, though, many viewed international trade agreements as having brought positive transformation to the lives of tens of millions of people. Consider, for example, Bangalore, an Indian city of about 6 million people, which has undergone a remarkable economic transformation in recent times. Bangalore is now one of the leading cities in the production of computer software. The rapid increase in jobs in the software and information technology industry has brought prosperity to an increasing number of workers in Bangalore. Similar stories can be told about U.S. trade with many countries in the world. Every day, people in countries like China, Germany, Korea, Japan, and Sri Lanka buy U.S. products: Caterpillar tractors, iPhones, Microsoft software, Boeing 747s, and Merck pharmaceuticals. At the same time, Americans drive cars made in Germany and Japan, watch television on Korean-produced TVs and laptops, play tennis wearing Nike shoes made in Korea, or go swimming in Ocean Pacific swimsuits made in Sri Lanka.

Even though international trade clearly has both supporters and detractors among politicians and voters, economists are much more in agreement about the benefits and positive impacts of international trade. From the very early days of economics as a subject, Adam Smith and David Ricardo emphasized that there are huge gains from trade between nations. Today, economists continue to point to the benefits from international trade noting, for example, that the North American Free Trade Agreement brought better economic policies and higher incomes than would have been possible in the U.S., Canada, and Mexico without NAFTA.

gains from trade

Improvements in income, production, or satisfaction owing to the exchange of goods or services.

In this chapter we learn what economic theory has to say about why people benefit from international trade. First, international trade allows different countries to specialize in what they are relatively efficient at producing, such as pharmaceuticals in the United States or electronic equipment in Malaysia. Second, international trade gives firms such as Merck access to a large world market, enabling them to invest heavily in research and reduce costs by concentrating production. This chapter explores the reasons for these **gains from trade** and develops two models that can be used to measure the actual size of these gains. In the process, we will also see that even though there are overall gains to the economy, trade does impact some groups negatively.

These distributional impacts will help us better understand the difference between international trade *theory*, which describes the gains from trade, and international trade *policy*, which often seems to seek to restrict trade despite those gains. From David Ricardo working in the British parliament to repeal protectionist trade laws 150 years ago to the debates over the "Buy American" clause in the 2009 stimulus bill to today's desire to renegotiate all existing trade agreements to get a better deal for Americans workers, the goal is the same: to understand the gains from trade and achieve the economic gains from trade in practice in a democracy.

1. TRENDS IN INTERNATIONAL TRADE

international trade

The exchange of goods and services between people or firms in different nations.

International trade is trade between people or firms in different countries. Trade between people in Detroit and Ottawa, Canada, is international trade, whereas trade between Detroit and Chicago is trade within a country. Thus, international trade is just another kind of economic interaction; it is subject to the same basic economic principles as trade between people in the same country.

International trade differs from trade in domestic markets, however, because national governments frequently place restrictions, such as **tariffs** or **quotas**, on trade between countries that they do not place on trade within countries. For example, the Texas legislature cannot limit or put a tariff on the import of Florida oranges into Texas. The **commerce clause** of the U.S. Constitution forbids such restraint of trade between states. But the United States can restrict the import of oranges from Brazil. Similarly, Japan can restrict the import of rice from the United States, and Australia can restrict the import of Japanese automobiles.

tariffs
A tax on imports.

quotas
A government limit on the quantity of a good that may be imported or sold.

commerce clause
The clause in the U.S. Constitution that prohibits restraint of trade between states.

International trade has grown much faster than trade within countries in recent years. Figure 29.1 shows the exports for all countries in the world as a percentage of the world gross domestic product (GDP). International trade has doubled as a proportion of the world's GDP during the last 40 or so years. Why has international trade grown so rapidly? What economic or technological forces have led to this increase in globalization?

One reason that international trade has grown so rapidly can be attributed to the dramatic reduction in the cost of transportation and communication. The cost of air travel fell to $0.095 per mile in 2000 from $0.87 per mile in 1930, and the cost of a three-minute phone call from New York to London fell to $0.24 in 2002 from $50 in 1960 (adjusting the 1960 prices for general inflation). The use of shipping containers to move vast amounts of cargo across the ocean on giant container ships dramatically lowered shipping costs, in some cases by over 95% compared to having to load and unload individual loads of goods. Use of e-mail and access to the Internet, unheard of in 1960, have reduced the cost of shipping "information" to a degree that is almost unfathomable to quantify compared to the 1960s.

FIGURE 29.1 World Trade as a Share of GDP

The faster growth of trade compared with GDP is probably due to the reduction in trade restrictions and the lower cost of transportation, both characteristics of greater globalization.

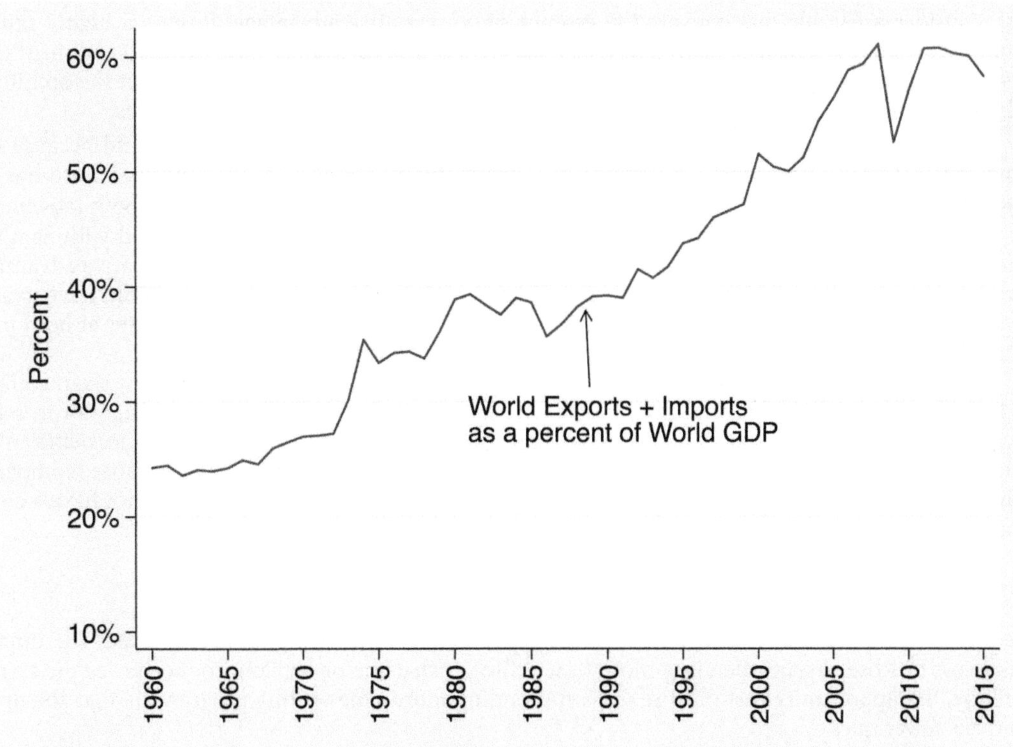

Source: World Bank (http://data.worldbank.org/)

The most important reason that trade has expanded so rapidly, however, is that government restrictions on trade between countries have come down. Western European countries have integrated into a single market called the European Union. Canada, Mexico, and the United States have agreed to integrate their economies into a free trade area, where the term free indicates the elimination of restrictions on trade. Previously closed economies have opened themselves to world trade through major political and economic reforms. Inspired by the rapid growth of export-oriented countries in Asia like Korea and Malaysia, other governments in Asia and South America in places such as Argentina, Bangladesh and Chile have opened their economies to competition and foreign trade. The formerly closed economies in Eastern Europe, the Russian Federation, and, especially, China have joined the World Trade Organization, an international organization that has outlined the rules under which virtually all global trade takes place today. Large multinational firms have built complex global supply chains, for example bringing in raw materials from Africa to manufacturing plants in Asia to produce cellular phones that are programmed with software written in the United States and sold to consumers in Europe. Understanding the economic reasons underpinning these global trade patterns is our first task for this chapter.

REVIEW

- The basic principles of economics apply to international trade between people in different countries.
- Governments have a greater tendency to interfere with trade between countries than with trade within their own country.
- International trade has grown rapidly in recent years because of reduced transportation and communication costs and, especially lower government barriers to trade.

2. COMPARATIVE ADVANTAGE

comparative advantage

A situation in which a person or country can produce one good at a lower opportunity cost than another person or country.

According to the theory of **comparative advantage**, a country can improve the income of its citizens by allowing them to trade with people in other countries, even if the people of the country are less efficient at producing all items.

2.1 Getting a Gut Feeling for Comparative Advantage

First, consider a parable that conveys the essence of comparative advantage. Rose is a highly skilled computer programmer who writes computer-assisted drawing programs. Rose owns a small firm that sells her programs to architects. She has hired an experienced salesman, Sam, to contact the architects and sell her software. Thus, Rose specializes in programming, and Sam specializes in sales.

absolute advantage

A situation in which a person or country is more efficient at producing a good in comparison with another person or country.

You need to know a little more about Rose. Rose is a friendly, outgoing person, and because she knows her product better than Sam does, she is better than Sam at sales. We say that Rose has an **absolute advantage** over Sam in both programming and sales because she is better at both jobs. But it still makes sense for Rose to hire Sam because her efficiency at programming compared with Sam's is greater than her efficiency at sales compared with Sam's. We say that Rose has a comparative advantage over Sam in programming rather than in sales. If Rose sold her programs, then she would have to sacrifice her programming time, and her profits would fall. Thus, even though Rose is better at both programming and sales, she hires Sam to do the selling so that she can program full time.

All this seems sensible. One additional part of the terminology, however, may at first seem confusing but is important. We said that Rose has the comparative advantage in programming, not in sales. But who does have the comparative advantage in sales? Sam does. Even though Sam is less efficient at both sales and programming, we say that he has a comparative advantage in sales because, compared with Rose, he does relatively better at sales than he does at programming. A person cannot have a comparative advantage in both of only two activities.

Opportunity Cost, Relative Efficiency, and Comparative Advantage

opportunity cost

The value of the next-best forgone alternative that was not chosen because something else was chosen.

The idea of comparative advantage also can be explained in terms of **opportunity cost**. The opportunity cost of Rose or Sam spending more time selling is that she or he can produce fewer programs. Similarly, the opportunity cost of Rose or Sam spending more time writing programs is that she or he can make fewer sales.

Observe that, in the example, Sam has a lower opportunity cost of spending his time selling than Rose does; thus, it makes sense for Sam to do the selling rather than Rose. In contrast, Rose has a lower opportunity cost of spending her time writing computer programs than Sam does; thus, it makes sense for Rose to write computer programs rather than Sam.

Opportunity costs give us a way to define comparative advantage. A person with a lower opportunity cost of producing a good than another person has a comparative advantage in that good. Thus, Rose has a comparative advantage in computer programming, and Sam has a comparative advantage in sales.

Comparative advantage also can be explained in terms of relative efficiency. A person who is relatively more efficient at producing good *X* than good *Y*, compared with another person, has a comparative advantage in good *X*. Thus, again, we see that Rose has a comparative advantage in computer programming because she is relatively more efficient at producing computer programs than at making sales compared with Sam.

From People to Countries

Why is this story about Rose and Sam a parable? Because we can think of Rose and Sam as two countries that differ in efficiency at producing one product versus another. In the parable, Rose has a comparative advantage over Sam in programming, and Sam has a comparative advantage over Rose in sales. In general, *country A has a comparative advantage over country B in the production of a good if the opportunity cost of producing the good in country A is less than in country B, or, alternatively but equivalently stated, if country A can produce the good relatively more efficiently than it can produce other goods compared with country B.* Thus, if you understand the Rose and Sam story, you should have no problem understanding comparative advantage in two countries, which we now examine in more detail.

2.2 Productivity in Two Countries

Consider the following two goods: (1) vaccines and (2) televisions. Different skills are required for the production of vaccines and televisions. Vaccine production requires knowledge of chemistry and biology, and the marketing of products for which doctors make most of the choices. Producing televisions requires knowledge of electrical engineering and microcircuitry, and the marketing of goods for which consumers make most of the choices.

In the example used in this chapter, Korea has a comparative advantage in an electronic good (television sets), and the United States has a comparative advantage in a pharmaceutical (vaccines). Thus, with trade, the electronic good will be produced in Korea, as shown in the left-hand photo, and the pharmaceutical good will be produced in the United States, as shown in the right-hand photo.

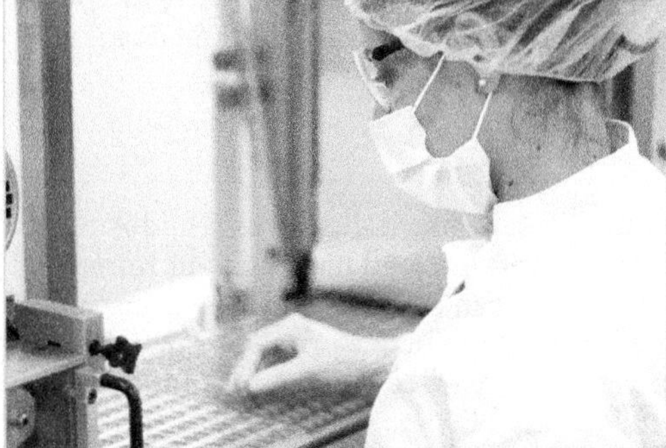

Electronics versus Pharmaceuticals

Source: humphery / Shutterstock.com

Table 29.1 provides an example of productivity differences in the production of vaccines and televisions in two different countries, the United States and Korea. Productivity is measured by the amount of each good that can be produced by a worker per day of work. To be specific, let us suppose that the vaccines are measured in vials, that the televisions are measured in numbers of television sets, and that labor is the only factor of production in making vaccines and television sets. The theory of comparative advantage does not depend on any of these assumptions, but they make the exposition much easier.

TABLE 29.1 Example of Productivity in the United States and Korea

	Output per Day of Work	
	Vials of Vaccine	*Number of Television Sets*
United States	6	3
Korea	1	2

According to Table 29.1, in the United States, it takes a worker one day of work to produce six vials of vaccine or three television sets. In Korea, one worker can produce one vial of vaccine or two television sets. Thus, the United States is more productive than Korea in producing both vaccines and television sets. We say that a country has an *absolute advantage* over another country in the production of a good if it is more efficient at producing that good. In this example, the United States has an absolute advantage in both vaccine and television set production.

The United States, however, has a comparative advantage over Korea in the production of vaccines rather than television sets. To see this, note that a worker in the United States can produce six times as many vials of vaccine as a worker in Korea but only 1.5 times as many television sets. In other words, the United States is relatively more efficient in vaccines than in television sets compared with Korea. Korea, being able to produce television sets relatively more efficiently than vaccines compared with the United States, has a comparative advantage in television sets.

Observe also how opportunity costs determine who has the comparative advantage. To produce three more television sets, the United States must sacrifice six vials of vaccine; in other words, in the United States, the *opportunity cost of one more television set is two vials of vaccine.* In Korea, to produce two more television sets, the Koreans must sacrifice one vial of vaccine; in other words, *in Korea, the opportunity cost of one more television set is only one-half vial of vaccine.* Thus, we see that the opportunity cost of producing television sets in Korea is lower than in the United States. By examining opportunity costs, we again see that Korea has a comparative advantage in television sets.

An American Worker's View

Because labor productivity in both goods is higher in the United States than in Korea, wages are higher in the United States than in Korea in the example. Now think about the situation from the point of view of U.S. workers who are paid more than Korean workers. They might wonder how they can compete with Korea. The Korean workers' wages seem very low compared with theirs. It does not seem fair. But as we will see, comparative advantage implies that U.S. workers can gain from trade with the Koreans.

A Korean Worker's View

It is useful to think about Table 29.1 from the perspective of a Korean worker as well as that of a U.S. worker. From the Korean perspective, it might be noted that Korean workers are less productive in both goods. Korean workers might wonder how they can ever compete with the United States, which looks like a productive powerhouse. Again, it does not seem fair. As we will see, however, the Koreans also can gain from trade with the Americans.

2.3 Finding the Relative Price

To measure how much the Koreans and Americans can gain from trade, we need to consider the *relative price* of vaccines and televisions in Korea and the United States. The relative price determines how much vaccine can be traded for televisions and, therefore, how much each country can gain from trade. For example, suppose the price of a television set is $200 and the price of a vial of vaccine is $100. Then two vials of vaccine cost the same as one television set; we say the relative price is two vials of vaccine per television set.

Another example of relative prices may be helpful:

Price of U2 concert ticket = $45.

Price of U2 t-shirt = $15.

Relative price = three t-shirts per concert ticket.

Relative Price without Trade

First, let us find the relative price with no trade between the countries. The relative price of two goods should depend on the relative costs of production. A good for which the cost of producing an additional quantity is relatively low will have a relatively low price.

Consider the United States. In this example, a day of work can produce either six vials of vaccine or three television sets. With labor as the only factor of production, six vials of vaccine cost the same to produce as three television sets; that is, two vials of vaccine cost the same to produce as one television set. Therefore, the relative price should be two vials of vaccine per television set.

Now consider Korea. Electronic goods should have a relatively low price in Korea because they are relatively cheap to produce. A day of work can produce either one vial of vaccine or two television sets; thus one vial of vaccine costs the same to produce as two television sets in Korea. Therefore, the relative price is one-half vial of vaccine per television set.

Relative Price with Trade

Now consider what happens when the two countries trade without government restrictions. If transportation costs are negligible and markets are competitive, then the price of a good must be the same in the United States and Korea. Why? Because any difference in price would quickly be eliminated by trade; if the price of television sets is much less in Korea than in the United States, then traders will buy television sets in Korea and sell them in the United States and make a profit; by doing so, however, they reduce the supply of television sets in Korea and increase the supply in the United States. This will drive up the price in Korea and drive down the price in the United States until the price of television sets in the two countries is the same. Thus, with trade, the price of vaccines and the price of television sets will converge to the same levels in both countries. The relative price therefore will converge to the same value in both countries.

If the relative price is going to be the same in both countries, then we know the price must be somewhere between the prices in the two countries before trade. That is, the price must be between two vials of vaccine per television set (the U.S. relative price) and one-half vial of vaccine per television set (the Korean relative price). We do not know exactly where the price will fall between one-half and two. It depends on the demand for vaccines and television sets in Korea and the United States. *Let us assume that the relative price is one vial of vaccine per television set after trade,* which is between one-half and two and is a nice, easy number for making computations. The calculation of the price with trade is summarized in Table 29.2.

TABLE 29.2 **The Relative Price (The relative price—vials of vaccine per television set—must be the same in both countries with trade.)**

	United States	Korea
Relative price before trade:	2 vials of vaccine per television set	1/2 vial of vaccine per television set
Relative price range after trade:	Between 1/2 and 2	Between 1/2 and 2
Relative price assumption:	1	1

2.4 Measuring the Gains from Trade

How large are the *gains from trade* because of comparative advantage? First, consider some examples.

One Country's Gain

Suppose that 10 U.S. workers move out of electronics production and begin producing pharmaceuticals. We know from Table 29.1 that these 10 U.S. workers can produce 60 vials of vaccine per day. Formerly, the 10 U.S. workers were producing 30 television sets per day. But their 60 vials of vaccine can be traded for television sets produced in Korea. With the relative price of one vial per television set, Americans will be able to exchange these 60 vials of vaccine for 60 television sets. Thus, Americans gain 30 more television sets by moving 10 more workers into vaccine production. This gain from trade is summarized in Table 29.3.

TABLE 29.3 **Changing Production and Gaining from trade in the United States and Korea**

	United States (10 workers)		
	Change in Production	*Amount Traded*	*Net Gain from Trade*
Vaccines	Up 60 vials	Export 60 vials	0
Television sets	Down 30 sets	Import 60 sets	30 sets

	Korea (30 workers)		
	Changes in Production	*Amount Traded*	*Net Fain from Trade*
Vaccines	Down 30 vials	Import 60 vials	30 vials
Television sets	Up 60 sets	export 60 sets	0

The Other Country's Gain

The same thing can happen in Korea. A Korean manufacturer can now hire 30 workers who formerly were working in vaccine production to produce television sets. Vaccine production declines by 30 vials, but television production increases by 60 sets. These 60 television sets can be traded with Americans for 60 vials of vaccine. The reduction in the production of vaccine of 30 vials results in an import of vaccine of 60 vials; thus, the gain from trade is 30 vials of vaccine. The Koreans, by moving workers out of vaccine production and into television set production, are getting more vaccine. This gain from trade for Korea is summarized in Table 29.3. Observe that the exports of television sets from Korea equal the imports of television sets to the United States.

Just Like a New Discovery

International trade is like the discovery of a new idea or technique that makes workers more productive. It is as if workers in the United States figured out how to produce more television sets with the same amount of effort. Their trick is that they actually produce vaccines, which then are traded for the television sets. Like any other new technique, international trade improves the well-being of Americans. International trade also improves the well-being of the Koreans; it is as if they discovered a new technique, too.

2.5 A Graphic Measure of the Gains from Trade

The gains from trade because of comparative advantage also can be found graphically with production possibilities curves, as shown in Figure 29.2. The figure has two graphs—one for the United States and the other for Korea. In both graphs, the horizontal axis has the number of television sets and the vertical axis has the number of vials of vaccine produced.

Production Possibilities Curves without Trade

The solid lines in the two graphs show the production possibilities curves for vaccines and television sets in the United States and in Korea before trade. To derive them, we assume, for illustrative purposes, that the United States has 10,000 workers and Korea has 30,000 workers who can make either vaccines or television sets.

If all the available workers in the United States produce vaccines, then total production will be 60,000 vials of vaccine (6 x 10,000) and zero television sets. Alternatively, if 5,000 workers produce vaccines in the United States and 5,000 workers produce television sets, then total production will be 30,000 vials of vaccine (6 x 5,000) and 15,000 television sets (3 x 5,000). The solid line in the graph on the left of Figure 29.2 shows these possibilities and all other possibilities for producing vaccines and television sets. It is the production possibilities curve without trade.

Korea's production possibilities curve without trade is shown by the solid line in the graph on the right of Figure 29.2. For example, if all 30,000 Korean workers produce television sets, a total of 60,000 television sets can be produced (2 x 30,000). This and other possibilities are on the curve.

The slopes of the two production possibilities curves without trade in Figure 29.2 show how many vials of vaccine can be transformed into television sets in Korea and the United States. The production possibilities curve for the United States is steeper than that for Korea because an increase in production of one television set reduces vaccine production by two vials in the United States but by only one-half vial in Korea. The slope of the production possibilities curve is the opportunity cost; the opportunity cost of producing television sets in the United States is higher than it is in Korea.

FIGURE 29.2 Comparative Advantage

On the left, Americans are better off with trade because the production possibilities curve shifts out with trade; thus, with trade, Americans reach a point like *C* rather than *A*. The gains from trade because of comparative advantage are equal to the distance between the two production possibilities curves—one with trade and the other without trade. On the right, Koreans also are better off because their production possibilities curve also shifts out; thus, Koreans can reach point *F*, which is better than point *D*. To reach this outcome, Americans specialize in producing at point *B* and Koreans specialize in producing at point *E*.

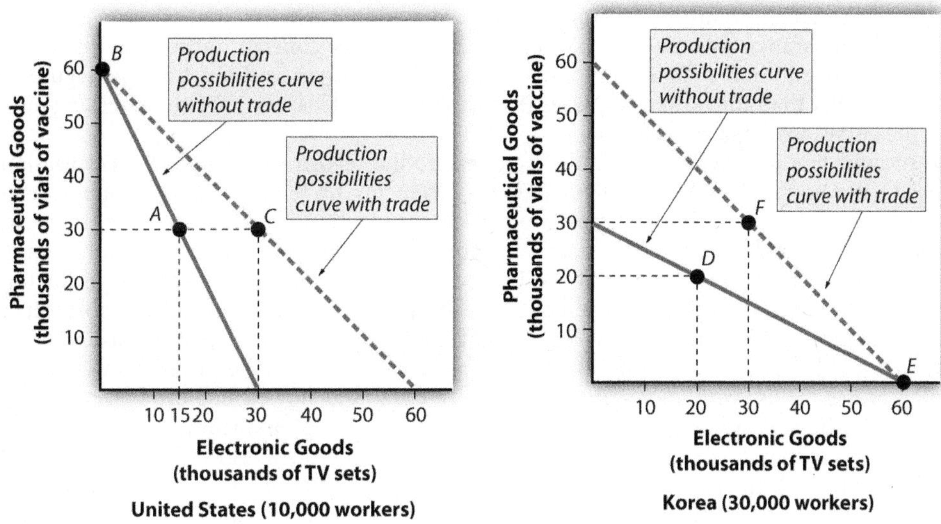

Production Possibilities Curves with Trade

The dashed lines in the two graphs in Figure 29.2 show the different combinations of vaccine and television sets available in Korea and the United States when trade exists between the two countries at a relative price of one vial of vaccine for one television set. These dashed lines are labeled "production possibilities curve with trade" to contrast them with the "production possibilities curve without trade" label on the solid line. The diagram shows that the production possibilities curves with trade are shifted out compared with the curves without trade.

To see how the production possibilities curve with trade is derived, consider how the United States could move from point *A* to point *C* in Figure 29.2. At point *A*, without trade, Americans produce and consume 15,000 television sets and 30,000 vials of vaccine by having 5,000 workers in each industry. Now suppose all U.S. workers move out of television set production into vaccine production, shifting U.S. production to zero television sets and 60,000 vials of vaccine, as shown by point *B*. Then by trading some of the vaccine, Americans can obtain television sets. As they trade more vaccine away, they move down the production possibilities curve with trade: one less vial of vaccine means one more television set along the curve. If they move to point *C* in the diagram, they have traded 30,000 vials of vaccine for 30,000 television sets. Americans now have 30,000 television sets and are left with 30,000 vials of vaccine. By producing more vaccine, the Americans get to purchase more television sets. The distance from point *A* (before trade) to point *C* (after trade) in Figure 29.2 is the gain from trade: 15,000 more television sets.

It would be possible, of course, to choose any other point on the production possibilities curve with trade. If Americans prefer more television sets and fewer vials of vaccine, they can move down along that dashed line, trading more of their vaccine for more television sets. In general, the production possibilities curve with trade is further out than the production possibilities curve *without* trade, indicating the gain from trade.

Observe that the slope of the production possibilities curve with trade is given by the relative price: the number of vials of vaccine that can be obtained for a television set. When the relative price is one vial per television set, the slope is negative one because one less vial gives one more television set. If the relative price were one-half vial per television set, then the production possibilities curve with trade would be flatter.

The gains to Korea from trade are illustrated in the right-hand graph of Figure 29.2. For example, at point *D*, without trade, Koreans produce 20,000 television sets with 10,000 workers and, with the remaining 20,000 workers, produce 20,000 vials of vaccine. With trade, they shift all production into television sets, as at point *E* on the right graph. Then they trade the television sets for vaccine. Such trade allows more consumption of vaccine in Korea. At point *F* in the right diagram, the Koreans could consume 30,000 vials of vaccine and 30,000 television sets, which would be 10,000 more of each than before trade at point *D.* As in the case of the United States, the production possibilities curve shifts out with trade, and the size of the shift represents the gain from trade.

This example of Americans and Koreans consuming more than they were before trade illustrates *the principle of comparative advantage: By specializing in producing products in which they have a comparative advantage, countries can increase the amount of goods available for consumption.* Trade increases the amount of production in the world; it shifts out the production possibilities curves.

Increasing Opportunity Costs: Incomplete Specialization

One of the special assumptions in the example we have used in Table 29.2 and Figure 29.2 to illustrate the theory of comparative advantage is that opportunity costs are constant rather than increasing. It is because of this assumption that the production possibilities curves without trade in Figure 29.2 are straight lines rather than the bowed-out lines that we studied in Chapter 1. With increasing opportunity costs, the curves would be bowed out.

The straight-line production possibilities curves are the reason for complete specialization, with Korea producing no vaccines and the United States producing no television sets. If opportunity costs were increasing, as in the more typical example of the production possibilities curve, then complete specialization would not occur. With increasing opportunity costs, as more and more workers are moved into the production of vaccine in the United States, the opportunity cost of producing more vaccine will rise. And as workers are moved out of vaccine production in Korea, the opportunity cost of vaccine production in Korea will fall. At some point, the U.S. opportunity cost of vaccine production may rise to equal Korea's, at which point further specialization in vaccine production would cease in the United States. Thus, with increasing opportunity costs and bowed-out production possibilities curves, specialization most likely will be incomplete. But increasing opportunity cost does not change the principle of comparative advantage. By specializing to some degree in the goods for which they have a comparative advantage, countries can increase world production. Substantial gains are realized from trade, whether between Rose and Sam or between America and Korea.

REVIEW

- Comparative advantage shows that a country can gain from trade even if it is more efficient at producing every product than another country. A country has a comparative advantage in a product if it is relatively more efficient at producing that product than the other country.
- The theory of comparative advantage predicts that gains from trade can be realized from increasing production of the good for which a country has a comparative advantage and from reducing production of the other good. By exporting the good for which it has a comparative advantage, a country can increase consumption of both goods.
- Comparative advantage is like a new technology in which the country effectively produces more by having some goods produced in another country.

3. REASONS FOR COMPARATIVE ADVANTAGE

What determines a country's comparative advantage? There are some obvious answers. For example, Central America has a comparative advantage over North America in producing tropical fruit because of weather conditions: Bananas will not grow in Kansas or Nebraska outside of greenhouses.

In most cases, however, comparative advantage does not result from differences in climate and natural resources. More frequently, comparative advantage is due to decisions made by individuals, by firms, or by the government in a given country. For example, a comparative advantage of the United States in pharmaceuticals might be due to investment in research and in physical and human capital in the areas of chemistry and biology. An enormous amount of research goes into developing technological know-how to produce pharmaceutical products.

In Korea, on the other hand, less capital may be available for such huge expenditures on research in the pharmaceutical area. A Korean comparative advantage in electronic goods might be due to a large, well-trained workforce that is well suited to electronics and small-scale assembly. For example, the excellent math and technical training in Korean high schools may provide a large labor force for the electronics industry.

Comparative advantages can change over time. In fact, the United States did have a comparative advantage in television sets in the 1950s and early 1960s, before the countries of East Asia developed skills and knowledge in these areas. A country may have a comparative advantage in a good it has developed recently, but then the technology spreads to other countries, which develop a comparative advantage, and the first country goes on to something else.

Perhaps the United States' comparative advantage in pharmaceuticals will go to other countries in the future, and the United States will develop a comparative advantage in other, yet unforeseen areas. The term dynamic comparative advantage describes changes in comparative advantage over time because of investment in physical and human capital and in technology.

3.1 Labor versus Capital Resources

To illustrate the importance of capital for comparative advantage, imagine a world in which all comparative advantage can be explained through differences between countries in the amount of physical capital that workers have to work with. It is such a world that is described by the Heckscher-Ohlin model, named after the two Swedish economists, Eli Heckscher and Bertil Ohlin, who developed it. Ohlin won a Nobel Prize for his work in international economics. The Heckscher-Ohlin model provides a particular explanation for comparative advantage.

Here is how comparative advantage develops in such a model. Suppose the United States has a higher level of capital per worker than Korea. In other words, the United States is **capital abundant** compared with Korea, and—what amounts to the same thing—Korea is **labor abundant** compared with the United States. Pharmaceutical production uses more capital per worker than electronics production; in other words, pharmaceutical production is relatively **capital intensive**, whereas electronics production is relatively **labor intensive**. Hence, it makes sense that the United States has a comparative advantage in pharmaceuticals: The United States is relatively capital abundant, and pharmaceuticals are relatively capital intensive. Conversely, Korea has a comparative advantage in electronics because Korea is relatively labor abundant, and electronics are relatively labor intensive. Thus, the Heckscher-Ohlin model predicts that if a country has a relative abundance of a factor (labor or capital), it will have a comparative advantage in those goods that require a greater amount of that factor.

capital abundant

A higher level of capital per worker in one country relative to another.

labor abundant

A lower level of capital per worker in one country relative to another.

capital intensive

Production that uses a relatively high level of capital per worker.

labor intensive

Production that uses a relatively low level of capital per worker.

3.2 The Effect of Trade on Wages

An important implication of the Heckscher-Ohlin model is that trade will tend to bring factor prices (the price of labor and the price of capital) in different countries into equality. In other words, if the comparative advantage between Korea and the United States was due only to differences in relative capital and labor abundance, then trade would tend to increase real wages in Korea and lower real wages in the United States.

More generally, trade tends to increase demand for the factor that is relatively abundant in a country and decrease demand for the factor that is relatively scarce. This raises the price of the relatively abundant factor and lowers the price of the relatively scarce factor. Suppose the United States is more capital abundant than Korea and has a comparative advantage in pharmaceuticals, which are more capital intensive than electronics. Then with trade, the price of capital will rise relative to the price of labor in the United States. The intuition behind this prediction—which is called **factor-price equalization**—is that demand for labor (the relatively scarce factor) shifts down with trade as the United States increases production of pharmaceuticals and reduces its production of electronic goods. Conversely, the demand for capital (the relatively abundant factor) shifts up with trade. Although no immigration occurs, it is as if foreign workers competed with workers in the labor-scarce country and bid down the wage.

factor-price equalization

The equalization of the price of labor and the price of capital across countries when they are engaging in free trade.

Because technology also influences wages and productivity, it has been hard to detect such movements in wages because of factor-price equalization. The wages of workers in the industrial world with high productivity resulting from high levels of technology remain well above the wages of workers in the developing world with low productivity resulting from low levels of technology.

In other words, changes in technology can offset the effects of factor-price equalization on wages. If trade sufficiently raises technological know-how, then no one has to suffer from greater trade. In our example of comparative advantage, U.S. workers are paid more than Korean workers both before and after trade, because their overall level of productivity is higher. Workers with higher productivity will be paid more than workers with lower productivity even in countries that trade.

Factor-price equalization can explain another phenomenon—that is, the growing wage disparity in the United States during the past 25 years, in which the wages of high skilled workers have risen relative to the wages of less-skilled workers. The United States is relatively abundant in high-skilled workers, and developing countries are relatively abundant in low-skilled workers. Thus, high-skilled workers' wages should rise and low skilled workers' wages should fall in the United States, according to factor-price equalization. In this application of factor-price equalization, the two factors are high-skilled workers and low-skilled workers.

REVIEW

- Comparative advantage changes over time and depends on the actions of individuals in a country. Thus, comparative advantage is a dynamic concept.
- International trade will tend to equalize wages in different countries. Technological differences, however, can keep wages high in high-productivity countries.

4. GAINS FROM EXPANDED MARKETS

In the introduction to this chapter, we mentioned the gains from trade that come from larger markets. Having discussed the principle of comparative advantage, we now examine this other source of the gains from trade.

4.1 An Example of Gains from Trade through Expanded Markets

Let us start with a simple example. Consider two countries that are similar in resources, capital, and skilled labor, such as the United States and Germany. Suppose Germany and the United States both have a market for two medical diagnostic products—magnetic resonance imaging (MRI) machines and ultrasound scanners. Suppose the technology for producing each type of diagnostic device is the same in each country. We assume that the technology is identical because we want to show that trade will take place without differences between the countries.

Figure 29.3 illustrates the situation. Without trade, Germany and the United States each produce 1,000 MRIs and 1,000 ultrasound scanners. This amount of production meets the demand in the two separate markets. The cost per unit of producing each MRI machine is $300,000, and the cost per unit of producing each ultrasound scanner is $200,000. Again, these costs are the same in each country.

FIGURE 29.3 Gains from Global Markets

In this example, the technology for producing MRI machines and ultrasound scanners is assumed to be the same in the United States and Germany. In the top panel, with no trade between the United States and Germany, the quantity produced in each country is low and the cost per unit is high. With trade, the U.S. firm increases its production of MRIs and exports to Germany; the German firm increases its production of ultrasound scanners and exports to the United States. As a result, cost per unit comes down significantly.

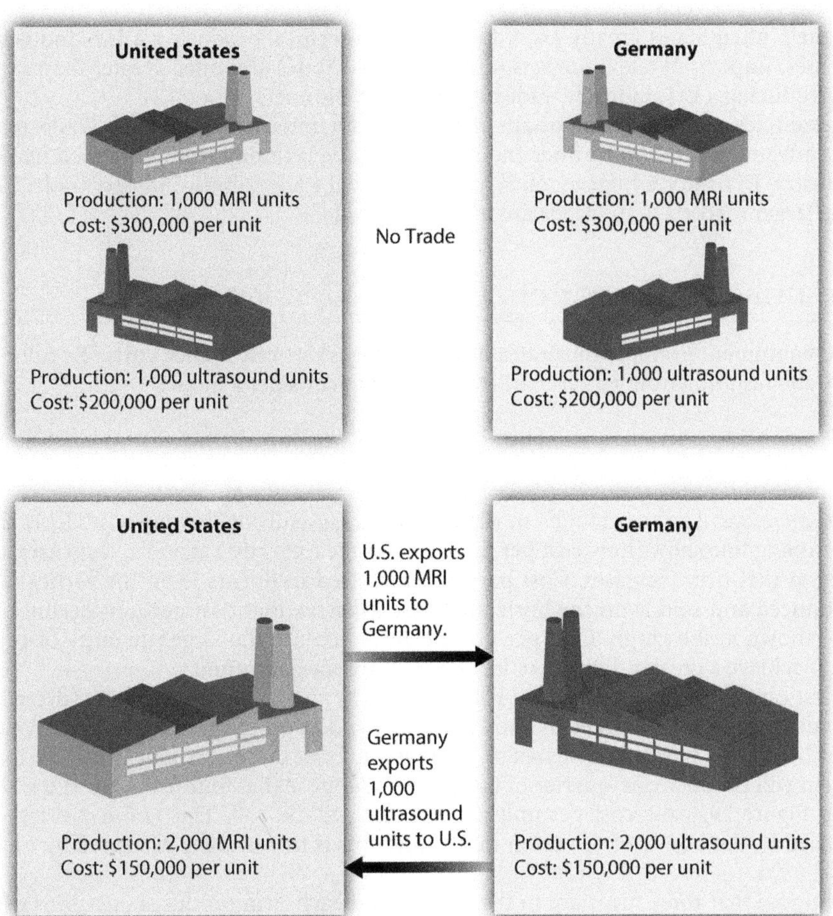

Effects of a Larger market

Now suppose that the two countries trade. Observe in Figure 29.3—and this is very important—that the *cost per unit* of producing MRIs and ultrasound scanners *declines as more are produced.* Trade increases the size of the market for each product. In this example, the market is twice as large with trade as without it: 2,000 MRIs rather than 1,000 and 2,000 ultrasound scanners rather than 1,000. The production of MRIs in the United States can expand, and the production of ultrasound scanners in the United States can contract. Similarly, the production of ultrasound scanners in Germany can expand, and the production of MRIs in Germany can contract. With the United States specializing in production of MRIs, the cost per unit of MRIs declines to $150,000. Similarly, the cost per unit of ultrasound scanners declines to $150,000. The United States exports MRIs to Germany so that the number of MRIs in Germany can be the same as without trade, and Germany exports ultrasound scanners to the United States. The gain from trade is the reduction in cost per unit. This gain from trade has occurred without any differences in the efficiency of production between the two countries.

Note that we could have set up the example differently. We could have had Germany specializing in MRI production and the United States specializing in ultrasound scanner production. Then the United States would have exported ultrasound scanners, and Germany would have exported MRIs. But the gains from trade would have been exactly the same. Unlike the comparative advantage motive for trade, the expanded markets motive alone cannot predict the direction of trade.

Intra-industry Trade versus Inter-industry Trade

intra-industry trade

Trade between countries in goods from the same or similar industries.

inter-industry trade

Trade between countries in goods from different industries.

MRIs and ultrasound scanners are similar products; they are considered to be in the same industry, the medical diagnostic equipment industry. Thus, the trade between Germany and the United States in MRIs and ultrasound scanners is called **intra-industry trade**, which means trade in goods in the same industry.

In contrast, the trade that took place in the example of comparative advantage was **inter-industry trade**, because vaccines and television sets are in different industries. In that example, exports of vaccines from the United States greatly exceed imports of vaccines, producing a U.S. industry trade surplus in vaccines. Imports of television sets into the United States are much greater than exports of television sets, producing a U.S. industry trade deficit in television sets.

These examples convey an important message about international trade: Trade resulting from comparative advantage tends to be inter-industry, and trade resulting from expanded markets tends to be intra-industry. In reality, a huge amount of international trade is intra-industry trade. This indicates that creating larger markets is an important motive for trade.

4.2 Measuring the Gains from Expanded Markets

The medical equipment example illustrates how larger markets can reduce costs. To fully describe the gains from trade resulting from larger markets, we need to consider a model.

A Relationship between Cost per Unit and the Number of Firms

Let us examine the idea that as the number of *firms in a market of a given size increases, the cost per unit at each firm increases.* The two graphs in Figure 29.4 are useful for this purpose. In each graph, the downward-sloping line shows how cost per unit (or average total cost) at a firm decreases as the quantity produced at that firm increases. Cost per unit measured in dollars is on the vertical axis, and the quantity produced and sold is on the horizontal axis. Observe that cost per unit declines through the whole range shown in the graph. Cost per unit declines because the larger quantity of production allows a firm to achieve a greater division of labor and more specialization.

Focus first on the graph on the left of Figure 29.4. The total size of the market (determined by the number of customers in the market) is shown by the bracket on the horizontal axis. We assume that the firms in the market have equal shares of the market. For example, if four firms are in the market, then each firm will produce one-quarter of the market. Suppose that four firms are in the market; then, according to Figure 29.4, the cost per unit at each firm will be $30. This is the cost per unit for the quantity labeled by the box "1 of 4," which means that this is the quantity produced by each one of the four firms.

Now, suppose that three firms are in the market and each firm produces one-third of the market. The cost per unit at each firm will be $25, as shown by the box labeled "1 of 3" in Figure 29.4. Cost per unit at each firm is lower with three firms than with four firms in the market because each firm is producing more—that is, one-third of the market is more than one-fourth of the market. Continuing in this way, we see that with two firms in the market, the cost per unit is $20. And with one firm in the market, the cost per unit is $10. In sum, as we decreased the number of firms in the market, each firm produced more and cost per unit decreased. If the number of firms in the market increased, then cost per unit at each firm would increase.

The Effect of the Size of the Market

Now compare the graph on the left of Figure 29.4 with the graph on the right. The important difference is that the graph on the right represents a larger market than the graph on the left. The bracket in the right hand graph is bigger to show the larger market.

FIGURE 29.4 Cost per Unit: The Number of Firms and Market Size

(1) The market on the right is larger than the market on the left. Hence, cost per unit is lower on the right with the larger market. (2) Regardless of the size of the market, cost per unit declines as the number of firms declines.

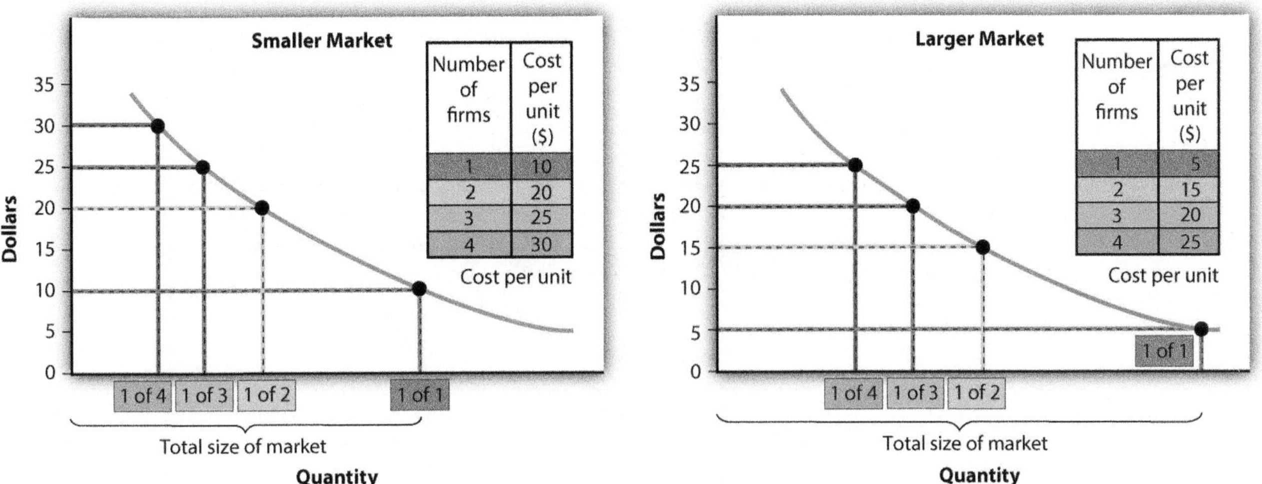

By comparing the graph on the left in Figure 29.4 (smaller market) with that on the right (larger market), we see that an increase in the size of the market reduces cost per unit at each firm, holding the number of firms in the industry constant. For example, with one firm in the market, cost per unit is $5 for the larger market compared with $10 for the smaller market. Or with four firms, cost per unit is $25 for the larger market compared with $30 for the smaller market. Compare the graphs in Figure 29.4. As the market increases in size, each firm produces at a lower cost per unit.

Figure 29.5 summarizes the information in Figure 29.4. It shows the positive relationship between the number of firms in the market, shown on the horizontal axis, and the cost per unit at each firm. As the figure indicates, more firms mean a higher cost per unit at each firm. (Be careful to note that the horizontal axis in Figure 29.5 is the *number* of firms in a given *market*, not the quantity produced by a given firm.) When the size of the market increases, the relationship between the number of firms in the market and the cost per unit shifts down, as shown in Figure 29.5. In other words, as the market increases in size, cost per unit declines at each firm if the number of firms does not change.

A Relationship between the Price and the Number of Firms

A general feature of most markets is that as the number of firms in the market increases, the price at each firm declines. More firms make the market more competitive. Thus, a relationship exists between the price and the number of firms, as shown in Figure 29.6. As in Figure 29.5, the number of firms is on the horizontal axis. The curve in Figure 29.6 is downward sloping because a greater number of firms means a lower price.

FIGURE 29.5 The Relationship between Cost per Unit and the Number of Firms

The first four points on each curve are plotted from the two tables in Figure 18.4 for one to four firms; the other points can be similarly obtained. Each curve shows how cost per unit at each firm rises as the number of firms increases in a market of a given size. The curve shifts down when the size of the market increases.

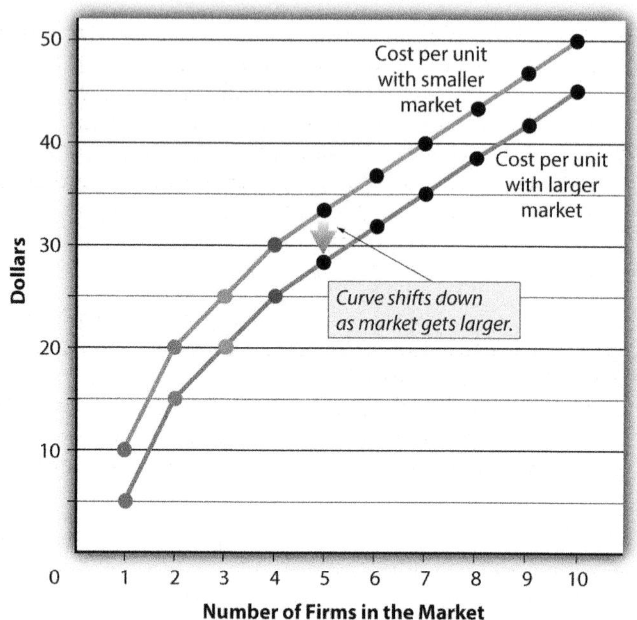

Equilibrium Price and Number of Firms

In the long run, as firms either enter or exit an industry, price will tend to equal cost per unit. If the price for each unit were greater than the cost per unit, then new firms would have a profit opportunity, and the number of firms in the industry would rise. If the price were less than the cost per unit, then firms would exit the industry. Only when price equals cost per unit is a long-run equilibrium achieved. Because price equals cost per unit, the curves in Figure 29.5 and Figure 29.6 can be combined to determine the price and the number of firms in long-run equilibrium. As shown in Figure 29.7, the industry arrives at a long-run equilibrium when the downward-sloping line for Figure 29.6 intersects the upward-sloping line (for the smaller market) from Figure 29.5. At this point, price equals cost per unit.

FIGURE 29.6 The Relationship between the Price and the Number of Firms

As the number of firms increases, the market price declines. This curve summarizes this relationship.

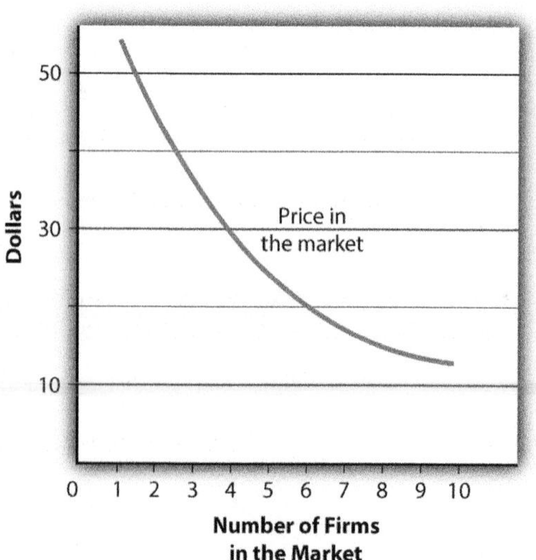

Corresponding to this long-run equilibrium is an equilibrium number of firms. More firms would lower the price below cost per unit, causing firms to leave the industry; fewer firms would raise the price above cost per unit, attracting new firms to the industry. Figure 29.7 shows how the possibility of entry and exit results in along-run equilibrium with price equal to cost per unit.

Increasing the Size of the Market

Now let us see how the industry equilibrium changes when the size of the market increases because of international trade. In Figure 29.8, we show how an increase in the size of the market, perhaps resulting from the creation of a free trade area, reduces the price and increases the number of firms. The curve showing the cost per unit of each firm shifts down and out as the market expands; that is, for each number of firms, the cost per unit declines for each firm. This brings about a new intersection and a long-run equilibrium at a lower price. Moreover, the increase in the number of firms suggests that product variety will increase, which is another part of the gains from trade.

The North American Automobile Market

The gains from trade because of larger markets arise in many real-world examples. Trade in cars between Canada and the United States now occurs even though neither country has an obvious comparative advantage. Before 1964, trade in cars between Canada and the United States was restricted. Canadian factories thus had to limit their production to the Canadian market. This kept cost per unit high. When free trade in cars was permitted, the production in Canadian factories increased, and the Canadian factories began to export cars to the United States. With more cars produced, cost per unit declined.

FIGURE 29.7 **Long-Run Equilibrium Number of Firms and Cost per Unit**

A condition for long-run equilibrium is that price equals cost per unit. In this diagram, this condition is shown at the intersection of the two curves.

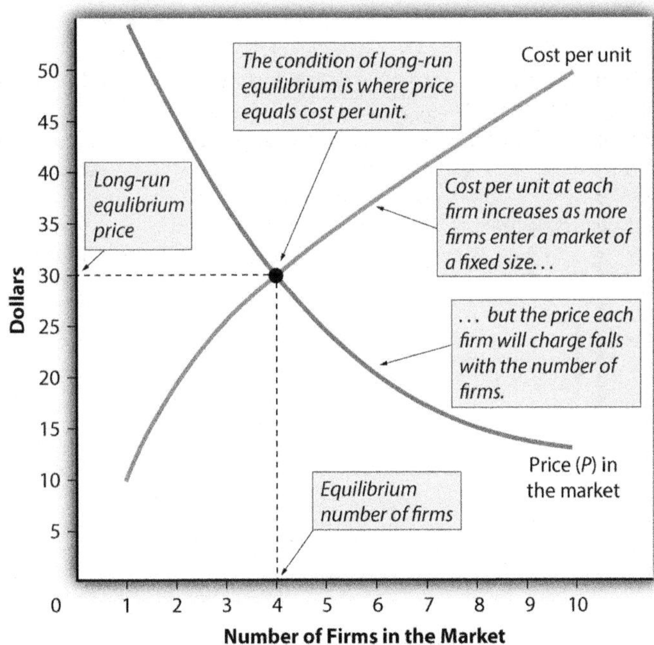

REVIEW

- Lowering cost per unit through the division of labor requires large markets. International trade creates large markets.
- A graphical model can be used to explain the gains from international trade; the model shows that a larger market reduces prices.

5. TARIFFS AND QUOTAS

In a democracy, a big difference exists between having a good economic idea and implementing the idea in practice. Even if you have the greatest economic idea in the world, you have to spread the word, convince people, debate those in opposition, and even compromise if the idea is to be voted on favorably, is to be signed into law, or is to serve as the basis for an international agreement. In spite of all the benefits from international trade that we have discussed, governments use many methods to restrict international trade. Policies that restrict trade are called *protectionist policies* because the restrictions usually protect industries from foreign imports.

Examining the economic impact of trade restrictions helps you understand why some industries lobby for protectionist policies. As you delve into the economic analysis, think about whether a protectionist policy would help or hurt you. If the United States restricts trade in clothing, how would this restriction affect U.S. clothing producers, foreign clothing producers, U.S. retailers that sell clothing, and U.S. consumers who buy clothing? How would the restriction affect U.S. employment in clothing production and the price of clothing? We will see that trade restrictions create winners and losers, but that the gains for the winners will be smaller than the losses of the losers. That is, the losses from trade restrictions outweigh the gains, creating dead weight loss. You also can check your understanding by considering the removal of an existing trade restriction. Again, winners and losers will result from the removal of trade restrictions, but the gains for the winners will be larger than the losses for the losers. Removing trade restrictions therefore eliminates dead weight loss.

FIGURE 29.8 **Gains from Trade Because of Larger Markets**

When trade occurs, the market increases from the size of the market in one country to the combined size of the market in two or more countries. This larger market shifts the upward-sloping line down because cost per unit for each firm is lower when the market is bigger. In the long-run equilibrium at the intersection of the two new curves, the price is lower and more firms are in the market. With more firms, more variety is achieved. Lower price and more variety are the gains from trade.

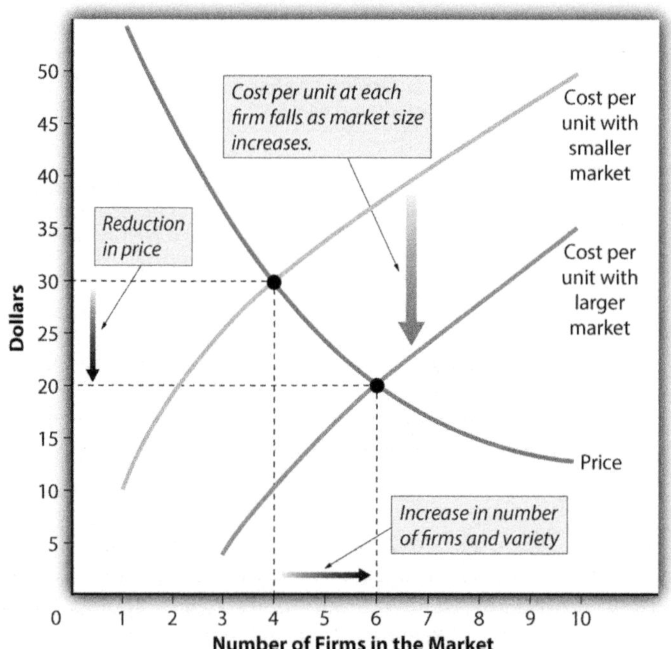

5.1 Tariffs

The oldest and most common method by which a government restricts trade is the *tariff*, a tax on goods imported into a country. The higher the tariff, the more trade is restricted. An **ad valorem tariff** is a tax equal to a certain percentage of the value of the good. For example, a 15 percent tariff on the value of goods imported is an ad valorem tariff. If $100,000 worth of goods is imported, the tariff revenue is $15,000. A **specific tariff** is a tax on the quantity sold, such as $0.50 for each kilogram of zinc.

ad valorem tariff

A tax on imports evaluated as a percentage of the value of the import.

specific tariff

A tax on imports that is proportional to the number of units or items imported.

The economic effects of a tariff are illustrated in Figure 29.9. We consider a particular good—laptop computers, for example—that is exported from one country (China, for example) and imported by another country (the United States, for example). An *import demand curve* and an *export supply curve* are shown in Figure 29.9. The *import demand curve* gives the quantity of imported goods that will be demanded at each price. It shows that a higher price for imported goods will reduce the quantity of the goods demanded. A higher price for imported Chinese-produced Lenovo laptop computers, for example, will lead to a smaller quantity of Lenovo laptops demanded by American firms. Like the standard demand curve, the import demand curve is downward sloping.

FIGURE 29.9 The Effect of a Tariff

A tariff shifts the export supply curve up by the amount of the tariff. Thus, the price paid for imports by consumers rises and the quantity imported declines. The price increase (upward-pointing smaller arrow) is less than the tariff (upward pointing larger arrow). The revenue to the government is shown by the shaded area; it is the tariff times the amount imported.

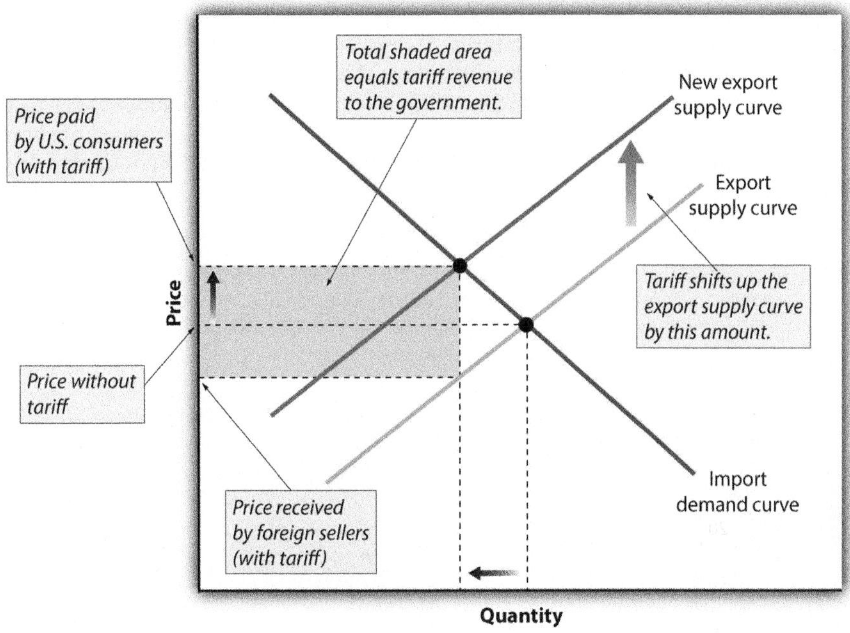

The *export supply curve* gives the quantity of exports that foreign firms are willing to sell at each price. In the case of laptop computers, the export supply curve gives the quantity of computers that Chinese producers are willing to sell in the United States. The supply curve is upward sloping, just like any other supply curve, because foreign producers are willing to supply more computers when the price is higher.

In equilibrium, for any single type of good, the quantity of exports supplied must equal the quantity of imports demanded. Thus, the intersection of the export supply curve and the import demand curve gives the amount imported into the country and the price.

When the government imposes a tariff, the supply curve shifts up, as shown in Figure 29.9. The tariff increases the marginal cost of supplying computers to the United States. The amount of the tariff in dollars is the amount by which the supply curve shifts up; it is given by the length of the larger arrow in Figure 29.9.

The tariff changes the intersection of the export supply curve and the import demand curve. At the new equilibrium, a lower quantity is imported at a higher price. The price consumers pay for laptop computers rises, but the increase in the price is less than the tariff. In Figure 29.9, the upward-pointing small arrow shows the price increase. The larger arrow, which shows the tariff increase, is longer than the small arrow along the vertical axis. The size of the price increase depends on the slopes of the demand curve and the supply curve.

The price received by suppliers equals the price paid by consumers less the tariff that must be paid to the government. Observe that the price received by the sellers declines as a result of the tariff.

The amount of revenue that the government collects is given by the quantity imported times the tariff, which is indicated by the shaded rectangle in Figure 29.9. For example, if the tariff is $100 per computer and 10 million computers are imported, the revenue is $1 billion. Tariff revenues are called *duties* and are collected by customs.

The tariff also has an effect on U.S. computer manufacturers. Because the tariff reduces imports from abroad and raises their price, the demand for computers produced by import-competing companies in the United States increases. This increase in demand will raise the price of U.S. computers. Thus, consumers pay more for both imported computers and domestically produced computers.

5.2 Quotas

Another method of government restriction of international trade is the *quota.* A quota sets a limit, a maximum, on the amount of a given good that can be imported. The United States has quotas on the import of ice cream, sugar, cotton, peanuts, and other commodities. Foreigners can supply only a limited amount of these goods to the United States.

The economic effect of a quota is illustrated in Figure 29.10. The export supply curve and the import demand curve are identical to those in Figure 29.9. The quota, the maximum that foreign firms can export to the United States, is indicated in Figure 29.10 by the solid orange vertical line labeled "quota." Exporters cannot supply more goods than the quota, and, therefore, U.S. consumers cannot buy more than this amount. We have chosen the quota amount to equal the quantity imported with the tariff in Figure 29.9. This shows that if it wants to, the government can achieve the same effects on the quantity imported using either a quota or a tariff. Moreover, the price increase in Figure 29.10, represented by the arrow along the vertical axis, is the same as the price increase in Figure 29.9. Viewed from the domestic market, therefore, a quota and a tariff are equivalent. If the quota is set to allow in the same quantity of imports as the tariff, then the price increase will be the same. Consumers will pay more for imports in both cases, and the demand for domestically produced goods that are substitutes for imports will increase. The price of domestically produced computers also will increase if a quota is set on foreign produced computers.

Seattle, 1999 The goal of the World Trade Organization (WTO) is to reduce trade barriers. But not everyone agrees with the goal, as the protest against the WTO meeting in Seattle reminded us. Although large antitrade protests have been less common in recent years, protectionist or isolationist sentiments continue to build as people worry about competition from China and other developing countries.

Source: www.flickr.com, CC-SA

FIGURE 29.10 The Effects of a Quota

A quota can be set to allow the same quantity of imports as a tariff. The quota in this figure and the tariff in Figure 18.9 allow the same quantity of imports into the country. The price increase is the same for the quota and the tariff. But, in the case of a quota, the revenue goes to quota holders, not to the U.S. government.

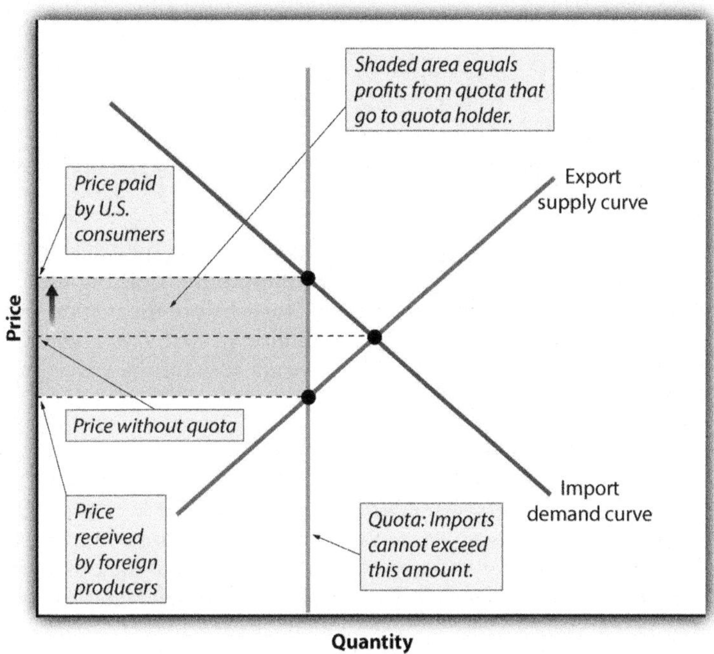

Then what is the difference in the effects of a tariff and a quota? Unlike the situation with a tariff, no revenue goes to the government with a quota. The difference between the price that the foreign suppliers get and the higher price that the consumers pay goes to the holders of the quota—the ones who are allowed to import into the country. Foreign countries frequently hold the quotas. The revenue the quota holders get is indicated by the shaded rectangle in Figure 29.10. It is equal to the quantity imported times the difference between the price paid by the consumers and the price received by the producers. The size of that rectangle is identical to the size of the rectangle showing the revenue paid to the government in the case of the tariff in Figure 29.9.

On January 1, 2005, the 1973 Multi Fibre Arrangement, a set of quotas on textiles and apparel, expired. This system of global quotas restricting imports added an estimated 20 percent to the cost of clothing, while benefiting companies in places like the Philippines that specialized in supplying clothing under this quota system. The lifting of the quotas created widespread fears among U.S. and European Union clothing manufacturers about the flood of cheap Chinese apparel into these markets. A coalition of U.S. producers claimed that 650,000 jobs were at risk. Since then, the European Union and the United States have both struggled to find a solution that will work for China and for domestic manufacturers, retailers, and consumers.

After the expiration of the quotas, exports from China surged, adding to downward pressure on prices of clothing in the United States. In contrast, exports from countries like the Philippines and Sri Lanka, that previously had quotas, have suffered. The surge in exports from China has caused U.S. clothing producers to lobby for new quotas though U.S. clothing retailers are opposed to them. If you were determining trade policy, how would you view this trade-off between U.S. clothing prices and U.S. clothing production?

5.3 The Cost of Trade Restrictions

Trade barriers, such as tariffs and quotas, distort prices and reduce the quantity consumed, benefiting domestic producers at the expense of domestic consumers and foreign producers. For example, the United States imposes quotas on sugar to increase the price of domestic sugar beets and sugar cane. Producers receive $1 billion a year in additional surplus as a result of higher prices, but U.S. consumers lose $1.9 billion, for a net loss of$.9 billion to the United States.

The Multi Fibre Arrangement, which ended in January 2005, was another trade restriction that had substantial implications for U.S. consumers. The estimated loss to U.S. consumers was $24 billion a year, and the cost to the U.S. economy was around $10 billion a year.

REVIEW

- The most common ways for government to restrict foreign trade are tariffs and quotas. Each has the same effect on price and quantity.
- With a tariff, the revenue from the tariff goes to the government. With a quota, that revenue goes to quota holders.
- Trade restrictions alter the allocation of resources in the economy and are significant sources of dead weight loss.

6. THE HISTORY OF TRADE RESTRICTIONS

revenue tariffs

An important tax whose main purpose is to provide revenue to the government.

As discussed, tariffs are the oldest form of trade restriction. Throughout history, governments have used tariffs to raise revenue. **Revenue tariffs**, whose main purpose is raising revenue, were by far the most significant source of federal revenue in the United States before the income tax was made constitutional by the Sixteenth Amendment to the U.S. Constitution in 1913 (see Figure 29.11). Revenue tariffs are still common in developing countries because they are easy for the government to collect as the goods come through a port or one of a few checkpoints.

6.1 U.S. Tariffs

Tariffs are a big part of U.S. history. Even before the United States was a country, a tariff on tea imported into the colonies led to the Boston Tea Party. One of the first acts of the U.S. Congress placed tariffs on imports. Figure 29.12 summarizes the history of tariffs in the United States since the early 1800s.

From the Tariff of Abominations to Smoot-Hawley

Tariffs were high throughout much of U.S. history, rarely going below 20 percent in the nineteenth century. In addition to raising revenue, these tariffs reduced imports of manufactured goods. The tariffs offered protection to manufacturers in the North but raised prices for consumers. Because the South was mainly agricultural and a consumer of manufactured goods, a constant dispute arose between the North and the South over these tariffs.

FIGURE 29.11 Tariffs as a Share of Total Federal Revenue

The first tariff, passed in 1789, represented nearly all of the federal government's revenue; 200 years later, tariff revenues were only about 1 percent of the total.

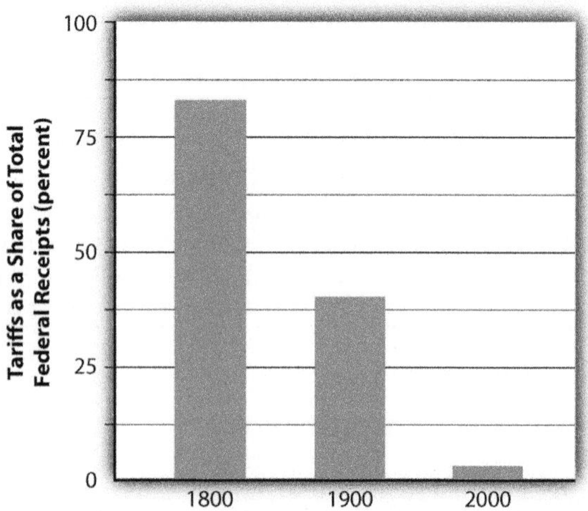

The highest of these tariffs was nicknamed the "tariff of abominations." This tariff, passed in 1828, brought the average tariff level in the United States to more than 60 percent. The tariff made purchases of farm equipment much more expensive in the southern states. It almost led to a civil war before the actual Civil War, as the southern states threatened to secede. Because the tariff was so high, however, it soon was repealed, and for the next 10 years tariffs were relatively low by nineteenth-century standards.

The most devastating increase in tariffs in U.S. history occurred during the Great Depression. The **Smoot-Hawley tariff** of 1930 raised average tariffs to 59 percent. Congress and President Hoover apparently hoped that raising tariffs would stimulate U.S. production and offset the Great Depression. But the increase had precisely the opposite effect. Other countries retaliated by raising their tariffs on U.S. goods. Each country tried to beat the others with higher tariffs, a phenomenon known as a **trade war**. The Smoot-Hawley tariff had terrible consequences. Figure 29.13 is a dramatic illustration of the decline in trade that occurred at the time of these tariff increases during the Great Depression. The Smoot-Hawley tariff made the Great Depression worse than it would have otherwise been.

Smoot-Hawley tariff

A set of tariffs imposed in 1930 that raised the average tariff level to 59 percent by 1932.

trade war

A conflict among nations over trade policies caused by imposition of protectionist policies on the part of one country and subsequent retaliatory actions by other countries.

From the Reciprocal Trade Agreement Act to the WTO

The only good thing about the Smoot-Hawley tariff was that it demonstrated to the whole world how harmful tariffs can be. To achieve lower tariffs, the Congress passed and President Roosevelt signed the *Reciprocal Trade Agreement Act* in 1934. This act was probably the most significant event in the history of U.S. trade policy. It authorized the president to cut U.S. tariffs by up to 50 percent if other countries would cut their tariffs on a reciprocating basis. The reciprocal trade agreements resulted in a remarkable reduction in tariffs. By the end of World War II, the average tariff level was down from a peak of 59 percent under Smoot-Hawley to 25 percent. The successful approach to tariff reduction under the Reciprocal Trade Agreement Act was made permanent in 1947 with the creation of a new international organization, the *General Agreement on Tariffs and Trade* (*GATT*). GATT was set up to continue the process of tariff reduction. During the half-century since the end of World War II, tariffs have continued to decline on a reciprocating basis. By 1992, the average U.S. tariff level was down to 5.2 percent.

In 1995, GATT was transformed into the **World Trade Organization (WTO)**, which continues to promote reciprocal reductions in tariffs and other trade barriers. But the WTO also has authority to resolve trade disputes between countries. For example, in 2002, the United States imposed a tariff on imported steel arguing that a surge in imports had hurt domestic steel manufacturers. Several affected countries then filed suit at the WTO arguing that the tariffs were in violation of the agreed upon trading rules. The WTO sided with these countries and ruled against the United States, which meant that other nations would be cleared to impose retaliatory tariffs on U.S. goods unless the steel tariff was lifted. In late 2003, the United States dropped the tariff that it had imposed. This dispute resolution authority has led to complaints that the WTO represents a loss of sovereignty for individual countries. On the other side of the argument, by resolving this steel import dispute, the WTO avoided a trade war between the countries impacted by the U.S. tariff.

World Trade Organization (WTO)

An international organization that can mediate trade disputes.

FIGURE 29.12 History of Tariffs in the United States

This chart shows the ratio of tariff revenues to the value of imports subject to tariffs measured as a percentage. This percentage is a measure of the average tariff excluding goods not subject to any tariff.

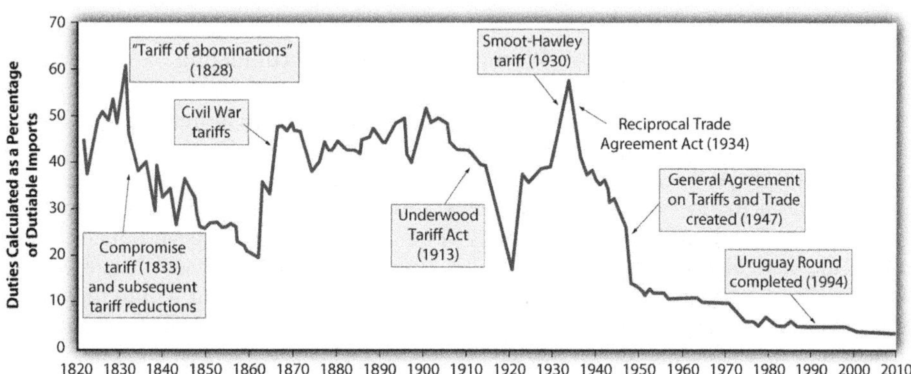

Antidumping Duties

No history of U.S. tariffs would be complete without a discussion of antidumping duties. **Antidumping duties** are tariffs put on foreign imports as a penalty for dumping. When a firm sells products in another country at prices below average cost or below the price in the home country, it is called dumping. Dumping can occur for many reasons. For example, the firm might want to sell at a lower price in the foreign market than in the home market because the demand in the foreign market is more elastic. If so, consumers in the foreign market benefit. But some people argue that dumping is a way for firms in other countries to drive domestic firms out of business and thereby gain market share and market power. Regardless of motive, in the United States and other countries, dumping is illegal; the penalty is a high tariff—the antidumping duty—on the good that is being dumped. Steel is one of

antidumping duties

Tariffs put on foreign imports as a penalty for dumping.

the industries protected with antidumping duties in the United States, at a cost to consumers of as much as $732,000 per job protected, about 10 times what a steelworker earns.

Many economists are concerned that antidumping duties, or even the threat of such duties, place serious restrictions on trade. They reduce imports and raise consumer prices. Moreover, they frequently are used for protectionist purposes. Firms in industries that desire additional protection can file dumping charges and request that tariffs be raised. Frequently, they are successful. Thus, an important issue for the future is how to reduce the use of antidumping duties for restricting trade.

FIGURE 29.13 Decline in World Trade during the Great Depression

This circular graph, used by Charles Kindleberger of MIT, illustrates how world trade collapsed after tariffs increased during the Great Depression. The distance from the middle of the graph to the point on each spoke is the amount of trade (in millions of dollars) during each month.

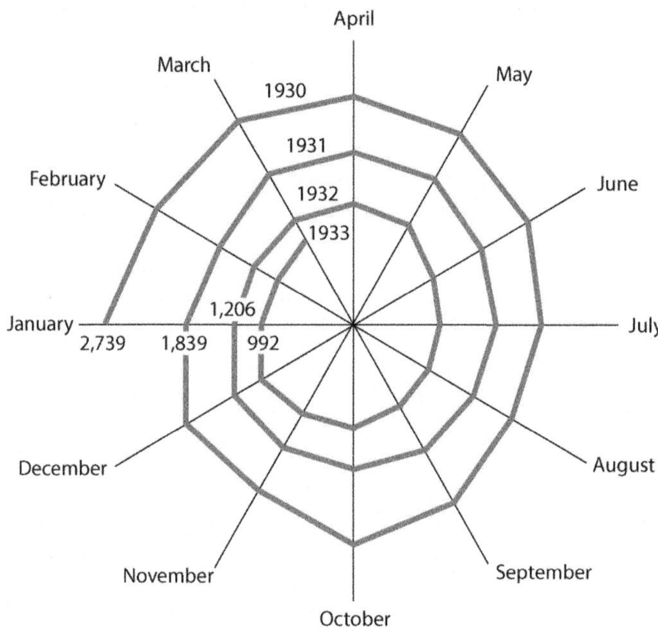

The Rise of Nontariff Barriers

nontariff barriers

Any government action other than a tariff that reduces imports, such as a quota or a standard.

As tariffs were being reduced in the post–World War II period, a conflicting trend began to emerge. Some of the other methods of restricting trade—called **nontariff barriers** to trade—grew in popularity. Nontariff barriers include anything from quotas to quality standards aimed at reducing the import of foreign products. Nontariff barriers may have arisen as a replacement for tariffs in response to political pressure for protection of certain industries.

Quality and performance standards sometimes are nothing more than barriers to trade. Some standards may have a good purpose, such as safety or compatibility with other products, but others do not. Consider the Canadian plywood standards for building construction, which keep out U.S. plywood. The Canadians argue that the standards are needed to satisfy building requirements in Canada, but Americans argue that plywood that does not meet the Canadian standards works just as well. A safety restriction against U.S.-made baseball bats in Japan during the 1980s is another example. Most Americans viewed the bats as perfectly safe and viewed the Japanese safety standard as a restriction on trade.

Quality and performance standards, therefore, are a tricky problem because governments can argue that they are imposed to improve economic conditions in their own country. The U.S. Food and Drug Administration (FDA) does not allow untested drugs into the United States even though foreign governments deem them safe. The FDA argues that the restriction is necessary to protect consumers, but foreign governments view it as a trade restriction. Although such a standard does seem like a trade barrier, in reality, it is a matter of dispute.

REVIEW

- Tariffs were used by governments to raise revenue long before income taxes were invented.
- Tariffs have been used for protectionist purposes in several important instances in U.S. history. Manufacturing firms in the North were protected by tariffs at the expense of consumers of manufactured goods, many of whom were in the South.
- The Smoot-Hawley tariff of the 1930s was one of the most harmful in U.S. history. It led to a trade war in which other countries raised tariffs in retaliation.
- Tariffs have come down since the 1930s. In recent years, however, nontariff barriers to trade have gone up.

7. ARGUMENTS FOR TRADE BARRIERS

Are there any good economic arguments for trade barriers? Let's examine some of the arguments that typically are made.

7.1 High Transition Costs

When an industry shrinks as a result of the removal of restrictions on trade, the cost of adjustment in the short run may be quite large, even if other industries grow. Those who lose their jobs in the protected industry, even temporarily, suffer. In the short run, it is difficult to retrain workers. Workers who are laid off as the industry shrinks cannot move easily to another industry. Many have to retire early. Retraining is possible, but it takes time and is difficult for older workers.

Phaseout of Trade Restrictions

Some people argue that these costs are so high that we should not reduce trade barriers. But there is a better approach. These costs of adjustment are a reason for a slow phaseout of trade barriers. *Phaseout* means that trade barriers are reduced a little bit each year. A slow phaseout of trade barriers was part of the North American Free Trade Agreement (NAFTA) between Canada, Mexico, and the United States. This agreement called for a phaseout period of 10 to 15 years, depending on the product. For example, some tariffs were scheduled to be cut by 25 percent in the first year, 50 percent after five years, and 100 percent after 10 years. The purpose of the slow phaseout was to allow production to shift from one industry to another slowly. The intention was to adjust the workforce through attrition as workers normally retired.

Trade Adjustment Assistance

Another approach is to use *trade adjustment assistance*, which refers to transfer payments to workers who happen to be hurt because of a move to free trade. Unemployment insurance and other existing transfer programs may go a long way toward providing such assistance. Because society as a whole benefits from free trade, some increased resources can be used to help the workers who bear the brunt of the adjustment. In other words, the extra income that can be obtained by trade may be used to ease the adjustment.

Transition costs are not a reason to avoid free trade. They are a reason to phase out the restrictions on trade gradually and to provide trade adjustment assistance to workers as needed. The discussion and debate regarding free trade in the 2016 election shows what happens if not enough attention is paid to issues like trade adjustment assistance. The workers losing their jobs in the manufacturing industries in the geographic middle of the country are not able to find jobs in the expanding information technology sectors of the West Coast or the bio-technology boom on the East Coast. Without robust transfer programs, these individuals see little obvious benefit from trade (the access to cheaper goods from abroad is not always visible and, even if it were visible, may be scant consolation to someone who lost their job) and in a democratic society find their voice by casting votes for candidates who seem to speak their language. Purely economic arguments about increased efficiency, enhanced consumption possibilities, etc. will not be able to win over policymakers in a country where the median electoral-college voter seems to view trade as having had a negative impact on his or her life.

7.2 The Infant Industry Argument

infant industry argument

The view that a new industry may be helped by protectionist policies.

One of the earliest statements of the **infant industry argument** in favor of trade restrictions was put forth by Alexander Hamilton in 1791 in his *Report on Manufactures*. Hamilton argued that manufacturing firms in the newly created United States should be protected from imports. Once the industries were established, they could compete with foreign imports. But as they got started, they needed protection until they reached a certain scale.

A danger with the infant industry argument is that the protection may last long after it was initially justified. In Latin America, for example, infant industry arguments were used to justify import protection in the 1950s. These barriers to trade, however, lasted long after any kind of reasonable infant industry argument could be made.

7.3 The National Security Argument

A nation's security is another argument for trade restrictions. The national security argument is that the country needs to be able to produce certain goods, such as special metals, computers, ships, or aircraft, in time of war. If the country does not have an industry that produces them, it could be at a severe disadvantage.

Firms can use these national security arguments, however, to seek protection from foreign imports. Japanese rice farmers, for example, made national security arguments for protection from rice imports. In fact, the rice restriction has little to do with national security because rice can be imported from many different countries. In the United States, the textile industry has argued on national security grounds that it needs protection because it provides military uniforms made from U.S. textiles.

It is important to examine alternatives to trade restrictions before applying the national security argument and restricting trade. For example, rather than restricting rice imports, the Japanese could store a large amount of rice in case of a war emergency. Or if the United States really thought that uniforms were a national security issue, it could store millions of extra uniforms rather than restrict textile imports. In fact, the United States does have stockpiles of many rare minerals and metals needed for national defense production.

7.4 The Retaliation Argument

Threatening other countries or retaliating against them when they have trade restrictions is another possible reason to deviate from free trade. If the United States threatens the Japanese by saying that it will close U.S. markets, this may encourage Japan to open its markets to the United States. Thus, by retaliating or threatening, it is possible to increase international trade around the world.

Those seeking protection, however, also can use the retaliation argument. Those in the United States who are most vocal about retaliation against other countries frequently are those who want to protect an industry. Many economists worry about threats of retaliation because they fear that other countries will respond with further retaliation, and a trade war will occur.

7.5 The Foreign Subsidies Argument

If foreign governments subsidize their firms' exports, does this justify U.S. government subsidies to U.S. firms to help them compete against the foreign firms?

Foreign subsidies to foreign producers are a particularly difficult issue. If foreign subsidies lower the price of U.S. imports, then U.S. consumers benefit. If Europe wants to use taxpayer funds to subsidize aircraft manufacturers, then why not enjoy the lower-cost aircraft? Foreign subsidies enable industries to thrive more for political reasons than for economic ones. From a global perspective, such government intervention should be avoided, because it hurts consumers by encouraging less economically efficient production and, ultimately, higher prices.

7.6 Environment and Labor Standard Arguments

During the 1990s, a new type of argument against reducing trade barriers emerged: that tariffs or quotas should not be removed against countries with weak or poorly enforced environmental protection laws and labor standards, such as child labor laws and workplace safety laws. Because such laws and standards generally are weaker in developing countries than in industrial countries, this argument frequently opposes reducing trade barriers to the imports of goods from relatively poor countries. For example, this argument is made by people who are against reducing tariffs on imports of Brazilian oranges into the United States.

Environmental and labor standard arguments are of two main types. First, some people argue that holding back on the reduction of trade barriers until countries change their environmental and labor policies is a good way to persuade these countries to change. An important counterargument, however, is that low trade barriers lead to improvements in environmental and working conditions. History has shown that as their income grows, people become more concerned with the environment and their working conditions; people in deep poverty do not have the time or resources to deal with such issues. Thus, by raising income per capita, lower trade barriers can improve the environment and the workplace. Moreover, more effective and cheaper technologies to improve the environment or increase safety become available through trade.

A second type of argument is that it is difficult for workers and firms in the industrial countries to compete with those in the developing countries who do not have to pay the costs of complying with environmental protection laws. By keeping trade barriers high, however, income growth may not be sufficient to address the environmental problems in developing countries, so the differences in the law persist.

7.7 The Public Health Argument

In 2008, hundreds of Chinese infants reportedly were being poisoned by tainted milk products that contained an industrial chemical known as melamine. This led to the withdrawal of various types of food products that were made from Chinese milk and milk powder. The European Union banned the importation of Chinese-made soy-based products for infants, and the United States halted the import of all milk-based products from China. The public health scare came only a couple of years after disruptions to trade in chicken stemming from outbreaks of bird flu in countries like Brazil and Thailand.

Such episodes lead to calls for limits on imports of food and medicine from countries whose quality control standards may not be as stringent as in the importing country. But such episodes are not limited to food products from developing nations. The export of beef from the United Kingdom to Europe was banned after an outbreak of "mad cow disease" in the mid-1990s. The European Union restricts the importation of U.S. beef that comes from cattle injected with growth hormones. Many African nations have resisted importing genetically modified seeds and grain despite the promise of more drought-resistant, higher-yield varieties that can improve farm productivity.

The public health arguments for trade restrictions present a complicated issue. On the one hand, few people would argue against a temporary halt in food imports following a scandal like the melamine incident or after an outbreak of disease like the avian flu. Such bans, once put in place, often tend to linger on for years, long after the source of the problem has been identified and addressed. And, sometimes, the arguments seem motivated more by the desire to protect domestic firms than consumer health, an example being the need to protect U.S. consumers in Detroit from buying pharmaceuticals produced just across the border in Ontario, Canada.

7.8 The Political Economy of Protection

Firms seek protection from foreign competition simply because the protection raises their profits. But the firms may use any of the above arguments to justify their case. In a famous satire of firms seeking protection from foreign competitors, a French economist, Frederic Bastiat, wrote more than 150 years ago about candlemakers complaining about a foreign rival—the sun. The candlemakers in Bastiat's satire petitioned French legislators to pass a law requiring the closing of all shutters, curtains, and blinds during the day to protect them from this competition. The behavior Bastiat described seems to apply to many modern producers who seek protection from competition.

Firms seeking protection frequently are successful in part because they spend a lot more time and money lobbying the U.S. Congress than do the people who would be hurt by the protection. Even though consumers as a whole benefit more from reducing trade barriers than firms in the protected industry are harmed, each consumer benefits relatively little, so spending a lot of time and money lobbying is not worthwhile. It is difficult to get enough votes to remove trade barriers when a few firms each have a lot to lose, even though millions of consumers have something to gain.

REVIEW

- Transition costs, environmental and labor standards, national security, infant industry, and retaliation are some of the arguments in favor of trade restrictions. Each has the possibility of being used by protectionists.
- Although many arguments in favor of trade barriers have been put forth over the years, in each case, we have better ways to deal with the problems raised. The case for free trade holds up well in the debates when the economic rationale for the gains from trade is applied correctly and understood.

8. HOW TO REDUCE TRADE BARRIERS

Viewed in their entirety, the economic arguments against trade restrictions seem to overwhelm the economic arguments in favor of trade restrictions. The economic arguments in favor of free trade have been in existence for more than 200 years. The recommendation of early economists such as Adam Smith and David Ricardo was simple: Reduce trade barriers.

It was not until many years after Smith and Ricardo wrote their recommendations, however, that they were translated into a practical trade policy. Then, as now, political pressures favoring protection made the repeal of trade barriers difficult. Hence, a carefully formulated trade policy is needed to reduce trade barriers. Next we consider a variety of approaches.

8.1 Unilateral Disarmament

One approach to removing trade barriers in a country is simply to remove them unilaterally. Making an analogy with the arms race, we call this policy *unilateral disarmament.* When a country unilaterally reduces its arms, it does so without getting anything in arms reduction from other countries. With unilateral disarmament in trade policy, a country reduces its trade barriers without other countries also reducing their trade barriers. Unilateral disarmament is what Smith and Ricardo recommended for England.

The problem with unilateral disarmament is that some individuals are hurt, if only temporarily, and it is hard to compensate them. Of those who gain, each gains only a little. Of those who lose, each loses a lot. The political pressures that the losers exert are significant. As a result, unilateral disarmament is rarely successful in the industrial countries as a means of reducing trade barriers.

8.2 Multilateral Negotiations

multilateral negotiations

Simultaneous tariff reductions on the part of many countries.

An alternative to unilateral disarmament is **multilateral negotiations**, which involve simultaneous tariff reductions by many countries. With multilateral negotiations, opposing political interests can cancel each other out. For example, import-competing domestic industries that will be hurt by the reduction of trade barriers, such as textiles in the United States or agriculture in Europe and Japan, can be countered by export interests that will gain from the reduction in trade barriers. Because consumers will gain, they are also a potential counter to protectionism, but they are too diffuse to make a difference, as we just discussed. With multilateral negotiations, interested exporters who gain from the reduction in barriers will push the political process to get the reductions.

Multilateral negotiations also balance international interests. For example, to get developing countries to remove their barriers to imports of financial and telecommunications services, the United States had to agree to remove agricultural trade barriers in the United States.

Uruguay Round

The most recently completed round of multilateral negotiations, opened in 1986 and completed in 1993.

Doha Development Round

The latest round of multilateral negotiations opened in November 2001 in Doha, Qatar.

Multilateral trade negotiations have taken place in a series of negotiating rounds, each of which has lasted several years. During each round, the countries try to come to agreement on a list of tariff reductions and the removal of other trade restrictions. Since 1947, eight rounds of negotiations have taken place. The most recently completed round was the Uruguay Round, named after the country where the first negotiations occurred in 1986. The **Uruguay Round** negotiations ended in 1993. Since 2002, the United States has been involved in negotiations for another global trade round, called the **Doha Development Round**. As with all such multilateral negotiations, this round is proving to be long and difficult and still is not finished.

The reduction in tariffs through multilateral negotiations under GATT has been dramatic. Tariffs have declined to below 3 percent on average in the United States with the implementation of the Uruguay Round agreement. Recall that this compares with nearly 60 percent in the mid-1930s.

Most-Favored-Nation Policy

Multilateral negotiations almost always are conducted on a *most-favored-nation* (*MFN*) basis. MFN means that when the United States or any other country reduces its tariffs as part of a multilateral trade agreement, it reduces them for everyone. Since the late 1990s, the term *normal trade relations* (*NTR*) frequently has been used in place of MFN because it is a more accurate description of the policy. In the twenty-first century, if a country is not granted MFN or NTR status, the United States imposes very high tariffs on the country. For example, concern about human rights in China has led some to argue that the United States should not grant MFN or NTR status to China. Without MFN or NTR, tariffs on Chinese imports to the United States would be about 60 percent.

8.3 Regional Trading Areas

Creating regional trading areas is an increasingly popular approach to reducing trade barriers. For example, NAFTA, the free trade agreement between the United States, Canada, and Mexico, removes all trade restrictions among those countries. An even wider free trade area covering the whole Western Hemisphere has been proposed.

Regional trading areas have some advantages over multilateral approaches. First, fewer countries are involved, so the negotiations are easier. Second, regional political factors can offset protectionist pressures. For example, the political goal of European unity helped establish grassroots support to reduce trade barriers among the countries of Europe.

Trade Diversion versus Trade Creation

Regional trading areas have disadvantages, however, in comparison with multilateral reductions in trade barriers under GATT. **Trade diversion** is one such disadvantage. Trade is diverted when low-cost firms from countries outside the trading area are replaced by high-cost firms within the trading area. For example, as a result of NAFTA, producers of electronic equipment in Southeast Asia have to pay a U.S. tariff, while producers of the same equipment in Mexico do not have to pay the tariff. As a result, some production will shift from Southeast Asia to Mexico; that is viewed as trade diversion from what might otherwise be a low-cost producer. The hope is that **trade creation**—the increase in trade resulting from the lower tariffs between the countries—will outweigh trade diversion.

trade diversion

The shifting of trade away from the low-cost producer toward a higher-cost producer because of a reduction in trade barriers with the country of the higher-cost producer.

trade creation

The increase in trade resulting from a decrease in trade barriers.

Free Trade Areas versus Customs Unions

An important difference exists between two types of regional trading areas: **free trade areas (FTAs)** and **customs unions**. In both, barriers to trade between countries in the area or the union are removed. But external tariffs are treated differently: Under a customs union, such as the European Union (EU), external tariffs are the same for all countries. For example, semiconductor tariffs are exactly the same in France, Germany, and the other members of the EU. Under an FTA, external tariffs can differ for the different countries in the FTA. For example, the United States' external tariffs on textiles are higher than Mexico's. These differences in external tariffs under an FTA cause complications because a good can be shipped into the country with the low tariff and then can be moved within the FTA to the country with the high tariff. To prevent such external tariff avoidance, *domestic content restrictions* must be incorporated into the agreement. These restrictions say that for a product to qualify for the zero tariffs between the countries, a certain fraction of the product must be made within the FTA. For example, under NAFTA, the majority of parts in television sets and automobiles must be manufactured in Canada, Mexico, or the United States for the television or car to qualify for a zero tariff.

free trade areas (FTAs)

An area that has no trade barriers between the countries in the area.

customs unions

A free trade area with a common external tariff.

9. END-OF-CHAPTER MATERIAL

9.1 Conclusion

Few economists disagree with the proposition that tariffs, quotas, and other trade barriers reduce the economic well-being of a society. In fact, polls of economists show that they disagree less on this proposition than on virtually any other in economics. This unanimity among economists was reflected in the debate over NAFTA in the United States. Every living Nobel Prize–winning economist endorsed the agreement to eliminate tariffs and quotas among Canada, Mexico, and the United States.

In this chapter, we first focused on the economic gains to the citizens of a country from international trade. We noted two reasons for such gains: comparative advantage and larger markets that reduce cost per unit. Both reasons apply to trade within a country as well as to international trade. We also showed how to measure the gains from trade because of comparative advantage and larger markets.

This chapter also shows that despite the benefits that come from trade, many restrictions on international trade still exist. Although few economists disagree with the proposition that tariffs, quotas, and other trade barriers reduce the economic well-being of a society, political pressure continues to erect new trade barriers or to prevent the existing ones from being removed.

It is important to point out that the benefits of international trade go well beyond economic gains. International trade sometimes puts competitive pressure on governments to deliver better policies. Within the United States, competition between states can make regulatory and tax policies more efficient. Similarly, competition can make regulatory policies in countries more efficient. International trade also can improve international relations. Trade enables Americans to learn more about Southeast Asians or Europeans or Latin Americans. This improves understanding and reduces the possibilities for international conflict. Developing international trade with China might have even reduced the possibility of another cold war or new international conflict in the future. If many people have an economic stake in a relationship, they will not like a military action that threatens that relationship. Thus, the need for good trade policies to reduce trade barriers is likely to increase rather than decrease in the future. The challenge is to develop a means for conducting international trade policy in a world with many sovereign governments, each of which is free to formulate its own policy.

Key Points

1. According to the principle of comparative advantage, countries that specialize in producing goods for which they have a comparative advantage can increase world production and raise consumption in their own country.
2. The gains from trade resulting from comparative advantage can be shown graphically by shifting out the production possibilities curve.
3. The relative price of two goods with trade is between the relative prices in the two countries without trade.
4. Comparative advantage is a dynamic concept. If people in one country improve their skills or develop low-cost production methods through research, they will alter the comparative advantage.
5. If differences in the relative abundance of capital and labor are the reason for differences in comparative advantage, then international trade will tend to equalize real wages.
6. Lower cost per unit in larger markets is another key reason for gains in trade. When the size of the market increases, the price declines, more firms enter the market, and product variety is greater.
7. Despite the economic arguments put forth in support of free trade, plenty of restrictions on trade still are in place in the world.
8. Tariffs and quotas are the two main methods of restricting international trade. They are equivalent in their effects on prices and imports.
9. Tariffs were originally a major source of government revenue but are relatively insignificant sources of revenue in the twenty-first century. Quotas do not generate any revenue for the government. The quota holders get all the revenue.
10. National security and infant industry are two of the main arguments frequently put forth in support of trade barriers. In most cases, they are overwhelmed by the arguments in favor of reduced trade barriers.
11. Eliminating restrictions on trade unilaterally is difficult because of the harm done to those who are protected by the restrictions. Regional trading areas and multilateral tariff reductions attempt to reduce trade barriers by balancing export interests against import-competing interests.
12. Free trade areas and customs unions both create trade and divert trade.

QUESTIONS FOR REVIEW

1. What is the difference between absolute advantage and comparative advantage?
2. What is the difference between the production possibilities curve before trade and after trade?
3. In what sense is comparative advantage a dynamic concept?
4. Why might costs per unit decline when the market increases in size?
5. What is the difference between interindustry trade and intraindustry trade?
6. In what sense are a tariff and a quota equivalent?
7. What is the infant industry argument in favor of trade protection?
8. Why is unilateral disarmament a difficult way to reduce trade barriers?
9. How do multilateral negotiations or regional trading areas make the reduction of trade barriers easier politically?
10. Why might a regional trade agreement cause trade diversion?

PROBLEMS

1. Bill and Hillary are two very smart lawyers who also have an active interest in public policy. Bill can write a law paper in three months or a policy paper in one month. Hillary can write a law paper or a policy paper in one month. Bill and Hillary like each other a lot and would like to get married. However, because the marriage of two lawyers often is fraught with difficulty, they decide that one of them should write law papers and the other should write policy papers.
   a. Draw a production possibilities curve for Bill and one for Hillary.
   b. Who has an absolute advantage in writing law papers? In writing policy papers?
   c. Who has a comparative advantage in writing law papers? In writing policy papers?
   d. Explain how to reconcile your answers to (b) and (c).
2. Suppose that the United States has 200 million units of labor and Mexico has 100 million units, and that the production of wheat and strawberries per unit of labor in the United States and Mexico is as follows:

	Wheat	Strawberries
Mexico	1 bushel	3 pints
United States	2 bushels	3 pints

   a. What is the shape of the production possibilities curve for each country? What does this shape imply about the nature of the trade-off between wheat and strawberries? Is this a realistic assumption? Explain.
   b. Which country has a comparative advantage in wheat production? Why?
   c. With free trade between the United States and Mexico, is it possible that 1 bushel of wheat will trade for 1 pint of strawberries? Why or why not?
   d. Suppose the free trade price is 1 bushel of wheat for 2 pints of strawberries. Draw a diagram indicating the production possibilities curve with and without trade.
3. Suppose there are two goods, wheat and clothing, and two countries, the United States and Brazil, in the world. The production of wheat and clothing requires only labor. In the United States, it takes one unit of labor to produce four bushels of wheat and one unit of labor to produce two items of clothing. In Brazil, it takes one unit of labor to produce one bushel of wheat and one unit of labor to produce one item of clothing. Suppose the United States has 100 units of labor and Brazil has 120.
   a. Draw the production possibilities curve for each country without trade. Which country has the absolute advantage in each good? Indicate each country's comparative advantage.
   b. In what range will the world trading price ratio lie when these countries open up to free trade? Will both countries be better off? Why? Show this on your diagram.
4. Comparative advantage explains interindustry trade in different goods between countries. How do economists explain intraindustry trade, that is, trade in the same industry between countries? Why might people in the United States want to buy German cars, and Germans want to buy cars from the United States?

5. Suppose that each firm in an industry has the total costs shown below.

Quantity of Output	Total Costs (dollars)
1	50
2	54
3	60
4	68
5	80
6	90
7	105
8	112

   a. Suppose that the quantity demanded in the market is fixed at four. Calculate the average total cost for each firm when one, two, and four firms are in the industry. Draw a diagram indicating the relationship between average total cost and number of firms.
   b. Suppose the quantity demanded in the market expands because of an opening of trade and is now fixed at eight. Draw a diagram similar to the one in part (a) indicating the relationship between average total cost and the number of firms. Why does the opening of trade cause this shift in the curve?

6. The following relationship between price, cost per unit, and the number of firms describes an industry in an economy.

Number of Firms	Cost per Unit ($)	Price ($)
1	10	90
2	20	80
3	30	70
4	40	60
5	50	50
6	60	46
7	70	43
8	80	40
9	90	38
10	100	36

   a. Graph (1) the relationship between cost per unit and number of firms and (2) the relationship between price and number of firms. Why does one slope up and the other slope down?
   b. Find the long-run equilibrium price and number of firms.
   c. Now suppose the country opens its borders to trade with other countries. As a result, the relationship between cost per unit and the number of firms becomes as follows in the next table. Find the long-run equilibrium price and number of firms.
   d. What are the gains from expanding the market through the reduction in trade barriers?

Number of Firms	Cost per Unit ($)
1	5
2	10
3	15
4	20
5	25
6	30
7	35
8	40
9	45
10	50

7. Suppose French wine suddenly becomes popular in the United States. How does this affect the price and quantity of imports of French wine? Suppose the U.S. wine industry lobbies for protection. If the government imposes a tariff to restore the original quantity of imports, what will happen to the price of French wine in the United States? Show how much tariff revenue the government will collect.
8. India has a 70 percent tariff on imported chocolate.
   a. Sketch a diagram to show the impact of this tariff on the price of imported chocolate in India.
   b. Suppose India cuts the tariff to zero but imposes a quota that results in the same high price for imported chocolate. Show this in a diagram.
   c. From the government's perspective, is it better off with a tariff or with a quota? Explain.
9. Suppose the president of a nation proposes a switch from a system of import quotas to a system of tariffs, with the idea that the switch will not affect the quantity of goods imported. Who will be in favor of the switch? Who will oppose it?
10. Suppose the U.S. government has decided that for national security reasons, it must protect the machine tools industry. Name two ways in which the government can accomplish this goal. Which policy would you recommend? Why?
11. Suppose the North American Free Trade Agreement causes the United States to import lumber from Canada instead of from Finland, even though Finland is a lower-cost producer than Canada. Identify and explain this phenomenon.
12. Assume that several hundred independent farmers in Argentina are the only producers of a rare plant that is used for medicinal purposes around the world. Imagine that you are an economic adviser to the Argentine government. The president asks you to find a way to capture some of the economic rents from the production of this rare plant, so that more profits stay in Argentina. Your job is to design a trade policy that accomplishes the president's goal. Explain verbally what your trade policy would be, how it would affect quantity and price in the market, and how it would affect all the players in this market.

CHAPTER 30
International Finance

Money serves a vital role as a medium of exchange in an economy. Money facilitates economic transactions within a country by eliminating the need for the double coincidence of wants. When it comes to transactions that take place across countries that use different moneys, however, a complication arises. When a supermarket chain in the United States wants to buy beef from Argentina or when a company in France wants to buy computers from the United States, for example, they typically have to exchange their own currency for the foreign currency before completing the transaction. The rate at which one currency can be exchanged for the other, also known as the **exchange rate**, plays an important part in deciding whether an economic transaction between countries will occur.

exchange rate
The price of one currency in terms of another in the foreign exchange market. We express the exchange rate as the number of units of foreign currency that can be purchased with one unit of domestic currency.

Source: Shutterstock.com

How are exchange rates set? For many countries, the value of their currency is determined by supply and demand conditions in the foreign exchange market. The foreign exchange market is a global market. Any time, day or night, the market in foreign currencies is open somewhere in the world. When the market closes for the day in Tokyo, it is just opening in London. When it closes in London, it is just opening in San Francisco. When the market closes in San Francisco, it is getting ready to open again in Tokyo. The total sum of money being traded on the foreign exchange market over a period of one week exceeds the volume of global foreign trade for a year. In this chapter, we illustrate how the exchange rate, the price of foreign currency, is determined in the foreign exchange market. As you will soon see, some unusual features of the foreign exchange market lead exchange rates to be a volatile price.

Some countries have adopted a "fixed" exchange rate regime in which the country fixes its currency to another. We will demonstrate how a fixed exchange rate system works, and what the consequences are of choosing a fixed exchange rate that artificially favors either buyers of foreign goods or sellers of domestic goods. This explanation will help us understand the policy disputes that arose over the past decade between the United States and China regarding China's decision to limit the movements of its currency and keep the value of its currency low. We will also study the European Economic and Monetary Union (EMU) or Eurozone, where a group of countries replaced their own currencies with a new single currency in 1999. After more than a decade of successful operation, a financial crisis in several countries in 2010 and 2011, including Greece and Portugal, has led to considerable tension within the Eurozone and a burgeoning debt crisis in Greece that has, on numerous occasions, created a scenario whereby Greece would exit the currency union (a "Grexit"), which in turn would spark a contagious exodus that would bring the currency union to its knees.

Understanding how exchange rates are determined, what the consequences of sharp movements in exchange rates are for an economy, knowing what happens to a small economy like Greece or Portugal when they are part of a currency union or what happens to a large economy like China when it fixes its exchange rate to make its goods artificially more attractive to the rest of the world, are all extremely important for better understanding the world economy.

1. EXCHANGE RATES

1.1 Important Definitions

Conceptually, an exchange rate between two currencies is a simple idea: It is the price of one country's currency in terms of another on the foreign exchange market. Confusion regarding exchange rates is common, and often stems from a lack of consistency regarding how the exchange rate is defined. For instance, some newspapers will report the exchange rate between the dollar and the euro as $1.25 per euro but report the exchange rate between the dollar and the yen as 120 yen per dollar. When you then read about the exchange rates going "up" or "down," the connotation of what "up" and "down" means differs depending on whether we are talking about an exchange rate written as dollars per foreign currency or foreign currency per dollar.

Here, we define the exchange rate as a number of units of foreign currency that are needed to purchase one unit of the domestic currency, or, in other words, the price of a unit of domestic currency in terms of foreign currency. If the United States is the domestic economy, then the exchange rate with the euro will be expressed as 0.80 euros per dollar rather than as $1.25 per euro.

appreciation

An increase in value of a currency.

depreciation

A decrease in a value of a currency.

An increase in the exchange rate signifies that the domestic currency has increased in value (and the foreign currency has decreased in value) because it takes more units of foreign currency to buy a unit of domestic currency. This is called an **appreciation** of the domestic currency. Conversely, a decrease in the exchange rate signifies that the domestic currency has decreased in value (and the foreign currency has increased in value) since it takes fewer units of foreign currency to buy a unit of domestic currency. This is called a **depreciation** of the domestic currency.

We can use the exchange rate to convert the price of goods from one currency to another. For example, if a BMW costs 40,000 euros and the exchange rate between Germany and the United States was 0.8 euros per dollar, then the price of the BMW to someone in the United States is (40,000 euros)/(0.8 euros per dollar) = $50,000. Similarly, the price of a $2,000 Apple computer to someone in Germany would be $2,000 x 0.8 euros per dollar = 1,600 euros.

1.2 Exchange Rates and Net Exports

As we discussed in Chapter 19, changes in the exchange rate change the price that people in one country have to pay for the other country's goods. Consider the example about the BMW and the Apple computer and suppose that the dollar appreciates from 0.8 euros per dollar to a value of 1 euro per dollar. Then, the price of the 40,000 euro BMW will now be $40,000 instead of $50,000. Similarly, the $2,000 Apple computer would now cost 2,000 euros in Germany instead of 1,600 euros.

All else equal, then an appreciation of the domestic currency makes foreign goods cheaper at home and domestic goods more expensive abroad, whereas a depreciation of the domestic currency makes foreign goods more expensive at home and domestic goods cheaper abroad. We can conclude, therefore, that an appreciation of the domestic currency leads to more imports and fewer exports, that is, it decreases net exports, whereas a depreciation of the domestic currency leads to more exports and fewer imports, that is, it increases net exports.

Changes in the exchange rate are not the only reason why domestic goods may be more or less expensive compared with foreign goods. So, even when the exchange rate does not change, a higher rate of inflation in the domestic economy than in the foreign economy will make domestic goods more expensive abroad, driving down net exports. Conversely, a higher rate of inflation in the foreign economy than in the domestic economy will make domestic goods cheaper abroad, increasing net exports.

Changes in the exchange rate are not the only reason why domestic goods may be more or less expensive compared with foreign goods. So, even when the exchange rate does not change, a higher rate of inflation in the domestic economy than in the foreign economy will make domestic goods more expensive abroad, driving down net exports. Conversely, a higher rate of inflation in the foreign economy than in the domestic economy will make domestic goods cheaper abroad, increasing net exports.

REVIEW

- An exchange rate between two currencies is the price of one country's currency in terms of another on the foreign exchange market. The convention here is to define the exchange rate in terms of foreign currency units per unit of domestic currency.
- An increase in the exchange rate signifies that the domestic currency has increased in value, also called an appreciation of the domestic currency. A decrease in the exchange rate signifies that the domestic currency has decreased in value, also known as a depreciation of the domestic currency.
- All else equal, a depreciation of the domestic currency makes foreign goods more expensive at home and domestic goods cheaper abroad. This implies an increase in net exports. Conversely, an appreciation of the domestic currency leads to a decrease in net exports.
- Even when the exchange rate does not change, a higher rate of inflation in the domestic economy will make domestic goods more expensive abroad, driving down net exports. Conversely, a higher rate of inflation in the foreign economy will make domestic goods cheaper abroad, increasing net exports.

2. EXCHANGE RATE DETERMINATION

Because the exchange rate as we defined it is simply the price of domestic currency (in terms of foreign currency), then we should be able to understand how that price is determined by analyzing the foreign exchange market using the familiar supply–demand framework.

Figure 30.1 demonstrates how to use a standard supply–demand framework to analyze the foreign exchange market. Because the exchange rate is simply the price of domestic currency, we can quickly draw a parallel with the regular supply–demand analysis. When the price of domestic currency is high (low), the quantity of domestic currency demanded will be low (high), resulting in a downward-sloping demand curve. Similarly, when the price of domestic currency is high (low), the quantity of domestic currency supplied will be high (low), resulting in an upward-sloping supply curve. The demand for domestic currency here is coming from those who have foreign currency that they wish to exchange into domestic currency, while the supply of domestic currency is coming from those who have domestic currency that they desire to convert into foreign currency.

When the demand for domestic currency rises or the supply of domestic currency falls, all else equal, domestic currency will appreciate—that is, the price of domestic currency rises. When the demand for domestic currency falls or the supply of domestic currency rises, all else equal, the domestic currency will depreciate—that is, the price of domestic currency falls. This simple supply–demand framework allows us to make two key predictions about what determines the behavior of exchange rates in the economy. The two predictions are (1) that interest rate differentials affect the behavior of exchange rates in the short run and (2) that price differentials for goods determines the behavior of exchange rates in the long run.

FIGURE 30.1 **Supply and Demand model of the Foreign Exchange Market**

The exchange rate is the price of domestic currency (expressed in terms of foreign currency). The quantity of domestic currency demanded (in exchange for foreign currency) varies inversely with the price of domestic currency (the exchange rate). The quantity of domestic currency supplied (in exchange for foreign currency) varies directly with the price of domestic currency (the exchange rate). The resulting equilibrium exchange rate is given by e_0 and the quantity of domestic currency exchanged for foreign currency is given by Q_0.

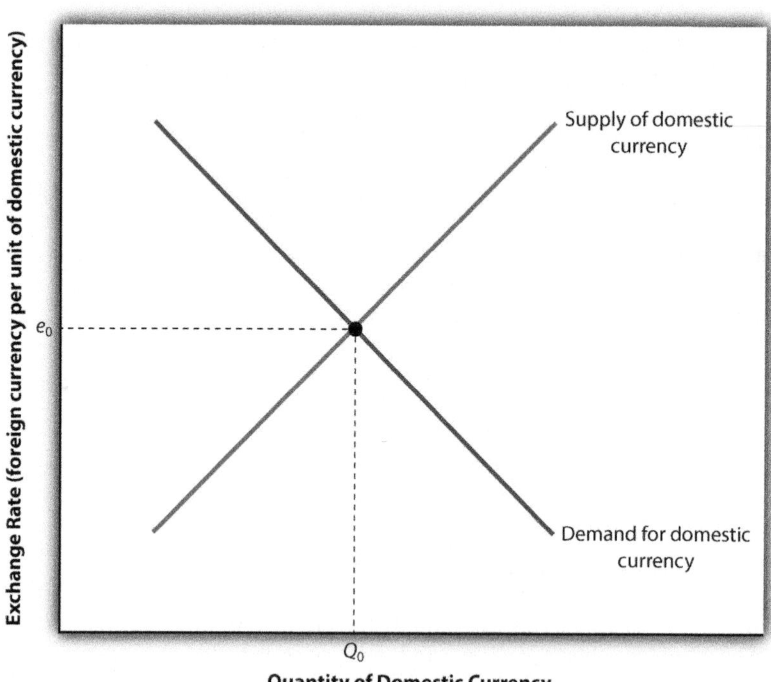

In practice, you have to be careful in using a traditional supply–demand model to analyze the foreign exchange market. In a traditional goods market, like the market for oranges, the factors affecting demand, such as the income levels of consumers, the price of apples, or the health benefits of drinking orange juice, likely will be quite distinct from the factors affecting supply, such as the costs of transportation or winter weather conditions in Florida. This means that we can analyze the impact of a particular event on the orange juice market by considering whether it would shift the demand curve or the supply curve. In the foreign exchange market, however, the factors affecting demand and factors affecting supply are likely to be much less distinct. For instance if an economy experiences some political unrest, this unrest would lead to both a decrease in the demand for domestic currency as well as an increase in the supply of domestic currency.

2.1 Interest Rate Differentials and Short-Run Exchange Rate Movements

In the short run, investors operating in the global foreign exchange market decide where to place their funds to get the highest return. The funds they invest are highly mobile; tens of millions of dollars worth of foreign currency can be moved from one country to another in a matter of seconds by means of a few keystrokes or a mouse-click. The movement of funds around the world to receive the highest return creates a link between interest rate differentials and the behavior of the exchange rate.

For example, suppose that the interest rate in the United States rises by more than the interest rate in Japan. International investors will find investing in financial assets in the United States that pay this higher interest rate to be more attractive, which in turn will lead to an increased demand for dollars and an appreciation of the dollar. Similarly, if the interest rate in the United States fell relative to the interest rate in Japan, then international investors will find investing in financial assets in the United States to be less attractive. This scenario will lead to a decreased demand for dollars and a depreciation of the dollar.

Figure 30.2 shows how interest rate differentials are correlated with the exchange rate. The rise of the dollar with respect to the British pound in the early 1980s and its subsequent decline in the late 1980s are highly correlated with the rise in U.S. interest rates in the early 1980s and the subsequent decline in the late 1980s.

FIGURE 30.2 Interest Rate Differentials and the Exchange Rate, 1980–2010

In the short run, investors operating in the global foreign exchange market decide where to place their funds to get the highest return. When the interest rate in the United States rises by more than interest rate in another country (in this example, the United Kingdom), international investors will move money to the United States; this will lead to an appreciation of the dollar. Similarly, if the interest rate in the United States falls relative to the interest rate in another country, then international investors will move money out of the United States; this will lead to a depreciation of the dollar.

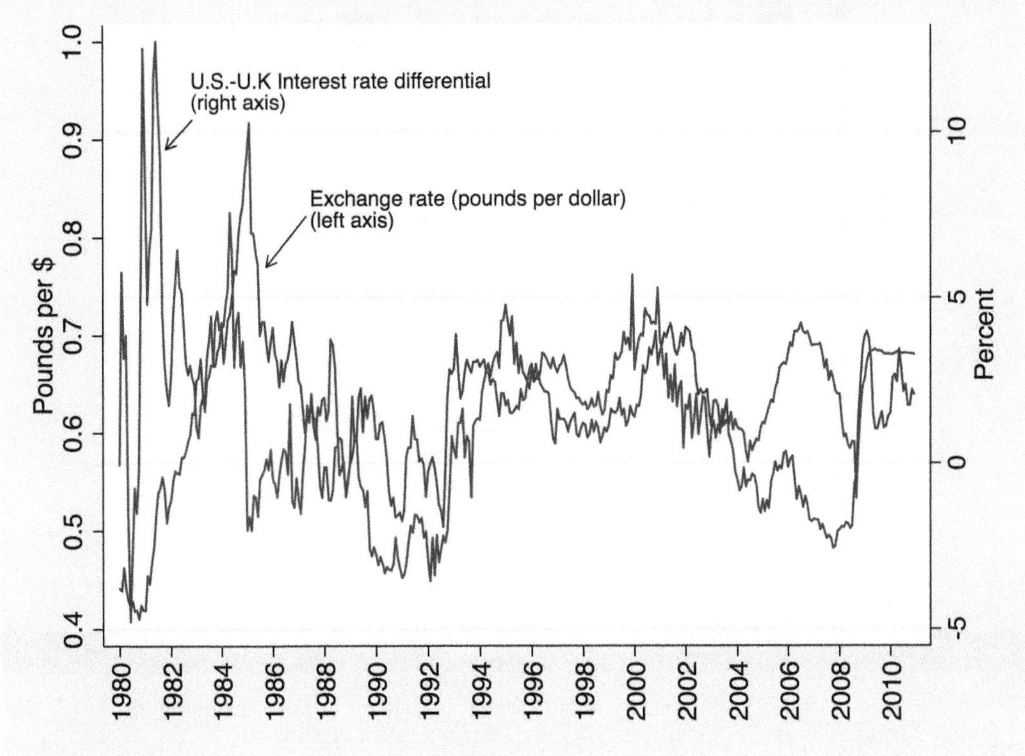

Source: Authors' calculations using IMF data

2.2 Price Differentials and Long-Run Exchange Rate Movements

If transport costs are low, and people are not prevented from buying whatever they want, the same commodity in two countries will sell for about the same amount; this is called the **law of one price.** The idea that the law of one price will hold for many different products is what underlies the theory of **purchasing power parity (PPP)**, which states that the exchange rate will adjust to equalize the price levels of two economies. The intuition here is that if PPP did not hold, then people would buy goods and services in the country where they are cheap, transport them to the country where they are expensive, and make a profit. This can only happen if the transportation costs are low and the goods and services can in fact be shipped from one country to another. The cost of shipping some goods (cement, milk) can be very high, whereas other products, especially services such as a haircut, may not be tradable across countries. The more nontradable goods and services are, and the higher transportation costs are, the less likely it is that PPP will hold.

PPP works better over long periods of time than over short periods. PPP predicts that when the domestic inflation rate exceeds the foreign inflation rate for a long period of time, then the domestic currency must depreciate over that time period so that domestic goods prices do not rise faster than foreign goods prices, when measured in the same currency. Conversely, PPP predicts that when the foreign inflation rate exceeds the domestic inflation rate, then the domestic currency must appreciate over time to ensure that foreign goods prices do not rise faster than domestic goods prices, when measured in the same currency.

Figure 30.3 shows how inflation differentials are correlated with the exchange rate in the last twenty-five years for a group of the United States' largest trading partners as predicted by the theory.

law of one price

The notion that if transport costs are low, and people are not prevented from buying whatever they want, the same commodity in two countries will sell for about the same amount when measured in the same currency.

purchasing power parity (PPP)

A theory that states that the exchange rate will adjust to equalize the price levels of two countries.

FIGURE 30.3 Purchasing Power Parity, 1980–2010

As predicted by PPP, the U.S. dollar has appreciated against countries with high inflation (Brazil, India) and depreciated against countries with low inflation (Germany, Japan) while remaining essentially unchanged against countries with similar inflation (the United Kingdom).

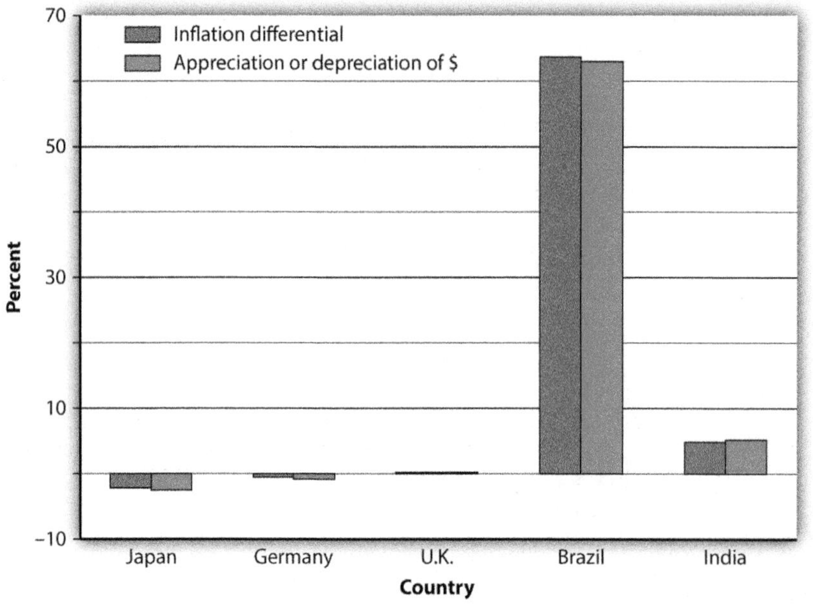

REVIEW

- Because the exchange rate is the price of domestic currency (in terms of foreign currency), we can use the supply–demand framework to understand how the exchange rate is determined.
- When the demand for domestic currency rises or the supply of domestic currency falls, all else equal, the domestic currency will appreciate. When the demand for domestic currency falls or the supply of domestic currency rises, all else equal, the domestic currency will depreciate.
- The supply–demand framework predicts that interest rate differentials affect exchange rates in the short run and that price differentials for goods affect exchange rates in the long run.
- International investors move their funds around the world to get the highest return. If the interest rate in the United States rose relative to the interest rate in Japan, then international investors would find financial assets in the United States more attractive, leading to an appreciation of the dollar. Conversely, a fall in U.S. interest rates would lead to a depreciation of the dollar.
- PPP states that the exchange rate will adjust to equalize the price levels of two economies. PPP predicts that the domestic currency will depreciate over time when the domestic inflation rate exceeds the foreign inflation rate so that domestic goods prices do not rise faster than foreign goods prices when measured in the same currency. Conversely, PPP predicts that the domestic currency will appreciate over time when the foreign inflation rate exceeds the domestic inflation rate.

3. FIXED EXCHANGE RATES

flexible exchange rate policy

A policy in which exchange rates are determined in foreign exchange markets and governments do not agree to fix them.

In our analysis thus far, we assumed that a country's currency was freely traded on the foreign exchange market and that the exchange rate was freely determined by the actions of the buyers and sellers in that market. The United States is an example of a country that follows a **flexible exchange rate policy**, allowing the value of its currency to be determined this way. In such a system, the exchange rate is likely to fluctuate quite substantially, as illustrated in Figure 30.4 for the euro–dollar exchange rate between 2000 and 2016.

But throughout history, governments have exercised substantial control over the exchange rate system. Governments who want to tightly control the value of their currency adopt a **fixed exchange rate policy**, whereby the government announces a fixed rate at which the central bank will exchange domestic currency for foreign currency. The implications of a fixed exchange rate system for monetary policy were explored in Chapter 27; here we focus more on how such a system operates.

fixed exchange rate policy
A policy in which a country maintains a fixed value of its currency in terms of other currencies.

In the early nineteenth century, Britain adopted a gold standard under which the government pegged the price of gold at a fixed price of about 4 British pounds per ounce of gold. In 1879, the United States joined the gold standard, agreeing to buy or sell gold at a rate of about $20 an ounce. Because both currencies were tied to gold, the exchange rates between the pound and the dollar were also tied together at a rate of about $5 per British pound. From the end of World War II through the early 1970s, the Bretton-Woods system linked the currencies of the world's largest economies to the U.S. dollar at a set value, while the dollar in turn was linked to gold at a price of $35 per ounce of gold. A more modern example was in Argentina during the period from 1992 to 2002, when the Argentinean government set up a system that fixed the Argentinean peso to the U.S. dollar at a rate of one to one by agreeing to hold enough U.S. dollars to convert all peso currency notes into dollars.

3.1 The Role of Reserves

Typically, the fixed exchange rate policy applies to a single foreign currency. The central bank therefore needs to have stocks of domestic currency (which every central bank has) and stocks of the foreign currency (also known as foreign currency reserves). Although reserves could theoretically be held in the form of any currency, typically, most foreign exchange reserves are held in terms of the currency to which the country is fixing its currency.

When a participant in the foreign exchange market comes to the central bank and exchanges domestic currency for foreign currency, the central bank's holdings of foreign currency reserves go down and their holdings of domestic currency go up. Conversely, when a participant in the foreign exchange market comes to the central bank and exchanges foreign currency for domestic currency, the central bank's holdings of foreign currency reserves go down and their holdings of domestic currency go up.

FIGURE 30.4 Fluctuations in the Euro–Dollar Exchange Rate

Since its introduction in 1999, the euro has fluctuated against the dollar, sometimes quite dramatically. After an initial period of depreciation, the euro underwent a sustained appreciation from 2002 until 2008. The dollar appreciated during the recession in the United States. After end of the recession, as individual Eurozone countries such as Greece and Portugal began to run into difficulty, the Euro began to depreciate against the dollar.

Figure 30.5 shows the exchange rate between the U.S. dollar and the Chinese renminbi between 2000 and 2010. The Chinese exchange rate was pegged to the dollar until 2005 when it was allowed to appreciate. China then returned to a fixed exchange from 2008 to 2016, around the period of the financial crisis. Beginning in 2010, the Chinese government again ended the peg and let their currency appreciate, but it is clear that they still were exercising a great deal of control over the exchange rate, which is less volatile than the euro–dollar rate shown in Figure 30.4.

3.2 Overvaluation and Undervaluation

A fixed exchange rate is unlikely to equal the rate that would prevail in a flexible exchange rate system without central bank involvement. Recall that in a flexible exchange rate system the prevailing exchange rate would be the rate at which the quantity supplied of domestic currency on the foreign exchange market equals the quantity demanded. Suppose that rate happens to be 20 units of foreign currency per unit of domestic currency, and consider what would happen in the two scenarios in which the government fixes the exchange rate (1) at a value that is higher than 20 or (2) at a value lower than 20.

FIGURE 30.5 **Lack of Fluctuations in the Yuan–Dollar Exchange Rate**

In contrast to the euro–dollar exchange rate the yuan–dollar exchange rate looks much more tightly controlled. Between 1999 and 2005, the exchange rate was fixed at 8.28 yuan per dollar. After 2005, China agreed to let the yuan appreciate but controlled the pace of that appreciation quite tightly. When the recession of 2008/09 hit, China again kept the exchange rate from appreciating only to relax their control again and resume the slow appreciation after the crisis ended. However, in the last two years the Chinese currency has shown signs of depreciation against the dollar.

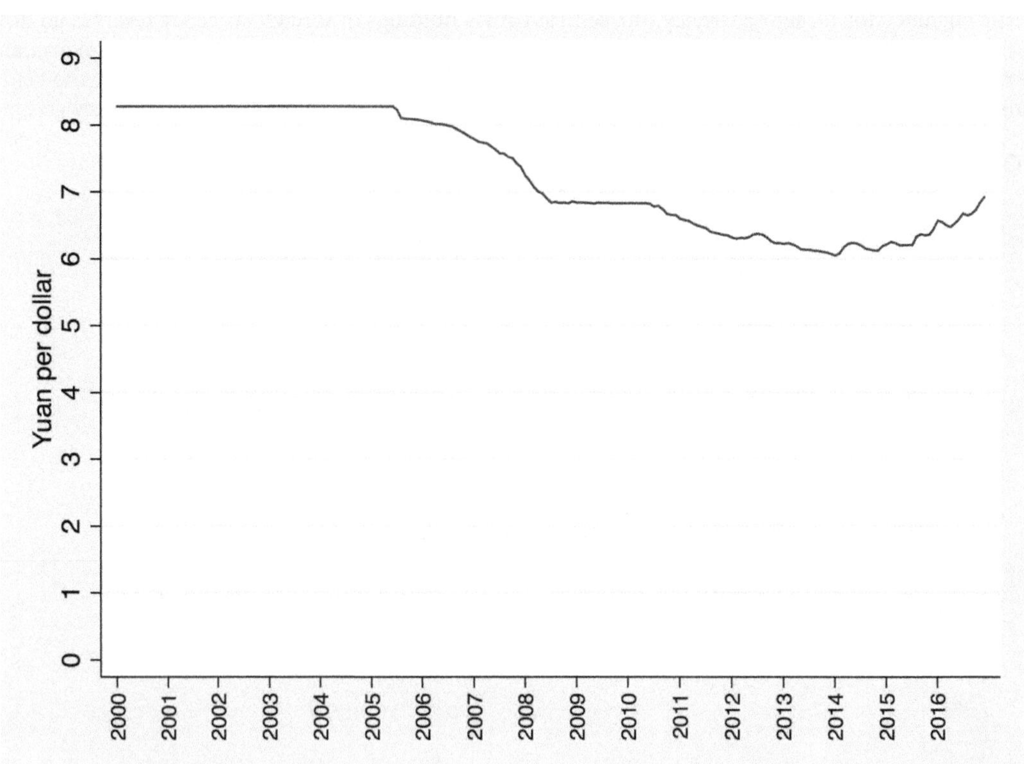

overvalued

A currency is said to be overvalued if the fixed exchange rate system makes the domestic currency artificially more valuable.

First, consider the case in which the central bank wants to fix the value of the domestic currency at a value of 25 units of foreign currency per unit of domestic currency. As you can see in Figure 30.6, this implies an excess supply of domestic currency. The central bank will see its foreign exchange reserves decrease because more people want to hand in domestic currency to the central bank in exchange for foreign currency. Because the fixed exchange rate makes the domestic currency artificially more valuable, we say that the domestic currency is **overvalued**.

Why would a government want to overvalue its currency? Well, by making the domestic currency artificially more valuable, consumers and importers in the economy will benefit from having access to cheap foreign goods. Conversely, exporters will suffer because their goods will be artificially more expensive to foreign buyers.

Next, consider the case in which the central bank wants to fix the value of the domestic currency at a value of 15 units of foreign currency per unit of domestic currency. In this case, because the fixed exchange rate makes the domestic currency artificially less valuable, we say that the domestic currency is **undervalued**. As you can see in Figure 30.7, this implies an excess demand for domestic currency, and the central bank will see its foreign exchange reserves increase rather than decrease because more people want to exchange foreign currency for domestic currency.

undervalued

A currency is said to be undervalued if the fixed exchange rate makes the domestic currency artificially less valuable.

A government would want to undervalue its currency because exporters in the economy will benefit from their goods being more attractive to foreign buyers, as a result of the domestic currency now artificially being less valuable. In contrast, consumers and importers would suffer because goods produced in other countries would cost more.

FIGURE 30.6 An Overvalued Fixed Exchange Rate

Suppose that the exchange rate that would prevail in the market under a flexible exchange rate regime was 20 units of foreign currency per unit of domestic currency. Now suppose that the central bank wants to fix the value of the domestic currency at a value of 25 units of foreign currency per unit of domestic currency. This implies that there is an excess supply of domestic currency (equivalent to an excess demand for foreign currency). The central bank's foreign exchange reserves will decrease as a result.

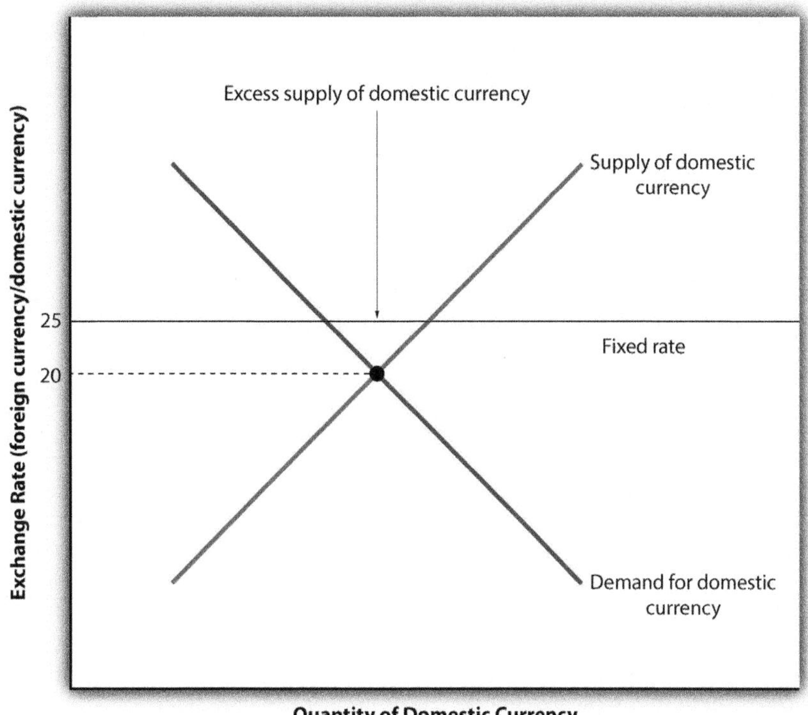

FIGURE 30.7 An Undervalued Fixed Exchange Rate

Suppose that the exchange rate that would prevail in the market under a flexible exchange rate regime was 20 units of foreign currency per unit of domestic currency. Now suppose that the central bank wants to fix the value of the domestic currency at a value of 15 units of foreign currency per unit of domestic currency. This implies that there is an excess demand for domestic currency (equivalent to an excess supply of foreign currency). The central bank's foreign exchange reserves will increase as a result.

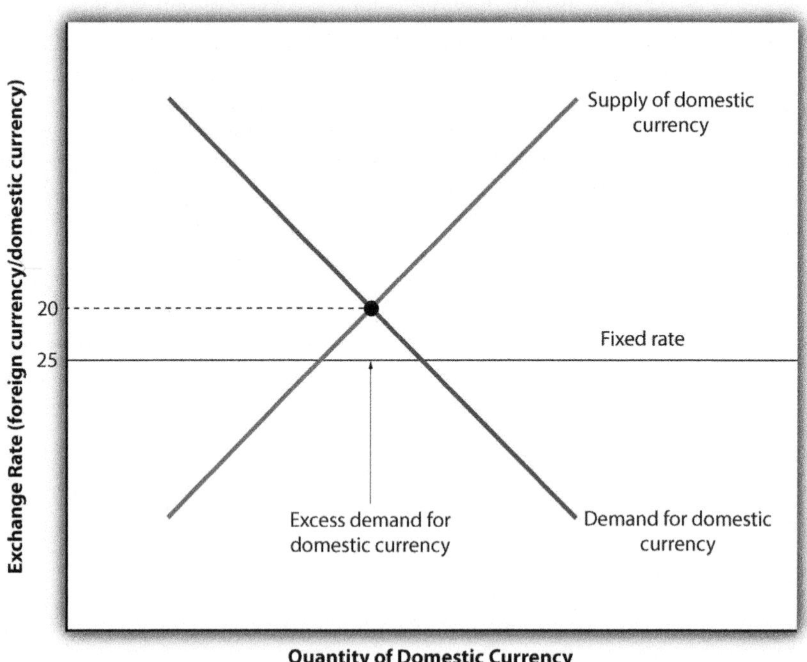

3.3 Consequences of Sustained Overvaluation

So what happens when the overvaluation continues? The central bank will continue to run down its foreign exchange reserves and correspondingly increase its domestic currency holdings. Having too few foreign exchange reserves is a serious problem because it means that the fixed rate cannot be sustained—when the central bank runs out of reserves, it cannot maintain the fixed exchange rate anymore. When the central bank does not have enough foreign exchange reserves, it is forced to do one of three things:

devaluation

When a fixed exchange rate is adjusted so that the domestic currency is worth less than it used to be.

1. Change the fixed rate to make the currency less overvalued—so move it from 25 units of foreign currency per unit of domestic currency to a new fixed rate that is closer to 20 units of foreign currency per unit of domestic currency. This is called a **devaluation** of the domestic currency, the fixed exchange rate analog to a depreciation.
2. Abandon the fixed exchange rate regime and move to a flexible exchange rate regime. In this case, the exchange rate will again move closer to 20 units of foreign currency per unit of domestic currency but will no longer be fixed.
3. Acquire more foreign exchange reserves sufficient to meet the excess demand. This approach usually is successful only if the underlying overvaluation is temporary.

In practice the situation is often more drastic. Suppose the government is forced to devalue from say 25 to 20 in the above example. If you had money in the domestic economy and you knew that the exchange rate was going to jump from 25 units of foreign currency per unit of domestic currency to 20 units of foreign currency in a few days, what would you do? Well, you would try to get your money out of the domestic economy as quickly as possible—if you had 1 million units of domestic currency, you could convert it into 25 million units of foreign currency and then, after the devaluation, convert it back to 1.25 million units of domestic currency and earn a nice profit. This means that many people will be rushing to convert domestic currency into foreign currency when it looks like the central bank is running into difficulty with its foreign exchange reserves.

This type of a panic in which everyone stampedes to exit the domestic currency and acquire foreign currency was fairly common in the 1980s and 1990s, with the notable examples being the East Asian currency crisis of 1997, the European currency crisis of 1991–1992, and the Argentinean crisis of 2001.

3.4 Consequences of Sustained Undervaluation

Undervaluation creates a different set of problems than overvaluation. Undervaluation occurs when governments want to favor certain sectors of the economy (exporters trying to sell goods abroad) over other sectors (importers and consumers who benefit from cheap goods from abroad).

The result of sustained undervaluation is that the central bank will see its foreign exchange reserves grow. Having too many foreign exchange reserves may seem like a positive development that can help countries avoid the panic associated with running out of reserves that occurred in past episodes of currency crises. But undervaluation has adverse longer-term implications. When the central bank keeps handing out domestic currency for foreign currency, it is increasing the domestic money supply. Increases in the domestic money supply imply a rise in inflation as people bid up the price of domestic goods, services, and assets. It also means that the central bank has to manage its growing holdings of foreign exchange reserves. Additionally, foreign economies will exert substantial political pressure if they are unhappy with the fact that another country is using the exchange rate to favor its own exporters at the expense of foreign exporters.

FIGURE 30.8 Foreign Reserves in China, 1990–2010

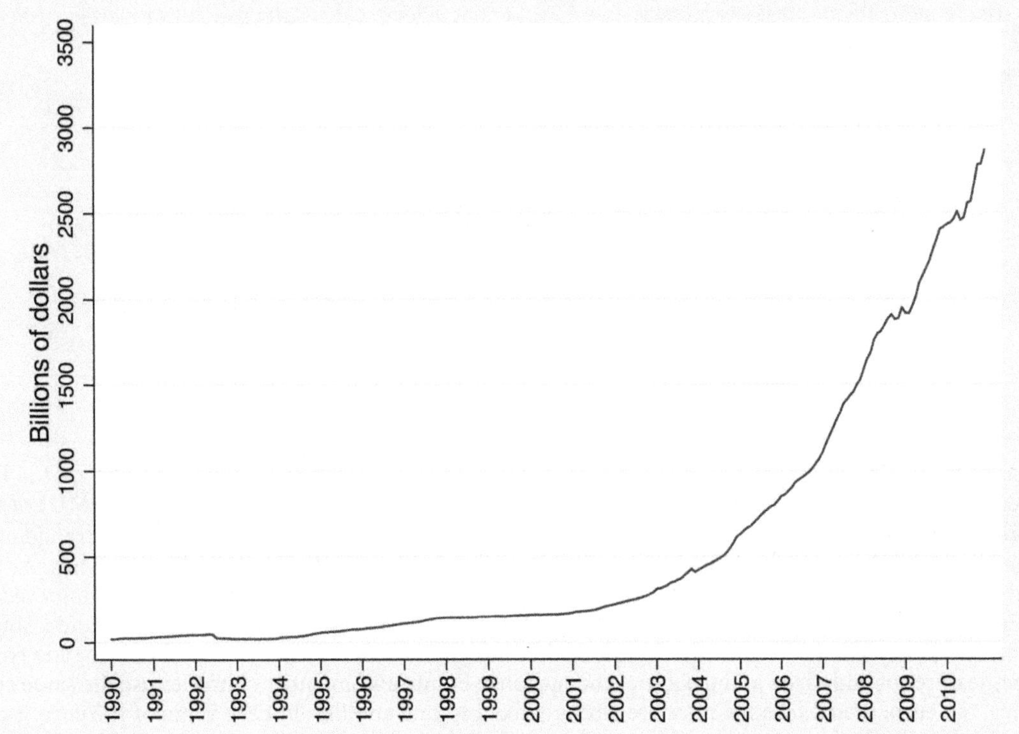

If the central bank feels that it has too many foreign exchange reserves, it will change the fixed rate to make the currency less undervalued, for example, by moving it from 15 units of foreign currency per unit of domestic currency to closer to 20 units of foreign currency. This is called a **revaluation** of the domestic currency, the fixed exchange rate analogy to an appreciation. Foreigners will now want to rush into an economy when they can acquire another currency at a rate of 15, rather than waiting and paying 20 units per unit of domestic currency after a revaluation.

revaluation

When a fixed exchange rate is adjusted so that the domestic currency is worth more than it used to be.

Similarly, people in the domestic economy who were looking to acquire foreign currency now will prefer to wait, because they can get only 15 units of foreign currency per unit of domestic currency today but potentially get closer to 20 units by waiting. This further decreases the supply of, and increases the demand for, domestic currency and drives foreign exchange reserves even higher. The central bank will be faced with ever escalating problems from inflation and be more inclined to revalue its currency. This revaluation, in turn, will lead to an even more dramatic rise in the number of people wanting to acquire domestic currency, leading to another stampede, albeit to the entrance this time.

Undervaluation was one of the key pillars of China's remarkable economic transformation, which began in 1978 with the economic reforms instituted by Deng Xiaoping. China aimed to achieve high rates of economic growth by focusing on exports and on attracting foreign direct investment (FDI), and thus embarked on a series of devaluations in the 1980s as the yuan per dollar exchange rate changed from 1.5 in 1980 to 2.8 by 1985, 4.7 by 1990, 8.5 by 1995, and finally settling at 8.28 in the late 1990s. The rate then stayed unchanged at this level till the mid-2000s, as you can see from Figure 30.8.

During this period, China's economy grew rapidly, with per capita gross domestic product (GDP) growth rates averaging around 7 to 9 percent. Even more impressive growth rates could be found in China's foreign exchange reserves, which increased from $19 billion in 1990 to $157 billion in 2000 to almost $700 billion at the time the 8.28 rate came to an end in mid-2005. But even afterwards, it is clear that China is carefully controlling its currency appreciation by buying dollars whenever it felt the Chinese currency was appreciating too much. The result is a dramatic rise in China's holdings of dollar reserves which had reached close to $3 trillion shortly after the global recession of 2008/09.

REVIEW

- A flexible exchange rate policy allows the exchange rate to be freely determined in the foreign exchange market. In a fixed exchange rate policy, the government sets the exchange rate at which the central bank will exchange domestic currency for foreign currency.
- To implement a fixed exchange rate system, the central bank needs to have foreign currency reserves. The level of foreign reserves increases when the central bank hands out domestic currency in exchange for foreign currency and decreases when the central bank hands out foreign currency in exchange for domestic currency.
- A government may choose to overvalue its currency by choosing a fixed exchange rate that makes the domestic currency artificially more valuable. Typically, this is done so that consumers and importers in the economy will benefit from having access to cheap foreign goods.
- A government, instead, may choose to undervalue its currency by choosing a fixed rate that makes the domestic currency artificially less valuable. A government may want to undervalue its currency to help exporters sell more goods to foreign buyers.
- A sustained overvaluation will cause a central bank to run down its foreign exchange reserves, set off a panicked rush to convert domestic currency into foreign currency, and lead to a currency crisis.
- A sustained undervaluation will lead to an increase in the domestic money supply, resulting in higher inflation. Foreign economies will exert political pressure if they are unhappy with the impact of the fixed exchange rate policy on their exporters.

4. CURRENCY UNIONS

currency union

An arrangement whereby a group of countries adopt a common currency in place of their individual currencies.

One of the most significant economic developments of the twenty-first century, and one that is frequently in the news, is the creation of the Eurozone, the Economic and Monetary Union (EMU) of the European Union. The Eurozone is the most prominent example of a **currency union**, an arrangement whereby a group of countries adopt a common currency in place of their individual currencies. At the end of 2016, the Eurozone, which started with 11 member countries had expanded to be composed of 19 independent sovereign nations that have united to adopt a common currency (the euro) and a single monetary policy maker for the whole region (the European Central Bank, ECB). The Eurozone combines features of both fixed and flexible exchange rates: Because all member countries use the same currency, the euro, their exchange rates are strongly fixed to one another, but the value of the euro is determined by the forces of supply and demand in the foreign exchange market.

Some countries in the European Union—the Czech Republic, Hungary, Poland, and Romania—have expressed interest in joining the Eurozone but have not yet been admitted. Other countries in the European Union—Denmark and Sweden—would be admitted into the Eurozone easily but do not want to join. At the same time, concerns have arisen that some Eurozone countries (Greece) want to leave, or could even be made to leave, the currency union as it struggles with a deep economic downturn that has devastated its economy. Why does a currency union lead to such a divergence of opinion among countries? We hope to answer this question by exploring how a currency union works and understanding the consequences of entering a currency union.

The origins of the EMU go back many years, but perhaps the most important development was the Treaty of Maastricht, which was signed in 1992. The Maastricht Treaty laid out the criteria that European Union countries would have to meet to enter the EMU and adopt the euro as the common currency. Among the criteria required were that all admitted countries have inflation rates that were within 1.5 percentage points of the three lowest inflation rates among member countries; that they have long-term interest rates that were within 2 percentage points of the three lowest interest rates among member countries; and that they have budget deficits that did not exceed 3 percent of GDP and government debt that did not exceed 60 percent of GDP. These conditions attempted to ensure that the economies of the member countries would converge to a similar state, in the hope that this would make the currency union function better.

On January 1, 1999, 11 countries embarked on what the Economist magazine then called "an awfully big adventure." The 11 founding countries that made up the EMU were Austria, Belgium,

Finland, France, Germany, Ireland, Italy, Luxembourg, the Netherlands, Portugal, and Spain. They were joined by Greece in January 2001, by Slovenia in January 2007, by Malta and Cyprus in January 2008, by Slovakia in January 2009, Estonia in January 2011, Latvia in 2014 and most recently by Lithuania in 2015 making a grand total of 19 members. All domestic currencies have ceased to exist in these member countries.

The 19 countries that form the EMU have chosen not only to adopt the euro but also to cede monetary policy decisions to a central bank for the entire region. Since January 1, 1999, monetary policy-making decisions for the EMU have been vested in the ECB. The ECB together with the existing member central banks form a system known as the Eurosystem. The member central banks took on a role similar to that played by the regional Federal Reserve Banks in the U.S. Federal Reserve System. The ECB is headquartered in Frankfurt. Wim Duisenberg, a Dutch central banker, was chosen as the first head of the ECB. He was followed by Jean-Claude Trichet, a French central banker who in turn was succeeded by the current governor Mario Draghi, an Italian central banker.

As we discussed in Chapter 27, the ECB policy instruments are Eurozone-wide and do not relate to a particular country. In other words, the ECB cannot set one interest rate in Germany and a different interest rate in France. Instead, it decides on the appropriate euro-wide interest rates in setting monetary policy. This is an important feature of a currency union: Individual countries no longer have the ability to control their monetary policy, and the monetary policy appropriate for the region may not be appropriate for an individual economy. For example, shortly after the EMU's inception, the ECB embarked on an expansionary monetary policy because the region as a whole struggled during the global economic slowdown in 2000/01. But individual countries in the region, like Ireland, were growing fairly rapidly at the time and actually would have preferred a less expansionary policy than appropriate for the entire region. Conversely, in 2011, the ECB wanted to move to a less expansionary policy because of concerns about rising inflation. But this had adverse consequences for Greece, Ireland, and Portugal, which were struggling with weak economic growth.

This type of disconnect is likely to be particularly problematic for smaller economies in the region because their economic outcomes will have little impact on the Eurozone aggregates that the ECB uses to set policy. Table 30.1 provides a set of weights indicating the contribution of member countries to euro-area economic aggregates. These weights reflect the relative size of consumption in the economy. As you can see, Germany, France, Italy, and Spain together account for about three-fourths of the Eurozone and the remaining 15 countries combined count for as much as France does in terms of how much they contribute to euro-area aggregates. So a recession in a smaller economy, like Ireland or Greece, at a time when the large economies like France and Germany are growing rapidly will not result in any help for the smaller economies from the ECB and will lead to growing tensions within the union.

TABLE 30.1 Contributions of Each Member Country to Euro-Area Aggregates (consumption-based weights)

Country	Weight	Country	Weight	Country	Weight
Germany	28.0%	Greece	2.3%	Slovenia	0.4%
France	20.6%	Portugal	2.2%	Luxembourg	0.3%
Italy	17.5%	Finland	1.9%	Latvia	0.25%
Spain	11.3%	Ireland	1.4%	Cyprus	0.2%
Netherlands	5.1%	Slovakia	0.7%	Estonia	0.15%
Belgium	3.8%	Lithuania	0.4%	Malta	0.1%
Austria	3.4%				

So why are so many smaller nations eager to join the Eurozone? Because many benefits accrue to these smaller economies, including greater trade and investment flows with a common currency. Moreover, uncertainty about future appreciation and depreciation is removed, as are transaction costs from exchanging one currency for another. This enhances travel and trade across borders.

These basic concepts help us understand why some member countries may want to leave the Eurozone and why some countries still want to join. To be sure, the Eurozone may not allow some of these countries to join because they have not met the convergence criteria laid down in the Treaty of Maastricht, and other countries are perfectly happy not to join because they value their own monetary policy autonomy.

REVIEW

- A currency union is an arrangement whereby a group of countries adopts a common currency in place of their individual currencies. The EMU is the most prominent example of a currency union in the world in the twenty-first century.
- The EMU began in 2001 when 11 countries that had met the convergence criteria laid out by the Treaty of Maastricht adopted a common currency (the euro) in place of their individual currencies and ceded monetary policy-making authority from their national central bank to the newly formed ECB.
- In a currency union, individual countries no longer have the ability to control their monetary policy. The monetary policy appropriate for the region may not be appropriate at all for the domestic economy. This is particularly true when a smaller economy in the region has conditions that diverge from conditions for the region as a whole.
- The primary benefits for a currency union are the prospects for greater trade and investment flows among the member countries because they all use the same currency. Another important change is the elimination of transaction costs from having to exchange one currency for another.
- In the near future, the Eurozone will have interesting developments because some countries may want to be admitted to the EMU, and at the same time, existing member countries may want to leave the EMU.

5. END-OF-CHAPTER MATERIAL

Key Points

1. An exchange rate is a rate at which one currency can be exchanged for the other. The convention used in this chapter defines the exchange rate in terms of foreign currency units per unit of domestic currency.
2. Because the exchange rate is the price of domestic currency (in terms of foreign currency), we can use the supply–demand framework to understand how exchange rates are determined.
3. When there is excess demand for the domestic currency in the foreign exchange market, the domestic currency appreciates. When there is excess supply of domestic currency in the foreign exchange market, the domestic currency depreciates.
4. The supply–demand framework allows us to predict that the country whose interest rate increases will see an appreciation of their currency in the short run and that the country with a higher rate of inflation will see a depreciation of their currency in the long run.
5. In a fixed exchange rate system, the government sets the exchange rate at which the central bank will exchange domestic currency for foreign currency using reserves of foreign and domestic currency.
6. If the fixed exchange rate makes the domestic currency artificially more valuable, we say that the domestic currency is overvalued; if it makes the domestic currency artificially less valuable, we say that the domestic currency is undervalued.
7. A government may want to overvalue its currency so that consumers and importers in the economy will benefit from having access to cheap foreign goods. Conversely, a government may want to undervalue its currency so that exporters in the economy will benefit from their goods being more attractive to foreign buyers.
8. A sustained overvaluation will lead to a crisis situation in which the government runs out of reserves and is forced to take drastic action. A sustained undervaluation can lead to inflation in the longer term.
9. A currency union is an arrangement whereby a group of countries adopts a common currency in place of their individual currencies. The primary benefits of a currency union are the prospects for greater trade and investment flows among the member countries because they all use the same currency and thus avoid transaction costs related to the exchange of currency.
10. In a currency union, individual countries no longer have the ability to control their monetary policy. The monetary policy appropriate for the region may not be appropriate for all the economies in the region.

QUESTIONS FOR REVIEW

1. What is the relationship between the exchange rate and net exports?
2. How are exchange rates related to interest rate differentials in the short run?
3. How are exchange rates related to inflation differentials in the long run?
4. What does it mean when we say that a country has "fixed its exchange rate"?
5. Why might a country want to undervalue its currency?
6. What are the adverse consequences of a decision to undervalue?
7. Why might a country want to overvalue its currency?
8. What are the adverse consequences of a decision to overvalue?
9. Why did the countries that formed the Economic and Monetary Union have to satisfy the Maastricht convergence criteria?
10. What is the main advantage of joining a currency union? What is the main disadvantage?

PROBLEMS

1. Suppose a Toyota costs 2 million yen, and a Caterpillar tractor costs $300,000. If the exchange rate between Japan and the United States was 80 yen per dollar, calculate the price of the Toyota to someone in the United States and the price of the tractor to someone in Japan.
2. Now suppose the exchange rate changes to 100 yen per dollar. Which currency has appreciated? What happens to the price of the Toyota to someone in the United States and the price of the tractor to someone in Japan? Then redo this exercise, assuming the exchange rate changed to 75 yen per dollar, instead of 100 yen per dollar.
3. Draw a supply–demand diagram, like Figure 30.6, that provides a visual depiction of an exchange rate that is fixed at an overvalued rate. Suppose this country is in danger of running out of reserves so that investors begin to fear a devaluation is looming. Show the resulting impact on foreign exchange reserves on your diagram.
4. Now draw a supply–demand diagram, like Figure 30.7, which provides a visual depiction of an exchange rate that is fixed at an undervalued rate. Suppose this country is concerned about rising inflation and investors have begun to expect that a revaluation is looming. Show the resulting impact on foreign exchange reserves on your diagram.
5. Why is a sustained undervaluation of a currency different from a sustained overvaluation of a currency, in terms of how quickly the policy maker will have to change the fixed rate?
6. What are some of the signs that can lead one to conclude that China's currency may be undervalued?
7. Using the information given in Table 30.1, explain why the European Central Bank may respond differently to a shock that hits an economy like Greece or Ireland (but not the rest of the euro area) than it would to a shock that hits an economy like Germany or France (but not the rest of the euro area).
8. Conduct an Internet search to find out which country is the most likely candidate to join the Economic and Monetary Union (EMU) next. What are the pros and cons for that country from joining the EMU, particularly in light of the travails of countries like Greece that are in the EMU currently?

Index

Notes

Notes